In memory of Bella Golden, 1896–1997,

an American Jewish woman

of courage and imagination

and

To three generations of American Jewish women,

Ida Tatelman Hyman, Toby and Merle Hyman,

and Judith Hyman Rosenbaum and Adina Hyman Rosenbaum

Contents

Volume I

Volume II

Alphabetical List of Entries

Editorial Advisory Board

Editors' Preface

This encyclopedia aims to recover the rich history of American Jewish women and to make visible their diverse accomplishments. Women have been absent from most accounts of the Jewish past, whose paradigms were set by male experiences. Particularly in Jewish encyclopedias, women scarcely make an appearance, and when they do, it is most often as the wives of famous men. Even in American women's reference works, Jewish women remain invisible as Jews because their Jewishness is not considered relevant to their achievements. Thus American Jewish women are not constructed as a category of knowledge. This encyclopedia rectifies this loss and provides a usable past for American Jewish women.

Unlike many reference works that largely summarize and organize existing information, this encyclopedia does more. It actually generates new knowledge and understanding of the history of American Jewish women and their contribution to American society. As we've learned from working on this project, Jewish women have shaped critical aspects of American culture and American Jewish life. We anticipate that scholars as well as other users of this work will make new discoveries in reading these volumes. Many of the topical entries bring women into the forefront of our historical consciousness, as do individual biographies. Similarly, the juxtaposition of extraordinarily diverse figures makes clear the wide range of Jewish women's activities in the United States.

This encyclopedia began in 1994 when the American Jewish Historical Society and Ralph Carlson, the publisher of the award-winning *Black Women in America: An Historical Encyclopedia*, agreed to collaborate on a comparable endeavor for American Jewish women and invited us to serve as its editors. As friends and colleagues, we shared an enthusiasm for as well as complementary scholarly expertise in the history of American Jewish women. We recognized the significance of the project and welcomed the opportunity to shape a field of knowledge. We also considered Jewish history to be severely flawed due to its ignorance of Jewish women's experiences. We understood that knowledge empowers, and we sought to give this and coming generations of women the tools to participate in designing their future.

The proposal for the encyclopedia also came at one of those propitious academic moments. Hyman was putting the finishing touches on a new comparative study of Jewish women in the modern world, *Gender and Assimilation in Modern Jewish History: The Roles and Representation of Women*. Increasingly, she was drawn to women's history as a subject of study and source of self-understanding. In this journey, she was returning to a field of inquiry begun very early during her graduate school days when she coauthored the path-breaking *The Jewish Woman in America* in 1976. Moore had just completed a book on American Jews in the postwar period, *To the Golden Cities: Pursuing the American Jewish Dream in Miami and L.A.*

Creating an encyclopedia is always a difficult

task. In the case of an encyclopedia on American Jewish women, the difficulties are compounded by basic questions of definition. Who is an American Jewish woman? Both adjectives require discussion. As used in this encyclopedia, America refers to the United States. Seeing the United States as a nation of immigrants, we have included women who were born and educated abroad, including those who immigrated as adults. In the case of refugees fleeing Nazi persecution in the 1930s, we have also included women whose major accomplishments were behind them when they arrived on these shores but who were integrated into American culture. We also consider as American a few women who grew up and were educated here but went on to make their mark on the world elsewhere. Most prominent in this category is Golda Meir, Israel's prime minister from 1971 to 1974.

Defining who is a Jew proved to be even more challenging. We did not limit ourselves to a definition based on Jewish law, which attributes Jewishness to any child of a Jewish mother but not a Jewish father. We accepted as Jewish a woman whose father or mother was a Jew or who was a convert to Judaism, provided that she identified as a Jew or was perceived as such by her contemporaries. When both parents were Jewish, we included some women who rejected their Jewish identity or considered it irrelevant to their lives. Conversion to another religion, a path chosen by a few women in the encyclopedia, was treated as part of a woman's Jewish biography, that is, her explicit rejection of Judaism. Conversion is, after all, an aspect of the modern Jewish experience.

We could not include every woman who deserves to be in the encyclopedia. We developed criteria that emphasized accomplishment. To complement a focus on well-known and influential figures, we were sensitive to regional and professional diversity as well as contribution to Jewish communal life and American civic activity as volunteers. Since this is a historical encyclopedia, preference was given to women whose lives were over. However, because so many Jewish women did not arrive in the United States until the beginning of the twentieth century, we decided that without living women we would have a truncated historical encyclopedia that slighted recent decades of significant achievement. Our guidelines called for limiting entries on living women to those age sixty or above. Of course, there are exceptions to every rule. In the fields of sports and entertainment, individuals often achieve fame at a relatively early age. Occasionally a woman slightly younger than sixty received an entry because we are confident that her place in history is secure. We also made exceptions for women in national politics. But we recognize that any selection process is flawed and that some individuals who merited inclusion in the encyclopedia were overlooked. Clearly, this is not a comprehensive encyclopedia; in particular, women of accomplishment in mid-career do not receive recognition. However, some of these women wrote entries, and therefore brief biographies of them can be found in the notes on contributors.

In addition to 800 individual biographies, the encyclopedia contains 110 topical essays. These range from synthetic overviews of immigration and assimilation in specific periods to historical accounts of Jewish women's organizations. The encyclopedia also has interpretative essays on women's roles in Jewish and American culture as well as in the several denominations of Judaism. Each entry reflects the individual viewpoint of its author. We made an effort to survey Jewish women's participation in various fields where many of them were active, such as literature, art, and scholarly disciplines. Unfortunately, we did not succeed in finding contributors for every field we sought to survey because these include areas where basic research still remains to be done. However, biographies are indexed by area of endeavor as well as by name so that readers can identify individuals in a particular field.

A project of this magnitude could not have reached completion without the valuable assistance of many people. First, we are extraordinarily grateful to the hundreds of contributors who graciously volunteered their time and expertise to research and write entries. Foremost among them are the members of our editorial board who helped to shape the content of the encyclopedia, suggested contributors, occasionally reviewed entries in their fields, and wrote entries themselves. Then there are many reference librarians and archivists who provided information and guided contributors to appropriate sources. We appreciate their help.

We were fortunate to work with professional staff who were dedicated to the project. Michael Feldberg, director of the American Jewish Historical Society, set the encyclopedia in motion and remained committed to its progress. Without Ralph Carlson's vision, the encyclopedia would not have come into being. First as publisher and finally as project director, he shepherded the complex process of producing these two volumes. At Routledge, Inc., Colin Jones, president, and his associates, in particular Maud Andrew, have worked energetically to produce the encyclopedia. Our managing editors Lisa Hacken, Sarah Rosen, and

Jonathan Korzen effectively carried out their responsibilities for coordinating the many contributors and their entries. Michele Siegel, a Vassar College Ford Fellow, provided valuable aid over one summer. Without the indefatigable efforts of Harriet Feinberg, who matched many entries with appropriate contributors, the encyclopedia would not have been completed in so short a time.

Two sources generously supported publication of the encyclopedia at critical moments. The Hassenfeld Family Foundation underwrote the first staff positions that led to the initial organization of the project. Barbara Dobkin came forward near the end of the project with a gift that permitted the encyclopedia to survive.

We are most grateful to them for acknowledging the significance of this work.

We want to conclude by thanking members of our families, who wrote entries, offered advice, encouraged us, and sustained us when the going got rough. We found the task of creating this encyclopedia to be enormously challenging and rewarding. We were impressed at the number of extraordinary women we met. We trust that readers will share our excitement in meeting these women and interpreting their lives.

Paula E. Hyman
Deborah Dash Moore

Sponsor's Preface

Founded in 1892, the American Jewish Historical Society is the nation's oldest ethno-religious historical organization. For more than a century, the Society has served as the primary preserver and interpreter of the Jewish historical experience in America. Its massive archives and outstanding library have served as the basis for much of the important scholarship in the field of American Jewish history. The Society's publications, including its quarterly journal and various monographs, have served to establish American Jewish history as a field of scholarly inquiry.

Thus, it is in keeping with a tradition of leadership in the field that the Society sponsors this pathbreaking two-volume historical encyclopedia on the history of American Jewish women. It is also with great pride that the Society joins with Routledge, Inc., editors Paula E. Hyman and Deborah Dash Moore, the editorial board and the contributors to bring the scholarship and learning contained in these pages to light. It is our goal and our hope that the study of American Jewish women's contributions to American and Jewish life will forever more be fully appreciated.

The Society extends particular gratitude to Paula E. Hyman and Deborah Dash Moore. This project required enormous energy, perseverance, commitment, exactitude and good will. Both editors brought extraordinary amount of each of these virtues to the project. Future generations of scholars in American, Jewish, and women's history owe them an enormous debt.

The Society is very grateful to the Hassenfeld Family Foundation for its essential and substantial support at the inception of this project. Without the Foundation's commitment, this project would never have been undertaken. Barbara Dobkin helped sustain the project at a critical moment, when without additional support years of labor and creativity might have been for naught.

The original idea to create this encyclopedia was Ralph Carlson's. His vision was that the publication would present new knowledge, be filled with remarkable images, and pay tribute to an extraordinarily creative and underappreciated group: American Jewish women. With the help of many others, Ralph has been able to realize his vision. The Society is grateful to him for making us central to its realization.

Waltham, MA
August, 1997

Reader's Guide

This encyclopedia consists of 910 entries, 800 of which are biographies of individual Jewish women and 110 of which deal with other topics. These two types of entries are integrated in this set and are presented in one alphabetical sequence. There is a complete list of all the entries in the front of this volume.

If you are interested in knowing about women in specific fields of endeavor (music, education, etc.), you should consult the Classified List of Biographical Entries at the end of Volume II.

The bibliographies at the end of the entries provide the sources the author drew upon for information and also provide suggested materials for additional reading. Commonly cited sources are abbreviated and a list of these abbreviations is included at the front of this volume.

The names of entries that are mentioned in other entries are printed in small caps the first time they occur in an entry.

Abbreviations

The following abbreviations are used for sources
that are frequently cited in the bibliographies to the entries.

AJA   Hebrew Union College—American Jewish Archives. *American Jewish Archives.* Volume 1 (1948) to present.

AI   *American Israelite*

AJH   American Jewish Historical Society. *American Jewish History.* Volume 68 (1978) to present.

AJHQ   American Jewish Historical Society. *American Jewish Historical Quarterly.* Volumes 51–67. 1961–1978

AJYB   Jewish Publication Society of America. *The American Jewish Year Book.* Philadelphia: American Jewish Committee, 1899 to present.

BDEAJ   Rosenbloom, Joseph R. *A Biographical Dictionary of Early American Jews.* Lexington: University of Kentucky Press, 1960.

BEOAJ   Glassman, Leo M., ed. *Biographical Encyclopaedia of American Jews.* New York: Maurice Jacobs & Leo M. Glassman, 1935.

CCARYB   Central Conference of American Rabbis. *Yearbook of the Central Conference of American Rabbis.* New York: Central Conference of American Rabbis, 1891–.

DAB   Johnson, Allen et. al., eds. *Dictionary of American Biography.* New York; Scribners', 1946–.

EJ   *Encyclopedia Judaica.* Jerusalem: Keter Publishing House Ltd, 1971–72.

JE   Singer, Isidore, ed. *The Jewish Encyclopedia.* New York: Funk and Wagnalls, 1901–1906.

NAW   James, Edward T., et. al, eds. *Notable American Women, 1607–1950.* Cambridge, MA: Harvard University Press, 1971.

NAW: modern   Sicherman, Barbara and Carol Hurd Green, eds. *Notable American Women, The Modern Period, A Biographical Dictionary.* Cambridge, MA: Harvard University Press, 1980.

NYTimes   *New York Times*

PAJHS   American Jewish Historical Society. *Publications of the American Jewish Historical Society.* Volumes 1–50. 1893–1960.

UJE   Landman, Isaac, ed. *The Universal Jewish Encyclopedia.* New York: The Universal Jewish Encyclopedia, 1939–1943.

WWIAJ   *Who's Who in American Jewry, 1926.* New York: Jewish Biographical Bureau, Inc., 1927.

   Who's Who in American Jewry, 1928. 2nd ed. New York: Jewish Biographical Bureau, Inc., 1928.

   Simons, John, ed. *Who's Who in American Jewry,* Volume 3, 1938–1939. New York: National News Association, Inc., 1938.

WWWIA   *Who Was Who in America.* Volumes 1–8. Chicago: Marquis, 1943–1985.

Photo Acknowledgments and Credits

Much of the photo research that made possible the splendid variety of images in these volumes was carried out by Hillary Mac Austin, Kirsten Fermaglich, Felicia Herman, Laura Lieber, and Adam Sol. We wish to thank them for their dedication and imagination. Curators at several photo archives provided help above and beyond the call of duty. We would like to single out for praise Kathy Spray at the American Jewish Archives, Dawne Baer at the American Jewish Historical Society, Linda Mack Schloff at the Jewish Historical Society of the Upper Midwest, Marie-Hélène Gold at the Arthur and Elizabeth Schlesinger Library on the History of Women in America, Joy Kingsolver at the Chicago Jewish Archives, Erika Gottfried of the Tamiment Institute Library, and Laura O'Hara at the Western Jewish History Center.

We have listed below the addresses of institutions with photographic collections on American Jewish history, which we drew upon for the *Encyclopedia*.

Jacob Rader Marcus Center
of the American Jewish Archives
3101 Clifton Avenue
Cincinnati, Ohio 45220-2488

American Jewish Historical Society
2 Thornton Road
Waltham, MA 02154

Chicago Jewish Archives
Spertus Institute of Jewish Studies

618 South Michigan Avenue
Chicago, IL 60605

Western Jewish History Center
Judah L. Magnes Museum
2911 Russell Street
Berkeley, CA 94705

YIVO Institute for Jewish Research
555 West 57th Street, Suite 1100
New York, NY 10019

Three sources were especially useful to us for images of American Jewish women. They are:

The Arthur and Elizabeth Schlesinger
Library of the History of Women in America
Radcliffe College
Ten Garden Street
Cambridge, MA 02138

Bettye Lane Photography
Studio 501 D
463 West Street
New York, NY 10014

Joan Roth Photography
215 East 80th Street
New York, NY 10021

Photographs which we secured from contributors to the *Encyclopedia* or from other institutions are so credited. Photos without credits are from private collections.

Jewish Women in America

A

ABARBANELL, LINA (1879–1963)

Though she sang but one season and one role at New York's Metropolitan Opera—Hänsel, in the company's first staging of Humperdinck's *Hänsel und Gretel* (premiere: November 25, 1905)—Lina Abarbanell's place in American opera was secured when Leonard Bernstein dropped her name in the scat chorus of his one-act *Trouble in Tahiti*. This opera is dedicated to fellow composer and mentor Marc Blitzstein, who had married Abarbanell's daughter Eva in 1933. After becoming the best-known exponent of Viennese operetta style in America, Abarbanell made an effective transition to American theater, contributing to it every talent for which her thorough European training had prepared her.

Lina Abarbanell was born on January 3, 1879, in Berlin, Germany, to Paul and Marie Abarbanell. A descendant of an eminent Sephardi family, Paul Abarbanell was a leading theater conductor. His daughter first sang in public at the age of seven. She later received both dramatic and vocal training, and appeared in numerous civic theaters in Germany. At fifteen, Abarbanell made her debut with the Berlin Court Opera, where she sang the role of Adele in *Die Fledermaus* over a hundred times. She performed all over Europe and gave command recitals before Austrian, Bavarian, and Persian royalty.

Abarbanell's success lay in lighter musical fare and operetta. Composers such as Oscar Straus, Franz Lehár, and Edmund Eysler wrote for her expressive soubrette voice. She made about twenty recordings in 1903 and 1904, only four of which appear to have survived. In 1905, Heinrich Conried, general manager of the Metropolitan Opera, invited her to sing the role of Hänsel and to perform at his Irving Place Theater, where she delighted his German-speaking audiences.

After that season, Abarbanell and her husband, journalist Eduard Goldbeck, settled in America with their daughter Eva (b. 1901). For a time she flirted with Christian Science; from a Jewish point of view she can be considered totally assimilated.

Abarbanell toured the country for almost thirty years, singing her way through frothy Viennese-inspired confections such as *The Geisha, Madame Sherry, The Red Canary, The Silver Swan, Flora Bella, The Grand Duke, Enter Madame,* and *The Student Prince.* Sheet music publishers placed her photograph on the covers of numbers such as "Every Little Movement Has a Meaning All Its Own," which she had popularized. Her greatest triumph came in the role of Hanna in Lehár's *The Merry Widow*, which she played for weeks on end, the press doting on her at every turn.

Abarbanell stopped singing in 1934 after the death of her husband, but she did not leave the theater. She became a well-known casting director, Broadway producer, and occasional director, for years as partner to Dwight Deere Wiman. Among the shows she cast were *I Married an Angel, Street Scene,*

A queen of operettas and lighter musical fare, Lina Abarbanell was a European success before taking America by storm early in the twentieth century. [New York Public Library]

the famous *Porgy and Bess* that toured the world in the early 1950s, and the film version of *Carmen Jones*.

Marc Blitzstein and Abarbanell remained close friends long after Eva, Blitzstein's wife and Abar-

banell's daughter, died in 1936. Abarbanell cast Blitzstein's opera *Regina* in 1949 and his musical *Juno* in 1959, when she had already passed the age of eighty.

Lina Abarbanell continued working in the theater almost until the day she died, on January 6, 1963.

BIBLIOGRAPHY

Abarbanell, Lina. Papers. Theater Collection, New York Public Library, Lincoln Center; *AJYB* 24:112; Goldbeck, Eva. Papers. Marc Blitzstein Collection, State Historical Society of Wisconsin, Madison; Gordon, Eric A. *Mark the Music: The Life and Work of Marc Blitzstein* (1989), and "The Met's First Hänsel." *Opera News* (December 24, 1983): 30–31; Obituary. *NYTimes*, January 8, 1963, 8:7; *UJE*; *WWWIA* 6.

ERIC A. GORDON

ABRAMOWICZ, DINA (b. 1909)

Renowned for her remarkable skills as a reference librarian, Dina Abramowicz has built an impressive library collection at the YIVO Institute for Jewish Research, where she has worked since 1947. Her scholarship and expertise, praised by readers and writers alike, have been celebrated by both library and cultural achievement awards.

Born in Vilna, Russia (today Lithuania), on May 8, 1909, Abramowicz was raised in a culturally rich, multilingual home. Her father, Hirsh Abramowicz, was an educator, Yiddish author, and member of the Jewish Labor Bund. Her mother, Anna (Schreiber) Abramowicz, came from a prominent family of worldly *maskilim*. Abramowicz attended Yiddish and Polish gymnasia in Vilna, and received an M.A. in humanities (philosophy, Polish literature) from Stefan Batory University (1936). She was assistant to the head librarian of the [Jewish] Central Children's Library of Vilna (1939–1941), and worked in the Vilna Ghetto Library during the Nazi occupation (1941–1943). After the ghetto was liquidated, she escaped from a deportation train and served with a Jewish partisan unit until liberation in 1944. Her mother perished at Treblinka in 1943; her younger sister survived the war in France, and her father was already on a visit to the United States in the summer of 1939.

In 1946, when Abramowicz came to the United States, she resumed her career as a librarian, first at Smith College from 1946 to 1947 and subsequently at the YIVO Institute for Jewish Research. In 1953, she received an M.S. from the Columbia University School of Library Service. Her positions in the YIVO library have included assistant librarian (1947–1962), head librarian (1962–1987), and reference librarian. Abramowicz's areas of expertise include Yiddish literature (including literature in English translation and children's literature), modern Eastern European Jewish history and culture, and the Nazi Holocaust. She has published numerous studies, bibliographies, book reviews, and topical articles.

During her tenure at YIVO, she has greatly expanded the library's collection, adding books and journals in many languages. Her professional memberships include the American Library Association, the Association for Jewish Studies, and the Association of Jewish Libraries.

In recognition of her outstanding ability to assist readers—whether in person, over the phone, or by mail, Abramowicz has been awarded the Dr. Chaim Zhitlowsky Prize (Yiddisher Kultur Farband, 1987), the Dr. Berl Frimer Prize for Cultural Achievement (Congress for Jewish Culture, 1992), and the Leonard Wertheimer Multicultural Public Library Service Award (Public Library Association of the American Library Association, 1994).

SELECTED WORKS BY DINA ABRAMOWICZ

"Ethnic Survival in the New World: Yiddish Juvenilia." *Wilson Library Bulletin* 50, no. 2 (1975): 138–145; "Di Geto-Biblyotek in Vilne" [The ghetto library of Vilna]. In *Lite (Lithuania)*. Vol. 1, edited by Mendel Sudarsky, Uriah Katzenelenbogen, and J. Kissin (1951), cols. 1671–1678; "The World of My Parents: Reminiscences." *YIVO Annual* 23 (1996): 105–157; "The YIVO Library." *Jewish Book Annual* 24 (1967–1968): 87–102; "Yom Kippur, 1941–1945: Memories of the Vilna Ghetto." *Jewish Frontier* 14, no. 1 (1947): 18–22.

BIBLIOGRAPHY

Axelrod, Toby. "People: Like Books in Her Care, Librarian Is a Survivor." *The Jewish Week* (November 9, 1990): 2, 39; Sharlet, Jeff. "Keeper of a Civilization." *The Book Peddler/Der Pakn-treger* 21 (Spring 1996): 9–21.

ZACHARY M. BAKER

ABRAMOWICZ, IRMA MAY
see MAY, IRMA

ABZUG, BELLA (b. 1920)

Born in the Bronx on July 24, 1920, Bella (Savitzky) Abzug predated women's right to vote by one month. A fighter for justice and peace, equal rights, human dignity, environmental integrity, and sustainable development, Bella Abzug has advanced human goals and political alliances worldwide.

Most recently, as cocreator and president of the Women's Environmental and Development Organization (WEDO), a global organization, Abzug galvanized and helped transform the United Nations agenda regarding women and their concerns for human rights, economic justice, population, development, and the environment. WEDO represents the culmination of her lifelong career as public activist and stateswoman.

Known by her colleagues as a "passionate perfectionist," Bella's idealism and activism grew out of childhood influences and experiences. From her earliest years, she understood the nature of power and the fact that politics is not an isolated, individualist adventure. A natural leader, although a girl among competitive boys, she delighted in her prowess at marbles, or "immies." When the boys tried to beat her or steal her

To generations of researchers in Jewish studies, the name of Dina Abramowicz was synonymous with "Jewish librarian." She was the reference librarian who knew where to find the answers. [YIVO Institute]

*As a young teenager, Bella Abzug delighted her elders with the brilliance of her prayers
and her ability to read Hebrew and daven. She is shown here in 1991 during the famous "Feminist Seder,"
which had been taking place every year since 1976. On her right is* PHYLLIS CHESLER *and
on her left is* LETTY COTTIN POGREBIN, *two of the original "Seder Sisters." [Joan Roth]*

marbles, Abzug defended herself fiercely with un-matched skill. She also played checkers, traded base-ball cards, climbed trees, became a graffiti artist, and understood the nuances, corners, and risks of city streets, which were her playground.

In synagogue with her maternal grandfather, Wolf Taklefsky, who was her babysitter and first men-tor, Bella's beautiful voice and keen memory delighted her elders with the brilliance of her prayers, and her ability to read Hebrew and daven [pray]. Although routinely dispatched to the women's place behind the *mechitzan* [curtain separating women from men in a place of prayer], by the time she was eight, she was an outstanding student in the Talmud Torah school she attended, and a community star.

Her Hebrew school teacher, Levi Soshuk, recruited her to a left-wing labor Zionist group, Hashomer Hatzair [the young guard]. By the time she was eleven, Bella and her gang of socialist Zionists planned to go to Israel together as a kibbutz community. In the meantime, they were inseparable and traveled throughout New York City, hiked in the countryside, danced and sang all night, went to free concerts, museums, the theater, picnics, and meetings. Above all, they raised money for a Jewish homeland—with Abzug in the lead. At subway stops, she gave impassioned speeches, and people tended to give generously to the earnest, well-spoken girl. From her first gang, Bella learned about the power of alliances, unity, and alternative movements.

Hitler came to power the year her father Emanuel died, and Bella emerged as an outspoken thirteen-year-old girl-child willing to break the rules. Prohibited by tradition from saying kaddish for her father in synagogue, Bella did so anyway. Every morning before school for a year, she attended synagogue and davened. The congregants looked askance and never did approve, but nobody ever stopped her. She just did what she needed to do for her father, who had no son—and learned a lesson for life: Be bold, be brazen, be true to your heart. She advised others: "People may not like it, but no one will stop you."

Bella never doubted that her father would have approved. Manny Savitzky adored his daughters. The butcher whose shop bore his personal mark of protest during and after World War I—"The Live and Let Live Meat Market" in the Clinton-Chelsea section of Manhattan—had a profound impact on his daughter's vision. Protest was acceptable; activism took many forms. After all, he had learned to tolerate Bella's pack of socialist Zionist friends who kept her out all night from the age of eleven. There was always music in her parents' home. Her father sang with gusto, her sister, Helene (five years older), played the piano—the grand piano that filled the parlor—and Bella played the violin. Every week, the entire family, including grandparents, congregated around music, led in song by her father.

Bella's mother also supported her rebellion—all her rebellions. Esther Savitzky appreciated her younger daughter's talents and encouraged her every interest. By the age of thirteen, a leader in the crusade for women's rights, equal space, dignity, and empow-

erment for girls was in active training. According to her mother, "Battling Bella" was born bellowing. A spirited tomboy with music in her heart and politics in her soul, beautiful, energetic Bella was vastly popular, and studious.

She continued violin lessons through high school. From Talmud Torah she went to Florence Marshall Hebrew High School after classes at Walton, and to the Teachers Institute at the Jewish Theological Seminary after classes at HUNTER COLLEGE. She earned additional money for her family by teaching Hebrew, and also committed herself to political activities. Elected class president at Walton High School in 1937 and student government president of Hunter College in 1941, Bella made a profound impression on teachers, contemporaries, and history.

As student council president at Hunter College, she opposed the Rapp-Coudert committee, which sought to crush public education and was on a witch-

The first woman elected to Congress on a women's rights/peace platform, Bella Abzug cast her first vote for the Equal Rights Amendment. [Library of Congress]

hunt against "subversive" faculty. A political science major, Bella was active in the American Student Union and was an early and ardent champion of civil rights and civil liberties. At Hunter, she was at the center of a permanent circle of friends who remained political activists and lifelong champions of causes for women, peace, and justice. Journalist Mim Kelber, who first met Bella at Walton, was editor of Hunter's student newspaper the *Bulletin*, remained a political partner, cofounded WEDO, and now edits its impressive newsletter and publication series.

With her brilliant college record and leadership awards, Bella won a scholarship to Columbia University Law School. (Harvard, her first choice, turned her down—its law school did not accept women until 1952.) Her record at Columbia was splendid. She became an editor of the *Law Review*, and her reputation as tough, combative, diligent, and dedicated grew. In addition, two new enthusiasms entered Bella's life during law school: poker and Martin Abzug.

She met Martin Abzug while visiting relatives in Miami after her graduation from Hunter. At a Yehudi Menuhin concert for Russian war relief, she saw a young man staring and smiling at her. They met; they dated; he left for the service; they corresponded. Upon his return, he wanted to party. She wanted to study. He would meet her at midnight at the law library. A writer, Martin Abzug knew how to type; she never did. Martin typed her briefs and promised that even when they married and had children she would continue to work—her major hesitation about marriage.

They married on June 4, 1944. The son and partner of an affluent shirt manufacturer (A Betta Blouse Company), who published two novels and later became a stockbroker, Martin encouraged all of his wife's interests and ambitions—including those that were demonstrably dangerous during the McCarthyite years of the Cold War. He admired her integrity, vision, and combative style, and until his death remained her steadfast supporter. For forty-two years, their marriage, based on love, respect, and a generosity of spirit unrivaled in political circles, enabled Bella's activities.

Immediately after law school, Bella joined a labor law firm that represented union locals. Routinely overlooked when she entered an office to represent the United Auto Workers, or the Mine, Mill and Smelting Workers, or local restaurant workers, she decided to wear hats. Hats made all the difference when it came to recognition and even respect, and they became her trademark.

For fifteen years, Abzug, her husband, and their two daughters—Eve Gail, called Eegee, born in 1949, now a sculptor and social worker; and Isobel Jo, called Liz, born in 1952, now an attorney and political consultant—lived in Mount Vernon, an integrated suburb that the parents believed the girls would benefit from. When the family moved to Greenwich Village, a center of urban activity, everybody was happier.

During the 1950s, Bella Abzug was one of very few independent attorneys willing to take "Communist" cases. With Martin's encouragement, she opened her own office, and defended teachers, entertainment, radio, and Hollywood personalities assaulted during the witch-hunt.

She also defended Willie McGee. In an internationally celebrated case, McGee, a black Mississippian, was falsely accused of raping a white woman with whom he had a long-term consensual relationship. Abzug appealed the case before the Supreme Court and achieved two stays of execution when she argued that "Negroes were systematically excluded from jury service." But she did not achieve a change of venue, and after the third trial and conviction, all appeals were denied.

On her trip south to Jackson for the special hearing board appointed by Mississippi's governor, Abzug never thought much about her personal safety, even though she was pregnant at the time. She realized she was in trouble, however, when the hotel room she had booked was denied her and no other room made available. When a taxi driver offered to take her fifteen miles out into the country to find a place to stay, she returned to Jackson's bus station and spent an unsettling night. At court the next morning, she argued fervently for six hours on behalf of racial justice, protesting the clear conspiracy to deny Willie McGee's civil rights, as well as the long tradition of race prejudice and unfair discrimination. To cancel his death sentence, she argued in 1950, would restore faith in U.S. democracy throughout the world. Despite worldwide publicity, protest marches, and Abzug's fervent plea to prevent another legal lynching, McGee went to the electric chair. Abzug had a miscarriage, but her dedication to the cause of justice was strengthened by her days in Mississippi.

In 1961, Abzug and her Hunter circle (Mim Kelber, AMY SWERDLOW, and Judy Lerner) joined others (including Dagmar Wilson, Claire Reid, and Lyla Hoffman) to create Women Strike for Peace. For the next decade, they lobbied for a nuclear test ban treaty, mobilized against Strontium-90 in milk, and protested against the war in Indochina. During the 1960s, Abzug became a prominent national speaker against the poverty, racism, and violence which mocked the promise of democracy in America.

A leading reform Democrat, a successful attorney, a popular grass-roots activist, Abzug was urged to run for Congress, which she agreed to do at the age of fifty in 1970. Stunning and galvanizing, with her hats and her homilies, she became a household symbol for dramatic change. Representing Greenwich Village, Little Italy, the Lower East Side, the West Side, and Chelsea, she was the first woman elected to Congress on a women's rights/peace platform. New York agreed, "This woman's place is in the House—the House of Representatives." And so, her daughter Eve proclaimed: "We got her out of our house and into your House."

A creative powerhouse for good, Abzug understood "pork," alliances, and the contradictions of leadership. Representing women, justice, and peace, she cast her first vote for the Equal Rights Amendment. As a member of the Committee on Public Works and Transportation, she brought more than $6 billion to New York State in economic development, sewage treatment, and mass transit, including ramps for people with disabilities and buses for the elderly.

As chair of the Subcommittee on Government Information and Individual Rights, she coauthored three important pieces of legislation: the Freedom of Information Act, the Government in the Sunshine Act, and the Right to Privacy Act. Abzug's bills exposed many secret government activities to public scrutiny for the first time. They allowed her and others to conduct inquiries into covert and illegal activities of the CIA, FBI, and other government agencies. The first member of Congress to call for Nixon's impeachment, Abzug helped journalists, historians, and citizens to combat the disinformation, misinformation, and generally abusive tactics that marked so much of the Cold War and blocked for so long the path toward human rights.

Above all, Abzug achieved splendid victories for women. She initiated the congressional caucus on women's issues, helped organize the National Women's Political Caucus, and served as chief strategist for the Democratic Women's Committee, which achieved equal representation for women in all elective and appointive posts, including presidential conventions. She wrote the first law banning discrimination against women in obtaining credit, credit cards, loans, and mortgages, and introduced pioneering bills on comprehensive child care, Social Security for homemakers, family planning, and abortion rights. In 1975, she introduced an amendment to the Civil Rights Act to include gay and lesbian rights.

Reelected for three terms, Abzug served from 1971 to 1977 and was acknowledged by a *U.S. News & World Report* survey of House members as the "third most influential" House member. In a 1977 Gallup poll, she was named one of the twenty most influential women of the world. That pipe-smoking Republican lady of the House, Millicent Fenwick, once said that she had two heroes, women she admired above all: Eleanor Roosevelt and Bella Abzug. They shared one thing, Fenwick said: They meant it! Women of vast integrity, they spoke from the heart, and they spoke truth to power. Although she agreed politically with Abzug on virtually nothing, Fenwick explained, Abzug was her ideal.

After Abzug was defeated in a four-way primary race for the Senate in 1976 by less than one percent, President Carter appointed her chair of the National Commission on the Observance of International Women's Year, and later cochair of the National Advisory Commission for Women.

Her hats are a metaphor for the way Bella Abzug has lived her life: boldly, championing the causes of women's rights, the environment, and world peace. [Bettye Lane]

Active in the UN Decade for Women conferences in Mexico City (1975), Copenhagen (1980), and Nairobi (1985), Abzug became an esteemed leader of the international women's movement. She also led the fight against the obnoxious Zionism Is Racism resolution passed in 1975, which was finally repealed in 1985 in Nairobi. Long active in supporting Israel, especially in Congress and in Israeli-U.S.-Palestine peace efforts, she insisted that Zionism was a liberation movement. Always controversial, her definition of Zionism embraced the international peace movement represented in Israel by Shulamith Aloni and others who promoted the peace process.

During this time, Abzug's not-for-profit advocacy organization, Women USA Fund, organized with Brownie Ledbetter, Patsy Mink, Gloria Steinem, Maxine Waters, and Mim Kelber, published educational materials and created the Women's Foreign Policy Council, which led to the creation of WEDO.

In November 1991, WEDO convened the World Women's Congress for a Healthy Planet. Fifteen hundred women from eighty-three nations met in Miami, Florida, to produce the Women's Action Agenda for the twenty-first century. This agenda became the platform for action at UN conferences preparing for the Fourth World Congress on Women (held in September 1995 in Beijing) and created an international women's caucus that transformed the thinking and policies of the UN community. Since 1991, Abzug has promoted the program around the world.

In the face of personal medical challenges, including breast cancer and heart disease, Abzug continues to confront global problems of poverty, discrimination, and the violent fallout of this "bloodiest century in human history." As chair of New York City's Commission on the Status of Women (1993–1995), and in partnership with Greenpeace and WEDO, she launched a national grass-roots campaign against cancer called "Women, Cancer and the Environment: Action for Prevention."

She eats macrobiotically, swims regularly, and plays poker fiercely, maintains a loving relationship with her daughters, with whom she shares a vacation home, and entertains her countless and loving friends (her "extended family") with her great good humor and her love of song. Her friendships with people from Hollywood to New York are legion. Woody Allen directed her in *Manhattan*, she played alongside Shirley MacLaine in *Madame Sousatzka*, and her magical rendition of "Falling in Love Again" inspired feminist troubadour Sandy Rapp to compose a ballad, "When Bella Sings Marlena." One line of the song reads, "On the second refrain of 'moths to the flame,' spirits fill the room."

Shameless about enlisting her friends and colleagues to her causes, Abzug is known for her boundless generosity. An indefatigable force for global survival, her mission, her challenge, and her legacy are clear:

> It's not about women joining the polluted stream. It's about cleaning the stream, changing the stagnant pools into fresh, flowing waters.
> Our struggle is [against] violence, intolerance, inequality, injustice.
> Our struggle is about creating sustainable lives, and attainable dreams.
> Our struggle is about creating violence-free families, . . . violence-free streets, violence-free borders.
> Our call is to stop nuclear pollution. Our call is to build real democracies not hypocracies. Our call is to nurture and strengthen all families. Our call is to build communities, not only markets. Our call is to scale the great wall around women everywhere.

Bella Abzug's understanding of the need for an international network of women working across this troubled planet for decency, justice, and peace has fortified a global sisterhood never before imagined. With a song in her throat and a very high heart, Abzug is a boundless source of hope for the future. She lives every day to the fullest and blesses every day with the spiritual fervor of her responsibility and commitment to all people—one life, one weave.

SELECTED WORKS BY BELLA ABZUG
Bella!, edited by Mel Ziegler (1972); *Gender Gap: Bella Abzug's Guide to Political Power for American Women*, with Mim Kelber (1984)

BIBLIOGRAPHY
Faber, Doris. *Bella Abzug* (1976); Swerdlow, Amy. *Women Strike for Peace: Traditional Motherhood and Radical Politics in the 1960s* (1993).

BLANCHE WIESEN COOK

ACKERMAN, PAULA (1893–1989)

At the turn of the twentieth century, a young girl from Pensacola, Florida, named Paula Herskovitz dreamed of one day becoming a medical doctor. Believing that the medical profession was unsuitable

In 1950, Paula Ackerman became the first woman to assume spiritual leadership of a mainstream American Jewish congregation. [American Jewish Archives]

Valedictorian of her high school class in 1911, Ackerman was offered a scholarship to Sophie Newcomb College in New Orleans, but because of her father's refusal to let her pursue a medical career, she declined it. Financial difficulties later required that she help support her family, so she became a private music instructor and high school Latin and math teacher. She also taught at Beth-El, led the congregational choir, and began a seven-year courtship with its newly hired rabbi, Dr. William Ackerman. Married in 1919, they soon left Pensacola for a better paying rabbinic position in Natchez, Mississippi. In 1924, they moved with their fifteen-month-old son, Billy, to Meridian, Mississippi, which for almost fifty years remained Paula Ackerman's home.

During her husband's tenure as rabbi of Temple Beth Israel, a Reform congregation in Meridian with a membership of approximately 150 families, Paula Ackerman taught preconfirmation classes and led religious services when her husband was ill or out of town. Still, she was unprepared for the congregation's request, less than a month after William Ackerman's death in November 1950, that she succeed him. Her initial response was that they should hire a formally trained rabbi with greater Judaic knowledge. Having received informal permission from Maurice Eisendrath, president of the Union of American Hebrew Congregations (the Reform Movement), the congregation persisted, and, by January, she accepted, viewing the invitation as both a divine call to service and an opportunity "to plant a seed for enlarged activity for the Jewish woman." Soon after, Eisendrath withdrew his approval, maintaining that in discussing the matter with other rabbis he had concluded that congregational leaders unqualified to discharge full rabbinical duties would create more problems than they would solve. His letter, apparently, was ignored, for, as the congregation's president had already informed him, in the eyes of "practically all of the members of our congregation she is qualified, and we want her."

From January 1951 through the fall of 1953, Paula Ackerman served as Temple Beth Israel's spiritual leader, conducting services, preaching, teaching, and performing marriages, funerals, and conversions. In so doing, she achieved the distinction of becoming the first woman to assume religious leadership of a mainstream American Jewish congregation. Attracting international attention from the press, she was erroneously labeled "America's first Lady Rabbi."

After retirement, Ackerman remained active on city, state, and national religious and cultural boards and traveled throughout the United States, lecturing

for women, her father insisted that she abandon her dream. Yet decades later, she embarked upon a career he no doubt would have found equally unsuitable: she became a spiritual leader.

Paula (Herskovitz) Ackerman was born on December 7, 1893, to Joseph and Dora Herskovitz. Ackerman later described her mother as a pious woman who imbued her home with Jewish teachings and values. Her father, raised in a traditionally religious home in Romania, initially intended to provide a Hebrew education for his sons only. Having long since abandoned the Orthodoxy of his youth, however, and recognizing his daughter's great desire to study, he hired a local Orthodox rabbi to tutor his three children to supplement their weekly religious education at Temple Beth-El, the Reform congregation of which they were members.

on religious themes. In 1962, she agreed to become spiritual leader of Temple Beth-El in her hometown of Pensacola until a new rabbi could be found. Six months later, she returned full-time to Meridian, subsequently moving to Pensacola (1970), Atlanta (1981), and Thomaston, Georgia (1985).

In 1986, at a special ceremony held at The Temple in Atlanta, the Union of American Hebrew Congregations formally recognized her pioneering contribution to Jewish communal life. Paula Ackerman died in Thomaston on January 12, 1989.

BIBLIOGRAPHY

Ackerman, Paula. Papers. American Jewish Archives, Cincinnati, Ohio, and Sermons (1915–1953). Private possession of Dr. William Ackerman; *Reform Judaism in America: A Biographical Dictionary and Sourcebook.* Edited by Kerry Olitzky, Lance Sussman, and Malcolm Stern (1993); Umansky, Ellen M. "Reform's Lost Woman Rabbi: An Interview with Paula Ackerman." *Genesis* 2, no. 17 (June/July 1986) 3: 18–20; Umansky, Ellen M., and Dianne Ashton, eds. *Four Centuries of Jewish Women's Spirituality: A Sourcebook* (1992).

ELLEN M. UMANSKY

ADLER, BARBARA OCHS (1903–1971)

A proud United States citizen and active civic leader, Barbara Ochs Adler was a committed advocate for social welfare. Her life's work, which combined important contributions to both Jewish and American social service organizations, paints a portrait of a woman who strongly identified herself as both Jewish and American.

Barbara (Stettheimer) Adler was born on January 14, 1903, daughter of Walter Stettheimer of San Francisco. Her father was a prominent businessman, and her parents were quite active in the San Francisco social scene. Adler grew up in California and attended Stanford University, where she studied theater and drama.

In 1922, six months before graduation from Stanford, she left school and married Julius Ochs Adler, who at the time was a major in the army reserve and the vice president and treasurer of the New York Times Company. The marriage brought Barbara Adler to New York City, where she developed many new interests and was profoundly influenced by her husband's illustrious military career. Julius Adler, born in Chattanooga, Tennessee, in 1892, traced his southern origins to Captain Julius Ochs, who came to the United States from Bavaria, and fought in the Mexican and Civil Wars, later migrating to Tennessee from Ohio in 1865. Major General Adler saw active duty in both world wars, received many honors and awards, and served as adviser to President Theodore Roosevelt. His father, Harry Clay Adler, was chairman of the board of directors and general manager of the *Chattanooga Times.* His mother, Ada Ochs Adler, was the sister of Adolph S. Ochs, who founded the *New York Times.*

Adler and her husband were members of Temple Emanu-El in New York City. Adler was a member of the executive committee of the Jewish Board of Guardians, which is presently the Jewish Board of Family and Children's Services. For many years, she represented this agency on the board of trustees of the Federation of Jewish Philanthropies of New York. Her work with these important Jewish philanthropic organizations revealed her great concern for the social betterment of Jews in need.

However, Adler also extended her philanthropic and civic efforts toward institutions and organizations that were not specifically Jewish in scope. During World War II, she served as chair of the New York City Defense Recreation Committee, a group that provided free entertainment to military servicemen passing through the city. She took great pride in her affiliation with this committee, and derived much satisfaction from its activities.

Adler was also fascinated by criminology, possessing a special interest in prison management and the treatment of criminal offenders. She was vice president of the Correctional Association of New York, which was successor to the Prison Association. As well, she served as a board member of the National Probation and Parole Association, and worked with the Social Service Bureau of the old magistrate's courts of the city. Through her involvement with these organizations, which were responsible for overseeing various aspects of the criminal justice system, Adler was able to participate actively in prison reform. In 1935, New York governor Herbert H. Lehman appointed her to the board of visitors of Westfield State Farm, a reformatory for girls at Bedford Hills, New York. In 1941, she was elected president of the correctional facility, and served in that capacity until approximately 1955.

Major General Adler died on October 3, 1955. The couple had three children: two daughters, Barbara A. Katzander and Nancy J. Adler, and a son, Julius Ochs Adler, Jr. After her husband's death, Adler continued her own philanthropic projects and took on some that were especially important to him, most notably the Lafayette Fellowship Foundation, which provided grants to selected French students to study in American universities.

Barbara Ochs Adler died in New York City on June 3, 1971, several days after suffering a cerebral hemorrhage at her home at 834 Fifth Avenue. She was sixty-eight years old. Her accomplishments as a civic leader and philanthropist bear witness to a life that, through social action, brought together both American and Jewish ideals.

BIBLIOGRAPHY

AJYB 73 (1972): 629; *Current Biography* (June 1948); *Current Biography Yearbook* (1956); Obituary. *NYTimes*, June 4, 1971, 38:1.

ANDREA BETH LIEBER

ADLER, CELIA (1889–1979)

Celia Adler's popularity as a Yiddish actress made her a force in the Yiddish art theater movement, where she succeeded despite her lack of a powerful male protector. She was acclaimed for her ability to combine pathos and charm, and those who witnessed her performances especially remember her talent for comedy.

Celia Adler's life was shadowed by her parents' divorce and the resulting feud that spilled over into the entire New York Yiddish theater world. She was born in New York on December 6, 1889, to Dina Shtettin Adler, who had left her Orthodox home to join the theater and who became the second wife of Jacob P. Adler, foremost actor of the Yiddish stage. Dina Shtettin Adler divorced her husband two years later, when he eloped with Sara Heine. Celia was raised by her mother and stepfather, the actor Siegmund Feinman. In need of work, "Madame Dina" continued to appear with Jacob Adler's troupe and brought her infant onstage as a prop at six months of age. At age four, Celia Adler played a role in *Der Yidisher Kenig Lear* [The Jewish King Lear], especially written for her by Jacob Gordin.

Educated in New York public schools, Adler originally planned to become a teacher. But after BERTHA KALICH praised her performance in Sudermann's *Heimat*, she resumed her acting career as Celia Feinman in 1909. She and her mother played in London's Pavilion Theatre, and in 1910, they toured Poland together.

That year, there were at least five Yiddish theaters operating in New York City: the Thalia, the New York People's Theater, the Liptzin, the Lyric, and the Liberty. When Boris Thomashefsky offered her a contract as understudy for his New York People's Theater, she signed on as Celia Adler. Years later she recalled in her autobiography the years she went from one temporary contract to another because of the difficulty actresses faced in a male-dominated theater world.

Adler's big break came when she was selected to tour with Rudolph Schildkraut in Shomer's *Eikele Mazik*. Subsequently, she played several seasons with Anschel Shur at the Arch Street Theater in Philadelphia, and returned to New York at David Kessler's invitation to play the Second Avenue Theatre. In 1918, Maurice Schwartz hired her for his Yiddish Art Theater. Others in the troupe included Jacob Ben-Ami, Ludwig Satz, BERTA GERSTEN, and Lazar Freed, whom she married. The couple later divorced. Schwartz was putting on as many as thirty-five plays per season, with actors ad-libbing their way through sketchy plots, aided by the prompter. Adler was usually cast as a weeping maiden or desperate mother. Then, Adler and Ben-Ami persuaded Schwartz to

In a show business career that, incredibly, spanned eight decades, Celia Adler was a mainstay of the Yiddish theater. [New York Public Library]

stage a serious drama. The resulting performance, Peretz Hirschbein's *Farvorfn Vinkl* [Forsaken nook], became a hit and was hailed by critics as "the foundation stone of the Yiddish art theater in America."

After this success, however, Schwartz returned to his former repertory and acting style. Under the leadership of Ben-Ami, a group of actors, including Celia Adler, broke away, founding the Jewish Art Theater (*Naye Teater*) in 1919. Inspired by the Moscow Art Theater and the new trend to realism in drama, they developed a small literary repertoire with fully realized characterizations. They adopted a single Yiddish dialect to be used consistently and appointed a literary-artistic committee to choose the repertoire. They hired a professional director, Emanuel Reicher of the Deutsche Freie Buehne [German free stage], and engaged professionals to design the sets and lighting. The new theater's first season—including Hirschbein's *The Idle Inn* and Leo Tolstoy's *Power of Darkness*—was well reviewed in the *New York Times*. *Theatre Magazine* hailed the Jewish Art Theater as the high point in the development of Yiddish theater. But the troupe could not weather a disagreement with its financial backer. Reicher left to become director for the Theatre Guild, and Ben-Ami left for Broadway.

In the 1921–1922 season, Celia Adler, Ben-Ami, and Satz performed at the Irving Place Theater, and the following year Adler acted again under the direction of Maurice Schwartz, appearing as leading lady of the troupe. The 1923–1924 season found her appearing as guest star with Anschel Shur in Philadelphia and touring Europe and America with her brother-in-law Satz. In 1927–1928, Adler tried directing her own repertory company, varying this work with guest roles at the various Yiddish theaters in New York and Philadelphia. While at the Yiddish Art Theater in 1929–1930 at Philadelphia's Arch Street Theater, she encountered Jack Cone, an actor and theater manager she had known in childhood. As she relates it in her autobiography, she was about to decline an invitation to perform in Buenos Aires because of her fear of traveling there alone, when Cone suggested they marry so that he could accompany her. The couple joined those "vagabond stars" who traveled throughout South America playing cities, out-of-the-way towns, and agricultural colonies. At that time, Buenos Aires boasted five professional Jewish theaters.

Adler appeared in two films: *Abe's Imported Wife* and the 1937 production *Vu Iz Mayn Kind?* [Where is my child?], a reprise of the melodramatic tearjerkers of her earlier years. In 1938 she joined the Yiddish Dramatic Players, together with the new star of the Yiddish stage, Joseph Buloff.

In the 1920s and 1930s, Yiddish-language theater played out the dramatic transition from Old Country to new and the traumatic process of immigrant adjustment. Out of the emotional turmoil of the flight from Europe, trans-Atlantic migration, and translation to new world poverty, there arose the inventive, re-creative power of Yiddish theater. Through its medium, Jewish immigrants were able to reimagine their previous lives, their present poverty, and their dreams of a better life. But as the immigrants improved their economic status and moved away from the old centers of Jewish life, the troupes lost their earlier base of support in the Jewish neighborhoods. Inevitably, they broke up for lack of funds. While art theaters always have financial problems, the Yiddish art theaters suffered as well from the dispersal of their audience and the decrease in the number of Yiddish-speaking people. Adler made her loyalties clear. When she accepted a contract to appear in an English-language production of David Pinski's *The Treasure* at the Garrick Theater in New York, she wrote a letter to her fans via the *Yiddish World* explaining that her departure was temporary and promising to return to the Yiddish stage. Spanning the immigrant and "Yankee" generations, Adler was in the rear guard of Yiddish theater.

In the aftermath of World War II, Adler was contracted by the Jewish Welfare Board to entertain troops in American military camps. She presented a program of English and Yiddish songs, and later continued these concert appearances for civilian audiences off-Broadway. But Yiddish theater was dead by that time, not only in the United States but in Russia and Poland as well, where it was literally killed off by communist regimes. At age fifty-seven, Adler was called back to the stage by Ben Hecht, who cast her opposite Paul Muni (an old friend from Yiddish theater days) in his English-language play *A Flag Is Born*. Members of the cast included Marlon Brando, Quentin Reynolds, and Luther Adler. Scheduled to run four weeks, the play actually went thirty weeks. Later, Adler played a part in the film *Naked City*. After that contract, she writes, she was happy to sit back and enjoy her career as *Bobe* Tsili to her grandchildren, daughters of "my son the doctor" Selwyn (Zelig) Freed. At the time of her death on January 31, 1979, Adler was married to Nathan Forman.

BIBLIOGRAPHY

Adler, Celia. *Tsili Adler Dertseylt* (1959); *AJYB* 24:113; *EJ*; *EJ* necrology (1973–1982); Lifson, David S. *The Yiddish Theatre in America* (1965); Rosenfeld, Lulla Adler. *The Yiddish Theatre and Jacob P. Adler* (1988); Sandrow, Nahma.

Vagabond Stars (1977); *UJE*; *WWIAJ* (1938); Zylbercweig, Zalmen. *Leksikon fun Yidishn Teater* (1931).

JUDITH LAIKIN ELKIN

ADLER, HELEN GOLDMARK
(1859–1948)

Although as accomplished and intelligent as her well-known husband Felix, Helen Adler did not strive to forge an independent name for herself. Her hard work and accomplishments, however, benefited the many people with whom she came into contact throughout her life.

Helen Goldmark was born September 4, 1859, the eldest daughter of Regina (Wehle) and Joseph Goldmark, both of whom had immigrated to the United States in 1849. Her mother came from Prague with her affluent Jewish family, and settled in Madison, Indiana. Born in Poland, her father was educated in Hungary and at the University of Vienna medical school, and he had been a member of the Austrian parliament. He played an important part in the failed Revolutions of 1848, after which he fled the country. In 1868 amnesty enabled him to return to Austria and clear his name of criminal charges. Instead, he immigrated to the United States and lived out his life in Brooklyn. There, he built his medical practice and continued his chemistry research, which led to several patents. One of these allowed him to manufacture superior percussion cartridges for the Union Army during the Civil War, a coup for both his business and political loyalties. Several of Helen's nine siblings, notably Pauline, Henry, and JOSEPHINE [GOLDMARK], achieved prominence in their respective fields, and her other sister, ALICE BRANDEIS, married the Supreme Court justice.

Helen, nicknamed "Nell" or "Nellie," attended the Brooklyn Heights Seminary and passed Harvard's entrance exam, although at that time women could not attend Harvard. She was an extremely intelligent and articulate writer, and could write fluent German, excellent French, and some Italian. Her father embraced a rationalist anticlericalism, and so the family did not regularly attend synagogue, but Helen and her sister Christine often went to Dr. John M. Chadwick's liberal Unitarian church in Brooklyn. There she introduced herself to Felix Adler, the young philosopher and founder (1876) of the nascent Ethical Culture Movement [WOMEN'S LEAGUE FOR CONSERVATIVE JUDAISM], when he came to preach in 1879. They were married on May 24, 1880.

After her marriage, Helen Adler involved herself in the Ethical Culture Movement and her husband's work. She took notes on philosophical essays for her husband's use; wrote articles for the *Standard*, the organ of the Ethical Culture Society; and took a prominent part in the Women's Conference of the society. Helen Adler helped her husband establish the first model tenements at Cherry Street as well as the first free kindergarten in America, called the Working Man's School, and later the Ethical Culture School at Fieldston. She took an active part in the visiting nurses' service for the poor at the DeMilt Dispensary, the oldest clinic in the city, which Felix had initiated in 1877. With the assistance of a Dr. Koplik, she helped cut the infant death rate by having milk bottled safely at the Laboratory Department for Modified Milk for Tenement Babies, which Koplik and Adler founded in 1891. She accompanied her husband on numerous trips abroad, notably to Berlin in 1903 and to Oxford, where he was Hibbert lecturer in 1923, where she did independent research on the history of Hibbert and the lectureship. When her husband traveled without her, they exchanged loving and engaging letters, revealing a lifelong intimate partnership.

In favor of woman suffrage, but opposed to unlimited public roles for women, Helen Adler lent limited support to her feminist contemporaries. She bore five children—Waldo, Eleanor, Lawrence, Margaret, and Ruth—and believed a woman's most important task was child rearing. Yet she worried that women were not rigorous or exacting enough to attend to this task adequately, and set out to make child rearing a science. Perhaps at her husband's suggestion, in 1888, Helen Adler and five other mothers founded the Society for the Study of Child Nature (later the Child Study Association), to educate parents. In 1891, the Teacher Company published her pamphlet "Hints for the Scientific Observation and Study of Children," designed to teach mothers to monitor their children's development.

Felix Adler died in 1933 at age eighty-two. In later years, Helen Adler's interest in art led her to greater involvement with the Arts High School at Fieldston, and also to produce floral sketches, pottery, and textile designs, described by one admirer as "beautifully living" and the fruits of a "genuine artistic impulse." Helen Adler died on March 19, 1948, survived by her children and siblings.

SELECTED WORKS BY
HELEN GOLDMARK ADLER

"Dr. Adler's Meeting with the Vienna Ethical Society." *The Standard* 14 (1927–1928): 24–25; "Felix Adler." Manuscript Collection, Columbia University; *Hints for the*

Scientific Observation and Study of Children (1891); "The Life and Writings of Dr. Arthur Pfungst." *The Standard* 13 (1926–1927): 15–16.

BIBLIOGRAPHY

American Reformers. Edited by Alden Whitman (1985); Andress, Bart. "Fifty Years of Child Study." *The Standard* 25, no. 2 (1938–1939): 29–30; "Dr. Felix Adler Dies in 82nd Year." *NYTimes*, April 26, 1933, 15:1; Friess, Horace L. *Felix Adler and Ethical Culture: Memories and Studies.* Edited by Fannia Weingartner (1981); Goldmark, Josephine. *Pilgrims of '48* (1930); "Mrs. Felix Adler Dies at Age of 89." *NYTimes*, March 21, 1948, 60:2; *Woman's Who's Who of America.* Edited by John William Leonard (1914); *WWIAJ* (1926, 1928).

MICOL SEIGEL

ADLER, POLLY (1900–1962)

Polly Adler, owner of a notorious New York City bordello, had a clear goal: to become "the best goddam madam in all America." Her earlier plan had been to attend the gymnasium in Pinsk to complete the educa-

Polly Adler had planned to continue the education she began under her village rabbi in Yanow, Belorussia, but was sent to America instead. Once in the United States she developed a different goal—to become "the best goddam madam in all America." This shocking quote was part of the publicity campaign for her best-selling book A House Is Not a Home. *She is shown here at a book-signing party. [UPI/Bettmann]*

tion begun under her village rabbi. However, her father decided to send her ahead as the first link in a "chain emigration" that would eventually bring the entire family to the United States. Alone in a new country, the young Polly fell prey to sexual exploitation and learned to survive by criminal activity, a pattern of immigration and settlement common to a minority of single Eastern European Jewish women.

Born on April 16, 1900, Pearl (Polly) Adler was the eldest of two daughters and seven sons of Gertrude (Koval) and Morris Adler of Yanow, Belorussia. Adler's father was a tailor whose work provided comfortably for his family. When Pearl was twelve years old, her father sent her to friends in Holyoke, Massachusetts. She did housework while attending school to learn English. When World War I cut her off from her family—and the monthly stipend sent by her father—she moved in with cousins in Brooklyn, where she continued attending school as often as her job in a shirt factory allowed. At age seventeen, she was raped by her foreman. When she found herself pregnant by him, she had an abortion. After an argument with her scandalized relatives, Adler moved to Manhattan, where she continued to support herself by factory work.

In 1920, her roommate introduced her to a bootlegger who offered Adler her first opportunity in the business in which she would make her name. She began to keep an apartment furnished and paid for by the gangster. Whenever he and his married girlfriend were not there, Adler provided a rendezvous and procured women for his friends and for her own developing clientele. Her first arrest for operating a house of prostitution put an end to this arrangement in 1922. Adler used her savings to open a legitimate lingerie business, only to see it fail a year later.

Impoverished, Pearl—now Polly—returned to her career as a madam. She opened the first of a series of ever fancier bordellos. Later, she opened a resort in Saratoga Springs, New York, the summer retreat of the fashionable upper-class clients she so desired. Gangsters, among them "Dutch" Schultz and Lucky Luciano, rubbed elbows in her parlors with the Manhattan haut monde, all persuaded by Adler's well-orchestrated publicity campaign that "going to Polly's" was the perfect end to an evening. Her oft-investigated associations with underworld figures never really damaged her glamorous image. To the public, she remained the classic American madam—a feisty, albeit disreputable, victor over adversity.

Adler remained in business through most of World War II until her last arrest in 1943 (the charges were dismissed, as usual). She then retired to

Burbank, California, where she completed high school and enrolled in Los Angeles Valley College. She died of cancer in Los Angeles on June 9, 1962.

BIBLIOGRAPHY

Adler, Polly, *A House Is Not a Home* (1953); Berger, Meyer. "Miss Adler and Guests." *NYTimes Book Review*, June 14, 1953; Bullough, Vern. "Polly Adler." In *European Immigrant Women in the United States: A Biographical Dictionary*, edited by Judy B. Litoff and Judith McDonnell (1994); *DAB* 7; Gosch, Martin A. *The Last Testament of Lucky Luciano* (1975); Marcus, Jacob Rader, ed. *The American Jewish Woman, 1654–1980* (1981), and *The American Jewish Woman: A Documentary History* (1981); Mitgang, Herbert. *The Man Who Rode the Tiger: The Life and Times of Judge Samuel Seabury* (1963); *NAW* modern; Obituary. *NYTimes*, June 11, 1962, 65:2; "Pollyadlery." Review of *A House Is Not a Home*, by Polly Adler. *Newsweek* (June 8, 1953): 104; Weinberg, Sydney Stahl. *The World of Our Mothers: The Lives of Jewish Immigrant Women* (1988).

ANN MANN MILLIN

ADLER, RACIE (1872–1952)

Racie (Friedenwald) Adler was born in Baltimore, Maryland, on August 5, 1872, one of at least three daughters of Moses and Jane (Alborn) Friedenwald. She was of a distinguished and well-off German Jewish family whose members played important roles in the formation and direction of many major American Jewish institutions. Her grandfather Jonas, a successful businessman who had emigrated from Germany, was very active as a Jewish communal leader, as were his sons, who included the prominent ophthalmologist Aaron Friedenwald.

The details of Racie's life before her marriage at the age of thirty-three are unclear, beyond the fact that she was educated at Goucher College in Baltimore. She married a man of similar socioeconomic background, who was equally devoted to Jewish communal involvement. Indeed, shaped by her family's position in society and the nature of its public commitments, Adler was ideally suited to be the wife of Cyrus Adler, the Assyriology scholar and major Jewish communal figure she married in September 1905. Characteristically for a woman of her time and social position, she played a strong, supportive role for her husband and his career, often assisting him in his work and proofreading his manuscripts. She accompanied him on many of his travels abroad, to Egypt, Palestine, and throughout Europe. Among their friends and acquaintances, the Adlers counted many high-level members of government administration, including the Roosevelts, diplomats such as Oscar Straus, and illustrious Jewish families such as the Warburgs.

Their only child, Sarah, was born in 1906. Her life seems to have been modeled on her mother's. When she grew old enough, she, too, helped her father in his scholarly work, and in January 1932, she married Wolfe Wolfinsohn, also from an "aristocratic" German Jewish family.

During World War I, Adler served as division chief for the Liberty Loan, using her social position to secure millions of dollars worth of subscriptions. She also headed a Red Cross unit operating out of Dropsie College in Philadelphia. For many years after the war, she remained a supervisor of the North Philadelphia branch of the American Red Cross.

With war concerns over, Adler devoted much of her energy to specifically Jewish causes. She served for many years as the president of the Hebrew Sunday School Society of Philadelphia and on the local Jewish Welfare Board. Perhaps her most significant contribution was as one of the founding leaders of the Women's League of the Conservative Movement [WOMEN'S LEAGUE FOR CONSERVATIVE JUDAISM], which was established in 1918 by MATHILDE SCHECHTER, wife of the scholar Solomon Schechter. Adler served as vice president of the organization from 1918 to 1938, but she consistently declined to take the more visible position of president. Certain undertakings of the organization were particularly important to her, especially the building of Jewish student houses at the University of Pennsylvania and Temple University, both in Philadelphia, and at the Jewish Theological Seminary in New York. She not only strongly supported these projects, but she used her connections to obtain funding for them.

Due to poor health, Racie Adler was forced to retire prematurely from her active involvement in the Women's League, but remained an honorary vice president from 1938 until her death in Philadelphia on March 20, 1952. She was remembered as a gracious society woman and a warm hostess who was devoted to the Jewish Theological Seminary and its students. Her efforts on their behalf, through the Women's League, facilitated the functioning and development of that central American Jewish institution.

BIBLIOGRAPHY

Adler, Cyrus. *I Have Considered the Days* (1941); *AJYB* 54:538; National Women's League of the United States of America. *They Dared to Dream: A History of the National Women's League, 1918–1968* (1967); Obituary. *NYTimes*, March 21, 1952, 23:4; *Women's League Outlook* 22, no. 4 (May 1952): 8–9.

LISA EPSTEIN

ADLER, SARA (1858–1953)

Although her reputation as an artist must have benefited from the association with her husband, Jacob P. Adler, Sara Adler was an admired actress and a strong presence on the Yiddish stage. Born in Odessa about 1858, the daughter of Pessye and Ellye Levitsky, Sara (Levitsky) Adler was educated in Russian-language schools. She made her stage debut at age eight as Amalia in Schiller's *The Robbers*. After winning a scholarship to study voice at the Odessa Conservatory, she decided on a stage career. The Jewish Theater Circle hired her as a between-acts divertissement, singing Russian songs. After learning Yiddish, she joined the troupe of Moishe Heine-Haimovitch (Maurice Heine) and studied with the Viennese stage director Gritzkopf. While on a tour of Russia, she married Heine. The banning of Yiddish theater and other restrictions on Jews in Russia led the troupe to relocate to London, where hardship almost caused the young actress to abandon the profession. After Heine joined forces with Jacob P. Adler, the combined troupes went to America in 1883, where, as Madam Heine, she became leading lady in Shomer's *The Orphans*. After divorcing Heine, she joined Jacob Adler, who was with the Finkel-Feinman-Mogulesko troupe, becoming their principal actress for both dramatic and operetta roles. She married Adler in 1891, following his divorce from Dina Shtettin, becoming his third wife.

At the turn of the century, the Yiddish stage was devoted to vaudeville and melodrama—tawdry entertainment for the masses of Jewish immigrants who had little time and less money to educate themselves in the arts. In 1891, Jacob Adler made a historic break from *shund* (trash) theater by staging and appearing in *Siberia*, a drama by Jacob Gordin. Serious Yiddish theater, which dates from that performance, reached its apotheosis in *Der Yidisher Kenig Lear* [The Jewish King Lear], a play that remained in the Adler repertoire for thirty years. Sara played the role of Teitele. Along with BERTHA KALICH, Ester Kaminska, and Keni Liptzin, Adler developed other serious character roles for women in plays by Gordin, H. Leivick, and Peretz Hirschbein. Together, they helped use the theater to play out the immigrant drama and to introduce their audience to the world's dramatic repertoire in translation. Immense public adulation followed the Adlers, and by the first decade of the new century they had achieved financial success. Their home on East 72nd Street became a mecca for Jewish artists and intellectuals.

Jacob Adler's numerous offspring were put on stage as soon as they could walk. The five children

Despite their tempestuous relationship, Sara Adler and her husband, the theatrical impresario Jacob P. Adler, worked together to change the face of Yiddish theater in America. [American Jewish Archives]

Sara bore—Frances (1892), Jay (1896), Julia (1899), STELLA [ADLER] (1902), and Luther (1903)—went on to careers in theater. Marital and artistic turbulence, infidelities, separations, and reconciliations punctuated Jacob and Sara Adler's marriage but did not always interrupt their appearances together. Sara dealt with continuous domestic disarray in a variety of ways. At one time, she entered a sanatorium to recover her peace of mind after one of her husband's infidelities. At another, she took a lover herself and, striking out on her own, made plans to establish a rival theater. A bout of tuberculosis diverted these plans, and eventually she returned home to Jacob Adler.

Her major roles included Mina in Kobrin's *Mina*, Fania Zorchis in Gordin's *Emese Kraft* [True power], Batsheva in Gordin's *The Homeless*, the woman in Gordin's *The Stranger*, Beata in Gordin's *Elisha ben Avuya*, Gittele in Libin's *Broken Hearts*, the mother in Marcovich's melodrama *A Mother's Tears*, Nora in Ibsen's *A Doll's House*, Yelena in Tolstoy's *Kreutzer Sonata*, and the gypsy in Tolstoy's *Resurrection*. Adler performed actively until 1928 in both New York and the "provinces." In her eightieth year, she performed the third act of *Resurrection* at a benefit performance, where a critic compared her with Eleanora Duse. She died in New York on April 28, 1953.

BIBLIOGRAPHY

AJYB 55:454; *DAB* 5; *EJ;* Obituary. *NYTimes,* April 29, 1953, 29:1; Rosenfeld, Lulla Adler. *The Yiddish Theatre and Jacob P. Adler* (1988); Sandrow, Nahma. *Vagabond Stars* (1977); *UJE;* Zylbercweig, Zalmen. *Leksikon fun Yidishn Teater* (1931).

JUDITH LAIKIN ELKIN

ADLER, STELLA (1902–1992)

At Stella Adler's death in 1992, Robert Brustein wrote in *The New Republic,* "Stella Adler's death . . . represents a major loss in the pantheon of theater greats. Through the strength of her convictions, the integrity of her character, and the brilliance of her mind, Adler embodied the art of the dramatic profession and remained an influential figure throughout a career that spanned most of the century."

Stella Adler was born February 10, 1902, in New York City, the youngest daughter of Jacob P. and SARA ADLER, the foremost actors of the Yiddish stage at the turn of the century. The fourth among five siblings (Frances, Jay, Julia, and Luther) and younger than her known half-siblings (Charles, Abe, and CELIA ADLER), Adler was enlisted in her father's troupe as a toddler. At age four, she took the part of one of the young princes in Shakespeare's *Richard III,* and at age nine she played the young Spinoza. Her education in New York City public schools always took second place to rehearsals and performances. She played Naomi in *Elisha ben Avuya* at the Pavilion Theatre in London in 1919, and on her return to the United States had a commercial hit as Butterfly in *The World We Live In.* In the 1920s, Adler achieved star status on the Yiddish stage, appearing in over a hundred roles in such plays as *Jew Süss, God of Vengeance,* and *Liliom,* as well as in classics by Shakespeare and Tolstoy, with the foremost actors of the Yiddish theater, including David Kessler, Siegmund Mogulesko, BERTHA KALICH, Keni Liptzin, and Jacob Ben-Ami. There followed a period of time on the road, including tours of Europe and Latin America. Back in New York, she enrolled at the newly established American Laboratory Theater school, where she studied with Richard Boleslavsky and Maria Ouspenskaya, who were then introducing their students to the revolutionary acting technique of Konstantin Stanislavsky. Already a veteran performer,

Adler said that the Laboratory Theater, with its roots in the Moscow Art Theater, "opened her up" and gave her a new life.

It was at the Laboratory Theater that she met Harold Clurman and Lee Strasberg, who had also come for acting lessons. In 1931, Clurman, Strasberg, and Cheryl Crawford formed the Group Theatre. Their intent was to create an ensemble of players, directors, designers, and writers to produce socially relevant plays that would provide an alternative to commercial theater. To develop true ensemble acting, they decided that everyone connected with a production—playwright, actor, stage designer—had to come to agreement on the meaning and perspective of the play. Strasberg directed the training of the actors based on the methods learned at the American Laboratory Theater, stressing "affective memory"—the active recall of incidents in the actor's own life to power her emotion on stage. Clurman invited Adler

In challenging herself and everyone around her—including, at one point, Stanislavsky—Stella Adler extended the legacy of her famous theatrical family, rejuvenated the study of acting in America, and in the process inspired entire generations of performers. [New York Public Library]

to join the new theater, initiating a love-hate relationship between the highly individualistic star and the communally committed Group. Although she has written that Clurman was her savior, Adler hated having to submerge her personality into the ensemble, rotating between starring roles and bit parts. Clurman maintained that the discipline was healthy, but Adler felt that the women in the company were coerced into going along with the men. Recalling Adler years later, Clurman described her at this time as "poetically theatrical, reminiscent of some past beauty in a culture I had perhaps never seen, but that was part of an atavistic dream. With all the imperious flamboyance of an older theatrical tradition—European in its roots—she was somehow fragile, vulnerable, gay with mother wit and stage fragrance."

The earliest members of the group included some thirty actors and playwrights, many of whom went on to stardom, including Morris Carnovsky, Clifford Odets, and Franchot Tone. Elia Kazan joined later as an apprentice. Group Theatre productions, including *The House of Connelly*, *Night over Taos*, and *Success Story*, were highly praised by the critics, and Method acting was launched in the United States. Adler married Clurman, but she split from Strasberg over their differing interpretations of Stanislavsky's teachings.

Despite critical and personal success in Odets's 1935 play, *Awake and Sing*, Adler was not satisfied with the Method or with the way her career was going. Taking a leave of absence from the company, she traveled to Europe, where she felt energized by the new theatrical techniques being developed in the Soviet Union. In Paris, she challenged Stanislavsky himself. According to her memoir, she accused him of having ruined the theater. He responded that perhaps she had not understood his method correctly, and (possibly on the strength of the Adler family legend) gave her several weeks of private instruction. Apparently, he expressed surprise that directors in America were still teaching theories that he had abandoned, such as the use of affective memory to activate a role. Adler, reinforced now by Stanislavsky, believed that conjuring up real-life personal tragedies in order to exhibit anguish on stage was "sick." "Don't use your conscious past," she urged the company on her return. "Use your creative imagination to create a past that belongs to your character." According to Group members, her formal presentation of the revised theory galvanized them and improved their work. Adler now began giving acting classes herself. Her last appearance with the Group Theatre was in 1935, in another Odets play, *Paradise Lost*.

In 1937, Adler took off for Hollywood, where she made several films: *Love on Toast*, *Shadow of the Thin Man*, and *My Girl Tisa*. Glamorized by the makeup artists and baptized "Ardler" by the flaks, she seemed a long way from the Yiddish theater dramas of her childhood. Later, she was associate producer on several MGM films, such as *DuBarry Was a Lady*, *Madame Curie*, and *For Me and My Gal*. In 1938, she returned to the Group for a season to direct several plays, including the critically acclaimed production of Odets's *Golden Boy*, which she took to London and Paris. In the 1940s, she was back on Broadway, taking the role of Catherine in Max Reinhardt's *Sons and Soldiers*, as Zenaida in Leonid Andreyev's *He Who Gets Slapped*, and as Mme. Rosepettle in Arthur Kopit's black comedy *Oh, Dad, Poor Dad, Mamma's Hung You in the Closet and I'm Feeling So Sad*. She reprised the latter role in 1961, as her last professional appearance.

Throughout the years, Adler was building her reputation as a theatrical director. In 1956, she directed the Paul Green/Kurt Weill antiwar musical *Johnny Johnson*. She became well known especially for developing the talent of new young actors. Deploring American acting standards, she criticized contemporary actors for not understanding what theater is about. She began teaching at Erwin Piscator's Dramatic Workshop at the New School for Social Research in the early 1940s. After some years, she left to establish the Stella Adler Theater Studio, where she designed a curriculum that included not only speech, voice production, and makeup, but play analysis, characterization, and acting styles. In the workshops that were central to the curriculum, students improvised or performed scenes before an invited audience of theater professionals. Adler taught her students to build characters out of the material provided in the playwright's text, within the context of the historical period presented in the play, and motivated by the actors' imagination rather than by their personal experiences.

By the 1960s, the renamed Stella Adler Conservatory of Acting numbered more than a dozen faculty and included among its more famous students Eddie Albert, Margaret Barker, Warren Beatty, Robert De Niro, and Marlon Brando. The latter wrote the laudatory introduction to Adler's book *The Technique of Acting*. During the 1966–1967 academic year, Adler was an adjunct professor of acting at Yale University's School of Drama. The New School for Social Research awarded her a doctor of humane letters degree, and Smith College granted her a doctor of fine arts degree in 1987.

Witnesses to Adler's workshop performances recall them as the most energetic in New York. Her teaching style can be seen in a video recorded in 1989, in which she exemplifies her own advice to students: "Get a stage tone, darling, an energy. Never go on stage without your motor running." Filmed in part in her Manhattan apartment, the video presents an energetic and witty woman who looks thirty years younger than her eighty-plus years. Clurman, who went on to become a Broadway impresario and theater critic, describes this apartment in his own video as being decorated in a style that was "part Venetian, part Madame Pompadour."

Adler married several times, the first time at age eighteen to Horace Eleascheff, with whom she had a daughter, Ellen. That marriage ended in divorce. In 1943, she married Harold Clurman, a union that was creatively productive but which also ended in divorce in 1960. Her third husband, Mitchell Wilson, a physicist and novelist, died in 1973. Adler died in Los Angeles on December 22, 1992.

Unlike her older half-sister Celia Adler, who remained in the Yiddish theater, with its roots in Europe and the nourishing soil of the immigrant generation, Stella Adler entered the larger world of the English-speaking American theater. From the older tradition, she brought her passionate attachment to the craft and her profound understanding of the dynamics of the profession, learned at the knees of its greatest practitioners, her parents. American-born and educated, she made the transition to the English-language stage successfully at a time when Yiddish theater was dying. Far from leaving the Yiddish experience behind, she used its strengths to develop her own persona and acting skills, and had the intelligence to modify these through her experience with Stanislavsky. More important for the development of theater in America, she transmitted the new acting techniques to her students and energized a generation of younger actors who shared her passion for the theater.

SELECTED WORKS BY STELLA ADLER

Awake and Dream. Videorecording (1989); *The Technique of Acting* (1988); "The World of My Parents: Reminiscences." *YIVO Annual* 23 (1996).

BIBLIOGRAPHY

Brustein, Robert. "Stella Adler." *The New Republic* 208 (February 1, 1993): 52–53; Clurman, Harold. *The Fervent Years* (1945); *Contemporary Theatre, Film and Television.* Vol. 3 (1986); *Current Biography Yearbook* (1985); *EJ*, s.v. "Adler"; Robinson, Alice M., et al., eds. *Notable Women in the American Theatre. A Biographical Dictionary* (1989); Rosenfeld, Lulla Adler. *The Yiddish Theatre and Jacob P. Adler* (1977); Sandrow, Nahma. *Vagabond Stars: A World History of Yiddish Theater* (1977); *UJE*, s.v. "Adler"; *WWIAJ* (1938).

JUDITH LAIKIN ELKIN

ADLERBLUM, NIMA (1881–1974)

Nima Hirschenson Adlerblum was a writer, educator, and early Zionist activist in New York, whose life began and ended in Jerusalem. She wrote widely on philosophy, education, Jewish philosophy, and American history, contributing to encyclopedias and scholarly journals.

She was born in Jerusalem on August 4, 1881, the daughter of Rabbi Hayim Hirschensohn and Eva (Hacohen) Hirschensohn. Her mother was the daughter of Rabbi Benjamin Shaul Hacohen, who had come to Jerusalem in 1858, and had headed the Etz Chaim Yeshiva. Adlerblum's paternal grandfather, Jacob Mordechai Hirschensohn, was a famous scholar who established yeshivahs in Safed and in Jerusalem. Her father was a scholar and publisher as well as an associate of Eliezer Ben-Yehuda. The oldest of five children, she maintained close contacts with her siblings, especially her sisters, TAMAR DE SOLA POOL, TEHILLA LICHTENSTEIN, cofounder and leader of the Jewish Science movement, and Esther Taubenhaus, founder of the campus Hillel association at Texas A&M University in College Station. Adlerblum left Jerusalem when her family went to Constantinople, probably in 1892. She then studied in Paris at the Alliance Israelite Francaise.

Adlerblum's father came to the United States in December 1903, and became rabbi to five congregations in Hoboken, New Jersey. His daughter Nima followed the next year. Adlerblum studied at Columbia University, receiving her B.A., M.A., and doctorate. Her master's essay in 1907 was written on "The Hebrew conception of suffering analyzed and compared with those of the Greeks with a brief sketch of the conception of suffering developed by Christianity." Her 1926 doctoral dissertation was on Gersonides, the early fourteenth-century philosopher also known as the Ralbag, and was entitled "A Study of Gersonides in His Proper Perspective." The focus of her approach to Jewish philosophy and to the Jewish philosophers on whom she wrote—including Gersonides, Judah Halevi, and Bachya Ibn Pakuda—was that Jewish philosophy had to be viewed as an expression of Jewish organic life, rather than studied in relation to Greek philosophy or medieval scholasticism.

Adlerblum's philosophical orientation, in particular her educational philosophy, was influenced by John Dewey, with whom she worked closely. Like Dewey, she placed great emphasis on environment and experience, believing that "a child must be taught life through action, by the adoption of different purposes and projects." She was active in promoting and disseminating Dewey's ideas in Latin America, and in 1948, she was chair of the international committee for the celebration of Dewey's ninetieth birthday.

Adlerblum wrote a book on the Jewish holidays, *A Perspective of Jewish Life Through Its Festivals* (1930), in which she placed emphasis on the idealism in Judaism: "The vision of certain ideals give to a people self-consciousness, coherence, and its own way of thinking. By grasping the vision of a nation we can penetrate into its history and philosophy." She believed that, for the Jewish people, the "moral life is the sole purpose of existence."

She worked closely with Rabbi Leo Jung of New York, and contributed to many of his volumes in the Jewish Heritage Series. In the volume entitled *The Jewish Woman* (1934), she wrote the concluding chapter, "The Elan Vital of the Jewish Woman." In it, she said that Jewish women through history had maintained Judaism by faithfulness to its ideals and vision.

Adlerblum was strongly influenced by the life of her paternal grandmother, Sara Bayla Hirschensohn, whom she remembered from her early years in Jerusalem. In the volume *Jewish Leaders*, edited by Leo Jung, she wrote about her grandmother in "Sara Bayla and Her Times," describing her piety and her energy, and particularly her role in the expansion of the Jewish community of Jerusalem in the second part of the nineteenth century.

Influenced strongly by nineteenth-century romanticism, she wrote about the "Romance of Judaism," which for her was "woven out of God, land and people, fused together into an organic spiritual life." For Adlerblum, Jewish history started with the promise of the land to Abraham. "The transformation of the physical land into the holy land—such was the Jewish dream. It is a dream which has become the chief motive power in the formation of Jewish consciousness . . . expressing the very essence of Jewish existence."

Zionism was a strong part of her life and thought. She founded the national cultural and educational program of HADASSAH and was its national and cultural chair, and a member of its national board from 1922 to 1935. Her sister Tamar de Sola Pool was later national president of Hadassah. She enjoyed a warm friendship with HENRIETTA SZOLD and corresponded with her on the role of Zionism and of Hadassah in Jewish life. Her reports as national cultural chair expressed her views on Zionism very strongly. For her, Palestine "is the starting point as well as the final goal of Jewish destiny. In making Palestine the starting point, we shall do away with the artificial abstraction of orthodoxy and reform and deal with Jewish life as something integral into which we are born and which we can carry with us throughout the larger world." In keeping with her role as one of the first children in Jerusalem (together with the children of Eliezer Ben-Yehuda) to use Hebrew on an everyday basis, she fostered the study of Hebrew as a modern language.

Adlerblum was also very involved in the welfare of Jews in other countries. In 1934, she wrote a report on conditions in Germany. In 1935, she wrote a report on Jewish adjustment in the Soviet Union, and made a study of the problems of minority nationalities in Eastern Europe. According to family sources, she was asked by an American Jewish organization to help 250 Jewish refugees from Hitler who had escaped to Italy, where they were imprisoned. She flew to Rome and obtained their release.

While growing up in Jerusalem, Adlerblum had been betrothed at age eight to a boy five years her senior whom her father had brought into his house and adopted. The boy lived with them for many years, but the two did not marry. On May 14, 1914, she married Israel S. Adlerblum, an insurance consultant and active Zionist worker. They had one daughter, Ivria.

In 1971 she returned to the land of her birth with her husband and lived first in Herzliya and then in Jerusalem until her death on July 25, 1974.

SELECTED WORKS
BY NIMA ADLERBLUM

"A Perspective for the Study of Jewish Philosophy." *Journal of Philosophy* 20, no. 17 (1923); *A Perspective of Jewish Life Through Its Festivals* (1930); "A Reinterpretation of Jewish Philosophy." *Journal of Philosophy* 14, no. 7 (1917); *A Study of Gersonides in His Proper Perspective* (1926); "The Elan Vital of the Jewish Woman." In *The Jewish Woman*, edited by Rabbi Leo Jung (1934).

BIBLIOGRAPHY

EJ (1973–1982); Obituary. *NYTimes*, August 2, 1974, 30:4; *UJE*; *Who's Who in World Jewry* (1972); *WWWIA*, 6; *WWIAJ* (1926, 1928, 1938).

JENNIFER BREGER

ADVERTISING AND CONSUMER CULTURE

In the twentieth century, Jewish women played a disproportionate role in the development of American consumer culture because of a combination of factors. For one, American industry became increasingly consumer-oriented, and consumer industries were comparatively open to small entrepreneurs. For another, Jewish immigrants and their children tended to display strong entrepreneurial tendencies.

One of the most significant shifts in American business took place in the last decades of the nineteenth century with the emergence of the "modern corporation," which sought to attract and retain consumers through new forms of packaging, marketing, and advertising. These decades also witnessed the rise of the great department stores and mail-order companies. In addition, whole new consumer industries developed rapidly after the 1870s, particularly cosmetics, women's ready-made clothing, and resorts. Unlike certain other fields, such as packaged foods, which were dominated by several huge firms, these new areas remained open to entrepreneurs with limited capital. Underlying all of these specific business developments was the nation's preeminence as a consumer-oriented economy and society. The constantly increasing demand of a rapidly growing and comparatively affluent population made the United States a mecca for enterprising merchants and manufacturers.

As elsewhere, Jews in America were disproportionately involved in commercial pursuits, ranging from clothing to furniture to real estate to movies. One of the outstanding features of the populous Jewish neighborhoods in New York City during the great era of immigration was the corresponding density of retail stores of all types. As well, street markets in these neighborhoods became so sophisticated that they sold specialized luxuries such as fur coats.

Although the popular stereotype of the Jewish merchant is of a man,
there were many American Jewish women who succeeded as entrepreneurs.
Shown here is Fannie Cohen in front of her grocery store in St. Paul, Minnesota, about 1915.
[Jewish Historical Society of the Upper Midwest]

While the great majority of merchants and entrepreneurs were men, Jewish women gained an unusual entree into this field of activity. There were two essential reasons for their participation. First, Jewish women traditionally had been more involved in commerce than women of most other groups. It is significant that the well-known and often repeated passage from Proverbs about the "Woman of Valor" depicts a wife and mother who buys vineyards while keeping her family properly fed, clothed, and nurtured. Whereas most ethnic groups had fairly conservative views about the propriety of women being involved in the public sphere, Jews seemed to accept an extraordinary degree of female participation in political, organizational, economic, intellectual, and public leisure activities. Thus, the idea of women being active in the selling of goods did not threaten Jewish sensibility and customs. In fact, the important role of women in commerce, which seemed to persist in Eastern Europe, increased during periods of economic duress. During the period of mass emigration, eyewitness

Often husband and wife worked together to build a successful business. Here Tillie Novick and her husband Falick (and their son) are shown in front of their coppersmith shop on West 12th Street in Chicago, around 1913.

accounts of Jewish life in the Pale of Settlement attested that women were frequently involved in trade.

Second, Jewish women seemed to be particularly responsive to the sophisticated new material world they discovered in America. The turn-of-the-century New York Yiddish press abounded with references to the enthusiasm of Jewish women, even the newly arrived, for the latest styles of dress and interior decoration. Furthermore, there were certain clear contrasts between Jews and other groups in respect to the consumption of goods. Advertisements of major American companies such as Borden's and Nabisco appeared more rapidly in the Yiddish press than in the foreign-language newspapers of other immigrants, suggesting that these companies quickly identified Jews, and especially Jewish women, as a strong prospective market for national brands. This attraction to new kinds of products and pleasures also contributed to the rapid development of a resort culture among Jews, which set them apart not only from other immigrants but from virtually all Americans of similarly modest means. From a combination of distinctive cultural, economic, and social characteristics, therefore, Jewish women emerged as potent agents of assimilation who identified the use of new products as an important way of participating in American life.

Published research on women in American business is still scarce. As a result, many commercial ventures by Jewish women throughout the twentieth century have barely been traced. Given that some of the most famous businesswomen, such as JENNIE GROSSINGER and HELENA RUBINSTEIN, have not yet been treated by scholarly biographies, it is not surprising that women of regional reputation—owners of retail stores, restaurants, and inns, as well as caterers of kosher and other foods—remain obscure or unknown in the historical record. Since the colonial period, Jewish women in America have done business as small-scale merchants and proprietors, and as manufacturers of light consumer goods both on the frontier and in the big cities. A number of them achieved major regional reputations, such as BEATRICE FOX AUERBACH, who headed the G. Fox and Co. department store of Hartford (dubbed the "Center of Connecticut Living Since 1847") from 1938 to 1965, Rose Blumkin, owner of Nebraska Furniture Mart of Omaha from 1937 to 1983, and Hannah Levy, co-owner of Denver's Fashion Bar chain of clothing stores from 1933 through the 1980s. Others represented significant successes in American business, such as Sylvia Weinberger, who produced and distributed kosher chopped liver throughout the Northeast from 1955 to 1989,

Beginning around the turn of the century, major American companies began to appeal explicitly to Jewish women. The dual-language Passover Cook Book *depicted here was published by Borden's Farm Products in 1940, but it is typical of advertising material the company began to produce some thirty years earlier.*

and particularly Tillie Lewis (originally Myrtle Ehrlich), who introduced the Italian pomodoro tomato to California in the 1930s and owned and operated a major canning business until 1966. The focus of the following survey, however, will be on women of national reputation in the marketing of nonedible consumer products or services. In the fields of resorts, women's wear, cosmetics, toys, film-production, and advertising, Jewish women have stood among the nation's most significant entrepreneurs and executives.

The fascination of New York's Jewish immigrants with the idea of the vacation produced a rich resort life in the Catskill Mountains, home to Grossinger's, one of the country's most renowned resorts. In the early twentieth century, the Jewish vacation was viewed as an escape for mothers from the drudgery of housekeeping in the congested immigrant city. Husbands typically sent their wives and children to the mountains, joining them on weekends. Given the strong female presence in the holiday settings, it is not surprising that a woman rose to become the quintessential resort entrepreneur. Innkeeping was a common occupation among the Jews of Eastern Europe,

and the Galician-born Jennie Grossinger had ancestors on both sides of her family who had served as innkeepers or estate managers. Her development as an entrepreneur took place within the framework of a family business that began in 1914 when the Grossinger family bought a small farm in Ferndale, New York, and opened a boardinghouse for vacationing immigrants. By the late 1920s, situated on a new, larger property, the successful Grossinger's Hotel and Country Club included sixty-three acres of woodland and a lake. In the highly personalized business of resort proprietorship, Jennie Grossinger established herself not only as a capable business manager, but more importantly as a hostess whose warmth and concern for her guests' comfort were instrumental in building up a loyal clientele over the years.

Taking charge of the family business after her father's death in 1931, Grossinger produced the model of a total resort experience for the average as well as the affluent consumer. From its early days, the complex included a bath in every room, still a notable luxury in the 1920s, and a huge dining room that seated four hundred. It also offered menu selections, a

The motto of Jennie Grossinger's resort was "Grossinger's Has Everything." One specialty that was available even to those who did not venture to her wooded grounds in the Catskills was her wine. A label is reproduced here. [Peter H. Schweitzer]

dance band, camp activities for children, winter sports such as ice skating, uniformed bellmen, and other amenities that would become standard in the area's hotels. To this enterprise, Grossinger added a host of "extras," including art classes, free honeymoons to couples who had met at Grossinger's, winter "reunions" of summer guests, convention facilities, vacations donated to charities for raffle and door prizes, and a constant circuit of talented and ultimately famous entertainers, with the innovative practice of booking a different act every night. Grossinger's also became famous for its stable of professional athletes who trained and gave lessons at the resort, including tennis star Jack Kramer and swimming great Florence Chadwick. At its peak, Grossinger's had 600 rooms, a dining room that seated 1,700 people, two kitchens—one for meat and one for dairy—a nightclub with two stages, a post office, an airport, a ski slope, an Olympic-sized swimming pool, a golf course, and a riding academy, as well as a space for Jewish and Christian religious services. Fittingly, its slogan was "Grossinger's Has Everything." Although changing vacation patterns among Americans would lead to the resort's decline after the 1960s and its closing in 1986, Jennie Grossinger had presided over and personified the ultimate democratic luxury resort of the early and mid-twentieth century.

Like the kosher resort business, the women's clothing and cosmetic industries in America were born during the period of mass migration from Eastern Europe. Similarly, they offered Jewish women entrepreneurial opportunities based on both the female orientation and the newness of the field. The innovations of businesswomen in clothing and cosmetics generally consisted of creative combinations of marketing and product creation.

One of the most significant innovations in women's clothing during the twentieth century was the modern brassiere, whose development and marketing owed much to the initiative of IDA COHEN ROSENTHAL. Like Grossinger, Ida Cohen grew up in a family that supported itself by running a business, in this case a general store that her mother operated in a shtetl near Minsk (Russian Poland). She immigrated to America in 1905, and within a decade emerged as a successful dressmaker in Hoboken, New Jersey, and later in Manhattan. In 1921, she made the bold stroke of creating a partnership with an English high-fashion designer, Enid Bissett. Unhappy with the defeminizing styles of the decade, Rosenthal and Bissett, with the assistance of Ida's husband, William Rosenthal, concentrated on making a brassiere that would fit rather than constrict the bosom. The simple cotton bra they created was initially marketed as a free bonus to accompany every dress purchased. Quickly, however, demand stimulated the trio to form the Maiden Form Brassiere Company in 1923.

After 1929, the flapper disappeared and the urban vogue returned to a fuller, more feminine look, which was propitious for Maidenform sales. The support bra also acquired new appeal when women were called to work in heavy industry during World War II. In addition to bras, the company began manufacturing girdles, lingerie, and swimwear, and it would ultimately become one of the nation's largest makers of women's foundation garments. In the postwar era, the company reached new heights of marketing with one of the best-known advertising campaigns of the time. In one of a series of similar ads, a vital young women dressed in a bra and boxing shorts appears with the slogan "I dreamed I was a knockout in my Maidenform bra." Although she was the force behind the company's effective marketing strategies, Rosenthal assumed the chairmanship of Maidenform only after her husband's death in 1958, and she continued to supervise retail sales until her own death fifteen years later.

In contrast to the immigrant-based experience of Rosenthal, who started out working as a dressmaker, the most conspicuous Jewish women in the post–World War II clothing industry entered as designers or purchasing agents, many of whom were college educated. The career of Linda Wachner provides an illustration. Born in 1946, the daughter of a New York fur salesman and a homemaker, Wachner graduated from the University of Buffalo and went immediately into retail buying, working in the 1970s as a bra-and-girdle buyer for Macy's. Success in this arena led to a series of executive positions. Wachner became a vice president of Warnaco's lingerie division and then made a dramatic move to Max Factor, where, as president of the U.S. division, she restored a flagging business in a five-year period (1979–1984). In 1986, she and a partner engineered a hostile takeover of the Warnaco Group, Inc., which controlled a large share of the women's undergarment market, including such prestigious brands as Warner's, Olga, Valentino, Scaasi, Ungaro, Bob Mackie, and Fruit of the Loom. Emerging as chairman, president, and CEO of Warnaco, Wachner became one of the highest-paid and most powerful businesswomen in America in the 1990s. Her success as an executive was based not only on her driving ambition but also on her keen marketing sense, renowned within the industry.

The careers of Ida Rosenthal and Linda Wachner show something of the generational difference among Jewish entrepreneurs, and a parallel is found in the fashion business. ESTELLE SOMMERS, the founder of the Capezio brand of dance wear, and designer Anne Klein both came of age before World War II and went directly into business without a college education. Sommers started out as a small-scale proprietor, opening a dance-supply store in Cincinnati that she transformed in the 1960s into the Manhattan-based Capezio Dance-Theater Shops. Anne Klein, whose original name was Hannah Golofski, started her career at age fifteen with a job as a free-lance sketcher at a New York wholesale house. After the war, she formed a company with her first husband, Ben Klein, designing and marketing junior clothes. She won acclaim for pioneering the change in junior-sized garments from traditionally frilly styles to a sleeker, more sophisticated look. In 1968, she formed Anne Klein and Company and continued to distinguish herself as an innovator, producing high-style casual wear for women and packaging her designs in interchangeable parts that the customer could arrange to make an outfit. At the time of her death in 1974, her clothing lines ranked among the finest in the country.

In stark contrast to Sommers and Klein, the most important Jewish women in the post–World War II clothing industry—Diane von Furstenberg and Donna Karan—represented the affluent background of the postwar generation. They entered a fashion business that was already highly developed, and made significant innovations attuned to a new generation's demand for both professional wear and more sophisticated leisure wear. Both women were born after World War II, both attended college, and both had careers marked by high-powered entrances into the fashion marketplace.

Von Furstenberg (born Diane Simone Michelle Halfin), a Belgian, strode into the field in 1970 when she unveiled a distinctive collection to rave reviews by the New York press. Within a few months of opening her Seventh Avenue showroom in 1972, her company was earning wholesale revenues of $1.2 million. Five years later, her clothing line and "signature" accessories were earning a gross income of over $142 million. Having licensed her name to a number of manufacturers, she withdrew from the fashion business in 1983, only to return in 1990 out of disappointment with the products that were bearing her signature. Her marketing success quickly resumed, with new lines of clothing priced for the average consumer and a new emphasis on factory-to-customer marketing and on products for the Avon direct-marketing company. Von Furstenberg's name was one of the most well-known in the fashion industry. She was noted for producing simple yet elegant wrap-around dresses and shirtwaists at a time when the women's market had few attractive alternatives to either the highly informal styles of the youth culture or the formalwear of the elite.

The daughter of a custom tailor and a fashion model, Donna Karan entered the fashion business as an assistant to Anne Klein. After Klein died in 1974, Karan developed a reputation for herself by sustaining the Anne Klein label. In 1985, Karan started her own company, designing comfortable, feminine clothes for executives. The collection was immediately successful, and Karan boosted her reputation further in 1989 by launching an even more popular, moderately priced line, DKNY (Donna Karan New York). Karan's merchandise was noteworthy for departing from the male-styled executive suits that had initially accompanied women into the business and professional worlds. More than most designers, Karan maintained close contact with all phases of product development and attributed her success in part to the fact that she made clothes with an ordinary woman's body, rather than a model's, in mind. Her extraordinary ability to produce fashionable, functional, and boldly feminine outfits led one industry analyst to state that Karan was "the only world-class woman designer this country has developed."

Perhaps even more dramatically than in the clothing business, Jewish women have played an outstanding role in the development of the cosmetics industry. The names of Helena Rubinstein and ESTÉE LAUDER became virtual synonyms for cosmetics in twentieth-century America. The bold careers of these entrepreneurs reflected the burgeoning of an immense new industry. Their immigrant backgrounds proved significant, for both started out in business with a product from the world of their European Jewish relatives.

Rubinstein was born in Cracow, Poland, the daughter of a prosperous wholesale food broker. Her mother had a strong interest in feminine beauty, and gave Helena important lessons about preserving the health of one's skin. Even more critical to Rubinstein's career was the moisturizing cream her mother obtained from a chemist named Jacob Lykusky for the use of her family. When she left home to live with relatives in Australia, Rubinstein took twelve pots of Lykusky's face cream with her. In Australia's dry climate, Rubinstein's cream quickly became popular, and in 1902 she opened a beauty salon in Melbourne. The salon was unique because it not only marketed skin cream but also provided consultations on skin care and beauty. The extraordinary success of this salon allowed Rubinstein to leave Australia for Europe in 1904 with $100,000 in profits, which she would invest in salons in both London (1908) and Paris (1912). She left the Melbourne business in the hands of two of her sisters, a practice she would continue with her European salons when she immigrated with her husband and two children to the United States in 1915. By this time, she had already pioneered the modern, full-fledged cosmetics salon, which included such innovations as treatments for skin marred by acne and on-site professional massages as a beauty service.

Rubinstein perceived the American market as huge in potential, not only because of its size and affluence, but also because the restraint and modesty of American women, compared to Rubinstein's European clients, was about to give way to much more sophisticated habits. By 1917, she had established salons in New York City, San Francisco, Boston, and Philadelphia, starting with the City of Paris store in San Francisco. One of the marketing innovations she introduced in America was the sale of her products in department stores. This created yet another precedent-setting change: personal training of department store clerks by Rubinstein herself, who was concerned about maintaining a high quality of service to the customer. In-store training of clerks would become a basic marketing feature in the cosmetics industry, as would Rubinstein's use of women as traveling sales representatives to demonstrate products in local stores. Rubinstein was also responsible for intro-

ducing a complex level of specialization into the cosmetics field. During her European period, she received fairly extensive training in the chemistry of skin lotions and employed many chemists, dermatologists, and other specialists throughout her career. Her company marketed hundreds of new beauty and medicinal products. Emphasizing diet, exercise, and massage as well as cosmetic treatments, Rubinstein originated the "total" approach to beauty and conceived of her work as having a scientific foundation. Her international success made her one of the wealthiest and most celebrated entrepreneurs of the twentieth century. After her death, control of the company passed to Rubinstein's niece Mala Rubinstein.

Careful to conceal her birthdate, Estée Lauder was born Josephine Esther Mentzer sometime before World War I, the child of affluent Central European Jews who had settled in Corona, New York. From early childhood, Lauder was interested in beauty and skin care. Her mother's brother, who was a skin specialist, brought with him from Europe a special recipe for skin cream, and he taught Lauder how to make it in a laboratory constructed in a stable behind the Mentzer house. The young Estée launched her career by marketing this cream through Florence Morris's beauty salon on the Upper East Side. It was here that she first jarred and labeled the cream with her own name, and created a line of face powder, lipstick, and eyeshadow. In addition to selling these products, she did makeup on customers while they were waiting for their hair to dry. Intent on expanding as rapidly as possible, Lauder opened up and hired staff for makeup counters at other locations, including hotels and resorts on Long Island. Her business began its spectacular climb in 1946, when Saks Fifth Avenue ordered and quickly sold out a large shipment of Lauder cosmetics. A tireless marketer, Lauder toured the country visiting both large and small department stores, where she set up counters, trained clerks, and established a rigorous policy of personal appearance and service among them. She also spent time persuading personnel in women's departments to steer customers to her beauty counter. She placed samples with fashion and beauty editors of local newspapers and magazines, and personally guided the print and broadcast advertising of her new concessions. In this period of expansion, Lauder used a number of marketing techniques that ultimately became conventions in the industry: giveaway samples, gifts-with-purchase, and direct mailings of invitations to women to visit the Lauder counter. In 1953, Lauder began selling Youth Dew, a bold fragrance that marked the company's entrance into the perfume business and that earned more than $150 million by 1985. By 1995, Estee Lauder, Inc., was registering annual sales of $2.9 billion and commanding about 40 percent of the upscale cosmetics market.

One of the firm's critical successes was the 1968 introduction of the 117-product Clinique line of fragrance-free, allergy-tested cosmetics. Clinique was promoted by means of an innovative in-house advertising campaign, headed by a former editor of *Vogue* who had been lured away from the magazine to serve as Lauder's advertising chief. Creating a new look in cosmetics advertising, the ads featured "still-life" photographs of Clinique bottles next to a glass with a toothbrush in it, underlined by the caption "Twice A Day." The stark ads, noteworthy for their lack of female models and references to age or life-style, fit Lauder's concept of the product line as one that was scientifically developed to suit the skin of anybody at any age.

Estée Lauder, Inc., remained essentially a family business, with Lauder's two sons and several grandchildren and other relatives inducted into executive positions.

In addition to fashion-related industries, Jewish businesswomen have been attracted to the field of children's dolls, toys, and games. The two toy companies that would end up as America's largest by the late twentieth century—Mattel and Hasbro—were both founded by Jews, and the former depended primarily on the marketing ability of RUTH HANDLER, who created the most monumental success in the history of brand-named toys, the Barbie doll.

The tenth child of Polish immigrants, Ruth Mosko (originally Moskowicz) was born in Denver, Colorado. She was raised by a sister who was twenty years her senior and who owned a successful drugstore and soda fountain. It was in partnership with her husband, Elliot Handler, that Ruth made her own successful venture in business. In 1939, the couple began selling Plexiglas knickknacks that Elliot manufactured in a small shop. As would be the case for the rest of their careers, Ruth handled the marketing of merchandise while Elliot concentrated on design and production. She started an informal partnership with Elliot and a former partner of Elliot's in plasticware, Harold "Matt" Matson. The company, called "Mattel" from the two men's names, began by manufacturing picture frames but quickly moved on to wooden doll furniture. When the wartime ban on plastics ended, Elliot, recognizing the ukulele fad of the time, developed a very popular plastic toy called the Uke-a-Doodle, which Ruth began marketing in 1947. Two years later, Mattel began production of a line of plas-

tic music-making toys that made the company's fortune and established its position as a leader in the industry. The next successful product line consisted of cap guns and "Winchester" rifles, as well as a repeating-fire "Burp Gun" modeled on the one used by paratroopers—the first Mattel product advertised on television.

Handler's astute understanding of the potential role of television for marketing was one of the primary reasons for Mattel's success in the industry. In 1955, Walt Disney invited the Handlers (Matson had sold out his share of the company) to be a sponsor of the new Mickey Mouse Club show. Their decision to do so had a strong effect on the toy business, which suddenly shifted from being a seasonal industry, focused on Christmas shopping, to one that experienced a year-round demand because of direct appeals to children during daily and weekly television shows. Furthermore, confronted with a time lag between the appearance of the television ad and the rush of retail orders, Mattel developed its own "retail detail," employed to visit stores all over the United States in order to report directly to the head office about demand, bypassing the longer information route through jobbers and representatives. Mattel sales nearly tripled between 1955 and 1958, and the new visibility of the company that came with television was magnified by the introduction of the Barbie doll in 1959. An adaptation of a risqué German doll for adults that Handler saw on a trip to Europe, Barbie had an odd combination of sophistication and innocence that distinguished it sharply from other dolls on the market. By 1969, the Barbie Fan Club had over 1.5 million members in the United States alone, and Mattel controlled over 10 percent of the nation's toy market. The Barbie collection, which quickly came to include a number of relatives and friends, such as boyfriend Ken, was constantly adapted to reflect changes in social attitudes and fashions. It thus possessed extraordinary longevity in the faddish toy market, and even acquired a cult status within American popular culture. In 1967, Mattel marketed one other highly popular line, the Hot Wheels die-cast metal miniature cars, which became the company's second biggest-selling product after Barbie. The Handlers left the company and the toy business in 1975 because of legal problems connected with alleged financial malfeasance by Ruth.

A small but not insignificant segment of the toy business has been the Jewish religious and educational market, which stimulated the entrepreneurial success of Diana Forman's Bible Dolls in the 1940s and 1950s. A rabbi's wife, Forman envisioned rejuvenating

RUTH HANDLER's "Barbie Doll" was one of the most successful toys ever created.
In the 1960s, Barbie had a secretary to answer the twenty thousand fan letters a week she received
and her fan club in the United States numbered 1.5 million members. This publicity photo was taken in 1984
at the International Barbie Doll Collector's Club celebration of Barbie's 25th anniversary.
[UPI/Corbis-Bettmann]

the Jewish home in America by selling novel and artistic Jewish items. She created a series of dolls representing biblical figures and packaged each one with a vial of soil from Israel, a few ornaments, and a "storyette" that taught a moral lesson. The products of the Bible Doll Company of America were sold by major department stores, and the business was sufficiently lucrative to attract a buyout by the Madame Alexander Doll Company in the 1950s.

With the notable exception of the Albert Lasker Agency, Jews did not play a major role in the American advertising industry until the second half of the twentieth century. In the early 1900s, the most prominent Jewish woman in the ad business was HELEN WOODWARD, who may have been the first woman to serve as an account executive in the industry. Born in 1882 in New York City, she lived on the Upper East Side until the family moved to Boston, where she attended the Girls' Latin School, a college-preparatory public school. Her career in advertising started in 1903 with a clerical job in the Hampton Agency, a

leader in the field. She gained some experience writing advertising copy for a publishing company, and in 1908 began working for the *Women's Home Companion*, one of the biggest-circulation magazines of the day. For *WHC* she inaugurated a "girls' club" whose purpose was to sell subscriptions. Her next job was a major promotional campaign for the *Review of Reviews*, writing the advertising for the first published volumes of Matthew Brady's Civil War photos. In 1912, she went to work for the Presbrey Advertising Agency, one of the premier agencies in the nation. This was an achievement, for the few women who worked as ad copywriters in those years were employed by department stores, not agencies. At Presbrey, she was put in charge of the *Review of Reviews* account, and created a new style of copywriting for books, emphasizing their content rather than their binding and external appearance. She used this approach to launch O. Henry's collections of short stories just before World War I. She married writer and historian William Woodward in 1913 and retired from the advertising business in 1923, spending the next four decades as a free-lance writer. Her pioneering role in the advertising business had a large impact, for the autobiographical account of her career, *Through Many Windows* (1926), was widely referred to by vocational counselors as a model for aspiring young women.

In the post–World War II period, the most significant woman in American advertising was SHIRLEY POLYKOFF, whose career involved both the shift toward hair-dyeing and the candid exaltation of blondeness that marked the consumer taste of American women between the 1950s and 1970s. Long fascinated by advertisements, which she believed served as models of American life for immigrants, the Brooklyn-born Polykoff started out as a copywriter for a local women's specialty shop in the 1920s, and moved on to hold the top fashion-writing job in Bamberger's and Kresge's department stores in Newark, New Jersey. In the 1940s, Polykoff, who retained her maiden name in business, wrote ads for the Frederick-Clinton Agency, specializing in copy for women's shoes but also producing the renowned musical advertisement "Chock Full o' Nuts, the heavenly coffee." By 1955, she had built up an impressive résumé, which attracted an offer from the prestigious agency Foote, Cone & Belding. Within her first few days, Polykoff was given a new account, that of the fledgling Clairol company, for which she created the famous "Does She Or Doesn't She?" slogan. The Clairol campaign was almost a test case for advertising methods because the idea of hair-dyeing was not socially acceptable. Polykoff's ingenious campaign centered on a mother-and-child motif in order to nullify any connotations of cheapness or promiscuity that might be associated with the product. Within a few years, the percentage of women using hair colorings rose from about 7 percent to about 50 percent.

In the 1950s and 1960s, Polykoff created several other memorable slogans for Clairol products: "Is it true blondes have more fun?," "If I've only one life, let me live it as a blonde!," and "The closer he gets, the better you look!" The television ad for "The closer he gets" campaign, which showed a young couple running to meet each other across a distance and culminated with the man picking up the woman, had a large impact on other campaigns and entered the popular culture as a cliché of the romantic encounter. Her final Clairol slogan, created just before her retirement from Foote, Cone & Belding in 1973, was "To know you're the best you can be." Reflecting the rise of feminism and the end of the "Does She Or Doesn't She" era, it too became a classic that reverberated through American culture. Recognized with two "firsts" at the Inter-national Film Festivals in Cannes and Venice, Polykoff was the highest-paid employee and senior vice president at Foote, Cone & Belding, as well as the first living woman elected to the American Advertising Hall of Fame. She enjoyed a final decade of success as head of her own advertising agency, retiring in 1984.

As was the case in advertising, Jews were first among women to assume positions of top authority in the motion picture industry. Sherry Lansing, whose mother was a refugee from Nazi Germany, graduated summa cum laude in theater from Northwestern University in 1966, enjoyed a brief modeling career, and then went to work as a script reader in Hollywood. By the late 1970s she became vice president of creative affairs at Metro-Goldwyn-Mayer and then vice president of production at Columbia Pictures. In 1980, Lansing was appointed president of the feature-film division of Twentieth Century–Fox, thereby becoming the first woman to be placed in charge of production at a major studio. In 1983, she left Fox to be an independent producer. She was responsible for a number of highly successful films, including *Kramer vs. Kramer* (1979), *Fatal Attraction* (1987), and *Indecent Proposal* (1993).

Dawn Steel began working in Hollywood in 1978, where she rapidly moved from a minor position in the merchandising department of Paramount to that of production chief. In 1987, Steel became the president of Columbia Pictures, succeeding Lansing as the most powerful woman in Hollywood. Partly as a result of her difficult personality, Steel was let go by Columbia in 1991 and, like Lansing, became an independent producer. She produced or collaborated on the production of such popular movies as *Flashdance* (1983), *Beverly Hills Cop* (1984), *Top Gun* (1986), and *The Untouchables* (1987).

A survey of the role of Jewish women in American consumer business over the twentieth century reveals that entrepreneurial pioneering tended to be relegated to the older generation. Those who can be regarded as founders or trailblazers of an industry—Grossinger, Rosenthal, Rubinstein, Lauder, Handler—were shaped by the immigrant context. Without exception, these women came from families with significant commercial experience, they collaborated with husbands and other family members, and they had the instinct or foresight to focus their talents on consumer industries that were in an early stage of development. In this respect, their generation benefited from the fact that the period of Jewish immigration coincided with the formative era for new consumer industries. The most influential women in the latter part of the century—such as Linda Wachner and Donna Karan—generally worked their way up within the retail, managerial, and executive ranks of a highly developed consumer economy. The many college-educated women entering corporate advertising, marketing, and retailing in the 1980s and thereafter would follow their lead.

BIBLIOGRAPHY

General background on Jewish women and their response to the American consumer economy is provided by Andrew R. Heinze, *Adapting to Abundance: Jewish Immigrants, Mass Consumption and the Search for American Identity* (1990); for a survey of the subject of Jewish women in business, see Irene D. Neu, "The Jewish Businesswoman in America," *American Jewish Historical Quarterly* 66 (September 1976): 137–154. There are also significant references in Daniel Pope and William Toll, "We Tried Harder: Jews in American Advertising," *American Jewish History* 72 (September 1982): 26–51.

Bibliographical information about women with their own entries in this publication is included with each individual entry. For information on Linda Wachner, see *Working Woman* (May 1992) and the company profile of Warnaco in *International Directory of Company Histories*, vol. 12. On Anne Klein, see *NYTimes*, March 20, 1974, *Newsweek* (April 1, 1974), and *Time* (April 1, 1974); Donna Karan, *New Yorker* (November 7, 1994), *Vogue* (June 1994), *NYTimes Magazine* (May 4, 1986), *Cosmopolitan* (October 1988), *Savvy Woman* (September 1989); Diane von Furstenberg, *Biographical Dictionary of American Business Leaders*, *Los Angeles Times*, August 31, 1995, *Newsweek* (March 22, 1976). On Diana Forman, see Jenna Weissman Joselit, *The Wonders of America* (1994), 82–84.

ANDREW R. HEINZE

ALBERT, MILDRED ELIZABETH LEVINE (1905–1991)

"M.A." and "The Mighty Atom," as Mildred Albert was called, charmed the fashion world as an international fashion consultant, lecturer, columnist, and radio and television personality.

The youngest of four children of Russian Jewish immigrant parents, Elizabeth (Sugarman) and Thomas Levine, Mildred was born in Russia on January 14, 1905, and grew up in Roxbury, Massachusetts. Her father was a builder and real estate developer in Brookline. She was about to enter the Sargent School of Physical Education (now part of Boston University) when she met James Albert, a freshman at Harvard. After meeting at "The Crest" at Winthrop, Massachusetts, where their families summered, they began a courtship that lasted throughout their college

years. In 1926, Mildred graduated and began teaching gym classes at Somerville High School in Massachusetts, while James Albert continued his education at law school. After they married in 1928, Albert worked at Florence Street Settlement House in the South End of Boston, where she taught art, dance, and literature to women and teenagers. The couple had three children: Justine Iris (Joy), born in 1930; Jeanne Marion, born in 1931; and Robert Alan, born in 1933.

The idea for creating the first finishing school in New England came to Albert when she was teaching posture at Massachusetts General Hospital. Among the enthusiastic students was the daughter of a prominent Boston family, to whom Albert taught good posture and etiquette in preparation for the debutante's "coming out" party. The results were so successful that Albert was asked to give private lessons to several of the young woman's friends. In 1936, with those six women as her first pupils, Albert created a finishing school called the Academie Moderne. Many thought she was foolish to begin this venture in the middle of the Depression, but her husband and father supported

An internationally known entrepreneur in the modeling industry who was dubbed Boston's "First Lady of Fashion," Mildred Albert was also a philanthropist and media personality who strongly identified with Jewish history and culture. [Jeanne Davis]

her. Her course included more than lessons on poise, proper walking, and good diction. She also developed students' cultural tastes by taking them to museums and ballet performances.

When some former finishing school students sought her advice for modeling at their Junior League fashion shows, she decided to open a separate school for women who wanted to become career models. In 1944, she cofounded Hart Model Agency and Promotions, Inc., with Muriel Williams Hart and her husband, Francis Hart. During those years, Albert also began covering major designer fashion shows. She became Boston's "First Lady of Fashion," initiating around-the-pool fashion shows, luncheon fashion shows, and the first cocktail fashion shows. In addition, she organized the first Million Dollar Back Bay Fashion Show for the Back Bay Association. Innovative in her business, Albert set up a six-week fashion course for brides in 1959. In 1981, she sold both businesses, but remained dean emeritus to the school and consultant to the agency.

In addition to her entrepreneurial successes, Albert enjoyed a secondary career as a media personality. She had a weekly WEEI radio program, "Youthful Loveliness," in the late 1930s, and a WCRB program, "Fashion As I See It," in the 1960s through the 1970s. In the 1980s, she continued to report on fashion shows for the CBS *Good Day Show*. Late in life, she covered fashion shows and various benefits for *The Tab* newspapers.

A legendary figure in the fashion world, Albert shared her name and money as a generous philanthropist. She coordinated fashion shows for various charities such as the National Foundation for Infantile Paralysis, the March of Dimes, and UNICEF. She was an overseer of the Wang Center for the Performing Arts and a cofounder of the Boston Arts Festival.

Albert was also involved in Jewish life. While only somewhat religiously observant, she identified strongly with Jewish history and culture. In the late 1920s, she taught Sunday school at Temple Israel in Boston, and served on the board of the Hebrew Teachers College in Boston in the 1920s and 1930s. While Albert identified herself more as a cultural Jew, she never hid her Judaism during her work with the predominantly non-Jewish society world.

Albert received numerous awards for her work from institutions such as Public Action for the Arts, Boston University, Sargent College, the National Foundation for the March of Dimes, and the USO Greater Boston Soldiers and Sailors Committee.

The year 1990 was not the first year of an official date of honor for Mildred Albert. On October 29,

1986, Massachusetts governor Michael S. Dukakis issued a proclamation honoring her. That year, she celebrated the fiftieth anniversary of the Academie Moderne. At age eighty-two, she was quoted as saying, "I'm not retiring. . . . I wouldn't dream of stopping. . . . I believe if you retire, you die." Energetic until the end, Albert died in Boston on August 26, 1991.

BIBLIOGRAPHY

Albert, Mildred Elizabeth (Levine). Papers. Schlesinger Library, Radcliffe College, Cambridge, Mass.; Davis, Jeanne. Interview with the author, April 5, 1994.

SARA ALPERN

ALBERT, MIRIAM (1920–1976)

Miriam Albert's very active life was based in two cities, Chicago, where she was born on September 6, 1920, and Washington, D.C., where she died after a brief illness on August 10, 1976. She received her college education at Wright Junior College, the University of Chicago, and Northwestern University, studying psychology and office management.

At the time of her death, Albert was marking her thirtieth anniversary as a member of the staff of B'NAI B'RITH WOMEN. Her affiliation with B'nai B'rith began as a volunteer when she joined the B'nai B'rith Youth movement in Chicago in 1940. She rose through the ranks to become the first national president of B'nai B'rith Young Women, at that time a B'nai B'rith youth group, in 1946. In that year she also joined the professional staff of B'nai B'rith Women, the first year of its existence as an organization independent of B'nai B'rith. Until that time, women's participation in that men's organization had been limited to forming auxiliary groups. Albert became assistant director of B'nai B'rith Women in 1952 and served as executive director from 1959 until her death. At that time, the organization had a professional staff of thirty-seven and a membership of 150,000. Eulogies and obituaries reflect her great dedication to B'nai B'rith Women, her strong, calm style of leadership, and her personal warmth and generosity.

B'nai B'rith Women has contributed signficantly to Jewish life both in the United States and in Israel, with programs involving human rights, Jewish education, community service, and youth activities. The course of Miriam Albert's involvement with the movement charts the expansion of women's roles in the organizational life of American Jewry.

BIBLIOGRAPHY

AJYB 78:538; *B'nai B'rith Messenger,* August 20, 1976; *National Jewish Monthly (B'nai B'rith)* (October 1976); *NYTimes,* August 11, 1976, 38:5; *Washington Post,* August 11, 1976; *Women's World (B'nai B'rith)* (August/September 1976).

LISA EPSTEIN

ALCOTT, AMY (b. 1956)

Golfer Amy Alcott has had a long and illustrious career. One of the greats of ladies' golf, she was still a force on the tour in 1996, at the age of forty.

Amy Alcott was born February 22, 1956, in Kansas City, Missouri. She grew up in California, daughter of an orthodontist and a mother who imbued her daughter with a sense of life as art. Golf moved to the center of Alcott's life when she was nine years old. Recognizing her remarkable talents, the local golf club allowed her special privileges on the course. In 1975, forgoing college, she joined the Ladies Professional Golf Association (LPGA) tour. From then until 1986, she was able to claim at least one tour victory every year. She has won four major championships, including three Nabisco Dinah Shore tournaments. In 1980, she won the U.S. Women's Open by nine strokes.

Alcott has often been a high-spirited feature of the LPGA tour. Two of her three "Dinah" victories were celebrated with dives into a pond. When she was asked what she would do with her winnings from a tour event sponsored by the Archdiocese of Trenton, New Jersey, she joked about giving the money to the United Jewish Appeal. At the JAL Big Apple Classic in 1995, she played the last hole wearing a goofy hat complete with fake dreadlocks. But her life has also been marked by sadness. Her father died in 1981, when she was only twenty-five years old. Her mother died ten years later. It was after her mother's death that Alcott took up painting as an avocation that would come to rival her dedication to golf.

In 1983, Alcott became the sixth golfer to win $1 million on the LPGA tour. In each of three separate seasons (1979, 1980, and 1984), she won four tournaments. She has also won three of the four modern major championships, a feat exceeded only by Pat Bradley. In 1986, she was awarded the Founders Cup, which recognizes altruistic contributions to the betterment of society by an LPGA member. In 1988, she had her best year yet, with fifteen top-ten finishes and $292,349 in earnings. That year she became the third member of the LPGA to pass the $2 million mark in earnings over a career.

That same year, Alcott began to attract an annoying sort of attention when it was realized that she was only three wins away from inclusion in the LPGA Hall of Fame. According to the rules of that organization, a golfer must win two major championships and more than twenty-nine tournaments for automatic inclusion. By 1991, Alcott had won two more tournaments, putting her only one win away. In 1995, the honor was proving elusive for three golfers—Alcott, Beth Daniel, and Betsy King. In that year, the closest Alcott came to a win was a tie for fifth. Still, it was one of only four winless seasons in her twenty years on the tour.

By 1996, King had won her place in the Hall of Fame, but Alcott and Daniel were still under the gun. Daniel had won thirty-one tournaments but only one major. Alcott had five majors and twenty-nine total.

The Hall of Fame issue has put a considerable amount of pressure on Alcott, but she has shunned sympathy. "It needs to be hard," she says. "It should be tough." But she goes on to declare that the rules should be changed because "there's nothing out there for the younger players to strive for." She is referring to the fact that the number and quality of players have so increased that winning thirty tournaments for a golfer who joins the tour in the 1990s will be virtually impossible. She also declared in 1995, "In my mind, I had a hall-of-fame career five or six years ago." A great many people would agree with her.

Alcott currently lives in Santa Monica, California, and is hoping for a career in broadcasting when she retires from golf.

BIBLIOGRAPHY

Garrity, John. "Golf Plus: Not a Bad Life." *Sports Illustrated* (October 2, 1995); LPGA Profiles, Internet; Molinet, Jason. "Alcott Makes Run for Hall of Fame." *Newsday,* July 21, 1995; "Beth Daniel, Betsy King and Amy Alcott." *Gannett News Service,* June 12, 1995.

KATHLEEN THOMPSON

ALEXANDER, BEATRICE (1895–1990)

Best known as Madame Alexander, Beatrice Alexander became acquainted with doll making while watching her father repair dolls in his shop. She observed at an early age how important dolls were to children, and how often the poorly made or fragile dolls were impossible to mend. It was in her father's doll hospital, the first of its kind in the United States, that Alexander learned her craft. Beatrice Alexander established her doll business in her home in 1923, and since then the Madame Alexander Doll Company has created more than 5,000 different dolls. Employing more than 650 people at its factory in Harlem, New York, the Alexander Doll Company is one of the largest doll manufacturing companies in the United States. Alexander believed that dolls play a vital educational role in a child's early development, and thus she created doll collections based on historic events, literature, music, art, and film. Madame Alexander Dolls, as they are called, are on permanent display at the Smithsonian Institution, the Brooklyn Children's Museum, the New Delhi Museum, and other museums worldwide.

Beatrice Alexander was born in New York City in 1895 to Russian immigrant parents. At the suggestion of her mother, she began to make dolls during World War I. The decrease in imported dolls created a shortage, and young Beatrice felt sympathy for children whose dolls could not be repaired or replaced. Her first project was the "Red Cross Nurse" rag doll with innovative, hand-painted, three-dimensional facial features. In 1923, she began to sell the dolls she had made on her kitchen table. By the late 1920s, she obtained a $5,000 loan to move her operations to a shop area. In the 1930s she began making dolls with lifelike details.

During this same period, the Alexander Doll Company obtained the trademark for a cloth Alice in Wonderland doll, a cloth series of Little Women characters, and a cloth series based on characters from Dickens's novels. A turning point for the Alexander Doll Company came in 1935, when the Canadian government granted the doll manufacturer the license to make Dionne Quintuplet dolls. The success of these dolls provided financial stability for the company and encouraged expansion. With the invention of synthetics in the 1940s, Alexander changed her materials to plastic and created dolls with vinyl heads and hair that could be styled. The demand for these dolls increased. Alexander obtained trademarks for well-known characters and public figures such as Scarlett O'Hara, Margaret O'Brien, Jacqueline Kennedy, Coco Chanel, Marlo Thomas, and various Disney characters.

During the period 1951–1954, the Alexander Doll Company was honored with the Fashion Academy Gold Medal. Also during this period, the British government requested dolls of the queen and her daughters. The 1953 coronation was reproduced in a set of thirty-six dolls dressed in exact detail copies of the royal family and honored guests, including Winston Churchill. This unique collection, valued then at $25,000, was donated to the Brooklyn Children's Museum.

In 1965, the Alexander Doll Company was honored by Ambassador Arthur Goldberg for its International Collection of United Nations Dolls. In 1968, the Smithsonian chose for its collection the "Madame Doll," representing the Revolutionary War, and the "Scarlett O'Hara" doll, based on the Civil War saga. Alexander dolls have received numerous awards from the doll industry, including the Doll of the Year Award (DOTY). In 1986, Madame Alexander was honored with the DOTY Lifetime Achievement Award.

Madame Alexander was also known for her philanthropic activities, which included work for B'nai B'rith, the Weizmann Institute, Harvard University, and the Massachusetts Institute of Technology. She was a devoted Zionist and was a charter member of the Women's League for Israel, which establishes homes for immigrants and disadvantaged youth in Israel. She served as vice president and was elected to the council of trustees of that organization. A rose garden was dedicated in her name at one of the league's homes in Jerusalem.

Beatrice Alexander was the wife of Phillip Behrman, with whom she had a daughter, Mildred. Mildred grew up in the business, as did her son, William Alexander Birnbaum. Although the company was sold in 1988, William Birnbaum remained president until 1994. Beatrice Alexander died at age ninety-five on October 3, 1990.

BIBLIOGRAPHY

Obituary. *NYTimes*, October 5, 1990; Press package, Madame Alexander Doll Company, NYC.

JULIE ALTMAN

ALLEN, ANNA MARKS (1800–1888)

"May you live to be a credit to yourself, a comfort and blessing to your parents, and the pride and protector of your sisters," wrote the educator and social activist Anna Allen to her nephew Lewis. In many ways, these words encapsulate her own life, which she devoted to the protection and betterment of the lives of Jewish women and children.

Allen was one of a group of Philadelphia Jewish women who established and ran the first independent

Jewish charitable societies in the United States. She was treasurer of the Female Hebrew Benevolent Society (founded 1819) for forty years and, for a time, its director as well. In 1838, along with REBECCA GRATZ, she founded the first Hebrew Sunday school in America, and in 1855, she started the Philadelphia Jewish Foster Home and Orphan Asylum, serving as its president until 1867. These institutions were later duplicated by Jewish women throughout America.

Anna was born in Sing Sing (now Ossining), New York, on March 30, 1800. Her father, Michael Marks (1761–1829), came to America from London in 1772. He married Jochebed (Johavith) Isaacks (1767–1852), also from England, in Newport, Rhode Island, in 1786. Anna was the sixth of nine children and the third daughter born to the couple. On December 10, 1823, she married Lewis Allen, Jr. (1793–1841), a Philadelphia merchant. He had come to the United States from London with his father in 1805. They had seven children: Amelia Johaveth (b. 1824), Lewis Marks (b. 1827), Henry Samson (b. 1828), Michael Mitchell (b. 1830), Benjamin Wolff (b. 1833), Charles Chauncy (b. 1835), and Alfred Hart (birthdate unknown).

The Allen family was prominent in early Philadelphia Jewish life. Anna Allen's father-in-law was president of Congregation Mikveh Israel from 1811 until his death in 1815, and her husband served as president of the congregation from 1834 until his own death in 1841. Though the offices of congregational life were restricted to men at that time, women of Allen's social position developed new ways to participate in the public life of the Jewish community. In particular, they tried to address the educational and spiritual needs of less fortunate Jewish women and children, whose numbers rose throughout the nineteenth century due to increased emigration from Europe. The growth of Jewish women's charitable societies closely mirrored developments among American Christian women, who, like their Jewish counterparts, seized upon newly emerging patterns of religious organization in America to establish a niche for themselves within the public sphere.

In 1875, Allen left Philadelphia for New York City, where she lived until her death on June 30, 1888. Anna Marks Allen's life work is a testament to her devotion to the Jewish community, and an important chapter in the history of women's contributions to the development of American Jewish life.

BIBLIOGRAPHY

Allen, Anna. Letter to Lewis Allen. Philadelphia, June 28, 1858. Ashton, Dianne. " 'Souls Have No Sex': Philadelphia Jewish Women and the Challenge of America." In *When Philadelphia Was the Capital of Jewish America*, edited by Murray Friedman (1993); Marcus, Jacob R. *The American Jewish Woman: A Documentary History* (1981); Markens, Isaac. *The Hebrews in America* (1888); Morais, Henry Samuel. *The Jews of Philadelphia* (1894); Stern, Malcolm H. *First American Jewish Families* (1991); *UJE*; Wolf, Edwin, and Maxwell Whiteman. *The History of the Jews of Philadelphia from Colonial Times to the Age of Jackson* (1957).

JAY M. EIDELMAN

ALSCHULER, ROSE HAAS
(1887–1979)

"Life is a mirage and life is an effort—and the fullness of life for every individual depends on the strength and beauty of his vision and the strength and beauty of his effort." These words are from the first paragraph of *I Believe—Today*, written by Rose Haas

As both a writer and a founder and administrator of nursery schools in the Chicago area, Rose Alschuler helped pioneer the study of early childhood education. [American Jewish Archives]

Alschuler in the 1920s. Alschuler was a prolific writer, lecturer, and educator, and in the later part of her life, she contributed to the development and growth of the State of Israel.

Rose was the third child of Mary (Greenebaum) and Charles Haas, born on December 17, 1887, and raised in Chicago. One of her aunts was HANNAH GREENEBAUM SOLOMON. Rose was educated at Vassar College (1905–1906) and the University of Chicago (1904–1905, 1906–1907). In 1907, Rose Haas married Alfred Alschuler, a famous architect, who was the first to use reinforced concrete in Chicago and designed numerous synagogues and public buildings. They had five children: Marion (b. 1909), Frances (1910–1986), Alfred S., Jr. (b. 1911), Richard (1915–1989), and John (b. 1918).

When the children were young, Rose Alschuler became very interested in the education of preschool and kindergarten children. She initiated a kindergarten program in Chicago that included her two older children and a child study group for couples.

Alfred and Rose Alschuler moved to Winnetka, a suburb of Chicago, in 1915, at a time when there were very few Jewish people living in the suburbs. Alschuler was a founding member, the first secretary (1922–1928), and a teacher for the first Sabbath school of North Shore Congregation Israel, the first Reform synagogue in the northern suburbs.

In 1922, Alschuler and her cousin Charlotte Kuh started the Children's Community School, the first nursery school in Chicago. It closed in 1926. From 1926 to 1931, Alschuler was the organizer and director of the Franklin Public School, the first nursery school to be affiliated with the Chicago Board of Education and the first public nursery school in the United States. The Elizabeth McCormick Fund provided health care and the Institute for Juvenile Research did case studies and provided psychological support for the school, which was under the auspices of the Chicago Woman's Club. In 1931, the school moved to Chicago Normal College, and Rose Alschuler continued her involvement until she moved in 1941.

Alschuler organized and was director of the following nursery schools: Winnetka Public School Nursery and Junior Kindergarten (1928–1940); Garden Apartment Nursery School (1928–1933), a project endowed by Julius Rosenwald; and eighteen Work Projects Administration nurseries (1933–1940). In 1930, Alschuler was a member of the Committee of the Infant and Preschool Child of the White House Conference on Child Health and Protection.

Alschuler was the chair for the Opportunity Through Education Round Table at the International Congress of Women held in Chicago in 1933. From 1938 to 1940, Alschuler was one of only two women who sat on the board of directors for the Federation of Jewish Charities of Chicago. While on the board, she focused on Jewish education. Alschuler was the first North Shore chair of the North Shore United Jewish Appeal in 1940–1941.

After her husband's death, she relocated to Washington, D.C., where she became chair of the National Commission for Young Children from 1941 to 1943, and was also a consultant for the Federal Housing Authority from 1941 to 1944.

After World War II, Alschuler traveled numerous times to Israel and became active in soliciting for Israel Bonds. Alschuler was instrumental in developing the concept of parlor meetings, which became a successful means to solicit funds for Israel Bonds. Alschuler's work helped to change the anti-Zionist attitude that was prevalent among many of the affluent Jews living in the northern suburbs of Chicago.

She published four books and numerous articles. An international guest speaker at early childhood education conferences, she appeared on radio broadcasts, and in 1955 she was highlighted on the Columbia Broadcasting System radio and newspaper series *This I Believe*.

Rose Haas Alschuler lived a full and active life that combined the role of motherhood with a career in the pioneer field of early childhood education. Her high level of expertise enabled her to become a popular speaker and respected writer. In response to the Holocaust and her visits to Israel, Alschuler's focus shifted to supporting the State of Israel through philanthropic work. Rose Haas Alschuler died on July 4, 1979.

SELECTED WORKS BY ROSE HAAS ALSCHULER

Bits and Pieces of Family Lore. Family history (1962); *Children's Center* (1942); *Painting and Personality: A Study of Young Children,* with LaBerta Hattwick (1947); *Play—The Child's Response to Life* (1937); *Two to Six* (1933).

BIBLIOGRAPHY

Alschuler, Rose Haas. Papers. Special Collections Department, University of Illinois, Chicago; Cutler, Irving. *The Jews of Chicago from Shtetl to Suburb* (1966); Lebeson, Anita Libman. *Recall to Life—The Jewish Woman in America* (1970); Marcus, Jacob R. *The American Jewish Woman* (1981); McCree, Mary Lynn. *Oral History Interview with Rose Haas Alschuler* (1973). Edited by Richard H. Alschuler (1985); Obituary. *Chicago Tribune,* July 6, 1979; Walton, Clyde C., ed. *Illinois Lives: The Prairie State Biographical Record* (1969); *Who's Who in World Jewry* (1972); *Who's Who of American Women* 1 (1958–1959); *WWIAJ* (1926, 1928, 1938).

SANDRA K. BORNSTEIN

AMERICAN, SADIE (1862–1944)

From 1893 to 1916, Sadie American and the NATIONAL COUNCIL OF JEWISH WOMEN were virtually synonymous. As one of the founders of the council, its first corresponding secretary (1893–1905), and later the paid executive secretary of the organization (1905–1914), American functioned as executive director, organizing local sections across the United States, representing the group at national and international meetings, and taking care of the routine work that building the organization required. In addition to these national duties, she also served as president of the council's New York section and was instrumental in establishing the organization's reputation as an effective agency for assisting Jewish immigrants. Yet her years of work on behalf of the organization were not without controversy. She resigned as executive secretary in 1914 and severed all ties with the council in 1916.

The same force of personality that enabled Sadie American to become a leader in the creation and success of the NATIONAL COUNCIL OF JEWISH WOMEN *would ultimately lead to a permanent rift between her and that organization. [American Jewish Historical Society]*

Sadie American was born on March 3, 1862, in Chicago, Illinois. She was the only child of Oscar American, a German immigrant and successful merchant, and Amelia (Smith), a native of New York. Educated in Chicago's public schools, she received a high school diploma, but, by her own account, was not allowed to attend college. Virtually nothing else is known of her personal life. She noted in an autobiographical sketch written about 1916 that she was involved in volunteer social service work as a young girl, but stated that as an adult family illness prevented her involvement in public work for many years.

American's intensive participation in both Jewish and non-Jewish organizations began in earnest in 1891. In that year, she became a member of the organizing committee of the Jewish Women's Congress, which was to be held in conjunction with the Chicago World's Fair of 1893 (the Columbian Exposition). The purpose of the congress, organized by fellow Chicagoan HANNAH GREENEBAUM SOLOMON, was to emphasize the role of women in American Jewish religious life, and to lay the groundwork for a national organization of Jewish women that would work to overcome Jewish illiteracy and inspire women to greater religious activity.

American was one of the most enthusiastic advocates of a national organization. The organizing committee chose her to deliver the final paper on the last day of the congress, calling for the formation of a national organization named—after some parliamentary maneuvering—the National Council of Jewish Women. Hannah Solomon was elected president by acclamation; Sadie American was elected corresponding secretary. This was the beginning of her council career.

But the National Council of Jewish Women was not American's only commitment. In the Jewish community, she became a club leader at the newly established Maxwell Street Settlement, working with young Eastern European Jewish immigrants, and she began to teach Sunday school at her own congregation, Sinai Temple. In the wider community, she became a member of the Women's Club of Chicago and eventually chair of its committee on permanent vacation schools and playgrounds. She wrote two papers based on her research. She was also a vice president and director of the Illinois Consumers' League, and president of Chicago's League for Religious Fellowship. In short, her involvement in the National Council of Jewish Women represented only a small part of her commitment to furthering the progressive social reforms of the late nineteenth and early twentieth centuries.

For the twenty-three years she was active in the council, American was a forceful, articulate spokesperson on behalf of the organization. The minutes of the triennial conventions, beginning in 1896, reveal the depth of her influence. She reported at length on her efforts to organize sections, told of the extensive correspondence she engaged in with Jewish women around the country as groups sought to become council affiliates, and detailed the statistics that showed the growing membership. All of these activities revealed her dedication to the council's success. For many Jewish women in the United States and Europe, she *was* the National Council of Jewish Women. On many occasions, she traveled both across the country and abroad to represent the council at other meetings of both Jewish and non-Jewish women's organizations.

In the last half of 1900, American left Chicago and moved to New York City with her mother. Her father did not accompany them; by June 1900, he was a patient in the Eastern Illinois Hospital for the Insane in Kankakee. American was soon involved with the council's New York section and became its president in 1902, a position she held until 1916. During her tenure as president, the New York section instituted immigrant aid programs that helped moved the national organization's focus away from religion and into social welfare. As she had in Chicago, American devoted much of her time in New York to civic organizations.

As the years passed, however, American became a figure of controversy because of her opinions and her personality. She was first attacked for her support of Sunday Sabbath observance, but members still reelected her as corresponding secretary at the 1900 triennial convention. She then came under increasing criticism for her sometimes brusque manner and autocratic style. A growing number of council members felt that she had become a liability rather than an asset to the organization. But despite this opposition, American was reelected corresponding secretary at both the 1903 and 1905 triennial conventions and appointed executive secretary in 1905. She held the latter position until the 1914 convention in New Orleans, when she could no longer deflect the criticism of her actions and her manner. Rather than face a constitutional change that closely circumscribed the position of executive secretary, she resigned. She continued to serve as the New York section's president until 1916, when her term ended and she was defeated for reelection.

Without American's organizational skills and articulate advocacy of the National Council of Jewish Women's purpose, the group would have disappeared

in its infancy, as did many other women's organizations early in the twentieth century. Sadie American passionately believed in the founding ideals of the council: that a group of Jewish women could come together to promote Jewish observance as well as social service. When the promotion of Jewish observance became too controversial, she helped council leaders to see that philanthropic service to the Jewish and non-Jewish communities would be the organization's most important contribution to American life. She had a strength of personality that made many people uncomfortable, but it was this strength that enabled her to accomplish her life's work.

Sadie American died in New York City on May 3, 1944.

SELECTED WORKS BY SADIE AMERICAN

"The Movement for Small Playgrounds." *American Journal of Sociology* 4 (1898–1899): 159–170; "The Movement for Vacation Schools." *American Journal of Sociology* 4 (1898–1899): 309–325; "Phases of Modern Education: XI—Vacation Schools." *Education* 26 (1906): 509–518, 614–623.

BIBLIOGRAPHY

AJYB 7 (1905–1906): 34–36, 24:115, 46:333; *American Hebrew* (1893–1916); *American Jewess* (1895–1898); American, Sadie. Papers. National Association of Jewish Social Workers, American Jewish Historical Society, Waltham, Mass., and National Council of Jewish Women, Library of Congress, Washington, D.C.; Elwell, Ellen Sue Levi. "The Founding and Early Programs of the National Council of Jewish Women: Study and Practice as Jewish Women's Religious Expression." Ph.D. diss., Indiana University, 1982; *JE*; Obituary. *NYTimes*, May 4, 1944, 19:3; *Reform Advocate* (1893–1901); Rogow, Faith. *Gone to Another Meeting: The National Council of Jewish Women, 1893–1993* (1993); *UJE*.

MARTHA KATZ-HYMAN

AMERICAN JEWESS, THE

The American Jewess, published from April 1895 to August 1899, was the first independent English-language magazine published by and for Jewish women in the United States. Founded and edited by writer, journalist, and clubwoman ROSA SONNESCHEIN, the magazine emerged from the network of activism created by late nineteenth-century middle-class Jewish clubwomen, particularly those from the NATIONAL COUNCIL OF JEWISH WOMEN (NCJW). *The American Jewess* also contributed to the NCJW by acting as a public forum promoting and supporting its activities and ideals.

Sonneschein, a clubwoman and writer active in Jewish and general women's associations in St. Louis, first asserted the need for a magazine that would connect American Jewish women across the country in a speech at the May 1893 Press Congress, held during the World's Columbian Exposition in Chicago. During a decade in which Jewish women's associations, especially synagogue sisterhoods, multiplied rapidly, Sonneschein's enthusiasm was particularly apt. In September 1893, also during the exposition, several prominent Jewish clubwomen, led by HANNAH GREENEBAUM SOLOMON, held the Jewish Women's Congress, bringing together participants from across the United States to discuss literature, philanthropy, and Judaism. Sonneschein likely garnered moral and financial support for *The American Jewess* from among these women and, in turn, lent her support to the NCJW, the organization they created.

In April 1895, Sonneschein began publishing *The American Jewess* from offices in Chicago. In 1896, Lucien Bonheur, well connected in New York financial and Jewish philanthropic circles, became Sonneschein's business partner and the business manager for the magazine. Bonheur opened New York offices and worked to bring in new sources of advertising and patronage, and thus improve the magazine's finances. Probably due partially to Bonheur's efforts and partially to the growing membership of the NCJW, the magazine's circulation reached the high figure of 29,000 subscribers.

Throughout its run, *The American Jewess*, in appealing to its intended audience of middle-class Jewish clubwomen, offered features both common to mainstream women's magazines and specifically geared to Jewish women. Short fiction and columns on popular medicine, music and art, household management, and fashion appeared in nearly every issue along with news of and commentary on the NCJW and other Jewish female philanthropic and social reform efforts, biographical sketches of prominent Jewish club and professional women, and articles by well-known rabbis and Jewish community leaders.

In its articles and editorials, *The American Jewess* discussed issues of fundamental concern to members of the NCJW and other middle-class Jewish women's groups. *American Jewess* writers argued for expanded roles for women in the synagogue and Jewish community. They promoted, most often in a limited way, both the benefits of women's education—particularly religious education—and the propriety of (some) women's work outside the home. Reflecting the ambivalence of the Jewish community, *The American Jewess* featured articles both in favor of and opposed to greater political rights for women. Some argued for suffrage in the same vein as they argued for a greater role in the synagogue—as extending women's moral guidance to the public sphere, where it was needed. More writers, however, including Sonneschein, believed that for American women—for middle-class women, in any case—suffrage was unnecessary. The gains that women had made through their club work and social positions convinced them that emancipation was a fact, not an unmet goal, except perhaps, some argued, in the religious sphere, where work remained to be done.

In addition to these kinds of articles, *The American Jewess* explicitly allied itself with the work of the NCJW. Within the first months of publication, Rosa Sonneschein declared a natural affinity between the NCJW and *The American Jewess* and, as "a woman to women," offered her magazine's aid to the organization's work. Several times, she proposed to turn the magazine into the NCJW's official publication, a move that the organization's leaders never accepted. Still, Sonneschein continued to demonstrate support for the organization by publishing progress reports from NCJW national leaders, minutes from local sections, and papers originally read before various NCJW meetings, and by reporting and editorializing on important NCJW events and prospective directions for the organization.

Like the NCJW, *The American Jewess* conveyed the middle-class belief in an essentially domestic vocation for American Jewish women, which included the transmission of Jewish tradition to their families in order to ensure group survival in modern America. As well, within the terms of this vocation, *The American Jewess* vigorously advocated the enlarged role for women in the Jewish community for which Jewish clubwomen in the 1890s worked.

Although Sonneschein expressed enthusiasm for the NCJW's success, because the magazine did retain independence from the organization, she also did not hesitate to make *The American Jewess* a forum for her critiques of it. She commended the NCJW for its philanthropic works but argued that it had the potential to fulfill a needed service to the American Jewish community by pursuing a religious mission. To this end, *The American Jewess* praised the NCJW's religious education work and called for more emphasis on Jewish observance. In the wake of the NCJW 1896 convention, at which NCJW president Hannah Solomon retained her position over the objections of more traditionally oriented members who argued that her observance of a Sunday Sabbath made her unfit to preside over a Jewish organization, Sonneschein

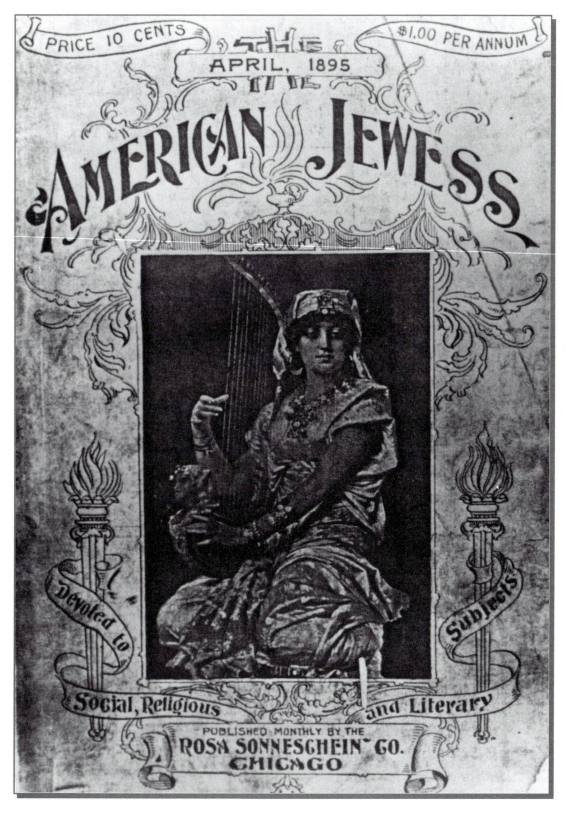

The American Jewess *was the first independent English-language magazine published by and for Jewish women in the United States. Pictured here is the cover of the first issue.*
[American Jewish Archives]

increasingly criticized the NCJW in the pages of *The American Jewess*. Though she supported Solomon's presidency, Sonneschein nevertheless deplored what she perceived as Solomon's devaluing of the traditional (Saturday) Sabbath, viewing it as symptomatic of religious division and inconsistency within the NCJW.

In 1896, Sonneschein also proposed that the NCJW take up the cause of Zionism as a means to gain members among the mass of immigrant Jewish women and thus become a truly representative national organization. That the NCJW did not pursue either a religious mission or Zionism, thus seemingly rejecting Sonneschein's recommendations, further fueled her criticism. This growing discord between Sonneschein and NCJW members likely contributed to the folding of *The American Jewess*.

Despite the gains in advertising and patronage that resulted from Bonheur's stint as business manager, financial difficulties prompted Sonneschein to seek more help for *The American Jewess*. In 1898, new managers took control over the magazine's publication, though Sonneschein remained as editor. To the disappointment of the management, subscription support for the magazine declined, so much so that it had to fold in August 1899. In her angry valedictory editorial, Rosa Sonneschein blamed the magazine's demise on its former subscribers, who, she believed, had become ashamed of receiving a Jewish magazine such as *The American Jewess* at home.

BIBLIOGRAPHY

The American Jewess (1895–1899); Berrol, Selma. "Class or Ethnicity: The Americanized German Jewish Woman and Her Middle Class Sisters in 1895." *Jewish Social Studies* 47 (1985): 21–32; Goldman, Karla. "Beyond the Gallery: The Place of Women in the Development of American Judaism." Ph.D. diss., Harvard University, 1993; Kuzmack, Linda Gordon. *Woman's Cause: The Jewish Woman's Movement in England and the United States, 1881–1933* (1990); Lichtenstein, Diane. *Writing Their Nations: The Tradition of Nineteenth-Century American Jewish Women Writers* (1992); Loth, David. "The American Jewess." *Midstream* 31 (1985): 43–46; Porter, Jack Nusan. "Rosa Sonnenschein [sic] and *The American Jewess*: The First Independent English Language Jewish Women's Journal in the United States." *American Jewish History* 67 (September 1978): 57–63, and "Rosa Sonnenschein and *The American Jewess* Revisited: New Historical Information on an Early American Zionist and Jewish Feminist." *American Jewish Archives* 32 (1980): 125–131; Rogow, Faith. *Gone to Another Meeting: The National Council of Jewish Women, 1893–1993* (1993); Sochen, June. *Consecrate Every Day: The Public Lives of Jewish American Women, 1880–1980* (1981); Sonneschein, Rosa. "The American Jewess." *The American Jewess* 6 (February 1898): 205–208, and "The National Council of Jewish Women and Our Dream of Nationality." *The American Jewess* 4 (October 1896): 28–32.

JANE H. ROTHSTEIN

AMERICAN JEWISH CONGRESS

Women have played an important part in the American Jewish Congress (AJCongress) since the organization was first established after World War I. American Jewish leaders originally convened a Jewish Congress in December 1918 in order to represent the interests of the war-torn Jewish communities of Eastern Europe at the postwar peace conference. Although AJCongress organizers hoped to create a vehicle of American Jewish unity, from the outset the AJCongress movement drew its strongest support from the ranks of American Zionism and from within the Eastern European immigrant community. This constituency probably contributed to the AJCongress's acceptance of women's involvement. While women in the more established and genteel German Jewish community tended to conform to the same model of middle-class domesticity as their non-Jewish counterparts, many Jewish women from Eastern Europe arrived in the United States with a tradition of active participation in the marketplace, the family economy, and the politics of the Jewish labor movement.

The leadership of the AJCongress also helped to encourage women's participation. Fully committed to the democratic idealism of progressive politics, AJCongress leaders such as Rabbi Stephen S. Wise and Louis D. Brandeis were strong supporters of women's rights, especially female suffrage. Moreover, as champions of greater democracy in Jewish communal life, AJCongress advocates could not have excluded women without provoking accusations of hypocrisy. These commitments were evident during the election of Jewish Congress delegates in 1917, in which Jewish women enjoyed the right to vote and to run as candidates—three years before American women gained the unrestricted right to vote under the Nineteenth Amendment.

The original American Jewish Congress was disbanded in 1920, after receiving the report of its delegation to the peace conference in Versailles. Immediately thereafter, the organization was reestablished on a permanent basis under the leadership of Stephen S. Wise. During the 1920s, the AJCongress devoted most of its modest resources to aiding

Eastern European Jewry and advancing the Zionist cause.

The rising tide of political anti-Semitism in Europe and the United States during the 1930s brought new challenges for the AJCongress, which quickly joined other American Jewish communal organizations in the fight against fascism. Early in this critical decade, in 1933, LOUISE WATERMAN WISE founded the Women's Division of the American Jewish Congress. Like her husband, Stephen, Louise Wise was a leader of the AJCongress and a progressive reformer. In 1914, she had organized the Child Adoption Committee of the Free Synagogue, the first agency specializing in Jewish adoptions. The Women's Division she established and led was dedicated to the same objectives as the general division of the American Jewish Congress: the protection of Jewish rights at home and abroad, the advancement of American democracy, the elimination of racial and religious discrimination in the United States, the enhancement of Jewish identity, and the promotion of Zionism.

Many of the officers and members of the Women's Division were married women who worked outside the home as unpaid volunteers. Louise's daughter, Judge JUSTINE WISE POLIER, who became president of the Women's Division shortly after her mother death in 1947, was an exception. She enjoyed a long and successful career on the benches of the Domestic Relations Court of New York City and the New York State Family Court. While the New York metropolitan area and its environs remained the center of organization and leadership, over the years AJCongress women launched local chapters in a wide range of cities, including Albany, Hartford, Philadelphia, Cleveland, Cincinnati, Indianapolis, Chicago, Detroit, Los Angeles, Miami Beach, St. Louis, Baltimore, Washington, D.C., and Norfolk, Virginia. During the postwar period, when increasing numbers of American Jews left the cities for the suburbs, chapters of the Women's Division blossomed in the bedroom communities outside of New York City, Boston, Newark, and other urban centers.

During the 1930s and 1940s, members of the Women's Division dedicated themselves to helping the victims of Nazi aggression in Europe. After Hitler came to power in Germany, Louise Waterman Wise transformed three townhouses owned by the Jewish Institute of Religion into refuge houses, which furnished food, temporary shelter, educational programs, and other necessities of life to thousands of Jews fortunate enough to reach the United States. Beginning in 1939, Women's Division volunteers sewed and knitted clothing and blankets for refugees, wounded soldiers, and civilians in Europe. AJCongress women also helped to administer a foster parent program, through which American Jews could help to provide food, clothing, and medical care to Jewish children in Europe who had lost one or both parents during the war. In order to support the American military effort, Women's Division members sold United States war bonds. In addition, after the Japanese attack on Pearl Harbor, one of the refuge houses in New York City was converted into a defense center, which offered accommodations, meals, recreation, and training courses to American servicemen.

After 1948, AJCongress women turned their energies toward the new State of Israel. In cooperation with the Israeli government, the Women's Division sent large shipments of toys and educational materials to the Jewish state, where these goods were in short supply. Women's Division members across the United States continued to produce clothing, which helped to clothe young Israeli immigrants. By the end of the 1950s, when this effort was superseded by the growing strength and productivity of the Israeli textile industry, American Jewish Congress women proudly claimed to have shipped over 90,000 children's garments to Israel. Women's Division members also worked on behalf of the Jewish state by selling tens of thousands of dollars worth of Israel Bonds and playing a prominent role in the annual campaigns of the United Jewish Appeal.

At the same time, AJCongress women sought a direct and personal connection with the Jewish state that material aid and fund-raising could not supply. In 1954, the AJCongress Women's Division established the Louise Waterman Wise Youth Center in Israel. The youth center, intended as a memorial to the founder of the Women's Division and her lifelong dedication to child welfare and Jewish nationalism, was constructed in western Jerusalem, not far from the grave of Theodor Herzl. Working closely with Israeli officials, the youth center offered special programs designed to help new immigrants adjust to Israeli society. Young Jews originally from North Africa received special instruction in English, mathematics, and other subjects under the center's auspices. In addition, the center furnished lodging for American Jews visiting Israel, provided leadership training for young Israelis, and housed educational and cultural projects for Jewish and Arab youth. Within a relatively short time, the programs of the Louise Waterman Wise Youth Center expanded to include thousands of Israelis and non-Israelis each year.

The AJ Congress sponsored the first international Jewish Women's Conference in 1988 in Jerusalem.
The women from New York brought a Torah as a gift to the women of Israel.
These two photos portray the Torah in an informal and in a formal setting.
[Joan Roth]

During the late 1950s and early 1960s, the Women's Division began to sponsor tours to Israel for AJCongress members and their families. These trips, like the youth center, were designed to strengthen the emotional bonds between AJCongress members and the people and land of Israel. Participants in the Women's Division tours met Israelis from all walks of life, including government officials, educators, well-known cultural figures, and leaders of the Arab community. Their itinerary included visits to kibbutzim, schools and universities, the Knesset, factories, Arab and Druze villages, and a wealth of religious and archaeological sites. Women's Division members especially enjoyed the opportunity to observe the programs of the Louise Waterman Wise Youth Center on a firsthand basis. In addition, these trips generally included excursions to a series of European cities, where AJCongress members toured sites of Jewish historical and cultural importance and conferred with European Jewish leaders. Women's Division leaders hoped that these personal interactions with Israeli and European Jews would enhance AJCongress members' commitment to the concept of *klal Yisrael*, or Jewish peoplehood.

As devoted Zionists, AJCongress women took direct action when they perceived a threat to Israel.

During the 1964–1965 World's Fair in New York City, AJCongress members, including Women's Division vice president JACQUELINE LEVINE, were arrested for picketing an anti-Israel mural at the Jordan Pavilion. After the Six-Day War in 1967, as American Jews became even more ardently committed to assuring Israel's safety, Women's Division officials concerned themselves with battling the influence of anti-Israel propaganda on Jewish college students. At the same time, the Women's Division called for negotiations between Israel and its Arab neighbors aimed at establishing a permanent peace in the Middle East.

On the home front, the leaders and members of the Women's Division dedicated themselves after 1945 to advancing the AJCongress's liberal civil rights program. During the late 1940s and 1950s, AJCongress women organized rallies to muster public support for the enactment of state legislation against discrimination in employment, public accommodations, and education. Justine Wise Polier and other Women's Division officials assumed leadership positions in national and New York state committees established to fight residential segregation. Women's Division members were also active in state and local civic organizations dedicated to eliminating racial discrimination in the public schools. During the early and mid-1960s, officers and members of the Women's Division took part in civil rights marches and lent material support to the African-American civil rights organizations leading the freedom struggle in the Deep South. In communities across the country, AJCongress women worked through local school boards and civic organizations to implement tutoring, job placement, and voter registration programs.

Women's Division members similarly lent their strength to the AJCongress's campaign to expand protection for civil liberties. During the postwar anticommunist crusade, local chapters of the Women's Division sponsored demonstrations to protest measures, such as the McCarran-Walter Immigration Act (1952), which violated fundamental principles of due process. Women's Division members were especially active in their local communities as champions of the AJCongress's fight to keep the public schools free from religious sectarianism. During the early 1950s, Women's Division members in New York mobilized parents, community activists, and civic organizations against the state's program of released-time religious instruction. While they were ardent supporters of federal aid to education, AJCongress women instigated letter-writing campaigns against measures that extended federal support to parochial schools or otherwise conflicted with strict separation between church and state.

In conjunction with their commitment to civil liberties, the Women's Division of the American Jewish Congress maintained a long tradition of involvement in issues of peace and international relations. Like their counterparts in the AJCongress's general division, Women's Division members were stalwart supporters of the United Nations. Women's Division representatives worked closely with the American Association for the United Nations, and lobbied the United States Government to ratify various UN treaties and conventions, especially those that promised to protect human rights. During the 1960s and 1970s, the Women's Division helped to organize letter-writing campaigns against nuclear testing, the arms race, and the antiballistic missile program, and urged that tax dollars allocated for nuclear weapons development be redirected toward education and other domestic social programs. At the same time, AJCongress women became increasingly concerned about the persecution of Jews in the Soviet Union. Beginning in the mid-1960s, Women's Division leaders and other AJCongress officials took an active part in conferences, protest rallies, and mass meetings designed to focus attention on Soviet anti-Semitism. In cooperation with other organizations, the Women's Division pressured the United Nations to consider Soviet anti-Semitism as a human rights issue.

Their commitment to international peace and human rights prompted many AJCongress women to become vocal opponents of the war in Vietnam. Beginning in the mid-1960s, the Women's Division issued a series of resolutions calling for peace. Members of the Women's Division, including Jacqueline K. Levine, who chaired the AJCongress's National Peace Committee, played an important part in the agency's antiwar efforts. Leaders of the Women's Division urged AJCongress members to write letters to President Lyndon B. Johnson, members of Congress, and United Nations ambassador Arthur Goldberg protesting the bombing campaigns in Vietnam and calling for an end to the war. In 1967, the Women's Division collaborated with the Americans for Democratic Action and SANE in a petition drive demanding peace negotiations. Women's Division members, including the organization's top leadership, took part in numerous antiwar demonstrations throughout the duration of the war.

During the 1960s and 1970s, partly as a result of their participation in the civil rights and antiwar movements, AJCongress women joined in the fight for women's equality. Since the 1930s, the Women's Division had served as an effective vehicle for social and political action. Its members, however, had consistently emphasized that their particular role was to build support for AJCongress policies and programs on the community level, through local school boards, as participants in parent-teacher associations, and especially in their capacity as mothers. By the 1960s, women within the AJCongress—like women active in other Jewish community organizations—increasingly rejected this separate sphere and demanded equal power and responsibility in Jewish communal life. In 1966, Women's Division president Virginia Snitow led a successful effort to gain a small but significant increase in representation for Women's Division members on the AJCongress Executive Committee. At the same time, Women's Division leaders, including Virginia Snitow and Jacqueline K. Levine, called for greater women's participation in other communal agencies, such as the President's Conference of Major Jewish Organizations and the Council of Jewish Federations and Welfare Funds (CJFWF), which were largely, if not entirely, male-dominated.

AJCongress women faced several obstacles, however, in their struggle for equality within the Jewish community. First, positions of authority were frequently awarded to wealthy donors, who tended to be successful businessmen. Second, some women were ambivalent about their traditionally separate position within the American Jewish Congress and the organized Jewish community as a whole. While women activists increasingly wanted to play an equal part in the policy-making process, some were reluctant to sacrifice the valuable ties they had established within separate women's divisions, auxiliaries, and organizations. Over time, however, Jewish leaders came to recognize that it would be difficult to attract younger Jews—both women and men—to communal organizations segregated by sex, and that the relegation of women to separate auxiliaries directly contravened the principles of liberty and equality upon which their agencies were founded. As a result, beginning in the 1970s, efforts were made to bring greater numbers of women into leadership positions within Jewish communal organizations. In 1972, Naomi B. Levine, who had previously served on the AJCongress's legal staff and as director of the Women's Division, became the agency's first female executive director. Jacqueline K. Levine, who began her long career in Jewish communal service by joining the AJCongress Women's Division, moved on to leadership positions with the AJCongress, the CJFWF, and the National Jewish Community Relations Advisory Council.

Women within the AJCongress also pushed the organization to take a strong stand in support of women's rights within the broader society. Starting in the late 1960s and early 1970s, the Women's Division issued resolutions from its biennial conventions that called for the total elimination of discrimination against women in employment, education, housing, politics, civil law, and jury service. The Women's Division advocated strong enforcement of the 1964 Civil Rights Act, which prohibited discrimination by sex as well as by race, and demanded the enactment of state laws mandating equal pay for equal work and the passage of an Equal Rights Amendment to the United States Constitution. Both the Women's Division and the AJCongress as a whole took an uncompromising position in favor of reproductive freedom. AJCongress officials called for the repeal of all laws restricting women's right to choose and took special note of the unfair impact of anti-abortion laws on poor women. After the Supreme Court decided *Roe* v. *Wade* (1973), AJCongress leaders expressed their strong approval of the ruling and testified before Congress against measures intended to nullify the decision. In more recent years, the AJCongress has joined with other Jewish communal and religious organizations in political demonstrations in defense of reproductive rights.

Throughout the postwar period, AJCongress women worked to sustain Jewish identity and culture.

During the 1940s and 1950s, the AJCongress sponsored studies to determine the most effective methods for helping Jewish children to develop psychologically sound self-images despite the presence of anti-Semitism in American culture. Programs developed by the Women's Division emphasized mothers' responsibility for transmitting Jewish values to their children. Members of local chapters organized study groups, holiday parties, music festivals, and other special activities dedicated to celebrating and imparting Jewish history and culture. Even as they became more active in the broad social movements of the 1960s and 1970s, AJCongress women confirmed their long-standing commitment to Jewish continuity. In the late 1960s, the Women's Division, the AJCongress's Commission on Jewish Affairs, and the Herzl Institute cosponsored a School for Jewish Parent Education, one of several programs designed to stem the tide of assimilation among Jewish youth by providing instruction in Jewish religion, history, music, and art.

The Women's Division was discontinued as a separate section after approximately fifty years of service. The AJCongress's support for women's rights and feminism within the Jewish community has continued, however, under the auspices of the Commission for Women's Equality, which was founded in 1984. Among its many projects, the commission has worked to create an international network of Jewish feminists, to serve as a vocal advocate for abortion rights, and to raise consciousness within the Jewish community about domestic violence, pay equity, and other issues of particular importance to women. Feminist Centers established by the AJCongress in various cities have become a forum for exploring women's equality within the Jewish religious context.

BIBLIOGRAPHY

Baum, Charlotte, Paula Hyman, and Sonya Michel. *The Jewish Woman in America* (1975); Cohen, Steven M., Susan Dessel, and Michael Pelavin. "The Changing (?) Role of Women in Jewish Communal Affairs: A Look into the UJA." In *The Jewish Woman: New Perspectives*, edited by Elizabeth Koltun (1976); *EJ*, s.v. "American Jewish Congress" and "Wise, Stephen Samuel"; Fishman, Sylvia Barak. *A Breath of Life: Feminism in the American Jewish Community* (1993); Frommer, Morris. "The American Jewish Congress: A History, 1914–1950." 2 vols. Ph.D. diss., Ohio State University, 1978; Glanz, Rudolph. "The Eastern European Jewish Woman." In *The Jewish Woman in America: Two Female Immigrant Generations, 1820–1929*. Vol. 1 (1976); Kuzmack, Linda Gordon. *Woman's Cause: The Jewish Woman's Movement in England and the United States, 1881–1933* (1990); Marcus, Jacob Rader. *The American Jewish Woman: A Documentary History* (1981); Pogrebin, Letty Cottin. *Deborah,*

Golda, and Me (1991); Svonkin, Stuart. "Jews Against Prejudice: American Jews and the Intergroup Relations Movement from World War to Cold War." Ph.D. diss., Columbia University, 1995; Urofsky, Melvin I. *A Voice That Spoke for Justice: The Life and Times of Stephen S. Wise* (1982); Waldman, Lois. Telephone interview with author, August 29, 1995; Women's Division of the American Jewish Congress. Papers. American Jewish Historical Society, Waltham, Mass.

STUART SVONKIN

AMERICAN MIZRACHI WOMEN
see **AMIT**

AMIR, NAOMI (1931–1995)

"I may not be perfect, but parts of me are excellent" read the badge on a big teddy bear physician Naomi Amir gave her young disabled patients to cuddle. The sentiment reflected her medical philosophy, which made her a pioneer in pediatric neurology. She treated children with a wide range of disabilities, including sleep problems, encephalitis, and autism, but her special interests were epilepsy, cognition (including neuro-metabolism), dysphasia, and developmental disorders. In her work, Amir stressed that the infant or child must be seen in the context of his or her Israeli family: Jewish or Arab, secular or religious.

Naomi Kassan Amir was born in Chicago on January 23, 1931, the first daughter and second child of Eva (Dushkin) and Shalom Kassan, an American mother and Palestinian father. Her mother, born into an Eastern European immigrant family, was one of the new generation of Jewish American woman who achieved careers of their own as social workers. Her father belonged to the elite of pre-state Jewish Palestine. At the age of four, her family moved to Palestine, where her father served as a judge in the legal service of the British mandate. After a year and a half, her mother and her children returned to the United States for a year. Following a second year in Palestine in 1938, Eva Kassan settled in New York City with the children. Naomi developed a strong bond with her mother during her youth.

After graduating from the Bronx High School of Science, she received her B.A. from New York University and then completed New York University Medical School in 1952. "I always knew I wanted to be a doctor," she said. "Madame Curie was my role model." She also never doubted that she could combine marriage with a career or that she would settle in Israel.

She came to Israel in 1953 to begin her residency in neurology at the Hadassah-Hebrew University Medical Center. She chose neurology "because it is a human-oriented aspect of science that deals with human functions, with learning and teaching, and with the organization of the brain." On March 27, 1955, she married Shlomo Amir. They had three children, immediately testing Naomi Amir's conviction that she could combine marriage, motherhood, and career. Their daughter Anat was born in 1957, followed by two sons, Ilan (b. 1959) and Gideon (b. 1964).

After completing her residency at Hadassah Hospital in Jerusalem, Naomi Amir decided to specialize in the diagnosis and treatment of children with neurological problems. This new field was not recognized in Israel, but Amir was fortunate to find a mentor in Dr. Helena Kagan, head of pediatrics at Bikur Holim Hospital in Jerusalem. Kagan gave her the support and counsel Amir needed in a medical world where women were a small minority. The religious hospital, serving a large Orthodox clientele, also proved advantageous because she received a small room where she set up her neurological clinic away from the pediatric wards.

Realizing that she needed additional training, Amir took a clinical fellowship at New York's Neurological Institute of Columbia Presbyterian Medical Center, working with Professor Sidney Carter. There she met a Swiss neurologist, Isabelle Rapin, with whom she subsequently collaborated. They jointly edited *Behavior and Cognition of the Child with Brain Dysfunction* (1991). Amir spent two years in New York, where she recognized the gap between pediatric neurologists who might diagnose and treat chronic handicaps and pediatricians who concentrated on developmental growth.

When she returned to Israel, in 1968, she was determined to bridge that divide and set up the first pediatric neurology rehabilitation day care center and nursery school. In 1979, she expanded this rehabilitation center for brain-damaged children into a full pediatric neurological service. Amir provided diagnosis, multidisciplinary evaluation, and intervention for static neurological conditions together in one place. Most interested in metabolic changes, Amir worked not just with clinicians administering therapy but also with researchers contributing to the field of neuroscience.

In 1990, Amir moved with her team of seven experts to Sha'arei Zedek Hospital in Jerusalem, which gave her an entire wing in a well-equipped new building. Amir also worked at the Spafford Clinic in the Old City, where she treated Moslem Arab children, and at the Mukassed Hospital on the Mount of Olives. She recognized that parental assessment of a child's abilities depended on their family history and that effective treatment could not be taken without family screening. She also understood the political dimensions of her medical work. "Even if governments don't always see eye to eye," she said, "I use my profession to bring people together."

Dr. Naomi Amir became ill with cancer, but she continued to run the department from her sickbed. Three days before her death on January 4, 1995, she gave precise instructions for the continuation of her work. Many of her patients undoubtedly felt personally bereaved by her loss. A young girl whom she had helped face life with a severe disability wrote in a condolence letter: "She taught me not to feel like a victim." Naomi Amir gave this gift to thousands of her patients as she established the field of pediatric neurology in Israel.

BIBLIOGRAPHY

Amir, Naomi, and Isabelle Rapin. *Behavior and Cognition of the Child with Brain Dysfunction* (1991); *Israeli Women of Achievement* (1989); Layish, Naomi. Tribute to Dr. Naomi Amir. Memorial Booklet; Obituary. *Jerusalem Post*, February 15, 1995.

DEBORAH DASH MOORE

AMIT

Established in 1925 to create vocational schools for religious girls in Palestine, AMIT, an American-based religious Zionist organization, has helped shape the educational and social welfare landscape in the State of Israel.

In May 1925, largely through the efforts of founder BESSIE GOTSFELD, the Mizrachi Women's Organization of America (known today as AMIT) was established as a confederation of women's groups hitherto operating as auxiliaries of the men's religious Zionist Mizrachi organization.

AMIT IN ISRAEL

AMIT's first project, Beth Zeiroth Mizrachi in Jerusalem, opened its doors in 1933 as the first vocational high school for girls in the country. One of the school's original staff members, Nechama Leibowitz, who taught there until 1952, subsequently achieved international renown as a Bible scholar and commentator.

A second Beth Zeiroth Mizrachi was established in 1938 on Dov Hos Street in Tel Aviv. In addition to its educational function, the school served, in April 1948, as the site of the historic meeting at which the Actions Committee of the World Zionist Organization adopted a resolution to declare the State of Israel upon the departure of the British mandatory power.

Having established its niche in religious vocational education, AMIT reached a turning point in 1943 with the arrival of several "Teheran children" on the doorstep of its Jerusalem school. These children, part of a group of some eight hundred boys and girls who had escaped from Europe and traveled on foot through the Soviet Union to Persia, had been brought to Palestine by the Youth Aliyah rescue movement. Most were from religious homes, and there were few available resettlement facilities that could carry on their religious education. AMIT undertook this role as a formal participant in Youth Aliyah and rapidly established a series of child-care facilities to house the flood of youngsters who arrived after World War II and especially following the establishment of the State of Israel. These facilities included several homes for younger children and two youth villages, the Mosad Aliyah Youth Village in Petach Tikvah, established in 1944, and Kfar Batya in Raanana, established in 1947 in honor of Bessie Gotsfeld. The AMIT youth villages have produced numerous well-known figures, among them education minister Zevulun Hammer, a former teacher at Mosad Aliyah, and Kfar Batya alumna Yaffa Eliach, the Holocaust scholar who curated the "Tower of Faces" at the U.S. Holocaust Memorial Museum in Washington, D.C.

Kfar Batya also witnessed the first arrival in the Jewish state of a group of Ethiopian Jewish students, who took part in a teacher training course (1955–1956) and then returned to their country under an agreement between the Israeli government and Emperor Haile Selassie. AMIT's exposure to the Ethiopian Jewish culture helped prepare the organization for its subsequent absorption of youngsters arriving with Operations Moses (1984) and Solomon (1991).

Within its dual role, AMIT gradually expanded during the three decades following the establishment of the State of Israel, opening another Beth Zeiroth Mizrachi in Beersheba, several community centers, and three teachers' seminaries. In the early 1980s, this expansion was dramatically accelerated by two events.

First, in 1981, the organization was designated as the Israeli government's official network (Reshet) for religious technological education. This moved the existing AMIT schools into the nationwide public religious education system and initiated the incorporation by AMIT of more than twenty additional schools in municipalities throughout the country between 1981 and 1996. AMIT thus became a prominent national voice in religious public education in Israel.

Second, in 1983, two existing AMIT children's homes were combined in the newly constructed AMIT Beit Hayeled in Gilo, Jerusalem. Beit Hayeled introduced a new concept in Israeli child care for youngsters from dysfunctional homes: It housed boys and girls age eight to fourteen in nine surrogate-family units. Each unit comprised twelve children, a married couple serving as surrogate parents, and a young woman performing national service. These surrogate families received extensive on-site support services while creating a genuine family environment. Beit Hayeled's success led to the establishment by AMIT of three satellite surrogate-family homes for younger children and to the transformation in 1994 of the teenage living quarters at the AMIT Youth Village in Petach Tikvah into a surrogate-family residence. Due to the salutary effects of this living arrangement, the village was awarded the Ministry of Education's Religious Education Prize in 1996 for its achievements with troubled teenagers.

AMIT today maintains thirty-four educational and child-care facilities in Israel. These include a Pre-Army Yeshivah in Safed, which provides a one-year post–high school course of study focusing on religious practices and interpersonal relationships in the army. Like the AMIT "Curriculum on Tolerance and Unity," which was implemented in all the AMIT high schools following the assassination of Prime Minister Yitzhak Rabin in 1995, the Pre-Army Yeshivah fosters amicable relations between observant AMIT alumni and their nonobservant colleagues.

AMIT IN THE UNITED STATES

AMIT is the largest religious Zionist organization in the United States, with some 80,000 members in 475 chapters across the country. It has maintained organizational autonomy since 1934, when—in an initiative highly unusual among women in the religious community—it declared its independence from the men's Mizrachi organization at a Mizrachi convention in Detroit, Michigan. Subsequent changes of name have reflected this autonomy, and the organization dropped the word "Mizrachi" entirely in 1983, when it adopted the name AMIT.

Although adhering to the tenets of religious Zionism, AMIT is a nonpolitical organization, with no administrative or financial ties to the National Religious Party in Israel. It is a constituent organization of the World Zionist Organization and the Conference of Presidents of Major American Jewish Organizations, participates in fund-raising for the United Jewish Appeal, Israel Bonds, and the Jewish National Fund, and has Non-Governmental Organization status at the United Nations.

In addition to providing membership services to its chapters and councils throughout the country, AMIT offers public programming on matters of interest to the Jewish community at large through annual psychological seminars, Days of Learning, and symposia on issues confronting Jewish women in the 1990s. It also publishes the quarterly magazine *AMIT*, which addresses Jewish and Israel-oriented topics.

BIBLIOGRAPHY

"Fifty Years," special section in *The American Mizrachi Woman* (September–October 1975); Goldfeld, Leona. *Bessie* (1981); Hammer, Zevulun. Letter to AMIT (undated. Received September 4, 1996); Head, Lee, and Annette Renick. "Fifty Years of Partnership: AMIT Women and Youth Aliyah," *AMIT Woman* (March–April 1984): 16+.

RUTH RAISNER

AMSTERDAM, BIRDIE (1901–1996)

Birdie Amsterdam was the first woman elected to the New York State Supreme Court. Justice Saul Streit, chairman of the Board of Justices, described the fifty-six-year-old judge as the "first lady of our judiciary" when he administered the oath to her on January 6, 1957. Amsterdam later declined a seat on the appellate court, preferring to remain a trial judge, hearing predominantly civil cases. Occasionally, she sat in criminal court. She was reelected to a second fourteen-year term and served until 1976.

Born March 25, 1901, on the Lower East Side of Manhattan, where she lived the rest of her life, Birdie Amsterdam was the second child and first daughter of Joseph and Essie (Sperling) Amsterdam's six children. Joseph Amsterdam was a classical trumpet player who made a living in the fur business. She had three brothers, Alton and Bernard, who became doctors, and Irving, who was a pharmacist. Her sister Ruth became a nurse, and her sister Sybil Chizner also became a lawyer. The family belonged to a Conservative synagogue.

After completing Hunter College High School, Amsterdam went to City College in 1918–1919 to study banking and accounting. She worked during the day in the records and accounting department of Mount Sinai Hospital and went to New York University Law School at night, graduating with an LL.B. in 1922. Admitted to the bar in 1923, she set up an independent practice and, in 1935, formed a partnership with Milton Sanders, her sister Ruth's husband.

The law firm of Amsterdam and Sanders lasted until 1939, when she went on the municipal court bench.

Amsterdam was an experienced jurist when she was seated on the state supreme court bench in 1957. She was the first woman to sit on the municipal court bench, serving from 1940 until 1954, and in 1954 she became the first woman appointed to the city court. In the election of 1955, the Democratic Party swept the judiciary, and she was elected to a full term on the city court.

Her professional and volunteer activities were lifelong and wide-ranging. She took a leadership role in bar associations, as well as religious, educational, and charitable organizations. During World War II, she led the Lower East Side war bond drive. She was a Democrat and a Tammany Hall district coleader of the Manhattan Democratic Club. A gifted speaker, she traveled some but was wholly dedicated to the law and the legal profession. Her career was her life.

Amsterdam's brief marriage to Dr. Robert Dunn ended in divorce. For many years she lived with Ruth and Judge Milton Sanders. Ever devoted to and admired by her family and community, she was ninety-five when she died of cardiac arrest in New York City on July 8, 1996. She is buried in Mount Zion Cemetery, in Queens, New York.

Judge Birdie Amsterdam was an exemplary jurist. Her thirty-six years on the bench dispelled any doubt as to a woman's judicial temperament and ability to dispense justice and maintain the rule of law.

BIBLIOGRAPHY

NYTimes, November 9, 1955, January 7, 1958, and July 10, 1996; Sanders, Milton, and Ruth Sanders. Interviews with author, June 1996; Thomas, Dorothy. *Women Lawyers in the United States* (1957).

DOROTHY THOMAS

In a career of firsts, Birdie Amsterdam's most notable was her election as the first woman justice of the New York State Supreme Court. [YIVO Institute]

ANARCHISTS

The Jewish anarchist women's movement in America has largely been associated with the name of EMMA GOLDMAN, but her political beliefs were not representative of the majority of members. For Goldman, individual fulfillment and personal liberation were at the heart of the anarchist project, and she had little faith in trade union activism. By contrast, most Jewish women anarchists, while deeply committed to transforming a whole way of life, gave priority to the struggle against oppression by employers, a struggle in which labor organizations played an essential role.

The first Jewish anarchist organization was formally set up as a result of the Haymarket bombing in 1886 and the subsequent trial of the accused anarchists. The inception and growth of the Jewish anarchist movement in the United States were inseparable from the mass immigration of Jews from Eastern Europe starting in 1881. Jewish immigrants from the czarist empire had been schooled in Russian radical politics of the nineteenth and early twentieth centuries—a period when the revolutionary movement and the anarchist project cooperated against tyrannical oppression by the czar. Jews participated actively in the Russian populist movement (*Narodnaya Volya*) and in assassination attempts against a succession of government officials and against the czar. Women anarchists like Vera Zasulich, Vera Figner, and Gesia Helfman provided role models for the young generation of Jewish women in the Russian Pale of Settlement who were receptive to secular and political involvement. Some of the women who participated in

ROSE PESOTTA *belonged to an anarchist group within the* INTERNATIONAL LADIES GARMENT WORKERS UNION.
She is shown here (left, foreground) with Seattle strikers in March of 1935.
[ILGWU Archives, Cornell University]

Jewish radical circles and in anticzarist agitation at the time of the 1905 revolution came subsequently to the United States.

The development of anarchist ideas in czarist Russia as well as German theoretical thought, as exemplified in Johann Most's German-language paper *Freiheit* published in the United States, had an important influence on the Jewish immigrant working class. The anarchist movement gained followers from the fertile ground of the densely populated Jewish immigrant centers, where poverty, sweated labor, and declining wages in the seasonal needle trades were a trademark of immigrant life. The ideology of the movement was based on a struggle against the tyranny of capitalism, on social equality, individual liberty, and the promotion of positive communitarian ideals. These ideals included the free association of individuals and groups without the intervention of the coercive state and social institutions.

Jewish anarchists, both men and women, participated in immigrant labor organizations in most American cities. Emma Goldman, as well as ROSE PESOTTA, Marie Ganz, MOLLIE STEIMER, and many rank-and-file women, had all worked and been active in the needle trades. Goldman had participated in the 1890 cloakmakers strike and in the unemployment demonstrations in 1894. Rose Pesotta, Anna Sosnovsky, Fanny Breslaw, and Clara Rotberg Larsen belonged to an anarchist group within the INTERNATIONAL LADIES

GARMENT WORKERS UNION (ILGWU) and the Amalgamated Clothing Workers of America, which published between 1923 and 1927 *Der Yunyon Arbeter* [The union worker] at the height of the rivalry with the communists. Pesotta, who rose to become the only woman on the board of the ILGWU in the 1930s, concentrated her efforts on unionizing Jewish and gentile women workers in the needle trades, as well as workers in other industries. She dedicated her life to promoting more democratic union structures and the advancement of women in the union hierarchy. The goals of women organizers often brought them in conflict with male union leadership, as well as with fellow anarchists who viewed unionism as a mere palliative.

The union provided its members with a community where work struggles were combined with a social life. The anarchists created enclaves in the form of circles and organizations that represented uniquely anarchist concerns around education, culture, and a different way of life. The self-contained groups, however, maintained their roots within the Jewish community. Over twenty such anarchist organizations were branches of the Workmen's Circle, the Jewish fraternal order. The extensive links with the community muted some of the early expressions of anarchist defiance against religious authority when the early anarchists' notorious Yom Kippur balls were subsequently abandoned.

Women anarchists participated actively in these community-building efforts, as well as in another central project, the education of children and adults. Commitment to the abolition of authority extended into this domain too. Schools that emphasized the dignity of the child and the development of the child's potential in a free and natural setting were the means to prepare members of the future anarchist society. The educational concerns that the anarchists shared with nonanarchist radicals resulted in the flowering of the Modern School movement between 1910 and 1958. The Ferrer Center in New York became in the years prior to World War I a cultural center that attracted progressive educators and the artistic avant-garde. The ideas of progressive education provided the focus and the inspiration for the anarchist colony movement: Stelton (1915) and Mohegan (1923) colonies in New York and the Sunrise (1933) project in Michigan. These mostly Jewish settlements, which were labeled by the outside world as "red" and inhabited by "free lovers," as in the case of Stelton, were set up around a school and were also experiments in alternative living to promote an anarchist life-style. Stelton ran a cooperative garment workshop and a cooperative food store.

The leading journal of the anarchist movement *Di Fraye Arbeter Shtime* [The free voice of labor] (1890–1976)—which in its heyday before the Bolshevik Revolution had a circulation of 30,000—reflected the labor concerns of its membership. On occasion, the journal also provided a forum for women writers and poets. ANNA MARGOLIN, FRADEL SHTOK, and YENTE SERDATSKY contributed in its pages to the exploration of women's concerns, their lives and psychology.

Jewish women anarchists were at the forefront of radical campaigns that combined forces with gentiles and civil liberties activists to curb abuses of state power. Pauline Turkel organized a rally in Madison Square Garden on behalf of Tom Mooney and Warren Billings in 1917. Pesotta campaigned for the release of Mooney from prison in 1934. Other practical causes that they took up included the amnesty of anarchists in Russia in 1911 by the Anarchist Red Cross. Hilda Adel helped to organize the Political Prisoners' Defense and Relief Committee in 1918 to help protesters who had been arrested for opposing United States intervention in World War I. Rose Pesotta, Emma Goldman, Rose Mirsky, and many others worked tirelessly in the defense of Sacco and Vanzetti in the 1920s.

The violent strand of anarchism, which remained an undercurrent of the mainstream movement until the assassination of President William McKinley in 1901, was subsequently renounced by most anarchists, including Emma Goldman and *Di Fraye Arbeter Shtime*. An assassination attempt on the life of John D. Rockefeller, Jr., the perpetrator of the Ludlow massacre in 1914, was the exception. Marie Ganz, a young Jewish immigrant, tried to assassinate him in 1914, but the attempt was foiled. She was one of the militant Jewish anarchists who were inspired by the ideas of the Wobblies (Industrial Workers of the World) and the upsurge of anarcho-syndicalism starting in 1905 and continuing through the period of World War I. In 1914, their activities included organizing the unemployed in New York City and anti-Rockefeller agitation in Tarrytown, New York. Becky Edelsohn, Helen Goldblatt, and Lillian Goldblatt were in the forefront of these confrontational activities.

A similar group set up a separate New York collective whose clandestine publication *Der Shturm* [The storm] (1917–1918) and subsequently *Frayhayt* [Freedom] (1918), which agitated against the war, defended the Bolshevik Revolution, and opposed American intervention in Russia, included Mary Abrams, Mollie Steimer, Hilda Adel, Clara Rotberg Larsen, and Sonya Deanin. Some of these women were employed in the garment industry, and Abrams had been in the TRIANGLE SHIRTWAIST FIRE. The New York groups joined with supporters from *Mother Earth*, representing the views of Emma Goldman and Alexander Berkman, to organize militant demonstrations against United States participation in the war, which often culminated in violent confrontations with the police.

The campaign to oppose the draft conflicted with the forces of *Di Fraye Arbeter Shtime*, which followed Kropotkin in its support of the war. A more formidable enemy was the U.S. Government. Opposition to the war and direct action advocated by *Frayhayt* were brutally suppressed through the 1918 Sedition Act. In 1919, the anarchist movement became the target of government persecution with many members being imprisoned and eventually deported, among them Emma Goldman and Mollie Steimer.

The anarchist movement declined as a result of other ideologies competing for the loyalty of the labor movement. For instance, the Bolshevik Revolution drew support from within the ranks of the Jewish immigrant workers in the 1920s, as did the New Deal ideology of the 1930s. However, Jewish anarchist cells and publications continued to exist. Much later, there was a brief upsurge of interest in anarchism among women in the 1960s, when Goldman became an icon again. Her ethics of personal and sexual liberation found many followers in the women's movement. However, since the 1930s, the appeal of anarchism had given way not only to New Deal ideology, but also to the pro-Zionist orientation of many among American Jewry, which was accompanied by a decline in the use of Yiddish and the waning of the Jewish labor movement.

BIBLIOGRAPHY

Avrich, Paul. *Anarchist Portraits* (1988), and *Anarchist Voices. An Oral History of Anarchism in America* (1995), and *The Modern School Movement: Anarchism and Education in the United States* (1980); Leeder, Elaine J. *The Gentle General: Rose Pesotta, Anarchist and Labor Organizer* (1993); Marsh, Margaret S. *Anarchist Women, 1870–1920* (1981); Pratt, Norma Fain. "Culture and Radical Politics: Yiddish Women Writers in America, 1890–1940," in *Women of the Word: Jewish Women and Jewish Writing*, edited by Judith Baskin (1994); Shepherd, Naomi. *A Price Below Rubies: Jewish Women as Rebels and Radicals* (1993).

HADASSA KOSAK

ANNENBERG, SADIE CECILIA (1879–1965)

"If you love something, you will find a way to care for it, whether it is a person or an institution." This was the personal credo of Sadie Cecilia Annenberg, loving wife, dedicated mother, and philanthropic contributor to educational, political, and Jewish causes.

Born in New York City on June 3, 1879, Sadie Cecilia (Friedman) Annenberg was the daughter of a retail shoe salesman who later moved his family to Chicago. The small, round, fiery-haired Sadie married a "lean, hungry wolf," Moses (Moe) Louis Annenberg, on August 20, 1899. While her husband pursued opportunities in the newspaper industry, Annenberg bore nine children: Diana (who died at age five), Esther, Pearl, Janet, Enid, Walter, Leah, Evelyn, and Harriet.

In 1907, the Annenbergs moved to Milwaukee, where Moe established his own news distribution agency by pawning some of his young wife's jewelry for $700 and borrowing another $1,500. Sadie is credited with inspiring a mail-order business that made the Annenbergs millionaires by their thirties. Moe recalled, "I asked my wife what among household articles of a durable nature she found herself buying oftenest. She answered quickly—teaspoons. I decided to try this. . . . My wife was right. Every woman in creation seemed to want these spoons. . . . Little Woman [Moe's nickname for Sadie] . . . made us a fortune."

By all accounts, the Annenbergs' marriage was happy. The couple differed only when it came to religion. "Little Woman" was observant; she faithfully attended synagogue and kept a kosher home. Her husband, however, rejected his ties to Judaism.

In 1917, when Moe took a job with William Randolph Hearst, the family relocated to New York. By 1920, the Annenbergs were dividing their time between a Manhattan apartment and a Long Island estate. Though fashion-conscious and well-dressed, Annenberg was "a simple woman . . . at home in the kitchen." In 1926, Moe left Hearst to build his own publishing empire, which included the *Philadelphia Inquirer*.

In 1939, Moe and his only son, Walter, were indicted by the federal government for tax evasion. To avoid public humiliation, Annenberg and her daughters waited in a nearby hotel as the verdict was handed down. Moe was found guilty of one charge of tax evasion. He also agreed to pay the United States Treasury $9.5 million. Her husband's incarceration caused

Sadie Annenberg's husband Moe credited her with the idea that made them millionaires, and she used that money to support numerous causes, including the State of Israel. She is shown here with Bernard Baruch receiving the Williamsburg Settlement Award in 1956.

Annenberg great pain, but she weathered the dishonor in silence. Moe Annenberg was released in June 1942; one month later, he died.

Before his death, Sadie Annenberg had become involved in philanthropic activities. Her support of the same causes as financier Bernard Baruch won his friendship. In the arts, she was the benefactor of the Sadie Cecilia Annenberg Music School of the Williamsburg (Brooklyn) Settlement House. She received the school's gold medal of appreciation in 1956.

In the political realm, Annenberg was a major contributor to Senator Richard M. Nixon's campaigns. When he became vice president, Nixon hosted a dinner in his home in her honor.

Annenberg made several gifts to the State of Israel, including the establishment of the Sadie C. Annenberg Soil and Irrigation Institute at Gilat. In 1960, she donated $250,000 to the United Jewish Appeal to develop arable land in the Negev. In 1962, her family honored her by giving a $1 million grant to the Albert Einstein College of Medicine at Yeshiva University in New York City. In June 1965, each of her eight children pledged $1 million toward the construction of the Mount Sinai School of Medicine.

On July 6, 1965, Annenberg died in her home in New York. Her influence lives on in the philanthropic activities of Walter Annenberg, who continues to champion the kind of causes that excited his mother's generosity.

BIBLIOGRAPHY

AJYB (1967): 531, s.v. "Necrology"; Annenberg, Moses L. Obituary. *NYTimes*, July 21, 1942, 19:1; Cooney, John E. *The Annenbergs* (1982); *DAB* 3: 19; *EJ*; Fonzi, Gaeton. *Annenberg: A Biography of Power* (1970); Fischel, Jack, and Sanford Pinsker, eds. *Jewish American History and Culture: An Encyclopedia* (1992); Obituary. *NYTimes*, July 7, 1965, 37:4.

THEA DIAMOND

ANSHEN, RUTH NANDA (b. 1900)

"It is the ideas I generate which captivate and hold the imagination of the scholars who write for me. I do not simply edit their work. I create ideas." True. Ruth Nanda Anshen, philosopher, lecturer, and author, has been an "intellectual instigator" for such writers of genius and eminent thinkers as physicist Albert Einstein, theologian Paul Tillich, philosopher Alfred North Whitehead, psychoanalyst Erich Fromm, scientist Jonas Salk, and anthropologist Margaret Mead. While illuminating the fields of education, science, literature, history, and the humanities, Anshen is self-admittedly not an expert in these fields, yet Anshen possesses the unique ability "to extrapolate an idea in relation to life."

Ruth Nanda Anshen, born in Lynn, Massachusetts, on June 14, 1900, is the daughter of Jewish Russian immigrants. Her mother, Sarah Yaffe Anshen, lived to age ninety-seven and was a prolific poet. Her father, Louis J. Anshen, was a translator of religious works who made a fortune syndicating precious stones. Anshen married Dr. Ralph Howard in January 1923 and bore one daughter, Judith Anshen.

Anshen's lifelong obsession with "the unitary structure of all reality" flowered when she was a Ph.D. candidate at Boston University in the late 1930s, studying under Alfred North Whitehead. In Cambridge, while attending the Harvard Tercentenary in 1936, she was distressed that the brilliant ideas presented by scholars from all over the world, for example, physicist Albert Einstein and geneticist J.B.S. Haldane, stood in sterile isolation. To Anshen, they did not seem to respect one another as experts in their fields. They confused while intending to enlighten. It was at that point that Anshen began her lifelong obsession to discover a thematic hypothesis: to develop a "unitary principle under which there could be subsumed and evaluated the nature of man and the nature of life, the relationship of knowledge to life." Anshen sought such a thesis in 1941 in her first of a collection of thought-provoking texts on universal themes by the twentieth century's greatest minds. Entitled the Science of Culture Series, the project would span two decades. Physicists Albert Einstein and Niels Bohr, novelist Thomas Mann, and Alfred North Whitehead served on the board of editors. Einstein expressed his enthusiasm for the project when he told Anshen, "It's a very good plan. You want the future to come sooner." This series included *Freedom: Its Meaning* (1940) and *The Family: Its Function and Destiny* (1949) with contributions from Whitehead, Tillich, John Dewey, and Einstein. The overriding purpose of the series was to ferret out kindred spirits and to show that science, fiction, philosophy, and every other discipline must work together if the world's problems are ever to be solved. Anshen was increasingly motivated to compile a series of books on universal themes. Shortly afterward, Anshen edited a ten-volume series, Perspectives in Humanism; a thirty-volume series, Religious Perspectives, and a thirty-volume collection of intellectual autobiographies titled Credo Perspectives. In 1953, Anshen began her World Perspective Series, which included *The Art of Loving* by Erich

Fromm and *Letters from the Field* by Margaret Mead. At last count, the various series had been translated into over forty-four languages.

Throughout her active intellectual life, Anshen developed a mysterious harmony and "symbiotic relationship" with scholars during her extensive travels to universities around the globe, as chair of the Nature of Man seminar at Columbia University in New York, and as a member of the Royal Society of Arts in London.

Once depicting herself as a woman deeply concerned over the problems people have created for themselves, and a social observer shocked by modern people's empty consumer mentality, Anshen devoted her life and career to counterbalancing a proliferation of facts and data by developing a consciousness of courage, integrity, responsibility, and ethical values.

SELECTED WORKS BY RUTH NANDA ANSHEN
The Family: Its Function and Destiny (1949); *Freedom: Its Meaning* (1940).

BIBLIOGRAPHY
Giusto, Joanne. "Ruth Nanda Anshen. *Publishers Weekly* 213 (1978): 10–12; Teich, Mark. "Editing Einstein." *Omni* (July 1988): 24–110; *WWIAJ* (1938); *Who's Who of American Women* (1991).

SUSAN WYCKOFF

ANTIN, MARY (1881–1949)

"I thought it [a] miracle," exclaimed Mary Antin in her best-selling autobiography, *The Promised Land*, written when she was just thirty years old, "that I, Mashke, the granddaughter of Raphael the Russian, born to a humble destiny, should be at home in an American metropolis, be free to fashion my own life, and should dream my dreams in English phrases." This best-selling author and lecturer, champion of free and open immigration, celebrated in her life and work the immigrant experience and the boundless opportunity of America.

Born in Polotsk in the Russian Pale of Settlement on June 13, 1881, to Israel Pinchus and Esther (Hannah Hayye) (Weltman) Antin, Maryashe Antin was the second of six children. For a brief period in her childhood, while the family business flourished, she learned with private tutors. But serious illness left the business in ruins. In 1891, unable to earn a living, her father set off, along with hundreds of thousands of others, to seek his fortune in America.

While their mother shouldered alone the burden of caring for the family, Antin and her elder sister found themselves apprenticed out to work. After three long years, their father managed to save enough to send for his wife and children. In the early spring of 1894, Esther Antin and her children left Polotsk bound for Boston.

While America never did deliver on its dream of prosperity to Israel Antin—his various business ventures generally failed—it did deliver on its promise of equal opportunity. Education kept the American dream alive for Maryashe—now Mary—and her younger siblings. Years later, when she wrote of the day they marched proudly off to school, she claimed that in "the simple act of delivering our school certificates . . . [my father] took possession of America."

Like other immigrant children, in the days when grade levels were determined by competence in English rather than by age, thirteen-year-old Antin squeezed herself into a desk meant for a kindergarten child. Her intelligence and evident literary gifts quickly impressed her teachers. Eager to show how much an immigrant child could accomplish in only four months, one of them sent Antin's composition entitled "Snow" to *Primary Education*. Seeing her name in print for the first time, Antin determined to become a writer.

Guided by her teachers, she vaulted through grammar school in four years. At the same time, she began to fulfill her literary ambition. Publication of her poems in Boston newspapers made her a local celebrity. At her grammar school graduation in 1898, her remarkable career was held up "as an illustration of what the American system of free education and the European immigrant could make of each other." To those who championed the nation's capacity to assimilate the immigrant and the immigrant's capacity to enrich America, Mary Antin became a symbol.

Knowing of the family's desperate need to put all hands to work to make ends meet, Hattie L. Hecht, a local Jewish communal leader, persuaded Philip Cowen, editor of the *American Hebrew*, to arrange for the publication of Antin's first book. In the summer of 1894, the thirteen-year-old, an inveterate letter writer, had described to an uncle the family's journey. Translated from the Yiddish and owing to a misprint of the name of her town, these letters became *From Plotzk to Boston* (1899). Income from the book's sales enabled Antin to continue her education at Boston's premier female high school, Girls' Latin School, and to dream of the day when she would enter college.

But school, writing, and household chores did not occupy all her time. On a field trip sponsored by Hale House, a South End settlement home, she met the geologist Amadeus William Grabau (1870–1946), the

From Russian immigrant to best-selling author to friend of Teddy Roosevelt, Mary Antin was an advertisement for the American Dream. [American Jewish Archives]

son and grandson of German-born Lutheran ministers. The two fell in love and were married in Boston on October 5, 1901.

Amadeus Grabau went from Harvard University, where he had completed his doctorate, to the faculty of Columbia University. There Antin fulfilled her dream of attending college, studying at Columbia's Teachers College (1901–1902) and at Barnard College (1902–1904), but without finishing a degree. And before too long the birth of their only child, Josephine Esther, completed the domestic portrait.

But despite her new family, Antin's ambitions for authorship did not wane. While most of her poems remained unpublished, JOSEPHINE LAZARUS—a tran-

scendentalist, sister of the poet EMMA LAZARUS, and a member of Antin's new circle of friends—convinced her to write her autobiography. Josephine Lazarus's death in 1910 spurred Antin to begin. In September 1911, the *Atlantic Monthly* published Antin's "Malinke's Atonement," a remarkable short story set in Polotsk about an impoverished nine-year-old "ignorant female" who, after a daring test of faith, wins access to the forbidden—an education "the same as a boy." Two months later, the *Atlantic Monthly* published the first installment of what became her best-known work, *The Promised Land* (1912).

In *The Promised Land*, Antin sketched her life in Polotsk and Boston. Espousing the myth of the American dream, she showed how the idea of America ran counter to the economic, political, and cultural oppression of Europe. She pointed to her own adolescent success as proof of the abundant opportunities held out to immigrants who abandoned the old to embrace wholeheartedly the new. *The Promised Land* brought her nationwide fame, selling nearly 85,000 copies before her death.

Antin continued writing short stories for the *Atlantic Monthly* and opinion pieces for *Outlook*. In the same year that *The Promised Land* appeared, she campaigned for Theodore Roosevelt's presidency. The former president's friendship confirmed what she had for so long asserted—that nothing stood in the way of the immigrant in America. And Roosevelt revealed his own debt to their friendship when he wrote that he became a zealous supporter of woman suffrage precisely because of his association with women like Mary Antin.

From 1913 to 1918, Antin traveled throughout the United States lecturing, often to Jewish organizations, on the themes set forth in *The Promised Land*. In the book, she not only celebrated the American dream, but also, perhaps surprisingly, championed Zionism. Although earlier she had found that her Jewish heritage paled before the American past that now belonged to her, she never repudiated her Jewish identity. Despite her intermarriage, her ardent quest for Americanization, and her abandonment of the piety of the Eastern European shtetl, she argued in the Zionist magazine *The Maccabaean* that "when I take my stand under the Zionist banner," it "is in no sense incompatible with complete civic devotion" to America. Perhaps her return visit to Polotsk after her marriage—a visit about which little is known—fueled these sentiments.

In 1914, she followed the success of *The Promised Land* with her last full-length work, *They Who Knock at Our Gates*, a polemic against the movement to restrict immigration. Although well received, this work was less popular than her autobiographical musings.

America's entry into World War I resulted in a serious personal crisis that permanently changed her life. While she threw herself into lectures for the Allied cause, her husband expressed his pro-German sympathies forcibly, causing a severe rift in their household. In 1918, worried over their estrangement, Antin suffered an attack of what was then diagnosed as neurasthenia, from which she never fully recovered. The illness caused her to retire from public life. By 1919, when Amadeus Grabau's pro-German sympathies had made his situation at Columbia untenable, he and Antin had separated. The following year, he left for China. Although the couple later corresponded, illness and war kept Antin from visiting Peking, where her husband died in 1946.

After the separation, Antin left New York for Massachusetts. She divided her time among a social service community in Great Barrington known as the Gould Farm, her family's home in Winchester, and her own apartment in Boston. She was hospitalized briefly and also worked as a hospital social worker. Subsequently, attracted by Rudolph Steiner's anthroposophy, she tried in "The Soundless Trumpet" (1937), one of her very few late essays, to convey the power of these new mystical insights—but without much success.

Mentally alert, but physically an invalid in her final years, Mary Antin resided with her younger American-born sisters. She died of cancer on May 15, 1949, in Suffern, New York.

Numerous memoirs and novels have recounted the Jewish immigrant experience since *The Promised Land* was first published in 1912. Nevertheless, for its celebration of America and how it transformed the foreign-born Maryashe into Mary Antin, author, citizen, and interpreter of the immigrant experience to her fellow Americans, Antin's autobiography remains the quintessential work of its genre.

SELECTED WORKS BY MARY ANTIN

"The Amulet." *Atlantic Monthly* 111 (January 1913): 177–190; "First Aid to the Alien." *Outlook* 101 (June 29, 1912): 481–485; *From Plotzk to Boston* (1899); "His Soul Goes Marching On." *Berkshire Courier*, May 14, 1925; "House of One Father." *Common Ground* 1 (Spring 1941): 36–42; "How I Wrote 'The Promised Land.' " *NYTimes*, June 30, 1912, 392; "The Lie." *Atlantic Monthly* 112 (August 1913): 177–190; "Malinke's Atonement." *Atlantic Monthly* 108 (September 1911): 300–319; *The Promised Land* (1912); "The Soundless Trumpet." *Atlantic Monthly* 159 (May 1937): 560–569; *They Who Knock at Our Gates: A Complete Gospel of Immigration* (1914); "A Woman to Her Fellow-Citizens." *Outlook* 102 (November 2, 1912): 482–486; "The Zionists' Bit." *The Maccabaean* (February 1918): 40; "A Zionist's Confession of Faith." *The Maccabaean* (February 1917): 157–158.

BIBLIOGRAPHY

AJYB 24:115, 51:519; *BEOAJ; DAB; EJ*; Koppelman, Susan. "Mary Antin." *Dictionary of Literary Biography Yearbook 1984* (1985); Nadell, Pamela S. Introduction to *From Plotzk to Boston* (1985); *NAW* (1971); Obituary. *NYTimes*, May 18, 1949, 27:3; *WWIAJ* (1926, 1928, 1938); *WWWIA* 6.

PAMELA S. NADELL

APPEL, ANNA (1888–1963)

Anna (Khane) Appel, a highly acclaimed character actress, straddled the Yiddish- and English-language worlds of theater, film, and television. Excelling in both comic and dramatic roles, she was especially acclaimed for the versatility of her mimic art. A tall woman with an expressive round face, Appel became noted for her mother roles.

On May 1, 1888, Anna was born in Bucharest, Romania, where her parents, Bernard and Jeanette (Schaeffer) Bercovici, owned a hotel. Anna went to primary and secondary schools and studied Yiddish privately until the family's immigration to Montreal, Canada, in 1902. Drawn to acting since early childhood, she joined a Yiddish amateur dramatic club in Montreal. After moving to New York in 1904, she became a member of a Yiddish vaudeville company. According to Appel, her family was so furious that they sat shiva for her. In 1906, she married Yiddish vaudeville actor Isadore Appel, with whom she had a daughter, Helen. Their marriage ended with his death in 1909. In 1915, she married Dr. Sigmund Ben-Avi and was widowed a second time in 1924. Her son, Avrum Ben-Avi, born in 1916, became a faculty member at the New York University Graduate School of Psychology. Appel's third partner was Morris Ross.

After her first husband's death, Appel continued to play in Yiddish vaudeville until 1916, when she joined Jacob P. Adler's company for one season. Her success began in 1918, when she, along with CELIA ADLER, BERTA GERSTEN, Jacob Ben-Ami, and others, formed the original company of Maurice Schwartz's Yiddish Art Theater in New York. A regular cast member until 1928, she continued to perform with the company off and on until its demise in 1950. Among her noteworthy performances were in Sholem Aleichem's *Dos Groyse Gevins* [The big win], Hirschbein's *A Farvorfn Vinkl* [The secluded nook], Shaw's *Mrs. Warren's Profession*, and Gorky's *The Lower Depths*.

During the 1920s and 1930s, Appel appeared in the Yiddish films *Yizker* [Prayer of remembrance] (1924) and *Broken Hearts* (1926), both featuring the actors of the Yiddish Art Theater. Later followed *Grine Felder* [Green fields] (1937), *Yankl der Shmid* [The singing blacksmith] (1938), and *Amerikaner Shadkhen* [American matchmaker] (1940). In Hollywood, she appeared in *Faithless* (1933) and was featured in *The Heart of New York* and *The Symphony of Six Million*, both 1932 melodramas set on Manhattan's Lower East Side.

At age forty, Appel debuted on the English-language stage with a starring role in *Poppa* (1928). During her ensuing thirty-year career in English, she performed in *Did I Say No?* (1931) and *Awake and Sing* (1936), as well as in such Broadway productions as *Good Neighbor* (1941), *All You Need Is One Good Break* (1950), the revival of *Abie's Irish Rose* (1954), in which she enjoyed outstanding success, *Highway Robbery* (1955), *Comic Strip* (1958), and *The Golem* (1959), which marked her final Broadway appearance. Anna Appel's last public appearance was on television in 1961. She died in New York on November 19, 1963.

Praising Appel for her performance in *Good Neighbor*, critic Brooks Atkinson wrote: "She probably could act the telephone book, if necessary, for she has great strength as an actress and great warmth as a person."

BIBLIOGRAPHY

American Jewish Biography (1994); "Apel, Khane." *Leksikon fun Yidishn Teater* [Lexicon of the Yiddish theater]. Vol. 1, edited by Zalmen Zylbercwaig (1931); Appel, Anna. Archival materials. Billy Rose Theatre Collection, New York Public Library, Lincoln Center, NYC, and Yiddish Theatre and Photo Collection, YIVO Institute for Jewish Research, NYC; Ehrenreich, Chaim. "Khane Apel: Ire Groyse Mayles: A Vort af Ir Frishn Keyver" [Anna Appel: her great qualities: A word at her fresh grave]. *Forverts* (November 29, 1963): 8; Hoberman, J. *Bridge of Light: Yiddish Film Between Two Worlds* (1991); "Khane Apel: Balibte Yidishe Shoyshpilerin, Tot Tsu 75 Yor" [Anna Appel: Popular Jewish actress, dead at 75]. *Forverts* (November 21, 1963): 1; Mukdoyni, A. *Teater* (1927); *Notable Names in American Theatre* (1976), s.v. "Necrology"; Obituary. *NYTimes*, November 21, 1963, 39; *Who's Who in Hollywood, 1900–1976* (1976), s.v. "Late Players"; *WWIAJ* (1938).

NINA WARNKE

ARBUS, DIANE (1923–1971)

Diane Arbus changed how the world looks at photographs and how photographs look at the world.

Best known for her pictures of "freaks" and eccentrics such as "The Jungle Creep," "The Marked Man," and nudists, she also changed the world of children's fashion photography and celebrity photography. She was alternately described as shy, sweet and girlish or coldly aggressive and "as tough as any man" in her field. Friends and colleagues were amazed by her ability to relate to her subjects, her openness and vulnerability with them. On the other hand, some people who posed for her found her to be manipulative, bossy, and cold. In a 1985 article titled "The Hostile Camera," Calvin Bedient said of her: "She is a modernist heroine, braving the dark places of psychology, her only shield her camera, an eye that would not flinch."

Diane was born on March 14, 1923, to Gertrude (Russek) and David Nemerov. She was the second of three children, between elder brother Howard and younger sister Renee. All the Nemerov children grew up surrounded by the trappings of wealth and success. Their maternal grandparents started the Russeks fur stores their father now ran. Their only contact with their father's side of the family (the poor immigrant Nemerovs) was when they would spend Passover in Brooklyn with David Nemerov's parents. Later in life, Diane would frequently refer to the atmosphere of wealth in which she grew up. "I was confirmed in a sense of unreality. All I could feel was my sense of unreality," she told interviewer Studs Terkel (in 1969). Her later career could be summed up as a constant search for the "reality" she was forbidden to see as a child.

Diane and her siblings attended the progressive Fieldston School. At fourteen, Diane met nineteen-year-old Allan Arbus, who was working in the Russeks art department. They immediately fell in love and became intensely involved with one another. Though her parents tried to discourage the affair (much as her grandparents had tried to stop her parents), Diane and Allan continued to meet clandestinely for the next four years. On April 10, 1941, when she was just eighteen, Diane and Allan Arbus were married by a rabbi. Her parents, faced with this fait accompli, gave their blessing to the marriage. The Arbuses were married for twenty-eight years, although they separated after nineteen, and had two children, Doon (b. 1945) and Amy (b. 1954).

In 1946, after Allan returned from World War II, the couple decided to pursue a career as fashion photographers. David Nemerov gave them their first job, the account with Russeks Furs. Over the next ten years the Allan and Diane Arbus Studio became very successful, with Diane conceiving the style of the shoot and Allan handling the technical side. Allan, for his part, always encouraged Diane to take her own pictures and pursue her own creativity. Diane herself credited Allan as being "my first teacher." However, Diane hated the world of fashion photography and began to suffer increasingly from depression (as had her mother). In 1957, she quit styling the Arbus Studio photo shoots.

Moving into the world of independent photography was not easy for her. Diane Arbus was extremely shy, which hampered her ability to approach strangers on the street to ask them to pose. In addition, pursuing her own career went against the model of women at the time. As her daughter Amy has remarked: "Ma had always thought all her life was about helping Pa do his thing. It took her a long time to adjust."

By 1960, Diane and Allan Arbus had separated, though Allan continued to be a major emotional support in her life. He also continued to assist Diane with her photography and taught her the technical side of the art.

To develop herself as a photographer, Arbus first enrolled in Alexey Brodovitch's workshop, but she quit soon after she started. Her next attempt was more successful. In 1958 she enrolled in Lisette Model's class at the New School. In Model, Arbus found her mentor and a lifelong friend. Model helped her identify and accept what subjects she wanted to photograph—what Doon Arbus later called "the forbidden." Art critic Peter Bunnell has said that Arbus "learned from Model that in the isolation of the human figure one can mirror the essential aspects of society."

In 1959, she met her second mentor, Marvin Israel, and he quickly became one of the major influences in her life. He supported her ideas and pushed her to pursue them even further. He advised her on which photograph to choose from a contact sheet and introduced her to people he thought would influence her or help her career. In 1961, he became the art director of *Harper's Bazaar* and was able to publish her work as well.

Perhaps because of Model's and Israel's support, Arbus began to use her fear as opposed to being frozen by it. Throughout the rest of her life she would talk of her photography as an adventure and the fear as a stimulus. Her biographer Patricia Bosworth notes, "Her terror aroused her and made her *feel;* shattered her listlessness, her depression. Conquering her fears helped her develop the courage she felt her mother had failed to teach her." Driven by her curiosity and fear, Arbus began to haunt the places that would define her as a photographer: Hubert's Freak Museum in Times Square, Coney Island, gay nightclubs, and the tenements of Brooklyn and Manhattan. She began her life as a self-described "collector," viewing her work as "a sort of contemporary anthropology."

In the late summer of 1959, Arbus took her portfolio to *Esquire* magazine and showed it to Harold Hayes, the articles editor. Hayes was "bowled over by Diane's images. . . . Her vision, her subject matter, her snapshot style were perfect for *Esquire,* perfect for the times; she stripped away everything to the thing itself. It seemed apocalyptic." A few months later, Arbus was asked to do a photo essay on the nightlife of New York for a special *Esquire* issue on the city, published in July 1960. It contained Diane Arbus portraits of six "typical" New Yorkers, titled "The Vertical Journey: Six Movements of a Moment Within the Heart of the City."

"The Vertical Journey" marked the beginning of her career as a solo commercial photographer. Over the next eleven years Diane Arbus would publish over 250 pictures in more than seventy magazine articles. Her most frequent supporters in the publishing world were *Esquire, Harper's Bazaar,* and two London publications, the *Sunday Times Magazine* and *Nova.* Her work also appeared in *New York, Show, Essence,* the *New York Times, Holiday, Sports Illustrated,* and the *Saturday Evening Post.*

Throughout her career Diane Arbus hoped to break the pattern that bound most photographers. She tried to make a living from magazines while still maintaining her integrity and pursuing her style and interests, and to some degree she succeeded. Her serious artwork and her magazine work were never as separate and distinct as that of most other photographers.

As the magazine assignments and her friendships with Lisette Model and Marvin Israel began to help Arbus feel more confident, she developed her own singular approach to photography, both artistically and technically. In 1962, Arbus changed her camera from a Leica to a Rolleiflex. The negatives were less grainy and gave her the clarity she wanted. The square frame of this new camera became a signature of her later work. In 1964, she began using a Mamiya C33 camera along with her Rollei. She used the Mamiya with a flash, which gave her subjects the exposed and vulnerable look that became another signature of her style. By 1970, she was taking photographs with a Pentax.

In 1965, three of Arbus's early pictures were included in a show at the Museum of Modern Art called "Recent Acquisitions." Arbus was hesitant and concerned, as she would be throughout her career, about the public's reaction. She was right. Yuben Yee, the photo department's librarian, would come in early every morning to wipe the spit off of the photos. When Arbus learned of this, she left town for several days. As Yee said, "People were uncomfortable—threatened—looking at Diane's stuff."

Over this period, Arbus was getting work from magazines to do portraits of the famous and a few children's fashion shoots. She also received two Guggenheim Fellowships, in 1963 and 1966, to pursue her private work. While still taking photos of "freaks" and eccentrics, she was moving into other areas of identity. She began taking pictures of twins and triplets, of families and couples in Central Park, of the uptown and downtown art scenes and of nudist camps.

In 1967, the Museum of Modern Art asked Arbus to contribute to "New Documents," a major exhibit of modern photography. Again, she was hesitant about putting her work on public display. At the same time, she became tremendously excited by the possibility for future work, which she hoped the exhibit might generate.

The critical response was generally positive, although Chauncy Howell of *Women's Wear Daily* called it "grotesque." Robert Hughes of *Time* said, "Arbus is highly gratifying." In the *New York Times*, Jacob Deschin wrote, "Even her glamour shots . . . look bizarre. . . . At the same time there is occasionally a subtle suggestion of pathos, now and then diluted slightly with a vague sense of humor. Sometimes, it must be added, the picture borders close to poor taste."

Unfortunately, although the "New Documents" exhibit did bring Arbus to the attention of the London *Sunday Times Magazine*, her fear that the exhibit might lead to the public misunderstanding her work was realized. With the notoriety of the "New Documents" show, Diane Arbus became more firmly established as the "freak" photographer, and publishers became increasingly shy of using her to photograph the subjects of their stories. A further blow to her commercial career came with the controversy over the "Viva pictures."

In December 1967, Arbus was hired by the newly created *New York* magazine to photograph the actress Viva. Arbus ultimately gave the magazine several nude photographs of Viva, which were published in the April 29, 1968, issue. Viva, who felt she had been misled and lied to by Arbus, threatened a lawsuit but later dropped it. The public and advertisers were so upset that the magazine lost over a million dollars in advertising, most of which never returned to the publication. Journalist Tom Morgan says that those pictures were "watershed pictures. They broke down the barriers between private and public lives."

In 1968, she was hospitalized with hepatitis. (She had suffered from it before, in 1966.) Weakened from the illness, she felt that she was losing her strength and independence. She became increasingly depressed. In 1969, her marriage to Allan Arbus was formally ended by divorce and the Arbus Studio was closed.

By 1970, Diane Arbus had become a legend among young photographers. She was teaching classes and workshops and giving lectures—generally not something she enjoyed, but she was in demand and needed the money. That year she won the Robert Levitt Award from the American Society of Magazine Photographers for outstanding achievement. She also began what would be one of the final projects of her career, taking pictures of mentally retarded adults at a home in Vineland, New Jersey. At first these photos seemed to exhilarate her, but soon she grew to hate the Vineland pictures, because she felt that the shots were "out of control."

Beyond her dismay over those photographs, there was the attention brought on by success. The May 1971 issue of *Artforum* had published a portfolio of her pictures. Walter Hopps of the Corcoran Gallery in Washington, D.C., had persuaded her to agree to exhibit her work at the Venice Biennale in the summer of 1972. These projects only seemed to panic and depress her further. "She did say over and over again that now that she was getting better known people *expected* things of her and she didn't want anyone to expect things from her since she didn't know what to expect from herself and never would."

Suffering from extreme depression, caught between her fear of fame and her need for money, and at a crossroads in her work, Diane Arbus committed suicide in her apartment on July 26, 1971, leaving the words "last supper" written across that date in her journal. Marvin Israel discovered the body on July 28.

A posthumous exhibit was mounted at the Museum of Modern Art in 1972, then traveled around the United States and Europe. Since her death three books of her photographs have been published: *Diane Arbus: An Aperture Monograph*, *Diane Arbus: Magazine Work*, and *Untitled*. For many years she remained a cult figure, and it was not until the 1980s that her work came to be generally accepted. Her impact and influence will never again be considered marginal. She changed not only photography but how we identify each other as human beings.

BIBLIOGRAPHY

Arbus, Doon, and Marvin Israel, eds. *Diane Arbus: Magazine Work* (1984); Bedient, Calvin. "The Hostile Camera: Diane Arbus." *Art in America* (January 1985); Bosworth, Patricia. *Diane Arbus* (1984); Bunnell, Peter. "Diane Arbus." *Print Collectors Newsletter* (January/February 1973); Deschin,

Jacob. "People Seen as Curiosity." *NYTimes*, March 5, 1967, sec. 2, p. 21; *Diane Arbus: An Aperture Monograph* (1972); Morgan, Susan. "Loitering with Intent: Diane Arbus at the Movies." *Parkett* 47 (1996); *NAW* modern; Spring, Justin. "Diane Arbus." *Artforum* (February 1992).

HILLARY MAC AUSTIN

ARENDT, HANNAH (1906–1975)

A political theorist with a flair for grand historical generalization, Hannah Arendt exhibited the conceptual brio of a cultivated intellectual, the conscientious learning of a German-trained scholar, and the undaunted spirit of an exile who had confronted some of the worst horrors of European tyranny. Her life was enriched by innovative thought and ennobled by friendship and love. Although her books addressed a general audience from the standpoint of disinterested universalism, Jewishness was an irrepressible feature of her experience as well as a condition that she never sought to repudiate.

Hannah Arendt was born on October 14, 1906, in Hanover, in Wilhelmine Germany. Raised in Königsberg, she was the only child of Paul and Martha (Cohn) Arendt, both of whom had grown up in Russian-Jewish homes headed by entrepreneurs. Arendt's childhood was punctuated with grief and terror. Her father, an engineer, died of paresis (syphilitic insanity) when Hannah was seven, and episodic battles between Russian and German armies were fought near their home soon thereafter. Her mother married Martin Beerwald in 1920, providing Hannah with two older stepsisters, Eva and Clara Beerwald.

After graduating from high school in Königsberg in 1924, Arendt began to study theology that fall with

Original, controversial, and daring, the philosophical works of Hannah Arendt divided Jewish thinkers but left their indelible mark on sociopolitical theory in the twentieth century. She is pictured here at a Hillel symposium at the University of Maryland in 1965.
[American Jewish Historical Society]

Rudolf Bultmann at the University of Marburg. Also on the faculty was the young philosopher Martin Heidegger, whose lectures, which would form the basis of *Sein und Zeit* [Being and time] (1927), were already inspiring allegiance to and interest in the emerging *Existenzphilosophie*. Her brief but passionate affair with Heidegger, a married man and a father, began in 1925 but ended when she went on to study at the University of Heidelberg with Karl Jaspers. A psychiatrist who had converted to philosophy, he became her mentor.

In September 1929, Arendt married Günther Stern, who wrote under the name of Günther Anders. That year, she also completed her dissertation on the idea of love in the thought of St. Augustine and earned her doctorate. However, the rising anti-Semitism afflicting the German polity distracted her from metaphysics and compelled her to face the historical dilemma of German Jews. By writing a biography of Rahel Varnhagen, a Jewish salon hostess in Berlin in the early 1800s, Arendt sought to understand how her subject's conversion to Christianity and repudiation of Jewishness illuminated the conflict between minority status and German nationalism. *Rahel Varnhagen: The Life of a Jewish Woman* was not published until 1958. By then, Arendt's great historical subject was no longer the question of whether Jews were fit to enter the salons, but the question of whether Jews were fit to inhabit the earth.

As the National Socialists grasped power, Arendt became a political activist and, beginning in 1933, helped the German Zionist Organization and its leader, Kurt Blumenfeld, to publicize the plight of the victims of Nazism. She also did research on anti-Semitic propaganda, for which she was arrested by the Gestapo. But when she won the sympathy of a Berlin jailer, she was released and escaped to Paris, where she remained for the rest of the decade. Working especially with Youth Aliyah, Arendt helped rescue Jewish children from the Third Reich and bring them to Palestine.

In Paris, she met Heinrich Blücher, a formally uneducated Berlin proletarian, a communist who had been a member of Rosa Luxemburg's defeated Spartacus League, and a gentile. After both had divorced, Arendt married Blücher on January 16, 1940. When the Wehrmacht invaded France less than half a year later, the couple was separated and interned in southern France along with other stateless Germans. Arendt was sent to Gurs, from which she escaped. She soon joined her husband, and in May 1941, both managed to reach neutral America, where her mother was able to reunite with them. While living in New York

during the rest of World War II, Arendt envisioned the book that became *The Origins of Totalitarianism*. It was published in 1951, exactly a decade after she arrived in the United States and the same year she secured United States citizenship.

From two separate launching pads, Arendt's career as an American intellectual took off. Her writing appeared early in Jewish journals such as *Jewish Social Studies*, and she was befriended by the editor and historian Salo W. Baron and his wife, Jeanette M. Baron. In magazines such as *Jewish Frontier* and *Aufbau* [Reconstruction], Arendt argued on behalf of a Jewish army and expressed the hope that Arabs and Jews might live together in a postwar Palestinian state. She also served as an editor at Schocken Books, a German Jewish publishing firm that reestablished itself in New York and in Palestine, and brought to the attention of English readers the diaries of Franz Kafka and the fin de siècle Jewish polemics of Bernard Lazare. After the Holocaust, Baron put Arendt in charge of Jewish Cultural Reconstruction, the effort to locate and redistribute the shards of Judaic artifacts and other treasures that had been salvaged from a doomed civilization. Her second launching pad was a circle of mostly leftist intellectuals associated with *Partisan Review*, especially non-Jews such as Dwight Macdonald and Mary McCarthy. The critic Alfred Kazin, however, was also invaluable in enhancing the prose of *The Origins of Totalitarianism*, the work that made Arendt an intellectual celebrity in the early years of the Cold War.

No book was more resonant or impressive in tracing the steps toward the distinctive twentieth-century tyrannies of Hitler and Stalin, or in measuring how grievously wounded Western civilization and the human status itself had become. She demonstrated how embedded racism was in Central and Western European societies by the end of the nineteenth century, and how imperialism experimented with the possibilities of unspeakable cruelty and mass murder. The third section of her book exposed the operations of "radical evil," arguing that the huge number of prisoners in the death camps marked a horrifying discontinuity in European history itself. Totalitarianism put into practice what had been imagined only in the medieval depictions of hell. In the 1950s, *The Origins of Totalitarianism* engendered much doubt, especially by drawing parallels between Nazi Germany and Stalinist Russia (despite their obvious ideological conflicts and their savage warfare from 1941 to 1945). The parallelism continues to stir skepticism in some readers, especially because of the unavailability and unfamiliarity of Russian sources when the book was researched and written. But Arendt's emphasis on the plight of the Jews amid the decline of Enlightenment ideals of human rights, and her insistence that the Third Reich was conducting two wars—one against the Allies, the other against the Jewish people—have become commonplaces of Jewish historiography. Much of her book is stunningly original, and virtually every paragraph is ablaze with insight. More than any other scholar, Arendt made meaningful and provocative the idea of "totalitarianism" as a novel form of autocracy, as springing from subterranean sources within Western society, but pushing to unprecedented extremes murderous fantasies of domination and revenge. An expanded edition of *The Origins of Totalitarianism* was published in 1958, taking into account the Hungarian Revolution of two years earlier.

Arendt's next three books—*The Human Condition* (1958), *Between Past and Future* (1961), and *On Revolution* (1968)—could be characterized by a yearning to reconstruct political philosophy rather than to explore the devolution of political history. Remarkably enough, in 1963 she also published what proved to be the most controversial work of her career: *Eichmann in Jerusalem.* In 1960, Israeli security forces had captured the S.S. lieutenant colonel who had been responsible for transporting Jews to the death camps. The following year, he was tried in Israel, where Arendt covered the trial as a correspondent for *The New Yorker.* Her articles were then revised and expanded for *Eichmann in Jerusalem.*

Her portrayal of a bureaucrat who did his duty and followed orders, rather than a raving ideologue animated by demonic anti-Semitism, was strikingly original. Far from embodying "radical evil," Eichmann exemplified "the banality of evil," Arendt argued—and thus the danger could not be confined to the political peculiarities of the Third Reich. While accepting the validity of Israeli jurisdiction and considering the Israeli court's verdict imposing the death sentence on Eichmann just, Arendt also offered her own justifications for capital punishment. Eichmann had not wanted to share the earth with the Jews; therefore, the Jewish state had no reason to share the earth with him. Almost in passing, she also claimed that fewer than six million Jews would have died if the Jewish councils had not collaborated to various degrees with Nazis like Eichmann. Even anarchy and noncooperation would have been better, she stated, than the effort to act as though the occupiers were traditional anti-Semites who might somehow be bribed or appeased. Her attribution of some responsibility for the catastrophe to the councils (*Judenräte*) not only met sharp criticism, but also provoked a considerable historical literature that investigated the behavior of

Jewish communities under Nazi occupation. The subsequent debate has often reinforced the picture of venality, delusion, fear, and selfishness that Arendt briefly presented.

The storm over the book's apparent elevation of Eichmann's character and denial of Jewish innocence frayed whatever bonds still tied Arendt to the organized Jewish community. Some segments mounted a propaganda campaign against the arguments that she advanced. Although *Eichmann in Jerusalem* is hardly free of factual error or bias, Arendt's critics tended to miss her subtlety and to ignore the relation between her book and the grandeur of her philosophy. She held the victims of the Final Solution accountable for inadequate and ill-conceived political action, and offered the perpetrators a measure of empathy and an effort to understand—lest the horrors be repeated under different historical conditions. But Arendt also wrote as though the modernization associated with the rise of mass society made problematic the classical injunction to think clearly and to act according to conscience. Partisanship and nationalism (even sometimes on behalf of Jews) had obscured the ideals of rational speech and meaningful deeds that she especially celebrated in *The Human Condition.* But nearly all of her books suggest a struggle to reclaim the possibilities of freedom grounded in the sense of a shared world.

According to Arendt, then, Eichmann had done evil not because he had a sadistic will to do so, nor because he had been deeply infected by the bacillus of anti-Semitism, but because he failed to think through what he was doing (his *thoughtlessness*). This theory led Arendt to conceptualize the neo-Kantian meditations on judgment in her posthumously published lecture collection *The Life of the Mind* (1978). While in Aberdeen, Scotland, to deliver these Gifford Lectures, she suffered a heart attack. A second coronary failure on December 4, 1975, while entertaining Salo and Jeanette Baron in her New York City apartment, proved fatal. (Blücher, to whom *The Origins of Totalitarianism* had been dedicated, had died in 1970.)

For well over two decades, Hannah Arendt was one of the nation's most prominent intellectuals. However, she was also a notoriously private person who shielded herself as ferociously from interviewers and television cameras as she resisted Anglo-American philosophical tendencies such as pragmatism, empiricism, and liberalism. The first woman to become a full professor (of politics) at Princeton University, she subsequently taught at the University of Chicago, Wesleyan University, and finally the New School for Social Research. Her articles in the *New York Review of Books* in the 1960s and early 1970s criticized military intervention in Vietnam and the abuses of executive power associated, for example, with the "imperial presidency." Her books exerted a major impact on political theory, particularly in North America, Europe, and Australia, where scholarly conferences and subsequent anthologies have been devoted to her work (as have over a dozen other books and numerous dissertations). In 1975, the Danish government awarded Arendt its Sonning Prize for Contributions to European Civilization, which no American and no woman before her had received. Her life even inspired a roman à clef, Arthur A. Cohen's *An Admirable Woman* (1983), possibly because her allure was more than austerely intellectual—her suitors included Hans J. Morgenthau, Leo Strauss, and W.H. Auden, who was homosexual.

While her work has not yet been given any major feminist readings, Arendt's critical intelligence has enriched Jewish studies. Jewish identity was so inescapable an aspect of her sensibility that, when beginning a lecture in Cologne less than a decade after World War II, she announced: "I am a German Jew driven from my homeland by the Nazis." Her thought also registered the impact of Bernard Lazare, whose polemics combined hostility to anti-Semitism with opposition to the timorous parvenus who often fancied themselves the representatives of the Jewish masses. As her friend Mary McCarthy once recalled, Israel was "the prime source of her political concern," and Arendt remarked that "any real catastrophe in Israel would affect me more deeply than anything else." When such a disaster was avoided in 1967, the victory of the Israel Defense Forces in the Six-Day War thrilled her.

Yet her own knowledge of Judaism was apparently slight, and not always accurate. Arendt died unconsecrated by a religious ceremony (her ashes are buried at Bard College, where Blücher taught), and the obituary in the *New York Times* tersely noted that she had "no religious affiliation." Her dissertation topic had been a Christian saint, and she later wrote dazzlingly on the goodness of Jesus. Yet it could be argued that the primary influences upon her thought were Hellenic philosophy—and German philosophy itself. Arendt denied harboring any special love for the Jewish people (*ahavat Yisrael*). Since Diaspora Jewry had been denied the public space in which she believed human excellence should be cultivated, Arendt admitted that she could neither admire nor "love" a collective so deprived of political possibilities. By 1950 or so, her disappointment with the dead-on-arrival idea of a binational state in the Near East quietly distanced her from the organized Jewish community, whose resources would henceforth be mounted on behalf of Jewish sovereignty in Palestine.

Although Arendt deeply appreciated the refuge that the United States provided (an appreciation that its academic institutions and audiences reciprocated by recognizing her gifts), it is difficult to detect any significant American influences upon her work. Arendt was supremely a product of Weimar culture. She had its awareness of both the brilliance of Jewish achievement and the fragility of the Jewish status. She shared its modernist sense of the disrupted ties to the classical heritage that her own political philosophy helped to elucidate, and its apocalyptic pessimism. Finally, she reflected its disdain for the petty compromises of electoral politics, and its valorization of creative thought and cosmopolitanism that transcend the tastes of the masses. Like Heidegger, she was entranced by the poetic and philosophical resources of the German language, and in 1967, the Deutsche Akademie für Sprache und Dichtung honored the excellence of her German prose. Like many other Jewish intellectuals, Arendt noticed the strangeness of the familiar and sought to clarify the senselessness of modern history. But like very few others, Arendt managed to stamp with individual authority a body of work that is saturated with speculative daring.

SELECTED WORKS BY HANNAH ARENDT

Between Past and Future (1961); *Eichmann in Jerusalem: A Report on the Banality of Evil* (1963); *The Human Condition* (1958); *The Jew as Pariah: Jewish Identity and Politics in the Modern Age.* Edited by Ron H. Feldman (1978); *The Life of the Mind* (1978); *Men in Dark Times* (1968); *On Revolution* (1963); *The Origins of Totalitarianism* (1951); *Rahel Varnhagen: The Life of a Jewish Woman* (1958).

BIBLIOGRAPHY

AJYB 77:591; Arendt, Hannah. Manuscript collections. Deutsches Literaturarchiv [German literary archive], Marbach, Germany, and Manuscript Division, Library of Congress, Washington, D.C.; Barnouw, Dagmar. *Visible Spaces: Hannah Arendt and the German-Jewish Experience* (1990); *DAB* 9 (1994): 40–43; *EJ*; *NAW* modern; Obituary. *NYTimes*, December 6, 1975, 1:8; Petuchowski, Elizabeth, and Janet L. Dotterer. "Arendt, Hannah." In *Jewish-American History and Culture: An Encyclopedia* (1992); Robinson, Jacob. *And the Crooked Shall Be Made Straight: The Eichmann Trial, the Jewish Catastrophe and Hannah Arendt's Narrative* (1965); Whitfield, Stephen J. "Hannah Arendt and Apocalypse." *Michigan Quarterly Review* 26 (1987): 445–458, and *Into the Dark: Hannah Arendt and Totalitarianism* (1980); *WWIAJ* 6; Young-Bruehl, Elisabeth. *Hannah Arendt: For Love of the World* (1982).

STEPHEN J. WHITFIELD

ARNOLD, EVE (b. 1913)

When she wrote that "a photographer must have a passionate, personal approach," Eve Arnold could have been describing herself. Celebrated as much for her candid portraits of the famous as for her sensitive photographs of the disadvantaged, Arnold has embraced "the chance for personal expression and spontaneity photography gives me."

Largely self-taught, Arnold was the first American woman to be accepted into Magnum Photos, a cooperative photography agency that in the 1950s helped photographers gain artistic and financial control of their work. Inspired by Magnum members such as Robert Capa and Henri Cartier-Bresson, Arnold took photographs for major newsmagazines such as *Life*. Her well-known studies of China, women, political figures like Senator Joseph McCarthy and Malcolm X, and movie stars like Joan Crawford and Marilyn Monroe have placed her among the top American photographers.

Arnold was born in Philadelphia in 1913, one of nine children in a family of poor Russian immigrants. Growing up in the Orthodox Jewish tradition, which forbids the making of graven images, she came to her vocation by chance. As a medical student in the 1940s, she was given a camera by a boyfriend. Thus began her love affair with film. She managed a photo processing plant and took a photography class with Alexey Brodovitch at the New School for Social Research in New York City in 1952. She launched her career with her class project, an unconventional, spontaneous study of fashion in Harlem.

With her husband and son Frank (b. 1948), Arnold moved to Long Island, where she began a ten-year photographic study of a founding family of Brookhaven Township. After suffering a miscarriage, she combated depression by photographing births. During the 1950s, she covered a Republican national convention and the McCarthy hearings. In the 1960s, she moved to England, where her marriage ended. At that time, she photographed English subjects, traveled to the Soviet Union, and documented the American civil rights movement.

Arnold favored topics of social concern, but also shot still photographs on movie sets to support herself and her son. In 1971, she made a film called *Women Behind the Veil*. However, she preferred still photography and began to produce books in the mid-1970s. Her many books of photography include *The Unretouched Woman* (1976), *Flashback: The Fifties* (1978), *In America* (1983), *Private View: Inside Baryshnikov's American Ballet Theatre* (1988), *All in a Day's Work* (1989), *In Britain* (1990), *The Great British* (1994), and

Eve Arnold: In Retrospect (1995). Her 1980 work *In China* was named a Notable Book by the American Library Association. Both it and *Marilyn Monroe: An Appreciation* (1987) were featured as Book-of-the-Month Club selections.

Arnold is also noted for the incisive written texts that accompany her photographs. Her articles and pictures have appeared in such magazines as *Look*, *Harper's*, *Geo*, *Stern*, *Epoca*, the *Sunday Times* (London) magazine, and *Paris Match*.

She has mounted one-woman shows at the Brooklyn Museum (1980), London's Knoedler Gallery (1987) and National Portrait Gallery (1991), and New York's International Center of Photography (1995). Her work has been included in group exhibitions as well.

Arnold's long career charts the significant changes in American photojournalism, from the candid black-and-white shots of the 1950s to the innovative color compositions of more recent years. Her stirring portraits make a remarkable artistic contribution to twentieth-century photography.

SELECTED WORKS BY EVE ARNOLD
All in a Day's Work (1989); *Eve Arnold: In Retrospect* (1995); *Flashback: The Fifties* (1978); *The Great British* (1994); *In America* (1983); *In Britain* (1990); *In China* (1980); *Marilyn Monroe: An Appreciation* (1987); *Private View: Inside Baryshnikov's American Ballet Theatre* (1988); *The Unretouched Woman* (1976); *Women Behind the Veil* (1971). Film.

BIBLIOGRAPHY
Contemporary Authors. New Revision Series. Vol. 31: 13–14; *Contemporary Photographers* (1982, 1995); *The Dictionary of Art.* Edited by Jane Turner. Vol. 20 (1986).

EMILY MEYER POMPER

ARNSTEIN, MARGARET GENE (1904–1972)

Margaret Gene Arnstein was a principal architect of the American nursing profession. Renowned for her work in public health, Arnstein also advanced nursing education and research. She was born in New York City on October 27, 1904. Her parents, Leo and Elsie, were second-generation Americans of German Jewish descent. Arnstein had an older sister and two younger brothers. The family participated in Jewish culture, but was not religiously observant.

The Arnstein family was active in Progressive Era reforms. After graduating from Yale University and becoming successful in business, Leo Arnstein served as president of Mount Sinai Hospital and as New York City's welfare commissioner. He was also on the Henry Street Settlement's board of directors. Elsie Arnstein was part of the settlement's vocational advisory service. The founder of the Henry Street Settlement and of public health nursing, LILLIAN WALD, was a family friend who inspired Margaret to become a nurse.

Arnstein completed her primary education at the Ethical Culture School in New York City and graduated from Smith College in 1925. Although her parents wanted her to become a physician, Margaret's interest lay in nursing. She enrolled in the New York Presbyterian Hospital School of Nursing, where she received her diploma in 1928. In 1929, she earned an M.A. in public health nursing from Columbia University.

Arnstein worked for five years with the Westchester County Health Department. She then returned to school, earning an M.A. in public health from the Johns Hopkins University in 1934. She spent eight years in the Communicable Disease Division of the New York State Department of Health (1934–1937, 1940–1943), where she designed and implemented innovative nursing research. Her vision for the profession was that nurses should be involved in research and health policy in addition to patient care.

In 1943 Arnstein's public health endeavors broadened to the international arena. She was hired by the United Nations to develop nursing services for World War II refugees. In 1946, Arnstein entered the newly created U.S. Public Health Service Division of Nursing. She served in several high-ranking posts and became division chief in 1960.

Throughout the 1950s and 1960s, Arnstein engaged in major international initiatives. She surveyed health issues abroad, worked with the World Health Organization, and directed the first International Conference on Nursing Studies. She authored books and numerous articles on nursing and public health.

In 1966, Arnstein left the Public Health Service to spend a year as professor of public health nursing at the University of Michigan. She then accepted the deanship of the Yale University School of Nursing. Under her leadership, Yale became a center for excellence in nursing education. Toward the end of her career Arnstein's contributions were widely recognized. She received several honorary degrees and in 1966 was the first woman to receive a Rockefeller Public Service Award. In 1971, the American Public Health Association awarded her its highest honor: the Sedgewick Memorial Medal. Arnstein retired in 1972 after becoming ill with cancer. She died in New Haven on October 8, 1972.

SELECTED WORKS BY MARGARET GENE ARNSTEIN

Communicable Disease Control, with Gaylord Anderson (1941); "Communicable Disease in Wartime." *Public Health Nursing* (April 1943): 194–196; *A Guide for National Studies of Nursing Resources* (1953); "Nursing in UNRRA Middle East Refugee Camps." *American Journal of Nursing* 45 (1945): 378–381; "Research for Improved Nursing Practices," with L. Petry and P. McIver. *Public Health Reports* (February 1952):183–187; "Surveys Measure Nursing Resources," with L. Petry and R. Gillian. *American Journal of Nursing* 49 (1949): 770–772.

BIBLIOGRAPHY

Arnstein, Margaret Gene. Archival material relevant to public service. Division of Nursing, United States Public Health Service, Rockville, Maryland; Arnstein, Margaret Gene. Personal papers. National Nursing Archives, Mugar Library, Boston University, Boston; Fondelier, Shirley H. "Margaret Gene Arnstein." In *American Nursing: A Biographical Dictionary*, edited by Barbara Sicherman and Carol Hurd (1988); Green, Ilene Kantrov, and Harriette Walker. "Margaret Gene Arnstein." In *Dictionary of American Nursing Biography*, edited by Vern Bullough, Olga Maranjian Church, and Alice P. Stein (1988); *NAW* modern; *NYTimes*, October 9, 1972, 34:4; *WWWIA* 5.

CYNTHIA CONNOLLY

ARONS, JEANNETTE (1881–1960)

"And Mrs. Arons gave in full measure of herself." These words from a history of the Brooklyn Section of the NATIONAL COUNCIL OF JEWISH WOMEN (NCJW) characterize Jeannette Arons's dedication to the welfare of the Jewish community. In conjunction with the Brooklyn Section and national offices of the NCJW, she worked tirelessly to expand and improve the work of this prominent service organization.

Jeannette (Lederman) Arons was born in Brooklyn on July 14, 1881, to Samuel and Minnie (Celler) Lederman. Her brother was Captain Jerome A. Lederman (USNR). After graduating from high school, she took college extension courses. On June 5, 1905, she married Mark Salomon. He died in 1916. She entered into a second marriage, with Abraham H. Arons, on January 18, 1917.

In the 1938 edition of *Who's Who in American Jewry*, Arons is designated a social worker and vice president of a child guidance clinic. Whether or not she was a professional social worker or her office was a child guidance clinic, one of many mental health facilities for children, it is clear that her work, professional or voluntary, was directed toward the needs of the Jewish community.

As the president of the Brooklyn Section of the NCJW from 1918 to 1925, Arons "gave in full measure of herself," expanding and developing new areas of activity for her section and widening the scope of her service with her work at the national office. Her concerns spanned many areas from public health to the problems of people with disabilities to the education of immigrant women. During her presidency, classes in English and citizenship for immigrant women became part of a joint project of the NCJW and the New York City Board of Education.

Her lifelong relationship with NCJW began in the early 1900s. In 1914, as part of a NCJW program, Arons was a volunteer probation officer in juvenile court, caring specifically for Jewish children in trouble. She moved from the Brooklyn Section presidency to become a member and chair of many committees on the national level, including the Farm and Rural Work Programs, and the vice-chair of the national executive committee.

Although most of her activity centered on her commitment to the National Council of Jewish Women, Arons also worked for other organizations, including the Women's Division Federation of Jewish Philanthropies, the Welfare Council of New York, the Pan-Pacific Women's Association U.S. Mainland Committee, and the Sisterhood of Congregation Beth Israel Anshei Emes.

In 1924, the Brooklyn Section established the Jeannette L. Arons Scholarship Fund to assist underprivileged girls to continue their pursuit of education. In the mid-1930s, Arons personally presented the scholarships to three Jewish girls, two art students and a student at the Women's Medical College of Pennsylvania.

Jeannette Arons died on July 2, 1960. She published no important papers. She left no memoirs in esteemed archives. But, like many other Jewish women, she left a legacy of service to the community in which she lived.

BIBLIOGRAPHY

"Brooklyn Section National Council of Jewish Women: A History," and Brooklyn Section, National Council of Jewish Women and Council Home for Jewish Girls (Amalie Seldner Memorial). Annual reports (May 1, 1933–January 1, 1935, and January 1, 1935–January 1, 1936); *The First Fifty Years: A History of the National Council of Jewish Women, 1893–1943*; National Council of Jewish Women newsletters (January 1933, March 1933, November 1934, October 1935, December 1935, 1936); Rogow, Faith. *Gone to Another Meeting: The National Council of Jewish Women, 1893–1993* (1993); *WWIAJ* (1926, 1938).

RONA HOLUB

ARPEL, ADRIEN (b. 1941)

Adrien Arpel, a pioneering entrepreneur in the skin-care industry, was born in Jersey City, New Jersey, on July 15, 1941. She believes that "when you're happy with yourself you make those around you happy," and "when you're honest with yourself first you are honest with everyone." This philosophy has served her well in her life and in her work. Launching a business devoted to women's skin care in 1959 with $400 she had earned from baby-sitting, Arpel is now president and CEO of Adrien Arpel, Inc., an enterprise with approximately 500 salons across the United States and Canada. Her mother, Ada Stark, of Polish extraction, was born in Montreal, Canada, and her father, Samuel Joachin, of Russian heritage, was born in the United States. Her parents met and married in the United States. Arpel has an older sister, Marilyn.

Arpel graduated from high school in 1959 and attended Pace University. She married Ronald Monroe Newman in New York City in 1960. The couple has one child, Lauren, who now works in both of her parents' businesses.

Arpel describes herself as becoming an entrepreneur as soon as she left high school. When she was very young, she regarded cosmetics as a kind of magic. She decided to venture into the facial and cosmetics business after receiving conflicting advice from staff selling cosmetics in department stores. None of the salespeople could detail the ingredients in their products or could explain how these products might improve the customer's skin. Arpel concluded that these saleswomen were selling cosmetics without being sufficiently knowledgeable about their products. She realized that there was a need in the cosmetics marketplace for a business that would educate the consumer, helping her understand how to care for her skin, and what products she needed to use at home. She decided to provide customers with a licensed cosmetologist who understood the most beneficial ingredients in skin-care products. A licensed cosmetologist could counsel women in nature-based products in a comfortable setting. Adrien Arpel also pioneered the concept of the makeover, now widely available in the cosmetics and skin-care business.

Arpel felt her busy clients would best be served in a convenient, private salon in a department store. Thus, she began offering her salon facials in major department stores, such as Macy's and Bloomingdale's, where she was also the first to provide a place for her clients to sit in a cosmetics department.

A clever marketer and a creative product developer, Arpel has developed a niche market for the professional skin-care expert. She sells her own brand of skin-care products and makeup, which are used during the salon treatments. Arpel's marketing strategy is to encourage customers to try her products before they buy them and to educate them in their own skin care.

From age eighteen, Arpel was determined to succeed in business. She is part of a large informal network of female executives who are friends as well as colleagues. She also has a true partnership with her husband, who runs a successful display business.

Arpel has written several beauty books and has won many professional industry awards. She was honored by Bloomingdale's in 1987 as a legend in the cosmetics industry. On November 17, 1988, Pace University praised her "high level of professional success and concern for the well-being and advancement of the community and the exemplary representation of the ideals and mission of Pace University."

Although Arpel is not a formally observant woman, she is very conscious of her Jewish heritage. She cherishes the value of a close family and considers the emphasis on the centrality of family as part of her Jewishness. She and her husband are close to their daughter, son-in-law, and grandchildren. They see each other often, take trips together, and celebrate the major Jewish holidays as a family.

BIBLIOGRAPHY

Allen, Margaret. *Selling Dreams: Inside the Beauty Business* (1981); Arpel, Adrien. Interview by author. NYC, July 20, 1995; "Adrien Arpel—A Legend in Aesthetics." *Dermascope* (July/August 1986): 3–4; Bergman, Joan. "Bloomie's Loves Arpel." *Stores* 69 (May 1987): 116–117; Gallani, Bess. "Salons Treat Clients to Feel of Luxury." *Advertising Age* 56 (February 21, 1985): 18+.

SARA ALPERN

ART

American Jewish women have made major contributions to the art world as artists, photographers, gallery owners, museum curators, art critics, art historians, and collectors at least since the beginning of the twentieth century. Tracing the development of this group in previous centuries is difficult because biographical documentation concerning American women in the art world is scarce and the existing material rarely mentions religious origins. Since most of the artists involved do not deal with explicitly Jewish themes, and many changed their names or adopted their husbands' names, deciding which American women artists are Jewish often involves guesswork. Whereas this poses a problem for the researcher, it also indicates to what extent these artists have integrated into the general fabric of American art and society.

The desire to become fully American, which characterizes all immigrant groups, is true of Jewish immigrants as well, and even more so of their children, who often felt ambivalent toward their parents' foreign accents and customs. Jewish artists—many of whom were immigrants or descendants of immigrants—also experienced the complex dilemmas of acculturation. Their decisions as to whether or not to express their Jewish identity in their art often reflect or exacerbate inner conflicts related to their perception of their position in American society. An installation titled *Postcolonial Kinderhood* (1994) by Elaine Reichek (b. 1943) exposes the tensions inherent in assimilation and the burden of secrecy that it entails. Reichek, who grew up in an assimilated environment of German Jews who tried to espouse all things American, re-creates her childhood bedroom with all the props that composed its simulated American genealogy. Yet, within the traditional American trappings, messages that expose what had been repressed in a conspiracy of silence begin to surface: for example, the samplers and towels are embroidered with subversive stitches that spell out Reichek's hidden identity—"JEW."

The problems of exposure and repression discerned in Reichek's installation preoccupy many American Jewish women artists. Mapping the oscillations between affirmation and denial of specific facets of their identity reveals a progression from denial to affirmation first of gender issues and only later of ethnic or religious components. The initial negation of particularistic aspects of identity through the use of a "universal" language of art, often consisting of neutral subject matter or an abstract style, was a strategy that allowed Jewish women to integrate into the dominantly male American art world. In a field known more for sexual bias than for religious discrimination, the crucial problem for most of these artists was gender rather than Judaism. From the beginning they demanded to be taken seriously as artists. Later, particularly since the

1970s, they emphasized the value of women's experiences and created visual images to express them, while trying to deconstruct the predominantly male canon and to search for alternative narratives.

This development is reflected in the professional names Jewish women artists selected. For example, at the beginning of the century, THERESA BERNSTEIN preserved her Jewish family name, but abbreviated Theresa to "T," obscuring her female identity. This maneuver led to her receiving an invitation to join a group of highly regarded male artists, which was withdrawn as soon as they discovered she was a woman. The case of LEE KRASNER (née Lena Kreisner) is more complex. She Americanized her name to Lenore Krassner in the 1920s because she had always felt that the synagogue discriminated against women. However, the purpose of the subsequent change in the 1930s from Lenore to Lee—a sexually neutral name—was to hide her identity as a woman. In contrast, in 1969 or 1970, Judy Gerowitz (née Cohen) changed her name to JUDY CHICAGO, affirming her identity as an independent woman divested of "all names imposed upon her through male social dominance."

In general, two major influences caused American Jewish women artists to reaffirm their Judaism. The first was the Nazi persecution of Jews and the Holocaust, which, from the late 1930s through the mid-1950s, led male and female artists to assert their Jewish identity through depictions of Jewish genre, biblical themes, and—rarely in the case of the women—scenes of slaughter and the camps. After this point, such expressions were rare until the 1970s, when they appeared in art either for personal reasons or as a result of commissions. Since then, the subject has become increasingly important, both among survivors, who begin to express their memories (e.g., Edith Altman, Alice Lok Kahane, Vera Klement, Kitty Klaidman, and Daisy Brand), and among children and grandchildren of survivors and refugees, who deal with their family histories (e.g., Mindy Weisel, Debby Teicholz, and Deborah Davidson).

The second influence that triggered a reaffirmation of Jewish identity in art relates to general cultural and social trends within American society. During the last decades, the concept of America as a melting pot was gradually replaced by visions of a multicultural society based on ethnic diversity, and the concept of a "universal" art reflecting a master-narrative was challenged by the belief in the necessity of pluralistic art forms that would express the multiple perspectives from which human experience may be viewed. Consequently, art dealing with ethnic and religious spe-

cificities became accepted as valid and significant. Following these trends, which postdate the interest in female identity, a growing number of artists began to explore their identities as Jews. These ideas have manifested themselves in exhibitions such as *Memories of Childhood, so we're not the Cleavers or the Brady Bunch* (1994–1997) curated by Bernice Steinbaum, which expresses the diversity of American society by including Jewish-American, African-American, Native American, Japanese-American, and Chinese-American artists. A shift in the curatorial policies of New York's Jewish Museum also reflects this "ethnic" trend. After years of promoting American avant-garde art, the museum mounted five major exhibitions that explore aspects of Jewish identity in modern art, two curated by men—Avram Kampf's *The Jewish Experience in Art of the Twentieth Century* in 1975–1976 and Norman Kleeblatt's *Too Jewish?* show in 1996—and three shows on contemporary American Jewish art curated by Susan Tumarkin Goodman in 1982, 1986, and 1993. Whereas the earliest of these exhibitions included only three American women, in the latest, after growing exposure in Goodman's shows, over half the participants were women, clearly demonstrating the radical change that had taken place in the position of American Jewish women artists during the last two decades.

The following discussion combines a chronological overview with a survey of some of the major Jewish women artists who have contributed to the visual arts in the United States.

PROFESSIONAL ORGANIZATIONS

At the beginning of the century, very few American Jewish women were professional artists. As their numbers slowly increased during World War I, many of them joined the National Association of Women Painters and Sculptors, founded in 1889, usually preserving their Jewish names and sometimes even stressing their religion. For instance, LOUISE WATERMAN WISE first exhibited under the name Mrs. Stephen S. Wise (an uncommon procedure in this group), to stress that her husband was a famous Reform rabbi. Others, such as Bernstein, served on the association's juries in the 1920s, while Bena Frank Mayer later served on its board of directors. The New York Society of Women Artists, founded in 1925 as a more professional, avant-garde, and radically feminist group, included ever-increasing numbers of Jewish artists, several of whom were among its founders (e.g., Bernstein and Minna Harkavy) and leaders: Bena Frank Mayer was twice elected president and, from the

1940s on, Ethel Katz served as both president and honorary president.

This active role in the organization of feminist art activities continued in the late 1960s and through the 1970s, a decade of great upheaval and change. For example, Nancy Spero was one of the founders of WAR (Women Artists in Revolution) established in 1969 to pressure museums and galleries to show the work of women artists, and Brenda Miller was active in the 1970 ad hoc committee that demanded equal opportunity for women at the Whitney Museum's annual exhibitions. In 1971, Miriam Schapiro and Judy Chicago established the first Feminist Art Program at the California Institute of the Arts in Los Angeles, and in 1972, Barbara Zucker and Dottie Attie were among the founding members of AIR (Artist in Residence), the first women's cooperative gallery in New York. Jewish women also played an active role in numerous publications and feminist venues, as well as in feminist art scholarship. In fact, it was Linda Nochlin's groundbreaking article "Why Have There Been No Great Women Artists?" of 1971 that launched the debate on women's art and set the parameters of feminist art history.

These feminist groups were not, however, these artists' only affiliations. Jewish women also participated in and exhibited with general artists' groups and held solo shows. For instance, in the 1930s, Krasner, RUTH GIKOW, and Lucienne Bloch were active in the Artists' Union and painted murals for the WPA—a field considered a masculine domain. In the 1940s, Krasner and Perle Fine were active in the avant-garde Abstract American Artists group. In 1938, Harkavy was one of the founding members of the New York Sculptors Guild, which was run for many years by Dorothea Schwarz Greenbaum, who was also active in founding the Artists Equity Association in 1947. Gikow was a founding member of the National Silkscreen Society, and June Wayne founded and directed the Tamarind Lithography Workshop in Los Angeles. Parallel to the rise of the women's movement in the late 1960s, the number of American Jewish women artists increased greatly, as did their contributions to contemporary American art.

THE FIRST GENERATIONS

FLORINE STETTHEIMER (1871–1944) and Theresa Bernstein (b. 1896) exemplify the diversity in origins and milieus that characterized American Jewish women artists in the early twentieth century. Stettheimer, born into a wealthy, assimilated New York German Jewish family that had been in the United States for generations, spent part of her childhood in Germany. Rejecting marriage on feminist grounds, she enrolled in the Art Students League in 1892 and traveled in Europe from 1898 to 1914, painting in an academic style. Back in New York during World War I and inspired in part by her recently developed hatred of Germany, in her late forties she changed her conservative "European" style to a neo-naive "American" style with strong Fauve colors and mannerist elongations, through which she depicted New York life and culture in a lightly satirical manner. Although proud to be a Jew, she did not express Judaism in her art, as there was little experience of it in her life.

Theresa Bernstein's parents were from Vienna, but she was born and studied art in Philadelphia, exhibiting in New York galleries and at the National Academy of Design by 1913, and holding her first solo show in 1919. Her contact with Jewish circles and her adhesion to Zionism grew after her 1919 marriage to the artist William Meyerowitz. However, while he depicted Jewish themes and experimented with cubism, she concentrated on landscapes and scenes from American life painted in an Ashcan School style, using bright colors. She rarely painted Jewish subject matter.

The number of American Jewish women artists rose in the 1920s and 1930s, and their activities expanded from painting into sculpture. Many of them adhered to a naturalistic style and depicted the life around them. Like their male counterparts, but to a lesser degree, during the 1930s and 1940s they expressed political sentiments in their art, reacting to national and international events. Thus Anita Weschler's stylized sculptures of this period express both her antiwar stance and her patriotism, while Berta Margoulies sculpted women and children tensely awaiting news following a mine disaster. Minna Harkavy (1895–1987), born in Estonia, also sculpted *An American Miner's Family* in 1931, and reacted to the Holocaust in her 1939 statue of a sad mother and child, titled *Lamentations,* and in her later *The Last Prayer.* Rivka Angel (née Angelovitch), born in Russia in 1899, was so worried as to the fate of the family she had left behind that she used her naivist style to paint *Hunger* and *Children Burning in a Fiery Furnace.*

Ruth Gikow (1915–1982), who depicted subjects such as *The Tenement Fire* of 1939, is a good example of this socially conscious group. After marrying Jack Levine, she combined her roles as artist, wife, and mother by having a studio at home, a solution she found frustrating. This combination of roles is

another series, *The Barque*, the figures that embark on a journey across the sea, leaving others behind, evoke an archetypal voyage to the underworld. On another level, they seem to reflect Frank's early experiences of immigration and rootlessness. Moreover, in her monumental *Horse and Rider* of 1982, the broken and tormented body of the rider recalls the charred bodies of war victims, while the double-headed Apocalyptic horse merges Rousseau's *War* with medieval visions of death to express a post-Holocaust version of horror.

The clay sculptures of Grace Bakst Wapner also reflect her concern with universal themes. The archetypal figures in her *Dyads* series, reminiscent of prehistoric art, seem to be involved in the timeless drama of human relationships. The biblical scenes included in this series stress interdependence between women and men, Jews and non-Jews. For example, *Ruth and Naomi* stresses the friendship and loyalty between women of all creeds. Several works related to *Abraham* evoke the primal conflicts among sacrifice, faith, and paternal love. In a recent work, Wapner joined the contemporary movement by American women to redefine Jewish rituals so as to foster equality between the sexes. Inspired by a feminist seder, she created *Elijah and Miriam Cups*, which complement each other like yin and yang. Their texture and shape evoke the ancient pottery of the Middle East, thus combining biblical roots with contemporary American Jewish culture.

Universal concepts pertaining to human relationships and interdependence are also expressed in the paintings of Selina Trieff (b. 1934). Trieff paints herself in various guises, identifying as male and female, human and animal, mythical and biblical creatures, who embark on existential journeys, in search of meaning. Only in hindsight, years after she painted her gallery of Self-as-Other figures, did the artist realize that they were "eternal wanderers," related to the experience of the Jewish people.

Audrey Flack (b. 1931) turned from abstraction to the figure in the 1950s to explore her identity as a woman and artist. In the 1960s, she painted the "unimportant" but strong American women she admired as opposed to powerful men such as Hitler and Rockefeller, who determined the fate of the world. Her photorealist paintings of the 1970s express different facets of her life: She identified as an artist with the Spanish Baroque sculptor Luisa Ignacia Roldàn, as the mother of an autistic child with the weeping Madonna, as a fragile woman with Marilyn Monroe, and as a Jew with the victims of the Holocaust. Following an illness, she turned to mysticism, framing Christian and Hindu images with Jewish ones

in *A Course of Miracles* of 1983: On the "west" side, a photograph of Albert Einstein and a European Jewish candlestick flank a statue of Christ; on the "east" side, an Old Testament with a Bezalel-style silver cover stands beside a photograph of Baba, a Hindu philanthropist. This interdenominational, multicultural imagery is also found in her sculptures in which she returns to strong women, creating feminist idols that affirm women's healing and inspiring powers.

Flack's concern with female divinity was earlier explored by other women artists, some of whom were Jewish. The centrality of this theme during the 1970s is reflected in the dedication of the Spring 1978 issue of the feminist journal *Heresies* to the Great Goddess, with the lead article by Gloria Feman Orenstein, "The Reemergence of the Archetype of the Great Goddess in Art by Contemporary Women." In numerous photographs, performances, and ceremonies created from the early 1970s on, Mary Beth Edelson reformulated archaic rituals based on a feminist quest for spirituality. The artist's search for a spiritual matrilineage was complemented by a parallel quest for human role models. Her 1971 poster offers a humorous and biting revision of Leonardo's *Last Supper* in which living American women artists replace Leonardo's all-male cast of Christ and the apostles. Sixty-seven other women artists frame this iconic image to make it a powerful political statement combating the discrimination against women in the art world and rebutting the assertion that there are no great women artists. At the same time that Edelson re-created Leonardo's masterpiece, Dottie Attie (née Laibow, b. 1938) was applying a related revisionist strategy vis-à-vis the neoclassical paintings of Ingres and other masterpieces of Western art. By focusing on fragments of these works and attaching various texts to the visual images, Attie offered innovative interpretations of the well-known masterpieces, exposing erotic, violent, and taboo aspects that are often the hidden subtext of canonical works.

Parallel to these feminist activities in New York, in Los Angeles Miriam Schapiro (b. 1923) and Judy Chicago (b. 1939) collaborated with their students to create art that expressed women's lives from a new perspective, exploring taboo issues such as vaginal imagery, menstruation, and lesbianism. *Womanhouse*, an avant-garde site installation, is an example of their use of collaborative projects to challenge the accepted notion of the individual artist-genius that had been used to explain the dearth of great women artists. Aiming to bestow significance on women's experiences and to give value to women's chosen art forms, they defied the hierarchic distinction between high art

JUDY CHICAGO *is shown here with the Brooklyn Museum of Art's installation of her work* The Dinner Party, *which includes a table set for thirty-nine illustrious women of the past, with runners and napkins that document their achievements and significance.*
[Bettye Lane]

and crafts, launching the pattern and decoration movement.

Schapiro continues to explore these ideas, integrating fans, kimonos, quilts, and lacy aprons into her art, thus evoking its connection to her artistic foremothers. Her *Collaboration Series* states her indebtedness to women of the past by celebrating the works of artists such as Mary Cassatt, Frida Kahlo, and the Russian avant-garde women of the early part of the century. While Schapiro's feminism plays a major role in her art, and her American identity surfaces in her frequent use of the quilt, her Jewish identity is rarely discernible. The few exceptions are her synagogue stained glass windows of *The Four Matriarchs*, and two autobiographical quilts, each of which includes a menorah. Her complex relationship with Judaism is evinced by her contribution to an exhibition about childhood memories. Rather than address her own biography, Schapiro invented an alter ego, Alexandra, a child artist who celebrates Hanukkah and installs a shrine for Anne Frank in her bedroom/studio.

Another leading innovator in the pattern and decoration movement is Joyce Kozloff (b. 1942), whose many public projects reflect her environmental and social concerns. Eschewing conventional hierarchies imposed by Western art, Kozloff often bases her works on the decorative arts of non-European cultures. A recent project deals with city maps: In her feminist map of Paris, the city streets are renamed after famous French women. In *Naming II* of 1996—her first overtly Jewish work—the streets of New York City are renamed after Jewish women.

The collaborative trend that Schapiro and Chicago advocated found its most elaborate expression in projects initiated by Chicago. *The Dinner Party*, completed in 1979, included a triangular dinner table set for thirty-nine illustrious women of the past, who were each given a sculpted place setting and embroidered runners and napkins that documented her achievements and significance. In addition, the names of 999 women "swallowed up by history" were inscribed on the floor where this ceremonial meal took place. Chicago's *Birth Project* (1980–1985) consisted of eighty-five embroidered, quilted, crocheted, and woven parts produced by volunteers to celebrate the personal and archetypal creative powers of women. In the late 1980s, Chicago rediscovered her Jewish identity. In her *Holocaust Project* (1993), she associates the Holocaust with other atrocities and injustices, placing Jewish victims alongside Gypsies, African Americans, Native Americans, and lesbians.

EXPOSING AGGRESSION

This tendency to incorporate images from the Holocaust within a broader political framework had antecedents in the work of artists such as Joan Snyder, Nancy Spero, and Ida Applebroog (née Horowitz, b. 1929). These artists continued and developed the political involvement and social commitment displayed by their counterparts during the 1930s and 1940s.

Although she began as an abstract expressionist, Joan Snyder (b. 1940) forcefully expressed both her Jewish identity and her political and feminist concerns in her art. Works such as *Resurrection* of 1977 deal with women as victims of violence, rape, and murder, while others, such as *Boy in Afganistan* and *Boy in Africa*, protest the suffering of helpless children in underprivileged third world countries. From her early *Grandma Cohen's Funeral Painting* of 1964 to *Morning Requiem with Kaddish* of 1987–1988, Snyder referred openly to her Jewish background. *Women in Camps* of 1988 reflects the artist's compassion for women and children as well as her awareness of her Jewish roots. The work juxtaposes photographs of Jewish concentration camp inmates with those of Palestinian women in refugee camps. Underlining this visual analogy is a text that is integrated into the composition: "women with babies, bags, grandmas wearing babushkas and scarves and yellow stars . . . the moon shone in Germany, the moon shone in Palestine and men are still seeking final solutions."

Nancy Spero (b. 1926) has been politically active both as a radical feminist artist and as a militant American antiwar activist. Although she incorporated references to the Holocaust such as swastikas, Stars of David, and images of crematoria into her anti-Vietnam *War Series* (1966–1970), her identity as a Jew was relegated to the background. In the 1990s, she overtly confronted the problem of Jewish victimization in her installations of *The Ballad of Marie Sanders, the Jew's Whore*, based on a 1934 ballad by Bertholt Brecht about a German woman tortured for having sexual relations with a Jew. In these works, Brecht's text is accompanied by an image of a naked, gagged-and-bound woman based on a photograph discovered in the pocket of a Gestapo officer, and related to Spero's earlier series *The Torture of Women*. To this she appended other photographic images of Jewish women, such as those who fought in the Warsaw

ghetto and Israeli women of the peace movement, as well as quotations from the poetry of Nelli Sachs and Irena Klepfisz.

Another artist who protested against the Vietnam War was Nancy Grossman (b. 1940), whose 1976 *Gunman* became an icon of the dehumanizing effects of male aggression. Like Spero's, Grossman's work exposes the abusive and oppressive nature of power. Yet, while Spero's work is usually directed against specific political events, Grossman's sculptures are generalized statements, pertaining to the nether aspects of the human condition. Her powerful leather figures display a violent dialectic between oppression and aggression, which stems from deep-seated emotions that may be traced to her formative childhood experiences. Grossman's family life was dominated by repressed anti-Semitism and xenophobia, and constant conflict between two oppositional systems of belief: Her father was a religious Jew, her mother a Catholic who converted to Judaism. Grossman herself received a religious Jewish education within the fold of her mother's Catholic family. Her constant struggle to define her identity, coupled with her persistent sense of being forever an outsider, clearly informs her art. Moreover, her use of sewing, zippers, leather, and other materials related to the clothing industry may also be seen as a reaction to the family garment business in which she was obliged to work from an early age. Hence, in contrast to Schapiro's and Chicago's celebration of women's crafts, Grossman's use of sewing materials has an oppressive quality.

Susan Rothenberg (b. 1945) also expresses this general sense of violence and angst in her art, but does so through images of horses, which she began to paint in 1974 after the birth of her daughter. Toward the end of that decade, parallel to the breakup of her marriage, her horses became more and more tormented: She merged animal and human elements together and painted agonized heads and fragmented bodies. After undergoing psychotherapy in 1983, Rothenberg began to depict her family and memories of her childhood, exposing her Jewish identity only in an occasional title, such as *Papa Cohen*.

REVISIONING THE FEMALE BODY

One of the major themes explored by women artists in the last decades has been the female body. Since the female nude was seen as the major vehicle by which male artists transformed women into sex objects, women artists were eager to reclaim it and assert their position as subjects rather than objects. Thus, the nudes of Joan Semmel (b. 1932) completely alter the accepted perspective through which the female body is traditionally viewed. Semmel painted her own body "from the object's eye"—the vantage point from which one sees one's own body. Her depictions of heterosexual sex posit equality between men and women, while her latest paintings of the aging female body critique the age discrimination that characterizes American culture.

Nancy Fried, who contributed a lesbian dwelling to the *Womanhouse* project, began to explore her body image following a serious illness. Her powerful terracotta *Self-Portraits*, created after a breast and her ovaries were removed, reject the norms of ideal beauty imposed by society on the female body. Fried uses her own experience of the fragility of her body and her fear of death to explore a wide range of human emotions related to loss, death, and mourning.

Toward the end of her life, literally on her deathbed, HANNAH WILKE (1940–1993, née Arlene Hannah Butter) explored similar terrain in her art. Wilke's work developed over the years as an exploration of the female body—usually her own: its beauty and scars, its status as an object, its fragility and final demise. She began with a series of photographs and performances, *Starification Object Series S.O.S.* of 1974–1975, in which her body was exposed as an object of desire but also "scarred" with pieces of chewing gum shaped in vaginal forms. Wilke explained one aspect of these scars as reminders that "as a Jew, during the war, I would have been branded and buried had I not been born in America." A series of colorful chocolate figurines of her own nude body titled *Venus Pareve* (1985) offers Wilke's humorous view of her identity as a Jewish female. In a 1984 installation, titled *Support, Foundation, Comfort*, Wilke used nude photographs of herself and her mother, who was dying of breast cancer, to explore their close mother-daughter bond, the mortality of the human body, and Jewish mourning rituals. The artist's final series, ironically titled *Intra-Venus*, is based on a painful documentation of her own bouts with cancer, the unsuccessful medical interventions, and her fatal physical deterioration. It is a bold and unflinching view—full of black humor—of the female body that failed, and of the human spirit that never lost the desire to live, to understand, and to create.

The sublimation of bodily injury into art that is manifest in Wilke and Fried is also found in the art of Susan Weil (b. 1930). As a child, she was badly burned in a boat explosion that claimed her brother's life. Left with scars and a limp, she created fragmented images, which she distanced from herself through her media and ostensible subject matter. In the early 1950s, she collaborated with her first husband, Robert Rauschenberg, on evocative images created by exposing

blueprint paper covered by parts of the body to the sun. Later, she explored the dynamics of motor control through images of walking and jumping in which one leg is darkened, and explored a sense of physical balance by setting cutout figures parallel, at angles, and perpendicular to a wall, an idea she developed in performances in which dancers walked on the walls. In the 1970s, she worked with sea horizons and skies whose shapes remain unchanged whether painted on taut, slack, or partially crumpled materials. These works both affirm the stability of the world despite cataclysms, and show that the "body," whole or damaged, reflects the same basic truths. This reading is reinforced by a series in which hands emerge from crumpled materials, which thus evoke injured body images.

In addition to Wilke and Weil, many Jewish women—among them Eleanor Antin (née Fineman, b. 1935), Rachel Rosenthal (b. 1926), and Carolee Schneemann (b. 1939)—made significant contributions to the genre of performance art, often relying on biographical material and sometimes exposing aspects of their Jewish background.

While experimenting with found objects, such as boots set in different narrative configurations, Eleanor Antin began to explore her identity as a woman and to critique the social construction of the feminine. Her 1972 *Carving: A Traditional Sculpture* is composed of 148 nude photographs of the artist at different stages of dieting, literally molding her body to conform to society's ideals, while in her videotape *Representational Act* she puts on makeup, reshaping her face. In other works from the 1970s, Antin re-created herself with the aid of costumes into a range of other personae, male and female. Only in the 1980s did she begin to explore her Jewish identity, reviving Yiddish theatrical representations of the shtetl with the aid of film.

Like Antin's *Carving* and Wilke's use of gum and chocolate, many of Rachel Rosenthal's performances deal with food, specifically stressing abnormal food intake. Rosenthal's obsessive approach to food relates not only to the female body but also to her well-to-do childhood in Europe before World War II. Two other performances deal with her feeling of guilt for having escaped from Nazi-occupied Europe in 1940. In *My Brazil* of 1979, she invented two alter egos who remained in Europe during the war, one of whom became active in the resistance while the other remained in hiding. In *Leave Her in Naxos* of 1981, she shaved her head to resemble both a collaborator and a Jewish concentration camp inmate.

Among the younger generation of performance, video, and multimedia artists who explore the female body, the work of Dorit Cypis stands out. Born in

Israel in 1951, she arrived in the United States as a child. She renders the female body as a fragmented and re-created entity, an evolving site composed of memories and emotions.

Several of the artists discussed above used their art and their own bodies to protest against the objectification of women in American society. The work of BARBARA KRUGER (b. 1945) uses different methods to expose the insidious way American media images control our minds, reinforce racism and misogyny, and mold the concept of "self" as a stereotypical gendered body. Using techniques that emulate commercial graphics, Kruger deconstructs the invisible structures that shape the hierarchies and accepted "truths" of American consumer society. Dara Birnbaum (b. 1946) uses video images related to commercial television to uncover hidden power structures in a similar way. Her work warns us of the possibility that everything we do is influenced by the powerful forces of the media. Sherrie Levine (b. 1947) appropriates the works of other artists, undermining concepts such as "originality" and "authenticity" in a way that questions the basic premises upon which modern art and culture are founded.

The recent works of Deborah Kass (b. 1952), Beverly Naidus (b. 1953), Rhonda Lieberman (b. 1960), Ilene Segalove (b. 1950), and Nurit Newman (b. 1962), shown together at the *Too Jewish?* exhibition of 1996, also react against the media-oriented, superficial consumer society that America has become, yet they do so from a specifically Jewish vantage point. They deal with the stereotypical Jewish nose, the Jewish American Princess who is also an obsessive shopper, and the definitive Jewish heroine produced by popular culture, Barbra Streisand. In these works, the unattainable desire to conform to the American female ideal, epitomized by the shapely, blonde Barbie doll, evokes a sense of conflict, frustration, and pain, articulated with the aid of a "Jewish" brand of ironic, self-effacing humor.

CONCLUSION

Being an American Jewish woman means different things to different people and manifests itself in diverse ways in the lives and work of individual artists. Theoretically, since art is an expression of self, facets of one's personal identity are necessarily invested in artworks. At times, aspects of an artist's American and/or female and/or Jewish identity may be clearly discerned in her work. In other cases, however, these cannot be easily traced either by the viewer or by the artist herself. Since American Jewish women artists are not a homogeneous group, their art defies catego-

rization in stylistic, thematic, or any other terms. Yet, whether or not they choose to express American, Jewish, or female aspects of their identity, and regardless of how they decide to do so, numerous Jewish women artists have been making continuous and significant contributions to the visual arts in America.

BIBLIOGRAPHY

Ankori, Gannit. Interviews with artists; Archives of American Art, Smithsonian Institution. Documents and interviews; Broude, Norma, and Mary D. Garrard, eds. *The Power of Feminist Art: The American Movement of the 1970s, History and Impact* (1994); Chicago, Judy. *Through the Flower: My Struggle as a Woman Artist* (1982); Elderfield, John. *Frankenthaler* (1989); Gouma-Peterson, Thalia. *Breaking the Rules: Audrey Flack, a Retrospective, 1950–1990* (1992); *From the Inside Out: Eight Contemporary Artists*. Exhibition catalog. Jewish Museum, NYC, June 13–November 14, 1993; Herrera, Hayden. *Mary Frank* (1990); *Jewish Themes/Contemporary American Artists*. Exhibition catalog. Jewish Museum, NYC, June 2–September 12, 1982; *Jewish Themes/Contemporary American Artists II*. Exhibit catalog. Jewish Museum, NYC, July 15–November 16, 1986; Kleeblatt, Norman L., ed. *Too Jewish? Challenging Traditional Identities* (1996); Kleeblatt, Norman L., and Susan Chevlowe, eds. *Painting a Place in America: Jewish Artists in New York, 1900–1945* (1991); Landau, Ellen G. *Lee Krasner* (1995); Lippard, Ludy R. *Overlay: Contemporary Art and the Art of Prehistory* (1983); Munro, Eleanor. *Originals: American Women Artists* (1979); Museum of Modern Art Library, New York. Artist Files Catalogues; Nemser, Cindy. *Art Talk: Conversations with Fifteen Women Artists* (1995); Nochlin, Linda. *Women, Art, Power and Other Essays* (1988); Raven, Arlene. *Nancy Grossman* (1991); Rosen, Randy, and Catherine C. Brawer. *Making Their Mark: Women Artists Move into the Mainstream, 1970–1985* (1989); Roth, Moira, ed. *The Amazing Decade: Women and Performance Art in America, 1970–1980* (1983); Rubinstein, Charlotte Streifer. *American Women Artists: From Early Indian Times to the Present* (1982); *Susan Weil, Painter/Sylvia Whitman, Dancer—Two Notebooks* (1976); Wilke, Hannah. *Intra Venus* (1995); Wilson, Laurie. *Louise Nevelson, Iconography and Sources* (1981); *Woman's Art Journal*. Edited by Elsa Honig Fine (1980–1996).

ZIVA AMISHAI-MAISELS
GANNIT ANKORI

ARTHUR, BEA (b. 1926)

"Let's face it," actress Bea Arthur told an interviewer in 1985, "nobody ever asked me to play Juliet." At five feet, nine and a half inches, with a deep voice and commanding presence, Arthur has instead made her career playing "strong women" who speak their own minds and control everyone around them.

Although these women have included such formidable characters as Yente in *Fiddler on the Roof* and Vera Charles in *Mame*, Arthur will probably always be best known for portraying liberal Maude Findlay, the "women's libber" who stuck it to Archie Bunker on television's *All in the Family* and then dominated her own situation comedy, *Maude*, throughout the 1970s. Arthur's imperious and controversial Maude left a lasting imprint on American television and feminism.

Born Bernice Frankel in New York City on May 13, 1926, Arthur was the middle child of Phillip and Rebecca Frankel's three daughers. When Arthur was eleven, her father's financial troubles led him to move the family to Cambridge, Maryland, to run a clothing store. As one of the only Jews in a segregated southern city, as well as the tallest girl in all her school classes, Arthur faced anti-Semitic rejection, considered herself a "misfit," and grew up "painfully shy." She spent much of her time reading movie magazines and dreaming of becoming "a little, short, blonde movie star." To hide her insecurities, Arthur developed a mean Mae West impression and won the title of "wittiest girl" in her class at Cambridge High School. After two additional years at private Linden Hall High School, Arthur studied at Blackstone College, a junior college in Virginia, and then graduated from the Franklin Institute of Science and Arts.

After working for a year as a medical laboratory technician in Cambridge, Arthur left for New York "to become someone else." She entered the New School's famous Dramatic Workshop to study with Erwin Piscator, along with classmates Harry Belafonte, Walter Matthau, Rod Steiger, and Tony Curtis. Although Piscator admired her height and deep voice and cast her in the leading role in classic plays like *Taming of the Shrew* and *Lysistrata*, Arthur was unable to find professional work in classical theater and instead began her career singing in nightclubs and reading bit parts on Sid Caesar's *Show of Shows*. Despite a number of years without professional success, Arthur was personally happy. She married a fellow Piscator student, actor, and director Gene Saks, on May 28, 1950, and the two entered domestic bliss making audition rounds together.

Bea Arthur's career took off when she landed the role of Lucy Brown in the long-running off-Broadway hit *The Threepenny Opera* in 1954. Receiving excellent reviews, Arthur was soon in demand as a character actress. Critics praised her for her "skillfully devastating" satire and claimed that she "ooze[d] comic command" in her various roles on and off Broadway. In 1964, she created the role of Yente the Matchmaker in *Fiddler on the Roof* on Broadway, and in 1966, she won the Tony Award for best supporting actress for her portrayal of the acid-tongued Vera Charles in *Mame*, directed by her husband.

Despite her successes on Broadway, however, Arthur won her genuine celebrity status when Norman Lear, the creator of *All in the Family* and a long-time admirer of Arthur, persuaded her to do a guest spot on the show in 1971. Appearing as Maude, Edith's limousine-liberal cousin, Arthur skewered Carroll O'Connor's Archie and won the immediate attention of CBS executives. Lear worked with Arthur to create a spin-off series, *Maude*, which premiered in 1972 and quickly moved into the top ten in the Nielsen ratings, winning Arthur an Emmy in 1977. In its six seasons, the show explored a host of controversial topics, including alcoholism and psychoanalysis, but it was Maude's decision to have an abortion that broke television taboos, sparked loud protest, and propelled the show's popularity in the liberal political environment of the early 1970s. As Maude, Bea Arthur inspired many female viewers as she came to symbolize the growing women's movement, portraying a woman who "looked real . . . [who] said what she felt and could tell her husband to go to hell."

Maude's outspoken liberalism and controlling nature marked her as a stereotypical Jewish mother in the minds of some critics. Arthur and Saks insisted in 1972, however, that the show's creators had intentionally made Maude a WASP matron because, "if you made her Jewish . . . her courage in fighting bigotry would be personal instead of ideological." Although this assertion reflects television writers' (and perhaps Arthur's) uneasiness with Jewish identity, it also yields a grain of truth. Had Maude been labeled "a Jewish mother," her courage and fiery independence probably would have been caricatured as insignificant nagging. The decision to make Maude a WASP allowed her to be a "prototypical woman" and thus an icon of the women's movement.

In real life, Bea Arthur's attitude toward feminism was much more ambivalent than that of her alter ego. In the early 1970s, Arthur insisted that she did not understand the women's movement: "I've never felt that being a wife and mother isn't enough." Interviews portrayed her as a gentle, unpretentious woman deeply tied to her husband and two adopted sons, and nothing like the threatening Maude. By 1978, however, the series had produced tensions that shattered Arthur's longtime marriage to Gene Saks, and in later interviews, Arthur actually adopted the language of the women's movement: "I don't think I ever truly believed in marriage anyway," she told an interviewer in 1985. "I guess marriage means that you're a woman and not a . . . person."

During her long and distinguished career on stage, screen, and television, Bea Arthur's most significant role, from the point of view of popular culture, was the feminist icon Maude in the Norman Lear television series of the same name. [New York Public Library]

Befitting her new status as a single, older woman, Bea Arthur created a new television character in the 1980s: Dorothy Zbornak, the divorced schoolteacher of *The Golden Girls*. From 1985 to 1992, Arthur played Dorothy as the sharp-tongued leader of four older women who lived together in Florida, coping with aging while looking for love and enjoying female friendship. This realistic, funny portrayal of senior citizens won the series a loyal older audience and helped Arthur garner a second Emmy in 1988.

Despite her continued identification with the theater in the 1990s, it is clearly television audiences that have most warmly embraced Bea Arthur's "strong women," and it is through television that Arthur has most influenced American culture. On *Maude*, Arthur helped break down television barriers and normalize topics like abortion and alcoholism as subjects for open discussion. Perhaps even more important,

Arthur's distinctive portrayals of Maude and Dorothy have shaped American women's conceptions of themselves. The sharp-tongued heroine who does not conform to cultural standards of youthful beauty or wifely duty but who holds herself tall and speaks her mind has been a rarity in American popular culture. Bea Arthur embodied this rarity and created a role model for many American women.

BIBLIOGRAPHY

Breslauer, Jan. "Arthur, Arthur." *Los Angeles Times,* October 8, 1995; *Current Biography* (December 1973); Flatley, Guy. "Gene, for Heaven's Sake Help Me!!" *TV Guide* (November 18, 1972); Harmetz, Aljean. "Maude Didn't Leave 'Em All Laughing." *NYTimes,* December 10, 1972, and "NBC's Golden Girls Gambles on Grown-Ups." *NYTimes,* September 22, 1985; Hentoff, Nat. "New Candor in Old America." *Village Voice,* September 28, 1972; Hodenfield, Jan. "Maude Meets Mame," *New York Post,* March 9, 1974; Honeycutt, Kirk. "We Ran Out of Controversy." *NYTimes,* April 16, 1978; "Maude Fraud." *People* (November 17, 1975): 35–38; Oppenheimer, Dabby. "Maude Minces No Words." *Lady's Circle* (November 1974): 22+; Renold, Evelyn. "Bea Arthur." *New York Daily News,* October 13, 1985; Stone, Judy. "She Gave Archie His First Comeuppance." *NYTimes,* November 19, 1972.

KIRSTEN FERMAGLICH

ASKOWITH, DORA (1884–1958)

Dora Askowith, author, historian, and college educator, believed that a knowledge of Jewish women's history would serve as a catalyst for organization, activism, and moral leadership. She taught women at HUNTER COLLEGE for a total of forty-five years, and wrote that she was anxious to teach college students Jewish history because they were "poorly versed in the history of their own faith."

Dora Askowith was born August 30, 1884, in Kovno, Russia, to Jacob Baruch and Sarah Golde (Arenovski) Askowith. Her family immigrated to the United States in the same year. Little is known of Askowith's early years attending grammar school in Boston, or of her upbringing with her siblings, Charles, Saul S., Herbert, Bathsheba, and Pearl B. (Yoffa).

Dora Askowith graduated from Girls' High School in Boston in 1902, and from its advanced course in 1903. She continued her education, receiving a B.A. from Barnard College in 1908 with general and departmental honors in history and anthropology. In the following fall, Askowith began studying medieval and modern history, sociology, and philosophy at Columbia University. Askowith counted Professors

James T. Shotwell, Richard J.H. Gottheil, William W. Rockwell, Solomon Schechter, Louis Ginzberg, Alexander Marx, and Cyrus Adler as her advisers and mentors in her studies. She earned an M.A. in 1909, and a Ph.D. in political science in 1915. Askowith also studied and conducted research abroad at the American School for Oriental Research (Jerusalem), the American Academy (Rome), and in Syria, Egypt, Central Europe, France, and England.

Askowith began teaching in New York City in 1908. She was an instructor at P.S. 18 in the Bronx for one year, and a history teacher at Morris and Wadleigh High Schools for three years. By the time she completed her graduate studies, Askowith had already instructed Hunter College students in history for three years. She taught at Hunter from 1912 to 1957. Askowith's courses at Hunter, the New School for Social Research, and several New York and Massachusetts synagogues, schools, and cultural associations included topics such as ancient civilization; biblical history; comparative religion; cultural, political, and religious history; and social ideals.

Askowith's first book-length publication was her doctoral dissertation, *The Toleration and Persecution of the Jews in the Roman Empire: Part I: The Toleration of the Jews Under Julius Caesar and Augustus* (1915). By her own admission, this work dealt more with comparative religion and Jewish communal life than with legal or political history. Subsequently, Askowith contributed chapters to two books, one entitled "Prolegomena: Legal Fictions or Evasions of the Law" in *Jewish Studies in Memory of Israel Abrahams* (1927) and one on the life and work of scholar-politician Luigi Luzzatti in his *God in Freedom* (1930). Askowith's second book, *Three Outstanding Women* (1941), celebrated the lives and accomplishments of MARY FELS, REBEKAH KOHUT, and ANNIE NATHAN MEYER, and highlighted Askowith's own commitments to a Jewish homeland in Palestine, to ending poverty and oppression, to woman suffrage and higher education, and to strong female Jewish role models. Additionally, Askowith wrote and published over a hundred articles on historical and biographical themes, including "The Earliest Jewish Settlers of Cape Cod" (1953), a nod to her summer residence. In the last years of her life, Askowith collaborated with Professor H.L. Friess on a map of world religions, and began writing a book on government and religion and an autobiography.

Askowith devoted herself not only to scholarly pursuits, but also to community organization and activism. She founded and advised the Hunter Menorah Society (the forerunner to campus Hillel associations) from 1913 until 1957 and advised other Hunter student groups. She was a member of the Palestine Oriental Society, Zionist Organization of America, Jewish Historical Association, American Historical Association, and League of Women Voters. Her latter affiliation may have spurred Askowith to help found the Women's Organization for the AMERICAN JEWISH CONGRESS. Not only was she the organization's first national director, she articulated its purpose and method of organization in *A Call to the Jewish Women of America* (c. 1917). This manifesto invoked the memories of Jewish heroines from biblical times through her own day and the sense of privilege, responsibility, and moral guardianship of her Jewish American sisters in calling for their participation in the struggle for equal rights for women and for world Jewry. She asserted that the unique history of Jewish women would inspire them to put their "mighty force" to work for social justice.

Dora Askowith died in a New York hospital after a protracted illness on October 23, 1958. In her quiet and modest fashion, she looked to the past in imagining a future of harmony, equality, and morality shaped by American Jewish women.

SELECTED WORKS BY DORA ASKOWITH
A Call to the Jewish Women of America (c. 1917); "The Earliest Jewish Settlers of Cape Cod." Paper presented at a meeting of the American Jewish Historical Society, February 1953; "The Life and Work of Luigi Luzzatti." In *God in Freedom: Studies in the Relations Between Church and State*, edited by Luigi Luzzatti (1930); "Prolegomena: Legal Fictions or Evasions of the Law." In *Jewish Studies in Memory of Israel Abrahams* (1927); *Three Outstanding Women: Mary Fels, Rebekah Kohut, Annie Nathan Meyer* (1941); *The Toleration and Persecution of the Jews in the Roman Empire: Part I: The Toleration of the Jews Under Julius Caesar and Augustus* (1915).

BIBLIOGRAPHY
Askowith, Dora. Correspondence with Dr. Judah Filch, August 1956. Collection I-75, box 3. Association for Jewish Education Papers. American Jewish Historical Society; Obituary. *NYTimes*, October 25, 1958, 21:2; *UJE*; *Wilson Library Bulletin* 33 (December 1958): 265; *WWIAJ* (1928, 1938).

ADINAH S. MILLER

ASSIMILATION OF NINETEENTH-CENTURY JEWISH WOMEN

Scholars have conventionally considered the nineteenth century the German era in the American Jewish history. Between 1820 and 1880, more than 200,000 immigrants from German lands arrived in the United States. Besides German Jews, this transatlantic movement also included migrants from ethnically Czech, Hungarian, Polish, and Baltic territories that at that time remained under German political control or cultural influence. Because German Jews were a decisive majority among the immigrants and because, together with their American-born children, they played a central role in the assimilation/Americanization of their communities almost until World War I, they are the focus of this article.

In the social science literature on immigration and ethnicity, the term *assimilation* has been assigned various meanings. In contrast to the conventional understanding of this concept in which Old Country bonds, customs, and attachments are gradually replaced by mainstream American ways, assimilation is viewed here as a process whereby blended or *ethnic*—in this case, Jewish-American—identities, life-styles, and patterns of social relations emerge in the interplay between the immigrant group's traditions and resources and those of the host society as they are adapted and used by the immigrants in pursuit of their goals. The contingency on the assimilation process on the social actors and their environment allows flexibility and variety in the ethnic blends, depending on the social-historical conditions in which they take shape.

Two related social circumstances in particular influence the forms and contents of ethnic blends as they evolve in specific periods and locations. Coined by sociologist Milton Gordon, the term *ethclass* denotes the inescapable class nature of assimilation. More recently, a similar idea of assimilation's inherent *genderedness* was elaborated by Paula Hyman. *Class-genderethnicity* may be used to denote this assimilation process, pointing to the historically situated gender and ethnic specificity of class position and class and ethnic specificity of gender roles and relations.

The assimilation-as-ethnicization of German Jewish women occurred as they confronted and acted upon the opportunities and constraints of the American environment by adapting, mixing, and reconfiguring their Jewish and the American class-gender role expectations, activities, and symbolic resources. German Jewish immigrants in America had a double cultural identity since the Jews' assimilation in Germany had progressed through the nineteenth century, and the later they left their home country, the more likely they were to have been such cultural hybrids.

The process of assimilation as ethnicization of German Jewish women throughout the nineteenth century was influenced from the outside by the larger American environment, in particular the voluntary and democratic character of its social associations, and by its political culture and practice based on the prin-

ciples of individual liberty. On the inside, two major developments in the American German Jewish society were shaped by the Americanization of its female members. The first was the embourgeoisement of German Jews that resulted from the fortuitous convergence of the demands of the expanding American economy with the supply by the Jews of particular skills and sociocultural resources. This upward movement on the mainstream socioeconomic ladder made the middle-class Anglo-Protestant women the reference model for the assimilation-ethnicization of their German Jewish counterparts.

The second development was the emergence of American REFORM JUDAISM modeled in considerable part on contemporary American middle-class Protestantism in whose philosophy and institutional functioning the women occupied a position significantly different from that prescribed by the traditional (Orthodox) Jewish religion. As these two developments made it possible for women to assume new, ethnic-American roles and activities in their homes and immigrant communities, the women, in turn, transformed, or Americanized, private and public spheres of the German Jewish society. These reciprocal transformations were cumulative, building upon the preceding changes.

Most of the German Jews who began to arrive in the United States in increasing numbers in the 1820s and 1830s were pushed out of their small towns by the economic modernization of Central Europe and, specifically, the structural relocations that undermined their livelihoods that had been drawn from petty trading in rural areas. An additional hardship and reason for emigration was the prohibition against marrying without sufficient means imposed by the newly instituted legal limitations on Jewish marriage. Young single men constituted the majority of immigrants, especially in the initial phase of transplantation, before they established themselves sufficiently to bring over their families or to marry. These young single men with entrepreneurial skills joined the west- and southbound frontier movement of native-born Americans and contributed to the early dispersal of German Jewish communities across the United States. This was quite a different pattern from the much greater urban concentration both of their Sephardi predecessors and their Eastern European followers to America.

Peddling, followed by the establishment of a stationary business, was the typical occupation of German Jewish immigrants during the first decades of their settlement in America. As in the Old Country, wives actively participated in the family economy

*As in the Old Country, Jewish women in nineteenth-century America often actively participated
in the management of family stores. This family scene depicts Bibo & Co. (probably in San Francisco), around 1890.
[Western Jewish History Center]*

either by managing the family stores or (an American novelty created to accommodate single immigrants) by running boardinghouses. The primary preoccupation of immigrant family members during this initial adaptation to the new environment was, first, securing economic self-sufficiency and, second, gradually growing the business and improving the material standard of living. These efforts absorbed a substantial share of the women's time and energy, especially because American free-for-all capitalism invited and rewarded the vigorous entrepreneurial efforts of new immigrants.

Women devoted whatever time remained to their homes and families, and to social and charitable activities in the Jewish immigrant community. The traditional Jewish view of the female as "naturally" pious and motivated mainly by concern for others, primarily for her family's well-being in the home, coincided to a large extent with the role model of the "true woman" that prevailed in mainstream American society in the early nineteenth century. But the characteristics of

contemporary American society and the particular circumstances of not-quite-settled Jewish immigrants made the scope and form of women's domestic piety change or ethnicize soon after they arrived in America.

The main American innovation in religious observance introduced by the immigrants shortly after their arrival in the United States was its significant diminution. In the home, religion as practiced by women meant, first and foremost, the trimming down or even elimination of kashrut—the time-consuming and complicated observance of Jewish dietary laws. Particularly consequential in this development was the appearance, for the first time for most of the women in the religious sphere, of individual choice whether to use more- or less-strict ways of managing the kitchen. This erosion in women's traditional piety was primarily a response to the new circumstances of their own lives as well as of the collective situation of German Jewish immigrants in America. They were also responding to the fluidity of the larger (host) society in the making and the voluntary basis of its operation. As well, the immigrants frequently moved, settled in residential dispersion, and lacked rabbinic leadership. Although religious "from the roots," to use BARBARA MYERHOFF's apt phrase, most of them, especially the early arrivals, did not have much Jewish education.

Another, related factor that contributed to the attrition in observance by Jewish women of traditional home religious rituals was the increased influence of Reform Judaism. Its philosophical and practical purpose was to modernize Jewish religion by eliminating the characteristics that set apart its practitioners from mainstream (Christian) society. Originated in Germany at the beginning of the nineteenth century by Jewish philosophers as the emancipation project "from within," Reform Judaism found in liberal-democratic America a particularly hospitable ground and, among Americanizing German Jews, eager followers. Because of close ideological links with the Reform movement in Germany, however, the modernizing effects of American Reform Judaism, in this case, loosening home religious observance and letting women decide the scope and "grasp" of their piety, must be considered, during the early nineteenth century, as both Americanizing and Germanizing. The latter influence was strengthened, at least temporally, by the arrival from Germany in the 1840s and 1850s of Jewish immigrants who were more educated in mainstream German culture.

Together with the increase in the flexibility of women's piety practiced at home, an incipient development in the middle of the nineteenth century began to refocus the central role of the woman and the home and family in the preservation of Jewishness in America. Combining elements of Jewish tradition and influences of the dominant middle-class American culture, especially the model of the segregated, male-public and female-private spheres, the ascending gender ideology of German Jewish immigrant society called on the woman, viewed as endowed with natural moral sense, to act as the main agent and carrier of Jewish tradition and made the home into the center of moral-religious education and the well of Jewish spirituality. Although this Americanized-ethnicized role model assigned women to their gender-specific sphere, as they established themselves in it, they saw and acted on the possibilities to redraw the boundaries and undertake new and different initiatives.

Besides piety and good care of the home as primary obligations, the nineteenth-century American female role model called upon women to do charitable work for the sick and the needy. In this case, too, the overlapping gender prescriptions of the American

ideal and the Jewish commandment of *tzedaka*, charitable deeds, aided the immigrant women's acculturation to the dominant society's gender role model. Yet both the American (specifically, Protestant American) moral ideal of "the charitable woman" and, parallel to it, the Jewish one, were being challenged and modified, as it were, from below by the very actors whose gender roles they defined. For immigrant women, this challenge-and-modify process involved at the same time ethnicization of traditional Jewish ways.

The major American innovation in this area was the gradual transformation of the traditional *hevrot nashim*, informal women's groups devoted to the fulfillment of the obligation of *tzedaka*, into self-governing voluntary philanthropic women's organizations. This change at once reflected and expressed the collective ascent of German Jewish immigrant families from the ranks of petty entrepreneurs into mainstream middle-class merchants and their acculturation to the dominant middle-class life-styles that had accelerated since mid-century.

The most common kind of women's charity work in the German Jewish immigrant communities during the early nineteenth century, the activities of *hevrot nashim*, included, besides the traditional ritual preparation of the dead (females) for burial, visiting the sick, assisting migrants, and charitable relief for the poor. But by the 1820s and 1830s, initiated by upper-middle-class Jewish women in larger cities, a new ethnic organization had appeared, American in form and Jewish in content, which by the 1850s became the dominant institutional channel of women's charitable work—the Ladies' Hebrew Benevolent Society.

Jewish women's benevolent societies continued to perform the traditional functions of the *hevrot nashim* but in significantly modified ways. These associations were based on voluntary membership rather than obligation, and their operation was based on written by-laws and established democratic procedures rather than informal interactions. In another important innovation, society members controlled their own financial means, which were generated by dues-paying subscribers and by another American novelty, fund-raising events such as "dime parties," theatricals, or "strawberry socials." Ladies' benevolent societies contributed such income to the needs of their congregations.

Whereas initially female benevolent associations were affiliated with synagogues and often had male chief officers, with time, both reflecting and contributing to Jewish women's growing sense of personal and collective autonomy, they became independent and were managed solely by their female members. The first nonsynagogual female Jewish society was founded in 1819 by REBECCA GRATZ, a member of the Philadelphia Jewish upper class and an exceptionally independent-minded woman for her time. Such autonomous and self-governing Jewish women's benevolent associations proliferated earlier and more quickly in America's West where societal structures were more flexible and people's ways less fixed than in the more settled East.

The gradual separation of Jewish female philanthropic societies from the synagogues as a cause-and-effect of women's increased sense of personal and collective autonomy was also a reflection, inside the acculturating German Jewish group, of the broader processes of secularization and institutional differentiation of American society. The appearance, by mid-century, of secular middle-class Jewish female clubs exemplified these developments. Their quick spread in German Jewish communities was further facilitated by the considerable amount of free time gained by middle-class housewives as they retreated from economic activities. Modeled after the sociocultural associations of middle-class Anglo-American women, but addressing German Jewish-American concerns and interests, these clubs are a good illustration of class-gendethnicization of German Jewish women's lives in nineteenth-century America. The first such club, the United Order of True Sisters, was founded in 1846 in New York and by 1851 had spread to Philadelphia, Albany, and New Haven. Its purpose was mutual help (structured after the male B'nai B'rith fraternal lodge founded three years earlier), gaining knowledge about "current arts and affairs" as well as "foster[ing] solidarity among the women [of the club]." As they grew, German Jewish women's clubs added to their activities study circles whose purpose was self-education in Judaic lore and philanthropic pursuits that with time turned into social work.

Characteristic of this transformation of Jewish women's traditional mitzvah of *tzedaka* into independent and self-governing voluntary associations with multiple purposes was that it was a quiet revolution, a major change in the sociocultural order accomplished without its breakdown. The female agents of this transformation did not explicitly challenge the separate-spheres model, but, as did their American Protestant sisters, they redrew the boundaries and thus altered the landscape of the female domestic realm by moving it into the public sphere of their ethnoreligious communities.

As women entered into the sphere of the secular public life of German Jewish communities, another important process with similar consequences was taking place in mid-century—the female entry into the realm that had been the exclusive preserve of men, the synagogue and public religious functions. In the transformation of congregational charities into organized philanthropy, the women themselves had been primary actors enabled by the American conditions and encouraged by the rabbinic leaders of the Reform movement. The latter were more directly instrumental in integrating women into the synagogue—an idea that was the integral component of the religious philosophy of Reform Judaism as formulated by its rabbinic leaders, especially Isaac Mayer Wise and David Einhorn, the authors of two programmatic texts of American Reform, *Minhag America* (1857) and *Olat Tamid* (1858), respectively.

Among the implemented changes with the greatest impact on the entrance by women into Reform Judaism's public religious sphere were the desegregation of the sexes in the synagogues by the introduction of family pews, the admission of women into the minyan (the ten adults necessary for public prayers to take place), and Jewish education for girls, all of which significantly increased women's participation in religious services.

These and other innovations of Reform Judaism conceptualized in the late 1840s to early 1850s by German-born and -trained rabbis should be interpreted as simultaneously Germanizing and Americanizing. The latter, in this case the influence of contemporary developments in middle-class American Protestant churches, was reflected in the steady increase in women's attendance at religious services, so that their numbers first equaled and then exceeded those of men. Another effect of the influence of American-Protestant practices on Jewish "public religion" was, supported by Reform rabbis, a takeover by second-generation women of the religious education of children in the Sunday schools. In turn, Jewish women's presence and active participation in the public religious sphere had transformed—Americanized—the latter.

These reciprocal transformations, too, were taking place not through the rejection by Jewish women of the female sphere as defined by the dominant model of gender roles but by a quiet alteration of accepted understandings as they extended into the synagogue women's domestic responsibility for the preservation of Jewishness in the home and the family. That it was, precisely, the *Americanization* of the synagogue that, by making women active participants in its religious activities, contributed to the *preservation of Jewish tradition* in America is a good illustration of the accommodation of change and continuity in the process of ethnicization.

New developments in American society and in German Jewish communities during the last three decades of the nineteenth century invited new initiatives on the part of Jewish women that, building on the transformations begun earlier in the century, further advanced their Americanization-as-ethnicization. In three areas these developments brought about the most visible changes in women's position and activities: (1) the rapid urban-industrial growth of the United States and technological advances, resulting in a greater material affluence and new life-styles for the American middle class; (2) the progressive "feminization of religion" in the American Protestant and German Jewish-American, middle-class societies; and (3) further specialization and, especially, professionalization of public-sphere activities of American, including German Jewish middle-class women.

A greater surplus of free time gained by American middle-class women in the 1870s to 1890s as the result of general increase in the economic affluence and the mechanization of many household tasks and the proliferation of commercial entertainment, such as vaudeville theaters, dance halls, amusement parks, and the first moving pictures, changed the life-styles of entire families and their individual members. A distinct and important American innovation in the life-styles of second-generation German Jewish families, which was both the result and a cause of increased economic affluence and substantially increased women's free time, was a significant decrease in the number of children they bore on the average (two to three) compared to middle-class Protestant American women.

American material innovations introduced by German Jewish women into their middle-class homes included technological novelties such as bathtubs, plumbing, washers, radios, parlor furnishings, and fashionable clothing. Jews, especially women, were apparently particularly concerned with clothing as a symbol of American middle-class status. They were also uncommonly capable and experienced in the clothing business, a "Jewish" trade specialty. The piano, a necessary feature of the typical American middle-class parlor, in Jewish homes was an ethnic expression of both German Jewish tradition and American middle-class membership.

Cultural (material and symbolic) and social ethnicization of family life-styles allowed by increased

In the late nineteenth century, with a flood of immigrants from Eastern Europe entering the United States,
organizations were formed to aid in their acculturation. This group of women (and men)
is identified as "Ellis Island Missionaries." [American Jewish Historical Society]

middle-class affluence and new developments in household and entertainment technologies that had been introduced and managed by women included innovations such as the use of Jewish-American cookbooks for confirmation receptions, invitation dinners, and Purim dance parties, and family vacations in Germany (by now an ethnic rather than Germanizing activity). Active involvement of middle-class German Jewish women in settlement houses in the education of recently arrived Eastern European Jewish immigrant women in the American way of life, including modern cooking, sanitary habits, and scientific management of the home, can also be viewed as the expression of Americanization in a double sense. The ways of middle-class American women had been learned by their German Jewish sisters, who, in turn, were passing them on to their fellow ethnic gendermates.

The progressive secularization of mainstream American social institutions and popular culture and, within American German Jewish society, the shrinking scope of the sacred in people's everyday lives as Reform Judaism significantly diminished and voluntarized religious observance, caused Jewish religious leaders to rely more than before on women for help. Echoing the American (Protestant) notion of womanhood as the natural wellspring of spirituality, Reform rabbis called upon Jewish women, "more responsive," in the words of Rabbi Kaufmann Kohler, the main architect of the Reform movement's Pittsburgh Platform (1885), "to the tender appeals of religious duty," to become "the saviors of Jewish religion." Similar normative representations of women as the bearers of Jewish tradition had come from the women themselves during their organizational meetings, in Jewish-American publications, and in literary works.

Declaring women to be Judaism's saviors indicated the major reversal—the culmination of a long-term process of Americanization-as-ethnicization begun in the early 1800s—of traditional Jewish gender roles, wherein women were defined at best as men's helpmates. In the home, middle-class German Jewish women—mostly second generation and much better educated in Judaism than their immigrant mothers—had assumed control of children's religious education, supervised their confirmation studies, and suggested interesting readings on Jewish religion.

Perhaps more dramatic because it lay in traditional male territory was the further redrawing of gender boundaries in synagogue life. Women as "saviors of Jewish religion" had assumed many diversified responsibilities as officers of religious school boards, and through fund-raising, community, educational, and sociocultural activities of temple sisterhoods. Organized locally in the 1880s and 1890s, they formed a national federation in 1913. The most far-fetched, indeed, revolutionary challenge to traditional gender roles in Jewish public religion was, parallel to contemporary developments in middle-class American Protestantism, a debate in the rabbinic and lay (including women) Reform circles in the 1890s concerning women's ordination. Although it was not formally instituted until 1972, at the turn of the century, particularly in the more open West, unordained women preachers (RAY FRANK was the most famous) conducted services in West Coast Jewish communities where there were no rabbis.

Three features of the expanding public nature of Jewish women's activities came into sharp relief at the close of the century. First, Americanization of women's roles involved at once innovations in the scope and content of their undertakings *and* purposeful action to preserve Jewish tradition. Second, illustrating ethnicization again as the fusing of continuity and change, even quite radical reconfigurations of traditional gender roles were presented by female advocates of these innovations in the rhetoric of familiar domesticity. Evocations of the biblical images of the "Mothers of Israel" following in the footsteps of Jochebed, Miriam, and Deborah in the representations of women's expanding presence and responsibilities in the forum, of Jewish public religion sustained in observers and participants alike a sense of the continuity of Jewish tradition. Third, whereas the assumption by women of new and important responsibilities in public religion, the area of great symbolic importance for Jewish identity, had Americanizing-ethnicizing effects by enhancing their sense of individual and collective (gender) self-worth and shared purpose, these new responsibilities and enhanced self-esteem of women reciprocally transformed, or Americanized-ethnicized, the ideas and practices of Reform Judaism.

In the secular public forum, new avenues for German Jewish women's pursuits in the late nineteenth century were opened, on the one hand, by the professionalization of American middle-class women's education, especially in the fields of teaching and social work, and, on the other hand, by the ideology and practice of Progressive reform movement to which lay and clergy, middle-class Americans, Protestant and Jewish Reform, actively committed themselves. Aimed at eradicating urban poverty and crime and (re)instituting social justice when it fell victim to predatory capitalism, the Progressive reform movement had been an outspokenly moral campaign and as such naturally appealed to women in whose gender role model moral vocation occupied central place. This affinity between women and social reform combined with professional training in social work and education and with the sociocultural capital accumulated in the earlier phase of women's club work—organizational experience, self-confidence, and gender support networks—greatly facilitated the creation in the 1890s of what Robyn Muncy has called "a female dominion in the American Reform." Urban neighborhoods, swelling at the turn of the century with new immigrants from Southern and Eastern Europe, provided a ready target for middle-class women reformers. The attention of German Jewish women educators and social workers naturally turned to recent Jewish arrivals from Russia and Austro-Hungary who had settled in densely populated immigrant sections in New York and other large cities in the East and Midwest.

The main foci of German Jewish women's activities and a new institutional sphere under their autonomous control were neighborhood settlement houses, among the most renowned, LILLIAN WALD's Henry Street Settlement (founded in 1893) and the CLARA DE HIRSCH HOME FOR WORKING GIRLS (1897) in New York. The programs of settlement homes managed by German Jewish women combined American and Jewish elements. The former, modeled after the activities of the American Protestant institutions, in particular the prototypical Chicago Hull House of Jane Addams, included vocational training programs for working immigrant girls and education in American middle-class female skills such as household science, personal hygiene, and etiquette and refinement. The latter were the ways of proper Jewish womanhood taught to Eastern European immigrant girls, including the modern kosher kitchen, observance of Jewish holidays, and morals and appropriate Jewish gender attitudes.

Inspired by the new science of philanthropy propagated by American Protestant social workers and by specifically Jewish purposes, the first nationwide Jewish women's organization in America, the NATIONAL COUNCIL OF JEWISH WOMEN (NCJW), actively joined settlement work. NCJW was founded in 1893, during a Jewish Women's Congress organized under the auspices of the World's Parliament of Religions held at the Chicago World's Fair. The Jewish Women's Congress itself, its key speakers (single women who were teachers and social workers), and its discussion topics which ranged from "Religion in the Home" to "Women as Wage Workers" and "Women Against Child Factory Labor", exemplified a new development in the Americanization-as-ethnicization of German Jewish women's social position and their activities.

NCJW set as its main objectives solidification of members' religious-cultural identity through the systematic study of Judaism and religious and educational work among Jewish working-class children and youth. In consultation with leaders such as Jane Addams and Lillian Wald, the council opened settlement houses in immigrant neighborhoods in more than one dozen cities. As perceived by NCJW, the goal of its settlement work resembled ethnicization, namely, "gradual assimilation and the recognition of the need to create a sense of continuity between the old and the new in an atmosphere of mutual respect, toleration, and understanding," as stated in Faith Rogow's *Gone to Another Meeting*.

The NCJW's settlement work led to the involvement of its members in mainstream American public institutions such as schools, juvenile courts, and medical centers. These institutions fell, by and large, in the purview of the domestic care-and-nurture sphere that constituted the then recognized culturally female dominion. NCJW leaders themselves insisted that social welfare work, within and without the German Jewish community, was simply an extension of motherhood. But even when justified as falling into the domestic sphere, further redrawing of the boundaries of Jewish women's public activities by the inclusion of the realm outside the ethnic community constituted the next important step in their assimilation. In collaboration with American Protestant clubwomen, council locals joined political campaigns for women's causes such as improved education and job opportunities for women, and Progressive social justice crusades for delegalization of child factory labor, minimum wages, and humane working conditions. At the same time, in a reconfirmation of the hybrid general (American) and particular (Jewish) assimilation that had characterized German Jewish women's adaptation in America since the beginning of the nineteenth century, NCJW pursued its own ethnic agenda (contradictory to the concerns expressed by middle-class American Protestant clubwomen), by defending the open-door immigration policy of the U.S. Government, and by lobbying for the improvement of living conditions of immigrant families in urban centers.

The adherence of late nineteenth-century middle-class American women to the accepted notions of womanhood in public self-representations and in interpretations of their expanding public activities, namely, making women's moral sensibility the justification for their responsibility for the perfection of society, has been dubbed by scholars as "domestic feminism." German Jewish women did not differ in their approach from their American Protestant sisters. They, too, presented themselves and their activities in terms of the then prevailing concept of femininity, which, in their case, included a distinctive Jewish component. Turn-of-the-century Jewish domestic feminism, however, testified to the long distance traveled by German Jewish women from *hevrot nashim* of the 1820s to the greatly augmented scope and diversified forms and content of their religious and secular activities, gains in personal autonomy and self-confidence, the emergence of a collective identity based on class-gendethnicity, and a sense of public responsibility.

Facilitating these changes in women's lives were long-term influences of the democratic functioning of American society and the principle of individual rights informing its laws and culture. The transformation during the nineteenth century of American German Jewish society, especially its collective ascent to the middle class and the economic and cultural consequences thereof, and the emergence and spread of Reform Judaism also significantly contributed to the changes in women's lives.

Conversely, as their activities expanded and self-confidence strengthened, the women transformed the German Jewish community as well. The American German Jewish community of the 1900s in which middle-class women hosted receptions in their parlors, managed public religious life as saviors of Judaism, busied themselves as professional social workers, organized women's congresses, and collaborated with American Protestant women in political campaigns differed dramatically from its "grandmother" of seventy-five years earlier in which women were mainly preoccupied with caring for numerous children at home, helping their husbands in family stores, and traditional *tzedaka* in the congregation. Jewish women Americanized-ethnicized themselves and their communities not solely as agents of change, however, but also simultaneously as agents for the preservation of Jewish tradition.

BIBLIOGRAPHY

Baum, Charlotte, Paula Hyman, and Sonya Michel. "Assimilation Was Their Goal: The German Jewish Woman in America." In *The Jewish Woman in America* (1976); Blair, Karen. *The Clubwoman as Feminist: True Womanhood Redefined, 1868–1914* (1980); Cohen, Naomi. *Encounter With Emancipation: The German Jews in the United States,* 1830–1914 (1981); Diner, Hasia. *A Time for Gathering: The Second Migration 1820–1880* (1992); Glanz, Rudolph. *The Jewish Woman in America: Two Female Immigrant Generations, 1820–1929.* Vol. 1, *The Eastern European Jewish Woman,* and Vol. 2, *The German Jewish Woman* (1976); Goldman, Karla. "The Ambivalence of Reform Judaism: Kaufmann Kohler and the Ideal Jewish Woman." *AJH* 4 (1990): 477–499; Golomb, Deborah Grand. "The 1893 Congress of Jewish Women: Evolution or Revolution in American Jewish Women's History?" *AJH* 1 (1980): 52–67; Gordon, Milton. *Assimilation in American Life* (1964); Hargrove, Barbara, Jean Miller Schmidt, and Sheila Greeve Davaney. "Religion and the Changing Role of Women." *The Annals of the American Academy of Political and Social Science* 480 (1985): 117–31; Heinze, Andrew. *Adapting to Abundance: Jewish Immigrants, Mass Consumption, and the Search for American Identity* (1990); Hyman, Paula. *Gender and Assimilation in Modern Jewish History: The Roles and Representations of Women* (1995); Kuzmack, Linda Gordon. *Woman's Cause: The Jewish Woman's Movement in England and the United States, 1881–1933* (1990); Marcus, Jacob Rader, ed. *The American Jewish Woman: A Documentary History* (1981); Meyer, Michael. *Response to Modernity: A History of the Reform Movement in Judaism* (1988); Morawska, Ewa. "The Sociology and Historiography of Immigration." In *Immigration Reconsidered: History, Sociology, and Politics,* edited by Virginia Yans-McLaughlin (1990); Muncy, Robyn. *Creating a Female Dominion in American Reform, 1890–1935* (1991); Nadell, Pamela, and Rita Simon. "Ladies of the Sisterhood: Women in the American Reform Synagogue, 1990–1930." In *Active Voices: Women in Jewish Culture,* edited by Maurie Sacks (1995); Rogow, Faith. *Gone to Another Meeting: The National Council of Jewish Women, 1893–1993* (1993); Sinkoff, Nancy. "Educating for 'Proper' Jewish Womanhood: A Case Study in Domesticity and Vocational Training, 1897–1926." *AJH* 3 (1988): 572–599; Sochen, June Miller. *Consecrate Every Day: The Public Lives of Jewish American Women, 1880–1980* (1981); Strauss, Herbert. "The Immigration and Acculturation of the German Jew in the United States of America." *Leo Baeck Institute Year Book* (1971): 63–96; Toll, William. "A Quiet Revolution: Jewish Women's Clubs and the Widening Female Sphere, 1870–1920." *AJA* 1 (1989): 9–26; Welter, Barbara. "The Feminization of American Religion: 1800–1860." In *Clio's Consciousness Raised,* edited by Mary Hartman and Lois Banner (1974); Wenger, Beth. "Jewish Women and Voluntarism: Beyond the Myth of Enablers." *AJH* 1 (1989): 16–36.

EWA MORAWSKA

ASSIMILATION OF TWENTIETH-CENTURY JEWISH WOMEN

Jewish women began to assimilate into American society and culture as soon as they stepped off the boat. Some started even earlier, with reports and dreams of the *goldene medine*, the golden land of liberty and opportunity. Very few resisted adapting to the language and mores of the United States; those who did often returned to Europe. Well over 90 percent stayed, even those who cursed Columbus's voyage and subsequent European settlement in North America. In their choice of paid employment and household labor, as well as through their attitudes toward love and marriage and in their methods of child rearing, immigrant women provided the first models of American Jewish womanhood for their daughters.

If assimilation began with immigration, it did not stop with the maturation of a native-born generation. Studies of assimilation often focus on the children of immigrants born in America or brought over when young: the second generation. The attitudes and behavior of the second generation in comparison to its immigrant parents reveal the extent of its adaptation to America and commitment to a distinctive Jewish way of life. Similarly, the third generation, with immigrant grandparents, often offers a touchstone to vouchsafe whether Jews and Judaism can survive in freedom. How these generations speak, eat, earn a liv-

ing, vote, dress, observe religious practices, and rear their children, not to mention where they live and whom they marry, are data to interpret their assimilation. A continuum exists between Jews whose distinctiveness from other Americans appears in each of these categories and Jews who resemble their fellow Americans in everything except name or self-identification as a Jew. Often stages are postulated on the path of assimilation, suggesting that some changes—such as language, dress, education, and ways of earning a living—precede other, more difficult changes—such as those involving family, including religious observance and choice of marriage partner. Occasionally, a generation may get stuck on the path, unwilling or unable due to anti-Semitism to continue to adapt. Even more rarely, members of a generation may reverse their steps, moving away from assimilation toward greater Jewish distinctiveness.

Scholars of assimilation disagree in their interpretations of Jewish assimilation in America. Initially many saw a straight-line path to complete assimilation: They expected Jews to disappear as a separate group in American society. For them, intermarriage is the final step. Others argue for the transformative

Jewish women were anxious to participate in American democracy. This group (all women, some dressed as men) campaigned for suffrage (with signs in English and Hebrew). [Peter H. Schweitzer]

power of assimilation, suggesting that the process of adaptation stimulates Jews to acquire and invent new ways to maintain their identity in America. Still other scholars imagine Jews as a symbolic social group, discounting the significance of religion and ethnicity. Some emphasize the importance of religious distinctiveness, of Jews as non-Christian dissenters in America; they often consider religious observance more important than marriage partner. Almost all agree that politics, place, and period influence assimilation, and that assimilation is an interactive process involving Jews on one side and non-Jewish Americans on the other. There is less unanimity on the significance of gender in assimilation; until recently, many scholars ignored gender as a category of analysis. To date, no comprehensive study of gender and Jewish assimilation in twentieth-century America exists, despite pioneering work by Paula Hyman.

Since immigration usually initiated the process of Jewish assimilation in America, the concept of generational change remains useful. Second-generation Jewish women, growing up in immigrant households but attending public schools and with access to American popular culture, encountered at least two different understandings of gender roles. Their mothers embodied Jewish womanhood, although its dimensions could be quite diverse; their teachers and popular female cultural figures represented American womanhood. Often these contrasting versions of what it meant to be a woman created conflict as daughters struggled to develop an American Jewish womanhood acceptable to themselves and to their mothers. Differences between second-generation mothers and their third-generation daughters were less striking because the former spoke English, had studied in public school, and often were middle class. As a result, both mothers and daughters often agreed on acceptable gender roles. Friction returned with the third and fourth generations. Changes in American definitions of appropriate gender roles, especially after the rise of the new women's movement of the 1960s, usually provoked this conflict rather than contrasts between Jewish and American constructions of gender.

If generation removed from immigration helps locate Jewish women in the assimilation process, it provides neither chronology nor historical framework for social, cultural, and religious change. Over the course of the twentieth century, four different, overlapping cohorts of Jewish women can be identified. Their paths of assimilation suggest alternative ways of defining American Jewish womanhood. The first group of women, the Yankees, came of age during the Progressive Era. Their parents emigrated during the

nineteenth century, many of them from the German states; a few were descendants of old Sephardi families. The second cohort, the women of World War II, grew to maturity during the Depression. Their parents were part of the mass immigration of Eastern European Jews that ended in 1924. The third group, the baby boomers, reached their adulthood during the era of the Cold War and civil rights movement. Their parents usually were native born, although some were the children of refugees from Nazi Europe and survivors of the Holocaust. The most recent cohort, the orphans of history, grew up in the age of Star Wars with little Jewish historical consciousness or sense of connection to a Jewish past. Not only their parents, but their grandparents, are native born. Many scholars would argue that they offer the best evidence of Jewish assimilation in America.

YANKEES: 1900–1960

Autobiographies suggest that this group of American Jewish women grew up well integrated into their Jewish families, comfortably embedded in American communities scattered throughout the United States. Many enjoyed the luxuries of middle-class family patterns in which mothers managed the household, sometimes with the assistance of servants, and children received an education. Despite a lack of zeal among Jews to educate daughters as they did their sons, Yankee Jewish women often benefited from expanding educational opportunities for American women. Many went to high school or normal school; a handful of determined women like JESSICA BLANCHE PEIXOTTO or FANNIE HURST attended college. The rise of the women's movement opened horizons for middle-class white women, including Jewish women. Even if they were not sufficiently radical as META POLLACK BETTMAN to support the woman suffrage movement, they recognized that their lives did not need to be bounded by marriage and motherhood. Social feminism, the idea that woman's particular strengths in caring for the vulnerable required that she leave her home and enter public life, attracted many Jewish women and provided a rationale for organizational activity.

Indeed, Yankee Jewish women created most of the national, mass membership Jewish women's organizations of the twentieth century. A sense of security as American Jews coupled with a desire to improve the world and educate themselves propelled this group into the mainstream of American women's activities. In addition to participating in the women's movement, they joined the club movement as did HANNAH SOLOMON. They pioneered in the settlement house movement as did MINNIE LOW and LILLIAN WALD. They helped spark the consumer movement like HELENE P. GANS. Together with such leaders as Ella Altschuler and Zerlina Hirsh Bilder, they supported the peace movement. And they established specifically Jewish venues to change the Jewish world. An encounter with Jewish immigrants from Eastern Europe, whose distinctiveness set them apart from other Americans, often stimulated action. Some Yankees saw immigrants as needy cousins, while others feared that their poverty and radicalism might incite anti-Semitism. These Jewish women tried to help by alleviating poverty and teaching American ways of living. For some, like JOSEPHINE LAZARUS, meeting immigrants inspired a romantic identification with Jewishness that strengthened their commitment to live as Jews. The NATIONAL COUNCIL OF JEWISH WOMEN (NCJW), an organization that took up the challenge of helping immigrant Jewish women, appeared first on the scene in 1893. HADASSAH, the Women's Zionist Organization, followed in 1912. Then came the founding of synagogue sisterhoods, first the Reform NATIONAL FEDERATION OF TEMPLE SISTERHOODS, followed by the WOMEN'S LEAGUE FOR CONSERVATIVE JUDAISM. Later Orthodox women established Mizrachi Women, for Zionists, and Emunah, a sisterhood. The diversity of Jewish women's organizations reflected differing religious and ideological stances. A commonality of belief in voluntarism and the power of women working together in women's organizations united them.

Organizational activism represented only one response of the Yankee cohort to changing gender roles. Other Yankee Jews grasped opportunities for educated women to pursue careers to further individual dreams as writers, artists, lawyers, scholars, educators. A few, like BLANCHE WOLFE KNOPF, transformed Jewish women's traditional economic activity as partner with her husband in business (usually some form of commerce or manufacture) into a modern occupation previously closed to women—in this case, as director of the publishing firm Alfred A. Knopf. An open and optimistic society dissolved conventions constraining determined and talented Jewish women who sought alternatives to marriage and motherhood. Facing relatively few obstacles specific to Jews, these women forged personal careers. For many, such goals took them away not only from any Jewish distinctiveness but even from any Jewish identification. Writers as different as GERTRUDE STEIN and THYRA SAMTER WINSLOW shaped cultural worlds for themselves that relegated Jewishness largely to a fact of birth and upbringing. Others found inspiration in their Jewish

background that encouraged them to pursue political and social activism. Figures like JEANETTE GOODMAN BRILL, who served as a municipal judge in New York City, and JULIA RICHMAN, who was the first woman to serve as an assistant superintendent of New York City's public schools, felt an intimate connection between their desire for careers in public service and their Jewish heritage. For them, new gender roles available to women—both married and single—did not translate into a form of assimilation that distanced them from other Jews or the Jewish community.

Only a minority of the Yankee group built the infrastructure of Jewish women's organizations or pioneered in developing new careers for women, but their significance outweighs their numbers. In both cases they established important precedents for the masses of second-generation American Jewish women coming of age during the Depression. These precedents included a tradition of American Jewish voluntarism and activism accompanying marriage and child rearing as well as the recognition that talent and perseverance could bring rewards of independence. By their activities and presence, leaders of the Yankee cohort indicated possibilities available to Jewish women in America. Individual expression and fulfillment could be achieved by middle-class women; less obvious were the personal sacrifices.

Leaders stood out in contrast to the majority, most of whom married Jews and raised children, and confined their activities to socializing within their class. Their Jewish religious observance usually took place at home on holidays and important times during the life cycle. Many also enthusiastically celebrated American holidays, especially Thanksgiving, and for some, Christmas and Easter. REFORM JUDAISM appealed to the majority as an American form of Judaism. In keeping with their middle-class position and urban residence in the Northeast, Midwest, and far West, the Yankee cohort usually supported the Republican Party, especially its progressive wing, when they received the vote. For most, Judaism was a family matter, not an issue of ideology or ethnicity. Although these Jewish women sought to replicate the integrated experience of their own childhoods, their children discovered anti-Semitic discrimination rather than an open society.

WOMEN OF WORLD WAR II: 1930–1990

In contrast to the tens of thousands of Jewish women in the Yankee group, the cohort of World War II included hundreds of thousands. Their very numbers changed the character of their assimilation. For example, following in the footsteps of Julia Richman, thousands of Jewish women joined the ranks of New York City public school teachers in the interwar decades. In 1920, 26 percent of new teachers were Jews, and a decade later, 44 percent were Jews. By the 1940s and 1950s, Jewish women were the vast majority of all public school teachers in New York City, which had at that time the world's largest public school system. As a result, Jewish teachers discovered that their essentially American occupation brought them into daily contact with other Jewish women. Their collective assimilation made teaching a distinctively Jewish vocational choice—indeed, it led New Yorkers to call teaching "the Jewish profession." Their numbers also swelled the ranks of active unionists. Similarly, wholesale adoption of birth control by this cohort of women dramatically changed the Jewish birth rate from one of the highest among immigrant groups to one of the lowest among urban ethnic groups. Thus these Jewish women made low fertility a characteristically Jewish attribute, along with a high

marriage rate of over 90 percent. In politics, their enthusiastic support of New Deal liberalism, especially its internationalism and social welfare policies, led to its identification with Jewish women. In many ways, this cohort overshadowed the singular achievements of the Yankee group, and its choices of gender roles often came to be considered typically American Jewish patterns, obscuring earlier alternatives.

Yet the women of World War II found far fewer options available than their predecessors. Society became more restrictive for Jews. Even as women achieved the right to vote in 1920, Congress limited immigration through legislation designed to reduce decisively the number of Eastern European Jews entering the country. Patterns of anti-Semitic discrimination became more widespread and acceptable, including exclusion of Jews from schools of higher education, white-collar employment, and residential neighborhoods. Substantial obstacles prevented Jewish women from assimilating into American society.

Many Jewish women (and men) learned how to become "Americans" through organized instruction. This 1934 photograph is captioned "Americanization Class, San Francisco." [Western Jewish History Center]

For example, job placement agencies occasionally admitted that "it was a waste of time to send Jewish women to the New York Telephone company and to the large insurance companies." In contrast to public school teaching, "it was common knowledge that 'the phone company was part of the Catholic Church,'" as Ruth Markowitz reported in *My Daughter, the Teacher.* In addition, most of the women of World War II grew up in working-class homes in large urban neighborhoods—New York City and Chicago accounted for half, and 75 percent lived in just five cities. They shared crowded apartments with many brothers and sisters. Ambitious and eager to achieve independence, they found themselves tied to family responsibilities, their horizons hemmed by neighborhood boundaries. Immigrant mothers expected daughters to help them; only those who enjoyed a modicum of economic security could afford to encourage their daughters to seek individual fulfillment. Pathways out of the neighborhood through education, employment, and talent

existed, but reaching them often required extra measures of determination and ambition.

Given the obstacles, the number of Jewish women who succeeded in such diverse fields as art and science, literature and law, politics and business, as well as entertainment and education, is impressive. They include outstanding figures like Nobel Prize winner ROSALYN SUSSMAN YALOW and U.S. Supreme Court justice RUTH BADER GINSBURG. Jewish women also shaped the growing field of Jewish education, writing history books and Bible stories, filling the ranks of Sunday and Hebrew school teachers, and contributing to the rise of Hanukkah as an American Jewish holiday alternative to Christmas. Their creativity as writers helped to generate a substantial body of American Jewish literature. Diverse Jewish women's voices, from the earthy stories of GRACE PALEY to the class conscious ones of TESS SLESINGER, allowed not only for individuality to emerge but also for a sense of common concerns. Among recurring themes is the tension

Synagogue auxiliaries instilled "American" values by staging numerous patriotic pageants during the 1940s. This presentation, entitled "My Country 'Tis," was put on in the Temple of Aaron in Saint Paul, Minnesota, by the Women's League on January 3, 1940. [Jewish Historical Society of the Upper Midwest]

between mothers and daughters, the struggle to find one's own voice and one's own way of expressing American Jewish womanhood, as in TILLIE OLSEN's poignant novella, *Tell Me a Riddle*. Few writers seek to replicate their mother's Jewishness, whether that appears as a competent *baleboste* (household manager) or a dedicated radical. Instead they strive to articulate a new way of understanding motherhood, marriage, and what it means to be an American Jewish woman. The desire to be part of mainstream American society remained strong among this group, perhaps because of difficulties gaining access and acceptance. When barriers fell in the postwar decades and Jewish women received recognition for their individual accomplishments, many discovered that their self-consciousness as outsiders endured despite new respect and influence.

For the vast majority who retired from paid employment upon marriage or the birth of their first child, American Jewish womanhood meant blending middle-class mores with a modified Jewish traditionalism focused on family and community. Even the minority who received a college education assumed that their lives should focus on fulfilling the duties of wife and mother. Their decision to leave paying jobs to marry and raise children reflected their acceptance of American gender norms. Immigrant Jewish women assumed that they would have to contribute to the family income, though they rarely did that by taking work outside the home—a pattern their daughters rejected as soon as feasible. Most of the women of World War II shouldered responsibility for passing on Jewish traditions to their children despite their own lack of formal Jewish education. Here, again, they adopted American mores that placed religion within the feminine domain. Since they knew very little about Judaism, though they accepted religion as the basis of Jewish distinctiveness, they usually turned to Jewish professionals to give their children a Jewish identity. This meant joining a synagogue, usually a Conservative one, when the children were old enough to attend Hebrew or Sunday school. Thus women increasingly attended synagogue services on the holidays, sitting together with their husbands and children. As mothers, this generation prepared Jewish foods learned from their mothers, though only a minority maintained kosher kitchens.

The tradition of volunteer activism established by Yankee cohort leaders took hold as the women of World War II left the large cities for suburban neighborhoods and a measure of affluence. Jewish women flocked to join Hadassah, NCJW, the synagogue sisterhoods, as well as smaller national women's organizations like WOMEN'S AMERICAN ORT, the AMERICAN JEWISH CONGRESS Women's Division, B'nai B'rith Women, and PIONEER WOMEN. Their numbers swelled the organizations' membership lists. Through these organizations they gained an education in politics and ideology, as well as practical experience in fund-raising and political action, and leadership training for those who desired it. Like their predecessors, these Jewish women also joined Parent-Teacher Associations and a variety of secular voluntary organizations. Many enjoyed socializing with female Jewish friends at home over cards or coffee and cake. When BETTY FRIEDAN discovered "the problem that has no name" in 1963 and its cure—feminism—Jewish women also joined the National Organization for Women. Many subsequently decided to return to the paid labor force after their children left home; a minority continued to work outside the home throughout their lives.

Gender roles adopted by the women of World War II, even by those who felt they had no opportunity to choose, reflected their eagerness to become American women and their discovery that they remained Jewish women. Anti-Semitism and the Holocaust slowed their trajectory of assimilation. As the poet MURIEL RUKEYSER testified in her poem, "To be a Jew in the twentieth century" was both a burden and a gift, but neither could be refused without terrible cost. The cultural critic SUSAN SONTAG also bore witness to the Holocaust, writing many years later of "a negative epiphany" upon seeing photographs of the concentration camps. "Indeed," she writes in *On Photography* (1977), "it seems plausible to me to divide my life into two parts, before I saw those photographs (I was twelve) and after." Thus even when anti-Semitism eased in the postwar period and the State of Israel offered an alternative image of Jews than that of victims, few American Jewish women of this cohort dissociated themselves from other Jews or from an identity as a Jew.

Yet unlike their mothers, the women of World War II suffered from stereotypes widely purveyed in popular culture. Produced and popularized largely by men, often their sons but occasionally their husbands, the stereotypes mocked these American Jewish women as the epitome of nouveau riche crassness. From their mink coats and jewels, to their ornate taste in home furnishings, to their overladen tables of food, to their enthusiasm for fund-raising to help suffering Jews in Israel, to their child-rearing patterns that induced guilt but avoided physical violence, to their ambitions for their sons and daughters, little in their way of life was not a potential target of mockery. Only with the rise of Jewish feminism in the 1970s did a reevaluation begin of the women of World War II.

BABY BOOMERS: 1950–PRESENT

Until the recent appearance of the orphans of history, the baby boomers served as the touchstone of Jewish assimilation in America. The first cohort to include large numbers of third-generation Jewish women, as well as second- and fourth-generation, its social and cultural patterns provided critical data to interpret the meaning and character of assimilation. The women of World War II clearly remained Jewish in their social and family life, as well as occupational and residential patterns. As the group bearing witness to the two outstanding Jewish events of the twentieth century—the destruction of European Jews and the establishment of the State of Israel—it remained bound to its Jewish identity. By contrast, baby boomers grew up in a society of suburban comfort that included the luxury of privacy and a room of one's own. In their world Israel was an accepted reality and European Jewry and its Jewish culture did not exist. Education, including college and postgraduate study, became an accepted norm for Jewish daughters as well as sons. Self-expression, careers, individuality, became available to Jewish women. A 1990 survey found almost 60 percent of the baby boomers employed full time and only 4 percent not employed. Few obstacles impeded their assimilation. In fact, they faced an America that more closely resembled the one encountered by the Yankee cohort than the America their mothers knew. New opportunities for women opened, fueled by the second wave of the women's movement in which Jews played an important part. In 1965, the United States even liberalized its immigration laws, though it did not return to the almost totally unrestricted situation that existed prior to 1921.

Unlike their predecessors, baby boomers received a formal Jewish education. A significant minority became bat mitzvah, a new ritual originated by the women of World War II for their daughters to mark their coming of age just as bar mitzvah symbolized a son's maturity. As feminism became a popular political movement, those women who had acquired Jewish learning began to press for equal access to positions of Jewish leadership, including the rabbinate. The first women rabbis came from this generation, products of both changing American gender roles and expanding Jewish education for women. Other women, like SHOSHANA CARDIN, who became the first woman elected to head the Conference of Jewish Federations, sought leadership positions within the Jewish communal infrastructure. Some women expressed dissatisfaction with positions in separate women's organizations; others attacked the tradition of voluntarism established by the Yankee cohort and enthusiastically embraced by

the women of World War II. Such battles between two groups of Jewish women reflected the impact of the new women's movement and its challenge to previously accepted gender roles, exactly the roles adopted by the women of World War II. Baby boomers did not categorically reject marriage and motherhood—in fact, a majority married and bore children—but they did question patriarchal assumptions behind relegating women to such tasks and then subordinating them. A smaller number of radical lesbian feminists challenged the entire notion of the heterosexual family and argued for new understanding of the family based on love, commitment, and caring rather than sexuality. Some, like Irena Klepfisz, also turned to the Jewish community, demanding recognition and inclusion. Changing gender roles available to American women registered forcibly within Jewish institutions.

Most baby boomers were too busy pursuing careers, participating in politics—from mainstream parties to those of the New Left to various factions of the feminist movement—and eventually marrying, to seek leadership positions within Jewish life. The opportunities available to them as talented, highly educated, hard-working, articulate women led many to ignore most Jewish issues, except for Israel and the Holocaust. Integrating easily into American life, benefiting from programs of affirmative action, moving out of areas of Jewish concentration in occupations and residence to jobs and homes throughout the United States but particularly in California and the South, they increasingly distanced themselves from family networks of their youth. Many found such freedom exhilarating; others regretted the loss of Jewish connections but did not return to patterns of the previous generation. In ever-increasing numbers, they chose to marry non-Jews, breaking radically with earlier traditions but bringing their behavior as women in line with that of Jewish men. In the homes they created, Jewish observance centered almost exclusively around holidays. Passover and Hanukkah, which could be celebrated at home, were the most popular, outranking the previously popular high holy days of Rosh Hashannah and Yom Kippur. Jewish cuisine similarly appeared only on holidays. As with the previous cohort, few kept kosher kitchens.

Like their predecessor, baby boomers produced impressive numbers of writers, lawyers, artists, educators, professors, businesswomen, entertainers, physicians, and psychologists. Even as they continued to influence Jewish education, they played critical parts in shaping the new fields of women's studies and Jewish studies. In 1996, for example, there were over 200 members of the women's caucus of the Association of Jewish Studies, an indication of even more widespread presence since neither the association nor the ten-year-old caucus included all women working in Jewish studies. Scholarship of baby boomers in the social sciences, including history, sociology, and anthropology, greatly expanded the work of earlier pioneers like HORTENSE POWDERMAKER and GERTRUDE HIMMEL-FARB. Indeed, the entry of Jewish women into academia resembles the enthusiastic embrace of public school teaching by New York City women of World War II. Both occupations gave women flexible schedules to allow them to combine marriage and motherhood with a successful career; both occupations also provided opportunities to blend intellectual pursuits with mentoring. As with public school teaching, Jewish women brought to academia a radical élan that often found expression in support of unionization, affirmative action, collective bargaining, and curriculum reform.

Unlike their predecessor, baby boomers included large numbers of women estranged from Judaism and Jewish life; numbers of these chose to reverse their steps on the path of assimilation. Some returned to strict religious observance, finding a meaningful alternative to the alienation of contemporary society in orthodox Judaism with its sexual segregation. These *ba'alot teshuva* challenged by their choices the majority embrace of a feminism that affirmed women's equality with men. Even among Orthodox women, demands for opportunities to study sacred rabbinic texts and for female prayer quorums reflect the influence of American feminism. The phenomenon of return was not limited to those who opted for orthodoxy. Within the Reform and Conservative movements, women adopted patterns of increased religious observance, including keeping the Sabbath and a kosher home, as well as heightened ritual participation at home and in the synagogue. A few baby boomers sought to recover the radicalism of immigrant mothers and the ideological and cultural tradition of Jewish secularism connected with Yiddish. Others experimented with personal forms of spirituality to express their understanding of Jewishness. Occasionally such mainstream liberal Jews as members of the Reconstructionist Movement adopted the writing of figures like MARGE PIERCY and JUDY CHICAGO, who had made reputations in secular America respectively as a feminist writer and artist. By including their poetry in the Sabbath prayer book, Reconstructionists transformed these personal reflections into collective expressions of Jewish spirituality.

Such contradictory trends—movements of return and Jewish leadership coupled with distancing from Jewish organizational life and dispersion throughout the United States as well as increasing intermarriage—provoked sustained debate among scholars over how to interpret the baby boomers' assimilation. Measures of continuity with the previous cohort include Jewish women's strong support for political liberalism associated with the Democratic Party, despite the changed content of that liberalism. Widespread marriage, despite increasing rates of divorce, and childbearing, albeit of fewer children and at an older age, can be seen as evidence of continuity or discontinuity. Elements of discontinuity involve adoption of different gender roles. Many baby boomers focus on their careers as much (or more) as on their families. Religious behavior offers diverse evidence for increased commitment based on formal knowledge, symbolic gestures, and accelerating dissaffection and dissociation. Many scholars turn to the most recent cohort, the orphans of history, to buttress their analysis of the most significant assimilation trends of the baby boomers.

ORPHANS OF HISTORY: 1980–PRESENT

While it is impossible to predict with certainty the paths of assimilation this last cohort will take, certain choices seem clear as the century draws to a close. Raised in affluence and security, in which anti-Semitism was a topic in history books and not a living reality, this group of Jewish women faces an openness and opportunity for individual and collective accomplishment unmatched in any previous cohort. Higher education has become the norm and advanced degrees are far from unusual. A fluidity in gender roles in America yields a wider array of choices than in the past. The idea of a Jewish construction of womanhood is itself contested, further expanding possibilities for this cohort largely unburdened by historical memory, personal, collective, or symbolic. As a result, increasing numbers have postponed both marriage and motherhood. How many will choose to forgo both cannot yet be determined, but age of marriage is rising rapidly as is age at birth of a first child. Careers increasingly serve as a focus of identity, although there are signs of a return to voluntarism. Politics remains important, but this group is not defined by its commitment to feminism as were the baby boomers. Many view the women's movement as past, though they appreciate reaping its benefits. An articulate minority criticizes the movement's mistakes. The Holocaust continues to provide an emotional and spiritual anchor; by contrast, Israel is important for the identity of only a minority, often those most committed to Jewishness.

Unlike previous cohorts, the orphans of history include a significant minority of women of mixed parentage. When these women choose to identify and act as Jews, they introduce new perspectives drawn from Christianity as well as other religions and cultures. Often what attracts them to Judaism differs from the values of third-, fourth-, and fifth-generation American Jewish women. How they will influence the character of assimilation remains to be seen.

Over the twentieth century Jewish women have followed diverse paths of assimilation in America. At times the majority society largely dictated their choices; at other times they faced an array of opportunities so that their own cultural values proved critical to the road taken. Irrespective of the receptivity of American society to Jews, Jewish women have always had to confront the issue of gender and the need to reconcile Jewish gender roles with American norms. The difficulty of reconciliation periodically stimulated Jewish women to challenge American gender roles. Yet despite impressive achievements in fashioning successive versions of American Jewish womanhood, Jewish women continue to be the butt of cruel jokes, such as those about the Jewish American Princess or JAP. Such stereotyping suggests that American Jewish women differ from other women of their socioeconomic class, that they remain outsiders in cultural style despite their accomplishments, and that Jewish men do not necessarily share their understanding of desirable gender roles.

The assimilation of Jewish women during the twentieth century provides perhaps more evidence of continuity than disruption. Each cohort accepted the centrality of marriage and motherhood; child rearing and transmitting culture to the next generation remain vital tasks. Each group also understood Judaism to be a religious culture rooted in family life. The tradition of political activism similarly endures, even as the issues changed. Yet American Jewish women at the end of the twentieth century look very different from those one hundred years ago. But then, so does America.

BIBLIOGRAPHY

Baum, Charlotte, Paula Hyman, and Sonya Michel. *Jewish Women in America* (1976); Fishman, Sylvia Barack. *A Breath of Life: Feminism in the Jewish Community* (1993); Friedan, Betty. *The Feminine Mystique* (1963); Hyman, Paula. *Gender and Assimilation in Modern Jewish History: The Roles and Representation of Women* (1995); Markowitz, Ruth Jacknow. *My Daughter, the Teacher: Jewish Teachers in the New York City Schools* (1993); Rukeyser, Muriel. "Letter to the Front." *The Collected Poems of Muriel Rukeyser* (1979); Sontag, Susan. *On Photography* (1977, 1990).

DEBORAH DASH MOORE

AUERBACH, BEATRICE FOX
(1887–1968)

People who shopped or worked at G. Fox and Company in Hartford, Connecticut, from the 1930s to the 1960s have fond memories of Beatrice Fox Auerbach and her department store. Many enjoyed the benefits of her merchandising innovations and progressive employment policies. Her customers enjoyed services such as personal shoppers, free home delivery, and toll-free telephone ordering long before these services were standard in other department stores. Because Auerbach believed in training programs and promotion from within, employees could achieve steady advancement and job security. Ahead of her time, Auerbach did not limit these opportunities to white workers. Beginning in 1942, G. Fox hired African Americans for sales and executive track positions. Auerbach was a talented executive, and G. Fox and Company became the largest privately owned department store in the country.

Born in Hartford, Connecticut, on July 7, 1887, Beatrice Fox Auerbach was the first of two daughters of Moses and Theresa (Stern) Fox. It was a merchandising family—Moses Fox was the son of Gerson Fox, founder of the Hartford emporium that bore his name. Although she attended several schools and traveled widely, Beatrice did not earn a degree from any school or college. In 1911, she married George Auerbach, whose family owned a department store in Salt

Thanks to Beatrice Auerbach, the word service *became synonymous with the G. Fox and Company department store in Hartford, Connecticut. An entrepreneur who was ahead of her time, Auerbach implemented progressive policies that were as good for her employees as they were for her customers. She is shown here with Eleanor Roosevelt. [Schlesinger Library, Radcliffe College]*

Lake City. After her father's store burned in 1917, the young couple returned to Hartford to help Moses Fox rebuild, and George Auerbach became secretary and treasurer of the expanded G. Fox store.

While raising two daughters (Georgette, b. 1916, and Dorothy, b. 1919), Auerbach remained interested in the business activities of her father and husband. After George Auerbach's sudden death in 1927, she helped her now elderly father for what she thought would be a short time, but she enjoyed the work and proved to be a skillful merchandiser. Upon her father's death in 1938, she became president of G. Fox and Company, and directed its operations until she sold it to the May Company in 1965.

Auerbach's success in becoming a respected professional woman inspired her to help others attain success as well. She established and funded the Service Bureau for Women's Organizations in 1945 to teach members of those groups how to conduct meetings, coordinate activities, and lobby effectively. She was also interested in helping other women enter her field with professional preparation. Between 1938 and 1959, she collaborated with the Connecticut College for Women (now Connecticut College) in a retailing program that used her store as the laboratory in which classroom theories were practiced.

For Auerbach, G. Fox and Company and Hartford were inextricably part of each other, and her philanthropic giving through the Beatrice Fox Auerbach Foundation was generous and widespread, with gifts to many of the city's cultural organizations, hospitals, and institutions of higher education. She was a member of Temple Beth Israel, founded by her grandfather, and on the board of Hebrew Union College in Cincinnati, continuing her family's interest in REFORM JUDAISM. She was widely honored for her executive abilities and philanthropy, and received several honorary degrees and many awards.

Beatrice Fox Auerbach died in Hartford on November 29, 1968. She was uninterested in personal publicity and agreed to interviews only if they related to her store or philanthropic activities. She would be pleased to learn that the service for which G. Fox and Company was famous is now the stuff of legend in Connecticut, and that residents of the Hartford area still mourn the store's closing.

BIBLIOGRAPHY

Case, Linda. "The Very Private Life of Beatrice Fox Auerbach." *Hartford Courant, Northeast Magazine* section, May 4, 1986, 12–24; Dove, Roger. "Inside A Great Store: Hartford's G. Fox & Co." *Hartford Courant*, April 10–17, 1955; Koopman, Georgette [daughter of Beatrice Fox Auer-bach]. Telephone interview with author, May 1996; "Leaders Extol Mrs. Auerbach." *Hartford Courant*, December 1, 1968; "Mrs. Beatrice Fox Auerbach, 81, Retailer and Philanthropist, Dies." *NYTimes*, December 1, 1968, 86:2; *NAW* modern; Silverman, Morris. *Hartford Jews, 1659–1970* (1970); *WWIAJ* (1938); *WWWIA* 5, 8.

SANDRA WHEELER

AUTOBIOGRAPHY

"I was born, I have lived, and I have been made over. Is it not time to write my life's story?" So begins *The Promised Land*, by MARY ANTIN, one of the best-known autobiographies penned by an American Jewish woman. Since the publication of Antin's classic work in 1912, there has been a virtual outpouring of autobiographical writing by American Jewish women. Accounts of the immigrant experience, of feminist and/or activist involvement, of the changing role of women in Jewish and American life, as well as literary and political autobiographies, Holocaust survival narratives, and coming-of-age memoirs are all categories of autobiography to which American Jewish women have contributed copiously.

This plethora of female Jewish autobiographical writing is especially striking given that scholars know of only a handful of autobiographies by Jewish women before the twentieth century. Several sociohistorical factors contributed to the rise of American Jewish woman's autobiographical writing during this period. At the turn of the century, middle-class American Jewish women, like their gentile counterparts, began to turn away from the tenets of Victorian "True Womanhood" and became increasingly involved in the women's movement—in the campaign for female suffrage, birth control, and greater educational/vocational opportunities for women. As the status and role of women in American and Jewish life began to change, more and more American Jewish women turned to autobiographical writing as a means of documenting these changes and addressing questions of American, Jewish, and female identity. Harriet Lane Levy's *920 O'Farrell Street* (1947) and Sophie Ruskay's *Horsecars and Cobblestones* (1949) offer personal views of Jewish girlhood just before the role of women began to be questioned. Autobiographical works by women such as LILLIAN D. WALD, founder of the Henry Street Settlement (*The House on Henry Street*, 1915, and *Windows on Henry Street*, 1934); ANNIE NATHAN MEYER, founder of Barnard College (*Barnard Beginnings*, 1935, and *It's Been Fun*, 1951); and her sister MAUD NATHAN, an activist for female suffrage and social welfare (*Once Upon a Time and Today*, 1933) tell stories of Jewish women's contributions to various social and feminist causes, while memoirs by Council of Jewish Women founder HANNAH SOLOMON (*Fabric of My Life*, 1946) and immigrant educator and activist REBEKAH KOHUT (*My Portion*, 1925, and *More Yesterdays*, 1950) offer specific insights into the development of Jewish women's organizations.

Eastern European Jewish immigration to America in the late nineteenth and early twentieth centuries provided an even greater impetus for autobiographical writing. In a 1927 introduction to Rebekah Kohut's first book, *My Portion*, HENRIETTA SZOLD (an important activist and scholar in her own right) offers an explanation of this phenomenon. Szold contends that for Jews in general, and Jewish women in particular, to begin writing autobiography, they needed first to discover the self—to free themselves from the staunchly communal perspective that had been forced upon them by centuries of collective persecution. The emancipation of the Jews in Europe in the eighteenth and nineteenth centuries abetted this process of self-discovery. Under these new historical circumstances, Jews began to assimilate into European culture and thus to feel the need to write the story of their enlightened, transformed lives. The waves of immigration to America provided even more dramatic stories of self-transformation. Crossing over to the promised land of opportunity and upward mobility, Jewish men and women began to make themselves over, to discover or invent new selves. Many Jewish men and women turned to writing autobiography as a means of chronicling this metamorphosis and coming to some understanding of the ambiguous relationship between the Old World and the New, between Jewishness and Americanness. For Jewish women immigrants, the new opportunities for education and advancement available to them in America only heightened these questions of identity and relationship with the past. If life in the European shtetl did not always afford Jewish women the narratives of transformation and the consciousness of self that are the preconditions for autobiographical writing, the journey across the sea from poverty to opportunity, from female shtetl ignorance to American learnedness and literariness, certainly did.

Some of these immigrant women autobiographers chose to tell of this journey in their mother tongue of Yiddish. In *Mayn Lebens-Veg* [My life path] (1948), Yiddish writer/activist Rokhl Kirsch Holtman tells of her immigrant journey from Russia to New York, her many literary and left-wing political activities, as well as her various travels throughout the world. *Baym Fentster fun a Lebn* [At the window of life]

(1966) by poet ALIZA GREENBLATT offers a Yiddish prose account of life in both the Old World and the New, interspersed with poems relating to various stages of her life. Likewise, fiction writer Fannie Edelman's memoir *Der Shpigl fun Lebn* (1948), translated into English and published as *The Mirror of Life* in 1961, recalls her childhood in Galicia as well as her new life in New York, where she met her "industrious hardworking" husband, and realized an ambition "that did not enter [her] mind while [she] was in the old world: that of being a writer."

For others, the English language was an integral part of the autobiographical narrative of transformation. Mary Antin's *The Promised Land*, is an unabashed celebration of the English language and of America. It is based, in part, on *From Plotzk to Boston* (1899), Antin's earlier account of her voyage from Russia to America, written as a series of Yiddish letters to her uncle when she was thirteen years old and then translated into English when she was eighteen. *The Promised Land* tells of Antin's life in the Russian Pale of Settlement, her immigration to America, and her cultural/spiritual rebirth as an American citizen and writer. Like many other immigrant autobiographers, Antin represents her immigrant experience in lofty, quasi-biblical terms as an exodus from the bondage of Eastern Europe to the promised land of America. George Washington becomes her Moses; the public library, her temple. The miraculous educational and vocational opportunities that are scattered in Antin's path are compared to manna in the desert. America becomes not merely a country, but a grand spiritual legacy that she—unlike her older brother and sister who are sent to work to support the family—is privileged to inherit. Indeed, while the Antin family often stoops beneath the immigrant burdens of poverty, Mary Antin herself is singled out for success, "passed on from hand to hand by ready teachers" and benefactors and welcomed into genteel American society.

My Mother and I (1917) by ELIZABETH STERN tells a similarly ebullient story of Americanization, although Stern is somewhat more candid about the price an immigrant woman pays to become an American. Like Antin, Stern proves to be a gifted student and writer. However, in contrast to Mary Antin, who develops her American identity very much apart from her family, Elizabeth Stern develops her authorial and autobiographical "self" alongside her mother, her greatest ally and supporter. Indeed, Stern's writing career begins in her mother's kitchen, where she sits composing letters for her illiterate immigrant neighbors to their relatives in the Old Country, her mother always at her side helping her with the more difficult compositions.

Eventually, however, Elizabeth's talents and aspirations draw her away from her mother's kitchen. On her first day of high school, when her fellow students gasp at the sight of the lunch her mother prepared for her, a newspaper-packed mélange of gefilte fish and potatoes, Elizabeth resolves to throw away all the lunches her mother gives her in the trash can outside the school. Slowly but surely, Elizabeth begins to discard not only the physical, but also the emotional, products of her mother's kitchen, replacing her mother's friendship with her American-born high school and college friends. From then on, Elizabeth, who moves to New York to study social work and marries an American-born man, becomes allied with a model of feminine identity completely different from that of her mother's. "To my eyes," Stern writes, "my mother's life appeared all at once as something to be pitied—to be questioned."

Through writing about her own life, Stern attempts to make peace with the loss of her past. In a subsequent fictional autobiography entitled *I Am a Woman–and a Jew* (1926), which she published under the pseudonym Leah Morton, Stern revisits this past and changes the end of the story. This pseudonym, composed of a biblical first name and a gentile/American family name, highlights Stern's desire to reinvent her original autobiographical account—to pit her newfound American identity against her Jewish past and come to some sort of resolution. In this revision of her life story, Leah, like Elizabeth, pursues an education against her father's wishes, drifts away from her beloved mother, and marries an American-born man—this time, a gentile. Ironically, it is the flagrant act of marrying out of the faith that leads Leah to reembrace her Jewish identity. If *My Mother and I* is the story of Elizabeth's estrangement from her past, *I Am a Woman–and a Jew* represents an attempt on the part of a onetime assimilationist to reassess the importance of her past and make sense of her identity as "a woman and a Jew." Leah's search for the meaning of her Jewishness is accompanied by her struggle to balance her literary, personal, and professional aspirations, her career objectives with her responsibilities as a mother. At first, writing is Leah/Elizabeth's means of escaping the Jewish ghetto and taking possession of the American dream. Later it becomes a means of reaffirming the various aspects of her identity, of reconnecting not only with America, but also with the spiritual nourishment of her beloved mother, as well as the scholarship of her rabbinical father, for "writing can be preaching too," Stern/Morton writes, "as fervent and holy as that from the pulpit."

The act of writing takes on a hallowed quality in other autobiographies by immigrant Jewish women. For Elizabeth Hasanovitz, author of *One of Them: Chapters from a Passionate Autobiography* (1917), writing offers an opportunity both to embrace the promise of America and to reinforce her solidarity with her fellow immigrant workers. When Hasanovitz is paid by an industrial efficiency expert to write her book—an account of her experiences as an immigrant Jewish sweatshop worker and labor activist—she feels at long last that she has found America. "And so I have emerged," she writes, "and risen 1800 feet above the sea level; amidst high mountains trimmed with red, green and yellow trees—bright life Oriental rugs." Hasanovitz quickly reproaches herself, however, for lifting herself above the lot of the common worker, thus reaffirming her commitment to the broader workers' struggle for "that wonderful dawn!"

In *I Came a Stranger: The Story of a Hull-House Girl*, Hilda Polacheck offers a similarly enthusiastic account of the relationship between writing and the promise of America. In Polacheck's case, a successful composition written for an English class at Jane Addams's Hull House earns her a partial scholarship to attend the University of Chicago. Polacheck never finishes her degree. Eventually she marries and moves to Milwaukee, where she dedicates herself to her husband, children, and volunteer activities. But when her husband dies and she is beset by the financial problems endemic to the Depression, writing again becomes her lifeline, as she finds a job on the Illinois Writer's Project, writing articles on various social welfare subjects connected with her Hull House experiences.

Likewise, *I Belong to the Working Class*, the autobiography of writer/activist ROSE PASTOR STOKES, offers an example of the way the act of writing helps the author claim and clarify her American immigrant working-class identity. Stokes's unfinished autobiography tells of her escape from the grind of a Cleveland cigar factory to a job as a reporter for the woman's page of the New York–based *Der Yidishes Tageblat*. In her capacity as a reporter, she is sent to interview millionaire philanthropist James Graham Phelps Stokes, whom she eventually marries in storybook fashion. The Cinderella plot unravels, however, when aristocratic James begins to disagree with Rose's brand of radical socialism and Rose becomes increasingly uncomfortable among the riches of the Stokes family. In one scene in the autobiography, Rose tells of her search through the thousands of books in the Stokes family library for a book "which tells of how the poor can do away with their poverty," only to find one volume after another "about great men." Stokes's autobiography, in which she affirms her allegiance with "the poor, the sick, the needy, and the suffering," is her attempt, albeit quixotic, to write the sort of socially conscious book that she had been looking for.

The autobiography and autobiographical fiction of ANZIA YEZIERSKA (who used Rose Pastor Stokes's life story as the subject of her first novel, *Salome of the Tenements*, 1923) perhaps best illustrates the relationship between the act of writing and the immigrant quest for the American dream. Unlike Antin and Stern, who spearheaded their literary careers with the writing of an immigrant autobiography, Yezierska was first and foremost a fiction writer, so much so that in reading her autobiography *Red Ribbon on a White Horse* (1950) it is somewhat difficult to tease out fact from fiction. In much of her writing, Yezierska tells and retells the story of her own struggle to become an American writer. Yezierska's hunger for self-expression remains unsatisfied even in her autobiography in which she tells of her emergence from East Side poverty to Hollywood, where she was given two lucrative contracts for film adaptations of her first two books. As her autobiography shows, Yezierska continually doubts her success, ruminates over her female immigrant identity and her relationship with the patriarchal religion of her rabbinic father, and struggles to find a proper place for her writing and her "self" in American culture. Too "green" for the New World, and yet too American for the Old, Yezierska occasionally finds her American home in her writing, although more often than not, the world of writing proves to be a place of exile as well.

Living My Life (1931), the autobiography of anarchist EMMA GOLDMAN, provides an even more extreme example of female exile. An immigrant from Lithuania, Goldman tells of her anarchist convictions and her disillusionment with America. Staunchly opposed to all traditional social and sexual values, she leaves her husband, travels around the country preaching her anarchist gospel, and participates in an assassination plot and other illegal activities that result in her imprisonment and eventually, her deportation to Soviet Russia. Goldman arrives in Russia ready to embrace the revolution and to serve her "beloved *matushka*," only to be disillusioned once again by Lenin's regime. Exiled both from America and from her Russian motherland, Goldman wanders from place to place in search of an ideal anarchist way of life, ending her life in St. Tropez, where she writes her autobiography.

In keeping with the wandering and subversive nature of her life, Goldman's autobiography takes readers into various forbidden spaces and places. Unlike Antin and Yezierska, who omit all discussion in their autobiographies of their relationships with their husbands, their children, and their attitudes toward sexuality (Antin refers obliquely to her husband as "one of her learned friends," and Yezierska makes veiled references to her affair with philosopher John Dewey), Goldman speaks freely about almost every stage and issue of her sexual history: her sexual awakening, her experience of being date-raped as a young woman, her various lovers, her inability to conceive children, her attitudes about marriage, birth control, and so on. As Betty Ann Bergland notes, what is so remarkable about this long, often rambling text is that in addition to entering into these forbidden private spaces, Goldman also claims a place for women in such public spaces as the lecture and union halls, and the political arena.

Of course, not all immigrant autobiographies present such a radical vision of American Jewish female life. Goldie Stone's *My Caravan of Years: An Autobiography*, Etta Byer's *Transplanted People*, Hilda Polachek's *I Came a Stranger*, Fannie Edelman's *Der Shpigl fun Lebn*, and Aliza Greenblatt's *Baym Fentster fun a Lebn* all concern themselves with issues of professional and personal aspiration and yet endorse the idea of marriage and the traditional family.

What is perhaps even more fascinating is the extent to which seemingly revolutionary or iconoclastic narratives, when examined closely, reaffirm traditional stereotypes and conventional gender roles. *The Autobiography of Alice B. Toklas* by GERTRUDE STEIN, an account of Stein's expatriate life in Paris, written as if from the mouth of her lesbian domestic partner, ALICE B. TOKLAS, is a case in point. On the one hand, the frequent references in the *Autobiography* to Stein's literary genius and her importance as the central figure in Parisian modernism represent a kind of breakthrough: Here is a (Jewish lesbian) woman unabashedly claiming her position as a great modern artist. Of course, Alice B. Toklas's position in the narrative complicates this reading. Throughout the *Autobiography*, Toklas plays the role of wife/female domestic catering to Stein's masculine genius. At the end of the *Autobiography*, Stein mocks Toklas's domesticity outright, suggesting that Toklas title her autobiography "Wives of Geniuses I Have Sat With." Toklas is so much the stereotypical "wife of genius" that she cannot even muster the intelligence to write her own life story. Stein, the real genius, must do it for her. In the end, the *Autobiography* reinforces the same heterosexual stereotypes that it seemed at first to oppose.

A Peculiar Treasure (1940), the autobiography of writer EDNA FERBER, poses a similar problem. On the one hand, Ferber provides an inspiring, iconoclastic account of Jewish female professional success. Despite the advice of an early acquaintance that she "try to do something decent, like teaching school," Ferber becomes a reporter in Milwaukee, working for three years "like a man," and then becomes a best-selling author, beginning with her stories of Emma McChesney, an American businesswoman. On the other hand, by describing her professional life as man's work, Ferber indirectly reinforces the notion that work is a male domain, and that a working woman must shrug off something of her feminine identity in order to gain admittance into this realm. Ferber herself never married or had children. Her autobiography offers little mention of a romantic or personal life. Although she insists she knows "no woman with whom she'd want to exchange places," it is clear that she pays a price for her "masculine" career.

My Life (1975), the autobiograpy of former Israeli prime minister GOLDA MEIR, who emigrated from America to Palestine in 1921, presents yet another account of the pitfalls of living and working "like a man." Meir's political involvements repeatedly take her away from her husband and children. Over and over again in the memoir, she reproaches herself for failing to be a good wife and mother while she pursued a career in public service. Ironically, however, when reflecting on her political career, Meir insists that her "being a woman never hindered her in any way at all," that it never caused her "unease" or made her "think that men are better off than women." Her denial of the relevance of gender in politics belies the extent to which she had to efface her femininity to get where she did in Israeli political life.

Works like Edna Ferber's *A Peculiar Treasure* and Golda Meir's *My Life* are significant today precisely because of the criticism that they provoke. What has emerged as a result of these eight or nine decades of Jewish women's autobiography is a kind of Jewish American woman's autobiographical tradition, in which writers refer to and/or challenge the version of Jewish/American/female identity and life presented by their predecessors. In the same way that Rebekah Kohut invokes such biblical "foremothers" as Sarah and Deborah, and writer Annie Nathan Meyer invokes the inspiration of her poet relative EMMA LAZARUS, contemporary autobiographers celebrate and/or debate the achievements of their predecessor autobiographers. In *Generation Without Memory: A Journey in Christian America* (1981), a personal meditation on the problem of Jewish identity in America, novelist ANNE ROIPHE contrasts her assimilated American perspective with the pious outlook of Glikl of Hameln, a European businesswoman and mother who wrote her memoirs in Yiddish in the late seventeenth and early eighteenth centuries. In *Deborah, Golda and Me* (1991), feminist activist and *Ms.* magazine founder LETTY COTTIN POGREBIN refers to Golda Meir as a "fantasy mother," and yet calls her to task for failing to take possession of her entire identity and for "opting out" of her womanhood. Likewise, in her exquisitely thoughtful and nuanced immigrant autobiography, *Lost in Translation: A Life in a New Language* (1989), Eva Hoffman lovingly recalls her predecessor Mary Antin, and yet criticizes her for being too optimistic in her depiction of the immigrant experience—for foregrounding "certain parts of her own experience, and [throwing] whole chunks of it into the barely visible background."

Where they do not explicitly refer to the work of their predecessors, contemporary Jewish women autobiographers often—consciously or unconsciously—revisit the primary themes of earlier women's autobiographies. *My Mother and I* by Elizabeth Stern, *Of Woman Born: Motherhood as Experience and Institution* (1976) by ADRIENNE RICH, *In My Mother's House* (1983) by KIM CHERNIN, and *Fierce Attachments* (1987) by VIVIAN GORNICK all deal with complicated, sometimes "love-hate" Jewish mother-daughter relationships. Gornick, Rich, and KATE SIMON, in her companion memoirs, *Bronx Primitive: Portraits in Childhood* (1982) and *A Wider World: Portraits in Adolescence* (1986), all touch upon many of the same sexual-political issues treated in Emma Goldman's *Living My Life*. Shulamit Soloveitchik Meiselman's *The Soloveitchik Heritage: A Daughter's Memoir* provides a history of the famous Soloveitchik rabbinic dynasty. In it, Meiselman considers some of the same issues concerning a modern woman's role in the rabbinic world that are treated in Rebekah Kohut's *My Portion* and in a self-published memoir by Esther Bengis entitled *I Am a Rabbi's Wife* (1935). Finally, Isabella Leitner's Holocaust-immigration memoir *Saving the Fragments* tells the story of her arrival in America following her liberation from Auschwitz, in language that roughly approximates the celebratory tones of Antin's and Stern's immigrant autobiographies. Arriving in the United States on V-E Day, Leitner writes, "We cannot believe that we are in the center of modern man's most momentous day. To arrive in America on the very day the war ends is too much for us to demystify." Of course, Leitner's use of the word "demystify" hints at the quasi-illusory nature of the American dream, thus recasting Antin's picture of America. The Jewish female immigrant experience, the changing role of women in American and Jewish life, issues of female sexuality and gender relations, and the act of writing as a kind of liberation or religious redemption are issues that continue to be treated by contemporary American Jewish women, part of an unfolding tradition of American Jewish women's autobiography.

BIBLIOGRAPHY

Antin, Mary. *From Plotzk to Boston* (1899), and *The Promised Land* (1912); Bengis, Esther. *I Am a Rabbi's Wife* (1935); Berg, Gertrude, with Cherney Berg. *Molly and Me* (1961); Bergland, Betty Ann. "Reconstructing the Self in America: Patterns in Immigrant Women's Autobiographies." Doctoral diss., University of Minnesota, 1990; Beyer, Etta. *Transplanted People* (1955); Chernin, Kim. *In My Mother's House* (1983); Cohen, Rose. *Out of the Shadow* (1918); Davidson, Jo. *Between Sittings: An Informal Autobiography* (1951); Dawidowicz, Lucy S. *From That Place and Time: A Memoir* (1989); Demiturk, Emine Lale. "The Female Identity in Cross-Cultural Perspective: Immigrant Autobiographies." Doctoral diss., University of Iowa, 1986; Edelman, Fannie. *The Mirror of Life* (1961), and *Der Shpigl fun Lebn* (1948); Feldman, Rivke. *A Mames Bukh* (1950. Translated as *Mother's Book*, 1950); Ferber, Edna. *A Kind of Magic* (1963), and *A Peculiar Treasure* (1949); Goldman, Emma. *Living My Life* (1931); Gornick, Vivian. *Fierce Attachments* (1987); Greenblatt, Eliza. *Baym Fenster fun a Lebn* (1966); Grossinger, Jennie, as told to Harold Taub. *Waldorf in the Catskills* (1950); Guggenheim, Marguerite. *The Informal Memoirs of Peggy Guggenheim* (1946); Hamburger, Estelle. *It's a Woman's Business* (1939); Hart, Sara L. *The Pleasure Is Mine: An Autobiography* (1947); Hartman, May. *I Gave My Heart* (1960); Hasonovitz, Elizabeth. *One of Them: Chapters from a Passionate Autobiography* (1917); Heilbrun, Carolyn G. *Writing a Woman's Life* (1988); Hilf, Mary Asia, as told to Barbara Bourns. *No Time for Tears* (1964); Hoffman, Eva. *Lost in Translation: Life in a New Language* (1989); Holtman, Rokhl. *Mayn Lebens-Veg* (1948); Hurst, Fannie. *Anatomy of Me: A Wanderer in Search of Herself* (1958); Jastrow, Marie. *Looking Back: The American Dream Through Immigrant Eyes* (1986), and *A Time to Remember* (1979); Kazin, Alfred. "The Self as History: Reflections on Autobiography." In *The American Autobiography: A Collection of Critical Essays*, edited by Albert Stone (1981); Kern, Janet. *Yesterday's Child* (1962); Kohut, Rebekah Bettelheim. *More Yesterdays: An Autobiography* (1950), and *My Portion* (1927); Kositza, Rachel Anna. *Zikhroynes fun a Byalistoker Froy* (1964); Lang, Lucy Robbins. *Tomorrow Is Beautiful* (1948); Leader, Pauline. *And No Birds Sing* (1931); Leitner, Isabella. *Saving the Fragments: From Auschwitz to New York* (1985); Levy, Harriet Lane. *920 O'Farrell Street* (1947); Lifschutz, E. *Bibliography of American and Canadian Jewish Memoirs and Autobiographies* (1970); Lindheim, Irma. *Parallel Quest* (1962); Marcus, Jacob Rader. *The American Jewish Woman: A Documentary History* (1981); Meir, Golda. *My Life* (1975); Meiselman, Shulamit Soloveitchik. *The Soloveitchik Heritage: A Daughter's Memoir* (1995); *Memoirs of Glückel of Hameln.* Translated with notes by Marvin Lowenthal (1932); Meyer, Annie Nathan. *Barnard Beginnings* (1935), and *It's Been Fun* (1951); Nathan, Maud. *Once Upon a Time and Today* (1933); Olney, James. *Autobiography: Essays Theoretical and Critical* (1980); Picon, Molly, as told to Ethel Clifford Rosenberg. *So Laugh a Little* (1962); Pogrebin, Letty Cottin. *Deborah, Golda and Me: Being Jewish and Female in America* (1991); Polachek, Hilda Satt. *I Came a Stranger: The Story of a Hull House Girl.* Edited by Dena J. Polachek (1989); Popkin, Zelda. *Open Every Door* (1956); Pratt, Norma Fain. "Culture and Radical Politics: Yiddish Women Writers in America," in *American Jewish History* (September 1980. Reprinted in *Women of the Word: Jewish Women and Jewish Writing*, edited by Judith Baskin); Rich, Adrienne. *Of Woman Born: Motherhood as Experience and Institution* (1976); Roiphe, Anne. *Generation Without Memory* (1981); Rubin, Steven J. "American Jewish Autobiography 1912 to the Present." In *Handbook of American Jewish Literature*, edited by Lewis Fried (1988), and *Writing Our Lives: Autobiographies of American Jews, 1890–1990* (1991); Rubinstein, Helena. *My Life for Beauty* (1966); Ruskay, Sophie. *Horsecars and Cobblestones* (1949); Simon, Kate. *Bronx Primitive: Portraits in Childhood* (1982), and *A Wider World: Portraits in Adolescence* (1986); Smith, Sidonie. *A Poetics of Women's Autobiography* (1987); Solomon, Hannah Greenebaum. *Fabric of My Life* (1946); Spacks, Patricia. *Imagining a Self: Autobiography and Novel in Eighteenth-Century England* (1976); Stein, Gertrude. *The Autobiography of Alice B. Toklas* (1933); Stokes, Rose Pastor. *I Belong to the Working Class.* Edited by Herbert Shapiro and David L. Sterling (1992); Stone, Goldie. *My Caravan of Years: An Autobiography* (1945); Talbot, Rose. *No Greater Challenge* (1955); Tucker, Sophie. *Some of These Days* (1945); Wald, Lillian. *The House on Henry Street* (1915), and *Windows on Henry Street* (1934); Wengeroff, Pauline. *Memoiren Einer Grossmutter: Bilder aus der Kulturgeschichte der Juden Russlands im 19. Jahrhundert* (1913–1919); Yezierska, Anzia. *Red Ribbon on a White Horse* (1950); Zierler, Wendy. "Border Crossings: The Emergence of Jewish Women's Writing and the Immigrant Experience." Doctoral diss., Princeton University, 1995; Zunser, Miriam Shomer. *Yesterday* (1978).

WENDY ZIERLER

AXMAN, SOPHIE CAHN (1865–1945)

Sophie Cahn Axman was an articulate and opinionated Progressive reformer, a member of the Jewish elite with an uncompromising drive to improve her people.

She was born July 29, 1865, in Washington, D.C., to Joseph and Carrie (Friedenwald) Cahn. After graduating from Mrs. Fröhlich's School in New York, she married Charles David Axman, then a clothing merchant. The

Axmans lived in Kansas City, where Sophie founded the Free Kindergarten for poor Jewish children. After the Spanish-American War, Charles sold his business and went to work for a short time in Cuba. Shortly after the turn of the century, the couple moved back to New York City, where Charles soon joined the prestigious banking house Ladenburg, Thalmann, and Company, and Sophie Axman threw herself wholeheartedly into philanthropy and criminal reform.

Sophie Axman first worked as a "visitor" for United Hebrew Charities (UHC), presumably to ascertain poor Jewish households' worthiness for aid from UHC and educate mothers in matters of household management and child rearing. In 1902, she became the editor of UHC's magazine, *Charity Work*, and continued to write or edit it through its name change in 1903 to *Jewish Charity* until late 1904. She involved herself in charitable and religious work, speaking at the first convention of the NATIONAL COUNCIL OF JEWISH WOMEN, the Jewish Chautauqua Society in Atlantic City, and the Winter School of Philanthropy in New York City and on Blackwells Island (now Roosevelt Island). During this period she wrote for *House Beautiful* magazine and wrote pamphlets on work among children. In her written work, Axman displayed a profound identification with her coreligionists and the lordly concern for the poor of a confident, upper-class woman.

By 1904, Axman and her husband and son Laurence were living in the Educational Alliance's East Side House. Under the alliance's auspices and through her own energetic initiative, Axman had begun to work as a probation officer for Jewish boys. She also administered the East Side House residence, which was an object of contention among Educational Alliance workers. Some thought it should be a true settlement house, inviting neighborhood participation and performing extensive social work, while others regarded it as simply a residence for alliance staff. After a conflict that may have been related to Axman's dedicated committment to social work, she withdrew and the family moved to a private residence on New York's Upper East Side. Axman continued her probation work, but moved from the children's to the special sessions court, whose convicted and accused were housed at the Manhattan House of Corrections, otherwise known as "The Tombs." From 1906 until her retirement in 1923, Axman labored there, earning the sobriquet "The Angel of the Tombs."

Axman's son Laurence became a prominent attorney, and her husband, Charles, continued his banking work until shortly before he died in 1937. Sophie Cahn Axman lived her last years at the Park Central Hotel in Manhattan, until her death in on March 2, 1945, at age seventy-nine.

SELECTED WORKS BY SOPHIE CAHN AXMAN

Charity Work 2, no. 1 (December 1902), and 2, no. 6 (July–August 1903), edited by Sophie Axman; *Jewish Charity*, edited with Lee K. Frankel and Joseph Jacobs (October 1903–July/September 1904); "Jewish Charity." *Jewish Charity* 1 (October 1903): 1–5; "The Northeast End." *Jewish Charity* 1 (October 1903): 16; "Probation Work Among Boys." *Charity Work* 2, no. 6.

BIBLIOGRAPHY

AJYB 7 (1905–1906): 37, 47 (1945–1946): 518; "Charles D. Axman, Retired Banker, 87." *NYTimes*, December 7, 1937, 25:4; Educational Alliance. Minutes. Board of Directors, Educational Alliance, NYC (1904–1906); "Mrs. Charles Axman." *NYTimes*, March 3, 1945, 13:5.

MICOL SEIGEL

B

BA'ALOT TESHUVA

Much of what we know sociologically about contemporary Jewish women's religious experiences comes from qualitative studies of Orthodox Jewish women in which gender is a central category of analysis. Since the division of gender roles is the sharpest in the Orthodox community, this group provides a ready resource for exploring the pivotal role of gender in shaping the religious life of Jews. In 1991, the first two book-length sociological studies of Jewish women were published: Debra Renee Kaufman's *Rachel's Daughters: Newly Orthodox Jewish Women* and Lynn Davidman's *Tradition in a Rootless World: Women Turn to Orthodox Judaism*. Both books begin with the experiences of *ba'alot teshuva* (Jewish women not brought up as Orthodox who have decided to become Orthodox as adults) and explore how these women negotiate within traditional religious institutions in order to find a meaningful place for themselves. Both authors develop an analysis of the meaning of Orthodoxy from the point of view of women and the reasons contemporary secular women are attracted to it.

The *ba'alot teshuva's* decision to explore Orthodox Jewish ways of life represents one possible solution to current widespread questions about women's proper roles. The structural changes in American society in the past thirty years, in particular the changing demographics of women's educational, occupational, marital, and childbearing patterns, have occasioned a debate in our culture about women's nature and social roles similar to the late nineteenth-century "woman question" that followed the Industrial Revolution. Within our society, there are a wide variety of competing definitions and prescriptions for women's roles, far more than there are for men's roles. Traditionalists clash with women's liberationists, and even within the various feminist communities there are numerous alternative visions. Women may now choose among the numerous variants of the "radical" solution (which creates alternative structures of meaning outside the framework of mainstream society), the liberal feminist approach (which seeks equality in the public sphere), and the "traditional" model (which emphasizes the centrality of woman's place in the home). The women who choose Orthodoxy might well espouse liberal feminist solutions for the workplace, but are content to embrace the traditional option for their personal lives.

In her interview-based study of married *ba'alot teshuva* who had been Orthodox for several years, Kaufman presents the women's perspectives on their role in Orthodoxy. Despite their acceptance of traditional roles, these women do not necessarily view themselves as second-class citizens of the Jewish community. Rather, they turn their devalued status in the secular world into a higher status by adopting the roles that the Orthodox community offers. Orthodoxy appeals to *ba'alot teshuva* precisely because of its positive valuation of the feminine and the female in the context of the nuclear family. Kaufman concludes that there are strong similarities between *ba'alot teshuva* and radical feminists, since both groups participate in sex-segregated communities that celebrate gender differences.

Davidman, in her comparative ethnographic study of modern Orthodox and Lubavitch Hasidic communities, also found that in the context of the confusion about gender and family norms in the wider society, Orthodoxy appealed to the new recruits because it offered clarity about gender and prescriptions for family living. Her findings suggest, however, that *ba'alot teshuva* are not postfeminist, as Kaufman contends, but rather, these women are attracted to Orthodoxy because they see it as a socially legitimate alternative to feminism. Instead of the feminist program of broader gender definitions, sexual liberation, emphasis on careers, and acceptance of a variety of family patterns, Orthodox Judaism proposes clearly circumscribed gender norms, control of sexuality, assistance in finding a partner, and explicit guidelines for nuclear family life.

The two types of Orthodox communities she studied differed greatly in their willingness to blend traditional conceptions with modern gender ideals. Davidman shows how these differences led to the attraction of different types of women to each setting. The Lubavitch Hasidic community, which prohibits premarital physical contact between women and men, publicly eschews birth control, and trivializes women's interest in professionalism, attracts relatively young women who are not yet established in careers or independent lives. In contrast, the modern Orthodox community offers a complex blend of the traditional and modern that attracts single, professionally established, independent adults who are seeking assistance in forming nuclear families.

Both Davidman and Kaufman state that *ba'alot teshuva* find Orthodox Judaism appealing precisely because it offers a conception of femininity in which women's roles as wives and mothers are honored and seen as central. Nevertheless, as sociologists of religion point out, there is a "fit" between religious institutions and the needs of the individuals who seek them out. Thus, newly Orthodox women are attracted to the Orthodox vision of Jewish womanhood that best suits their life circumstances. Modern Orthodox rabbis articulate a vision of femininity that not only prioritizes women's roles in the home but also allows women to seek secondary fulfillment in other spheres, such as careers. This conception matches with the needs of the women in the modern Orthodox community Davidman studied, who described themselves as being "settled" at work but wishing to develop a role and identity at home. The Lubavitch rabbis, in contrast, offer a definition of femininity that focuses exclusively on women's roles as wives and mothers. This vision is attractive to the Lubavitch *ba'alot teshuva*, who seek one all-embracing role. In the context of a differentiated society, these diverse groups of women are able to seek out those religious communities that validate their life choices and give them meaning.

These two studies, in which women are the primary focus, build on but also extend in a feminist direction an earlier book about newly Orthodox Jewish women and men, Herbert Danzger's *Returning to Tradition: The Contemporary Revival of Orthodox Judaism.* Danzger reported that most of the newly Orthodox are women and that women are more likely than men to turn to a religious way of life out of a desire to have a family. He provides a gendered analysis of the different routes by which women and men enter the world of Orthodoxy. Many of the men were religious seekers who ventured into yeshivahs to seek deeper knowledge. The women were less likely to be on a spiritual quest; they tended to become Orthodox through synagogue programs and marriage. However, although Danzger's study offers important insights into gender differences, most of his research focuses on male yeshivahs, so that his database on women is much scanter. Regrettably, he also does not always make explicit at what point his discussion includes women and where it refers to men only, thereby making it more difficult to ascertain the distinctive experiences of *ba'alot teshuva* (female) and *ba'alei teshuva* (male).

Ba'alot teshuva are seeking a sense of self-rootedness in a larger continually existing community with a past and a future. They are also in search of an ordered sense of self on a personal level: They are often troubled by the confusion over gender in the wider society and by the lack of comfortable patterns for forming nuclear families. Critics of contemporary culture see the "deinstitutionalization" of the private realm—the transformations in society's norms for courtship, marriage, sexuality, and child rearing—as leading to a sense of anomie and discomfort that provides fertile ground for the growth of spiritual movements, Orthodox Jewish ones included.

BIBLIOGRAPHY

Danzger, Herbert. *Returning to Tradition: The Contemporary Revival of Orthodox Judaism* (1989); Davidman, Lynn. *Tradition in a Rootless World: Women Turn to Orthodox Judaism* (1991); Kaufman, Debra Renee. *Rachel's Daughters: Newly Orthodox Jewish Women* (1991).

LYNN DAVIDMAN

BACALL, LAUREN (b. 1924)

Lauren Bacall's 1944 Hollywood debut in *To Have and Have Not* catapulted this young Jewish actress into instant stardom. Costarring with her husband-to-be, Humphrey Bogart, Bacall soon became known for "The Look"—downturned head, eyes looking up, suggestive of a young woman sexually wise beyond her years. She and Bogart were one of Hollywood's most famous couples, both on screen and off, and Bacall was famous for her characterizations of women whose strong will complemented, rather than detracted from, their sexual attraction. Throughout her career in Hollywood, Bacall has felt economic and social pressure to relinquish a Jewish identity, a demand complicated by her strong allegiance to her first-generation Jewish immigrant family.

Lauren Bacall was born Betty Joan Perske on September 16, 1924, to William Perske and Romanian-born Natalie (Weinstein) Perske. She spent her earliest years in Brooklyn. When she was six years old, her parents divorced, and she and her mother relocated to Manhattan. At age eight, her father stopped his weekly visits, and they remained estranged for the rest of his life. As an only child, Bacall was brought up in the close-knit, extended Weinstein family. In addition to her mother, Natalie Bacal (who changed her and her daughter's last name to the Romanian version of Weinstein), Bacall was especially close to her grandmother Sophie, aunt Renee, and uncles Charlie and Jack and their spouses. Her maternal grandfather, Max Weinstein, had started life in America as a pushcart peddler and quickly earned enough to buy a small candy store in the Bronx. He died at age fifty-five, but Sophie Weinstein managed the candy store successfully enough to send her sons to City College to get law degrees. Natalie Bacal worked as a secretary.

While a student at Julia Richman High School, Bacall took Saturday acting classes at the New York School of the Theater. For a year after high school, she attended the American Academy of Dramatic Arts until economic circumstances forced her to find employment. While looking for work in the theater, Bacall held jobs as a model on Seventh Avenue and as an usher on Broadway. She finally landed a few small roles, but still had to make ends meet by working as a model, this time for *Harper's Bazaar*. After seeing Bacall on the cover of the magazine, Slim Hawks suggested to her producer husband, Howard, that he invite the young woman to Hollywood for a screen test. This invitation was Bacall's big break.

After her initial role in *To Have and Have Not*, having used the name Lauren Bacall, she costarred

In spite of Hollywood's anti-Semitism, "The Look" and her on- and off-screen relationship with Humphrey Bogart combined to make Lauren Bacall a film star. She later returned to her roots on Broadway to great acclaim. [New York Public Library]

with Bogart, whom she married in 1945, in *The Big Sleep* (1946), *Dark Passage* (1947), and *Key Largo* (1948). In 1949, the couple had a son, Stephen, and in 1952 a daughter, Leslie. While committed to her role as wife and mother, Bacall also found time to star in a number of movies, including *Young Man with a Horn* (1950), *How to Marry a Millionaire* (1953), and *Designing Woman* (1957). Humphrey Bogart died in 1957 of throat cancer.

At loose ends in Hollywood without Bogart, Bacall accepted an offer to return to her first love, the theater, in a show called *Goodbye Charlie* (1960). Moving back to New York, Bacall established herself as a consummate stage actress, starring in *Cactus Flower* (1966–1968), *Applause* (1970, 1972, 1973), and *Woman of the Year* (1981–1982). She received Tony Awards for her roles in the latter two shows. While living in New York, Bacall married the actor Jason Robards, Jr. During their marriage (which lasted from 1961 to 1969), she gave birth to her third child, Sam. Bacall won the National Book Award for her autobiography *By Myself* (1979). Her second book, *Now*, was published in 1994.

Lauren Bacall was never known by moviegoers as a "Jewish actress." Indeed, Warner Brothers' first press release on Bacall incorrectly indicated that her family had been in the United States for several generations and implied that they were from the upper echelons of society (and therefore not Jewish). Bacall also deferred to Bogart in the decision to raise Stephen and Leslie as Episcopalians. Aware of the prejudice against Jews expressed by many people in power in Hollywood, Bacall—one of the few Jewish leading ladies of the studio system—did not loudly proclaim her roots. Yet, according to her autobiography, she always felt proud of her Jewish heritage, which was rooted primarily in her love for the Weinstein family. Her values and identity as a Jewish woman were firmly fixed by her upbringing in their midst.

SELECTED WORKS BY LAUREN BACALL
By Myself (1979); *Now* (1994).

FILMOGRAPHY
All I Want for Christmas (1991); *Appointment with Death* (1988); *The Big Sleep* (1946); *Blood Alley* (1955); *Bright Leaf* (1950); *Cobweb* (1955); *Confidential Agent* (1945); *Dark Passage* (1947); *Designing Woman* (1957); *The Fan* (1981); *Gift of Love* (1958); *Harper* (1966); *Health* (1980); *How to Marry a Millionaire* (1953); *Le Jour et la Nuit* (1996); *Key Largo* (1948); *The Mirror Has Two Faces* (1995); *Misery* (1990); *Mr. North* (1988); *Murder on the Orient Express* (1974); *My Fellow Americans* (1996); *Ready to Wear* (1994); *Sex and the Single Girl* (1965); *The Shootist* (1976); *A Star for Two* (1991); *To Have and Have Not* (1944); *Two Guys from Milwaukee* (1946);

Woman's World (1954); *Written on the Wind* (1956); *Young Man with a Horn* (1950).

TELEVISION
"Applause" (1973); "Blithe Spirit" (1956); "Dinner at Eight" (1990); "A Foreign Field" (1993); "From the Mixed Up Files of Mrs. Basil E. Frankweiler" (1995); "Lions, Tigers, Monkey and Dogs" (1979); "A Little Piece of Sunshine" (1989); "Perfect Gentlemen" (1977); "Petrified Forest" (1955); "The Portrait" (1992).

THEATER
Applause (1970, 1972, 1973); *Cactus Flower* (1966–1968); *Goodbye Charlie* (1960); *Sweet Bird of Youth* (1985, 1986); *The Visit* (1995); *Woman of the Year* (1981, 1982); *Wonderful Town* (1977).

BIBLIOGRAPHY
Hyams, Joe. *Bogart and Bacall: A Love Story* (1975); Quirk, Lawrence J. *Lauren Bacall: Her Films and Career* (1986).

KIM KLAUSNER

BAERWALD, EDITH JACOBI (1878–1965)

It was Edith Jacobi Baerwald's fascination with New York City and her humanitarian vision that inspired her to commit her life to social action.

She was born in 1878 to the prominent Jacobi family of San Francisco. Her parents had both come to America from Germany. Her mother's family, the Brandensteins, settled in San Francisco as peddlers during the time of the California Gold Rush. Her father came to America as an immigrant, ultimately settling with his brother in California as a wine merchant. The two Jacobi brothers established a successful wine-selling business in San Francisco, and both married Brandenstein sisters.

When Edith was nearly twelve years old, she and her family began to spend summers in New York City. Enthralled with New York even at that young age, she expressed a desire to attend school on the East Coast. Therefore, it was in New York City, as a volunteer at the University Settlement on the Lower East Side of Manhattan, that she developed a passion for helping others through social work.

Although Baerwald was born into a privileged, upper-class family, her wealth did not isolate her with respect to social class. She was deeply interested in the social structure of New York City, and recognized her ability to contribute to the lives of others less fortunate than herself. She considered volunteer work a social obligation, and poured her time and tireless energy into numerous projects. She especially loved her work as a dance teacher at the Lower East Side settlement houses, where she developed friendships with Jewish women of social and economic backgrounds quite different from her own. Even after the demise of those dance clubs, she and a group of young Jewish women she had met at the University Settlement continued their friendship. They would meet regularly for coffee or for a meal, often at Baerwald's elegant home—a world apart from that of the settlement houses.

Although surrounded by men from prominent families with impressive backgrounds, she led an active and independent life, and did not choose to marry until age thirty. In 1908, she married Paul Baerwald, a partner in the brokerage firm of Speyer and Brothers in London. Baerwald, born in Germany, came to New York in 1898 from England, where he had been an active Jewish philanthropist. A founding member of the Joint Distribution Committee (JDC), a major American agency for the relief of distressed Jews overseas, he shared his wife's commitment to social activism and concern for those in need. A partner in the New York firm of Lazard Frères from 1907 to 1930, he retired in order to devote himself full-time to philanthropy. During their life together and after her husband's death at age eighty-nine on July 2, 1961, Baerwald remained actively involved with the JDC and the Federation of Jewish Philanthropies. She was a founding member of the Greater New York United Jewish Appeal, and served as honorary chair of its Women's Division. In addition, she served as a member of the Mount Sinai Hospital Women's Auxiliary Board for more than thirty years, and was honorary vice president of the Girls and Boys Service League.

Paul and Edith Baerwald had four children: a son, Herman, and three daughters, Pauline Falk, Jane Aron, and Florence Doubilet. The Baerwald children carried on their proud family tradition of philanthropy through continued affiliation with the Federation of Jewish Philanthropies and the Joint Distribution Committee. In addition, Pauline Falk was president of Jewish Family Services and a founder of the New Lincoln School, an institution committed to progressive education.

Edith Jacobi Baerwald died at age eighty-seven on August 8, 1965, in Neptune, New Jersey. Through her deep appreciation for the humanity of all people, she recognized the important role social work could play in bettering the lives of poor and oppressed Jews and non-Jews in the United States and Europe. While she considered it her duty as a woman of means to bring assistance to those in need, her accomplishments were driven by a profound sense of personal commitment and respect for those whose lives she touched.

BIBLIOGRAPHY

AJYB 67 (1966): 531; Falk, Pauline. Interview with author, October 8, 1996; *NYTimes*, July 3, 1961, and Obituary. August 10, 1965, 29:4.

ANDREA BETH LIEBER

BAIRD, CORA (1912–1968)

Cora Baird was half of the world-renowned Bil & Cora Baird Marionettes.

She was born Cora Eisenberg on January 26, 1912, in New York City to Morris and Anne (Burlar) Eisenberg. As a toddler, she was nicknamed "Jimmy Canigo" by her family because, according to her sister, "That's all she ever said: 'Gimme!' and 'Can I go?'"

She attended HUNTER COLLEGE, where she pursued her interest in theater. After college, she studied dance with Martha Graham and was accepted as member of the prestigious Group Theatre, whose roster included Elia Kazan, Clifford Odets, Sanford Meisner, and Morris Carnovsky (who, thirty years later, narrated the Baird production of *L'Histoire du Soldat*). She taught the Graham dance technique at the Toy Theater and performed in a number of their productions. She appeared on Broadway in *Noah* with Pierre Fresnay of the Comédie Française and with Eva Le Gallienne's Civic Repertory Theatre.

In 1937, while working on a production of *Dr. Faustus* directed by Orson Welles, Cora performed the voices of the seven deadly sins. It was during this production that she met Bil Baird, who had created the puppets of the sins. They were married four weeks later on January 13, 1937. After their marriage, she decided to give up her career in the "legitimate" theater and join Bil in his troupe, where she became a full partner. The company became Bil & Cora Baird Marionettes. "My own backyard became a lot more interesting than traipsing the streets for eleven months to get two weeks work, so I switched." According to friends, after their meeting, Bil's female puppets began to look more and more like Cora. Together, they played the vaudeville circuit, produced shows for the Swift Pavillion at the 1939 World's Fair, created

Though she studied dance with Martha Graham and was a member of the legendary Group Theatre, Cora Baird found her ultimate destiny linked with her husband and the Bil & Cora Baird Marionettes. Together they performed for vaudeville, Broadway, television, and industrial film audiences, entertaining and teaching hundreds of thousands of children and adults.

and performed numerous industrial shows, and were part of the Broadway production of the Ziegfeld Follies of 1941.

During the 1940s and 1950s, the Bairds produced a string of industrial films teaching children about nutrition (*The Story of Wheat, Gardening Is Fun*), how to use the telephone (*Party Lines, Adventures in Telezonia*), hygiene, and food handling (*A Boy and His Cow*).

In the 1950s, the Bairds produced shows using the new technology called television. Their biweekly fifteen-minute programs, *Life with Snarky Parker* and *The Bil Baird Show*, created formats for children's programming that have endured to the present day, in addition to appearing regularly on *The Morning Show* and *The Ed Sullivan Show*. An interesting sidebar to this period (the McCarthy era) was the opportunity for Cora Baird to employ the talents of artists who had been blacklisted from employment in areas of the entertainment industry that were considered more "legitimate" than children's entertainment. In addition to their TV shows, the Bairds produced live children's shows that appeared on Broadway (*Davy Jones' Locker, Ali Baba and the Forty Thieves, The Man in the Moon*).

In 1965, the Bairds realized a longtime dream when they opened the Bil Baird Theatre. This was the first Actors Equity repertory theater created exclusively for puppets. The theater ran continuously for eleven years under the auspices of the American Puppet Arts Council, a nonprofit organization that Cora was instrumental in creating, dedicated to furthering the art of the puppet in this country. A total of twenty-eight productions were staged and somewhere in the neighborhood of 240,000 children and adults were introduced to the enchanting world of the puppet.

The Bairds toured India, Afghanistan, and Nepal for the United States Information Agency and toured Russia for the U.S. Cultural Exchange program that was one of the first acts of both countries beginning the end of the Cold War. Cora was moved immensely by the people of these countries and the hardships with which they lived. In India, she was stunned by the "spirit of people who maintained such dignity in the face of such incredible poverty." In Russia, she was moved to tears and visibly shaken when she was "very unofficially" shown a synagogue that had been closed and boarded up. She was incredulous at the concept of "outlawing of a faith."

Cora was diagnosed with lung cancer in the mid-1960s. For the majority of those years, she continued to perform in the shows presented at the Bil Baird Theatre. She performed for the last time in *Winnie the Pooh*, in December 1967, a week before her death.

BIBLIOGRAPHY
NYTimes, December 7, 1967, 52:4; *WWWIA* 5.

PETER B. BAIRD

BAIS YA'ACOV SCHOOLS

Bais Ya'acov schools in the United States continue a Jewish educational movement for girls that began in Poland in 1918 and spread throughout Eastern

Europe in the years before World War II. The name, meaning "House of Jacob," comes from the verse "House of Jacob, come ye, and let us walk in the light of the Lord" (Isa. 2:5).

The now legendary seamstress Sarah Schenirer created an unprecedented formal Jewish education curriculum for girls in order to curb the influence of the strictly secular education that most Jewish girls in Eastern Europe were receiving. Schenirer's ultimate goal was to keep Jewish women within the fold of traditional Judaism by educating them from an early age. In the most famous statement supporting Jewish women's education at that time, the Hofetz Hayim (Rabbi Israel Meir HaCohen, head of the yeshivah in Radin, Lithuania) not only advocated the idea of formally educating girls in religious topics (most previous Jewish education for girls had consisted of oral traditions handed down from mother to daughter) but also expanded the parameters of that education to include Pirkei Avot, a nonlegal tractate of the Mishnah.

Schenirer ran her schools independently, teaching from her home in Cracow, Poland, and aided by young girls who subsequently went to other Jewish communities to establish schools. After two years, Bais Ya'acov was taken over by Agudat Yisrael in Poland, an Orthodox political party. Under the auspices of the Agudat Yisrael, Bais Ya'acov expanded greatly: By 1925, there were thirty schools across Eastern Europe, the *Bais Ya'acov Journal* was published more regularly, seminars were instituted for the training of Bais Ya'acov teachers, and summer camps were established. Three types of Bais Ya'acov schools taught girls of various ages: all-day schools in large cities (secular and Jewish studies), afternoon schools in small towns (Jewish studies only), and vocational and business high schools (only a few, in very large cities). Other organizations related to the Bais Ya'acov schools were established, such as B'nos (Daughters of Agudat Yisrael) and Batya, both providing social and cultural activities for Jewish girls. Support for Bais Ya'acov in Britain and the United Stated came chiefly from more liberal Orthodox elements of the Jewish community.

In addition, under the influence of Agudat Yisrael, which brought in both male and female administrators with modern training from Western Europe, the Bais Ya'acov movement combined modern forms of instruction with traditional content. New buildings were state-of-the-art and pedagogical methods were contemporary, but the content remained strictly traditional. Bais Ya'acov teachers taught girls not only the specific prayers and duties which Jewish women were expected to know but presented secular subjects as if they, too, were part of Judaism. Literature was a venue for teaching the values of Jewish living, and the wonder of God's creation was the underlying theme for science classes.

In the United States, Bais Ya'acov schools—now sometimes called Beth Jacob schools—were developed by Orthodox Jews recently immigrated during and after World War II. Still supported by Agudat Yisrael, the first American Bais Ya'acov school was an elementary day school established in 1937 in the Williamsburg section of Brooklyn; there also were after-school Bais Ya'acov programs for girls who attended public schools. Following the European model of training their own teachers, Bais Ya'acov established a seminary in 1945, a parochial high school in 1948, and another high school in Borough Park in 1958. Schools spread from Brooklyn to Washington Heights and the Lower East Side, with a curriculum of Bible, Jewish history, and Jewish laws and customs. By the early 1960s, there were eighteen Bais Ya'acov elementary and secondary schools, all but two in New York.

In America, where so many Jews focused on living the "American dream," Bais Ya'acov schools contributed to the endeavor within certain Orthodox Jewish communities to protect their girls from assimilating influences. While other Orthodox Jewish parents sent their daughters to colleges and universities, Bais Ya'acov parents discouraged theirs from pursuing secular education. As other Orthodox Jews created a particularly American version of traditional Judaism by combining contemporary popular culture and dress with the observance of Jewish law, the families associated with Bais Ya'acov schools struggled to hold on to a pure, traditional world, free of the assimilating influences of American society. Today, Bais Ya'acov schools are associated with the traditionally, or strictly, Orthodox Jews in the United States.

BIBLIOGRAPHY

Dansky, Miriam. *Rebbetzin Grunfeld: The Life of Judith Grunfeld, Courageous Pioneer of the Bais Yaakov Movement and Jewish Rebirth* (1994); Greenberg, Blu. "Schenirer, Sarah." *The Encyclopedia of Religion*; Gurock, Jeffrey S. *The Men and Women of Yeshiva: Higher Education, Orthodoxy and American Judaism* (1988); Rosengarten, Sudy. *Worlds Apart: The Birth of Bais Yaakov in America, A Personal Recollection* (1992); Rubin, Devora, comp. *Daughters of Destiny: Women Who Revolutionized Jewish Life and Torah Education* (1988); Weissman, Deborah. "Bais Ya'acov: A Historical Model for Jewish Feminists." In *The Jewish Woman: New Perspectives*, edited by Elizabeth Koltun (1976); Weissman, Deborah R. "Bais Ya'acov, A Women's Educational Movement in the Polish Jewish Community: A Case Study in Tradition and Modernity." Master's thesis, New York University (1977).

LAUREN B. GRANITE

BAIZERMAN, EUGENIE (1899–1949)

Artist Eugenie Baizerman rarely exhibited her work and never sold a painting during her lifetime. According to her husband, sculptor Saul Baizerman, although she sought a quiet life to focus on her work, she nevertheless experienced an inner turmoil that manifested itself in the free, expressionistic colors of her canvases.

Born Eugenie Silverman on October 14, 1899, in Warsaw, Poland, the artist grew up in Bessarabia and Odessa, Russia. Her family, from the Caucasus region, had artistic inclinations. Her grandfather collected Near Eastern art objects, while her mother was a semi-professional actress. Her father, a language teacher, would habitually desert the family for long periods of time.

To encourage her artistic talent, the Silvermans hired an art teacher who taught Eugenie a fine style of drawing and shading influenced by the ornamental design work then in vogue. She also studied at the Odessa Art School. When she was fourteen, the family immigrated to the United States. In New York City, she continued to study art at the National Academy of Design and later at the Educational Alliance, a settlement house located on the Lower East Side. Her student work, though finely drawn, was static and subdued in color, showing little of the dynamism that would mark her mature work.

In 1920, she met her future husband, the sculptor Saul Baizerman. The couple traveled to Italy and Paris, where Baizerman's sense of color was awakened. She began to paint in a neo-pointillist style, covering canvases with bright dots. Around 1927, her mature style, characterized by short strokes of vivid color, emerged. She would paint under artificial light in the evenings, since her days were occupied with work in a garment factory and with caring for her daughter, Ugesie.

Fruits, flowers, and childhood memories of naked women bathing in the Black Sea were frequent subjects of Baizerman's art. The garment factories where she worked were another source of inspiration. Toward the end of her life, she created landscape paintings of the deserts and mountains of Arizona.

In her canvases, the riotous colors create a constant tension between surface and depth, between foreground figures and the background. Recognizable forms such as nudes and still-life objects seem to occupy the same plane as the decorative background created by stippled brushstrokes. The artist often compared painting to music. The dynamic effects of her technique present sensations of color and tone in movement.

The Artists Gallery was a great champion of her work, mounting one-woman exhibitions in 1938 and 1950, a husband-and-wife show in 1948, and a retrospective in 1961. A posthumous exhibition was held at the Krasner Gallery in 1964. More recently, her work was displayed at the Zabriskie Gallery in 1988. The Whitney Museum of American Art and the Museum of Modern Art in New York City have paintings by Baizerman in their collections.

Eugenie Baizerman died suddenly in New York City on December 30, 1949, at age fifty.

BIBLIOGRAPHY

Baizerman, Saul. "Eugenie Baizerman and Her Art," April 17, 1950. Artist's file. Museum of Modern Art Library; *EJ*; Gerdts, William H. *Women Artists of America, 1707–1964* (1965); Hills, Patricia, and Roberta K. Tarbell. *The Figurative Tradition and the Whitney Museum of American Art: Paintings and Sculpture from the Permanent Collection* (1980); Obituary. *NYTimes*, December 31, 1949, 15:5, and January 1, 1950, 43:1.

SUSAN CHEVLOWE

BAKER, BELLE (1896–1957)

Belle Baker has been described as a famed torch singer and vaudeville star, as well as a Yiddish, Broadway, and motion picture actress. Among the songs associated with her are "Eili, Eili" and "My Yiddishe Mama." Her style combined the warmth and tender lament of the Yiddish folk song with the modern jazz lyric.

Belle Baker was born in New York City on December 25, 1896, to Hyman and Sarah Becker. She was one of six children. At age eight she was singing for pennies on the street and sold flowers and newspapers. She was educated in public schools, which she left at age nine to make a living in a dress factory.

The stage was her goal. In 1910, she earned three dollars a week at the Peoples Music Hall. Jacob P. Adler, the famous Yiddish actor, heard her, and he hired her to play the part of a boy in his drama *The Homeless* and to sing songs between acts. She sang in the Lower East Side music halls and nightclubs. She later played the Yiddish theater and toured the United States many times.

Baker had a deep, resonant voice and achieved stardom at age twenty when she played the Palace Theatre, sharing the program with Sarah Bernhardt. She performed in the Hammerstein musical *Victoria* and in 1926 in Rodgers and Hart's musical *Betsy*. She appeared in several editions of the Ziegfeld Follies. In

A vaudeville "red hot mama" who could sing a Yiddish ballad and modern jazz with equal ease, Belle Baker introduced songs like "Blue Skies," "All of Me," and "Alexander's Ragtime Band" to the American public.

1933, she performed on radio for the Columbia Network and played music halls in England in 1935, where she danced with the Prince of Wales.

She was one of vaudeville's "red hot mamas" and introduced 163 songs, including "Blue Skies," "All of Me," "Cohen Owes Me $97," and Irving Berlin's "International Rag" and "Alexander's Ragtime Band."

A short, dark, plump woman, she made *Song of Love*, a movie released in 1929. Her last official appearance in public was on the television show *This Is Your Life* in 1955.

Baker was a member of the Deborah Jewish Consumptive Relief Society, Hebrew Convalescent Home, Hebrew Home of the Aged of Harlem, Home of the Daughters of Jacob, Jewish Consumptive Relief Society (Denver), Beth Abraham Home for Incurables, Hebrew Orphan Home, and Temple Beth El (Belle Harbor, Long Island), and served on the council of the American Federation of Actors and the Jewish Theatrical Guild of America.

She was married three times. She married Lou Leslie, a vaudeville actor, in 1913; the marriage ending in divorce in 1919. She then married Maurice Abrahams, a songwriter, on February 16, 1920. They had one son, Herbert Joseph Baker, who became a television and film scriptwriter. He adopted his mother's maiden name for his professional career. Maurice Abrahams died in 1931. Her third marriage, on September 21, 1937, to Elias E. Sugarman, editor of *Billboard*, ended in divorce in 1941.

Belle Baker lived most her life in New York, spending her last years in Beverly Hills, California. She suffered a heart attack in her Beverly Hills home on April 28, 1957, and died shortly thereafter in Cedars of Lebanon Hospital at age sixty-two. She was survived by her son, two brothers, and three sisters.

BIBLIOGRAPHY

AJYB 24:116, 59:474; Lifson, David S. *The Yiddish Theatre in America* (1965); Obituary. *NYTimes*, April 30, 1957, 29:1; *UJE*; *WWIAJ* (1926, 1928, 1938).

OLIVER B. POLLAK

BALABANOFF, ANGELICA
(1878–1965)

Angelica Balabanoff was one of the best-known and widely beloved figures of European socialism in the early decades of the twentieth century. She left home at age nineteen to study in Belgium, and began a lifetime of travel and activism that was to center around the politics of the Second International and bring her into contact with a fascinating range of political figures, including Rosa Luxemburg, Clara Zetkin, Leon Trotsky, V.I. Lenin, EMMA GOLDMAN, Alexander Berkman, and Benito Mussolini. During and after World War I, she was a major figure of the left wing of the Socialist movement and a member of the Zimmerwald Group. She returned to Russia after the Revolution of 1917 and served as an officer of the Comintern before becoming disillusioned by the authoritarianism and corruption of the Bolshevik regime.

Born in Chernigov, near Kiev, in the Ukraine, in 1878, the youngest of sixteen children, seven of whom had died before she was born, Angelica was raised to be the "crown of the family." Her family was quite wealthy—her father was a landowner and businessman—and she was educated at home by a series of governesses and tutors. From early youth, Balabanoff was troubled by the privileges she and her family enjoyed, reporting in her autobiography that she "cringed with shame" at the way the servants regularly humiliated themselves before her and her parents. She attributed her own rebelliousness and commitment to the cause of social justice not to any influence of her Jewish heritage (about which she makes no mention in her autobiography), but to these experiences at home, and her sense of an "unbridgeable abyss" between herself and her "despotic" mother.

She left home in 1897 to study at the Université Nouvelle in Brussels, an institution known for its radicalism. There, she hoped to learn how to translate her passion for social justice into more practical strategies for aiding the downtrodden. Through the combination of classes at the university and meetings at the socialist-sponsored People's House, she met and was deeply influenced by George Plekhanoff and a variety of other Russian and Italian emigrés, who befriended her and introduced her to many of the major figures of the Second International. After doing research in the library of the British Museum, she returned to Brussels, receiving a doctorate in philosophy and literature from the Université Nouvelle. She then went to Leipzig, and on to Rome, where she studied with the Italian Marxist philosopher Antonio Labriola and began what was to be a lifelong relationship with the Italian (and, ultimately, international) socialist movement.

From 1901 to 1902, she worked with Italian immigrant workers in Switzerland, and organized among young women who had been recruited by the Swiss to be a docile labor force. Although she was hostile to feminism, which she viewed as bourgeois, she was deeply committed to addressing the needs of working-class women as well as men—needs she believed would be best met through socialist transformation. She was extremely successful as both a speaker and a journalist. Elected to the executive committee of the Italian Socialist Party in Switzerland, she served as its official representative to congresses of the Second International in 1907 and 1910. Also during this period, she met and befriended a poor Italian emigré, Benito Mussolini, helping him to find work and introducing him to socialist clubs in which he, too, became active.

In 1910, she left Switzerland for Italy, where she began her active involvement in the Italian socialist movement. In the ensuing years, she was elected to the party's Central Committee; served as coeditor of the party's official organ, *Avanti;* and increasingly came to support the more revolutionary (antireformist) wing of the Italian Socialist Party. Disillusioned by the failure of socialist internationalism in 1914, she helped to found and remained active throughout the war in the Zimmerwald movement, an organization of socialists protesting imperialism and demanding immediate peace. Her fluency in many languages, combined with her strong commitment to international socialism and her popularity as a public

At an early age, Angelica Balabanoff rejected the privileged life into which she had been born and turned to socialism. She would become one of the leading spokespersons of that cause, in the process associating with political notables such as EMMA GOLDMAN, *V.I. Lenin, and Benito Mussolini. [Schlesinger Library]*

speaker, made her an indispensable figure at socialist conferences and conventions.

Although she rejected Lenin's call for socialist revolutions to end the war, she returned to Russia in 1917 to help rally international support for revolutionary Russia. Despite her reservations (which she shared with Emma Goldman and Alexander Berkman, during their exile in Russia), she became secretary of the Communist International in 1919, but was removed from that position after about a year for opposing the corrupt and manipulative tactics of Lenin and Zinoviev.

Early in 1921, she left Russia forever. In the ensuing years, she suffered from a continuing campaign of slander on the part of Lenin and his associates. After living for a while in Vienna and in Paris, she spent the years of World War II in New York City, where she became friends with Norman Thomas and was an occasional contributor to *Socialist Review.* Balabanoff dedicated herself to awakening the American population to the dangers of Italian fascism, publishing *The Traitor: Benito Mussolini and His "Conquest" of Power,* as well as her autobiography, *My Life as a Rebel.* At the end of the war, she returned to Italy, where she continued to be active in the Italian Socialist Party. She died in Rome on November 25, 1965.

SELECTED WORKS BY
ANGELICA BALABANOFF

Impressions of Lenin (1964); *My Life as a Rebel* (1938); *The Traitor: Benito Mussolini and His "Conquest" of Power* (1942–1943).

BIBLIOGRAPHY

The Continuum Dictionary of Women's Biography; Florence, Ronald. *Marx's Daughters: Eleanor Marx, Rosa Luxemburg, Angelica Balabanoff* (1975); Mullaney, Marie Marmo. *Revolutionary Women: Gender and the Socialist Revolutionary Role* (1983); Obituary. *NYTimes,* November 26, 1965, 37:3; *UJE;* Wolfe, Bertram D. *Strange Communists I Have Known* (1966).

MARTHA ACKELSBERG

BAMBER, GOLDE (1862–193?)

Described as a stiff Victorian woman from an old Boston Jewish family, Golde Bamber applied her education and cultured upbringing to become one of Boston's pioneer social reformers and educators among the city's Eastern European immigrants.

Born in Boston in 1862, Bamber was raised among the city's small, elite German Jewish community. In 1879, she graduated from the Boston University's School of Oratory and began teaching elocution lessons privately and at the Young Men's Hebrew Association. But the great tide of Eastern European immigrants that exploded Boston's Jewish population from approximately five thousand in 1880 to forty thousand by 1900 drew Bamber's attention, and she joined the female Jewish leadership in Boston dedicated to relieving the immigrants' poverty and preparing them for life as fully integrated American citizens.

Invited by LINA HECHT in 1889 to evaluate Hecht's new Jewish Sunday school, Bamber instead recommended a program that would teach immigrant girls skills in sewing and cooking, as well as provide a basic American and Jewish education. In January 1890, the Hebrew Industrial School for Girls (HIS) opened with twenty pupils on Hanover Street in Boston's North End. Funded by Lina and Jacob Hecht, Bamber served as the school's superintendent and director for four decades. In 1892, its partner Hebrew Industrial School for Boys opened on Chambers Street in Boston's West End. In their first five years alone, Bamber's schools trained more than twelve hundred children to be "wage earners, breadwinners,

and self-respecting citizens," overcoming initial opposition within the Jewish community to vocational training and manual labor. Educational clubs, vocational classes, even a "Soap and Water" club, taught good citizenship, self-sufficiency, American manners and morals, and the foundations of Jewish knowledge and culture. The school's motto, "A good Israelite will make a better citizen," summarized Bamber's conviction that Jewish and American traditions were compatible and productive, and not antithetical as Boston's virulent anti-immigration movement argued. Much of Boston's non-Jewish leadership agreed.

The HIS's successes garnered financial and political support from Boston's leading Brahmin philanthropists and institutions, including Unitarian Revered Edward Everett Hale who asserted that "the much-dreaded Russian Jew . . . because he has been welcomed with wisdom and kindness, proves to be . . . a model emigrant." Bamber's HIS, along with Boston's North Bennett Street Industrial School, served as a pioneering model for the entire settlement house movement in the Northeast. Bamber's own achievements were recognized by Massachusetts Governor Curtis Guild, who appointed her a trustee for the Lyman School for Boys.

Bamber kept her own education current with her innovations. During the 1890s and early 1900s, she studied vocational guidance and social work with Frederick Allen at Harvard College and Simmons College of Social Work. By the end of World War I, the settlement house approach of the HIS had run its course, and Bamber changed her school with the times. In 1922, the school's name changed to the Hecht Neighborhood House, and with funds from the bequest of Lina Hecht, purchased a Charles Bullfinch–designed house on Bowdoin Street in the West End. Bamber served as director until her retirement in 1930, introducing one of the nation's first nursery schools there in 1925 and transforming the institution from a vocational and educational institution for Jewish children and women to a full-service, nonsectarian community center for the West End's broadly mixed ethnic population.

Golde Bamber was a leader in the emergence of a young, educated, professional class of Jewish women—both from established and immigrant families—who worked cooperatively to create Boston's new charitable and educational infrastructure for the early twentieth century. Bamber envisioned, institutionalized, and directed new educational structures for the new social landscape. Her pioneering work influenced settlement house, vocational, Jewish, and nursery school education well beyond Boston and well beyond her lifetime.

BIBLIOGRAPHY

Bamber, Golde. "Russians in Boston." *Lend a Hand* 8 (1892): 168–172; Combined Jewish Philanthropies of Greater Boston. Papers. American Jewish Historical Society, Waltham, Mass.; Hecht Neighborhood House. Papers. American Jewish Historical Society, Waltham, Mass.; Solomon, Barbara Miller. *Pioneers in Service: The History of the Associated Jewish Philanthropies of Boston* (1956).

ELLEN SMITH

BAMBERGER, FLORENCE (1882–1965)

Educational administrator, professor, and author, Florence Bamberger devoted her life and career to developing and implementing her progressive views on teaching, teacher education, and scientific educational supervision. Her commitment to supervisory models of pedagogy continues to influence schools of education today.

Florence Bamberger was born on October 19, 1882, in Baltimore, Maryland, to Ansel and Hannah (Eilau) Bamberger. She was educated at Columbia University, receiving a B.S. from Columbia Teachers College in 1914, an M.A. in 1915, and a Ph.D. in 1922.

Bamberger's early career in the Baltimore public school system led to her position as the first female school supervisor in Baltimore. In 1916, she launched a long association with Johns Hopkins University, beginning as an instructor of education in 1916 and becoming in 1924 the first woman elected to the faculty of the school of philosophy as a full professor. From 1930 to 1937, Bamberger served as the executive secretary of the executive committee of the Johns Hopkins College for Teachers, and in 1937, she was appointed director of the College for Teachers.

A prolific contributor to educational journals, she also wrote several books in the field. Bamberger lectured on parental education under the auspices of the Child Study Association of America and taught pedagogy courses at the Universities of Pennsylvania and Chicago. Bamberger focused her life around her professional concerns and commitment to improving education for children. She maintained numerous professional affiliations, including the National Society for Study of Education, the National Society of College Teachers of Education, the National Education Association, the Baltimore Educational Society, and the American Academy of Political and Social Science. Her membership in Phi Beta Kappa, the American Association of University Women, the International Peace Council, and the Baltimore League of Women Voters reflected her political interests in women's achievement and influence.

After retiring from Johns Hopkins, she taught at several private elementary schools in Baltimore and served as the chair of the board of trustees of the William Deiches Fund, an organization providing scholarships to Baltimore public school students. In later years, Bamberger's work centered on designing curricula for teacher training.

Florence Bamberger died in Baltimore on December 18, 1965.

SELECTED WORKS BY FLORENCE BAMBERGER

Effect of Physical Make-Up of the Book on Children's Selection (1922); *Guide to Children's Literature*, with A.M. Broening (1931); *Syllabus Guide for Observation of Demonstration Lessons* (1938).

BIBLIOGRAPHY

AJYB 24:116; Bamberger, Florence Eilau. Files. Maryland Room, Enoch Pratt Free Library, Baltimore, Md.; *BEOAJ*; *EJ* (1972); Helmes, Winifred G., ed. *Notable Maryland Women* (1977); Marcus, Jacob Rader. *The American Jewish Woman, 1654–1980* (1981); *NYTimes*, December 2, 1926, February 13, 1928, May 18, 1938; "Personalities and Projects: Social Welfare in Terms of Significant People." *Survey* 86 (December 1950): 564–565; *UJE*; *WWIAJ* (1926, 1928, 1938).

MELISSA KLAPPER

BARA, THEDA (1890–1955)

Long before Mae West, Greta Garbo, Marlene Dietrich, Jean Harlow, and Madonna vamped their way across the silver screen, there was Theda Bara—the original celluloid "vamp."

Born Theodosia Goodman on July 22, 1890, in Cincinnati, she was the daughter of Bernard Goodman, a Jewish tailor from Chorsel, Poland, and Pauline Louise Françoise de Coppet, who was Swiss of French descent. Bara had an older brother named Marque and a younger sister named Lori.

At age eighteen, she decided to become an actress and moved to New York City. Seven years later, she became known throughout the country as the sex goddess of the silent screen. Between 1915 and 1919, she starred in forty films as a deadly seductress, ushering in the age of the "vamp," a word that came to be used as both noun and verb. In movies with such titles as *Sin, Destruction, The Serpent, Salome,* and *Cleopatra,* she played exotic and wicked characters who lured helpless men to their ruin.

"A horribly fascinating woman" is the way one review heralded the arrival of the scandalous Theda Bara in A Fool There Was, *the movie that made her an overnight sensation. Her novalike career as the first "vamp" of the silver screen was all but over in five years. [New York Public Library]*

Her fame began in 1915, when director Frank Powell discovered her and asked her to star in a Fox Film Company production titled *A Fool There Was*. Realizing that her career on the stage was not progressing, she reluctantly accepted. Concerned about casting an unknown actress alongside the well-known Broadway star Edward Jose, William Fox, head of Fox Film Company, staged the first ever sensationalized publicity campaign. Fox's press agents promptly changed Theodosia Goodman's name and origins. "Theda Bara," they announced, was an anagram for "Arab Death." Born in the shadow of the Sphinx, they claimed, she was the daughter of a French artist and his Arabian mistress. In reality, Theda was a contraction of Theodosia, and Bara came from her maternal grandfather's name, François Baranger de Coppet.

A Fool There Was was based on Porter Emerson Browne's 1909 stage melodrama, which in turn was based on Rudyard Kipling's poem "The Vampire." Kipling had been inspired by Sir Edward Burne-Jones's painting of the same name. The story revolved around a temptress who squeezed everything out of men—money, dignity, and finally life itself.

Little did Fox have to worry about casting the unknown Bara—she was an overnight sensation. The *New York Dramatic Mirror* wrote: "Miss Bara misses no chance for sensuous appeal in her portrayal of the Vampire. She is a horribly fascinating woman, vicious to the core, and cruel. When she says 'Kiss me, my fool,' the fool is generally ready to obey and enjoy a prolonged moment, irrespective of the less enjoyable ones to follow."

Her large black eyes, accentuated by heavy kohl makeup, set off her rounded, dead-white face. Elaborate props such as a tiger-skin rug and a long gold cigarette holder embellished her exoticism, as did her penchant for veils, crowns, large hoop earrings, and bronze bangles. With her long, dark hair and voluptuous figure draped in low-cut gauzy gowns, the vamp perpetuated a familiar stereotype of European passion and exoticism. At the same time, the character created a popular image of women as sensual yet powerful. The vamp dominated and triumphed over men, and contrasted sharply with the clean-cut WASPish characters portrayed by Mary Pickford and Lillian Gish.

Bara scandalized the mores of the middle classes. Meetings held across the country put the burgeoning film industry on trial and focused on Theda Bara—the vampire, the wickedest woman in the world, as she was billed by Fox. Of one film, a critic wrote, "Were the National Board of Censorship possessed of any judgment whatsoever, this is the kind of picture it should place the ban of its disapproval upon." Local boards issued edicts condemning her films.

But her popularity was unstoppable. In 1915 alone, she starred in eleven pictures. Labeled "Hell's Handmaiden," she received two hundred letters a day, including over a thousand marriage proposals. Adoring fans named their babies after her. Her movies ran continuously, sometimes playing six times a day.

Some fans failed to distinguish Bara from her fictionalized roles. One bitter moviegoer wrote, "It is such women as you who break up happy homes." Bara replied, "I am working for my living, dear friend, and if I were the kind of woman you seem to think I am, I wouldn't have to." Another, a criminal defendant, claimed that he killed his mother-in-law after viewing one of Bara's films.

Bara defended her role: "The vampire that I play is the vengeance of my sex upon its exploiters. You see, I have the face of a vampire, but the heart of a feministe." But she also worried about the image she perpetuated: "I try to show the world how attractive sin may be, how very beautiful, so that one must be always on the lookout and know evil even in disguise." Besides, she added, "Whenever I try to be a nice, good little thing, you all stay away from my pictures."

Fox refused to renew her contract after 1919. More significantly, by 1920 the movie industry had reached a larger public. Filmmakers such as Cecil B. DeMille cleaned up the vamp image for a wider audience. No longer menacing or mysterious, stars like Clara Bow and Louise Brooks exuded a cleaner image of sex and sexuality.

After 1919, Bara did some stage work and starred in two more films in 1925 and 1926. In 1921, she married director Charles Brabin. Their marriage lasted until her death on April 7, 1955. Theda Bara created, with her characterization of the vamp, a seminal and enduring image of female sexuality in American popular culture. Tragically, *A Fool There Was* is the only one of her films that has survived intact.

BIBLIOGRAPHY

AJYB 24: 117; Bodeen, Dewitt. "Theda Bara: The Screen's First Publicity-made Star Was a Woman of Sensibility." *Films in Review* 19 (May 1968): 266–287; *DAB* 5; Ewen, Elizabeth. *Immigrant Women in the Land of Dollars* (1985); Koszarski, Richard. *An Evening's Entertainment: The Age of the Silent Feature Picture, 1915–1928*. In *History of American Cinema Series*. Vol. 3 (1990); MacCann, Richard Dyer. *The Stars Appear* (1992); *NAW* modern; Obituary. *NYTimes*, April 8, 1955; Zierold, Norman. *Sex Goddesses of the Silent Screen* (1973).

SUZANNE WASSERMAN

BARIGHT, CLARICE (1881–1961)

Known to her contemporaries as the "Lady Angel of the Tenement District," Clarice Baright was a social worker and a trailblazing attorney who combined these skills as an advocate for the rights of New York City's children and its poor. In a career spanning the first half of the twentieth century, Baright fought for reforms in the style and spirit of the Progressive Era, while earning the distinctions of serving as the second female magistrate in New York City history and of being among the first few women admitted to the American Bar Association.

The only child of Jewish parents, Elizabeth and Shussman Margoles, Baright was born Sadie Margoles in Vienna, Austria, in 1881. Her family immigrated to New York's Lower East Side when she was three years old. After graduating from New York University as a young adult,, she returned to Europe to study social conditions and then enrolled in the night division of

New York University's law school in 1903. Although she was not a candidate for a law degree, and never received one, she was admitted to the New York State Bar Association in 1905.

The following year Clarice married insurance agent George Frances Baright, the son of a Protestant minister. George had two daughters from a previous marriage, Gertrude and Dorothy, whom Baright embraced as her own. For the next ten years she devoted herself to the problems of juvenile delinquency, combining fieldwork with theoretical endeavors such as authoring works on the psychology of child crime and developing and promoting the idea of a juvenile police force.

Baright's hard work in this area was recognized in 1915, when she was recommended for a seat on the bench of the New York City Court of Special Sessions

Without benefit of a law degree, Clarice Baright was admitted to the New York State Bar Association and as a lawyer worked to protect citizens' rights and solve the problem of juvenile delinquency. Though often mentioned as a judicial candidate, she was appointed only once, serving a thirty-day term.
[Library of Congress]

in the Family Court division. Her candidacy was rejected at this time by Mayor John Mitchel, so Baright threw her energies into the practice of law, reputedly becoming the first woman to try a case before an army general court-martial. After gaining admission to the New York State and American Bar Associations in 1916 and 1919, respectively, she further distinguished herself in 1925 by serving as legal adviser to the Metropolitan Housewives League and other civic groups fighting for improvements in the then privately owned subway system.

Baright's career took an even more public turn later that year, when she was appointed by Mayor John Hylan to the same court from which she had been denied a seat a decade earlier. While this appointment made her New York's second female magistrate, she served only a thirty-day term as a replacement for one of the other judges, who was ill. Seeking a more permanent judicial position, she was passed over by Mayor James Walker for the same court in 1927 and by Governor Herbert Lehman for a New York State Supreme Court vacancy in 1934. Undeterred, Baright remained active in politics, generally supporting and advising Democratic candidates.

She also kept up an active legal practice, maintaining an affiliation with the law firm Markewich and Null, which later became Markewich, Rosenhaus, Beck, and Garfinkle. She became a formal member of this firm in 1950, and remained one until her retirement from legal practice in 1958. Her death in January 1961 brought to a conclusion a life filled with both accomplishments and disappointment. Unable to secure more than a temporary position in government, Baright was nevertheless a crusader for women in the legal profession and a vigorous and effective advocate for social justice.

BIBLIOGRAPHY

Krone, Judith P. "Clarice Margoles Baright." Advanced reference paper, Emory University, December 1979; "Mrs. Baright, Ex-Lawyer, Author, Dies." *New York Herald Tribune*, January 9, 1961, 25; "Mrs. Baright, 75, A Former Judge." *NYTimes*, January 9, 1961, 39:2; *UJE*.

I. SCOTT MESSINGER

BARON, SADI MURIEL (1889–1961)

Like many mothers of celebrities, Sadi Muriel Baron might be considered famous because of her child, rather than because of her own personal accomplishments. Baron was the mother of Dr. Richard Raskind, who became one of the most famous American male-to-female transgender personalities when he was transformed into Dr. Renée Richards in 1976. However, Baron was herself a success story. Baron was a pioneering neurologist and psychiatrist who maintained her own private practice well into the 1950s. Indeed, one might argue that perhaps Renée derived her strength and determination to follow her heart after the example set by her mother.

Born on April 1, 1889, Baron grew up in Bryn Mawr, Pennsylvania, the elder of two daughters. Her religious father pushed her toward a medical career as would have been traditional with a Jewish firstborn son. As a consequence, she maintained a defiant, headstrong identity as a professional Jewish woman throughout her life. This was evident in her educational accomplishments. Baron graduated at the top of her high school class, was among the top graduates of Bryn Mawr College, and was first in her class at the Women's Medical College of Pennsylvania in Philadelphia.

In the late 1920s, after her medical training, Baron became the first female resident at Columbia-Presbyterian Medical Center's Neurological Institute in New York City. During this time, Baron married Dr. David Raskind, who had established a successful medical practice in Long Island City, and the couple moved to Sunnyside, Queens. Baron refused to take her husband's last name, since she felt that to do so would undermine her struggle against traditional notions of what a good Jewish wife was "supposed" to be. In 1929, she gave birth to a daughter, Michael, and in 1934 to a son, Richard. According to Renée Richards's revealing autobiography, *Second Serve* (1983), during his early life as Richard, he never discussed his gender dysphoria with his mother, with whom he enjoyed an intimate, though often strained, relationship.

Although Baron had always planned to become a neurosurgeon, in 1937 she decided to abandon her aspirations—and what she considered neurosurgery's exclusive world of male privilege—to become a psychiatrist. In 1939, the Baron-Raskind household relocated to Forest Hills, Queens. During the 1940s, Baron not only maintained a successful private practice from her own home, but served on the faculty at Columbia-Presbyterian's Department of Psychiatry. Baron also became active in several public health agencies, where she used her talents as a skilled clinician and administrator to counsel poor and low-income families in Queens. After a lifetime of professional achievement, Baron was diagnosed with rectal cancer and died, less than a year later, on August 12, 1961.

BIBLIOGRAPHY

BEOAJ; Richards, Renée, with John Ames. *Second Serve: The Renée Richards Story* (1983); Obituary. *NYTimes*, August 14, 1961, 25:3; *Who's Who of American Women* (1961).

DAVID SERLIN

BARR, ROSEANNE *see* ROSEANNE

BARRON, JENNIE LOITMAN (1891–1969)

Even as a schoolgirl, Jennie Loitman Barron ignored society's limits and set high goals for herself. In her long career as a lawyer and a judge, and in her lifelong work for women's rights, she set many precedents for women in Massachusetts and across the United States.

Jennie Loitman Barron was born on October 12, 1891, to Russian immigrant parents Fannie and Morris Loitman. She was one of four daughters and grew up in Boston's West End with few material benefits. "Money isn't important," her mother told her. "It can be lost or stolen. Learning is the thing that enriches your spirit—and that, no one can take from you." Jennie never forgot that advice.

Out of necessity, she worked part-time while attending high school. In spite of the hours away from her studies, she graduated as valedictorian from Girls' High School in Boston at age fifteen and went straight to college. Selling books door to door and teaching Americanization classes at night did not postpone her graduation. In fact, she earned a four-year degree from Boston University in only three years, and was awarded her law degree two years after that. In 1914, she received her master of law from the same university, one of the few women to earn such a high degree.

"It's a 365-day-a-year job," Jennie Barron said of her appointment as the first woman on the Massachusetts Superior Court in 1957. That work ethic allowed her to break a number of gender barriers in her career, both on state and national levels. She is pictured here with her grandchildren in 1942. [Schlesinger Library]

While still at college, Jennie joined the suffragist movement. She organized and became the first president of the Boston University Equal Suffrage League, marching with her fellow members in parades and giving soapbox speeches. Even after women had gained the right to vote in 1920, she continued working for women's rights. She was a delegate to the National Committee of Uniform Laws Regarding Marriage and Divorce in 1930, and lobbied for the right of women to serve as jurors.

After being admitted to the Massachusetts bar in 1914, she opened her own law practice in Boston. Unlike many other committed suffragists, she supported America's involvement in World War I and became executive secretary of the Liberty Loan Bond Committee. Just before the end of the war, in June 1918, she married her childhood sweetheart, Samuel Barron, also a Massachusetts lawyer. By the end of that year, the couple opened up a joint practice, Barron and Barron. Their partnership lasted until 1934, when Jennie Barron was appointed assistant attorney general of Massachusetts.

Beginning with that first appointment, Barron broke many barriers. She was the first woman to try a major criminal case in her state. A few years later, in 1937, she was named associate justice of the Boston Municipal Court, the first woman to serve as a full-time justice in Massachusetts. She was the first mother on the Boston School Committee, and the first female United States delegate to the United Nations Congress on Crime and Juvenile Delinquency. In 1957, she was the first woman to be appointed justice of the Massachusetts Superior Court.

"It is a 365-day-a-year job," Barron said, "because when not in court there are decisions to be written, citations to be looked up, problems to be pondered."

In spite of her demanding job, Barron found time and energy to accept international appointments, travel all over the world, and raise three daughters, Erma, Deborah, and Joy. She remained close to her expanding family, gathering them at her Sabbath table every Friday night. In 1959, already a grandmother, she was awarded the National Mother of the Year Award by American Mothers, Inc.

Barron actively participated in numerous volunteer organizations. She was the first president of the Women's Division of the AMERICAN JEWISH CONGRESS, national board member of HADASSAH, and honorary president of Beth Israel Hospital and the Boston Women's Division of the American Jewish Congress. In addition, she was a director of the Home Owners Cooperative Bank and chair of the League of Women Voters.

In June 1968, Jennie and Samuel Barron were honored by hundreds of friends and public officials on the occasion of their golden wedding anniversary. Just one week later, Samuel Barron died. Jennie Loitman Barron died the following year, on March 28, 1969. She was seventy-seven years old and had remained on the bench until her heart attack the week before. In a previous statement about her work, Barron had defined as her goals "to make our city, our country better, to promote human brotherhood, to be good citizens." The crowd of dignitaries of all religions and political parties who attended her funeral attested to her success in achieving those goals.

BIBLIOGRAPHY

Barron, Jennie L. Papers. Schlesinger Library, Radcliffe College, Cambridge, Mass.; *BEOAJ*; *Boston Globe*, March 28, 1969; *EJ*; Kuzmack, Linda Gordon. *Woman's Cause: The Jewish Woman's Movement in England and the United States, 1881–1933* (1990); *NAW* modern; Obituary. *NYTimes*, March 30, 1969, 71:5; *UJE*; *WWIAJ* (1928 addenda, 1938).

EMILY TAITZ

BARSKY, EVANGELYN (1894–1936)

The screaming headline on the front page of the *Wilmington Journal Every Evening* on Monday, September 14, 1936, bespoke Evangelyn Barsky's importance to the city and state: "MISS EVANGELINE [sic] BARSKY KILLED IN AUTOMOBILE MISHAP." The forty-two-year-old assistant city solicitor of Wilmington, Delaware, was the first Republican woman appointed to a legal post and, with Sybil Ward, one of the first two women lawyers regularly admitted to practice in Delaware. When the car her friend was driving took a curve at high speed, skidded on a wet road, and crashed into a telephone pole, Barsky's vibrant, successful life ended prematurely.

Born in Wilmington on March 31, 1894, Barsky was the youngest of four children and only daughter of Russian-born Nathan and Rose (Ostro) Barsky. As Nathan Barsky was a successful dry-goods merchant and realtor, the children did not have to struggle to obtain their education. Barsky and two of her brothers became lawyers. Her brother Joseph became a doctor.

Barsky went to Wilmington High School and then Goucher College, graduating with a B.A. in 1916. She continued at the University of Pennsylvania, earning an M.A. in 1918 and an LL.B. in 1922. During World War I, she was in the women's motor car corps, driving trucks and ambulances. She also taught school in Wilmington. Politically active with friends in the Democratic and Republican parties, she campaigned for the Republican Party and worked for the advancement of women. In 1936, she attended the Republican National Convention.

Delaware's progress in granting women equal rights was among the slowest in the nation. In 1920, the state did not ratify the Nineteenth Amendment granting women suffrage, and the whipping post was still legal. Not until a new section was added to the state constitution in January 1923, barring sex as a disqualification from holding office, were women able to practice law in the state. Delaware was among the very last states to admit women to the bar.

In February 1923, Barsky and Sybil Ward applied for admission to practice; they were admitted, and took the oath on March 26, 1923. Barsky practiced law with her brother Victor from 1923 until she was appointed assistant city solicitor, taking office on July 2, 1935.

She was a member of the League of Women Voters, New Century Club, American Association of University Women, and the New Castle County, Delaware State, and American Bar Associations. Her parents were founders of Temple Beth Emeth and donors of a cottage to the Brandywine Sanitarium, and her mother was a founder of the Jewish Home for the Aged. Barsky took up where they left off by supporting these institutions.

This pioneer woman lawyer of Delaware, taken in the prime of life, was honored in death. Hundreds of people—family, ordinary citizens, and officials—led by Mayor Walter W. Bacon, attended Evangelyn Barsky's funeral. Flags were flown at half-staff throughout the city. After funeral services at the home she shared with her brother, Dr. Joseph Barsky, she was buried in Beth Emeth Memorial Park Cemetery.

BIBLIOGRAPHY

Frankel, Estella, and Mrs. Sigmund Schoor. Interviews with author, May 1958; Thomas, Dorothy. *Women, the Bench, and the Bar* (forthcoming); *Wilmington* (Delaware) *Journal Every Evening*, September 14, 1936.

DOROTHY THOMAS

BARTH, BELLE (1911–1971)

Belle Barth was born Annabelle Salzman in East Harlem, New York, on April 27, 1911. With three brothers, Moe, Abe, and Saul, and one sister, Paula, Annabelle had a virtual audience of siblings. Not much is known about her childhood, but recognition of her talent as a musician and comedian clearly came

early, as her performance as a student at Julia Richman High School demonstrates. Upon graduation from high school, she billed herself as a singer-pianist who also did impersonations. Singing her way through popular standards and performing imitations of SOPHIE TUCKER, Al Jolson, Harry Richman, and Gypsy Rose Lee kept Barth employed on the vaudeville circuit through the 1930s and 1940s.

The character of her act changed in the 1950s, when she began to mix her two talents—music and comedy—and added a splash of "red hot mama" for good measure. In other words, Barth capitalized on the emerging field of adult comedy that emphasized overtly sexual material. This sort of comedy teetered perilously on the brink of obscenity, and the police were often part of Barth's audience. However, as long as her acts were confined to small clubs, avoided religious gags, and maintained a one-liner approach, she avoided clashes with the law. In addition, Barth often delivered particularly vulgar references in Yiddish, a language familiar to its native speakers but exotic to the uninitiated. In either case, the result was less crude. Indeed, this interplay between crude and coy characterized her style. Critic Ron Smith points to this interplay as the element that made her comedy particularly effective: "She was especially good at contrasting a coquette's conversational sweetness with the sudden brawling howls of a Brooklyn bordello madam." Barth described her act: "She says dirty words in a cute way and everybody digs her the most."

Her upbeat rendition of herself did not take into account the personal difficulties that she endured. She married and divorced four times before finding companionship with George Martin, her fifth husband. In addition, she battled a drinking problem. Occasionally too drunk to tone down her act, Barth was arrested for obscenity.

Notwithstanding these personal struggles, she traveled the country and entertained others all her life. She produced a series of well-known comedy albums, the most popular being *If I Embarrass You Tell Your Friends*, recorded at her own Belle Barth Pub in Miami. Although she favored Miami as a venue, she traveled to New York, Las Vegas, and Los Angeles to perform through her fifties. She was working at Caesar's Palace in Las Vegas when she became ill in 1970. Belle Barth died of cancer one year later, on February 14, 1971, in Miami Beach, Florida.

DISCOGRAPHY

Battle of the Mothers, with Pearl Williams, Riot; *Belle Barth In Las Vegas*, Record Productions; *Book of Knowledge Memorial Album*, Laff; *The Customer Comes First*, Laff; *Hell's*

Belle, Laff; *Her New Act*, Riot; *I Don't Mean to Be Vulgar, But If It's Profitable*, Surprise; *If I Embarrass You Tell Your Friends*, After Hours; *If I Embarrassed You, Forget It*, Riot; *In Person*, Laugh Time; *My Next Story Is a Little Risqué*, After Hours; *Wild Wild Wild Wild World*, Record Productions.

BIBLIOGRAPHY

"Belle Barth." *Variety*, February 17, 1971; "Belle Barth Martin." *NYTimes*, February 16, 1971; Franklin, Joe, ed. *Joe Franklin's Encyclopedia of Comedians* (1979); Regan, David, ed. *Who's Who in Hollywood* (1992); Smith, Ronald L. *Comedy on Record: The Complete Critical Discography* (1988), and *The Stars of Stand-Up Comedy: A Bibliographical Encyclopedia* (1986), and *Who's Who in Comedy* (1992).

JOELLYN WALLEN

BARUCH, DOROTHY WALTER
(1899–1962)

In Dorothy Baruch's most widely recognized book, *One Little Boy*, she writes: "The thoughts and feelings of childhood are dark and deep. If they creep out inadvertently and we meet them with the shock of believing them abnormal, we do one kind of thing to a child. If we meet them with the embracing sympathy born of having already encountered them and seen them as natural we do another."

Baruch's foremost concern, expressed through a wide range of professional activities as an educator, author, psychologist, and community leader, was the healthy emotional development of the young child with the full understanding that physical, intellectual, and emotional development are all interrelated. She believed that the expression of the child's feelings and fantasies and their respectful acknowledgment by parents and teachers were crucial not only for the individual and the family, but also for life in a democratic society. She encouraged adults to help children find ways to rechannel feelings through such activities as dramatic play, the writing of stories, poems, and journals, and the use of art materials, all widely accepted techniques today.

Dorothy Walter Baruch was born on August 5, 1899, in San Francisco, California. She was the daughter of Clarence and Rosalie (Neustadter) Walter. She studied at Bryn Mawr College from 1917 to 1919 and the University of Southern California from 1919 to 1920. She earned both a B.E. (1930) and an M.E. (1931) from Whittier College, Broadoaks School of Education, and a Ph.D. from Claremont College (1937). She married Herbert M. Baruch on April 23, 1919. They had two children, Herbert and Nancy. On June 20, 1946, she married Dr. Hyman Miller.

She organized and directed the Gramercy Cooperative Nursery School (1924–1927) and did experimental work in children's language at the Normandie Nursery School (1929–1930), both in Los Angeles. She was a professor of education and director of the laboratory school at the Broadoaks School of Education, Whittier College, from 1930 to 1940. Along with teaching in-service teacher training courses in the Burbank and Los Angeles city schools (1940–1941), she organized and headed the public relations program for the National Association for Nursery Education from 1937 to 1941. During World War II she worked with the War Manpower Commission and headed the National Commission on Mobilization of Volunteers for Young Children (1941–1942). She was a special lecturer in interracial relations at Claremont College (1944–1945). In 1946, she opened a private practice as a consulting psychologist. She was an active member of many professional groups and lectured before public and professional conferences on parent and child education, child psychology, play therapy, psychosomatic aspects of allergies, and related subjects.

Along with many stories in children's magazines and many articles in professional journals and popular magazines, Dorothy Baruch wrote more than twenty books of fiction for children and was the consultant and coauthor of the Scott Foresman Basic Health and Safety Program Series for children. She wrote eleven nonfiction volumes, primarily for parents, on such topics as play therapy, discipline, prejudice, children in wartime, and sex education.

Dorothy Baruch was a member of B'nai B'rith and, in 1928, organized and directed a parent education department for the NATIONAL COUNCIL OF JEWISH WOMEN. In all that she did, Baruch strove to bring about greater understanding between parents and children of all backgrounds. Her practical, psychodynamically oriented thinking is echoed today in much current work in early education.

Dorothy Walter Baruch died in Los Angeles on September 4, 1962.

**SELECTED WORKS BY
DOROTHY WALTER BARUCH**

Glass House of Prejudice (1946); *How to Live with Your Teen-ager* (1953); *New Ways in Discipline: You and Your Child Today* (1949); *New Ways in Sex Education: A Guide for Parents and Teachers* (1959); *One Little Boy*, with Hyman Miller (1952); *Parents and Children Go to School: Adventuring in Nursery School and Kindergarten* (1939); *The Practice of Psychosomatic Medicine as Illustrated in Allergy*, with Hyman Miller (1956); *A Primer for and About Parents: Parents Can Be People* (1944); *Sex in Marriage: New Understandings*, with Hyman

Miller (1962); *You, Your Children and War* (1942); *You're Out of the Service Now: The Veteran's Guide to Civilian Life*, with Lee Edward Travis (1946).

BIBLIOGRAPHY

BEOAJ; *Book Review Digest 1952*. Edited by Mertrice M. James and Dorothy Brown (1953): 49; *Book Review Digest 1959*. Edited by Dorothy P. Davison (1960): 62; *NYTimes Book Review*, March 23, 1952, 10; *Something About the Author* 20 (1980): 6–8; *WWIAJ* (1938); *WWWIA* 4.

ANN HURWITZ

BAT MITZVAH

"The Friday night before the service my father decided what I was to do. I was to recite the blessings, read a portion of the Torah *sidra* . . . in Hebrew and in English and conclude with the blessing—and that was it. . . . And that was enough to shock a lot of people, including my own grandparents and aunts and uncles."

So reminisced JUDITH KAPLAN EISENSTEIN, the daughter of Rabbi Mordecai Kaplan, about her 1922 bat mitzvah ceremony, widely considered the first to have occurred in America. The bat mitzvah is the female equivalent of a boy's bar mitzvah, the ritual that signifies his entrance into religious majority at age thirteen. To mark the occasion, in the synagogue the boy is called to the Torah for the first time and, if the Sabbath is the chosen day, chants the haftarah, the prophetic portion of that week.

The bat mitzvah ritual was introduced into American Judaism as both an ethical and a pragmatic response to gender divisions in traditional Judaism. For boys, reaching religious majority occasioned a ritual ceremony in the synagogue, but for girls, attaining the status of adult received no communal attention. Jewish tradition declared a girl's majority to begin at age twelve, but her transition from child to adult was not reflected in the synagogue because women had no part in the public reading of the Torah except as listeners, segregated in the women's gallery. On the ethical plane, the new rite was designed to demonstrate that, in the modern age, women were considered equal with men. On the practical level, it provided a stimulus for educating women in Judaism as preparation for their presumed role as transmitters of Jewish culture and religious sensibility.

The bat mitzvah ceremony has its roots in developments in nineteenth-century Judaism of Western Europe and America. As Jews became exposed to Western culture in the nineteenth century, acquired a measure of political rights, and began the process of social integration, they adapted aspects of their religious tradition to the values of the larger society. Concerned that the limited roles of women within traditional Judaism might suggest that Jews were "orientals" rather than Westerners, Jewish leaders included girls in the new ceremony of group confirmation that they instituted. That ceremony generally took place as a ritual conclusion to one's Jewish education. Confirmation was a regular feature of the American Reform Movement by the second half of the nineteenth century. Its growing popularity displaced the individual bar mitzvah rite.

"No thunder sounded. No lightning struck," recalled Judith Kaplan Eisenstein of her history-making 1922 bat mitzvah ceremony, the first in America. She is pictured here at her second bat mitzvah ceremony, where she was honored by a number of prominent Jewish women, including BETTY FRIEDAN *and* LETTY COTTIN POGREBIN. *[Reconstructionist Rabbinical College]*

Because the Reform Movement diminished the importance of the bar mitzvah and because Orthodox Jews accepted the gender segregation of the traditional synagogue as a divine mandate, it fell to the Conservative Movement to struggle with the issue of the bat mitzvah ceremony. Committed to both tradition and modernity, Conservative Judaism became the most popular denomination among American Jews in the interwar years, when the children of Eastern European immigrants became the predominant group in the Jewish community. Even within the Conservative Movement, however, Kaplan's 1922 innovation had few immediate followers. A decade later, only a handful of synagogues had adopted the rite. By 1948, though, some form of bat mitzvah ceremony was held in about one-third of Conservative congregations, and by the 1960s, it had become a regular feature within the movement. Until the past decade or so, the ritual was most often not a precise parallel of the bar mitzvah. It was often held at Friday night services, when the Torah is not read. Even Judith Kaplan, whose bat mitzvah took place on Sabbath morning, read a passage in Hebrew and English from the printed Humash (first five books of the Bible), rather than from the Torah scroll, after the completion of the regular Torah service.

Although it was designed simply to offer public recognition of a girl's coming of age religiously, the bat mitzvah rite raised questions about the status of women within the synagogue. How could a girl be called to the Torah as a bat mitzvah and then never have such an honor again? In 1955, the Conservative Rabbinical Assembly's Committee on Jewish Law and Standards discussed the issue of extending *aliyot* (the honor of being called to the Torah) to women. A favorable minority opinion fostered the dissemination of this practice and paved the way for the full equality of women within the Conservative synagogue that gradually prevailed in the 1970s and 1980s.

Equality for women in the Reform Movement had sources other than the bat mitzvah, although there were some bat mitzvah ceremonies in Reform temples from 1931. The rehabilitation of ritual within Reform Judaism in recent decades has led to a greater attention to both the bat and bar mitzvah ceremonies as an important component of public worship. While in 1953 only 35 percent of Reform temples offered the bat mitzvah to their members, the ritual has since become close to universal.

With the emergence of Jewish feminism in the 1970s, the need to acknowledge the equality of women as Jews has led to the adoption of some type of

The bat mitzvah ceremony is now widely accepted in American Judaism. Some take place, however, in special locations. Yael Schneider is pictured above reading from the Torah at her ceremony near the Western Wall in Jerusalem. On her left is the prayer leader, Betsy Cohen-Kallus, and on her right is her mother, Susan Weidman Schneider. [Edith Robbins]

bat mitzvah ceremony by every American Jewish denomination from Reform to modern Orthodoxy. Because even within Reform, Reconstructionist, and Conservative Judaism women have generally enjoyed ritual equality for less than a generation, some adult women in the past fifteen years have also turned to the bat mitzvah ceremony as a way to expand their Jewish knowledge and skills and to signify their assumption of the rights and responsibilities of Jewish adulthood. Unlike younger celebrants, they often perform the ritual as members of a group.

The form of the bat mitzvah rite varies according to the custom of the particular denomination. In non-Orthodox synagogues the bat mitzvah, like her counterpart, may simply be called to the Torah and recite

*Many adult women have recently turned to the bat mitzvah ceremony as a way of expanding their Jewish knowledge
and skills and to signify their assumption of the rights and responsibilities of Jewish adulthood.
Pictured above is an adult class at Temple Israel in Great Neck, New York. The women are, from left to right:
Karen Commer, Susan Yellin, Ruthe Golden, Naomi Schulman, and Hermine Plotnick.*

the haftarah or may also chant the Torah portion and deliver a *devar Torah,* a talk based on the weekly reading. In Orthodox synagogues, the constraints of Jewish law prevent a girl from being called to the Torah, but some synagogues allow a bat mitzvah to give a *devar Torah* after the conclusion of the service or at a festive meal. In a few Orthodox communities a women's *tefilla* (prayer) group enables the celebrant to perform all the roles of a non-Orthodox bat mitzvah, with the exception of reciting the blessings. The once-radical innovation of the bat mitzvah has become widely accepted in American Judaism and symbolizes the changing roles of women in the American Jewish religious community.

BIBLIOGRAPHY

There has been little scholarly investigation of the bat mitzvah ceremony. For a historical study, see Paula E. Hyman, "The Introduction of Bat Mitzvah in Conservative Judaism in Postwar America." *YIVO Annual* 19 (1990): 133–146. For sociological studies of adult bat mitzvah experiences, see Stuart Schoenfeld, "Integration in the Group and Sacred Uniqueness: An Analysis of Adult Bat Mitzvah," in *Persistence and Flexibility: Anthropological Perspectives on the American Jewish Experience,* ed. Walter Zenner (1989), 117–133, and "Ritual and Role Transition: Adult Bat Mitzvah as a Successful Rite of Passage," in *The Uses of Tradition: Jewish Continuity in the Modern Era,* ed. Jack Wertheimer (1992), 349–376. For one version of Judith Kaplan Eisenstein's reflections on her bat mitzvah, see *Eyewitnesses to American Jewish History* 4, ed. Azriel Eisenberg (1982), 30–32. On the educational impact of bat mitzvah, see Cherie Koller-Fox, "Women and Jewish Education: A New Look at Bat Mitzvah," in *The Jewish Woman: New Perspectives,* ed. Elizabeth Koltun (1976), 31–42.

PAULA E. HYMAN

BAUER, MARION EUGÉNIE
(1882–1955)

An energetic champion of contemporary music, Marion Eugénie Bauer's work as a writer, teacher, and music advocate augments—perhaps even overshadows—her importance as a composer. Like many women composers of her generation, she focused her initial compositional activity on songs and piano solos. During the 1930s and 1940s, she completed several of her largest compositions.

Born on August 15, 1882, in Walla Walla, Washington, Marion was the youngest of seven children (four girls and three boys). The oldest, Emilie Frances (1865–1926), was Marion's first piano teacher, and she supported Marion both financially and emotionally.

Her parents, Jacques (Joe) Bauer (d. 1890) and Julia (not Julie as generally given) (Heyman) Bauer, were Jewish immigrants from France. Marion identified her father, band member in the Nineteenth Infantry during the Indian Wars and an amateur tenor, as the source of her interest and talent in music. Jacques Bauer was a storekeeper. Her mother, fluent in seven languages, was a respected educator who taught at Whitman College in Walla Walla (1882–1888) and then privately. Marion's parents were married at Beth Israel Synagogue in Portland, Oregon, in 1864.

Despite her Jewish roots, Marion Bauer seems to have been nonobservant in her adult life. A former student, Maurice Peress, maintained that Bauer practiced Christian Science while at New York University; Fredric Stoessel claimed she studied Christian Science "in her final days"; and in a 1923 letter she expressed a desire to publish a song appropriate for Christian Science service.

Although Bauer gave her birth date as 1887 (the date used in virtually all biographical publications), the census of 1887 identified Marion as four years old, and an extant birth announcement states that a daughter was born to the wife of Joe Bauer on August 15, 1882, in Walla Walla. In 1898 (not 1903 as she claimed), Marion completed her formal academic education with graduation from St. Helen's Hall in Portland, Oregon, the private high school where her mother taught German. By 1899, Marion Bauer had moved to New York to live and study with her sister, Emilie, a successful music critic, teacher, and occasional composer. She also studied piano and harmony with Henry Holden Huss. She went to Paris in 1906–1907, where she studied with Raoul Pugno, Louis Campbell-Tipton, Pierre Monteux, and, perhaps most notably, Nadia Boulanger, who also taught Aaron Copland and Leonard Bernstein. After returning to New York in 1907, she worked with Walter Henry Rothwell and Eugene Heffley, who remained a guiding musical influence until his death in 1925. Additional study trips to Europe included work with John Paul Ertel in Berlin (1910–1911) and André Gédalge in Paris (1923–1924).

Upon Emilie's death in 1926, Marion Bauer joined the faculty at New York University, where she taught music history and composition until 1951. In addition to this full-time position, she was affiliated with the Juilliard School from 1940 until her death, and during summers she taught at Mills College, the Carnegie Institute of Technology, and the Cincinnati Conservatory, and offered public lectures about contemporary music. For twelve summers intermittently between 1919 and 1944, the MacDowell Colony for composers, artists, and writers in Peterborough, New Hampshire, provided a supportive atmosphere for composition along with an opportunity to meet other important women composers such as Amy Beach, Ruth Crawford, and MIRIAM GIDEON.

Despite brief experiments with twelve-tone writing in the 1940s and 1950s, her music rarely ventures beyond extended tonality, emphasizing coloristic harmony and diatonic dissonance. Compositions, often with programmatic titles, are melodic in focus with energetic rhythms. Characterized in the 1920s as a left-wing modernist, by the 1940s her music was viewed as conservative yet well crafted. Bauer was a noted composer during her lifetime: Scores were published, and her music received many performances, including the 1947 premiere of *Sun Splendor* by the New York Philharmonic conducted by Leopold Stokowski.

In another time and place, Marion Bauer might have become a world-famous composer. As it is, her compositions are respected but play second fiddle to her work as a writer, teacher, and advocate of modern music. [New York Public Library]

Her strong support for American music and modern composers is evident in her active organizational affiliations, frequently as the only woman in a leadership position among these groups that included America's most prominent composers. She was a founding member of the American Music Guild (1921), the Society of American Women Composers (1925), the American Composers Alliance (1937), and the American Music Center (1939); secretary for the Society for the Publication of American Music; and a board member for the League of Composers and the American Composers Alliance. Her final years included recognition with a 1951 Town Hall concert devoted to her music, works featured on a Composers Forum concert in 1954, and an honorary doctorate from New York College of Music in 1954. An important writer about music, addressing both specialists and general readers, she was widely published in journals and the author of five published books.

Marion Eugénie Bauer died on August 9, 1955, in South Hadley, Massachusetts, where a rabbi conducted her memorial service.

SELECTED WORKS BY MARION EUGÉNIE BAUER

WRITINGS

Musical Questions and Quizzes: A Digest of Information About Music (1941); *Twentieth Century Music: How It Developed, How to Listen to It* (1933; rev. ed. 1947; reprint of 1st ed., 1978).

WITH ETHEL PEYSER

How Music Grew: From Prehistoric Times to the Present Day (1925; completely rev. 5th ed. 1939); *How Opera Grew: From Ancient Greece to the Present Day* (1956); *Music Through the Ages: A Narrative for Student and Layman* (1932; 3d ed. revised and enlarged by Elizabeth E. Rogers as *Music Through the Ages: An Introduction to Music History*, 1967).

BIBLIOGRAPHY

For an extensive, detailed listing of Marion Bauer's compositions, see Adrienne Fried Block and Carol Neuls-Bates, *Women in American Music: A Bibliography of Music and Literature* (1979). See *NAW* modern for a bibliography of writings about Bauer up to 1980.

Ammer, Christine. *Unsung: A History of Women in American Music* (1980); Edwards, J. Michele. "North America Since 1920," in *Women and Music: A History*, edited by Karin Pendle (1991), and "Bauer, Marion Eugénie," *The Norton/Grove Dictionary of Women Composers*, edited by Julie Anne Sadie and Rhian Samuel (1994); Fuller, Sophie. *The Pandora Guide to Women Composers: Britain and the United States, 1629–Present* (1994); Hisama, Ellie M. "Gender, Politics, and Modernist Music: Analyses of Five Compositions by Ruth Crawford (1901–1953) and Marion Bauer (1887 [sic]–1955)," Ph.D. diss., City University of New York (1996); Horrocks, Peggy A. "The Solo Vocal Repertoire of Marion Bauer with Selected Stylistic Analyses," D.M.A. diss. University of Nebraska (1994); *NAW* modern; Obituary. *NYTimes*, August 11, 1955; Pickett, Susan. Telephone and e-mail communication with the author (June–July 1996); Stewart, Nancy Louise. "The Solo Piano Music of Marion Bauer," Ph.D. diss., College-Conservatory of Music, University of Cincinnati (1990); *UJE*; *WWIAJ* (1938); *WWWIA* 3.

Archives holding significant collections related to Bauer include the Library of Congress, Mount Holyoke College, New York University, New York Public Library, American Composers Alliance, and American Music Center.

J. MICHELE EDWARDS

BAYES, NORA (c. 1880–1928)

Nora Bayes was an international singing star in vaudeville and musical comedy during the first twenty-five years of the twentieth century. Known as a willful and temperamental star, Bayes relied on her own charisma and popularity as she resisted managerial control and ignored the details of legal contracts. These traits and tactics matched those of other famous female vaudevillians such as Eva Tanguay who also refused to follow the rules set by theater administrators. In these battles with male businessmen and in her unconventional personal life, Bayes provides some flamboyant, indeed extreme, examples of the broad social changes happening in the United States in the early twentieth century, namely the questioning of traditional roles for women as well as the challenges to male political and economic power that marked the women's movement of the time.

Born to Elias and Rachel (Miller) Goldberg, she was originally named Dora but changed her name many times for her theatrical career before settling on Nora Bayes. The date of her birth and other details about her early life are sketchy. She gave Los Angeles as her place of birth, but other accounts list her birthplace as Chicago or Milwaukee. When Bayes was approximately eighteen years old and married to her first husband, Otto Gressing, an undertaker, she began to pursue her dream of a theatrical career. While living in Joliet, Illinois, with Gressing, she performed at amateur night at Hopkins' Theater in Chicago. Thus began a stage career as tumultuous and unpredictable as her personal life.

After performing for several years in vaudeville in the United States and earning acclaim with the hit song, "Down Where the Wurzburger Flows," written

She was a performer who changed names and husbands, broke contracts and producers, and joked about her Jewish background and those changed husbands. Ultimately, Nora Bayes was a free spirit whose main allegiance was to the public that adored her. [Library of Congress]

by Harry von Tilzer in 1902, she opened the bill at the Palace Theatre in London, England, in November 1905. When she returned to the United States, Florenz Ziegfeld helped establish her as a star when he recruited her for his *Follies of 1907*. Enjoying great success in the theater, Bayes divorced Gressing and married singer and dancer Jack Norworth in 1908. Bayes and Norworth then starred together in the *Follies of 1908*, which included a song they had written together—"Shine On, Harvest Moon." Though Bayes and Norworth worked well together on stage, their life offstage was strained. Bayes, who commanded higher salaries than Norworth, often treated him as her servant and resented his flirtations with other women.

Confident in her growing popularity, Bayes began to challenge the authority of theater managers and producers. She angered Florenz Ziegfeld, for example, when she walked out of the *Follies of 1909* largely because of her jealousy over the success of SOPHIE TUCKER's performance in this show. After Ziegfeld brought an injunction against Bayes that prevented her from performing for several months, Bayes returned to vaudeville even more popular than before, earning $2,500 a week. Critics noted that Bayes succeeded through her lush singing voice, her sensitivity

to her audience's tastes, and her willingness to make fun of herself, including jokes about her Jewish background and her failed marriages.

Divorced from Norworth in 1913, she married Harry Clarke, an actor, that same year; this marriage dissolved only two years later. Bayes achieved great success on the Keith vaudeville circuit, including a prosperous tour in 1914, but she began to chafe under Keith's powerful demands. Bayes broke her contract and thus gave up the lucrative bookings. Following her break with Keith, she launched her own two-hour, one-woman show in 1917, starred in the musical *Ladies First* in 1918, and then continued to perform in vaudeville in the England and the United States through 1927.

Bayes's fourth marriage—to actor Arthur Gordon (also known as Gordoni)—lasted two years, from 1920 to 1922. Her final marriage, in 1925, was to Benjamin Friedland, a wealthy New York businessman. She died of cancer at the Jewish Hospital in Brooklyn on March 19, 1928. She was survived by Friedland, her three adopted children (two boys and a girl), as well as brother Harry Goldberg and sister Ida Klein.

BIBLIOGRAPHY

AJYB 24:117; American Society of Composers, Authors and Publishers. *ASCAP Biographical Dictionary.* 4th ed. (1980); Bayes, Nora. Clipping files. Harvard Theatre Collection, Harvard University Library, Cambridge, Mass., and Scrapbooks. Robinson Locke Collection, New York Public Library at Lincoln Center, NYC; Claghorn, Charles Eugene. *Biographical Dictionary of American Music* (1973); Ireland, Norma Olin. *Index of Women of the World from Ancient to Modern Times* (1970); Kinkle, Roger D. *The Complete Encyclopedia of Popular Music and Jazz, 1900–1950* (1974); *NAW;* Obituaries. "Nora Bayes." *Variety,* March 14, 1928, and *NYTimes,* March 20, 1928, 27:3; Samuels, Charles, and Louise Samuels. *Once Upon a Stage: The Merry World of Vaudeville* (1974); Slide, Anthony, ed. *Selected Vaudeville Criticism* (1988); *UJE;* Westerfield, Jane T. "An Investigation of the Life Styles and Performance of Three Singer-Comediennes of American Vaudeville: Eva Tanguay, Nora Bayes and Sophie Tucker." Ph.D. diss., Ball State University (1987); *Who Was Who in the Theatre: 1912–1970* (1978).

M. ALISON KIBLER

BECK, EVELYN TORTON (b. 1933)

Evelyn Torton Beck is a professor of women's studies and Jewish studies, as well as an associate faculty member in the comparative literature program, at the University of Maryland, College Park (UMCP).

She is a scholar, a teacher, a feminist, and an outspoken Jew and lesbian on campus. With her energy and drive, the state flagship campus has become a more welcome place for Jewish, female, and homosexual students, faculty, and staff.

Evelyn Torton Beck was born in Vienna, Austria, on January 18, 1933, to Max and Irma (Lichtmann) Torton. Max Torton was born in Buzacz, Poland; Irma Torton was born in Vienna. The family, which includes Beck's younger brother, Edgar, survived the Holocaust and immigrated to the United States after the war, settling in Brooklyn, New York.

Evelyn and Anatole Beck married in 1954. Before divorcing in 1974, they had two children: Nina Rachel (b. 1955) and Micah Daniel (b. 1958). Nina, also a lesbian, has one child. Micah has one child, age eight. Beck has been married for many years to her partner, L. Lee Knefelkamp, a nationally known developmental psychologist and scholar of higher education.

Beck received her B.A. from Brooklyn College in 1954 and, a year later, her M.A. from Yale. In 1969, she completed her Ph.D. at the University of Wisconsin at Madison. She is currently completing a Ph.D. in clinical psychology (with an emphasis on feminist perspectives) at the Fielding Institute. Her *Wounds of Gender: Frida Kahlo and Franz Kafka*, focuses on common threads between Franz Kafka, the subject of her first dissertation, and Mexican artist Frida Kahlo. Another current book project, *Jewish Women and Anti-Semitism*, also combines her interest in Judaism, women's epistemology, and psychoanalysis.

Such eclectic interdisciplinary connections are the hallmark of Beck's scholarship, which has produced two major but very different contributions to Jewish scholarship: *Franz Kafka and the Yiddish Theater: Its Impact on His Work* and *Nice Jewish Girls: A Lesbian Anthology*. The latter was the first anthology of its kind, collecting poetry, essays, reminiscences, and short stories from a wide variety of women from the United States and abroad who are Jewish and lesbian. Beck is known as the "grandmother" of Yiddish at the Modern Language Assocation, where she started the Yiddish section in 1972, years before the current Yiddish revival. For many years, she was an active member of *B'not Esh* [Daughters of Fire], a Jewish feminist think tank composed of rabbis, therapists, theologians, social workers, and scholars who, collectively, formulate theory and create new, woman-affirming ceremonies.

Since the 1970s, Beck has published countless articles and delivered many conference papers and keynote speeches around the world. She has always been a proud and assertive Jewish activist. She was instrumental in transforming UMCP into a Jewish-sensitive campus and introducing many Jewish-content courses into the curriculum. Moreover, she was one of the first to recognize the need for lesbian inclusion in Jewish circles and for Jewish inclusion in feminist circles.

After graduating from the University of Wisconsin, Beck taught there for a dozen years. In 1984, she was recruited by UMCP to further develop their Women's Studies Program. When she stepped down as director in 1993, the program had become one of the most respected women's studies departments in the country, offering an undergraduate degree and a graduate certificate in women's studies.

In 1994, Evelyn Torton Beck received the university's Outstanding Woman of the Year Award, and received the Distinguished Scholar/Teacher Award the following year. She is on the advisory editorial board of *BRIDGES: A JOURNAL FOR JEWISH FEMINISTS AND OUR FRIENDS*.

SELECTED WORKS BY EVELYN TORTON BECK

Interpretive Synthesis: The Task of Literary Scholarship, with Jost Hermand (1975); *Jewish Women and Anti-Semitism* (forthcoming); *Kafka and the Yiddish Theater* (1971); *Nice Jewish Girls: A Lesbian Anthology* (1982); *The Prism of Sex: Essays in the Sociology of Knowledge*, edited with Julia A. Sherman (1979); *Wounds of Gender: Frida Kahlo and Franz Kafka* (forthcoming).

LIORA MORIEL

BEHREND, JEANNE (1911–1988)

In 1936, Jeanne Behrend, renowned pianist, music educator, and composer, received the Joseph Bearns Prize from Columbia University for her piano suite *A Child's Day*, and for her song cycle on poems by Sara Teasdale. Behrend debuted at Carnegie Hall in 1937, performing one of her own compositions. She continued throughout her life to appear as a soloist with major orchestras. Although Behrend wrote many works for piano, voice, orchestra, and chamber ensemble, her creative efforts received little of the recognition she had hoped for, and she stopped composing in the 1940s.

Behrend was born in Philadelphia on May 11, 1911, and died there on March 20, 1988. She studied piano with Josef Hofmann and composition with Rosario Scalero at the Curtis Institute of Music and graduated in 1934.

Fortunately, Behrend's contributions to American music did not cease with her compositional activity.

Instead, she turned her energies to the study and dissemination of North and South American music. She embarked on a U.S. State Department–sponsored concert tour of South America in 1945–1946, and in 1959–1960, she founded the Philadelphia Festival of Western Hemisphere Music. For her work with Brazilian music, she was awarded the Southern Cross by the Brazilian government in 1965.

Behrend taught piano and American music courses at the Curtis Institute, the Juilliard School, the Philadelphia College of Performing Arts, Temple University, the New School of Music in Philadelphia, and Western College, in Oxford, Ohio. She also edited collections of early American choral music, the songs of Stephen Foster, the piano works of Louis Moreau Gottschalk and his diaries *Notes of a Pianist* (1979).

BIBLIOGRAPHY

Cohen, Aaron I. *International Encyclopedia of Women Composers.* Vol. 1 (1987); Doyle, John G. "Jeanne Behrend." *The New Grove Dictionary of American Music*, edited by H. Wiley Hitchcock and Stanley Sadie (1986), and "Jeanne Behrend." *The New Grove Dictionary of Music and Musicians*, edited by Stanley Sadie (1988); Hostetter, Elizabeth Ann. "Jeanne Behrend: Pioneer Performer of American Music, Pianist, Teacher, Musicologist, and Composer." D.M.A. diss., Arizona State University (1990); Obituary. *NYTimes*, April 15, 1988; Slominsky, Nicolas. *Baker's Biographical Dictionary of Musicians* (1984); *Sonneck Society Bulletin* 14, no. 2 (Summer 1988): 86; *UJE*; *Who's Who in American Music: Classical* (1985).

JENNIFER STINSON

When her dreams of being recognized as a renowned composer went unrealized, Jeanne Behrend became a music scholar of international repute. [New York Public Library]

BELLANCA, DOROTHY JACOBS (1894–1946)

The *New York Times* described Dorothy Jacobs Bellanca as one of America's foremost women labor leaders. An outstanding union organizer and a captivating speaker, she was born in Zemel, Latvia, on August 10, 1894. Though she lacked formal ties to the Jewish community, many of the immigrants Bellanca organized were Jewish. The youngest of four daughters of Bernice and Henry Jacobs, she immigrated with her family to Baltimore in 1900, where her father worked as a tailor. Her mother died several years later. She attended Baltimore public schools. At age thirteen, she started work as a hand buttonhole sewer on men's coats. After one month of unpaid training, she began ten-hour workdays, earning three dollars a week.

At age fifteen, Dorothy organized female immigrant buttonhole makers into Local 170 of the United Garment Workers of America (UGW). In 1914, she led her union from the conservative UGW to the Amalgamated Clothing Workers of America (ACWA). She promoted class solidarity, but took particular interest in organizing women. She worked to convince men that unionizing women, a majority of the industry, benefited all workers.

She was one of five women (of 175 delegates) who attended the founding convention of the ACWA, where she promoted the need for a woman organizer. She became secretary of the Joint Board (the ACWA's central body in Baltimore) on October 21, 1915, and established the Education Department, paying particular attention to the experiences of women unionists. In 1916, the ACWA recognized her skills. She was the sole female nominated to serve on the seven-member General Executive Board (GEB) and in July, at age twenty-one, became the only woman vice president of a major trade union.

She undertook a wide range of tasks for the union. In 1917, she participated in major organizing campaigns in Philadelphia and New York. The same

One of America's foremost women labor leaders, in 1916 Dorothy Bellanca was the sole female nominated to serve on the General Executive Board of the Amalgamated Clothing Workers of America. That same year, at age twenty-one, she became vice president, the only woman vice president of a major trade union. [Cornell University, Kheel Center]

year the ACWA appointed her as a full-time woman's organizer. In that role, she promoted a union culture that involved members and families in activities beyond the shop. She regularly contributed to *Advance*, the ACWA's paper, which began publication in English in March 1917, and included articles in both Italian and Yiddish.

She married August Bellanca, an Italian ACWA labor leader, in 1918. She won reelection to the GEB in 1918 but stepped down after she married, though remaining active in the union. During the war, she encouraged unionization among uniform makers. In 1920, the Bellancas joined a special committee to organize "runaway" shops that evaded the union by moving their facilities into economically depressed areas. During the 1920s, Bellanca emerged as one of the most powerful women trade unionists. In 1922, August Bellanca became ill and his doctor recommended rest. The couple traveled abroad, because they knew they would need to leave the country in order to avoid union demands. Bellanca believed her

husband's contributions to the ACWA were unique, and she could be of greatest assistance to him, and thus the union, by leaving her own position and caring for her husband.

Bellanca favored the creation of a separate Women's Department within the ACWA, which the GEB invited Bellanca to direct upon its establishment in July 1924. She supported the good of the organization over individual interests. Consequently, she recommended disbanding the Women's Department after learning that Baltimore men resented it. The Women's Department dissolved in 1926. Though Bellanca still encouraged separate organizing activities targeting women, she opposed reestablishment of the Women's Department in 1928.

During 1933–1934, unions experienced a revival thanks to the New Deal. Bellanca set to work organizing women in rural areas of Pennsylvania, New Jersey, New York, and Connecticut. Bellanca was also involved in politics and helped found the American Labor Party (ALP) in 1936. Despite reservations some unionists had toward the Democratic Party, Bellanca supported Franklin D. Roosevelt's reelection campaign, because he was most supportive of workers' interests. In 1938, Frances Perkins, secretary of labor, asked Bellanca to serve on the Maternal and Child Welfare Committee. The same year, in an unusual move for women, Bellanca ran for Congress for Brooklyn's Eighth Congressional District, gaining the support of the ALP, Republican Party, City Fusion Party, Progressive Party, and Fiorello La Guardia. She supported federal housing programs, national health care, wages and hours law, and civil rights legislation. Incumbent Donald J. O'Toole, who won (133,998 to 118,000), sought to discredit Bellanca, noting that she lived in Manhattan, not Brooklyn, was not Italian, and had abandoned Judaism by marrying a Catholic. Soon after the start of World War II, Bellanca joined the Women's Policy Committee of the War Manpower Commission, concerned with incorporating women into war industries.

Throughout the 1940s, Bellanca served on numerous city, state, and federal committees. She was an adviser to the Department of Labor's Committee on Women in Defense Work (1940). She advocated protective legislation and opposed the Equal Rights Amendment, but supported equal treatment of trade union women. She served on the Labor Advisory Committee of the Department of Labor, as labor adviser to the International Labor Organization Conference, and on the New York Defense Council on Discrimination in Employment (1941). Other service included membership on a state commission on problems of women in wartime (1942); the New York State War Council Committee on Discrimination (1943), from which she and seven others resigned when Governor Thomas E. Dewey refused to support antidiscrimination legislation; and a committee to promote racial harmony in New York City. In 1940 and 1944, she was elected state vice-chair of the ALP. Bellanca was also active in the Consumers League of New York and the Women's Trade Union League. The Women's City Club recognized Bellanca in 1945 as one of thirty women who gave outstanding service to New York.

Bellanca developed multiple myeloma, tumors of the bone marrow, a painful and debilitating disease. The ACWA honored her at a special luncheon in 1944. She had hoped to attend the ACWA's first postwar convention in 1946, but was too weak. She died on August 16, 1946, just after her fifty-second birthday.

BIBLIOGRAPHY

AJYB 49:608; Asher, Nina Lynn. "Dorothy Jacobs Bellanca: Feminist Trade Unionist: 1894–1946." Ph.D. diss., State University of New York, Binghamton, 1982; Asher, Nina. "Dorothy Jacobs Bellanca: Women Clothing Workers and the Runaway Shops." In *A Needle, A Bobbin, A Strike: Women Needleworkers in America*, edited by Joan Jensen and Sue Davidson (1984); Bellanca, Dorothy Jacobs. Papers. Martin P. Catherwood Library, New York State School of Industrial and Labor Relations, Cornell University, Ithaca, New York; *DAB* 4; "Dorothy Bellanca—A Tribute." *Life and Labor Bulletin* 75, no. 3 (1946): 3; Marcus, Jacob. *United States Jewry: 1776–1985*. Vol. 4 (1993): 239–240; Markowitz, Ruth Jacknow. "Dorothy Jacobs Bellanca." In *European Immigrant Women in the United States*, edited by J. Litoff and J. McDonnell (1994); McCreesh, Carolyn Daniel. *Women in the Campaign to Organize Garment Workers, 1880–1917* (1985); *Nation* 163 (August 31, 1946): 227; *NAW*; Neidle, Cecyle. *America's Immigrant Women* (1976); Obituary. *NYTimes*, August 17, 1946, 13:3; Williams, Victoria. "Dorothy Jacobs Bellanca." *Labor Unity* 78, no. 2 (1992): 24+.

SUSAN L. TANANBAUM

BELLARINA, BELLA (1898–1969)

Unless they worked on the English-speaking stage, Yiddish actors were largely unnoticed by critics and the general media. Thus very little is known about the life of many of these wonderful artists who appeared before adoring audiences on the Lower East Side, Brooklyn, or the Bronx. Such is the case with Bella Bellarina, an actress who made her mark with the famous Vilna Troupe, a company dedicated to serious drama and avant-garde staging techniques.

Bella (Rubinlicht) Bellarina was born in Warsaw on July 15, 1898. Her father, Getzl Rubinlicht, was a real estate broker. Her mother, Tuna (Vinover) Rubinlicht, was a homemaker who cared for sixteen children, four of whom died in early childhood. Bellarina was the fifth in order of birth. She attended a girls' school, and at seventeen began taking classes in education at the university, presumably to become a teacher. Early on, however, she was drawn to the stage and appeared in various school productions.

In 1916, Bellarina enrolled in the Warsaw School of Drama. David Herman, future director of the Vilna Troupe, saw her perform there and urged her to join

Perhaps one of the most talented and versatile actresses of the Yiddish stage, Bella Bellarina has remained largely unknown because she did not make the transition to Broadway and Hollywood. [YIVO Institute]

several drama clubs in the city, among them the renowned *Artistisher Vinkl* [Artists' corner].

Her first role on the Yiddish stage was Fanitchke in Sholem Aleichem's play *Mentshn* [People]. In 1918, she became a member of the Vilna Troupe and toured in Europe for several years. In 1924, amid great anticipation, the company arrived in New York, where Bellarina was cast in such Yiddish classics as Ansky's *The Dybbuk*, Peretz Hirschbein's *Di Puste Kretchme* [The idle inn] and *Grine Felder* [Green fields], Jacob Gordin's *Mirele Efros*, as well as works by Leon Kobrin and David Pinsky.

While in America, Bellarina and her husband, Haim Schneyer Hamerow, an actor with the Vilna Troupe, decided to stay. In New York, she worked with, among others, Maurice Schwartz, the legendary producer, director, and actor, founder of the Vilna-patterned Yidisher Kunst Teater. In 1929, Bellarina and Hamerow became American citizens, which allowed them to return to Poland and reclaim their son, Theodore, who had been in the care of Bellarina's mother. The three returned to New York in 1930. Bellarina and Hamerow continued to tour for several more years with various companies in North and South America. However, the war and the steady decline of the Yiddish theater forced Hamerow into working in the garment district. Bellarina managed to survive by appearing at benefits and various social and cultural functions. Haim Hamerow died on July 24, 1961, and Bella Bellarina on February 1, 1969.

Bellarina played many important roles on the Yiddish stage, but she is best remembered for her portrayal of Tsine in *Grine Felder* and Leah in *The Dybbuk*. As Tsine, she played a peasant girl, a mischievous tomboy in love with a shy yeshivah student from a neighboring city. The role requires a great deal of energy and charm, and Bellarina had plenty of both. By contrast, Ansky's classic calls for an actress who can play a reserved, deeply religious young woman, secretly in love with a man she cannot marry. Both characters are beautiful women, but while Tsine's beauty is robust and earthy, Leah's is delicate, even fragile. Tsine is a happy-go-lucky country girl; Leah is a tragic hero. Bellarina was successful in both roles. However, Helen Beverly and Lili Liliana are better known as Tsine and Leah because they were cast in the 1937 screen adaptations of the Hirschbein and Ansky plays. Another reason for Bellarina's lack of popularity was her inability to play on the English-speaking stage and in English-language films. Critics agreed that her talents were equal to those of Ester Rokhl Kaminska, Ida Kaminska, MOLLY PICON, and

CELIA ADLER—widely recognized names from the golden age of the Yiddish theater. Bellarina remained relatively obscure since she never appeared on Broadway or in Hollywood. Her obscurity, however, does not diminish her great contributions to Yiddish culture in the United States.

BIBLIOGRAPHY

AJYB 71: 602; Hamerow, Theodore [son of Bella Bellarina]. Telephone interviews with author; Landis, Joseph, ed. and trans. *The Great Jewish Plays* (1972); Lifson, David. *Yiddish Theater in America* (1965); Obituary. *NYTimes*, February 2, 1969, 72:3; Sandrow, Nahma. *Vagabond Stars: A World History of the Yiddish Theater* (1977); Zylbercweig, Zalmen. *Leksikon fun Yidishn Teater* (1931).

MICHAEL TAUB

BENDER, ROSE I. (1895–1964)

Rose I. Bender's lifelong dedication to and support of a Jewish homeland began at an early age. She was taught the finest Talmudic traditions by her parents and was inspired by their love of Zion to become a guiding light for American Zionism and a Philadelphia Jewish community leader.

She was born in Philadelphia on December 22, 1895, one of four children of Joseph and Rachel Magil, originally from Lithuania. They were both Hebrew scholars and Zionists. She was descended from the Gaon of Vilna through her mother.

Rose graduated from Philadelphia High School for Girls and Gratz College of Jewish Studies. While still in high school, she organized the first Young Judaea Club in America and was its first president. Later she taught Hebrew and Sunday school classes. On June 24, 1917, she married a prominent lawyer, Oscar G. Bender, and had two daughters.

In 1927, Bender became a member of HADASSAH and later national chairman of fund-raising. She was a delegate to the 1939 World Zionist Congress. When she became executive director of the Zionist Organization of Philadelphia in 1945, she was the first woman in the United States to hold such a prestigious position.

Well before the present-day women's liberation movement, Rose I. Bender, though lacking a college education, was able to transcend barriers and use her considerable abilities to fulfill herself and make significant contributions to Zionism and the Jewish community.

Rose I. Bender died on November 4, 1964.

BIBLIOGRAPHY

AJYB 66:572; Bender, Rose I. Papers, 1929–1946. MSS. 20, Box 1, Folder 1, Balch Institute, Philadelphia, and MS 80–774, American Jewish Archives, Cincinnati, Ohio; *NYTimes*, November 5, 1964, 45:5.

LILY SCHWARTZ

BENEDEK, THERESE (1892–1977)

Therese Benedek was among the pioneers of psychoanalysis, first in Germany and then in the United States. She developed expertise in psychosomatic medicine, sexual dysfunction, and family dynamics, but she is best known for her work on the psychosexual development of women.

Born on November 8, 1892, in Eger, Hungary, Therese (Friedmann) Benedek was the third of four children of a traditional Jewish family. Her father was Ignatius Friedmann, a merchant, and her mother was Charlotte (Link) Friedmann. Although neither her brother nor her two sisters attended university, she graduated from the University of Budapest in 1919 with a doctorate in medicine. After training as a pediatrician in Budapest and Bratislava, she decided to become a psychoanalyst instead.

In 1919, she married a Hungarian Protestant, Tibor Benedek, a dermatologist and academic researcher. The following year they moved to Germany, and she became a research assistant in the Neurological-Psychiatric Clinic of the University of Leipzig. A member of the Berlin Psychoanalytic Society, she opened up the first private psychoanalytic practice in Leipzig in 1921 and became a training analyst. In 1926, she gave birth to a son, Thomas; three years later, a daughter, Judith, was born. With nannies and governesses raising her children, she continued her psychotherapeutic practice and published on the problems of motherhood.

She was reluctant to leave Germany after the Nazi takeover because, she insisted, "I am not a Jew, I am a Hungarian!" and "I will not go uninvited to another country." But in 1936, her husband persuaded her to accept Franz Alexander's invitation to become training analyst of the Chicago Institute of Psychoanalysis. Despite serious language difficulties, she obtained her American medical license in 1937. She became an American citizen in 1943, but always spoke and wrote English with a distinct Hungarian accent. After the war, she refused to visit either Germany or Hungary, although she and her husband traveled frequently in Europe.

Benedek's career combined therapy, training, and research. She played a central role in the development of psychoanalysis in the United States, while serving as supervising analyst and member of the research staff of the Chicago Institute of Psychoanalysis for thirty-four years. She was president of the Chicago Psychoanalytic Society from 1958 to 1959. Her best-known work, *Psychosexual Functions in Women*, which deals with the emotional response of women to the fluctuations of hormones during the sexual cycle, appeared in 1952. Much of her finest research on parenthood, family life, and depression was completed in her seventies. Even after her retirement in 1969, she maintained a private practice, although by then her hearing was impaired and she had difficulty walking. In 1972, for her eightieth birthday, the Therese Benedek Research Foundation was established in her honor.

Although she was not an observant Jew and her husband attended church regularly, Therese Benedek never formally left the Jewish community. She devoted her life to her career and was considerably more successful in the United States than her husband. A lively but reserved and self-assured person, she was valued for her feminine, motherly qualities and viewed as a cultivated lady with Old World charm. She maintained close ties with her extended family and became a doting grandmother in her later years. Three years after her husband's death, she died of a heart attack on October 27, 1977.

SELECTED WORKS BY THERESE BENEDEK

Depression and Human Existence, with E.J. Anthony (1975); *Insight and Personality Adjustment* (1946); *Parenthood. Its Psychology and Psychopathology*, with E.J. Anthony (1970); *Psychoanalytic Investigations: Selected Papers* (1973); *Psychosexual Functions in Women* (1952).

BIBLIOGRAPHY

EJ (1983–1985); Fermi, Laura. *Illustrious Immigrants.* 2d ed. (1971); *International Biographical Dictionary of Central European Emigres,*, Vol. 2, part 1 (1980): 78; *NYTimes*, October 27, 1977, 26:4; Peters, Uwe Henrik. *Psychiatrie im Exil* (1992); Stevens, Gwendolyn, and Sheldon Gardner. *The Women of Psychology.* Vol. 2 (1982): 46–48; Weidemann, Doris. *Leben und Werk von Therese Benedek 1892–1977* (1988).

HARRIET PASS FREIDENREICH

BERENSON, SENDA (1868–1954)

Known as the "Mother of Women's Basketball," Senda Berenson pioneered women's basketball as the director of the physical education department at Smith College in Northampton, Massachusetts.

The "Mother of Women's Basketball" Senda Berenson is shown here (in the long dress) with Smith College students. She conducted the first official game of women's basketball (pitting Smith sophomores against the freshmen) on March 22, 1893. [Naismath Memorial Basketball Hall of Fame]

She was born Senda Valvrojenski in Vilna, Lithuania, on March 19, 1868. Her father, Albert Valvrojenski, immigrated to the United States in 1874, settled in Boston, became a peddler, and changed the family's name to Berenson. Berenson was a frail seven-year-old when she immigrated to Boston in 1875 with her mother, older brother Bernard, and younger brother Abie. Senda Berenson's two sisters, Elizabeth and Rachel, were born in Boston in 1878 and 1880, respectively.

According to biographer Betty Spears, "Mr. Berenson demanded that the family become Americanized as quickly as possible. He insisted that the family speak only English and that they sever all connections with the Jewish religion. . . . In 1880, Mr. Berenson became an American citizen, making the entire family American citizens."

Weak and delicate throughout her childhood, Berenson was tutored by her father in reading and languages. She was unable to complete her training at the Boston Conservatory of Music because of her health. In an effort to improve her strength and vigor,

she attended the Boston Normal School of Gymnastics in Boston from 1890 to 1892. There she was trained in anatomy, physiology, and hygiene to teach gymnastics. Then, at age twenty-three, she began her teaching career at Smith College.

Within a year after joining the staff at Smith College, Berenson read about a new game then called "Basket Ball" that had been invented as a class exercise for boys. She observed the game being played at the YMCA Training Center in Springfield and attended a physical education conference at Yale University. At that convention, she met the game's inventor, Dr. James Naismith, and received his encouragement to adopt the sport as a team exercise for her female students. Women of that time did not participate in team sports, which were viewed as too strenuous. They did participate in individual sports such as horseback riding, hiking, rowing, swimming, golf, fencing, archery, and tennis.

On March 22, 1893, Berenson conducted the first official game of women's basketball, pitting the Smith sophomores against the freshmen. At that game, no male spectators were allowed. The new game soon swept the country, and by 1895, there were hundreds of women's basketball teams. The success of basketball also opened the door to other team sports programs for women.

At a time when women did not hold leadership positions in sports, Berenson wrote and developed the official rule book for women's collegiate basketball as well as numerous articles on the new sport. The first official publication of its kind, *Basket Ball for Women*, was published by the Spalding Athletic Library in 1901, with Berenson as its editor. She continued to edit the rules until the 1916–1917 issue. Many of the rules that she developed for women's basketball were the standard ones used for seventy years.

In 1905, Berenson was appointed chair of the basketball rules committee of the American Association for the Advent of Physical Education, the forerunner of the National Association for Girls and Women in Sports, whose mandate was to study the various interpretations of women's basketball rules. She served on this committee until 1917.

On January 15, 1911, Berenson married Herbert Vaughn Abbott, an English professor at Smith College. She resigned her post at Smith and became the director of physical education at Burnham School, a private girls' school, where she remained until 1921.

Senda Berenson died in Santa Barbara, California, on February 16, 1954. In 1984, her contributions to basketball were recognized when Senda Berenson Abbott became the first woman to be inducted into the Basketball Hall of Fame in Springfield, Massachusetts.

BIBLIOGRAPHY

National Basketball Hall of Fame. *Class of 1995 Yearbook* (1995); Berenson, Senda. Archives. Smith College, Northampton, Mass.; *DAB* 5; *EJ* (1983–1985); Hill, Edith N. "Pioneer Women in Physical Education." *The Research Quarterly Supplement* (October 1941): 658–665; Read, Phyllis J., and Bernard L. Witlieb. *The Book of Women's Firsts* (1992): 47; Spears, Betty. "Senda Berenson. New Woman: New Sport." *Coaching Women's Basketball* (December/January 1992), and "Senda Berenson Abbott. New Woman: New Sport." In *A Century of Women's Basketball: From Frailty to Final Four* (1991).

RUTH GURSKY

BERG, GERTRUDE (1899–1966)

For a generation of Americans, Gertrude Berg embodied Jewish motherhood in a series of radio, television, stage, and film performances. She is best remembered as the creative force behind the Goldbergs, a fictitious Jewish family who lived in an apartment at 1038 East Tremont Avenue in the Bronx. In addition to her matriarchal public persona, Berg was also a one of the first American women to work as a writer and producer of radio and television situation comedy.

The only child of Diana and Jacob Edelstein, Gertrude (Edelstein) Berg was born October 3, 1899, in New York City. Her childhood was divided between New York and Fleischmanns, a town in the Catskills, where her family ran a resort hotel. Here she made her first forays into producing and writing shows by creating entertainments for the hotel's guests. (Her hotel experience no doubt also inspired *The House of Glass*, a short-lived radio series about a Catskills resort that Berg produced for NBC in 1935.) While working in the Catskills, she met Lewis Berg. They were married in 1919 and were eventually parents to a son and a daughter.

After graduating from Wadleigh High School, Berg took extension courses in playwrighting at Columbia University. She tried her hand at the new genre of radio drama and eventually convinced NBC to broadcast her series by reading a sample script to network executives. From the late 1920s through the mid-1950s, the Goldbergs made appearances on radio, stage, television, and film. In addition to playing Molly, the family matriarch, Berg produced and scripted the Goldbergs' various outings. On radio, *The Rise of the Goldbergs* aired on NBC Blue from 1929 to 1934, and then on CBS from 1938 to 1945, making it one of the longest-running series in the medium. Berg presented the Goldbergs live on tour in 1934, and in a

Broadway play, *Me and Molly*, in 1948. Following a half-hour television play based on the radio series broadcast on NBC's *Chevrolet Tele-Theatre* in October 1948, *The Goldbergs* became one of the first situation comedies on American television in 1949 on CBS, and continued to appear on different networks until 1954 (CBS, 1949 to 1951; NBC, 1952 to 1953; DuMont, 1954). Unlike several other series, *The Goldbergs* made a successful transition from radio to television. Rating reports compiled by the A.C. Nielsen Company counted it among the ten most popular programs in the 1949–1950 television season. Berg received an Emmy for her portrayal of Molly in 1950. *Molly*, a film version of the Goldberg family, appeared in 1951. During its final season (1954–1955), the formerly live series was filmed and syndicated to local stations.

In these various manifestations, the Goldbergs offered a genial portrait of domestic life, centered, like most situation comedies, around a series of minor disruptions that were handily resolved by the end of each installment. At the same time, the Goldbergs

When she created Molly Goldberg and the Goldberg family for radio, stage, TV, and film, Gertrude Berg introduced middle-class Jewish life to millions of Americans.

offered millions of Americans an image of a second-generation American family whose Jewishness was, for the most part, a matter of comical speech—singsong rhythms, inverted syntax, malapropisms, with only the occasional Yiddish interjection ("nu?" and "oy!"). On *The Goldbergs*, integration into the American "mainstream" prevailed over immigrant Jewish particularism. Thus, while a portrait of George Washington hung prominently in the Goldbergs' living room on the television series, a samovar sat discreetly on a sideboard at the back of the dining room. Explicitly Jewish figures and issues appeared in occasional episodes: For example, Jan Peerce sang "Kol Nidre" on a radio broadcast for the High Holidays; Molly prepared gefilte fish in a 1955 telecast. But during their final season, the Goldbergs symbolically completed their Americanization (and "rise" into the middle class) by moving from their Bronx apartment to the fictitious suburb of Haverville.

The televised version of *The Goldbergs* is perhaps best remembered for an off-screen incident—the blacklisting of actor Philip Loeb (who played Molly's husband, Jake) by anticommunist activists in 1951. Although Berg defended Loeb, she eventually yielded to pressure from CBS and the program's sponsor, who threatened to cancel *The Goldbergs* if she did not replace Loeb with another performer. Unable to find work as an actor, Loeb committed suicide in 1955.

Berg's inviting, matronly persona of Molly Goldberg extended beyond the narrative confines of the various Goldberg family comedies. At the beginning and end of the television series, Berg often appeared leaning out a window of the family's Bronx apartment and spoke directly to the camera, telling viewers about the virtues of her sponsor's product, whether it was Sanka decaffeinated coffee or electrical appliances manufactured by RCA. (During the episodes Molly often leaned out the same window to talk to one of

The quintessential Jewish mother to millions of television viewers, Molly Goldberg (Gertrude Berg) is shown here in a scene from the film Molly, *presumably giving out a taste of chicken soup.*

her neighbors. Molly calling out, "Yoo hoo, Mrs. Bloom!" became something of a national catch phrase.) This device not only enabled Berg to establish an intimacy with the television audience, transforming the viewer's television set into a neighbor's window, but also conflated Berg and Goldberg in the public consciousness. This fusion of performer and character appeared as well in *The Molly Goldberg Cookbook*, written by Berg and Myra Waldo in 1955, in which Molly offered Jewish recipes and homey advice.

Following the cancellation of the series, Berg continued to perform her Jewish matriarch in other venues. On *The Gertrude Berg Show* (originally titled *Mrs. G. Goes to College*; CBS, 1961–1962) she portrayed Sarah Green, a widow who becomes a college student. Berg also received the Tony Award in 1959 for her portrayal of Mrs. Jacoby in *A Majority of One*, a Broadway comedy by Leonard Spigelgass about the relationship between a Jewish widow and a Japanese widower, both of whom had children who died during World War II.

The character of Molly Goldberg—an endearing but somewhat scatterbrained homemaker whose good intentions often led to comic mishaps—was not unlike her contemporary, Lucille Ball's Lucy Ricardo on *I Love Lucy*. The Goldberg persona that Berg created masked her own talents, professionalism, and intelligence. Behind this image of a simple housewife and mother stood one of the few women (along with Ball) who maintained creative control over her work in American broadcasting for decades.

In her memoirs, *Molly and Me*, written in 1961 with her son, Charney, Berg attributed her success in show business to her family's background in the hotel business, which taught her to be accommodating toward guests and to avoid offending them. Thus, during a period in American history when Jews were the object of considerable suspicion and discrimination, she managed to introduce a Jewish family as charming, if comical, guests into millions of American homes.

Gertrude Berg died in New York City on September 14, 1966.

BIBLIOGRAPHY

Berg, Gertrude, and Charney Berg. *Molly and Me* (1961); Berg, Gertrude, and Myra Waldo. *The Molly Goldberg Cookbook* (1955); Brooks, Tim, and Earle Marsh. *The Complete Directory to Prime Time Network TV Shows 1946–Present* (1988); Lipsitz, George. "The Meaning of Memory: Family, Class, and Ethnicity in Early Network Television Programs," *Camera Obscura* 16 (January 1988): 79–117; Marc, David. "Comic Visions of the City: New York and the Television Sitcom," *Radical History Review* 42 (1988): 49–63; Obituary. *NYTimes*, September 15, 1966, 43; Sapoznik, Henry. "Broadcast Ghetto: The Image of Jews on Mainstream American Radio," *Jewish Folklore and Ethnology Review* 16, no. 1 (1994): 37–39.

JEFFREY SHANDLER

BERKSON, LIBBIE SUCHOFF (1891–1970)

"Hoy, hoy, Yefefia, bat yarim Modinia." "Aunt Libbie" Berkson, a pioneer of Jewish education, led this song every summer at the start of Friday night *zmirot* singing at Camp Modin for girls. Generations of campers who attended Camp Modin were influenced by her spirit and leadership.

Libbie Suchoff Berkson was born on November 17, 1891, the fourth of six children, in Luptsch, a town near Minsk. Her father, Benjamin Suchovitsky, was a medical worker. He died when Libbie was nine years old. With her mother, Dina (Cahan), and her one sister and four brothers, she immigrated to the United States in 1903. The family settled on the Lower East Side of New York City. There, Libbie learned English so that she spoke it with no European accent. She attended New York public schools, received her B.A. degree from HUNTER COLLEGE in 1911, became a teacher in the New York public schools, and received her M.A. from Teachers College, Columbia University in 1915.

While still in college, she became involved in youth work. She was the first director of the Anti-Mission League, an organization that provided educational activities for Jewish children. This was the beginning of her lifelong career of leadership in that field. As one of the original members of Samson Benderly's program of Jewish education, she was director of the League of Jewish Youth, which was created to provide informal Jewish education to adolescent girls. While with the Benderly group, she met Isaac B. Berkson, the educational philosopher, administrator, and professor. They were married on November 27, 1919, and subsequently had three children, Dina (b. 1922), Carmel (b. 1924), and Gershon (b. 1931). From 1922 to 1927, Libbie Berkson also worked as a teacher and then became director of a Hebrew high school in Philadelphia.

In June 1922, with Alexander and Julia Dushkin and Albert and BERTHA SCHOOLMAN, Libbie and I.B. Berkson conceived the original idea of a summer "camp with the Jewish ideal." The camp was located in Canaan, Maine. When the Berksons became its sole owners in 1942, Libbie assumed the main responsibility.

The camp retained its strong Jewish spirit, daily religious services in the Conservative tradition, and a strictly kosher kitchen—a major accomplishment for a camp in Maine in those days. She continued to direct Camp Modin until her retirement in 1958.

When I.B. Berkson became a member of the executive committee of the Jewish Agency in Palestine under the British Mandate from 1928 to 1933, the family lived in Talpioth, Jerusalem, where Libbie Berkson became involved in the organization of the first experimental Hebrew kindergarten. She also was a member of the Palestine Council of HADASSAH, and later established a teahouse in Jerusalem (the Al Cos Te, now the popular Atara in Jerusalem). During these years, despite her strong affection for Palestine, she also traveled repeatedly to the United States to continue running Camp Modin, and ultimately the family returned to the United States permanently in 1935.

After her retirement from Camp Modin, she remained active with "her projects," now completely focused on Israel. She helped with Mi Yeled l'Yeled, a project in which American children provided funds to buy books for children in Israel. She also worked with Nogah Hareuveni during the initial stages of establishment of Neot Kedumim, now one of Israel's leading educational centers.

"Aunt Libbie" died on August 3, 1970, after a long illness and a final trip to Israel.

BIBLIOGRAPHY

Dushkin, Alexander M. *Living Bridges: Memoirs of an Educator* (1975); Skirball, Henry Franc. "Isaac Baer Berkson and Jewish Education." Ed.D. diss., Columbia University Teachers College, NYC (1977); Winter, Nathan H. *Jewish Education in a Pluralist Society: Samson Benderly and Jewish Education in the United States* (1966) *WWIAJ* (1938).

GERSHON BERKSON

BERLER, BEATRICE (b. 1915)

Beatrice Berler returned to school at the age of forty-five and became an award-winning translator of Spanish-language novels and history. Her work as a literacy activist has earned her national recognition.

Beatrice "Beady" Berler is the child of Ukrainian immigrants Clara Bichman and Max Goldenblank. Born in Brooklyn in 1915, Beady spent her first two years in New York before moving to Miami, Florida, with her parents and younger brother Aaron. In 1932, she graduated from Miami Senior High School and became a buyer for a store specializing in ladies' intimate apparel. She worked in women's fashion for twelve years in Florida and briefly in Tennessee. In 1945, she married Albert Berler, a real estate investor, and they settled in San Antonio, Texas.

After continuing to work in women's sportswear for ten years, in 1956 she decided to pursue a college and graduate education. Berler earned a B.A. and an M.A. in foreign languages and history from Trinity University in San Antonio. Her master's thesis, "The Mexican Revolution: Its Reflection in the Novel," was published in part in *Hispania*. In addition, she has cotranslated three novels—*The Underdogs, Trials of a Respectable Family*, and *The Firefly*—by Mariano Azuela, the eminent Mexican author.

Aside from these publishing achievements, Berler has also become a renowned community activist. As president of the Brandeis University National Women's Committee from 1971 to 1973, she directed and organized sixty-five thousand members in the effort to raise funds for the Brandeis libraries. Simultaneously, in 1971 she began a collaborative project with federal judge William S. Sessions to provide reading material to correctional institutions. The Brandeis women's committee, through Berler's leadership, channeled over four million leisure reading books to thirty federal correctional institutions. In recognition of her efforts, the Federal Bar Association of San Antonio honored Berler in 1975 for Outstanding Community Services. And, in October of 1980, Norman Carlson, director of the Federal Bureau of Prisons, acknowledged the donation of these most needed paperbacks at a formal ceremony held in Washington, D.C.

In 1987, Mayor Henry Cisneros and the entire San Antonio City Council named Berler a benefactor of the city for her idea to raise funds for the San Antonio Public Library. With her help, over $64,000 was raised in four weeks, and this is now a yearly project. In addition, the Texas Library Association Awards Committee selected Berler as its recipient of the 1987 Outstanding Service to Libraries Award because of her innovative approach to outside funding for the San Antonio Public Library. In February 1988, the National Conference of Christians and Jews honored her with its Brotherhood Award.

Berler continues to translate and publish books. In 1988, she published *The Conquest of Mexico*—a modern rendering of William H. Prescott's history—and in 1993 the New York Public Library gave a special award to her translation of *Ellos Vienen . . . La Conquista de Mexico* [They are coming . . . The conquest of Mexico], by José López Portillo, former president of Mexico.

Berler served as a member of Brandeis University's board of trustees from 1971 to 1973 and is currently a fellow of the university. In addition to her innumerable academic and civic achievements, throughout the years numerous children from San Antonio and throughout the country have "adopted" Berler as their grandmother, confidant, and special friend.

SELECTED WORKS BY BEATRICE BERLER

"Azuela y La Veracidad Histórica." *Revista Ibero-Americana* (February 1966): 189–305; *The Conquest of Mexico: A Modern Rendering of W.H. Prescott's History* (1988); *El Epistolario y Archivo de Mariano Azuela* [The letters and archives of Mariano Azuela]. Compiled and edited by Beatrice Berler (1969. Reprint, 1993); *El Epistolario y Archivo de Mariano Azuela: Documentos Adicionales* [The letters and archives of Mariano Azuela: Additional documents]. Compiled and edited by Beatrice Berler (1996); "The Mexican Revolution: Its Reflection in the Novel." Master's thesis, Trinity University, San Antonio, Texas (1965).

TRANSLATIONS

Los de Abajo [The underdogs], by Mariano Azuela. Translated by Beatrice Berler, with Frances Kellam Hendricks (1979); *Ellos Vienen . . . La Conquista de México* [They are coming . . . The conquest of Mexico], by José López Portillo. Translated by Beatrice Berler (1992); *Hispanoamérica, sus Razas y Civilizaciones* [Hispanic America and its civilizations], by Edmund S. Urbanski. Translated by Beatrice Berler, with Frances Kellam Hendricks (1978); *La Luciérnaga* [The firefly], by Mariano Azuela. Translated by Beatrice Berler, with Frances Kellam Hendricks (1964); *La Revolución de la Iglesia en América Latina* [The revolution of the Latin American church], by Hugo LaTorre Cabal. Translated by Beatrice Berler, with Frances Kellam Hendricks (1978); *Latina America y el Mundo* [Latin America and the world], by Leopoldo Zea. Translated by Beatrice Berler, with Frances Kellam Hendricks (1969); *Las Tribulaciones de Una Familia Decente* [The trials of a respectable family], by Mariano Azuela. Translated by Beatrice Berler, with Frances Kellam Hendricks (1979).

BIBLIOGRAPHY

Dictionary of International Biography (1988); *Who's Who in American Women* (1997); *Who's Who in Religion* (1989); *Who's Who in the Southwest* (1996); *Who's Who in World Jewry* (1989).

ROSE ANN MILLER

BERLIN, FANNY (1852–1921)

A courageous, motivated pioneer in medicine, in the late 1800s Fanny Berlin became one of the first Jewish women to practice surgery in the United States.

Fanny Berlin was born Stefanija Berlinerblau in 1852, in Cherson, Ukraine. Determined to be useful to society by becoming a physician, she and a friend persuaded their parents to allow them to travel to Zurich, Switzerland, where they joined a colony of Russian women who were studying medicine at the University of Zurich. She entered the Faculty of Medicine in 1870, but in 1873 the Russian government banned any further study by women in Zurich. Fanny completed her medical studies in 1875 at the University of Bern. She was described at that time as intelligent, calm, helpful, and idealistic.

Following graduation, Fanny Berlinerblau, as she was still known at that time, decided to continue her studies in the United States. In 1877, she was appointed resident physician at the New England Hospital for Women and Children in Boston, Massachusetts, and in 1879 joined the hospital staff as one of four women surgeons. The New England Hospital was administered by Dr. Marie Zakrzewska, a physician who felt strongly that women doctors could be successful only in a hospital led and staffed by women physicians.

Women doctors were not able to practice in other hospitals in Boston and were not accepted in the Massachusetts Medical Society, so in 1878 a group of ten women physicians, including Berlin, formed their own New England Women's Medical Society. It was not until 1885 that Fanny Berlin and the other female physicians could join the Massachusetts Medical Society.

In 1881, the *American Journal of Obstetrics* published an article by Fanny Berlin titled "Three Cases of Complete Prolapsus Uteri Operated upon According to the Method of Leon Le Fort." By this time, Berlin had become respected for her surgical expertise in performing laparotomies. She became chief surgeon at the New England Hospital and remained there until 1894, when she resigned to devote full-time to private practice.

Berlin used her linguistic skills in helping the many foreign-born people in Boston, and contributed actively in the advancement of women in medicine. She retired from private practice in 1916, as her vision deteriorated in her later years.

Fanny Berlin died in Boston on September 4, 1921, respected for her medical skills and her compassion for her patients.

BIBLIOGRAPHY

Bonner, Thomas Neville. *To the Ends of the Earth* (1992); Drachman, Virginia G. *Hospital with a Heart* (1984); Ehrenfried, Albert. *A Chronicle of Boston Jewry* (1963); Meijer, J.M. *Knowledge and Revolution* (1955); Rohner, Hanny. *Die Ersten 30 Jahre des Medizinischen Frauenstudiums an der Universität Zurich 1867–1897* (1972); Tiburtius, Franziska. *Erinnerungen einer Achtzigjährigen* (1929); *UJE*.

JUDITH CHASIN

BERNARD, JESSIE (1903–1996)

Jessie Bernard once wrote of feminism, "Once you 'catch it,' it makes all the difference in how you see the world." Bernard's feminist "epiphany" came at age sixty-seven at a meeting of the Woman's Caucus of the American Sociological Association in the spring of 1969. Already the best-known woman sociologist of her generation, she quickly became an important voice of American feminism.

Born Jessie Sarah Ravitch in Minneapolis on June 8, 1903, she was the third of four children of David and Bessie Kanter Ravitch (later Ravage), Jewish Romanian immigrants. Modestly successful, her father worked his way from dairy deliveryman to real estate broker. Having arrived in the 1880s before her future husband, Bessie had toiled in the New York garment district and reportedly once marched in a woman's rights parade. But to Jessie, her mother's "complete satisfaction" in marriage robbed her of personality. Her youthful heroine was instead her maternal grandmother who lived with the family, dispensed discipline, and "set the Jewish stamp on our home."

In 1923, Jessie earned a B.A. at the University of Minnesota, and in 1924 an M.A. for a thesis on "Changes of Attitudes of Jews in the First and Second Generation." There she also met Luther Lee Bernard, a sociology professor two decades her senior, whom she married on September 23, 1925. Stormy from the start, their union limited her opportunities for more than a decade, as they followed Luther's peripatetic career before settling finally at Washington University in St. Louis in 1929. During these years, Jessie Bernard unsuccessfully pursued a literary career, earned a Ph.D. from Washington University in 1935, and was research assistant for the Bernards' jointly written *Origins of American Sociology* (1943). Separating from Luther in 1936, she worked in Washington for four years before returning to her marriage and a teaching post at Lindenwood College. In 1947 both Bernards were appointed to Penn State, from which she retired in 1964. They had three children, Dorothy, Claude, and David, whom Jessie Bernard raised as a single parent following her husband's death in 1951.

Throughout her early years, Bernard struggled with her Jewish heritage, changing her given middle name "Sarah" to "Shirley" in high school and listening to her older sister lecture the family on "American" food and life-style. Luther's openly hostile attitudes toward Jews, her family in particular, blighted their marriage. As she worked her way through her own conflicted feelings, she wrote extensively on Jewish culture and her own "bicultural identity" as a "Jew in a WASP world." In 1938, she joined the Society of Friends.

As a sociologist, Bernard specialized in the family, sexuality, and gender, often anticipating new approaches in a fast-changing discipline. Her most widely discussed books were *Academic Women* (1964), *The Future of Marriage* (1972), and *The Female World* (1981). Methodologically, she moved from a narrowly quantitative approach to a critique of the alleged male bias of this position, and thematically, from a resigned acceptance of women's traditional role to an analysis of the "female world" that historically has limited women's opportunities.

Bernard's many honors included election as president of the Eastern Sociological Society (1953) and the Society for the Study of Social Problems (1963), and vice president of the American Sociological Association (1953–1954). In retirement, she served as visiting professor at Princeton (1959–1960) and elsewhere, and received several honorary degrees and almost annual awards from various professional organizations. A personal, more permanent legacy, however, is preserved in the many letters she received during the 1970s and 1980s from dozens of younger women sociologists for whom she served as mentor and role model.

Jessie Bernard died in Washington, D.C., on October 6, 1996.

SELECTED WORKS BY JESSIE BERNARD

Academic Women (1964); *American Community Behavior* (1949. Rev. ed. 1952); *American Family Behavior* (1942); "Biculturality." In *Jews in a Gentile World*, edited by Isacque Graeber and Steuart H. Britt (1942); *The Female World* (1981); *The Female World from a Global Perspective* (1987); *The Future of Marriage* (1972); *The Future of Motherhood* (1975); *Marriage and Family Among Negroes* (1966); "My Four Revolutions." *American Journal of Sociology* 78 (1973): 773–791; *Origins of American Sociology*, with Luther L. Bernard (1943); *Remarriage: A Study of Marriage* (1956); *Self-Portrait of a Family* (1978); *The Sex Game* (1968); *Social Problems at Midcentury* (1957); *The Sociology of Community* (1972); *Women and the Public Interest* (1971).

BIBLIOGRAPHY

Bannister, Robert C. *Jessie Bernard: The Making of a Feminist* (1991); Bernard, Jessie and Luther L. Bernard. Papers. Labor Archives, Pennsylvania State University Library, University Park; Deegan, Mary Jo. "Jessie Bernard." In *Women in Sociology: A Bio-bibliographical Sourcebook* (1991); Howe, Harriet. "Jessie Bernard." *Sociological Inquiry* 64 (1994): 10–22; Lipman-Blumen, Jean. "Jessie Bernard—A 'Reasonable Rebel.'" *Gender and Society* 2 (1988): 271–273; Obituaries. *NYTimes*, October 11, 1996, B9, and *Washington Post*, October 10, 1996, E4.

ROBERT BANNISTER

BERNAYS, ANNE FLEISCHMAN
(b. 1930)

Anne Bernays's work as novelist and nonfiction writer is notable for its literary quality and as a running commentary on manners and customs. She comes from a background of high achievement.

Her parents, Edward L. Bernays, a nephew of Sigmund Freud, and Doris E. Fleischman, were successful pioneers in the field of public relations. Anne Bernays was born in New York City on September 14, 1930, and raised in privileged circumstances. Bernays attended the Brearley School from 1939 to 1948 before going on to Wellesley College and graduating in 1952 from Barnard College, which she favored for its urban setting and social diversity. During these years she developed a critical distance from her parents' confidently articulated opinions. After college, she worked briefly for *Town and Country* and then as managing editor of *Discovery*, a magazine of new writing. This brought her into contact with the literary and social culture of Greenwich Village and defined her subsequent career.

In 1954, she married biographer Justin Kaplan; they had three daughters and live in Cambridge, Massachusetts. In 1962, she published *Short Pleasures*, the first of her eight novels. The most recent, *Professor Romeo* (1989), applied her eye and idiom to the subject of sexual harassment. The *New York Times Book Review* featured it on page one and listed it as a notable book of the year. In Bernays's fifth novel, *Growing Up Rich*, she wrote about being Jewish in America. Its young, orphaned heroine traverses the vexed territory between "Our Crowd" and Russian Jewry, New York's Upper East Side and suburban Brookline, Massachusetts, and the opposed policies of assimilation and separateness they represent. *Growing Up Rich* received the Edward Lewis Wallant Award for its contribution to American Jewish life. By this time, Bernays had come to reject her father's claim that to be Jewish was purely elective. Although far from religiously observant, she has been increasingly active as a board member of such ventures as the Vilna Center for Jewish Heritage and the Jewish Film Festival, both based in Boston.

In addition to her novels, Bernays has written dozens of reviews, travel and opinion essays for national publications, as well as two nonfiction books: *What If? Writing Exercises for Fiction Writers* (1990, with Pamela Painter) and *The Language of Names* (1997, with Justin Kaplan). She has taught at several institutions, from 1992 to 1995 at the College of the Holy Cross as Jenks Professor of Contemporary Letters and, more recently, at Boston University's College of Communications. Active in the literary and artistic community, she founded and for many years served on the executive board of PEN/New England. She is on the advisory board of the National Writers Union and has also been chair of the board of trustees of the Fine Arts Work Center in Provincetown, near her summer home in Truro. She is a member of the Century Association in New York.

Bernays is a dedicated swimmer, walker, traveler, singer, and player of word games as well as an enthusiastic grandmother. She has managed to resolve many of the tensions of being a Jew, a woman, and a writer in America.

SELECTED WORKS BY
ANNE FLEISCHMAN BERNAYS

Growing Up Rich (1975); *The Language of Names*, with Justin Kaplan (1997); *Professor Romeo* (1989); *Short Pleasures* (1962); *What If? Writing Exercises for Fiction Writers*, with Pamela Painter (1990).

BIBLIOGRAPHY

Contemporary American Authors; *Who's Who in America*.

JUSTIN KAPLAN

BERNHARD, DOROTHY LEHMAN
(1903–1969)

Dorothy Lehman Bernhard was a civic leader and philanthropist who was a staunch and tireless supporter of children in need. With roots in two of New York's most prestigious German Jewish families, she dedicated her time, energy, and family wealth to over thirty human service, public welfare, cultural, and social organizations. Her contributions were widely recognized, including receiving the Child Welfare League of America's first Child Welfare Award from Eleanor Roosevelt in 1962.

The oldest child of Arthur Lehman and ADELE LEWISOHN LEHMAN, Dorothy was born in New York City on April 22, 1903. She and her two younger sisters, HELEN (BUTTENWIESER) and Frances (Loeb), grew up in a tightly knit extended family that lived, worked, socialized, and vacationed together. Although they were not particularly religious, the entire family proudly embraced Jewish values and identified very strongly with Jewish traditions of helping those in need. With models like her parents, uncles Herbert and Irving Lehman (governor and chief justice of the Court of Appeals in New York State, respectively), and grandfathers Mayer Lehman and Adolph Lewisohn (major business magnates and philanthropists), Dorothy absorbed a deep commitment to helping others and addressing social needs.

She graduated from the Horace Mann School in 1920, attended Wellesley College for one year, and married investment banker Richard Jaques Bernhard in 1923. They had two children, Robert Arthur (b. 1928) and William Lehman (b. 1931). In the late 1930s, in response to the rise of Hitler and the persecution of the Jews, the Lehman family established a fund to aid distant relatives in Germany to emigrate, and Bernhard managed these efforts, including providing direct assistance in resettlement, job finding, and addressing other social needs upon the refugees' arrival.

Although she did not have any formal training in social work, Bernhard became deeply involved in both the provision of services and giving support and direction for the field. She was a moving force in child welfare, devoting thirty years to the Child Welfare League of America, holding the role of president from 1957 to 1962 and vice president for various terms totaling thirteen years. She served on the board of the Citizens Committee for Children of New York City for over twenty years and was active in the Jewish Child Care Association, where she was vice president (1940–1942) and chaired their Foster Home Bureau. Not only was she was a vocal advocate for the deinstitutionalization of foster care, she also exhibited a deep personal commitment serving as a foster parent herself.

In the field of social work, she was a board member and chair of the HUNTER COLLEGE School of Social Work Advisory Committee and served on national and international councils of social work. Bernhard's contributions to these fields were also recognized through public appointments. She was a member of the New York State Board of Social Welfare from 1942 to 1947, was appointed to the New York City Advisory Board on Public Welfare by Mayor Robert F. Wagner in 1960, and served on other city and state committees.

Her diverse activities in Jewish communal organizations included being a trustee of the Federation of Jewish Philanthropies, a board member of the New York Association for New Americans, an honorary vice president of the Associated YM-YWHA's of Greater New York (formerly known as the YMHA), a member of the publications committee of *Commentary* magazine, and a long-time member of Temple Emanu-El. In addition, Bernhard was a notable art collector, was a benefactor to the Metropolitan Museum of Art, was appointed to the board of the New York Philharmonic, and promoted international understanding through her fifteen-year involvement in the Institute of International Education.

Dorothy Lehman Bernhard was a leader in the field of social welfare in New York City. While her actions were rooted in Jewish values, they transcended religious and ethnic barriers. Following her death from cancer on March 6, 1969, her dedication, leadership, and unfailing concern for others, particularly children, were widely lauded.

BIBLIOGRAPHY

AJYB 71:602; Bernard, Jacqueline. *The Children You Gave Us: A History of One Hundred Fifty Years of Service to Children* (1973); Bernhard, Robert A. Oral History Collection. UJA-Federation of Jewish Philanthropies of New York, 1985; Birmingham, Stephen. *Our Crowd: The Great Jewish Families of New York* (1967); Buttenwieser, Helen L. Oral History Collection. UJA-Federation of Jewish Philanthropies of New York, 1977, 1982; Loeb, John Langeloth, Frances Lehman Loeb, and Kenneth Libo. *All in a Lifetime: A Personal Memoir* (1996); Obituary. *NYTimes*, March 7, 1969, 34:1; *WWWIA* 5; *Who's Who of American Women*. 6th ed. (1971).

JENNIFER ROSENBERG

BERNSTEIN, ALINE (1880–1955)

In the world of theater, Aline Bernstein is remembered as one of the most important designers of the first half of the twentieth century. In the world of literature, she is remembered for loving, not wisely but too well, one of the great writers of her time, the young Thomas Wolfe.

Born December 22, 1880, Aline Bernstein was the daughter of noted actor Joseph Frankau and his wife, Rebecca Goldsmith. She grew up in a boardinghouse run by Rebecca's sister Mamie, surrounded by actors and laughter. Her mother died when she was eleven and her father when she was sixteen. For the next few years, she and her younger sister Ethel were shunted around among relatives. They had no stable home, but Bernstein found a sense of belonging when she walked the streets of the Lower East Side. "My Jewishness runs through me like a strain of gold," she would say later in life. After graduating from the School of Applied Design, she met and married Theodore Bernstein. Ethel moved in with the couple, and the three of them were never again apart.

In 1911, the two sisters began to volunteer their time at the Henry Street Settlement House, where Alice and IRENE LEWISOHN were developing a theater. Soon Aline was the main designer at the Neighborhood Playhouse. In *Aline*, Carole Klein writes that the playhouse was called, "admiringly, 'a woman's theater,' and newspapers reporting their progress announced that: 'No man has anything whatsover to do with it except by invitation.'" It was the first New York theater to design and make all of its own costumes, props, and scenery. Indeed, critic John Gassner has said that the profession of "scene designer" originated at this small, innovative community theater that produced the early works of such writers as Clifford Odets, Elmer Rice, and even Eugene O'Neill.

During this time, Bernstein also gave birth to two children, Theodore (b. 1904) and Elda (b. 1906). She found great satisfaction in the role of wife and mother. In her early forties, she realized that the deafness which was part of her family's genetic legacy was becoming severe. She learned to read lips and carried on.

In the 1923–1924 season, Bernstein' strikingly original design for *The Little Clay Cart* at the Playhouse and her work with Norman Bel Geddes in the creation of hundreds of costumes for Max Reinhardt's production of *The Miracle* on Broadway consolidated her reputation as a designer. She began to design show after show, raiding museums for warrants of authenticity and traveling to Europe to gather materials. On her return from one of the European journeys she

One of the greatest theatrical designers of the American theater, Aline Bernstein is often remembered for her stormy relationship with writer Thomas Wolfe. [New York Public Library]

met and fell in love with twenty-five-year-old Thomas Wolfe. Her passion was thoroughly reciprocated, and a new stage in her life began.

For the next five years, Bernstein and Wolfe waged a war on many fronts, not the least of which was between themselves. They also fought Wolfe's inner demons, which were many. Bernstein nurtured him while he struggled to create his monumental first novel, *Look Homeward, Angel.* On another front, Aline fought to keep her passion for Wolfe from destroying her marriage and family. She was helped in this difficult battle by her husband's sensitivity and understanding and by the loving equity she had accumulated in twenty-three years of dedication to him and their children.

In 1928, Eva Le Gallienne approached Bernstein about becoming resident designer for her new theater, the Civic Repertory Company. Bernstein threw herself into the project, enabling the cash-poor group to function as a true repertory company by designing a unit set with movable parts that could be adapted easily to a variety of plays.

Wolfe's breakup with Bernstein in 1930 left both of them shattered. She went into a depression that threatened her family life in a way her affair had never done. He went into an emotional tailspin from which he never completely recovered. He wrote about her and her family in two novels and several short stories, and they continued a rocky friendship for years, in spite of a latent vein of anti-Semitism in Wolfe that he would mine when he most wanted to hurt her. When he died at the age of thirty-eight, the last words he said were a cry for Aline.

With time, Bernstein recovered. She founded the Costume Museum, which later became part of the Museum of Modern Art, and began writing, receiving critical acclaim for her work. May Sarton wrote of her novel *The Journey Down,* "I was up all night reading your book. It is a beautiful piece of work, with the intensity, texture and peculiar sustained excitement of a poem."

Bernstein won a Tony Award for her costume design for the opera *Regina* in 1949, when she was seventy. It was one of four shows she did that season. In 1953 she did the costumes for the Off-Broadway production of *The World of Sholom Aleichem.* She died in New York on September 7, 1955.

BIBLIOGRAPHY

Houghton, Norris. "The Designer Sets the Stage." *Theatre Arts* (February 1937); Klein, Carole. *Aline* (1979); *NAW*; Obituary. *NYTimes*, September 7, 1955.

KATHLEEN THOMPSON

BERNSTEIN, REBECCA THURMAN (1896–1987)

In 1968, Rebecca Thurman Bernstein was awarded the Eleanor Roosevelt Humanities Award by the Israel Bond organization. She was cited in the November 19, 1968, *Portland (Maine) Press Herald* for "her outstanding contributions over many years to the human values of the people of Portland." Concern for the human condition was the focus of Bernstein's long and productive life.

Rebecca (Thurman) Bernstein was born in Boston, Massachusetts, on April 14, 1896, the second child of Russian immigrants, Jacob and Bella (Rabinowitz) Thurman. Jacob was a flour merchant and founded Thurman and Company, which is still operated by family members. She had an older sister, two younger sisters, and two younger brothers.

Jacob believed that his daughters, as well as his sons, should be well educated; thus five of the six children earned graduate degrees. Rebecca's older sister, Anna, was a dentist; younger sister, Esther, was a schoolteacher; brothers Aaron and Harold were a doctor and merchant, respectively. One sister, Sarah, married and did not go to college.

Rebecca attended Boston schools. One of 10 women in a class of 113, she received her LL.B from Boston University Law School in 1917, graduating magna cum laude, and received her LL.M., also from Boston University, in 1918. She was a member of the Massachusetts and Maine bars.

For several years after her graduation Rebecca worked for Thurman and Company. On June 24, 1922, she married Israel Bernstein, a Portland, Maine, lawyer. After she married, Rebecca Bernstein devoted her life to her family and to the Portland community.

Bernstein was proud of her Jewish heritage and worked for many Jewish causes, but her interests were not limited to or by her Jewishness. She was admired and respected by the greater community as well as the Jewish community. She belonged to the NATIONAL COUNCIL OF JEWISH WOMEN and served as president of the Portland and New England Sections and also on the national board. She served as vice president of the Jewish Federation, and as a life director of Portland's Jewish Community Center.

Health and social issues that affected all citizens were her prime concern. She was an early member of the Birth Control League. She served as a director of the Community Chest, the precursor of the United Fund. She was a life board member of Child and Family Services and a member of the women's board of Portland's largest hospital, Maine Medical Center.

An accomplished speaker, Bernstein frequently addressed community groups about health and social issues and often testified before legislative committees about those issues. She received many honors and commendations for her work, including Portland College Club Woman of the Year (1966), Eleanor Roosevelt Humanities Award (1968), Distinguished Community Service Award from the University of Maine (1969), and from the Portland Section of the National Council of Jewish Women (1975). She also served on the boards of the Portland Public Library and Westbrook College.

Bernstein was a member and director of the College Club of Portland. She established the College Club Remembrance Fund for gift scholarships, requesting that, in addition to memorial gifts, people donate to the fund to celebrate happy events. The interest was to be given to female scholarship students so that they might enjoy small luxuries not otherwise available to them. This thoughtful gesture epitomizes Bernstein's care for and affirmation of the human spirit.

Rebecca and Israel Bernstein had two children. Their son, Sumner Thurman Bernstein, is a lawyer and senior partner of Bernstein, Shur, Sawyer and Nelson, the Portland firm founded by his father. He is, as was his mother, active in civic affairs. Their daughter, Helen Barbara Bernstein Wasserman, is a community activist and volunteer.

Rebecca Thurman Bernstein died at age ninety-one on December 22, 1987. Her husband died in 1967.

BIBLIOGRAPHY

Bernstein, Sumner T. Interview with author, Portland, Maine, August 1, 1996; College Club of Portland. *Mosaics of the College Club of Portland 1900–1995* (1995); Hagopian, Margo. Telephone conversation with author, Portland, Maine, August 23, 1996; "Local Woman to Receive Eleanor Roosevelt Award." *Portland (Maine) Press Herald*, November 19, 1968; "Rebecca Bernstein, Community Leader." *Portland (Maine) Press Herald*, December 23, 1987; *WWIAJ* (1938).

SANDRA HARTFORD

BERNSTEIN, THERESA (b. 1890)

An artistic career lasting over eighty years and spanning the twentieth century might seem a worthwhile achievement in itself, but to Theresa Bernstein, longevity is just "an accident of nature." Only art matters. Painter, printmaker, teacher, poet, celebrated raconteur, and art activist, Bernstein has been an

Though her greatest acclaim came early in her career, Theresa Bernstein's life and art have virtually spanned the twentieth century. She is shown here in 1924 with her painting Sunset Hour. *[Library of Congress]*

enduring fixture in the art worlds of New York and the summer colony at Gloucester, Massachusetts.

The only child of European immigrants Isidore and Anne (Ferber) Bernstein, Theresa was born in Philadelphia on March 1, 1890. She graduated from the Philadelphia School of Design for Women (now the Moore College of Art and Design) in 1911 (the college awarded her an honorary doctorate in 1992). The following year, her father, a textile manufacturer, moved the family to New York City. Bernstein rounded out her art education at the Art Students League, where she studied with William Merritt Chase. In 1919, she married artist William Meyerowitz, a Russian emigré. They had one child, a daughter who died in infancy. Meyerowitz died in 1981.

Although not a formal member of the Ashcan School, Bernstein shared with it a passion for "modern" subject matter, to which she added a radically expressive manner. She embraced urbanism and popular culture with enthusiasm, painting such subjects as the cinema, trolleys and the elevated trains, and Coney Island. She exhibited at the MacDowell Club and had a major show at the Milch Gallery in 1919. Her harbor views and beach scenes painted in blazing Fauve-like color attracted equal interest among the young modernists of Gloucester.

After the 1920s, her reputation waned for many reasons, chief among them a decreased interest in realistic subject matter. There followed a lifetime of steady, consistent work in her signature style—work that was exhibited, reviewed, and (sometimes) purchased, but that did not achieve great critical acclaim. Renewed interest in Bernstein's art was sparked by the women's movement, which recognized the quality and originality of her work and her historic contribution to early twentieth-century American art.

As a woman crossing the gender threshold at the beginning of the new century, Bernstein experienced the excitement of that moment but was not spared the indignity of discrimination. Either paying a reluctant compliment or implying criticism, reviewers often described her work as having a "masculine" style. Whatever the gender construction of her style, she *saw* as a woman, incorporating into her art types and activities ignored by others, such as women at work, women artists, and suffragist parades.

Although Jewish subject matter was not a specialty of Bernstein's, her works in this genre are among her most profound and moving. Her tropism for community aspects of life led her to depict such subjects as weddings and synagogue services. An ardent Zionist, Bernstein attended the first Zionist meeting in America in Madison Square Garden in 1923, an experience she transformed into the painting *Zionist Meeting, New York* (1923, National Jewish Fund). Fully assimilated and completely at ease with American culture, Bernstein nevertheless maintained close touch with her Jewish roots and visited Israel many times. Raised in what she referred to as a secular household, she later took on the greater religious observance of her husband.

Works by Theresa Bernstein are scattered across the country in many different venues, from prestigious private collections such as the Manoogian Collection to small personal caches in Gloucester, where, in the early days, she may have bartered a painting for food or fuel oil. The Mannheim, Pennsylvania, post office boasts a Bernstein mural from the 1930s. Major works are also held by the Jewish Museum, the Cape Ann Historical Association, the Museum of the City of New York, the National Museum of Women in the Arts, the Montclair Art Museum, and the Archer M. Huntington Art Gallery at the University of Texas.

SELECTED WORKS BY THERESA BERNSTEIN
Israeli Journal (1994); *The Journal* (1991); *The Poetic Canvas* (1989); *The Sketchbook* (1992); *William Meyerowitz: The Artist Speaks* (1986).

GROUP EXHIBITIONS
American Women Artists: The 20th Century. Knoxville Museum of Art (1989–1990); *Cultural Roles: William Meyerowitz, Theresa Bernstein and Peter Blume.* Jewish Museum (1995–1997). *The Genius of the Fair Muse: Painting and Sculpture Celebrating American Women Artists 1875 to 1945.* Grand Central Art Galleries, Inc., New York (1987); *New York Themes: Paintings and Prints by William Meyerowitz and Theresa Bernstein.* New-York Historical Society (1983); *Painting a Place in America: Jewish Artists in New York 1900–1945.* The Jewish Museum (1991); *The Paintings and Etchings of William Meyerowitz and Theresa Bernstein.* Cape Ann Historical Association (1986); *Women's Caucus for Art Honor Awards.* National Museum of Women in the Arts (1991).

RECENT ONE-PERSON EXHIBITIONS
Echoes of New York: The Paintings of Theresa Bernstein. Museum of the City of New York (1990); *Theresa Bernstein.* Smith-Girard, Stamford, Conn. (1985); *Theresa Bernstein: Expressions of Cape Cod and New York, 1914–1972, A* *Centennial Exhibition.* The Stamford Museum and Nature Center (1989); *Theresa Bernstein, People and Places: A Retrospective.* The Philadelphia Museum of Judaica (1995).

BIBLIOGRAPHY
Burnham, Patricia M. "Theresa Bernstein." *Woman's Art Journal* 9, no. 2 (Fall 1988/Winter 1989): 22–27, and *Theresa Bernstein, People and Places: A Retrospective.* Exhibition brochure. The Philadelphia Museum of Judaica (1995); Cohen, Michelle. *Echoes of New York.* Exhibition brochure. Museum of the City of New York (1990); Jackson, Girard. *Theresa Bernstein.* Exhibition catalog. Stamford (1985), and *Theresa Bernstein: Expressions of Cape Cod and New York, 1914–1972, A Centennial Exhibition.* Exhibition catalog. Stamford Museum and Nature Center (1989); Kleeblatt, Norman, and Susan Chevlowe. *Painting a Place in America Jewish Artists in New York 1900–1945.* Exhibition catalog. The Jewish Museum in cooperation with Indiana University Press (1991); Lozowick, Louis. *100 Contemporary American Jewish Painters and Sculptors* (1947); *Who's Who in American Art* (1995–1996): 98–99.

PATRICIA BURNHAM

BETH JACOB SCHOOLS
see BAIS YA'ACOV SCHOOLS

BETTMAN, META POLLAK
(1880–1955)
Meta Pollak Bettman was an untiring volunteer in Jewish and civic causes. She was born in Cincinnati, Ohio, on April 19, 1880, one of five children—three brothers and a sister—to Emil and Carrie (Benjamin) Pollak. Her father, born in Vienna in 1846, immigrated to America in 1865. His business ventures included a grocery store, jobbing crockery, and a scrap iron and steel company. Meta attended Cincinnati High School and did postgraduate work in languages, art, music, philosophy, and history. She married Irvin Bettman, a clothing manufacturer, on April 2, 1903. They had two sons and a daughter.

Bettman was one of the founders and, for many years, an officer of the St. Louis Section of the NATIONAL COUNCIL OF JEWISH WOMEN and served on the national board of directors. She was active during World War II, providing training for refugees from Nazi-dominated countries. She participated in civic affairs for the Missouri Association for Criminal Justice, St. Louis Women's Symphony Committee, St. Louis League of Women Voters, Red Cross, Clothing Bureau of Citizens Committee on Relief and Unemployment, and Citizens School Board Committee.

On August 18, 1955, Meta Pollak Bettman died at age seventy-five in St. Louis, Missouri, after a long illness.

BIBLIOGRAPHY

AJYB 58:475; *BEOAJ*; Obituary. *NYTimes*, August 20, 1955, 17:4; Pollak, Emil. Papers. *AJA*; Rogow, Faith. *Gone to Another Meeting: The National Council of Jewish Women, 1893–1993* (1993); *WWIAJ* (1926, 1938).

OLIVER B. POLLAK

BILAVSKY, GLIKA (1884–1964)

As an actress on the Yiddish stage, Glika (Degenshteyn) Bilavsky participated early on in the renaissance of secular Yiddish culture in the twentieth century.

Bilavsky was born on January 23, 1884 (or on May 6, 1891, according to one source) into a prosperous family engaged in agricultural trade. She was a niece of Nahum Sokolow, the Zionist leader and Hebrew writer. She did not receive a traditional Jewish education, but attended a public elementary school in her hometown of Glechine, Congress Poland, and continued her education at a middle school (*pro-gimnaziia*) in Warsaw.

In 1907, Glika fled Poland with her fiancé, Morris Bilavsky, a fellow Yiddish actor and member of the illegal Bund (General Jewish Workers' Union in Lithuania, Poland, and Russia). The two married and settled in Copenhagen, Denmark, where they established an amateur Yiddish theater group that later turned professional. Bilavsky also studied drama and debuted both on the Danish stage and in the Danish cinema in 1920. During their fifteen-year residence in Copenhagen, the couple traveled frequently to Sweden and Norway to appear in Yiddish productions.

In 1921, Bilavsky and her husband immigrated to New York City. Over the following four decades, Bilavsky played occasionally on the Yiddish stage, lectured, and was active in HADASSAH, United Jewish Appeal, and the women's auxiliary of Mizrachi, as an organizer of its Yiddish-speaking branches. Glika Bilavsky died on April 4, 1964, in New York City.

BIBLIOGRAPHY

AJYB 66: 572; *Leksikon fun Yidishn Teater*, s.v. "Glika Bilavksy," and "Moris Bilavsky"; Lifson, David. *The Yiddish Theater in America* (1965); Obituary. *Forverts* (April 6, 1964); Sandrow, Nahma. *Vagabond Stars: A World History of Yiddish Theater* (1977).

TONY MICHELS

BILDERSEE, ADELE (1883–1971)

A feminist before her time, Adele Bildersee was an advocate for women in education. Born to Barnett Bildersee, a businessman, and Flora (Misch) Bildersee in New York City on September 4, 1883, the oldest of three children who all became respected educators, she devoted her life to scholarship and research. Her parents were also born in New York, to a family of Russian Jewish descent that had migrated first to England and then to the United States in the early nineteenth century. Her sister, Dorothy, became a school principal in Brooklyn, and her brother, Isaac, was an associate superintendent of schools, who is memorialized by a junior high school in Canarsie that bears his name.

Adele Bildersee was a serious young woman and dedicated student who graduated with the first class from HUNTER COLLEGE, then an all-women's college, in 1903. After Hunter College, she went on to receive an M.A. in 1912 and a Ph.D. in 1932 from Columbia University. In her early days, she was a teacher in the public schools of New York City and then became an

From contributing to the establishment of Brooklyn College to writing Bible textbooks for Jewish children, Adele Bildersee was always committed to the education of the young.

English instructor at Hunter High School in 1907. In 1910, she joined the faculty of Hunter College and was named assistant professor of English in 1921. Her book *Imaginative Writing: An Illustrated Course for Students*, published in 1927, was a widely used text.

Bildersee distinguished herself as a prominent figure at Brooklyn College, which she helped found. With establishment of a Brooklyn branch of Hunter College in 1926, she was appointed acting dean of women. In 1932, Bildersee became dean of women in the newly established Brooklyn College, a position she held until she was named dean of students in 1938. In addition to her role as dean, she served as director of admissions from 1944 until her retirement in 1954. Bildersee continued to teach English throughout her entire tenure as an administrator. On her retirement, she was awarded an honorary doctorate of humane letters and the title of dean and professor emerita.

Always serious and conservative, Bildersee was a music lover who believed that anything more recent than Schubert marked the onset of the modern era with sounds too dissonant for her taste. A dedicated lover of nature, she took pains to catalog for her great-nieces and -nephews the wildflowers and birds that she observed on her nature walks. Sunday strolls in the lovely Brooklyn Botanic Garden, located directly opposite her home, were a source of aesthetic joy and restoration of spirit.

Bildersee was also known for her interest in Jewish biblical history. She was principal of the Temple Beth-El religious school in Manhattan and produced several textbooks for Jewish children, such as *The Bible Story in the Bible Words* and *Jewish Post Biblical History Through Great Personalities*. After her retirement from Brooklyn College, at age seventy, she published *The Hidden Books: Selections from the Apocrypha*.

Adele Bildersee died at age eighty-eight on November 19, 1971. Thomas Evans Coulton, in his book about Brooklyn College, *A City College in Action*, said of Bildersee, "It was to the students, their social and emotional life, that Adele Bildersee gave her particular attention. Ever a faithful and devoted officer and teacher, she fostered their clubs, their newspaper, their dances, their interfaith movements, and the Country Fair . . . and took the first steps in establishing a program of personal counseling for them. She carried with her in full measure the very special gift of a deep concern for youth."

SELECTED WORKS BY ADELE BILDERSEE

The Bible Story in the Bible Words. 6 volumes (1924–1930); *The Hidden Books: Selections from the Apocrypha for the General Reader* (1956); *Imaginative Writing: An Illus-* *trated Course for Students* (1927); *Jewish Post-Biblical History Through Great Personalities from Jochanan ben Zakkai Through Moses Mendelssohn* (1918).

BIBLIOGRAPHY

AJYB 24:121; *BEOAJ*; Bildersee, Adele Sarah [greatniece]. Personal recollections; Coulton, Thomas Evans. *A City College in Action: Struggle and Achievement at Brooklyn College, 1930–1955* (1955); *EJ*; Obituaries. *Brooklyn College Alumni Bulletin* (Winter 1972), and *Long Island Press*, November 20, 1971, and *New York Daily News*, November 20, 1971, and *New York Post*, November 20, 1971, and *NYTimes*, November 20, 1971 34:4, and *Newsday*, November 20, 1971; *UJE*; *WWIAJ* (1926, 1928, 1938) ; *WWWIA* 5.

ADELE SARAH BILDERSEE

BING, ILSE (b. 1899)

In Paris in 1932, a critic called Ilse Bing the "Queen of the Leica." Her work in photojournalism, fashion, and advertising utilized this new camera, fast film, and darkroom techniques of polarization and cropping. The resulting photographs diminished the distinction between commercial and artistic photography. Her work was highly influential in France in the 1930s when many émigré artists were energized by the cross fertilization of disciplines that contributed to modern photography.

Louis and Johanna (Katz) Bing's daughter was born in Frankfurt on March 23, 1899. They were affluent and occasionally observant Jews who provided their daughter with a liberal education including music and art. In 1920, Ilse Bing entered the University of Frankfurt to study mathematics and physics. By 1923, her interests had changed, and she was in Vienna studying art history. She returned to the University of Frankfurt in 1924 to pursue a doctorate. In 1929, she purchased a new Leica, became devoted to photography, and abandoned her studies. Family and friends ostracized her for working at the *Frankfurter Illustrierte* as a photo essayist, a job they considered to be menial. She immersed herself in this new work and in developing her artistic abilities. As Ilse Bing told Nancy Barrett in a 1985 interview, "I didn't choose photography, it chose me. . . . Now over 50 years later, I can look back and explain it. In a way it was the trend of the time; it was the time when you started to see differently . . . the beginning of the mechanical device penetrating into the field of art." She struggled to fuse representation and abstraction. Her work consistently challenged the line between art and commercial photography. She saw beauty in subjects others did not notice. She focused attention on materials, surfaces, architectural spaces, nuances of movement, and texture. Her lifelong love of mathematics and science always informed her work.

Moving to Paris in 1930, Bing instantly loved the city. She participated in the avante-garde movement that affected all aspects of creative life: exhibitions, journals, performances. The leaders were largely self-taught émigré artists such as Man Ray, André Kertesz, Pavel Tchelitchev, Germaine Krull, and Florence Henri. Tchelitchev commissioned Bing to photograph a ballet, *Errante*, using only ambient light. The results were acclaimed. The Leitz Corporation was so impressed that they sent her new wide-angle and tele-photo lenses for experimentation. She worked for the fashion designer Schiaparelli, *Harper's Bazaar, Vu,* and various weekly newspapers. After Hitler's rise to power in 1933, she refused to work for German magazines. She built a successful career doing architectural, advertising, theater, and portrait photography. Her art photography was shown in leading galleries and exhibitions. By 1932, her work was exhibited in New York at Julien Levy's gallery.

In 1936, she was invited to New York by the author Hendrik Willem Van Loon. Her popularity brought commissions, a one-person show, meetings with photographer Alfred Stieglitz, and a job offer at *Life* magazine. She returned to Paris in 1937 to marry Konrad Wolff, a pianist and musicologist. That year Beaumont Newhall selected her work for his important 1937 photography exhibition at the Museum of Modern Art. Bing did less work in the late 1930s, describing herself as fulfilled and accomplished, yet searching for something different. In 1940, she was jailed in France by the Vichy government at Camp Gurs, but she was able to immigrate to New York the following year.

Ilse Bing struggled to forge a new life among many talented refugees. By 1947, she had found a new style using an electronic flash and a large-format Rolleiflex. Her scale was larger, and her subjects projected a sense of isolation and stillness. A decade later she was working exclusively in color, doing all her own developing. Her work was highly praised, but in 1959 she stopped photographing. Instead, she wrote poetry in German, French, and English and constructed collages often using old photographs. Bing's work was rediscovered after being included in a 1976 exhibition at the Museum of Modern Art and a subsequent exhibition at the Witkin Gallery. A retrospective exhibition of her work was organized by the New Orleans Museum of Art in 1985, followed by exhibitions at the International Center of Photography in

New York, the Baltimore Museum, and Musée Carnavalet in Paris. In 1993, the National Arts Club awarded her their Gold Medal for photography.

Ilse Bing's legacy is her photographs. Many images fascinate because they eloquently represent vanished lives, events, and places. She developed a mature style characterized by strong diagonals and an overhead axis, reflective surfaces, focused pools of light, clarity of textures, and regrouping of real objects out of their context. Her photographs convey a strong sense of time continuing, not as a moment frozen. Her dominant aesthetic is grounded in constructivism, but in Paris she forged this with a sensibility learned from the surrealists, dadaists, and neo-romantics. After fifty years, her vision remains compelling. She leaves work rich in craftsmanship and aesthetics upon which others can build. She was an artist who seized the moment and is recognized as a pioneer in the birth of modern photography.

BIBLIOGRAPHY
Barrett, Nancy C. *Ilse Bing: Three Decades of Photography* (1985); Bing, Ilse. *Numbers in Images* (1976), and *Words as Visions* (1974); Rosenblum, Naomi. *A History of Women Photographers* (1994); Sullivan, Constance. *Women Photographers* (1990); Witkin, Lee D. *A Ten Year Salute* (1979).

JANE KAMINE

BIRTH CONTROL MOVEMENT

The dedicated commitment of great numbers of American Jewish women to this country's long and controversial crusade to legalize birth control had its origins in 1912, when the movement's formidable pioneer Margaret Sanger—baptized a Catholic, and married to a Jew, but by then calling herself a socialist—was working part-time as a visiting nurse in the immigrant districts of New York City's Lower East Side. What she came to identify as an "awakening" occurred in the service of a young Jewish woman named Sadie Sachs, whom Sanger assisted through the complications of a self-induced septic abortion. Countless times through her fifty-year career as a reformer, she would repeat the saga of Sachs's broken plea for reliable contraception and the doctor's callous rejoinder that she tell her husband "to sleep on the roof." Returning several months later to find Sachs dying of septicemia, Sanger resolved to pursue fundamental social change.

Barrier and chemical contraception—including condoms, cervical caps, womb veils, and douches—

had circulated widely in America in the nineteenth century, precipitating a dramatic decline in fertility. This development, in turn, fueled a national preoccupation with moral and social purity. During the 1870s, the federal government and almost every state adopted far-reaching obscenity statutes that criminalized contraception and abortion and prohibited the distribution of information or products intended to promote their use.

Named after their principal architect and chief enforcer, Anthony Comstock, these laws did not succeed in suppressing the traffic in contraception, but did push it underground, out of the jurisdiction of government bodies that might have regulated price and quality. Consequently, physicians, looking to consolidate their scientific authority, defamed once-common practices. Middle-class fertility continued to decline as the result of private arrangements, but the poor—especially the growing numbers of immigrant poor—were disadvantaged because they often could neither afford contraception nor understand the many popular subterfuges through which it was sold.

Margaret Sanger first drew support from labor organizers and other leftists. "No Gods, No Masters," the rallying cry of the Industrial Workers of the World, became her personal and political manifesto. Even as the two women jousted for celebrity and quarreled over personal differences, Sanger, inspired by EMMA GOLDMAN's forceful doctrines, published *The Woman Rebel* (1914), a radical journal that encouraged personal autonomy for women through the use of "birth control," a phrase she invented to give them an easy way of talking about a delicate subject in public.

Spurred on to renewed militancy by the tragic death of her young daughter from pneumonia, Sanger opened the country's first birth control clinic in 1916 behind the curtained windows of a tenement storefront in the Brownsville district of Brooklyn. Handbills advertised the location in English, Yiddish, and Italian. Led by the determined ROSE HALPERN, the mothers of Brownsville quickly rose to Sanger's defense when the facility was closed down in its second week of operation.

Following a high-profile trial, Sanger's sister Ethel Byrne, a nurse at Mount Sinai Hospital in New York, was sentenced to one month's imprisonment in the workhouse on Blackwell Island (now Roosevelt Island), where she made headlines and secured her release through a hunger strike modeled on the attention-getting exploits of the British suffragists. Fania Mindell, a Jewish social worker, was fined fifty dollars for handing out illegal information. Charged with the more serious crime of actually fitting as a birth con-

trol device a Mizpah Pessary, which was then commonly sold in pharmacies as a womb support, Sanger was handed and served a full month's jail term.

Attorney Jonah Goldstein's appeal of her conviction, however, did establish a medical exception to the New York State birth control prohibitions. Doctors (though not nurses, as Sanger had hoped) were granted the right to prescribe contraception for health reasons, a development that determined the future course of the movement. Free-standing clinics became the model for the distribution of contraception, despite the continued reluctance of the country's medical establishment to support them. The American Medical Association did not officially endorse birth control until 1937, well after these facilities had demonstrated the efficacy of the rubber-spring diaphragm and spermicidal jelly regimen that Sanger first smuggled to the United States from Europe.

The victory for woman suffrage had been achieved through the efforts of women oriented to activism and looking for a new cause. Birth control, Sanger argued, would enhance the opportunities of women beyond the promises of economic reformers on the one hand and of suffragists on the other. It would be a tool for the fundamental redistribution of power. Women would achieve personal freedom by experiencing their sexuality free of consequence, just as men have always done. But in taking control of the forces of reproduction, they would also lower birthrates, alter the balance of supply and demand for labor, and therein accomplish the revolutionary goals of workers without the social upheaval of class warfare. Bonds of gender would transcend divisions of ethnicity, race, or class. The refusal of women to bear children indiscriminately would alter the course of history.

In 1921, Sanger founded the American Birth Control League, which subsequently became the Planned Parenthood Federation of America. Still, no matter how much she toned herself down, she remained a target of repression. A lecture at New York City's Town Hall was closed down by police ostensibly acting on orders of political authorities under pressure from powerful Catholic church officials. Subsequent appearances in Albany, Syracuse, and Boston were canceled or interrupted. These incidents sustained her image as a daring, romantic figure and earned her the moral and political support of progressive leaders of New York's Protestant and Jewish communities, including Rabbi Stephen Meyer Wise, a leader of the Jewish Reform Movement, and Samuel Rosenman, a young Jewish assemblyman from New York City, who would subsequently serve as a principal adviser to President Franklin Delano Roosevelt.

Reform doctrine in the Protestant and Jewish faiths allowed for relativism in matters of sexuality and for reasonable differences of individual conscience in family size. The rabbis had long ago encouraged sentiment in marriage and recognized the virtues of sexual expression in promoting human happiness. Within one generation, average Jewish family size declined to national norms and subsequently fell below them. By contrast, the Catholic church in these years closed ranks around a traditional morality rooted in ancient Augustinian canons demanding individual discipline and self-sacrifice. Divorce, contraception, and abortion were absolutely enjoined, as they remain today. Birthrates among American Catholics dropped markedly only after the introduction of the pill in the 1960s.

In 1923, Sanger established the Birth Control Clinical Research Bureau (later renamed the Margaret Sanger Bureau) in New York, which became the prototype for a network of facilities that developed with local sponsorship in major cities around the country. These pioneering clinics provided a range of services including contraception, gynecology, sex education, marriage counseling, and infertility advice. Their professional staffs included many Jewish women doctors and social workers who could not secure professional placements elsewhere.

The gifted HANNAH STONE, M.D., ran the Sanger clinic in New York and, with her husband Abraham, wrote the groundbreaking *Marriage Manual*, one of the best-selling sexual advice books of its era. LENA LEVINE, M.D., took over upon Stone's early death in 1941. Rachelle Yarros, M.D., a resident of Hull House, opened the first clinics in Chicago. BESSIE MOSES, M.D., ran a facility in Baltimore, as did Sarah Marcus, M.D., in Cleveland, and Nadine Kavinoky, M.D., in Los Angeles. Detroit's first clinic was supported by women from the Jewish labor movement.

Despite these achievements, the birth control movement stalled, stymied by the cost and complexity of reaching those most in need, engulfed by internal dissension, and overwhelmed by the barrage of opposition it provoked. Birthrates plummeted in the face of economic crisis, precipitating a backlash against women's rights, much like what had happened years earlier. Politicians shied away from moral controversy. Physicians feared the specter of socialized medicine that the clinics came to represent.

Moreover, eugenic concerns for the promotion of physical and mental fitness that had once been highly regarded by many progressives quickly deteriorated into an excuse for the control of undesirables on the straightforward basis of ethnicity or race. One of birth control's most credible arguments during these years was that sensible programs of social reform ought to address the manner in which biological factors, as well as environmental ones, affect human health, intelligence, and opportunity.

Sanger saw new possibilities for helping the poor through comprehensive programs of preventive social medicine. Having worked as a midwife, she was especially sensitive to the individual and social costs of diseases transmitted from mother to child during pregnancy as the result of inadequate nutrition and prenatal care. But she also endorsed prevailing views about society's obligation to prevent the transmission of ostensibly genetic defects, and she supported state statutes then under consideration that called for the forced sterilization of individuals in institutions for the "feeble-minded," a commonly used term identifying mental retardation. Despite a scientific foundation that has proved largely specious and insupportable on moral grounds, eugenic interventions gained a broad constituency, culminating in a nearly unanimous decision of the Supreme Court in *Buck* v. *Bell* (1927) that upheld Virginia's sterilization statute. Voting with the majority were Chief Justice Oliver Wendell Holmes and the country's first Jew on the court, Louis Brandeis.

Many eugenicists opposed birth control on the grounds that middle-class women should have more babies, not fewer. Sanger, instead, disdained the idea that a "cradle-competition" existed between rich and poor, native and immigrant, or black and white. She distinguished between individual applications of eugenic principles and cultural ones and spoke out against immigration prohibitions that promoted ethnic or racial stereotypes with a biological rationale. She saw birth control as an instrument of social justice, not of social control.

By the 1930s, however, the perverse application of eugenic principles under Nazi Germany had virtually discredited this kind of thinking on all grounds, and the reputation of anyone associated with it, however tenuously, was tarnished. As Americans reeled under the pressure of economic and social crisis, Sanger tried to reinvent her movement, abandoning the term "birth control" for "family planning," a friendlier concept, and urging that it be legalized and incorporated into government programs. Tying her cause to the New Deal's enthusiasm for social and economic reconstruction, she created a national lobby that mobilized thousands of constituencies, including such significant Jewish ones as the United Synagogue of America and the Union of American Hebrew Congregations. But opposition from an increasingly politically powerful Catholic church held sway on Capitol

Hill and at the White House. Bending to political considerations, the New Deal—unlike other advanced social democracies, such as England, France, and Sweden—denied birth control a place in America's social welfare and public health agenda.

Her legislative initiative having failed, Sanger, along with Hannah Stone, did prevail in a federal appellate court decision in the case of *U.S. v. One Package* (1936) that actually licensed physicians to import contraception and to use the federal mails for its transport. But the ruling did not override remaining state prohibitions in Connecticut and Massachusetts. It was not until the landmark 1965 decision of the Supreme Court of the United States in *Griswold v. Connecticut* that constitutional protection was granted to the private use of contraceptives by married couples. Seven years later in *Eisenstadt v. Baird* that privacy was extended to the unmarried.

During the 1950s, Sanger joined forces with another prominent American Jew to produce the oral, anovulant birth control pill. She introduced the scientific entrepreneur Gregory Pincus of Worcester, Massachusetts, to Katherine Dexter McCormick, heiress to an agricultural equipment fortune, who provided his initial research funds. The following decade, as Sanger lay dying in an Arizona nursing home, Alan Guttmacher, M.D., a distinguished Jewish gynecologist at Mount Sinai Hospital in New York, assumed the presidency of the Planned Parenthood Federation of America, a post in which he helped facilitate government funding when President Lyndon Johnson's Great Society provided the first public support of contraceptive services for the poor.

BIBLIOGRAPHY

The principal archival resources for the American birth control movement are housed at the Library of Congress in Washington, D.C., and at the Sophia Smith Collection of Smith College, Northampton, Massachusetts.

Chesler, Ellen. *Woman of Valor: Margaret Sanger and the Birth Control Movement in America* (1992); Cott, Nancy F. *The Grounding of Modern Feminism* (1987); Degler, Carl N. *In Search of Human Nature: The Decline and Revival of Darwinism in American Social Thought* (1991); Gordon, Linda. *Woman's Body, Women's Right: A Social History of Birth Control in America* (1978); Kennedy, David M. *Birth Control in America: The Career of Margaret Sanger* (1970); Kevles, Daniel J. *In the Name of Eugenics: Genetics and the Uses of Human Heredity* (1985); Moore, Gloria, and Ronald Moore. *Margaret Sanger and the Birth Control Movement, A Bibliography, 1911–1984* (1986); Piotrow, Phyllis Tilson. *World Population Policy: The United States Response.* (1973); Reed, James. *From Private Vice to Public Virtue: The Birth Control Movement and American Society Since 1830* (1978); Rosenberg, Rosalind. *Divided Lives: American Women in the Twentieth Century* (1992); Sanger, Margaret. *An Autobiography* (1938), and *The Pivot of Civilization* (1922), and *Woman and the New Race* (1920).

ELLEN CHESLER

BLAUSTEIN, HENRIETTA GITTELSON (1871–1965)

Freed from domestic duties by her husband's success in business, Henrietta Gittelson Blaustein, like many other wealthy Jewish women, was able to give generously of her time to charitable, religious, and civic organizations. The Blausteins were active in the Oheb Shalom Congregation of Baltimore, which had been founded in 1853. Henrietta Blaustein was a member of the Oheb Shalom Sisterhood, and in 1956, contributed $500,000 to the synagogue building fund to construct the Blaustein Auditorium. Blaustein was a member of many other Jewish organizations, including the American Jewish Committee, the American Jewish Joint Distribution Committee, and the Baltimore Council of Jewish Women.

Born on January 16, 1871, Henrietta was only fourteen years old when in 1885 she left her native Riga in Latvia and immigrated to Baltimore, Maryland, where she joined members of her family who had been living there for more than one hundred years. She was part of the larger migration of Jews from Eastern Europe and the Soviet Union to America in the late 1880s that transformed Baltimore's small, predominantly German Jewish community. In 1891, six years after arriving in the United States, she married Louis Blaustein, two years her senior, who had emigrated in 1888 from Russia. Within a year of their marriage, Henrietta gave birth to their first son, Jacob. The couple had three more children: two daughters, Fanny and Ruth, and a second son who died at a young age. In 1892, Louis Blaustein began to work as a kerosene peddler for Standard Oil in Baltimore, and by 1910, he had become an executive in the company. That year, he left Standard Oil, and with his son Jacob, he founded the American Oil Company. Innovations in oil distribution and experiments with new types of gasoline made the new company highly successful. In 1924, Pan American Petroleum and Transport Company paid $5 million for a half interest in American Oil, and the two merged in 1933.

This wealth allowed the Blausteins to contribute generously to both secular and Jewish charities. When Louis died in 1937, his will stipulated that $500,000 be used to endow the Louis and Henrietta Blaustein Foundation. She served as chairperson of the board of the foundation from its creation until her death on December 8, 1965, at age ninety-four, and played an active role in its grant-making endeavors. In 1951, the Foundation awarded $1 million to the Sinai Hospital at the Jewish Medical Center in Baltimore to build an obstetrical and gynecological building, a gift that at the time was the largest individual contribution ever made to a Jewish organization.

In addition to being involved with Jewish concerns, Blaustein was a devotee of the arts and contributed both time and money to the Baltimore Museum of Art. She also loved symphony music and, until the last two years of her life, never missed a performance of either the Baltimore Symphony or the Philadelphia Orchestra.

Henrietta and Louis Blaustein inculcated their children with their priorities to Jewish community work and charitable enterprise. All three of their children and their spouses are actively involved in Jewish and civic organizations and established private charitable foundations.

BIBLIOGRAPHY

AJYB 67:532; Cahn, Louis F. *The History of Oheb Shalom, 1853–1953* (1953); *EJ*; *Baltimore Evening Sun*, December 9, 1965; "The Forbes Four Hundred." *Forbes* (October 16, 1995): 284; *News American*, December 9, 1965; Obituaries. Maryland Jewish Historical Society, source unknown, and *NYTimes*, December 9, 1965, 47:2.

IDANA GOLDBERG

BLOCH, BLANCHE (1890–1980)

Blanche Bloch was a pioneer on behalf of women in music. Her efforts date back to the early 1930s when she was a founding member of the New York Women's Orchestra.

Blanche Bloch was born in New York on December 20, 1890, the daughter of Godfrey and Jeanette Estelle (Fried) Bloch. She received her education at the Academy of the Visitation, in Mobile, Alabama, with private piano study in New York City, Vienna, and Berlin. She was a special student at Columbia University's Teachers College, and also studied conducting with Chalmers Clifton of the National Orchestra Association.

Bloch was married to Alexander Bloch, the violinist and conductor, who was a student of the famous violinist Leopold Auer. She was his accompanist when he made his 1913 New York debut, and the couple performed in concerts for the next ten years, specializing in violin and piano sonatas. They had two children, Alan Edward and Janet Elizabeth.

Bloch was on the music faculties of Rollins College, 1936 to 1943, and the Out-of-Door School in Sarasota, Florida, 1934 to 1937. She wrote two mystery books, *The Bach Festival Murders* and *The Strange Case of Mr. Crawford*, as well as numerous articles. She also wrote the libretto for *Roeliff's Dream*, a children's operetta composed by Alexander Bloch.

Blanche Bloch died of cancer on March 5, 1980, in Hillsdale, New York, after a long career as a concert pianist, educator, and writer.

SELECTED WORKS BY BLANCHE BLOCH

The Bach Festival Murders (1942); "Music: The Leaderless Orchestra." *Nation* 127, no. 3307 (1928): 556; "Music on the Air." *Nation* 128, no. 3335 (1929): 670–671; "Olga Samaroff." *Woman's Journal* 14 (1929): 24; *Roeliff's Dream*. Libretto (1932); *The Strange Case of Mr. Crawford* (1948).

BIBLIOGRAPHY

"Blanche Bloch, a Pianist and Writer of Mysteries." *NYTimes*, March 7, 1980, D14; *Contemporary Authors*. Edited by Frances Locher. Vols. 97–100. (1981), s.v. "Bloch, Blanche"; Derdeyn, Marjorie. Telephone interview with author, May 1, 1996; "Pianist and Mystery Writer Blanche Bloch Dead at 89." *Chicago Tribune*, March 8, 1980, sec. 1, p. 19; *WWIAJ* (1938); *Who's Who in World Jewry* (1965), s.v. "Bloch, Blanche."

HARRIETT RANNEY

BLOCK, ANITA (1882–1967)

Anita Block helped to found one of the first socialist newspapers in the United States, the *New York Call*, serving as the editor of its women's page and as its drama critic from 1903 until 1923, when the paper closed during the antiradical, anti-immigrant sentiment following World War I.

She was born in New York City on August 22, 1882, the daughter of Herman and Henriette (Florsheim) Cahn. Her father had immigrated to the United States from Germany some years before and made his living by writing about finance and economics. Her socialist parents gave her little education in Judaism. As an adult, she rejected all religion in order to seek a universal ethic that would unite the people of the world. She graduated with a B.A. from Barnard College in 1903 after completing a senior thesis on dramatic realism in the plays of Henrik Ibsen. The subject evoked discomfort and disdain from her instructors, who commented, in her words, "that no nice girl would dream of reading Ibsen." Drama became a lifelong study. Soon after graduation, she married lawyer S. John Block, who died in 1955, and together they became members of the American Socialist Party.

At the *Call*, Block directed the Sunday women's page, an institution at the paper that featured subjects of social and political interest to women. As she recalled, "It was probably the only woman's page which never printed a recipe or a fashion note." She also noted that it was the first page in the country to present the views of Margaret Sanger, an early advocate of birth control. Block also served as the paper's drama critic, and after the *Call* ceased publication in 1923, she continued to write about theater for other newspapers and various magazines. She traveled to Europe and searched the United States for obscure playwrights worthy of public attention and became the Theatre Guild's reader of foreign plays in 1926. She also wrote a book on the subject.

In *The Changing World in Plays and Theatre* (1939) Block argues that plays should be read as literature and not simply experienced in performance, that fine drama lives on the page though it may be displayed in the theater. Her subjects include a discussion of the world war in contemporary drama, sexual morality in plays, and a survey of theater in Soviet Russia in which she ruminates "to what new horizons drama is pointing in the one country that has advanced to a new social order." Block said of Americans that they tended to be more impressed with the show than the content. "In this country," she told a reporter, "we never face facts; we try to escape from their unpleasantness. We are neither socially, politically nor economically minded." She called Eugene O'Neill's *Strange Interlude* the only American play good enough to stand with the great European dramas.

Anita Block died in New York City on December 11, 1967. Though never Jewish in religious practice, Block remains one of the most accomplished contributors to the culture of Jewish socialism in New York.

BIBLIOGRAPHY

Block, Anita. *The Changing World in Plays and Theatre* (1939); Obituary. *NYTimes*, December 13, 1967, 47:1; *UJE*.

STEVEN STOLL

BLONDELL, JOAN (1906–1979)

A beautiful and accomplished stage and screen actress, Blondell was born on August 30, 1906 (some accounts say 1909) on Manhattan's Upper West Side.

The daughter of vaudeville comics Eddie and Kathryn Blondell, she got whatever schooling she could in whatever city her parents happened to be performing. She made her debut in the family show at age one. Blondell toured all over the United States, Europe, Australia, and China with the troupe, then settled in Dallas, Texas, where she joined a stock company in 1926. Her sister Gloria was also an actress.

Blondell came to New York City after she won a "Miss Dallas" beauty contest in Texas. Her performance in the 1929 Broadway musical *Penny Arcade*, which also featured James Cagney, caught the attention of Warner Brothers, who signed both of them in 1930. The studio adapted the play for the screen, renaming it *Sinners' Holiday*.

Throughout the 1930s, Blondell remained in Hollywood, working for Warner Brothers, often playing second lead, in the role of the wisecracking but good-natured working-class gal. At Warner, she gained recognition as the indefatigable gold digger in films such as *Blonde Crazy* and *Footlight Parade*. Though she worked hard, like most actresses in that era, she felt the studio underutilized her talent—particularly her affinity for light comedy. While audiences appreciated

A wisecracking beauty, Joan Blondell spent most of her career as the quintessential Hollywood second lead.

the assured optimism her characters possessed on-screen, it was her self-deprecating humor that sustained her offscreen.

Blondell left Warner Brothers in 1938 and began to freelance, acting smaller parts in a number of Fox and MGM films and, later, television. She mainly played character roles, such as Aunt Cissy in the 1945 production of *A Tree Grows in Brooklyn* with director Elia Kazan. In 1951, Blondell received an Academy Award nomination for her performance in *The Blue Veil.* She appeared in three television series in the 1960s and 1970s: *The Real McCoys, Here Comes the Bride,* and *Banyon.* In 1972 she wrote the novel *Center Door Fancy,* a work of thinly disguised fiction based on her own career.

Blondell was married to cinematographer George Barnes from 1933 to 1935, to actor Dick Powell from 1936 to 1945, and to producer Mike Todd from 1947 to 1950. She had one son, Norman, with Barnes, and a daughter, Ellen, with Powell. She died in Santa Monica, California, on December 25, 1979, of leukemia.

FILMOGRAPHY

Adventure (1946); *The Amazing Mr. Williams* (1939); *Angel Baby* (1961); *Back in Circulation* (1937); *Big Business Girl* (1931); *Big City Blues* (1932); *Big Daddy* (1969); *Blonde Crazy* (1931); *Blondie Johnson* (1933); *The Blue Veil* (1951); *Broadway Bad* (1933); *Broadway Gondolier* (1935); *Bullets or Ballots* (1936); *Central Park* (1932); *The Champ* (1979); *Christmas Eve* (1947); *The Cincinnati Kid* (1965); *Colleen* (1936); *Convention City* (1933); *The Corpse Came C.O.D.* (1947); *The Crowd Roars* (1932); *Cry Havoc* (1943); *Dames* (1934); *The Desk Set* (1958); *Don Juan Quilligan* (1945); *East Side of Heaven* (1939); *Famous Ferguson Case* (1932); *Footlight Parade* (1933); *For Heaven's Sake* (1950); *The Glove* (1978); *God's Gift to Women* (1931); *Gold Diggers of 1933* (1933); *Gold Diggers of 1937* (1936); *Good Girls Go to Paris* (1939); *Goodbye Again* (1933); *Grease* (1978); *The Greeks Had a Word for Them* (1932); *Havana Windows* (1933); *He Was Her Man* (1934); *I Want a Divorce* (1940); *Illicit* (1931); *I've Got Your Number* (1934); *The Kansas City Princess* (1934); *The Kid from Kokomo* (1939); *The King and the Chorus Girl* (1937); *Kona Coast* (1968); *Lady for a Night* (1942); *Lawyer Man* (1933); *Lizzie* (1957); *Make Me a Star* (1932); *Millie* (1931); *Miss Pacific Fleet* (1935); *Miss Pinkerton* (1932); *Model Wife* (1941); *My Past* (1931); *Night Nurse* (1931); *Nightmare Alley* (1947); *Off the Record* (1939); *The Office Wife* (1930); *Opening Night* (1977); *The Opposite Sex* (1956); *Other Men's Women* (1930, 1931); *The Perfect Specimen* (1937); *The Public Enemy* (1931); *The Reckless Hour* (1931); *Ride Beyond Vengeance* (1966); *Sinners' Holiday* (1930); *Smarty* (1934); *Sons o' Guns* (1936); *Stage Struck* (1936); *Stand-In* (1937); *Stay Away from Joe* (1968); *Support Your Local Gunfighter* (1971); *There's Always a Woman* (1938); *This Could Be the Night* (1957); *Three Girls About Town* (1941); *Three Men on a Horse* (1936); *Three on a Match* (1932); *Topper Returns* (1941); *The Traveling Saleslady* (1935); *A Tree Grows in Brooklyn* (1945); *Two Girls on Broadway* (1940); *Union Depot* (1932); *Waterhole 3* (1967); *We're in the Money* (1935); *Will Success Spoil Rock Hunter?* (1958); *The Woman Inside* (1980).

BIBLIOGRAPHY

Blondell, Joan. *Center Door Fancy* (1972), and Clippings file. New York Public Library for the Performing Arts. New York; Bowers, Ron. "Joan Blondell." *Films in Review* 23, no. 4 (April 1972); Katz, Ephraim. *The Film Encyclopedia* (1979); Mordden, Ethan. *Movie Star: A Look at the Women Who Made Hollywood* (1983); *Picturegoer and Film Weekly* (December 23, 1939): 10–11; Quinlan, David. *Quinlan's Illustrated Registry of Film Stars* (1981); Rigdon, Walter, ed. *Who's Who of the American Theatre* (1966); Thomas, Nicholas, ed. *International Dictionary of Films and Filmmakers.* Vol. 3, *Actors and Actresses* (1992); Thomson, David. *A Biographical Dictionary of Film.* 3d ed. (1994); *UJE.*

ALYSSA GALLIN

BLOOMFIELD ZEISLER, FANNIE
see ZEISLER, FANNIE BLOOMFIELD

BLUM, HELEN ABRAHAMS
(1886–1958)

Artist and community activist Helen Abrahams Blum was born August 17, 1886, in Philadelphia to Simon and Theresa Abrahams. She was educated in the Philadelphia public schools and awarded a four-year board of education scholarship in 1902. She attended the School of Design for Women in Philadelphia from 1902 to 1905 and received her diploma in 1906, at which time she was recognized with an alumnae prize for artistic excellence. From 1909 to 1912, she studied at the Academy of Fine Arts under Elliot Daingerfield, Hugh Breckenridge, and Henry Snell. On January 17, 1917, she married Alexander A. Blum. The couple had two children: Audrey Anthony and Robert Alex Blum.

Blum exhibited in various galleries throughout the country, notably the Philadelphia Art Club in 1909 and the Wanamaker Art Show in 1910, and was active in the New York City art community. In 1915, her still-life painting in oil was purchased for the permanent collection of the Fellowship of the Academy of Fine Arts. A specialist in portraiture, Blum sold some of her portraits to William Chase, noted artist and teacher.

Blum's talents extended to designing scenery and costumes for the Little Theater Movement. She also managed, staged, and acted in many plays and pageants for various Jewish religious organizations in Philadelphia. She authored a short story and wrote numerous articles. As well as being a fellow of the Pennsylvania Academy of Fine Arts and a member of the Rodolph Shalom Sisterhood, she was very active in the international peace movement.

Helen Abrahams Blum died on December 24, 1958, in Queens, New York.

BIBLIOGRAPHY

Blum, Helen Abrahams. Files. Pennsylvania Academy of Fine Arts, Philadelphia; Petteys, Chris. *Dictionary of Women Artists: An International Dictionary of Women Artists Born Before 1900* (1985); *WWIAJ* (1926, 1928, 1938).

HARRIET L. PARMET

BLUME, JUDY (b. 1938)

The perennially best-selling author Judy Blume is a rare phenomenon in children's literature. Almost seventy million copies of her books have been sold worldwide. Her young fans pass around her books and compare notes, cram her mailbox with up to two thousand letters a month, and buy her books with great fervor. At the same time, her books are frequently subject to censorship. Blume's works are characterized by emotional and sexual candor, total empathy with the concerns of childhood, and a direct colloquial tone, which all give her readers the sense that she knows all their secrets.

Judy Blume was born on February 12, 1938, in Elizabeth, New Jersey, to Esther (Rosenfeld) and Rudolph Sussman, a dentist. When Judy was in third grade, she moved with her mother and her older brother David to Miami Beach, where the climate would help David recuperate from a kidney infection. Her father, to whom Blume was especially close, stayed behind in New Jersey, running his practice.

Blume has described her childhood home as culturally Jewish rather than religious. Her father had six brothers and sisters, almost all of whom died while Judy was growing up, and she has said, "a lot of my philosophy came from growing up in a family that was always sitting shivah."

She graduated from New York University in 1960 with a B.A. in education. She married lawyer John M. Blume in 1959, the year her father died. Her daughter Randy Lee was born in 1961, and son Lawrence Andrew in 1963. She divorced Blume in 1975, moved to Princeton, New Jersey, and later lived in London, England. In 1976, she married physicist Thomas A. Kitchens and moved to Los Alamos, New Mexico. She divorced her second husband in 1979 and moved to New York in 1981. In 1987, Blume married writer George Cooper.

Blume began writing after her children started nursery school in the mid-1960s. Although she had

There have been efforts to ban her children's books from libraries for their emotional and sexual candor. Judy Blume must be doing something right, however. Her readers are devoted to her and have bought more than seventy million copies of her books. [Library of Congress]

published two short stories, she received as many as six rejection slips a week for two and a half years before Reilly and Lee accepted her picture book, *The One in the Middle Is the Green Kangaroo* (1969). Her next book, *Iggie's House* (1970), was written in the course of a writing class she took at New York University.

The tremendous success of *Are You There God? It's Me, Margaret* (1970) was a turning point for Blume. She acknowledges that it was the first book she gave herself permission to write from her own experience, and it was then that she began to grow "as a writer and as a woman." In the novel, Margaret Ann Simon, the child of a Jewish mother and a Christian father, asks God for direction in choosing a religion, and prays that she will soon get her period. When the story ends, Margaret is stuffing her bra with cotton balls. She has explored various religions but has chosen none.

Blume, who had no idea she was breaking any barriers with the novel, was surprised at the efforts to have her book banned from libraries. However, the *New York Times Book Review* ranked it as one of the best children's books of the year, and it remains one of her most popular titles.

Blume's great popularity can be attributed to her compassionate treatment of a range of subjects that concern her readers. Her books for younger children, such as *Tales of a Fourth Grade Nothing* (1972), *Otherwise Known as Sheila the Great* (1972), and *Blubber* (1974), deal with problems of sibling rivalry, self-confidence, and social ostracism. Books for teenagers, such as *Are You There God? It's Me, Margaret* (1970), *Deenie* (1973), and *Just as Long as We're Together* (1987), consider matters of divorce, friendship, family breakups, and sexual development. *Starring Sally J. Freedman as Herself* (1977) and *Tiger Eyes* (1981) explore issues of death and loss. *Forever* (1975) is the story of a young woman's first love and first sexual experience. In each of her books, Blume's characters confront their feelings of confusion as they begin to search for a resolution for their problems.

Blume has said that she vividly remembers the questions and emotions of her own youth and that she attempts to show readers they are not alone in their fears and confusion. He&r books read like diaries or journals, and the reader is drawn in by the narrator's self-revelation. Blume's work is laced with realistic personal details, from a child's breakfast menu to sleepwear fashions.

While Blume's work is popular with readers, critics have frequently asserted that the author's readable style, with its emphasis on mundane detail, lacks the depth to deal with the complex issues that she raises.

However, the overall evaluation of Blume's work is ultimately determined by her loyal and enthusiastic readership. Her emotional adventure stories give her young readers a reference point from which to examine and discuss their own feelings.

Blume has also written two novels for adults which share the writing style and empathetic tone of her juvenile fiction: *Wifey* (1978), concerning a woman's search for fulfillment in her life and marriage, and *Smart Women* (1983), about a divorced woman trying to cope with single motherhood and new relationships.

In 1986, Blume published an anthology of letters she had received from readers called *Letters to Judy: What Your Kids Wish They Could Tell You* (1986). The book is an attempt to help parents see life through their children's eyes. Furthering this end, Blume established the KIDS Fund in 1981 to develop programs that encourage communication between parents and teens and that foster parent-child discussions through books.

Judy Blume has received countless state and local awards for her books, as well as the International Reading Association Children's Choice Award (1981), an American Book Award nomination for *Tiger Eyes* (1983), the Eleanor Roosevelt Humanitarian Award and Children's Choice Award—Favorite Author (1983), and the Margaret A. Edwards Award (1996).

SELECTED WORKS BY JUDY BLUME

Are You There God? It's Me, Margaret (1970); *Deenie* (1973); *Forever* (1975); *Fudge-a-Mania* (1990); *Here's to You, Rachel Robinson* (1993); *Iggie's House* (1970); *It's Not the End of the World* (1972); *The Judy Blume Diary* (1981); *Just as Long as We're Together* (1987); *Letters to Judy: What Your Kids Wish They Could Tell You* (1985); *The One in the Middle Is the Green Kangaroo* (1969); *Otherwise Known as Sheila the Great* (1972); *The Pain and the Great One* (1984); *Smart Women* (1984); *Superfudge* (1980); *Tales of a Fourth Grade Nothing* (1972); *Then Again, Maybe I Won't* (1971); *Tiger Eyes* (1981); *Wifey* (1977).

BIBLIOGRAPHY

Contemporary Authors, New Revision Series. Vol. 37; *Contemporary Literary Criticism*. Vol. 30; Cooper, George. Telephone interview with author, January 10, 1997; *Current Biography* (1980); Decter, Naomi. "Judy Blume's Children." *Commentary* (March 1980): 65–67; *Dictionary of Literary Biography*. Vol. 52 (1986); Lipsyte, Robert. "A Bridge of Words." *The Nation* 233, no. 17 (November 21, 1981): 551–53; Sutton, Roger. "Forever . . . Yours." *School Library Journal* (June 1996): 25–27; Weidt, Maryann N. *Presenting Judy Blume* (1990).

AMY GOTTLIEB

BLUMENTHAL, FLORENCE MEYER
(1875–1930)

Florence Meyer Blumenthal, an extraordinary philanthropist and arts patron, organized her own arts foundation in Paris, and donated millions of dollars to established institutions and public charities in America and France.

Born in Los Angeles in 1875 to Eugene and Harriet (Newmark) Meyer, she was the third of eight children. Eugene Meyer was a dry-goods merchant from Strasbourg; his sister married Zadoc Kahn, the Grand Rabbi of France. Harriet Newmark was the daughter of the Los Angeles lay rabbi, Joseph Newmark, who had founded New York's Elm Street Synagogue before heading west to California in 1851. Florence's older sisters Rosalie and Elise joined San Francisco's Jewish elite and married Sigmund and Abraham Stern, nephews of Levi Strauss. Her younger brother Eugene became the president and publisher of the *Washington Post*.

In 1898, at age twenty-three, she married international financier George Blumenthal. Many of her philanthropic efforts were made in conjunction with her husband. The couple had three homes: a Park Avenue apartment, a large house in Paris, and a villa in the South of France. In 1916, to display their growing art and furniture collection, they moved into a mansion at 50 East 70th Street that was designed to look like a fifteenth-century Italian villa. From 1911 to 1938, the Blumenthals gave three million dollars to Mount Sinai Hospital, one of New York's prominent German Jewish institutions, including a sum allotted for a wing in memory of their only child, George, Jr., who died as a young boy.

Florence Blumenthal's generosity extended across the Atlantic as well. In 1919, she initiated her most ambitious charitable endeavor. She organized the American Foundation for French Art and Thought in Paris to discover young French artists, aid them financially, and in the process draw the United States and France closer together through art, thought, and literature. Juries of well-known artists, including Paul Signac and Aristide Maillol, awarded the prizes to fellow painters, sculptors, decorators, engravers, writers, and musicians. For the first few years of the foundation, each artist received six thousand francs a year for two years, but from 1926 until her death in 1930, Blumenthal increased the purse to ten thousand francs a year. From 1919 to 1954, nearly two hundred artists benefited from the foundation's grants.

In 1925, when George Blumenthal retired, the couple made their house in Paris their primary residence. In 1926, they gave sixty thousand dollars to the Children's Hospital in Paris; in 1928, one million dollars to the Metropolitan Museum of Art in New York. Several years later, George Blumenthal would leave their house on East 70th Street and all of its Roman, Gothic, and baroque art treasures to the Met as well. Their contributions to the Sorbonne in Paris, made over several years, exceeded $250,000. In 1929, the French government presented Blumenthal and her husband with the Legion of Honor in recognition of their altruism.

On September 21, 1930, at age fifty-five, Florence Meyer Blumenthal died of bronchial pneumonia at her home in Paris.

BIBLIOGRAPHY

Gauthier, Maximilien. *La Fondation américaine Blumenthal pour la pensée et l'art français* (1974); Narell, Irena. *Our City: The Jews of San Francisco* (1981); Obituary. *NYTimes* (September 22, 1930), 19:4; *UJE*.

MICHELE SIEGEL

BLUME-SILVERSTEIN, ELIZABETH *see* SILVERSTEIN, ELIZABETH BLUME

B'NAI B'RITH WOMEN

When the first permanent chapter of B'nai B'rith Women (BBW) was founded in 1909 in San Francisco, its aim was "to promote sociability among [B'nai B'rith] lodge members and their families." B'nai B'rith, American Jewry's oldest and largest fraternal and service organization, did not permit women's auxiliaries until 1897, when Ruth Lodge No. 1, Daughters of Judah, enjoyed a very brief existence.

In 1909, searching for a more permanent venue, the Columbia Auxiliary of B'nai B'rith announced a safe, socially acceptable goal: genteel entertainment, designed to attract the young, single adult members of B'nai B'rith with card parties, boating parties, picnics, and dances. Entertainment served as an effective icebreaker, easing the women into the more serious activities being undertaken by other women's groups across the country. Auxiliary members pressed for the official recognition by B'nai B'rith, but the men's Grand Lodge refused, setting a precedent that would continue for decades.

Membership in B'nai B'rith women's auxiliaries grew to 12,000 by 1935.
This photo of a luncheon of the Albany Park, Illinois, auxiliary was taken on May 22, 1939.
The term "auxiliaries" was dropped in favor of "chapters" in 1940. [Chicago Jewish Archives].

The Columbia Auxiliary was part of a movement by nineteenth-century American women who had begun to emerge out of the home and into the public sphere partly by creating their own voluntary social and charitable associations. Jewish women followed the pattern of their Christian peers by forming Jewish women's groups. Some of these groups became associated with male-run synagogues and charitable and fraternal organizations; one group, the NATIONAL COUNCIL OF JEWISH WOMEN, was independent.

Before the outbreak of World War I, over a dozen B'nai B'rith women's auxiliaries were scattered from San Francisco to New Jersey. They expanded into cultural activities, philanthropy, and community service, such as financial support of orphanages and homes for the elderly. Their announced aims were to perpetuate Jewish culture, enrich their communities, and ensure the religious survival of their sons and daughters.

Their unannounced goals included sociability and the first steps toward personal independence.

Most women's auxiliaries included male members as "mentors" or trustees. The men's motives were often highly personal. One "mentor" noted that men attended auxiliary meetings to "seek, like Ponce de León, the 'spring of eternal youth.'" Despite their appreciation for the female sex, however, the men permitted only two representatives at Grand Lodge meetings—"a voice, but no vote."

World War I changed the women's pattern of service. As men went off to war, American women expanded their work and volunteer activity by serving in hospitals, settlement houses, offices, and factories. B'nai B'rith auxiliary members, like other women, rushed into patriotic volunteer activity. They filled women's wartime roles, which had been growing since the Crimean War: entertaining and knitting for soldiers, rolling surgical dressings, nursing in military hospitals, helping ambulance crews, and even driving ambulances themselves. They also started their own fund for the relief of Jews in Europe.

The growing emphasis on service activities brought the number of new auxiliaries to seventeen by the end of the war. B'nai B'rith Women was not directly involved in the suffragist movement, but women's activism seems to have influenced the group. By 1929, the beginning of the Great Depression, six thousand women belonged to eighty-three auxiliaries.

The 1920s and 1930s saw the rise of social conservatism in the United States and fascism in Europe. Women who had won the vote now returned to the nineteenth-century women's tradition of exercising political influence through voluntary associations. BBW membership increased accordingly, reaching 12,000 women in 103 auxiliaries by 1935. Despite their growing political force, however, the women failed in their renewed bid for B'nai B'rith Supreme Lodge official recognition.

In 1940, the term "auxiliaries" was dropped in favor of "chapters," and the Women's Districts formally organized the Women's Supreme Council as a national coordinating body for the districts and chapters. Judge Lenore Underwood Mills of San Francisco was elected the first national president. A formal liaison with B'nai B'rith was established, and the groundwork was laid for auxiliary representation at B'nai B'rith commissions and conventions.

As Nazi persecution of European Jews increased and war drew closer, the auxiliaries engaged in relief work for Jewish victims. At the same time, America's isolationism, social anti-Semitism, and sympathy for fascism in some quarters, particularly in the U.S. State Department, made it particularly important to Jewish organizations that they prove their patriotism. Eager to demonstrate their support for America, some auxiliaries embarked on civil defense projects before the attack on Pearl Harbor.

At the beginning of World War II, BBW included 248 chapters with more than 40,000 members, and produced its first monthly publication, *B'nai B'rith Women*. In 1941, voteless women delegates protesting their status created a stir at the B'nai B'rith Supreme Lodge convention.

As America entered the war, BBW chapters threw themselves into the war effort: They sold bonds, knitted and sewed, and rolled bandages. They provided USO-type entertainment for servicemen. They donated collapsible wheelchairs, bookmobiles, portable radios, and other recreational equipment to military hospitals. The organization received a citation from the U.S. Treasury Department for its sale of war bonds.

But the war years were also a period of emancipation for women. In an era when Rosie the Riveter was a national heroine, BBW members drove ambulances and worked in armament factories. BBW helped recruit and assist military service women. The organization also focused on the women's concern for Jews in Europe, sending money to London for refugee orphans and Jewish working girls whose homes had been destroyed. Mourning President Franklin Roosevelt's death in 1945, B'nai B'rith Women established the Four Freedoms Library in the B'nai B'rith building in Washington, D.C.

B'NAI B'RITH GIRLS

The war also brought to a peak the organization's great interest in serving young girls. In 1927, it created Junior Auxiliaries, also called Girls' Auxiliaries, BB Junior Leagues, and BZB (a substitute for AZA, the Aleph Zadik Aleph group for boys). Junior activities were primarily educational, religious, and recreational. During World War II, these youth groups contributed to the American and Canadian war effort.

B'nai B'rith Women saw B'nai B'rith Girls as a favorite child. "These young women are our daughters, who we hope will take our places . . . in promoting the ideals we work for," said Mrs. Louis Perlman, the national chair of junior girls in 1941. Perlman worked to establish a national girls' group similar to Aleph Zadik Aleph. In 1942, the AZA accepted BBW's proposal to make B'nai B'rith Girls a national organization, and to form the B'nai B'rith Girls Youth Commission, governing both AZA and BBG. By 1944, B'nai B'rith Girls formally achieved national status.

ISRAEL

By the end of 1944, B'nai B'rith Women counted over a hundred thousand members, and moved toward strengthening the work in Palestine that it had begun during the war. Members raised $1 million, plus food, clothes, and equipment to assist the fledgling State of Israel in 1948. The Children's Home there was turned over to B'nai B'rith leaders in 1943. B'nai B'rith Women assumed responsibility for its maintenance. Expanding the home over the years, BBW reopened the original building in 1972 as a residential treatment center for emotionally disturbed boys, which it still maintains. BBW also continues to provide a network of social services in Israel.

The Dolls for Democracy program of B'nai B'rith Women used dolls representing famous personalities in American and world history in their schoolroom lectures. Shown here in 1957 is Mrs. Louis B. Perlman, the president of the organization, with Eleanor Roosevelt and the doll made in her likeness.
[UPI/CORBIS-BETTMANN]

THE POSTWAR YEARS

America's postwar idyll nursed a decade that swung gradually between traditionalism and rebellion. Men returned from war, and the mostly male-run businesses boomed. Women returned to children, service clubs, and the suburbs. Women's small victories came quietly. The long battle for a vote in the traditionally male B'nai B'rith organization was won in 1953, when, for the first time, women delegates voted at the B'nai B'rith Supreme Lodge convention.

Sympathetic to the influx of postwar immigrants, BBW undertook a variety of projects, particularly in human relations and prejudice reduction. In cooperation with the Anti-Defamation League of B'nai B'rith, the organization sponsored interfaith seminars, developed school curricula in prejudice reduction, and introduced its popular Dolls for Democracy program in diversity for elementary school children in 1954. These dolls from different ethnic backgrounds are part of a program to teach tolerance.

Social service projects ranged from helping displaced persons to assisting the American Tuberculosis Association, to providing donors for blood banks. During this period, support of B'nai B'rith Hillel organizations on college campuses began, as BBW raised funds to furnish Hillel buildings and sponsor Hillel programs.

In 1957, membership totaled 132,000 women in 768 chapters in the United States and Canada, with 41 chapters in foreign countries. The organization's name was changed officially to B'nai B'rith Women. Headquarters were moved to the new B'nai B'rith building in Washington, D.C., which houses the Four Freedoms Library maintained today by B'nai B'rith International.

TRANSITION TO FEMINISM

The 1960s became the turning point in B'nai B'rith Women's activism. Inspired by the presidency of John F. Kennedy, BBW became involved in the War on Poverty's anti-illiteracy and antipoverty programs, as well as in the needs of senior citizens, including senior housing. However, the burgeoning women's movement and the early Jewish feminist movement of the 1970s became even more critical influences, turning the organization toward feminist issues.

In 1971, a year before *Ms.* magazine's first issue was published, former New York congresswoman BELLA ABZUG was given an award at the BBW District One Convention. Lamenting women's exclusion from political power, she called for delegates to "challenge a way of life that has oppressed 53 percent of the population—women." Abzug's award illustrated B'nai B'rith Women's new focus on political activism for women's issues. At the convention, members urged greater opportunities for women to hold political office and to participate equally in appointive posts at all levels, called for business and industry to count volunteer experience as qualification for job entry, and urged public and private support of day-care centers.

BBW transformed itself into a politically conscious and activist feminist organization, campaigning for such issues as free choice in abortion, equal Social Security benefits for women, assistance for the displaced homemaker, women's and infants' health care, and reducing teenage pregnancy. The organization also focused on programs to meet the growing needs of women on their own, career women, older women, and young family women juggling families and careers.

The members advocated national health insurance, improving the image of women in the media, curbing teenage pregnancy, and improving the legal status of homemakers. B'nai B'rith Women became the first Jewish organization to back the Equal Rights Amendment in 1971, and members campaigned steadily for the amendment's ratification. BBW became a nongovernmental organization with consultative status at the United Nations, and participated in the UN World Conference for Women.

At the same time, BBW continued its Jewish focus, particularly as a convener of the Women's Plea for Soviet Jews and Human Rights, and as an advocate for Jewish family issues, support for youth programs, and the BBW Children's Home outside Jerusalem.

JEWISH WOMEN INTERNATIONAL

By 1980, BBW had 114,000 members and 914 chapters in the United States and Canada with associate units overseas, and boasted some political influence on women's issues. Its members included the astronaut JUDITH RESNIK and Maryland House of Delegates representative Ida Ruben. Nevertheless, B'nai B'rith Women experienced a decline in membership similar to that of other volunteer organizations: It had lost fifteen thousand members since its height in the 1950s. As its *National Jewish Monthly* acknowledged, "The future for women's volunteer service organizations has never been more uncertain. As more and more women join, and remain in, the work force, and as their personal responsibilities increase, will they have the time and be willing to do volunteer work?"

In the late 1980s, BBW faced a takeover attempt by B'nai B'rith International (BBI). Some BBI leaders argued that men and women should be equal partners in B'nai B'rith International, and that a separate women's organization was unnecessary and out of step with the times.

But BBW believed that declining BBI membership and financial problems were the real reasons the men wanted to take over the women's organization. Moreover, BBW leadership felt that independence was critical, with more advantages than disadvantages in having an all-women organization, including more leadership opportunities for women. A struggle began, noted *Lilith*, "over who will attract and then speak for those Jewish women who want to affiliate with B'nai B'rith."

In September 1988, the BBI biennial conference, concerned with declining enrollment, decided that the organization should admit women. Following the BBI decision, BBW passed a resolution affirming its status as a separate legal entity identified with B'nai B'rith, thus pitting the organizations against each other.

B'nai B'rith International instituted what BBW saw as a "hostile takeover" attempt in January 1989. It ordered BBW to rescind the "autonomy" statement, and threatened litigation and expulsion of B'nai B'rith Women from the BBI "family." Negotiations failed, and BBW moved out of the B'nai B'rith building in November.

BBW argued that keeping its historical autonomy meant the continuation of a strong women's voice speaking out on women's and family issues. The critical issue, noted *LILITH*, was whether organizations such as B'nai B'rith International, "still largely led by men even after two decades of Jewish feminist activism, [would] ever take these issues as seriously as women must."

All attempts to avoid an organizational schism failed. Taking its case to the press, B'nai B'rith Women insisted that its concerns were to protect B'nai B'rith Women's organizational integrity, maintain its role in the B'nai B'rith International "family," secure continued use of the BBW name, and protect the BBI insurance coverage of BBW members and the pension coverage of its employees. Press reports sympathized with the women.

By fall 1990, BBW and BBI reached an agreement recognizing B'nai B'rith Women as an independent, self-governing organization affiliated with B'nai B'rith. BBW kept its name, recognizing its emotional ties to B'nai B'rith International, in return for a financial payment to the B'nai B'rith Youth Organization and Hillel.

B'nai B'rith Women fully declared its independence by changing its name to Jewish Women International in 1995. It announced its intention of continuing "cordial relations" with B'nai B'rith, and maintaining its support of the B'nai B'rith Youth Organization, Hillel, and the Anti-Defamation League.

Today, Jewish Women International continues its effective programs and political advocacy on issues of concern to women. Nevertheless, it struggles with the same dilemma as other women's organizations: the difficulty of recruiting new members from women juggling families and careers, with little time left for volunteerism. Yet, Jewish Women International is actively involving both younger and older members in three primary issues: Domestic violence; the emotional well-being of children, particularly in rescuing children from violence; and the expression of Jewish life and values, especially through Holocaust remembrance and prejudice awareness.

BIBLIOGRAPHY

A History of B'nai B'rith Women (1984); Joselow, Beth. "Women on Their Own." *National Jewish Monthly* (August–September 1980); Kuzmack, Linda Gordon. *Woman's Cause: The Jewish Woman's Movement in England and the United States, 1881–1933* (1990): 30; *Lilith* (Spring 1990): 4; Moore, Deborah Dash. *B'nai B'rith and the Challenge of Ethnic Leadership* (1981): 13; *B'nai B'rith Women's World* (April 1959, Winter 1990, Fall 1990, Summer 1993, Winter 1994, Summer 1994, Fall 1995, Spring 1996).

LINDA GORDON KUZMACK

BORG, MADELINE (1878–1956)

Madeline Borg was active in philanthropic work for over fifty years.

She was born in New York City on July 31, 1878. At Columbia University, she concentrated on the causes of juvenile delinquency. She was especially active in promoting psychiatric clinics as an integral part of the study of child behavior. Her major contribution was as founder of the Big Sister movement in America in 1912, an organization that provides young girls with companions and role models. In 1914, Borg helped to found the Jewish Big Sister movement. In 1939, she became president of the New York Federation of Jewish Philanthropies, one of the first women to hold such a post. Other positions she held included chair and member of the executive committee of the Jewish Board of Guardians of New York; member of the executive board of the American Jewish Committee; vice president of the National Probation and Parole Association, which helped prisoners upon their release; director of the Child Welfare League, which was active in the prevention of juvenile delinquency; vice-chair of the Mental Hygiene Committee of the State Charities Aid; member of the executive committee of the Girls' Service League of America; trustee of the Training School for Jewish Social Work; head of the Women's Division and vice president of the Federation for the Support of Jewish Philanthropic Societies of New York; president of the Montefiore Hospital Ladies' Auxiliary Society; and active officer in the Salvation Army.

In 1929, Governor Franklin D. Roosevelt appointed her a member of the New York State Old Age Pensions Committee. At the same time she was named to the executive committee of the New York City Crime Prevention Bureau. In 1939, she was a trustee of the New York World's Fair and active on several of its administrative committees.

Her husband, Sidney Cecil Borg, was a financier and civic and communal leader in New York City.

Madeline Borg died in New York City, on January 9, 1956.

BIBLIOGRAPHY

AJYB 58:475; *BEOAJ*; Obituary. *NYTimes*, January 10, 1956, 31:1; *UJE*; *WWIAJ* (1926, 1928, 1938).

JACK NUSAN PORTER

BOUDIN, ANNA PAVITT (1883–1959)

Upon her death in 1959, Anna Pavitt Boudin was remembered by the WOMEN'S AMERICAN ORT as "a woman of searching mind, of dignity, of true feeling for the Jewish people throughout the world on whose behalf she gave her energies and her talent." Her granddaughter Janet Neschis described Boudin as a pioneer—an elegant but imposing woman with an independent spirit whose interest was in helping others learn to help themselves. Boudin exemplified those qualities in her work in the field of dentistry and, most significantly, in her role in the founding and operation of ORT.

Anna Pavitt Boudin was born into a Jewish household in Mariampol, Poland, on July 15, 1883. In 1904, at age twenty-one, she joined thousands of other Jews emigrating from Russia and Eastern Europe to the United States to escape rampant prejudice and persecution.

Shortly after her arrival, she enrolled in the dentistry program at Columbia University, graduating in 1907. At the end of the nineteenth century, women were still largely excluded from dentistry because they were considered physically too weak. It is notable, therefore, that Boudin overcame that stereotype, but it is even more remarkable that she attained this professional status so quickly after immigration. She was one of eight women in her graduating class of thirty-nine students, and she went on to have a successful career as a dentist. In addition to maintaining her own private practice, Boudin was an active member in many professional organizations, such as the American Academy of Dental Medicine and the American Academy of Periodontology. She established the dental clinic at the New York Infirmary in 1924, and remained in charge of its dental division until 1956, when she became attending dentist emeritus, holding that post until her death in 1959.

Soon after her graduation from Columbia, she fell in love with Louis B. Boudin, a well-known leftist labor lawyer who wrote extensively on American constitutional law and Marxist economic theory. Boudin's first wife, Leah Kanefsky, had died of tuberculosis in 1906, leaving him a widower with two small children. On May 1, 1909, Louis Boudin married Anna Pavitt, who took over the role of mother to eleven-year-old Eleanor and five-year-old Vera. The new family's first years were spent in Brooklyn and, later, in midtown Manhattan. The Boudins spent their summers in a cottage in Cold Spring, New York, where they cooperatively owned land with several friends.

Through her husband, Boudin became acquainted with ORT, an organization that was first established in Russia in the 1870s and 1880s to help address the precarious economic condition of the Jewish population by promoting agricultural and industrial work through vocational training. However, pogroms and political reaction limited the work and success of the organization, and it was not until 1906, after the first Russian Revolution, that ORT was able to grow. It spread beyond Imperial Russia, following the Jewish diaspora into Europe and finally, in 1922, to the United States, where the American ORT Federation was organized in Manhattan. Among its founders was Louis Boudin. Five years later, in 1927, several American ORT Federation wives gathered in Anna Boudin's Brooklyn living room to start the Women's American ORT, with Boudin as its founding president. The organization focused on fund-raising for ORT, establishing schools for Jews in the United States and abroad, discouraging anti-Semitism, and promoting health care.

The Women's American ORT grew to be one of the largest Jewish women's organizations in the United States and the largest membership group within ORT worldwide. Boudin remained an active member throughout her life, serving on the national executive committee and the advisory board, even within weeks of her death. She was also an important contributor to the Bramson ORT Trade School in New York, which was established during World War II to help unskilled Jewish immigrants assimilate into the American economy by teaching them viable trades.

Anna Pavitt Boudin was diagnosed with cancer a few years after her husband's death in 1952. She chose to travel in Europe, rather than dwell on her illness. This decision, her granddaughter remembered, was indicative of her desire to be independent and active. When she finally became too ill to travel any longer, she returned to New York City, where she died on October 25, 1959.

BIBLIOGRAPHY

AJYB 62:449; Boquist, Constance, and Jeanette V. Haase. *An Historical Review of Women in Dentistry: An Annotated Bibliography* (1977); Louis B. Boudin Papers, Columbia University, NYC; Buhle, Paul. "Boudin, Louis B.," *Encyclopedia of the American Left*, ed. Mari Jo Buhle, Paul Buhle, and Dan Georgakas. 2d ed. (1992); "Dr. Anna Boudin, Founding President." *Women's American ORT News* 10, no. 2 (1959): 8; *Eighty Years of ORT: Historical Materials, Documents, and Reports* (1960); Neschis, Janet. Interview by author (October 9, 1996); Obituary. *NYTimes*, October 26, 1959, 29:5; "ORT America." *ORT Yearbook, 1987* (1987); Shapiro, Leon. *The History of ORT: A Jewish Movement for Social Change* (1980); U.S. Bureau of the Census. *Census Descriptions of Geographic Subdivisions and Enumeration Districts, 1920* (1978); "Women's American ORT Education for a Lifetime" (1995); *WWWIA* 3 (1960).

JENNIFER TAMMI

BOWLES, JANE (1917–1973)

"That genius imp, that laughing, hilarious, tortured elf" was how Truman Capote described the writer Jane Bowles, who, with her composer-writer husband Paul Bowles, became the center of an avant-garde circle in Morocco. Her darkly comic, original work was admired by writers such as Capote, Tennessee Williams, John Ashbery, and ALICE B. TOKLAS.

Bowles lived in Tangier from 1948 until her death, but her origins were less exotic. She was born in Manhattan on February 22, 1917, as Jane Stajer Auer, the only child of Claire Stajer of Hungarian Jewish parents and Sidney Major Auer of German Jewish parents. After attending public high school in New York, she went to private school in Massachusetts, where her fall from a horse broke an already weak right knee, causing permanent lameness. Before she was seventeen, she suffered prolonged physical pain and the unexpected early death of her father. At age forty, she endured a stroke whose effects darkened her remaining sixteen years.

She probably thought of herself as a lesbian before she met (1937) and married (1938) Paul Bowles, a bisexual writer and composer. They remained together after their sexual relationship ended, giving one another personal and professional support for over thirty-five years.

Bowles's only published novel, *Two Serious Ladies*, appeared in 1943 to mixed reviews. Several short stories were published before her play *In the Summer House* opened in New York. Included in *Best Plays of 1953–1954*, it was later twice revived. A collection of her short stories called *Plain Pleasures* appeared in 1966. *The Collected Works* were published during her lifetime in 1966 and reissued in 1978 as *My Sister's Hand in Mine*. Paul Bowles prepared the posthumous miscellany *Feminine Wiles* for publication in 1976. One novel, one full-length play, one short puppet play, and fewer than a dozen stories make up the slender corpus that has excited steady and serious critical response.

Bowles's fictional tone is never dark, although betrayal, sin, madness, and death inhabit her work. Her lucid, spare, rarely figurative style acquires both comic and disturbing reverberations. Her novel is characteristic. In it, "two serious ladies" pursue different unnerving journeys away from traditional women's lives.

Bowles's Jewishness was apparent in the Yiddish expressions that peppered her conversation, but beyond this display, she dealt with her heritage obliquely, if at all. Her fictional Spanish characters may represent a displacement of her Jewishness. They are voluble, gesticulating, anything but Anglo-Saxon. In the unfinished story "Andrew," Irish, Jews, and circus people are described as having "a foreign flavor" that both excites Andrew and makes him feel sick. As Jewish, lame, and lesbian, Bowles was a triple outsider

who could be mordantly self-mocking—referring to herself, for example, as "Cripple, the Kike Dyke." Perhaps her responsiveness to other languages is related to her outsider status; she became fluent in French, Spanish, and Arabic, the languages of the countries she lived in. Although her life touched major historical events, Bowles's fiction and drama are more attuned to cultural and psychological difference than to historical context or politics. Her stepfather, Julian Fuhs, was a Holocaust survivor. Her membership in the Communist Party was not an uncommon gesture in a period marked by cataclysmic social and political upheavals. However, her deathbed conversion to Catholicism is less credible. Jane Bowles died on May 4, 1973, and is buried in a Catholic cemetery—in an unmarked grave because her husband, unable to believe her conversion, would not allow a cross on it.

SELECTED WORKS BY JANE BOWLES
The Collected Works (1966). Reissued as *My Sister's Hand in Mine* (1978); *Feminine Wiles* (1976); *In the Summer House*. In *Best Plays of 1953–1954* (1955); *Out in the World: Selected Letters of Jane Bowles, 1935–1970*, edited by Millicent Dillon (1985, 1990); *Plain Pleasures* (1966); *Two Serious Ladies* (1943).

BIBLIOGRAPHY
Bowles, Paul. *Without Stopping* (1972); Dillon, Millicent. *A Little Original Sin: The Life and Work of Jane Bowles* (1981).

CLAIRE SPRAGUE

BOXER, BARBARA (b. 1940)

Barbara Boxer is currently one of the most influential liberal political figures in the country, having served in the United States Senate since 1992. Her visibility especially flows out of her vocal commitment to feminist causes.

Boxer was born on November 11, 1940, in Brooklyn to lawyer Ira R. Levy and homemaker Sophie (Silvershein) Levy, who were immigrants. After what she characterizes as a "Debbie Reynolds" type of life in the 1950s, she married Stewart Boxer in 1962 while a senior at Brooklyn College. The couple has two children. Doug, the elder, is a lawyer and an assistant deputy mayor in Los Angeles. Nicole, who works in the film business, married Hillary Rodham Clinton's brother Tony in a White House wedding in 1995.

Boxer's politicization was gradual. The same year she was married, a professor sexually harassed her—something she did not publicly disclose until the Anita

Hill–Clarence Thomas hearings that brought her national attention. In 1962, she organized tenants in her Brooklyn apartment complex to persuade a recalcitrant landlord to make necessary improvements.

After graduating from Brooklyn College in 1962 with a major in economics, Boxer hoped to become a stockbroker in order to put her husband through law school. No firm would hire her, so she had to study for the required exam while serving as a secretary. She was then able to ply her trade on Wall Street for three years.

In 1965, the Boxers moved to Greenbrae, in Marin County, California. The war in Vietnam and the assassinations of 1968 catalyzed her politicization. During the late 1960s and early 1970s, Boxer helped form a number of grassroots organizations involving education, day care, peace, and women's empowerment.

Boxer ran for political office for the first time in 1972, losing a race for the Marin County Board of Supervisors. She became a member of the Board of Supervisors in 1977 after working as a journalist and a congressional aide. She went on to be the first female president of the Board of Supervisors in 1981 and was then elected to Congress the following year.

In her decade in the House of Representatives, Boxer specialized in feminist issues, particularly abortion rights, and in exposing waste in defense spending. Yet it was the 1991 Supreme Court confirmation hearings for Clarence Thomas that were, and are, at the heart of Boxer's political life. Indeed, the narrative centerpiece of Boxer's biography/political testament, *Strangers in the Senate*, is Boxer leading the march of seven congresswomen over to the Senate to demand a full consideration of the charges of sexual harassment against Thomas.

The Hill-Thomas hearings provided the primary context for Boxer's election to the United States Senate in 1992 as part of the "Year of the Woman." That November, Californians elected another Jewish woman to the Senate, DIANNE FEINSTEIN, and new female senators from Illinois and Washington also joined the

As a congresswoman, Barbara Boxer led a march of seven of her female colleagues to the Senate to demand a full consideration of the charges of sexual harassment against Clarence Thomas by Anita Hill, during the 1992 confirmation hearings on his nomination to the Supreme Court. That November, as part of the Year of the Woman, she was elected to the Senate, along with another Californian, DIANNE FEINSTEIN. This group photo depicts the "Senate Women" in early 1993, with Hillary Rodham Clinton. From left to right are: Carol Moseley-Braun, Patty Murray, Barbara Mikulski, Hillary Rodham Clinton, Boxer, Feinstein, and Nancy Kassebaum. [White House Photograph]

Senator Boxer is shown here with Ambassador Stuart Eizenstat discussing how to trace the lost assets of victims of the Holocaust. [Office of Senator Boxer]

upper house. Domestic concerns ranging from gun control to children's programs to environmental protection have dominated Boxer's agenda in the Senate. She took a strong stand in favor of public hearings in the ethics case against Senator Bob Packwood, again demonstrating her commitment to feminist causes in general and making sexual harassment a visible political issue in particular.

Although she has won the Women of Achievement Award from the Anti-Defamation League and the Hannah G. Solomon Award from the NATIONAL COUNCIL OF JEWISH WOMEN, Boxer does not much publicly profess her religion. Indeed, *Strangers in the Senate* does not refer to her Judaism at all.

In many ways a classic Marin County liberal committed to individual liberties and government action on behalf of the underprivileged, Boxer is outside the national political mainstream. Boxer's feisty liberalism—with its strong feminist core—may stand her in good stead.

BIBLIOGRAPHY

Boxer, Barbara, and Nicole Boxer. *Strangers in the Senate: Politics and the New Revolution of Women in America* (1994); *Current Biography Yearbook* (1994): 63–66; *Who's Who in American Politics, 1995–1996* (1995).

ROBERT JOHNSTON

BRANDEIS, ALICE GOLDMARK (1866–1945)

A champion of progressive causes, Alice Goldmark Brandeis was outspoken on behalf of woman suffrage, industrial reform, organized labor, the legal rights of children, and the fledgling American Zionist movement.

She was born in 1866 in Brooklyn to Viennese immigrants Dr. Joseph and Regina Goldmark. Alice and her three sisters and one brother were raised in New York City. She married attorney Louis D.

Brandeis. The couple had two daughters, Susan (b. 1893), and Elizabeth (b. 1896).

The Brandeises moved to Boston, where Louis Brandeis's legal activism soon gained him a reputation as "the people's attorney," and Alice Brandeis assumed an increasing role advising him on strategies for promoting progressive causes.

After Louis was appointed to the U.S. Supreme Court in 1916, the Brandeises moved to Washington, D.C., where their home became a gathering place for liberal politicians and intellectuals. Despite their prominence, the Brandeises maintained a notoriously modest life-style; the Zionist leader and Chicago judge Julian Mack once joked that meals at the Brandeis home were so sparing that guests knew they should eat before and after each visit.

Alice Brandeis was not one to shy away from a controversial cause: She assisted in the campaign on behalf of anarchists Nicola Sacco and Bartolomeo Vanzetti, and embraced the third-party presidential campaign of Robert La Follette (1924). During World War II, Brandeis stirred some controversy by associating herself with militant critics of American policy toward European Jewry and Palestine.

Alice Brandeis died on October 11, 1945.

BIBLIOGRAPHY
AJYB, 48:485; Mason, Alpheus Thomas. *Brandeis: A Free Man's Life* (1946); Obituary. *NYTimes*, October 13, 1945, 15:3; Strum, Philippa. *Louis D. Brandeis: Justice for the People* (1984); Urofsky, Melvin I. *Louis D. Brandeis and the Progressive Tradition* (1981).

RAFAEL MEDOFF

BRANDEIS, MADELINE (1897–1937)

In her dedication to her 1929 book, *The Little Swiss Wood-Carver*, Madeline Brandeis, children's author and producer and director of travel films, sounded her unique multicultural note: "To every child of every land, / Little Sister, Little Brother, / As in this book your lives unfold, / May you learn to love each other." Until her untimely death, Brandeis traveled the world in search of stories to tell, aiming the lens of her camera at the lives of her characters.

Madeline (Frank) Brandeis was born on December 18, 1897, in San Francisco, to Albert and Mattie (Ehrman) Frank and attended Miss Burke's School there. She married E. John Brandeis on January 28, 1918, and had a daughter, Marie Madeline. Brandeis married a second time, to Dr. Joseph A. Sampson, on October 5, 1933. They lived in New York City.

Brandeis began her writing career at a time when children's literature was just coming into its own. The publication of dozens of her titles for children and adolescents, including the *Children of All Lands* series (1933) and the novel *Six Face the World* (1938), reflected the explosion in the quantity and quality of books for children that began in the 1920s and 1930s. In addition to illustrating her books with photographs from her travels, Brandeis took up the movie camera in her role as producer of eight motion pictures for children. Her work does not deal overtly with her own Jewish identity, although the themes of respect for different cultural and national heritages and of passing down family traditions and values resound in her books. In *The Little Swiss Wood-Carver*, the poor mountain boy of Switzerland keeps the memory of his artist father alive in his own work; and in *The Little Spanish Dancer* (1931), the young dancer is reminded of how her Spanish foremothers, despite persecution, secretly took their daughters into the dim light of caves in order to teach them the art of the dance.

Madeline Brandeis died on June 28, 1937, at age thirty-nine in Gallup, New Mexico, of injuries suffered in an automobile accident.

SELECTED WORKS BY MADELINE BRANDEIS
Adventures in Hollywood (1937); *Carmen of the Golden Coast* (1935); *Jack of the Circus* (1931); *Little Anne of Canada* (1931); *The Little Dutch Tulip Girl* (1929); *Little Farmer of the Middle West* (1937); *The Little Indian Weaver* (1928); *Little Jeanne of France* (1929); *Little John of New England* (1936); *The Little Mexican Donkey Boy* (1931); *Little Pepito of Central America* (1941); *Little Phillipe of Belgium* (1930); *Little Rose of the Mesa* (1935); *The Little Spanish Dancer* (1931); *The Little Swiss Wood-Carver* (1929); *Little Tom of England* (1935); *Little Tony of Italy* (1934); *Mitz and Fritz of Germany* (1933); *Shaun O'Day of Ireland* (1929); *The Wee Scotch Piper* (1929).

BIBLIOGRAPHY
Obituary. *NYTimes*, June 29, 1937, 21:2; *WWIAJ* (1938).

SUZANNE OSHINSKY

BRASLAU, SOPHIE (1902–1935)

Sophie Braslau was a leading contralto who debuted at the Metropolitan Opera in New York at age eleven.

She was born in New York City on August 16, 1902, the daughter of Dr. Abel and Alexandra (Goodelman) Braslau. Her parents, both from Russia, recognized early on the musical talent of their only child. Her father was on friendly terms with many musicians and often hosted visiting virtuosi. Sophie Braslau acknowledged that her musical inspiration came from a performance by soprano ALMA GLUCK at the old Mendelssohn Hall.

Her early musical training, which began at age five, was directed to becoming a concert pianist. She graduated from the Institute of Musical Art and continued under the training of Alexander Lambert, noted sponsor of young musical geniuses.

Signor A. Buzzi-Pecci, a voice teacher, who was often a visitor at the Braslau home, heard Sophie humming during piano practice. At the maestro's request, she sang, and he exclaimed, "Ah, here you have a contralto of operatic caliber, doctor, without knowing it." She studied three years with Buzzi-Pecci, then with Madame Marcella Sembrich, Gabriele Sibella, Herbert Witherspoon, Mari Marafioti, and others.

When she auditioned at the Metropolitan Opera with a group of seventeen other hopefuls, she won instant recognition and was granted a five-year contract.

She made her first appearance in a minor, off-stage voice role in *Parsifal* in 1913. Her real debut at the Metropolitan Opera House in New York occurred on November 28, 1913, when she sang the role of the Tsarevitch Feodora in Mussorgsky's *Boris Godunov*. The following year, she performed the part of

Sophie Braslau was a musical prodigy who made her New York Metropolitan Opera debut at age eleven and by eighteen had retired from opera. She went on to make Yiddish recordings and tour the United States and Europe but died at age thirty-three. [New York Public Library]

Mercedes in the revival of *Carmen* that Toscanini conducted in 1914. She performed in Leoni's *L'Oracolo*, Zandonai's *Francesca da Rimini*, Mozart's *Die Zauberflöte*, and Rimsky-Korsakof's *Le Coq d'Or*. She was lauded for her title role at the Met on March 23, 1918, in the world premiere of the opera *Shanewis* by Charles Wakefield Cadman. Her repertoire included all the standard operas in English, Russian, French, German, and Italian. She retired from opera in 1920.

Sophie Braslau was also part of the so-called Victor Quartet, which made operatic recordings. Her Yiddish records "Eili, Eili" (which was also popularized by BELLE BAKER) and "Yahrzeit" sold for $1.75 each in 1921. By 1926, she had toured the United States at least five times, appearing as a soloist with various symphony orchestras and at leading music festivals. She sang at fund-raisers such as the Omaha Hebrew Club campaign in 1921 to raise money for Jewish war sufferers. She toured Canada and the principal cities of Europe. Her last appearances were with the Philharmonic Society of New York in 1934.

She died on December 22, 1935, at age thirty-three. She had been ill for almost two years and bedridden for six months. Her eulogy was read by Olin Downes, the music critic of the *New York Times*. Among the honorary pallbearers were fellow musicians Sergey Rachmaninoff, Jascha Heifetz, Fritz Reiner, and José Iturbi.

BIBLIOGRAPHY

AJYB 24:124, 38:426; *BEOAJ*; Braslau, Sophie. Manuscript collection. Brooklyn Public Library, and Papers. Music Division, New York Public Library; *DAB* 1; *NAW*; Obituary. *NYTimes*, December 23, 1935, 19:1; *UJE*; *WWIAJ* (1926, 1938); *WWWIA* 1.

OLIVER B. POLLAK

BRAUN, SUSAN (1916–1995)

Susan Braun, recognizing the need for a new genre that combined dance and film, single-handedly set up a place where artists could come together and plan how to merge the ideas of choreographers and filmmakers. She founded Dance Films Association in 1956, an organization that presaged the ever-growing development of work between filmmakers and dancers, and that continues to provide a haven for these artists. Dancers are not only preserving their works on film, but are establishing a new medium, a dance and film evening, that merges the two art forms. The dancer can now make a second career—that of the filmmaker.

Susan Braun was born July 24, 1916, in New York City to Alfred and Georgina (Ballin) Braun. Alfred Braun, born in Hungary to Jewish parents, became a distinguished otolaryngologist after he immigrated to the United States. Georgina Braun, who had German roots, died when her daughter, an only child, was just two years old. Although Braun had a rigid "old world New York" upbringing on the Upper East Side of Manhattan, the world of music and painting enlightened her childhood. Although not religious by nature, she learned and maintained a great reverence for the symbolic rituals of all faiths. Her father executed many fine paintings, and her uncle Maurice Braun, a popular California artist, had quite an influence on her. Alfred Braun frequently took his daughter to the Metropolitan Opera, thus beginning her lifelong love of music. Braun attended the Parsons School of Design, Jamesine Franklin School of Professional Arts, and the Jessie Ansbacher Group at the Art Students League.

From 1949 until 1953, Braun studied Isadora Duncan dance technique with Anita Zahn, thereby discovering that dance would play a major part in her life. Having been trained for a career in art, she did an about-face and focused on dance. In the early 1950s, other than some 16mm films on Russian ballet, very little film documentation of dance existed. After having helped Daniel Livingston with the New York Dance Films Society, Braun started Dance Films, Incorporated, in 1956 when his organization folded. It soon became Dance Films Association, Incorporated, a not-for-profit service center for the dance and film community, and the first such center in the United States. She also created the Dance on Camera Festival, the first film/video/dance festival.

Susan Braun died in New York City on October 3, 1995. In her work, she crossed paths with and was admired and respected by almost all the luminaries of the dance and film world.

BIBLIOGRAPHY

Lipari, Victor. "A Singular Vision: Susan Braun and Dance Films Association." *Sightlines: The Journal of the American Film and Video Association* (Summer 1992): 26–27; Tish, Pauline. "Dance Films Association Is Still Growing." *Performing Arts Review* 10, no. 1 (1980): 85; Towers, Dierdre. "Susan Braun, 79, Dies." *Dance on Camera News* (September–October 1995): 1; *Who's Who of American Women* (1958–1959): 159.

VICTOR LIPARI

BRAVARSKA, ESTHER RUDA
see SHOSHANA, ROSE

BREGMAN, ELSIE OSCHRIN (1896–1969)

Elsie Oschrin Bregman was a psychologist most noted for her pioneering research on the measurement of mental ability and intelligence.

She was born on November 30, 1896, in Newark, New Jersey, to Aaron and Theresa (Goldstein) Oschrin. She graduated from Barnard College in 1918 and received her doctorate in psychology from Columbia University in 1922. She married Adolph Bregman, a metallurgical engineer, in 1919, and they had two daughters, Judith and Cynthia.

Bregman developed the first department-store sales testing and employee training program when she worked for R.H. Macy's from 1919 to 1921. She wrote several scholarly articles reporting on this aspect of her research: "Mental Tests for Retail Saleswomen," "Studies in Industrial Psychology," and "Application for Psychological Tests and Ratings in Industry." She also studied the intellectual ability of high school students and the possibility of predicting vocational success through testing. In 1933, she researched the mental abilities of student nurses, as reported in her monograph "Performance of Student Nurses on Tests of Intelligence."

In addition, she helped revise the Army's Alpha Test in the 1920s and 1930s with Edward L. Thorndyke. Both participated in a benchmark study published in 1926 titled *The Measurement of Intelligence*.

Bregman maintained a private practice in psychology in New York City from 1935 until 1962 and was active in the American Psychological Association, the Association of Consulting Psychologists, and the Institute of Educational Research of Teachers College, Columbia University, and was also a fellow of the American Association for the Advancement of Science.

Elsie Oschrin Bregman died on July 26, 1969, in New York City.

BIBLIOGRAPHY

BEOAJ; Obituary. *NYTimes*, July 26, 1969, 25:1; *WWIAJ* (1926, 1928, 1938).

ANNETTE MUFFS BOTNICK

BRENNER, ROSE (1884–1926)

"The Council concerns itself with the Jewish woman, in America, *and on her way to America*: in the city and on the farm lands: in need of adjustment to her environment and capable of contributing to the

President of the NATIONAL COUNCIL OF JEWISH WOMEN *from 1920 to 1926, Rose Brenner provided strong leadership, almost doubling the size of the organization. The NCJW has always championed both public service and the role of traditional motherhood. Brenner is the only unmarried woman ever to be president. [American Jewish Archives]*

enrichment of her environment." This statement by Rose Brenner, first formulated in 1921 at a board of managers meeting, embodied her philosophy during her tenure as president of the NATIONAL COUNCIL OF JEWISH WOMEN (NCJW), from 1920 to 1926.

Rose Brenner, the eldest of four daughters and two sons, was born on April 3, 1884, in Brooklyn, New York, to Judge Jacob and Louise (Blumeneau) Brenner. Jacob Brenner was a leader in local political, religious, and philanthropic endeavors. The middle-class family belonged to Reform Beth Elohim Temple. When Rose was almost eighteen years old, her mother died. She immediately assumed the responsibilities of helping to care for her siblings, the youngest of whom was only eight months old. She also assisted her father in his many activities. Even

with these additional duties, Rose Brenner entered Adelphi College and graduated with honors in 1908.

Soon after obtaining her college degree, Brenner accepted a chairmanship in the Brooklyn Section of the NCJW. She served as president of the section from 1912 to 1918. Under her administration, membership increased fivefold. New projects included religious study groups, sponsorship of a home for Jewish girls, and support of the war effort. Within the Brooklyn Section, Brenner organized a group of juniors. This led to the formation of the National Council of Jewish Juniors, which had its own constitution, officers, and biennial conventions. As president of the Brooklyn Section, Brenner designated the Sabbath nearest Purim as "Council Sabbath." This observance, adopted nationally in 1920, provided synagogues with the opportunity to recognize NCJW members, and women with the chance to participate in worship services in their own congregations.

Brenner was elected second vice president at the NCJW 1914 Triennial Convention, first vice president at the 1917 Triennial Convention, and national president at the 1920 Triennial Convention. She was reelected president at the 1923 Triennial Convention.

During her presidency, NCJW expanded numerically from 150 sections with 28,000 members to 235 sections with over 50,000 members. This growth was the result of increased publicity about the NCJW's work, attention to its resourceful and effective programs, and the continuation of volunteer efforts begun by women during World War I. Other secular women's groups showed corresponding growth during this period. The membership rise enabled the NCJW to develop a National Speakers Bureau, a Committee on Deaf and Hard of Hearing, and an enlarged Department of Immigrant Aid. It prepared and distributed courses on Jewish prayer and published the first Jewish prayer book in Braille.

Rose Brenner had shown keen interest in the Jewish immigrants who settled in America's rural communities. Through Brenner's initiative, delegates to the 1920 Triennial Convention created a Department of Farm and Rural Work that was separate from the immigrant aid work the NCJW had begun in the early part of the century to aid Jewish women and girls upon their arrival in America. This department became the second-largest NCJW program during the 1920s, reaching Jewish women and their families on nearly three thousand farms in eight states. It provided nurses to run preventive health care programs and, along with food and ritual objects, lecturers to stimulate observances of Jewish holidays. More than seven hundred Jewish children in rural areas participated in religious school classes, staffed by Hebrew teachers engaged by the NCJW.

Under Brenner's administration, the national board strengthened and energized the growing organization in several other ways. It began publication in 1921 of the quarterly *The Jewish Woman* and of the monthly *The Immigrant*. State and regional conferences were started in order to dispense information to those who could not attend national conventions, to aid geographically close sections in working together, and to provide a ladder of leadership for more members.

Rose Brenner appointed committees on foreign relations and on reconstruction to assist in post–World War I resettlement. As part of the reconstruction program, the NCJW helped to establish NCJW sections in Europe. They cooperated with the American organization in caring for thousands of refugees abroad and on their way to America. This groundwork led to the first World Congress of Jewish Women held in Vienna in 1923, and the election of NCJW leader REBEKAH KOHUT as president.

Rose Brenner was actively involved in other causes related to and outside of the NCJW. She taught religious school at Beth Elohim Temple for twenty years, served as president of its sisterhood, and was the first woman elected to the temple's executive board. Brenner was elected to the Brooklyn Board of Education and served as a director of the Women's Foundation for Health. As president of the NCJW, she represented the organization at the biennial meetings of the NATIONAL FEDERATION OF TEMPLE SISTERHOODS (NFTS) in 1921 and 1923. At her urging, the Conference Committee of National Jewish Women's Organizations was formed at the 1925 biennial meeting of the NFTS.

Under Brenner's stewardship, the NCJW initiated and broadened efforts to Americanize immigrants while encouraging their continued religious and ethnic identity. Its work on resettlement, citizenship, and peace efforts brought national and international recognition to the organization. Rose Brenner's leadership is also significant, since she was the sole unmarried woman to attain the presidency of the NCJW, an organization that had championed traditional Jewish motherhood alongside its commitment to public service.

Rose Brenner died suddenly at home on April 5, 1926, at age forty-two.

BIBLIOGRAPHY

AJYB 24:125, 29:117; Brenner, Rose. Papers. National Office, National Council of Jewish Women Collection, Manuscript Division, Library of Congress, Washington, D.C. Box I: 2–4, 35–36, 103; Campell, Monroe, and Willem Wirtz. *The First Fifty Years, A History of the National Council of Jewish Women, 1893–1943* (1943); *The Immigrant* (1921–1927); *The Jewish Woman* (1921–1927); Korelitz, Seth. "'A Magnificent Piece of Work': The Americanization Work of the National Council of Jewish Women." *AJH* 83, no. 2 (June 1995): 177–203; "Leader of American Jewish Womanhood Passes Suddenly." *The American Hebrew* (April 9, 1926): 721; National Council of Jewish Women. *Official Report of the . . . Triennial Convention . . . 1917, 1920, 1923, 1926*, and *Report of the Office of the Executive Secretary for the Eleventh Triennial, 1923–1926* (1926), and *Tenth Triennial Program and a Record of Council Achievements (1920–1923)* (n.d.); Rogow, Faith. *Gone to Another Meeting: The National Council of Jewish Women, 1893–1993* (1993); *UJE* 2:519–520.

PEGGY PEARLSTEIN

BRICE, FANNY (1891–1951)

One of America's great clowns, Fanny Brice built her career on a Yiddish accent and a flair for zany parody. In an era when ethnic comedy was the norm, she delighted audiences for more than forty years and won a following in almost every branch of American show business. During the fourth decade of her professional life, she became precocious radio brat "Baby Snooks," and that is the role for which she is most often remembered. Yet "Snooks" was only one of Brice's many inimitable characters and radio, the last of the entertainment forms in which her comic genius found expression. Before focusing exclusively on "the airwaves," she appeared in burlesque and vaudeville, drama, film, and musical revues (including nine *Ziegfeld Follies* between 1910 and 1936). Brooks Atkinson, longtime drama critic of the *New York Times*, called Brice "a burlesque comic of the rarest vintage" and acknowledged her achievement in comedy, a field men had previously dominated.

Born Fania Borach on October 29, 1891, Brice was the child of Jewish immigrants who had settled on New York's Lower East Side. Her mother, Rose Stern, left a small village near Budapest to come to America in 1877. Charles Borach, her father, set off from Alsace during the late 1870s or early 1880s. When they met in Manhattan, Rose was working at a sewing machine in a fur factory and Charles was a bartender in a Bowery saloon. They married in 1886, moved to Second Avenue, and produced four children in the next seven years: Philip ("Phil," born in 1887), Carolyn ("Carrie," born in 1889), Fania ("Fanny," born in 1891), and Louis ("Lew," born in 1893). By 1895, they had left the Lower East Side's congestion and crime for Newark, New Jersey.

One of the most popular stars of Florenz Ziegfeld's Follies, *Fanny Brice created the character Baby Snooks. Snooks led Brice to the radio stardom she desired. [New York Public Library]*

The Borachs bought a saloon that Charles Borach turned over to his wife's efficient management and gambled away the money she worked so hard to earn. Tiring of the unequal partnership, she left her indolent husband and took her children to Brooklyn

(c. 1902). Charles Borach followed them to New York and drifted into a series of odd jobs. When he died in 1912, he had lost virtually all contact with his family. Brice, who accepted the estrangement from her father as irrevocable, would mirror her mother's experience. Like Rose Stern, she would marry unwisely and unhappily. She, too, would be a working mother, a single parent, whose relentless drive assuredly came from necessity as well as ambition.

A chronic truant who ended her formal education sometime during or after the eighth grade, Brice yearned for a career in show business.

Performing in *The Transatlantic Burlesquers* (1907–1908) as chorus girl Fanny Borach, she joined the cast of *The Girls from Happyland* for the 1908–1909 season. Although the show was poorly received, it was a landmark in her career because it marked her first appearance as Fanny Brice, the name she used for the rest of her life. She explained in a 1946 interview that she was tired of being called "Borax" and "Boreache" and chose Brice, the surname of a family friend, to prevent further teasing. She was also, undoubtedly, trying to seem less ethnic, less foreign, and less Jewish, thereby broadening her appeal. In 1908, she did not know that she would shortly find fame as an entertainer by exploiting her Jewishness and caricaturing her ethnicity.

In Max Spiegel's *The College Girls* the following season, she had her first sizable role. Cast as Josie McFadden, she won praise for the specialty number she performed in the show's second act, particularly her rendition of "Sadie Salome, Go Home." It was, in her words, "a Jewish comedy song" by Irving Berlin, who must have known it would suit the lanky teenager with the big nose and wide mouth when he suggested it. An outrageous spoof of Salome dancing, a phenomenon once described as "the phoniest craze to hit show business," the song was the first Brice performed with a Yiddish accent. In so doing, she was giving American audiences what they wanted. Ethnic comedy was still very much in vogue in the early years of the twentieth century, and minority groups were parodied by the popular arts. Racial and ethnic stereotypes appeared in serious dramatic fare and cavorted in burlesque and vaudeville. Although allegedly unable to speak Yiddish, she could join the many non-Jews who succeeded as "Jew comics" by adopting the externals required for "Hebrew impersonation." Just as Al Jolson could put on his makeup and perform in blackface, Brice could assume the accent and the mannerisms for Yiddish dialect comedy. With Sadie, she created the first of her many memorable characters and found the performance style that became her

Described by Brooks Atkinson, longtime drama critic of the New York Times, *as "a burlesque comic of the rarest vintage,"
Fanny Brice is shown here in some of her characteristic "mugging" faces.*

signature, a style based on deft parody, broad physical humor, and an accent used brilliantly for comic effect.

She also attracted the attention of producer Florenz Ziegfeld, Jr., who hired her for his *Follies of 1910*. When he did, he was certainly not adding another lovely showgirl to his stable. Although far from unattractive by today's standards, the tall, slender, Semitic-looking Brice did not conform to the prevailing notion of feminine beauty. Yet, paradoxically, Ziegfeld provided the setting that displayed her comic talents to best advantage. If she could not be the prettiest girl on the stage, she would be the funniest. She was literally built for comedy.

It was not until she hired songwriter Blanche Merrill after several disappointing seasons that she developed into the "character comedienne" she had promised to be with "Sadie Salome." They began collaborating in

1915, and Merrill, who specialized in writing for women, created material that suited her. In spite of her *Follies* success, Brice wanted to develop her talents as a dramatic actress. Her attempts to do so foundered. The vehicle she unfortunately chose in 1918 was *Why Worry?*, a theatrical hodgepodge in which she floundered as waitress Dora Harris. Even the last-minute addition of two wonderful Merrill songs ("I'm an Indian" and "I'm a Vamp") could not salvage Brice's performance. She would be similarly disappointed in 1926 when she thought David Belasco's production of the banal *Fanny* would establish her reputation as a serious actress and, instead, saw her efforts dismissed by the critics who referred to the show irreverently as "What Brice Glory?" and "Fanny's Worst Play."

On October 18 Brice finally married the man she loved after a six-year relationship. She had met handsome and sophisticated Jules Wilford "Nick" Arnstein in 1912 and said she fell in love with him as soon as she saw his seven toothbrushes and monogrammed silk pajamas in the bathroom of his hotel suite. Contrary to her glowing perception of him, the Norwegian-born Arnstein was a con man and a criminal who operated under a number of aliases and failed at everything he attempted, including the wiretapping that sent him to Sing Sing in 1915 and the bond theft that led him to Leavenworth in 1924. Oblivious to his character flaws, she was also undeterred by the discovery that he was already married. (Brice herself had impulsively married barber Frank White in 1910 while touring with *The College Girls*, but never lived with him and obtained a divorce in 1913.)

After Arnstein's divorce in 1918, he and Brice married. They had two children, Frances (b. 1919) and William (b. 1921), but life was far from idyllic. In 1920, "Nicky" was accused of orchestrating a Wall Street bond robbery. Convinced of his innocence, Brice financed his trial and lengthy appeal, endured the attendant notoriety, and remained loyal to him during his incarceration. They finally divorced in 1927, after his release from Leavenworth, on account of his flagrant infidelity. He disappeared from their lives more abruptly than Charles Borach had vanished from Brice's.

From 1918 to 1927, Brice worked hard and steadily on the stage. (She performed into the seventh month of both her pregnancies, returning to rehearsals soon after the birth of each child.) She appeared in three more editions of the *Ziegfeld Follies*, four other Ziegfeld shows, and two non-Ziegfeld productions. She made several records, produced *Is Zat So?* and *The Brown Derby*, and filled the remaining time with lucrative vaudeville engagements. She refined her craft as a comic artist, describing herself as "a cartoonist working in the flesh," and caused a sensation in *The Ziegfeld Follies of 1921* with an uncharacteristically serious selection, "My Man," designed to capitalize on her tumultuous relationship with Arnstein. Instead of the animated parody she typically offered, she stood almost motionless, sang without a funny accent, and created the illusion that she was sharing her own painful experience. The moving song always produced a powerful emotional effect on audiences who clamored for it.

Brice had some of her best comic material in the *Follies of 1921*, including spoofs of Ethel Barrymore in *Camille* and the memorable song "Second Hand Rose." Yet dissatisfied with being "just a comic," Brice still sought acceptance as a serious actress in a starring vehicle. In 1923, tired of being a sight gag, she

decided to have cosmetic surgery on her nose. Algonquin wit DOROTHY PARKER quipped that Brice had "cut off her nose to spite her race," and there was probably far more truth to that acerbic statement than Brice ever acknowledged. However legitimate her dramatic aspirations, she was motivated in part by her wish to escape from the ethnicity of her comedy. She seems to have decided that her Yiddish-accented routines had become too limiting, particularly in the xenophobic and racist climate of the 1920s when prejudice against ethnic groups was very real. She had escaped from Borach fifteen years earlier; at thirty-two, thanks to medical advances made during World War I, Protestant prettiness might actually be attainable.

Disappointed both with the results of the surgical procedure and the response to her attempts at more serious material, Brice accepted the inevitable and returned to comedy. Determined to find a starring vehicle that would catapult her into the nation's consciousness, she turned to film. Even with her new nose, she did not have the kind of face Hollywood loved. But she could sing and since Al Jolson's 1927 triumph in *The Jazz Singer*, Hollywood needed voices. Promoted by Warner Brothers as a "female Jolson," Brice became the first woman to star in a sound motion picture. Much to her dismay, she did not duplicate Jolson's success. Audiences across America simply could not relate to her Yiddish accent and comic mannerisms. Although she would make six movies in all, film stardom eluded her and she claimed she never felt comfortable in front of the camera.

The year 1929 brought another critical failure in the musical *Fioretta* and in another marriage. Songwriter and aspiring impresario Billy Rose became her third husband in a civil ceremony on February 8 at Manhattan's City Hall. Brice's friends considered the union a mismatch, and her children compared the short, stocky Rose unfavorably to their handsome father. Nevertheless, the thirty-seven-year-old Brice seemed happy about the marriage. "I was never bored with Billy," she later reminisced. They shared a passionate commitment to show business, and she spent the next two years performing in the musical revues her husband created to showcase her talent, *Sweet and Low* (1930) and *Crazy Quilt* (1931). She also began a successful series of radio broadcasts and achieved her greatest stage triumphs in the *Ziegfeld Follies of 1934* and *1936*.

In these posthumous editions of the *Follies* produced by the Shuberts, Brice created some of her most brilliant comic characters. From "Soul Saving Sadie" (a spoof on evangelist Aimee Semple McPherson) to "Countess Dubinsky" (an outrageous parody of stripteasing and fan dancing) and "Modernistic Moe" (an antic burlesque of modern dancer Martha Graham), Brice had never been funnier. With her humorous accent, mobile face, and wonderfully expressive body, in Billy Rose's words, "she stood out like a bagel in a loaf of white bread." Her amusing sketches included two in which she appeared as terrible toddler "Baby Snooks" and delighted audiences with her thoroughly believable impersonation, complete with hair ribbon, starched pinafore, ankle socks, and Mary Janes.

"Snooks" would lead Brice to the radio stardom she desired. In 1937, with her marriage to Billy Rose disintegrating, she moved to California. They were divorced on October 27, 1938. Beginning in November, she launched a new career on radio with a popular weekly program broadcast across the country. Instead of her gallery of comic creations, she played only "Baby Snooks," the one character who did not require an accent of any kind. With anti-Semitism rampant in the United States and Europe, even Brice, admittedly uninformed about world events, must have realized that a Yiddish accent was probably not the best way to win a national following. "Schnooks," as she liked to call her, ensured a much wider appeal.

Brice suffered a serious heart attack in July 1945 but was well enough to resume her radio show in the fall. The profitable series continued until 1948, when she went off the air during a highly publicized contract dispute caused by fierce competition from the latest technological marvel to arrive on the show business scene: television. Rather than take a salary cut, Brice refused to work and began an autobiography she would not live to complete. Returning to radio in 1949, she continued happily wreaking havoc as Snooks. She had no interest in making the transition to television and, ironically, was contemplating retirement when she had a stroke on May 24, 1951. She died in Los Angeles, five days later, without regaining consciousness.

Reminiscing in her memoirs, Brice acknowledged the price professional women often pay for success: "If you have a career, then the career is your life. The hell with anything else. It is the biggest part of you and you can be married, have children, have a husband, but it isn't enough for you because the career is always there in your mind, taking the best out of you which you should give to your husband and kids." Yet, in what would have been the conclusion of her planned autobiography, she declared, "I made most things happen for me, and if they were good, I worked to get them. If they were bad, I worked just as hard for that. But I am not sorry. I will tell anybody that and it is the truth. I lived the way I wanted to live and never did what people said I should do or advised me to do." Ambitious, tenacious, and tough, a survivor in a ruthless business where fame is especially ephemeral, she achieved greatness when she accepted her comic gifts and abandoned her desire to become a serious actress.

Critics frequently noted the "pronounced Jewish flavor" of her performances, and it is tempting to attribute a great deal of significance to Brice's Jewishness. Although she worked with a Yiddish accent for many years on stage and screen, however, her routines were only superficially "Jewish" and did not stem from a deep sense of ethnic or religious identity. A performer in the dialect comedy tradition, Brice often played to the prejudices of the period, but mocking Jewish values was not generally part of her comic world and she was careful not to offend Jewish audience members. Even as the quintessential Jewish mother in the monologue "Mrs. Cohen at the Beach," she managed to avoid vicious satire. Brice's expressive delivery, coupled with her great warmth as a performer, humanized the stereotype and rounded the caricature into a character.

A truly popular entertainer, Fanny Brice worked hard to establish a rapport with her audiences. She did not deal with upsetting topics or controversial events, and people did not look to her for an evening of corrosive social commentary. A deft satirist capable of adroitly lampooning a variety of contemporary subjects, she seemed entirely uninhibited in performance, and her name always meant laughter, hilarious antics, and great fun. Whether spoofing ballerinas, opera singers, movie vamps, child stars, or nudists, her zany comedy made her special, and her lunatic creations inspired endless delight. A brilliant clown and a consummate professional, Brice was a genuinely funny woman who turned to show business, like so many other children of immigrants, and fulfilled the American dream.

SELECTED WORKS OF FANNY BRICE

"Fannie of the *Follies*," as told to Palma Wayne. Parts 1, 2, and 3. *Cosmopolitan* (February, March, April 1936); "The Feel of the Audience." *Saturday Evening Post*, November 21, 1925.

FILMOGRAPHY

Be Yourself. United Artists (1930); *Everybody Sing.* MGM (1938); *The Great Ziegfeld.* MGM (1936); *My Man.* Warner Brothers (1928); *The Ziegfeld Follies.* MGM (1946).

DISCOGRAPHY

Fanny Brice-Helen Morgan: Rare Originals by Two Legendary Pioneers of Theatre and Tin Pan Alley. RCA Victor LPV 561. Rodgers and Hammerstein Archives of Recorded

Sound at Lincoln Center; *Great Personalities of Broadway: The Original Great Performances*. RCA Camden CAL 745. Rodgers and Hammerstein Archives; *The Original Funny Girl: Fanny Brice Sings the Songs She Made Famous*. Audio Fidelity AFLP 707; *The Original Torch Singers: Fanny Brice, Ruth Etting, Libby Holman, Helen Morgan, 1928–1935*. Take Two Records TT 207; *Ziegfeld Follies of 1934*. Recorded live at the Shubert Theatre in New Haven, Conn., March 16, 1935. Rodgers and Hammerstein Archives.

BIBLIOGRAPHY

AJYB 24:125, 53:523; Atkinson, Brooks. *Broadway* (1974); Brice, Fanny. Papers. Billy Rose Theatre Collection, New York Public Library at Lincoln Center, and Harvard Theatre Collection, Harvard College Library, Cambridge, Mass., and Theatre and Music Collection, Museum of the City of New York; *BEOAJ*; Busch, Niven, Jr. "Firesign." In *Twenty-One Americans* (1930); Cantor, Eddie. *Take My Life* (1957), and *Ziegfeld—The Great Glorifier* (1934); *Current Biography* (1947); *DAB* 5; Dunning, John. *Tune in Yesterday— the Ultimate Encyclopedia of Old-Time Radio* (1976); Farnsworth, Marjorie. *The Ziegfeld Follies: A History in Text and Pictures* (1956); Goldman, Herbert G. *Fanny Brice: The Original Funny Girl* (1992); Green, Abel, and Joe Laurie, Jr. *Show Biz from Vaude to Video* (1951); Green, Stanley. *The Great Clowns of Broadway* (1984); Grossman, Barbara W. *Funny Woman: The Life and Times of Fanny Brice* (1991); Harmon, Jim. *The Great Radio Comedians* (1970); Katkov, Norman. *The Fabulous Fanny: The Story of Fanny Brice* (1953); Kutner, Nanette. "If You Were Daughter to Baby Snooks." *Good Housekeeping* (March 1943); Laurie, Joe, Jr. *Vaudeville: From the Honky-Tonks to the Palace* (1953); *NAW* modern; Nelson, Stephen. *"Only a Paper Moon": The Theatre of Billy Rose* (1987); Obituary. *NYTimes*, May 30, 1951, 21:1; Seldes, Gilbert. "The Daemonic in the American Theatre." *The Dial* (September 1923); Spiegel, Irving. "Having to Do with Baby Snooks." *NYTimes*, April 22, 1945; Sheppard, Eugenia. "Life with Mother." Interview with Frances Brice Stark. *New York Herald Tribune*, March 22, 1964; *UJE*; *Who's Who in the Theater*, 11th ed. (1952); *WWIAJ* (1926 addenda, 1928, 1938); *WWWIA* 3; Zeidman, Irving. *The American Burlesque Show* (1967); Zolotow, Maurice. "Baby Snooks." Parts 1 and 2. *Cosmopolitan* (September, October 1946).

BARBARA W. GROSSMAN

BRIDGES: A JOURNAL FOR JEWISH FEMINISTS AND OUR FRIENDS

Drawing on the traditional Jewish values of justice and repair of the world and insights honed by the feminist, lesbian, and gay movements, seven Jewish women began to publish *Bridges: A Journal for Jewish Feminists and Our Friends* in 1990.

Bridges evolved from a nationally distributed Jewish feminist newsletter called *Gesher* [Hebrew for "bridge"] started in 1988 by Ruth Atkin and ADRIENNE RICH for the National Feminist Task Force of New Jewish Agenda. Atkin, Rich, Elly Bulkin, and Clare Kinberg—all previously editors of lesbian or Jewish feminist publications—with Rita Falbel, Ruth Kraut, and Laurie White, began publishing *Bridges* as an editorially independent journal of fiction, poetry, essays, visual art, and reviews. By 1996, the eight-member core editorial group included women from the United States and Canada. *Bridges* has a circulation of three thousand. Bound like a book, with a spine wide enough to contain the periodical's name, issue number, and publication date, each volume is designed to have a permanent place on bookshelves.

Bridges is an explicitly Jewish participant in a multi-ethnic feminist movement. It connects Jewish women who are active in antiracist, economic justice, peace, lesbian/gay, and Jewish renewal movements; integrates analyses of racism and classism into Jewish-feminist thought; and makes connections across generations, countries, and languages by publishing archival material and writing in different Jewish languages and in translation. It publishes substantive essays on such topics as campus organizing, the Holocaust, Jewish women's rituals, incest, dis/ability, and Israel and Palestine. *Bridges* also publishes work by men and non-Jewish women of particular relevance to its focus.

Among *Bridges'* key contributions has been its insistence on the multiplicity of Jewish experiences and identities within a context that values different voices, histories, and languages. Although most contributors are Ashkenazi Jews, *Bridges* readers have read the words of Sephardic Jews Rita Arditti and Loolwa Khazzoom; Latina Jews Marjorie Agosín (Chile), Ruth Behar (Cuba), Renée Epelbaum (Argentina), and Aurora Levins Morales (Puerto Rico); and several Jews by choice. The pages of *Bridges* have contained translations—alongside the original—of contemporary writing (the Hebrew poetry of Dahlia Ravikovitch; Yiddish fiction by Blume Lempel) and archival writings (Yiddish fiction and poetry by YENTE SERDATSKY, KADIA MOLODOWSKY, Abraham Sutzkever, and others), as well as an article by Irena Klepfisz on women thinkers and activists from the Yiddish world of Eastern Europe.

Bridges provides a rare space in the Jewish community: one where lesbian and working-class voices can be heard consistently, heterosexual and middle/upper-class identities are not viewed as norms, and dialogues can appear between allies—lesbian and heterosexual, poor/working-class and middle/upper-class. From the outset, *Bridges* has featured work by Jewish

Depicted here is the Bridges *editorial board meeting in July 1992.*
Front row, left to right: ADRIENNE RICH, *Fai Coffin, Ruth Atkin; back row,*
left to right: Clare Kinberg, Rita Falbel, Helene Lipstadt, Elly Bulkin, Ruth Kraut, and Tobi Mae Lippin.
[Tova Stabin]

lesbians, including Christie Balka, Joan E. Biren (JEB), Elana Dykewomon, Marcia Freedman, and Melanie Kaye/Kantrowitz. *Bridges* has increasingly addressed issues of class. It added a "Working Class Words" column as a regular feature, coordinated by tova, and published a special section ("Making Our Lives Visible: Poor and Working-Class Women Speak Out") that included discussions of cost sharing, class and race, red diaper babies, and other topics.

Bridges had made a distinct contribution both to the feminist and the Jewish presses. In aiming to publish materials of durable quality and interest, it has become an ongoing, twice-yearly anthology of politics, art, history, and spiritual concerns.

ELLY BULKIN

BRILL, JEANETTE GOODMAN (1889–1964)

Jeanette Goodman Brill was Brooklyn's first woman magistrate and the second woman magistrate appointed in New York City. She was born on Essex Street on the Lower East Side of New York City in 1889 to Sam and Sarah Goodman. She was the only daughter and had many brothers.

As teacher, lawyer, judge, writer, community activist, camp director, mother and wife, woman, and Jew, her accomplishments were many. The central theme that ran through all of her activities was social justice and welfare, primarily focusing on children, adolescents, and women. Her interests and accomplishments were shaped by her heritage as a child of

Eastern European Polish immigrant parents and the Progressive movement with its focus on maternalism.

Jeanette grew up on the Lower East Side, where she attended a commercial school, then taught at the Manhattan Preparatory School on East Broadway during the day and attended classes at night to obtain her Regent's diploma. Afterward, she attended classes at Brooklyn Law School while she continued teaching. She graduated in 1908 and was admitted to the bar two years later, when she became twenty-one years old. Her granddaughter stated that her determination to become a lawyer and render justice came from her firsthand knowledge of poor people in her

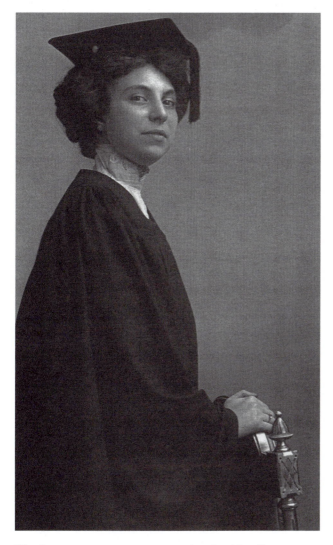

The first woman magistrate appointed in Brooklyn, Jeanette Brill spent her life as a social activist dedicated to improving the lot of children, adolescents, and women. [Jane Nusbaum]

neighborhood. She was married to attorney Abraham Brill in 1911. They practiced law together until his death in 1950 in their firm, Brill Bergenfield and Brill, at 50 Broadway. They had two children, Helen Claire Brill Gordimer and Herbert Baer Brill, both of whom became lawyers.

In 1923, Brill was the first woman appointed to serve as a deputy assistant on the state attorney general's staff, where she handled labor and compensation matters. She was appointed to the Magistrate's Court in Brooklyn in 1929 by Mayor James J. Walker to fill an unexpired term and was reappointed to a full ten-year term in 1931. In a 1933 address to a reunion of the HUNTER COLLEGE class of 1904, she said that more women were needed on the bench as they were particularly able to deal with cases involving women, children, and family affairs; however, at the completion of her term, she was not reappointed by Mayor Fiorello La Guardia. During her time on the bench, she was a strong supporter of the Adolescent Court in Brooklyn, established as a social experiment in 1935 for youths age sixteen to eighteen. She was the co-author with E. George Payne of *The Adolescent Court and Crime Prevention* (1938), a book about her experience with the Adolescent Court. While on the bench, Brill attended New York University School of Education at night and received a B.S. in psychology and sociology in 1938. After her retirement, she continued to practice law.

Brill was very active in Democratic politics, serving as president of the Madison Democratic Club in Brooklyn and as campaign manager for congresswoman Edna Kelly. Eleanor Roosevelt and Al Smith were her friends.

Her community activities related to Judaism, women and children, and social welfare. She was president of the Brooklyn Child Guidance Clinic and the Community Service League. During the Depression, the league canvassed local residents and employers to procure positions for women and men with families to support, and it opened a child guidance clinic in 1929, one of the first community clinics in the country. She was a member of the Federation of Jewish Women's Organizations, the NATIONAL COUNCIL OF JEWISH WOMEN, and the Brooklyn Business and Professional Women's Club, and was vice president of the Brooklyn Federation of Jewish Charities.

In the 1930s, she founded Camp Kinni Kinnic for girls in Poultney, Vermont, which she ran with her son for over thirty years. As a camp director, she is remembered as a strong, charismatic leader who was influential in shaping many campers' lives.

In 1960, when Judge Brill became the first woman to receive the certificate of the Brooklyn Bar Association "in commemoration of fifty years of the practice of her profession," she recalled that women lawyers got pretty rough in their long fight for equality. "The judges and lawyers were very unkind to us."

Judge Jeanette Goodman Brill died in Brooklyn on March 30, 1964.

BIBLIOGRAPHY

AJYB 66:573; Brill, Edith [daughter-in-law of Jeanette G. Brill]. Telephone conversation with author; Brooklyn Bar Association. Telephone conversation with author; Brooklyn Historical Association. Telephone conversation with author; Brooklyn Law School. Telephone conversation with author; Gordimer, Richard [grandson of Jeanette G. Brill]. Telephone conversation with author; *Journal American*, April 1, 1964, and January 31, 1956; *NYTimes*, October 14, 1934, sec. II, p. 1:6, and June 9, 1938, 19:1, and May 1, 1941, 25:6; Obituary. *New York Herald Tribune*, April 1, 1964, and *NYTimes*, March 31, 1964, 35:3; Roth, Barbara Gordimer [granddaughter of Jeanette G. Brill]. Telephone conversation with author; Roth, Warren [great-grandson of Jeanette G. Brill]. Telephone conversation with author; *UJE*; *WWIAJ* (1938).

JANE NUSBAUM

BRIN, FANNY FLIGELMAN
(1884–1961)

Although named as one of the ten most influential clubwomen in America in 1934, Fanny Fligelman Brin saw no paradox between her national stature and her husband's expectation that she be present when he came home for his noontime meal. In this melding of civic and domestic responsibilities, Brin is emblematic of her generation of American clubwomen. A riveting public speaker, masterful politician, skilled organizer, and administrator, Brin, who served two terms as president of the NATIONAL COUNCIL OF JEWISH WOMEN (NCJW), 1932 to 1938, is best remembered for her work on behalf of world peace during the interwar years.

She was born in 1884 in Berlad, Romania, and emigrated with her mother and stepsister three months later. Her father, John, had a yeshivah education; her mother, Tony Friedman, had some background in French. The family settled in Minneapolis, where another daughter and three sons were born. John eked out a living in a jewelry and watch repair business. Tony, the practical one, encouraged her daughters' educational aspirations, and both attended college.

Fanny was an award-winning debater, and after graduating Phi Beta Kappa from the University of Minnesota in 1906, taught in country and city schools. She married Arthur Brin, a prosperous glass manufacturer, in 1913. He was an active member of many Jewish fraternal and service organizations. The Brins had three children: Rachel (b. 1915), Howard (b. 1919), and Charles (b. 1923). They lived most of their married life in an upper-class neighborhood in Minneapolis. With the help of a cook and an upstairs maid, Fanny started her career of unpaid public service.

She was invited to join a variety of exclusive cultural clubs, apparently experiencing no anti-Semitism. Her interest in peace issues is evident in her work within and outside of the NCJW. In 1921, she directed world disarmament activities in Minneapolis. Three years later, she was both president of the Minneapolis Section of the NCJW and chair of its national subcommittee on peace. Her efforts on this subcommittee continued when she became national president (1932–1938), resulting in the organization spending more time on peace issues than social service.

Through NCJW peace work, she became involved with the National Committee on the Cause and Cure of War (NCCCW), founded in 1926 by Carrie Chapman Catt. Brin served on the executive board of the NCCCW for fifteen years. She effectively mobilized Minneapolis public opinion for the Kellogg-Briand Pact and, in 1931, for world disarmament. In 1944, she called together thirty-six Minneapolis women's groups to form the Women's UN Rally, a focal point of United Nations Week activities. She also helped found the World Affairs Council and Center at the University of Minnesota. The capstone of her peace career was being chosen alternate consultant on the United States delegation to the United Nations conference in San Francisco in 1945. A few years later Parkinson's disease disabled her, and she died on September 4, 1961.

Brin was a latecomer to Zionism, and she drew upon Judaism for humanistic rather than ritualistic themes. A daughter of her era, she felt that privileged women could educate and persuade society of the linkage between democracy and peace.

BIBLIOGRAPHY

AJYB 64:492; Brin, Fanny Fligelman. Papers. Minnesota Historical Society, St. Paul; Brin, Ruth. "She Heard Another Drummer: The Life of Fanny Brin and Its Implications for the Sociology of Religion." Master's thesis, University of Minnesota (1972); Obituary. *NYTimes*, September 7, 1961, 35:1; Stuhler, Barbara. "Fanny Brin: Woman of

Her six years as president of the NATIONAL COUNCIL OF JEWISH WOMEN *(1932–1938) and her efforts on behalf of world peace*
led Fanny Brin to be named one of the ten most influential clubwomen in America in 1934.
She is shown here in 1933 at HANNAH SOLOMON*'s seventy-fifth birthday party.*
From left to right are: Brin, Jane Addams, Solomon, and Mrs. Gerson Levi.
[National Council of Jewish Women]

Peace." In *Women of Minnesota: Selected Bibliographic Essays,* edited by Barbara Stuhler and Gretchen Kreuter (1977); *UJE; WWIAJ* (1926, 1938); *WWWIA* 7.

LINDA SCHLOFF

BRIN, RUTH F. (b. 1921)

Ruth F. Brin is one of the liturgical pioneers of the post–World War II era. In the 1950s, when most Jewish women still seemed content with their traditional subordinate role in public worship, Ruth Brin was already at work modernizing traditional Jewish prayers and texts, and offering new interpretive readings and original poetry reflecting her own religious experience. Her liturgical innovation bore fruit.

Today it is difficult to find a Reform, Conservative, or Reconstructionist prayer book or anthology that does not include one or more of her writings, and many individual synagogue services throughout the United States and Canada make use of her work. She is the first woman, and one of the few American-born writers, of whom this can be said.

In a writing career that has spanned more than fifty years, Ruth Brin's published works have included four books of poetry and prayers, five worship services, five children's books, dozens of scholarly and historical articles that have appeared in more than thirty periodicals, and librettos for Cantor Charles Davidson's "The Hush of Midnight" (1970) and "Kristallnacht" (1988). She founded *Identity,* a Jewish literary magazine, in 1966 and edited it for five years.

She taught Jewish studies at the University of Minnesota and Macalester College and continues to write book reviews for the *Minneapolis Star Tribune*. She has served on numerous boards of directors, including the Minneapolis Urban League, League of Women Voters, NATIONAL COUNCIL OF JEWISH WOMEN and HADASSAH, and she is a founder and board member of Mayim Rabim, a new Reconstructionist synagogue in Minneapolis. She chaired the Head Start program for children in her area, and continues her volunteer activities working with young children at a day care center.

Brin has described her own work as "a personal search for the ultimate reality, the wonder, the mystery, the meaning that most of us call God." She has been called "one of the few truly authentic Jewish poets" writing today, and her work has been described as "a spiritual feast" and "a resource for people seeking faith or engaged in helping others understand and make sense out of their traditions." Charles Silberman says Brin has been "responsible for creating an atmosphere conducive to liturgical innovation and experimentation." Reviewers have commented on Brin's propensity for mentioning her Minnesota locale, which reminds the reader that her poems and prayers are not detached and otherworldly, but rather are reflections of a wife, mother, community activist, poet, and scholar.

Born on May 5, 1921, in St. Paul, Minnesota, Ruth (Firestone) Brin was the third child and only daugher of Milton and Irma (Cain) Firestone. Her mother's family was from Germany and France (Alsace). Her father's family was of Hungarian-Jewish descent. Brin's two older brothers were an attorney and a doctor. Her father, an attorney, was a graduate of Northwestern University Law School, and her mother was a graduate of Vassar College. Both were Reform Jews and very active in the Jewish community. Her father served on the Ramsey County Welfare Board during the Depression years.

Ruth graduated from Vassar College Phi Beta Kappa in 1941. On August 6, 1941, she married Howard Brin, a 1941 graduate of Harvard. While he served in the U.S. Army, she worked for the War Production Board in Washington, D.C. from 1942 to 1944, and then returned to Minneapolis with him after the war. Howard managed the family business, Brin Glass Company, and became a leader in the Jewish community. He died on June 1, 1988.

Ruth Brin earned an M.A. in American studies from the University of Minnesota in 1972, and received the Kter Shem Tov [Crown of a Good Name] award, comparable to an honorary doctorate, from the Reconstructionist Rabbinical College in June 1985. The college library maintains a complete collection of her published work.

The Brins' four children are Judith Brin Ingber (b. November 5, 1945), author of *Victory Dances, A Biography of Fred Berk* and founder, choreographer, and dancer with the internationally known Voices of Sepharad; Aaron Brin (b. September 3, 1948), administrator at an organic farm cooperative in Wisconsin; David Brin (b. September 29, 1950), a cellist, composer, and magazine editor in San Francisco; and Rabbi Deborah Brin (b. October 8, 1953), a chaplain, teacher, and hospice supervisor in Albuquerque, New Mexico.

SELECTED WORKS BY RUTH F. BRIN

Butterflies Are Beautiful (1974); *David and Goliath* (1977); *Harvest: Collected Poems and Prayers* (1986); *The Hush of Midnight*, with Cantor Charles Davidson (1967); Amim Records, 1970; *Interpretations for the Weekly Torah Reading* (1965); *Kol Haneshamah Sabbath and Festival Prayer Book* (1994); *My Heart Is in the East* (dramatic script) (1970); *A Rag of Love* (1971); *The Shabbat Catalogue* (1978); *The Story of Esther* (1976); *A Time to Search: Poems and Prayers for Our Day* (1959); *Wildflowers* (1982); *Women in Social Reform* (1977).

BIBLIOGRAPHY

Greenberg, Sidney, and Jonathan Levine. *Likrat Shabat* (1981); Harlow, Jules, ed. *Bond of Life: A Book for Mourners* (1975); Plaut, Rabbi W. Gunther, Bernard J.H. Bamberger, and William W. Hallo, eds. *The Torah: A Modern Commentary* (1981); Riemer, Rabbi Jack. *Wrestling with the Angels: Jewish Insights on Death and Mourning* (1995); Silberman, Charles. Introduction to *Harvest: Collected Poems and Prayers*, by Ruth F. Brin (1986).

RHODA LEWIN

BROD, RUTH HAGY (1911–1980)

Ruth Hagy Brod was a versatile and peripatetic career woman who worked for nearly fifty years as a journalist, publicist, literary agent, television host, and government antipoverty official.

Known professionally as Ruth Geri Hagy, she was born on May 31, 1911, in East Harlem, New York City, to Abraham and Jeanette (Rapaport) Fleischman. She grew up in Chicago, where she developed as a musical prodigy, giving piano recitals at age six. She studied music at Crane Junior College in Chicago and received a bachelor's degree in music at the Chicago College of Music in 1929.

She then turned from music to journalism. At age twenty-five, she moved to Hollywood, where she was an editor for the Macfadden movie and radio magazines from 1936 to 1938.

From Hollywood, she moved to Philadelphia, where she wrote features for the *Philadelphia Ledger* from 1938 to 1941. Over the years, she worked for the *New York Graphic*, the *Chicago Daily American*, the *Chicago Daily Times*, the *Chicago Daily News*, and the *Philadelphia Bulletin*. She also worked as a radio reporter and documentary filmmaker.

During World War II, she served as publicity director for the United War Chest campaigns and was a member of the women's advisory board executive committee for the U.S. Savings Bond division of the U.S. Treasury from 1942 to 1946.

After the war, she became women's editor of the *Philadelphia Bulletin* in 1946. While there, she initiated the Bulletin Forum, which she developed in 1952 into the "College News Conference." The Sunday programs featured a panel of college students who questioned prominent figures in politics, labor, and government.

In 1961, she traveled to Latin America and served as an educational television adviser to the Colombian government while producing a Peace Corps documentary film. She also produced a television series on Asian women and was a correspondent in Southeast Asia for the now-defunct North American Newspaper Alliance. She was a Far East correspondent for NBC Radio Press International and others.

In 1962, she returned to New York. There, she formed Ruth Hagy Productions and News Service. In the mid-1960s, she was asked to develop JOIN (Job Orientation in Neighborhoods) and served as special assistant to Mayor Robert F. Wagner. In the late 1960s, she was the founder-director of the Mayor's Coordinating Council under Mayor John V. Lindsay.

As a book author, her choice of topics was offbeat. She coauthored *The Edgar Cayce Handbook of Health Through Drugless Therapy* and *Ena Twigg, Medium*.

As a literary agent, she took on two famous clients each of whom came to a violent end: Allard K. Lowenstein, a former United States congressman and civil rights activist who was slain in March 1980, and James Hoffa, the Teamsters union leader, whose memoirs she was negotiating to publish at the time of his disappearance (1975).

Ruth Hagy Brod was widowed twice. Her first husband was Anatol Frikin, whom she married in 1929, and with whom she had a daughter, Sybil Joan (Lefferts). She married Lewis Hagy in 1932. She married Ed Albert Thomas Brod in 1954. She died of lung cancer on May 9, 1980, at age sixty-eight, in Freeport, Bahamas.

Ruth Brod did not focus on specifically Jewish issues in her career, but as a woman and a Jew, she paved the way for a greater role for women in journalism and public service.

SELECTED WORKS BY RUTH HAGY BROD
The Edgar Cayce Handbook of Health Through Drugless Therapy, with Harold J. Reilly (1975); *Ena Twigg, Medium*, with Ena Twigg (1972).

BIBLIOGRAPHY
Contemporary Authors (1981); Obituary. *NYTimes*, May 11, 1980; *WWWIA 7*; *Who's Who of American Women* (1965, 1967).

LINDA HERSKOWITZ

BRODBECK, MAY (1917–1983)

May Brodbeck was among the foremost American-born philosophers of science. Regarding science as a search for truth and moral well-being, she devoted her life to exploring fundamental questions about individuals and society. Her anthology with Herbert Feigl, *Readings in the Philosophy of Science* (1953), was known throughout the world of philosophy. Her anthology *Readings in the Philosophy of the Social Sciences* (1968) became a benchmark in the field. A feminist, she was a prominent philosopher, teacher, and administrator who received many honors: she was a Fulbright scholar (1962–1963), president of the Western Division of the American Philosophical Association (1972–1973), and fellow at the Center for Advanced Study in the Behavioral Sciences (1981–1982).

Born in New Jersey on July 26, 1917, May was the first of two children. Her parents, Louis and Etta (Brager) Schachter, divorced when she was young. She grew up with the privations of the Great Depression, took a commercial course in high school, and worked to put herself through New York University at night, receiving a bachelor's degree in chemistry in 1941. She married Arthur Brodbeck about this time, but they divorced in 1949. She taught high school chemistry and later participated in the Manhattan Project for development of the atomic bomb during World War II. She attended graduate school at the University of Iowa. There, under Gustav Bergmann, she took her master's degree (1945) and her doctorate (1947) in philosophy. She then taught philosophy at the University of Minnesota, chairing the department of philosophy from 1967 to 1970. She was dean of the graduate school at the University of Minnesota from 1972 to 1974 and then returned to the University of Iowa as Garver Professor of Philosophy and vice president for academic affairs and dean of the faculties. At this time, outside of exclusively women's colleges, this was the highest position attained by a woman in the academic world. Among her achievements at the University of Iowa were creating the Council on the Status of Women and founding one of the first women's studies programs in America. She left administration in 1981 and retired in 1983. The University of Iowa has established a chair in liberal arts in her name.

Brodbeck's early writings concentrate on questions of scientific method and the logic of scientific explanation. She defended a conception of science as a rigorous, objective enterprise whose scope includes the human as well as the natural sciences. Her later writings examine the complex relations between mind and body, developing an idea of parallelism that rejects any simple reduction of the mental to the physical as well as any simple division of the two into separate domains. Her discussions of human nature are free of ideology and focus instead on consciousness and complex biological structure to differentiate human beings from computerlike machines. As she put it, " [A] robot can do everything a man can do, but it cannot be everything a man can be." Her work anticipates contemporary discussions over what it means to be a physical thing that is also alive and free.

May Brodbeck died in California on August 1, 1983.

SELECTED WORKS BY
MAY BRODBECK

"Logic and Scientific Method in Research on Teaching." In *Handbook of Research on Teaching,* edited by N.L. Gage (1963); "Mind: From Within and from Without." *Proceedings and Addresses of the American Philosophical Association* 45 (1972): 42–55; *Philosophy in America: 1900–1950* (1952. Reprint 1972); *Readings in the Philosophy of Science,* edited with H. Feigl (1953); *Readings in the Philosophy of the Social Sciences,* editor (1968).

BIBLIOGRAPHY

Addis, L. "Memorial Minutes: May Brodbeck 1917–1983." *Proceedings and Addresses of the American Philosophical Association* 57 (1983): 503–504; *Directory of American Scholars* (1974, 1978, 1982); *The Philosopher's Index; Who's Who in America* (1972–1973 to 1982–1983); *Who's Who of American Women* (1958–1983).

ARTHUR FINE

BRONER, ESTHER M. (b. 1930)

Novelist, playwright, ritualist, and feminist writer, Esther M. Broner was born on July 8, 1930, in Detroit, Michigan, the daughter of Paul Masserman, a journalist and Jewish historian, and Beatrice (Weckstein) Masserman, once an actress in Yiddish theater in Poland. Educated at Wayne State University, where she received her B.A. and M.A, and later served as a professor of English and writer-in-residence, she completed her Ph.D. at Union Graduate School in 1979.

Before she was twenty years old, she married artist Robert Broner. The couple had four children, two of whom were twins. Before any of the children turned five years old, Esther Broner had written autobiographically about the passions of everyday life and about her Jewish heritage.

Beginning with her 1968 experimental novel *Journal/Nocturnal,* Broner articulates forceful and original views of women's experience. With the publication of *Her Mothers* in 1975, Broner emerged as a leading feminist writer whose characters were bitter, fearless, and uproariously funny. "It's a gentle book and yet a savage one," one reviewer wrote, about the birth, nurturance, and rebirth of all women. Her novel *A Weave of Women* (1978) combined Jewish and feminist themes to achieve a mystical, surreal, and hilarious vision of women who invent a new society. This pair established Broner as a writer of enduring masterpieces that expressed but were not contained by the feminist movement.

Marking her presence in the academic world, she edited with Cathy Davidson a collection of scholarly articles, *The Lost Tradition: Mothers and Daughters in Literature* (1981). Broner and Davidson began their collaboration in 1975 at the Midwest Modern Language Association meeting when members of the women's caucus voted to hold a special workshop on mothers and daughters in literature at their next convention.

In 1982, Esther and Robert Broner moved to New York City. There she joined and helped shape a thriving community of Jewish feminists, becoming a ritualist who invented new rites of passage to mark the new era. In the spring of 1976 Broner published "Women's Haggadah" in *Ms.* magazine. Published as a book in 1994, this more direct engagement with Jewish tradition carried her writing into a more explicitly autobiographical direction. Her memoir *The Telling: The Story of a Group of Jewish Women Who Journey to Spirituality Through Community and Ceremony* (1993) gives a historical overview of her previous ten years and provides an instructional guide to Jewish feminism.

In two books that described her reaction to first her father's and then her mother's deaths, Broner continued this combination of compelling autobiography and acute feminist critique of Jewish ritual. *Mornings and Mourning: A Kaddish Journal* (1994) narrates her day-to-day struggle to join a local minyan in the year following her father's death. *Ghost Stories* (1995) tenderly relates and gives meaning to her mother's death. Both works draw on Broner's capacity for self-transcendence through wildly improbable humor and deeply committed spirituality.

Broner's work as a dramatist began early in her career with *Colonel Higginson* (1968) and *The Body Parts of Margaret Fuller* (1976), which draws on her interest in American literary history. In 1982 she adapted *A Weave of Women* to the stage and she later completed *Letters to My Television Past* (1985), *The Olympics* (1986), and *Half-a-Man* (1989), which were staged in New York City, Los Angeles, and Detroit. Her short stories have appeared in dozens of periodicals.

Novelist and playwright Esther Broner is perhaps best known in the Jewish world as the author of The Women's Haggadah.

In addition to Wayne State University, she has taught at the University of California, Los Angeles; the University of Haifa, Israel; Hebrew University, Jerusalem; Oberlin College; and Sarah Lawrence College. She and her husband live in New York City.

SELECTED WORKS BY ESTHER M. BRONER

The Body Parts of Margaret Fuller (1976); *Colonel Higginson* (1968); *Ghost Stories* (1995); *Half-a-Man* (1989); *Her Mothers* (1975); *Journal/Nocturnal* (1968); *Letters to My Television Past* (1985); *The Lost Tradition: Mothers and Daughters in Literature*, edited with Cathy N. Davidson (1981); *Mornings and Mournings: A Kaddish Journal* (1994); *The Olympics* (1986); *The Telling: The Story of a Group of Jewish Women Who Journey to Spirituality Through Community and Ceremony* (1993); *A Weave of Women* (1978); "Women's Haggadah." *Ms.* (Spring 1976); *The Women's Haggadah* (1994).

BIBLIOGRAPHY

Davidson, Cathy N. *Guide to American Women Writers.* Vol. 1; *Jewish Book Annual* (1981); Witenko, Barbara. "Feminist Ritual as a Process of Social Transformation." Ph.D. diss., New York University, 1992.

KATHRYN KISH SKLAR

BROOK, CLAIRE (b. 1925)

Claire Brook is a writer, editor, and composer whose career is most distinguished by her work in publishing. She was managing editor of RILM Abstracts of Music Literature from 1968 to 1969. She then became associate music editor at W.W. Norton in 1969 followed by promotion to music editor in 1973. Ultimately, she became vice president at Norton in 1979, a post she held until her retirement in 1992.

A native of New York, Brook received her education at the City University of New York, earning her bachelor's degree in 1945, and at Columbia University, from which she received her master's degree in 1947. Following her university education, she studied with Nadia Boulanger in Paris in 1947–1948. In the 1950s, in part because of the difficulties faced by women composers, she gave up her career in composition in favor of publishing. More recently, however, she has returned to composition and published "Four Songs from 'Six Significant Landscapes'" in 1995 as part of the series *Art Songs by American Women Composers*.

Brook has been married to musicologist Barry S. Brook since 1958. She has two children with her first husband, Seymour Mann. Though Brook was not raised in an observant Jewish home, she describes her upbringing as culturally and politically Jewish, and she raised her own children to be aware of their Jewish heritage.

In addition to the "Four Songs," Brook's publications include a series of musical guides to European countries (coauthored with Elaine Brody) entitled *Music Guide to Austria and Germany, Music Guide to Great Britain, Music Guide to Belgium, Luxembourg, Holland and Switzerland,* and *Music Guide to Italy.* She is also coeditor (with E. Clinkscale) of *A Musical Offering: Essays in Honor of Martin Bernstein.*

In 1982, Brook received the Distinguished Alumni Award from the Aaron Copland School of Music at Queens College and in 1987, the ASCAP/Vincent Persichetti Award for Service to Music. She is a member of the American Music Center, the College Music Society, the American Institute of Verdi Studies, the American Musicological Society, and the Music Library Association.

Brook's contributions have been most notable in publishing. She attained the position of vice president at one of the most prestigious publishing firms in the United States. In addition, her appointment as the sole music editor at Norton in 1973 was a significant accomplishment for a woman at that time. Brook has championed the continued publication of music books by commercial publishing houses because of their significant contribution to the field and despite their marginal commercial potential. She continued through her career to strike a necessary balance between specialized and commercial music books as well as recognizing the potential of changing technologies for publishing, such as the inclusion of recordings with music textbooks. Thus, in her publishing career, she has made a significant mark in the field of music.

SELECTED WORKS BY CLAIRE BROOK

"The Book Publisher and Recordings." In *The Phonograph and Our Musical Life,* edited by H. Wiley Hitchcock (1980); "Four Songs from 'Six Significant Landscapes.'" In *Art Songs by American Women Composers* (1995); *Music Guide to Austria and Germany,* with Elaine Brody (1975); *Music Guide to Belgum, Luxembourg, Holland and Switzerland,* with Elaine Brody (1976); *Music Guide to Great Britain,* with Elaine Brody (1975); *Music Guide to Italy,* with Elaine Brody (1977); "Music Publishing Today—A Symposium." *Notes* 32, no. 2 (December 1975): 243–248; *A Musical Offering: Essays in Honor of Martin Bernstein,* with E. Clinkscale (1977).

BIBLIOGRAPHY

Who's Who in American Music: Classical. 2d ed. (1985).

LAURIE BLUNSOM

BROTHERS, JOYCE (b. 1929)

During a public career spanning more than forty years, Dr. Joyce Brothers made the unlikely journey from housewife to celebrity quiz show contestant to the nation's best-known media psychologist. On her first venture into television in 1955 as a contestant on *The $64,000 Question,* the most popular quiz show of its day, Brothers won the viewing public's notice for her knowledge of boxing, an expertise that seemed unusual for the petite woman who also held a doctorate in psychology. Her instant celebrity led to a television show of her own, as well as radio programs and syndicated newspaper and magazine columns.

Joyce Diane (Bauer) Brothers was born in New York City on October 29, 1929, into the middle-class household of Morris K. and Estelle (Rappaport) Bauer, both attorneys. Joyce and her younger sister Elaine, who also practiced law and is now a judge, grew up in Far Rockaway, Queens. She credited her

The quiz show The $64,000 Question *was the unlikely launching pad for the career of psychologist Dr. Joyce Brothers. Her enduring popularity, however, has been no fluke, as her straightforward style has touched a chord with millions of people. [Library of Congress]*

parents with instilling in their daughters a desire for achievement and respect for hard work. Their Jewish faith also imparted a sense of ethics and a belief in God. At twelve years of age, she worked in a camp for disturbed children, gaining great satisfaction from helping others. After graduating from Far Rockaway High School in 1943, she entered Cornell University, majoring in psychology. She took her B.S. degree with honors in 1947, and then enrolled at Columbia University, where she did graduate work in behavior and personality. While attending Columbia, she was an assistant in psychology as well as a teaching fellow and instructor at HUNTER COLLEGE.

Shortly after receiving her M.A. degree on July 4, 1949, she married Milton Brothers, a medical student. She continued with research and teaching, earning a Ph.D. in 1953 with a doctoral dissertation on anxiety avoidance and escape behavior measured by the action potential in muscle. By this time, her husband had completed medical school and she was pregnant. When their only child, Lisa, was born, Brothers chose to remain at home to raise her daughter according to her own beliefs about child rearing. However, this decision reduced the couple's income to the fifty dollars a month her husband received for his medical residency.

In late 1955, to relieve the financial strain, Brothers decided to try out for the popular television show *The $64,000 Question*, which frequently selected contestants with novel areas of specialization. The attractive psychologist, who had become an expert on boxing to please her husband, as she explained it, was an instant favorite. With the determination that has characterized her entire career, Brothers studied volumes of a boxing encyclopedia to enhance her already considerable knowledge. After seven weeks on the show, she became the second person and only woman to win the $64,000 top prize. Two years later, Brothers appeared on a successor program, *The $64,000 Challenge*, which matched the contestant against experts in the field. Again, Brothers walked off with the maximum prize. "I had enough to promise myself I'd never do things I didn't want to do again," she recalled. When hearings were held in 1959 about corruption on *The $64,000 Question*, Brothers's honesty was documented. She later revealed that the producers had wanted her off the show, but she had frustrated their intentions by answering the difficult questions they had expected would defeat her.

After her victory on *The $64,000 Question*, Brothers remained in the public eye, first as cohost on *Sports Showcase*, and as a popular guest on many television talk shows. Then, in 1958, NBC offered Brothers her own afternoon talk show, initially called *The Dr. Joyce*

Brothers Show, devoted to counseling viewers on child rearing, love, marriage, and sex. It was an instant success; when Brothers began receiving more than a thousand letters a week, the show was syndicated nationally. In less than a year, she added a late-night show on which she was one of the first to discuss such previously taboo subjects as sexual satisfaction, frigidity, menopause, and impotence. Within a short time, she had a live call-in program on WMCA and was appearing on programs of other networks. A syndicated column ran in 350 newspapers, and a monthly column in *Good Housekeeping*, initiated in 1963, is still a feature of the magazine. Several of her books, including *What Every Woman Should Know About Men* (1982), sold well.

Currently, Brothers has a daily program on NBC Radio/Westwood Radio Network and is a contributing editor or staff writer on several journals. She is a long-standing member of the Federation of Jewish Philanthropies, and in 1964 was named a Woman of Achievement by the Federation of Jewish Women's Organizations. In 1968, she received a merit award from Bar-Ilan University.

Brothers clearly filled a need. Conforming in many ways to the dominant image of women in the 1950s and early 1960s, Brothers described herself as a mother, wife, and psychologist last. Yet her apparent observance of the status quo permitted her to delve into some of the issues that many Americans were concerned about without seeming to threaten the established order. While some psychologists criticized her for giving advice without having adequate knowledge of the patients, others believed she helped people by showing them that their problems were shared by others. Brothers herself claimed that she only linked her viewers with the information available in psychological literature.

Brothers's world was shaken in 1989 by the death from cancer of her husband of thirty-nine years. "I had never really experienced grief before," she explained, "and although the pain was enormous, I became much more sensitive to others." After her initial reaction, she recovered by returning to the habits of a lifetime and using what she had learned to help other women surmount their own grief. Buoyed by the support of her daughter (an ophthalmologist), son-in-law, and four grandchildren, Brothers wrote of her gradual return from suicidal thoughts to a satisfying, productive life. The book she wrote describing this journey, *Widow* (1990), would be the most personal and the most popular of her ten books. It was excerpted in many journals, and Brothers again became a sought-after speaker on television and radio talk shows. The thousands of letters she received from grateful women, she explained, "made my own pain not only bearable but worthwhile."

As the most durable of popular psychologists, Joyce Brothers has kept her finger on the pulse of what many Americans—particularly women—are concerned about. From bringing up children to putting the "romance" back into marriage to coping with the death of a loved spouse, she has dealt with familiar, universal issues, couching her advice in jargon-free, commonsense language. She helped to make such previously unacceptable topics as sexuality and menopause subject to a more open discourse; equally important, she made the seeking of help from a psychological "expert" respectable.

SELECTED WORKS BY JOYCE BROTHERS

What Every Woman Should Know About Men (1982); *Widow* (1990).

BIBLIOGRAPHY

Contemporary Authors 15 (1984): 120–121; *Current Biography* (1971): 62–68; Rodgers, J.E. "Psychologists at Home: How They Live." *Psychology Today* 26 (July-August 1993): 48–53; *Who's Who in America* (1991).

SYDNEY STAHL WEINBERG

BRUCH, HILDE (1904–1984)

Hilde Bruch is recognized as one of the world's leading authorities on emotional problems relating to eating, thanks to her research on obesity in children and her innovative approach to the treatment of anorexia nervosa.

Born on March 11, 1904, in the small German town of Dülken on the Lower Rhine, Hilde Bruch was the third of seven children. Her father, Hirsch Bruch, a successful cattle dealer, and her mother, Adele (Rath) Bruch, belonged to the local Jewish community. Like her two sisters and four brothers, Hilde attended a one-room Jewish elementary school before commuting to a girls' high school in a nearby town in order to prepare for university. Although she wanted to become a mathematician, the uncle who financed her education after her father's death convinced her that medicine was a more practical choice for a Jewish woman. She studied in Würzburg, Freiburg, Cologne, and Munich, and received her doctorate in medicine from the University of Freiburg in 1929.

After obtaining her medical license, Bruch accepted an assistantship at the University of Kiel, and in 1930, she transferred to the University of Leipzig, where she continued her research and training until 1932. Due to anti-Semitism, she gave up her aspirations for an academic career in Germany and established a private pediatric practice near Düsseldorf. Soon after the April 1, 1933, anti-Jewish boycott, she decided to immigrate to England.

Bruch worked in London for a year at the East End Maternity Hospital and the Child Guidance Clinic. She left for the United States in September 1934, and quickly found a job at Babies Hospital in New York, obtaining her pediatric license in 1935 and her American citizenship five years later. On a fellowship from the Josiah Macy, Jr., Foundation, she began her groundbreaking research on obesity in children in 1937. Between 1941 and 1943, she studied psychiatry at Johns Hopkins University in Baltimore and underwent psychoanalytic training with FRIEDA FROMM-REICHMANN and Harry Stack Sullivan. Upon returning to New York, she established a private practice in psychoanalysis and became affiliated with the College of Physicians and Surgeons at Columbia University, where she was appointed clinical associate professor in 1954 and professor in 1959. In 1964, she accepted a position as professor of psychiatry at Baylor College of Medicine in Houston, Texas, where she remained even after her retirement in 1978. Before leaving New York, she had purchased a Rolls-Royce because she refused to "kowtow to Texas Cadillacs."

Hilde Bruch was an outspoken individualist who relished her independence and rebelled against any form of authoritarianism. She helped rescue her mother and several of her siblings from Nazi Germany, but many members of her family perished during the Holocaust. In 1946, she adopted her orphaned nephew, Herbert Bruch, who had survived the war in England. Although she returned for several visits, she felt extremely uncomfortable in postwar Germany.

Bruch published numerous scholarly and popular studies on obesity, schizophrenia, and psychotherapy training, but over the years her research focused increasingly on the underlying causes of anorexia nervosa. Her collected work *Eating Disorders* is considered a definitive work on this subject.

Although afflicted with Parkinson's disease, she continued to see patients and play an active role as an emeritus faculty member until her eightieth birthday. She was the recipient of numerous academic honors and awards, including the President's Citation for Meritorious Contributions to the Clinical Services, Baylor College of Medicine (1978); the William A. Schonfeld Award for Contribution to Psychiatry, American Society for Adolescent Psychiatry (1978); the Golden Doctoral Diploma, Medical Faculty of

Albert-Ludwig University of Freiburg (1978); the Mount Airy Gold Medal Award for Distinction and Excellence in Psychiatry (1979); the Nolan D.C. Lewis Award for Contributions to Psychiatry (1980); the American Psychiatric Association Founders Award (1981), the Agnes Purcel McGavin Award, American Psychiatric Association (1981); the Joseph B. Goldberger Award in Clinical Nutrition, American Medical Association (1981). She died in Houston on December 15, 1984.

SELECTED WORKS BY HILDE BRUCH

Don't Be Afraid of Your Child (1952); *Eating Disorders: Obesity, Anorexia Nervosa and the Person Within* (1973); *The Golden Cage: The Enigma of Anorexia Nervosa* (1978); *The Importance of Overweight* (1957); *Learning Psychotherapy. Rationale and Ground Rules* (1974).

BIBLIOGRAPHY

Brumberg, Joan. *Fasting Girls* (1988); Dick, Jutta, and Marina Sassenberg, eds. *Jüdische Frauen im 19. und 20. Jahrhundert: Lexikon zu Leben und Werk* (1993): 82–84; Dickstein, Leah J., and Carol C. Nadelson. *Women Physicians in Leadership Roles* (1986): 123–130; Heitkamp, Reinhard. "Hilde Bruch (1904–1984), Leben und Werk." Medical dissertation, University of Köln (1987); *International Biographical Dictionary of Central European Emigres*, Vol. 2, part 1 (1980): 158; Peters, Uwe Henrik. *Psychiatrie im Exil* (1992): 331–341; "Psychiatric Lecture Series Honors Dr. Hilde Bruch." *Inside Baylor Medicine* (April 1979); Stevens, Gwendolyn, and Sheldon Gardner. *The Women of Psychology*, Vol. 2 (1982): 164–166; *WWWIA* 8.

HARRIET PASS FREIDENREICH

BRUNSWICK, RUTH MACK
(1897–1946)

Psychoanalyst Ruth Mack Brunswick participated in the development of Freudian theory in the 1920s and 1930s as a sounding board for Sigmund Freud's ideas. As colleague, disciple, patient, interpreter, and liaison to the American psychoanalytic group, her tact in proposing contributions to Freud's thinking won her ideas a rare acknowledgment. First to use the term "preoedipal" in print, she was one of the women who called to Freud's attention the importance of the earliest relationship with the mother, the prelude to the father-centered oedipal events that are central to Freud's theory of the neuroses. She was a pioneer in the attempt to understand the experience of psychotic

Pioneer psychoanalyst Ruth Mack Brunswick was chosen by Sigmund Freud to take over treatment of the "Wolf-Man," the patient who was the subject of one of Freud's most important and publicized cases. [Matilde B. Stewart]

patients and character-disordered patients within a psychoanalytic framework.

Freud chose Brunswick to treat the "Wolf-Man"—the patient who was the subject of Freud's most elaborated and important published case—when new symptoms unstabilized the patient years after his work with Freud.

Ruth Mack was born in Chicago on February 17, 1897, the only child of Julian William and Jessie (Fox) Mack. Her father was born in San Francisco but, like her mother, was raised in Cincinnati; both were descendants of old German Jewish immigrant families. Julian Mack was a Zionist, a prominent Reform Jew, and a philanthropist. He was a distinguished liberal jurist, one of the original juvenile court justices in Cook County, Illinois.

She attended Radcliffe College, graduating in 1918. Denied admission to Harvard Medical School because she was a woman, she received her medical education at Tufts University, graduating cum laude in 1922. Soon after, she was accepted for psychoanalysis in Vienna by Sigmund Freud. Thus began a long professional association and friendship.

Ruth Mack was married while a junior at Radcliffe, in 1917, to Hermann Ludwig Blumgart, who became a leading cardiologist and later the director of Boston's Beth Israel Hospital. They divorced in 1924. In Vienna in 1928, she married Mark Brunswick, a composer and later a professor of music at the City University of New York. Their daughter, Mathilde Juliana Brunswick (Stewart), is a clinical social worker. Ruth and Mark Brunswick divorced in 1945.

Ruth Brunswick was an active member of the Vienna Psychoanalytic Society and an instructor in its Psychoanalytic Institute. She later taught at the New York Psychoanalytic Institute. She served on the editorial board of the *International Journal of Psychoanalysis*.

After the Austrian Anschluss in 1938 she devoted considerable energy to providing affidavits that enabled Jewish psychoanalysts to procure American visas. Her mastery of this process provided a model to others to rescue their Jewish colleagues.

Upon returning to the United States, she practiced psychoanalysis in Manhattan. But her time after leaving Vienna was marked by significant personal and health problems. Her physical suffering led to uncontrolled use of opiates. She died an untimely death on January 24, 1946, at age forty-eight, after a fall.

SELECTED WORKS BY
RUTH MACK BRUNSWICK

"The Analysis of a Case of Paranoia." *Journal of Nervous and Mental Disease* 70 (1929); "The Preoedipal Phase of Libido Development." *Psychoanalytic Quarterly* 9 (1940); "A Supplement to Freud's History of an Infantile Neurosis." *International Journal of Psychoanalysis* 9 (1928).

A small collection of Brunswick's notes and papers are in the Freud archives at the National Archives, Washington, D.C. Film footage taken by Mark Brunswick of the Freuds, Brunswicks, and others of the Freud circle is preserved in the Freud Museum in London.

BIBLIOGRAPHY

Appignanesi, Lisa, and John Forrester. "The Friendship of Women." In *Freud's Women* (1992); *DAB* 4; Freud, Sigmund. *Female Sexuality* (1961), and *New Introductory Lectures* (1961); Gardiner, Muriel. *Code Name "Mary"* (1983), and *The Wolf-Man by the Wolf-Man*, editor (1971); *NAW*; Nunberg, Herman. "In Memoriam, Ruth Mack Brunswick." *Psychoanalytic Quarterly* 15 (1946); Roazen, Paul. "The Women." In *Freud and His Followers* (1975); "Ruth Brunswick: Freud Associate." *NYTimes*, January 26, 1946, 13:3.

LYLE L. WARNER

BRYANT, LANE *see*
MALSIN, LANE BRYANT

BULLOWA, EMILIE M. (c. 1869–1942)

"Our democracy doesn't work if the people who can't afford to give compensation for legal aid can't get justice." With this declaration, lawyer Emilie M. Bullowa expressed her liberal viewpoint and charitable approach to people from all walks of life. Indeed, Bullowa put words into action, utilizing her professional and financial success for various humanitarian purposes.

She was born around 1869 to Morris and Mary (Grunhut) Bullowa of New York City. Her father, a merchant, had come to the United States from Lubenz, Czechoslovakia, around 1850. Emilie studied in New York public schools, including the Training School; she was privately taught languages, music, and art. She then attended the Normal College (later HUNTER COLLEGE). Both of Bullowa's parents died before she turned twenty, and, as the eldest of eleven children—some of whom were ill and required nursing—she took charge of her brothers and sisters. In doing so, she postponed her own legal career, not entering law school until each child was established in school. This sacrifice for her family foreshadowed a lifetime of selfless devotion to those in need.

Finally, in 1900, Bullowa graduated from the Law College of New York University and was admitted to the bar. In that same year, she and her brother

Ferdinand opened their own law office in New York called Bullowa and Bullowa, specializing in admiralty law. The firm dealt with the maritime legal affairs of foreign shipping lines. After Ferdinand died in 1919, Emilie continued practicing until her retirement in 1941.

Bullowa earned a reputation for being a great trial lawyer. Lawyers and others admired her ability to convince judges and juries of her cases. In 1919, she established a new point in the law of libel. Her colleagues, as well as many judges, respected her attitude as a woman in a field then dominated by men: She took pride in being a lawyer, rather than in being a *female* lawyer.

From 1916 until 1922, Bullowa was president of the Women Lawyers Association of New York City. When she helped to take the organization to a national level in 1922, she was elected president of the now-named National Association of Women Lawyers. She became a member of the platform committee of the Women's Democratic Union in 1924, and served as chairman of various committees of the American Bar Association. She was also a member of the committee on citizenship of the New York County Lawyers Association, a position which led to her being selected as a judge in an essay contest on the United States Constitution sponsored by the *New York Times*. In addition, Bullowa was affiliated with the New York Medical College and Hospital for Women, first as a member of its board of directors and then, from 1921 until her death in 1942, as its president.

More than just a remarkably skillful lawyer, Bullowa was an outstanding citizen, using her talents and money to help those in need. She remarked, "It is just as important to help people in their rights as in their health and their housing." She never turned away clients who were unable to pay. In her later years, she mainly focused on contract and surrogate cases, in order to help those who could not afford legal aid. After World War I, she inherited a château in France, which she gave to the French War Relief; she also adopted several French war orphans. During World War II, she donated a mobile kitchen unit to the British War Relief Society in New York and once again adopted children, this time British.

In 1941, nearing retirement, Bullowa donated two thousand law volumes collected by her brother to the legal library of the Criminal Courts branch of the Legal Aid Society. When she retired in early 1942, she gave the British War Relief Society all of her office furniture. She also left $25,000 in her will toward the upkeep of the Legal Aid Society.

Bullowa was known as a modest, quiet person, who championed the American form of government.

An enthusiastic gardener in her spare time, she especially enjoyed cultivating roses and lilies. She was religiously affiliated with the Central Synagogue in New York City.

Emilie Bullowa died on October 25, 1942, at about age seventy-three. In an era when women usually engaged in philanthropic and social activism through their husbands, and when few women were educated in the professional fields, Emilie M. Bullowa stood out as an independent and successful lawyer who used her resources for the benefit of the underprivileged.

BIBLIOGRAPHY

AJYB 45: 382; *National Cyclopedia of American Biography* 31 (1944); Obituary. *NYTimes*, October 26, 1942, 15:3.

TAMAR KAPLAN

BUNZEL, RUTH LEAH (1898–1990)

Ruth Leah Bunzel began her career as anthropologist Franz Boas's secretary and became an accomplished anthropologist herself. She broke new ground in her research on the artist and the creative process among the Zuni, her pioneering work on the Mayas in Guatemala, and her comparative study of alcoholism in two villages in Guatemala and Mexico.

Ruth Leah (Bernheim) Bunzel, the youngest of four children, was born in New York in 1898, and lived on the Upper East Side of Manhattan with her parents, Jonas and Hattie Bernheim, of German and Czech heritage. Her father died when Ruth was ten years old, and she was raised by her mother, who had inherited money from her family's Cuban tobacco-importing business. Ruth's mother raised the children in a Jewish household that was largely acculturated to American ways. The family spoke English at home, but Ruth's mother encouraged Ruth to study German at Barnard College. Ruth, however, changed her major because of the political atmosphere surrounding World War I and received a B.A. in European history from Barnard in 1918.

Talking about the choices that bright young people confronted in the 1920s, Bunzel wrote that some went to Paris seeking freedom, some aligned with radical workers and sold the *Daily Worker* on street corners, and others turned to anthropology to "find some answers to the ambiguities and contradictions of our age and the general enigma of human life." She saw anthropology as a means to understand not only others but also ourselves.

Having taken a course with Boas in college, Bunzel succeeded ESTHER GOLDFRANK as his secretary and editorial assistant at Columbia University in 1922. In 1924, she accompanied anthropologist Ruth Benedict to western New Mexico and east-central Arizona to study the Zuni people, and followed Boas's suggestion to give up typing and begin her own research on a topic that interested him, the artist's relationship to work. Critical of ethnographers who often ignored women as subjects in their fieldwork, Bunzel felt that "society consisted of more than old men with long memories." She was drawn to the Zuni because women were the potters and had considerable societal power.

Bunzel began graduate study in anthropology at Columbia University. In 1929, she received her Ph.D. with the publication of a landmark book on the artistic process, *The Pueblo Potter.* Rather than focusing on the objects of art, Bunzel was the first anthropologist to analyze artists' feelings, their relationship to their work, and the process of creativity. To understand how artists work within the confines of traditional styles, Bunzel apprenticed herself to Zuni potters, and among them she became a respected, skilled potter.

Visiting the Zunis intermittently between 1924 and 1929, Bunzel was a sensitive fieldworker, respecting local factionalism and esoteric ceremonies. Bunzel's focus on the individual and the degree of aesthetic freedom an individual had in a given culture influenced her writing on Zuni kachina (ancestral spirit) cults and mythology, ceremonialism and religion, and poetry. A prolific scholar, she also contributed an understanding of Zuni cosmology and social organization by producing important work on Zuni values, language, culture, and personality. Deeply influenced by Boas and Ruth Benedict, Bunzel's work, in turn, provided much of the material for Benedict's synthesis of Zuni in *Patterns of Culture.* In addition to the Zuni, Bunzel wrote about the Hopi, Acoma, San Ildefonso, and San Felipe Pueblo Indians of the southwestern United States.

Bunzel was one of the first American anthropologists to work in Guatemala, and she published a monograph on the Chichicastenango community in highland Guatemala in 1952. Reflecting both her interest in culture and personality studies and the neo-Freudian influence of psychoanalyst Karen Horney, she also wrote a comparative study on alcoholism in Chamula in Chiapas, Mexico, and in Chichicastenango. Her research, supported by a Guggenheim Fellowship (1930–1932), looked at psychological factors that led to different patterns of drinking in two communities. She also focused on the role alcohol played in the Indians' subjugation and how haciendas profited by keeping Indians in debt. Her study on alcoholism was the first anthropological writing on this subject.

Bunzel went to Spain to perfect her Spanish and to gain background information for her southwestern Indian studies and was there when the Spanish Revolution broke out. During World War II, from 1942 to 1945, Bunzel worked for the Office of War Information in New York and London. From 1946 to 1951, Bunzel participated in the Research in Contemporary Cultures Project, directed by Ruth Benedict, which specialized in Chinese cultures. She had participated in seminars led by Abraham Kardiner (1936 and 1937) held at the New York Psychoanalytic Institute and Columbia University, which influenced her postwar national character study.

Bunzel taught sporadically at Columbia University throughout the 1930s, but she became an adjunct professor in 1954 until her retirement in 1972. She then spent two years as a visiting professor at Bennington College. Bunzel earned a modest living teaching and felt she had never obtained full-time work because she was a woman. Others have attributed her marginal position, in part, to hostility between Boas and Ralph Linton, who became chair of the anthropology department at Columbia.

Throughout the 1950s and 1960s, she worked with other colleagues against the proliferation of nuclear weapons. Bunzel was a private person with several lifelong relationships, mostly with female colleagues. She lived much of her life on Perry Street in Greenwich Village, never leaving New York and Columbia University for long periods, except to do field research. She died in 1990 of cardiac arrest. Her detailed fieldwork and writing are known for their great sensitivity and quality and remain an enduring legacy of her anthropological accomplishment.

SELECTED WORKS BY RUTH LEAH BUNZEL

"Art." In *General Anthropology,* edited by Franz Boas (1938): 535–588; "Chamula and Chichicastenango: A Reexamination." In *Cross Cultural Approaches to the Study of Alcohol,* edited by Michael W. Everett, Jack O. Waddell, and Dwight B. Heath (1976); *Chichicastenango, a Guatemalan Village* (1952); "The Economic Organization of Primitive Peoples." In *General Anthropology,* edited by Franz Boas (1938): 327–408; "Further Notes on San Felipe." *Journal of American Folklore* 41 (1928) 592; *The Golden Age of American Anthropology,* with Margaret Mead (1960); "Introduction to Zuni Ceremonialism." *Bureau of American Ethnology BAE Annual Report* 47: (1932) 467–554; "The Nature of Katcinas." *BAE Annual Report* 47 (1932): 837–1006. Reprinted in *Reader in Comparative Religion,* edited by A.W. Lessa and

Evon Vogt (1958): 401–404; "Notes on the Katcina Cult in San Felipe." *Journal of American Folklore* 41 (1928): 290–292; *The Pueblo Potter: A Study of Creative Imagination in Primitive Art* (1929); "Psychology of the Pueblo Potter." In *Primitive Heritage,* edited by Margaret Mead and Nicolas Calas (1953): 266–275; "The Role of Alcoholism in Two Central American Cultures." *Psychiatry* 3 (1940): 361–387; "The Self-effacing Zuni of New Mexico." In *The Americas on the Eve of Discovery,* edited by Harold Driver (1964): 80–92; "Zuni." In *Handbook of American Indian Languages.* Part 3, edited by Franz Boas (1933): 385–515; *Zuni Texts* (1933); *Zuni Ceremonialism: Three Studies.* Edited by Nancy J. Parezo (1992); "Zuni Origin Myths." *BAE Annual Report* 47 (1932): 545–609; "Zuni Ritual Poetry." *BAE Annual Report* 47 (1932): 611–835. Reprinted as *Zuni Ceremonialism: Three Studies* (1992).

BIBLIOGRAPHY

Babcock, Barbara A., and Nancy J. Parezo. "Ruth Bunzel, 1898–." *Daughters of the Desert: Women Anthropologists and the Native American Southwest, 1880–1980. An Illustrated Catalogue* (1988): 38–43; Bunzel, Ruth Leah. File. Wenner-Gren Foundation, New York City; Caffrey, Margaret M. *Ruth Benedict: Stranger in this Land* (1989); *EJ*; Fawcett, David M., and Teri McLuhan. "Ruth Leah Bunzel." In *Women Anthropologists: A Biographical Dictionary,* edited by Ute Gacs, et al. (1988): 29–36; Hardin, Margaret A. "Zuni Potters and The Pueblo Potter: The Contributions of Ruth Bunzel." In *Hidden Scholars: Women Anthropologists and the Native American Southwest,* edited by Nancy J. Parezo (1993): 259–270; Howard, Jane. *Margaret Mead: A Life* (1984); Murphy, Robert F. "Ruth Leah Bunzel." *Anthropology Newsletter* 31, no. 3 (March 1970): 5; Parezo, Nancy J. Introduction to *Zuni Ceremonialism: Three Studies,* by Ruth L. Bunzel (1992): vii–xxxix; Woodbury, Nathalie F.S. "Bunzel, Ruth Leah." In *International Dictionary of Anthropologists,* edited by Christopher Winters (1991).

CYNTHIA SALTZMAN

BUTTENWIESER, HELEN LEHMAN (1905–1989)

A distinguished attorney who specialized in adoption and foster care issues and represented child welfare agencies and the children under their care, Helen Lehman Buttenwieser was born on October 8, 1905, and grew up in a Jewish family prominent in New York banking and philanthropic circles. Her mother was Adele Lewisohn, a suffragist and daughter of Adolph Lewisohn, who had made a fortune in copper. Her father was banker Arthur Lehman, whose brothers were Herbert H. Lehman, governor of New York, and Irving Lehman, a judge on the Court of Appeals. Her husband, Benjamin J. Buttenwieser, was a member of the banking firm of Kuhn, Loeb & Co. and a United States assistant high commissioner in Germany after World War II. They had four children.

A graduate of Horace Mann School for Girls and Connecticut College (1926), she studied for a year at the New York School of Social Work and then entered child guidance work as a volunteer. While raising her family she served as board member (1929–1945) and then president of Madison House Settlement on New York's Lower East Side, in posts to which Mayor James J. Walker appointed her on the Commission on Social Welfare (1929–1932), and as trustee (1930) of the Widowed Mothers Pension Fund and of the Citizens Committee for Children. As a Jewish Big Sister, she testified in many court cases concerning children and women's rights. This experience led her to think about becoming a judge in Children's or Domestic Relations Court (now Family Court). While this plan remained unfulfilled, she took the first step, enrolling in New York University Law School in 1933.

Buttenwieser graduated in 1936, one of only twelve women in her class. A distinguished legal career, in which she accumulated many firsts for women, followed. She was the first woman hired at Cravath, Swaine & Moore, although the firm insisted that she remain in an office by herself for her first year and expected her to leave when she became pregnant. As a staff member of the Legal Aid Society, she served two months in the society's Criminal Court Office in Manhattan, work then deemed "inappropriate for women." Later, as a member of her own firm of Lindau, Robbins, Buttenwieser & Backer, she was active in the Association of the Bar of the City of New York, a member of the Democratic State Committee (15th Assembly District), the first woman chair of a standing committee of the Bar Association of the City of New York, and the first woman to serve on the board of Title Guarantee & Trust Co. (appointed in 1949).

In 1946, Buttenwieser pioneered in the movement to correct abuses in adoptions. Reports of a black market in babies and of babies remaining in foster care so long that they became too old for placement led three groups—the Welfare Council of New York City, the United Hospital Fund, and the New York Academy of Medicine—to form a New York City Committee on Adoptions and appoint Buttenwieser its chair. Its report, issued in 1948, recommended major reforms in the adoption and foster parent system, including prompt notification of appropriate public agencies of couples' intentions to adopt, authorized investigations of homes of presumptive adoptive parents, and establishment of procedures for terminating unsuccessful adoptions and for preventing placements of children for profit.

An avid civil libertarian, Buttenwieser was the first woman chair of the Legal Aid Society board and a trustee of the New York Civil Liberties Union. When Alger Hiss, convicted of perjury in a spy case in 1949, sought to overturn his conviction in 1950, Buttenwieser became his counsel; later, she helped bail out an accused Soviet spy, Dr. Robert Soblen, who later fled to Israel. She was a board member of the Legal Defense Fund of the National Association for the Advancement of Colored People. During the 1960s, her prior civil liberties work was used against Mayor Robert Wagner, whom she was supporting. In the 1970s, she presented amicus curiae briefs to the United States Supreme Court challenging the government's right to terminate Aid to Families with Dependent Children on the basis of a mother's sexual behavior. In an interview given shortly before her death, she characterized her career as "just a way of life." "I never thought of a career," she said. "I wanted to go to law school, so I went to law school. I wanted to practice law, so I practiced law. I didn't ever stop to say did I want to do something—I just did it." Throughout her life in the law she served as an important role model for many women attorneys.

BIBLIOGRAPHY

Buttenwieser, Helen Lehman. Papers. Schlesinger Library, Radcliffe College; *NYTimes, passim,* 1932–1989.

ELISABETH ISRAELS PERRY

C

CAJE

While the post-Holocaust generation of Jewish educators was predominantly male, today the field of Jewish education is predominantly female. Growing enrollments in Hebrew schools in the late 1960s and early 1970s created a teacher shortage with college students swelling the ranks of Jewish educators. They organized themselves into enthusiastic student groups such as the World Union of Jewish Students, whose American branch, known as the Network, created gatherings such as the Women's Conference, which sparked the beginning of the Jewish feminist movement. They began to lobby for greater emphasis on Jewish education in the Council of Jewish Federations' allocations and for a less top-down structure within the profession. In 1976, Cherie Koller-Fox and Jerry Benjamin, both students at the Harvard School of Education, called for and ultimately chaired a Jewish Students Network conference on Jewish education. Held in August 1976 at Brown University, it was called the "Conference on Alternatives in Jewish Education" because, in Koller-Fox's words, "the basic conference philosophy was to offer as many of the alternative approaches to teaching in one particular area as possible, and to communicate that there was a wide range of choices available in Jewish pedagogy."

The following year at Rochester, New York, a permanent organization called the Coalition for Alternatives in Jewish Education was formed and the initials CAJE now stood for both the organization and the conference. The annual conferences, dubbed by Seymour Rossel as "the Jewish Woodstock," brought together a diverse spectrum of the Jewish community for multiple workshops on every aspect of the Jewish curriculum with many items on the Jewish communal agenda. The organizational name was changed to the Coalition for the Advancement of Jewish Education in 1987, reflecting the evolving position of the group in the Jewish organization world.

Annually, the conference is convened on a university campus in rotating quadrants of the United States and twice, in 1988 and 1996, in Israel. With approximately two thousand delegates (75 percent of whom are women) in attendance at most conferences, participants choose from over five hundred sessions of varying lengths, addressing contemporary and historical issues of pedagogy and content. Many innovative concerns such as family education and women's issues were introduced at CAJE.

Many prominent women figures were introduced at the CAJE conferences. Among them were Debbie Friedman and Peninnah Schram. Debbie Friedman is a cantor, liturgical composer, and proponent of spiritual healing whose career began in Jewish summer camps, and is now known nationally for her recordings. Peninnah Schram, originally the head of the storytelling network, is now the doyenne of Jewish American storytellers and has published numerous

*Debbie Friedman, the cantor, liturgical composer, and proponent of spiritual healing,
is shown here leading a CAJE chorale at one of their annual conferences. [Lawrence Salzmann]*

collections of these tales. The evening programs offer many of the famous names on the American Jewish and Israeli scene. A media center constantly reviews the latest software and videos. The Educational Resource Center presents the contents of a Curriculum Bank. The Exhibit Center allows teachers to peruse and buy textbooks, academic Judaica books, educational aids, and Jewish arts and crafts.

During the year, CAJE sponsors regional conferences; publishes curriculum materials, often referring to the latest current events; twenty-nine Networks for members of common interests; and a professional journal three times a year called *Jewish Educational News*. *Jewish Educational News* focuses on continuity, a common area of concern, and columns entitled "Teen Experience" and "College Program." CAJE is still responding to grass-roots needs: A 1993 Task Force for Educator Empowerment is committed to building the profession. To do this, CAJE must now, according to Rosalyn Bell, the CAJE publications coordinator, "build a profession with high standards, proper com-

pensation, retention of personnel, intellectual rigor, and creativity."

BIBLIOGRAPHY

Bell, Rosalyn [publications coordinator of CAJE]. Conversations and e-mail with author, July 1, 1996, September 11, 1996, September 13, 1996, and "The Greening of a Dream." *Outlook Magazine* (Summer 1994); Benjamin, Jerry, and Cherie Koller-Fox. Interviews by author, July 1995, September 5, 1996, and "Reflections on a Movement a Making." *Sh'ma* 8-156 (September 1, 1978); Flexner, Paul. Conversations with author; Koller-Fox, Cherie. "The Empowerment of the Jewish Teacher: Founding of the Coalition for Alternatives in Jewish Education." *Studies in Jewish Education*. Vol. 7, *Origins: The Beginnings of Jewish Educational Institutions. The Hebrew University of Jerusalem: The Melton Centre for Jewish Education in the Diaspora* (1995): 213–258; Rosenblatt, Gary. "A New Boost for Jewish Education." *Baltimore Jewish Times*, July 4, 1980; Rossel, Seymour. "CAJE: A Short History." *CAJE 20 1995 Program Book* (1995): 32–38.

ROSIE ROSENZWEIG

CALISHER, HORTENSE (b. 1911)

Hortense Calisher has been a significant presence in American letters for over forty years, producing novels, short stories, and memoirs of striking originality and intelligence. A relatively late bloomer—she published her first story in 1948 at age thirty-seven—Calisher's output has been impressive: six collections of short stories and novellas, twelve novels, and two autobiographies. She has received much critical recognition for her work, including O. Henry Awards for her stories, a National Book Award nomination, two Guggenheim Fellowships, honorary doctorates, and a National Endowment for the Arts Lifetime Achievement Award (1989). She has served as president of American PEN (1986–1987) and of the American Academy and Institute of Arts and Letters (1989–1990). Yet despite the high regard in which the literary community holds her, popular fame has not followed. Calisher's novels are densely textured works that have earned her the label "writer's writer." If there is anything her critics can agree on, it is that she is a consummate stylist.

Hortense Calisher was born in New York City on December 20, 1911, the elder of two children of Joseph Henry and Hedwig (Lichstern) Calisher, a German Jewish emigré twenty-two years her husband's junior. Calisher's grandfather, born in 1832, was a leader in the Richmond, Virginia, synagogue; he and his family moved to New York City in the late 1800s. Calisher's father, born in 1861, possessed "a towering pride in his Jewishness and in his southernness" (*Herself* 59). An autodidact who, his daughter imagined, may have spoken Hebrew with a drawl, Joseph Calisher was a manufacturer of perfumes, soaps, and talcs. He and his future wife, a native of Frankfurt, Germany, met at the Saratoga races in upstate New York. The portrait of him that emerges from Calisher's autobiographical stories is of a southern fin de siècle dandy as intent on the art of living well as on making a living. Hedwig Calisher, on the other hand, was a steely minded perfectionist for whom hard work and respectability were life's cornerstones. Reminiscing about her household, Calisher observed that its clashes of cultures and personalities were "bound to produce someone interested in character, society, and time" (*Current Biography Yearbook*)—in other words, a writer.

In the very depths of the Depression, in 1932 Calisher graduated from Barnard College with a major in English and a minor in philosophy. She then worked for the New York Department of Public Welfare, visiting 175 families a month. In 1935, Calisher married engineer Heaton Heffelfinger. They had two children, Bennet, now deceased, and Peter, "a kind of art ombudsman," in his mother's words.

Calisher spent the 1940s moving from one suburb to another. It was a period of estrangement, as she recounts in her memoir, *Herself*: "As a New Yorker I am out of it in one way, as a Jew in another (almost all engineers at this time were, like my husband, Christians). And as a secret artist (for I continue writing poems in between the housework) in a third way, perhaps the most significant" (28–29). Eventually, Calisher turned to writing stories, the first of which she composed in her head while walking her son to school. "The Middle Drawer," which appeared in *The New Yorker* in July 1948 and won an O. Henry Award, is the first of a dozen autobiographical stories. Three years later, in 1951, the publication of her first book of stories, *In the Absence of Angels*, established her reputation as a formidable presence in American fiction.

With major life and career changes in the 1950s, Calisher came into her own as a writer. She and her husband divorced. She was twice a Guggenheim Fellow (1952 and 1955), and in 1956–1957 she was an adjunct professor of English at Barnard College. This was the first of over a dozen adjunct or visiting professorships she has held. In 1958, she was a U.S. Department of State American specialist's grantee to Southeast Asia, traveling extensively and giving lectures. On May 23, 1959, Calisher married the writer Curtis Harnack, past president (1971–1987) of the artists' colony Yaddo.

Continuing to write and publish short stories, Calisher spent several years writing her first novel, *False Entry* (1961). Spanning decades and worlds—from an upper-middle-class Jewish family of Golders Green, London, to a Klan-dominated Alabama town, and, finally, to a New York City version of the London family—the novel marked a major shift in Calisher's fiction. What most bewildered many longtime readers of Calisher's short stories was the complexity of style and form. Cast as his memoir, the novel is an ambitious attempt to explore an intricate, even Jamesian, consciousness. Never content simply to repeat past successes, Calisher would continue in future novels to stretch the bounds, formally and stylistically.

The 1960s saw a great creative outburst: four novels and three collections of novellas and short stories. Calisher's second novel, *Textures of Life* (1963), is a domestic novel of manners exploring the initiations into life undergone by young newlyweds. True to form, Calisher followed it, in 1965, with a very different work. *Journal from Ellipsia*, an antic novel of interplanetary encounters, explores the often uneasy relationship between science and the humanities.

Eight years after her first novel, Calisher published its companion, *The New Yorkers* (1969). In this sprawling social drama, the focal point is the New York Jewish family introduced in *False Entry*. Here, as throughout Calisher's fiction, it is character rather than racial or ethnic backgrounds that most engages her. Jewishness is a given rather than a dramatic element.

In the 1970s, Calisher turned to more recognizably contemporary subjects. The coming of age of two New Yorkers is told in *Queenie* (1971) and *Eagle Eye* (1973). *Standard Dreaming* (1972) and *On Keeping Women* (1977) dramatize middle-aged identity crises. During this decade, Calisher also published an atypical memoir, *Herself* (1972), a mix of reminiscences, essays, reviews, and musings. In 1975, her *Collected Stories* appeared to predominantly enthusiastic reviews. Curiously, many of the critics who preferred her stories to her novels cited contradictory criteria. Some praised the stories for their intricate plots, others for the richness of characterization as opposed to plot. The wide divergence of critical response underscores Calisher's impressive imaginative and formal range.

In 1983, at age seventy-two, when most novelists are hardly breaking new ground, Calisher published perhaps her most ambitious novel, *Mysteries of Motion*. Her work throughout the 1980s only confirmed her reputation as a writer with a voracious imagination and searing intelligence. In 1985, she published *Saratoga, Hot*, a collection of "little novels," and in 1986, *The Bobby-Soxer*, the only one of Calisher's novels set in a small American town. A year later Calisher published *Age*, an unflinching yet elegant novel about old age. Calisher's second memoir, *Kissing Cousins* (1988), followed. For the first time since the autobiographical stories, Calisher wrote of her household's unique blend of German and southern Jews, of northern and southern sensibilities. Her most recent novel, *In the Palace of the Movie King* (1994), is further proof of her impressive creative powers.

Ironically, the protean nature of this writer may have contributed to her work not being better known. She cannot be neatly categorized as primarily a "writer's writer," a Jewish writer, or a New York writer. Instead, she continues to spin out new variations on a theme that is both universal and deeply personal.

SELECTED WORKS BY HORTENSE CALISHER

Age (1987); *The Bobby-Soxer* (1986); *The Collected Stories of Hortense Calisher* (1975. Reprint 1984); *Eagle Eye* (1973); *False Entry* (1961); *Herself* (1972); *In the Absence of Angels* (1951); *In the Palace of the Movie King* (1994); *Journal from Ellipsia* (1965); *Kissing Cousins* (1988); "The Middle Drawer." *The New Yorker* (July 1948); *Mysteries of Motion* (1983); *The New Yorkers* (1969); *On Keeping Women* (1977); *Queenie* (1971); *Saratoga, Hot* (1985); *Standard Dreaming* (1972); *Textures of Life* (1963).

BIBLIOGRAPHY

Calisher, Hortense. Letter to author, May 21, 1995; *Current Biography Yearbook* (1973): 75; Snodgrass, Kathleen. *The Fiction of Hortense Calisher* (1993), and "Hortense Calisher: A Bibliography, 1948–1986." *Bulletin of Bibliography* 45 (March 1988): 40–50; *Who's Who of American Women* (1993–1994).

KATHLEEN SNODGRASS

CAMPS, JEWISH *see* SUMMER CAMPING

CANTORS

By the end of the nineteenth century, Jewish women in America had taken on significant roles in the rapidly developing cultural phenomenon of Yiddish American theater. Not only were they performing as stars in a wide range of dramatic productions, but they were singing all sorts of Jewish songs, including the religious hymns and liturgical chants, and newer music of spiritual significance. For example, Sophie Karp (1861–1906) introduced a Yiddish ballad written especially for her, "Eili, Eili" [My God, My God], with text material derived from Psalm 22 and other Jewish prayers. The song became a favorite solo of many other female performers of that day, including the renowned actor BERTHA KALICH and opera singers SOPHIE BRASLAU and Rosa-Raisa. In 1918, the popular singer-actor Regina Prager starred in a successful musical production, *Di Khazinte* [The lady cantor]. Throughout the early decades of the twentieth century, vaudeville programs featured women who sang Jewish selections, especially Yiddish folk songs and holiday melodies. Special prayers like *Kol Nidre* [All vows], *Eyl Moley Rakhamim* [God of mercy], and a variety of well-known Sabbath *zmirot* [spirituals] were available on player-piano rolls, in published sheet music arrangements, and on commercial recordings, and women were publicly singing such music.

Not only did they perform Jewish spiritual music, but some women also arranged and composed suitable religious songs. For example, Mana-Zucca (Augusta Zuckerman, 1891–1981) wrote a number of such works, including a highly popular anthem, *Rakhem* [Have compassion]. In 1926, the popular songwriter and performer Solomon Smulewitz (otherwise known as Solomon Small) put a photograph of his young

Cantor Nancy Abramson is shown here at the March 1994 Community Feminist Seder,
sponsored by MA'YAN: The Jewish Women's Project.
More than two hundred women attended. [Joan Roth]

daughter clad in a prayer shawl and cap on the sheet music cover of his published song, "Bar Mitzvah." Actor MOLLY PICON, early in her long career, played comic girl-boy-girl roles, singing characteristic traditional Jewish tunes. Increasingly, gifted female musicians were participating in the religious musical expression of American Jewry. This practice soon became a viable challenge to the concept of isolating *kol isha* [voice of woman] in observant Jewish life. By the 1930s, except at Orthodox synagogues, women sat with men and intoned the prayers in congregational unity. They were featured singers in religious choirs, and often sang the solos. Women had always sung in their homes, but now they sang at public rituals, and the music they sang was well beyond that of the usual range of Jewish women's songs. All Jewish music was becoming a domain to be shared with men. Then, in the second half of the twentieth century, the tragedy of the Holocaust made each and every Jewish voice much more precious.

In 1948, the School of Sacred Music was established at the Hebrew Union College–Jewish Institute of Religion (HUC–JIR) for the formal academic training of cantors and music educators, in order to better serve the Reform branch of Judaism. Soon after, in 1952, the Jewish Theological Seminary of America (JTS) inaugurated its own Cantors Institute and College of Liturgical Music on behalf of its particular constituency, Conservative Judaism. Yeshiva University also began to add courses in Jewish musical study, and in 1964 formally established its Cantorial Training Institute to serve strictly Orthodox congregations. Along with these three schools for cantorial studies, three professional cantorial membership groups were also formed: the Reform-based American Conference of Cantors, the Conservative-based Cantors Assembly of America, and the Orthodox-based Cantorial Council of America. Additionally, there remains an American organization of cantors established late in the nineteenth century, the Jewish Cantors Ministers Association. Those members continue to abide by the time-honored European training tradition dating back to the Talmudic era, that of oral transmission from individual cantor to apprentice. Until the 1970s the entire cantorate was still deemed a male profession.

In 1968, SALLY J. PRIESAND was accepted for rabbinic training at HUC–JIR, and she was ordained in 1972 as the first female rabbi in America. Until that time, women had enrolled and been accredited at the School of Sacred Music at HUC–JIR for studies in liturgical music in order to serve congregations as music teachers and choral leaders. Following the ordination of a female rabbi, the Reform Movement of Judaism also began to accredit female music students for formal cantorial studies. In 1975, Barbara Ostfeld-Horowitz was ordained the first female cantor, a landmark event. She received immediate pulpit placement following graduation and was promptly inducted into the American Conference of Cantors. Early on, Ostfeld-Horowitz had become interested in Jewish music, and she was active as a youngster in Reform temple activities. She admired the ministerial roles of rabbi and cantor, and after high school in Oak Park, Illinois, came to New York. Despite the then daring nature of her ambition, she applied for cantorial training at the School of Sacred Music. Upon her acceptance, she chose to train in both the fully traditional as well as Reform liturgical music services. During her four-year program of full-time studies, she served at various pulpits. Currently, she serves a Reform congregation in the greater Buffalo area, and enjoys being a cantorial and educational minister to her congregation, an active role model to women, a dedicated Jewish musician, and a wife and mother whose husband shares her pulpit duties as a cantor-educator. By 1995, when she received a special twenty-year honorary award at HUC–JIR graduation services, ninety-four other women cantors had graduated from that school. Scattered throughout the country, most of them are in full duties, the rest hold part-time positions, but all are cantorially employed. In reflecting upon her chosen profession, Ostfeld-Horowitz writes, "Women cantors have altered the way in which prayer is offered, heard, and received."

In 1980, the JTS began admitting women for rabbinic training in the Conservative branch of Judaism. Meanwhile, women had been attending classes at the College of Jewish Music at JTS since the late 1950s, and over the years some had been granted formal degrees in sacred music. Finally, in 1984, two of those students, Erica Lipitz and Marla Rosenfeld Barugel, applied and were permitted to prepare for ordination as hazans. They were granted that status by the Cantors Institute of the JTS in 1987. Both were placed at congregations, and since then a number of other women have completed and received cantorial designation. Currently, admission at the College of Jewish

Music is open to both women and men for cantorial training in a five-year, full-time educational study track. However, there remain differences in the status of female cantors in the Conservative Movement, and much depends upon a particular congregation. Moreover, until recently, the Conservative professional organization, the Cantors Assembly of America, did not formally grant admission to female cantorial graduates. This reflects the abiding, strong reservations that many of its members hold concerning acceptance of women functioning in cantorial pulpits. Albeit in less measure, American Conservative congregational leaders are also divided ideologically regarding the role of female rabbis. In age-old Judaic tradition, the rabbi was viewed as a religious teacher-scholar and spiritual interpreter-counselor, and only in America has that office assumed a more active ministerial role at the religious services. In contrast, however, the traditional role of the American cantor has remained that of *shaleach tzibbur*, the leader for ritual duties and musical guider-inspirer of congregational prayer. Therefore, issues are still hotly debated regarding women's exemption from, or active practice in, mandatory observance of the 613 principles of faith (male injunctions); the counting of women in a minyan for a proper order of service; and of course the matter of *kol isha*, woman's voice in divine worship. No woman has been permitted admission to the Orthodox cantorial training at Yeshiva University, nor is that likely ever to happen.

Two nonacademic affiliated organizations are presently involved with the roles of women in synagogue music. The American Guild of Organists has a mixed constituency of liturgical musicians, not only men and women, but also Jews and non-Jews. The guild endeavors to offer a wide range of Jewish musical guidance to its membership. The Women Cantors Network is in essence a female counterpart to the still-functioning Jewish Cantors Ministers Association, the traditionally oriented group whose membership remains entirely male.

The Women Cantors Network was founded by Cantor Deborah Katchko-Zimmerman in 1981. It gathered together a group of twelve women then serving as cantors or actively seeking that professional goal. By 1996, the active membership roster had grown to ninety. Katchko-Zimmerman was typical of those who needed such an organization. Granddaughter of an eminent European cantor, most of whose family had perished in the Holocaust, she was trained privately by her cantor father. She then auditioned and secured a fully active position at a Conservative congregation in Connecticut, but felt isolated from the male cantorate. Soon she was joined in spearheading the network by Doris Cohen, a former liturgical soloist with composer and conductor Sholom Secunda and a privately trained cantor serving at a Reform pulpit in New York City. The core group grew rapidly to function as an outreach support group, with annual study conferences and a regular newsletter. The network also works for the nationwide recognition and employment of properly qualified female cantors, whether from one of the cantorial schools or by private traditional means of instruction.

Though debate continues regarding the female cantorial profession, women's voices increasingly come forth from pulpits in America, leading congregations in all the year-round calendar and life-cycle observances of the Jewish faith. They train and lead choirs, arrange and compose liturgical works, present special Jewish music programs, and attend to a great many duties as music educators, including the training of girls and boys to assume their religious responsibilities of bat and bar mitzvah.

ACADEMIC CATALOGS
FOR CANTORIAL STUDIES

Cantors Institute of the Jewish Theological Seminary of America, NYC; School of Sacred Music of Hebrew Union College–Jewish Institute of Religion, NYC.

IRENE HESKES

CARDIN, SHOSHANA S. (b. 1926)

It was an indication of things to come when eleven-year-old Shoshana Shoubin stood outside Baltimore's most popular movie theater one Sunday in 1938, collecting money for the Jews settling in the land of Palestine. In a single afternoon she filled two canisters with coins donated by people who responded to her persuasive determination, and as a result, young Shoshana was rewarded with a prize from Keren Kayemet.

These days Shoshana Shoubin Cardin is doing much the same thing—but on an entirely different scale. A savvy, tough, and elegant woman known by presidents, dictators, and almost everyone else simply as Shoshana, she has become perhaps the most widely respected and successful lay leader in the Jewish community of the 1980s and 1990s.

In the process, this woman, who has refused to challenge the title "chairman" just because she is a woman, and who fought the National Organization for Women in the 1960s and 1970s when she felt it was degrading the value of women's contributions as home-

Shoshana Cardin is an iconoclastic political activist whose guiding principle has been to serve the Jewish people. Though a supporter of women's rights, she has locked horns with feminists, not to mention prime ministers and presidents. [United Israel Appeal]

makers and volunteers, has broken the glass ceiling over almost every major national and international Jewish organization.

Shoshana's early years were modest in financial resources but rich in family and *yiddishkeit*. She was born in Tel Aviv on October 10, 1926, and emigrated with her parents just over a year later. The Shoubin family settled in Baltimore, Maryland, in the East Baltimore section, which was then a predominantly Jewish neighborhood peopled by recent immigrants.

She earned a B.A. in English at UCLA in 1946, after three years at Baltimore's Johns Hopkins. She met Jerome Cardin on a blind date and married him in 1948 when she was nearly twenty-two. While her husband finished law school and began his career, which later included real estate development, she taught public school. She began substitute teaching and became a tenured teacher of seventh and eighth grades in the Baltimore public school system. Pregnant women were not allowed to teach, so Cardin quit when she was expecting the first of her four children: Steven, Ilene, Nina, and Sanford.

The belief that *kol Israel arevim ze le'ze*, that all the Jewish people are responsible for one another, is the principle on which Cardin has built her career of service and one she instilled in her children. Cardin takes pride in the fact that three of her children—a speech pathologist working as a Jewish educator; a Conservative rabbi and editor of the Jewish intellectual newsletter *Sh'ma;* and an attorney working as the head of a Jewish family foundation—are deeply committed to serving the Jewish community.

While home with her young children, Cardin continued the career of volunteer work she had begun so young and was soon invited to sit on the boards of directors of local nonprofit organizations. She also became president of Maryland's Federation of Jewish Women's Organizations, a position she used to foster awareness of racial inequality at a time, in 1960 and 1961, when the Jewish community was just getting involved with the civil rights movement. "It was unusual for women in the southern tradition to be political activists," she recalls of the controversy sparked by her invitation to a local Hispanic politician to come speak to the group.

In 1967 she served as a delegate to Maryland's Constitutional Convention, and in 1968 she was invited to join Maryland's Commission for Women, which she chaired from 1974 to 1979. Beginning in 1976, she worked as an activist to change federal and state laws pertaining to women's ability to obtain credit. In 1976 and 1977, Cardin testified at hearings in Maryland and Washington, D.C., and played a central role in convincing legislators to allow women to obtain credit in their own name. Cardin served as commissioner of Maryland's Commission on Human Relations from 1979 to 1982 and as chair of Maryland's State Employment and Training Council from 1979 to 1983.

She was offered a job touring the country for banks to teach women about their rights and was nominated to serve on the Federal Reserve Board but turned down both opportunities "because my husband traveled a lot and my family came first." That kept her close to home for a time, where she devoted her bountiful energy and talent for organizing and leading people to local Jewish and civic groups. She became deeply involved with Baltimore's Jewish Community Center and instituted a permanent cadre of volunteers to support its work.

In 1984 she became the first woman elected president of the Council of Jewish Federations (CJF), the umbrella organization for the groups that raise money and coordinate social and educational services in 189 North American Jewish communities. It was during her time at the helm of CJF, which lasted until 1987, that her husband was convicted of stealing $385,000 from a Maryland savings and loan. After serving one year of his fifteen-year prison term, he was diagnosed with lung cancer and granted medical parole. He died in 1993.

During her CJF presidency and afterward, as chairman of the organization's Who Is a Jew Committee, Cardin played a critical role in unifying the Jewish community's leadership in opposition to proposed changes in Israel's Law of Return. Cardin met more times than she can remember with the heads of the Israeli coalition government, Yitzhak Shamir and Shimon Peres, and ultimately played a seminal role in convincing them to jettison the legislation, which would have altered the law that states that anyone born to a Jewish mother or converted to Judaism may immigrate to Israel and be granted immediate citizenship, and would have required that all conversions be approved by the Orthodox rabbinate. "I can't believe how many times I've challenged presidents and prime ministers," she says, chuckling.

From 1988 to 1992, Cardin served as chairman of the National Conference on Soviet Jewry. In May 1989, she led a small delegation that held, for the first time, a meeting with Soviet leaders, including the head of OVIR, the emigration office in the former Soviet Union. Rudolph Kusnetzov was responsible for the fact that more than eleven thousand refuseniks were prohibited from leaving the former communist nation, and it was from that meeting and the several that followed with Cardin, in Copenhagen and Helsinki, that the restrictions on remaining refusniks began to be loosened and emigration soared.

In December 1990, she was elected to head the Conference of Presidents of Major American Jewish Organizations, a coalition of several dozen of the largest and most influential Jewish organizations whose role is to represent the Jewish community's interests to the U.S. Government. She is the only woman to have held that role.

It was while in that position that she interceded with President George Bush in September 1991, after he made remarks implying that he was being victimized by Jewish lobbying efforts to get the American government to guarantee $10 billion in loans the Israeli government was seeking to borrow on the international market, to fund the resettlement of the hundreds of thousands of Jews from the collapsing Soviet Union who were pouring into the Jewish state.

After some thirteen hundred Jews spent the day lobbying their congressional representatives to release the loan guarantees, Bush angrily told reporters at a White House press conference that he was just "one lonely little guy" opposing them. Cardin wrote to the president, calling his remark "disturbing." In short order Bush apologized for sounding "pejorative."

Since 1994 Cardin served as chairman of the United Israel Appeal, the organization that allocates the money raised in the United States for Israel to the Jewish Agency for Israel, which distributes the funds to the recipient agencies in the Jewish state. She also worked as national chair of the Jerusalem 3000 Committee, which coordinated activities in the United States for the Israeli capital's trimillennium, was national vice-chair of the United Jewish Appeal, and served on the board of governors and executive of the Jewish Agency for Israel and on the board of directors of the American Jewish Joint Distribution Committee, which aids distressed Jewish communities all over the world. She sits on the executive committee of the Council of Jewish Federations and is past chairman of CLAL (the National Jewish Center for Learning and Leadership), which is devoted to promoting religious pluralism.

Cardin says that her commitment to Jewish peoplehood has fueled the work she has done. "The most important message I have wanted to give people has been the importance, the pride and the responsibility, the blessing of being Jewish. That's what gives me the strength to challenge what I have challenged and bring about change where I could."

BIBLIOGRAPHY

Cardin, Nina Beth [daughter of Shoshana S. Cardin]. Interview with author, November 1996; Cardin, Shoshana S. Interview with author, November 1996; Goldberg, J.J. *Jewish Power* (1996); Jewish Telegraphic Agency archives.

DEBRA NUSSBAUM COHEN

CARNEGIE, HATTIE (1886–1956)

We have the loveliest women in the world in this county and wherever there are beautiful women there will be beautiful clothes. To show the American woman herself off to best advantage—that has always been my aim and that is my real biography.

—Hattie Carnegie

Hattie Carnegie led a fashion empire that set the pace of American fashion for nearly three decades. She imported Paris designs, produced custom designs

She couldn't sew or cut a pattern herself, yet Hattie Carnegie's sense of style and taste sparked her rise from humble beginnings as a Jewish immigrant to the creator of a fashion empire around a distinctly "American" look. [Library of Congress]

and a ready-to-wear collection, and sold other designers' ready-to-wear. Even women who could not afford to buy Carnegie originals felt the influence of her style in the many mass-market copies of her work. Carnegie made numerous trips to Paris every year, buying and importing the models of designers such as Vionnet, Lanvin, Chanel, Dior, Molyneux, and Schiaparelli.

Hattie Carnegie was born Henrietta Kanengeiser, the second of seven children, on March 15, 1886, in Vienna, Austria. In 1892, she immigrated with her family to New York's Lower East Side. She changed her name to Carnegie by 1909, naming herself after the richest person in America, Andrew Carnegie. In 1927, she married Major John Zanft, a childhood friend from the Lower East Side, after two other brief marriages. Zanft was involved in the motion picture industry; he was a former vice president of Fox Films.

Carnegie formed a partnership with Rose Roth, a seamstress, in 1909. They started a custom clothing and millinery shop on East 10th Street in New York City. By 1913, they had incorporated and moved their shop to a more fashionable location, on West 86th and Riverside Drive. During this time, fashion leaders Mrs. Harrison Williams and Mrs. William Randolph Hearst became her clients. In 1918, Carnegie bought out her partner. In addition to selling her own designs, she began to travel to France and bring back Parisian fashions that she restyled and remodeled for her American customers.

Over the next twenty years, Carnegie traveled to Paris as many as seven times a year to study and buy current fashions. In 1923, Carnegie moved her business to a townhouse at 42 East 49th Street. This location remained the seat of her custom business. The store sold furs, jewelry, lingerie, perfumes, and accessories in addition to clothing. The Carnegie look embodied total perfection, and her accessories were as much a part of the "look" as the clothing. In the 1940s, she created the Blue Room, where she sold her own and other manufacturers' ready-to-wear lines. Her innovative Jeune Fille department (created in 1941) provided lower-priced clothing for her younger customers.

In 1925, I. Magnin was the first store to buy Hattie Carnegie designs wholesale. These designs carried the I. Magnin label and the Hattie Carnegie label. Carnegie is known as the first custom designer to create special collections for a ready-to-wear label for wholesale trade. "Hattie Carnegie Originals" were produced in Carnegie's own factories. She ran her wholesale business at 711 Fifth Avenue.

Carnegie could not sew or cut a pattern herself, but she had an eye for gathering talented people to work for her. Many of the designers who worked for Hattie Carnegie emerged as important designers and arbiters of style on their own. Pauline Potter (later Baroness Philippe de Rothschild), Norman Norell, Claire McCardell, James Galanos, Jean Louis, and Travis Banton all began their careers under the direction of Carnegie. Acting as a great editor of style and taste, Carnegie brought out the best of her designers' talents. Carnegie maintained regular customers among America's most prominent socialites and Hollywood and Broadway stars. Clients included the Duchess of Windsor, Barbara Hutton, Clare Booth Luce, Constance Bennett, Tallulah Bankhead, Joan Crawford, Gertrude Lawrence, and Norma Shearer. Her best known works were her "little Carnegie suits." Carnegie's suits typified a style that was neither youthful nor matronly, but very feminine and very neat—the "Carnegie Look." Carnegie claimed in 1951 that "there is really no 'Carnegie Look,' there is only the 'you' look. My clothes are built to show off the woman who wears them. I like them to be simple, complicated and simple, to move well, to move with the times and a little ahead of them. The dress itself should never take over. On the contrary a woman should feel so at ease in her clothes that she can forget all about them" (Lambert).

In 1948, she received the Coty American Fashion Critics Award. She received the United States Army's highest civilian award for designing the Women's Army Corps uniforms.

Hattie Carnegie died at age sixty-nine on February 22, 1956, in New York. Her multimillion dollar fashion business continued into the 1970s, but the strength of Carnegie's personal dynamism and leadership was so closely identified with the company that it was difficult for it to continue successfully without her. Two of Carnegie's brothers had worked closely with her in her business. Tony managed the wholesale dress business, and Herman managed her financial affairs.

The Carnegie look defined the American desire for a style that is discreet, simple, and sophisticated. Her career began at a time when Americans looked almost entirely to French haute couture for direction. When French fashion became unavailable during World War II, Carnegie continued producing high-quality clothing with the best American fabrics and designers. Carnegie's work as a great editor of French haute couture for the American market as well as her extraordinary record of recognition and development of American talent place her firmly at the forefront of the development of American style in the twentieth century.

BIBLIOGRAPHY

Bauer, Hambla. "Hot Fashions by Hattie." *Collier's* (April 16, 1949); *DAB* 6; "Hattie Carnegie." *Current Biography* (October 1942); "Hattie Carnegie: American Style Defined." Exhibition. The Museum of the Fashion Institute of Technology, NYC (February 16–April 27, 1996); Lambert, Eleanor, "Hattie Carnegie: Biography." Press release. New York Dress Institute (1951); "Luxury, Inc." *Vogue* (April 15, 1928); Milbank, Caroline Rennolds. *New York Fashion: The Evolution of American Style* (1989); *NAW; New York and Hollywood Fashion: Costume Designs from the Brooklyn Museum Collection* (1986); Obituary. *NYTimes*, February 23, 1956, 27:1; Steele, Valerie. *Women of Fashion: Twentieth Century Design* (1991); *WWWIA* 3.

DENNITA SEWELL

CASPARY, VERA (1899–1987)

Novelist and screenwriter Vera Caspary wrote in her autobiography, *The Secrets of Grown-Ups* (1979): "This has been the century of The Woman and I know myself fortunate to have been part of the revolution. In another generation, perhaps the next, equality will be taken for granted. Those who come after us may find it easier to assert independence, but will miss the grand adventure of having been born a woman in this century of change."

Vera Louise Caspary was born on November 13, 1899, in Chicago, Illinois, the daughter of Paul and Julia (Cohen) Caspary. Her paternal grandfather fled Germany during the 1848 Revolution. Her maternal grandfather emigrated from Amsterdam by way of England. She had a sister, Irma, fifteen years her senior, and two older brothers, Arthur and Danny. Her father was a buyer for a department store. Caspary was educated in Chicago public schools. On October 5, 1949, she married I.G. Goldsmith, a film producer born in Vienna.

Caspary worked as a stenographer, a copywriter, the director of a mail order school for such courses as ballet lessons and writing photoplays (before writing any of her own), the editor of *Dance Magazine* (1925–1927), and a free-lance author and screenwriter from 1927 until her death. She wrote twenty published novels and was a prolific screenwriter for Hollywood films.

In her best-known work, *Laura*, first written as a novel, Caspary went beyond the traditional murder mystery. With its brilliantly constructed plot involving complex characters interacting on multilevels, this might well be considered the first psychothriller. The 1944 film, directed by Otto Preminger and starring Gene Tierney in the title role, has become a classic. She received awards from the Screen Writers Guild in 1948 for *A Letter to Three Wives* and in 1967 for *Les Girls*.

Caspary was an unconventional, independent woman, despite her conventional, Jewish middle-class background. She supported herself, and later her widowed mother, at a time when few women had careers of their own. The female characters in her novels and plays are strong, emancipated women. Her analyses of what drives her villains and victims alike are objective and evenhanded. In her screenplays, Caspary displayed an apt ear for dialogue and allowed the characters to reveal themselves through their own words and actions, producing realistic portraits on a wide range of social levels. Beginning with her first novel, *The White Girl* (1929), about an African-American woman who moves north to Chicago, where she passes as white, Caspary concerned herself with issues of prejudice and class consciousness in twentieth-century America.

Her autobiography provides a sensitive yet unsentimental retrospective of the twentieth century, highlighting such broad topics as the New York scene of the roaring twenties, gangster Chicago, the world in the grip of the Depression, American intellectuals embracing (and becoming disillusioned by) communism, the romanticizing of the Spanish Civil War, Hollywood studios, London during World War II, the first reactions to the concentration camps, postwar Europe, and Hollywood in the McCarthy era.

Caspary described herself and her husband as two who "scorned the practice of religion but shared contempt for Jews who denied their heritage." Her respect for that heritage shows in her insistence on the dignity of all. It adds poignancy to her community's reaction to the Leopold-Loeb murder case, to her description of the atmosphere in Britain following the victory brought by the bombings of Hiroshima and Nagasaki, and to her encounter with a bigoted Texan on her return voyage to America after the war. And that heritage surely fostered her proud independence. The characters Caspary created and the life she lived do indeed define "the grand adventure of having been born a woman in this century of change."

Vera Caspary died of a stroke on June 13, 1987.

SELECTED WORKS BY VERA CASPARY

NOVELS

Bedelia (1945); *A Chosen Sparrow* (1964); *The Dreamers* (1975); *Elizabeth X* (1978); *Evvie* (1960); *False Face* (1954); *Final Portrait* (1971); *The Husband* (1957); *Ladies and Gents* (1929); *Laura* (1943); *The Man Who Loved His Wife* (1966); *The Murder in the Stork Club* (1946); *Music in the Street* (1930); *The Rosecrest Cell* (1967); *Ruth* (1972); *Stranger Than Truth* (1946); *Thelma* (1952); *Thicker Than Water* (1932); *The Weeping and the Laughter* (1950), republished as *The Death Wish* (1951); *The White Girl* (1929).

AUTOBIOGRAPHY

The Secrets of Grown-Ups (1979).

PLAYS

Blind Mice, with Winifred Lenihan (1930); *Geraniums in My Window*, with Samuel Ornitz (1934); *Laura*, with George Sklar (1945); *Wedding in Paris* (1954).

SCREENPLAYS

Bachelor in Paradise (1961); *Bedelia* (1946); *The Blue Gardenia*, with Charles Hoffman (1953); *Claudia and David*, with Rose Franken and William Brown Meloney (1946); *Easy Living*, with Preston Sturgis (1937); *Les Girls*, with John Patrick (1957); *Give a Girl a Break*, with Albert Hackett and Frances Goodrich (1954); *I Can Get It for You Wholesale*, with

Abraham Polonsky (1951); *I'll Love You Always* (1935); *Lady Bodyguard*, with Edmund L. Hartmann and Art Arthur (1942); *Lady from Louisiana*, with others (1941); *A Letter to Three Wives*, with Joseph L. Mankiewicz (1949); *Out of the Blue*, with Walter Bullock and Edward Eliscu (1947); *Scandal Street*, with Bertram Millhauser and Eddie Welch (1938); *Service Deluxe*, with others (1938); *Sing, Dance, Plenty Hot*, with others (1940); *Three Husbands*, with Edward Eliscu (1950).

BIBLIOGRAPHY

Evory, Ann, and Linda Metzger, eds. *Contemporary Authors. New Revision Series*. Vol. 9 (1983); Kinsman, Clare D., ed. *Contemporary Authors*. Vols. 13–16 (1975); Obituary. *NYTimes*, June 17, 1987; Reilly, John M., ed. *Twentieth-Century Crime and Mystery Writers* (1980); Rothe, Anna, ed. *Current Biography* (1948); *UJE*.

ANN KNEAVEL

CEDAR KNOLLS SCHOOL FOR GIRLS

In November 1911, a group of Jewish women convened under the auspices of the New York Jewish Protectory and Aid Society, an organization that had been founded in 1902 to address the problem of Jewish juvenile delinquency. The women, many of whose husbands were associated with the society, resolved to provide "for the care of delinquent girls of our faith." Among those spearheading this effort were MADELEINE BORG, JULIA RICHMAN, Florence Lowenstein Marshall, ALICE DAVIS MENKEN, Sissie Strauss Lehman, Mrs. Arthur Sachs, and Adele Neustadt Schiff.

Alarmed by reports of the growing numbers of young females arraigned in New York City's children's courts, the concerned women advocated the establishment of a Jewish girls' correctional facility comparable to the existing Hawthorne School. This Jewish reformatory for boys had opened in May 1906 in Hawthorne, New York. The school, one of the first such institutions in the country, was built on the "cottage," or group living, plan and was widely acclaimed for its emphasis on rehabilitation, rather than punishment, in the treatment of troubled youngsters.

Working independently, though in consultation with the Hawthorne School directors, the women founders raised the necessary funds and established the Cedar Knolls School for Girls (CK) in 1913. Financed by private donations and city subsidies, the residential school (originally known as the Council Home for Jewish Girls) operated out of temporary quarters in Bronxville, New York. In August 1917, Cedar Knolls moved to its own building on the Hawthorne campus.

The initial group of seventeen girls admitted to the school were aged twelve to sixteen and were generally referred by the children's courts, individuals, or organizations. The girls were committed to Cedar Knolls and other institutions for a variety of reasons, including disorderly conduct, peddling, "improper guardianship," "malicious mischief," "incorrigibility," "immorality," stabbing or assault, and petty larceny. These young women, according to longtime CK president Madeleine Borg, were "not hardened criminals, but only children deprived of their natural heritage and rights. . . . it was our duty to assist [them]."

CK directors strove to rehabilitate their students through basic education, vocational training, religious instruction, wholesome recreation, and, most importantly, moral guidance. Girls were required to complete the regular course of study mandated by the New York City Board of Education. They also received instruction in various vocational subjects, including hand and machine sewing, embroidery, knitting, millinery, typing, and, later, hairdressing. The school's Jewish character was reflected in its Sabbath and holiday services, weekly classes in Hebrew, Bible, and biblical history, and confirmation ceremonies for the girls.

Beyond formal instruction, the girls enjoyed many recreational activities, such as clubs, storytelling, music, gardening, dramatics, instructive talks, weekly campfire gatherings, Girl Scout programs, physical exercise, and dancing. They were also responsible for daily upkeep of the school, and through cleaning, cooking, laundering, and sewing the girls prepared for their future domestic roles.

In all aspects of the program, the emphasis was on cooperation, teamwork, and mutual responsibility. Directors were determined to teach their highly individualized students to function as part of a group.

The CK's well-to-do women managers strove to govern by kindness and were dedicated to their mission. They clearly saw themselves as benefactors, patrons, and role models for their young charges. Borg commented in 1917, "We have always borne in mind the importance of surrounding these girls with women of refinement and ideals who, both by precept and example, would influence the girls to a loftier viewpoint of life."

The women involved in this work attributed rising Jewish juvenile delinquency to the difficulties experienced by immigrants as they adjusted to life in the United States. Of the 145 girls enrolled in Cedar Knolls between 1909 and 1921, 109 were foreign-born, while only 36 were American-born. As Borg explained in 1913:

The problem of the delinquent Jewish girl is the most recent issue.... The Jews ... with their strong religious principles and ... high ... ideals as to the chastity of their persons, thrown into new surroundings, where the customs of the country are strange and incomprehensible to them, amid different economic conditions, where the struggle for mere existence is so keen, find many of their cherished beliefs slipping away from them as impossible and impracticable.

In particular, female reformers and philanthropists pointed to the following factors as contributing to Jewish juvenile delinquency: incompatibility between immigrant parents and their American-born children, lack of religious education, overcrowding in immigrant neighborhoods, bleak home environments resulting in girls' attraction to the excitement of cabarets or dance halls, inadequate vocational training in the schools that reduced young women's wage-earning capacity, and few parks and playgrounds available for wholesome recreation.

As stated in the 1922 annual report of the Jewish Board of Guardians, CK was designed for delinquent girls who required "more regular and systematic treatment than preventive agencies can give." However, the women managers were quick to recognize the multidimensional nature of their work. Many branched out into related areas, in addition to their involvement with the school. Some joined or supervised the growing Big Sister movement, one of the most important preventive programs in the treatment of juvenile delinquency. As Big Sisters, they offered guidance to large numbers of young girls referred to them by parents, schools, the courts, charities, and social service agencies. In addition, the managers of CK went on to train volunteers through lecture courses on child psychology and development that were organized by synagogue sisterhoods and settlement houses. Other women connected with CK became involved with the Lakeview Home for Unmarried Mothers, a project of the Jewish Protectory and Aid Society with the cooperation of the NATIONAL COUNCIL OF JEWISH WOMEN. Moreover, the school's paid probation officer, as well as women volunteers, represented Jewish girls in New York City's juvenile courts.

By 1930, CK had expanded considerably, housing fifty girls. The length of time spent in the institution varied, depending on each girl's circumstances and progress. Most were released to their parents or relatives and were able to find suitable employment. Many eventually married and established their own households.

As the population of the combined Hawthorne/Cedar Knolls School gradually changed to include more emotionally disturbed and socially maladjusted youngsters, the institution focused on individualized treatment. In order to meet the needs of these students, the school established its first psychiatric clinic in 1935.

By the late 1980s, the Hawthorne/Cedar Knolls School, now coeducational, served some 170 youngsters, aged eight to twenty-two, both Jewish and non-Jewish. The school is still in existence, and the treatment program, now sponsored by the Jewish Board of Family and Children's Services, continues to provide troubled boys and girls with a "cottage" group-living experience, clinical counseling services, special education, and recreational activities.

CK directors took great pride in their achievements on behalf of delinquent girls. As MADELINE BORG (who was also among the founders of the Jewish Board of Guardians, and its president from 1942 to 1951) observed, "Our aim in creating our Home is to give to these girls who have been denied through circumstances the privileges to which every child is entitled, an opportunity to readjust themselves and to return to the community as useful and self-respecting members" (Borg, 1917).

BIBLIOGRAPHY

Borg, Madeline. Jewish Protectory and Aid Society. Annual reports, 1911, 1913, 1917; Cedar Knolls School. Archival collection. Jewish Division, New York Public Library; Jewish Board of Guardians. Annual report, 1922; Menken, Alice D. *Tales of One City—A Few Selected Stories to Illustrate the Rehabilitation of the Morally Handicapped: A Study in Social Services* (1924): 24–25; Morris, Robert, and Michael Freund. *Trends and Issues in Jewish Social Welfare in the United States, 1899–1952* (1966); Rischin, Moses. *The Promised City: New York's Jews, 1870–1914* (1962).

REENA SIGMAN FRIEDMAN

CHARREN, PEGGY (b. 1928)

Peggy Charren, founder of Action for Children's Television (ACT), took on the burgeoning television industry of the 1970s and won. She was honored for her efforts in 1995 when she received a Presidential Medal of Freedom for her work on behalf of quality television programming for children. In August 1996, she stood with President Bill Clinton when he announced that the television industry had agreed to abide by the advocates' interpretation of 1990 legislation linking licensing to children's educational programming.

Peggy Charren, founder of Action for Children's Television, was honored for her efforts in 1995 when she received a Presidential Medal of Freedom for her work on behalf of quality television programming for children. [Peggy Charren]

She was born Peggy Walzer on March 9, 1928, to Ruth Rosenthal of Manhattan and Maxwell Walzer of Brooklyn. Her grandparents had come to the United States from Germany and Russia before the turn of the century. She had a liberal, middle-class upbringing "where the idea of caring for others and their plight was part of life. Many Jewish families felt this way because of what happened to the Jews. My grandfather was a doctor with many poor patients. My family was always involved in the political process."

Her mother, a pianist, had won a scholarship to the Juilliard School of Music, but married instead and instilled a love of music in her and her sister, Barbara, who was three years younger. Peggy majored in liberal arts at Connecticut College, graduating in 1949. She became director of the film department at station WPIX-TV in New York City. In 1951, when she was twenty-three years old, she married Stanley Charren, an engineer. The couple lives in Cambridge, Massachusetts, and has two daughters and four grandchildren.

She did not start out to be an advocate, but while at home with two young daughters, she was concerned by the lack of children's educational programming and the prevalence of violent and product-related shows designed primarily to sell toys to young audiences. Drawing on experience gained in her job at a television station, her skill for organizing, and her boundless energy, she founded, in 1968, Action for Children's Television (ACT), a nonprofit organization dedicated to encouraging more diversity in television choices for children.

She realized that the Communications Act of 1934, which states that in return for a license to use the broadcast spectrum a station must serve the public interest, could be used as leverage to promote educational television programs. In response to ACT's efforts, Congress passed the Children's Television Act in 1990, requiring each television station to provide some programs specifically designed to educate children or risk losing its license. It took six more years to get the industry to pay attention, however. Although ACT closed in 1992, Peggy Charren continued to work on the issue, and in 1996, with the help of President Clinton and the Federal Communications Commission, the rules were strengthened to mandate at least three hours of children's programming per week before a station license would be renewed.

Prior to founding ACT in 1968, Charren was director of the Creative Arts Council of Newton, Massachusetts. She owned and operated Quality Book Fairs, a company that organized children's book fairs, and Art Prints, a gallery specializing in graphics.

She is a visiting scholar at Harvard University's Graduate School of Education and received the Helen Homans Gilbert Award from Radcliffe College. She has received numerous honorary degrees.

She received the Annenberg Public Policy Center Award from the University of Pennsylvania for lifetime contribution to excellence in children's television and a Women That Make a Difference Award from the International Women's Forum (both in 1996), a Peabody Award in 1992, and a National Academy of Television Arts and Sciences Emmy in 1988. She was also honored by the Consumer Federation of America with the Consumer Service Award in 1994, the Great Friend to Kids Award from the Association of Youth Museums in 1994, and the Daniel Marr Boys and Girls Club Tribute to Women Award in 1997.

SELECTED WORKS BY PEGGY CHARREN

Changing Channels: Living Sensibly with Television, with Martin W. Sandler (1983); Television, Children and the Constitutional Bicentennial (1986); The TV-Smart Book for Kids, with Carol Hulsizer (1986).

BIBLIOGRAPHY

Boston Globe, March 17, 1996; Charren, Peggy. Interview with author; Christian Science Monitor, April 11, 1996; Contemporary Authors (1992); Schoenebaum, Eleanor W. Political Profiles: The Nixon/Ford Years (1979); Who's Who in America (1976–); Who's Who of Advertising; Who's Who of American Women. 11th–18th eds.; Who's Who of Entertainment. 2d ed.

JANET BEYER

CHERNIN, KIM (b. 1940)

Ranging from poetry to investigations of women's eating disorders, from fictional autobiography to the story of a voice, Kim Chernin's works radiate the "spiritual politics" she considers the essence of her Jewishness. Born May 7, 1940, in the Bronx to Paul Kusnitz, an engineer, and ROSE CHERNIN, a radical organizer, Chernin was profoundly influenced by her family's experience as Russian-Jewish immigrants and their commitment to Communist ideals. Chernin spent the first five years of her life in New York, but when her older sister died the family moved to Los Angeles.

A declared radical after high school, Chernin traveled to Europe and Russia to study the Communist political system she idealized. She entered the University of California at Berkeley severely disillusioned, however, and met and married David Netboy in 1958. Chernin then traveled with her husband to

England and Ireland, studying for a time at Oxford and Trinity College in Dublin, where her daughter, Larissa Nicole, was born in 1963. Returning to California, Chernin received her B.A. with honors from the University of California in 1965. Her marriage to Netboy ended in divorce, as did a later marriage to Robert Cantor. After spending nine months in an Israeli kibbutz (1971), Chernin returned to Berkeley, where she began a writing and consulting practice. In 1982 she met Renate Stendhal, now her life partner. In 1990 she earned an M.A. in psychology from New College of California. Chernin still resides in Berkeley, which she says provides a necessary immigrant and radical atmosphere for her work as writer, teacher, and therapist.

Chernin's literary innovations, blended with a poetic and political focus on women's psychology and spirituality, have helped radicalize American women's culture. Her most famous book, *In My Mother's House*, weaves a narrative of multiple voices to produce both a tale of contemporary mother-daughter encounters and a family history that traces back through several generations of Eastern European Jewish women to the Russian shtetl. Chernin has also written poetry, novels, and an autobiographically framed series focusing on women's search for spirituality through food, psychotherapy, and the body. *Sex and Other Sacred Games*, written with Stendhal, uses two narrating voices plus letters and journals to create a stunningly intellectual and uniquely female story of a spiritual and erotic relationship.

Chernin's most recent work consolidates her interests in gender, spiritual politics, and literary form. *Crossing the Border*, a novel dealing with Jewish-Arab conflict through sexual relationships, and *A Different Kind of Listening*, which traces Chernin's psychoanalysis, completely subvert traditional modes of storytelling. *My Life as a Boy: A Woman's Story*, *In My Father's Garden*, and Chernin's recently completed tale of Cecilia Bartoli's voice synthesize the psychological, ethnic, spiritual, and literary aspects and richness of her work. Chernin's use of the self as living laboratory has dramatically expanded the potential of American prose while recording one Jewish American woman's lifework in "the politics of the small."

SELECTED WORKS BY KIM CHERNIN

Cecilia Bartoli: The Passion of Song, with Renate Stendhal (1997); *Crossing the Border: An Erotic Journey* (1994); "Current Trends in Psychoanalysis: Social Constructivism," with Michael J. Bader. *Tikkun* (1993); *A Different Kind of Listening: My Psychoanalysis and Its Shadow* (1995); *The Flame-Bearers: A Novel* (1986); *The Hunger Song* (poems, 1982); *The Hungry Self: Women, Eating, and Identity* (1985); *In My Father's Garden: A Daughter's Spiritual Journey* (1996); *In My Mother's House: A Daughter's Story* (1983); "A Matter of Attitude." In *The Erotic Edge: Erotica for Couples* (1994); *My Life as a Boy: A Woman's Story* (1997); *The Obsession: Reflections on the Tyranny of Slenderness* (1981); "The Politics of the Small." *Tikkun* (1993); *Reinventing Eve: Modern Woman in Search of Herself* (1987); *Sex and Other Sacred Games: Love, Desire, Power and Possession*, with Renate Stendhal (1989).

BIBLIOGRAPHY

Barker-Nunn, Jeanne. "Telling the Mother's Story: History and Connection in the Autobiographies of Maxine Hong Kingston and Kim Chernin." *Women's Studies* 14, no. 1 (1987): 55–63; Chernin, Kim. Telephone interviews with author (May 18, 1992; May 1, 1996); *Contemporary Authors* (1983); Faderman, Lillian. "Clouded Hindsight." *Los Angeles Times*, February 27, 1994, 10; Gagnier, Regenia. "Feminist Autobiography in the 80's." *Feminist Studies* 17 (Spring 1991): 135–148; Jamison, Kay Redfield. "Physician, Know Thyself." *Washington Post*, March 19, 1995, 5; Mantell, Suzanne. "PW Interviews Kim Chernin." *Publishers Weekly* 228, no. 1 (July 5, 1985): 72–73; Penn, Shana. Review of *Sex and Other Sacred Games*. *Women's Review of Books* 7, no. 6 (March 1990): 28; Waldron, Karen. "Kim Chernin." *American Women Writers: Supplement*. Edited by Carol Hurd Green and Mary G. Mason (1994).

KAREN E. WALDRON

CHERNIN, ROSE (1901–1995)

Ambivalent about Judaism, passionately Marxist, charismatic, courageous, Rose Chernin devoted a great deal of her life to securing the rights of disenfranchised citizens: the unemployed of the Depression, farmworkers without a union, black home buyers thwarted by redlining, and other foreign-born leftists, like herself, who faced deportation in the 1950s.

Rochele Chernin was born in 1901 in Chasnik, Russia. She was renamed Rose when she and her three younger siblings, renamed Celia, Gertrude, and Milton, and their mother, Perle, landed at Ellis Island in 1913. They were met by Chernin's father, Max, after five years of separation. The family moved to Waterbury, Connecticut, where Chernin's father opened a dry-goods store. Her mother stayed home, suffering from her isolation in an unfamiliar world. Upon finishing grade school in Waterbury, Connecticut, fourteen-year-old Rose Chernin worked on a munitions assembly line. Chernin, a foreign-born, unskilled laborer, boldly requested admission to Crosby, the local preparatory school, over the local trade school. It was at Crosby that Chernin first met Paul Kusnitz, also from a Russian Jewish family. He introduced

Chernin to socialist ideas through the newspaper the *New York Call.*

Chernin's education was jeopardized when her father deserted the family and moved to Canonsville, Pennsylvania, where he opened another store. Resolutely, young Rose Chernin threatened him with jail if he did not send for his wife and their four younger children, who now included baby Lillian. Chernin herself wanted to stay in Waterbury to complete high school. In 1921, after her mother and siblings left for Pennsylvania, Chernin graduated and went to New York City. She entered HUNTER COLLEGE and found work in a perfume factory. All around her, Chernin saw New Yorkers organizing against unfair labor practices and dismal living conditions. Drawn to join them, she became active in a political group called the Russian Club, a commitment that precluded her continuing to study at Hunter. She left college, regretting that decision always.

At age twenty-two, Rose Chernin heard from Paul Kusnitz, who had since received a degree in engineering from the Massachusetts Institute of Technology. On June 20, 1925, they married. Their happy marriage was based on the couple's common socialist interests and mutual respect. They moved to the Bronx, and Paul began working on the subway. Shortly thereafter, her mother was placed, involuntarily, by her father, into a state psychiatric hospital in Binghamton, New York. Aghast at the conditions there, Rose Chernin successfully arranged for her mother's release, the first of many such battles she would fight on behalf of those weakened by unjust treatment and unable to defend themselves.

In 1929, at the beginning of the Great Depression, Chernin and Kusnitz had their first child, Nina. As a young mother, Chernin organized pickets to protest price gouging in poor neighborhoods, led tenant negotiations, and supported rent strikes. She also helped form unemployed councils, petitioning congressional representatives to provide either more jobs or unemployment insurance. In 1932, Rose Chernin joined the Communist Party, campaigning for election as alderwoman in the Bronx. Then Kusnitz lost his job. The family moved to the Soviet Union, where Kusnitz worked on the Moscow subway, while Chernin worked in a publishing house.

On a visit to Los Angeles in 1934, Chernin saw fourteen communist activists like herself arrested and tried under the Criminal Syndicalist Laws, which outlawed organizing. Hearing the prisoners' call for her help, Chernin decided to stay in California and form a defense committee. Within the year, the prisoners were released. By this time, Rose Chernin had decided that she could not give up her work in America. Kusnitz returned from Moscow, and once again the family lived together in the Bronx.

Their second daughter, KIM CHERNIN, was born in 1940. Soon Chernin was asked to become the organizational secretary for the Communist Party of the Bronx. But in 1944, tragedy struck when Nina died of Hodgkin's disease. Rose Chernin retreated from political work, and the family moved to California, determined to leave the place associated with their profoundest sorrow.

Two years later, when African-American neighbors in Los Angeles had a cross burned on their property, Chernin began organizing to protect housing rights. Renewed in her work, Chernin spearheaded a campaign to support Henry Carlisle, a British-born movie writer targeted for deportation as a communist. Once again visible in the people's struggle, Chernin became executive secretary of the Committee for the Protection of the Foreign Born, which she founded in 1950. Rose Chernin's known success as an organizer led to her arrest in July 1951, when she was charged with forming a conspiracy to overthrow the government. With her bail set at $100,000, Chernin remained in jail until February 1952 when the trial began. Six months later, she was convicted, sentenced to five years in prison, jailed again, but released on bail five weeks later.

Not long after, Chernin was subpoenaed to appear before the House Un-American Activities Committee, but she refused to give the names of other communists. Another denaturalization proceeding followed, this time with the Immigration and Naturalization Service attempting to deport Chernin by arguing that when she applied for United States citizenship in 1928, she intended to join the Communist Party, thus violating the Smith Act of 1940. However, the judge refused to denaturalize her, reprimanding the government for having presented no evidence of her guilt. By 1957, the Supreme Court heard *Yates* v. *United States*, in which Rose Chernin was named. In a landmark decision, Chernin's earlier conviction was overturned, ruling the Smith Act unconstitutional.

In 1967, Paul Kusnitz died in a car accident. In 1983, she saw the publication of *In My Mother's House,* Kim Chernin's deeply touching memoir that captures Rose Chernin's Yiddish-inflected voice telling her sister's heroic story. Appropriately, her last years were spent in a Los Angeles retirement home that resembled a collective. Among the residents were aged leftist friends, delighted to see their old comrade among them.

Rose Chernin died of Alzheimer's disease on September 8, 1995, in Los Angeles, at almost ninety-four years of age.

BIBLIOGRAPHY

Chernin, Kim. *In My Mother's House: A Daughter's Story* (1983); Obituary. *NYTimes*, September 16, 1995, and *San Francisco Chronicle*, September 14, 1995.

JERILYN FISHER

CHESLER, PHYLLIS (b. 1940)

Phyllis Chesler, a radical feminist and liberation psychologist, is a prolific writer, seasoned activist and organizer, and committed Jew and Zionist. She is the author of eight books, including *Women and Madness* (1972), *Women, Money and Power* (1976), *About Men* (1978), *Mothers on Trial: The Battle for Children and Custody* (1986), *Patriarchy: Notes of an Expert Witness* (1994), and *Letters to A Young Feminist* (1998). She publishes in both popular and academic journals and is the editor-at-large for *On the Issues* magazine. Lecturing widely on women's legal rights and emotional health, Chesler also serves as an expert witness on women's and family issues.

Born on October 1, 1940, Chesler and her two younger brothers grew up in an Orthodox Jewish family in Borough Park, Brooklyn. Her mother, Lillian (Hammer), was a school secretary, and her father Leon was a truck driver. She traces her activism back to her experiences as a child when, at age eight, she joined Hashomer Hatzair, a Zionist youth organization, and later Ain Harod, a leftist Zionist youth group advocating Arab-Jewish kibbutzim. According to Chesler, when it became clear to her that, as an Orthodox Jew, she would not be bat mitzvahed, she broke from the formal aspects of Judaism.

Much of Chesler's university career has been spent at Richmond College, The College of Staten Island, part of the City University of New York (CUNY), where she is a tenured professor in psychology and women's studies. In addition to teaching at the college, Chesler has been active in the founding of the College Birth Control and Ob/Gyn Self-Help Clinic, the College Child Care Center, the Rape Counseling Project, and the Counseling for Battered Women Project. A cofounder of one of the first women's studies programs in the country and teacher of one of the first "accredited" women's studies classes, Chesler was instrumental in the creation of women's studies programs throughout the CUNY system.

Phyllis Chesler, author of the feminist classic Women and Madness, *revolutionized the way the mental health system treats women. In the 1970s, she cofounded the Association for Women in Psychology and the National Women's Health Network.* [Bettye Lane]

As a psychotherapist who completed her graduate work in psychology at the New School for Social Research, Chesler counts among her most prized accomplishments writing and "giving speeches that saved women's lives or sanity, and contributed to feminist awakening, among women and men." Her first book, *Women and Madness*, has sold two and a half million copies and has been translated into six languages. It is one of the earliest works of the modern American feminist movement to address issues such as the mistreatment of women, particularly in rape and incest; female role models; and spirituality in the mental health services.

Since the publication of *Women and Madness*, Chesler has advocated for change in the treatment of women in mental health services through the

Association for Women in Psychology (which she cofounded), the National Women's Health Network, and the National Center for Protective Parents in Civil Child Sexual Abuse Cases.

Chesler has always believed that "the kind of feminist I am has everything to do with my Jewish passion for justice." Her direct involvement with Jewish feminism began in 1971, when she encountered anti-Semitism on the Left and in the women's movement. She began to wear a large star around her neck to identify herself as Jewish. Her first visit to Israel in December 1972 began a long-standing connection with the then nascent Israeli feminist movement.

A participant in the 1973–1974 National Jewish Feminist Conference in New York City, Chesler first publicly wrote about being a radical feminist and a Zionist Jew in LILITH (winter 1976–1977). In that article she advocated the creation of "feminist sovereign space," drawing a parallel between feminism and Zionism. After attending the 1980 UN Conference on Women in Copenhagen, Chesler wrote a second article in *Lilith*, this time using a pseudonym, to expose the anti-Semitism of the conference. Chesler was one of the organizers of Feminists Against Anti-Semitism, a group that defined itself as Zionist and feminist and coordinated a panel on feminism and anti-Semitism for the 1981 National Women's Studies Association conference. In 1997 she was appointed the first Research Associate at Brandeis' International Research Institute on Jewish Women.

Chesler has been creating alternative rituals for Jewish holidays and life-cycle events since her involvement in the first feminist seder in New York City in 1975. She is active in the struggle for equal rights of access to women at the Western Wall as a founding member and a director of the Board of the International Committee for the Women of the Wall.

Married and divorced twice, Chesler has one son, Ariel David Chesler, who is a student at Brandeis University. A single mother who was diagnosed with chronic fatigue immune dysfunction syndrome in 1991, Chesler cautions, "holding one's own against patriarchy, just holding one's own, is not easy. Resisting it—building a resistance movement—takes all we have. And more."

SELECTED WORKS BY PHYLLIS CHESLER

About Men (1978); Foreword to *Jewish Women Speak Out: Expanding the Boundaries of Psychology* (1995), edited by Kayla Weiner and Arinna Moon; *Mothers on Trial: The Battle for Children and Custody* (1986); *Patriarchy: Notes of an Expert Witness* (1994); "Telling It Like It Was." *On the Issues* (Summer 1995); *Women and Madness* (1972); *Women, Money and Power* (1976).

BIBLIOGRAPHY

Chesler, Phyllis. Interview by author, November 1996; Cole, Ellen. "A Leader of Women" [Interview of Phyllis Chesler]. In *Feminist Foremothers in Women's Studies, Psychology and Mental Health*, edited by Phyllis Chesler, Esther D. Rothblum, and Ellen Cole (1995).

TAMARA COHEN

CHICAGO, JUDY (b. 1939)

For three decades Judy Chicago has melded politics with art through painting, sculpture, writing, and teaching.

Born Judy Cohen on July 20, 1939, in Chicago, Illinois, she later broke with patrilineal tradition by adopting the surname Chicago. To explain her seemingly innate belief in herself and her dismissal of sexist stereotypes, Chicago has pointed to the lack of gender bias in her family. An avid Marxist, Chicago's father, Arthur, encouraged his only daughter to participate in the political discussions that pervaded their middle-class home. Arthur, descended from twenty-three generations of rabbis—one of whom was the eighteenth-century Lithuanian rabbi the Gaon of Vilna—rejected Orthodox Jewish life. As a former dancer, Chicago's mother, May, prompted Chicago and her younger brother, Ben, to pursue artistic interests.

Chicago's art education commenced at the Art Institute of Chicago and continued at the University of California at Los Angeles, where she completed a master of fine arts degree in 1964. Her marriage to Jerry Gerowitz in 1961 ended abruptly when he was killed in a car accident two years later. Chicago explains that she turned to art for solace and produced minimalist sculpture—aspiring to gain acceptance from the male-dominated art world. Soon, however, she changed her objective: "I could no longer pretend in my art that being a woman had no meaning in my life" (*Through the Flower* 51). She began to examine what it meant to be both a woman and an artist. Wanting to aid other women on their artistic journeys, Chicago developed the Fresno Feminist Art Program at California State University in 1970. Artist Miriam Schapiro joined Chicago the following year, when the program was moved to the California Institute of the Arts in Valencia. Here female students relied upon personal experience for subject matter, culminating with the exhibition *Womanhouse* (1972). Via installation and performance, the Feminist Art Program transformed a dilapidated house into an environment expressing their individual perspectives as women.

With the women's movement in full swing, Chicago became increasingly disturbed by the absence of women from historical accounts. By 1976, Chicago had separated from her second husband, Lloyd Hamrol, and was conducting research that uncovered a wealth of significant women neglected by historians. She resolved to honor many such women in a monumental work, *The Dinner Party* (1974–1979). Hundreds of volunteers collaborated with Chicago to commemorate individual women through personalized place settings that are distributed around a large triangular table. Each setting consists of an embroidered runner and a vaginal/butterfly-designed ceramic plate. Such sexually dynamic imagery challenges feminine stereotypes, but also raises complex questions about essentialism. Undeniably a landmark in feminist art history, *The Dinner Party* continues to empower women while remaining controversial to this day.

Creating iconographic imagery where there had been little before is a pattern in Chicago's art. Upon realizing that the birthing process was seldom depicted in Western art, Chicago decided to portray it in a new communal endeavor, *The Birth Project* (1980–1985). She designed images of women in labor that were then translated into needlework by women across the country. The goal, asserts Chicago, was to recast the story of Genesis by challenging "the notion of a male god creating a male human being with no reference to women's participation in this process" (*Beyond the Flower*, 84–85).

Chicago altered her focus when she began to investigate the construction of masculinity and its

This detail from Judy Chicago's mixed-media work The Holocaust Project, *an image of a train going through the woods in Frankfurt, Germany, translates a historical truth into visual reality—"the indifference of the Allies, the Vatican and the International Red Cross to the transport of Jews to the death camps." [Donald Woodman]*

relationship to power in the painted series *Powerplay*. This course of inquiry led her to the tragedy of the Holocaust and her realization of the insufficient knowledge she had concerning this event as well as her heritage in general. Settling in New Mexico, Chicago planned to explore her Jewish identity in tandem with her soon-to-be husband, photographer Donald Woodman. By the time they were married on New Year's Eve, 1985, the couple had agreed to join their efforts in order to visually represent the Holocaust—a subject rarely broached in fine art. After years of study, Chicago and Woodman produced *The Holocaust Project: From Darkness into Light* (1985–1993), a mixed-media installation that confronts formidable issues surrounding the abuse of power and its horrific manifestations.

Looking to the future, Chicago is working on *Resolutions for the Millennium*. By reinterpreting traditional proverbs, she hopes to "present images of a world transformed into a global community of caring people" (*Beyond* 262). Indeed, as Chicago suggests, it is the Jewish concept of *tikkun*—the healing of the world—that consistently motivates her most profound art.

SELECTED WORKS BY JUDY CHICAGO

Beyond the Flower: The Autobiography of a Feminist Artist (1996); *The Birth Project* (1980–1985); *The Dinner Party* (1974–1979); *Embroidering Our Heritage: The Dinner Party Needlework* (1980); *Holocaust Project: From Darkness into Light* (1985–1993); *The Second Decade, 1973–1983* (1984); *Through the Flower: My Struggle as a Woman Artist* (1975).

BIBLIOGRAPHY

Bronx Museum of the Arts. *Division of Labor: 'Women's Work' in Contemporary Art* (1995); Jones, Amelia. *Sexual Politics: Judy Chicago's Dinner Party in Feminist Art History* (1996); Lippard, Lucy. *From the Center: Feminist Essays on Women's Art* (1976), and "Judy Chicago's 'Dinner Party.'" *Art in America* 68:4 (April 1980): 114–126; Mathews, Patricia. "Judy Chicago." In *North American Women Artists of the Twentieth Century: A Biographical Dictionary*, edited by Jules Heller and Nancy G. Heller (1995); *The Power of Feminist Art: The American Movement of the 1970s, History and Impact*, edited by Norma Broude and Mary D. Garrard (1994); Robinson, Marlee. "Judy Chicago." In *Contemporary Artists*, edited by Muriel Emanuel et al. 2d ed. (1983); Rubinstein, Charlotte Streifer. *American Women Artists: From Early Indian Times to the Present* (1982), and *American Women Sculptors: A History of Women Working in Three Dimensions* (1990).

Judy Chicago donated her papers to the Schlesinger Library at Radcliffe College in 1977.

DEBRA WACKS

Judy Chicago has melded politics with art through painting, sculpture, writing, and teaching. It is the Jewish concept of tikkun—the healing of the world—that motivates her. [Donald Woodman]

CHILDREN'S LITERATURE

It is hard to imagine the world of children's books without Jewish women writers. Gone would be *Jennifer, Hecate, MacBeth, William McKinley and Me, Elizabeth* (1967) and *From the Mixed-Up Files of Mrs. Basil E. Frankweiler* (1967) as conceived by Elaine L. Konigsburg. Barbara Cohen's famous Joe, *The Carp in the Bathtub* (1972), never would have splashed happily unaware that Passover was almost upon him. SYDNEY TAYLOR's *All-of-a-Kind Family* (1951) would not have introduced hundreds of thousands of children to the lives of five little girls in a Jewish immigrant family in New York. Hundreds of characters and situations familiar to and beloved by children around the world would not exist.

The majority of Jewish women writers are noted for their many books of broad general interest (E.L. Konigsburg, Katheryn Lasky, Johanna Hurwitz, Marilyn Sachs, Barbara Cohen, Sonia Levitin, CHARLOTTE ZOLOTOW), but few have not produced at least one or two books springing specifically from their own Jewish sensibilities and experiences. A select group have devoted themselves entirely to topics dealing directly with Judaism. Others have placed some of their most universally popular stories, whether emphasizing school adventures, social and ethical development issues, early childhood concerns, or family relationships, into settings where the families, attitudes, customs, and concerns are either peripherally or implicitly Jewish.

IN THE BEGINNING: 1930 TO 1960

American children's literature as a separate literary category is a recent phenomenon. American women writers began to produce generally preachy and/or sentimental works for young people in the eighteenth century, following upon previous moralistic, religious, and educational tracts, but no known American Jewish women writers for children emerged until the great waves of nineteenth- and twentieth-century immigration had quieted.

Jewish children in Europe historically had been introduced directly to text study and had learned their religion through practice and community. But in America in the early 1930s and on through the 1950s, writers like Sadie Rose Weilerstein, Lillian Freehof, Deborah Pessin, MAMIE GAMORAN, Shulamith Ish-Kishor, and ELMA EHRLICH LEVINGER produced biblical retellings, family fiction, legends, and nonfiction primarily designed to teach Judaism in this far different environment. Weilerstein's *Adventures of K'tonton* (1935), the tale of a thumbling boy and his doting observant parents, and Gamoran's *Hillel's Happy Holidays* (1939), also a family-based holiday guide, while recently thought of questionable literary merit, succeeded in accomplishing their apparent goal: coating Jewish knowledge with honey to help the learning go down. Ish-Kishor (1896–1977) was particularly proficient and prolific in producing Judaica for children, but her finest work was not to come until the 1960s, when *A Boy of Old Prague* (1963), a powerful historical novel about anti-Semitism in the 1600s, was named an American Library Association Notable Book. Later, *Our Eddie* (1969), a moving novel about a sensitive boy and his difficult father, won the 1969 Association of Jewish Libraries (AJL) Children's Book Award and was a 1970 Newbery Honor Book.

Beginning in the 1950s, some writers, such as Libby Mindlin Klaperman (1921–1982), who wrote primarily pedagogical works for Jewish educational publishers, also put out a few biographies or histories with general publishers. Others, like Dorothy Karp Kripke, author of the *Let's Talk About* series, remained focused on Jewish teaching tools. As the decade progressed, however, more children's books by Jewish women were published as broad-appeal trade books. A groundbreaking series in this pivotal time was the work of an author almost by accident, Sydney Taylor (1904–1978).

An actress and professional dancer with Martha Graham's company, Taylor had recorded the adventures of her family of five sisters for her daughter. Later, her husband, reading about a contest being conducted by Follett, submitted the manuscript without her knowledge. To her surprise, it won publication as *All-of-a-Kind Family* (1951), garnering awards and launching her on a new career. The several books containing the adventures of this warm New York immigrant family are still popular among children today. The last book in the series, *Ella of All-of-a-Kind Family* (1978), focusing on the eldest daughter as she faces difficult choices about her future, was published the year of Taylor's death. In 1979, AJL honored her posthumously for her body of work and renamed their annual Children's Book Award the Sydney Taylor Award in her memory.

After writing a number of sailing stories, in the early 1950s Nora Benjamin Kubie (1899–1988), inspired by living in an area rich in American history and by reading about Jewish involvement in the Revolution, wrote *Joel* (1952), one of the few children's novels presenting young Jews as active in the birth of this country. Later, Kubie went to Israel and began writing nonfiction works on the country and its archaeology, as well as Jewish children's historical fiction, including the award-winning *King Solomon's Navy* (1954).

The late 1950s saw only a few mainstream books about Jewish American boys and girls, among them Mina Lewiton's *Rachel and Herman* (1957), Leota Harris Keir's *Freckle Face Frankel* (1959), and Sydney Taylor's family novels.

THE ERA OF ISRAEL, UNREST, AND UNDERSTANDING: THE 1960s AND 1970s

Jewish women wrote many children's books during this period and built important reputations in the field.

Molly Cone (b. 1918), well known for her highly praised *Mishmash* (1962) series about a large and lovable dog, and for numerous other popular works for children and young adults, also produced important specifically Jewish materials: a holiday series for Crowell Publishing; a classic collection of original tales, *Who Knows Ten: Children's Tales of the Ten Commandments* (1965), and a series of storybooks called *Hear O Israel* (1972–1973), for the Union of Hebrew Congregations; and several trade-published books about Israel including *The House in the Tree: A Story of Israel* (1968), *You Can't Make Me If I Don't Want To* (1971), and *Dance Around the Fire* (1974). Cone won an AJL award for her contributions to children's literature (1972) and continued to write both general and Jewish fiction and nonfiction, including a work on Jewish identity and several on nature and ecology published in the 1990s.

In addition to novels and picture books, Malka Drucker (b. 1945) wrote a distinguished holiday series, winning recognition from the Southern California Council on Literature for Children and Young People in 1982. Miriam Chaikin (b. 1928), winner of the Sydney Taylor Award for Body of Work (1984), produced a lively group of books on the holidays, as well as a popular series of Molly books, readable stories with strong moral underpinnings, and, later, a number of cautionary tales about a lovable Orthodox boy named Yossi. Both the Molly and the Yossi stories brought the concept of *middos* books, books that teach overtly Jewish ethical lessons, into trade publication and distribution by making them enjoyable and relatively free of didacticism.

Immigrants are always making transitions, feeling out of place, learning to fit in, processing new experiences. So are children. Chaya Burstein with her Rifka books (*Rifka Grows Up*, 1977), Marietta Moskin with *Waiting for Mama* (1975), Anita Heyman with *Exit from Home*, (1977) and Carol Snyder with *Ike and Mama and the Block Wedding* (1979), all award winners, wrote hopefully about immigration near the beginning of the century, picturing a promising New Land. Rose Blue (b. 1931), whose work includes books on black children and *Grandma Didn't Wave Back* (1972), about old age and nursing homes, later wrote on a more sober note about contemporary transplanted Soviet Jewish immigrants in *Cold Rain on the Water* (1979). Her story ends sadly, lacking the sentimental nostalgia often present in tales about those who came earlier.

During the 1960s and 1970s, Jewish women writers, perhaps caught up in the increasing mood of social protest, ethnic pride, and emancipation for women, seemed to be writing more powerful juveniles about Israel, about immigration, about assimilation, and about the Jewish American child in the broader

society. Pluralism became a reality in children's literature, often made salable through the medium of folktale. Not all families were perfect, and the "problem novel" dealing with death, divorce, drugs, and disillusionment did not leave Jewish families inviolate. Even those novels dealing with the past, harkening back to immigrant days, were more honest about confronting the problems involved in the transition. Marilyn Sachs's *Call Me Ruth* (1982) won an AJL Award by showing a young girl's desperate effort to become Americanized. As she tries to emulate her WASP teacher and disown her Yiddish-speaking union firebrand mother, we see the exploitation of immigrant workers, the courage of sweatshop organizers, and the tension caused in families where New World children and Old World parents have different goals and values.

Barbara Cohen's first published work was the classic *Carp in the Bathtub*, but Cohen (1932–1992) also became known for her insightful intermediate and young adult novels about alienation, resolution, Jewish identity, and survival. *King of the Seventh Grade* (1982) is about a rebellious boy, son of an intermarriage, who finally chooses to become a Jew and celebrate his bar mitzvah. *Thank You Jackie Robinson* (1974), *My Name Is Rosie* (1978), and *The Innkeeper's Daughter* (1979) are loosely based on the lonely lives Cohen and her siblings led as children of a Jewish innkeeper in a small anti-Semitic town. As in *Bitter Herbs and Honey* (1976), the story of a young girl whose ambitions for herself are far different from those of her immigrant parents, the struggle is one against constraints, with resultant anger and guilt, all emotions universally recognizable to any child. Cohen's interests included Israel, folklore, and social concerns. *The Secret Grove* (1985) is told by a grown Israeli soldier sadly remembering when, as a boy, he shared a moment of friendship and an orange with an Arab boy who may now be his enemy. In *Unicorns in the Rain* (1980), Cohen forecast an increasingly armed society and set it in a mythic environment based on the story of Noah; in *The Long Way Home* (1990), Cohen confronted honestly the fears raised in a family of girls when the mother develops breast cancer.

After publishing an earlier historical novel, *The King's Persons* (1963), under her own name, Joanne Greenberg (b. 1932) who is also an adult novelist, used the pseudonym Hannah Green to confront harsh realities in *I Never Promised You a Rose Garden* (1964), a controversial and startling work for young adults about her own adolescent mental problems. A later, also largely autobiographical children's novel, which stunned readers by departing from previous stereotypes of the Jewish family as being warmly nurturing, was *Summer of My German Soldier* (1973) by Bette Greene (b. 1934). This World War II story of an abusive Jewish family in Arkansas, whose unhappy daughter finds her only friends in an escaped German POW and a supportive housekeeper, created quite a backlash but was critically acknowledged and has remained popular with young readers who feel equally isolated and misunderstood. Following a sequel, Greene wrote other, far lighter works set in the South but without Jewish content.

Hila Colman began her writing career in 1957 and has written prolifically ever since, primarily for adolescents. She explored the runaway generation of the 1960s (*Claudia, Where Are You?*, 1969), troubled mother-daughter relations (*Sometimes I Don't Love My Mother*, 1977), and remarriage and its difficulties (*Weekend Sisters*, 1985). The daughter of a well-to-do Jewish family, Colman based two novels, *Rachel's Legacy* (1978) and *Ellie's Inheritance* (1979), loosely on her own mother's rise from immigrant child to successful clothing designer and businesswoman, her early death, and its effect on the family's fortunes and her daughter's development.

Norma Klein (1938–1989) and Gloria D. Miklowitz (b. 1927) also dealt with modern life's issues honestly. Klein, the daughter of a Freudian psychoanalyst, found many of her books regarded as very unconventional, especially her first novel, *Mom, the Wolf Man and Me* (1972), in which the heroine's mother is unmarried. The book, written for middle-aged readers, was forced into the young adult category by the irregularity of this situation, but Klein nonetheless felt lucky and said she was sure she and many of her contemporaries, such as JUDY BLUME, were published only due to the delayed influence of the 1960s when openness and boldness were encouraged. Klein's work, like that of many other Jewish women writers, while not often overtly Jewish in content, is informed by an urban sensibility reflecting authorial worldviews.

Gloria Miklowitz first published in 1964 for younger children. By the late 1970s, she was writing for young adults, exploring such difficult subjects as rape in *Did You Hear What Happened to Andrea?* (1979). Racism, nuclear holocaust, AIDS, abuse, and religious cults are among the topics she has tackled in highly readable novels. Of particular Jewish interest is *Close to the Edge* (1983), the story of a half-Jewish girl in a wealthy Los Angeles family whose inner emptiness makes a mockery of her "golden girl" image until, while grudgingly playing piano at a Jewish senior center at Venice Beach, she begins to learn

about courage, resiliency, and love from the old Jews she meets there.

A number of other writers began to write during this period, producing many books and building their careers throughout the 1980s and 1990s. Among them are Sue Alexander, whose *Nadia the Willful* (1983) is a timeless story of loss, grief, and healing; Judy Blume; Charlotte Herman, author of *The Difference of Ari Stein* (1976), *Our Snowman Had Olive Eyes* (1977), and *What Happened to Heather Hopkowitz* (1981); Johanna Hurwitz, author of *Once I Was a Plum Tree* (1980) and many other works; and Norma Fox Mazer, whose output was considerable during the 1970s and whose novel *After the Rain* (1987) deals sensitively with a young girl's relationship with her grandfather. The question of Jewish identity and assimilation is central to many of these works, and grandparents figure largely in a number of the books listed here, emphasizing the importance of traditions and of family ties, however imperfect.

Judith Viorst (b. 1931), best known for poetry and journalism, also wrote many children's books filled with warm understanding and humor. Among the best known are *The Tenth Good Thing About Barney* (1971), a classic picture book about the death of a beloved pet, and *Alexander and the Terrible, Horrible, No Good, Very Bad Day* (1972). Other poets who became well known for a large body of children's books were MAXINE KUMIN, who occasionally wrote with Anne Sexton, and Myra Cohn Livingston (1926–1996), whose output included volumes of poetry selected and/or composed for children, anthologies, and critical texts such as *The Child as Poet: Myth of Reality*. Livingston won numerous awards for her contributions to making poetry an important part of children's education and literature and was an outstanding educator at UCLA for many years.

HOLOCAUST AND SURVIVAL

The 1970s saw a great many works on the Holocaust by American writers, Jewish and non-Jewish, many by writers born in Europe who escaped either just before or just after World War II, eventually becoming naturalized Americans. Among the latter was Esther Rudomin Hautzig (b. 1930) whose award-winning *The Endless Steppe: Growing Up in Siberia* (1968) tells of her Polish family's arrest by the Soviets and exile to the Altai region of Siberia, where they survived for six years while the Nazis destroyed the family left behind. Hautzig's works include other books of Jewish interest, among them *A Gift for Mama* (1981), *Remember Who You Are: Stories About Being Jewish* (1990), and *Riches* (1992).

Sonia Levitin (b. 1934) published *Journey to America* in 1970, basing it on her family's flight from Berlin when she was three and their subsequent lives as refugees. While she avoids heavy-handedness and many of her picture books and novels contain humor or are folkloric in mood, early exposure to danger and separation influenced the author's concerns and often have led her to deal with serious subjects such as war, aging, love, sacrifice, and freedom. Honors have been given Levitin for such varied work as *Journey to America*, the western *No-Return Trail* (1978), the murder mystery *Incident at Loring Grove* (1988), and *The Return* (1988), about a young Ethiopian Jewish girl's trek to Israel. Ironically, among Levitin's numerous awards was the Catholic Children's Book Prize in Germany.

Doris Orgel (b. 1929) began her career retelling European tales for children. Her original work includes poetry, picture books, middle-grade fiction, and young adult novels. One of her best-known works, however, is *The Devil in Vienna* (1978), an AJL Award winner inspired by her own family's flight from Vienna in the late 1930s. In it, the friendship between two girls is tested as Lieselotte's family becomes rabidly Nazi and Jewish Inge's family frantically tries to escape. A Disney TV film titled *Friendship in Vienna* was based on this book.

Johanna De Leeuw Reiss (b. 1932), born in Holland, wrote two fictional books, *The Upstairs Room* (1972) and *The Journey Back* (1976), based on the years she and her sister spent hidden from the Nazis by a Christian couple in their farmhouse and on what happened to them after they were freed. Reiss's vivid recollections of these experiences, told through the eyes of a ten-year-old child, won acclaim from both Jewish and secular organizations. Marietta Moskin also lived in Holland, but began writing while interred in camps; her Holocaust novel *I Am Rosemarie* (1972) reflected her wartime experiences.

American-born Marilyn Sachs (b. 1927), a prolific and much-prized author, is known for her realistic family novels and accurate depiction of the travails of childhood and adolescence. Many of her family stories are set in New York in a Jewish milieu, and her first book, *Amy Moves In* (1964), waited ten years for publication until the time was ripe for its honest portrayal of an imperfect family. Socially conscious in her life and much of her work, Sachs based her *Call Me Ruth* (1982) on an actual textile workers' strike; *Thunderbird* (1985) protests against nuclear weapons; and *At the Sound of the Beep* (1990) deals with the homeless. Her Holocaust novel *A Pocket Full of Seeds* (1973) was based on the life of a friend and tells of a young French girl who spends the war hidden in a boarding school.

Judith Kerr's family left Germany in time; their story is told in *When Hitler Stole Pink Rabbit* (1971) and continued in *The Other Way Round* (1975) and *A Small Person Far Away* (1978).

Jane Yolen (b. 1939), noted for works of fantasy, describes the horrors of a Nazi concentration camp as experienced by a contemporary child in her powerful award-winning time-travel novel *The Devil's Arithmetic* (1988). *Briar Rose* (1992) is another Yolen story with Jewish meaning underlying the fantasy. Olga Levy Drucker's *Kindertransport* (1992), Aranka Siegal's *Upon the Head of the Goat: A Childhood in Hungary, 1939–1944* (1981), and Isabella Leitner's *The Big Lie: A True Story* (1992) are all successful in depicting this difficult topic for young readers.

Overviews of the period include *A Nightmare in History* (1987) by Miriam Chaikin and *Smoke and Ashes* (1988) by Barbara Rogasky.

PICTURE BOOKS
WORTH A THOUSAND WORDS

Barbara Cohen, before writing novels, in 1972 penned *The Carp in the Bathtub*, an ageless "don't eat my pet for the holiday" picture book, which has appeared in over four hundred collections and pedagogical anthologies. Subsequently, Cohen produced outstanding picture books on biblical themes (*The Binding of Isaac*, 1978), holidays (*Yussel's Prayer*, 1981; *Here Come the Purim Players!*, 1984), and Israel (*The Secret Grove*, 1985), winning the 1981 Sydney Taylor Body of Work Award. *Molly's Pilgrim* (1983), a Thanksgiving story about Russian immigrants, relates the American holiday to the Jewish holiday of Sukkoth and was made into a short live-action film, which won an Academy Award in 1985. *Make a Wish, Molly* (1993) was published posthumously.

Charlotte Zolotow (b. 1915), author and editor, is one of the most well-known Jewish women writers who do not write on specifically Jewish themes. She made her mark exploring in picture books the universal world of children's lives and emotions. One theme important in Zolotow's work is that of family generations and heritage. Gentle works like *The Sky Was Blue* (1963) and *This Quiet Lady* (1992) show that although people change through time, feelings remain the same. In her classic *My Grandson Lew* (1974), she broke ground as one of the first authors to address, in picture books, the forbidden topic of death. Zolotow tells of a small boy, wakened by memories of his dead grandfather, relieving his grief by talking about his sense of loss with his mother. Another important topic she broached was that of sex-role rigidity. In *William's Doll* (1972), William's father and friends believe that liking to play with dolls is just for girls; his wise grandmother knows better.

Miriam Cohen (b. 1926) is best known for writing warmly reassuring works such as *Will I Have a Friend?* (1967) and *The New Teacher* (1972), both illustrated by Lillian Hoban.

Other Jewish women contributed greatly to the world of picture books, both as writers and as illustrators. Artist-writer MARILYN HIRSH (1944–1988) was best known for her books on Jewish themes, especially folktales, village life, the adventures of Jewish immigrant children, and Jewish holidays. She produced over thirty books, some of them Indian folktales while in India in the Peace Corps, and in 1980 won the first Sydney Taylor Body of Work Award given by AJL. Among her best-known titles are *Where Is Yonkele?* (1969) and *Could Anything Be Worse?* (1974); she also illustrated books by other authors, such as David Adler's *The House on the Roof* (1976).

Beverly Brodsky (b. 1941) contributed her bold visions and dramatic text to a number of picture books of Jewish import, including *Jonah* (1977), *Secret Places* (1979), and a stunning picture book for older children, *The Golem* (1975), a powerful study of the famous Jewish legendary protector gone amok.

Karla Kuskin (b. 1932) has been writing and illustrating her own works, as well as providing art for other writers, since her first book, *Roar and More*, in 1956. Known for rhythmic verse and drawings that appeal to a child's sense of humor, her body of work includes only two works that might be thought specifically of Jewish import: *The Animals and the Ark* (1958) and *Jerusalem, Shining Still* (1987), a work illustrated by David Frampton's woodcuts and designed to make the city's history accessible to all children. Marc Simont illustrated her well-received *The Philharmonic Gets Dressed* (1982), called "a symphony in words and pictures," in which 105 orchestra members bathe, shave, dry their hair, and go forth from their homes to meet and make beautiful music.

Margot Zemach (1931–1989) was primarily an illustrator, often of folktale adaptations by her husband, Harve, and many stories and tales by various well-known writers including Isaac Bashevis Singer and Yuri Suhl. However, she also adapted tales herself, the most Jewish of which was *It Could Always Be Worse: A Yiddish Folktale* (1976). She was winner of a Fulbright scholarship, various honors, and the Caldecott Medal in 1974.

Anita Lobel (b. 1934), Polish-born survivor of a German concentration camp, married Arnold Lobel,

himself an author and illustrator of children's books, in New York after she immigrated. Since 1965, she has written and illustrated many wonderfully theatrical picture books, as well as illustrating texts by her husband. Their joint venture *On Market Street* (1981) was a 1982 Caldecott Honor Book.

Sheila Greenwald (b. 1934) wrote and illustrated a number of middle-school books, many of them featuring Rosy Cole, an imaginative and trouble-prone heroine whose best intentions often go awry.

Patricia Polacco (b. 1944) draws on her Russian background for many of her picture books, and her AJL Award winner *The Keeping Quilt* (1988) reflects her Jewish heritage as well. Cross-cultural friendship between an old Jewish woman and a young African American boy is the focus of *Mrs. Katz and Tush* (1992), and the support diverse neighbors gave each other when the Oakland fire struck during the Jewish holiday of Sukkoth is emphasized in *Tikvah Means Hope* (1994). Polacco's work is a good example of how today's Jewish women writers and artists transcend stereotypes and leap cultural divides in trade books.

Jane Breskin Zalben (b. 1950), watercolor artist and author of a number of novels, moved Jewish holiday books into the mainstream with *Beni's First Chanukah* (1988), the first of her series for preschoolers. This book and its successors successfully adapted the popular tradition of depicting small animals in cozy family settings and made Zalben a favorite for laptime read-alouds.

An important development in 1975 was the founding of Kar-Ben Copies, Inc., a small Jewish children's press, by two women, Judye S. Groner and Madeline Wikler, who first wrote, illustrated, published, sold, packed, and mailed the kind of Jewish-content books they wanted for their children. The publishing house they founded has become an important mainstream house, with a large backlist of universally appealing picture books, all with Jewish themes, now widely distributed by major chains.

THE 1980S AND 1990s

Sandy Asher (b. 1942) published two books of Jewish import in 1980: *Summer Begins*, raising questions of censorship and religious freedom, and *Daughters of the Law*, about a young girl, a child of a survivor, trying to understand her Jewish identity in the face of her mother's repressed memories. Barbara Girion (b. 1937), after writing several popular books for younger children in the late 1970s, moved to works for adolescents, among them several with Jewish settings. *A Tangle of Roots* (1979) shows how a Jewish high school girl and her father cope when the mother of the family dies; *Like Everybody Else* (1980) is a funny story of a bat mitzvah girl whose children's-writer mother becomes notorious after writing a *very* adult novel; *A Handful of Stars* (1981) tells of the impact of epilepsy on a high schooler; and *A Very Brief Season* (1984) contains short stories about the conflicts of teenaged girls during that brief time preceding adulthood.

Fran Arrick, Jan Greenberg, Johanna Hurwitz, Sheila Solomon Klass, Kathryn Lasky, Marilyn Levy, Lois Ruby, Jan Slepian, and Hilma Wolitzer are among the writers who produced a number of well-received children's and young adult novels during this period. Their stories continue to focus on the insecurities of life, on fitting in, on the importance of family, on the difficulties inherent in human relationships, and on problems of their time. Arrick's *Chernowitz* (1981) deals with anti-Semitism and revenge; Ruby deals with charismatic religion versus rational Judaism in *Miriam's Well* (1993) and with neo-Nazi youth movements and their powerful attraction in *Skin Deep* (1994). Jan Slepian's *The Alfred Summer* (1980) and *Lester's Turn* (1981), based on her mentally retarded, epileptic, hemiplegic brother, demonstrates her frequent theme of how difficult but how important it is for people to connect with each other. Slepian often addresses the challenges of mental and physical handicaps; in *Risk n' Roses* (1990), Skip, the "normal" daughter of a Jewish family, struggles with her longing to be accepted by other kids and her loyalty to her retarded sister. Susan Goldman Rubin also deals sensitively and well with a young retarded Jewish girl in *Emily Good as Gold* (1993), the story of Emily's effort to become more independent of her overprotective family as she enters adolescence.

A new development in the 1990s was a resurgent interest in storytelling and the resultant popularity of Jewish tales, both individually and in collections. Among women writers well known in this area are Barbara Diamond Goldin and Peninnah Schram.

Yaffa Ganz, an Orthodox American woman now living in Israel, has written a number of excellent books on Jewish traditions and customs, as well as the Savta Simcha series, featuring a Hebrew-speaking Mary Poppins–type grandmother evocative of Israeli surroundings and humor.

Doris Faber (b. 1924), Nancy Smiler Levinson (b. 1938), and Rhonda Blumberg (b. 1917) are best known for nonfiction. Faber's biographies and studies of politics are noteworthy; Levinson, who has also written fiction, has won awards for her historical studies; and Blumberg has won numerous accolades for her works on American historical movements and

eras. Biographies on famous Israelis include Malka Drucker's life of Eliezer Ben-Yehuda (1986), Hazel Kranz's work on HENRIETTA SZOLD (1987), and Ida Cowan's story of spy Sarah Aaronsohn. Chaya Burstein's *A Kid's Catalog of Israel* (1988) and Barbara Sofer's *Kids Love Israel; Israel Loves Kids* (1988) introduce children to various facets of Israeli history, geography, and life.

CONCLUSION

Jewish women have written for children about both general and specific concerns. For instance, in the literature of the 1970s, Israel was often a symbol, offering a sense of purpose and belonging in an era of social unrest and confusion. Suzanne Lange's *The Year* (1970) and Gloria Goldreich's *Lori* (1979) are examples in which restless young girls find personal growth and understanding amidst the uncertainties and pressures of living in Israel. Lillian Hoban's *I Met a Traveler* (1977) also shows Israel vividly through the eyes of an eleven-year-old heroine whose unconventional mother has taken her there to live. Today's authors more often emphasize the need for peace, such as in *When Will the Fighting Stop? A Child's View of Jerusalem* (1990) by Ann Morris and Lilly Rivlin and *Neve Shalom-Wahat Al Salaam: Oasis of Peace* (1993) by Laurie Dolphin and Ben Dolphin.

Other authors are dealing with spiritual issues, family relationships, understanding Jewish history, and the shifting place of women in Judaism and in the larger society. Most, however, are simply writing to help children understand themselves and the world in which they live. Informed by the Jewish focus on family, inspired by the need to communicate feeling, meaning, and purpose, uplifted by their inherently Jewish sense of the absurdity and irony of things, they write.

It is interesting to note that *Children's Books and Their Creators*, edited by Anita Silvey (1995), an important guide to children's literature, lists other ethnic groups (Japanese-American Children's Books, African-American Children's Literature, etc.), but Jewish-American children's literature is absent as an ethnic or cultural category. We have been absorbed. No longer a minority group, our literature is considered so mainstream it need not be set out from the rest. To the extent that this indicates that children of all kinds are reading books about all kinds of children, this bodes well. American children will be aware of Judaism, sensitive to Jewish immigrants and pioneers and their place in American history. Children will read mysteries with Jewish settings and humorous books with Jewish flavor. General fiction by Jewish writers may be infused with a subtle sensibility reflecting our Jewish heritage and values.

On the other hand, writers who have focused on Jewish themes, even outstanding writers published by general trade houses, are missing from this "invitation to the finest of twentieth-century children's literature." Perhaps this is one reason why recent trends show fewer books with specifically Jewish settings or themes. Books with strong Jewish roots or influence may become rare commodities if Jewish women writers assimilate into the marketplace. We can only hope they will not join the mainstream at the expense of the rich heritage they have so often portrayed so well.

BIBLIOGRAPHY

Children's Books: Awards and Prizes, Including Prizes and Awards for Young Adult Books. Compiled and edited by the Children's Book Council (1985); David, Enid. *A Comprehensive Guide to Children's Literature with a Jewish Theme* (1981); Frischer, Rita Berman. "The Bar/Bat Mitzvah Book." In *The Schocken Guide to Jewish Books: Where to Start Reading About Jewish History, Literature, Culture and Religion*, edited by Barry W. Holtz (1992), and "Israel in Children's Books." In *Ariel: The Israel Review of Arts and Letters* 99/100 (1995): 100–113; Grossman, Cheryl Silberberg, and Suzy Engman. *Jewish Literature for Children—A Teaching Guide* (1985); Jurich, Marilyn. "*Once upon a Shtetl.*" In *The Lion and the Unicorn: A Critical Journal of Children's Literature* l, nos. 1 and 2 (1977): 9–25; Kirkpatrick, D.L., ed. *Twentieth-Century Children's Writers.* 2d ed. (1983); Nodelman, Perry. "Children's Literature: 1900 to the Present." In *The Oxford Companion to Women's Writing in the United States*, edited by Cathy N. Davidson and Linda Wagner-Martin (1995); Posner, Marcia W. "Fifty Years of Jewish Children's Books in the *Jewish Book Annual.*" In *Jewish Book Annual: The American Yearbook of Jewish Literary Creativity.* Vol. 50 (1992–1993) 5753: 81–98, and "A Search for Jewish Content in American Children's Fiction." Abstract of doctoral diss., New York University (1980); Rudman, Masha Kabakow. *Children's Literature: An Issues Approach* (1995); Silvey, Anita, ed. *Children's Books and Their Creators: An Invitation to the Feast of Twentieth-Century Children's Literature* (1995); *Something About the Author—Autobiography Series.* Miscellaneous volumes; Wacker, Jill. "Children's Literature: 1650 to 1900." In *The Oxford Companion to Women's Writing in the United States*, edited by Cathy N. Davidson and Linda Wagner-Martin (1995).

RITA BERMAN FRISCHER

CHOCHEM, CORINNE (1905–1990)

Best remembered for her contribution to Jewish cultural life and for her unique ability to inspire those around her, Corinne Chochem had a distinct impact on Hebrew folk dance, both in her teaching and her two books, *Palestine Dances* (1941) and *Jewish Holiday Dances* (1948), the latter an original work for which Leonard Bernstein, Darius Milhaud, Ernst Toch, and Tedesco wrote music based on the original folk tunes. Studying in Israel in 1950, she met and married the painter Yehoshua Kovarsky, and began to study painting. Later in life, under the name of Kovarska, she found fulfillment as a painter with several exhibits in Los Angeles. She used both acrylics and ink. Her final black period was exhibited in New York in 1987.

Corinne Chochem was born in Zwanitz, Russia, in 1905 to Esther (Gendelman) and Mendel Chochem. The family immigrated to the United States in 1920 and settled in Newark, New Jersey, where she taught Hebrew and dance at a Montessori school. Vitally interested in dance, she went to Palestine in 1930, where she worked on a kibbutz while researching folk dance. After studying with Martha Graham, Louis Horst, and Carmelita Maracci, she found Pauline Koner and discovered a kindred spirit. Frail, but with tremendous energy, Chochem founded the Rikud Ami dance group, taught at the Jewish Theological Seminary, the University of California, and as guest artist at the Hillel Foundation at Cornell University. Her sister, Fanya Sage, was also a dancer. She also had a brother, Ben Charles. Corinne Chochem and her husband settled in Los Angeles in 1953, where she concentrated on her special talent: dance for children. Kovarsky died in 1967, and Chochem began a career as a painter. She died in 1990.

PAULINE KONER

CIVIL RIGHTS MOVEMENT

The image of Rita Levant Schwerner (b. 1942), the grieving but stoic widow of the disappeared Michael Schwerner, remains emblematic of the sacrifices made for the southern civil rights movement. In the popular mind, it is well known that two Jewish men—Schwerner and Andrew Goodman—along with their black colleague James Chaney, were murdered in Mississippi in 1964. What most people do not know is that Andrew Goodman had been in Mississippi for one day when he was killed. Rita Schwerner had been working with her husband for six months to open a civil rights project in Meridian when he was targeted for murder by a white supremacist gang. Despite her grief and because of her passionate political commitment, Rita Schwerner managed to point out to the media that the only reason they noted James Chaney's death was because he was murdered with two white men. Failure to recognize Rita Schwerner as an

Rita Schwerner and her husband, Michael, had been working in the civil rights movement in Mississippi for six months when he, along with Andrew Goodman and their African-American colleague James Chaney, was murdered. She was the person who emphasized to the media that they were paying attention to Chaney's death only because he was killed with two white men. She is pictured here testifying before the credentials committee of the Democratic Party at the 1964 convention on behalf of the Mississippi Freedom Democratic Party. [UPI/Corbis-Bettmann]

activist in her own right reinforces the invisibility of all the Jewish women who put themselves on the line to fight racism in the civil rights movement.

Despite widespread awareness of significant contributions to the movement by Jewish women, the documentary record and public perception reflect the roles and experiences of men. Scholarship in American Jewish history, civil rights history, and women's studies does not directly address the contributions of Jewish women. Nor does it ask what Jewish cultural influences primed young Jewish women to respond (in numbers disproportionate to their representation in the population) when the civil rights movement put out the call.

The kinds of roles Jewish women played helped build the infrastructure of a remarkably effective movement that did miraculous things with slender resources. They managed and connected people, money, resources, and information. Jewish women worked as campus organizers, fund-raisers, demonstrators and desegregators, voter registration workers, fieldworkers and organizers, Freedom School teachers, strategists, communications coordinators, human resource managers, economic cooperative organizers, typists, cooks, and sympathetic listeners. Among Jewish women professionals who volunteered their skills were law students and lawyers, doctors, and social workers.

Jewish women who found their way to the southern movement had to juggle multiple senses of identity. They were simultaneously relatively privileged, well-educated northern students who could choose to come south to work in a social justice movement; they were the children of Jews struggling to assimilate into American society without losing their Jewish connection; they were women from families and a culture that both encouraged and limited their life choices; they were white women in a movement led most visibly by black men; they were competent and experienced women willing to take action before the feminist movement made it legitimate to do so; and they were secular Jews in a black Christian movement working in the anti-Semitic and virulently racist and sexist South.

With commitment, courage, and individual initiative, a number of northern Jewish women went to the South even before the 1963, 1964, and 1965 summer projects provided an organizational framework for recruiting northern white college students. In 1960, New Yorker Dorothy Miller (b. 1938) learned and practiced nonviolent resistance techniques, going to jail in Miami during a summer workshop sponsored by the Congress of Racial Equality (CORE). She returned to Atlanta in 1961 to do research for the Southern Regional Council. A volunteer for the nascent Student Nonviolent Coordinating Committee (SNCC), founded in 1960, Miller later joined its staff. Because of her writing skills, she was assigned to work with Julian Bond to build SNCC's communications and outreach efforts. She and her future husband, Robert Zellner (SNCC's first white field secretary), remained among SNCC's inner circle until 1967, when it was decided that the SNCC staff should be all black.

Carol Ruth Silver (b. 1938) responded to CORE's 1961 radio call for freedom riders, and she was the only woman on her biracial freedom-riding bus. Arrested in Jackson, Mississippi, on June 7, 1961, Silver spent the next forty days in jail. After the first few days, she was joined by thirteen more white women freedom riders, over half of them Jewish. The young women entertained themselves by reading, doing exercises, and playing chess (Silver had fashioned a chess set out of white bread). They had a party that included the hora. More important, they had philosophical discussions about nonviolence, learned to collaborate with black women activists jailed in nearby (segregated) cells, and developed the sensitivity and skills to be northern white allies in a black-led southern movement.

Having grown up in a woman-headed household that included her black music teacher, Faith Holsaert (b. 1943) had acquired some of these skills already. Yet she was only eighteen years old when she went to the South for the first time to participate in a Baltimore sit-in. A Barnard College freshman, she spent Christmas break 1961 in jail. In the summer of 1962, Holsaert left school for a year to work with SNCC in Albany, Georgia, on one of the movement's first mass voter registration campaigns. One of the few white women fieldworkers in the South before the 1964 summer project, Holsaert may have been SNCC's first Jewish woman field organizer.

Jewish women's organizational skills enabled them to play critical coordinating roles for the movement. Roberta Galler (b. 1936) was a founder and first executive secretary of Chicago Friends of SNCC. After doing fund-raising, organizing, and press outreach in Chicago for several years, SNCC's Lawrence Guyot asked Galler to come to Mississippi in the fall of 1964 to open the first statewide office of the Mississippi Freedom Democratic Party (MFDP). She arrived after the failure to seat the MFDP delegation (which contended it was more representative of Mississippi's Democratic citizens than the all-white delegation) at the Atlantic City Democratic National Convention. Galler worked around-the-clock with colleagues to lay the groundwork for MFDP's Congressional Challenge, which would attempt to oppose the seating of the all-white Mississippi delegation. Galler worked on a variety of projects in the South until 1968.

Jewish women professionals also contributed their skills to the southern movement. Law clerk ELIZABETH HOLTZMAN (a future member of the United States House of Representatives) was involved in the defense of the "Albany Nine," a group of activists from Albany, Georgia, indicted by the federal government in 1963. Among those indicted was Joni Rabinowitz, another Jewish woman activist and the daughter of radical lawyer Victor Rabinowitz.

Dr. June Finer (b. 1935) spent the summer of 1964 working with the Medical Committee for Human Rights (MCHR) in Mississippi. She returned the following year to work as MCHR's southern coordinator, assigning tasks to the many volunteer doctors, nurses, and psychologists who came to the South to provide support. FLORENCE HOWE (b. 1929), a professor at Goucher College, coordinated the Blair Street Freedom School in Jackson, Mississippi, in the summer of 1964. Howe, who went on to establish the Feminist Press, attributes her groundbreaking work in women's studies to lessons learned in Mississippi.

In another type of role, Jewish mothers organized Parents of SNCC groups around the country and were instrumental in fund-raising. Gertrude (Trudy) Orris (b. 1916) ran the New York Parents of SNCC group and spent much time on the phone with the Atlanta office, monitoring developments in the South and trying to get media and government attention focused there. At her New York home, Orris hosted young black activists from all over the South, arranging for their housing, medical care, and fund-raising events.

Some Jewish women volunteers stayed on after the 1964 Summer Project, while others came to the South in 1965. From January to June 1965, Harriet Tanzman (b. 1940), one of the few white women fieldworkers for Martin Luther King, Jr.'s Southern Christian Leadership Conference, worked in Selma, Alabama. She taught literacy and practical skills to small groups of mostly black women, some of whom went on for training that enabled them to teach their own literacy classes. Elaine DeLott (b. 1942), coordinator of federal programs for the Council of Federated Organizations (Mississippi's civil rights umbrella group), helped organize an okra cooperative in Batesville, Mississippi, that was in existence for fifteen years.

Jewish women who went to the South for the civil rights movement demonstrated a willingness to put their bodies on the line to fight racism. This was a very transgressive act on a number of levels. First, it remains extraordinary for any white person in the United States to be a "race traitor," risking his or her life to fight racism. Second, for women, going to the South directly challenged traditional gender roles before the second wave of the women's movement made such challenges less individualized acts. Finally, going to the South required negotiating Jewish cultural and political ambivalence about becoming visible as critics of American society. This was precisely what many of the women's second-generation parents, engaged in the project of assimilation and upward mobility, most feared, even as they recognized that their daughters were acting with the moral values they had learned at home.

Despite varying degrees of alienation and/or identification with Judaism, Jewish backgrounds, traditions, politics, and values did shape the worldviews and commitments of Jewish women civil rights activists. Some but not all were children of Old Left families, whose activism was in keeping with family values. Others came from liberal Democratic families who retained a sense of *tikkun olam* (Hebrew for "repair of the world"), which suggests a special Jewish concern with social justice.

Women such as Vivian Leburg Rothstein (b. 1946), the child of refugees from Nazism, and Trudy Orris, then an Army wife who had visited the newly liberated concentration camps in Germany in 1946, directly tie their antiracist activism to close encounters with the Holocaust.

Other facets of mid-century American Jewish life fostered identification of Jews with the black struggle. One dimension is the closeness of many of Jewish women activists' families to poverty and struggle. Carol Ruth Silver and Barbara Jacobs Haber (b. 1938) both had fathers who had earned law degrees but were forced to work at odd jobs to support their families. Several women came from divorced, woman-headed households, which only highlighted their "otherness" in the 1950s.

Sometimes a sense of "otherness" came with feeling marginalized as Jews. Some future civil rights workers experienced blatant anti-Semitism, often for the first time when they went away to college. In the 1950s, Florence Howe was the only Jewish graduate student at Smith College; there was one black student as well. Howe remembers overhearing the leaders of her dorm planning a party. "Do we have to invite the Jew and the colored?" they asked.

Many future Jewish women activists experienced a contradiction between the Jewish familial expectation of attaining higher education and the 1950s cultural norm in which women were supposed to stay home and raise families. Furthermore, Jewish women have traditionally been expected to work and to take care of family businesses, albeit to facilitate men's Talmud study and spiritual development. This meshed nicely with the need for Jewish women (as northern white women) to play significant but heretofore invisible roles in the black-led civil rights movement.

In reflecting on the Holocaust, a number of future Jewish women activists saw the movement as an opportunity to fight back. It offered a chance to take risks, to expand their possibilities as women, and to fight economic oppression and racism. Given Jewish ethical imperatives, going to the South gave Jewish women a powerful context in which to act upon their own moral visions.

BIBLIOGRAPHY

Blumberg, Rhoda Lois. "White Mothers as Civil Rights Activists: The Interweave of Family and Movement Roles." In *Women and Social Protest*, edited by Guida West and Rhoda Lois Blumberg (1990); Bond, Julian. "The Politics of Civil Rights History." In *New Directions in Civil Rights Studies*, edited by Armistead Robinson and Patricia Sullivan (1991); Cagin, Seth, and Philip Dray. *We Are Not Afraid: The Story of Goodman, Schwerner and Chaney and the Civil Rights Campaign for Mississippi* (1988); Carson, Clayborne. *In Struggle: SNCC and the Black Awakening of the 1960s* (1981); Crawford, Vicki L., Jacqueline Anne Rouse, and Barbara Woods, eds. *Women in the Civil Rights Movement: Trailblazers and Torchbearers, 1941–1965* (1990); Dittmer, John. *Local People: The Struggle for Civil Rights in Mississippi* (1994); Evans, Eli. *The Provincials: An Informal History of Jews in the South* (1973); Evans, Sara. *Personal Politics; The Roots of Women's Liberation in the Civil Rights Movement and the New Left* (1980); Huie, William Bradford. *Three Lives for Mississippi* (1968); Kaufman, Jonathan. *Broken Alliance: The Turbulent Times Between Blacks and Jews in America* (1988); Kaye/Kantrowitz, Melanie. *The Issue Is Power: Essays on Women, Jews, Violence and Resistance* (1992); Lawson, Steven. "Freedom Then, Freedom Now: The Historiography of the Civil Rights Movement." *American Historical Review* 96 (April 1991): 456–471; Lyon, Danny. *Memories of the Southern Civil Rights Movement* (1992); McAdam, Doug. *Freedom Summer* (1988); May, Elaine Tyler. *Homeward Bound: American Families in the Cold War Era* (1988); Prell, Riv-Ellen. "Why Jewish Princesses Don't Sweat: Desire and Consumption in Postwar American Jewish Culture." In *The People of the Body: Jews and Judaism from an Embodied Perspective*, edited by Howard Eilberg-Schwartz (1993); Rothschild, Mary Aickin. *A Case of Black and White: Northern Volunteers and the Southern Freedom Summers, 1964–1965* (1982); Schultz, Debra L. "We Didn't Think in Those Terms Then": *Narratives of Jewish Women in the Southern Civil Rights Movement, 1960–1966* (forthcoming); Shapiro, Edward S. *A Time for Healing: American Jewry Since World War II* (1992); Waxman, Chaim. *America's Jews in Transition* (1983).

DEBRA L. SCHULTZ

CIVIL WAR

Like their gentile neighbors, North and South, Jewish women figured in the history of the Civil War (1861–1865) in two ways. As the wives, mothers, and daughters of men in military service, they shouldered a range of responsibilities brought on by wartime exigencies. As community activists, they involved themselves in home-front activities to minister to the soldiers directly and to raise money for the troops. Both of these classic forms of women's participation in war tended to generate little in the way of documentation, and thus historians studying the involvement of Jewish women in the Civil War and the impact of the war on Jewish women have a sparse body of primary sources upon which to draw.

Approximately ten thousand Jewish men served in the armies of the United States and the Confederacy. With seven thousand soldiers enlisted in the Union forces and three thousand on the side of the Confederacy, Jews served in the military far out of proportion to their number in the population. As in any war, the engagement of men in the military put a tremendous strain on loved ones left behind, and the over five hundred Jewish men who lost their lives in the war created widows, orphans, and bereaved parents whose later lives were shaped by their losses. More immediately during the war, just about each one of the ten thousand men in uniform represented a breadwinner absent from the family economy. Jewish women no doubt had to fill in, both emotionally and financially, for the absent male.

That the war placed a burden on Jewish women can be ascertained from the fact that in a number of communities, like Baltimore, Cincinnati, New Orleans, and Philadelphia, the local Jewish female benevolent associations turned almost all of their attention during the war years to the specific needs of Jewish women whose sons and husbands had gone off to the military. The Jews of Washington, D.C., placed an appeal in the *Jewish Messenger* to the Jews of New York in which they noted, "Unlike you in New York, we have no fund to support the families of poor soldiers, and the unhappy consequence is, the wives and the children of these poor men are in *abject want.*"

However compelling the anecdotes about Jewish women's suffering during the war, the history of the impact of the Civil War on Jewish women and their families and communities remains to be written. The one full-length book that treats the Jews and the Civil War, the 1951 study by Bertram W. Korn, *American Jewry and the Civil War,* paid scant attention to the home front. It dealt with women and the impact of the war upon them only anecdotally in passing. Later

studies, like Harry Simonhoff's *Jewish Participants in the Civil War* (1963), Irving Katz's *The Jewish Soldier from Michigan in the Civil War* (1962), Robert Shostek's *The Jewish Community of Washington, D.C., During the Civil War* (1967), and Mel Young's *Where They Lie: The Story of the Jewish Soldiers of the North and South* (1991), offered no fundamental improvement and did not reflect any of the changes in the writing of history that increasingly focused on the analysis of community, family, and gender.

Details about the ways in which the Civil War affected Jewish community life have surfaced occasionally in a plethora of single-city studies. Historians of the Jewish people of diverse communities like Atlanta, Baltimore, Buffalo, Chicago, Syracuse, Rochester, Utica, and elsewhere considered the Civil War a significant moment in local Jewish affairs. Usually, however, the authors of these studies have limited themselves to naming the Jewish men of these communities who participated in the war, or they have discussed the impact of the war on the local Jewish economy. For example, for Jewish communities in cities like Buffalo and Rochester, where most Jews made a living in tailoring and other aspects of garment making, the war represented a tremendous economic boon. Jewish tailors and merchants in these cities received government contracts to make uniforms, and their marginal enterprises prospered. No doubt, Jewish women participated in this economic transformation, since the earlier, more marginal tailoring establishments functioned as family-based enterprises, with wives and daughters sewing and selling alongside the men. These community histories also have not examined this change in Jewish business in the context of women's experiences, and so provide little specific information and no analysis of the impact of the war on women.

The Civil War memoir of Marcus Spiegel, born in 1829 in Abeheim, Germany, constitutes one of the few documents that hint at the impact on a wife and family of a Jewish husband's military service and his death in battle. Spiegel served as second lieutenant in the 67th Ohio Volunteer Infantry and then as colonel in the 120th Ohio Infantry. He sent a steady stream of letters to his wife, Caroline, a convert to Judaism, up to the time of his receiving a mortal wound on April 30, 1864. These letters, published in 1981 as *Your True Marcus: The Civil War Letters of a Jewish Colonel,* provide an occasional glimpse into the impact of the war on Caroline Spiegel. In a letter marked "Strictly private," Marcus addressed his "good, lovely and abused Wife!" He explained, "I speak truly when I say 'abused Wife'; a Woman as good and lovely, as saving and industrious, as kind a wife and good mother as you are should [not] be left alone hundreds of miles from her husband who loves her more and with more fervor, zeal, and devotion . . . with 3 small children and one coming, or that he should leave her at all." More prosaically, on February 17, 1862, he begged her to send him a pair of boots as well as "something nice to eat in the Box. . . . A bottle of something to drink won't hurt anybody." As Spiegel lay dying from his wound, he reportedly wept to the surgeon, "This is the last of the husband and father, what will become of my poor family?" The scattered details offered by *Your True Marcus*, however sparse, represent one of the few personal insights into the life of a Jewish soldier in the Civil War and the involvement of his wife back home in his military service.

Organized Jewish women's activities on the community level in a number of cities, in both the North and the South, to sustain the war effort have received more, although still inadequate, attention. In Philadelphia, the women of Congregation Mikveh Israel turned the synagogue into a hospital, and the various Jewish women's sewing societies began to produce uniforms for men in the Union Army. At the annual exercises of the Hebrew Sunday School Society in 1863, the hazan, Sabato Morais, called upon the women of the congregation to make an even greater contribution to the Union cause. Morais publicly read a letter he had received from Mary Rose Smith, head of the Visiting Committee of the Women's Branch of the United States Sanitary Commission, requesting that a woman from the congregation be appointed to represent Mikveh Israel to the Sanitary Commission. The women of the congregation met and elected Matilda Cohen to take on this responsibility, and under her auspices the women of the congregation formed themselves into the Ladies Hebrew Relief Association for the Sick and Wounded Soldiers. Celia Meyers became the president of this group, and within a month 250 women had joined. By the war's end, this organization had sent ten crates of supplies to the Sanitary Commission. Additionally, in Philadelphia, as in many other cities on both sides of the conflict, Jewish women participated in communitywide, interdenominational fund-raising fairs. A group of nine young Jewish women who had formed themselves into a club called Alert provided the embroidery and needlework to be sold at the fair.

While less information is currently available about Jewish women's activities in other cities, Philadelphia Jewish women did not differ from their sisters elsewhere. Bits of information from numerous other cities confirmed that Jewish women partici-

pated, as Jewish women, in a wide range of charitable functions to support war efforts across America. Three Jewish women in Detroit helped found the interdenominational Ladies' Soldiers' Aid Society. The wives of members of New York's Temple Emanu-El sewed uniforms for the Union soldiers, of a quality "far better," according to the *New York Times*, "than some specimens turned off from the contractors' shelves." A young Jewish woman in Columbus, Georgia, belonged to the Soldiers Aid Society and spent time in the Columbus Hospital tending the ill and dying. She actually taught one of these dying soldiers to read and write in order to divert him from thinking about his pain. A Jewish woman in Washington, D.C., wrote of the activities of the women of the Washington Hebrew Congregation and noted, "As in all wars the ladies of Washington aided the overtaxed hospital personnel. . . . The daughters of my late grandparents, the Reverend [Abraham] Simon and Hannah Mundheim, were among these good Samaritans." Simon Wolf reported in the *Jewish Messenger* of May 6, 1864, about a Sanitary Fair in the capital city that "the Hebrew Society's Table is credited for $756.95; and . . . the entire receipts were only $10,661.47. . . . All honor to our fair Jewesses!"

Indeed, given the tremendous involvement of Jewish women with charitable work, it is reasonable to assume that most of the Jewish home-front contributions in terms of organizing fairs, preparing bandages and lint, sewing uniforms, visiting the sick and wounded, looking after the needs of orphans and widows, and providing hospitalities for Jewish soldiers represented the activities primarily of women.

The labors of Jewish women for the Civil War cause aroused little conflict, and their activities unified one community after another, as Jews expressed their solidarity with their adopted homes, specifically as Jews. The only controversy that flared occurred in Rochester, New York, where the president of Congregation Berith Kodesh, obviously a man, since women neither belonged to nor held office in synagogues, protested the participation of Jewish women in the local bazaar as Jews. *The Jewish Record* picked up on this theme and asked its readers why "pretty Jewesses" were distinguished in their charitable and patriotic endeavors from other women.

This incident conflicted with the widespread praise that non-Jews, women and men, and Jewish men, during the war and in subsequent generations, offered to Jewish women for their communal leadership. Herbert Ezekiel's 1915 comments to the Rimon Lodge of the B'nai B'rith of Richmond, Virginia, may have typified the overwhelmingly positive reactions toward the efforts of Jewish women, when he acclaimed the Jewish women of Richmond, who "fed the hungry, clothed the poor, nursed the sick and wounded and buried the dead. The wives and mothers and sisters did valiant work in the hospitals."

These two exceptional cases do not, however, challenge the basic assertion that the Civil War represented a notable moment in the history of Jewish women because of the economic and emotional burden it placed on them, on the one hand, and the central role that women played in mobilizing Jewish home-front activities, on the other. These two phenomena represent an unstudied aspect of American Jewish history and one of tremendous consequence.

BIBLIOGRAPHY

Bodek, Evelyn. "'Making Do': Jewish Women and Philanthropy." In *Jewish Life in Philadelphia, 1830–1940*, edited by Murray Friedman (1983): 143–162; Ezekiel, Herbert. *The Jews of Richmond During the Civil War* (1915); Katz, Irving I. *The Jewish Soldier from Michigan in the Civil War* (1962); Korn, Bertram W. *American Jewry and the Civil War* (1951); Massey, Mary E. *Bonnet Brigades* (1966); Shosteck, Robert. *The Jewish Community of Washington, D.C., During the Civil War* (1967); Simonoff, Harry. *Jewish Participants in the Civil War* (1963); Young, Mel. *Where They Lie: The Story of the Jewish Soldiers of the North and South Whose Deaths— [Killed, Mortally Wounded or Died of Disease or Other Causes] Occurred During the Civil War, 1861–1865* (1991).

HASIA R. DINER

CLARA DE HIRSCH HOME FOR WORKING GIRLS

Concerned about the welfare of young working girls in New York City at the turn of the twentieth century, a group of Jewish leaders, mostly women, founded the Clara de Hirsch Home for Working Girls in May 1897. The original board of directors consisted of eleven women and two men. Funds were supplied by the Baroness de Hirsch, who had written to her friend Oscar Straus, the German Jewish political activist and philanthropist, a year earlier expressing her interest in such a project. The baroness donated $200,000 for the construction of the home and pledged additional funds to maintain it once completed. After a few years in temporary quarters, the home was permanently established on East 63rd Street in Manhattan.

Directors of the Clara de Hirsch Home provided their young, largely immigrant charges with comfortable lodging, vocational training, and social activities. Their mission, as they saw it, was to "improve [the girls'] mental, moral and physical condition, and train them for self-support."

The Clara de Hirsch Home became a model for similar trade schools throughout the country and was one of many charitable organizations established by "uptown" Jews, primarily of German origin, who had established themselves in the United States by the mid-nineteenth century, on behalf of their Eastern European immigrant coreligionists. Most of the home's directors were drawn from New York's German Jewish community. Rose Sommerfeld, who was the home's resident director from 1899 through 1926 and who had a profound impact upon its development, was a German Jewish woman from Baltimore. Sommerfeld's background and experience were similar to those of many female settlement workers of her day. She was middle-class, unmarried, and dedicated to her work with the underprivileged. Before coming to the home, she had been associated with the NATIONAL COUNCIL OF JEWISH WOMEN, the Frank Free School (for Russian Jewish children), and the Daughters of Israel Working Girls Home in her native city.

Sommerfeld was involved in every aspect of the home's program, and took a personal interest in its residents and staff members. As SARAH STRAUS wrote of her in the home's annual report of 1901, Sommerfeld took responsibility for "the moral and material welfare of the girls under her charge [and] by her rare judgment and tact she wins their respect, love and confidence." And, as Straus added in 1905, Sommerfeld "is wont to be considered a personal friend of each girl who has lived in the home."

Girls were referred to the home by various individuals and groups, both Jewish and non-Jewish. Among these were the National Conference of Jewish Charities, synagogue sisterhoods, the Hebrew Orphan Asylum, the Hebrew Sheltering Guardian Society, the National Council of Jewish Women, Educational Alliance, Charity Organization Society, the New York City Department of Charities and Board of Education, and the settlement houses. In many cases, the referring organization, or the home itself, provided scholarships to cover the girls' tuition and living expenses (amounting to three dollars a week for each). The home opened with accommodations for 13 girls; by 1912–1913, over 140 girls lived at the home, more than 70 of whom were trainees.

The home offered boarding facilities for working women, age sixteen to thirty, who were either orphans or had no relatives in the city. Its training department instructed girls over age fourteen, most of whom were also residents of the home, in either "domestic science" (housework, cooking, laundry, mending, etc.) or "industrial skills," such as hand sewing, machine sewing, dressmaking, and millinery. Students enrolled in one of these departments for a twelve-month course of study, which also included elementary education (especially English-language instruction) and physical exercise. Many girls also supplemented this curriculum with board of education lecture courses or typing and stenography classes outside the home. In addition, the girls were responsible for daily cleaning of their own rooms, as well as basic upkeep of the home.

Jewish religious instruction was also incorporated into the home's program. While the home was open to non-Jews, these were to constitute no more than 10 percent of the total number of residents. Jewish boarders and trainees celebrated Jewish holidays, such as Hanukkah, Purim, and Passover. They attended Sabbath services on Friday evenings (using the Reform *Hebrew Union Prayerbook*), and were encouraged to attend nearby "uptown" synagogues, using seats provided for them by the trustees. However, the home, while kosher, was not strictly observant and provided only minimal religious education, consisting of one hour of biblical history a week.

In addition to formal education and vocational training, young residents participated in a variety of social and cultural activities. They could choose from several literary and social clubs (including cooking, millinery, "physical culture," English, and German) and enjoyed musical and dramatic performances (particularly an annual minstrel show performed by the girls themselves). The young women had access to a library, evening lectures on a wide array of topics, and weekly teas, when the superintendent read aloud to the boarders while they sewed. The girls especially looked forward to frequent outings to museums, concerts, the theater, and parks. During the summer months, they were treated to boat trips, campfires, and picnics, and were sent to various camps, including the home's own Welcome House Vacation Home in Long Branch, New Jersey, which provided rest and recreation to girls in need of gaining weight and restoring their health. On Sunday evenings, residents were encouraged to invite male visitors to join them in social dancing; as a result, according to the home's 1909–1910 annual report, "the 'dance hall,' with its attendant evils, has no attraction for them."

This reference to the "dance hall" reflects the concern of the home's directors with the safety and sexual morality of young working women. Like their colleagues in the settlement house and working girls' club movements, these women of the German Jewish elite sought to provide their charges with the means to earn a decent livelihood. They would then be able to help support their families and cultivate their self-respect. Most importantly, the women reformers hoped to protect their charges from the evils of city life, especially growing numbers of white slave traffickers who were known to lure innocent and desperate immigrant girls into prostitution.

This was the motivation behind the establishment, in May 1904, of a Home for Immigrant Girls by a group of women connected with the Clara de Hirsch Home. The new home provided temporary shelter for girls who had no one to meet them upon their arrival in the country, were unable to locate their relatives, or lacked sufficient funds to reach their destinations. An agent representing the National Council of Jewish Women met the girls at Ellis Island and brought them directly to the home, where they received information and guidance.

In their efforts to guide and protect immigrant Jewish girls, the home's directors seem to have been motivated by genuine sisterly concern, as well as by their class and ethnic interests. As members of the German Jewish community, they were anxious to Americanize their charges, and to "lift" them out of poverty into middle-class respectability. In the context of the home's program, this meant training girls in domestic skills in the hope that they would internalize American middle-class ideals regarding a "woman's place." Despite the attention given to "industrial training," girls at the home were prepared to be self-supporting before marriage, but ultimately to be good wives and mothers. Many, the benefactresses noted proudly, returned to the home to celebrate their weddings.

It was this value system that prompted the home's directors to steer their young charges into domestic service. In the nineteenth century, such positions were widely regarded as safe and appropriate for lower-class women. They would also provide graduates with the skills needed to eventually establish their own homes. Some historians such as Nancy Sinkoff have suggested that the home's directors were also interested in training domestics to staff their own households. Whatever the motivations of the directresses, the home's residents tended to reject domestic service for various reasons, generally preferring work in the garment trades.

Upon "graduation" from the home, girls found work as domestics, cooks, chambermaids, waitresses, infant nurses, seamstresses (in the garment shops), singers, actresses, bookkeepers, or sewing teachers (especially in orphan asylums). Some qualified for positions as teachers, factory forewomen, or supervisors at other institutions, such as the Temple Emanuel Sisterhood Day Nursery and the Jewish Industrial Home for Girls in Philadelphia.

Despite their class biases and sometimes patronizing attitudes, the home's directors provided their charges with marketable skills. Beyond that, they succeeded in creating an appealing home life for young women who had largely been deprived of this experience. As a reporter for the *Hebrew Standard* wrote in 1907, "The girl . . . enjoys many home-like privileges, for it is a home in the truest sense of the word. The rooms are well-lighted and well heated and the young woman, after many hours of work, comes home and finds much good cheer awaiting her. . . . In all [the girls] are a happy crowd."

Over time, the home's program was gradually modified in response to changing conditions. As immigration declined, and greater educational opportunities became available to the city's young women, the directors decided, in 1926, to close their trade school. Beginning in the 1930s, the home sheltered growing numbers of young European Jewish refugees, as well as self-supporting students of various New York educational institutions.

In July 1960, the home's board of directors sold its building on East 63rd Street and, a year later, concluded a merger agreement with the 92nd Street YMHA. The home contributed its assets toward the construction and maintenance of a new residential building that would accommodate two hundred women. It was completed in 1967.

BIBLIOGRAPHY

Baum, Charlotte, et al. *The Jewish Woman in America* (1976); Clara de Hirsch Home for Working Girls. Annual Reports: 1901, 1905, and 1909–1919; Archival Collections. Jewish Division, New York Public Library, and 92nd Street YM-YWHA, NYC; Glanz, Rudolf. *The Jewish Woman in America: Two Female Immigrant Generations, 1820–1929.* Vol. 2 (1977); Rischin, Moses. *The Promised City: New York's Jews, 1870–1914* (1962); Rothman, Sheila. *Woman's Proper Place: A History of Changing Ideals and Practices, 1870's to the Present* (1978); Sinkoff, Nancy B. "Educating for 'Proper' Jewish Womanhood: A Case Study in Domesticity and Vocational Training, 1897–1926." *American Jewish History* 77, no. 4 (June 1988): 572–599; Welter, Barbara. "The Cult of True Womanhood, 1820–1860." In *The American Family in Social-Historical Perspective,* edited by Michael Gordon (1973); "The Work of the Clara de Hirsch Home." *Hebrew Standard* (April 5, 1907): 30.

REENA SIGMAN FRIEDMAN

CLUB MOVEMENT

Jewish clubwomen emerged in America between 1880 and 1920 as part of a comprehensive social transition. Jews—women as well as men—evolved from a series of scattered ethnic enclaves primarily of German origin into a more cohesive and politically active portion of a decidedly American middle class. The activities of clubwomen were responses to the social pressures placed upon them. As the source of family nurture, they were pressured by rabbis to study the Jewish religion so they might protect their children from conversion to Christianity or a drift into atheism. As the heirs of a tradition of maternal charity, they suddenly faced an influx of immigrants whose immense economic, educational, and health care needs presented unprecedented challenges.

To meet these challenges, clubwomen refined their tradition of charitable obligation first into volunteer aid to Jewish strangers and then into formally organized and professionally administered social settlement work. They also redefined the religious and civic meaning of American Judaism. While rabbis may have encoded the tenets of Reform Judaism in documents like the Pittsburgh Platform (1885), clubwomen implemented the new emphasis on meaningful ceremonial and social reform. In addition, while rabbis may have shared pulpits with liberal Protestant ministers, Jewish clubwomen worked with Protestant social reformers like Jane Addams, Florence Kelley, and Margaret Sanger to demonstrate that the new "mission of Israel" was to make the needs of children and women part of the new Progressive political agenda.

SOCIAL AND POLITICAL SETTING

Even more so than in Germany and Britain, the growth of very large American cities dominated by industrial production facilitated the unprecedented migration and mobility of people. Unlike their counterparts in Germany or England, American Jewish women matured in cities that were themselves both ethnically diverse and very rapidly expanding. Without a titled elite like the Montefiores and Rothschilds in Britain or legally incorporated Jewish communities as in Central Europe to provide publicity and funding, the wives and daughters of merchants across America organized their social circles to create institutions to direct newcomers. They were forced by the new scale of life, by the very magnitude of impoverished immigrant communities, to extend familial protection to strange women and children.

The political context within which clubwomen organized shaped the gender roles they redefined and the programs they offered to their new clients. While their clubs grew from different cultural traditions than those of upper-middle-class Protestant women, they were part of an effort by elite women to assert their own autonomy while learning to understand and working to resolve the problems of newcomers. American Jewish clubwomen were not so much being afforded entry to an ongoing bourgeois culture as being asked to share in an effort by elite women to manage a shift in life's scale and its cultural diversity. Nevertheless, they differed from Protestant clubwomen in being culturally akin to the clients toward whom their efforts were directed. While sharing many class interests with Protestant clubwomen, they remained institutionally separate and socially absorbed in the Jewish community.

To appreciate the rapid and complex shift in gender roles forged by clubwomen, it is first helpful to examine the ethnic setting from which clubwomen emerged. Clubwomen were generally the daughters of immigrant German Jews who had scattered across the United States. Most of their fathers were merchants or artisans along the major American trade routes, from New York to New Orleans and San Francisco. Their mothers were usually the daughters of village families, who were accustomed to frequent childbearing and responsibility for large households. In German hometowns, Jewish families were usually legally organized into a self-supporting community. Charity was the responsibility of the *gemeinde*, or community, supplemented by women who volunteered to assist poor families personally and materially.

In the United States, German Jewish immigrant women continued some of the traditions of their hometowns. They tended to marry young to men considerably older than themselves and to have large families. As the wives of merchants, however, they could afford to hire servants to help care for their own children. But since the Jewish communities were not legal entities, the women had to form benevolent societies to assist one another with emergency household needs. Care of sick women and their children, burial of the dead, and raising funds to send widows and young children back to their paternal families were part of the personal service immigrant women gave to one another. In small towns, Ladies Hebrew Benevolent Societies held annual Strawberry Festivals or sponsored whist parties to help pay the mortgage and provide accessories for the synagogue.

By the late 1880s, the ladies benevolent societies in larger cities had to respond to the needs of Eastern European families who were complete strangers. The immigrants lived in a distant part of an enlarged city, spoke a different language—Yiddish rather than German or English—practiced a variant form of Judaism, and had different family traditions. The women of the benevolent society saw the immigrant families as being at the starting point of a process that combined acculturation to American social norms and liberalization of Jewish identity. As the newcomers proliferated, the benevolent society assigned a member to visit their homes in the immigrant district to ascertain the extent of family needs.

By the mid-1880s, the daughters of benevolent society families had become adults. They had assimilated an American bourgeois style of young womanhood, which usually included the equivalent of a high school education, perhaps family vacations in Germany, and a smattering of knowledge about the Old Testament. Unlike their mothers, they saw no need to marry in their teens or very early twenties, or to have large families. Manuscript census data for cities like Portland, Oregon; Galveston, Texas; and Charleston, South Carolina in 1900 and 1910 show that American-born Jewish women under age forty created a family pattern similar to that of their Protestant peers. On the average, these women married in their mid-twenties to men four to seven years older than themselves and usually had only two or three children. The family usually owned its home and had a servant to help with family chores. In addition, over 20 percent of women in their thirties in these sample cities were unmarried at a time when many American college-educated women did not marry.

For these women, Jewishness usually meant a sense of communal responsibility for charity work combined with a broader knowledge of secular literary issues. Women like Henrietta and HANNAH SOLOMON were not only active members of the Reform Temple Sinai but also the first Jewish women invited to join the Chicago Woman's Club in 1877. By 1887, JENNIE FRANKLIN PURVIN and her friends formed the Chicago Women's Aid, initially to visit the Jewish sick at Michael Reese Hospital. But their interests soon expanded. As Jewish matriarchs, they raised money to expand Michael Reese Hospital and to bring Jewish nurses to Chicago. As genteel American women, they formed study circles to discuss literature like the work of George Eliot.

YOUNG WOMANHOOD

In Charleston, South Carolina, in 1889, Rabbi David Levy and the married women of the Reform Congregation Beth Elohim adapted, on a small scale, the idea of women's communal responsibility to meet

Benevolent societies responded to the needs of new immigrants and those less fortunate than themselves.
They were "true sisters" to their Jewish brethren in need. [Peter H. Schweitzer]

new social conditions. The young, unmarried women of the congregation desired to use their time more productively, while city authorities observed an influx of poor Jews with social needs. So forty-five unmarried sisters and cousins from age sixteen into their early thirties formed a club called the Happy Workers "to care for as many poor [Jewish] children as the funds will allow." As some of the women married, they retained membership, but motions in the 1890s to open the club to married women or to admit girls under age sixteen were defeated.

For Charleston to have poor Jewish children must have been a startling anomaly. In 1880, only a handful of Eastern European Jews lived in the city, and most of these had successful businesses. A few daughters from these families even belonged to the Happy Workers. But after 1890, several hundred Eastern European Jewish families arrived and settled among poor African Americans living near the wharves along North King Street. The Happy Workers formed committees to visit these newcomers. A few widows or deserted wives and their children were temporarily "adopted," with the women given medical care and the children given clothing, medicine, or eyeglasses. The context within which this charity was given, however, reflected the class tensions that cut through ethnic loyalties. The Happy Workers' meetings combined routine business and sewing of garments for their wards with moralistic discussions of women who were not responding appropriately to the proffered aid. Some women were judged incapable of budgeting funds properly, while other "clients" balked at classes in sewing that were supposed to make them self-sufficient. More than one client informed the Happy Workers that she no longer wished to receive support.

Over the years, the Happy Workers accumulated a small endowment and contributed to projects like kindergartens or night school classes for Jewish children and women. As the era of extensive spinsterhood came to an end, the Happy Workers amended their charter and accepted married members, but they continued to think of their work as genteel charity. They did not see themselves acquiring professional expertise, affiliating with Protestant women with similar goals, or interacting in some formal way with civil authorities. The Happy Workers had developed a very traditional outlet for a new Jewish social strata—unmarried, genteelly educated young women—but it did not connect them to the larger world of professionalized acculturation and social control that young women in larger, more dynamic cities felt able to build.

"PERSONAL SERVICE"

A more comprehensive program to meet the needs of poor newcomers was organized by women at the Reform Temple Emanuel in San Francisco. In 1893, the depression left many immigrants, including Eastern European Jews, unemployed. Rabbi Jacob Voorsanger encouraged the women of his congregation to form a Sisterhood for Personal Service to provide immediate relief and to help men and women find work. The term "personal service" symbolized a step away from simple benevolence toward self-conscious social and personal reform. As used by Robert Woods of Boston, the leading theorist of settlement work, it referred to the way college graduates would reside among immigrants to gather accurate data on their social pathologies and to bring to them knowledge about modern urban services. Personal service would help reintegrate a crumbling social order. But for SADIE AMERICAN, a resident social worker at the Maxwell Street Settlement who would soon help found the Council of Jewish Women, it connoted the reintegration of a confused Jewish identity. For her, personal service extended beyond benevolence by requiring socially comfortable Jewish women to study Jewish history and ethics, so they might understand their responsibility for reknitting a fragmented ethnic community. As clubwoman SERAPHINE PISKO, a fund-raiser and later chief administrator of the National Jewish Hospital in Denver, noted, personal service meant learning about the Jewish past as personified in the immigrants, as much as it meant bringing to immigrants America's ideas about individualism, citizenship, and health care.

In San Francisco, the Emanuel Sisterhood for Personal Service soon developed broad plans. Unlike the Happy Workers, the sisterhood consisted of married women with well-established social roles. But in a cosmopolitan city, they faced an apparently permanent problem of acculturating an unprecedented number of Jewish strangers. Even as the depression abated, they turned their club to meet the long-term needs of immigrants. By 1897, they acquired a building in the immigrant district, where mothers could find child care while they were instructed in modern ideas about heath care, nutrition, and child rearing. Members of the sisterhood also intended to intervene in the child-rearing process. They organized a club for the daughters of immigrant families, and they allowed Sidney Peixotto, the son of Temple Emanuel's president, to organize a similar club for boys. The boys, especially, were to receive vocational instruction not yet available in the public schools, as well as practical lessons in civic participation.

As a woman's club, the sisterhood assumed responsibility for what they saw as a permanent problem—the protection of young Jewish women who lacked families. The newly organized Council of Jewish Women in New York would soon focus on the lures of prostitution to young Jewish girls. But the sisterhood in San Francisco took responsibility for girls released at age sixteen from the regional Jewish orphan home maintained by the district lodge of the B'nai B'rith. The sisterhood helped them find work, rented a house to shelter them, and then constructed a new building that by 1920 could house about thirty-three young women at a time. During 1921, for example, seventy-one girls were accommodated, and fifty-seven more had to be turned away. The responsibility for supervising the home and for providing additional classes in personal hygiene, nutrition, home finance, and child rearing fell on the resident social worker. In 1916, Ethel Feinemen, who had been trained in social work by Jacob Billikopf in Kansas City and had spent a year at the University of Chicago and at Hull House, was hired as the first Jewish full-time resident social worker on the West Coast. In a little over twenty years, the sisterhood had learned the difference between ladies' philanthropy and professional social work.

THE CLUB MOVEMENT

Institutionalized club work among Jewish women received national coordination in the formation of the Council of Jewish Women in 1893. During preparation for the Chicago World's Fair, Hannah Solomon was invited to organize a Jewish Women's Congress under the auspices of the World's Parliament of Religions. She did so because rabbis had neglected Jewish women when organizing presentations on Judaism. But she decided to hold the Jewish Women's Congress in the Religion Building rather than in the Women's Building in order to avoid confronting the issue of women's rights within Judaism. Instead, Jewish women demonstrated their professional expertise in discussing cultural and social issues. Women spoke not only about themes that reinforced traditional roles, like "Women in the Bible" and "Religion in the Home," but also about "Women as Wage Workers" and "Women Protesting Persecution."

Equally important, single women with training as schoolteachers and social workers, like JULIA RICHMAN, Julia Felsenthal, and Sadie American, gave major addresses. American's address summarized and rebutted the criticisms of women's new club work and explained why the Jewish community needed the new work of women beyond the home and the sisterhood.

Women, she conceded, did and would do different work from men, but where men refused to see problems, women had to act. At the same time, Jews in America were and would remain a separate cultural entity, and Jewish women needed to organize to help immigrant women and children adjust. To provide this leadership, American Jewish women, through their local social networks, needed to understand how Jewish heroines had taken the initiative in the past and how they now could be guided to study and resolve modern problems.

After the World's Fair, Solomon and American organized the NATIONAL COUNCIL OF JEWISH WOMEN. They hoped to interest women's networks all over the country to initiate study circles that would turn Reform Judaism to social activism on behalf of women and children. By 1896, fifty council sections had enrolled four thousand members. At first, the sections differed from the benevolent societies or ladies aid work because of the study circles. In fact, at first a number of council sections felt that social service was the responsibility of the Ladies Aid, while their responsibility was to read and study. But unlike the reading circles at early Protestant women's clubs, the council sections revitalized the members' religious and cultural identity. This focus was in part a response to the charge from rabbis that Jewish women were neglecting the religious education of their children. But the context of club work, in expanding cities with impoverished Jewish immigrants, soon led energized women to refocus on the social problems to which American had first pointed.

BRIDGING THE GENERATION GAP

The council sections, though dominated by married women, welcomed unmarried women as well. Council organizers could see through the work of American and Felsenthal that guidance for immigrants should be entrusted to women with formal education and expertise, not only to those who had raised their own families. The small section organized in Seattle in 1900 had a large majority of married women, but of the new women recruited between 1901 and 1906, half were unmarried. By 1906, in a much larger section in San Francisco, 20 percent of the 621 members were unmarried.

Generally, single women were more sensitive to the new directions in women's lives. In San Francisco, for example, JESSICA PEIXOTTO, who had just earned a doctorate in sociology at the University of California with a dissertation on European socialism, led the Philanthropic Committee through comprehensive readings on the English Poor Laws and on Engels's

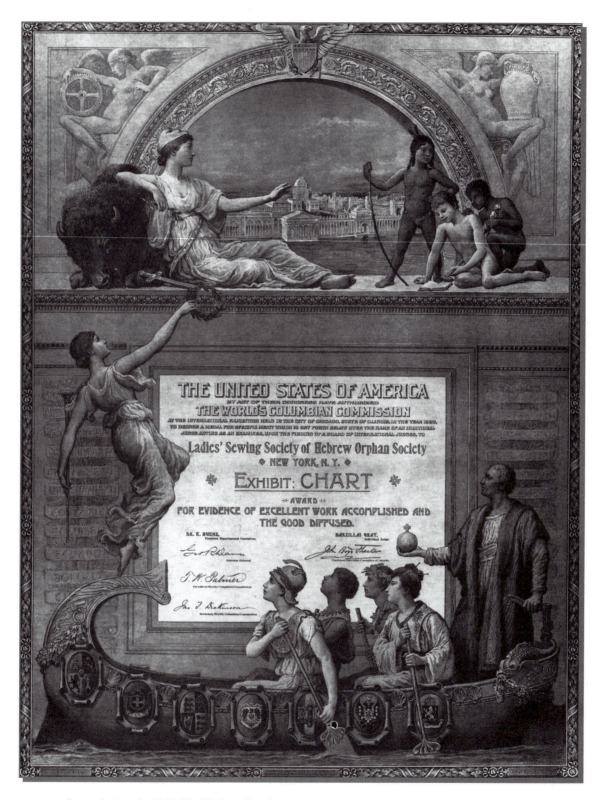

It was during the 1893 World's Fair that the NATIONAL COUNCIL OF JEWISH WOMEN was founded.
One of the central goals of the council was to promote social activism. But, as this plaque from the fair
honoring the New York City "Ladies' Sewing Society of Hebrew Orphan Society" shows, there were
already local organizations dedicated to ameliorating social problems among the Jewish population.
[American Jewish Historical Society]

By 1896, three years after the organization was founded, the NATIONAL COUNCIL OF JEWISH WOMEN
*had fifty sections around the country and more than four thousand members. This photograph
of past presidents of the Portland, Oregon, section was taken in 1910.*

study of slum housing in London. In 1901, the Terre Haute section listened to a paper by Helen Arnold on "The Continued Misconception of a Woman's True Sphere." A discussion followed in which each member was required to express her views. Regrettably, no transcript survives, but the minutes suggest that members were searching for alternative projects to augment their goals.

As the sections turned to settlement work, in part to combat the influence of Protestant "missions" to immigrant districts, a rough division of labor occurred between the older married women and the younger unmarried women. Older women usually taught domestic skills, while unmarried women organized clubs for boys and girls, taught Sunday school classes, and organized the religious ceremonies that highlighted their version of an Americanized Judaism. They also seemed more resilient in coping with the disrespect they occasionally encountered in the settlement houses from adolescent boys in immigrant families. As the settlement work of the council sections became more sophisticated, married women usually acted as liaisons with public agencies like schools and

city councils, and as "friendly visitors" in the homes of families whose children were under the jurisdiction of the juvenile courts. A network of unmarried women was encouraged to acquire professional training and usually provided the medical, dietetic, and "case work" expertise utilized to instruct immigrant women and their daughters.

By 1920, the Council of Jewish Women represented the epitome of what Jewish clubwomen had hoped to achieve. Their national leaders like American and BELLE MOSKOWITZ were recognized as experts on the causes of prostitution, while the council sections had established clubs and other family support services to prepare young women for employment and motherhood. Local and national federations of women's clubs expected the officers of council sections to speak for the Jewish community on social welfare issues. Within the Jewish community, council sections had bridged the generation gap. They had defined honorable work for unmarried young women by creating a network that led from volunteer social service to professional social work. They were also safeguarding Judaism as a modern, ceremonially focused religious community in which women could play as distinctive a role as men.

BIBLIOGRAPHY

Blair, Karen J. *The Clubwoman as Feminist: True Womanhood Defined, 1868–1914* (1980); Council of Jewish Women. Minute books and section files. AJA, Cincinnati, Ohio, and Denver Section. Records. Rocky Mountain Jewish Historical Society, University of Denver, and Portland Section. Records. Oregon Jewish Historical Society, Portland Jewish Community Center, and San Francisco Section. Records. Western Jewish History Center, Berkeley, Calif., and Seattle Section. Records. Suzzalo Library, University of Washington; Daniels, Doris G. *Always a Sister: The Feminism of Lillian D. Wald* (1989); Emanu-el Sisterhood for Personal Service. Records. Western Jewish History Center, Berkeley, Calif.; Hyman, Paula E. *Gender and Assimilation in Modern Jewish History: The Roles and Representations of Women* (1995); Israels, Belle Linder. "The Way of the Girl." *The Survey* (July 3, 1906): 486–497; Kaplan, Marian A. *The Making of the Jewish Middle Class: Women, Family and Identity in Imperial Germany* (1991); Kuzmack, Linda Gordon. *Woman's Cause: The Jewish Woman's Movement in England and the United States, 1881–1933* (1990); Muncy, Robyn. *Creating a Female Dominion in American Reform, 1890–1935* (1991); Perry, Elizabeth Israel. *Belle Moscowitz: Feminine Politics and the Exercise of Power in the Age of Alfred E. Smith* (1987); Pisco, Seraphine. Letters. National Jewish Hospital Records, Rocky Mountain Jewish Historical Society, University of Denver; Portland Ladies Hebrew Benevolent Society. Records. Oregon Jewish Historical Society, Portland Jewish Community Center; Purvin, Jennie Franklin. "The Chicago Woman's Aid" (1914) and "The Place of the Council of Jewish Women among the Jewish Women's Organizations of Chicago" (1921). Jennie Franklin Purvin Collection, AJA, Cincinnati, Ohio; Rogow, Faith. *Gone to Another Meeting: The National Council of Jewish Women, 1893–1993* (1993); Seattle Ladies Hebrew Benevolent Society. Records. Suzzalo Library, University of Washington; Toll, William. "A Quiet Revolution: Jewish Women's Clubs and the Widening Female Sphere, 1897–1920." *AJA* 41, no. 1 (Spring/Summer 1989): 7–26, and "Gender, Ethnicity and Jewish Settlement Work in the Urban West." In *An Inventory of Promises: Essays in Honor of Moses Rischin*, edited by Jeffrey Gurock and Marc L. Raphael (1995); Wenger, Beth S. "Jewish Women of the Club: The Changing Public Role of Atlanta's Jewish Women." *AJH* 76, no. 3 (March 1987): 311–333, and "Jewish Women and Voluntarism: Beyond the Myth of Enablers." *AJH* 79, no. 1 (Autumn 1989): 16–36.

WILLIAM TOLL

COALITION FOR THE ADVANCEMENT OF JEWISH EDUCATION *see* CAJE

COHEN, AUDREY (1931–1996)

Audrey Cohen, founder and president of Audrey Cohen College in New York City, was an internationally recognized educator who stood at the vanguard of education and social policy for almost forty years. Impelled by a vision of a better world, she developed a system of education based on the principle that people learn best when they use their learning to achieve purposes that improve the world.

Born on May 14, 1931, in Pittsburgh, Audrey Cohen was the daughter of Abe and Esther (Morgan) Cohen, both religiously observant Jews. She was raised in Pittsburgh and graduated magna cum laude from the University of Pittsburgh and did postgraduate work at George Washington University and Harvard University. In 1958, she founded Part Time Research Associates, a social science research corporation employing only women. Early on, Cohen recognized the need for college-educated women to have flexible work schedules allowing them to care for their families.

While living in New York City during the early 1960s, Cohen focused on developing training programs to meet the requirements of the emerging service economy. In 1964, she founded the Women's Talent Corps, an organization that designed new jobs for the service economy (including the first paralegal and educational assistant positions) and combined study with on-the-job training. Building upon that organization's dramatic success in assisting low-income women, Cohen and her colleagues then developed an entirely new approach to education. They envisioned education as a continuum extending from kindergarten to the graduate level, with each level achieving, in the world outside of the classroom, a purpose that was crucial to life and work.

In 1964, the Talent Corps developed into a private, fully accredited coeducational institution of higher learning initially called the College for Human Services and later renamed Audrey Cohen College. By 1979, the college was offering bachelor's degrees in the human services. In 1983, the college initiated a business degree program, and in 1988, it began offering a master's program in administration. Also in 1983, the college's Purpose-Centered System of Education® began to be adapted for elementary and secondary education.

Audrey Cohen received numerous awards in recognition of her educational work, including the Mina Shaughnessy Scholarship Award from the United States Office of Education, the Outstanding Leadership in Higher Education Award from the Committee of Independent Colleges and Universities,

Dissatisfied with the training students were receiving for the emerging service economy, in the 1960s Audrey Cohen founded an organization that grew into Audrey Cohen College. [Audrey Cohen College]

the President's Award from the National Organization of Human Service Educators, and a doctorate of humane letters from the University of New England. During her lifetime, she published numerous articles and pamphlets. Her book, *To Build a Better World*, was completed shortly before she died.

Cohen had two daughters, Winifred Alisa Cohen and Dawn Jennifer Cohen Margolin, by her first marriage, to Mark Cohen. She is survived by them and her second husband, Dr. Ralph Wharton, a psychiatrist in private practice in New York City.

Cohen's commitment to educational reform demonstrated that she was a person of unusual courage, persistence, and vision. In addition to creating a new system of education, she instilled in others a willingness to inquire deeply into the proper goals and methods of learning.

BIBLIOGRAPHY

Cohen, Audrey. Archives. Audrey Cohen College, NYC, and *To Build a Better World* (1997); Obituary. *NYTimes*, March 12, 1996.

ANNIE LaROCK

COHEN, ELAINE LUSTIG (b. 1927)

The related fields of typography and graphic design played a vital role in the advent of modernism in early twentieth-century Europe, with many vanguard groups—better known for painting, sculpture, architecture, and manifestos—using design to test the practical application of their new modes of artistic production. The European avant-garde, imported to the United States by a wave of emigrés in the late 1930s, was embraced by a new breed of designers, eager to build upon the principles of an incipient "international style." Elaine Lustig Cohen, with her husband, Alvin Lustig, were among the most prominent graphic designers to adopt these advanced aesthetic concepts for use in the American market.

She was born on March 6, 1927, in Jersey City, New Jersey, to Elisabeth (Loeb) and Herman Firstenberg. She decided to study art at the H. Sophie Newcomb Memorial College of Tulane University after learning that one of the instructors at that school had trained under the Hungarian Bauhaus master László Moholy-Nagy. This early interest in what became known as International Constructivism stayed with her, informing both her painting practice and her daily occupation. She remained in Louisiana for two years before transferring to the University of Southern California, receiving a B.F.A. in 1948. The same year she married Alvin Lustig, and she began honing her craft in the company of her husband, long considered one of the foremost American practitioners of avant-garde typography and graphic design. Using canonical modernist devices such as sans-serif type, photomontage, and geometric planes of color, the Lustigs were able to introduce high modernist design principles into the traditionally conservative American graphic vernacular.

After her first husband's premature death in 1955, she continued to work as a major designer for Meridian and New Directions Books in New York throughout the late 1950s. She was also a pioneer in the field of architectural signage, working on such important modernist structures as Eliel and Eero Saarinen's General Motors Technical Institute in Warren, Michigan, of 1955; Ludwig Mies van der

Rohe and Philip Johnson's Seagram Building in New York of 1958; and interiors for the then little-known Richard Meier. Continuing her early training in the fine arts, she continued to paint—following the abstract constructivist party line—and has exhibited widely, most notably in 1979 as the first woman to show at the now-legendary Mary Boone Gallery. A retrospective of her paintings and photomontages was mounted at the prominent Manhattan gallery Exit Art in 1985.

In 1972, Cohen established Ex Libris—a Manhattan bookstore concentrating on rare printed materials of the European avant-garde—with the novelist and theologian Arthur Cohen (d. 1986), whom she had married in 1956. Her work is amply represented in the collection of the Cooper-Hewitt National Design Museum in New York, where a major retrospective of her graphic work was held in 1995.

BIBLIOGRAPHY
Blueprint (March 1995): 40–41; Cohen, Elaine Lustig. *Letters from the Avant-Garde: Modern Graphic Design*, with Ellen Lupton (1996); *Cooper-Hewitt National Design Museum Magazine* 2, no. 1 (Winter 1995): 8–10; *Metropolis* (March 1995): 95; *New York* (February 27, 1995): 140.

NOAH CHASIN

COHEN, ELIZABETH D.A.
(1820–1921)

"Insert M.D. after her name." This annotation to the 1888 admission records of Touro Infirmary illustrates the thirty-year struggle of the first woman physician in Louisiana to be recognized as an equal by her male colleagues.

Elizabeth D.A. Cohen was born on February 22, 1820, in New York City. Her parents, David and Phoebe Magnus Cohen, were of British descent. She was educated in New York City, where she met and married Aaron Cohen, a doctor, and gave birth to five children. According to interviews in the *New Orleans Times-Picayune*, the turning point in her life came when her young son died of measles. Elizabeth Cohen felt more could have been done to save the child and determined to "become a doctor myself and help mothers to keep their little ones well." When her husband moved to New Orleans to study surgery in 1853, the thirty-three-year-old Elizabeth Cohen took a daring step: She enrolled in the Philadelphia College of Medicine, the first women's medical school in the United States.

Diploma in hand, Elizabeth Cohen arrived in New Orleans in 1857, having distinguished herself by graduating fifth in a class of thirty-six. She became the fourteenth physician and the first woman to practice in Louisiana.

Cohen was interviewed for the *New Orleans Times-Picayune* daily newspaper twice in her long life, when she was ninety-three and on her hundredth birthday. Each time, "looking back through memory's haze," she praised the male doctors of her youth for accepting women practitioners without antagonism. "I worked with the doctors of those days through two epidemics of yellow fever, one in the year 1857 and one in [1878]. I attended to families through generations, and often the girl at whose coming into the world I had assisted, when grown to womanhood would engage me for a similar function." In truth,

In 1857, Elizabeth D.A. Cohen became the first woman physician to practice in Louisiana. In 1920, the year the Nineteenth Amendment was passed, the 100-year-old Cohen said, "I'm for votes for women."
[Touro Infirmary Archives]

Cohen's practice was mostly limited to women and children, and the city directory listed her as a midwife through the year 1867. In 1869, she was listed as a "doctress," and in 1876, nearly twenty years after her arrival in New Orleans, she was finally listed as a physician.

Widowed and alone after the death of her children, Cohen retired from practice in 1887 and entered Touro Infirmary in February 1888, as a resident of their Department of the Aged and Infirm, later called the Julius Weis Home for the Aged. She became a volunteer for the hospital, caring for the sewing and linen room. Her interest in current events and women's rights was evident even in old age. "I'm glad to see the girls of today getting an education. In my youth you had to fight for it. And I believe in suffrage, too—things will be better when women can vote and can protect their own property and their own children. Even if I am a hundred, I'm for votes for women."

Although no overt displays of Judaism are evident in what is known of her life, her adherence to her faith is clear in her choice of retirement residence, and in her own words to her brother, written in 1902: "I am not sure what I will have in the hereafter, so I am trying to enjoy what is given to me here . . . I am . . . trying my very best to be good according to my ideas of goodness—that is to live in the fear of God and keeping his ten commandments."

Elizabeth Cohen died on May 28, 1921, and was buried in Gates of Prayer Cemetery on Canal Street. She left her estate to the Julius Weis Home for the Aged.

BIBLIOGRAPHY

Blackmar, Mrs. K.K. "New Orleans First Woman Doctor." *New Orleans Daily Picayune*, January 26, 1913; Duffy, John, ed. *The Rudolph Matas History of Medicine in Louisiana* (1962); O'Brien, Sharon, ed. "The Attic Letters of Elizabeth D. A. Cohen, M. D." *Tourovues: The Magazine of Touro Infirmary* (Summer 1977); Samuels, Marguerite. "Woman Doctor Celebrates Her 100th Birthday." *New Orleans Times-Picayune*, February 22, 1920.

CATHERINE KAHN

COHEN, HELEN LOUISE
(1882–1957)

Helen Louise Cohen, an educator and author, made the study of drama more accessible and vibrant to countless numbers of high school students in the first half of the twentieth century. Although Judaism seemed to play only a small role in her adult life, it is Jewish culture and values that contributed to her regard for education and helped to shape her life's work.

She was born on March 17, 1882, in New York City to Gustavus Anker Cohen and Clara (Mayer) Cohen, German-American Jews. Helen earned her B.A. in English in 1903, at Barnard College, where she acted in a number of college productions. In 1905 she earned her M.A. in English, also at Barnard, and in 1915 she was awarded a Ph.D. in English at Columbia University. Her dissertation was entitled "The Ballade."

Like many young women who received graduate degrees, Cohen had pursued her career rather than marrying immediately upon graduation. In 1903, she had begun teaching English at Washington Irving High School. From 1909 to 1913, she was the deputy principal, and in 1914 she became the chair of the English Department. Cohen was also a lecturer at Columbia University's Extension School in 1914–1915 and taught summer school at Johns Hopkins University in 1924 and at Pennsylvania State College in 1929.

Through her widely used collections of plays for high school students, Cohen's impact reached far beyond Washington Irving High School. Although she had studied the medieval and Renaissance French ballade, Cohen believed that the study of modern drama, especially American plays, was particularly important for high school students. In many cases, she argued, formal education would end with high school graduation. Thus, pupils should study drama because it offered "the young worker" "diversion, solace, and inspiration." American plays might inspire a patriotism in students that would contribute to "the welfare of the native drama," and also spur creativity.

The introductions to the volumes of plays Cohen edited convey both a sense of excitement and passion for drama and a solid sense of how pupils should study and write plays. As modern drama was becoming an increasingly accepted art form, she hoped to convey to students how to be discriminating theatergoers.

Cohen's other professional activities included membership in the American Academy of University Women, the New York Academy of Public Education, the National Council of Teachers of English, the National Council of Administrative Women in Education, Phi Beta Kappa, and the School and Collegiate Conference on English. She was also an associate member of the legal advisory board in connection with the selective service law in New York for

1917–1918, and a personnel worker for the Military Intelligence Division in Washington, D.C., in 1918.

Cohen was married in 1934 to William Roswell Stockwell, the general manager of the Weil-McLain Company of Chicago, manufacturers of boilermakers. With her marriage, Cohen became part of the 3 percent of American Jews who intermarried in the 1930s. She died on July 18, 1957, and is buried in the Sleepy Hollow Cemetery in New York.

SELECTED WORKS BY
HELEN LOUISE COHEN

"The Ballade" (1915); *Educating Superior Students: Co-operative Studies Carried on Under the Auspices of the Association of First Assistants in the High Schools of the City of New York*, with Nancy G. Coryell (1935); *The Junior Play Book*, editor (1923); *Longer Plays by Modern Authors*, editor (1922); *Lyric Forms From France: Their History and Their Use* (1922); *More One-Act Plays by Modern Authors*, editor (1927); *One Act Plays by Modern Authors*, editor (1921).

BIBLIOGRAPHY

Cremin, Lawrence. *American Education: The Metropolitan Experience, 1876–1980* (1988); Lefkowitz, Helen Horowitz. *Alma Mater: Design and Experience in the Women's Colleges From Their Nineteenth-Century Beginnings to the 1930's* (1984); Solomon, Barbara Miller. *In the Company of Education Women: A History of Women and Higher Education in America* (1985); *UJE*; *WWIAJ* (1926, 1928, 1938).

RACHELLE E. FRIEDMAN

COHEN, JESSICA (JESSIE)
(1869–1945)

Jessie Cohen devoted the majority of her adult life to the Jewish press. Following an early career in the Cleveland, Ohio, public school system, she moved to Memphis, Tennessee, where she became the associate editor of that city's *Jewish Spectator*. She remained in that position for five years. Cohen left Tennessee to return to Cleveland as the editor of the *Jewish Review and Observer*. She remained as its editor until forced to retire due to ill health. Until her death, Cohen served as editor emeritus.

Jessie Cohen was born in Cleveland, Ohio, on July 11, 1869, the daughter of early Cleveland settlers Elias and Rachel Cohen. Her father was active in Great Lakes shipping. Jessie Cohen attended Cleveland public schools and graduated from Central High and the Cleveland Normal School, which became the School of Education at Case Western Reserve University.

Cohen was active in a number of organizations. She was a member of the NATIONAL COUNCIL OF JEWISH WOMEN and Temple Women's Association, and was an honorary member of the Cleveland Women's Writers Association. Jessie Cohen died at her home in Cleveland Heights, Ohio, on August 15, 1945.

BIBLIOGRAPHY

AJYB 6 (1904–1905): 75, 48:486; *Jewish Review and Observer* 17, no. 33 (August 17, 1945), 1:3; Obituary. *NYTimes*, August 17, 1945, sec. 2, 17:4.

LORI A. FERGUSON

COHEN, KATHERINE M.
(1859–1914)

Although few Jews were sculptors in nineteenth-century America, in part due to the biblical prohibition against creating graven images, Katherine Cohen, a sculptor from Philadelphia with elite academic training, exhibited figurative works, often of Jewish subjects, in an era when women and Jews achieved slight renown in the art world.

Katherine Cohen, the youngest of four children, was born in Philadelphia on March 18, 1859, to immigrant parents, Henry Cohen of London and Matilda (Samuel) Cohen of Liverpool. As a child, she had a private tutor and later attended the Chestnut Street Seminary. Cohen's art training lasted several years. She studied first in Philadelphia at the Pennsylvania Academy of Fine Arts under painter Thomas Eakins, and then worked at the Art Students League in New York City as an assistant in the atelier of Gilded Age sculptor Augustus Saint-Gaudens. In 1884, she opened her own studio in Philadelphia. In 1887, she went to Paris to work under sculptors Puech and Mercie, remaining in Europe for several years. While in Paris, she was elected an honorary member of the American Art Association. The academic jury chose her life-size sculpture *The Israelite* for the 1896 Paris Salon, a definitive sign of her arrival as an artist.

In 1893, on a visit to the United States, Cohen spoke on the "Life of Artists" at the Women's Pavilion at the World's Columbian Exposition in Chicago. Her speech described the daily struggles and triumphs of artists, defended their way of life, and commented on the potential of art in the United States. "When we arrive at the point that American art is better than anything we can get in Europe," she said, "then we shall stay at home to study.... We can all of us help the quick realization of this, if we encourage our boys and girls to cultivate their artistic tastes instead of scoffing at them as impractical and never likely to make them rich."

Comfortably situated in the community of Philadelphia's Jewish elite, the Cohen family was highly respected, even powerful, in the city's secular establishment. Before she left for Europe, Cohen illustrated *A Jewish Child's Book* for kindergartners, published by the Jewish Publication Society. Her book was one of the first Jewish children's books to be printed in color. She also chaired the choir at Mikveh Israel, the prominent Philadelphia synagogue. Her mother founded the Committee of Thirteen, which organized the art exhibit at Philadelphia's 1876 centenniel celebration. Her sister Mary was an author on Jewish subjects and a community organizer who addressed the Jewish Women's Congress at the 1893 Chicago World's Fair. Her brother, Charles, a merchant, was the president of the Philadelphia Chamber of Commerce and a trustee of Gratz College.

Not surprisingly, Cohen found many patrons to support her. Among her commissions were the design of the seal of Gratz College and portrait busts of prominent Philadelphia Jews, including Judge Mayer Sulzberger and businessman/philanthropist Lucien Moss. She further illustrated a strong choice of Jewish themes with her ambitious multifigured sculpture *Vision of Rabbi Ben Ezra*. However, her success did not necessarily mean she subscribed to cutting-edge developments of the contemporary art of her period. True to the tenets of academic classicism, she had little tolerance for the modern art emerging at the turn of the century and likened futurist and cubist depictions of a human eye to "a horrible distorted fish."

Katherine Cohen died in Philadelphia in December 1914 age fifty-five. Her 1893 Women's Pavilion speech evidenced her lifelong pursuit of and commitment toward art in which she stated, "An artist's chief grief is that life is too short for him to accomplish what he wants to do even in his own special line of work, and this is equally true of woman, for talent knows no sex."

SELECTED WORKS BY KATHERINE M. COHEN

A Jewish Child's Book [Illustrations] (1913); "Life of Artists." *The Congress of Women* (1894).

BIBLIOGRAPHY

AJYB 6 (1904–1905): 76, 17 (1915–1916): 219; *AJA* (April 1963): 48; *American Jewish Historical Society Quarterly* (Summer 1995); Cohen, Katherine M. Letters. Historical Society of Pennsylvania, Philadelphia; *JE*; *UJE*.

MICHELE SIEGEL

COHEN, NAOMI W. (b. 1927)

A prolific author and noted educator and academic, Naomi W. Cohen has achieved prominence as a historian of the United States and Jewish Americans.

She was born to Louis and Mary (Halkin) Wiener on November 13, 1927, in New York City. She received her B.A. from HUNTER COLLEGE in 1947 and her B.H.L. (bachelor of Hebrew letters) from the Seminary College of Jewish Studies in 1948. Also in 1948, she married Gerson D. Cohen, a Jewish historian who later became chancellor of the Jewish Theological Seminary of America (1983–1986). The couple had two children, Jeremy and Judith.

Naomi Cohen went on to earn a master's degree in 1949 and a Ph.D. in 1955 from Columbia University. In 1962, she was appointed assistant professor of history at Hunter College of the City University of New York. In 1968, she was made an associate professor, and became a full professor in 1973. She was also on the faculty of the Graduate Center of the City University of New York. She retired in 1996 and moved to Israel.

Cohen's research focuses on two main areas: twentieth-century American history and American Jewish history. Her numerous publications include: *Not Free to Desist: The American Jewish Committee, 1906–1966* (1972), *American Jews and the Zionist Idea* (1975), and *The Year After the Riots: American Responses to the Palestine Crisis of 1929–1930* (1988). She also edited *Essential Papers on Jewish-Christian Relations in the United States: Imagery and Reality* (1990).

Cohen is a member of many scholarly organizations, including Phi Beta Kappa, the American Historical Association, the Organization of American Historians, the Academic Council of the American Jewish Historical Society, the Association for Jewish Studies, and the Conference on Jewish Social Studies.

She entered the academic world at a time of heightened self-consciousness among Jewish scholars. Ethnic studies became prominent in the late 1960s, allowing Judaic and Semitic university departments to flourish. Professors in these new fields reflected on the best goals and methods for advancing such studies, and as a result, the Association for Jewish Studies was founded in 1969. The purpose of this self-regulating body was to monitor Jewish studies departments and to establish academic standards for undergraduate and graduate courses and programs in this field across the United States.

In 1960, American women began pushing seriously to be recognized as Judaic scholars; by 1978, only one female full professor was listed as a member of the Association for Jewish Studies, as opposed to 101 males. With her scholarship, Naomi W. Cohen has contributed a great deal to Jewish knowledge, culture, and self-awareness. While women are much more visible in Jewish studies departments today than they were even a decade ago, Cohen remains an exemplar of scholarly excellence and success for American Jewish women.

SELECTED WORKS BY NAOMI W. COHEN

American Jews and the Zionist Idea (1975); *Essential Papers on Jewish-Christian Relations in the United States: Imagery and Reality,* editor (1990); *Not Free to Desist: The American Jewish Committee, 1906–1966* (1972); *The Year After the Riots: American Responses to the Palestine Crisis of 1929–1930* (1988).

BIBLIOGRAPHY

Contemporary Authors. Edited by Hal May. Vol. 114 (1985); *Directory of American Scholars.* 8th ed. Vol. 1: History (1982); Ritterband, Paul, and Harold Wechsler. *Jewish Learning in American Universities* (1994); *Who's Who in World Jewry* (1978).

TAMAR KAPLAN

COHEN, NATALIE (b. 1912)

Because Natalie Cohen's life met the very essence of the definition of the "Georgia Women Sports Trailblazers," she was elected a charter member in 1996. Already a Hall of Famer, this crowning honor is only one of many received throughout her life recognizing Natalie Cohen as a woman who has made significant contributions to sports, forging paths for others to follow.

Born on June 9, 1912, Natalie Cohen, a lifelong resident of Atlanta, Georgia, was the only surviving daughter of Dewald A. Cohen of Atlanta and Meta Leinkauf Cohen of Mobile, Alabama. She was educated in the Atlanta public school system, graduating from Girls' High in 1930, and matriculated at University of California, Berkeley, graduating with a bachelor of arts degree in political science in 1934, with honors.

Her religious training stemmed from her parents and Sunday school at Atlanta's Hebrew Benevolent Congregation. A confirmant in May 1928, Cohen's lineage includes early members of the oldest Atlanta congregation through her great-grandfather Solomon Dewald and his daughter Dora Dewald, who married Henry Cohen. Henry Cohen's son, Dewald Cohen, Natalie's father, was president of the congregation during the World War II years between 1941 and 1944.

After graduation from the university, Cohen's first professional mentor was the beloved Pulitzer Prize–winner Ralph McGill, then the sports editor of the *Atlanta Constitution.* After an initial taste of sports

Natalie Cohen began playing tennis at age eight. Described as a "tennis legend," she has been involved in the game ever since, first as a player and then as an umpire.

journalism, Cohen commenced work in the federal government, at first with the Civil Service Commission district office from 1936 to 1940, then in the War Department Civilian Personnel Field Office (later of the Department of Army) and South Atlantic Engineer Division from 1941 to 1967. After retiring from federal service in 1967, Cohen started a new career as the first executive secretary of the Southern Tennis Association (STA), which she held until her second retirement in September 1980.

Described in articles as "Miss Tennis of Atlanta," a "tennis legend," and "USLTA woman of the month," Cohen began playing tennis at age eight. When she retired from play in 1994, she had won thirteen Georgia State Women's Open Double Championships and the Atlanta singles in 1949. In 1954, at age forty-two, she won the "grand slam" of local tennis by winning both the Atlanta City and Georgia State singles and doubles championships. Cohen was ranked number two in doubles by the STA.

Cohen was a certified umpire for over fifty years, a United States Tennis Association stadium umpire and referee. She was the first woman to serve as chair umpire for men's National Collegiate Athletic Association's Tennis Championships; the first southern woman to serve as chair umpire at Forest Hills; and chair of umpires, Southern Tennis Association and Georgia Tennis Association (GTA). She received the Marlborough Award from *World Tennis* in 1962. She was selected umpire of the year by STA in 1976; awarded the Jacobs Bowl by STA in 1977; was GTA umpire of the year in 1978; and became the recipient of the GTA Service Award in 1980. She is an STA, GTA, and Georgia Jewish Sports Halls of Fame member and was awarded the Presidential Sports Award by President Gerald Ford. As a volunteer, Natalie Cohen umpired local, regional, and national matches and was the first woman to umpire a professional match during the Jack Kramer tours in the 1950s.

Drawing upon her experiences in sports, she wrote and spoke on encouraging more active roles for women, particularly in tennis. Cohen's alma mater, the University of California at Berkeley, recognized her long-standing support by dedicating a seat in its stadium in her honor, and she was recognized in *International Tennis Who's Who*.

Outspoken for good sportsmanship and adherence to fairness in the application of the rules, she did not hesitate to write, "To kow-tow and break rules and regulations for a few favored players is wrong, wrong, wrong." She publicly reprimanded the famous Romanian tennis star, Ilie Nastase, while umpiring at his matches in Atlanta. Nastase, in a public apology that made the international news of the day, presented Cohen with a bouquet of roses.

SELECTED WORKS BY NATALIE COHEN

"Bitsy Grant Is Life Member of the Month." *Tennis USA* (April 1972); "My Point." *Tennis* (September 1977).

BIBLIOGRAPHY

Cohen, Natalie. Interviews by author, April 3, 1996, and September 26, 1996; *International Who's Who in Tennis* (1983); McDonald, Joe D. "Miss Tennis of Atlanta." *Net News* (October–November 1980); "Reminiscences of a Southern Old Blue." Regional Oral History Office, The Bancroft Library, University of California, Berkeley; Train, Sally. "Finding Missing Persons 'Elementary' for Cohen." *Tennis USA* 2, no. 13; Weiner, Beryl H. "Athlete Natalie Cohen Has Always Been Ahead of Her Time." *The Jewish Georgian* (May–June 1996); "Women of USLTA in Profile: Natalie Cohen Is a Fixture at SLTA Office." *Tennis* (December 1970).

BERYL H. WEINER

COHEN, NINA MORAIS (1855–1918)

Nina Morais Cohen distinguished herself as a writer, teacher, and community leader of her adopted home of Minneapolis, Minnesota. The daughter of a scholar and community leader, her life and work exemplified the ideals of her father, the longtime rabbi of Philadelphia's Mikveh Israel and founder of the Jewish Theological Seminary.

Named Bonina, or Tobah, at birth, the eldest child of Sabato and Clara Esther (Weil) Morais was born in Philadelphia, on December 6, 1855. Nina's father was an immigrant from Livorno, Italy, who served the London Jewish community for six years before arriving in Philadelphia in 1851. He held the post of rabbi of Mikveh Israel (succeeding Isaac Leeser) from 1851 until his death in 1897. Nina's mother, Clara Weil, was American-born, the daughter of a German immigrant.

Nina graduated from the Girls' Normal School, where her abilities in many subjects, especially literature, made her a popular tutor and teacher. She also served as a superintendent of the Southern Branch of Philadelphia's Hebrew Sunday School.

Clara Weil Morais died in 1872 when Nina was seventeen years old, and the remaining six children, two boys and four girls, ranged in age from twelve to three. Providing child-rearing assistance to her father may explain why Nina married relatively late in life, at age thirty. In 1885, she married Emanuel Cohen, a native of Carbondale, Pennsylvania, a small town northeast of Scranton. The two of them set out for Minneapolis in 1886.

Nina Cohen's reputation as an intellectual and champion of woman suffrage dates from her years in Philadelphia. She was an active writer, a contributor to Jewish and secular journals, a teacher, and a public speaker on literary as well as political topics. In Minneapolis, she, like her husband, rose to leadership in both the Jewish and non-Jewish communities. Her husband, an attorney and graduate of Williams College, became a successful insurance lawyer, was a member of the city's first Charter Commission, and was the local agent for the Baron de Hirsch Fund. Cohen's activities in the larger community included her unwavering support of woman suffrage. She hosted Susan B. Anthony when she visited Minneapolis. She was an organizer and charter member of the Woman's City Club, and also headed the Minneapolis campaign to raise funds for a memorial to Shelley and Keats to be built in Rome.

However, it was to the NATIONAL COUNCIL OF JEWISH WOMEN (NCJW) that Nina Morais Cohen devoted her greatest energies. In 1893, she attended the Congress of Religions in Chicago, organized as part of the World Columbian Exposition, and was present at the founding of the council. On her return to Minneapolis, she began to organize a local section, founded on July 25, 1894. A few months later, she helped to organize the St. Paul Section and to establish their study program. She served as president of the Minneapolis Section from 1894 to 1907, vice president for Minnesota, and led an ambitious study program devoted to biblical subjects, Jewish literature, and history. For thirteen years, Cohen conducted Saturday afternoon study sessions for NCJW members in her home, and she is credited with influencing and inspiring many future communal leaders.

Nina Morais Cohen's death on February 19, 1918, was marked by a prominent notice in the *Minneapolis Journal* signed by representatives of the National Council of Jewish Women, the Woman's City Club, Minnesota Woman Suffrage Association, the public library, and the College Women's Club—clear evidence of her influence and interests.

BIBLIOGRAPHY

AJYB 7 (1905–1906): 49; Friedman, Murray, ed. *Jewish Life in Philadelphia: 1830–1940* (1983); Marcus, Jacob R. *The American Jewish Woman: A Documentary History* (1987); "Memorial Resolution." *Minneapolis Journal*, February 23, 1918; Morais, Henry S. *The Jews of Philadelphia* (1894); Plaut, W. Gunther. *The Jews in Minnesota: The First 75 Years* (1959); Rogow, Faith. *Gone to Another Meeting: The National Council of Jewish Women, 1893–1993* (1993).

JUDITH E. ENDELMAN

COHEN, ROSALIE (b. 1910)

I have lived through most of this century and observed all the -isms: Communism, Socialism, Fascism, Nazism, Zionism . . . only Zionism survives. It has been a great privilege to devote my life to Zionism, the millennial dream of the Jewish people.

—Rosalie Cohen

Role model and mentor to a generation of young Jews, Rosalie Cohen has spent most of her life promoting Zionism and Jewish education in her hometown of New Orleans and on the national and international scenes.

She was born on May 27, 1910, in New Orleans. Her parents, Fanny (Brener) and Leon Palter, had emigrated separately from Bialystok, Russia, around 1905. Educated as a chemist and textile dyer in Russia, Leon Palter initially became a peddler in New Orleans and, in 1921, opened a furniture business called Universal Furniture House.

The seven-thousand-strong Jewish community in New Orleans (comprising less than 1 percent of the city's population) consisted overwhelmingly of second- and third-generation classical Reform Jews of German heritage. The Palters, by contrast, were Russian immigrants, Orthodox, and dedicated to Zionism. From an early age, Rosalie was taught about the importance of the Jews' homeland. As a child, she attended Zionist meetings with her parents. Between the ages of eight and sixteen, she studied the Torah and Hebrew daily, achieving fluency under the tutelage of the distinguished Russian Hebrew poet Ephriam E. Lisitzky. The Palters had helped to bring Lisitzky to New Orleans in 1918 from Milwaukee, where he had been teaching Hebrew to GOLDA MEIR. In his new base, Lisitzky established the Communal Hebrew School.

In 1929, at age nineteen, Rosalie Palter married Dr. Joseph Cohen, a surgeon and native New Yorker who shared her love of Zion. During their honeymoon, the couple attended the 1929 World Zionist Congress in Zurich, Switzerland, the historic meeting in which Zionists and non-Zionists were united in the newly formed Jewish Agency. The Cohens also visited Palestine, where they were incorrectly reported as having been slain during Arab-Jewish skirmishes.

Cohen studied at the Tulane University School of Journalism, developing eloquent written and oral skills in the process, and graduating with a B.A. in 1930. During World War II, she was employed as a Hebrew translator by the United States Department of Censorship. Starting in the 1940s, she began annual visits to the future State of Israel.

In New Orleans, Cohen worked to strengthen the intellectual and cultural life of the local Jewish community. She served as the first female president of the Greater New Orleans Jewish Federation from 1959 to 1961. She was a cofounder of the Jewish Community Center Senior Citizens Club in the late 1950s, the Home for the Jewish Aged in 1962, and Women in Federation in 1966. Believing that "Jewish education is the source of Jewish continuity," she focused particular attention on training future Jewish leaders (especially women) and on developing Jewish academic programs. She established the New Orleans Lemann Stern Young Leadership Group in 1960, whose purpose was to educate young Jewish women and men in leadership skills and philanthropy through exposure to national leaders and missions to Israel. Cohen's

Rosalie Cohen has devoted her life to promoting Zionism, both in her hometown of New Orleans and also on the national and international scenes. She is shown here introducing Eleanor Roosevelt at the launching of New Orleans's Israel Bonds Organization in 1951.

program philosophy eventually became a national model for federation leadership training.

She was responsible for several other educational programs for New Orleans Jewish women: a program at the New Orleans Enduring Heritage Institute (1965–1972), a forum for presidents of Jewish women's organizations (1980s), and a Torah study group (1985–1993). Her Shabbat table attracted eminent scholars, political thinkers, lay leaders, and travelers, who in turn have enriched the somewhat geographically isolated New Orleans Jewish community.

For her civic activities and leadership, she received the keys to the city from three different New Orleans mayors: Victor Schiro in 1960, Moon Lan-

drieu in 1971, and Marc Morial in 1996. She also received a Tulane School of Social Work Honorary Award in 1997.

At the national level, she was the first elected female vice president of the American Council of Jewish Federations (1963–1965). She was a founding member of the National Foundation for Jewish Culture (NFJC) in 1960. She helped to establish the NFJC's funding program for doctoral students of Jewish studies—a program that contributed to the dramatic increase in the number of chairs of Jewish learning at American universities from only three before 1960 to ten times that number today. Also in the early 1960s, Cohen served as national vice president of the Jewish Educational Services of North America, an organization dedicated to fostering Jewish grade-school education.

Since her first visits to Israel in the 1940s, Cohen has sought to promote Jewish education at an international level. In Israel, she worked with Professor Moshe Davis, chairman of Hebrew University's International Committee for University Teaching of Jewish Civilization. The committee has guided the development of departments and programs of Jewish studies around the world.

Cohen's talents as a leader and organizer, as well as her gracious southern manners, have been key assets in overcoming the obstacles she faced as a Zionist in a southern city and as a woman in a predominantly male Jewish national arena. Despite her ties with national and international Jewry, she particularly cherishes her New Orleans community, which has nurtured such eminent figures as Judah Touro, Judah P. Benjamin, and Rabbi Max Heller. Cohen herself has been a builder of this community, leading it from "the flight [from Israel] to the return," from the "abandonment [of Israel] to the embrace." As she said, "I have had a vision of what a Jewish community ought to be, and I felt I had a responsibility."

BIBLIOGRAPHY

"Assails the British on Palestine Riots—New Orleans Doctor Declares Soldiers Witnessed Murders Without Interfering." *NYTimes*, October 14, 1929; "Jewish Stalwart Excels as Leader." *New Orleans Times-Picayune*, January 21, 1995; "New Orleans Residents Recall Robin's Lasting Impression." *New Orleans Times-Picayune*, November 7, 1995.

ALICE YELEN

COHEN, ROSE GOLLUP (1880–1925)

Rose Gollup Cohen was the author of a 1918 autobiography detailing her childhood in Russia, immigration to the United States, and life on New York City's Lower East Side. *Out of the Shadow* offers one of the richest accounts of the experience of a Russian Jewish immigrant woman at the turn of the century.

Rose Gollup Cohen, born on April 4, 1880, was the daughter of Abraham (Avrom), a tailor, and Annie Gollup. The oldest child in her family, she grew up in a small village in what is today Belarus. The onset in the 1880s of attacks on Jewish communities and the expulsion of Jews from numerous Russian towns and cities made life increasingly intolerable for the Jewish

minority and contributed to the exodus of about two million Russian Jews between 1880 and 1914.

The Gollup family was part of this massive immigrant flow. As was common in the period, Rose's father migrated first in 1890, leaving his family behind. He worked and got a foothold for himself in New York City, and after a year and a half sent two prepaid steamship tickets to his family. In 1892, Rose and her unmarried aunt, Masha, joined him. A year later, her mother, two brothers, and two sisters followed.

Cohen provides a detailed view of sweatshop garment work. She recounts union organizing among the men of her shop, her attendance at a mass union meeting, and joining a union, probably the United Hebrew Trades. After the arrival of her mother and siblings, her story continues with accounts of a brief stint as a domestic servant, her rejection of a prospective suitor, and increasing health problems. During

Rose Gollup Cohen's groundbreaking 1918 autobiography, Out of the Shadow, *made her a literary celebrity. It painted a moving picture of a Russian Jewish woman's journey from persecution in her homeland to the garment sweatshops of New York's Lower East Side.*

one illness, she was visited by the noted settlement worker LILLIAN WALD. Through the settlement, she was referred to the uptown Presbyterian Hospital, and there she met wealthy non-Jews who sponsored summer outings for children of the Lower East Side. She worked successive summers at a Connecticut retreat established for immigrant children and, like others, found herself torn between the immigrant world of her family and broader American culture.

Wald helped the young Rose Gollup in yet another way, by referring her in 1897 to a cooperative shirtwaist shop under the direction of Leonora O'Reilly, later a board member of the National Women's Trade Union League. That work proved short-lived, but when O'Reilly began teaching at the Manhattan Trade School for Girls in 1902, she recruited Rose Gollup as her assistant.

Little is known about Cohen's later life. She married Joseph Cohen and stopped working when her daughter, Evelyn, was born. She continued her education after marriage, attending classes at Breadwinners' College at the Educational Alliance and the Rand School, there coming under the influence of Joseph Gollomb, a Russian Jewish immigrant novelist.

In addition to her autobiography, she wrote five short pieces published in New York literary magazines between 1918 and 1922. Her writing was received enthusiastically by contemporaries. Reviews in *The Outlook* and the *New York Times* were glowing. Lillian Wald and Leonora O'Reilly both praised the work as well. The book appeared in two European editions, French and Russian. A short story, "Natalka's Portion," was reprinted six times, including in the prestigious *Best Short Stories of 1922*. In addition, in the summers of 1923 and 1924 Cohen attended the Mac-Dowell Colony in Peterborough, New Hampshire. There she met the American impressionist painter Lilla Cabot Perry and the poet Edwin Arlington Robinson.

Her tragic death in 1925 at age forty-five under uncertain circumstances led ANZIA YEZIERSKA to write a thinly veiled short story about Cohen that ended in suicide. We may never know how she died, but her autobiography survives as Rose Gollup Cohen's legacy, a moving account of a cultural journey shared with many other Russian and Eastern European Jewish immigrant women at the turn of the twentieth century.

SELECTED WORKS BY ROSE GOLLUP COHEN

"My Childhood Days in Russia." *Bookman* (August 1918): 591–608; *Out of the Shadow* (1918. Reprint 1995); "To the Friends of 'Out of the Shadow.'" *Bookman* (March 1922): 36–40.

BIBLIOGRAPHY

Cohen, Rose Gollup. Letter to Lilla Cabot Perry. November 12 [?]. Perry Family Papers. Colby College Library, Waterville, Maine; Dublin, Thomas. Introduction to *Out of the Shadow*, by Rose Gollup Cohen (1995); MacDowell Colony. *Annual Reports* (1923, 1924); National Archives. U.S. Federal Manuscript Census of Population (1900). Microfilm T623, reel 1084, enumeration district 82, sheet 9; O'Reilly, Leonora. "Rahel and 'Out of the Shadow.'" *Life and Labor* (May 1919): 103–105; Yezierska, Anzia. "Wild Winter Love." *Century Magazine* 113 (February 1927): 485–491.

THOMAS DUBLIN

COHEN, SELMA JEANNE (b. 1920)

It has been Selma Jeanne Cohen's mission in life to make dance scholarship a respected field, taking its place with the study of the other arts both in society and, particularly, the university. As a writer, editor, and teacher, she has been a leader in transforming dance history, aesthetics, and criticism into respected disciplines. She encouraged and often trained those who are now working in these vital fields, so that dance is no longer viewed as mere entertainment, but is studied as a rich art on many levels, from the most elite to varieties of popular and folk expression, illuminating society in new and valuable ways. She is an internationalist, her Jewish heritage playing little part in her life or her approach to dance in the world.

Selma Jeanne Cohen was born in Chicago on September 18, 1920, the only child of Frank and Minnie (Skud) Cohen. With no intention of becoming a dancer, she studied ballet while attending the Laboratory School of the University of Chicago and later the university itself, receiving a B.A. in 1941 and a Ph.D. in English literature in 1946, with a dissertation on the poetry and thought of Gerard Manley Hopkins. She brought this rigorous intellectual training with the "Chicago Aristotelians" to dance scholarship. Two years of teaching English at the University of California at Los Angeles (1946–1948) made her realize that her real interests were in dance, so she worked and taught for several years with choreographer-teacher Eugene Loring before moving to New York in 1953, where she taught at HUNTER COLLEGE and the High School of the Performing Arts. At the high school, her students in dance history included the future dance company directors Arthur Mitchell, Bruce Marks, and Eliot Feld.

She had already begun writing about dance, including an important 1950 article, "Some Theories of Dance in Contemporary Society." She developed a

Though never a dancer, writer, editor, and teacher Selma Jeanne Cohen has almost single-handedly brought recognition to dance as a vital art form worthy of historical study and criticism. [New York Public Library]

close association with the American Society for Aesthetics as part of her struggle to make dance "visible" in many fields of scholarly endeavor. From 1955 to 1958, she was an assistant to John Martin, dance critic of the *New York Times*, and was one of the earliest women to write criticism for that paper. In 1962, she began a decade of teaching dance history and writing at the American Dance Festival, held at Connecticut College. This resulted in 1970 in the formation of a program to train professional dance critics, many of them journalists without any particular knowledge of the field assigned to cover dance.

In 1959, with A.J. Pischl, she founded *Dance Perspectives*, a quarterly journal specializing in monographs on a wide variety of dance topics written by leading scholars and practitioners. It set a high standard that served as a model for later journals in the field. She became sole editor from 1966 to 1976 and

used the journal to encourage a wider understanding of dance throughout the world. Individual issues dealt with ballet and modern dance, as well as dance in ancient Greece, India, Korea, Micronesia, Israel, and Ghana, popular entertainment, iconography, music, design, and even dance poetry. She also established the Dance Perspectives Foundation, which since 1973 has given the annual De la Torre Bueno Prize for the best dance book of the year, the most prestigious award in the field.

Dance Perspectives led her to undertake her great dream, a multivolume encyclopedia that would do for dance what *The New Grove Dictionary of Music and Musicians* has done for music: provide a concise and accurate source of information on all aspects of the art around the world. After many vicissitudes, *The International Encyclopedia of Dance* (sponsored by the Dance Perspectives Foundation) has at last been published.

Cohen continued teaching and gave seminars and advice on shaping the graduate program at the University of California at Riverside from 1966 to 1989. In 1974–1976, she offered summer seminars at the University of Chicago, and in 1977 at Sarah Lawrence. She was distinguished professor at Smith College in 1976–1977.

In addition to her many reviews and articles, her four books have made important and very different contributions to the field. In *The Modern Dance: Seven Statements of Belief*, seven leading choreographers discuss their approaches to the art. *Doris Humphrey: An Artist First* turns Humphrey's unfinished autobiography into a full examination of her life and work. *Dance as a Theatre Art* provides a carefully annotated anthology of dance writing from the Renaissance to the present. And *Next Week Swan Lake* is concerned with the varied aesthetic considerations suggested by a dance performance, based on a lifetime of watching and thinking about dance.

Cohen has also been active in many national and international organizations, attending and, on occasion, organizing conferences for the International Theater Institute, the American Society for Theater Research (ASTR), the International Federation for Theater Research, Conseil International de la Danse, the World Dance Alliance, and the American Society for Aesthetics (ASA). She served on the boards of ASTR and ASA. She was a founder of the Society of Dance History Scholars, which in 1994 established the Selma Jeanne Cohen Young Scholars Program to encourage students of dance history. In 1974, she received a Professional Achievement Award from the University of Chicago, and in 1981, the first Dance Magazine Award given to a dance historian.

SELECTED WORKS BY SELMA JEANNE COHEN

Dance as a Theatre Art: Source Readings in Dance History from 1581 to the Present, editor (1974); *Doris Humphrey: An Artist First*, edited and completed by Selma Jeanne Cohen (1972); *The International Encyclopedia of Dance* (1997); *The Modern Dance: Seven Statements of Belief*, editor (1966); *Next Week Swan Lake: Reflections on Dance and Dances* (1982); "Some Theories of Dance in Contemporary Society." *Journal of Aesthetics and Art Criticism* 9, no. 1 (September 1950): 111–118.

BIBLIOGRAPHY

Dorris, George. "Selma Jeanne Cohen." *Dance Chronicle* 18, no. 2 (1995); *Who's Who in America*, 1995.

GEORGE DORRIS

COHN, FANNIA M. (1885–1962)

In the first half of the twentieth century, Fannia M. Cohn was one of the leading Jewish women trade union activists in the United States. Drawing on her Russian Jewish cultural traditions, she pioneered in the development of educational programs within the INTERNATIONAL LADIES GARMENT WORKERS UNION (ILGWU). Ultimately, however, male opposition undermined her efforts and diminished her long-term significance. Her life offers evidence of the possibilities and limitations of women's activism in the American labor movement.

Fannia Cohn, the fourth of five children of Hyman (Chaim) and Anna (Rosofsky) Cohn, was born in Kletzk, in what is today Belarus. She came from a prestigious and wealthy Russian Jewish family, and her father managed a family flour mill. She was encouraged to read, was educated privately, and at age fifteen became involved in clandestine revolutionary activities.

In 1904, following a pogrom in which her brother was almost killed, she and her brother emigrated, using second-class steamship tickets purchased by wealthy cousins who were already living in New York. She worked at first as the representative of the American Jewish Women's Committee at Ellis Island. Eschewing further education and employment in her relatives' business, she took a job in 1906 as a sleeve-maker, with the clear intent of becoming involved in trade union work. In 1909, she was a founding organizer of ILGWU Local 41, a local for wrapper and kimono makers. In 1913, Cohn led a white goods strike and served as a delegate from the local to the ILGWU national convention.

She moved to Chicago in 1914, where she attended a school for labor organizers sponsored by the Women's Trade Union League. Dissatisfied with the courses offered at the University of Chicago, Cohn made her own arrangements to take private English lessons. She was soon working for ILGWU again, organizing dressmakers. In 1915, she helped lead a strike at a contract shop for Sears, Roebuck. In early 1916, she left Chicago and returned to New York City.

That same year, Cohn was elected vice president of the ILGWU, the first woman to serve in such a high office in that union. Reelected four times, she served ten years on the union's executive board. The position made Cohn a union policymaker, and in 1917, she launched ILGWU programs in workers' education, thus moving into the career niche that became her life's work. The ILGWU sponsored a Workers University at Washington Irving High School in New York City, and Cohn succeeded in establishing educational programs in other cities, including Boston, Chicago, Cleveland, and Philadelphia.

Fannia Cohn took part in a wide variety of workers' education activities. She was instrumental in the founding of Brookwood Labor College, the first residential workers' college in the United States. She was a founder and board member of the Manumit School, a school for workers' children in Pauling, New York. She also served on the board of the Workers' Education Bureau, an umbrella organization promoting activities in the area of workers' education. In the 1920s, she attended major international conferences on workers' education in Brussels and Oxford. She developed an international network of contacts and became widely known for her pioneering work in the field.

Despite her international notice, Cohn did not enjoy unqualified support within ILGWU circles. As a woman in a male-dominated union hierarchy and an idealist among bureaucratic functionaries, her efforts to promote workers' education met stiff opposition. She made enemies in the anticommunist 1920s by tolerating socialists and communists within the workers' education movement. She saw workers' education as a valuable aspect of trade unionism in its own right, while ILGWU officers saw it as a tool to build their own power. Male union leaders struck repeatedly at the independence of the educational institutions that emerged from Cohn's efforts. In 1928, the American Federation of Labor withdrew its financial support for Brookwood Labor College, accusing the college of permitting communists in its faculty and fostering anti-AFL sentiment among its students. In 1929, the AFL took over the Workers' Education Bureau, thus

Although male opposition undermined her efforts and diminished her long-term significance, Fannia M. Cohn was one of the leading Jewish women trade union activists in the United States during the first half of the twentieth century. [Cornell University, Kheel Center Archives]

turning that organization into a subordinate arm of organized labor.

Although a founder of educational activities within the ILGWU, Cohn never headed the union's education department. Her job titles varied, but for over forty years, the official head of her department was always someone else. She worked closely with Juliet Poyntz, Louis Friedland, and Alexander Fichandler, the first directors of the department, and often ran the department in fact, if not in name. But in 1935, when the ILGWU stripped her of her title as executive secretary and brought in an Englishman, Mark Starr, to head the department, Cohn's fury rose. She wrote to ILGWU president David Dubinsky, describing her demotion as "unwarranted" and "inhuman," an affront to the twenty-five years she had spent working for the union and her eighteen years guiding its educational efforts.

Increasingly, the union implemented a narrow program of labor education, rather than Cohn's broader vision of workers' education. ILGWU leaders desired obedient members and well-trained officers. Cohn's efforts had been geared to empowering rank-and-file members, awakening them to new intellectual and cultural currents, and stimulating them to become more active in union affairs. The union's male leadership did not share her vision; rather, they were threatened by it. Although Cohn continued to work within the education department until her retirement in September 1962, she was increasingly isolated in her work.

Cohn's life was her educational work. When the union cut funding for her projects, Cohn quietly raised money from family members to keep the activities going. She did not retire on her own; the union finally scheduled a testimonial dinner in her honor to force the issue. She was seventy-six years old at the time and lived only another three months. Although she was embattled during much of her career in the ILGWU, her work was appreciated beyond the ranks of union officialdom. Charles Beard praised her "splendid efforts in the field of labor education." ROSE PESOTTA, a noted ILGWU organizer and herself a vice president of the union, understood the contradictions of Cohn's life and work: "Fannia Cohn's service to our organization is only recognized by those on the outside who can dispassionately evaluate such unselfish efforts on the part of one person for the cause of worker's education.... She remains a tragic figure amidst her own fellow workers.... Were she a man it would have been entirely different."

Fannia M. Cohn died in New York City on December 24, 1962.

BIBLIOGRAPHY

Antonovsky, Anton. Papers. Box 115, YIVO Institute for Jewish Research, NYC; *Biographical Dictionary of American Labor Leaders* (1974); Cohen, Ricki Carole Meyers. "Fannia Cohn and the International Ladies' Garment Workers' Union." Ph.D. diss., University of Southern California, 1976; Cohn, Fannia. Papers. Rare Books and Manuscript Division, New York Public Library; ILGWU and Workers' Education Bureau. Papers. New York State School for Industrial and Labor Relations, Cornell University, Ithaca, N.Y.; *NAW* modern; Orleck, Annelise. *Common Sense and a Little Fire: Women and Working-Class Politics in the United States, 1900–1965* (1995); *Who's Who in Labor* (1946); Wong, Susan Stone. "From Soul to Strawberries: The International Ladies' Garment Workers' Union and Workers' Education, 1914–1950." In *Sisterhood and Solidarity: Workers' Education for Women, 1914–1984*, edited by Joyce L. Kornbluh and Mary Frederickson (1984).

THOMAS DUBLIN

COHN, FELICE (1884–1961)

Felice Cohn was one of Nevada's first women lawyers, an author of suffragist legislation in Nevada, and one of the first women admitted to the United States Supreme Court.

She was born May 14, 1884, in Carson City, Nevada, the daughter of pioneers Morris and Pauline (Sheyer) Cohn. Morris, a merchant, established the first creamery in Nevada, introduced alfalfa raising in the state, and engaged in mining. He owned more than eight thousand acres in Carson Valley and around Lake Tahoe.

Felice taught school at age fifteen and then attended Nevada State University and Stanford University, and graduated from Washington Law School. She was admitted to the Nevada Bar in 1902 and started to practice law at age eighteen. She was admitted to the California Bar in 1908. When admitted to the bar of the Supreme Court in 1916, she was the fourth woman with that distinction.

She served as court reporter for Ormsby County for eight years and took testimony for 147 days from Frank Wildes, a witness in the State Bank and Trust Company case.

She served as assistant U.S. attorney at Carson City, 1911 to 1912; special sales agent for the U.S. Land Office, 1914 to 1918; and U.S. hearings attorney, 1918 to 1922. She supervised land sales and mineral claims between the United States and the Southern Pacific and Union Pacific railroads in Colorado, Kansas, Oregon, and Oklahoma, resulting in over 100,000 acres being returned to the government. She was a frequent visitor at the White House and received the personal commendation of President Woodrow Wilson.

As president of the Non-Militant Suffrage Association (1912–1914), she authored the amendment extending the franchise adopted by the Nevada legislature in 1914. She worked for child labor amendments and foster home and adoption laws. She opposed separate income tax and all other legislation adversely affecting women and children.

She entered private practice in Reno in 1922, where she handled thousands of divorces. She practiced in Nevada, California, Utah, Wyoming, and Colorado. She was appointed a United States referee in bankruptcy in 1926, one of the first women in that position. Due to political infighting, she was removed in 1934 and was appointed national chair of the committee on ethics of the National Association of Referees in Bankruptcy. In 1931, she was the only practicing woman attorney in Nevada.

She served on several boards, including the Reno YWCA, where she was a trustee and their lawyer. She was Nevada vice president of the American Bar Association (1930–1931), vice president of the National Association of Women Lawyers, chairman of the legislative committee of the American Federation of Women's Clubs (1929), first president and organizer of the Nevada Federation of Business and Professional Women's Clubs, National Association of Referees in Bankruptcy, and charter member and president (1930–1931) of Nevada Native Daughters. She belonged to the International Association of Women Lawyers, Nevada Historical Society, Iota Tau Tau, Reno Branch of the United Nations, and was president of B'nai B'rith. She served on the American Red Cross board beginning in 1925, and was chairman of the home service committee for over fifteen years. She was supervisor of surgical dressings during World War II and was active in the USO.

Felice Cohn died after a short illness on May 24, 1961.

BIBLIOGRAPHY

American Women. The Standard Biographical Dictionary of Notable Women. Vol. 3 (1939–1940): 17; Cohn, Felice. Clipping file. Nevada State Historical Society, Reno; *WWIAJ* (1926, 1938).

OLIVER B. POLLAK

COHN, MILDRED (b. 1913)

A pioneer in using new technologies to measure organic reactions, Mildred Cohn has received many top awards in the fields of chemistry and biology. Early in her career, she surmounted prejudice against women and Jews.

Cohn was born in New York City on July 12, 1913, to Isidore and Bertha (Klein) Cohn. Her father, trained as a rabbi in Russia, became a "militant atheist" involved in the Yiddish culture movement in New York. He worked in the garment and printing industries. Mildred had a brother, Albert, two years older.

Graduating at age fourteen from public school, Cohn majored in chemistry at Barnard College, while taking all available courses in physics. She received a bachelor's degree in 1931 and, a year later, a master's degree in chemistry from Columbia University.

After passing a civil service exam for junior chemist, Cohn began to work at the National Advisory Committee for Aeronautics, a predecessor of NASA. She was given a position lower than the one she qualified for and was eventually banned from the laboratory because she was a woman, but she persevered in planning fuel-injection experiments that others carried out.

Cohn eventually returned to Columbia, where, under Harold Urey, she used isotopes to study reaction mechanisms. She received her Ph.D. in 1937, but still had difficulty finding work. According to Cohn, corporations seeking employees at Columbia posted notices, "Interviewing all Ph.D. candidates, male and Christian." Luckily, Vincent du Vigneaud hired her as a physical chemist, originally at Washington University and later at Cornell University Medical Center. She again worked on isotopes, initially measuring the deuterium content of water. Nine years passed before she could choose her own research, and twenty-one years passed before she received a university appointment.

In 1938, Cohn married physicist Henry Primakoff. She did not change her name, preferring, during World War II, to reveal her Jewish identity. The couple had three children: two daughters, Nina and Laura, who became psychotherapists, and a son, Paul, who became a scientist. Her husband died in 1983.

In 1946, she moved to Washington University, where she worked with Carl and Gerty Cori, a husband-and-wife team who allowed Cohn to pursue independent research. Among other endeavors, she analyzed enzyme-catalyzed reactions and built a mass spectrometer. In 1958, she was appointed associate professor.

In 1960, Cohn became a faculty member at the University of Pennsylvania, and was made full professor within a year. In 1964, she became the only woman to receive the American Heart Association's Lifetime Career Award, which provided generous support until she turned sixty-five. In 1978, the university appointed her the Benjamin Rush professor of physiological chemistry. She is currently a professor emeritus at the university.

Cohn was the first woman on the editorial board of the prestigious *Journal of Biological Chemistry*, where she was editor for ten years. Other honors include the American Chemical Society's Garvan Medal, the Franklin Institute's Cresson Medal, the International Organization of Women's Biochemists Award, the National Medal of Science, and Columbia University's Chandler Medal. She was president of the American Society of Biological Chemists.

Mildred Cohn started her career at a time of great innovation in physics. With her strong interest in physics, she reached new frontiers in understanding chemical reactions at the atomic level. She used innovative technologies—mass spectrometer, nuclear magnetic resonance, and electronic paramagnetic resonance—to elucidate organic reactions. Her research included metabolic studies, mechanisms of enzymatic reactions, ATP, and electron spin. Although she did not have a university appointment for two decades, she worked with scientists who were or would become Nobel laureates. Her low-profile jobs gave her not only flexibility to rear children, but also freedom for long-term projects that other scientists could not undertake, projects that eventually reaped rich rewards.

BIBLIOGRAPHY

American Chemical Society. Videotape. *American Men and Women of Science* (1992); Bailey, Martha J. *American Women in Science* (1994); Cohen, Harry, and Itzhak J. Carmin, eds. *Jews in the World of Science* (1956); Cohn, Mildred. "Atomic and Nuclear Probes of Enzyme Systems." *Annual Review of Biophysics and Biomolecular Structure* 21 (1992): 1–24, and personal interview with author, June 26, 1996; *EJ*; Gortler, Leon. "Mildred Cohn (1913–)." In *Women in Chemistry and Physics: A Biobibliographic Sourcebook*, edited by Louise S. Grinstein, Rose K. Rose, and Miriam H. Rafailovich (1993), and oral interview at the Chemical Heritage Foundation, Philadelphia, Pa.; *International Who's Who* (1993); *Who's Who in America* (1996); *Who's Who in Science and Engineering* (1994); *Who's Who of American Women* (1995–1995); *WWIAJ* (1980).

BETTY BARRER

COLLEGE STUDENTS

While Jews have traditionally placed a great deal of emphasis on education and learning, in the past they reserved the privilege of education primarily for their sons. Religious and cultural ideals assigning women's place to the home and family combined with societal sexism and anti-Semitism to make the course charted by Jewish women in pursuit of a college education rocky and in many cases inaccessible. In the last two decades, Jewish women in America have achieved parity with their male counterparts on college campuses, but only after many decades of struggle. Indeed, the obstacles facing all American women who sought to enroll in college institutions in the decades surrounding the turn of the century proved numerous, imposing, and at times, defeating. For Jewish women, anti-Semitism posed an added challenge that they had to conquer in order to receive the college education they sought.

THE BEGINNINGS OF FEMALE COLLEGE EDUCATION

While the mass immigration of Jews to the United States between 1881 and 1924 occurred at precisely the same time as the development of public education for the masses, Jewish males reaped the benefits of this educational movement in far greater numbers than did their Jewish sisters. While recent arrivals to the country sought to enhance their sons' chances of success in America by sending them to school and then to college, the same did not apply to daughters, whose chances of earning a living even with a college education appeared slight. Indeed, for most parents, the help provided by daughters within the household and the wages secured from outside work represented important contributions to the family in terms of putting food on the table and even paying the tuition required by their brothers' schools. Parents were not willing to forgo this financial and physical assistance supporting their daughters' quest for a college education.

This parental preference for sending sons to school while keeping daughters home was common to all religious groups, not just to Jews. In fact, although more Jewish males than females attended school at the turn of the century, Jewish women were more likely to receive an education than any other group of women in the Unites States. Jewish daughters often pursued an education while holding down jobs and helping with family chores. A study of night school attendees in 1910 revealed that although Jews comprised only 19 percent of the population in New York City, 40 percent of the women enrolled in night school were

Jewish. Still, this high number of women willing to pursue an education, even after a long day of work, did not translate into a significant Jewish female presence in college during the decades preceding and following the turn of the century.

In the 1870s and 1880s, less than 2 percent of women aged eighteen to twenty-one attended college. Strongly held societal beliefs that assigned woman's proper place to the home served as prescriptions against higher education for women. Of the small group of pioneers who did enroll in college, nearly all came from Protestant backgrounds. The few women who might have been Jewish either hid their religious identities or else blended in with their fellow collegians and thus escaped comment and notice on the basis of their religion. Amelia D. Alpinger, a student in the class of 1896 at the University of Illinois at Urbana-Champaign, served as the first Jewish female collegian to be identified according to her religion. A prominent student on campus, Alpinger played a visible role in many campus activities and served as a charter member of Pi Beta Phi sorority. Two years after she graduated, another identifiable Jewish female, GERTRUDE STEIN, graduated from the Harvard Annex, later Radcliffe College, the women's division of Harvard. Other than these two prominent women, the Jewish females who attended college during the latter decades of the nineteenth century and the first decade of the twentieth century did so in relative anonymity.

Because of their small numbers and relative invisibility as a group, Jewish students, and particularly the females among them, attracted little notice in terms of their religion from either their fellow students or outside society. Jewish members of the community, however, at times helped the few Jewish collegians to maintain their religious identities by inviting them to Passover seders and to share other celebrations with them. In some places, members of the Jewish Ladies Circle or other social organizations in the community helped Jewish students to take on their new collegiate identities without losing their sense of themselves as Jews. In other places, young Jewish women struggled alone to make their way through the intricacies of higher education, often finding it easier to forgo or suppress their Jewish identity to fit in better with the small number of female collegians surrounding them.

Although the number of Jewish women enrolled in colleges increased, according to the responses from a questionnaire distributed to colleges across the United States in June of 1916 by the Intercollegiate Menorah Association, Jewish women comprised only a tiny fraction of the college population. The survey also found that Jewish men attended college in a higher proportion than did their non-Jewish counterparts, while female Jews comprised only one-ninth the number of male Jews and attended college in numbers less than half of their non-Jewish female counterparts. While the study located only a tiny number of Jewish women enrolled at colleges nationwide, it found that at the all-women's colleges of the Northeast, such as Barnard, Radcliffe, Smith, Wellesley, Vassar, and Bryn Mawr, 335 Jewish women held 5 percent of the enrolled places.

Having few Jewish sisters accompanying them in their collegiate quests both harmed and aided Jewish women in the decades surrounding the turn of the century. While often spared the outright anti-Semitism directed at male Jews, Jewish women tended to face their struggles alone and had to combat more tacit forms of anti-Semitism. According to the Intercollegiate Menorah Association survey, while Jewish women participated along with other students in all branches of collegiate activities, many of them did so by hiding or simply not declaring their religious and cultural heritage.

By all accounts, the first Jewish female collegians performed well in their studies. In 1916, at Smith College, where Jews comprised only 3 percent of the student body, they won 9 percent of the Phi Beta Kappa keys awarded. In the same year, at Bryn Mawr College, although Jewish women represented only 4 percent of the senior class, they earned more than twice that percentage of the cum laude degrees awarded. In addition to earning notable marks, the early Jewish female collegians also took steps upon graduation to put their education to use. From 1914 to 1915, for example, 5.5 percent of the women registered at the Intercollegiate Bureau of Occupations were Jews, although Jewish women comprised a far smaller percentage of the female college population.

INCREASING NUMBERS, INCREASING STRUGGLES

The wave of immigration that accompanied the spread of mass education served to increase the Jewish population in the United States more than threefold. Between 1897 and 1917, the number of Jews in the country expanded from less than 1 million to more than 3.3 million, and the bulk of the new arrivals hailed from Eastern Europe. These new arrivals proved poorer, less educated, and less cultivated than their better assimilated German predecessors. When the children of these recent immigrants began to arrive in numbers on college campuses in the late 1910s and 1920s, their presence attracted greater societal and institutional notice and comment than had the earlier Jewish students.

The 1920s has been called a period of democratization in higher education, a time when the ivy gates opened en masse to students of less privileged and more racially and ethnically diverse backgrounds. Jewish women participated in this wave of expanding enrollment, joining the collegiate ranks in greater numbers and with increased visibility. By 1914, enough Jewish women attended Radcliffe College to form a Menorah Society, whose mission included spreading Jewish culture and ideas. Increasingly made aware by their fellow students and institutions of their identities as Jews, Jewish female students, buoyed by their strength in numbers, began to form organizations to aid themselves and their Jewish sisters in responding to and combating the rise in anti-Semitism and discrimination that accompanied their increased presence on campus.

Concurrent societal paranoia and fear of foreigners mixed with institutional concerns regarding the expanding number of Jewish students enrolled on campus to produce a wave of anti-Semitism that reached high proportions during the 1920s and 1930s. During these two decades and extending into the 1950s, students, alumni, and administrators of many institutions, eager to preserve the so-called Anglo-Saxon superiority of their colleges, instituted explicit and tacit policies both to limit Jewish enrollment and to restrict Jewish participation in campus activities.

Drawing upon popular "scientific" racial theories to justify their discriminatory policies, administrators of many institutions of higher education across the country created screening techniques to weed out Jewish applicants for admission. These institutional efforts to maintain an exclusive and "homogeneous" student body hurt Jews more than they did other ethnic and religious groups. Whereas Catholics and African Americans developed and maintained colleges specifically for their own students, Jews created few institutions of their own, preferring instead to enter the American mainstream through the same avenues as non-Jews.

In the 1920s and 1930s, prominent institutions such as Harvard, Yale, Princeton, and Columbia established admissions quotas and other practices for manipulating admission procedures to curb or even prevent the entry of Jewish students. Jewish women felt the ramifications of these policies when the Ivy "sister" schools, such as Barnard and Radcliffe, and the all-female institutions of many other schools began to copy the more prestigious institutions with their anti-Jewish stances. Indeed, while technically forbidden by state and national laws from imposing admission quotas based on race, religion, or ethnicity, the women's branches of many major state universities in the eastern and midwestern United States devised strategies to address a situation they labeled the "Jewish problem" by limiting, in a tacit manner, Jewish attendance at their institutions.

Prompted by concerns that a large Jewish attendance would make their institutions less attractive to the sought-after white Anglo-Saxon Protestant students, schools such as New Jersey College, the female coordinate of Rutgers, the State University of New Jersey, created a department of admissions whose representative would evaluate the personal background, leadership, breadth, and potential of prospective students. Ranking students by applying a set of subjective criteria enabled college administrators to weed out Jewish applicants who generally came with higher marks and scores than their non-Jewish counterparts, but who nevertheless were considered inferior enrollment material.

The explicit and more subtle discriminatory policies against Jewish female applicants proved effective. Between 1928 and 1932, for example, while the number of Jews in the northern New Jersey area increased dramatically and the number of Jewish students enrolled at Rutgers University more than doubled, the Jewish female enrollment at New Jersey College declined by more than a third, from 17 percent in 1928 to 11 percent in 1932. In 1930, moreover, while New Jersey College accepted 337 of the 635 females who applied, an acceptance rate of 61 percent, the admissions committee issued acceptances to only 50 of the 162 Jewish applicants, at a rate of 31 percent, despite the fact that the chair of the Committee on Admission and Freshman Work reported of the Jewish applicants that "their scholastic standing is usually better than that of other students" (Greenberg and Zenchelsky, 304). Harvard's sister school, Radcliffe College, joined New Jersey College in introducing screening policies to weed out Jewish candidates for admissions. Between 1936 and 1938, the women's college reduced the number of Jewish women it admitted by almost half, and cut the percentage of Jewish students enrolled among its ranks from 24.8 to 16.5, despite the fact that applications for admissions from Jewish women rose during the same period.

At New Jersey College, Radcliffe, and other institutions, deans of women and other powerful administrators adopted the practice of interviewing every student who applied and evaluating each on the basis of mental ability, character, personality, health, and background. This practice enabled administrators to single out for rejection the students whom they considered "undesirable," "crude," and "lacking in refinement," a high proportion of whom were often Jewish. When Jewish groups publicly pressured institutions to ease their restrictions, the schools under examination simply altered their processes of selection and placed limits on the number of commuter students they would admit. This policy proved an effective, if more subtle, approach to curbing Jewish admissions, as in the late 1920s and 1930s, a high proportion of Jewish women students commuted to their respective campuses.

In fact, a majority of the Jewish women arriving on campus between the two world wars did so on a daily basis. Preferring to keep their daughters close to home in the hopes of both saving money and keeping an eye on their female offspring, Jewish families played a major role in swelling the ranks of the commuter student population in schools located in New York and Boston. By 1934, Jews accounted for more than 50 percent of the New York female college student population. Although Jewish males felt subtly stigmatized by their peers for attending local institutions, their sisters found that attending schools like New York University and HUNTER COLLEGE, as commuters, represented a high achievement and brought them prestige within the young Jewish community.

Both the commuter students and their counterparts at distant colleges felt the dual sting of sexism and anti-Semitism from institutions unaccustomed to the visible presence of Jewish female collegians. Attending schools resistant to their presence proved difficult and at times lonely for women trying to earn a higher education. Indeed, the pressure to conform to collegiate ideals despite their religious differences and the desire to blend into campus environments suspicious of, or even hostile to, their presence created numerous crises of identity for Jewish women and other members of minority groups. Hounded by the knowledge that in order to fit in they had to hide their religious affiliation, yet conscious that such action would separate them from their own families and communities, Jewish female students struggled to find a way to make themselves belong on American college campuses in the early decades of the century.

The Jewish Greek system, sororities and fraternities, founded at the same time as Jewish students began to flock to universities, sought to aid the new collegians in their quest to belong. For many Jewish females, the religious-based sororities, created and developed by sisters of their faith in the 1910s, provided opportunities for campus involvement that might have otherwise been closed to them. The Jewish organizations served as an entrée into mainstream collegiate society, in part through the organizations' deliberate, collective mission to counter negative Jewish stereotypes. Teaching etiquette, manners, dress, sports, and upper-middle-class activities and mores, Jewish sororities and fraternities strove to make their members ideal representatives of American college students. Only through their Greek letter societies, Jewish sorority women argued, could they as Jews reach parity on campus with their non-Jewish counterparts. By placing a high level of emphasis on school loyalty and patriotism and on dispelling myths about Jews by their own deportment and behavior, the members of the Jewish Greek system sought to use their organizations as vehicles for personal as well as collective advancement.

The Jewish sororities attracted a high percentage of the female Jewish college population. A 1927 survey published by the *American Jewish Year Book* found that twenty-five thousand Jewish students were members of fraternities and sororities, 80 percent of membership in all Jewish student organizations. Yet, while these organizations drew many Jewish women into their ranks, the sororities restricted their membership to a chosen group of students. For those excluded from membership, the Jewish sororities served to exacerbate feelings of exclusion and discrimination—a sentiment that Hillel, a Jewish society formed at the University of Illinois in the 1920s, sought to alleviate. Created by a newly ordained rabbi to provide support for a Jewish student population lacking in direction and faith, Hillel sought to provide students with a religious, moral, and social outlet through an organization in which they could learn the principles of Judaism while cultivating themselves as individuals. In response to the selective Greek letter societies, Hillel opened itself to all Jewish students, embracing all brands of the faith without exclusion.

Hillel remained small at first, as the members of the highly developed Jewish Greek system treated the new organization with skepticism for its public assertion of Judaism. Used to hiding or at least downplaying their religion, the Jewish Greeks argued that the activist stance adopted by Hillel would make their own mission of assimilation more difficult. However, as discrimination on the part of the prestigious eastern schools caused increasing numbers of Jewish students to flock to campuses in the South and Midwest, Hillel soon spread to other institutions. By 1927, it boasted branches at Illinois, Wisconsin, Ohio State, Michigan, California, Cornell, West Virginia, and Texas.

A Jewish society formed at the University of Illinois in the 1920s, Hillel opened itself to Jewish students of all brands of the faith, without the exclusion of other Jewish campus organizations. Pictured here are students at Hillel's "Model Seder" at the University of Maryland in 1948. [American Jewish Historical Society]

THE ACTIVIST 1930s AND THE WAR

Jewish students played active and important roles in the student protest movement of the 1930s. In high numbers, they joined the newly developing peace and protest organizations. The American Student Union, the most prominent campus protest group of the time, thrived mainly on campuses populated by large numbers of Jewish students. Female Jews adopted a more political stance on campus than ever before. At Radcliffe, for example, they abandoned en masse their cultural organizations like the Menorah Club and dedicated their time and efforts instead to the more politically activist Avukah group.

The association of Jewish students with the protest movement served to increase displays of public anti-Semitism in college towns. Outraged citizens responded to what they perceived as the movement's socialist and communist leanings by charging the student members—and particularly the Jews among them—with anti-American tendencies. The rise of Nazism in Europe added to the pressures placed on Jewish collegians. Should they downplay their Judaism and thus escape the blame of those who said that the Jewish people had brought their hardships on themselves? Should they abandon the peace movement and turn their energies instead to opposing

Nazism and supporting Hitler's foes? Regardless of which course they chose to follow, Jewish students in the 1930s pursued their college degrees cognizant of the additional weight added to their shoulders by virtue of their religion.

Within the Jewish Greek system, the issue of what members should do in response to Nazism and the increase in anti-Semitic expression on the part of the American public prompted a great deal of discussion. Fiercely patriotic since their inception and wary of affiliating themselves too strongly with radical causes, Jewish sorority and fraternity leaders warned their sisters and brothers that all Jews would be judged by the members' behavior. Shying away from political action for fear of drawing public criticism, the Jewish Greek organizations chose instead to aid the Jewish cause by serving as "model" representatives of their faith. As Alpha Epsilon Phi national president Reba B. Cohen reminded her sorority sisters in 1939, "We can, as college women, best serve our people by creating better understanding between Jews and non-Jews, by paying special attention to our dress, manners, and speech, and by cooperating amongst ourselves" (Sanua, 17).

When America joined its European allies and entered the war in 1941, Jewish collegians rushed to join the cause. Although during the war years women outnumbered men on campus, the air of abnormality created by an absence of males who had previously dominated the campuses reminded female students of the temporary nature of this situation. Watching their male friends and brothers join the armed forces, Jewish female collegians turned their efforts to doing their part to help the American cause.

DOMESTICITY IN THE 1950s

As the veterans flocked to American colleges after World War II, Jewish and non-Jewish women became a smaller percentage of the college population than they had been either prior to or during the war. The number of female collegians increased in real numbers, from 601,000 in 1940 to 806,000 in 1950, but the percentage of female students declined, from 40.2 percent in 1940 to only 30.2 percent of all students in 1950. For Jewish women collegians in the aftermath of the war, sex as much as religion played a decisive role in shaping their college experiences.

Like non-Jewish women, the Jewish female collegians of the 1950s celebrated domesticity, beauty, and traditionally "womanly" concerns such as marriage and family. A B'nai B'rith survey of female college graduates, conducted from 1946 to 1959, found that female graduates of the period married young, often quitting school in the process, and bore children at an earlier age than had their mothers. The survey also found that Jewish women led this return to domesticity, marrying more quickly after graduation than their non-Jewish cohorts, although they waited longer than non-Jews to bear children.

The courses of study that colleges offered to female students in the 1950s both mirrored and shaped the revival of domesticity so celebrated by the American media at this time. Crowded out of the traditional liberal arts classrooms by male students eager to enter the corporate world of postwar America, high numbers of female students of all religions turned to "womanly" subjects such as health and education. In their choice of majors, however, Jewish women differed from other students. While non-Jewish women chose to major in disciplines like English and history, which would prepare them for teaching careers, and business administration and secretarial training in preparation for work as secretaries, Jewish women shied away from these subjects and majored instead in psychology, the social sciences, government and public administration, economics, and languages, in preparation for careers in health-related services and in the professions. Although many Jewish women, like all female graduates, adhered to the public celebrations of domesticity by passing over careers of their own to serve as homemakers and full-time mothers, they still pursued majors in areas where they, as Jews, would be likely to find jobs.

Although in their choices of majors Jewish women set themselves off from their non-Jewish counterparts, the importance of religion as a determinant of college experience declined in relative terms during the postwar years. While laws such as the 1948 Fair Education Practices Act in New York and, later, Title IV of the 1964 Civil Rights Act called for an end to discrimination on the basis of race, creed, color, or national origin, more tangible pressures worked to break down religious divisions on college campuses.

In the early 1950s, the Jewish sororities, and eventually the fraternities, succumbed to this pressure and dropped their religious affiliation. With their Jewish identity now historical rather than functional, the formerly Jewish sororities also removed the religious overtones from their celebrations and rituals. Now reluctant to take part in any Jewish activities for fear of being accused of sectarianism, Jewish sorority women shied away from Hillel and other explicitly faith-oriented groups. As a result of the removal of the sectarian clauses, the degree to which religion played a role in shaping the campus experiences of Jewish female collegians declined. At the same time, however, religious affiliation still played an important role in determining which students would be allowed to enroll in particular institutions of higher learning.

Despite state laws and governmental pressure, college institutions continued to impose quotas on Jewish enrollment in the years following the war. A 1950 study of seventy-six nonsectarian colleges in upstate New York revealed that nearly one-third of the schools still placed restrictions on the numbers of Jews and other minorities admitted, some in the form of quotas, others in outright rejection.

In spite of the obstacles they faced in winning admissions to certain institutions of higher learning, Jewish women continued to push for a college education. Indeed, Jewish students of both sexes flocked to campus during the 1950s, despite quotas. By 1960, 63 percent of Jewish men and women aged eighteen though twenty-four attended college. Despite the postwar decline in the percentage of females enrolled in institutions of higher education, the number of Jewish women matriculating continued to rise. By the mid-1960s, their numbers crept close to the figures for Jewish male attendance and for non-Jewish female attendance.

Like non-Jewish women, the Jewish female collegians of the 1950s celebrated domesticity, beauty, and traditional "womanly" concerns. Two couples are pictured here at a Hillel dance at the University of Maryland during the period. [American Jewish Historical Society]

RISING CONSCIOUSNESS—
IDENTITY IN THE 1960s AND 1970s

During the late 1960s, female collegians for the first time reached a level of parity with the number of men enrolled on college campuses across the United States. The 1972 passage of Title IX of the Educational Amendments Act added the weight of law to the equality of opportunity that college women had struggled so hard to achieve. For Jewish women, the heightened social, sexual, and ethnic consciousness on campus brought about by the student protest movement of the 1960s created a campus environment more favorable to their presence than had existed at any point in the century.

The civil rights movement and ensuing campus protests attracted Jewish students to their causes in high numbers. In fact, at a time when Jews comprised only 3 percent of the United States population and 10 percent of the college population, they served in the majority of leadership roles within the student protest organizations and made up between 33 and 40 percent of the active membership of the movement. Although Jewish women took less prominent roles than their brothers in the civil rights and protest movement, female collegiate Jews took more active posts in the burgeoning women's movement. Inspired by BETTY FRIEDAN and other prominent Jewish feminist leaders, Jewish female collegians awoke from a period of quiescence in the late 1960s and early 1970s and adopted more activist, politicized stances on issues such as feminism, abortion rights, and the Equal Rights Amendment.

By the early 1970s, Jewish women began to surpass their non-Jewish counterparts in terms of the percentage of females compared to males of the same religious faith. A study conducted in 1971 at the University of Maryland revealed that while females comprised 59 percent of the population of Jewish students, they made up only 47 percent of the non-Jewish student population. The study also determined that Jewish women maintained a greater sense of ethnic and religious identity than did their Jewish brothers. For example, the percentage of female Jewish students belonging to Hillel exceeded that of males by more than six percentage points (18.9 to 12.7). In addition, 66.7 percent of Jewish women declared that their dates were "usually or always" Jewish, compared to only 54.9 percent of males making the same claim. Finally, whereas 37.5 percent of Jewish women asserted that they would not intermarry, only 26.8 percent of the male Jews were willing to make this statement. Thus, in addition to outnumbering Jewish males on the Maryland campus, Jewish females, according to the study, possessed more developed senses of cultural and ethnic consciousness and religious affiliation than did their male counterparts.

With the Jewish Greek system on the decline for both males and females, the rise in celebrations of ethnicity and ethnic consciousness in the late 1960s and 1970s created an environment favorable to the growth and spread of new Jewish-identified organizations. Groups founded in support of Israel and dedicated to taking political stances on Jewish issues sprang up on campuses and claimed Jewish female support. Beneficiaries of a campus environment more supportive of their presence than ever before, Jewish women continued to flock to college in increased numbers and to play more prominent roles within campus life.

JEWISH FEMALE COLLEGIANS
IN THE 1980s AND 1990s

According to the Current Population Survey performed by the Department of Labor in 1990, by the late 1980s Jewish women had achieved a higher level of education than their non-Jewish white female counterparts. Whereas the study found that over half of the Jewish women in America held at least a bachelor's degree, and over 25 percent of Jewish women held a graduate or professional degree, by 1990 only 17 percent of white female non-Jews had received a bachelor's degree and less than 5 percent of them had earned a graduate or professional degree. This high level of educational achievement signaled a shift within the Jewish community away from drawing a distinction between the educational paths of female and male children. At the same time, though, while both Jewish males and females possessed higher levels of education than their non-Jewish white counterparts, Jewish men still outranked Jewish women in numbers of years of education. The 1990 study showed that whereas 49.5 percent Jewish women over eighteen had spent four or more years in college, more than 60 percent of their Jewish brothers had achieved this feat. And although more Jewish women than men held high school degrees, the percentage of men who had earned college degrees topped the percentage of women by more than fifteen, 66 percent compared to 50 percent.

In the late 1990s, the number of Jewish women receiving a collegiate education has reached a greater degree of parity with Jewish men. Approximately 125,000 Jewish women attend college, comprising 85 percent of the Jewish female population between the ages of eighteen and twenty-four. This number and percentage mirror the number and percentage of

Jewish men earning a college degree. In the last few decades of the twentieth century, Jewish women have overcome many of the obstacles to their collegiate success posed by religious and cultural opposition, sexism, and anti-Semitism. Although Jewish collegians still occasionally encounter pressures and discrimination as a result of their religion, Jewish women have succeeded in establishing a place for themselves in college campuses on a par with their Jewish brothers and ahead of their non-Jewish female counterparts.

BIBLIOGRAPHY

Baird, William Raimond. *Baird's Manual of American College Fratenities.* 7th ed. (1912; also, 10th–17th editions); Baum, Charlotte, Paula Hyman, and Sonya Michel. *The Jewish Woman in America* (1976); Brown, Francis J., ed. "Discriminations in College Admissions: A Report of a Conference Held under the Auspices of the American Council on Education in Cooperation with the Anti-Defamation League of B'nai B'rith, Chicago, Illinois, November 4–5, 1949." In *American Council on Education Studies* 14 (April 1950); Eagan, Eileen. *Class, Culture, and the Classroom: The Student Peace Movement of the 1930s* (1981); Fass, Paula S. *The Damned and the Beautiful: American Youth in the 1920s* (1977); Fishman, Sylvia Barack. *A Breadth of Life: Feminism in the American Jewish Community* (1993); Glazer, Nathan. *Remembering the Answers: Essays on the American Student Revolt* (1970); Greenberg, Michael and Seymour Zenchelsky. "Private Bias and Public Responsibility: Anti-Semitism at Rutgers in the 1920s and 1930s." *History of Education Quarterly* 33 (Fall 1993): 460–319; Gurock, Jeffrey S. *The Men and Women of Yeshiva: Higher Education, Orthodoxy, and American Judaism* (1988); Hartman, Moshe, and Harriet Hartman. *Gender Equality and American Jews* (1996); Horowitz, Helen Lefkowitz. *Campus Life: Undergraduate Cultures from the End of the Eighteenth Century to the Present* (1987); Koltun, Elizabeth, ed. *The Jewish Woman: New Perspectives* (1976); Lavender, Abraham D. "Jewish College Women: Future Leaders of the Jewish Community?" *The Journal of Ethnic Studies* 5 (1977): 81–90; Marcus, Jacob R. *The American Jewish Woman: A Documentary History* (1981); McWilliams, Carey. *A Mask for Privilege: Anti-Semitism in America* (1948). National Panhellenic Congress. Minutes of Fifteenth, Eighteenth, and Nineteenth Congresses (1917, 1923, 1926); Newcomer, Mabel. *A Century of Higher Education for American Women* (1959); Oren, Dan A. *Joining the Club: A History of Jews and Yale* (1985); Ritterband, Paul, and Harold S. Wechsler. *Jewish Learning in American Universities: The First Century* (1994); Rosin, Nurite. Telephone interview by author, January 13, 1997; Rosovsky, Nitza. *The Jewish Experience at Harvard and Radcliffe: An Introduction to an Exhibition Presented by the Harvard Semitic Museum on the Occasion of Harvard's Three-Hundred-Fiftieth Anniversary, September 1986* (1986); Rothman, Stanley, and S. Robert Lichter. *Roots of Radicalism: Jews, Christians, and the New Left* (1982); Sanua, Marianne. "Jewish College Fraternities and Sororities in American Jewish Life, 1895–1968: An Overview." Unpublished paper with accompanying notes; Sapinsky, Ruth. "The Jewish Girl at College." In *The American Jewish Woman: A Documentary History*, edited by Jacob R. Marcus (1981); Scheckner, Jeff. Telephone interview by author, January 13, 1997; Schneider, Susan Weidman. *Jewish and Female: Choices and Changes in Our Lives Today* (1985); Schoem, David, ed. *Inside Separate Worlds: Life Stories of Young Blacks, Jews, and Latinos* (1991); Schwartz, Howard. *Jewish College Youth Speak Their Minds: A Summary of the Tarrytown Conference* (1969); Shosteck, Robert. "Five Thousand Women College Graduates Report: Findings of a National Survey of the Social and Economic Status of Women Graduates of Liberal Arts Colleges of 1946–1949." B'nai B'rith Vocational Service Bureau (1953); Solberg, Winton. "Early Years of the Jewish Presence at the University of Illinois." *Religion and American Culture: A Journal of Interpretation* (Summer 1992): 215–245; Solomon, Barbara Miller. *In the Company of Educated Women: A History of Women and Higher Education in America* (1985); Toll, George S. "Colleges, Fraternities, and Assimilation." *Journal of Reform Judaism* (1985): 93–103; Wechsler, Harold S. *The Qualified Student: A History of Selective College Admissions in America* (1977).

DIANA B. TURK

COLONIAL ENTREPRENEURS: A QUARTET OF JEWISH WOMEN

Esther Pinheiro, Esther Brown, Rachel Luis, and Simja De Torres were widows, each held property, each was at one time or another a merchant. Although all lived in New York City for a time, none were born there. Pinheiro died on the Island of Nevis, and the other three in New York. All four have been overlooked by history. They have been included here because written records survive documenting their activities.

Brown left a will as well as a detailed inventory of her estate. De Torres and Luis left wills. De Torres seems to have been illiterate as far as English is concerned, leaving only her mark on her last testament. The others used their full signatures, though those of Luis and Brown are basically death scrawls done at the very last minute at their last breath. Thus, two or three seem educated, a rather high percentage for women of the colonial period. Of twenty-seven extant wills of Jewish men for the period, only six were unsigned.

There appears to be an identification with religion and religious institutions held in common by the group. De Torres left money to Congregation Shearith Israel and the synagogue in Kingston, Jamaica. Luis provided proceeds from the sale of household "furniture such as bed, bedding, chairs, table, and cubbard spoons" to be used to buy a "Shefer Tora" (Torah) for the New York congregation. Brown was "Penitent and sorry from the bottom of my heart for my sins past" and awaited forgiveness from God and hope of the "glorious resurrection on the last day." This curious Christian imagery was perhaps used by the clerk writing her will. De Torres and Luis both asked to be buried in the manner and ceremony of the "Jewish nation." The four witnesses to the Brown will, Joseph Bueno, Abraham De Lucena, Nathan Simpson, and Mordeci Gomez, took their oaths on the Torah, and she was buried "Decently" in the Bet Haim (Shearith Israel Cemetery).

Esther Brown (sometimes Hester) died on May 28, 1708, just after (or when) she signed her will. Her daughter Abigail was immediately made executrix. Widow Brown had married Saul Pardo (Brown is the Anglicized version), the first known hazan in New York and a merchant, who died in 1703. The couple had six children, four of whom, Josiau, Abigail, Sarah, and Simja, were alive at Esther Brown's death. They all died in Curaçao. Brown continued her husband's general merchandise business, not too unusual for colonial women. On March 22, 1708, she imported twenty-five gallons of rum from St. Thomas, aboard the sloop *Flying Horse*. She died two months later, it seems quite suddenly. The date of birth of one child is known: Josiau, in New York on September 22, 1694. Since she died some fourteen years later, she was then seemingly about thirty-five to forty years old at her death. Her inventory taken July 1, 1708, included furniture, one oval table, seven leather chairs, one "Ordinary Cubbard," a "Japan dressing box," and a large quantity of cloth, surely used in business, flannel, silk crape, damask, five pair of ordinary sheepskin gloves, four pair of coarse women's stockings, and twenty gallons of fine aniseed water plus an additional fifteen gallons "made here." The inventory was signed by Governor Edward Cornbury on July 14, 1708.

Simja De Torres, daughter of Moses de Silva, came to New York from Jamaica, though her place of birth is not known. Her year of birth is given as 1677. She was the wife of merchant Joseph De Torres, who died in 1724 in Jamaica. She too continued her husband's business, being active in the slave trade. On July 19, 1742, she imported three slaves. Earlier, on March 19, 1728, she had bought four slaves aboard the ship *Duke of Portland*, one of whom was under four years old and "one for my person," the latter thus being exempt from any import duty. She wrote her will on February 16, 1744, and it was probated November 13, 1746, De Torres having died October 23, 1746. In her will, she devised to her "nease" Rebecca Da Silva "one Negrow Girle," and to another "nease" Rachel Da Silva another "negro gireal." Still another "negro gireal" was given to still another "nease" Simja Da Silva. The remainder of her estate was given to her grandson, Moses Gomez. If Moses died before marriage or reaching age twenty-one, her estate went to her son-in-law, Daniel Gomez.

Esther Pinheiro, wife of Isaac Pinheiro (d. 1710), was married in Amsterdam in 1656. Her mother was Rachel Pinheiro, and the family was originally from Madrid. She received from her husband his Nevis plantations, "Negros," the profits of his mill, and the rest of his estate not devised to his five children, two boys and three girls. Eighteen slaves were listed by name. Before she left for Nevis, Pinheiro went into business. In 1707, she purchased from Governor Edward Cornbury a slave, Bastiana. In 1716 through 1718, either she or her ships were in Boston and New York, where they traded salt, molasses for timber, fish, and European goods.

Rachel Luis surely died right after signing her will on April 8, 1737. Money from her estate was to be used to purchase a Torah for Congregation Shearith Israel, while her executor, David Machado, provided money for an "Escaba" or memorial prayer. She seemingly left neither children nor family. At least a good part of her estate was derived from trade.

The lives of these four relatively obscure women touched many. Certainly, they contributed to history.

BIBLIOGRAPHY

Bloch, Julius M., Leo Hershkowitz, Kenneth Scott, and Constance Sherman, eds. *An Account of Her Majesty's Revenue in the Province of New York, 1701–1709* (1966); Emmanuel, Isaac S. *Precious Stories of the Jews of Curaçao, 1656–1957* (1975); Hershkowitz, Leo. *Wills of Early New York Jews, 1704–1799* (1967); Marcus, Jacob R. *The Colonial American Jew, 1492–1776* (1970); Verdooner, Dave, and Harman Snel. *Jewish Marriages in Amsterdam* (1995).

LEO HERSHKOWITZ

COLONIAL PERIOD

More so than some of their counterparts in England's Caribbean colonies, Jewish women in colonial North America occupied traditional positions and played traditional roles within the Jewish community as well as in the larger society. They could not serve in positions of leadership in either the Jewish or the general community, and they are not known to have had their own social organizations. Their primary occupation was that of homemaker, although, in an extension, several kept lodgings in which poorer Jewish individuals lived at the Jewish community's expense.

Marriage, the central event in the life of a colonial Jewish woman, occurred for the first time at an average age of twenty-three; men were approximately seven to ten years older. The exceedingly small size of the Jewish population in colonial North America necessitated choosing marriage partners not only from among the local population but also from among the Jewish communities located elsewhere in North America, in the Caribbean, and in England. Marriage thereby created networks of personal ties that spanned the Atlantic world. Such networks bestowed commercial advantage on the Jewish merchants who resided in each location and comprised the upper ranks of each Jewish community. The small size of the Jewish population also probably accounts for the occasional marriages with non-Jews, although Jewish women appear to have entered into such marriages less frequently than Jewish men did.

Women who married men from other parts of the Atlantic world might well remain in their home communities with their new spouses, but they might just as likely move to their husbands' communities, separated by great distances from their own parents, siblings, and friends. Participation by Jews in international commerce led to still other forms of family disruption and separation for colonial Jewish women. Merchant husbands traveled frequently and extensively, while sons were often posted to distant ports to act as commercial representatives for their families.

Families of means engaged private tutors for their daughters, but girls may have also attended the school maintained by the Jewish community, which taught secular as well as religious matter, although there is no direct evidence that they did. Evidence regarding the extent of literacy among them also is inadequate, but it appears from the wills of men who named their wives as their executrixes that many colonial Jewish women were quite literate and had been educated to the point of being capable of administering what in some cases were sizable estates.

Their presence as the executrixes of estates suggests, as well, that Jewish women had some experience in business matters, although few functioned as businesswomen in their own right. Although some owned land or kept lodging houses, and one in New York (Grace Levy Hays, 1690–1740) is known to have kept a retail store, the majority who were exposed to commercial affairs functioned primarily as ancillaries to their husbands, either by assisting them as clerks or by watching their businesses when they traveled. A comment by ABIGAIL FRANKS of New York in a letter to her son in 1745 exemplifies the prevailing norm: "As to wath relates to buissness I have Soe little knowledge of It that I Leave the Explainat[io]n of it interely to y[ou]r Father. . . ."

Jewish women in colonial America regularly received property and money in the form of bequests in the wills made by husbands, fathers, brothers, and other male relatives. Impoverished women also received funds, including dowries for marriage, through the communal allocations that were regularly made to the poor.

Orthodox practice prevailed within the walls of the synagogue, the community's primary institution, so that colonial Jewish women sat apart in an upstairs gallery during services and participated in worship in only a passive manner. Nonetheless, they made voluntary financial contributions to the synagogue and, when they made wills, bequeathed funds to it as well as to the Jewish community in general.

In contrast to Jewish women in the mainland colonies, those in England's Caribbean colonies had more visibility outside of the home. At Nevis, Esther Pinheiro owned several ships in her own right as well as in partnership with men as far away as Boston, and her ventures in international commerce spanned the Atlantic between 1710 and 1728. Jamaica's Jewish population during the eighteenth century included a small number of women who paid annual trade taxes, indicating that they had their own businesses. Women there comprised approximately one-third of the Jewish individuals who applied for and became naturalized under the terms of the Act of Naturalization passed by Parliament in 1740. And in Barbados, women by the end of the century paid the *finta*, the annual assessment imposed on all members of the Jewish community, setting the stage for efforts by female rate payers in the early nineteenth century to obtain a voice in communal governance.

BIBLIOGRAPHY

Congregation Nidhe Israel, Bridgetown, Barbados. Records. Spanish and Portuguese Jews' Congregation, London; Daniels, Doris Groshen. "Colonial Jewry: Religion, Domestic and Social Relations." *American Jewish Historical Quarterly* 66 (1976–77): 375–400; Hershkowitz, Leo, ed. *Wills of Early New York Jews (1704–1799)* (1967); Hershkowitz, Leo, and Isidore S. Meyer, eds. *Letters of the Franks Family (1733–1748)* (1968); Kingston Poll Tax Records (1792–1805). Jamaica Archives, Spanish Town, Jamaica; Kingston Vestry. Minutes (1744–1749, 1769–1770). Jamaica Archives, Spanish Town, Jamaica; Marcus, Jacob Rader. *The American Jewish Woman, 1654–1980* (1981), and *American Jewry—Documents—Eighteenth Century* (1959), and *The*

Colonial American Jew, 1492–1776, 3 vols. (1970); St. Catherine Poll Tax Records (1772–1774). Jamaica Archives, Spanish Town, Jamaica; Stern, Malcolm H. "The Function of Genealogy in American Jewish History." In *Essays in American Jewish History to Commemorate the Tenth Anniversary of the Founding of the American Jewish Archives under the Direction of Jacob Rader Marcus* (1958).

ELI FABER

COMDEN, BETTY (b. 1917)

Beginning with *On the Town* (1944) and continuing with *The Will Rogers Follies* (1991), Betty Comden's long career as librettist and lyricist for Broadway and Hollywood has included many classics of American musical comedy. With her partner Adolph Green, Comden has written lyrics and/or librettos for such hits of stage and screen as *The Barkleys of Broadway* (1949), *Singin' in the Rain* (1952), *Wonderful Town* (1953), *The Band Wagon* (1953), *Peter Pan* (1953), *Bells Are Ringing* (1956), the film version of *Auntie Mame* (1958), *Say Darling* (1958), *Applause* (1970), and *On the Twentieth Century* (1978).

Born Basya Cohen in Brooklyn, New York, on May 3, 1917, she was the second of two children in a comfortable middle-class family. Her father, Leo (Sadvoransky) Cohen, a lawyer, and her mother, Rebecca, an English teacher, were both Russian immigrants. The Cohens were observant Jews, keeping a kosher home and lighting candles on the Sabbath. At age five, however, teased about her name by neighborhood children, Basya Cohen began to call herself Betty. Fourteen years later, Betty and her older brother Nat, then a medical student, changed their names from Cohen to Comden. That same year, Betty Comden, always sensitive about her nose, had plastic surgery. In her autobiography, Comden, who has turned to Judaism sporadically in her adult life, comments that she still feels "uneasy in my skin," remaining insecure about aspects of her identity.

Betty Comden has always considered herself a performer. Comden first appeared on stage at the progressive Brooklyn Ethical Culture School, in a seventh-grade dramatization of *Ivanhoe,* in which she played the "Jewess" Rebecca. Teaching by dramatization was common at Ethical, and this early production is significant not only because it gave Comden her first experience of working in dramatic form and theatrical collaboration, but also because it represented to Comden a dichotomy between the clever brunette and the "beauteous" blonde heroine that appears in many of her later musicals. After attending Erasmus High School, Comden majored in drama at New York

While admitting to an insecurity about her Jewish identity, Betty Comden obviously does not have the same problem writing for the theater and film. She and her long-time partner Adolph Green have penned librettos and lyrics for such classics as "Singin' in the Rain," "Wonderful Town," and "Applause."
[New York Public Library]

University, graduating in 1938. Comden's professional career took off after meeting Green and JUDY HOLLIDAY shortly after graduating from New York University. With two other partners, the group formed The Revuers and began their career as a nightclub act in 1938, writing their own material and performing first at the Village Vanguard and eventually at clubs on both coasts. Twenty years later, Comden and Green's two-person act, *A Party with Betty Comden and Adolph Green,* won an Obie Award for Best Off-Broadway Musical.

In the eventful summer of 1938, Comden met Siegfried Schutzman, later Steven Kyle, whom she married three and a half years later. Comden's personal life has often had to take a backseat to her extremely successful career, but Kyle, an accomplished artist who ran Americraft, a store for decorative accessories in New York, always supported his wife's career, encouraging her to take risks and travel for her work. Comden and Kyle had two children: Susanna, whose birth in 1949 was commemorated in a composition by Leonard Bernstein called "Anniversary for Susanna Kyle," and Alan, born in 1953. After thirty-eight years of happy married life, Kyle died in 1979 of acute pancreatitis. Comden's son, Alan, suffered years of drug addiction and died of AIDS in 1990.

Comden's friends and collaborators have included the brightest stars of Hollywood and New York. Most important was Leonard Bernstein, with whom Comden had a close relationship dating back to the summer of 1938. In 1944, Comden and Green joined Bernstein and Jerome Robbins to write *On the Town*, the first great hit for each of the creative foursome, all still in their twenties. Directed by George Abbott, *On the Town* also featured Comden as Claire, the anthropologist, and Green as Ozzie, the sailor who looks like a prehistoric man. After many other successes, Comden and Green, in 1953, were asked again by George Abbott to work with Bernstein on music and lyrics for *Wonderful Town*, which won a Tony Award for Outstanding Musical, and for which Comden and Green won a Donaldson Award.

Comden's best work is about New York, which she portrays affectionately, always representing a human, personal experience of the big city, as in *On the Town*. In the same spirit, her work satirizes the glamour of show business, including Hollywood and the movies, which she also loves. *Singin' in the Rain* and *The Band Wagon* deflate the "stars" who grow too big for their britches with wit and compassion. In some ways, Comden herself seems not unlike her filmic creation Auntie Mame, both bohemian and dignified, with an incisive sense of humor and a penchant for playing roles. Comden's work privileges female characters who are clever, fast-talking, and humorous over tall, blonde, dumb starlets and narrow-minded debutantes who, in Comden's work, always lose their man. In the final analysis, Betty Comden is one of the most important librettists in the history of American musical comedy, contributing a wit informed both by her liberal Jewish upbringing and her implicit belief that women need to assert themselves creatively.

SELECTED WORKS BY BETTY COMDEN

The Bandwagon, with Adolph Green (1986); *Comden and Green Songbook*, with Adolph Green (1992); *Off Stage* (1995); *Singin' in the Rain*, with Adolph Green (1972).

BIBLIOGRAPHY

Robinson, Alice M. *Betty Comden and Adolph Green: A Bio-Bibliography* (1994); Styne, Jules. *Bells Are Ringing* (1957).

ALAN ACKERMAN

COMMUNISM

In the forty years following the Russian Revolution of October 1917, communism was the most dynamic force in American left-wing politics and a primary mobilizer of radical Jewish women. At the center of this movement lay the American Communist Party, which grew out of various radical factions inspired by the October Revolution. In December 1921, most of these groups came together as the Workers Party, renamed the Communist Party USA (CP) in 1930.

Jewish women, mostly Eastern European immigrants in New York City, helped to lead the communist cause and were a vital component of its rank and file. Notable leaders included ROSE WORTIS, a legendary labor organizer in the needle trades, ROSE PASTOR STOKES, a radical journalist elected to the Workers Party's central executive committee, and Betty Gannett, who joined the party as a teenager in 1923 and was appointed national education director of its Young Communist League in 1929. The majority of rank-and-file party members were garment workers or housewives. Many came to the party through the Jewish Federation, a Yiddish-language organization that originated in the Socialist Party and defected to the communists in 1922.

The Jewish Federation's mission was to preserve and invigorate revolutionary *yiddishkeit* through community-based cultural projects, work that found a generally comfortable home in the communist movement of the early 1920s. While nativism and racism surged in American society at large, ethnic communism flourished in the Workers Party. By the time the Yiddishists joined, the party contained a slew of other foreign-language federations as well. The Yiddishists gave the party a vital link to, and influence among, the large Jewish immigrant Left. The *Morgen Frayhayt*, the communist Yiddish-language daily established in New York in 1922, soon gained more readers than the whole Workers Party had members. In the mid-1920s, its circulation stood at about twenty-two thousand, while the party's national membership was about sixteen thousand (approximately 15 percent of it Jewish). The Jewish Federation spearheaded the creation of a rich network of ethnic summer camps, schools, choirs, and dramatic clubs. Jewish women—party members and larger numbers of sympathizers—were deeply involved in these efforts to keep left-wing *yiddishkeit* alive in a hostile America. In particular, the activists focused on projects aimed at the native-born children of immigrants.

In the second half of the 1920s, the Yiddishist communists lost ground both within and outside the

Workers Party. In 1925, in response to advice from the Soviet-led Communist International (Comintern), the party dissolved its foreign-language federations, and the Yiddishists' previously autonomous activities came under the control of party leaders for whom cultural work had a low priority. A second blow fell in 1928, when the Comintern urged its member parties to beware of alliances with the larger left and internal deviations from Bolshevism. This directive further diminished the resources available to Yiddishists in the Workers Party and subjected them to attack from non-Jewish members. As one woman recalled in an interview with historian Paul Buhle: "We weren't allowed to be proud that some great public figure was Jewish. . . . They used to laugh and complain about our having a bar mitzvah or celebrating the holidays." Then, in August 1929, the Yiddishists themselves undercut their outside support by defending the Comintern's endorsement of an Arab pogrom against Jews in Palestine and by inaugurating a series of anti-Zionist rallies in New York's Jewish communities. The communities retaliated with a boycott of the *Morgen Frayhayt* and with assaults on communist meetings. Despite these setbacks, most Yiddishist communists stayed with the party and continued their commitment to *yiddishkeit*, but their cultural work never regained its initial momentum—not even after a 1935 shift in Comintern policy prompted party leaders to exchange sectarianism for broad alliances with antifascist forces, including an array of English- and Yiddish-speaking Jewish organizations.

While the Yiddishist projects flagged, the late 1920s also saw some advances in community activism by Jewish communists, particularly women. Starting in Brooklyn's Brownsville district in 1926, communist activist housewives such as CLARA LEMLICH SHAVELSON and Kate Gitlow mobilized women in Jewish neighborhoods throughout New York City to protest exorbitant food and housing costs. In June 1929, this movement gave birth to the United Council of Working Class Women (UCWW). Though its membership was almost entirely Jewish until the mid-1930s, the UCCW was not officially an ethnic association. This departure from Yiddishist activism not only dovetailed with the Workers Party policy but also reflected a growing trend in Jewish communities. Increasingly, older immigrant Yiddishists were being outnumbered by younger, native-born leftists who were as self-consciously American as they were Jewish.

Many of these younger radicals aligned themselves with communism during the Great Depression and World War II, the heyday of both the Communist Party and Jewish women's involvement in its work.

The party swelled from just under ten thousand members in 1929 to about forty thousand in 1936 and to eighty-three thousand in 1943. Female membership expanded from about 15 percent in the early 1930s to 30 or 40 percent at the end of the decade and to about 46 percent in 1943. CP historians estimate, moreover, that almost half of the party's membership was Jewish in the 1930s and 1940s, and that approximately 100,000 Jews passed through the party in those decades of high member turnover. It seems safe to say, then, that Jewish women were one of the CP's largest sectors during the Depression and war years; and for each who was a "card-carrying" communist, there were several who took part in party-led mass organizations but did not belong to the party itself.

In addition to industrial workers and housewives, the new generation of Jewish women connected with the CP included a large number of college students, schoolteachers, office workers, and social service professionals. There was also a small but significant cadre of artists and intellectuals, such as playwright LILLIAN HELLMAN and anthropologist Eslanda Robeson, a Sephardic Jew who wrote and lectured on African affairs. In the early to mid-1930s, radical Jewish women were mainly engaged in neighborhood activism through unemployed councils and housewife movements such as the UCWW. Toward the end of the decade, their focus shifted to the labor movement, expanding beyond the traditional strongholds in the needle trades into newborn "red unions" such as the United Office and Professional Workers of America and to radical sectors of mainstream unions like the American Federation of Teachers. Jewish women also played important roles in communist-led student and youth movements, campaigns to defend civil liberties, and coalitions in solidarity with Spanish Republicans and the Soviet Union.

Radical activism extended far beyond New York City, which still had the largest proportion of Jewish communists but which was no longer their only stronghold. A second vital center was the CP's California branch, whose Jewish members included civil liberties leader Elaine Black Yoneda, labor leader Dorothy Healey, and a host of lesser-known women. Smaller groups of Jewish women worked with the party in cities and university towns throughout the Northeast, the Midwest, and parts of the South.

Jewish communists did much of their organizing among Jews, often through multiethnic movements, Jewish fraternal networks, coalitions of women's clubs, and the Yidishe Kultur Farband, founded in 1937. This work reflected the ethnic consciousness among Jewish communists and heightened their attention to the party's position on Jewish issues. For example, both the older Yiddishists and the younger, Americanized generation were especially proud of the Soviet Union's laws against anti-Semitism. They were pained by the Soviet peace pact with Nazi Germany from August 1939 to June 1941 and cheered by the party's post–World War II support for the establishment of a Jewish homeland in Palestine. The memoirs of Jewish women about communism suggest that these policies mattered not only in and of themselves, but also in terms of their effect on grass-roots organizing.

From 1946 to the mid-1950s, the Communist Party and its mass organizations were under unremitting attack from government, anticommunist labor leaders, and business associations. The most famous Jewish communist woman of this period was ETHEL ROSENBERG, who was convicted, along with her husband Julius, of espionage. As Jewish liberals, once friendly toward the CP, turned away, the Rosenbergs were executed in 1953. The "red scare" of the 1950s, along with political rifts within the party itself, reduced its membership from around eighty thousand at the end of World War II to about twenty-three thousand in 1955. Retreat gave way to utter chaos in 1956, when the Soviets revealed Stalin's crimes, Jewish communists in Poland denounced the Soviets for systematic anti-Semitism, and Soviet troops crushed the Hungarian revolt against Russian occupation. These events decimated the CP, which shrank to just three thousand members by 1958 and lost almost all of its mass following. The McCarthyists' determination to eliminate communism in the United States had been aided by the actions of communists in other countries.

Though the Communist Party survives to this day, it is smaller than ever in both size and influence. Rival communist factions, mostly Trotskyists and Maoists, have also receded following brief surges in the 1960s and 1970s. Jewish women remain a vital component of the American Left, but the communists among them are increasingly few and belong to an array of competing sects.

BIBLIOGRAPHY

Buhle, Mari Jo, et al., eds. *Encyclopedia of the American Left* (1990); Buhle, Paul. "Jews and American Communism: The Cultural Question." *Radical History Review* 23 (1980): 9–33; Chernin, Kim. *In My Mother's House* (1983); Coiner, Constance. *Better Red: The Writing and Resistance of Tillie Olsen and Meridel Le Sueur* (1995); Dennis, Peggy. *The Autobiography of an American Communist: A Personal View of a Political Life, 1925–1975* (1977); Draper, Theodore. *American Communism and Soviet Russia: The Formative Period* (1977); Foster, William Z. *History of the Communist Party of the United States* (1952); Gornick, Vivian. *The Romance of American Communism* (1977); Gosse, Van. "'To Organize in Every Neighborhood, in Every Home': The Gender Politics of American Communists Between the Wars." *Radical History Review* 50 (1991): 109–141; Healey, Dorothy, and Maurice Isserman. *Dorothy Healey Remembers: A Life in the American Communist Party* (1990); Isserman, Maurice. *Which Side Were You On? The American Communist Party during the Second World War* (1993); Johnpoll, Bernard K., and Harvey Klehr, eds. *Biographical Dictionary of the American Left* (1986); Murphy, Marjorie. *Blackboard Unions: The AFT and the NEA, 1900–1980* (1990); Naison, Mark. *Communists in Harlem during the Depression* (1985); *NAW*; *NAW* modern; Orleck, Annelise. *Common Sense and a Little Fire: Women and Working-Class Politics in the United States, 1900–1965* (1995); Philipson, Ilene. *Ethel Rosenberg: Beyond the Myths* (1988); Raineri, Vivian McGuckin. *The Red Angel: The Life and Times of Elaine Black Yoneda* (1991); Shaffer, Robert. "Women and the Communist Party, USA, 1930–1940." *Socialist Review* 9 (1979): 73–118; Shannon, David A. *The Decline of American Communism: A History of the Communist Party of the United States since 1945* (1959).

PRISCILLA MUROLO

CONE, CLARIBEL (1864–1929)

Immortalized in drawings by French modernists Pablo Picasso and Henri Matisse and in GERTRUDE STEIN's essay "Two Women," Dr. Claribel Cone was well known in her day as a charming, dignified, well-informed, self-assured, idiosyncratic, and highly independent woman with two passions, medical research and collecting art and artifacts.

Claribel Cone was born on November 14, 1864, to German immigrants Herman and Helen (Guggenheimer) Cone (Kahn), the fifth of thirteen children. Her father had immigrated to Richmond, Virginia, in 1846 and worked as a dry-goods peddler. Within ten years he settled in Jonesboro, Tennessee, became a co-owner of a grocery store, married, and began a family. In 1871, they moved to Baltimore, where Herman opened a wholesale grocery business and purchased an elegant, spacious home on Eutaw Place in 1880, becoming part of Baltimore's flourishing German Jewish community. On Herman Cone's retirement, his two oldest sons and business partners sold the grocery firm and went into the textile business, moving to Greensboro, North Carolina, in the 1890s and eventually building their own mills. Cone Mills prospered, becoming the world's leading producer of denim by the 1920s.

Young Claribel Cone loved to read and write, studied botany and German, and enjoyed playing the piano and painting watercolors. She graduated from the Baltimore Western Female High School in 1883. Though her parents encouraged marriage, Cone decided to study at the Women's Medical College of Baltimore to become a physician. First in her class, she graduated in 1890 and undertook postgraduate study at Johns Hopkins University, the University of Pennsylvania, and the Women's Medical College of Pennsylvania. She won one of five internships at the Philadelphia Blockley Hopital for the Insane. On returning to Baltimore in 1893, Claribel Cone announced that she preferred medical research and teaching to clinical practice. She secured a position as a lecturer in hygiene at the Women's Medical College of Baltimore. Appointed full professor in 1895, she taught pathology at the college until it closed in 1910.

Between 1903 and 1913, Claribel Cone traveled to Europe nearly every summer and spent several winters at the Senckenberg Pathological Institute in Frankfurt, Germany. Her research focused on tuberculosis and the behavior of fatty tissue under normal and pathological conditions. She worked in laboratories under several distinguished pathologists and published at least two articles but did not seem to consider herself a fully established professional in her field. She was grateful when mentors praised her work. "It is one of the most flattering and charming things that has ever happened to me in my life—to be approved of as woman and as worker by [Dr. E. Albrecht], one of the most talented yet critical and learned men in the world," she wrote to her sister Etta in 1910.

Claribel Cone's competing passion was collecting "beautiful things," which she said in 1928 that she had enjoyed "ever since I was a small girl and picked up all the shells I could find, reveling in their color and in their forms. In Paris in 1903, Leo and Gertrude Stein introduced their Baltimore friends Claribel and ETTA CONE to struggling artists Picasso and Matisse, encouraging the sisters to "indulge in romantic charity" and buy some of the artists' work. Drawing on their inherited yearly incomes of $2,400, the Cone sisters gradually purchased works by Picasso, Matisse, Cézanne, Renoir, Degas, Gauguin, Van Gogh, and others, selecting pieces to adorn the walls of their adjoining Baltimore apartments. After World War I, high profits at Cone Mills enabled the sisters to buy more expensive oil paintings. At Etta's death in 1949, their extensive and world-famous art collection featured over two hundred works by their favorite, Henri Matisse, spanning fifty-two years.

Cone continued to work and study with medical colleagues while living in Munich from 1914 to 1921.

Despite her delight in intellectual and social companionship, Cone always lived alone after she left the family home. Her Munich letters report nearly daily social engagements and frequent trips to the opera, concerts, and plays, though she commented in 1920, "On the whole I find things so much more satisfactory than people—people are interesting but you cannot live with them as satisfactorily as with things—things are soothing—if they are works of art—most people are overstimulating."

Though described by a nephew as a "freethinker," Claribel Cone was quite conscious of her identity as a Jew. She often commented on colleagues' ethnic identities and labeled herself a Jewess. Her family belonged to a local Reform temple, observed some religious holidays, and maintained strong ties with other German Jews, but, like many immigrant families, they emphasized Americanization, insisting that their children speak and write in English. Because she lived abroad much of her adult life, Cone's emotional and social connections to her community of origin are somewhat unclear, though her family generously supported Jewish institutions in Baltimore.

Claribel Cone's legacy, as she saw it, was her art and artifact collection. Aware of her declining health, she decided to leave her collection to Etta, her most trusted relative and friend. She expressed hope that, "if the spirit of appreciation of modern art in Baltimore should improve," Etta would will both collections to the Baltimore Museum of Art. She did so.

Claribel Cone died in Lausanne, Switzerland, on September 20, 1929.

BIBLIOGRAPHY

Balliett, Carl J., Inc. *World Leadership in Denims Through Thirty Years of Progress* (1925); Bonner, Thomas N. *To the Ends of the Earth: Women's Search for Education in Medicine* (1992); "Claribel Cone a Remarkable Woman." *Baltimore Evening Sun*, April 8, 1911; Cohen, Naomi W. *Encounter with Emancipation: The German Jews in the United States, 1830–1914* (1984); Cone, Claribel. Letters to Etta Cone, March 16, 1920, Munich, and September 8, 1910, Paris; Cone, Edward T. "The Miss Etta Cones, the Steins, and M'sieu Matisse." *American Scholar* 42 (Summer 1973): 441–460, and Oral interview, July 12, 1996; Cone, Sydney. Oral interview, July 18, 1996; *DAB* 4; *EJ*, s.v. "Cone"; Hirschland, Ellen B. "The Cone Sisters and the Stein Family." In *Four Americans in Paris: The Collections of Gertrude Stein and Her Family* (1970); Levy, Jane L. "Claribel and Etta Cone." Unpublished paper in author's possession (May 1995); *NAW*; Pollack, Barbara. *The Collectors: Dr. Claribel and Miss Etta Cone* (1962); Richardson, Brenda. *Dr. Claribel and Miss Etta* (1985), and Oral interview, August 22, 1996; Scarborough, Katherine. "Baltimore Collection Widely Known." *Sunday Sun Magazine*, Baltimore, April 15, 1928,

20; *"Send Us a Lady Physician": Women Doctors in America, 1835–1920*, edited by Ruth J. Abram (1985): Stein, Gertrude. *The Autobiography of Alice B. Toklas.* In *Selected Writings of Gertrude Stein*, edited by Carl Van Vechten (1946); *UJE*, s.v. "Cone"; *WWIAJ* (1926, 1928); Zweigenhaft, Richard L., and G. William Domhoff. *Jews in the Protestant Establishment* (1982).

SARAH S. MALINO

CONE, ETTA (1870–1949)

Though her formal education ended when she graduated from Baltimore Western Female High School in 1887, Etta Cone, often overshadowed by her more flamboyant sister CLARIBEL CONE, assembled with Claribel one of the major private art collections of the century. For years the sisters squeezed Matisses, Picassos, glorious textiles, and period furniture into the apartments they maintained and graciously displayed on Eutaw Place in Baltimore. Outliving Claribel by twenty years, Etta bequeathed their joint collections to the Baltimore Museum of Art.

Etta Cone was born on November 30, 1870, in Jonesboro, Tennessee, the ninth of thirteen children of Herman and Helen (Guggenheimer) Cone (formerly Kahn) and their third daughter. Both sides of the family were German Jews without much attachment to religious practice, though the elder Cones were synagogue members. Her family was well-to-do as the result of the business successes of her merchant father and later of her brothers Moses and Ceasar. Herman Cone's death in 1897 left her and Claribel with comfortable incomes, and after World War I they were wealthy.

Etta Cone's collecting began modestly but auspiciously in 1898 when she purchased five paintings by American impressionist Theodore Robinson for the family parlor. The Cone sisters' long friendship with Leo and GERTRUDE STEIN, whom they came to know as young people in Baltimore, was crucial to their collecting. Etta's taste in art was nurtured and excited by an intense month in the summer of 1901 that she and several friends spent in Italy with Leo Stein. From 1903 to 1906, both sisters spent considerable time in Paris with Gertrude and Leo and with their relatives Michael and Sally Stein. Diaries and letters document high spirits and shopping sprees. The fall and winter of 1905–1906 were key for the inception of the Cones' collection; Etta bought her first Matisse and her first Picasso from the artists and ventured further into textiles, jewelry, laces, and Japanese prints.

Moses Cone died in 1908. Etta, who adored her brother, went through a long period of grief. In 1912,

she resumed her summer trips to Europe, which featured ebullient Stein-Cone reunions. Yet only after World War I did the sisters start consciously building their collection, their summer buying alternating with winters in Baltimore. Their tastes were complementary, Claribel's often bolder.

Etta Cone's complicated relationship with Gertrude Stein included years of strong attachment, then feelings of hurt, then ambivalence. She typed the manuscript of *Three Lives* from Stein's handwriting in the winter of 1905–1906, while they were still close. But starting in 1907, as ALICE B. TOKLAS became Stein's life partner, the relationship became cooler.

Neither as a young woman nor later did Etta Cone participate actively in the diverse and lively Jewish organizational life of Baltimore; her meticulous record books, however, do show contributions to several Jewish charities. The opening of a letter to Gertrude Stein dated September 9, 1907, "Happy New Year to you, you heathen," combines Jewish identification with humorous distancing.

Claribel died in 1929. Etta gradually overcame grief and resumed her yearly buying trips, always accompanied by a young woman companion. She strengthened the collection with significant works of Corot, Manet, and Gauguin and developed an increasingly close friendship with Henri Matisse, who often set aside a few paintings he thought she would like in anticipation of her yearly visits. After 1938, she no longer traveled to Europe but still purchased art and gloried in showing visitors the collection. She died on August 31, 1949.

BIBLIOGRAPHY

Burke, Carolyn. "Gertrude Stein, the Cone Sisters, and the Puzzle of Female Friendship." *Critical Inquiry* 8, no. 3 (Spring 1982): 543–564; Cone, Etta. Archives and personal library. Baltimore Museum of Art; *DAB* 4; *EJ*, s.v. "Cone"; Fein, Isaac M. *The Making of an American Jewish Community: The History of Baltimore Jewry from 1773 to 1920* (1971); Hirschland, Ellen B. "The Cone Sisters and the Stein Family." In *Four Americans in Paris: The Collections of Gertrude Stein and Her Family*, edited by Margaret Potter (1970); *NAW*; Pollack, Barbara. *The Collectors: Dr. Claribel and Miss Etta Cone* (1962); Richardson, Brenda. *Dr. Claribel and Miss Etta* (1985); *UJE*, s.v. "Cone"; Wineapple, Brenda. *Sister Brother: Gertrude and Leo Stein* (1996); *WWIAJ* (1926, 1928).

HARRIET FEINBERG

CONFERENCE ON ALTERNATIVES IN JEWISH EDUCATION *see* CAJE

CONSERVATIVE JUDAISM

Women have played a pivotal role in Conservative Judaism throughout the twentieth century and have been instrumental on both the grass-roots and national levels in propelling the Conservative Movement to confront essential issues including Jewish education, gender equality, and religious leadership. The Conservative Movement's attention over the decades to issues such as the religious education of Jewish girls, the status of the *agunah* [deserted wife], equal participation of women in ritual, and the ordination of women has helped to shape the self-definition of Conservative Judaism and its maturation as a distinct denomination.

Solomon Schechter, president of the Jewish Theological Seminary (1902–1915), and his wife, MATHILDE SCHECHTER, were convinced of the indispensability of Jewish homemakers to the preservation of Judaism in the United States. After her husband's death, Mathilde Schechter extended their vision by founding the National Women's League in 1918 as the women's division of the United Synagogue of America. Through this organization, which is the coordinating body of Conservative synagogue sisterhoods, the Conservative Movement has promoted the perpetuation of Conservative Judaism in America through the home, synagogue, and community.

Mathilde Schechter believed in setting a personal example of Jewish living, and she was a powerful role model, especially for Jewish Theological Seminary (JTS) faculty wives and *rebbetzins* [rabbis' wives] who then influenced others. *Rebbetzins* throughout the century have served as important role models and experts for their congregants. They opened their homes for Sabbath and holidays, teaching by example the beauty of Jewish observance. Some served as guides to fledgling sisterhoods by supervising committees and programs, delivering *devar Torah* [sermonettes], and writing bulletin columns. They were particularly valuable in the area of kashrut, setting communal standards through their own home kitchens and teaching others the minutiae of keeping a kosher home.

The Conservative Movement experienced rapid growth in the interwar and post–World War II periods. During that time, congregational sisterhoods formed the backbone of the educational mission of the Conservative synagogue. Rabbis generally depended on these women for their loyal support of educational programming. Sisterhood women successfully took on many projects that greatly enhanced Conservative Jewish life in their synagogues, offering financial support as well as volunteer hours. They often took responsibility for assisting in Sunday and religious schools and were instrumental in organizing classes in Jewish living and observance for mothers. Typically, women also maintained the synagogue kitchen, both by ensuring kashrut and by serving as cooks and hostesses for the collations and luncheons that were the hubs of synagogue activities. Many groups also took it upon themselves to issue a sisterhood cookbook, a popular fund-raising project that demonstrated on a local level that it was possible to keep the highest standards of kashrut while cooking a wide variety of both Jewish and American-style dishes. Maintaining the synagogue gift shop, women were largely responsible for introducing Jewish ceremonial objects, as well as Jewish books and artwork, into the homes of Conservative Jews. Finally, these women were often instrumental in campaigns to decorate or refurbish synagogue buildings. Choosing curtains, carpeting, and wall hangings, women often set the tone for their synagogues through their dedication to its beautification. Eventually, many women moved up the ranks of synagogue administration from sisterhood to congregational leadership positions, where they have played active roles as officers of congregations throughout the United States and Canada.

The National Women's League provided inspiration on a national level for each of these local efforts through its publications and its leadership. For example, Betty Greenberg and Althea Osber Silverman shared their views on the beauty and spirituality of the Jewish home with other American Jewish women in "The Jewish Home Beautiful," a pageant first presented in the Temple of Religion of the World's Fair in 1940 and then published as a popular book by the National Women's League. Althea Osber Silverman with her *Habibi and Yow* and Sadie Weilerstein with her *K'tonTon* series became noted children's authors who made it easier for mothers to enrich their children's Jewish upbringing by providing adventurous, age-appropriate stories on Jewish customs and festivals. The combined efforts of all these women reinforced the message that one could both embrace American culture and transmit a full Jewish life to one's children. Through their writings, as well as through their lives, these women reassuringly illustrated that Conservative Jewish living was compatible with the aspirations of upwardly mobile women.

The National Women's League also played a crucial role in the national Conservative scene through its fund-raising capabilities. Responsible for collecting sufficient funds to open the Mathilde Schechter Residence Hall and, more recently, for refurbishing what is now called the Women's League Seminary Synagogue, these women made an important difference in the quality of life for students at the Jewish Theological Seminary.

Several difficult Jewish legal issues have long perplexed rabbinic leaders concerned about the inequality of women. The most difficult of these is that of the *agunah*, a woman whose husband has left her without issuing a Jewish divorce. She is unable to remarry as a result. The longstanding concern for the *agunah* is an important sign of the Conservative Movement's commitment to addressing the unequal treatment of women. The Law Committee tried for over twenty years to resolve the dilemma, and the first breakthrough came with the adoption of what came to be known as the "Lieberman clause" (1953), which made the Jewish marriage contract into a civil binding agreement that committed both husband and wife to abide by the recommendations of a Jewish court of law if their marriage ended. Though widely used throughout the Conservative Movement, it did not resolve the *agunah* problem. First, many rabbinic authorities hesitated bringing Jewish legal matters to the civil courts. Second, the civil courts have been reluctant to decide religious questions, even in states like New York that have laws prohibiting one spouse from impeding the remarriage of another. Therefore, the Joint *Bet Din* [Jewish court] of the Conservative Movement has, in recent years, become more aggressive in dealing with this problem, both by certifying Conservative rabbis qualified to write *gittin* [bills of divorce] and by using *hafkaat kiddushin* [annulment of marriage] as a tool against recalcitrant husbands. Based on a Talmudic text, though not universally accepted, *hafkaat kiddushin* is reserved for those severe cases where a Jewish divorce cannot be obtained, either because of the husband's extreme recalcitrance or his disappearance. The Joint *Bet Din* deals with each case individually and, where necessary, grants approval for a local *Bet Din* to annul the marriage. This approach has protected and aided women beyond what the Lieberman clause accomplished without abandoning a commitment to Jewish legal principles.

The Conservative Movement has long advocated equal education for both sexes, calling for primary Jewish education for girls at a time when girls traditionally were receiving little formal Jewish instruction. Similarly, on a more advanced level, the Teachers Institute of the Jewish Theological Seminary, founded in 1909, offered Jewish higher education to men and women on an equal basis. From 1915 on, it also offered a professional teacher-training curriculum that enabled women to prepare for careers in Jewish education.

The path of women from the periphery to the center of religious life began with the introduction of mixed seating in prayer services. By 1955, mixed seating characterized the overwhelming majority of Conservative congregations and served as a yardstick to differentiate them from Orthodoxy. The bat mitzvah, first introduced by Mordecai M. Kaplan in 1922 for his own daughter, became increasingly popular within the Conservative Movement. By 1948, approximately one-third of all Conservative synagogues had introduced such a ceremony. Bat mitzvah took different forms, including group rituals that resembled confirmation as well as individual ceremonies at the late Friday evening service, where the bat mitzvah girl generally chanted a haftarah. By the 1980s, most bat mitzvah ceremonies came to resemble a bar mitzvah, where girls are called to read from the Torah and chant a haftarah. The rapid growth of the bat mitzvah ceremony was also designed as an incentive to retain girls in the same supplementary religious school educational setting as boys. The Conservative Movement was challenged to accept the implications of this equality in education and obligation in places like Camp Ramah as well, where girls were given the opportunity to assume leadership roles in prayer services.

The Committee on Jewish Law and Standards of the Conservative Movement responded to the changing role of women in the synagogue by deciding to permit women to be called up for *aliyot* in 1955. At that time, the option was implemented in only a few synagogues in the Minneapolis area, but the precedent was established. In 1973, the Committee on Jewish Law and Standards passed a *takkanah* [enactment] that allowed women to count in a minyan equally with men. One year later, it adopted a series of proposals that equalized men and women in all areas of ritual, including serving as prayer leaders. Also in 1973, the United Synagogue of America, the Conservative Movement's congregational association, now called the United Synagogue of Conservative Judaism, resolved to allow women to participate in synagogue rituals and to promote equal opportunity for women for positions of leadership, authority, and responsibility in congregational life. From 1972 to 1976, the number of Conservative congregations giving *aliyot* [the honor of being called to the Torah] to women increased from 7 percent to 50 percent.

Grass-roots pressure for change intensified throughout the 1970s. In 1972, Ezrat Nashim, a group of young, well-educated women, most of whom were products of the camps and schools of the Conservative Movement, presented to the Conservative Rabbinical Assembly (CRA) a call for the public affirmation of women's equality in all aspects of Jewish life. They demanded that women be granted membership in synagogues, counted in a minyan, allowed full participation in religious observances, recognized as witnesses in Jewish law, allowed to initiate divorce, permitted and encouraged to attend rabbinical and cantorial school and perform as rabbis and cantors in synagogues, encouraged to assume positions of leadership in the community, and considered bound to fulfill all the mitzvahs (commandments) equally with men. This call evoked a sympathetic response from the rabbinate, and it precipitated widespread, often heated, divisive debate within the Conservative Movement and in the press over the next decade. Some women who wanted to become Conservative rabbis came to study at the seminary, and due to an unrelated academic reorganization effective with the 1974–1975 year, they were able to study in any class at their appropriate level. Preparing for ordination without being officially enrolled in the rabbinical school, they hoped that someday they would be ordained on the basis of their studies. In September 1977, the seminary's chancellor, Gerson D. Cohen, appointed a Committee for the Study of the Ordination of Women as Rabbis, which held hearings in cities throughout the country to obtain the perspective of the laity as well as the view of its professionals. The committee's final report of January 30, 1979, recommended, 11 to 3, that women be ordained, but the CRA voted 127 to 109 to take no action prior to the decision of the seminary faculty. Pressure increased when, one month later, seminary students organized GROW (Group for the Rabbinical Ordination of Women) in an attempt to organize political action and education. In 1979, the issue was brought to the seminary senate for a vote, but it was tabled when its divisiveness became apparent.

In 1983, the CRA decided to consider for membership Beverly Magidson, a graduate of Hebrew Union College. Her admission fell short of receiving the necessary three-quarters vote of rabbis present but had widespread support, an indication that such approval was imminent. This spurred the seminary to reconsider the issue, and on October 24, 1983, the seminary faculty voted thirty-four to eight, with one abstention and over half a dozen absent in protest, to admit women to the seminary's rabbinical school. The Jewish legal basis for their acceptance was the responsum of Rabbi Joel Roth (known as the *Roth Teshuva*), which held that individual women could become rabbis (and prayer leaders) if they chose to assume the same degree of religious obligation as men. Individuals opposed to the decision formed the Union for

Traditional Conservative Judaism, which became a separate group in 1990, changing its name to the Union for Traditional Judaism.

The first class to include women entered the seminary in the fall of 1984, and Amy Eilberg was the first woman ordained (1985). At the spring 1985 convention, the CRA voted to admit for membership Beverly Magidson and Jan Kaufman, also a graduate of Hebrew Union College. Their membership was made effective July 1, 1985, to enable Eilberg, the seminary graduate, to be the first woman admitted to the CRA. There are currently seventy-two women members of the CRA out of a total membership of almost fourteen hundred. This includes several in Israel and one in Latin America. Women's presence in the rabbinical school—they currently make up 38 percent of the student body—has had a dramatic impact on the nature of rabbinic education. According to Rabbi William Lebeau, the current dean of the rabbinical school, the inclusion of women's voices on a regular basis has immeasurably enriched the dialectic of traditional study.

The struggle for acceptance of women as cantors took a different course, since women had been eligible to study in the Cantors Institute since its inception in 1952 as candidates for bachelor's, master's, and doctorate of sacred music degrees. In 1987, seminary chancellor Ismar Schorsch announced that the Jewish Theological Seminary would confer the diploma of hazan to two women, Marla Barugel and Erica Lipitz. The Cantors Assembly voiced its disapproval and established a Committee of Inquiry to look into the question of admitting women. A resolution to admit women to the Cantors Assembly was defeated in 1988 (95 for, 97 against) and again in 1989 (108 for, 82 against, 2 abstentions) and 1990 (110 for, 68 against) because, although the majority of the assembly had turned in favor of admission, the resolution failed to receive the necessary two-thirds vote. Women were finally admitted in December 1990 as a result of a decision by the executive council of the assembly. Today women make up approximately 50 percent of the student body in the Cantors Institute. Thirty-eight of the 476 current members of the Cantors Assembly are women.

The *Roth Teshuva* guided the seminary synagogue until 1995, when Chancellor Schorsch announced that in the Women's League Seminary Synagogue the principle of full egalitarianism would be decisive in granting women religious status equal to that of men. Some students have agitated for liturgical change as well, challenging the Conservative Movement to address issues of sexism and patriarchy in the liturgy.

The Women's League Seminary Synagogue, for example, now permits the inclusion of the matriarchs along with the patriarchs in daily prayer at the discretion of the prayer leader.

After a decade in the rabbinate, women have begun to have an impact on the Conservative Movement. They occupy a number of pulpits throughout the United States, and even in Israel, though women, like their male counterparts, have chosen many diverse career options within the rabbinate. According to Rabbi Joel Meyers, executive vice president of the CRA, the past ten years have seen greater acceptance of women as rabbinic leaders by Conservative congregations. He maintains that the nature and challenges of rabbinic leadership are essentially the same for all rabbis, but that women are generally more concerned about quality-of-life issues in terms of their families and private lives, and are more likely to make adjustments in their careers for the sake of those concerns. Given the seniority system in terms of placement, women are just beginning to become eligible for positions in large congregations. Debra Newman Kamin is the first woman to serve as senior rabbi of a major Conservative congregation, Am Yisrael, in Northfield, Illinois (1995). The involvement of women rabbis in the law committee has begun to influence its decisions on many issues, including appropriate mourning rituals for women suffering a miscarriage or stillbirth.

Since 1986, the vast majority of Conservative synagogues have accorded women partial or full equality in religious services, although the official position of the Conservative Movement is to endorse both egalitarian and nonegalitarian services, and both options continue to be offered at the seminary, Camp Ramah, and United Synagogue events. There is a sense of women coming of age religiously, entering the mainstream of public Jewish religious life. Ceremonies for the naming of baby Jewish girls, performed in an ad hoc, experimental way by individuals for a generation, have now begun to enter the mainstream with the publication of the National Women's League's *Simhat-Bat: Ceremonies to Welcome a Baby Girl* (1994). It is no longer odd to see women reading Torah or donning Jewish religious garb for prayer. During the past twenty years, small numbers of Conservative women have begun to wear tallith [prayer shawl] and tefillin [phylacteries]. Some women prefer the traditional wool tallith with its black and white stripes, while others opt for more eclectic colors, fabrics, and shapes. Some women wear *kippot* [skullcap], but creative head coverings that conform to the shape of women's hair have also been developed in response to this growing demand. Though egalitarianism has not been universally embraced by the Conservative Movement, it is now the dominant position.

Certain Jewish legal issues have not yet been resolved, the most notable being the inadmissability of women as witnesses in Jewish legal matters. There is also great lack of uniformity on many of the changes that have been introduced. Taken as a whole, however, the Conservative Movement has made great strides during the twentieth century in positioning itself as committed both to Jewish law and to gender equality with respect to equality of education and of opportunity, and it has emerged both strengthened and more sharply focused as a result of this challenge.

BIBLIOGRAPHY

Cantors Assembly Minutes, 1987–1991; Cardin, Nina Beth, and David W. Silverman, eds. *The Seminary at 100* (1987); Fishman, Sylvia Barack. *A Breath of Life: Feminism in the American Jewish Community* (1993); Friedman, Reena Sigman. "The Politics of Ordination." *Lilith* 6 (1979): 9–15; Greenberg, Simon, ed. *The Ordination of Women as Rabbis: Studies and Responsa* (1988); Grossman, Susan, and Rivka Haut, eds. *Daughters of the King: Women and the Synagogue* (1992); Hyman, Paula E. "The Introduction of Bat Mitzvah in Conservative Judaism in Postwar America." *YIVO Annual* 19 (1990): 133–146; Joselit, Jenna Weissman. *The Wonders of America: Reinventing Jewish Culture, 1880–1950* (1994); Nadell, Pamela S. *Conservative Judaism in America: A Biographical Dictionary and Sourcebook* (1988); Siegel, Seymour, ed. *Conservative Judaism and Jewish Law* (1977); Sklare, Marshall. *Conservative Judaism: An American Religious Movement.* Rev. ed. (1972); Stone, Amy. "Gentleman's Agreement at the Seminary." *Lilith* (Spring/Summer 1977): 13–18; Wertheimer, Jack. *A People Divided* (1993), and ed., *The American Synagogue* (1987).

SHULY RUBIN SCHWARTZ

CONTEMPORARY JEWISH MIGRATIONS

SOVIET EMIGRATION

Over a quarter million Soviet Jews have settled in the United States since the mid-1960s, making it the largest Jewish immigrant wave since the 1920s. Women, who comprise 53 percent of this immigrant group, arrive in the United States with an unusually high degree of professional and technical skills. In contrast to 16.5 percent of American women who work as engineers, technicians, or other professionals, over two-thirds of Soviet Jewish emigré women had worked in these occupations prior to their arrival. As is consistent with their occupational status, Soviet Jewish women immigrants are also highly educated. Their average number of years of schooling is 14.2. Despite their high degree of educational and occupational attainment, women's salaries in the U.S.S.R. were only 57 percent those of men.

Due to economic need, as well as to a cultural expectation that women work, more than 60 percent of Soviet Jewish emigré women held full-time jobs in the American labor force in 1980. The types of jobs women received were different from those of their male counterparts. Thirty-eight percent of working women held managerial, professional, or technical positions, compared with 69 percent of men. Another 31 percent of the women emigrés were employed in clerical and sales jobs, compared with just 7 percent of Soviet Jewish male immigrants. Similar to their experience in their country of origin, Soviet Jewish women's earnings in the United States remain 57 percent of those of their male counterparts, a proportion only slightly below that of American women's earnings relative to those of men. Despite these income disparities and their lower job statuses than the ones they had in the U.S.S.R., 42.5 percent of Soviet Jewish women (versus 35.4 percent of men) are very satisfied with their work, and another 40.2 percent (versus 51.1 percent of men) reported being somewhat satisfied.

In addition to being satisfied with work, surveys show that Soviet Jewish women emigrés are content with other economic features of their new country. In the United States, they have attained better housing, higher incomes, and an overall higher standard of living than in the Soviet Union. They also report being satisfied with the Jewish component of their lives. Life in the United States is less dominated by anti-Semitism than in their former home.

In other realms, however, Soviet Jewish women immigrants find the quality of their lives deficient. Compared with the Soviet Union, most female Jewish immigrants find life in the United States to be less emotionally and intellectually fulfilling. They perceive cultural life as thinner in the United States, friendships as weaker, and their social status as lower. Their departure from their homes, then, was not motivated by discontent in their personal lives. Rather, anti-Semitism, combined with a desire to seek occupational and educational opportunities for themselves and their children, led the great majority of the Jewish emigré women, as well as men, to leave the U.S.S.R.

Detailed observations reveal another source of discontent among Soviet Jewish women immigrants.

Although the majority of Soviet emigrés are still part of two-income families, evidence suggests that upwardly mobile men are increasingly pressuring their wives to leave the labor force, undermining Soviet Jewish women's triple role as wife-mother-worker. Working had been such an integral part of Soviet Jewish women's identities that female emigrés were surprised when, upon their arrival, their social workers did not automatically expect them to work.

As wives and mothers, Soviet Jewish women marry young and have small families, with an average of 1.4 children. They often immigrate as part of extended families that include three generations. As a result, a high proportion of Soviet Jewish emigré families are multigenerational and include a very elderly population. Settling in the United States with elderly parents and grandparents is one sign of the permanent character of the Soviet Jewish immigration.

ISRAELI EMIGRATION

In contrast to Soviet Jews, most of the ninety thousand Israeli Jews who reside in the United States view themselves as sojourners. Most Israeli women did not want to leave their homes, and their refusal to assign a definition of permanence is one way to cope with the immigration decision.

Unlike Soviet Jewish women who see immigration as a way to improve their own lives, Israeli Jewish women, whether married to Israelis or Americans, place the onus of the immigration decision upon their husbands. For those married to Israeli men, they claim that they came to the United States because of their husbands' economic and educational goals, thus seeing themselves as adjuncts, rather than as active participants in their families' immigration decision. Israeli women married to Americans rationalize that for the sake of keeping their marriages intact, they had no choice but to follow their husbands back to the United States.

The perceived lack of responsibility and choice has shaped Israeli women's immigrant experiences in the United States. Often feeling wrenched away from families, friends, and jobs, Israeli women, particularly those married to Israelis and who have young children, suffer from homesickness and isolation in the United States. While their husbands develop social networks through work and school, the women often remain isolated at home, caring for their children in a new and unfamiliar environment.

Further compounding their isolation, a high percentage of female immigrants who had worked in Israel are not working in the United States. A survey of naturalized Israelis who live in New York reveals that only 4 percent of the women listed "housewife" as their occupation in Israel, while over one-third of the women indicated "housewife" in the United States. And many of those women who worked in the United States did so only part-time. Compared with Israeli men, Israeli women are more dissatisfied with America and less identified with their new country.

Although a large percentage of Israeli immigrant women are housewives, a much larger percentage have entered the paid labor force. According to 1990 census data, half of Israeli women in New York, and 59 percent of their Los Angeles counterparts, are employed. Of employed Israeli women in New York between the ages of twenty-five and sixty-four, 23 percent are managers and administrators, 33 percent work in either professional or technical fields, 11 percent are in sales, 20 percent are in clerical jobs, and 16 percent are self-employed. Nearly one-third of Israeli women in Los Angeles (versus 40 percent of men) have four or more years of college. Israeli women are a highly educated and skilled group.

In both New York and Los Angeles, Israeli women are nearly twice as likely as Israeli men to be in professional and technical jobs. In New York, slightly more than one-third of the women are in these fields, compared with 17 percent of the men. On the West Coast, 41 percent of the women are employed in professional or technical jobs compared with just 21 percent of the men. The overrepresentation of women in this category is probably due to the large number of Israeli women employed as Hebrew school teachers, as well as other types of professionals (e.g., mental health workers) within Jewish agencies.

Living in neighborhoods with other Israelis, meeting other Israeli women, and joining communal organizations offer emotional relief. In Los Angeles, for example, Israeli women become involved with Tzofim (Israeli Scouts), the AMI School (for learning Israeli Hebrew), as well as Israeli-oriented chapters of American Jewish organizations such as the Jewish Federation's Israeli Division, the Jewish Community Center's Israeli Program, the Hebrew-speaking chapter of B'nai B'rith, an Israeli chapter of WIZO (Women's International Zionist Organization), and ORT (Occupational Training and Rehabilitation). Other Israeli women in Los Angeles add synagogues to their organizational repertoire. Finding strategies for maintaining a Jewish identity for themselves and their families, either through secular activities with a national focus or through religious institutions, is a priority.

IRANIAN EMIGRATION

After the fall of Iran's Shah Riza Pahlevi in 1979, many Iranian Jews left their homeland for the United States, settling primarily in Los Angeles and New York. This was a permanent migration characterized by entire families moving to the United States.

In the United States, Iranian Jewish women are increasingly entering their ethnic economy through businesses that are operated both in and outside of their homes. According to ethnographic research, Moslem Iranian women are frequent customers of stores and businesses run by Jewish Iranian women, and Jewish women buy at Moslem women's shops as well. The sharing of many cultural traditions, including particular culinary predilections, has created new avenues of social interaction between these two groups of female immigrants. In Los Angeles, for example, Jewish and Moslem women participated together in building an elderly day center during the 1980s. In contrast to the American setting, Jewish women in Iran were more likely to confine their social interactions to the Jewish world.

Since their arrival in the United States, Iranian Jewish women have become involved with a variety of gender-specific organizations. In Los Angeles, women belong to Iranian chapters of national Jewish organizations such as HADASSAH, WOMEN'S AMERICAN ORT, and PIONEER WOMEN, as well as to synagogue sisterhoods. In addition, they founded the Iranian Jewish Women's Organization of Los Angeles in 1976, an organization that traces its roots to a 1947 women's organization in Iran. Among its many activities, the Iranian Jewish Women's Organization provides student loans, hosts lectures, raises money for Israel, gives an annual "Best Mother" award, and serves as a general philanthropic agency.

Through their wage-earning and domestic duties, Jewish women play central roles in shaping their group's adaptation to the United States. They contribute financially to their family economies, they have a large responsibility for managing their homes and for child rearing, and they are central actors in the communal realm.

BIBLIOGRAPHY

Collins, Beth, et al. "Family and Community Among Iranian Jews in Los Angeles." M.A. thesis, Hebrew Union College–Jewish Institute of Religion, Cincinnati, Ohio (1986); Dallalfar, Arlene. "Iranian Immigrant Women in Los Angeles: The Reconstruction of Work, Ethnicity, and Community." Ph.D. diss., University of California, Los Angeles (1989); Gold, Steven J. "Gender, Immigration and Social Capital Among Israelis in Los Angeles." *Diaspora* 4, no. 3 (1995): 267–301, and "Soviet Jews in the United States."

AJYB 94 (1994): 3–57; Lipner, Nira H. "The Subjective Experience of Israeli Immigrant Women: An Interpretive Approach." Ph.D. diss., George Washington University (1987); Markowitz, Fran. *A Community in Spite of Itself: Soviet Jewish Emigres in New York* (1993); Simon, Rita James, Louise Shelley, and Paul Schneiderman. "The Social and Economic Adjustment of Soviet Jewish Women in the United States." In *International Migration: The Female Experience*, edited by Rita James Simon and Caroline Brettell (1986).

SHELLY TENENBAUM

CONVERSION, *see* INTERMARRIAGE AND CONVERSION

COOKBOOKS

When you are searching for instructions on how to prepare the perfect pickled tongue, for hints on setting a festive Shabbat table, or a refresher course in the laws and lore of Passover, American Jewish cookbooks are an invaluable source of information on Jewish life. The first publicly available American Jewish cookbook was published in 1871. Esther Levy's *Jewish Cookery Book on Principles of Economy Adapted for Jewish Housekeepers with Medicinal Recipes and Other Valuable Information Relative to Houskeeping and Domestic Management* was an attempt to touch on most aspects of Jewish home life. While few of the hundreds of Jewish cookbooks written since attempt the breadth of this first work, American Jewish cookbooks capture the range of Jewish religious and cultural expression.

Jewish cookbooks include recipes for all manner of Jewish and American dishes as well as exotic, gourmet, and ethnic fare. They are far more than technical manuals. For some women the kitchen and its responsibilities represent limitations placed on them in Jewish society; other women, however, use food and cookbooks as a means of expression. Written primarily by and for women, these books present their authors' interpretations of and commitment to Judaism. The inclusion of traditional fare stresses attempts to maintain ties with the past, while recipes for smores and apple pie signify adoption of American culinary norms. Motherly voices retell the story of Hanukkah as an explanation of why we eat latkes. The frequent dedications to foremothers and/or offspring remind us that for many Jews food is an important means through which Judaism passes from generation to generation.

DEFINING AMERICAN JEWISH COOKBOOKS

American Jewish cookbooks include books dedicated to the preparation of fish as well as others that make suggestions on how to discipline your children. Indeed, no single criterion defines the American Jewish cookbook. Some can easily be identified as Jewish by the inclusion of the word "Jewish" in the title, such as *Jewish Cookery Book* or *Jewish Cook Book*. Others, such as *Chinese-Kosher Cookbook* or *The Yemenite Cookbook*, can be identified as Jewish by the use of Hebrew or Jewish terms. Volumes put out by groups with a Jewish affiliation can be included in the category of American Jewish cookbooks even when they focus on topics not specifically Jewish, such as desserts. Jewish cookbooks often stress ritual or religious issues as well as recipes for traditional Jewish dishes. But Jewish contents such as a sweet raisin-studded noodle kugel do not mark the book as Jewish in all cases. A general book on holiday entertaining may suggest a Hanukkah menu between those for Christmas and Kwanzaa. Some Jewish foods, such as challah—braided egg bread—that appeal to mainstream America palates appear regularly in general American collections. Particular attention to kashrut (Jewish dietary law) nonetheless remains a marker of uniquely Jewish cookbooks.

KASHRUT

Not all American Jewish cookbooks engage kashrut, but those that do define the concept broadly. Some authors adhere to traditional Orthodox legal standards. Books in this category sometimes serve as detailed guides to keeping a kosher kitchen. For Lubavitch women, the way to cook a brisket cannot be separated from the choice of a proper kosher butcher; neither aspect of the preparation can be neglected. In addition to a large presentation of Jewish recipes, including eight variations of gefilte fish, the Lubavitch Women's *The Spice and Spirit of Kosher-Jewish Cooking* describes aspects of religious law related to food, kitchen, and home.

Recipes for chicken in cream sauce, or other dishes that combine milk and meat, may not mean abandonment of kashrut but rather redefinition of the traditional term. *Aunt Babette's Cook Book*, which first appeared in 1889, includes instructions for skinning a hare and steaming shellfish. Though paying great attention to these and other traditionally forbidden foods, the author made clear that she was reinterpreting, not renouncing, kashrut. In her mind, "Nothing is 'Trefa' that is healthy and clean." Following this logic, she included recipes for ham but not for bacon. Other books' authors show no ideological attachment to kashrut but maintain a cultural connection to the concept by not mixing meat and milk or by providing kosher alternatives to recipes that do mix milk and meat.

PERSONAL COOKBOOKS

Everyone has an aunt or a friend who is always clipping and borrowing recipes. These collections, whether kept on scraps of paper in a box, on cards in a file, or in a book, are the essence of personal "cookbooks." Whereas a cook may or may not use all or any of the recipes found in a purchased collection, personal cookbooks reflect most closely the foods prepared in Jewish homes. Many collections remain the property of one individual cook. The Gold family story, however, told when a personal cookbook was made publicly available, suggests how personal cookbooks can connect generations. When Evelyn Gold's mother came to Canada from the Ukraine, she brought with her memories of food her mother had made and a good knowledge of Eastern European Jewish cooking. She applied this knowledge to the foods of Canada and through the years adapted numerous newspaper recipes to suit her taste. Later in life, she codified her eclectic collection of recipes and passed it on to her daughter. In 1994, Gold published this personal cookbook and dedicated it to the family's next generation. Thus Jewish food tastes formed over time in the Ukraine and adapted to North America passed down through a family and to others in this personal cookbook.

ORGANIZATIONAL COOKBOOKS

The organizational cookbook is an institution of American culture and Jewish life. Usually spurred by the desire and need to raise money, members of sisterhoods, women's organizations, or schools publish collections of recipes. Such projects allow broad membership participation as individuals contribute a favorite secret for preparing brownies or sweet and sour chicken. Additionally, such endeavors find a ready purchasing audience as members buy copies to see their name in print, send copies to relatives, or learn how to make the watercress soup Sylvia serves yearly at the sisterhood brunch.

The wide range of Jewish groups in North America is apparent in the diverse cookbooks these organizations produce. Some answer the specific needs of a particular community. *The When You Live in Hawaii You Get Very Creative During Passover Cookbook* highlights the community's kitchen. This project not only brought members together in its production but also provides some practical suggestions for Passover, such

as matzoh pie and hot-spicy zucchini latkes. A gay and lesbian congregation worked to have their cookbook reflect the diverse family constellations of its members, so, whereas most organizational cookbooks suggest quantities to feed four to eight, *Out of Our Kitchen Closets* provides meal plans for one, two, or many. Commonly, religious organizations concerned with observance include ritual information intended to guide members of the community.

Boston baked beans in collections from New England to burritos in those from the Southwest underscore the incorporation of local fare into America's Jewish homes. Even traditional dishes come under regional influence as southern cooks trade the walnuts traditionally used by Jews for the more easily available pecan. Some home cooks feel comfortable combining the unique elements of Jewish and regional cuisine for creative recipes such as catfish matzoh-ball gumbo.

Each organizational cookbook is arranged according to its own principles. Sometimes editors focus on Jewish themes such as the holiday cycle, Passover foods, or Shabbat cooking. Often food categories such as soups, meats, or salads dominate, with either a special section for Jewish foods or Jewish dishes sprinkled throughout. Not all Jewish organizations, however, concentrate on Jewish dishes.

COMMERCIAL COOKBOOKS

While the category of cookbooks put together and published by organizations is by far the largest of the publicly aware available type of American Jewish cookbook, commercially published cookbooks are more widely available. The latter are expected to reach a broad readership, whereas the former primarily circulate locally.

Since 1871, and the very limited success of the first Jewish cookbook published in the United States, the popularity of commercial cookbooks has mounted steadily. Today, numerous American Jewish cookbooks appear from both Jewish and general commercial presses and are widely available. Recently, even that first volume has been reprinted.

THE NINETEENTH CENTURY

Esther Levy saw her 1871 *Jewish Cookery Book* as a comprehensive guide for keeping a Jewish home. In the introduction, worried that young Jewish brides might not know how to instruct their maids in housekeeping matters, she included explanations of table setting and other points of etiquette. Working to counter the myth that "a repast, to be sumptuous, must unavoidably admit of forbidden food," she provided instructions for matzoh charlotte and ochre gumbo as well as other recipes that blended contemporary tastes and Orthodox kashrut observance.

Levy's book reflects the tastes and standards of her Philadelphia German Jewish community. German dishes such as pancake soup appear with both their original and translated names. Matzoh balls remain untranslated as *Matzo Cleis*. In contrast to the presence of German and English fare, Eastern European Jewish foods are noticeably absent. Levy's omission of gefilte fish, a dish she likely did not know, led later cookbook authors to question the manual's authenticity as a Jewish cookbook.

Writing under the pseudonym Aunt Babette, Bertha F. Kramer compiled in 1889 *Aunt Babette's Cook Book, Foreign and Domestic Resipst* [sic] *for the Household*. Unlike Levy's effort, this book went through multiple editions, several in the first year. Kramer claimed that her only intention in compiling this volume was to pass her secrets on to her daughters, but her attention to the extensive duties of a middle-class woman and the prominence of her German Jewish Reform publisher, Bloch Publishers, suggests a broader audience. Kramer made sure to provide instructions for all occasions from the grand wedding meal to the intimate "Koffee Klatch." Housewives looking to be the perfect hostess could turn to Aunt Babette for directions on running a "Pink Tea" with pink foods, pink linens, and pink aprons for maids.

EASTERN EUROPEAN JEWS ARRIVE

Gefilte fish finally gained its central place in American Jewish cuisine with the mass immigration of Eastern European Jews (1880–1924). The variety of new American Jewish cookbooks of this period addressed this new group and its Old World foodways.

Some books benignly explained how to prepare the multitude of unfamiliar foods that mystified recent arrivals. (Such volumes explained that the inside, not the peel, of the yellow fruit called a banana was to be eaten.) Other books, often authored by progressive reformers, aimed to change how immigrants approached cooking and teach them how to cook American style. *The Settlement Cook Book* out of Milwaukee also explained household skills from washing dishes and feeding invalids to the intricacies of preparing a feast for forty. Its detailed menus and explicit instructions made it a basic handbook for cultivating American habits and nutritional standards.

Other commercial cookbooks embraced the culinary style of this new community. Slow-fermenting beet rosl and plump meat-filled kreplakh began to show up with regularity among the new recipe collections. Assuming a traditional and Yiddish-speaking audience, the new cookbooks often presumed Orthodox kashrut standards, and many were written in Yiddish.

Major American food manufacturers saw Jewish immigrants as an important consumer market. They not only advertised in Yiddish for American products but also provided recipes advising how to use their products in Jewish dishes. Crisco and Manishewitz were some of the many manufacturers that produced Yiddish/English cookbooks. These bilingual cookbooks were popular with general presses as well. A Yiddish-speaking cook could learn basic English vocabulary by looking across at the translation. Additionally, these books allowed a Yiddish-speaking mother and an English-speaking daughter to work from the same recipe side by side, thus facilitating the mother-daughter transmission of culinary knowledge.

THE SCIENCE AND ART
OF JEWISH COOKING

Concerns about scientific approaches to nutrition, budgetary constraints, and proper hostessing have merged with Jewish considerations in the pages of many American Jewish cookbooks. One early example, the *Jewish Cook Book* published by Bloch Publishing Company, appeared first in 1918, later enjoying numerous editions and one major revision. Both the original author, Florence Kreisler Greenbaum, and Mildred Grosberg Bellin, author of the second version, were university-trained home economists. The two incarnations of this volume stress economy, nutrition, and Jewish dietary restrictions. Speaking as authorities on scientific approaches to cooking, these women reassured their readers that a Jewish diet was compatible with contemporary concerns.

Starting with Esther Levy's section on medicinal cures for everything from sore throats to diphtheria, American Jewish cookbooks have attended to health. By the 1920s, nutritional information was routinely being integrated into the body of menus and recipes. Today the complexity of dietary knowledge and health considerations can be seen in a variety of cookbooks that adapt Jewish dishes for diabetic, low-cholesterol, or vegetarian diets.

Other authors feared that Jewish wives would be drawn away from kashrut and Jewish customs by the delights of Christmas trees, Easter baskets, and other elements of non-Jewish living. Several well-known and respected women joined in the effort to reassure Jewish homemakers that a Jewish life-style could properly express full womanhood. On behalf of the

In terms of influence, Lizzie Kander was both the Julia Child and the James Beard of Jewish cooking. Her Settlement Cook Book *was privately printed in an edition of one thousand copies in 1901; by 1984, nearly two million copies had been sold. Pictured here is the dust jacket of the twenty-fourth edition (1941). [Collection of Barbara Kirshenblatt-Gimblett. Courtesy of the Jewish Museum, New York City]*

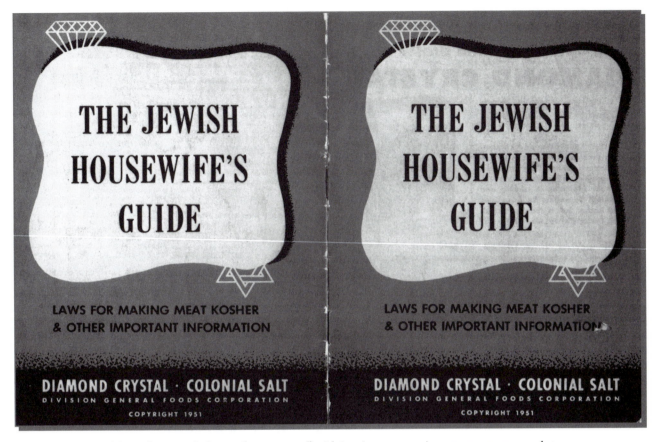

Major American food manufacturers saw Jewish immigrants as an important consumer market and often published pamphlets to help them adjust to American ways by using their products. The Jewish Housewife's Guide pictured above was published by General Foods and pushed their brand-name salt. [Peter H. Schweitzer]

National Women's League of Conservative Judaism, Betty Greenberg and Althea Silverman coauthored *The Jewish Home Beautiful*, the best-known book of this type. More than merely a recipe book, this volume includes a script for an elaborate musical and spoken pageant on Jewish living. Each section contains a photograph of a fancy table setting appropriate for marking the festivity of Jewish occasions. Even the Yom Kippur table, though lacking food, is beautifully laid out with silver candlesticks. This book was published multiple times and even served as a field guide to Jewish observance for American soldiers fighting in Europe during World War II.

If *The Jewish Home Beautiful* taught Jews how to bring American hostessing into their homes, *The Molly Goldberg Cookbook* brought Judaism into gentile homes. GERTRUDE BERG portrayed the beloved Molly Goldberg character, first on radio and then on television. Building on the popularity of the show, Berg (with Myra Waldo) wrote a Jewish cookbook that would appeal to the public at large. Published by the mainstream Doubleday Press, the book seamlessly weaves together Jewish and American holiday recipes, putting ethnic and national holidays on equal footing. Molly tells her readers, "Purim and Lent [are] close together, and in my neighborhood you'd be surprised how the recipes change from hand to hand and back and forth." Jews not only participate in America, but gentile Americans can also learn from Jews.

ETHNIC AND GOURMET COOKING

Into the 1960s, American Jewish cookbooks that wanted to include international fare chose dishes representative of the diversity of the world's Jewish communities: chunky Hungarian goulash, spicy Yemenite *memulaim*, or the typical Israeli *falafel*. But in the latter part of that decade, virtually all Americans developed an awareness of ethnic cultures and began to

*Many name-brand advertisers published bi-lingual materials promoting their products.
As a Jewish housewife, you can use recipes using Crisco by reading this cookbook
from front to back or back to front. [Peter Schweitzer]*

integrate foods from around the world into their diets. Jewish cooks concerned with kashrut, and working to keep up with culinary trends, encouraged diversification of American Jewish cookbooks. Starting with Bob and Ruth Grossman's series of Chinese, French, and Italian kosher cookbooks, many cookbooks attempted to merge the need of kosher cooks with the flavors and styles of ethnic food. Dishes such as matzoh lo mein highlight the uniqueness of the American Jewish kitchen.

This trend also encouraged the publication of cookbooks that reflect the diversity of the Jewish community in North America. Most American Jewish cookbooks represent the traditions of the Ashkenazi kitchen, but a growing number of Sephardi-oriented volumes, such as Copeland Marks's *Sephardic Cooking*, offer insight into the traditions of American descendants of North African, Arab, and Spanish Jews. In recent years, American Jews have written cookbooks reflecting their families' origins in countries such as Yemen, Italy, and India.

With the blossoming, in the 1970s, of cooking as a leisure activity in the United States, cookbook publication began to thrive, a trend that includes a growing number of Jewish cookbooks. Today's American Jewish cookbooks address all elements of cuisine from a quick Passover matzoh brei to a fancy Thai celebration for twenty. These gourmet collections suggest the degree to which even the most observant of Jews are integrated into the social pastimes of the United States.

Most recently there has been a trend to publish cookbooks that capture the history of Jewish cuisine. One popular volume of this type is *Jewish Cooking in America*, in which Joan Nathan brings together heirloom recipes, anecdotes about Jewish food, and historic photographs—thus highlighting the centrality of food in Jewish American life.

BIBLIOGRAPHY

Agabria, Hani, and Zion Levi. *The Yemenite Cookbook* (1988); Berg, Gertrude, and Myra Waldo. *The Molly Goldberg Jewish Cookbook*. 2d ed. (1955); Congregation Sha'ar Zahav. *Out of Our Kitchen Closets: San Francisco Gay Jewish Cooking* (1987); Congregation Sof Ma'arav. *The When You Live in Hawaii You Get Very Creative During Passover Cookbook* (1989); Gold, Evelyn. *You Made My Day: Four Generations of Kosher Cooking* (1994); Goldberg, Betty S. *Chinese Kosher Cooking. Middle Village* (1989); Grossman, Bob, and Ruth Grossman. *The Chinese-Kosher Cookbook* (1963), and *The Italian-Kosher Cookbook* (1964); Kander, Mrs. Simon. *The Settlement Cook Book* (1934); Kirshenblatt-Gimblett, Barbara. "The Kosher Gourmet in the Nineteenth-Century Kitchen: Three Jewish Cookbooks in Historical Perspective." *Journal of Gastronomy* 2/4 (1986–1987): 51–87, and "Jewish Charity Cookbooks in the United States and Canada: A Bibliography of 201 Recent Publications." In *Jewish Folklore and Ethnology Review* 9, no. 1 (1987): 13–18; Levy, Esther. *Jewish Cookery Book on Principles of Economy Adapted for Jewish Housekeepers with Medicinal Recipes and Other Valuable Information Relative to Housekeeping and Domestic Management* (1971); Lubavitch Women's Organization Junior Division. *The Spice and Spirit of Kosher-Jewish Cooking* (1977); Marks, Copeland. *Sephardic Cooking: 600 Recipes Created in Exotic Sephardic Kitchens from Morocco to India* (1992); Nathan, Joan. *Jewish Cooking in America* (1994); Shosteck, Patti. *A Lexicon of Jewish Cooking: A Collection of Folklore, Foodlore, History, Customs and Recipes* (1981).

RUTH ABUSCH-MAGDER

COPELAND, JO (1900–1982)

Jo Copeland was an innovative fashion designer who was noted for using unusual fabrics in unusual ways.

She was born in New York City on February 29, 1900, the third child of Samuel and Minna Copeland. Her mother, a talented pianist, died giving birth to Jo. Her father, a scholar, art lover, and traveling salesman, soon remarried, and there eventually were nine children in the family.

One of the earliest truly American designers, Jo Copeland rejected the tyranny of Paris to create exquisitely designed and crafted clothing for life in these United States. She is pictured here on the left at the 1967 wedding of her daughter Lois to Robert E. Gould, M.D. Jo Copeland designed the wedding dress. [Lois Gould]

Copeland's artistic temperament was recognized early, on a night of high drama. She was sent to do the dishes. Her stepmother waited for the comforting clatter of a mountain of plates sloshing in soapsuds. Instead, there came a forlorn, nonstop wail of artistic protest. Sam Copeland rushed into the kitchen. Jo was up to her elbows in suds, howling into the steam. He lifted her arms high above the sink and proclaimed, "These hands will never touch dishwater again!" And they never did.

Copeland attended the Art Students League and graduated from the Parsons School of Design. By age twenty, she was working as a designer and helping to put her older brothers through Harvard Law School. She married Edward Regensburg in 1923 (they divorced in 1944), and they had two children: Anthony and Lois (Gould). She married a second time, to Mitchell Benson, in 1953; this marriage also ended in divorce.

In the 1920s, when Copeland began her fifty-year career, there was no such thing as "American fashion." The best dresses made in the United States carried labels with names like "Parisian Modes," and they were copies of the latest Paris styles. Copeland helped lead the fledgling United States fashion industry out of slavery to Paris. She did travel to Paris and throughout Europe, but her creations were all her own, particularly what was called the "two-piece suit," worn without a blouse. Copeland would have quibbled: It wasn't a suit; it was a costume, an ensemble—a dress and jacket so artfully tailored, so subtly supported by fine silk underpinnings, that it did the work of suit, blouse, slip, and bra. A fabulous collar—fur, or lace encrusted with Austrian rhinestones—was actually part of the dress beneath. Unjacketed, a Jo Copeland costume was even more stunning.

Copeland once said that she designed "for the American woman, whoever she is." The woman she had in mind was in fact much like herself. She used her own figure—slim, with a tiny waist and narrow shoulders—as a model. Nor was a Jo Copeland creation cheap. But her customers, especially after the Depression, were starved for glamour, and they found it in Copeland's designs. As she put it, "My consistent approach was to strive for perfection with as little compromise as possible. I wanted to give women clothes that would enhance them, with a certain excitement. My clothes proved to have a long life, more than justifying their original cost."

Jo Copeland was on the faculty of the Fashion Institute of Technology, president of the Manhattan Industrial Home for the Blind, and the advisory board of the Girls' Club of New York. She was the recipient of many awards, including the Neiman-Marcus award for the best designer of the year (1944), a citation from the Philadelphia Museum of Art, and an award from the Federation of Jewish Philanthropies.

Jo Copeland died on March 20, 1982, in New York City.

BIBLIOGRAPHY

Obituary. *NYTimes*, March 21, 1982; *Who's Who in America* (1980–1981).

LOIS GOULD

COPELAND, LILLIAN (1904–1964)

Lillian Copeland was one of the greatest overall woman athletes in the mid-1920s. Born in New York City on November 25, 1904, she was the daughter of Minnie Drasnin, a housewife, from Grodno Poland. She was also raised by her stepfather, Abraham Copeland, the manager of a produce company, after the death of her father. She attended Los Angeles High School.

In 1926, Copeland held National Amateur Athletic Union championships in shot put, discus throw, and javelin throw, as well as world records for the discus and javelin throws. Copeland won every woman's track event that she entered while at the University of Southern California in the late 1920s.

A four-time national champion in the shot put, Lillian Copeland switched to the discus throw (since the shot put was not yet an Olympic event), setting a new world record at the 1928 Olympic trials. At these trials, she also ran the lead-off leg on the United States 400-meter relay team that set a new world record. Copeland went on to become one of the first women to win an Olympic medal (silver), for the discus throw.

Lillian Copeland received a B.A. degree in political science in 1930 and then curtailed her track activities to attend USC Law School. In 1931, she returned to competition and won national championships in both the shot put and the javelin throw. Copeland decided to concentrate on the discus throw for the 1932 Los Angeles Olympics. She placed third in the trials and sixth going into the finals. Nonetheless, a reporter for the *Los Angeles Record* stated, "Confidant, calm and perfectly poised, [she] made a perfect throw." For this effort Copeland won a gold medal and set new Olympic and world's records (133 feet, 1⅛ inches). Ruth Osburn, the teammate whose new discus-throw world record was eclipsed within a half hour by Copeland, graciously said, "She's been a great

The National Track and Field Hall of Fame has recognized the remarkable talents of all-around athlete Lillian Copeland, who won a gold medal in the Olympics in 1932 and boycotted the 1936 games in Berlin. [Amateur Athletic Union Foundation Library]

star for a long time and she deserves to be an Olympic champion."

After attending the University of Southern California Law School through the spring semester of 1934, Copeland traveled to the 1935 World Maccabiah Games in Tel Aviv, where she won the triple championship in the discus throw, javelin throw, and shot put. This was her last public appearance, since Copeland was one of many Olympic athletes who boycotted the 1936 Berlin Olympics.

Lillian Copeland joined the Los Angeles County Sheriff's Department in 1936 and worked there until her retirement in 1960. Her service included sixteen years as a Juvenile Bureau sergeant at the Firestone and Lennox stations. Copeland qualified as an expert marksman in 1938, scoring 274 points out of a possible 300 in a sheriff's department competition. She died in Los Angeles on July 7, 1964, following a long illness.

Lillian Copeland identified herself as a Jewish athlete when she paid her own way to attend the Second Maccabiah Games. And, in turn, Copeland was inducted into both the International Jewish Sports Hall of Fame in Netanya, Israel (1980), and the Southern California Jewish Sports Hall of Fame in Los Angeles (1991).

BIBLIOGRAPHY

Babcock, Muriel. "Lillian Copeland Closes Athletic Career in Glory." *Los Angeles Times*, August 3, 1932: 12; *BEOAJ*; Drasnin, Bob [cousin of Lillian Copeland]. Interview by author, January 1997; Frank, Stanley B. *The Jew in Sports* (1936); Gagnon, Cappy. "1932 Olympic Star Has Star in Her Future." *Newsletter of the Los Angeles County Sheriff's Department* (c. 1985); Hanley, Reid M. *Who's Who in Track and Field* (1973); Hoffman, David [Registrar of the USC Law School]. Interview by author, August 8, 1996; Huston, Ralph. "World's Champion Half-Hour." *Los Angeles Times*, August 3, 1932: 9, 12; Obituary. *NYTimes*, July 8, 1964, 35:1; Postal, Bernard. *Encyclopedia of Jews in Sports* (1955); Siegman, Joseph. *The International Jewish Sports Hall of Fame* (1992); Slater, Robert. *Great Jews in Sports* (1983), and "U.S. Olympic Star Copeland Dies at 60." *Los Angeles Times*, July 8, 1964; *UJE*.

MEL WACKS

CORCOS, LUCILLE (1908–1973)

Lucille Corcos was, for some thirty years, the doyenne of the "modern primitivist" trend on the American art scene. Her paintings, with their composite urban scenes, are often views into various buildings that the observer generally sees only from the outside and in passing; Corcos turns them inside-out before the eye of the viewer. The work is literally "revealing." As such, it is touching, witty, and thoroughly delightful to contemplate. Though Corcos paid little heed to conventions of scale and perspective, her work is far from abstract, and her renderings are painterly and nuanced.

The daughter of Amelia (Abrams) and Moroccan-born Joseph Corcos, the rabbi of Congregation Shearith Israel, New York's Spanish-Portuguese synagogue, Corcos made her earliest forays into the world of the fine arts creating illustrations for certificates celebrating special occasions in the lives of her father's congregants. Trained under Jean Matulka during the heyday of the Art Students League, Corcos began her professional career with a move from Manhattan to Brooklyn Heights, in 1929, where she produced several illustrated children's books, which editorial consensus deemed too sophisticated to publish. Frustrated, Corcos took the illustrations to the offices of *Vanity Fair*, where she received a cover commission on the spot. Her work subsequently became quite popular, and she illustrated a number of books for children as well as for adults. While their parents appreciated Corcos's elegant and charming compositions, children, no doubt, were drawn in by her playful sense of line, and many of her books quickly became classics. One example is the *Illustrated Treasury of Gilbert and Sullivan* (1940), which she conceived, and which rivals Gilbert's own *Bab Ballads* for its charming and sophisticated illustrations.

By the mid-1930s, Corcos was exhibiting widely, participating often in the Whitney Biennial; in the 1940s, her work was exhibited at the Metropolitan Museum of Art, the British Museum, the Art Institute of Chicago, the National Academy of Design, and many other museums. Later in life she exhibited at the Tel Aviv Museum of Art. She traveled extensively throughout Europe and South America and executed a significant public mural, which remains on view, in the Waldorf-Astoria in New York City.

Corcos was widely praised for her lack of self-consciousness and complete freedom of expression, for knowing the ropes of academic illusionism, yet rejecting it in her quest for spontaneity and freedom. Her ability to combine simplicity, intelligence, and creative flair in her work earned her a place with her contemporaries John Kane and Horace Pippin as an exemplar of a buoyant and playful, robust, nativist, unacademic tradition of naive art in America.

BIBLIOGRAPHY

Lucille Corcos, 1908–1973 (1992).

MARC EPSTEIN

COSER, ROSE LAUB (1916–1994)

In a life devoted to studying how social structure affects individuals, sociologist Rose Laub Coser made contributions to medical sociology, refined major concepts of role theory, and analyzed contemporary gender issues in the family and in the occupational world.

She was born in Berlin, Germany, on May 4, 1916. Her mother, Rachel Lea (Lachowsky) Loeb, was born near Kiev in the Ukraine. Her father, Elias Laub, was born in Poland and immigrated before World War I to Germany, where he became a printer and a publisher. Both parents were ardent socialists close to Rosa Luxemburg. They published Luxemburg's writings and named their first-born daughter in honor of her. In 1924, the family moved to Antwerp, Belgium, where Rose received a classical and multilingual education, continued to grow in a socialist environment, worked as a printer, and lost a younger sister to an accidental death. To escape the Nazi threat, the Laubs immigrated in 1939 to New York City, where Elias Laub acquired a print shop and occasionally published Yiddish books.

On August 25, 1942, Rose Laub married Lewis A. Coser, a fellow refugee who shared her commitment to socialism and who later became an eminent sociologist. The couple had two children, Ellen Coser Perrin, a professor of pediatrics at the University of Massachusetts Medical School, and Steven Coser, a computer scientist.

From 1943 to 1945, Coser studied philosophy at the École Libre des Hautes Études, a Parisian institution relocated during the Nazi years to the New School for Social Research in New York City. After serving as a research assistant to psychoanalyst and experimental child psychologist René Spitz and working for David Riesman on his study of political apathy that became *The Lonely Crowd* (1950) and *Faces in the Crowd* (1952), Coser studied at Columbia University with Robert S. Lynd and Robert Merton and completed a Ph.D. in sociology in 1957.

Her career path was not a straight one. She obtained her first full-time academic position at Wellesley College, in Massachusetts, where she remained from 1951 to 1959, advancing from instructor to assistant professor. For the next seven years, she was a research associate in the psychiatry department of the Harvard Medical School, and then became associate professor at Northeastern University. In 1968, both she and her husband obtained professorships in sociology at the State University of New York (SUNY) at Stony Brook. Joint positions for a couple were exceptional at that time, as Coser ironically described in a 1971 article, "On Nepotism and Marginality." In the course of her distinguished career, she worked both with her husband and independently.

Coser was president of the Society for the Study of Social Problems in 1973 and of the Eastern Sociological Society in 1984. She was also vice president of the American Sociological Association in 1985. She was one of the founders of the periodical *Dissent* and sat on the editorial boards of the *International Journal of Marriage and the Family* and *Gender & Society*, as well as on other publications.

Coser began her career with major contributions to medical sociology. In detailed case studies of mental and medical hospitals, she showed the effects of the bureaucratic organization of medical work on patients and staff. For example, where observability was institutionally structured, professional standards were higher. In expanding Merton's role theory, Coser emphasized ambiguity and multiplicity. Her study of the professional training of psychiatric residents demonstrated their ambiguous status as both physicians and students. As for multiplicity, Coser argued that a larger repertoire of roles gives the individual greater agency, better opportunities, and wider connections to the outside world. She staunchly defended the liberating potential of a broad modern public

world, far beyond the family and the narrow local community. She deplored the traditional restrictions placed on women and their confinement to the "greedy institution" of the family, an institution that demanded their total commitment. In her view, the lack of serious child-care policies enforced women's low status in society.

In *Dissent*, Coser expressed her passionate feminism and strongly defended affirmative action and social justice. She also initiated a class-action suit against SUNY at Stony Brook, on behalf of female faculty and staff, to redress wage discrimination.

After retiring as professor emerita from Stony Brook in 1987, Coser and her husband moved to Cambridge, Massachusetts. There, she became an adjunct professor at Boston College as well as distinguished visiting professor and then visiting scholar at the Henry Murray Center of Radcliffe/Harvard. She died on August 21, 1994, at age seventy-eight.

Coser was not religious, but she highly valued her Jewish cultural heritage. Her very first publication was a 1947 review of a book on anti-Semitism, and at the end of her life, she was working on a comparative study of Jewish and Italian women immigrants at the turn of the century. Her personal life was woven into her sociological work. Her quest for social justice, her defense of modernity, and her "sociological imagination" owe much to her identity as a woman and a Jew.

SELECTED WORKS BY ROSE LAUB COSER

Access to Power: Cross-National Studies of Women and Elites, coedited with Cynthia Fuchs Epstein (1981); "Affirmative Action: Letter to a Worried Colleague," *Dissent* 22 (Fall 1975): 207–210; "Alienation and the Social Structure." In *The Hospital in Modern Society*, edited by Eliot Freidson (1963); "The American Family: Changing Patterns of Social Control." In *Social Control: Views from the Social Sciences*, edited by Jack P. Gibbs (1982); "Anti-Semitism Reexamined," *The New Leader* (May 28, 1951): 23; "Authority and Decision-Making in a Hospital: A Comparative Analysis," *American Sociological Review* 23 (February 1958): 56–63; "Cognitive Structure and the Use of Social Space," *Sociological Forum* 1 (Winter 1986): 1–26; "The Complexity of Roles as a Seedbed of Individual Autonomy." In *The Idea of Social Structure: Papers in Honor of Robert K. Merton* (1975); "Evasiveness as a Response to Structural Ambivalence," *Social Science and Medicine* 6 (August 1967): 203–218; *The Family, Its Structure and Its Functions*, edited by Rose Laub Coser (1964; 2d ed., 1974); "The Greedy Nature of Gemeinschaft." In *Conflict and Consensus*, edited by Walter W. Powell and Richard Robbins (1984); "A Home Away from Home," *Social Problems* 4 (July 1956): 3–17; "The Housewife and Her Greedy Family," with Lewis A. Coser. In *Greedy Institutions*, edited by Lewis Coser (1974); *In Defense of Modernity: Complexity of Social Roles and Individual*

Autonomy (1991); "Insulation from Observability and Types of Conformity," *American Sociological Review* 26 (February 1961): 28–39; "Jonestown as Perverse Utopia," with Lewis A. Coser, *Dissent* 26 (1979): 158–263; "Laughter Among Colleagues: A Study of the Social Functions of Humor Among the Staff of a Mental Hospital," *Psychiatry* 23 (February 1960): 81–95; *Life Cycle and Achievement in America*, edited by Rose Laub Coser (1969); *Life in the Ward* (1962); "On Nepotism and Marginality," *American Sociologist* 6 (August 1971): 259–260; "On *The Reproduction of Mothering*: A Methodological Debate," with Judith Lorber, Alice S. Rossi, and Nancy Chodorow, *Signs* 6 (1981): 482–514; "Pockets of 'Poverty' in the Salaries of Academic Women," with Judith M. Tanur, *American Association of University Professors Bulletin* 64, no. 1 (1978): 26–30; "Political Involvement and Interpersonal Relations," *Psychiatry* 14 (May 1951): 213–222; "Portrait of a Bolshevik Feminist," *Dissent* 29 (Spring 1982): 235–239; "The Principle of Patriarchy: The Case of the Magic Flute," *Signs* 4 (Winter 1978): 337–348; "The Principles of Legitimacy and Its Patterned Infringement," with Lewis A. Coser. In *Cross-National Family Research*, edited by Mavin B. Sussman and Betty Cogswell (1972); "Role Distance, Sociological Ambivalence and Transitional Status Systems," *American Journal of Sociology* 72 (September 1966): 173–187; "A Social Disease," *Modern Review* 9 (November 1947): 714–719; "Some Social Functions of Humor," *Human Relations* 12 (May 1959): 171–182; "Stay Home, Little Sheba: On Placement, Displacement and Social Change," *Social Problems* 22 (April 1975): 470–480; "Suicide and the Relational System—A Case Study in a Mental Hospital," *Journal of Health and Social Behavior* 17 (December 1976): 318–327; "Time Perspective and the Social Structure," with Lewis A. Coser. In *Modern Sociology*, edited by Alvin M. Gouldner and Helen P. Gouldner (1963); *Training in Ambiguity: Learning Through Doing in a Mental Hospital* (1979); "Where Have All the Women Gone? Like the Sediment of a Good Wine They Have Sunk to the Bottom," in *Access to Power: Cross-National Studies of Women and Elites*, edited by Cynthia Fuchs Epstein and Rose Laub Coser (1981); "Why Bother: Are Research Issues of Women's Health Worthwhile?" In *Women and Their Health:*

Research Implications for a New Era, edited by Virginia Olesen (1977); "Women in the Occupational World: Social Disruption and Conflict," with Gerald Rokoff, *Social Problems* 18 (1971): 535–554; *Women of Courage* (forthcoming); "Women's Liberation: The Real Issues," *Dissent* 20 (Spring 1973): 224–230.

BIBLIOGRAPHY

Blau, Judith, and Richard Alba. "Empowering Nets of Participation," *Administrative Science Quarterly* 27 (1982): 363–379; Blau, Judith, and Norman Goodman, eds. *Social Roles and Social Institutions: Essays in Honor of Rose Laub Coser* (1991; 2d ed., 1995); Boldt, Edward D. "Structural Tightness, Autonomy, and Observability: An Analysis of Hutterite Conformity and Orderliness," *Canadian Journal of Sociology* 3 (1978): 349–363; Deegan, Mary Jo. *Women in Sociology* (1991); Coser, Lewis. Personal communications (December 23, 1995; February 13, 1996; June 17, 1997); Epstein, Cynthia Fuchs. "Rose Laub Coser 1916–1994." *Dissent* 42 (1995): 107–109, and "Obituary: Rose Laub Coser (1916–1994)," *Footnotes* 22, 8 (November 1994): 14; Hughes, Helen MacGill. *The Status of Women in Sociology, 1968–1972* (1973); LaGory, Mark. "Toward a Sociology of Space: The Constrained Choice Model," *Symbolic Interaction* 5 (1982): 65–78, and "The Organization of Space and the Character of the Urban Experience," *Publius: The Journal of Federalism* 18 (1988): 71–89; Moen, Phyllis, Robin W. Williams, Jr., and Donna Dempster-McCain. "Social Integration and Longevity: An Event History Analysis of Women's Roles and Resilience," *American Sociological Review* 54 (1989): 635–647; Stebbins, Robert A. "A Note on the Concept of Role Distance," *American Journal of Sociology* 73 (1967): 247–250; Warren, Donald I. "Power Visibility, and Conformity in Formal Organizations," *American Sociological Review* 26 (1968): 951–970; Wrong, Dennis. "Remembering Rose," *Dissent* 42 (1995): 109–110.

SUZANNE VROMEN

CROSS, AMANDA
see HEILBRUN, CAROLYN

D

DAILY, RAY KARCHMER (1891–1973)

Ray Karchmer Daily was a leader in Texas in the struggle for equal opportunities for women. She was born in Vilna, Lithuania, on March 16, 1891, to Kalman and Anna (Levison) Karchmer. The youngest of five children (Jack, Alex, Sidney, Nathan, and Ray), she immigrated to the United States with her parents when she was age fourteen. The family settled in Denison, Texas, where her father operated a business. In 1913, she become the first Jewish woman to graduate from a Texas medical school. After much difficulty, she found an internship at Women's Hospital in Philadelphia, the only hospital/medical school with a dormitory for women. Throughout her career she crusaded for adequate housing for female medical students. Her chosen specialty was ophthalmology, but there were no residence positions available in the United States for women. She finished her training in Vienna, Austria.

In 1914, Ray Karchmer returned to Houston to marry Dr. Louis Daily, an ear, nose, and throat specialist, whom she had met in medical school. Louis and Ray Daily were partners personally and professionally until his death in 1952. The couple had one son, Dr. Louis Daily, Jr., who joined his mother's practice after the death of his father.

A leader in the Houston medical community, Daily was the only woman physician among the founders of the Houston Academy of Medicine. She held many positions within the field of medicine, including president of the Houston Memorial Hospital staff.

In 1928, Ray Daily was elected to the Houston school board, the second woman to serve on the board. She served one term as president of the board and as president of the Texas School Board Association. As a member of the Houston school board, she became an advocate for those needing special care or suffering from discrimination in education. Daily promoted classes for those with reading disorders (today known as dyslexia). But it was her support for the federally funded free lunch program for needy children that led to a label of "communist" for Daily. She was denounced by anonymous individuals as a "Russian born Red Jewess" and put under FBI surveillance. The discrimination, born in the 1940s, climaxed in 1952 during the time of Senator Joseph McCarthy and the subsequent "red scare."

Ray Karchmer Daily died on March 7, 1973. She served her profession, her community, and her faith for over forty years in Houston, Texas. She worked for the rights of women and children, for equitable educational opportunities, and for a variety of socially progressive programs.

BIBLIOGRAPHY

Carleton, Don E. *Red Scare! Right-wing Hysteria, Fifties Fanaticism, and Their Legacy in Texas* (1985); McAdams, Ina

May Ogletree. *Texas Women of Distinction: A Biographical History* (1962); Ornish, Natalie. *Pioneer Jewish Texans: Their Impact on Texas and American History for Four Hundred Years, 1590–1990* (1989); Texas Jewish Archives. Barker Texas History Center, University of Texas, Austin, Texas; Winegarten, Ruthe, and Cathy Schechter. *Deep in the Heart: The Lives and Legends of Texas Jews* (1990); *WWIAJ* (1926, 1938).

SUZANNE CAMPBELL

DALSHEIMER, HELEN MILLER (1900–1974)

Helen Miller Dalsheimer was a distinguished leader in the Jewish community, both nationally and in her native Baltimore. She had a distinguished career as a volunteer whose contributions helped bring women, both volunteers and professionals, into positions of leadership previously occupied only by men.

She was born in Baltimore on April 16, 1900, the daughter of Sol and Minnie (Kaufman) Miller. Her father was a dealer in horses and later in the insurance business. She grew up with an older brother, Howard, in Baltimore, where she graduated from the Friends School in 1917, attended Goucher College from 1917 to 1919, and married Hugo Dalsheimer, business executive and philanthropist, in 1921. They had two sons, George and Roger, both of Maryland.

Helen Dalsheimer was deeply involved in the Baltimore Hebrew Congregation, where she was confirmed in 1914. She became president of the sisterhood in 1936, held other posts, and served as the first woman president of a major Jewish Reform congregation from 1956 to 1959. She was the first woman president of a community center, the Baltimore YM-YWHA (1947–1950) and of the World Federation of YMHAs and Community Centers in 1965. In her many lectures to diverse Jewish groups, her subject matter was frequently, "The role of women in . . ." She was the first Jewish woman to become a member of the board of Women's Hospital of Baltimore, where she served in many positions from 1939 to 1958. She was president of the NATIONAL FEDERATION OF TEMPLE SISTERHOODS (now Women of Reform Judaism) from 1953 to 1957. She held many board memberships and, with her husband, was a friend of prominent Jewish leaders. She wrote musicals and parodies for congregational events.

Helen Miller Dalsheimer died on December 25, 1974.

BIBLIOGRAPHY
AJYB 76: 513; Dalsheimer, Helen Miller. Archives. Baltimore Hebrew Congregation, Baltimore, Maryland; *Who's Who of American Women 1958–1959*.

NAOMI GOODMAN

DANCE: ISRAELI FOLK DANCE PIONEERS

An intense desire to share the joy of dance coupled with a strong identification with Israel and their Jewish roots profoundly affected a diverse group of American Jewish women. Each added a dimension to the flourishing of community Israeli dance activities, including regional festivals, workshops, performing groups, and weekly folk dance sessions. All were also involved in enriching Jewish education by developing dance resources or programs in day schools and summer camps.

Since biblical times, the Jewish community has used dance as an integral part of agricultural and religious celebrations and rituals. No matter where the community was dispersed, dance continued to be part of the wedding celebration.

At the turn of the century, the Zionist movement encouraged Jews to return to their homeland, and they brought dances with them. The hora, originally from Romania, perfectly expressed the closeness and equality of kibbutz pioneers as the dancers moved in a closed circle with arms around each other's shoulders. In early endeavors to create new songs and dances to reflect the reviving culture of Israel, pageants recreating nature festivals from biblical times were devised. There were no visual guides to the original dances, so appropriate movement had to be inferred from written descriptions. The various ethnic groups, including Yemenites, Kurds, Moroccans, Druze, and Arabs, also influenced the new dances. Festivals evolved, providing an opportunity to teach dances to others. Dance creators, inspired by celebrations and rituals of Judaism, a variety of movement and rhythmic styles brought from the diaspora, ethnic traditions, and the pulse of modern Israel, built an ever-increasing repertoire of Israeli folk dances.

With the establishment of the State of Israel, the American Jewish community experienced an awakening of pride and interest in new forms of Israeli culture. Today, Israeli folk dance enjoys a wider popularity than ever with programs on every continent for every age group. It appeals to people of all backgrounds, not only because of its energy and

Dvora Lapson was a pioneer in the development of Israeli folk dance. When she began her career in the 1930s, she was the only concert dancer creating movements based on Jewish themes: biblical folklore, Cabalistic mysticism, Hasidic joy, Zionist ideology, and Yemenite culture. [New York Public Library]

FRED BERK AND DVORA LAPSON

Two individuals can be singled out as pioneers in the development of Israeli folk dance: Fred Berk and Dvora Lapson.

In 1951, Fred Berk established the Jewish Dance Division at the 92nd Street Y in New York City and founded the Israeli Folk Dance Institute of the American Zionist Youth Foundation, through which he created the annual Israel Folk Dance Festival. His accomplishments became the model for Jewish dance educators.

Dvora Lapson was born in New York on February 16, 1907, into a family with a strong Jewish identity. Concurrent with her Jewish and secular education, she studied ballet and modern dance. When she began her career on the New York stage in the 1930s, she was the only concert dancer creating movements based on Jewish themes: biblical folklore, Kabbalistic mysticism, Hasidic joy, Zionist ideology, and Yemenite culture. This was truly a breakthrough for Jewish ethnic dance as an accepted art form. In 1934 she choreographed and performed as soloist in the first Hebrew opera, *The Pioneers*. Lapson received wide international acclaim for her work; in a series of prewar recitals in Poland, she was deemed *the* exponent of Jewish dance. Throughout her career, she was dance consultant to many performers and productions, including *Fiddler on the Roof* on Broadway.

As director of the Dance Education Department of the New York City Jewish Education Committee (later Board of Jewish Education), Lapson pioneered the concept of integrating dance into the Jewish school curriculum. This led to the Annual Dance Festival of Jewish Schools, which was held for some thirty years to culminate each year's achievements. As a consultant for the Israel Music Foundation, Folkcraft, and Tikva Records, Lapson further aided the educational process by producing recordings of Israeli folk dance music, supplemented with written dance descriptions, music notation, and the text and translation of the songs.

Another landmark opportunity for Jewish dance came about during the summers of 1951 and 1952, when Lapson was invited to teach at the University of the Pacific in Stockton, California. For the first time, university dance instructors and folk dance leaders from over twenty western and midwestern states were exposed to the dances, culture, and values of the Jewish people. This resulted in the international folk dance curriculum being broadened to include Jewish and Israeli folk dance. She died June 10, 1996.

varied ethnic qualities but also because of the warm, social atmosphere it generates. Beyond its recreational value, the direct emotional bond resulting from participation in this culturally based activity is a powerful tool for instilling long-term commitment to and respect for Judaism and Israel.

JOYCE MOLLOV

Joyce (Dorfman) Mollov, born in Winnipeg, Canada, on April 20, 1925, was influenced by both Lapson and Berk. As a child, she learned from Cantor Benjamin Brownstone to associate a sense of creative freedom with Jewish expression. Her interest in dance brought her to the Winnipeg School of Ballet, where she was later asked to teach and to join the Royal Winnipeg Ballet Company. Wanting to express herself in a Jewish context, she choreographed and directed the annual Young Judaea concerts. When Mollov left for New York, Sara Sommer, one of her dancers, replaced her. Sommer subsequently founded the Chai Folk Ensemble, widely regarded as one of the highest-level performing folk companies.

Mollov went to New York at the invitation of Lapson and the Jewish Education Committee. Through this organization, she taught in Hebrew schools, Yiddish schools, and day camps, and worked in the New York City public schools to stage Hebrew-language assemblies and represent Jews in intercultural events.

She also continued to perform, joining Fred Berk and KATYA DELAKOVA as part of the Hebrew Arts Committee and later in their Jewish Dance Guild. When they appeared at the 1946 HADASSAH convention in Boston's Symphony Hall, David Ben-Gurion was in the front row and later addressed the audience.

Mollov introduced the first dance program integrated into the curriculum of a Hebrew day school, at the Yeshiva of Central Queens in 1952. Students were trained in dance technique, improvisation, and creativity, as well as Jewish, Israeli, and international folk dance, and dance became a prominent element in all school activities: assemblies, graduations, holiday celebrations, park festivals, and parades. Her success resulted in first prize for this school's participation in the 1969 Salute to Israel Parade, an annual New York City event involving seventy-five thousand young marchers. This honor led to her being asked to serve as program coordinator of the parade, a role she used to integrate music, arts, and costume to further the concept of pageantry, which remains a defining feature of the parade to this day.

Mollov was founder and director of the Jewish Dance Ensemble, which originated in 1967 as the Choreographic Workshop in Jewish Dance and flourished for eleven years. The ensemble's pieces, beginning as imaginative movement generated through improvisational exercises, were molded through the collaborative efforts of its members to form visualizations of Jewish themes. The group appeared several times on network television, performed for the first Network Women's Conference in 1973, and from 1972 to 1977 toured a program entitled "Jewish Expression Through Dance" to colleges in the New York area.

Mollov was an adjunct lecturer at Queens College, where she taught a survey course on Jewish dance, from 1980 to 1984 and at Sarah Lawrence College in 1984. Beginning in 1980, she conducted lecture demonstrations on Jewish dance for colleges and adult studies programs. In July of 1986, she organized the Jewish Dance Educators Network as part of CAJE (the Coalition for Alternatives in Jewish Education) and edited their newsletter.

She also expressed her love of Jewish and secular dance through writing. Her articles appeared in *Dance Magazine* (October 1986), *Ballet News* (cover article, August 1984), and *Arabesque*, as well as in Jewish publications. Mollov continued to research and write on dance until her death on September 10, 1989. The Joyce Mollov Memorial Lecture and Performance, endowed by her family, has been held annually at Queens College since 1990 to recognize important dance artists and educators.

SHULAMITE KORNBERG KIVEL

Shulamite Kivel was born Salome Shulamite Diskind in Latvia on February 22, 1927. Her mother was Luba Dzenzelsky. Her father, Leib, was an educator and Hebraist. Shula, as she became known, held to her 1940 resolution, "If I survive, I will dance." She escaped via Belgium and France, running through the countryside. Alone in the fields, she had time to think and to decide what would give meaning to her life, if life ever became normal again. The answer was unconditional—dance.

Shula did survive and came to America, where she felt as if she had stepped out of a nightmare into a magic land where Jews were free. Now came the long struggle of becoming a dancer. She studied ballet with Valentina Belova and the American School of Ballet, and modern dance with the Graham School, José Limón, and the New Dance Group. She performed whenever possible, but there was always something missing. She could not reconcile the unresolved guilt of being a survivor and the dream of a land where all Jews are strong and proud.

Katya Delakova and Fred Berk provided a first step. Kivel worked with them, dancing to beautiful Jewish songs, old and new. They choreographed their feelings about their Jewish past and Jewish visions. It was a total involvement and became a way of life.

The pull to Israel became stronger, and in 1949 Shula made aliyah. This was the beginning of Israel as a state and a time of the ingathering of the exiles.

Shula spoke Hebrew and began to work for the Bureau of Education and Culture as a dance teacher. With a team of dance, music, and Hebrew teachers she went from camp to camp. To integrate emigrant children into a common culture, they worked to create Jewish holiday celebrations of grace and joy. The message was warmly embracing: "This is your dance, this is your song, this is your language." She also worked with the Sabra children in Tel Monda as a rhythmics teacher.

She married American college professor and author Leonard Kornberg in 1951 and returned to live in America, where they had two sons and a daughter. She continued working to integrate dance in educational settings, most often in Jewish schools, camps, and community centers. Creating innovative programs using whatever form of dance suited the situation best, drawing from folk, modern, and interpretive sources, she worked with every age group, from early childhood to college. Her goal was always to use dance to build emotional bridges to the Jewish experience.

As a codirector of the Jewish Dance Division of the 92nd Street Y in New York, Kivel taught classes, directed a teen performing troupe, and was coproducer and choreographer of the annual Hanukkah festival, *A Gift of Light*. She was in charge of dance at Camp Ramah in the Berkshires and Nyack and established the Forest Hills YM-YWHA Israeli dance program, with weekly Israeli folk dance sessions and a performing group. At Queens College, she organized the Hillel performing group. She was also a codirector of the Fred Berk Israeli Dance Workshop at Camp Blue Star in North Carolina. She taught modern dance at the Flushing YMHA, dance in early childhood for the Fieldston School Arts Program, and Israeli dance at the Torah Academy for Girls and the Hebrew Academy of Nassau County.

In her forty-five years of teaching, Shula touched many lives. As one student said: "It does not matter if it is snowing outside; in this room I feel as if there's sand under my feet, the sun is warm and I am free!" Widowed in 1963, Shula married Morton Kivel, a businessman, in 1969. She now resides in Florida, where she finds artistic expression through painting; dancers are her main subject matter.

SHIRLEY WAXMAN

Shirley Waxman was born on April 23, 1933, to Alex and Esther (Buchalter) Silbert. Her first exposure to Israeli folk dance was in 1945 while she was a member of the Hashomer Hatzair, a Zionist youth group, in Toronto. At an *Oneg Shabbat*, she was thrilled to see a new dance from Palestine, *Mayim*. As Waxman describes the experience: "There was such electricity in the air that I knew I had found my place. The warmth and feeling of everyone standing with their hands on each other's shoulders stayed with me permanently." At the age of fourteen she begin teaching Israeli dance at the Hamilton Jewish Community Center in Toronto. However, her desire to care for people led her to a career in nursing, and she was in the first graduating class of the Jewish General Hospital School of Nursing in Montreal.

In 1962, Waxman moved to the Washington, D.C., area. Burned out on nursing, she turned to Israeli folk dance for her second career. The sense of community, of *chevra*, motivated Waxman to devote eighteen years to Israeli folk dance, pioneering activities in the Washington area and inspiring many to become Israeli dance enthusiasts. She began teaching at the Arlington-Fairfax Jewish Congregation and initiated a dance program in northern Virginia Hebrew schools using folk dance as a tool to teach Jewish history. At the Jewish community center in Rockville, Maryland, she was director of the Israeli dance and folklore department for ten years and taught classes for preschoolers through senior citizens as well as for the handicapped. Waxman had a special interest in drawing boys to Israeli folk dance by emphasizing its energetic, athletic style. She founded the Kallil Teen Israeli Folk Dance Performing Troupe, which performed at the Kennedy Center as well as in Hebrew schools and festivals in communities in the Washington area and beyond.

Waxman established Washington's Annual Israeli Folkdance Festival in 1973 and was its director until 1985. The festival grew in scope to include two thousand participants and 350 performers. Underprivileged black preschoolers in Arlington, students at James Madison University, and members of the Mormon church were introduced to Israeli folk dance in her attempt to bridge cultural barriers. Waxman found that "Israeli folk dance is a good way to teach non-Jews something about Judaism. When you show Jewish dance comes from the Bible, it seems to open doors."

As choreography consultant to the folk dance ensemble at James Madison University, Waxman created a *Yemenite Wedding Suite* and *Simchat Torah (Eastern European) Suite*. She also organized and directed an Israeli folk dance performing group in northern Virginia that appeared at numerous community events including the Northern Virginia Folk Festival and the first three annual Washington Israel Folkdance Festivals.

As part of Waxman's work in Israeli folk dance, she designed and constructed authentic costumes.

This led to her third career, as a fiber artist and Jewish ceremonial crafts specialist. Her creations include Jewish ceremonial objects, synagogue art, decorative pieces, wearable art, and ethnic garments.

Waxman has traveled extensively in Israel and the United States to research folklore and to study with well-known choreographers and teachers. She has several publications to her credit, including magazine articles and *Israeli Folkdance for Early Childhood*, published in 1981 as part of a series of monographs and recordings for ethnic education commissioned by James Madison University.

RUTH BROWNS GUNDELFINGER

Ruth Browns Gundelfinger was born on May 13, 1929, in Montreal, Quebec, Canada. Her father, Samuel Browns, came from Vinitza, Russia, in the early 1900s. He had been a scrap-metal peddler and died when Ruth was just one year old. His death left Ruth's mother, Sara (Miller) Browns, destitute and responsible for Ruth and her three siblings, Morris, Issie, and Toby. On her tenth birthday, Ruth was invited to a party being held by the Zionist youth movement, Hashomer Hatzair. Ruth and her friends went and fell in love with the Israeli (at that time, Palestinian) dances and songs. She was too young to join the movement but insisted on attending for the music and dance every Friday and Saturday evening. In Montreal, Ruth finished the ninth grade and then, at age fifteen, began working as a bookkeeper.

At age twenty-one, she spent a year in Israel. Afterward she came to New York City, where she would stay for six years, dancing with Fred Berk and acquiring a basic repertoire of Israeli folk dances. From New York she went to San Francisco, where she began dancing with a group led by Grace West, a Protestant who felt an affinity for Israeli music and dance. West knew Ruth Browns from a Balkan dance group in New York and had been impressed with her teaching and leadership methods. Several months later, when West's schedule limited her ability to continue leading the group, the core members decided to continue on a cooperative basis with Florence Freehof as their leader. They chose the name Rikudom, a contraction of the Hebrew term for folk dance, *rikudei om*.

This unusual group, most of whose members were non-Jewish but had a deep interest in anything connected to Israel, ranged from high school students to grandparents. Each session began with singing Israeli songs. Rikudom was vital and spirited and grew to one hundred weekly participants plus a performing group with a core of twenty members, gaining recog-

nition as an ethnic folk dance group affiliated with the California Folk Dance Federation. In 1958, Ruth Browns was asked to teach at the Rikudom Israeli Folk Dance Group. Soon after, she began teaching at the Hillel Foundation in Berkeley and the Jewish community center in Palo Alto. In 1970, she spent another year in Israel. When she returned to San Francisco in 1971, she resumed teaching. Richard Gundelfinger came to dance with her group, and they married on March 16, 1974. (He died on May 31, 1989.)

Ruth Browns Gundelfinger pioneered several noteworthy projects and contributed greatly to stimulating interest in Israeli folk dance in northern California. In December 1969, she started the Cafe Shalom Israeli Folk Dance Group, a recreational group that began weekly meetings at the Jewish community center in San Francisco. She was the first person on the West Coast to initiate a Weekend Folk Dance Camp, bringing folk dance teachers from Israel to teach their own dances or dances of other choreographers. The camp, held in San Luis Obispo, has continued annually since 1972.

MOLLY SHAFER RUTZEN

Molly Abramow, the oldest of three children, was born on March 23, 1927, in Rochester, New York, to Sarah (Tepperman) and Nathan Abramow. Her education was well rounded. In addition to her study of tap, jazz, and modern dance, she holds a B.A. in Romance languages, an M.A. in education, and permanent New York State certification as a teacher of French and Spanish. In 1948 she wed Earl Shafer, a CPA. They had two sons and a daughter.

Raised with a strong sense of her Jewishness, Molly Shafer had first been exposed to Israeli folk dance as a child through the Zionist youth movement, Young Judaea. She was an enthusiastic participant in the week-long Fred Berk Israeli Dance Workshop held annually at Blue Star Camp in North Carolina from 1972 to 1992.

Shafer's initial theatrical experiences involved choreographing, writing, and directing musicals for Hadassah, the Cornell Study Club, and other organizations. In 1969, while working as a French and Spanish tutor and substitute teacher in the Brighton schools, she was hired to implement an Israeli dance program at Temple Beth El. "Since dance and music were a joy to me, when the opportunity arose, my hours at Beth El were increased and I dropped the language teaching." Within three years, she had initiated four extracurricular dance groups, for different ages, and two choruses. On a rotating basis, she also taught Israeli dance and music to all the classes in the school. Later, a class was added in which she taught talented high school students to teach, notate, and choreograph Israeli folk dance.

Encouraged by Berk, Shafer established and directed the first Rochester Israel Folk Dance Festival sponsored by Temple Beth El. The festival attracted high school and college groups from Syracuse, Ithaca, Elmira, Buffalo, and Albany to participate with the local groups. In response to Berk's emphasis on quality control, she visited all groups participating in the festival and supervised their choreography, costumes, and music. The festival continued annually under her direction for nineteen years. Several of Shafer's former students, including Barry Tempkin and Danny Gwirtzman, have gone on to careers in dance.

In addition to periodic teaching at Temple Sinai High School and Congregation B'rith Kodesh, Shafer taught Israeli dance and song for fifteen years at the Hillel School, the Hebrew Day School in Rochester. All of these teaching experiences included work with performing groups that participated in the festival.

Widowed in 1985, she retired in 1994 and in 1996 married Dr. Robert Rutzen.

GALE JACOBSOHN

Gale Jacobsohn was born in Cleveland, Ohio, to Isaac and Jeanne (Shedroff) Goldweber on September 18, 1933. She discovered folk dancing only as an adult. When her children were old enough, she signed up for a beginning folk dance class offered at the local Jewish community center. She quickly became addicted to folk dance—to the music and to learning about the cultures of many peoples of the world. Her labor Zionist background led her to believe that dancing other people's dances helped form a bond among peoples. She felt that Israeli folk dance had pulled her closer to her own Jewish Zionist roots.

Working mainly through the Hillel of Case Western Reserve University in Cleveland, she successfully developed an Israeli dance program, which attracted both Jewish students and young working adults who often had no other contact with Judaism or Zionism. Once the Hillel program was established, she formed the Hillel Israeli Dancers of Cleveland. The group, which performed in the Cleveland area and participated in festivals in other parts of the country from 1979 until 1989, reflected Jacobsohn's belief that dynamic Israeli dance presents a positive picture of modern Israel to the world at large. Through the Coalition for Alternatives in Jewish Education and the local mini-CAJE program, she has taught Israeli dance to teachers in the Cleveland area, thus enriching the local Jewish educational programs. From 1982 to 1984, as an artist-in-residence in the Cleveland area, she taught an appreciation of many cultures through international folk dance.

INBAL DANCERS IN AMERICA

Two Yemenite-Israeli women, both former principal dancers and soloists with the Inbal Dance Theatre of Israel, came to reside in the United States, where they have made significant professional contributions.

Hadasah Badoch Kruger had two world tours with Inbal, studied choreography with Louis Horst at the Martha Graham School, and had principal roles with the Batsheva Dance Company under Graham's direction. Since 1966, she has performed throughout the United States both as soloist and with her own company. She has been adjunct assistant professor of dance at the College of Staten Island in New York and was on the faculty of the Hebrew Arts School. Her teaching includes workshops and master classes in modern and Yemenite-Israeli dance as well as yoga. Additional credits include network television specials and Lincoln Center and City Center productions of *The King and I.* Her work incorporates authentic Yemenite movement, Israeli-Arabic motifs, and biblical themes.

MARGALIT OVED was a principal dancer with Inbal for fifteen years. Under Sol Hurok's management, she toured with Inbal for nine months, including performances in New York, Paris, and Australia. She came to reside in Los Angeles, where she taught dance at UCLA and created the Margalit Dance Company. She conducted master classes, workshops, and lecture demonstrations and toured as soloist and with her company throughout the United States and Israel. She recently returned to Israel to serve as director of Inbal.

DANCERS AS AUTHORS

CORINNE CHOCHEM immigrated to the United States as a child from Russia. She felt that dance was an important educational tool and was one of the first to concentrate on Israeli (then Palestinian) dance, leading a group from 1936 to 1945. Her dance training was with Martha Graham, Louis Horst, HELEN TAMIRIS, Mary Wigman, and Pauline Koner. She wrote two books on folk dance: *Palestine Dances!*, with Muriel Roth (1941), and *Jewish Holiday Dances*, set to poems by Alfred Hayes (1948). She also supervised several recordings of dance music.

Florence Freehof, based in San Francisco, conducted training classes for folk dance teachers and was

In addition to her performance career, CORINNE CHOCHEM *wrote two books on folk dance, one of which,* Jewish Holiday Dances, *was set to poems by Alfred Hayes. [New York Public Library]*

the first leader of the Rikudom group. Her books have provided valuable guidance and a source of material for Israeli dance teachers and enthusiasts. *Jews Are a Dancing People* (1954) gives the form, steps, and rhythmic description of many Jewish folk dances as well as their background. *Tips on Teaching Folk Dancing* appeared in 1958. *A Guide for Israeli-Jewish Folk Dancers* (1963) provides a complete bibliography of all printed works in the United States and Israel on this subject. She is also the author of *New Dances from Israel*, with translations and notation methods, and *Rhythm Games and Dances for Jewish Juniors*, which includes music and choreography based on Hebrew folk songs. Two articles by Florence Freehof appeared in the magazine *Let's Dance:* "The Dancing People of Israel" (July 1956) and "Customs and Costumes of the Jewish People" (August–September 1963).

BIBLIOGRAPHY

Most information was gathered from personal telephone interviews with and written personal histories written by Ruth Browns Gundelfinger, Gale Jacobsohn, Shulamite Kivel, Molly Shafer, and Shirley Waxman during the summer and fall of 1995. I have also drawn from my resources and personal knowledge as director of the Israeli Dance Institute and of the Jewish Dance Division of the 92nd Street Y. Additional references include:

Berk, Fred. "Workshop in San Francisco August 11–12, 1962." *Hora Magazine* 1, no. 1 (October 1962); Berk, Fred, ed. "Dvora Lapson—Pioneer of Jewish Dance in America." *Hora Magazine* 3, no. 2 (Winter 1971), and "Margalit Oved." *Hora Magazine* 4, no. 3 (Spring 1972); Fenster, Saul. "A History of the Rikudom Israeli Folk Dancers of San Francisco." *Hora Magazine* 40 (Summer 1984); Koner, Pauline. Corinne Chochem Kovarska obituary. *Dance Magazine* (January 1991); Mollov, Joyce. "For Those Who Wish to Pursue Their Ideals." *Hora Magazine* 41 (Winter 1984), and tape-recorded interview with Ruth Goodman, New York (August 3, 1989); Shafer, Molly. "Diary of a Dance Festival." *Hora Magazine* 30 (Spring 1978); Waxman, Shirley. "The Washington Israeli Folk Dance Festival." *Hora Magazine* 30 (Spring 1978); *Who's Who in World Jewry* (1965).

RUTH R. GOODMAN with
RUTH P. SCHOENBERG

DANCE, PERFORMANCE

Dance has always had a special place in the Jewish community because of its capacity to heighten communal and individual joy at weddings as prescribed in the Talmud, at bar and bat mitzvahs, and at other happy occasions. The Bible contains many mentions of dance in celebration of important holidays and Israelite victories. Jews have always danced with the Torah scrolls in processionals at the holiday of Simchat Torah, and there are movement processionals on other holidays as well as during the weekly Sabbath services. A very simple form of dance is even part of Jewish prayer, as the rhythmic rocking movement of *davening* literally embodies the notion of total devotion to God.

Jewish immigrants to the New World brought with them their ritual and celebratory dances. In both Ashkenazic and the minority Sephardic communities, as families began to assimilate, the traditional forms of Jewish dance, as well as its central role in communal life, became harder to maintain. Nonetheless, the bond between dance and Judaism remained strong, particularly as young women began to find their self-expression in the art of dance. Jewish American women have participated in all aspects of dance as performers, teachers, choreographers, company directors, producers, writers, researchers, dance critics, dance therapists, costumers, and lighting designers.

MODERN DANCE

American revolutionary individualism affected not only politics but also the art of dance, through the modern dance movement, which was created in the main by gentile dancers. Isadora Duncan was the first to break with the classical ballet world in the early 1900s. She was followed by Ruth St. Denis and Ted Shawn's Denishawn troupe, which nurtured Martha Graham, Doris Humphrey, and Charles Weidman, who in turn left to form companies in New York in the 1920s and 1930s.

The development of the American modern dance movement from the 1920s through the 1950s centered in New York City, which was also the site of America's largest Jewish community. Working-class and poor Jewish immigrant parents on the Lower East Side sought out culture and education in the arts for their children, often as a vehicle for assimilation. Ironically, many of these same parents disapproved when dance became their children's chosen profession.

Julia Levien was born in New York City in 1911 to Rashel Wetrinsky, a Yiddish poet, and Benjamin Levien, both from Russia. She is considered one of the premier teachers of the Isadora Duncan dance style and was one of the four core performers in the company of one of Duncan's adopted daughters, Irma Duncan. (The others, also Jewish, were Mignon Garlin, Ruth Fletcher, and Hortense Kooluris.) Levien found in Yiddish dance a style suited to express her own ideas. From 1945 to 1948, in New York, she choreographed for the Yiddish Folksbiene, part of the Workmen's Circle Theater Project. Through the Workmen's Circle connection, she toured throughout the United States with her solo dance shows. In the late 1940s, she partnered Benjamin Zemach, choreographer of Jewish dance programs. She also taught at Camp Boiberik and at the Sholom Aleichem House of Cooperative Living in New York City.

Another dancer in the Duncan style was ANNABELLE GAMSON, born Annabelle Gold in New York City, August 6, 1928. She began with Julia Levien and went on to perform on Broadway in Jerome Robbins's *On the Town* and in *Finian's Rainbow*. She also performed occasionally with ANNA SOKOLOW's concert group and American Ballet Theatre, but is best known as an interpreter of Duncan's dances, which she reconstructed and took on extensive tours.

Although Ruth St. Denis and Ted Shawn apparently discriminated against Jews and their important Denishawn company and schools had a quota system limiting Jewish students, Klarna Pinska succeeded in becoming one of St. Denis's protégés. Pinska was raised in a Jewish family in Winnipeg and saw Ruth St. Denis there on a vaudeville theater tour, then moved to California and worked as St. Denis's personal maid in exchange for classes. Eventually she taught at the Denishawn schools in Los Angeles and New York but performed only rarely, most notably in the 1930 Lewisohn Stadium concert presentation of St. Denis's *A Buddhist Festival*. In 1976, Pinska restaged Denishawn works for the Joyce Trisler Dance Company in New York.

Martha Graham, Ted Shawn's protégé, did not share his anti-Semitism. Graham left Denishawn with the German-American Louis Horst and started choreographing group works in 1926. In them she included Jewish dancers. From her early group would emerge Jewish choreographers including SOPHIE MASLOW, Anna Sokolow, and Lillian Shapero. PEARL LANG, from a later Graham Company period, also became a noted choreographer using Jewish themes. Other Jewish Graham dancers included Frieda Flier, Isabel Fisher, Miriam Cole, MARJORIE (Mazia) GUTHRIE, Nelle Fisher, Gertrude Shurr (who was Graham's assistant and went on to teach at the High School of Performing Arts in New York), Nina Fonaroff (who was Louis Horst's assistant and then went on to England), Elizabeth Halpern, Lilly Mehlman, Marie Marchowsky (who joined the New Dance Group), Lili Mann, Linda Margolies Hodes (who would bring Graham's work to Israel as part of the Batsheva Dance Company), Thelma Babitz, Sydney Brenner, Mattie Haim, Pauline Nelson (who went on to dance with HELEN TAMIRIS), Florence Schneider, Ruth White, Frima Nadler, Mary Radin, and Lillian Ray (also known as Rae Moses).

Another Denishawn dancer to start her own company was Doris Humphrey; she was also more open to Jewish dancers. Her troupe included Beatrice Seckler, Eva Desca, Eve Gentry (who helped to develop the Pilates exercise system), Saida Gerrard, Marion Scott, and Eleanor Schiel.

The Henry Street Settlement House, on New York's Lower East Side, offered many programs to help Americanize the immigrants, including dance classes. Although Alice (c. 1883–1972) and IRENE LEWISOHN (1892–1944) had professional training in dance and drama, their Orthodox Jewish father dissuaded them from stage careers. He did, however, allow them to work at the Henry Street Settlement, as he considered it a philanthropic endeavor. For twenty years, they produced pageants and festival celebrations, intended to give young participants pride in their ethnic backgrounds, as well as fully professional theater and dance offerings. In 1914, they built a 325-seat theater, in a separate building, which became known as the Neighborhood Playhouse. Blanche Talmud (b. c. 1900), who is pictured in the famous 1951 book *Twenty-five Years of American Dance*, was one of the important Jewish dance teachers at the Playhouse from the early 1920s into the 1940s. She was also a concert dancer, performing in Adolf Bolm's Ballet Intime performances in 1917, in a number of Alice Lewisohn's productions, including the 1926 dance piece *Burmese Pwe*, and in Humphrey-Weidman productions in 1931. Talmud's studies included Dalcroze eurhythmics in New York and Paris. Among the many talented Jewish women with admirable careers who began dancing at the Playhouse in Talmud's classes were Anna Sokolow, Sophie Maslow, Helen Tamiris, Edith Segal, and Lillian Shapero.

Anna Sokolow grew up on the Lower East Side, in the heart of the Jewish ghetto. Her personal experiences with poverty affected her ideas of social justice, later reflected in her choreography and politics. Sokolow joined Graham's company in 1930 and stayed until 1939, and during this period she began to perform her own work as well. She also collaborated with the New Dance League; Jewish dancers with this group included Sophie Maslow and Lily Mehlman. In the 1940s, Sokolow began to explore her Jewish heritage, creating *Kaddish* (1945), *The Dybbuk* (1951), *Rooms* (1955), and her elegy to the Holocaust, *Dreams* (1961). She also created a Purim pageant (1952) and an Israel Bonds program (October 1953) in Madison Square Garden.

In 1953, Jerome Robbins invited Sokolow to go to Israel to coach the gifted Yemenite Jewish dancers of the new Inbal Dance Company in modern and ballet technique and theater skills. She spent several years helping to mold Inbal into an internationally famous professional dance troupe. One of Inbal's lead dancers, MARGALIT OVED, left in 1965 and in 1967 began to teach at UCLA; she also directed her own company from 1971 to 1993 and was the subject of the Allegra Fuller Snyder film *Gestures of Sands*. She returned to Israel to direct Inbal from 1994 to 1996.

While in Israel, Sokolow also choreographed for a small repertory company called Bamat Machol and established her own company, the Lyric Theater (1963–1964). Ze'eva Cohen danced with Lyric and then returned to New York with Sokolow to become a featured performer in Sokolow's New York company, making her own mark first as a solo performer in the 1970s, and then with her own company, Ze'eva Cohen and Dancers. She has also choreographed for companies including the Boston Ballet, the Batsheva Dance Company of Israel, the Alvin Ailey Repertory Dance Company, Munich's Tanz Projekt, Pennsylvania Dance Theatre, and the Chicago Repertory Dance Ensemble. She founded the dance program at Princeton University, where she is professor of dance and continues as its dance coordinator.

Another of Blanche Talmud's dance students was Edith Segal (b. c. 1910). For twelve years she acted and danced at the Neighborhood Playhouse; afterward, she earned a scholarship with the ballet dancer Michael Mordkin, then began her own work—even though her immigrant mother disparagingly called her a *bummarke* [bum] for working in dance professionally. As early as 1930, her pageant *The Belt Goes Red* at Madison Square Garden celebrated the Soviet Union, which she would visit the next year; the theme was taken from the assembly line and alienated labor. William Kolodney of the 92nd Street Y was among the managers who refused to book her because of her far-left politics. (On the other hand, Kolodney, who chose all the performing groups presented at the Y for almost fifty years and was the director of its education department, welcomed many other Jewish dancers as teachers, students, and performers and made the 92nd Street Y one of the most important modern dance venues in the city.)

Segal often used Yiddish songs or Jewish music to accompany her dances. *A Jewish Family Portrait*, set to a *nigun* [wordless melody] and depicting an Ashkenazic family coming alive from a picture frame, is witty and poignant in its simplicity. She used Jewish themes, she said, because there was a lot of discussion about anti-Semitism; she wanted working people to see her dances and to help preserve Yiddish culture. Segal made her living teaching dance in Yiddish secular schools, occasionally performing, and teaching every summer from the 1930s to the 1970s at Camp Kinderland.

During the Depression, many dancers who allied themselves with the working class began to choreograph using themes about class struggle and issues of survival. Leftist and communist cooperative groups developed a genre of dance known as agitprop. The leftist Jewish dance critic Edna Ocko was allied with many of these Jewish dancers and championed their art and their causes, despite the generally critical attitude toward them. Many of the Jewish dancers who studied and performed with the important gentile modern dancers preferred to make political statements of their own in dance. For example, Graham company dancers Anna Sokolow, Lily Mehlman, and Sophie Maslow joined the Workers Dance League, and in 1934 they produced a concert of their own solo works.

Modern dance pioneer Hanya Holm, who had come to New York from the German expressionist dance company of Mary Wigman, had several Jewish students, including Nadia Chilkovsky and Miriam Blecher, who were also on the 1934 program. They had been at a rally of the unemployed when a young organizer was slain by the New Jersey police; this inspired them to launch a working-class organization for dance, the New Dance Group. Its slogan was "Dance is a weapon in the class struggle." Chilkovsky told reporters that they believed capitalism was tottering and that they were helping to overthrow it with dance.

By the mid-1930s, Jewish dancers created dances with humanistic concerns against war, fascism, censorship, and in sympathy for Spain as the rest of Europe edged toward war. Jewish dancers from Europe who managed to escape the Nazis in the 1940s included KATYA DELAKOVA, Claudia Vall, Pola Nirenska, and Trudy Goth. Their dance style and experiences were so different that more notice was given to American-raised Jewish dancers such as Sophie Maslow, Pauline Koner, and Helen Tamiris.

Sophie Maslow, like Sokolow, Segal, and Koner, started dancing at the Neighborhood Playhouse in Blanche Talmud's children's classes. Maslow remembers dancing as a child in Irene Lewisohn's orchestral production *Israel*, which gave her her first glimpse of the dancer Martha Graham. Maslow studied with Graham at the Playhouse and graduated from the three-year course of study there, which was compara-

ble to a conservatory-college arts program. Jean Rosenthal (b. 1912) was a fellow dance student in the program; she became an important lighting designer for dance and on Broadway. Miriam Blecher was also in the course. Like Anna Sokolow, Maslow went from the Neighborhood Playhouse to the Graham company. She danced there for eleven years; during that time, she also began choreographing her own works. She taught the Graham technique for the New Dance Group and from her students there, including Jewish dancers Muriel Mannings and Billie Kirpich, formed her first company. Maslow also used Anneliese Widman and Rena Gluck (who moved to Israel, danced with the Batsheva Company, and now directs the dance program of the Rubin Academy). Programs and choreography by Maslow were seen at, among others, the New Dance Group, the 92nd Street Y, and Madison Square Garden celebrations for the Jewish community.

Pauline Koner, born June 26, 1912, in New York City, started at the Neighborhood Playhouse, although she came to prefer studying with ballet master Mikhail Fokine and others, including Michio Ito. Her Jewish background includes memories of dancing with her grandfather on Simchat Torah on the Lower East Side with the observant men parading, holding flags, and dancing with the Torah scrolls. By the time she was fourteen years old she was teaching dance at the Workmen's Circle camp in the summers; although her parents considered themselves Jewish intellectuals, they still spoke Yiddish and were part of Yiddish New York culture.

Koner saw herself as a loner and did not join in the left-wing groups or dance companies of her time. Instead she created solo concerts and had success touring. Thematically she occasionally drew on Jewish ideas: *Voice in the Wilderness* takes its text from Isaiah. Koner's friend and fellow Jewish dancer CORINNE CHOCHEM went to Palestine and influenced Koner to travel there from 1932 to 1933; she also danced in Egypt and traveled to the Soviet Union in 1936. In 1945 Koner performed at the 92nd Street Y and met dancer Doris Humphrey, who had just begun directing the Y's dance education department in addition to continuing with her own company. In this period, Koner began to dance with Humphrey and with Humphrey's protégé José Limón; she was a soloist with the Limón company from 1946 to 1960. In 1964, Koner received the *Dance Magazine* Award and a Fulbright to teach in Japan. In 1979, she went back to Israel and staged *Cantigas* for the Batsheva Company. In 1985, she was awarded an honorary doctorate of fine arts from the University of Rhode Island. She has published two books, one on modern technique and the other an autobiography. She is the widow of the symphony conductor Fritz Mahler, whom she married on May 23, 1939.

Helen Tamiris, born in 1902, began her dance studies at the Neighborhood Playhouse around 1918. She later studied ballet at the Metropolitan Opera and with Mikhail Fokine, then joined the Metropolitan Opera ballet chorus. Her concert dance career began in 1927 and quickly established her as one of the premier contemporary choreographers. In 1930 she succeeded in organizing a repertory company with the choreographers Graham, Humphrey, and Weidman, with Louis Horst as musical director, in response to the high cost of self-producing concerts and continued for two seasons. Then she began the Tamiris Group and school. She rarely used Jewish themes in her work, but her dances reflected a commitment to social justice and responsibility learned growing up in a poor Jewish family. She was one of the first white choreographers to depict aspects of black life, as in her early works *Negro Spirituals* and *How Long Brethren?* In the summer of 1995, these two pieces were restaged and set audiences cheering at the American Dance Festival. In addition, Tamiris was posthumously given the Scripps Award, with the money going toward scholarships in her memory at the festival's important dance school.

During the Depression, when the federal government began to support the arts, Tamiris was instrumental in making dance a part of the Federal Theater Project (FTP). In 1935, as chairperson for the Dance Association, she convinced Hallie Flanagan, director of the FTP, to create an individual Federal Dance Project. Many of Tamiris's WPA dancers were Jewish, including Paula Bass, Pauline Bubrick (Tish), Florence Cheasnov, Mura Dehn, Fanya Geltman, Klarna Pinska, Selma Rubin, and Sue Ramos. In 1941 Corinne Chochem, her sister Fanya, and Sue Ramos performed with Daniel Nagrin, Tamiris's dance partner and husband.

Felicia Sorel (1904–1972) also worked in the WPA; Sorel was trained by Mikhail Fokine and danced at Radio City Music Hall. She became involved in, and eventually director of, the WPA Music Project's Opera Division. After the war she created theater works, including a television production of *The Dybbuk* for CBS in 1949.

Lillian Shapero was born on January 17, 1908, in New York City, into the observant Hasidic family of Jennie and Morris Shapero and was raised by her grandparents after her mother died. She always joined her grandfather in his little synagogue, where he encouraged her to participate in the songs and dance. After studying at the Neighborhood Playhouse and with Bird Larson and Michio Ito, she became a member of the first Martha Graham company in 1929, remaining until 1935. She danced the solo role in Graham's *Primitive Mysteries*. In 1933, she made a name for herself choreographing for Maurice Schwartz's Yiddish Art Theater production *Yoshe Kalb*; their association would continue with, among others, *The Wise Men of Chelm*, *The Water Carrier*, *The Three Gifts*, and *The Dybbuk*.

In addition to Jewish themes, Shapero used political themes in her dances. Her group dance *Dance for Spain—No Pasaran* was seen in the 1930s. She toured widely and performed in Paris, London, and Moscow, where she was the guest of the Soviet Theater Festival in 1937. The two types of dances she favored thematically were recognized in an October 18, 1943, review in the *New York World-Telegram* as "revolutionary dances on American themes and dances based on Jewish folklore." The concert being reviewed included *Dances of the Oppressed* and *Anti-War Dance*.

In 1952, her works were seen at Carnegie Hall, and the *Dance Observer* noted in its August–September issue that the music to her dances was composed by Maurice Rauch, conductor of the Jewish Peoples Philharmonic Chorus. He was also Shapero's husband. The reviewer commented that the performance was thrilling and that Shapero showed a great talent for group choreography and interesting contrapuntal themes that made the scenes lively and exciting theater. In the 1960s, Shapero, by now considered an authority on Jewish dance, traveled to Cleveland to stage a Jewish Community Center production of *The Dybbuk*. Shapero died on April 19, 1988.

Another favorite Jewish dancer who began in the Graham company was Pearl Lang, though later than Shapero, Maslow, and Sokolow. Born in Chicago in 1922, Lang grew up in a socialist home rich in Jewish culture; she was educated in the Workmen's Circle Yiddish schools. Lang's mother introduced her to dance when she was eight, and she had her first exposure to the Graham dance technique as a teenager. She received a scholarship to the Graham school in New York and joined the company in 1941. She remained for fourteen years, during which time, because of her charisma and technical prowess, she created leading roles in Graham masterpieces.

In 1952, she was selected by the Juilliard School to create her first group work, *Song of Deborah*. Since then she has choreographed over fifty works, often on Jewish themes, for her own company and has also been its leading dancer. Her company has appeared

HADASSAH (SPIRA EPSTEIN) *had an indelible influence on dance in America. Originally from Jerusalem, she came to the United States in 1924, at the age of fifteen. Her dance* Shuvi Nafshi *[Return, oh my soul] was described by Walter Terry in the* New York Herald Tribune *as "a dance of Biblical power in its projection of ecstatic reverence for the divine." [New York Public Library]*

throughout the United States and also in Italy, Holland, Denmark, Israel, and Canada. She has also choreographed for the Boston Ballet, the Netherlands National Ballet, and the Batsheva Dance Company (in 1982). Lang programs a Jewish work on every dance concert she creates. Twice she has received a Guggenheim Fellowship; in 1992 she won the National Foundation for Jewish Culture's Jewish Cultural Achievement Award, and in 1995 she received an honorary doctorate of fine arts from Juilliard.

An exotic presence in New York was a Jewish dancer from Jerusalem, HADASSAH (SPIRA EPSTEIN) (1909–1992). She came to New York in 1938 and made her professional debut in 1945. She studied with Jack Cole, La Meri, Nala Najan, and others from India and the Far East. Her own programs in Israeli, Javanese, Indian, and Balinese dance styles were seen through the mid-1970s. Her best-known work, *Shuvi Nafshi* [Return oh my soul], based on Psalm 116 to a liturgical hymn sung by Cantor Leibele Waldman, premiered at the 92nd Street Y on February 12, 1947. Other dances with Jewish themes included *Israeli Suite, The Cantor, The Wanderer,* and *Water.* Hadassah was also a beloved teacher, known for her warmth; she taught at and headed the ethnic dance department of the New Dance Group for many years.

Dancers who came from Europe brought with them both modern dance training and Jewish dance experience. Truda Kaschmann, who had worked with the German expressionist choreographer Mary Wigman, settled in Connecticut, where she taught Alwin Nikotais. In 1939, Katya Delakova (1915–1991) fled the Nazis and came to New York from her native Vienna, where she had worked with Jewish dancer Gertrud Kraus. In 1941 she was reunited with another Kraus performer, Fred Berk, whom she married. Together they formed the Delakova-Berk duo, which toured university campuses, Jewish Community

Centers, and other venues along the East Coast. They established the Jewish Dance Guild and the Jewish Dance Repertory Group and taught and also appeared at the Jewish Theological Seminary, the 92nd Street Y, and other Jewish venues from 1941 to the 1950. They performed in the displaced persons camps in Europe in 1948 and in Israel in 1949. After she and Berk divorced, she married Moshe Budmor, with whom she developed collaborative movement and music workshops and taught internationally and in the United States.

Claudia Vall, born in August 1910 in Zagreb, also studied and danced with Kraus in Vienna, and at Hellerau with Dalcroze as well. Vall came to the United States in 1940 and first partnered Fred Berk, then settled in Los Angeles, where she continued her professional studies with Michel Panaieff, taught children dance, and choreographed for KTLA-TV.

Pola Nirenska, born in Warsaw in 1911, studied in the Wigman schools in Berlin and Dresden, joined Wigman's dance group for a 1932–1933 tour to the United States, worked with Rosalia Chladek in Vienna, and received first prize for choreography and second prize for performance in the 1934 International Dance Competition in Vienna. After she was dismissed from the Wigman company because she was Jewish, she performed in Vienna and Switzerland and then fled to Britain, arriving in the United States in 1949. She worked with Humphrey and Weidman until she settled in Washington, D.C., where she performed, taught, and choreographed, influencing Liz Lerman and others. She died in Maryland, July 25, 1992.

Judith Berg Fibich was born in Lodz, Poland, in 1912. Although trained in the most modern expressionist style with Mary Wigman in Germany, she preferred to develop Hasidic-influenced works. She was active in the Jewish Art Theater in Warsaw and choreographed for Ida Kaminska and others. Most highly regarded is her choreography for the 1937 film version of *The Dybbuk*, created in Warsaw and recently restored at Brandeis University's National Center for Jewish Film. After the Nazi invasion of Poland, she escaped to Soviet Russia with her husband, Felix Fibich; in 1950, they immigrated to the United States, giving joint recitals in Carnegie Hall and the Brooklyn Academy of Music, and touring to Canada, Israel, and South America. Judith Fibich staged a Yiddish revival of *Rebecca, the Rabbi's Daughter* at Town Hall in New York City in November 1979. She died in New York on August 19, 1992.

An American-born dancer who became an expert in Jewish dance was Dvora Lapson, born in New York City in 1907. Though she began her dance studies with Fokine, by the late 1920s she had become enthralled with Jewish dance. Lapson became the premier exponent of Jewish dance for Jewish educators through her work with the Jewish Education Committee in New York. Among her projects was advising choreographer Jerome Robbins on Jewish dance for *Fiddler on the Roof* on Broadway. She also wrote about Jewish dance and was the primary author of the definitive article in the *Encyclopedia Judaica*, published in Israel.

Joyce Mollov was one of Lapson's dancers who worked with her at the Jewish Education Committee. Mollov also performed with the Delakova-Berk company. She received a master's degree in dance education from Columbia University, was an adjunct lecturer at Queens College, directed the Jewish Dance Ensemble from 1967 to 1978, and coordinated the Jewish Dance Network for the Congress on Alternatives in Jewish Education. Since 1990, a yearly program on Jewish dance has been held in her memory at Queens College.

After World War II, with the establishment of the State of Israel, Jewish dance became synonymous with Israeli folk dance. Naima Prevots (b. 1935), who grew up in a strongly Zionist and bilingual Hebrew-English home, studied at the Neighborhood Playhouse with Natanya Neuman and at the New Dance Group, and performed with Delakova and Berk; eventually she became a dance author and a dance educator as director of the dance program at American University. Prevots remembers the particular fervor of Jewish dance activities, especially Israeli folk dance performances, that accompanied the establishment of Israel. Like many of her contemporaries, she was a dance specialist in Jewish camps teaching Israeli folk dance, was a member of Hechalutz Hatzair, and made speeches and danced in the subway for the Jewish National Fund while she held the signature little blue-and-white can to collect pennies and nickels. She also recalled evenings of Israeli folk dance at New York's Jewish Theological Seminary and participating in Israeli folk dance performances at Ebbets Field.

Esther Nelson (b. 1928), an authority on children's dance classes and author of articles and books about young children and dance, also grew up in New York and danced with Delakova and Berk. Nelson's parents were International Workers Order Communists, and the family became part of the cooperative workers' housing built by like-minded Russian immigrants. The children went to Yiddish schools in the co-op, which also housed art studios and an auditorium for lectures and concerts. At the co-op Nelson studied with Julia Levien before joining Katya Delakova and Fred Berk. Other young women who studied and performed with Delakova include Rita Chazen, now teaching adults dance in Scarsdale, and Sheila Helman, who is the head of cultural arts in a New Jersey YMHA. Shulamite Kivel, who escaped the Nazis in her native Latvia, also performed with Delakova and Berk before specializing in Israeli folk dance at the 92nd Street Y and later in Florida.

Berk and Delakova centered their activities at the 92nd Street Y, where the dance offerings were very broad, including classes in modern, ballet, tap, ballroom, and Israeli and Jewish dance; it also served as a showcase for performers and resident companies. Berk created the Jewish dance department there; Doris Humphrey headed the dance education department, assisted in 1950 by Jewish dancer Eva Desca. The Y sponsored a contest known as Auditions, the winner provided with a free dance program at the Y. Nona Shurman, who was in Humphrey's company, was a winner, as were Emily Gluck and Emily Frankel and her husband, Mark Ryder; other Jewish winners included Miriam Cole and Rena Gluck. Trudy Goth, who came from Europe as a refugee, started producing dancers on a program known as the Choreographers Workshop and used the 92nd Street Y as a venue. Delakova and Berk's Jewish Dance Guild performed often. Some fifteen programs of Anna Sokolow's were presented at the 92nd Street Y between April 1936 and 1961. Pauline Koner had a certain amount of support from the Y. Others who appeared at the Y were Nina Fonaroff, Hadassah (in her first *Shuvi Nafshi*, 1947), Gloria Neuman (1951), Judith Martin and Company (1952), Marie Marchowsky (1952), Linda Margolies (later known as Linda Hodes), and Pearl Lang (whose *Song of Deborah* premiered there in 1948).

Another venue for dance was the Henry Street Playhouse on New York's Lower East Side, where Alwin Nikolais began a dance theater and school. Two of his best dancers, Phyllis Lamhut (b. 1933) and Gladys Bailin (b. 1930), were Jewish. Lamhut's mother brought her to Henry Street when she was fourteen, and she received her professional training from Nikolais and was one of his principal dancers for twenty years. In 1970, she incorporated her own company, the Phyllis Lamhut Dance Company, for which she has choreographed over a hundred works. She has received a Guggenheim Fellowship, sixteen choreography fellowships from the National Endowment for the Arts, and grants from the New York State Council on the Arts.

Gladys Bailin studied with Nikolais and performed in his troupe beginning in 1948. She was also a charter member of Murray Louis's troupe and has choreographed her own works, beginning in the 1950s. She teaches in Athens, Ohio, where she directs the Ohio University School of Dance.

Henry Street gave concert space to others who were Jewish: for example, a concert of Ellida Geyra's on February 19, 1956. Geyra also danced with Berk and Delakova and later moved to Israel, where she teaches and sponsors wide-ranging educational dance programs in Tel Aviv. Muriel Topaz, who was seen the same Henry Street program, later went on to direct the dance program at Juilliard and to be an editor at *Dance Magazine*.

Leah Harpaz studied with Dvora Lapson and Nikolais at Henry Street and performed with Benjamin Zemach's New York group and with Eve Gentry and Helen Tamiris. As a mature dancer she specializes in teaching the elderly (with Erna Lindner) and is active in the Israel Dance Library Association.

Later venues for modern dance in New York included Judson Church, which was home to experimental performances by Aileen Pasloff (b. 1931), who became a dance teacher at Bard College; Judy Dunn (1933–1983), who was an adventurous choreographer, a dancer with Merce Cunningham's avant-garde company, and a teacher at Bennington College; and Meredith Monk.

Modern dancers who made their careers outside of New York include Fannie Aronson (1903–1991), originally from Detroit. She studied at the famed Bennington summer school of dance and at the Dalcroze school in New York. After a brief period with the New Dance Group, she returned to Detroit, where she taught in the public schools and became a founding member of the Michigan Dance Council. She also taught and formed a performing company at the Jewish Community Center, and lectured and wrote about dance.

Tosia Munstock (b. 1907) was born in Germany and studied with Mary Wigman, moving to Detroit in 1927. She was active as a teacher for some sixty-five years and formed a company in 1934, the Rebelarts Dance Group.

Harriet Berg (b. 1924) has had a long career in the Detroit area. She studied dance at Wayne State University and in New York, and has taught at the Jewish Community Center of Metro Detroit since 1959 as well as at Marygrove College. She heads three companies: the Festival Dancers and the Renaissance Dance Company, in residence at the Jewish Community Center; and Madame Cadillac Dance Theatre, specializing in seventeenth- and eighteenth-century dance, in residence at the International Institute of Metropolitan Detroit since 1981. The latter company tours in France, and in 1993 Berg received an award from the French government for promoting French-American relations.

In Los Angeles, Ruth Zahava was a dance director for Jewish Community Centers in Los Angeles, organized the Jewish Folk Dance Council, and headed the Jewish Community Association modern dance ensemble in the 1940s and 1950s. In the introduction to her book *Jewish Dances*, Mordecai Kaplan, the important Jewish theologian, wrote: "The dance art undoubtedly possesses certain characteristics that render it uniquely adapted to become an entering wedge that would make way for all the other arts in Jewish life. It's the only one of the arts which not only engages the entire personality of the artist but transforms him into an instrument for convincing thoughts too deep for words."

Miriam Rochlin (b. 1920) was raised in Berlin and studied with Jutta Klamt until the Nazi period, immigrating to the United States in 1940. She worked with the Jewish dancer Benjamin Zemach from 1948 to 1967 as dancer, assistant director, and production manager. In addition to teaching for the Bureau of Jewish Education in Los Angeles, she produced the documentary *The Art of Benjamin Zemach* through the University of Judaism in 1967.

Ruth Clark Lert (b. 1913) also grew up in Berlin, where she received a diploma in dance before coming to the United States in 1936. She was an instructor for Eugene Loring's American School of Dance and became a recognized dance photographer, working in Los Angeles from 1956 to 1971. Her impressive collection of dance books, programs, and her own photographs was donated to the University of California at Irvine's Dance Library and Archives in 1993.

BELLA LEWITZKY (b. 1916) is well documented in Lert's photographic collection. Lewitsky was born to Russian Jewish immigrants in a utopian community in the Mojave Desert. As an adolescent she moved with her father to Los Angeles and began to study dance with Lester Horton, performing with his company for fourteen years. With Horton she choreographed *Warsaw Ghetto* and her only other Jewish-themed piece, *Heritage.* In 1947, she created Dance Theatre of Los Angeles with Horton and her husband. She formed her own company in 1966, which operated until 1995

and was considered one of the main dance institutions in California.

As a teacher, Lewitzky inspired Fanchon Shur, who was born in Chicago in 1935. After working in Los Angeles and marrying musician Bonia Shur, she settled in Cincinnati, where she and her husband create works together. Their *Taalit* has toured extensively throughout the United States.

ANNA HALPRIN established another dance institution in California, the Tamalpa Institute of San Francisco Dancers Workshop. She has received a Guggenheim Fellowship, several choreographic fellowships from the National Endowment for the Arts, and, in 1980, the American Dance Guild Award for outstanding contributions in dance. She studied dance with Graham, Holm, and Humphrey-Weidman, completed her formal education at the University of Wisconsin dance department, and moved to San Francisco in 1945. In the fall of 1955 she spent time in Israel. Halprin's major choreographic work began in 1959. Considered an innovator, she was interested in using dance in rituals and participatory public dance events and as a process for social change and health. She created dances in the beginning of her career with Jewish themes, including *Kaddosh*, commissioned by Temple Beth Shalom in 1960, but her most noteworthy work deals with healing and global concerns. In September 1995, her *Planetary Dance: A Prayer for Peace* was presented in Berlin to mark the fiftieth anniversary of the end of World War II.

Among the youngest generation of Jewish dancers is Liz Lerman, based in Washington, D.C. Her Liz Lerman Dance Company is multigenerational and multiracial. *Good Enough Jew*, choreographed by Lerman in 1990, is a multidimentional dance that is autobiographical, using layers of Jewish tradition. JoAnne Tucker, born in 1943 in Pittsburgh, studied with Tamiris and graduated from Juilliard, then earned her Ph.D. at the University of Wisconsin. Since 1978, she has directed and choreographed all the material with Jewish themes for her company Avodah Dance Ensemble, which travels extensively to synagogues and Jewish Community Centers. Liz Keen, who trained with Tamiris and danced in the Paul Taylor company before starting her own, now teaches dance composition at Juilliard.

BALLET

At the beginning of the twentieth century, audiences sought out ballet for its beauty and its grand reflection of elite European culture. Those interested in ballet studied with the classical teacher-choreographers such as Mikhail Fokine, Michael Mordkin, and Adolf Bolm in the 1910s and 1920s and performed in the main ballet companies, including the American Ballet Theatre (ABT), the Metropolitan Opera Ballet, George Balanchine's New York City Ballet, and even Radio City Music Hall's ballet company.

On the vaudeville stage, FANNY BRICE included among her characterizations a young Lower East Side woman who decides to become a ballerina. In other memorable skits, she satirized the Ballet Russe's *Swan Lake*.

Whether for economic, cultural, or political reasons, fewer Jewish women went into ballet than into modern dance. Toni Sostek (1937–1996), who trained at the Ballet Russe and ABT schools in New York, performed on Broadway in the 1950s, and taught ballet at Carleton College in Minnesota from 1971 until her death, believed that because ballets are filled with fairies, nymphs, castles, princes, and romantic stories, the dance form had less appeal for American women than the modern dance with its messages of strong emotions, socially relevant concerns, and independent thinking. The long years of ballet education, often with obeisance to the demands of a patriarchal teacher, likewise deterred American Jewish women.

However, a fount for Jewish dancers was the choreographer and ballet dancer Mikhail Fokine, and his children's classes in particular. His Jewish students in the 1920s included Nora Koreff (later Nora Kaye), Esther Rosen (who danced in the Radio City ballet company), Annabelle Lyon, Betty Eisner (renamed Betty Bruce, a headliner in Broadway shows), and Anne Wilson Wangh (who later danced with ABT).

Anne Wilson Wangh (b. 1918) wrote about her memories of studying with Fokine. Many Jewish mothers who, like Fokine, were immigrants from Russia, were steeped in ballet. Wanting their daughters to be cultured, they enrolled them with the master. Wangh remembers Rosa Feldman, who went to the Metropolitan Opera as a dancer, and Miriam Weiskopt, who became a teacher of the Fokine style. After performing with ABT, Wangh choreographed her own programs, became active in the National Dance Guild, and started the Israel Dance Library with Yemmy Strum, a noted teacher of children in New York. Both women moved to Israel and stayed active in the Israel Dance Library organization.

Nora Kaye, born Nora Koreff on January 17, 1920, is notable not only for her technical ballet mastery, but for her intensity of dramatic portrayals as the main interpreter of Antony Tudor's ballets.

Ruthanna Boris (b. 1918) received her early training at the Metropolitan Opera's school of ballet and in 1934 became one of the first students at Balanchine's School of American Ballet. She performed with the ABT and Balanchine's early company, in Agnes de Mille's Broadway productions, at Radio City Music Hall, at the Metropolitan Opera (1937–1942), with the Ballet Russe de Monte Carlo, and as a guest artist with the New York City Ballet. Boris is also an acclaimed ballet choreographer, who made her name choreographing *Cakewalk* in 1951 for ABT, and has taught at the University of Washington in Seattle.

Other ABT dancers who were Jewish include Muriel Bentley, Isabel Mirrow, Annabelle Lyon, and Miriam Golden. Bentley (b. 1920) attended the Metropolitan Opera ballet school, joined its corps in 1938, and then performed for more than fifteen years with ABT; she also danced in Robbins's Ballets USA company and in his Broadway shows. Mirrow married fellow ABT dancer Kelly Brown, and is mother to ABT dancer Leslie Browne and Ethan Brown. Annabelle Lyon (b. 1915) was trained by Fokine and at the School of American Ballet, and was a charter member of the company; she was also in de Mille's Broadway shows and in Balanchine's first company, and performed his early works, including *Serenade*. Miriam Golden, born in 1920 in Philadelphia, joined her teacher Catherine Littlefield's company in 1936 and then ABT as a charter member in 1940.

Jewish ballet dancers with Balanchine have included MELISSA HAYDEN, who danced with the Radio City Music Hall company and then with ABT before joining Balanchine's New York City Ballet in 1950, retiring in 1973. ALLEGRA KENT (b. 1937) trained with Bronislava Nijinska before coming to the School of American Ballet and joining New York City Ballet in 1953. One of the principals with the company until 1978, she is known especially for her work in Jerome Robbin's dances.

Barbara Weisberger (b. February 28, 1926, in Brooklyn to Herman and Sally Linshitz) was a student of Marion Horwitz Lehman and then the first child to study with George Balanchine at the newly formed American School of Ballet. She founded and directed the Pennsylvania Ballet in 1962 and also choreographed for it. She went on to direct the Carlisle Project from 1984 to 1996 to help develop ballet choreographers.

Raya Keen was a ballet dancer with Radio City Ballet Company, and she organized the first union participation for dancers there.

Rochelle Zide, born April 21, 1938, in Boston, performed with the Ballet Russe de Monte Carlo in the mid-1950s, achieving the rank of soloist. She was a principal dancer with the Robert Joffrey Ballet, served as artistic director of the Nederlands Dance Theater in 1973, and has been a dance professor at Adelphi University since 1975.

Outside of New York a very remarkable pair of sisters had an influence on ballet. Hermene (1902–1986) and Josephine (b. 1908) were born to Hanna (Lindeman) Schwartz, a sculptor, and Joseph Schwartz, a haberdashery owner. They studied ballet and modern dance with notable teachers in Chicago, New York, and Europe, and had professional experience, but made their mark in Dayton, Ohio, their hometown. They founded the Schwartz School of Dance, where individual lessons cost ten cents. Their Experimental Group for Young Dancers became the Dayton Theatre Dance Group in 1941 and the Dayton Civic Ballet in 1958, America's second-oldest regional ballet company. Built on both ballet and modern technique, it reflected a contemporary view. By 1972 the company was so fine it was invited to perform at the prestigious Jacob's Pillow Dance Festival and Central Park's Delacorte Theatre in New York City. By the late 1970s it had become a professional company and changed its name to the Dayton Ballet.

WRITERS AND RESEARCHERS

Just as with modern dance, there are a disproportionate number of American Jewish women writers and researchers specializing in dance.

Judith Chazzin Bennahum (b. 1937) was a student of Antony Tudor at the Metropolitan Opera Ballet School. She was a soloist with the Metropolitan Opera Ballet from 1959 to 1963 and danced in Agnes de Mille's Broadway show *Goldilocks* (1958–1959) and with the ballet choreographer Robert Joffrey. She has been a professor of dance at the University of New Mexico since 1975. Bennahum has written two books, *Dance in the Shadow of the Guillotine* and *The Ballets of Antony Tudor;* the latter won the prestigious De la Torre Bueno Prize. She was president of the Society of Dance History Scholars from 1986 to 1989.

SELMA JEANNE COHEN (b. 1920) received a Ph.D. from the University of Chicago before she began her pioneering work in dance history. She was editor and publisher of *Dance Perspectives* from 1960 to 1976, has written *Doris Humphrey*, *The Modern Dance*, and *Next Week Swan Lake*, and is overall editor of the *International Encyclopedia of Dance*.

Ann Barzel studied dance with Bolm in Chicago and Fokine in New York, received her B.A. from the University of Chicago, and taught ballet in Milwaukee from 1945 to 1961. Most noted as a dance reviewer for the *Chicago American, Ballet Review,* and *British Ballet Annual,* she became senior editor of *Dance Magazine* in 1936. She is also known for the extraordinary ballet performance films she made from 1937 into the 1960s. These archival films and her private dance collection were donated to Chicago's Newberry Library as the Ann Barzel Dance Archives.

LYDIA JOEL (c. 1920–1989) danced in Hanya Holm's company, became interested in dance photography and writing, and completely revolutionized *Dance Magazine*, which she edited from 1954 to 1968. She brought a new breadth to the coverage of dance, increasing the magazine's thematic scope to include all styles of dance, dance history, and dance education, and its geographic scope to cover the entire United States.

Marcia Siegel, dance critic of the *Hudson Review*, has written *Days on Earth*, *The Dance of Doris Humphrey*, and *The Shapes of Change: Images of American Dance*, is a founding member of the Dance Critics Association, and teaches dance at New York University.

Dawn Lille Horwitz received her B.A. from Barnard, her M.A. from Columbia, and her Ph.D. from NYU, and is an expert teacher in Labanotation and several aspects of dance history. Her writings include the book *Michel Fokine* as well as numerous articles in *Dance Research Journal, Ballet Review, International Dictionary of Ballet, Dance Chronicle, International Encyclopedia of Dance,* and others.

Judith Lynne Hanna, who holds a Ph.D. from Columbia University, is a specialist in dance ethnography and anthropology. She is especially known for her books *To Dance Is Human* and *Dance, Sex and Gender*. Barbara Palfy (b. 1936) danced in the company of Fred Berk at the 92nd Street Y and worked with Hadassah Badoch before her work as librarian in the Dance Collection of the New York Public Library at Lincoln Center, as associate editor for *Dance Chronicle*, and as chief copy editor for the *International Encyclopedia of Dance*.

BIBLIOGRAPHY

"American Dancer Well Received in Program of Revolutionary and Jewish Folk Dances." *New York World-Telegram*, October 18, 1943; Anderson, Jack. "Champion of Racial Justice When Little Prevailed." *NYTimes*, August 27, 1995, p. 22; Berk, Fred. *The Jewish Dance* (1960); Brin Ingber, Judith. "Dance." *Jewish-American History and Culture: An Encyclopedia*. (1992), and *Victory Dances: The Life of Fred Berk* (1985); Chochem, Corinne. *Jewish Holiday Dances* (1948); Cohen-Stratyner, Barbara Naomi. *Biographical Dictionary of Dance* (1982); *EJ*, s.v. "Dance"; Garafola, Lynn, ed.

"Of, by, and for the People: Dancing on the Left in the 1930s." *Studies in Dance History* 5, no. 1 (Spring 1994); Graff, Ellen. *Stepping Left: Dance and Politics in New York City, 1928–1942* (1997); Halprin, Anna. *Circle the Earth Manual* (1987); Hering, Doris. "The Jewish Dance Festival." *Dance Magazine* (1947); Hering, Doris, ed. *25 Years of American Dance* (1951); "Julia Levien." *Dance Magazine* (1945); Koner, Pauline. Interview with author, New York, June 7, 1995, and *Solitary Song* (1989); Lang, Pearl. Interview with Laurie Horn of *Miami Herald*, April 1, 1978; Lapson, Dvora. "The Chassidic Dance." *Dance Observer* (October 1937): 107, and "The Dance and Intolerance." *Dance Observer* (May 1940): 69, and "The Modern Hebrew Dance." *American Dancer* (1934); Levien, Julia. Interview with author, September 2, 1995; Martin, John. "Success Scored by Dance League." *NYTimes*, November 26, 1934, p. 16; Maslow, Sophie. Interview with author, New York, June 6, 1995; Nagrin, Daniel. "Tamiris in Her Own Voice: Draft of an Autobiography." *Studies in Dance History* (Fall/Winter 1989): 1–162; Nathanson, Lucille. Interview through Nassau Community College for the Oral History Archives of the Dance Collection of the Performing Arts Library at Lincoln Center, New York Public Library, December 14, 1976; Schlundt, Christina L. *Tamiris: A Chronicle of Her Dance Career 1927–1955* (1972); Segal, Edith. Interview for Oral History Archives of the Dance Collection of the Performing Arts Library at Lincoln Center, New York Public Library, January 14, 1991; Shelton, Suzanne. *Divine Dancer: A Biography of Ruth St. Denis* (1981); Sostek, Toni. Interview with author, Northfield, Minn., August 20, 1995; Stodelle, Ernestine. *Deep Song: The Dance Story of Martha Graham.* (1984); Terry, Walter. "Sophie Maslow." *New York Herald Tribune*, January 23, 1951; Tish, Pauline. "Remembering Helen Tamiris." *Dance Chronicles* (1994): 327–361; Tucker, JoAnne, with Susan Freeman. *Torah in Motion* (1990); Wangh, Anne Wilson. "Fokine's Jewish Ballet Mothers." *Israel Dance Annual* (1986): 35–39; Warren, Larry. *Anna Sokolow: The Rebellious Spirit* (1991), and *Lester Horton: Modern Dance Pioneer* (1977); Weisberger, Barbara. Interview with author, October 22, 1996; Wilder, Lucy. "Lillian Shapero and Her Group." *Dance Observer* (August–September 1952): 105; Zahava, Ruth. *Jewish Dances* (1950).

JUDITH BRIN INGBER

DARVAS, LILI (1902–1974)

International actress Lili Darvas won acclaim in her adopted country, the United States, on stage, in films, and on television. Born in Budapest on April 10, 1902, to Alexander and Berta (Freiberger) Darvas, both of whom were Jewish. She was educated at the Budapest Lyceum. She made her professional debut at age twenty, playing Juliet in Shakespeare's *Romeo and Juliet* at the Magyar Szinhas in Budapest. Married to one of Hungary's outstanding playwrights, Ferenc Molnár, Darvas appeared in a range of modern and classical works and became one of Budapest's leading actresses. Molnar, inspired by her talent, created a series of sparkling plays for her, including *Riviera*, *Olympia*, and *The Girl from Trieste*. In 1926, Darvas joined the acting troupe of the German impresario Max Reinhardt, even though she had learned to speak German only two years earlier, by reciting classical German verse plays for hours at a time.

She performed with Reinhardt's company in Vienna and Berlin and at the Salzburg Festival until 1938. Her roles included Beatrice in *Much Ado About Nothing*, Lady Milford in *Kabale und Liebe*, Vivie in *Mrs. Warren's Profession*, and Sadie Thompson in *Rain*. When Reinhardt's company traveled to New York in 1927, Darvas appeared as Titania in *A Midsummer Night's Dream*, as Faith in *Jedermann*, Lucille in *Danton's Tod*, and Beatrice in *The Servant of Two Masters*. Like other actors in the Reinhardt company, she gravitated to film work in the 1930s. Toward the end of her prewar European career, she played the title role in the film *Marie Baskirchev* (1936). Her next significant movie role would be in the MGM all-star musical *Meet Me in Las Vegas* in 1956.

Darvas's particular strength was her acting range. She combined the fetching qualities of an ingenue with the depth and mature allure of an experienced woman of the world. In 1938, she left Europe, immigrating to the United States, where she became a citizen in 1944.

In 1944, she made her Broadway debut as Peter Gray, the women's page editor of the *Herald Tribune*, in the play *Soldier's Wife*. Her performance led critic George Jean Nathan to praise her performance even as he wondered what a Hungarian was doing on the staff of that newspaper. The following season, she played Gertrude in Maurice Evans's famous "G.I." production of *Hamlet*. Throughout the 1950s and 1960s, Darvas worked steadily on the New York stage. She returned to Budapest to perform in a revival of *Olympia* in 1965 and made the film *Love* there five years later. Her last major Broadway stage role was that of Madame Neilsen in *Les Blancs* in 1970.

In 1951, she began a television career that would lead to roles in over a hundred programs. Her most significant television performance was in the title role of the National Educational Television Opera Theatre production of *Rachel La Cabana* in 1973.

Lili Darvas died on July 22, 1974. The theater critic Harold Clurman summed up her talent: "Lili Darvas' pulsating heartiness, a kind of paprika which

*An actor of international status who won praise for her range in both classical and modern works,
Lili Darvas performed in her native Hungary and later Germany before immigrating
to the United States. [New York Public Library]*

flavors the dismal and obscene with the dignity of sound human instincts, is a cause for rejoicing."

BIBLIOGRAPHY

All the Plays of Molnar (1937); Clurman, Harold. Review of *Happiness*. *The Nation* (November 27, 1967); *EJ*; Loggia, Marjorie, and Glenn Young. *The Collected Works of Harold Clurman* (1994); Nathan, George Jean. *The Theatre Book of the Year 1944–45* (1945); Obituary. *NYTimes*, July 23, 1974, 40:1; Rigdon, Walter, ed. *The Biographical Encyclopedia and Who's Who of the American Theatre* (1966); *WWWIA* 6.

THOMAS F. CONNOLLY

DAUM, ANNETTE (1926–1988)

"Feminists can and should have a significant role in promoting understanding and respect between Christians and Jews." These words of Annette Daum highlight her devotion to two causes: interfaith dialogue and feminism.

Born on June 29, 1926, in New York City to Joseph and Eva Posner, she attended Walton High School and went on to receive a bachelor's degree in statistics from HUNTER COLLEGE. She married Alfred Daum on October 12, 1947, and had three children: Elliot, Russell, and Sandra. In 1953, the Daums moved to Long Island, where they helped to found the North Shore Synagogue (Reform).

Interested in feminism yet deeply religious, Daum wished to bring Jewish and Christian women together so that they could share their insights on issues facing women of faith. However, she discovered to her dismay that many Christian and post-Christian feminists harbored anti-Judaic sentiments. She decided to become involved in fostering greater ties between women of the two faiths.

She became the coordinator of interreligious affairs at the Union of American Hebrew Congregations, and also served as the religious action consultant to the Commission on Social Action of Reform Judaism. With Deborah McCauley, she co-organized a task force on Jewish-Christian-feminist dialogue sponsored by the Feminist Theological Institute. As a member of the Catholic-Jewish Relations Committee of Long Island, she forged close ties with John Cardinal O'Connor of the New York Diocese. In addition, she edited the journal *Interreligious Currents* and wrote a number of articles about feminism and Judaism.

Besides promoting interreligious dialogue, Daum distinguished herself as a teacher. She created courses for religious teachers and students to promote greater awareness of gender inequality in learning materials and in religious liturgy. In one course called "Male and Female in Religion," she asked her students to create a nonsexist religious service for their school. While working at the Union of Hebrew Congregations, she staffed two task forces on gender equality, which created a glossary of substitute terminology for the Reform prayer book. For instance, the task forces proposed that the words "Heavenly Father" be replaced by "Heavenly One."

In her later years, Daum became increasingly involved with the North Shore Synagogue. After working with the sisterhood, she became the synagogue's first vice president and, later, its first female president (1968–1972). She also taught comparative religion at the synagogue's religious school. When she tried to retire from teaching after ten years, the students petitioned her to stay, saying that they would not continue without her. She yielded to their request for a few more years.

Annette Daum died of Hodgkin's disease on December 20, 1988.

SELECTED WORKS BY ANNETTE DAUM

"Blaming Jews for the Death of the Goddess." In *Nice Jewish Girls: A Lesbian Anthology*, edited by Evelyn Torton Beck (1989); "Essay Review." *Religious Education* 80, no. 1 (Winter 1985): 314–317; "How to Get What We Want by the Year 2000." *Lilith* 7 (1980): 19–20; "Jewish-Christian-Feminist Dialogue: A Wholistic Vision," with Deborah McCauley. *Union Seminary Quarterly Review* 38, no. 2 (1983): 147–190; "A Jewish Feminist View." *Theology Today* 41, no. 3 (October 1984): 294–300; "The Jewish Stake in Abortion Rights." *Lilith* 8 (1981): 12–17; "Preserving Catholic-Jewish Relations." *Tikkun* 2, no. 4 (September/October 1987): 53–55; "U.A.H.C. Meeting on Catholic-Jewish Relations." *Journal of Ecumenical Studies* 22, no. 3 (Summer 1985): 677–678.

BIBLIOGRAPHY

Daum, Alfred. Telephone interview by author, December 2, 1996; Fisher, Eugene. Review of *Jews and Christians: Teaching About Each Other. Union Seminary Quarterly Review* 38, no. 2 (1983): 243–248; Fishman, Sylvia Barack. *A Breath of Life: Feminism in the American Jewish Community* (1995); Schneider, Susan Weidman. "Feminists and Faith: A Discussion with Judith Plaskow and Annette Daum." *Lilith* 7 (1980): 14–17, and *Jewish and Female: Choices and Changes in Our Lives Today* (1984).

PAULANA LAYMAN

DAVIDSON, CARRIE DREYFUSS (1879–1953)

Founder and longtime editor in chief of *Outlook* magazine, Carrie Dreyfuss Davidson, born in Brooklyn, New York, on February 12, 1879, exemplified the often competing paradigms of Jewish homemaker and accomplished writer and community leader. Introduced to many in American Jewish society as the wife of renowned professor Israel Davidson of the Jewish Theological Seminary of America, this gifted woman eventually founded and fostered an array of significant organizations and publications.

Davidson's most lasting public contribution was as a founder and board member of the United Synagogue of America's National Women's League. In 1918, she joined with a small group of women to create the league as a national framework for the Conservative Movement's women's groups. In 1930, Davidson established the league's journal, *Outlook*, which remained under her editorial hand for almost twenty-four years. With the founding of the journal, Davidson took her place as a literary, religious, and political commentator for more than a generation of American Jewish women.

In the pages of *Outlook*, which included among its readers women and men who had no affiliation with the Conservative Movement, Davidson wrote about issues affecting the lives of Jews across the United States and the world. She gave voice to her strong convictions about the efficacy of early childhood education in both Jewish and other areas, her feelings about the position of the Jews, and Jewish women in particular, in the life of the nation, and her concern for persecuted Jews in other countries. Evident, too, were her stalwart convictions supporting a Judaism that was traditional and yet modern, and her deep devotion to Zionism. The latter was reinforced by her husband's sabbatical in 1926–1927, which allowed the Davidsons, with their daughters Gladdie and Jessica, to spend six months in Palestine. Carrie Davidson's views were conveyed through numerous articles and editorials and in a monthly book review column, the breadth of which showed its writer to be extraordinarily well read and intellectually discriminating.

Davidson demonstrated her concern for the global condition of Jewry through a number of other ventures, both political and cultural. During the 1930s, she was president of the Women's Division of Keren HaTarbut, the Palestine Hebrew Culture Fund, and treasurer of the American Pro-Falasha Committee. In the latter organization, where she was the only woman on the committee's board, Davidson was an early and vocal advocate for the acceptance of Ethiopian Jews, sometimes called "falasha," into the world Jewish community. She also took an active interest in the Jewish Theological Seminary's Women's Institute for adult education, and served on steering committees for the prestigious *Menorah Journal*.

Following her husband's death in 1939, Davidson devoted herself to preserving his memory. She took a two-year leave of absence from editorial duties at *Outlook* to write an informative, if uncritical, memoir of her husband's personal and academic life, entitled *Out of Endless Yearnings*. She also donated his 7,500-volume library on medieval Hebrew literature to New York's City College, establishing the Israel Davidson Memorial Library, and gave his collection of medieval manuscripts to the Jewish Theological Seminary. The Davidsons had two children, Jessica Davidson and GLADYS (DAVIDSON) WEINBERG.

Carrie Davidson died on December 17, 1953. A fitting testament to her work and her personal philosophy can be found in her own words, written only days before her death and published as a tribute in the pages of *Outlook*.

> A woman's best years for learning and doing are those in which she raises a family. . . . When the children were put to bed, I attended college courses; I gave all the time possible to organizational work—going out to speak, being president of two organizations, establishing a Talmud Torah, editing a publication, writing articles for various publications. . . . Though I am now long past seventy . . . I have not yet begun to live in the past. . . . Young women, build your future now!

SELECTED WORKS BY CARRIE DREYFUSS DAVIDSON

Out of Endless Yearnings (1946); *Outlook* (1930–1953).

BIBLIOGRAPHY

AJYB 56:569; Davidson, Carrie Dreyfuss. Henry Hurwitz/Menorah Papers. Box 9, folder 4, American Jewish Archives, Cincinnati, Ohio; Obituary. *NYTimes*, December 19, 1953, 15:4; *WWIAJ* (1938).

LAUREN B. STRAUSS

DAVIDSON, CECILIA RAZOVSKY
see **RAZOVSKY, CECILIA**

DAVIDSON, RITA CHARMATZ
(1928–1984)

Rita Charmatz Davidson led the vanguard for women in the state of Maryland, rising through the ranks of appointed local public service posts to the governor's cabinet and seats on both of Maryland's appellate courts.

A native of Brooklyn, New York, daughter of Michael and Eiga (Rokeach-Kochkovsky) Charmatz, Rita Charmatz Davidson attended local public schools. She had one older sister, Isabel Zackson. She attended Goucher College in Maryland and graduated with honors with a bachelor of arts degree in 1948. Thirty-one years later, Goucher conferred upon her an honorary doctor of laws degree. She graduated from Yale Law School in 1951 and was in private practice from 1951 through 1967 in Washington, D.C., and Montgomery County, Maryland.

Her career in public service was a series of hard-earned firsts. After serving as a member of the Montgomery County Board of Appeals from 1960 to 1964, she was the first person appointed to hold the position of county zoning hearing examiner (1967–1970), a position created largely as a result of a landmark decision of the Maryland Court of Appeals in a case which she brought as counsel for a civic association. Then she was appointed secretary of the Maryland Department of Employment and Social Services, later renamed the Department of Human Resources (1970–1972). In that position, she was the first woman in Maryland to serve on the governor's cabinet. In this post, her strong support of women's rights and the welfare of children led to the establishment of the Commission on the Status of Women within her department.

Maryland lawyer Rita Davidson's life was a series of firsts in her state, among them: the first woman to be appointed appellate judge, the first to be elected judge of the court of special appeals, and the first to sit on the state's highest judicial body—the Maryland Court of Appeals.

Reform congregation and served on the board of directors of the Mid-Atlantic region of the Anti-Defamation League for a number of years in the late 1960s and early 1970s. Her mother, Eiga Rokeach-Kochkovsky Charmatz, was born into a distinguished Lituanian family, with a line of rabbis and the founders of the Rokeach food manufacturing business on her paternal side. Her father's family was from Latvia. Judge Davidson's parents met in Russia and immigrated to the United States in the early 1920s. Once here, they did not participate actively in the Jewish community, but provided both Judge Davidson and her sister Hebrew tutoring at home.

On April 19, 1985, in a memorial tribute to Judge Davidson, Honorable Richard P. Gilbert, chief judge of the Maryland Court of Special Appeals, recalled that as an appellate judge, Rita Davidson "repeatedly demonstrated that she was not only a person of large intellect, but one of great compassion. . . . Any fair reading of the opinions signed Davidson, J., will lead to the obvious conclusion that Rita oftentimes marched to the beat of a different drum—her own. She established beyond doubt, through her writing and by her life, that she was philosophically a liberal, physically courageous, and mentally persistent."

BIBLIOGRAPHY

Davidson, David [husband of Rita Davidson]. Correspondence with author, February 18, 1996, and telephone conversation with author, June 5 and 13, 1997; *NYTimes*, November 13, 1984, B6; Thurlow, Katherine. "Profiles." *The Maryland Bar Journal* (June 1986): 25; "A Tribute to Judge Rita C. Davidson." *The Maryland Bar Journal* (June 1986): 13; *WWWIA*, 8; *Who's Who of American Women* (1972–1973): 200.

RUTH GURSKY

In November 1972, she was the first woman to be a Maryland appellate judge when she was appointed associate judge of the Maryland Court of Special Appeals. In November 1974, she held the highest elective office ever held by a woman in Maryland when she was elected judge of the court of special appeals. In January 1979, she was the first woman to sit on the Maryland Court of Appeals, the state's highest judicial body, when she was elevated to fill an interim vacancy. Thereafter, in November 1980, Judge Davidson was elected to a ten-year term as judge of the court of appeals. Sadly, her career was cut short by cancer, and she died at age fifty-six, after serving only four years of her term.

While Davidson's primary activities were based in the secular and political arena, she was affiliated with a

DAVIS, NATALIE ZEMON
(b. 1928)

Natalie Zemon Davis is a leading European historian, a pioneer in feminist studies, and one of the first women to assume a senior position in academic life. In 1987, when she served as president of the American Historical Association, the largest professional organization of historians in the United States, she became only the second woman ever to hold that post. Davis's work has enriched historical understanding by challenging the boundaries of scholarly inquiry and broadening the scope of the historical profession.

She graduated from Smith College in 1949, earned a master's degree from Radcliffe College in

1950, and received her Ph.D. from the University of Michigan in 1959. She began her teaching career at Brown University (1959–1963) and has held faculty positions at the University of Toronto (1963–1971) and the University of California at Berkeley (1971–1977). Davis joined the faculty of Princeton University in 1978, where she was the Henry Charles Lea professor of history from 1981 until her retirement in 1996. Davis was the Northrop Frye professor of literary theory at the University of Toronto in the fall of 1996. She has authored four books and over seventy articles.

She grew up in a middle-class Jewish family in Detroit, Michigan. She attended the Kingswood School for Girls, where she was one of only a few Jewish students. Her interest in history, as well as her leftist political allegiances, began to develop in high school and grew stronger in her college years. As a student at Smith College in the late 1940s, she participated in several political organizations, ranging from Marxist discussion groups to campaigns against racial discrimination. At the same time, as an honor student at Smith, she began to nurture her passion for historical research.

While still in college, Natalie Zemon married Chandler Davis, then a graduate student in mathematics. After completing college, she began her graduate studies at Harvard University, where she pursued social and cultural history and learned the fundamentals of archival research. In 1950, Davis continued her graduate work at the University of Michigan, while her husband accepted a position on the faculty.

The couple remained politically active, and both suffered the repercussions of the 1950s anticommunist backlash. Chandler Davis refused to sign the university's required anticommunist oath, and in 1953 was brought to testify before the House Un-American Activities Committee. His refusal to cooperate in the government witch-hunts resulted in his being dismissed from the faculty, blacklisted within the profession, and briefly imprisoned. Shortly before her husband's firing, Davis had spent several months in France, a period she described as initiating her "lifelong love affair with the archives." After returning from Europe, the government confiscated both the Davises' passports, making it impossible for her to continue any research abroad. Forced by circumstance to revamp her research agenda, Davis turned her attention to rare book collections in the United States. Throughout her career, Davis has continually broadened the intellectual scope of her work, examining the categories of class, gender, and religion,

and employing the methodological tools of history, anthropology, and literature within her scholarly repertoire.

Davis's early work explored the Protestant-dominated printing industry in sixteenth-century Lyon and set the stage for her investigation of the complex intersection of class, religion, and consciousness in early modern Europe. Her first book, *Society and Culture in Early Modern France* (1975), was a collection of essays covering a vast array of topics, including gender, social class, literacy, and religious culture in the early modern period. Many of her essays have become classics in the study of gender and social history. Davis has always displayed a remarkable ability to draw broad historical conclusions from the small details of daily life. In *The Return of Martin Guerre* (1983), Davis used sixteenth-century court records to craft a dramatic and revealing tale about Bertrande of Artigat and the impostor who posed as her husband, Martin Guerre. The book was widely read, and the story was popularized in an acclaimed film, made with Davis's contribution as historical consultant. In *Fiction in the Archives: Pardon Tales and Their Tellers in Sixteenth-Century France* (1987), Davis again brings archival sources to life, describing how common people accused of crimes explained their actions as they sought royal pardon. In a process Davis labeled "self-fashioning," she demonstrates how individuals of different classes, gender, and social status constructed meaning, identity, and culture. *Women on the Margins: Three Seventeenth-Century Lives* (1995) explores the lives of Glikl Bas Judah Leib, Marie de l'Incarnation, and Maria Sibylla Merian. In her examination of Glikl, the only Jewish woman among the three she studies in the book, Davis interprets Glikl's complex roles as businesswoman, wife, and mother. The corpus of Natalie Davis's work demonstrates her intellectual range and breadth, her ability to transcend disciplinary boundaries, and her innovative historical style.

Davis has always displayed a strong interest in the political and professional dimensions of the historical enterprise. As a young professor at the University of Toronto and the mother of three children, she pressed the university to make provisions for child care and recognize the needs of female employees and graduate students. Davis has also been vocal about the need for historians to conceive their work broadly, and not as part of an enclosed professional discourse. In her 1987 presidential address to the American Historical Association, Davis advanced the notion of history as dialogue. "My image of history would have at least two bodies in it," she explained, "at least two persons talking, arguing, always listening to the other as they gestured at their books."

While Davis's work has not been centered on Jewish issues, she has explored Jewish subjects in her research and cited her Jewish background as a factor shaping her identity as a historian. She recalled that feelings of being an outsider in the majority culture prompted her curiosity about social construction and identity. As a Jew and a woman, Davis gravitated toward exposing and bringing to life the histories of those groups often suppressed in traditional historical narratives.

Natalie Davis has emerged as one of the foremost historians of the twentieth century. Her scholarship and intellectual creativity have expanded the scope of historical inquiry, elicited new types of questions, and prodded the limits of research methodology. Davis's work has enhanced the study of gender, class, culture, religion, art, and literature, and helped to place all of those categories under the broad rubric of history. In addition to her many contributions to the historical profession, she has written in an accessible style and addressed contemporary issues, giving her ideas a wide audience beyond the limited realm of historians.

SELECTED WORKS BY NATALIE ZEMON DAVIS

"Anthropology and History in the 1980s: The Possibilities of the Past." *Journal of Interdisciplinary History* 12, no. 2 (Autumn 1981): 267–275; *Fiction in the Archives: Pardon Tales and Their Tellers in Sixteenth-Century France* (1987); "Ghosts, Kin and Progeny: Some Features of Family Life in Early Modern France." *Daedalus* 106, no. 2 (Spring 1977): 87–114; "History's Two Bodies." Presidential address, American Historical Association. *American Historical Review* 93, no. 1 (February 1988): 1–30; *The Return of Martin Guerre* (1983); "The Sacred and the Body Social in Sixteenth-Century Lyon." *Past and Present* 90 (February 1981): 40–70; *Society and Culture in Early Modern France: Eight Essays* (1975); *Women in the Margins: Three Seventeenth-Century Lives* (1995); "'Women's History' in Transition: The European Case." *Feminist Studies* 3 (Spring–Summer 1976): 83–93.

BIBLIOGRAPHY

Diefendorf, Barbara B., and Carla Hesse, eds. *Culture and Identity in Early Modern Europe (1500–1800): Essays in Honor of Natalie Zemon Davis* (1993); "Natalie Zemon Davis." In *Visions of History: Interviews with E.P. Thompson . . . by Marho*, edited by Henry Abelov et al. (1983); *Le Retour de Martin Guerre* [The Return of Martin Guerre]. Daniel Vigne, director. Société française de production cinématographique, producer. Paris, May 1982. New York, June 1983.

BETH WENGER

DAWIDOWICZ, LUCY S. (1915–1990)

In her essay entitled "What is the Use of Jewish History?" Lucy S. Dawidowicz wrote that *ahavat Yisrael*, the love of the Jewish people, was a crucial ingredient in writing Jewish history. She went on to say that "Some people think that the professional historian's personal commitments—to his people, his country, his religion, his language—undermine his professional objectivity. Not so. Not so, as long as historians respect the integrity of their sources and adhere strictly to the principles of sound scholarship. Personal commitments do not distort, but instead they enrich, historical writing."

Dawidowicz followed this dictum and was, throughout her life, a historian of her people.

Lucy (Schildkret) Dawidowicz was born to Max and Dora (Ofnaem) Shildkret on June 16, 1915, in

Historian and author Lucy S. Dawidowicz was a controversial figure not only because of her opinions about Jewish life and history but also because of her methodology. She was not afraid to immerse herself in the world of her people, believing her analyses could combine passion and objectivity.
[American Jewish Historical Society]

New York City. Her sister, Eleanor (Sapakoff), was born in 1921. Both of the Shildkret parents were recent immigrants from Poland, and despite financial difficulties, they were committed to furnishing their daughters with a strong education in both Jewish and secular subjects. Dawidowicz wrote later in life that she was profoundly influenced both by the rigorous curriculum offered at the Hunter College High School and the fine teachers she studied with at the Sholem Aleichem Mitlshul, a secular, Yiddishist supplementary school.

She entered HUNTER COLLEGE in 1932 and studied English literature. By the fall of 1936, she had graduated, entered a master's program in literature at Columbia University, and dropped out. She was unsure what to do with her life and increasingly concerned about the situation in Europe. In 1937, after working for one year, she reentered Columbia to pursue a master's degree in Jewish history. One year later, after having completed her course work and at the suggestion of her former teacher from the Sholem Aleichem Mitlshul, Jacob Shatzky, Lucy set off for a year of research in Vilna, Poland.

In the year that she spent in Vilna, working at the YIVO, the Institute for Jewish Research, she lived Jewish history. Her colleagues were major Jewish scholars and writers, and her home was the "Jerusalem of Lithuania" now in precipitous decline. The intellectual and social highlights of that year, as well as the growing tension culminating in her flight from Vilna only days before the Germans and Russians invaded, tied her to the place and the people. She spent the rest of her life commemorating the destroyed world she had so briefly known.

In 1940, Max Weinreich, a founder of the YIVO, who had also managed to escape the war in Europe, made New York his headquarters and asked Lucy to work for him. She gladly left her civil service job in Albany to join the staff at YIVO. For the next six years, she devoted herself to helping expand YIVO and to following the course of the war. During these years, she met Szymon Dawidowicz, a political refugee from Poland. They married on January 3, 1948.

When the war ended, Dawidowicz left her job and the Jewish history program at Columbia University, which she never completed, to enlist in the Joint Distribution Committee. She spent eighteen months in Germany, serving among Jewish survivors and helping to catalog the thousands of books confiscated by the Nazis. Back in New York, the American Jewish Committee (AJC) hired Dawidowicz as a research

analyst. In 1968, she was promoted to director of research. These were busy and exciting years at the AJC, where she worked with such scholars as Milton Himmelfarb and Marshall Sklare.

In 1969, Dawidowicz left the AJC to serve as an associate professor at Yeshiva University. By 1974, she was a full professor and held first the Paul and Leah Lewis Chair in Holocaust Studies and subsequently the Eli and Diana Zborowski Chair in Interdisciplinary Holocaust Studies. Throughout the 1970s and 1980s, Dawidowicz wrote books and articles and received numerous awards. In 1979, her husband died at home and under her vigilant care.

Lucy Dawidowicz's most important works are about Eastern European Jewry and the Holocaust, but she also wrote about contemporary issues and Jews in America. All of her works reflect her deep love of the Jewish people as well as her fierce and uncompromising opinions. Dawidowicz's most famous, important, and controversial book was *The War Against the Jews, 1933–1945* (1975). In this book, she articulated her major theories regarding the Holocaust and World War II. First and foremost, Dawidowicz was an intentionalist, arguing that the murder of European Jewry was, from the beginning, the goal of Adolf Hitler. She opposed the functionalists who believed that the Final Solution evolved as the war progressed. Another influential and controversial thesis taken in the book is that Jewish resistance would have been futile. She chronicled the activities of various underground movements, and dismissed those who criticized Jewish passivity.

The War Against the Jews provides a supremely organized history of the whole period. In 1976, Dawidowicz published the accompanying volume, *A Holocaust Reader*, a compilation of documents from the Holocaust. Together, both books offer a comprehensive, coherent portrait of the Holocaust from a Jewish perspective.

Dawidowicz's first book was also a compilation of documents. *The Golden Tradition: Jewish Life and Thought in Eastern Europe* (1967) contains letters, fiction, autobiography, and essays written by European Jews. Beginning with Hasidism and ending with Russian revolutionaries, the excerpts chosen cover a wide variety of topics and eras, covering the history of the Jews of Eastern Europe. The documents are contextualized in an eighty-page introduction. It is here that Dawidowicz narrates the history of the Jews of Eastern Europe. Within this framework she inserts references to the individuals whose documents will follow. The introduction lacks footnotes, as well as complexity, but serves as an appropriate outline. Overall, despite criticism that the documents chosen focus too much on the intellectual elite, *The Golden Tradition* is an invaluable sourcebook.

Along with devoting herself to longer projects, Dawidowicz actively disseminated her ideas by writing articles and essays on numerous subjects of historical and contemporary interest. These ranged from the Bitburg controversy, to Holocaust denial, to feminism, of which she did not approve. The majority of these were published in *Commentary*, and many were received with a storm of letters, both for and against her views. In 1977, Dawidowicz collected some of these essays in *The Jewish Presence: Essays on Identity and History*, and in 1992, shortly after her death, her longtime friend and editor Neal Kozodoy published *What Is the Use of Jewish History? Essays by Lucy S. Dawidowicz* (in which he also included an essay about her life and work). These books contain Dawidowicz's writing on such subjects as Jews in America, modern Jewish identity, and the repercussions of the Holocaust.

Dawidowicz's ongoing interest in these subjects also led to her publication of *On Equal Terms: Jews in America, 1881–1981* (1982) and *The Holocaust and the Historians* (1981). The latter book contains harsh critiques of many contemporary historians and prevailing theories and was widely discussed. At the time of her death, Dawidowicz was working on a comprehensive history of American Jewish life.

Dawidowicz's final book differs remarkably from the others. In *From That Place and Time: A Memoir, 1938–1947*, she wrote of her personal experiences beginning with her year in Vilna and ending with the eighteen months she spent in displaced persons camps in Germany. *From That Place and Time* is an elegant and powerful description of the vibrancy of Jewish life in Eastern Europe, the horrors of the war, and relations with survivors and perpetrators afterward. It simultaneously presents the formative moments in modern Jewish history and the formative moments in the life of its author.

Lucy S. Dawidowicz died on December 5, 1990, after devoting her life to writing about and teaching Jewish history.

SELECTED WORKS BY LUCY S. DAWIDOWICZ

From That Place and Time: A Memoir, 1938–1947 (1989); *The Golden Tradition: Jewish Life and Thought in Eastern Europe*, editor (1967); *The Holocaust and the Historians* (1981); *A Holocaust Reader*, editor (1976); *The Jewish Presence: Essays on Identity and History* (1977); *On Equal Terms: Jews in America, 1881–1981* (1982); *The War Against the Jews, 1933–1945* (1975).

BIBLIOGRAPHY

Bernstein, Richard. "Lucy S. Dawidowicz, 75, Scholar of Jewish Life and History, Dies." *NYTimes*, December 6, 1990, D21; Dawidowicz, Lucy S. Papers. American Jewish Historical Society, Brandeis University, Waltham, Mass.; "Dawidowicz, Lucy S. 1915–."*Contemporary Authors*, New Revision Series, vol. 18; *EJ* (1983–1985); Kozodoy, Neal, ed. *What Is the Use of Jewish History? Essays by Lucy S. Dawidowicz* (1992); Obituary. *AJYB* (1992); Sklare, Marshall. *Observing America's Jews* (1993).

ELIYANA R. ADLER

DEAN, VERA (1903–1972)

In the preface to her book *Builders of Emerging Nations* (1961), Vera Dean poses the question, "What makes a leader?" While the book goes on to discuss the important qualities necessary to be a leader in the political arena, the story of Vera Dean's life is a testament to her own leadership abilities. She helped shape American foreign policy and opinion on international relations, as both an educator and a writer.

She was born in St. Petersburg, Russia, on March 29, 1903, the eldest of three children. Her father, Alexander Micheles, was of German Jewish ancestry, while her mother, Nadine (Kadisch) Micheles, had been born in Russia to Polish and German Jews who had been baptized in the Russian Orthodox church. Vera's mother was educated in England and spent her time translating English novels into Russian. Her father spent eight years in the United States, sometimes working as a reporter for several Jewish newspapers in New York City. His connection to the United States would later have a great impact on his daughter's life.

Vera was tutored in several languages and became fluent in seven, including Russian, English, German, and French. Unfortunately, her education was hindered after 1917. During the Revolution in Russia, their connections with American companies forced the Micheles family to flee to Finland. They eventually made their way to London in 1919. From there, Alexander Micheles sent Vera to the United States, where she lived in Boston under the care of a guardian.

In America, Vera attended business school and worked as a stenographer. Wishing to pursue a higher education, she enrolled at Radcliffe College in 1921. She graduated Phi Beta Kappa in 1925. After receiving a Carnegie Endowment fellowship, she attended Yale University, where she earned an M.A. in international law in 1926. She then returned to Radcliffe, and in 1928 obtained a doctorate in the new and growing field of international law and relations. That same year, she became an American citizen.

Her career with the Foreign Policy Association began in 1928. It was here she pioneered the field of popular education in international relations.

In August 1929, Vera Micheles married William Johnson Dean, a New York attorney. When William Dean died in 1936, leaving her with two small children, Elinor and William, she immersed herself in her work. She directed research on foreign policy and edited several publications, including the bimonthly *Foreign Policy Bulletin*. During World War II, she denounced American isolationism and advocated collective security as a means of establishing world peace. Her influence was so great that the State Department invited her to advise the American delegation at the founding of the United Nations in 1945. She also worked as UN correspondent to India.

Dean published numerous books about international politics, including *Foreign Policy Without Fear* (1953) and *Builders of Emerging Nations* (1961). Her books ranged in theme from the importance of American integrity to politics in non-Western nations. She consistently emphasized the importance of America's influence as a world power, and fought to erase the stigma placed on the Soviet Union by Americans during the Cold War.

Dean's need to create awareness of international relations led her to adopt another role, that of educator. She began teaching in 1946 at Barnard College. She also taught at Harvard from 1947 to 1948 and at Smith College from 1952 to 1954, and she held various teaching positions at colleges throughout the country for short periods of time. At the University of Rochester, she directed the Non-Western Civilization Program from 1954 to 1961. In 1962, she accepted a position at New York University's Graduate School of Public Administration, where she taught seminars in international administration and political science of underdeveloped areas of the world. She remained a valuable part of the faculty at New York University until 1971.

Vera Dean died in New York City on October 10, 1972, of heart failure and a stroke. Her death marked the close of a full life devoted to the selfless endeavor of creating a more peaceful world.

BIBLIOGRAPHY

Micheles, Vera Dean. *Builders of Emerging Nations* (1961); *NAW* modern; New York University. Archives. *Graduate School of Public Administration Bulletin* (1962–1963); Obituary. *NYTimes*, October 12, 1972, 50:1.

NATALIE FRIEDMAN

DEAR ABBY *see* VAN BUREN, ABIGAIL

DIE DEBORAH

"German Israelites! So little is done in this country for the instruction and the intellectual entertainment of the ladies that we believe *Die Deborah* will be welcome to everybody.... [She will form] the connecting link in the chain of Judaism between America and Germany; she will give important service to those who do not read English and she will be welcome to everybody who venerates Judaism and who loves his mother tongue." With these words, the leading Reform rabbi, Isaac Mayer Wise of Cincinnati, introduced the periodical *Die Deborah* in 1855. Wise edited *Die Deborah* as a German-language supplement of the English-language weekly *The Israelite* (from 1874 on, *The American Israelite*). *Die Deborah* disbanded in 1902, two years after Wise died.

As the most important German Jewish newspaper in America, *Die Deborah* propagated a program of German identity, of bourgeois culture, and of Jewish Reform in which women were assigned a strategic place. The paper published essays on Jewish religion, culture, and history, and debates on education. Literature, mostly ghetto novels, was given a privileged place. While *Die Deborah* reported on Jewish issues from all over the world, it focused on news from Germany, and it gave special attention to the cultural life of the German immigrant community in America.

The contributors to *Die Deborah* understood their Germanness not as an ethnic identity, but as a cultural asset. They believed in German *bildung* [education]—in the harmonious formation of the intellect and of the character—and in a democratic and progressive society with high ethical standards. The articles in *Die Deborah* insisted that true religiosity and cultural refinement could be expressed best in the German language. In fact, long after Jewish immigrants from German-speaking lands had adapted English in other realms of life, they still considered German the language of the synagogue, the language of spirituality and morality, the language of the house, and the language of women.

Nineteenth-century middle-class culture ascribed to women a greater sense of religiosity and morality than men. In the German concept of *bildung*, notions of religiosity and cultural distinction converged. *Die Deborah* addressed Jewish women as "priestesses of the home," whose excellence was considered essential for the moral standard of the family, for bourgeois gentility and for the survival of Judaism. Being the educator of Jewish children was a woman's holiest task. A Jewish mother should encourage her child to be charitable, grateful, truthful, gentle, orderly, and punctual, and she should always be a good example. She should accustom her child to the synagogue and should read from the Bible or from religious tractates at home. According to *Die Deborah*, such behavior was apt to preserve "the venerable customs of Judaism."

Clearly, what was propagated as the virtues of Jewish family life were class specific, bourgeois values that had little to do with traditional Jewish housekeeping. By defining the Jewish religion not as a culture of male learning, such as traditional Judaism tended to perceive itself, but as a moral institution, Jewish women gained great prominence. For the contributors to *Die Deborah*, "the daughter of Israel" was the pillar on which the Jewish religion rested. *Die Deborah* was persistently concerned with religious education and secular schooling for Jewish women, and the journal advocated as well a greater role for women in the synagogue.

Many series portrayed women as Jewish national heroines and praised their achievements in the history of their people. In order to fulfill the legacy of historical Judaism, *Die Deborah* claimed, the social position of Jewish women needed to be improved. However, until the last decades of the nineteenth century, how far such an emancipation of Jewish women should go was highly controversial. Should, for example, girls leave the home for the sake of education, and should women's supposedly benevolent influence extend beyond the domestic setting? The contributors to *Die Deborah* saw education for Jewish girls as primarily moral training that would enable young women to withstand the seductions of materialism and atheism. Then, they would not only remain within Judaism, but would also infuse their children with morality.

The ideal of female domesticity, marriage, and motherhood remained the central point of reference in *Die Deborah* throughout its existence, but from the 1880s on, its emphasis on women's education and accomplishments of women in Jewish history encouraged women's activities outside the home, including professional careers. By then, *Die Deborah*, and also *The American Israelite*, were addressing the small elite of America's college-educated women. Moreover, Jewish women began to contribute in significant numbers to both journals. Male and female authors not only defended women doctors, lawyers, and other professionals, but they also expressed great pride in these Jewish women, claiming that a woman's education did not endanger, but enhanced, married life.

Finally, *Die Deborah* and *The American Israelite* supported women's suffrage. In fact, in the 1890s, the publications were similar in tone and content to the feminist AMERICAN JEWESS, America's first journal edited by a Jewish woman, ROSA SONNESCHEIN. Sonneschein had been married to Rabbi Solomon Hirsch Sonneschein, who was a close friend and coworker of Isaac Mayer Wise. However, *Die Deborah* and *The American Israelite* kept their distance from natural rights feminism. The women's rights that the journals advocated stemmed from Jewish women's alleged excellence as mothers and wives, and from their pivotal role in promoting religiosity, morality, and propriety.

The importance of *Die Deborah* declined after a few decades, when Jewish immigrants from German-speaking lands and their children preferred to read an English-language, rather than a German-language, newspaper. Women's issues, as well, were increasingly to be found in *The American Israelite*. This shift from *Die Deborah* to *The American Israelite* not only reflects Jewish integration into American society and culture, it also documents how German Jewish women found their way into the world of women's clubs, philanthropy, and middle-class feminism. Early American feminism, which was interconnected with evangelism, temperance, and Christian abolitionism, had little appeal for Jewish women. German cultural patterns, upward mobility, and an emphasis on women's importance in a modernized Judaism shaped the trajectory from enlightened ideals of Jewish womanhood of the 1850s to the "New Jewish Woman" of the turn of the century.

BIBLIOGRAPHY

Die Deborah. Complete set on microfilm, Hebrew Union College, Cincinnati, Ohio; incomplete set, New York Public Library.

Friedenberg, Albert. "Main Currents of American Jewish Journalism." *The Reform Advocate* (May 27, 1916): 503–523; Goldman, Karla. "The Ambivalence of Reform Judaism: Kaufmann Kohler and the Ideal Jewish Woman." *American Jewish History* 79, no. 4 (1990): 477–499; Goren, Arthur A. "The Jewish Press." In *The Ethnic Press in the United States: A Historical Analysis and Handbook*, edited by Sally M. Miller (1987): 203–228; Hyman, Paula E. *Gender and Assimilation in Modern Jewish History: The Roles and Representation of Women* (1995); Kaplan, Marion A. "Priestess and Hausfrau: Women and Tradition in the German-Jewish Family." In *The Jewish Family: Myths and Reality*, edited by Steven M. Cohen and Paula Hyman (1986): 62–81; Kuzmack, Linda Gordon. *Woman's Cause: The Jewish Woman's Movement in England and the United States, 1881–1933* (1990); Meyer, Michael A. "German-Jewish Identity in Nineteenth-Century America." In *The American Jewish*

Experience, edited by Jonathan Sarna (1986); Otto, Kerstin. "The Image of Women in Isaac M. Wise's 'Die Deborah', 1855–1874." Master's thesis, University of Cincinnati (1993); Vierhaus, Rudolf. "Bildung." *Geschichtliche Grundbegriffe: Historisches Lexikon zur politisch-sozialen Sprache in Deutschland,* edited by Otto Brunner, Werner Conze, and Reinhart Koselleck (1972); Wise, Isaac Mayer. *Reminiscences.* Edited by David Philipson (1901).

MARIA T. BAADER

DECTER, MIDGE (b. 1927)

"Nerve," according to activist-writer Midge Decter, is "the one thing all writers need." Her own career has demonstrated this principle several times over, as Decter's controversial opinions have put her at the center of public debates over issues such as feminism and foreign policy. A neoconservative who enjoys debunking cherished liberal beliefs, Decter has inspired both fury and respect among readers. Even those who disagree violently with her insist that hers is "an opinion to be reckoned with."

She was born Midge Rosenthal on July 25, 1927, one of three daughters of Harry and Rose (Calmenson) Rosenthal, in St. Paul, Minnesota. Her father owned a sporting goods store in which Midge helped as a clerk. She dreamed of becoming a writer as a young child; as a student at Central High School in St. Paul, she worked on the literary magazine. After high school, however, she stopped relying upon traditional educational venues for writing experience. She studied for one year at the University of Minnesota, then transferred to New York's Jewish Theological Seminary for two years, and later briefly attended New York University, but she never received a college degree.

Instead, she married Jewish activist Moshe Decter on September 7, 1947, and had two daughters before the marriage ended in divorce in 1954. After 1948, Decter began a career in publishing, working as secretary to the managing editor of *Commentary,* the journal published by the American Jewish Committee. On October 21, 1956, Decter married Norman Podhoretz, future managing editor of *Commentary* and had two more children, a girl and a boy.

Decter maintained a twenty-year career in publishing after her second marriage, working as an editor variously at *Midstream, Commentary,* the Hudson Institute, CBS Legacy Books, *Harper's, Saturday Review/ World,* and then finally at Basic Books until 1980. Despite this distinguished career, Decter became famous—or infamous—after writing three controversial works that blasted feminism and liberal child

rearing and passionately, if somewhat ironically, championed traditional domestic roles for women. In *The Liberated Woman and Other Americans* (1970) and *The New Chastity and Other Arguments Against Women's Liberation* (1972), Decter advanced the thesis that radical women who claimed they wanted freedom from male oppression were, in fact, afraid of growing up, having children, and taking on responsibility. According to Decter, women's liberation strove to "keep [a woman] as unformed, as able to act without genuine consequence, as the little girl she imagines she once was and longs to continue to be." In *Liberal Parents, Radical Children* (1975), Decter went further, attacking liberal theories of child rearing for producing these narcissistic, overindulged "radical" children, who believed they could change the world and take no responsibility for their actions.

Feminists and liberals predictably rejected Decter's conclusions. One reviewer called *The Liberated Woman and Other Americans* a "craftily contrived, meandering stream of words," while another concluded of *Liberal Parents, Radical Children*: "the book's point is nonexistent and its usefulness negligible." Critics took Decter to task for her conservative detachment and for her method of analyzing fictional types like "the Pothead," rather than specific individuals: "we cannot accept theories clothed in shadows." Yet Decter had numerous supporters. One conservative reviewer relished the author's "feisty, fighting" spirit and claimed that *Liberal Parents, Radical Children* was "a splendid stimulus to a critically needed self-examination." Even liberals with reservations found Decter's essays "illuminating and chastening" and "seriously and closely argued."

After playing her role as "the center of resistance to the [women's] movement" in the 1970s, Midge Decter began to emphasize issues of foreign policy in the 1980s. She became the executive director of the Committee for the Free World, a group of intellectuals who claimed that their goal was "to alter the climate of confusion and complacency . . . that has done so much to weaken the Western democracies." By holding conferences and monitoring news reports, this group hoped to publicize the threat they believed the Soviet Union posed to the Unived States and Israel.

Midge Decter's aggressive foreign policy complemented her iconoclastic critique of the women's movement. Like a number of Jewish liberals of the 1950s, Decter swung to the right in the 1970s, galvanized by a distaste for leftist politics that increasingly criticized Israel, supported affirmative action, and opposed Cold War interventionism. Decter continued

*Katya Delakova was an innovative dancer and choreographer who explored the
Jewish experience in her work, melding Eastern and Western traditions
with modern and folk styles. [New York Public Library]*

DENMARK, FLORENCE LEVIN
(b. 1932)

The existence of two autobiographies and two biographies attest to the importance of Florence Denmark's contributions to American psychology. However, none of these published materials mention the fact that she is Jewish, probably because she has never felt that her Jewish heritage is particularly salient to her. Nevertheless, like the work of other Jewish women of her generation, Denmark's contributions to psychology have been socially activist in nature. She is a founder of the field of the psychology of women, and has contributed much to its legitimization in terms of both scholarship and organizational leadership.

She was born on January 28, 1932, in Philadelphia, where she grew up as part of a large extended family. Her mother was a musician, and her father was a lawyer. Her sister became a physician. She describes her mother as the driving force behind her accomplishments.

She graduated Phi Beta Kappa from the University of Pennsylvania in 1952 with honors in two majors—history and psychology. She married Stanley Denmark, an orthodontist, within a year after receiving her B.A., but continued her graduate work at the University of Pennsylvania and received a Ph.D. in social psychology from that institution in 1958. After graduation, Denmark and her husband moved to New York City and had three children (a daughter and a mixed-sex set of twins). During this period, Denmark began to teach as an adjunct professor at Queens College, where she met Marcia Guttentag (another young mother) and began to collaborate on studies with her. Their research looked at the impact of college reentry on mature women, the effects of racial integration in preschool education, and the consequences of psychiatric labeling on immigrants.

In 1964, after six years of postdoctoral experience, Denmark was appointed an instructor at HUNTER COLLEGE. She remained at Hunter and was promoted to full professor there in 1974. In 1984 she received a distinguished professorship, and in 1988 she became the first Robert Scott Pace Professor at Pace University—an endowed chair. At that time she also became chair of Pace's department of psychology (a position she continues to hold).

Denmark was instrumental in establishing the psychology of women as a recognized and legitimate scholarly field. She helped get funding from the National Science Foundation and the National Institute of Mental Health for the first research conference in this field (held in Madison, Wisconsin, in 1975), which brought both senior and junior women together for extensive dialogue. The book that developed from this conference, *The Psychology of Women*, was considered an important resource for scholars. Denmark also coauthored one of the earliest text/readers in the field, *Woman: Dependent or Independent Variable?* She has written extensively about the disadvantaged status of women in psychology and has worked to help the field recognize women's neglected contributions to it. Recently, she coedited *Psychology of Women*, which contains insightful reviews of various aspects of the field contributed by leading scholars.

Denmark's organizational skills are superb. She was one of the founders of the American Psychological Association's Division on the Psychology of Women and its third president in 1975–1976. In 1980, she was elected the fifth woman president of the American Psychological Association (the first Jewish woman to hold this office). She has held many offices in national and international organizations and has received numerous awards.

Denmark believes "in empowering other women." Her support is appreciated by her many colleagues and former students, whom she has taught to aspire greatly and collaboratively.

SELECTED WORKS BY FLORENCE LEVIN DENMARK

"Autobiography." In *Models of Achievement: Reflections of Eminent Women in Psychology*, edited by Agnes N. O'Connell and Nancy F. Russo. Vol. 2 (1988): 279–293; "Contributions of Women to Psychology," with Nancy F. Russo. *Annual Review of Psychology* 38 (1987): 279–298; "Feminist and Activist." In *Feminist Foremothers in Women's Studies, Psychology, and Mental Health*, edited by Phyllis Chesler, Esther D. Rothblum, and Ellen Cole (1995); *Psychology of Women: A Handbook of Issues and Theories*, edited with Michele A. Paludi (1993); *The Psychology of Women: Future Directions of Research*, edited with Julia A. Sherman (1978); *Woman: Dependent or Independent Variable?*, with Rhoda K. Unger (1975).

BIBLIOGRAPHY

Denmark, Florence Levin. Correspondence with author, February 1997; Paludi, Michele A., and Nancy F. Russo. "Florence L. Denmark." In *Women in Psychology: A Bio-Bibliographic Sourcebook*, edited by Agnes N. O'Connell and Nancy F. Russo (1990): 75–87; Stevens, Gwendolyn, and Sheldon Gardner. *The Women of Psychology*. Vol. 2 (1982).

RHODA K. UNGER

DEREN, MAYA (1917–1961)

For a woman who was to transform film, it is fitting that Maya Deren was born in Russia in 1917, during the birth of the Revolution.

Born Eleanora Derenkowsky in Kiev, Ukraine, on April 29, 1917, the only child of Marie (Fiedler) and Solomon David Derenkowsky, she was named after Eleanora Duse, the eminent Italian actress.

With pogroms continuing in the Ukraine into 1922, Eleanora Derenkowsky's family fled to America. They landed in New York, and later joined family members in Ohio, while her father studied at Syracuse University for his American degree in medicine. A psychiatrist, Dr. Derenkowsky was appointed as an assistant physician at the Syracuse State School for Mental Defectives. In 1928, the Derenkowskys became naturalized American citizens and shortened the family name to Deren.

Deren attended both elementary and high schools in Syracuse. She spent 1930 to 1933 in Geneva, Switzerland, at the League of Nations' International School, where she pursued her desire to write. She returned to Syracuse in 1933, entering Syracuse University to study journalism and political science. There she met and married fellow student Gregory Bardacke, whose Russian Jewish family had moved to Harbin, China, Bardacke's birthplace, before immigrating to America. In 1935, Deren and Bardacke moved to New York City, where he became a union organizer. Both she and her husband were actively involved in the American socialist movement.

Many thought Deren's socialist leanings served as a replacement for Judaism. Her father, whom she adored, was agnostic. Clearly aware of her Jewish roots, she felt no affinity for her religion or culture. Though aware of problems for Jews in the world, Deren looked to socialism as the cure for such issues. Indeed, socialism allowed her to merge her Jewish identity into a universalist worldview. She rarely made reference to her Jewishness.

Apart from her political activities, Deren finished her B.A. degree at New York University in 1936. By 1938, she and Bardacke were divorced. At this juncture, Deren attended Smith College, completing her master's degree in English literature in June 1939.

First working as an editorial assistant, Deren was hired in 1940 as the secretary to choreographer Katherine Dunham, whom she joined on her cross-country road tour. Deren subsequently published an article entitled "Religious Possession in Dancing" for the journal *Educational Dance*. She parted from Dunham in 1942.

She started as a writer with an interest in dance, but Maya Deren would eventually be known as the "Mother of Underground Film" for her work in experimental cinema. [New York Public Library]

Living in Los Angeles with her mother, Deren met photographer Alexander Hackenschmied, who had fled the Nazis from his native Czechoslovakia. Having changed his name to Sasha Hammid, he worked as a motion picture photographer for the American newsreel *The March of Time*. She married Hammid in 1942.

Deren had continued to pursue her ambitions as a writer. She published poetry, essays, and newspaper articles. But with Sasha Hammid, she penetrated the world of film, becoming Maya Deren, avant-garde filmmaker.

Together, she and Hammid made the highly experimental *Meshes of the Afternoon* (1943). Immersed in symbolism—Deren's beloved father was, after all, a psychiatrist—the film tampers with past and present, time and place, and reality and fantasy in this interpretation of a frightening dream.

Deren and Hammid moved to New York, where Deren, often referred to as the Mother of Underground Film, continued her film career, focusing also on her interest in dance. Considered among the most important figures in the postwar development of personal independent films in the United States, Maya Deren defined her approach: "The great art expressions will come later, as they always have, and they will be dedicated, again to the *agony* and the *experience* rather than the incident."

Because of the inherent difficulty in distributing her experimental films, Deren became a self-promoter par excellence: she rented the Provincetown Playhouse in Greenwich Village, where she exhibited her films. In addition, she set up a distributing business from her home and established the Creative Film Foundation to provide cash awards and money for experimental filmmakers.

Eventually, Sasha Hammid and Maya Deren divorced. Deren received a Guggenheim Fellowship in 1946 for the purpose of traveling to Haiti in order to photograph Haitian dance. She remained for eighteen months, and became immersed in voodoo rhythms and rituals. She shot thousands of feet of film, but she never completed her envisioned film. Voodoo ceremony, however, remained an integral part of her life, as she continued to practice its rites in New York.

Maya Deren met her third husband, Teiji Ito, when he was only fifteen years old and she was in her thirties. Deren lived with the Japanese youth for many years, and eventually they married. He became a composer, at one point adding music to her earlier film *At Land* (1944). Maya Deren died of a cerebral hemorrhage on October 13, 1961, at age forty-four.

SELECTED WORKS BY MAYA DEREN

An Anagram of Ideas on Art, Form and Film (1946); "Cinematography: The Creative Use of Reality." In *The Avant-Garde Film: A Reader of Theory and Criticism*, edited by P. Adams Sitney (1978).

FILMOGRAPHY

At Land (1944); *Meditation on Violence* (1948); *Meshes of the Afternoon* (1943); *Ritual in Transfigured Time* (1946); *A Study in Choreography for the Camera* (1945); *The Very Eye of Night* (1959); *The Witches Cradle* (1943).

BIBLIOGRAPHY

Brakhage, Stan. "Maya Deren." In *Film at Wit's End: Eight Avant-Garde Filmmakers* (1989): 91–112; Clark, VeVe, Millicent Hudson, and Catrina Neiman. *The Legend of Maya Deren* (1984); Deren, Maya. Papers. Department of Special Collections, Mugar Memorial Library, Boston University; *NAW* modern; Obituary. *NYTimes*, October 14, 1961, 23:4; Renan, Sheldon. *An Introduction to the American Underground Film* (1967); Sadoul, Georges. *Dictionary of Film Makers* (1972); Vogel, Amos. *Film as a Subversive Art* (1974).

JUDITH E. DONESON

DEUTSCH, BABETTE (1895–1982)

"How to sustain the miracle / Of being, that like a muted bell, / Or like some ocean-breathing shell, / Quivers, intense and still?" asked Babette Deutsch in her poem "Quandary." Questions surrounding the miracle of life formed an important part of Babette Deutsch's poetry. She also published many novels and works of literary criticism, but she is best known for her poetry, which was greatly influenced by Jewish themes and culture.

Babette Deutsch was born in New York City on September 22, 1895, to parents of German Jewish descent, Michael and Melanie (Fisher) Deutsch. Except for brief trips abroad, she lived in New York City all her life.

Deutsch attended Barnard College at Columbia University, where she received her B.A. in 1917. While still an undergraduate, she began to publish her verse in various magazines. In 1919, her first volume of poetry was published, entitled *Banners*. Her second book of verse, *Honey Out of a Rock*, was published in 1928. This second work dealt with many biblical themes and reflected the influence of Jewish culture, as well as imagism and Japanese haiku.

On April 28, 1921, the young poet married Avrahm Yarmolinsky, a writer of Russian Jewish descent. They had two sons, Adam and Michael, and their marriage marked the beginning of a long and successful creative partnership. The couple translated several works of Russian poetry together, including the works of Pushkin. Deutsch, who was fluent in German, also translated the works of Rilke into English.

Deutsch was the author of several novels, among them *A Brittle Heaven* (1926), *In Such a Night* (1927), and *The Mask of Silenus* (1933). Her other literary contributions include children's novels, such as *I Often Wish* (1966) and *Tales of Faraway Folk* (1963). She was also well known as a literary critic, publishing many essays on modern poetry and editing the poems of Shakespeare (1946) and Samuel Taylor Coleridge (1967).

Deutsch was a well-respected educator. She lectured at the New School for Social Research from 1933 to 1935, and at Columbia University from 1944 to 1971. She also worked for two years as a lecturer at the Poetry Center of the Young Men's Hebrew Association in New York City.

Her committee work was an integral part of her role as a writer and teacher. She was a member of the advisory board for the National Book Committee, secretary for the PEN National Institute of Arts and Letters, as well as chancellor for the Academy of

Although she also wrote novels and literary criticism, Babette Deutsch was acclaimed for her poetry, which often drew upon Jewish themes for its power and lyricism. [New York Public Library]

to the Jewish community. Not only did she donate her time to organizations like the YMHA, but she also used her poetry as a medium for paying homage to her heritage. Deutsch was sensitive to the precarious and tragic situation of the Jews during the Holocaust. Her final three books of verse deal with her rage against the destruction and horror of World War II. Her poems about war also try to make some sense out of the evils of humankind: "A sage once said the mind of God forgets / Evil that men remember having done, as it remembers / The good that men do and forget."

Babette Deutsch died on November 13, 1982.

SELECTED WORKS BY BABETTE DEUTSCH

Banners (1919); *A Brittle Heaven* (1926); *Collected Poems, 1919–1962* (1963); *The Collected Poems of Babette Deutsch* (1969); *Honey Out of a Rock* (1928); *In Such a Night* (1927); *I Often Wish* (1966); *The Mask of Silenus* (1933); *Tales of Faraway Folk* (1963).

BIBLIOGRAPHY

American Women Writers. Vol. 1. Edited by Lina Maniero (1979); *BEOAJ*; *Contemporary Authors.* Vols. 1–4. Edited by James M. Etheridge and Barbara Kopala (1962); *EJ*; Obituary. *NYTimes*, November 15, 1982; *UJE*; *WWIAJ* (1928, 1938); *WWWIA* 8.

NATALIE FRIEDMAN

DEUTSCH, HELENE (1884–1982)

In 1923, Helene Deutsch became the first psychoanalyst to write a book about female psychology, called *Psychoanalysis of the Sexual Functions of Women* in English. Her interest in the subject, along with that of Karen Horney, helped to push her mentor Sigmund Freud, who did not like being left behind, into writing articles about female psychology. When Deutsch was completing her manuscript, she wrote to her husband, Felix, "It brings something new to this *terra incognita* in analysis—I believe, the first ray of light on the unappreciated female libido." For her to draw attention to the female libido in that era was implicitly to amend Freud's own outlook. At the same time, Deutsch was pioneering the importance of motherhood. Other psychoanalysts of the period, such as Otto Rank, Sandor Ferenczi, and Georg Groddeck, were also intrigued by the neglected role of mothering, but Deutsch was the one to insist on its special significance for female psychology. Although she always remained loyal to Freud's conceptual framework, her writings were an outgrowth of her own personal experiences and insight.

American Poets. She was a consultant for the Library of Congress from 1960 to 1966.

Babette Deutsch was the recipient of many honors and awards throughout her life. Her poetry won much acclaim early in her career. In 1926, *The Nation* awarded her its Poetry Prize. This was followed by a Julia Ellsworth Ford Foundation Prize for her critical work on Walt Whitman. In 1946, Columbia University bestowed upon her an honorary doctorate in literature, and her alma mater later recognized her as a distinguished alumna in 1977.

Babette Deutsch was one of the gifted women artists of her era who made a significant contribution

Deutsch was born on October 9, 1884, in Przemysl, Poland. Her parents were Jewish, but she also grew up as a Polish nationalist. As early as 1898, she was emotionally involved with a much older—and married—man, Herman Lieberman, who was a local Social Democratic leader. They had an affair that lasted for years, and, in her extreme old age, it seemed to Deutsch to be the one great romance of her life. Although formal schooling for women was almost impossible in late nineteenth-century Poland, she received private tutoring, which enabled her to enroll at the University of Vienna in 1907. There, she studied medicine and was, from the outset, interested in a psychiatric career.

While spending a year in Munich in 1910–1911, she finally broke off with Lieberman, who since 1907 had been a Polish deputy in the Parliament in Vienna. In Munich, she met her future husband, Felix Deutsch, in medical school, and the two were married in 1912. He was already a respected Viennese internist as well as a passionate Zionist.

At the University of Vienna, Deutsch became the student of neurologist Julius Wagner-Jauregg. Since women were not allowed to hold clinical psychiatric posts at the university, Wagner-Jauregg helped Deutsch to obtain a study position at the clinic of Emil Kraepelin in Munich in 1914. When World War I broke out, physicians were needed by the Austrian military, and Deutsch found new and welcome responsibilities being thrust upon her at Wagner-Jauregg's clinic. She worked unofficially as one of his assistants, a high post that, as a woman, she was not permitted formally to assume.

In the fall of 1919, she left Wagner-Jauregg's clinic in order to undertake a personal analysis with Freud in Vienna, which lasted about a year. She had given birth to a son, Martin, in 1917, and was feeling uncertain about herself as both a mother and a wife. She had been on the periphery of Freud's circle for some years, although she became a member of the Vienna Psychoanalytic Society only in February 1918. While for some students of Freud—particularly exceptionally talented male pupils—Freud could be a hindrance to their independent development, Deutsch found that Freud managed to release her most creative talents. She was able to write as Freud's adherent and at the same time fulfill her own needs for self-expression. Her professional audience responded to her work as that of one of the most prominent leaders in psychoanalysis. She was no mere imitator of Freud, but contributed her own insights within his system of thought. Later, in 1923–1924, she went to Berlin for a second analysis with Karl Abraham, where she also learned about the Berlin Psychoanalytic Institute's training facilities.

The 1920s were perhaps Deutsch's most creative period. Not only did she make some of her most notable psychological contributions during that decade, but she also emerged as one of the most successful teachers in the history of psychoanalysis. In 1924, she became the first woman to head a clinic, the new Vienna Psychoanalytic Training Institute, where she assessed all candidates who came to Vienna for instruction in analysis. In addition to her role on international training committees and her reputation as a lecturer, she was much sought-after as a training analyst and as a supervisor. Her seminars were remarkable and memorable experiences for students, and she trained a host of future psychiatrists and therapists, including the next generation of the most prominent "classical" analysts. Her 1930 book *Psychoanalysis of the Neuroses* was a memorable teaching aid.

In Vienna, Deutsch's caseload became two-thirds American and, in 1930, she briefly visited the United States to attend the First International Congress of Mental Hygiene held in Washington, D.C. By this time, she was considering relocation to the United States. One potential difficulty was finding a suitable position for her husband, a nonpracticing member of the Vienna Psychoanalytic Society who had also been Freud's personal physician when Freud first contracted cancer in 1923.

Boston, Massachusetts, appeared to offer the best opportunities for both Deutsches. A new facility, the Psychoanalytic Training Institute, was being established there at the same time that Dr. Stanley Cobb was creating a psychiatric department at the famous Massachusetts General Hospital. Cobb was interested in psychosomatic medicine, Felix's specialty, so he was eager to attract the couple. Helene came to Boston in the fall of 1935 with her son Martin, who then enrolled in college; a few months later, Felix finally decided to leave Vienna and arrived in Boston in January 1936.

Deutsch's mental stylishness and her reputation as a favored colleague of Freud earned her great respect at the Boston Psychoanalytic Training Institute. The analysts there had been mainly students abroad when she was already established as a teacher and lecturer. Although she was not eager once again to be involved in the politics of training students, she functioned as president of the Boston Psychoanalytic Society from 1939 to 1941.

During World War II, she wrote a two-volume work, *The Psychology of Women*, published in 1944–1945. While remaining loyal to Freudian psychoanalysis,

Deutsch added her special outlook on women's psychology, derived from her own personal experience and clinical observations. She wrote, for example, about women's inner conflict between motherliness and eroticism, a conflict that she herself experienced. She recognized that her preoccupation with her work had cost her a heavy price in terms of emotional closeness with both her husband and her son. With the advantage of hindsight, she emancipated herself from theoretical dogmatism and discouraged her students from following her example too closely.

Deutsch characteristically emphasized the realistic conflicts of young women. Her books were filled with female case histories of which other psychoanalysts of the time had limited knowledge. She was not afraid to sound old-fashioned about how sexual experience could take the place of love. She thought that in order to understand pathologic behavior correctly, we must first realize what constitutes normal development. The thrust of Deutsch's argument was that a woman's intensified inner life becomes a unique source of human superiority. She highlighted the sources of a woman's capacity to identify with others. Probably her most famous clinical concept was that of the "as if" personality, a false affect that was neither neurotic nor psychotic. To Deutsch, victimization was a central danger of female masochism, while intensified self-love could be a self-preserving counterweight, protecting a woman from her masochistic tendencies.

Karen Horney had caricatured some of Deutsch's writings in the 1930s, but Deutsch's position seemed secure by the early 1940s. Her temperament was so untruculent that she answered Horney's criticisms with only a few mild footnotes in *The Psychology of Women*.

Deutsch's old age was as remarkable as any other feature of her life. She kept on sustaining friends and acquaintances almost right up to her death in 1982 at age ninety-seven in Cambridge, Massachusetts. Her interest in other people helped keep her alive for a long time. After her husband died in 1964, Deutsch's publications seemed to accelerate. Her collection of essays called *Neuroses and Character Types* appeared in 1965 and two monographs were published as books in the late 1960s. Her autobiography, *Confrontations with Myself*, was pubished in 1973.

Deutsch retained her intellectual vitality right to the end. Typically, she questioned whether generations of analyzed people were any happier after their treatment. Privately, she thought that her own life had been ruined by too much denial. She believed that she had failed as a mother, which caused her to redouble her efforts with her two grandsons. She hid her tragic feelings from most people, who saw in her a joyful, fascinating, very competent woman with a seemingly inexhaustible supply of energy. If she had been more accepting of herself, she might have formulated ideas about human development and normality more in keeping with her own unconventional experience and enabled others to feel more at ease in defying conformist pressures.

SELECTED WORKS BY HELENE DEUTSCH

Confrontations with Myself: An Epilogue (1973); *Neuroses and Character Types: Clinical Psychoanalytic Types* (1965); *Psychoanalysis of the Neuroses* (1951); *A Psychoanalytic Study of the Myth of Dionysus and Apollo* (1969); *The Psychology of Women: A Psychoanalytic Interpretation.* Vol. 1: *Girlhood.* Vol. 2: *Motherhood* (1944–1945); *Selected Problems of Adolescence: With Special Emphasis on Group Formation* (1967); *The Therapeutic Process, the Self, and Female Psychology: Collected Psychoanalytic Papers.* Edited by Paul Roazen (1992); *Zur Psychoanalyse der weiblichen Sexualfunktionen* [Psychoanalysis of the sexual functions of women]. Edited by Paul Roazen (1923; translated, 1991).

BIBLIOGRAPHY

EJ; Roazen, Paul. *Freud and His Followers* (1975, 1992), and *Helene Deutsch: A Psychoanalyst's Life* (1985; reprint with new introduction, 1992), and "A Note on the Vienna Psychoanalytic Society: Felix Deutsch's Letters, 1923 and 1935." *Journal of the History of the Behavioral Sciences* (October 1984).

PAUL ROAZEN

DEUTSCH, NAOMI (1890–1983)

Naomi Deutsch, a leader in the field of public health nursing, was born on November 5, 1890, in Brno, Moravia, the second child of Rabbi Dr. Gotthard and Hermine (Bacher) Deutsch. With her parents, her brother Herman, and her sister Edith, she immigrated to Cincinnati, Ohio, where her brothers Eberhard and Zola were born. She graduated from Walnut Hills High School in 1908 and from the Jewish Hospital School of Nursing in 1912.

From 1912 to 1916, she worked at Irene Kauffman Settlement House in Pittsburgh, Pennsylvania. In 1916, she enrolled at New York City's Columbia University Teachers College, receiving a B.S. degree in 1921. From 1917 to 1924, she worked at the Henry Street Settlement, serving as supervisor, field director, and acting director. She applied for military service in World War I but was refused because of her place of birth. She also was a member of the American Red Cross Nursing Services (badge number 36,776).

Deutsch was the director of the San Francisco Visiting Nurse Association from 1925 to 1934 and began public speaking engagements as early as 1926. She became a lecturer in public health nursing at the University of California, Berkeley, in 1933 and in 1934 was appointed assistant professor and assumed full charge of the public health nursing course. She was invited to the White House Conference on Child Health and Protection in February 1931 and to the 1940 Conference on Children in a Democracy.

In 1935, Deutsch accepted the position of organizing and directing the Public Health Unit of the U.S. Department of Labor's Federal Children's Bureau in Washington, D.C. She became a staff member of the Pan American Sanitation Bureau in 1943. As principal nurse consultant, she collaborated in the development of health programs in the Caribbean and Central America and traveled extensively in the region. Returning to Columbia University Teachers College, she served as an associate in research in nursing education (1945–1946) and part-time instructor (1946–1950).

Deutsch was affiliated with numerous professional organizations during her career, among them the National League of Nursing Education, the California State Conference of Social Work, the American Nurses Association, the American Association of Social Work, the National Conference of Social Workers, and Delta Omega. She served at various times on the boards of the California State Nurses Association and the National Organization for Public Health Nursing, as president of the California State Organization for Public Health Nursing and the Social Workers Alliance of San Francisco, and on the governing council of the American Public Health Association. She was also a member of the League of Women Voters and worked with Planned Parenthood, staying active with these groups well into retirement.

She remained in New York City until 1973, when she moved to New Orleans, Louisiana, to share an apartment with her sister, who was in frail health. Deutsch died on November 26, 1983.

SELECTED WRITINGS BY NAOMI DEUTSCH

"Economic Aspects of Maternal Care." *Public Health Nursing* 31 (November 1939): 619–624; "Generalized Public Health Nursing Services in Cities." *American Journal of Public Health* 25 (April 1935): 475–478; "Promoting Maternal and Child Health: Public Health Nursing Under Social Security Act, Title V, Part I." With M.D. Willeford. *American Journal of Nursing* 41 (August 1941): 894–899; "Public Health Nursing in Programs for Crippled Children." *Public Health Nursing* 29 (January 1937): 10–15; "Public Health Nursing Under the Social Security Act: Development Under the Children's Bureau." With H. Hilbert. *Public Health Reports* 28 (September 1936): 582–585; "Role of Public Health Nurse in Service for Crippled Children." *Public Health Nursing* 29 (June 1937): 350–356; "What Every Health Officer Should Know: Public Health Nursing." *American Journal of Public Health* 28 (September 1938): 1087–1090.

BIBLIOGRAPHY

Binheim, Max, ed. *Women of the West* (1928); Bullough, Vern, O.M. Church, and A.P. Stein, eds. *American Nursing: A Biographical Dictionary* (1988); Bullough, Vern, L. Sentz, and A.P. Stein, eds. *American Nursing: A Biographical Dictionary* (1992); Hawkins, Joellen. "Naomi Deutsch." In *Dictionary of American Nursing Biography*, edited by M. Kaufman (1988); Howes, D., ed. *American Women, 1935–1940: A Composite Biographical Dictionary*. Vol. I (1941); Mayer, Susan L. "The Jewish Experience in Nursing in America: 1881 to 1955." Ed.D. diss., Teachers College, Columbia University (1996).

SUSAN MAYER

DIAMOND, SELMA (1921–1985)

"I do not discuss my age, height, weight, or other vital statistics. Other than that, shoot. I tolerate any kind of nonsense up until six o'clock. After that, I just want to be admired." In typical Selma Diamond fashion, the witty, wisecracking (with a voice she once described as sounding like Brillo), longtime comedy writer/actor held her own when warding off nosy interviewers. Best known as the crotchety, chainsaw-voiced bailiff Selma Hacker on television's *Night Court* from 1984 to 1985, Diamond embodied in her writing and her comedy routines the quintessential cynical, jaded character. Penning skits and jokes for some of the early greats of radio and television, she became one of the most famous and accomplished female comedy writers of her time.

Born in London, Ontario, in 1921 to a tailor and his wife, Diamond moved at a young age to Brooklyn, New York. After graduating from New York University, she started to write radio routines for Rudy Vallee and Jimmy Durante. She traced her ambition and talent to her grandmother, who had been a suffragette. Diamond, both hailed and criticized for her dry wit and tenacity in a male-dominated field, was proud to claim lineage from a woman who had fought for equal rights among men.

Despite being greatly outnumbered by men early in her career, she became one of the most successful writers for television. She noted that she was often

It was her wit, her wise-guy attitude, and, of course, that voice (which she described as sounding like Brillo) that made Selma Diamond a successful show biz writer and performer long before she landed the role of Selma Hacker on TV's Night Court. *[New York Public Library]*

hired only to provide the "female angle," but she was soon respected as an equal talent in the heretofore "boys' club" of comedy writing. At first, she said that male writers were afraid to tell off-color jokes in her presence. This was only one of the many hurdles she had to jump in order to prove herself. And prove herself she did. As she once observed, "There's no such thing as a woman comedy writer. I'm hired—and I'm fired—as a writer."

One of the most frequently discussed issues of her life was her status as a single woman. Again and again, she was asked why she never married. Ironically, her very first published piece of comedy writing was the mock news item called "How He Proposed," for which she was paid five dollars. Later in her career, she based much of her comedy on her life as a single woman. "The only reason for getting married," she once wrote, "is to have someone get up in the middle of the night to get you a drink of water."

She did not consider her single status to be a drawback or a flaw. On the contrary, not having to play wife or homemaker was an asset. During her career, she wrote for Groucho Marx, Sid Caesar, and Perry Como. She was a regular on Jack Paar's television show, where her dry wit earned her a place as a Goodman Ace Writer and the respect of her male employers, who had once told her that she was not equipped for the hectic life-style of a television writer. She proved them wrong, as she did every other naysayer.

Despite her success, Diamond did not become a household name until her role on *Night Court*. Some of her lesser-known acting roles include the voice of Spencer Tracy's wife in the movie *It's a Mad Mad Mad Mad World* and small parts in *My Favorite Year* and *All of Me*. She also appeared on stage in *Come Blow Your Horn*, *Barefoot in the Park*, and the musical *Follies*. Her television appearances included *The Tonight Show* and a role in the sitcom *Too Close for Comfort*. Selma Diamond died in Los Angeles in May 13, 1985.

BIBLIOGRAPHY

Cue (September 5, 1953); *Newark Evening News*, August 28, 1963; Obituary. *NYTimes*, May 14, 1985; *Sunday News*, January 19, 1964,

DEBORAH SCHNEIDER

DINNERSTEIN, DOROTHY (1923–1992)

Ever since its publication, Dorothy Dinnerstein's *The Mermaid and the Minotaur: Sexual Arrangements and Human Malaise* (1976) has been recognized as one of the most important contributions to modern feminist thought. The book, translated into at least seven languages, is widely used in women's studies courses and is an influential text outside academia as well. Comparing Dinnerstein's book to Simone de Beauvoir's *The Second Sex*, one reviewer declared that this seminal essay not only belongs in "every feminist library" but in the "library of every well-educated person."

Dorothy Dinnerstein was born in New York City on April 4, 1923, and spent her childhood in a Jewish neighborhood in the Bronx. Within this social and cultural context, she came to view her political activities as integral to her Jewish identity, believing that Judaism and socialism were inseparable.

This was in part her parents' legacy. Both of her parents were politically progressive Jews: her mother's family came from Bialystok, Poland, and her father's family emigrated from Minsk, Russia. Celia Moed

Dinnerstein, her mother, was an administrative assistant at the Bronx Family Court. Her father, Nathan Dinnerstein, was an architectural engineer, but lost his business early in the Depression. He worked thereafter as a bookkeeper in his brother-in-law's junkyard; he died before the Depression was over. Dinnerstein was married to Walter Miller, a poet and professor at New York University, and they had a daughter, Naomi May, born in 1955. Dinnerstein also had two stepdaughters, Nina and June Leherman, from her second marriage to the ethnologist David Leherman.

After graduating from Brooklyn College in 1943, she began graduate studies at Swarthmore College under mentors Wolfgang Kohler, father of Gestalt psychology, and Max Wertheimer. She went on to complete her Ph.D. in psychology at the New School for Social Research as a student of Solomon Asch, a prominent social psychologist. Dinnerstein would later recruit Asch to be the first director of the Institute for Cognitive Studies, which she cofounded at Rutgers University in Newark, New Jersey. She taught and researched at Rutgers for thirty years before retiring as a distinguished professor emeritus.

According to Dinnerstein's *Mermaid*, the roots of patriarchy and misogyny lie in women's traditional monopoly over child rearing. Departing from earlier feminist thinkers who viewed asymmetrical patterns of parenting as a symptom of societal oppression of women, Dinnerstein was among the first to claim that women's role as primary caretakers causes fear and loathing of women and of things culturally inscribed as "female." Combining insights taken primarily from Freudian psychoanalysis and Gestalt psychology, Dinnerstein argued that the infant's ambivalent relationship with his or her mother, who is both a nurturer and a disciplinarian, is the source of sexual, social, and ecological pathologies that are the content of "human malaise." Humans are unable to live in harmony with themselves, each other, and their environment.

The symbols of the mermaid and the minotaur represent "the pernicious prevailing form of collaboration between the sexes," the tacit consent of both men and women to sustain gender arrangements within which "both man and woman will remain semi-human [and] monstrous." Dinnerstein's style is bold, disrupting the expected language of academic discourse and is, in fact, a diversion from the scope and style of her early work, which was within the scientific tradition of empirical psychology. Dinnerstein admittedly tried to enrage the reader because she believed that a radical revision of gender roles is both possible and imperative if we are to preserve the human species. Although she contended that a greater equality between men and women in child rearing might hold the solution to many of our emotional and social problems, Dinnerstein was well aware of the formidable resistance to changing traditional practices, since these patterns of child rearing still serve "defensive psychological functions."

Dinnerstein's involvement in feminist politics reflected her particular interest in ecology and nuclear disarmament. She was an active participant in the Seneca Women's Peace Camp, Women's Pentagon Action, Demeter's Daughters, and in other aspects of the feminist peace movement. Ecological concerns were also paramount in *Mermaid*. Dinnerstein maintained that the abuse of nature ("Mother Nature") by human beings is closely tied to gender inequality. In later publications, environmental issues occupied an increasing role.

Before her untimely death in a car accident on December 17, 1992, Dorothy Dinnerstein was engaged in a new project about environmental issues. Under the working title "Sentience and Survival," she was exploring the ways in which human cognitive structures interfere with our taking appropriate actions to prevent world destruction. This work reflected her deep commitment, as explored in her political activism, to examine the genocidal tendencies in the human species, including the destruction of the environment, and what she saw as the inevitability of nuclear holocaust.

SELECTED WORKS BY DOROTHY DINNERSTEIN

"Afterward: Toward the Mobilization of Eros." In *Face to Face: Essays for a Non-Sexist Future*, edited by M. Murray (1983); "AL and Structural Interaction: Alternate or Complimentary Concepts?" *Adaption-Level Theory* (1971); "Contextual Determination of Apparent Weight as Demonstrated by the Methods of Constant Stimuli," with F. Curcio and J. Chinsky. *Psychonormic Society* 5 (1966); "Figural After-effects in Kinesthesis," with W. Kohler. In *Miscellaneous Psychologic*, edited by Albert Michotte (1947); "Interaction of Simultaneous and Successive Stimulus Groupings in Determining Apparent Weight," with T. Gerstein and G. Michel. *Journal of Experimental Psychology* 73 (1967); "Intermanual Effects of Anchors on Zones of Maximal Sensitivity in Weight Discrimination." *American Journal of Psychology* 45 (1965); "The Little Mermaid and the Situation of the Girl." *Contemporary Psychoanalysis* (1967); *The Mermaid and the Minotaur: Sexual Arrangements and Human Malaise* (1976); "On the Development of Associations," with H. Egeth. In *Psychologische Beitrage*, edited by J. Ceraso (1962); "Previous and Concurrent Visual Experience as Determinants of Phenomenal Shape." *American Journal of Psychology* 78 (1965); "Some Determinants of Phenomenal Overlapping," with

M. Wertheimer. *American Journal of Psychology* 70, no. 1 (1957); "The 'Source' Dimension of Second-Hand Evidence." *Journal of Social Psychology* 45 (1957); "Techniques for the Diagnosis and Measurement of Intergroup Attitudes and Behavior," with J. Harding et al. *Psychology* (1948); "What Does Feminism Mean?" In *Rocking the Ship of State: Toward a Feminist Peace Politics*, edited by A. Harris and Y. King (1989).

BIBLIOGRAPHY

Alford, C. "Psychoanalysis and Social Theory: Sacrificing Psychoanalysis to Utopia?" *Psychoanalysis and Contemporary Thought* 13, no. 4 (1990): 483–507; Bart, P. "The Mermaid and the Minotaur, a Fishy Story That's Part Bull." *Contemporary Psychology* 22, no. 11 (1977): 834–835; Baruch, E., and L. Serrano. *Women Analyze Women: In France, England and the United States* (1988); Burack, C. *The Problem of the Passions: Feminism, Psychoanalysis, and Social Theory* (1994); Chodorow, N., and S. Contratto. "The Fantasy of the Perfect Mother." In *Rethinking the Family: Some Feminist Questions*, edited by B. Thorne (1982); Eisenstein, H. "The Cultural Meaning of Mothering: II. The Mermaid and the Megamachine." In *Contemporary Feminist Thought* (1983): 79–86; Gottleibe, R. "Mothering and the Reproduction of Power: Chodorow, Dinnerstein and Social Theory." *Socialist Review* 14, no. 5 (1984): 93–119; Haaken, J. "Freudian Theory Revisited: A Critique of Rich, Chodorow, and Dinnerstein." *Women's Studies Quarterly* 2, no. 4 (Winter 1983): 12–15; Hirsch, M. "Mothers and Daughters." *Signs* 7, no. 11 (1981): 200–222; "The Mermaid and the Memories." *The Women's Review of Books* X:7 (April 1993): 7–8; Raymond, J. "Female Friendship: Contra Chodorow and Dinnerstein." *Hypatia* 1, no. 2 (Fall 1986); Snitow, A. "Thinking About *The Mermaid and the Minotaur.*" *Feminist Studies* 4, no. 2 (June 1978): 192–198; Steele, R. "Paradigm Lost: Psychoanalysis After Freud." In *Points of View in the Modern History of Psychology*, edited by C. Buxton (1985).

ALYSON COLE

DR. RUTH *see* WESTHEIMER, RUTH

DOLARO, SELINA (1849–1889)

A woman of gusto and talent, Selina Simmons Belasco Dolaro was an exceptional performer and single mother in late nineteenth-century England and America. Through her income from singing, dancing, acting, and writing, she raised and supported four children.

She was born in England on August 20, 1849, to Benjamin and Julia (Lewis) Simmons. Her father was a violinist at one of the city's opera houses, and as a young girl Selina received music instruction from his masterful colleagues. Barely a teenager, she entered the Paris Conservatory to continue studying music. In 1865, just sixteen years old, she married an Italian Jew of Spanish descent named Isaac Dolaro Belasco in Upper Kennington, England. Isaac's ancestral family name was Miara D'Olivares, but the Spanish Inquisition forced his family to take refuge in the Italian town of Belasco. D'Olivares then became Italianized to Dolaro. Five years later, Selina adopted the stage name Dolaro and made her debut in London at the Lyceum Theater in an Offenbach opera. She went on to appear in several London operas, most notably in the title role of the first English version of *Carmen*, and produced Gilbert and Sullivan's *Trial by Jury* herself at London's famous Haymarket Theatre.

In 1879, Dolaro arrived in New York and made her American debut as Carmen at the Academy of Music. Reviews were mixed. "She's impersonating a Spanish gypsy, yet she looks neither Spanish nor Gypsy," remarked one critic in *New York World* in 1880. The same year, a reviewer in *New York Spirit of the Times* praised her as a "plump and pleasing prima donna" who was "much more at home" performing burlesque and comic opera.

Dolaro's sharp and witty presence followed her offstage. In 1883, the *New York Herald* printed a quintessentially Victorian opinion piece from a Reverend Philip Germond, in which he denounced "play-acting as a godless life." Dolaro, irritated by his narrow-minded characterization, responded, "Had I not been 'launched' on this 'godless life,' I should probably have been a burden to some parish or perhaps launched on what I regard as indeed a godless life." She concluded her letter inquiring, "Is it not enough that we must slave as we do to earn the means to educate and train our children so as to enable them to become useful members of society without being assailed even from the pulpit with such outrageous slander?" Fueled by her tenacity, evidenced in her charged defense of the acting profession, Dolaro's determination was as integral to her success as her talent.

In 1873, while still in England, Selina Dolaro divorced her husband on the grounds of adultery and desertion, and she alone raised her two sons and two daughters on the income from her professional engagements. In addition to acting and singing, she wrote two plays, *Justine* and *Fashion*, neither of which was a success, a novel, *Belle Demonia*, and a book of poetry, *Mes Amours*, based on love letters she had received. Dolaro did not appear to be involved in late nineteenth-century New York's flourishing world of Yiddish theater or other Jewish cultural spheres. After a bout with tuberculosis, which lasted several years, Dolaro died at her home in New York on January 3, 1889.

A favorite with nineteenth-century London and New York audiences, Selina Dolaro was a multitalented performer whose spirit and tenacity enabled her to succeed on stage and at the same time raise four children. [New York Public Library]

This indefatigable woman, much admired by the public, seemed to reach near icon status with her London and New York audiences. One American newspaper's notice of her death read, "Evidently of Hebrew descent, she had a youthful beauty, the cleverness, and versatility of her race. . . . Both here and in London she was recognized as a veritable Queen of Bohemia."

BIBLIOGRAPHY

JE; Music and Drama, March 17, 1883; and *New York Spirit of the Times*, February 28, 1880, and July 17, 1880, and January 26, 1889; Robinson Locke Scrapbook Collection, vol. 368. New York Public Library, Lincoln Center; *UJE*.

MICHELE SIEGEL

DOLOWITZ, FLORENCE
(1879–1983)

Florence Dolowitz was a founder and lifelong leader of the WOMEN'S AMERICAN ORT (Organization for Rehabilitation and Training). She was born in a small town in Lithuania sometime in 1879, the exact date unknown. She was a precocious student, and, to further her education, she was sent with a brother-in-law to live with a childless uncle and aunt in the United States. When the nine-year-old arrived in the country, her destination had been shifted to another uncle. After a few years, she moved to New York City to join her two older sisters who had also emigrated and were now living on Henry Street.

Florence continued her schooling while helping her sisters with their neckwear piecework in their home. As a teenager, she attended classes run by the Davidson Society at the Educational Alliance. Thomas Davidson was an ardent advocate of "breadwinners' colleges," where the participants were both students and teachers. In this idealistic atmosphere, Florence met and married Alexander Dolowitz, one of the "breadwinners" who taught mathematics. He became an accountant and grew increasingly concerned about discrimination against Jews in hiring and academic admission policies. His work in this area led to his participation on a committee that greeted the first World ORT delegation that came to the United States. Thus began the Dolowitzes' interest in ORT.

Upon graduating from Normal College (now HUNTER COLLEGE), Florence Dolowitz became a teacher. Her interest in Jewish matters led her to study at New York's Jewish Theological Seminary. She and her husband contacted people from their Davidson Society days in their efforts to establish an American ORT and a separate Women's American ORT.

The first organizing meeting of the Women's American ORT was held at the home of ANNA BOUDIN, a Davidson link. Dolowitz was instrumental in getting the fledgling organization started. ORT's mission was to provide "help through work," vocational and agricultural training for young people in institutional settings, in order to improve the economic structure of European Jewish communities. By June 1922, the American ORT was established, and by 1927, so was the Women's American ORT.

Dolowitz quickly assumed a leadership position and helped the Women's American ORT to receive national status. She was elected national president in 1932, serving until 1937. She also served as a board member of the World ORT Union, the American ORT Federation, and the Conference of Jewish

Women's Organizations. In 1974, she was elected honorary national president of the Women's American ORT. She held the post until her death on July 26, 1983, in Brooklyn.

BIBLIOGRAPHY

AJYB 85:414; Obituary. *NYTimes*, July 26, 1983; *WWIAJ* (1938).

MIRIAM DINERMAN

DRABKIN, STELLA (1906–1971)

In her 1938 self-portrait, Stella Drabkin depicts herself with extraordinarily large eyes, widened to take in the world. Some thirty years later, in a haiku to accompany the multitype *Birds of Prey*, she wrote, "The eye of the eagle sees what you do not . . . aware as the artist." The application of the artist's eye was the constant in Stella Drabkin's varied undertakings as painter, printmaker, mosaicist, and author.

Born (Stella) Molly Friedman to Carlaman and Francesca (Seandel) Friedman in New York City, she worked as a commercial artist before attending the National Academy of Design in New York for one year. She was married on May 1, 1926, to Dr. David L. Drabkin, later chair of the department of biochemistry, Graduate School of Medicine, University of Pennsylvania.

In the early 1930s, the Drabkins moved to Philadelphia, and Stella Drabkin became integrally involved in the art community of her adopted city. She studied at the Philadelphia Graphic Sketch Club with Earl Sorter, an illustrator known for fine etchings of cityscapes. Drabkin herself did a number of prints of street life of Philadelphia. For example, in *Bargain Sale I and II*, *Pushcarts I and II*, and *Free Day at the Zoo*, all from the 1930s series *Old Philadelphia*, she concentrated on depicting working-class, ethnic neighborhoods.

In 1933, shortly after Drabkin's arrival in Philadelphia, she entered a painting in the Gimbel Competition. It was her inaugural exhibition outside of New York, and she was the recipient of first prize. Among other awards won over the years were the American Color Print Society Prize (1944), the Katzman Prize of the Print Club of Philadelphia (1955), and the New Jersey State Museum Purchase Prize (1967).

In an interview given in 1945 to *Art Alliance Bulletin*, Drabkin professed to have begun painting at the age of two. She also recalled the great pride and plea-

sure she felt when, in the first grade, her teacher held up her drawing for the class to admire. In the same interview she reports having no favorite medium, stating that "an artist should work in various medi[a], depending on the ideas he intends to express."

Stella Drabkin's work, both in process and in product, reflects a serious lifelong commitment to her art. Her career was marked by experimentation and technical innovation, particularly with the multitype. Multitypes were described by Drabkin as a development of the monotype, produced by printing multiple impressions and superimposing them one over the other, resulting in a variety of color, texture, and luminosity. Her early multitypes were made from glass plates, but by 1950 Drabkin was using plastic plates, enabling her to run first states through the etching process. Additionally, plastic plates allowed the combination of intaglio and relief methods. In the multitype process, the prints could go through twenty or more states.

Drabkin also experimented with tesserae, creating a series of mosaic panels on biblical themes. These panels are owned by the Philadelphia Free Library and were on exhibit there for a number of years. Although the art community in Philadelphia that Drabkin belonged to had a large Jewish membership, specifically Jewish subject matter is reflected in only a small portion of her work. Drabkin's subject matter in the 1950s and 1960s included the biblical personages Enoch, Elijah, Joseph, Solomon, and David. Biblical women did not appear in this series. Drabkin also produced works titled *Cabalist* and *Cabalist Drawings*, though for the most part her work reflects the general subject interests common at the time: street life (1930s), self-portraits (1930s, 1940s), circus and mime (1950s), or nature, with haiku (1960s). Drabkin designed the 1966 UNICEF calendar. In 1969 Drabkin's book, *Prints with Poems*, was published.

Stella Drabkin died on August 11, 1971. The following year, in 1972, the Stella Drabkin Memorial Award Fund was established, administered by the Art Alliance, in her honor.

BIBLIOGRAPHY

Art Alliance Bulletin (March 1945); Collins, J.L. *Women Artists in America* (1973); Drabkin, Stella. Artist's file. New York Public Library, and Philadelphia Free Library, and Print Department, Philadelphia Museum of Art; Fielding, Mantle. *Dictionary of American Painters, Sculptors, and Engravers*. 2d ed. (1986); Petteys, Chris. *Dictionary of Women Artists* (1985); *Who Was Who in American Art* (1985); *WWWIA* 6.

BETH HABER

DRESSER, LOUISE (c. 1882–1965)

Louise Dresser was a celebrated singer in vaudeville and musical comedy, as well as a star in early motion pictures. She adopted the stage name of Louise Dresser after the songwriter Paul Dresser, an acquaintance of her father, encouraged her to use his name as a strategy for her to gain greater recognition on stage. This ruse, along with several of Paul Dresser's famous songs, indeed improved Dresser's drawing power in vaudeville, and she was often believed to be the sister both of Paul Dresser and novelist Theodore Dreiser (Paul Dresser's brother). Known largely for her rendition of Paul Dresser's song "My Gal Sal," she also sang his "On the Banks of the Wabash."

Born Louise Josephine Kerlin to Ida and William Kerlin, Dresser turned to the stage at age fifteen or sixteen after the death of her father, a railroad engineer. In 1898, she married composer and actor Jack Norworth, and they performed together in vaudeville, where she reportedly earned $1,750 a week. In vaudeville, Louise Dresser, like many other white women, used African-American children—known on stage as "pickaninnies"—as a chorus of eccentric singers and dancers. For this vaudeville act, she was billed as Louise Dresser and her Picks.

Although Dresser's vaudeville engagements with her "pickaninnies" were but a small part of her varied career, they are nevertheless quite significant in relation to the history of Jewish women on stage. The white women associated with "pickaninny" acts traditionally used some type of racial masquerade, such as heavy racial dialect in their songs or blackface makeup. This appropriation of blackness was particularly popular with Jewish actors, including such famous Jewish female performers as SOPHIE TUCKER. Historians have noted that this racial borrowing helped Jewish performers establish an American identity. These racial disguises dramatized the remaking of ethnic identity but also reinforced derogatory stereotypes of African Americans. In this light, Dresser's career reveals broader patterns of assimilation and exclusion in turn-of-the-century American culture.

After vaudeville, Louise Dresser found success on Broadway. She starred with De Wolf Hopper in *Matinee Idol* (1910–1912) and had roles in *Broadway to Paris* (1912), *Potash and Perlmutter* (1913), and *Hello Broadway!* (1914).

Following her divorce from Norworth in 1908, Dressler married actor Jack Gardner in 1910. This marriage lasted until Gardner died in 1950. Louise Dresser is perhaps best remembered for her roles in the many films in which she played the wife of Will Rogers, including *State Fair* (1933) and *David Harum*

She wasn't related to Paul Dresser, though she sang his songs, or married to Will Rogers, though she played his wife in many films. Louise Dresser, however, used this confusion to her advantage in a long career that extended from the "pickaninny" shows of vaudeville to Broadway to Hollywood. [Library of Congress]

(1934). Dresser and Rogers were so closely linked in the minds of their fans that many believed they were actually husband and wife. Dresser also played Al Jolson's mother in *Mammy* (1930) and had leading roles in *The Goose Woman* (1925) and *The Scarlet Empress* (1934). She retired from motion pictures in 1937, and although she planned a revival of her career following the death of her second husband, her comeback was not successful. Louise Dresser died in Woodland Hills, California, in 1965, following surgery for an intestinal obstruction.

BIBLIOGRAPHY

Bordman, Gerald. *Oxford Companion to American Theatre* (1984); *DAB* 7; Dresser, Louise. Daniel Blum Collection. Clipping files. State Historical Society of Wisconsin, Madison, Wis.; Ewen, David, ed. *American Popular Songs: From the Revolutionary War to the Present* (1966); Halliwell, Leslie. *Filmgoer's Companion.* 4th ed. (1974); Ireland, Norma Olin. *Index to Women of the World from Anient to Modern Times* (1970); Katz, Ephraim. *Film Encyclopedia* (1979); "Louise Dresser." *NYTimes,* April 25, 1965, 87:3; "Louise Dresser." *Variety,* April 28, 1965; Ragan, David. *Who's Who in Hollywood* (1992), and *Who's Who in Hollywood, 1900–1976* (1976); Samuels, Charles, and Louise Samuels. *Once Upon a Stage—The Merry World of Vaudeville* (1974); Schuster, Mel. *Motion Picture Performers: A Bibliography of Magazine and Periodical Articles, 1900–1969* (1971); Slide, Anthony. "Louise Dresser." *Encyclopedia of Vaudeville* (1994); Springer, John, and Jack Hamilton. *They Had Faces Then: Super Stars, Stars and Starlets of the 1930's* (1974); Truitt, Evelyn Mack. *Who Was Who on Screen.* 3rd ed. (1983); *WWWIA* 4, 7.

M. ALISON KIBLER

DREYFUS, SYLVIA GOULSTON (1893–1942)

Sylvia Goulston Dreyfus, born November 12, 1893, was a prominent community activist in Boston. She was president of the Hecht Neighborhood House, a community outreach center (modeled after Jane Addams's Hull House in Chicago) that helped many Boston Jews and still exists to this day. She also was a trustee of the New England Conservatory of Music, sat on the advisory board of the Berkshire Music Festival, and was honorary chair of the Palestine Orchestra fund, an orchestra that later became the Israeli Philharmonic.

She was a friend of the famed Russian-American conductor Serge Koussevitzky, who from 1936 conducted Tanglewood's renowned summer music concerts. Dreyfus wrote a reminiscence of their friendship called "Conversation with Koussevitzky." She was also an accomplished bas-relief sculptor.

Sylvia Gouston Dreyfus died at age forty-nine in Boston on September 14, 1942. Her son, Carl Dreyfus of Brookline, Massachusetts, is also active in local communal affairs.

BIBLIOGRAPHY

AJYB 45:384; Dreyfus, Carl. Conversation with author, September 6, 1995; Dreyfus, Sylvia Goulston. "Conversation with Koussevitzky"; Obituary. *NYTimes,* September 15, 1942: 23:2.

JACK NUSAN PORTER

DRISHA INSTITUTE FOR JEWISH EDUCATION

Drisha Institute for Jewish Education was founded in 1979 by Rabbi David Silber to provide women with the unprecedented opportunity to engage in the serious study of traditional Jewish texts. At the time, Silber was a lone pioneer in his promotion of serious women's learning, and years later, Drisha continues to hold a unique spot in the world of higher Jewish education for women.

Silber, ordained by Yeshiva University's Rabbi Isaac Elchanan Theological Seminary in 1975, confesses that "I didn't realize at the time that I was doing something revolutionary."

What started as a few part-time classes has blossomed into a school with approximately 450 women taking weekly courses, studying full-time, or attending periodic lectures. Some of the women are college students taking a single night course, others are professionals who free up an hour for a weekly "lunch and learn" session. High school students from across the country and abroad travel to New York to spend five weeks of the summer at Drisha, learning intensively all day. Yet, despite the expansion of Drisha's original handful of classes into an extensive array of courses at all levels of instruction, Rabbi Silber still focuses on his original initiative to provide strong learning for women.

Drisha Institute was founded in 1979 to provide women with the opportunity to engage in the serious study of Jewish texts. Its impact on Jewish life is worldwide. [Drisha Institute]

"This is not only a feminist issue," he says. "It is a community issue. The more thoughtful and knowledgeable men and women we have active in the Jewish community, making good ethical decisions and setting good goals, the better community we have."

In the years since Drisha began to offer women a place of their own to engage in the study of Jewish texts, other schools have emerged that offer women similar opportunities for study. However, all of these institutions clearly define themselves along Orthodox lines. Drisha, on the other hand, is nondenominational and has made it a priority to meet the differing needs of its students.

Reni Dickman, who spent time at Drisha while studying to be a Reform rabbi, says she never felt uncomfortable as a Reform Jew in what many would consider a traditional or even Orthodox setting. "Even though we all came from different backgrounds," she notes, "we didn't talk about it. We just studied Torah; nothing else mattered and we were unified in that goal."

Drisha also is distinguished from other institutions in its commitment to providing women with the skills they need to study even the most difficult classical Jewish texts independently. Although this is evident in most of Drisha's classes, it is most striking in its revolutionary Scholars Circle program. Women who complete this rigorous program, which is akin to a program of rabbinic ordination granted within the Orthodox community, receive a certificate of recognition for dedicating three years to the intensive and advanced study of Talmud and halakah (Jewish law). Graduates of the Scholars Circle have gone on to teach honors Talmud at Jewish high schools, traditionally the domain of male rabbis.

Until Drisha "there was never an opportunity for traditional women to gain knowledge of central rabbinic texts, much less enough knowledge to study independently and to teach," says Noa Jeselsohn, a member of the Scholars Circle's second graduating class. The skills Jeselsohn acquired at Drisha prepared her to teach Talmud at Pelech, an innovative religious girls' high school in Jerusalem.

"The women we get in our programs are exceptional, but they are all special cases," Rabbi Silber stresses. "The day-school movement is not producing girls with the necessary skills and attitudes who say, 'I want to learn and teach.' It is vitally important to have women and men who are knowledgeable and open-minded in positions of educational leadership throughout North America. It is my hope that the Jewish community will provide opportunities for women, give them a voice and a platform and the respect which will enable them to serve as leaders in the Jewish community."

Since its inception, Drisha has provided a unique learning environment that encourages seriousness of purpose, free inquiry, and respect for the texts of our tradition. Drisha's impact on Jewish life is worldwide, as community awareness of the importance of women's learning grows, and as Drisha faculty, students, and alumnae serve as scholars, teachers, and role models in a wide variety of Jewish settings throughout the world.

LESLIE LAUTIN

DROPKIN, CELIA (1887–1956)

The explicitly sexual imagery and themes of Celia Dropkin's poems redefined the ways modern Yiddish poetry could depict relationships between women and men. Beautifully crafted lyrics, Dropkin's poems undo the poetic conventions implicit in their very forms and, with their anger and passion, call into question societal assumptions about love. These poems open up a woman's psyche in a voice that sounds contemporary in the 1990s. Even her poems about depression, about mother love, and about nature are infused with erotic energy. Best known for her poetry, Dropkin also published short stories and was an accomplished visual artist.

Celia (Zipporah) Levine Dropkin was born in Bobruisk, White Russia, on December 5, 1887. Her father, Yoysef-Yona Levine, was a lumber merchant who died of tuberculosis when Celia was a young child. Her mother, Feige Levine, from a distinguished family named Golodets, raised and educated Celia and her younger sister, Sima.

Until the age of eight, Celia studied traditional Jewish subjects with a *rebbetzin* [rabbi's wife]. She also received a secular education from her mother, a woman with artistic sensibility, attending a Russian school in Bobruisk and, later, the high school (gymnasium) in the neighboring city of Novosybko. According to Reysen's *Leksikon*, upon graduating from high school, Celia taught school in Warsaw and tutored privately. She wrote poetry in Russian as early as age ten. When she was seventeen, she went to Kiev to continue her studies. There, in 1906, she met the famous Hebrew writer Uri Nissan Gnessin (1881–1913), who encouraged her to continue writing poetry. Celia formed a passionate friendship with Gnessin, but he prevented it from becoming a romance because he was infected with tuberculosis. Unbeknownst to Celia at the time, his translation into

First in Russian and then in Yiddish, Celia Dropkin wrote finely crafted,
erotically charged poetry that viewed in a new way the relations between the sexes.
[American Jewish Archives]

Hebrew of her poem "The Kiss" was included without credit to her in a posthumously published novel.

With Gnessin, Celia traveled to Warsaw, where she lived for several months. In January 1908, she returned to Bobruisk. There, in 1909, she married Samuel (Shmaye) Dropkin, a Bund activist, originally from Homel (Gomel), Belarus. In February 1910, soon after their first child was born, Shmaye's political involvement forced him to flee the czarist authorities in Russia for the United States. In 1912, Celia and their son joined him in New York.

In New York with her husband, Celia Dropkin bore five other children. One daughter, Tamara, died in 1924 or 1925, as an infant. Her surviving children were John (b. 1910), Esther (b. 1913), Lillian (b. 1917), Henry (b. 1921), and Eva (b. 1926).

Although she began to meet Yiddish writers in New York, Dropkin continued to write poetry in Russian. In 1917, she translated some of her poems into Yiddish, including "The Kiss," which Gnessin had translated into Hebrew. These translations, her first Yiddish publications, appeared in *Di Naye Velt* and *Inzikh* (1920). Throughout the 1920s and 1930s, Dropkin's poems appeared in these and other avant-garde publications of the Yiddish literary movements, the Yunge and the Introspectivists: *Onheyb*, *Poezye*, and

Shriftn. Her poems of sex, love, and death shocked and seduced her contemporaries, who acclaimed her as a leading woman poet. She also received encouragement from more established Yiddish writers, such as Avraham Liessin, the editor of *Tsukunft*, who published her short stories, as well as her poems.

Despite her acclaim, only one book of Dropkin's poems was published in her lifetime: *In Heysn Vint* [In the hot wind] appeared in 1935. After her husband died, in 1943, Dropkin wrote a biography of him, which was never published. In her last years, Dropkin painted in oils and water colors, and took art courses at the Art Students League in Manhattan, with Kunyoshi and Levi. The last poem Dropkin herself published, "A Whistle Calls from Somewhere," appeared in *Tsukunft* (April 1953).

Celia Dropkin died on August 17, 1956. Three years after her death, Dropkin's children sponsored the publication of a new and expanded edition of her poetry, short stories, and paintings, also titled *In Heysn Vint* (1959). This second book includes the poems of the 1935 edition, as well as previously unpublished poems. A friend, Sasha Dillon, selected the manuscript materials and reordered all the poems for this volume. (Although the poet H. Leivik is credited as well, he was too ill to do this work.) Much later, one poem for which there seems to be no written text, "Shvere Gedanken" [Black thoughts], was discovered on a tape recording that Celia Dropkin had made. The translation of this poem was published in *Yidishe Kultur* (1990).

SELECTED WORKS BY CELIA DROPKIN

"Adam," "The Circus Dancer," "The Filth of Your Suspicion," "Like Snow on the Alps." Translated by Grace Shulman. In *Penguin Book of Modern Yiddish Verse*, edited by Irving Howe, Ruth R. Wisse, and Khone Shmeruk (1987): 241–245; "Adam," "The Circus Lady," "My Hands," "A Terror Was Rising in My Heart." Translated by Ruth Whitman. In *An Anthology of Modern Yiddish Poetry*, edited by Ruth Whitman (1995): 29–35; "A Dancer." Translated by Shirley Kumove. In *Found Treasures: Stories by Yiddish Women Writers*, edited by Frieda Forman et al. (1994): 193–201; *Dans le vent chaud: Bilingue yiddish-français*. Introduction and translation into French by Gilles Rozier and Viviane Siman (1994); *In Heysn Vint* (1935. Revised and expanded 1959); "Poem" and "Poem." Translated by Adrienne Rich. In *A Treasury of Yiddish Poetry*, edited by Irving Howe and Eliezer Greenberg (1969): 168–169.

BIBLIOGRAPHY

Dillon, Sasha. "Vegn Tsilye Dropkin." In Celia Dropkin, *In Heysn Vint: Poems, Stories, and Pictures* (1959): 263–269; Hadda, Janet. "The Eyes Have It: Celia Dropkin's Love Poetry." In *Gender and Text in Modern Hebrew and Yiddish Literature*, edited by Naomi B. Sokoloff, Anna Lapidus Lerner, and Anita Norich (1992): 93–112; Hellerstein, Kathryn. "From Ikh to Zikh: A Journey from 'I' to 'Self' in Yiddish Poems by Women." In *Gender and Text in Modern Hebrew and Yiddish Literature*, edited by Naomi B. Sokoloff, Anne Lapidus Lerner, and Anita Norich (1992): 113–143; Howe, Irving, Ruth R. Wisse, and Khone Shmeruk, eds. *The Penguin Book of Modern Hebrew Verse* (1987); *Leksikon fun der Nayer Yidisher Literatur.* Vol. 2 (1958): 540–541; Reyzen, Zalmen, "Celia Dropkin." *Leksikon fun der Literatur Prese un Filologye* (1926); Yeshurin, Yafim, "Tsilye Dropkin: Bibliografye" [Celia Dropkin: Bibliography]. In Celia Dropkin, *In Heysn Vint: Poems, Stories, and Pictures* (1959): 271–273.

KATHRYN HELLERSTEIN

DUBNOW-ERLICH, SOPHIA
(1885–1986)

Although the Jewish academic community has typically cast her as either the daughter of the historian Simon Dubnow or the wife of the Bundist leader Henryk Erlich, Sophia Dubnow-Erlich was in fact a poet, political activist, critic, translator, and memoirist in her own right. Her literary corpus tells the remarkable story of one Eastern European Jewish woman's entry into two very disparate spheres of activity. Over a lifetime spanning 101 years (44 years spent in the

United States), Dubnow-Erlich engaged in Jewish socialist party politics, on the one hand, and Russian Silver Age poetry, on the other.

Born on March 9, 1885, in Mstislavl, Belarus, she was the eldest child of Simon and Ida (Friedlin) Dubnow. At age five, she and her parents, along with siblings Olga and Yakov, moved to Odessa. Her father began to instruct her according to John Stuart Mill's educational system until age fourteen, when she entered a gymnasium. Upon graduation in 1902, she studied at the Bestuzhev Higher Courses in St. Petersburg, a four-year degree program equivalent to that of the university, offered to women with parental permission and the annual tuition of fifty rubles.

Simultaneously, she began her foray into both the literary and political worlds in 1904, when her first poem, "Haman and His Demise," appeared in the Russian Jewish weekly *Budushchnost'* [Future]. Her satire of the czar's minister of interior, Plehve, was immediately confiscated by the censors, while her proud father wrote the Zionist leader Ahad Ha'am: "Our daughter is the hero of the day." That same year, university officials expelled her from her courses for participating in a student protest. Undeterred, she entered the history-philology department of St. Petersburg University in 1905 and later studied comparative religion and the history of world literature at the Sorbonne (1910–1911).

Meanwhile, her family had moved to Vilna, the hotbed of Jewish politics in the Russian Empire, where she became an active member of the Social Democratic Labor Party and the Jewish Labor Party, and an antimilitarist propagandist. As she explained in her 792-page Russian-language memoir, "The anxiety of our generation was destined to become intertwined with the anxiety of our era." She sealed that fate in 1911 by marrying Henryk Erlich (1883–1941), a prominent leader of the leftist Bund in Poland.

In deed and in printed word, the couple worked to promote the ideals of Jewish cultural autonomy and socialist internationalism. Dubnow-Erlich, for instance, wrote for various Bund journals, including *Nashe Slovo* [Our word] and *Evreiskie Vesti* [Jewish news], during World War I and the Russian Revolution. By 1918, the political situation drove the Dubnow-Erlich and her husband to relocate to Warsaw, where they remained for over twenty years with their sons, Alexander and Victor. When Warsaw fell to the Nazis in 1939, Henryk Erlich was arrested by Soviet authorities, and Dubnow-Erlich moved her family to Vilna, where they lived until 1941. When she reached the United States in 1942, she learned of her husband's death and her father's murder by the

Nazis. Dubnow-Erlich remained politically active in her new land as well, advocating for civil rights and protesting the Vietnam War.

Despite the early sensation over her poetic debut, Dubnow-Erlich's writing career soared well into her nineties. She contributed over fifty poems, essays, and translations to Russian and Yiddish-language journals and newspapers on her dual interests in the high arts and politics, as well as producing three volumes of symbolist poetry, several histories on topics relating to the Bund, and a biography of her father. A sampling of her writings sheds light on the experiences of women in general and mothers in particular.

Sophia Dubnow-Erlich died on May 4, 1986, in New York. Her fascinating life and extensive literary oeuvre of varied genre, which has not yet been translated into English (except for Simon Dubnow's biography), deserves the full attention of students of history and literature alike. The tapestry of her life is woven into the very fabric of Eastern European Jewish history of the twentieth century.

SELECTED WORKS BY
SOPHIA DUBNOW-ERLICH

Biografye un Shriftn. Leyvik Hodes (Bund leader in Vilna in Yiddish). Edited by Sofie Dubnov-Erlikh (1962); *Di Geshikhte fun 'Bund'* (collective history of the Bund in Yiddish). 5 vols. Edited with Jacob S. Hertz, Gregor Aronson, et al. (1960–1981); *Garber-bund un Bershter-bund Bletlekh fun der Yidisher Arbeyter-bavegung.* Translated from the Russian by Khaim Shmuel Kazdan and Leyvik Hodes (history of two intercity Bundist unions in Eastern Europe in Yiddish) (1937); *Khmurner-bukh* (on Josef Leszczynski and the Bund in Poland in Yiddish). Edited with Leon Oler [Ohler] (1958); *The Life and Work of S.M. Dubnov.* Translated by Judith Vowles. Edited by Jeffrey Shandler (1991; original in Russian, 1950); *Mat'* (poetry collection on motherhood in Russian) (1918; reprint 1969); *Osenniaia Svirel': Stikhi* (poetry collection in Russian) (1911); *Stikhi Raznykh Let* (poetry collection in Russian) (1973); *Khleb i Matsa* [Bread and matzoh] (1994).

BIBLIOGRAPHY

Aaronson, G. Ia. "Dubnov-Erlikh, Sofie (9 March 1885–)." *Leksikon fun der Nayer Yidisher Literatur* 1 (1958): 466–467; Dubnow-Erlich, Sophie. Archives. YIVO, NYC, and Professor Kristi Groberg, University of Minnesota, Duluth; *EJ* 6:844–845, s.v. "Ehrlich, Henryk"; Groberg, Kristi A. "Dubnov and Dubnova: Intellectual Rapport Between Father and Daughter." In *Simon Dubnov 50th Yortsayt Volume*, edited by Avraham Greenberg and Kristi Groberg (1994), and "Dubnova, Sofiia Semenovna." *Dictionary of Russian Women Writers* (1994), and "Sophie Dubnov-Erlich." In *European Immigrant Women in the United States: A Biographical Dictionary*, edited by J.B. Litoff (1994); Obituary. *NYTimes*, May 6, 1986.

CAROLE B. BALIN

At age fifteen Ariel Kaufman roller-skated to her civil wedding ceremony to William Durant at New York's City Hall. She is shown here, sixty-one years and a shelf of books behind her, receiving the Presidential Medal of Freedom from Gerald Ford. [Gerald R. Ford Library]

DURANT, ARIEL (1898–1981)

Ida Kaufman was a recalcitrant student, but after observing a Ferrer Modern School class meeting in Central Park, New York City, she immediately enrolled herself and promptly fell in love with her teacher, William Durant, thirteen years her senior. On October 31, 1913, at age fifteen, she roller-skated to her civil wedding ceremony at City Hall. Her new husband, a gentile, renamed her Ariel after the Shakespearean character.

Ariel Durant was born Chaya (her English name was Ida) Kaufman on May 10, 1898, in the Jewish ghetto of Proskurov, or Chmelnitski, in the West Ukraine, to Ethel Appel, the stylish and poetic daughter of a biblical scholar, and Joseph Kaufman, a struggling clothing salesman who subsequently immigrated to America in search of a better life for his family. With six children (Ariel was the fifth), her mother soon managed to reunite the family after a forced quarantine in England. In New York the family sold newspapers and moved constantly.

In *Will and Ariel Durant: A Dual Autobiography*, Ariel identifies with her mother's "full and intense personality" and describes her mother's plight with sympathetic poignancy. After the birth of a seventh child, Ariel's worn-out mother denied her husband any further intimacies, and later moved out to pursue her bohemian and socialist interests. She maintained her ties to her family, however. When Durant married, her mother's uncle objected so violently to Ariel's being given "to a Godforsaken Gentile" that frantic Ethel borrowed money to return to Proskurov so that the "good Moishe Lebe should [not] think ill of her," only to be interned in Russia because of the outbreak of World War I. Using their influence, the American consul in Odessa arranged for safe passage home in August 1915.

Like her mother, Ariel Durant rebelled against her domestic isolation, and biked to Boston, but eventually beckoned to her husband to retrieve her. Later, when left at home with daughter Ethel and adopted son Louis while Will traveled to lecture, teach, and write, she frequented the bohemian haunts of Greenwich Village, making "loans" to numerous aspiring artists.

Ariel Durant helped organize the material for the first five volumes of Will Durant's opus, *The Story of Civilization*, a multivolume concise popular summary of human history. She pleaded with him to do justice to the medieval Jews in *The Age of Faith* (vol. 4, 1950), so Will also included an insightful essay on the roots of anti-Semitism. Because of her numerous contributions, Will insisted they share authorship. She coauthored *The Age of Reason Begins* (vol. 7, 1961), *The Age of Louis XIV* (vol. 8, 1963), *The Age of Voltaire* (vol. 9, 1965), *Rousseau and Revolution* (vol. 10, 1967), and *The*

Age of Napoleon (vol. 11, 1975). They also coauthored *The Lessons of History* (1968), *Interpretations of Life* (1970), and *Will and Ariel Durant: A Dual Autobiography* (1977).

Even though some scholars criticized the Durants for inaccuracy, they received worldwide acclaim, including the Pulitzer Prize (1968, for *Rousseau and Revolution*), the Presidential Medal of Freedom, medallions from the French government, and the 1963 Huntington Hartford Foundation Award for Creative Writing. Ariel Durant received an honorary LL.D. from Long Island University, as well as several subsequent honorary doctorates. The *Los Angeles Times* awarded Durant the 1965 Woman of the Year Award in Literature. During her life, she met the intellectual, political, and popular leaders of the day, including Albert Einstein, Franklin D. Roosevelt, and Charlie Chaplin. Ariel Durant died in Los Angeles, California, on October 25, 1981, just two weeks before her husband.

BIBLIOGRAPHY

Almanac of Famous People. 5th ed. (1981); "Ariel Durant, Historian, Is Dead: Wrote 'The Story of Civilization.'" *NYTimes*, October 28, 1981, B4, D26; *Contemporary Authors. New Revision Series.* Vol. 4; Durant, William. "The Mind and Heart of the Jew, 500–1300." *The Age of Faith*, vol. 9 of *The Story of Civilization* (1950); Siefert, Susan E. "Ariel Durant." In *American Women Writers from Colonial Times to the Present: A Critical Reference Guide*, edited by Lina Mainieri (1979); *WWWIA* 8.

ROSIE ROSENZWEIG

E

EARP, JOSEPHINE SARAH MARCUS (1861–1944)

Impulsive, adventurous, and outspoken, Josephine Sarah Marcus Earp ran away from home when she was seventeen years old. Two years later, she joined destinies with western lawman, gambler, and entrepreneur Wyatt Earp. For forty-seven years, they roamed the West, mingling with well-known westerners on both sides of the law. Her name was rarely in print until her published memoir revealed an overlooked western folk heroine, long on daring, short on propriety, and, of all things, Jewish.

The third of four children, Josephine Sarah (Marcus) Earp was born in Brooklyn, New York, in 1861 to German-Jewish immigrants Sophie and Hyman (Henry) Marcus. When she was seven years old, the family moved to San Francisco. In 1879 the Pauline Markham Theater Company came to town, and Josephine slipped away with the troupe. In the Arizona Territory, she fell for Johnny Behan, a divorced, bankrupt politico. Her family retrieved her, but Johnny followed and convinced her gullible parents of his honorable intentions. In May 1880, she joined him in Tombstone, Arizona, but they did not marry.

Her gaze shifted to thirtyish, tall, handsome, and laconic Wyatt Earp, who, despite his common-law wife, stared back. Their romance blazed through the shoot-out at the O.K. Corral (the Earp brothers were key participants) and related trials and vendettas. After Tombstone, the couple lived in other western boomtowns, Nome, Los Angeles, and intermittently, San Francisco, at times with Josephine Earp's parents. In the 1920s, financially aided by her sister, Henrietta, the couple seesawed between mining and oil ventures in southern California, promoting a movie about Wyatt Earp's lawman exploits and writing his life story. The unpublished manuscript intrigued journalist Stuart Lake, who projected his own Wyatt Earp biography. After Wyatt Earp died in 1929, warfare exploded between Josephine Earp and Lake. Issues included his commercialized depiction of her husband and unflattering portrayal of her. *Wyatt Earp, Frontier Marshal*—deleterious passages stricken—came out in 1931 and fueled fifty years of Wyatt Earp mania, pro and con, in print and film.

Josephine Earp's contribution, *I Married Wyatt Earp*, written with Mabel Earp Cason and Cason's sister Vinola Earp Ackerman, and edited by western writer Glenn Boyer, was published in 1967. Boyer had fine-tuned her facts, and now other researchers are working on his facts. Notably, the cover photograph, a discreet cameo of young Josephine Earp, is in dispute. Boyer long maintained that Johnny Behan took the photo of her in Tombstone in 1880. Challengers say Boyer adapted it from a full-length, near-nude portrait of early twentieth-century vintage, copyrighted in 1914 and circulated by a novelty card company.

When her husband died, Earp buried his ashes in the Marcus family plot in the Little Hills of Eternity, near San Francisco. Josephine Sarah Marcus Earp died in 1944, and her remains now rest with his. But the collision of Jewish and cowboy cultures that epitomized their union goes on. Wyatt Earp enthusiasts have made the gravesite the most visited in that Jewish cemetery and once even stole the tombstone.

BIBLIOGRAPHY

Boyer, Glenn G. *Wyatt Earp: Facts Volume Two, Childhood and Youth of Wyatt's Wife, Josephine Sarah Marcus* (1996), and *Wyatt Earp's Tombstone Vendetta* (1993); Earp, Josephine Sarah Marcus. *I Married Wyatt Earp*, with Mabel Earp Cason and Vinola Earp Ackerman. Edited by Glenn G. Boyer (1967), and Papers. American Jewish Archives, Cincinnati, Ohio, and Stuart N. Lake Collection, The Huntington Library, Department of Manuscripts, San Marino, Calif.; Hutton, Paul Andrew. "Showdown at the Hollywood Corral: Wyatt Earp and the Movies." *Montana: The Magazine of Western History* 45 (Summer 1995): 2–31; Lake, Stuart N. *Wyatt Earp, Frontier Marshal* (1931); Marcus, Jacob R. *The American Jewish Woman: A Documentary History* (1981); Marks, Paula Mitchell. *And Die in the West: The Story of the O.K. Corral Gunfight* (1989); Morey, Jeffrey J. "The Curious Vendetta of Glenn G. Boyer." *National Association for Outlaw and Lawman History, Inc. Quarterly* 18, no. 4 (October–December 1994); Rochlin, Harriet, and Fred Rochlin. *Pioneer Jews: A New Life in the Far West* (1984); Tefertiller, Casey T. "Wyatt Earp: O.K. or Not O.K." *Image Magazine, San Francisco Examiner*, October 17, 1993; Tritten, Larry. "Looking for a Legend and Finding Wyatt Earp." *Washington Post*, June 20, 1993, E1, E8, E9; Waters, Frank. *The Earp Brothers of Tombstone* (1962).

HARRIET ROCHLIN

EASTERN EUROPEAN IMMIGRATION

Of all Jewish immigrants to the United States from 1886 to 1914, 44 percent were women, far more than for other immigrants groups arriving during the heyday of mass immigration. The more than two million Jews from the Russian Empire, Romania, and Austria-Hungary who entered the United States in the years 1881 to 1924—when the American government imposed a restrictive quota system—came to stay. Only 7 percent chose to return to Europe, as opposed to about 30 percent of all immigrants. Jewish immigrants intended to raise American families. Ashkenazi (European) Jewish culture and American values as conveyed by social reformers as well as by advertising, and the economic realities of urban capitalist America, all influenced the position of women in immigrant Jewish society in America. Jewish immigrant women shared many of the attributes of immigrant women in general, but also displayed ethnic characteristics.

Immigrant Jews, both female and male, arrived in America with considerable experience of urban life in a capitalist economy. Unlike many other migrants to America's shores, they had not been peasants in the old country. In the northwest section of Russia's Pale of Settlement, the western provinces to which Jews were restricted, they accounted for 58 percent of the total urban population. In the Pale as a whole, Jews constituted 38 percent of those living in cities or towns, though only 12 percent of the total population. Similarly, more than a third of the population in urban communities in Galicia were Jews, as were 20 percent in Romania's provincial capitals. Women worked alongside men, supporting their families primarily through petty commerce, selling all kinds of produce in the marketplace, and also through artisan trades such as shoemaking and tailoring. In the small number of traditional families where husbands devoted themselves to studying Torah, women bore the major responsibility as breadwinners for their families.

Settling primarily in the cities of the East Coast, in crowded, tenement-filled districts that were often called "ghettos," many Jewish immigrants worked in the burgeoning garment industry, in shops often owned by descendants of an earlier immigrant wave of Central European Jews. Others took advantage of their commercial background in the market towns and cities of Eastern Europe to become peddlers, hoping that their entrepreneurial skills would lead to prosperity. Although immigrant Jewish males arrived in the United States with less cash than the average immigrant, they inserted themselves into the economy largely as skilled workers and peddlers, while most newcomers began their working lives in America as unskilled laborers.

Even though the mass migration of Jews from Eastern Europe was a "family migration," the process of leaving the Old World for the New often temporarily disrupted families. Jews engaged in chain migration, in which one member of an extended family secured a place in the new country and then bought a ticket for siblings so that they could settle in America. Oftentimes, married men set out in advance to prepare the way economically and planned for their wives and children to join them once they were settled. Sometimes the delay in reuniting the family stretched into years, compelling women to raise their

Some energetic immigrant Jewish women contributed to the family economy by becoming entrepreneurs.
Faga Rasa ran a tobacco shop in Chicago. She is shown on the right, holding a child.
This photo was taken around 1898. [Chicago Jewish Archives]

children alone and to take on the full responsibility of arranging a transoceanic voyage. The outbreak of World War I, for example, left Rachel Burstein with her three children in the Ukrainian town of Kamen-Kashirski while her husband labored in America, having returned there from a prolonged visit with his family that began in 1913. Only after six and a half years of separation did Rachel and her children succeed in reaching Ellis Island, where they were quarantined for two weeks, before coming to their final destination of Chelsea, Massachusetts. Hershl, now Harry, Burstein made no effort to meet them at Ellis Island or at the train station in Boston. As their daughter, Lillian Burstein Gorenstein, then age twelve, wrote in her memoirs years later, "On both sides were lines of people waving. . . . No one waved to us" (169).

Once settled in America, women and men worked together to sustain their families. Because Jewish men were more successful than other immigrants in earning enough to support their households, albeit with the help of their teenage children, fewer married immigrant Jewish women worked outside the home than all other married American women, immigrant or native. Immigrant families could not survive, however, on the father's wages alone. Until they had children old enough to enter the labor market, women had to supplement their husbands' wages while caring for their households. They did so by working at home, taking in piecework and especially cooking and cleaning for boarders. In fact, more immigrant Jewish households had boarders than any other immigrant group. A 1911 governmental study found that in New

York City, for example, 56 percent of Russian Jewish households included boarders, as compared with 17 percent of Italian households. Other Jewish women assisted their husbands in "mom and pop" stores—grocery stores, candy stores, cigar stores—which were generally located close to the family's living quarters. Mothers ran back and forth between their customers in the store and the food cooking in their ovens, balancing their conflicting responsibilities. In most official documents, these women appear simply as housewives, but their labor was crucial to the family economy.

Almost all the women worked, of course, but their work patterns depended on their domestic obligations. Married women had full responsibility for managing the household, and the obligations of mothers were particularly heavy. Indeed, women and men alike assumed that wives would quickly develop skill in stretching their husband's wages; their role as baleboostehs [efficient housewives]—shopping, cooking, and cleaning—complemented their husbands' role as breadwinners.

Some energetic immigrant Jewish women contributed to the family economy by becoming entrepreneurs. Female pushcart peddlers were a familiar sight in immigrant neighborhoods. As the sociologist Louis Wirth wrote in his 1928 book *The Ghetto*, "In accordance with the tradition of the Pale, where the women conducted the stores . . . women are among the most successful merchants of Maxwell Street [in Chicago]. They almost monopolize the fish, herring and poultry stalls" (236). Other women provided the initiative for their families' economic success. One immigrant woman in New York City, for example, put her skills at bargaining and cooking to work in running a restaurant, whose profits were invested in real estate. In the early 1890s, Sarah Reznikoff, mother of the writer Charles Reznikoff, persuaded a garment manufacturer to give her the opportunity to show what fine ladies' wrappers (loose dresses) she could sew at home. She soon persuaded him to hire as her partner her cousin Nathan, who later became her husband. Sarah made the decisions about hiring and firing workers. She convinced Nathan to become a foreman, in charge of eighty-six machines. When her husband's fortunes failed years later, when their children were in school, she learned how to make hats and established a successful millinery business into which she brought her husband and brother. That business sustained the family while the children were growing up. Although she clearly had more business sense than her husband, she was content to recede into the background once she had laid the foundation for a family

enterprise. No such reluctance to take center stage characterized Anna Levin, who immigrated to Columbus, Ohio, in 1914. She began by selling fish in a garage. Within a decade, her store, which now also sold poultry, fruits, and vegetables, was so successful that her husband gave up his carpentry work to join her in the business.

Yet, varied household responsibilities filled most women's daily routines, even those women involved in business. With fewer grandmothers and aunts available than was the case in the home country, and with mandated public education that kept older children at school, child care was burdensome. Keeping a crowded tenement flat clean and orderly in a grimy industrial city required much scrubbing. Laundry for the family had to be managed in cramped indoor conditions in cold-water flats. Limited family budgets forced housewives to spend hours circulating among stores and pushcarts looking for the best bargain. Literature written by the children of immigrant women praised their self-sacrifice as well as their capacity to cope with economic hardships, sometimes sentimentalizing the mothers in the process of acknowledging the difficulties of their lives. The critic Alfred Kazin typifies this view of the immigrant Jewish mother:

> The kitchen gave a special character to our lives: my mother's character. All my memories of that kitchen are dominated by the nearness of my mother sitting all day long at her sewing machine. . . . Year by year, as I began to take in her fantastic capacity for labor and her anxious zeal, I realized it was ourselves she kept stitched together. (66–67)

Many autobiographies and oral history interviews as well as fictional accounts have also commented on the central role played by mothers in the emotional life of the family.

Before marriage, most adolescent girls and young women worked to contribute to their families' support. Like their fathers and brothers, they found jobs in the garment industries, especially the ladies' garment trades. Because the wage scale and division of labor were determined by gender, immigrant daughters earned less than their brothers. Working full-time in garment shops, they earned no more than 60 percent of the average male wage. They worked in crowded and unsanitary conditions in both small workshops and larger factories. Their hopes for improving their economic circumstances lay in making an advantageous match, while their working brothers aspired to save enough to become petty entrepreneurs. Moreover, immigrant sons occupied a privileged place in the labor market in comparison with their sisters. In New York in 1905, for example, 47 percent of immigrant Jewish daughters were employed as semiskilled and unskilled laborers; only 22 percent of their brothers fell into those ranks. Conversely, more than 45 percent of immigrant sons held white-collar positions, while less than 27 percent of their sisters did. The roles and expectations of daughters within the family also differed substantially from those of their brothers. Even when they were working in the shops and contributing to the family's income, girls were also expected to help their mothers with domestic chores.

The gendered expectations regarding work and the lower salaries that women earned made mothers particularly vulnerable when no male breadwinner could be counted upon. Women were more likely to be poor than were men. Widows with small children and few kin in America found it impossible to earn enough to feed and house their children. Wife desertion, sometimes referred to as the poor man's divorce, became more frequent than in Europe. The *Jewish Daily Forward*, the most popular American Yiddish newspaper, printed the pictures of deserting husbands in a regular feature called the "Gallery of Missing Husbands." The separation of families in the migration process and the poverty of immigrant workers spurred husbands to abandon their families. The personal and cultural divide between husbands and wives who had immigrated to America at different times occasionally became too wide to bridge.

Jewish philanthropic associations in the early 1900s spent about 15 percent of their budgets assisting the families of deserted wives, and still more on the families of widows. Jewish communal leaders responded to these social problems not only through direct provision of charity, but also by establishing the National Desertion Bureau to locate recalcitrant husbands and orphanages to house poor children. No more than 10 percent of residents of orphanages in the immigrant period were actually orphaned of both parents; rather their surviving parent was unable to care for them. The case of the family of ROSE SCHNEIDERMAN, the labor leader, was typical. After the death of her tailor husband from the flu, Rose's pregnant mother was compelled temporarily to place her two sons, and briefly Rose, in New York's Hebrew Orphan Asylum while she cared for her newborn infant.

Despite the differential they experienced in wages and social mobility because they were female, young immigrant women reveled in the freedom that wage-earning work conferred. As one proudly declared years later in an interview, "The best part was when I

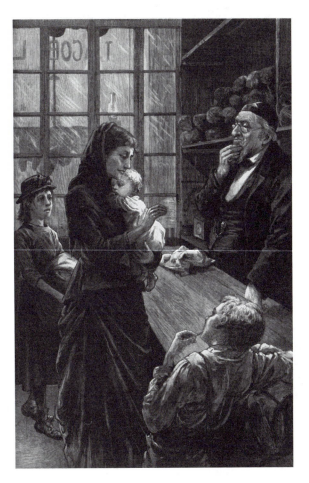

Wife desertion, sometimes referred to as the poor man's divorce, became more frequent in the United States than in Europe, often leaving women destitute. This linecut from Frank Leslie's Illustrated Newspaper *(February 9, 1889) is captioned "Pawning the Wedding Ring." [Peter H. Schweitzer]*

got a job for myself and was able to stand on my own feet" (Krause 296). Although immigrant daughters were expected to hand over most of their wages to their parents, and to accept this obligation to their families, they also developed a sense of autonomy, as they decided what small portion of their wages to keep back for their own needs. Like other urban working-class girls, they took advantage of the leisure-time activities that the city made available: dance halls, movies, amusement parks, cafes, and theater. Their sense of autonomy, reinforced by their participation in the labor force, extended to courtship and marriage. The custom of chaperonage disappeared in America, perhaps because the parents of young immigrants often remained behind in Europe, and young immigrant men and women considered it their right to choose their own spouses.

The years spent at work between the end of formal schooling and marriage contributed to the Americanization, and particularly the politicization, of immigrant daughters. Young Jewish women preferred to work in larger factories, where they came in contact with a more varied work force than in smaller shops and where they experienced a female community of their peers. Most importantly, they participated in the labor movement that became a powerful force within immigrant Jewish communities. In fact, their activity helped to shape the nascent Jewish labor movement, as young women activists, demonstrating in picket lines, repeatedly confronted the authorities.

Young immigrant women and immigrant daughters were reared with the sense that the world of politics was not reserved for men alone. Although the public religious sphere of the Jewish community had been closed to women in Eastern Europe, they participated in the public secular sphere of economic and political life. Radical socialist movements like the Bund were not as egalitarian as their rhetoric suggested, but they did recruit women as members. Unlike the women of some ethnic groups who were closely supervised by their men folk, immigrant Jewish women attended lectures and political meetings alone and often discussed the issues of the day. Gentile observers commented that Jewish working women were not concerned simply with their own tasks or skills. With confidence in their right to act politically, they demonstrated a great interest in labor conditions in general and in the left-wing political movements that addressed working-class problems. The immigrant Jewish community, particularly through the Yiddish press, validated their political involvement, providing support for female-led kosher meat boycotts and rent strikes as well as for woman suffrage.

Although the male Jewish leaders in the nascent garment industry unions, the INTERNATIONAL LADIES GARMENT WORKERS UNION and the Amalgamated Clothing Workers, did not accept women as their peers and discriminated against those who sought leadership roles, women in fact galvanized the Jewish labor movement. In the years immediately before World War I, the union movement achieved the stability that had eluded it until then, largely due to women worker militance. The UPRISING OF THE 20,000, the massive 1909 strike of women in the ladies' garment trade, initiated a period of successful labor activism among Jewish workers. Women took their place on the picket lines and suffered arrest along with their male colleagues. Female activists such as Rose Schneiderman, PAULINE NEWMAN, FANNIA COHN, and CLARA LEMLICH SHAVELSON, along with

others, devoted themselves to the cause of improving the economic conditions and the status of workers. They helped to introduce concern for workers' education and recreation into the American labor movement. Jewish women probably contributed more than a quarter of the total increase in female members of all labor unions in the United States in the 1910s.

The political interest and sophistication of young immigrant Jewish working women continued even when they quit the garment workshops upon marriage. Within immigrant Jewish communities, older women with families engaged in political activity on the local level. From the 1890s through the 1930s, they spoke out and demonstrated on issues that directly affected their roles as domestic managers. When Margaret Sanger opened a birth control clinic in the heavily immigrant Jewish neighborhood of Brownsville, Brooklyn, Jewish housewives thronged to it, even though dispensing birth control information was then illegal. They organized boycotts in response to rising meat prices and conducted rent strikes to protest evictions and poor building maintenance. When New York state held elections on female suffrage in 1915 and 1917, they canvassed their neighbors, going from house to house to persuade male voters of their moral claim to enfranchisement. Because they had fewer institutional affiliations than men, women often have been omitted from scholarly examination of the Jewish community. Yet women found in their neighborhoods, in the streets and stoops where they spent their days, a sense of community that nourished their political activity.

Although immigrant Jews kept their children in school longer than other ethnic groups, they invested more heavily in the education of their sons than their daughters. *McClure Magazine*'s 1903 story of Bessie, a department store girl with a brother in City College of New York, was not atypical. This family strategy made sense when women's labor force participation was tied so closely to their marital status. But it also frustrated the dreams of many immigrant girls who had defined the freedom of America as the opportunity of studying as long as they liked.

As immigrant Jewish families prospered, they kept children of both sexes in school. The youngest in the family usually had the best chance of getting an education, irrespective of gender. MARY ANTIN, a precociously successful immigrant who wrote her autobiography at age thirty, recognized her privileged experience in comparison with her older sister's. As she noted in *The Promised Land*, "I was led to the schoolroom, with its sunshine and its singing and the teacher's cheery smile; while she was led to the workshop, with its foul air, care-lined faces, and the foreman's stern command" (199). Even for the children of the most successful immigrants, however, social mobility was gendered. Sons went to college to become doctors or lawyers, while daughters attended normal school to become teachers. Of course, most immigrant sons did not even graduate from high school in the years before World War I; they became businessmen. Most immigrant daughters entered the world of white-collar work as saleswomen or commercial employees. They became schoolteachers in large numbers only in the interwar years, and only in a city like New York that allowed married women to keep on teaching. When they married, they became housewives, although the Depression compelled many to find employment, at least temporarily.

Because traditional Jewish culture valued education, and because their need to go to work thwarted their aspirations for attending high school and perhaps college, many immigrant Jewish women chose to supplement their meager formal education by taking advantage of free public evening classes and lectures organized by settlement houses, unions, and Yiddish cultural organizations. They saw in education the key to the freedom that America symbolized. As one woman who arrived in America as an adolescent in 1906 reminisced in her old age, "I told my parents, 'I want to go to America. I want to learn, I want to see a life, and I want to go to school'" (Kramer and Masur 8). Sociological studies conducted both before World War I and in the 1920s documented the disproportionately large numbers of immigrant Jewish women in evening courses. In Philadelphia in 1925, for example, 70 percent of night school students were Jewish women. Many immigrant Jewish women, therefore, had the opportunity to acquire the secular education of which they had been deprived by a combination of economic conditions and governmental discrimination in their countries of origin. But many found that the straitened economic circumstances of their lives prevented them from achieving their dream. As one woman who arrived in America as an adolescent before World War I reflected years later, "I always wanted education. I never got it" (Weinberg 167).

Women had even fewer opportunities for Jewish education. The traditional exemption of women from formal Jewish study continued in the American immigrant community. Although only a quarter of immigrant Jewish children received any Jewish education, the situation of girls was particularly bleak. A 1904 study found that on the Lower East Side, there were 8,616 male students in traditional Jewish supplementary schools, but only 361 girls. In 1917, the situation

had improved; one-third of the students enrolled in Jewish schools in New York City were female. But they received a more meager education than their brothers, often limited to Sunday school. A handful of girls did receive excellent Jewish education as well as training to be Hebrew teachers, as educational reformers like Samson Benderly found that they could introduce innovations more easily in schools for girls than in schools for boys. Only as Jewish communal leaders became aware that the Jewishness of the children of the immigrants could not be taken for granted, however, did they focus on the education of girls. Since middle-class Americans considered women to be more sensitive to religion than men and expected mothers to teach moral values to their children, Jews soon realized that the Jewish education of girls was critical to the transmission of Jewish identity to the younger generation.

The public space of the immigrant synagogue, as was the case in Eastern Europe, was reserved largely for men. We still know little about the religious practice of immigrant women in America. Women's religious expression seems to have remained domestic. As so much Jewish observance is home-centered, immigrant housewives were responsible for the Jewish ambience of the entire household. Even in families whose traditional observance had lapsed, women prepared a special family dinner for Friday evening and made sure that appropriate foods were available on Jewish festivals.

Despite their political activity and secular knowledge, immigrant Jewish women were generally perceived by social reformers, both gentile and Jewish, to be obstacles to the successful Americanization of their families. Since they typically spent their days in their own households, they were presumed to be transmitters of Old World values. Recently, historians have revealed a far more complex role for women in the adaptation of immigrant Jews to American conditions.

Immigrants took the first steps toward becoming American when they put on ready-made American clothes. Working in garment factories and therefore familiar with the latest fashions, which changed more dramatically in ladies' than in men's wear, young women were often the first to outfit themselves in American styles and influenced the entire household's clothing purchases. But dressing well did not mean spending a fortune. Jewish women became adept shoppers and learned how to put together a fancy outfit at little expense. As immigrants experienced upward social mobility, a wife's clothing and jewelry signified the family's success. Women purchased more than the family's clothing. As domestic managers, they did most of the household shopping. As new consumer items became available and their husbands achieved economic success, Jewish women had numerous opportunities to select American merchandise, ranging from Uneeda Biscuits to parlor furniture, all widely advertised. Mass marketers used the Yiddish press to target Jewish housewives as consumers, perhaps aware of Jewish men's relative economic success compared to other immigrant workers. Because of their long experience with the marketplace in Eastern Europe, and the cultural value of shrewd bargaining as a marker of the successful *baleboosteh*, immigrant Jewish women apparently became effective consumers. They introduced large numbers of American products into their homes, making them more American in the process.

American Jewish social reformers, the middle-class and highly acculturated descendants of earlier waves of immigration, recognized the potential of immigrant women as agents of assimilation, but felt that they needed to be directed to exert appropriate influence on their families. The social reformers impressed on immigrant mothers the values of cleanliness, social order, and class deference in order to turn them into good Americans. The eagerness with which Jewish social reformers embraced this task resulted from their realization that gentile Americans were unlikely to distinguish between different types of Jews. The new immigrants were so numerous and visible in their Yiddish-speaking ghettos, so conspicuous in their radical politics, that they threatened to displace the prosperous, respectable German Jewish banker or merchant as the representative Jew in the popular imagination. In short, they worried that immigrant foreignness would provoke anti-Semitism. For American Jewish social reformers, teaching appropriate gender roles to the immigrants from Eastern Europe involved curtailing what reformers considered the "deviant" behavior of immigrant women by making them Americans on the middle-class model.

Social reformers particularly feared disreputable behavior on the part of women as likely to contaminate the reputation of all Jews. This led Jewish women reformers to focus on the disturbing issue of Jewish prostitutes and, to a lesser extent, Jewish pimps. Although relatively few Jewish women were involved in prostitution, the fact that 17 percent of women arrested for prostitution in Manhattan between 1913 and 1930 were Jewish prompted serious concern. Furthermore, Jewish prostitutes and pimps were a stock-in-trade of purveyors of anti-Semitism. Similarly, reformers recognized the presence of unwed mothers among immigrants as a sign of family breakdown.

When the NATIONAL COUNCIL OF JEWISH WOMEN addressed these issues by stationing a dock worker at ports of entry to protect immigrant Jewish women and girls traveling alone from procurers, or by establishing the Lakeville Home for Unwed Mothers, they sought to ameliorate the situation of unfortunate women. Male-dominated Jewish organizations seemed to be motivated as much by concern for the prevention of anti-Semitism as by the victimization of Jewish women. For all Jewish social welfare providers, evidence of women's deviant behavior shook one of the foundation stones of the Jewish claim to moral superiority, the reputation of the Jewish family for unblemished purity.

Jewish social reformers shared the prejudices of their class. They sought not only to train women for their domestic roles as respectable wives and mothers. Because they were dealing with their social inferiors, they also aimed to teach their clients that workers should respect their "betters" in the middle class and that women should defer to men. The CLARA DE HIRSCH HOME FOR WORKING GIRLS, which was at the same time a boardinghouse and a vocational school, limited its training to marketable skills that were also of use to women as homemakers, such as hand and machine sewing, dressmaking, and millinery, even though it recognized that its working-class clientele would have to support themselves through wage labor and would benefit economically by learning diverse skills. The girls at the school resoundingly rejected the home's program in domestic service. Unlike the directors of the institution, they did not presume that their class status was fixed; they thought America promised middle-class comfort to all who worked hard. They also shared a Jewish disdain for domestic service, which was culturally devalued by Jewish migrants from both Central and Eastern Europe. The Hebrew Orphan Asylum went even further than the Clara de Hirsch Home. The asylum supervised discharged adolescent girls and discouraged them from seeking employment, such as working as waitresses or salesgirls in department stores, that might lead to immorality. Although the Educational Alliance, the largest Jewish settlement house in New York City, could not control its clientele as did the residential facilities, it devised programs to inculcate appropriately American behavior in youth. The alliance provided different recreational programs for boys and girls. Boys were encouraged to join competitive athletic teams whose success in meets with other settlement houses might refute the stereotype of Jewish males as weak and cowardly. A similar program did not exist for girls. Instead, they were taught housekeeping and cooking so that they might, in the words of the institution's 1902 annual report, "cultivate a taste for those domestic virtues that tend to make a home-life happier and brighter" (Educational Alliance 21).

Immigrant Jewish writers of Yiddish-language advice manuals also appear to have recognized the influence of wives and mothers on the members of their families. Their books addressed a primarily female audience and focused on issues assumed to fall within women's domain, such as child rearing, fashion, table manners, and birth control. As Chaim Malitz noted in his 1918 book entitled *Di Heym un di Froy* [The home and the woman], "Take away the mother from the home, and there remains no home" (41). Ironically, male purveyors of advice literature singled women out for attention, because they felt women had not yet succeeded in their task as agents of Americanization. Yet the authors acknowledged that women were the family members most likely to introduce middle-class standards of behavior and taste into their homes. Women could transform their husbands and children into Americans.

Oral history interviews and memoirs suggest that immigrant women, in fact, used their domestic position to mediate between home life and the public world of school, work, and recreation. Daughters, in particular, have commented upon how their mothers supported their aspirations and desires for independence and education. Women's fiction, too, often depicts immigrant mothers as wielding their influence, not always successfully, to mitigate a father's rigid religious traditionalism that would deny their daughters freedom to choose a spouse or to go off to study. Some historians and cultural critics lament what they perceive as a transfer of power within the immigrant Jewish household from the father to the mother, but they share with those who write positively about the immigrant mother a recognition of her centrality in her home.

Women who immigrated to America from Eastern Europe discovered their lives stamped by the economic, social, and cultural impact of their migration. Although the cultural tradition the immigrants brought with them permitted women more autonomy than was the case among other immigrant groups, economic circumstances constricted Jewish women living on the Lower East Side. Moreover, Americans' understanding of success in America limited women's aspirations. Americans assumed that if a married woman engaged in paid work, she was not appropriately feminine, and her husband was a failure. This meant that volunteer social work became the main

outlet for the creative energies of Eastern European immigrant Jewish women who enjoyed the luxury of leisure time and sought meaningful work. These Eastern European immigrant women followed a similar path of an earlier generation of women who founded Jewish women's organizations like HADASSAH and the National Council of Jewish Women. Eastern European immigrant women also set up a host of local organizations, ranging from day nurseries to maternity hospitals to old-age homes. Hopes that immigrant women had harbored for themselves were often transferred to the younger generation. As Sarah Reznikoff concluded in her memoir, "We are a lost generation. . . . It is for our children to do what they can" (99).

BIBLIOGRAPHY

PRIMARY SOURCES

Antin, Mary. *The Promised Land* (1912. Reprint, 1969); Educational Alliance. *Annual Report of 1902*; Gorenstein, Lillian. "A Memoir of the Great War, 1914–1924 (In Memory of my beloved brother, Morris)." *YIVO Annual* 20 (1991): 125–183; Kramer, Sydelle, and Jenny Masur, eds. *Jewish Grandmothers* (1976); Marcus, Jacob Rader, ed. *The American Jewish Woman: A Documentary History* (1981); Reznikoff, Sarah. "Early History of a Seamstress." In *Family Chronicle*, edited by Charles Reznikoff (1963); Schneiderman, Rose, with Lucy Goldthwaite. *All for One* (1967).

SECONDARY SOURCES—BOOKS

Baum, Charlotte, Paula Hyman, and Sonya Michel. *The Jewish Woman in America* (1976); Bristow, Edward. *Prostitution and Prejudice: The Jewish Fight Against White Slavery, 1870–1939* (1983); Ewen, Elizabeth. *Immigrant Women in the Land of Dollars: Life and Culture on the Lower East Side, 1890–1925* (1985); Friedman, Reena Sigman. *These Are Our Children: Jewish Orphanages in the United States, 1880–1925* (1994); Glanz, Rudolf. *The Jewish Woman in America: Two Female Immigrant Generations, 1820–1929.* Vol. 1, *The Eastern European Jewish Woman* (1976); Glenn, Susan A. *Daughters of the Shtetl: Life and Labor in the Immigrant Generation* (1990); Heinze, Andrew. *Adapting to Abundance: Jewish Immigrants, Mass Consumption and the Search for American Identity* (1990); Hyman, Paula E. *Gender and Assimilation in Modern Jewish History: The Role and Representation of Women* (1995); Joselit, Jenna Weissman. *The Wonders of America* (1995); Kazin, Alfred. *A Walker in the City* (1951); Kessner, Thomas. *The Golden Door: Italian and Jewish Immigrant Mobility in New York City, 1880–1915* (1977); Orleck, Annelise. *Common Sense and a Little Fire* (1995); Raphael, Marc Lee. *Jews and Judaism in a Midwestern Community: Columbus, Ohio, 1840–1975* (1979); Smith, Judith E. *Family Connections: A History of Italian and Jewish Immigrant Lives in Providence, Rhode Island, 1900–1940* (1985); Weinberg, Sydney Stahl. *The World of Our Mothers* (1988).

SECONDARY SOURCES—ARTICLES

Hyman, Paula E. "Gender and the Immigrant Jewish Experience in the United States." In *Jewish Women in Historical Experience*, edited by Judith R. Baskin (1991), and "Immigrant Women and Consumer Protest: The New York Kosher Meat Boycott of 1902." *American Jewish History* 70, no. 1 (1980): 91–105; Kessler-Harris, Alice. "Organizing the Unorganizable: Three Jewish Women and Their Union." In *Class, Sex, and the Woman Worker*, edited by Milton Cantor and Bruce Laurie (1977); Krause, Corinne Azen. "Urbanization Without Breakdown: Italian, Jewish, and Slavic Immigrant Women in Pittsburgh." *Journal of Urban History* 4, no. 3 (1978): 291–306; Kuznets, Simon. "Immigration of Russian Jews to the U.S.: Background and Structure." *Perspectives in American History* 9 (1975): 35–124; Sinkoff, Nancy B. "Educating for 'Proper' Jewish Womanhood: A Case Study in Domesticity and Vocational Training, 1897–1926." *American Jewish History* 77, no. 4 (1988), 572–599.

PAULA E. HYMAN

EBIN, S. DEBORAH (1888–1974)

S. Deborah Ebin was a national community and Zionist leader who devoted her life to the advancement of Jewish education and Zionist ideals. A dynamic orator, fund-raiser, and world traveler, she was fluent in several languages and versed in the Talmud, making her a formidable figure in American Jewish life.

She was born in 1888 in Syracuse, New York, to Polish-born rabbi Aaron M. and Pearl (Drob) Ashinsky. Rabbi Ashinsky was a founder of the Mizrachi movement in the United States and Canada. She was the eldest of five daughters and two sons. She spent her early years in Detroit, Michigan, and Montreal, Canada, where her education included the study of French and Latin. At the turn of the century, the family settled in Pittsburgh, where she attended Madam De Wolfe's Academy and was privately tutored in Hebrew and Talmudic studies—not a common practice for Jewish women at the time. In later years, Ebin's memorable speeches often included Talmudic references.

In 1907, she married the Russian-born rabbi Nachman Ebin. The young couple lived in Scranton, Pennsylvania, and Cleveland, where Deborah Ebin cofounded the Cleveland chapter of HADASSAH with HENRIETTA SZOLD. The Ebins also lived in Buffalo and eventually settled permanently in Brooklyn. They had one daughter, Freda, and two sons, David and Judah.

Rabbi Ebin was a prominent rabbinic and Zionist leader involved in Jewish education and Zionist causes. After his death in 1943, Deborah Ebin was

Deborah Ebin cofounded the Cleveland chapter of HADASSAH *with* HENRIETTA SZOLD. *In 1943 she became American Mizrachi Women's (*AMIT*) chair of National Youth Aliyah, the agency responsible for the largest mass migration of Jewish children to Palestine during and after the war. [Jeanette K. Schechter]*

approached by Rabbi Meire (Berlin) Bar-Ilan (after whom Bar-Ilan University was named) to become involved with the women's Mizrachi movement in the United States. Ebin agreed to follow in her father's footsteps, becoming the chairman of a child restoration project sponsored by American Mizrachi Women. The project was aimed at helping European Jewish children to immigrate to Israel during and following World War II. Ebin coined the phrase "child restoration" to describe the physical and spiritual rehabilitation of young refugees from Hitler's Europe. She worked closely with Kfar Batya, a children's village founded by BESSIE GOTSFELD in Ranaana, Israel, and universally recognized for its work with Jewish youths.

In 1943 Ebin became American Mizrachi Women's chair of National Youth Aliyah, the agency responsible for the largest mass migration of Jewish children during and after World War II. Ebin embarked on an extensive schedule of speaking engagements and activities throughout the United States and other countries. She visited Israel and Europe, including child detention centers in Cyprus. She also organized Mizrachi Women chapters in the Netherlands and Mexico.

Ebin represented the women's Zionist movement at many international meetings, including the World Zionist Congress and the World Youth Aliyah Conferences of 1939 and 1951. As national president of American Mizrachi Women from 1954 to 1956, she met with U.S. Government leaders, including President Harry S. Truman, to whom she presented the organization's America-Israel Friendship Award in Kansas City in 1955.

She remained active in Jewish causes until her death on September 23, 1974, in New York City.

BIBLIOGRAPHY

AYJB 76:513; Chaleff, Joanne, and Dina Dyckman, and Herzl Eisenstadt, and Ruth Jacobson. Conversations with author, September 1996; Golub, Mollie F. "AMW Expands to Meet the Ingathering of the Exiles." *American Mizrachi Woman* (September–October 1975); Swiss, Irwin A., and H. Norman Shoop. *Rabbi Aaron M. Ashinsky: Fifty Years Study and Service* (1935); *NYTimes*, May 28, 1943; Obituary. *NYTimes*, September 25, 1974, 42:4, *WWIAJ*.

JEANETTE K. SCHECHTER

EDELMAN, LILY (1915–1981)

A preeminent authority on adult education and multiculturalism, Lily Edelman spent her life encouraging others to read and think about people of different cultures and faiths. Through her writings, the reviews and anthologies she edited, and the adult education courses she taught and planned, she challenged individuals to examine both their own religious faith and society. Drawing upon her own heritage, she wrote a popular children's book, *The Sukkah and the Big Wind* (1956) about the Jewish holiday of Sukkoth, and *Israel: New People in an Old Land* (1958) was based on her many trips to Israel.

Lily Judith (Pokvidz) Edelman was born on September 2, 1915, in San Francisco, California, to Morris and Rachel (Margolis) Podvidz. She married Nathan Edelman on May 30, 1936, and had one child, Jean Louise, who is now deceased. She received a B.A. in 1936 from HUNTER COLLEGE, where she was elected to Phi Beta Kappa. In 1938 she received an M.A. from Columbia University, and in 1954, she earned a diploma in adult education from Columbia University Teachers College.

Edelman's multicultural educational writings, *Mexican Mural Painters and Their Influence in the United States* (1938) and *Music in China and Japan: Classroom*

Material (1940), published by the Service Bureau for Intercultural Education, led to a position as the education director of the East & West Association (1941–1950), an organization founded by novelist Pearl S. Buck. In addition, she wrote *The People of India: Who They Are, How They Live, What They Like, What They Are Thinking* (1943). Edelman worked as a freelance writer and editor for the U.S. State Department in the Overseas Information Program, New York City (1950–1952), and for the United Synagogue of America, now called the United Synagogue of Conservative Judaism (1954–1957). She was also the executive secretary of the National Academy for Adult Jewish Studies, New York City (1953–1957). During the 1950s, she published several cultural history books for young people, including *Japan in Story and Pictures* (1953) and *Hawaii, U.S.A.* (1954). In 1957 she joined the staff of B'nai B'rith in Washington, D.C., and held a series of positions that joined her interest in adult education with her interest in writing and editing: She was editorial associate, director of adult education, national program director, and director of the lecture bureau for B'nai B'rith, as well as editor of the Anti-Defamation League bulletin *Face to Face* and *Jewish Heritage*. She served as book editor of the *B'nai B'rith National Jewish Monthly*. She also edited the book *Face to Face: A Primer in Dialogue* and *Jewish Heritage Reader* and she coedited the Jewish Heritage Classics series. Edelman joined with Goldie Adler in 1967 to compile an anthology of the writings of Rabbi Morris Adler, *May I Have a Word With You?*, and compiled *Questions for Modern Jews: Pros and Cons on Current Issues* with Edward E. Grusd. In 1970 she worked with Elie Wiesel to translate from the French *A Beggar in Jerusalem* and *One Generation After*. She was an active member of B'nai B'rith Women, the Adult Education Association, the Maryland Association of Adult Education, the National Council on Adult Jewish Education, the Jewish Book Council, and Phi Beta Kappa.

Lily Edelman, a dynamic and much-sought-after lecturer, committed her life to learning, to teaching, and to understanding multicultural society. She died in New York City on January 22, 1981.

SELECTED WORKS BY LILY EDELMAN

A Beggar in Jerusalem, translated from French with Elie Wiesel (1970); *Face to Face: A Primer in Dialogue*, editor (1967); *Hawaii, U.S.A.* (1954); *Israel: New People in an Old Land* (1958. Rev. ed. 1969); *Japan in Story and Pictures* (1953); *Jewish Heritage Reader*, editor (1965); *May I Have a Word with You?*, with Goldie Adler (1967); *Mexican Mural Painters and Their Influence in the United States* (1938); *Music in China and Japan: Classroom Material* (1940); *One Generation After*, translated from French with Elie Wiesel (1970);

The People of India: Who They Are, How They Live, What They Like, What They Are Thinking (1943); *Questions for Modern Jews: Pros and Cons on Current Issues*, with Edward E. Grusd (n.d.); *The Sukkah and the Big Wind* (1956).

BIBLIOGRAPHY

AJYB 83:353; *Contemporary Authors.* Vols. 61–64 (1976), and Vol. 102 (1981); Obituary. *NYTimes,* January 27, 1981, B19; *Something About the Author: Facts and Pictures About Authors and Illustrators of Books for Young People.* Vol. 22 (1981); Tuchman, Maurice S. Interview by author, July 29, 1996; Ward, Martha E., et al. *Authors of Books for Young People.* 2d ed. (1971), and *Authors of Books for Young People.* 3d ed. (1990); *Who's Who in World Jewry* (1981): 178.

HELENE L. TUCHMAN

EDINGER, TILLY (1897–1967)

Tilly Edinger made her mark as one of the leading vertebrate paleontologists of the twentieth century. Her pioneering work in paleoneurology, the study of fossil brains, established her international reputation as the outstanding woman in her field.

Born on November 13, 1897, in Frankfurt-am-Main, Germany, Tilly Edinger was the youngest of three children of a wealthy Jewish family. Her father, Ludwig Edinger, was a well-known medical researcher and the founding director of the Frankfurt Neurological Institute. Her mother, Anna (Goldschmid) Edinger, was a prominent social activist and feminist. Her brother, Fritz, was killed during the Holocaust; her sister, Dr. Dora Lipschitz (Lindley), immigrated to the United States.

After studying at the Universities of Heidelberg and Munich, Tilly Edinger received her doctorate in natural philosophy from the University of Frankfurt in 1921, having written a dissertation on the skull and cranium of a fossil reptile. Her father objected to women pursuing a professional career, and her mother regarded fossil research as merely a hobby. Nevertheless, she continued working as an unpaid research assistant in the university's institute for paleontology until 1927, when she became curator of fossil vertebrates at the Senckenberg Museum. She also served as a part-time assistant in the Frankfurt Neurological Institute after her father's death, but she was happy to resign, rather than be fired, in 1933, since she greatly preferred studying the comparative brain anatomy of fossils to analyzing human brains.

After the Nazis came to power in 1933, Edinger encountered increasing difficulties because she was Jewish. She was able to continue curating for five more years, but her nameplate was removed from her office door, and she often had to use a side entrance. In 1938, the museum dismissed her, and she left for England in May 1939. While waiting for her American visa, she needed to earn money to support herself and translated German medical papers into English.

In recognition of her important scientific publications, the Museum of Comparative Zoology of Harvard University offered her a research position. She arrived in the United States in 1940 and became an American citizen in 1945. At Harvard, she continued her groundbreaking research on fossil brains, publishing a major book on the evolution of the horse brain and many controversial articles, as well as comprehensive bibliographies of her field. Her work proved the necessity of studying the brain's evolution based on fossil evidence, rather than by comparing modern species. She received a Guggenheim Fellowship (1943–1944) and an American Association of University Women Fellowship (1950–1951). She was also president of the Society of Vertebrate Paleontology (1963–1964).

Edinger taught zoology for a year at Wellesley College, which also bestowed upon her an honorary degree, as did the University of Giessen (1957) and the University of Frankfurt (1964). But most of her career was devoted to research. She was described as feisty, strong-willed, and opinionated, but also warm-hearted. Due to a severe hearing impairment, she experienced increasing difficulty communicating with colleagues and students, and often engaged in extended monologues. However, even after her retirement in 1964, she continued her writing and worked in an advisory capacity.

Tilly Edinger always retained a sense of loyalty to her native town of Frankfurt-am-Main, but toward the end of her life she considered Boston her true home. She died on May 26, 1967, at age sixty-nine, a day after having been hit by a Harvard-owned truck in Cambridge.

SELECTED WORKS BY TILLY EDINGER

Bibliography of Fossil Vertebrates, Exclusive of North America, 1509–1927, with A.S. Romer, N.E. Wright, and R.V. Frank. 2 vols. (1962); *The Evolution of the Horse Brain* (1948); *Die Fossilen Gehirne* [Fossil brains] (1929); *Paleoneurology, 1804–1966: An Annotated Bibliography* (1975).

BIBLIOGRAPHY

Aldrich, Michele L. "Women of Geology." In *Women of Science,* edited by G. Kass-Simon and Patricia Farnes (1990); *American Men of Science* (1944): 501; Backhaus-Lautenschläger, Christine. *Und standen ihre Frau: Das Schicksal deutschsprachiger Emigrantinnen in den USA nach 1933*

(1991); Edinger, Tilly. Archives. Tilly Edinger Collection (AR-1267/4182 and 551/1479), Leo Baeck Institute, NYC, and Museum of Comparative Zoology Library, Harvard University, Cambridge, Mass; *EJ*; Hofer, H. "In Memoriam Tilly Edinger." *Gegenbaurs Morphologisches Jahrbuch* 113, no. 2 (1969): 303–313; *International Biographical Dictionary of Central European Emigres.* Vol. 2, part 1 (1980): 236; Kaznelson, Siegmund, ed. *Juden im Deutschen Kulturbereich* (1959): 423; *Lexikon der Frau.* Vol. 1: 872; *NAW* modern; Obituary. *NYTimes*, May 29, 1967, 25:2; Patterson, Bryan. Foreword to *Paleoneurology*, by Tilly Edigner (1975); Romer, A.S. "Tilly Edinger, 1897–1967." *News Bulletin, Society of Vertebrate Paleontology* (October 1967): 51–53; Rossiter, Margaret W. *Women Scientists in America: Before Affirmative Action, 1940–1972* (1995); Tobien, H. "Tilly Edinger." *Palaontologische Zeitschrift* 42 (1968).

HARRIET PASS FREIDENREICH

EDUCATION *see*
COLLEGE STUDENTS; HIGHER EDUCATION ADMINISTRATION; JEWISH EDUCATION; TEACHING PROFESSION; VOCATIONAL TRAINING SCHOOLS; WORKING WOMEN'S EDUCATION

EDUCATION OF JEWISH GIRLS IN AMERICA

The secular and religious education of Jewish girls in America has very modest roots. Initially perceived as seamlessly bound together, over the course of nearly three and a half centuries, the general and Jewish education of Jewish girls took separate paths, crossed, and on occasion entered into conflict with each other. Secular education of Jewish girls has consistently expanded, but the path of Jewish education has been inconsistent.

EARLY HISTORY

The first Jewish settlers to North America in the seventeenth century, Sephardim from the Caribbean, provided rudimentary instruction to their own children, usually in the home, occasionally employing tutors. In the late eighteenth century, education began to move out of the home, and the children of now-established Jews, boys and girls, went to dame schools (a combination child care and primary school run by women, often in their homes) and private schools (a few linked to synagogues) where they received a general education.

Boys were tutored in Jewish subjects in preparation for bar mitzvah by religious leaders in towns with established synagogues, such as New York, Newport, Philadelphia, and Charleston. Girls, except if a parent elected to provide tutoring, received virtually no formal instruction in Jewish subjects. A girl's Jewish knowledge was to be acquired by listening, observing, and modeling her own religious beliefs and practices on those of her mother.

When large-scale Jewish emigration from German lands was under way in the 1820s, 1830s, and 1840s, the battle over primary school for girls was being fought and won in most settled parts of the United States. At the end of the American Revolution, few schools admitted girls. By the middle of the nineteenth century, almost as many girls as boys attended elementary (common) schools, and by the 1870s the achieved educational level of girls had surpassed that of boys.

Rapidly rising elementary school enrollments in the decades surrounding the turn of the nineteenth century were largely fueled by the growth in female school attendance. It was argued that to carry out their adult roles as mothers and homemakers, girls needed a strong basic education, especially so they could educate their own children.

Coeducational, graded classes taught by women were rapidly becoming the norm by the 1840s. The perceived special female talent for teaching young children, coupled with women's willingness to work for wages much lower than those of men, led to the entry of women into teaching. Common school education enabled them to do so. By the middle of the nineteenth century in the northeast United States, over half of all teachers were women, a proportion that would grow to about 70 percent nationwide by century's end. The substantial demand for teachers generated by the great common school movement in the first half of the nineteenth century set in motion a dynamic that was sustained well into the twentieth century: the need to educate more women, and to higher academic levels, to meet the nation's demand for teachers.

The wide-scale acceptance of coeducation and the feminization of teaching went hand in hand. And the feminization of teaching and enhanced educational opportunities for girls and women were also intimately related. There was a close relationship between and among growing school enrollments of girls, increased demand for women teachers, and the rise in secondary education for girls at the female seminaries created by Emma Willard, Mary Lyons, Harriet Beecher, and others in the 1820s and 1830s.

Women used the education they acquired, even if modest, to transform themselves into educators. This process became a recurrent theme in the story of the education of American women, Jews and gentiles. Teaching became among the very first occupations open to women. It would prove to be of great advantage to women's education that they were gender stereotyped into an occupation that required academic preparation. Each time American society sought to broaden the education of its children or raise the quality of teaching and learning, it had to enhance the education of women, who came to dominate classroom teaching. And these higher levels of education could be used beyond the confines of school to enlarge and respond to opportunities in other fields as they opened to women.

American Jewish women were very much part of the same dynamic landscape. Unlike Catholics who largely rejected the Protestant-controlled common schools as anathema to their religious beliefs, most Jews accepted the common school ideal. Jewish girls benefited from the expansion in educational opportunities for all girls in the American common school. More equivocal, however, was the Protestant character of common schooling. If secular schooling was to take place in a Christian-influenced environment, supplementary Jewish education was needed to counter Christian influences.

There was a long history of supplementary Jewish schooling in the colonial and federal periods to draw upon, but such schools served boys almost exclusively. If girls received no Jewish instruction, their formal religious training and informal models would be increasingly pan-Protestant—based on Bible readings from the Old and New Testaments, and Protestant prayers and hymns led by Protestant women teachers who served as their religious role models. The Jewish community could no longer rely exclusively on a mimetic process for girls to learn their female Jewish roles: Imitation could as readily lead to assimilation and conversion as to retention and knowledgeable Jewish participation.

The urban, immigrant poor were of intense interest to Protestant Christian missionaries, many of whom were women staunchly committed to the evangelical religious movements of the age. In the 1830s in Philadelphia, such missionaries turned their attention to poor Jewish immigrants. The ecumenical Christianity, moral instruction, and literacy training of the common school classroom could be brought by missionaries directly to the children of Jewish neighborhoods, boys and girls believed to be dwelling in ignorance and darkness. Christian missionaries offered poor Jewish mothers charity (food and clothing) and in return offered to educate their children in Sunday schools. Philadelphia, home of the American Sunday School Union (1825), was a city well prepared to give these children a limited basic education linked to Protestant religious and moral instruction. Philadelphia's Jewish community had to respond.

Led by REBECCA GRATZ, a group of Philadelphia women rose to the dual challenge: the need to counter missionary efforts among Jews and the need for a Jewish education to supplement the general (and Christian-influenced) education received by most Jewish children. These Jewishly committed women were themselves poorly schooled in Jewish subjects but were imbued with the American vision of "women" as pious, spiritual, and possessing a gift for teaching the young. With years of public charitable activity behind them as members of the Female Hebrew Benevolent Society, they were prepared publicly to defend Jewish interests by founding a Sunday school in 1838 based upon the model of the Protestant Sunday school.

The Hebrew Sunday school offered perhaps the first opportunity for American Jewish women to teach Jewish subjects. Lacking teaching materials, they adopted the Protestant Sunday School Union catechism as the basis of their religious and moral instruction, blotting out overtly Christian passages. They used the King James Bible because English was the language of teachers and students and there was no alternative Jewish translation.

The Hebrew Sunday school enrolled boys and girls, American-born and immigrant. Through this very model of an American institution, Americanized Jewish women responded to the Protestant challenge to their Jewish community. By providing formal Jewish teaching to girls, they implicitly acknowledged that the mimetic process was insufficient for educating girls Jewishly. The Hebrew Sunday school embraced the American practice of coeducation and placed women teachers at the head of the class. Since many of the Sunday school's pupils went to other schools during the week, it reinforced the supplementary nature of Jewish education and legitimized the separate study of secular and religious subjects. It framed Judaism as an American religion that was compatible with, and complementary to, the American day school.

The Sunday school curriculum presented Judaism as a religion with a catechism to master, Bible stories to mine for moral lessons, and religious practices compatible with American life. This Jewish education, taught in English, was worlds apart from European concepts of Jewish studies tied to Talmud and Torah, taught by men and generally reserved for males.

The Sunday school, which spread rapidly to Richmond, Charleston, Savannah, and other Jewish communities, circumvented traditional halakic practices regarding the status and roles of women in Judaism. Women served as teachers and as defenders of the Jewish community in the face of forces promoting assimilation of the young into American Protestant society. The teachers of the Hebrew Sunday school explicitly used the school to recruit new young women into Jewish school teaching. As was already the case in the American common school, the education of girls led to women becoming educators in Jewish schools.

JEWISH EDUCATION IN NEW YORK CITY

In New York City in the 1840s and 1850s, the course of Jewish education, for boys as well as girls, was tied to the relationship between the city's Jews and its public schools. German Jewish immigration in this period made New York City America's largest Jewish community. The new arrivals found the city's schools divided by class and religious denominations. Parents with even modest means sent their children to private, usually church-related schools. Free public education, common throughout the rest of New York State and most of the northeast United States, was not provided in New York City until 1842. Free education was available at charity schools, especially those of the Public School Society, a philanthropy with an overtly Protestant character that was organized early in the century to offer instruction to the city's poor.

New York City's small public school system also had a decidedly Protestant cast: Readings from the New Testament, Protestant prayers, and primary readers with stories of a clearly Protestant nature offended Catholics as well as Jews. Many Jewish parents, especially among new immigrants, did not want to expose their children to Christianizing influences in either private or public school. The need of these parents to educate their children, coupled with the lack of viable alternatives, gave rise to pressures to found Jewish day schools. In 1842, B'nai Jeshurun, the city's first Ashkenazi synagogue (1824) organized a day school that existed for five years. Three German congregations, Ansche Chesed in 1845, followed immediately thereafter by Rodeph Shalom and Shaarey Hashamayim, founded day schools. These three schools, which briefly merged under the leadership of Max Lilienthal, were joined by four other congregational day schools in the early 1850s. By 1854, there were seven day schools enrolling over 850 students.

With the exception of B'nai Jeshurun, the day schools enrolled both boys and girls. Girls accounted for about one-third of enrollments, a proportion of Jewish school enrollments (day and supplementary) that, with a few percentage points of variation, has been relatively constant to the present time. These schools offered both secular and religious studies at the elementary school level. At that time, schools were divided into multiple-year classes (not year-by-year grades): one at the primary level and two at the grammar level. In general, boys and girls were placed in a coeducational primary class but were then assigned to sex-segregated grammar classes. Women taught the primary secular (English) subjects, and men taught all religious (Hebrew) subjects (primary and grammar) and secular grammar classes. While it would appear that boys and girls followed a common curriculum, there was gender differentiation: Girls received instruction in sewing and needlework and boys in cantillation of Torah and haftarah. The presumed adult roles of men and women within the Jewish community now seemed to permit, if not yet require, Jewish as well as general education for girls. But the presumed nature of adult participation, at least in the public religious realm, was still divided on gender lines and hence the differentiated studies.

The congregational day schools arose, in part, to provide an alternative to the Christian-influenced public schools and to offer secular instruction of higher quality than could be provided by means of the "monitorial" system, then employed by the free public schools. Monitorial schools were organized into huge classes of several hundred children, with limited instruction provided by student monitors under the direction of a single teacher. While learning was limited, it kept costs low and hence instruction could be provided free of charge. However, even parents with limited means elected to send their sons and daughters to private, usually church-affiliated, schools with smaller classes, and, in the case of Jewish parents who sent their children to congregational schools, the smaller classes were also free from overt Christian influences.

In addition to congregational schools, private Jewish day schools were founded in New York in the same period. Several were boarding schools that served Jewish families outside New York City. The first day school for girls was founded by the Palache sisters in 1840 and served boarders as well as day students. Max Lilienthal, after leaving Congregation Ansche Chesed, founded a school for boys (1849), which was taken over by the Rev. Mr. Henry in 1855 when Lilienthal moved to Cincinnati. In 1851, Adolph Loewe founded a boys' school, and sometime before 1860, Mrs. Bondy founded a school for Jewish girls. These schools, which charged higher fees than the congregational schools, tended to serve a wealthier community and were modeled on upper-class Protestant private schools in the city. Like the congregational schools, they included both general and Jewish instruction.

Jewish day schools, especially those sponsored by congregations, served a largely immigrant community, but they were not modeled on Jewish education in Europe. They reflected a Jewish Enlightenment concept of education in which Jewish children received instruction related to both the Jewish and contemporary secular worlds. These schools, however, were very much a product of the American educational environment. They recognized the need for the education of girls and placed children in coeducational classes in the early grades. They offered a secular curriculum, with English as the language of instruction. And they employed women as teachers.

CATECHISM

Much reliance was placed on catechisms in the study of religion. Acknowledging that few Jewish boys and fewer girls (given gender-differentiated curricula) would gain sufficient Jewish knowledge to study Talmud or Hebrew legal codes, the question-and-answer method of the catechism, popular in the American Sunday school, was adopted as a direct approach to teaching Jewish beliefs and moral values. Jewish catechisms had been published in Europe and brought to America in English translation in the early nineteenth century. The first American Jewish catechisms were written and published around 1840, hence available for adoption by day schools in the 1840s and 1850s.

CONFIRMATION

At mid-century, Lilienthal introduced a new practice to the American Jewish community: confirmation of boys and girls. The bar mitzvah was denied to girls, which undercut the incentive to educate girls Jewishly. Lilienthal's Shavuoth-linked confirmation ceremony, first held in 1846, was preceded by five months of twice-weekly classes for the participating twelve-year-old girls and boys. Criticized by more-Orthodox congregants, and suspended due to unrelated congregational politics, the confirmation was adopted by Temple Emanu-El in 1852 and resumed by Ansche Chesed in 1860. Although now held at a slightly older age, confirmation continues in many congregations, especially Reform, and was an early acknowledgment of the importance of Jewishly educated women.

CHANGES IN PUBLIC EDUCATION

Changes in New York State's education laws in 1851 and 1855, and changes in the nature of public education in New York City, addressed many of the concerns of Jewish parents. Local school boards were granted the powers to choose instructional materials, and reading from the Bible was made discretionary. The ward system of public education in the city meant that local concerns could be brought to bear on elected ward trustees. Overt Christian religious influences were considerably diluted, especially in wards with concentrations of Jewish families. In addition, in the 1850s the city's public schools did away with the monitorial system, and organized class sizes became closer to those in private schools: one teacher for each group of thirty to thirty-five children. The vibrant congregational day school sector of the 1840s and 1850s evaporated overnight. The seven congregational day schools that flourished in 1855 collapsed by 1856.

Jewish parents apparently were ready to accept the division of secular and religious instruction for their sons and daughters. Jewish parents rapidly abandoned congregational day schools in favor of free public schools, although the private boys' and girls' Jewish day schools continued to function and absorbed some of the students formerly enrolled in congregational schools. Most Jewish parents, it would appear, had been more concerned with shielding their children from Christian influences than with providing them with a Jewish education.

Most Jewish children in New York City, like those throughout the United States, now received their secular schooling in public schools. Jewish education, if received at all, was offered in supplementary schools or by private teachers who scheduled instruction after school hours. Jewish girls were especially affected. While continuing to receive a general education in the public schools, many, probably the majority, received little or no Jewish instruction. For those American Jews who embraced then-emerging Reform Judaism, the Reform Sunday school provided girls with a limited Jewish education but presumably an education considered adequate for their anticipated adult Jewish roles. But even Jewish girls who did attend Sunday school received the better part of their education in a secular setting, influenced by American ideas and values, gender role expectations, and concepts of religion and civic virtue as embodied by their American (generally women) teachers.

OLD TRADITIONS VERSUS
THE LURE OF AMERICANIZATION

For Orthodox Jews, especially newly arriving immigrants from Eastern Europe, efforts were made to adopt and adapt European educational models of

Jewish education. The first Talmud Torah was opened in New York City in 1857 and, by 1890, hundreds of heders had been established. A typical heder enrolled forty to fifty boys, often in wretched physical quarters, after public school hours to learn mechanical reading of Hebrew, siddur, Humash, and Mishnah.

As inadequate as the Jewish education was for boys, the state of Jewish education for girls was worse. Since there were no European models of Jewish schooling for girls, the education of Jewish girls was largely neglected. In Eastern Europe, the mimetic tradition, coupled in many cases with home tutoring, provided girls with the knowledge, skills, and affective attachments they needed to live as Jewish women. Jewishness was as much cultural as intellectual. Hence, for Eastern European Jews, the natural and informal process of cultural transmission carried along with it religious identity and beliefs, group attachment, lifeways, and gender-defined roles. Since Jewish women had few religious responsibilities outside the home and no obligation to study religious texts in Hebrew (although there was a considerable religious and later popular literature in Yiddish intended for a substantial female audience), little or no formal provision was made to educate girls. It was assumed that home and community in America would nurture the head and heart of Jewish girls as they had in the old world.

The opening of a Christian mission school in 1864 on New York's Lower East Side, home of many of New York's poorest immigrant Jews, spurred the Jewish community to action, as an earlier mission school had done in Philadelphia in 1838. Eleven established congregations met and organized the Hebrew Free School Association, which opened its first school in 1865, a day school teaching general and Jewish subjects. Many in the already established Jewish community opposed a day school, arguing that it segregated Jewish immigrant children and made it more difficult to assimilate them into American society. Additional free schools, all supplementary schools, were opened and the day school was closed in 1872. Attendance at a public school became a precondition for enrollment at a Hebrew free school.

The free schools were more popular with girls than boys. Poor immigrant parents, many Orthodox, preferred the traditional instruction of the heder for their sons to the free schools' lessons on morality, manners, vocationalism, and Americanization. However, lacking a European precedent for daughters, these same parents seemed more disposed to experiment with a new curriculum when it came to their daughters' educations.

The Hebrew Free School Society joined in 1889 with other Lower East Side agencies to form the Educational Alliance, the main vehicle for uptown, established Jews to help downtown immigrants. Ostensibly the alliance was to assume responsibility for the religious instruction it inherited from the free schools, whose enrollments had reached five thousand in 1899, its last year of operations. In practice, however, the alliance served primarily as a settlement house, with a focus on social, economic, and cultural assimilation, not religious education, and it paid little attention to the Jewish education of Lower East Side boys or girls.

As the great wave of new Jewish immigrants to America gathered force in the last decades of the nineteenth century, settled Jews became increasingly concerned with the poor Jews of the tenement districts. Out of a complex mix of self-interest and self-lessness, established Jews greatly expanded their missionary–social work efforts. Charity work among the Jewish poor became a major expression of one's religiosity and identity as a Jew, especially among Reform Jewish women of the upper classes. Their mixed motives yet strong commitment are captured in the record of the first Jewish Women's Congress held in Chicago in 1893: "And who are there to lend a helping, nay, a saving hand here? The women of America! The religiously enlightened matrons of our country, delivered from the oppressor's yoke, must dive into the depths of vice to spread culture and enlightenment among our semi-barbaric Russian immigrants, not insusceptible to the keen edge of the civilizer's art."

In New York City, MINNIE LOUIS, president of the sisterhood of Temple Emanu-El, led her colleagues downtown to make home visits to immigrant families. Out of these visits emerged the Visiting Trained Nurses (which, under LILLIAN WALD, became the Henry Street Settlement) and, in the early 1880s, the Down-Town Sabbath School, later the Louis Downtown Sabbath School. Initially it provided one-day-per-week Jewish religious instruction to girls of the Lower East Side, but it expanded to daily technical-vocational instruction for girls in 1887. Passing through several additional changes, it became the Hebrew Technical School for Girls in 1899. What started as a school to bring religious education to Jewish girls who otherwise had few such opportunities was transformed into a vocational program to serve what came to be considered the more pressing need to help female Jewish immigrants adapt to a modern, enlightened, but economically demanding America.

At the turn of the twentieth century, parents as well as the Jewish charitable community—Reform and

Orthodox—were ambivalent about and even neglectful of Jewish education for girls. On the other hand, there was strong commitment to secular education for Jewish girls. Established Jews, often in close collaboration with American public schools, directed the children of immigrants into the public schools. In addition, such factors as compulsory education laws, which usually required a school to offer a general education curriculum taught in English; lack of resources in the Eastern European Orthodox community to found an alternative Jewish school system that would simultaneously meet state education laws and the demands of Torah and Talmud; conflicting tendencies within the immigrant community (secular, religious, socialist, Yiddishist, Zionist, assimilationist, etc.); the legal requirement for educating girls as well as boys; the lack of appropriate European models; and the natural desire of the children of immigrants to want to become "Americans" resulted in an overwhelming proportion of Jewish children entering American public schools. By World War I, over 275,000 Jewish children in New York City attended public schools and fewer than 1,000 attended the city's three all-male yeshivahs.

Established Jews saw the public schools as their allies in efforts to transform immigrant children into model Americans. The established Jews set out to modernize these children and give them religious enlightenment, teach them the vocational skills needed for the contemporary economy, replace their Yiddish with English, rid them of "oriental" superstitions, beliefs, and lifeways, and through all these, they believed, facilitate their successful integration into American society.

The emerging division of American education into separate secularized public schools and complementary but independent religious schools served the needs of established Jews. They wanted to sever the ethnic-religious amalgam that characterized Eastern European Jews. American nationality was to replace ethnic Judaism, and a reformed religion would replace an oriental, Old World halakic Judaism. The public schools would have primary responsibility for making over the children of immigrants into true Americans, and a new, modern Jewish education would transform Old World religious beliefs and practices into a modern Jewish religion better suited to the American milieu—one in which all citizens shared in a common secular-civil culture while individuals embraced compatible, but separate, religious denominations.

Jewish identity was to be religious rather than national. Public school would shape the immigrant child's American cultural identity, and Jewish education would inculcate religious faith and moral character. For many established Jews, that transformed religion was to be more like American Reform Judaism than the minhag Eastern European immigrants had brought with them.

By 1900, the elementary school attendance of American girls was about that of boys, and at the secondary level more women than men graduated from high school. For middle- and upper-class girls, high school was a socially acceptable place to spend one's teen years, and for young women intending to teach, high school was a necessary step into teaching, one of the few careers open to them. Boys, however, could enter many fields without a high school diploma.

Brothers often shouldered aside sisters when it came to college entrance, but Jewish girls, with a public school education behind them, did go on to college in the early decades of the twentieth century, usually as day students in municipal colleges and generally in the fields of education or social work. In New York City, many attended the Normal School (later HUNTER COLLEGE) or one of the three public teacher-training schools.

Boys' and girls' public education was strikingly similar. Girls were taught sewing and home economics and boys were taught shop, acknowledging presumed differences in adult roles. But the academic curriculum was largely the same, both in elementary and high school. In elementary school, boys and girls almost always sat in the same classes and learned the same subjects. Even in high school, which enrolled only a small proportion of young people, boys and girls generally attended the same coeducational classes and sat for the same examinations. More girls than boys may have entered commercial programs, and more boys than girls may have entered vocational programs, but many girls and boys selected the more traditional liberal arts–college preparatory curriculum, which was not gender differentiated.

Jewish girls in American public schools, especially at the elementary level, were exposed to the potent model of the American woman teacher. The mimetic tradition was alive and well, but now it was in the service of cultural transformation rather than conservation. Mary F., a student in the New York City schools early in the twentieth century, recalled the influence of her American teachers. "I think they were a different breed . . . the way they acted, dressed, and so on. I think I got [to know American practices] that way, there was a certain thing—very retiring. See, my Jewish background is to be outgoing and to yell and scream and do everything. And I think the one big thing that I learned is to behave and to be retiring, not to be pushy. I think I learned that from my teachers. I think that's an American trait." Jewish girls also acquired a new set of American aspirations that could be satisfied only by mastering American culture. Mamie T, a seventh-grade student on the Lower East Side, wrote of her class "Trip to Riverside Drive," published in her school magazine in 1917. "It was a bright, clear Sunday afternoon when [my teacher, classmates, and I] got on the Fifth Avenue bus at Washington Square. We immediately felt the change of atmosphere. . . . In less than an hour, we were in the regions of those who have always been in our dreams, presenting us with cups of gold and pearls, and offering us a dwelling place, similar to those they possessed. So you needn't be surprised when I say that we were eagerly looking for the houses that would perhaps be ours in the future. . . . As soon as we returned to the East Side, we first realized how poor and congested the people lived in our section of the city."

It was not a nostalgic dream of Europe that spurred these girls, but the bright prospects of America. And public school—American school, which could prepare them for modern women's roles—provided the opportunity to get up and out. Sara Z., in her nineties and a veteran of fifty years as a New York City schoolteacher, reflected on her own life and education. "My [immigrant] father was a very learned man, and he believed that the man counts, the woman doesn't, and I was more or less of a revolutionary. The woman has to count. Well the brothers counted, as I remember, and the women didn't count, and we said, Yes, that the women do count, and that is why I went to [college]." She followed a path from Ellis Island to public school, teacher's college, and back to the public school classroom—a path followed by thousands of Jewish women in the twentieth century. But her formal Jewish education was nonexistent. She set her sights, chose her path, and did not look back. "Certainly the boys studied Hebrew but the girls studied if they wanted to. I didn't study Hebrew. I said, 'I'm an American—I have to study English.' And I did. And that's how I came to go to Hunter College."

In fact, few Jewish children received any religious education in the period prior to World War I. As Alexander Dushkin reported in his study of New York City Jewish education, fewer than one in four children in 1917 received any Jewish education, dropping to only one in six girls. More children would have received some Jewish education during their childhood than were enrolled in any given year, but it is clear that the Jewish education, especially of girls, was largely neglected. The experience of Mary F., so strongly influenced by her public school teachers, is representative of her times. "Yes, my father wanted me to read, thank God he did, the Hebrew alphabet, which I remember to this day. I was about nine and I wanted to be out in the street, playing, but my father used to drag us in . . . and this Rabbi would come. He probably got ten cents for the lessons and every day, maybe it lasted a year, I used to read from the Good Book. . . . Yes, the Rabbi would come, dum-de-dum, and out he'd go!" The peddler *melamed* [teacher], going from door to door with siddur and Humash in hand, teaching boys and girls their aleph-beth, or the Old World rabbi confronting scores of boys in a basement heder, stood in stark contrast to the modern public school, with its imposing building and its corps of well-trained American teachers.

Jewish children, but especially girls, lacked a Jewish education to complement their public schooling. American life, observed and imitated in public schools, was reinforced in the streets, public entertainment, magazines, and libraries, as well as in the casual process of window shopping, going on uptown outings and, later, watching movies and listening to the radio. And for those whose employment was outside immigrant districts, their work lives gave them the opportunity to observe, practice, and perfect American lifeways. The public schools also indelibly reinforced children's adoption of the English language. It was English that conveyed a new cultural world, new manners, social conventions, tastes, embedded values and beliefs, and daily discoveries.

The absence of public Jewish ritual or study roles for girls and women in the Eastern European immigrant community reduced the perceived need to educate them Jewishly. Most immigrant parents were concerned with discharging the religious obligation of preparing their sons for bar mitzvah. But no such obligation was felt to extend to their daughters. It was assumed that girls would learn their adult roles by observing their mothers. The Jewish education of girls had to compete for the little time left in a girl's life after public school with baby-sitting, piano lessons, settlement house clubs, and socializing on the front stoop. From the vantage point of young girls, they knew they could compete with boys on nearly equal footing in public schools, win prizes, and aspire to be teachers. But when it came to Jewish learning, immigrant Jewish girls were assigned a separate, unequal status. And with few things the adult Jewish woman was expected to do that required formal Jewish learning, there was little incentive to study and master Jewish subjects.

EMBRACING OLD TRADITIONS AND AMERICANIZATION

The need to provide a modern Jewish education to American Jewish children was recognized early in the twentieth century by many Jewish leaders, especially those connected with the Kehillah of New York. Samson Benderly, the father of modern American Jewish education, was invited to New York to form the Bureau of Jewish Education in 1910. The dual task of Jewish educators, as he saw it, was to Americanize their students while simultaneously building a viable Jewish culture in America. Jewish education, he argued, should be "complementary to and harmonious with the public system."

The new Jewish education that Benderly, Rabbi Mordecai Kaplan, and others set out to create was to prepare Jewish youth for active participation in a bicultural world. Heavily influenced by Cultural Zionism and strongly embracing the Hebrew language, they were optimistic regarding the possibility of a Jewish renascence in America. Benderly and Kaplan set out to identify and attract the best and brightest Jewish college graduates of the day to the field of Jewish education and provide them with professional training at the Teachers Institute of the Jewish Theological Seminary and at Teachers College, Columbia University. While most of "Benderly's boys" were men, young women such as Rebecca Aronson Brickner, LIBBIE SUCHOFF BERKSON, and Dvora Lapson were also recruited to the bureau.

The bureau recognized that a modernized concept of women's role in the American Jewish community was critical and set out to enlarge the Jewish educational opportunities of girls. Experimental programs for girls at the elementary level were developed, followed by girls' (ages eleven to fourteen) Hebrew preparatory schools, and Hebrew high schools (the Marshaliah schools). By the 1920s, the bureau had created what may have been the first Jewish school "system" for girls, from elementary to the Teachers Institute, a program that attracted more women than men. Based on American institutional models, the bureau actively embraced the American practice of training and employing young women as teachers. This new adult role for Jewish women who had been born into an Eastern European immigrant community served as a goal and motivation for pursuing a Jewish education in America. And the growing presence of Jewishly educated women helped to redefine female Jewish roles. In 1922, the first bat mitzvah was celebrated by Rabbi Kaplan's eldest daughter, a ceremony that went beyond confirmation and opened a possibility for girls that became a reality for many as the twentieth century progressed.

The demise of the New York Kehillah after World War I led to a drastic reduction in the activities of the New York Bureau of Jewish Education. Most of the young people it had recruited and trained could not be retained. They scattered across America, helping to establish and run city Bureaus of Jewish Education. Between 1915 and 1938, bureaus were started in fifteen cities, and, in four of these, Hebrew teachers' colleges were founded to train modern Jewish educators, men and women.

SECULAR JEWISH EDUCATION

Not all Jewish education directed at Jewish children was religious. In the early decades of the twentieth century, secular Jewish movements proliferated in the New World. Often Yiddish-language oriented and including bundists, socialists, anarchists, Yiddish culturalists, Zionists, and nationalists, education became critical to each group as it sought to establish itself in America and propagate its ideas and faith among a new generation of Jewish youth. In 1910, the first Yiddish secular school was opened by the Labor Zionists (the National Radical School, later known as the Jewish folk schools). In 1913, the coeducational Sholom Aleichem schools, which eschewed an overt political position and focused on Jewish culture and the Yiddish language, were organized.

The largest Yiddish-language school system was founded in 1918 by the Workmen's Circle. These "after-school" schools promoted both socialism and Jewish nationalism, with Yiddish as the critical vehicle for communicating Jewish knowledge and understanding and ensuring Jewish cultural autonomy. By 1934, the Workmen's Circle had established 104 schools (elementary and secondary) in 42 cities in the United States and Canada, which enrolled over 6,000 students, nearly 58 percent of whom were girls. They maintained a teacher-training institute to prepare male and female teachers, ran national educational conferences, and supported a summer camp. Though now greatly reduced in number and influence, for decades the Workmen's Circle provided an extended range of educational programs (kindergarten through teacher training) to boys and girls, which served as a potent secular Jewish complement to the public schooling received by its students.

ORTHODOX EDUCATION

Most Jewish children in the twentieth century, if they received a Jewish education, did so in congrega-

The need to provide a modern Jewish education to children was recognized early in the twentieth century by many Jewish leaders. The above photo shows a Hebrew kindergarten in Boston around 1920. [American Jewish Historical Society]

tional after-school programs or Sunday schools. But Orthodox Jews in New York and elsewhere grew increasingly concerned with the limited Jewish education available to their sons and daughters. Many felt supplementary education inadequate. In the 1880s, Orthodox educators founded a boys' yeshivah that emphasized Torah and Talmud but also offered secular studies to meet state education laws.

New York's Orthodox were first able to send their daughters to day schools in the late 1920s. The Center Academy was established in 1927 as a coeducational elementary school at the Brooklyn Jewish Center, then a modern Orthodox congregation that served an upper-middle-class community and gravitated toward Conservative Judaism. The Center Academy, headed by a woman principal, defined itself as "a progressive school for the American Jewish child." The coeducational Yeshiva of Flatbush was opened in 1928, followed shortly by the all-girls' Shulamith School in 1929. These schools, along with the coeducational Ramaz School in Manhattan (1937), offered both secular and religious instruction, seeking to inte-

grate the modern with the classical, Jewish with American. Except for the Center Academy, which sought to be Jewish but theologically neutral, these schools were religiously Orthodox. However, they all supported cultural Zionism and the Hebrew language. In an important sense, they attempted to prepare students for the bicultural world envisioned by the new Jewish educators within one Jewish institution rather than splitting responsibility between public and Jewish schools.

THE MODERN DAY SCHOOL

Modern day schools are clearly distinguished from European yeshivahs by their rejection of Yiddish and its replacement by English and Hebrew; the coeducational practice of most of these schools; the high level of Jewish instruction provided to girls, including in many cases the study of religious texts previously considered inappropriate and proscribed by traditional Orthodox practice; the employment of women teachers; and the high regard for secular studies. In addition, even to this day, most of their graduates go

Modern Jewish day schools are usually coeducational and provide a high level of Jewish instruction to girls. Although the above photograph is obviously posed, the classroom clearly emphasizes the importance of learning Hebrew. [American Jewish Historical Society]

on to American colleges and universities rather than to higher rabbinic training.

Jewish day schools, now numbering about six hundred in towns and cities throughout the United States, are a growing American Jewish phenomenon. While three-quarters are under Orthodox auspices, the Conservative and Reform branches of Judaism also sponsor day schools. In an American environment in which public education has been questioned by some and religious education has become increasing relevant to many, the private religiously sponsored day school—Catholic, Protestant, and Jewish—is a common sight on the American educational landscape. Jews who at one time strenuously opposed Jewish day schools as a form of self-imposed segregation and looked to the public schools as the best means of integrating Jews into American life are now confronted by a much more variegated educational-religious landscape. While most Jewish children still attend public schools, over 11 percent attend Jewish day schools. And unlike the beginning of the twentieth century, girls are now almost as likely as boys to attend day schools. In the 1980s, about 41 percent of Jewish children were enrolled in all forms of Jewish schooling, approximately 72 percent in after-school programs and 28 percent in day schools.

ULTRA-ORTHODOX EDUCATION

In addition to the modern Jewish day school there is a second, potent, Jewish day school sector sponsored by the ultra-Orthodox who arrived in America in small numbers before World War II and in larger

numbers following the Holocaust. They brought with them models of settlement and education that conformed with their desire to separate themselves as best they could from the secular world. They rejected the models of American Jewish day schools developed by the modern Orthodox Jews, schools that sought to synthesize the Jewish and the modern, and established their own yeshivahs that focus on Jewish texts and Jewish learning, and incorporate secular studies only to the degree that they minimally satisfy state compulsory education laws.

For ultra-Orthodox Jews, schools are integral to their efforts to protect their children from the perceived evils of secular America. Jewish education can do battle with the antireligious, assimilating, and secularizing forces of modern education, represented especially by public schools. And girls as well as boys are to be saved from public education.

The Orthodox community in Eastern Europe had neglected the formal Jewish education of its girls, allowing many to attend secular government schools and even church-run schools. In 1917, Sarah Schenirer founded the BAIS YA'ACOV school for girls in Cracow, Poland, to provide a religiously acceptable alternative to secular schooling. Jewish girls from Orthodox families were being educated for life in a modern, Western-oriented, secular society—poor preparation for marriage and motherhood in a strictly observant Jewish community. With the support of several prominent rabbis, most notably the Hofetz Hayim, Schenirer was able to overcome initial opposition to a girls' school and, under the wing of Agudat Yisrael, the Bais Ya'acov school system grew rapidly.

Ultra-Orthodox Jews who immigrated to the new world in the 1930s carried with them the Bais Ya'acov model and established such a school in Williamsburg, Brooklyn, in 1937. Other schools followed in the 1940s, joined by girls' secondary schools. The curriculum of Bais Ya'acov and later Bais Rivka (run by the Lubavitch Hasidim) focuses on Jewish studies but also includes secular, English-language classes to meet state requirements. However, consistent with ultra-Orthodox beliefs, girls' Jewish studies are limited to the written law, excluding nearly all of the oral law. For boys, Talmud, the oral law, forms the very essence of their study. Such study is believed to be a religious obligation for men, but not for women. For men, Torah study is as much a religious as an intellectual activity: Learning becomes a means to perceive God's will.

Ultra-Orthodox girls, traditionally excluded from all study, were now to study Torah (the written law) and secular subjects but not the oral law. Secular study, lacking precedent in the Orthodox world, either for men or women, and considered of decidedly lesser value compared to the study of Jewish texts, was readily incorporated into the schooling of girls. The study of the written law and the literature dealing with morality and piety were not entirely foreign to women, since women had long read and studied an altered and abridged form of the Torah (with commentary) in Yiddish (*Ts'ena Ureena*) and Yiddish-language pietistic writings. But Talmud remained beyond the scope of learning for ultra-Orthodox girls in Europe and later in America.

Whereas Jewish religious reformers, Maskilim as well as Reform, saw schools as positive modernizing forces, and the modern Orthodox saw schools as the arena within which modernity and tradition could be synthesized, the ultra-Orthodox saw education as the means to conserve their beliefs and lifeways, a defense against the modern world, a way of ensuring separation rather than integration, and a way to reinforce stringent adherence to halakic prescriptions.

For the first time in the history of Jewish settlement in America, a community of Jews, the ultra-Orthodox, sought to use schools as a defense against America and not as a means to incorporate Jews into American society. Integration clearly was and still is the goal of Jews who place their children in public schools for secular studies and in supplementary Jewish schools for a religious education. But it is also true for Jews who established modern day schools: Their children may not go to class with gentiles, but the curriculum of such schools seeks to incorporate and integrate the secular and the Jewish, and to educate children, boys and girls, for roles in the larger American society. The ultra-Orthodox reject cultural integration. Their goal is to establish a separate community of believers devoted to stringent adherence to halakic Judaism.

The education of Jewish girls in America today is as heterogeneous as the Jewish community of which they are a part. By far, the largest number attend public schools and secular colleges and universities. Many receive no Jewish education at all. But American Jewish girls now have Jewish educational opportunities broader and more available than ever before and a full range of adult Jewish roles in which to actively employ their Jewish studies, including rabbi, cantor, Judaica scholar, and Jewish educator. Women study Torah and Talmud and have become acknowledged scholars. The only limits to what women can study or the adult roles they can perform are set by the status of women in the branch of Judaism into which they are born or in which they choose to participate.

BIBLIOGRAPHY

Ashton, Dianne. "The Feminization of Jewish Education." *Transformations* 3, no. 2 (Fall 1992): 15–23; Brumberg, Stephan F. *Going to America, Going to School: The Jewish Immigrant Public School Encounter in Turn-of-the-Century New York City* (1986); Dushkin, Alexander M. *Jewish Education in New York City* (1918); Grinstein, Hyman B. *The Rise of the Jewish Community of New York, 1654–1860* (1945); Gurock, Jeffrey S. *The Men and Women of Yeshiva: Higher Education, Orthodoxy, and American Judaism* (1988); Hyman, Paula, E. *Gender and Assimilation in Modern Jewish History: The Roles and Representations of Women* (1995); Kaestle, Carl F. *Pillars of the Republic: Common Schools and American Society, 1780–1860* (1983); Pilch, Judah, ed. *A History of Jewish Education in America* (1969); Rury, John L. *Education and Women's Work: Female Schooling and the Division of Labor in Urban America, 1870–1930* (1991); Soloveitchik, Haym. "Rupture and Reconstruction: The Transformation of Contemporary Orthodoxy." *Tradition* 28, no. 4 (Summer 1994): 64–130; Tyack, David B., and Elizabeth Hansot. *Learning Together: A History of Coeducation in American Public Schools* (1992); Weissman, Deborah. "Education of Jewish Women." *EJ Yearbook, 1986–87* (1987).

STEPHAN F. BRUMBERG

EINSTEIN, HANNAH BACHMAN (1862–1929)

Hannah Bachman Einstein was a rare example of a volunteer philanthropic activist who achieved stature in both the Jewish and gentile social welfare communities. Her lobbying efforts in Albany made her known to the larger professional and volunteer establishment and the group of male Jewish leaders who controlled New York Jewish philanthropy allowed her into their leadership circle. She combined the skill and knowledge of a professional with the dedication of a volunteer.

Hannah Bachman Einstein was born in New York City on January 28, 1862, the first child of a German Jewish family. Her parents, Fanny (Obermeyer) and Herman Bachman, raised her in the German Reform tradition and emphasized social justice issues. They attended Temple Emanu-El, the most prominent German Jewish Reform temple in New York City. The Reform tradition became the religious form of choice for German Jews who sought ways of modernizing Judaism in the American setting. English was the language of the temple, with Friday night or (in some cases) Sunday morning as the time for the main worship service. A shortened prayer service, emulating the Protestant service, became the standard form, with the rabbi delivering a sermon in either German or English.

Hannah graduated from the New York Chartier Institute and shortly thereafter, on June 23, 1881, married William Einstein, a woolens manufacturer. The Einsteins established residence in New York City and became active members of Temple Emanu-El. The couple had two children, a son William, and a daughter Marion. In 1890, the temple created its sisterhood organization, and Einstein became an active member. In 1897, she became president, a position she held for twenty-five years.

It was as sisterhood president that Einstein visited the homes of the newly arriving immigrants and came to the conclusion that direct relief provided by the temple was insufficient to deal with the enormous variety of social problems faced by the immigrants. In 1899, as president of the New York Federation of Sisterhoods, she gained additional experience traveling around the state.

In order to improve her own education, she took courses in 1900–1901 in sociology at Columbia University and the New York School of Philanthropy. This experience confirmed her secular progressive and Jewish belief that private philanthropy and volunteer activity could not alleviate society's ills. Government was the only agency that had the resources to do so. She joined with other reformers to lobby the New York State Legislature for widowed mothers' pensions. One of her colleagues in this effort, with whom she worked closely, was newspaper reporter SOPHIE LOEB. Both Einstein and Loeb supported woman suffrage as well as social welfare issues. Between 1909 and 1915, Einstein and Loeb worked diligently for the adoption of the state law that would provide a subsidy to widowed mothers, so that they could care for their children without working outside of the home. Einstein believed strongly in the role of the family in creating healthy and contributing citizens, and she believed that motherhood was a full-time occupation.

In 1913, the state appointed her chair of its committee to investigate the issue. In the final drafting of the law, the focus became child welfare rather than mothers' pensions. Einstein's committee wrote the Child Welfare Law of 1915, which became the model for all states' laws on this subject. Einstein played an active role in the administering of the law. She also lobbied within the Jewish community for the projects she supported. In recognition of her high profile in social welfare, she became the first woman to sit on the board of the United Hebrew Charities. During this period, she held the position of president of the New York State Association of Child Welfare Boards.

Hannah Bachman Einstein died in New York on November 28, 1929.

BIBLIOGRAPHY

AJYB (1905–1906); Einstein, Hannah Bachman. Papers. American Jewish Archive, Cincinnati, Ohio; Kohut, Rebekah. *My Portion* (1925); Kuzmack, Linda Gordon. *Woman's Cause: The Jewish Woman's Movement in England and the United States, 1881–1933* (1990).

JUNE SOCHEN

EISEN, THELMA ("TIBY") (b. 1922)

Tiby Eisen was an outstanding center-fielder in the All-American Girls Professional Baseball League (AAGPBL) of the 1940s and 1950s, starring for nine years in the only professional women's league in the game's history.

Thelma "Tiby" Eisen was born in Los Angeles on May 11, 1922, the daughter of New Yorker Dorothy (Shechter) Eisen and Austrian immigrant David Eisen. From age fourteen, she played on top-notch softball teams in Los Angeles, starting with the Katzenjammer Kids, named for manager George Katzman.

Baseball was not her entry into pro sports, she explained: "In 1940, they tried to start women's professional football in Los Angeles. After they got a couple of teams together, city council said women could not play football in L.A. I was a fullback on one of the teams, and we traveled to Guadalajara. They filled the stadium."

In 1944, Eisen was one of six Los Angeles athletes chosen to try out for the All-American baseball league, and she won a spot on the Milwaukee team. In her first season, her team won the league championship. The next year the team relocated to Grand Rapids, Michigan. "When we walked down the street people would ask for our autographs, ask us where we were from. They wanted to know all about us," she said. "It was big time in these small towns."

At first, Eisen's ballplaying drew a mixed reaction from family members.

We played a big charity game in Chicago for a Jewish hospital. My name and picture were in every Jewish paper. My uncle, who had said, "You shouldn't be playing baseball—you'll get a bad reputation, a bad name," was in the stands, and he was just bursting with pride that I was there.

Eisen's best season was in 1946, when she made the all-star team, leading the league in triples and stealing 128 bases for Peoria. In 1949, she was picked

*In 1995, center-fielder "Tiby" Eisen was voted one of the top twenty greatest players
in the All-American Girls Professional Baseball League, where she played
from 1944 till 1952. [Thelma Eisen]*

for an all-star team that toured Latin America. In 1995, the authoritative *Total Baseball* encyclopedia named her one of the league's twenty greatest players.

In 1947, Eisen was traded for Faye Dancer, the woman Madonna's character was based on in the movie *A League of Their Own*. The league, which operated from 1943 to 1954, was largely forgotten before the movie, but since its release in 1992 renewed interest in the league has inspired new books, documentaries, and baseball cards.

Eisen made $400 a month, "good money," she said, at a time when banks paid women only $60 a month. Before she joined the league, she had applied for work at the Bank of America, which sponsored a softball team in L.A. "You'd work for the bank, then play for the team. I had my interview, but I never heard from them," Eisen recalled. "My girlfriend, who played on the team, told me they didn't hire me because I was Jewish—but she only told me that twenty years later because she didn't want to hurt my feelings."

Eisen has said she did not encounter anti-Semitism in the AAGPBL, and there were other Jewish players: Anita Foss, Blanche Schachter, and Margaret Wigiser. She did recall one anecdote:

> Once when I was playing for Fort Wayne, I was out in the outfield and I thought there were three out. There were only two, but I was coming in from the outfield. The manager Bill Wambsganss was waving, "Go back, go back." And he turned to one of the players sitting at the bench and said, "I never heard of a Jew that couldn't count."

After Eisen left the AAGPBL in 1952, she settled in the Pacific Palisades area of Los Angeles and starred on softball's world champion Orange Lionettes until 1957.

In 1993, she was elected to the board of directors of the AAGPBL's Players Association, which established an exhibit at the Baseball Hall of Fame, raises funds for reunions, and records the stories of the women who played. Eisen feels strongly about the importance of this work:

> We're trying to record this so we'll have our place in history. It's important to keep our baseball league in the limelight. It gets pushed into the background, so people almost don't know it happened. Women have been pushed into the background forever. If they know about our league, perhaps in the future some women will say, "Hey, maybe we can do it again."

BIBLIOGRAPHY

Eisen, Tiby. Interviews by author, 1996; *Total Baseball: The Official Encyclopedia of Major League Baseball.* Edited by John Thorn et al. (1995, 1997).

DAVID SPANER

EISENSTEIN, JUDITH KAPLAN (1909–1996)

Before she was thirteen years old, author, composer, and musicologist Judith Kaplan Eisenstein was already a significant figure in Jewish history. The eldest of four daughters born to Lena (Rubin) and Rabbi Mordecai Menachem Kaplan, the founder of Reconstructionist Judaism, Judith Kaplan was the first young woman to celebrate a bat mitzvah in America, on March 18, 1922.

Neither of her parents was American-born. Kaplan, born on September 10, 1909, in Sventzian, Lithuania (near Kovno), arrived in the United States at age eight, after a year in Paris. In addition to rabbinic ordination from the Jewish Theological Seminary, he earned a degree from City College (New York City) and received graduate training at Columbia University in philosophy and sociology. Lena Rubin, born in Friedrichshaven, Germany (near the Polish border), was brought to New York as a three-year-old child.

Judith was precocious intellectually—she learned to read English at age two and a half and began studying Hebrew at age three—and musically—between the ages of seven and eighteen, she studied at the Institute of Musical Art (now the Juilliard School) in New York. She also attended the Jewish Theological Seminary Teachers Institute and Columbia University's Teachers College, where she received her B.S. (1928) and M.A. (1932) in music education. A brief marriage to Albert Addelston, on June 28, 1932, ended in divorce in Reno, Nevada, in September 1933. On June 10, 1934, she married Ira Eisenstein, then assistant rabbi at her father's synagogue, the Society for the Advancement of Judaism.

From 1929 until 1954, Judith Kaplan Eisenstein taught music pedagogy and the history of Jewish music at Jewish Theological Seminary Teachers Institute. Where teaching and performing materials did not exist, she created them. Her publications include the first Jewish songbook for children, *Gateway to Jewish Song* (1937), *Festival Songs* (1943), *Songs of Childhood* (with Frieda Prensky, 1955), *Heritage of Music: The Music of the Jewish People* (1972), as well as five cantatas on Jewish themes written with Ira and two song cycles, all written between 1942 and 1974. In

*She earned a place in Jewish history by becoming the first American woman to celebrate a bat mitzvah.
Judith Kaplan Eisenstein would later contribute to her culture as a successful composer and musicologist,
publishing the first Jewish songbook for children. She is shown here in the early 1930s embarking
on a trip with her family. From left to right are: her sister Naomi; her mother, Lena; her husband,
Rabbi Ira Eisenstein; Judith; her father, Rabbi Mordecai Kaplan; and, her sisters Selma and Hadassah.*
[Reconstructionist Rabbinical College]

1987, she created and broadcast a thirteen-hour radio series on the history of Jewish music.

In 1959, at age fifty, Eisenstein entered the School of Sacred Music of Hebrew Union College–Jewish Institute of Religion (HUC–JIR), where she received her Ph.D. (1966) with a dissertation on "The Liturgical Chant of Provencal and West Sephardic Jews in Comparison to the Song of the Troubadours and the Cantigas." She then taught at HUC–JIR (1966 to 1979) and at the Reconstructionist Rabbinical College in Philadelphia (1978 to 1981).

The Eisensteins retired to Woodstock, New York, in 1981, and to Silver Spring, Maryland, in 1995. They have two daughters, Miriam Rachel Eisenstein, a lawyer with the U.S. Justice Department, and Ann Nehama Eisenstein, a therapist in private practice in New York, and one grandson. A son, Ethan Jacob, was institutionalized very young with severe mental retardation.

Judith Kaplan Eisenstein began her adult life as an important figure in Jewish history. Talented and superbly literate in both Jewish and musical tradition, she expanded the understanding, enjoyment, and dissemination of the music of the Jewish people. She died on February 14, 1996.

SELECTED WORKS BY JUDITH KAPLAN EISENSTEIN

Festival Songs (1943); *Gateway to Jewish Song* (1937); *Heritage of Music: The Music of the Jewish People* (1972, 1990); *The Music of the Jewish People.* Set of thirteen audiotapes (1987); *Our Bialik,* with Ira Eisenstein (1945); *Reborn: An Episode with Music,* with Ira Eisenstein (1952); *The Sacrifice of Isaac: A Liturgical Drama* (1972); *The Seven Golden Buttons: A Legend with Music,* with Ira Eisenstein (1947); *Shir ha-shahar* [Song of the Dawn] (1974); *Songs of Childhood,* with Frieda Prensky (1955); *Thy Children Shall Return,* with Ira Eisenstein (1954); *What Is Torah,* with Ira Eisenstein (1942).

BIBLIOGRAPHY

Obituary. *NYTimes,* February 15, 1996.

PAULA EISENSTEIN BAKER

ELION, GERTRUDE ("TRUDY") BELLE (b. 1918)

Gertrude ("Trudy") Belle Elion's greatest legacy is the thousands of lives touched by the drugs she and her associates developed for the treatment of leukemia, gout, rejection of transplanted organs, and herpes, among other disorders.

Elion was born on January 23, 1918, in New York City, to Lithuanian immigrant dentist Robert and Bertha (Cohen) Elion. Her father came from a long line of rabbis. Elion's intellect manifested itself at an early age; she was a voracious reader and an excellent student, graduating from Walton High School at age fifteen. Despite her father's losses in the 1929 stock market crash, she was able to continue her education by qualifying for tuition-free HUNTER COLLEGE. The death of her beloved grandfather from stomach cancer, coupled with her aversion to animal dissection, led her to choose chemistry as "a logical first step in committing myself to fighting the disease." Her younger brother Herbert chose engineering and physics.

Elion received her B.A. summa cum laude in 1937 but found work opportunities scarce for a woman chemist. After several unfulfilling jobs she entered graduate school at New York University, receiving her M.S. in 1941. During this period, she also suffered the death of her fiancé and never married. The manpower shortage of World War II proved a boon for Elion, as she found work as a quality control chemist at Quaker Maid Company, and then as a research chemist at Johnson & Johnson. She finally found a rewarding and challenging career in 1944 as a research chemist at Burroughs Wellcome, a noted pharmaceutical company, initially as assistant to George H. Hitchings, and later as head of experimental therapy, a post she held until her retirement in 1983. Elion never completed a Ph.D. She began the doctoral program at Brooklyn Polytechnic but was forced to leave after two years when the college dean made her choose between her education and her job.

At Burroughs Wellcome, Elion and her associates exploited the biochemical differences between normal cells and rapidly dividing, pathogenic cells such as cancer, bacteria, and viruses in order to develop new drugs. More specifically, purine compounds and their derivatives were used to inhibit the growth of such cells by blocking the synthesis of certain nucleic acids. This work resulted in chemotherapies for leukemia, immunosuppressive drugs for kidney transplants (azathioprine), treatments for gout, lupus, and severe rheumatoid arthritis, and the important antiviral drug acyclovir used to treat herpes. In addition, the tech-niques developed by Elion resulted in the development of the AIDS treatment AZT. Elion, Hitchings, and British chemist Sir James Black (discoverer of beta-blockers) shared the 1988 Nobel Prize for Physiology or Medicine "for their discoveries of important principles for drug treatment."

In addition to the 1988 Nobel Prize and twenty honorary doctoral degrees, Elion has received the Garvan Medal from the American Chemical Society (1968), the Sloan-Kettering Institute Judd Award (1983), the American Chemical Society Distinguished Chemist Award (1985), the American Association of Cancer Research Cain Award (1985), the American Cancer Society Medal of Honor (1990), and the National Medal of Science (1991). She is a member of the National Academy of Sciences, the American Academy of Pharmaceutical Scientists, the American Chemical Society, and the American Association for Cancer Research, of which she was president in 1983–1984. She has also served on the boards of the National Cancer Institute, the American Cancer Society, and the Multiple Sclerosis Society. In 1991, she was the first woman inducted into the National Inventors Hall of Fame.

SELECTED WORKS BY GERTRUDE BELLE ELION

"Antagonists of Nucleic Acid Derivatives. VI. Purines," with George H. Hitchings and Henry Vanderwerff. *Journal of Biological Chemistry* 192 (1951): 505–518; "Interaction of Anticancer Drugs with Enzymes." In *Pharmacological Basis of Cancer Chemotherapy* (1975); "The Purine Path to Chemotherapy." *Science* 244 (1989): 41–47; "Selectivity of Action of an Antiherpetic Agent, 9-(2-hydroxyethoxymethyl) guanine." *Proceedings of the National Academy of Sciences* 74 (1977): 5716–5720; "The Synthesis of 6-Thioguanine," with George H. Hitchings. *Journal of the American Chemical Society* 77 (1955): 1676.

BIBLIOGRAPHY

American Men and Women of Science, 1992–1993. 18th ed. Vol. 2 (1992); Bailey, Martha J. *American Women in Science* (1994); Biesele, John J., et al. "Studies on 2,6-Diaminopurine and Related Substances in Cultures of Embryonic and Sarcomatous Rodent Tissues." *Cancer* 4 (1951): 186–197; "Drug Pioneers Win Nobel Laureate." *New Scientist* 20 (October 22,1988): 26–27; "Garvan Medal—Gertrude B. Elion." *Chemical and Engineering News* 46, no. 3 (1968): 65; Graham, Judith, ed. *Current Biography Yearbook* (1995); Holloway, Marguerite. "The Satisfaction of Delayed Gratification." *Scientific American* 265 (October 1991): 40–44; Marx, Jean L. "The 1988 Nobel Prize for Physiology or Medicine." *Science* 242 (1988): 516–517; McGrayne, Sharon Bertsch. *Nobel Prize Women in Science* (1993); Schlessinger, B.S., and J.H. Schlessinger, eds. *The

Who's Who of Nobel Prize Winners 1901–1990. 2nd ed. (1991); St. Pierre, Stephanie. *Gertrude Elion: Master Chemist* (1993); Yount, Lisa. *Contemporary Women Scientists* (1994).

KRISTINE LARSEN

ELLIOT, "MAMA" CASS (1941–1974)

Called the Earth Mother of Hippiedom by fellow band member John Phillips, Cass Elliot brought charm and vocal muscle to a stormy and transitional period of American music history. In flowery print dresses of the mid-1960s, made tentlike to accommodate her great size, Elliot, born Ellen Naomi Cohen on February 19, 1941, in Baltimore, grew to fame with the tightly harmonic vocal group the Mamas and the Papas. During their three-year reign at the top of popular music charts, the Mamas and the Papas melded folk and psychedelic styles in a quartet whose half-dozen remembered songs still evoke a time prior to the 1968 Chicago Democratic National Convention, when hippie ideologies of communal living and relaxed standards of dress and demeanor had not yet divided the recording industry or the nation along fierce political lines. In 1966, the Mamas and the Papas made their television debut, singing "California Dreamin'" on the variety show *The Hollywood Palace*. It was broadcast to American soldiers in Vietnam, and host Arthur Godfrey sent "our boys" a message of hope.

Cass Elliot looked like the mother of a commune, photographed lounging on the grass, a bottle of wine at her side. The band's familial names lent credence to the public image that their lives were one continuous summer picnic. Papa John Phillips, baritone and songwriter, was a gangly opposite to his wife, Michelle Phillips. Michelle Phillips's delicate beauty offset the robust Mama Cass. Rounding out the quartet was tenor Denny Doherty, who shared the band's penchant for long hair and brightly colored clothing. Musically, the Mamas and the Papas created a sound never duplicated in American pop music. Their harmonies, indebted to the power of Elliot's voice, resemble a distant, often eerie echo that suddenly appears to be closer than it sounds. "California Dreamin'," "Monday, Monday," and "I Saw Her Again Last Night," all written by John Phillips, remain staples of both AM radio and elevator music circuits, an honor never bestowed on songs by the band's hard-edged contemporaries Janis Joplin and Jimi Hendrix. But even within the Mamas and the Papas' lush harmonies, the candor of Cass Elliot's voice is conspicuous.

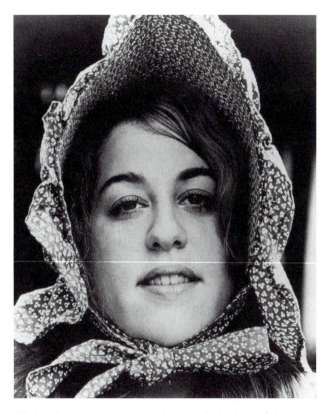

With a clear, penetrating voice that was the linchpin of the musical group the Mamas and the Papas, and a girth that was almost as legendary, "Mama" Cass Elliot will forever be identified as an earth mother of the 1960s. [New York Public Library]

Though very much a California band, the members of the Mamas and the Papas found each other through the folk music network in New York. Elliot had had her own group, Cass and the Big Three, and had been a member of the Mugwumps with Doherty before joining John Phillips's new band at St. Thomas in the Virgin Islands, where the quartet perfected its sound in sunlight and penury. One of the Mamas and the Papas' biggest hits, the autobiographical chronicle "Creeque Alley," details the genesis of the band down to John Phillips's American Express card, which sustained all four until they arrived in Los Angeles and were immediately signed to a recording contract at Dunhill Records in 1965.

Although always overweight, Cass Elliot appeared comfortable with her size, and allowed it to inspire a few of John Phillips's lyrics. Verses of "Creeque Alley" conclude with the refrain, "No one's getting fat except Mama Cass." In his autobiography, Phillips says Elliot repeatedly tried to lose weight, but such worries never penetrated her public persona. A solo

LP called "Bubblegum, Lemonade, and . . . Something for Mama" features Elliot in a white baby dress seated on a wicker chair looking positively enormous. Labeled "the queen of L.A. pop society in the mid-sixties" by *Rolling Stone*, Elliot lived in a home in Laurel Canyon once owned by Natalie Wood. She surrounded herself with famous and soon-to-be famous peers in the recording industry, including David Crosby, Stephen Stills, Graham Nash, and Joni Mitchell. Elliot was first married to James Hendricks, of Cass and the Big Three, with whom she had a daughter, Owen Vanessa, in 1967, and again briefly to Baron Donald von Wiedenman in 1971.

Elliot's solo career began in 1968 with the release of the Mamas and the Papas song "Dream a Little Dream of Me." Solo performing deprived her of the opportunity to serve the sumptuous harmonies that made the quartet distinctive, although "Dream a Little Dream" remains the clearest indication of her gift. She released eight albums as a solo artist (one as part of a duet with former Traffic member Dave Mason), but none was successful. Cass Elliot contented herself with a career in cabaret, and in the early 1970s was a frequent guest on television programs like *The Hollywood Squares*. Ironically, she was a guest host on *The Tonight Show* as the nation learned of Janis Joplin's death. Soon afterward, Elliot died after completing a show at the London Palladium on July 29, 1974. Speculation that Elliot choked on a sandwich has bound her musical legacy with her weight in perpetuity, a turn of events Cass Elliot might have heartily enjoyed.

SELECTED WORKS BY CASS ELLIOT

RECORDINGS WITH THE BIG THREE
The Big Three (1963); *The Big Three Featuring Cass Elliot* (1969); *Live at the Recording Studio* (1964).

RECORDINGS WITH THE MUGWUMPS
The Mugwumps (1967).

RECORDINGS WITH THE MAMAS
AND THE PAPAS
Deliver (1967); *Historic Performance at the Monterey International Pop Festival* (1968); *If You Can Believe Your Eyes and Ears* (1966); *The Mamas and the Papas* (1966); *People Like Us* (1971); *Present The Papas and the Mamas* (1968).

SOLO RECORDINGS
Bubblegum, Lemonade and . . . Something for Mama (1969); *Cass Elliot* (1971); *Dave Mason and Cass Elliot* (1971); *Compilation: Mama's Big Ones* (1971); *Don't Call Me Mama Anymore* (1973); *Dream a Little Dream* (1968); *Make Your Own Kind of Music* (1969); *The Road Is No Place for a Lady* (1972).

BIBLIOGRAPHY

Fong-Torres, Ben. "John: 'It Sounded Like the Mamas and the Papas.'" *Rolling Stone* (June 10, 1971): 1, 6–7; Helander, Brock. *Rock Who's Who* (1982); Kloma, William. "Has Success Spoiled Supergroup." *NYTimes*, 1968; Phillips, John. *Papa John* (1986); Phillips, Michelle. *California Dreaming: The Story of the Mamas and the Papas* (1986); Rockwell, John. "A Hearty Performer." *NYTimes*, July 30, 1974, 36:2; Ward, Ed. *Rock of Ages: Rolling Stone History of Rock and Roll* (1986).

PETER TABACK

ELSTER, SHULAMITH REICH
(b. 1939)

In the 1980s, when she served as headmaster of the Charles E. Smith Jewish Day School in suburban Washington, D.C., Shulamith Elster was often referred to as the dean of Jewish education.

The eldest daughter of Anna (Machlis) Reich, a Hebrew teacher, and Rabbi Paul Reich, Shulamith Reich Elster was born on May 19, 1939, in Norfolk, Virginia, where her father was rabbi of Beth-El (Conservative). As a teenager, Shulamith was one of the founders of United Synagogue Youth. Graduating from New York University in 1958 with a degree in sociology/anthropology, she taught confirmation class at New York's B'nai Jeshurun Congregation during the school year and spent summers on the staff of Camp Ramah, a breeding ground for leadership in the Conservative Movement. She received an M.A. in secondary school education from Teachers College (Columbia University) in 1959, after which she taught social studies in the New York City public schools. That year she married Sheldon Elster, a rabbinical student at the Jewish Theological Seminary. When he assumed a pulpit in Youngstown, Ohio, she became an associate professor of social sciences and communications at Youngstown State University, where she was also the faculty adviser to the Jewish Student Union from 1964 to 1968. They have three children: Jonathan, Elana Beth, and Adam Jeremy.

In 1968, the family moved to the suburbs of Washington, D.C., and enrolled their oldest child in the Solomon Schechter Day School, then a fledgling school in Silver Spring, Maryland. It was as a day school parent that Elster's career in Jewish education started its climb. She served in volunteer positions at the school, pursued doctoral studies at George Washington University (Ed.D. 1975), and became a part-time school counselor at Schechter. In 1978, with two other women, she founded Binder, Elster, Mendelson and Wheeler, Inc., a career counseling firm that emphasized service to women. She was also the codirector of career guidance programs of Wider Opportunities for Women in Washington, D.C.

The Solomon Schechter Day School continued to grow, and in 1979, Elster became the assistant principal of the upper school. By that time, the school had become a community day school called the Charles E. Smith Jewish Day School. In 1982, she was appointed the school's headmaster. It was under Elster's tutelage that the school grew to over a thousand students and 150 faculty. She is credited with turning the school into a model day school and gaining international recognition for its excellent programs in general and Jewish studies. During Elster's tenure at the school, over five hundred students graduated. Some of them were admitted to the finest universities in the United States.

With the school as her résumé, Elster was invited to become the chief education officer of the newly established Council for Initiatives in Jewish Education in 1991. The organization was established by the Commission on Jewish Education in North America to implement its report, "A Time to Act," its Jewish continuity agenda for the 1990s. In 1993, Elster was invited to found a graduate program in Jewish education at Baltimore Hebrew University, where she is currently associate professor of education.

BIBLIOGRAPHY

Developing Options (1979); "No More Prizes for Building Arks." *Women's League Outlook* (1991); "Rabbi, Teacher, Preacher-Leader?" *Proceedings of the Rabbinical Assembly* (1991); *Self-Assessment for Career Planning.* U.S. Department of Health and Human Services (1981).

JAN CARYL KAUFMAN

EMMA LAZARUS FEDERATION OF JEWISH WOMEN'S CLUBS

The Emma Lazarus Federation of Jewish Women's Clubs (ELF), a progressive women's group, grew out of the Emma Lazarus Division, founded in 1944 by the Women's Division of the Jewish People's Fraternal Order of the International Workers Order (IWO). Formed to provide relief to wartime victims, but especially to combat anti-Semitism and racism and to nurture positive Jewish identification through a broad program of Jewish education and women's rights, the Emma Lazarus Division attracted a membership of leftist, largely Yiddish-speaking women, many of the immigrant generation. Among its founders was CLARA LEMLICH SHAVELSON, the young woman who had called for the general strike of garment workers that sparked the 1909 UPRISING OF THE 20,000. Shavelson and other organizers believed that, because of the Holocaust, thousands of women had become "newly aware of themselves as Jewish women," but they urgently needed "history, self-knowledge as Jews, and cultural products" that could sustain the fight against fascism. In its early years, the division offered fellowships for fiction and history on Jewish themes. It also supported a home for French war orphans and a day nursery in Israel, and championed a broad range of women's issues.

In 1951, after the New York State attorney general initiated proceedings against the IWO as a subversive institution, the division reorganized as the independent Emma Lazarus Federation of Jewish Women's Clubs. Although some leaders broke with the Communist Party, the ELF did not relinquish its radical commitments. Throughout the 1950s, the ELF emphasized the progressive voice of labor as the hallmark of democracy, and called for coexistence with the Soviet Union. While Khrushchev's revelations about Stalinist terrors and other information about the country's virulent anti-Semitism shocked the ELF, leaders like the executive directors, June Croll Gordon and Rose Reynes (who became director after Gordon's death), continued to hope that the U.S.S.R. would not discriminate against Jews and other ethnic minorities.

The terrors of McCarthyism, which stigmatized many Jewish radicals as "un-American" communists, contributed to the Emmas' desire to claim their own Jewish identity by promoting a progressive, secular Jewish heritage. In the early 1950s, the ELF focused attention on two Jewish women whose achievements they believed symbolized two different directions. The ELF commissioned EVE MERRIAM to write a biography of poet and essayist EMMA LAZARUS. For the ELF, Lazarus's "universal scope," coupled with her support for Jewish culture and women's freedom, made her an admirable symbol of secular, humanistic values. Every year, the Emmas celebrated Lazarus's birthday with a trip to Liberty Island. They succeeded in having the cities of New York and Miami declare an Emma Lazarus Day and arranged a commemorative medal to honor her. Basing their program on Lazarus's work, the Emmas hoped to give "leadership to women in Jewish communities in our own time in the same spirit as Emma Lazarus did in hers."

In 1954, the ELF published a biography of ERNESTINE ROSE by Yuri Suhl. Although Rose's work as social reformer, abolitionist, and suffragist was not

The Emma Lazarus Federation was committed to a wide variety of progressive causes, springing from their belief in and dedication to their own identification as Jews, as women, as workers, and as Americans. [American Jewish Archives]

Jewish-oriented, the ELF claimed her as the first Jewish woman reformer in the United States. To the ELF, Rose's work on behalf of abolition and women's rights and against anti-Semitism demonstrated the "interrelationships between Jew and non-Jew, Negro and white, men and women." Like Lazarus, she was seen to combine Jewish patriotism with a broader humanism.

The ELF also wrote outlines of REBECCA GRATZ, LILLIAN D. WALD, SOPHIE LOEB, and PENINA MOÏSE. Interested in the broader history of American women, it developed curricula on the contributions of dissident women from Anne Hutchinson to ETHEL ROSENBERG, and on the role of America's working women in the Lowell mills and garment sweatshops. In 1954, it commissioned artist Philip Reisman to do a mural of the 1909 mass meeting at Cooper Union, depicting Clara Lemlich at the center. The five-by-seven-foot painting was donated to the INTERNATIONAL LADIES GARMENT WORKERS UNION in 1982. The ELF also commemorated the anniversary of the uprising of the

Warsaw Ghetto, paying tribute to the women who took part in the antifascist resistance, as well as those who helped establish the State of Israel.

The links between women's rights and the abolitionist and civil rights movements was of special interest. The ELF wrote about such black women leaders as Sojourner Truth, Ida B. Wells, Harriet Tubman, Frances Ellen Harper, Rosa Parks, and Autherine Lucy. Its most important contribution was the pamphlet "Women in the Life and Time of Abraham Lincoln," a reprint of the proceedings of a conference held by the National Women's Loyal League in 1863, with an introduction by Daisy Bates, leader of the desegregation struggle at Little Rock High School.

In 1951, the ELF joined in a statement of principle with the Sojourners for Truth and Justice, a black women's group. The Emmas made a regular financial contribution to the Sojourners, and the groups met at an annual luncheon. During the 1950s and 1960s, the ELF sent truckloads of food and clothing to the South and joined boycotts and sit-ins. In 1963, the ELF initiated a multiyear petition campaign for the United States to ratify the Genocide Convention, which had been adopted by the UN General Assembly in 1948 and subsequently signed by seventy-five nations; it considered this campaign its most important political project.

The ELF five-point program, adopted in 1951, established lasting goals. While the promotion of Jewish culture was considered the "number one project," other goals included the elimination of anti-Semitism and racism, the campaign for women's rights, support for the State of Israel, and world peace and consumers' issues. The ELF tracked and protested the resurgence of neo-Nazism throughout the United States and abroad (its blind spot remained the public disregard of Soviet anti-Semitism), continued as the sole support of the day-care center it had established for the Jewish and Arab children of working mothers in Israel, engaged in a vigorous campaign for a statute of limitation against the deportation of foreign-born Americans, became a cofounder of the Museum of Immigration on Liberty Island, and supported numerous peace efforts and organizations.

Women's issues were always central to ELF interest. It worked continuously to bring women's history, especially Jewish women's history, to a wide public. After the advent of second-wave feminism in the 1960s, the ELF joined women's rights organizations to support the Equal Rights Amendment and advocated for working women's and minority women's interests.

With chapters in Brooklyn, the Bronx, Boston, Los Angeles, San Francisco, Chicago, Philadelphia, Detroit, Miami, Rochester, Newark, Jersey City, Lakewood, and Toms River, New Jersey, the ELF maintained its educational and political activities for almost forty years, attracting approximately 4,000 to 5,000 members in 100 clubs at its peak. Affected by the graying of the membership, the transformation of women's work, and the development of the women's movement, the Emma Lazarus Federation of Jewish Women's Clubs disbanded in 1989, though some individual clubs remained. It had been, according to its leaders, the "only Jewish women's organization that encourages mass action, the movement of people," a "progressive organization."

While all of its varied projects sprang from a dedicated core of Jewish identity, members' pride in their ethnicity did not hamper, but in fact promoted, their identification as women, workers, and Americans. As proclaimed in the ELF's 1951 constitution, the enhancement of Jewish culture was proposed "as a part of the whole multi-national culture of American life." "We are a part of American life generally, and of the Jewish community in particular," one ELF president reaffirmed, as well as a member of the "family" of women's organizations. In this manner, the Emmas asserted the importance both of "unity as Jews, unity in variety" and the "special approach" needed to solve women's problems.

BIBLIOGRAPHY

Antler, Joyce. "Between Culture and Politics: The Emma Lazarus Federation of Jewish Women's Clubs and the Promulgation of Women's History, 1944–1989." In *U.S. History as Women's History: New Feminist Essays*, edited by Linda K. Kerber, Alice Kessler-Harris, and Kathryn Kish Sklar (1995); Emma Lazarus Federation of Jewish Women Clubs. Papers. American Jewish Archives, Cincinnati, Ohio.

JOYCE ANTLER

ENGEL, KATHARINE (1898–1957)

When Katharine Engel's alma mater, Smith College, conferred upon her its first honorary degree for Jewish achievement in 1950, the citation praised Engel's "sensitive understanding of the many complex problems which confront the immigrant to this country." A renowned emigré expert and Jewish communal leader who devoted much of her career to resettling displaced European Jewry, Engel was also an outspoken critic of McCarthyism and a tireless advocate of immigration reform.

Katharine (Asher) Engel was born on October 27, 1898, in New Haven, Connecticut, the daughter of Pauline (Housman) and Harry Asher, who was a prominent lawyer, founder of two local financial institutions, and president of the local board of education. Katharine's only sibling was Harry Asher, Jr.

A cum laude, Phi Beta Kappa graduate of Smith College (1920) and class alumnae president until 1933, she undertook a course of graduate study in English at Oxford University from 1921 to 1923. On January 14, 1926, she married Irving M. Engel, a New York City lawyer who became internationally prominent as a champion of human rights. The couple had one daughter, Susan Katharine.

Katharine Engel became extensively involved with private and governmental organizations in 1946. In that year she was elected chair of the National Committee on Service to Foreign Born and chair of the board of directors and executive committee of the United Service for New Americans, a position she held until 1948, becoming honorary president from 1951 until 1954. In 1946 she was also director of the

Greater New York United Jewish Appeal, later joining the national body's executive and administrative committees (1946–1948) and the Women's Division Executive Committee (1946–1949). In the same year Engel was vice president of the NATIONAL COUNCIL OF JEWISH WOMEN. She served as its national president from 1949 to 1955, and as president of the New York Section from 1955 until her death.

An influential policy adviser, Engel was appointed to the Women's Advisory Committee on Defense Manpower in 1951. She was then appointed to the New York State Committee on Refugees in 1955, after long-standing service to the National Committee on Immigration Policy.

Over the years, Engel was also director of the New York Association for New Americans and Self-Help for Emigrés from Central Europe; honorary vice president of the Jewish Publication Society; vice president of the Hebrew Immigrant Aid Society; vice chair of the 1951 Bond Drive for Israel; associate chair of the Jewish Tercentenary Committee; and a member of the National Committee for UNESCO, the board of governors of the American Friends of Hebrew University, the Crusade for Freedom, and the YWCA Centennial Committee.

After a respected career of public service, Katharine Engel died in New York City on March 30, 1957.

SELECTED WORKS BY KATHARINE ENGEL

"Diplomatic Passport to Panama." *The Council Woman* 14, no. 5 (1952): 7–8; "Five Years as Council President." *The Council Woman* 17, no. 2 (1955): 2–3; "This I believe . . ." *The Council Woman* 15, no. 2 (1953): 9; "We Launch a Freedom Campaign!" *The Council Woman* 14, no. 1 (1952): 1–2.

BIBLIOGRAPHY

AJYB 59:474; National Council of Jewish Women. "In Memoriam—Katharine Asher Engel." *The Council Woman* 19, no. 2 (1957): 2; Obituary. *NYTimes*, March 31, 1957, 88:3; *Who's Who in America* (1952–1953, 1954–1955, 1956–1957); *Who's Who in World Jewry* 3 (1955); *WWWIA* 3.

ESTELLE C. WILLIAMS

EPHRON, NORA (b. 1941)

Nora Ephron has used her refreshing wit, biting sarcasm, and ability to make the mundane entertaining to write her way into the lives of millions. Heeding her mother's advice that "everything is copy," Ephron draws upon her own experiences—childhood dreams, anxieties about her flat chest, and her two divorces—in her articles, books, and screenplays.

Beginning as one of America's most incisive essayists, Nora Ephron eventually followed in the footsteps of her screenwriter parents. Screenplays led Ephron to yet a third career as a successful film director. [Schlesinger Library]

Born in New York City on May 19, 1941, to the playwriting and screenwriting team of Henry and PHOEBE EPHRON, Nora was the eldest of four sisters, three of whom have become writers. Her education as a writer began early. The Ephrons relocated to Los Angeles when Nora was three years old, and she grew up immersed in the liberal Hollywood writing community. After graduating from Beverly Hills High School, Ephron left Los Angeles to attend Wellesley College, accompanied by her mother's advice to avoid sororities and organized religion. Upon receiving her bachelor's degree in 1962, Ephron moved to New York City to pursue a career in journalism. She began working as a reporter at the *New York Post*, and then made a name for herself as a contributing editor and columnist at *Esquire* magazine, later working as senior editor and columnist until 1978. Ephron was also a contributing editor at *New York* magazine from 1973 to 1974.

Nora Ephron became famous for her sharp tongue and for fearlessly asserting herself in her reporting. She wrote funny, personal, and sardonic pieces on feminist concerns and pop culture phenomena. Her first collection of essays, *Wallflower at the Orgy*, appeared in 1970, followed by *Crazy Salad: Some Things About Women* in 1975. Ephron then took on the press in her 1978 collection *Scribble Scribble: Notes on the Media*. The 1991 *Nora Ephron Collected* is a compendium of her most famous essays.

While Ephron professes to be bad at making things up, she is not bad at creating irony and comedy from her own life experiences. She wrote of her first marriage to comedy writer Dan Greenburg and of the end of her second marriage to *Washington Post* reporter Carl Bernstein in the 1983 best-selling novel *Heartburn*, which was adapted into a movie of the same name in 1986. In her largely autobiographical fiction, Ephron draws upon her cultural Jewish identity, as she often writes about Jewish characters.

Turning to screenwriting in 1983, Ephron received an Academy Award nomination for the film *Silkwood*, which she wrote with Alice Arlen. She collaborated with Arlen again to write *Cookie* in 1989. That same year, the screenplay for *When Harry Met Sally* was nominated for both an Academy Award and the British Academy of Film and Television Arts award for best screenplay. Ephron's fourth screenplay was *My Blue Heaven* in 1990. Ephron collaborated with her sister Delia on the 1992 screenplay *This Is My Life*, the film on which Nora Ephron made her directorial debut. Ephron received her third Academy Award nomination for the screenplay of the 1993 film *Sleepless in Seattle*, which she both cowrote and directed. In 1994 Nora and Delia again collaborated on the screenplay for *Mixed Nuts*, which she also directed. Nora Ephron directed the comedy *Michael* in 1996.

Nora Ephron is a member of the Writers Guild of America, the Authors Guild, the Directors Guild of America, and the Academy of Motion Picture Arts and Sciences. Ephron's two sons from her marriage to Bernstein, Jacob and Max, now live with her and her husband, writer Nicholas Pileggi, in New York City.

SELECTED WRITINGS BY NORA EPHRON

BOOKS
   Crazy Salad: Some Things about Women (1975); *Heartburn* (1983); *Nora Ephron Collected* (1991); *Scribble, Scribble: Notes on the Media* (1978); *Wallflower at the Orgy* (1970).

SCREENPLAYS
   Cookie, with Alice Arlen (1989); *Mixed Nuts* (1994); *My Blue Heaven* (1990); *Silkwood*, with Alice Arlen (1983); *Sleepless in Seattle* (1993); *This Is My Life*, with Delia Ephron (1992); *When Harry Met Sally* (1989).

BIBLIOGRAPHY
   Bennetts, Leslie. "Nora's Arc." *Vanity* 55 (February 1992); Gross, Amy. "Some Things About Nora Ephron." *Vogue* 173 (May 1983): 287; Kornbluth, Jesse. "Scenes from a Marriage." *New York* 16 (March 1983): 40–43; *Marquis Who's Who* (1994); Martin, Judith. "Heartburn: A Diagnosis." *Vogue* 173 (May 1983): 286; Nonkin, Lesley Jane. "Take One." *Vogue* 182 (January 1992): 144–147; Thompson, Anne. "The Ten Most Powerful Women in Showbiz." *Glamour* 93 (January 1995): 114–115.

TOBIN BELZER

EPHRON, PHOEBE (1914–1971)

Phoebe (Wolkind) Ephron was born in the Bronx on January 26, 1914, to Louis Wolkind, a manufacturer, and Kate (Lautkin) Wolkind. She had one brother, Harold Wolkind. A graduate of James Monroe High School and HUNTER COLLEGE, she met Henry Ephron in 1933, while both were summer camp counselors. Shortly after, Henry Ephron proposed to her. "I expect to be a good playwright soon and I have no time for courtship," he declared. "Let me read one of your plays," replied his future wife. For nearly forty years, Phoebe and Henry Ephron were literary collaborators, cowriting successful Broadway plays and Hollywood films, and had four daughters, Nora, Delia, Amy, and Hallie. Their first play, *Three's a Family* (1943), was based on the experiences raising their firstborn, NORA EPHRON. Soon after, they moved to Los Angeles and cowrote the scripts for many major motion pictures, including *There's No Business Like Show Business*, *Carousel*, and *Captain Newman, M.D.*, which was nominated for an Academy Award. *Desk Set*, the 1957 movie starring Spencer Tracy and Katharine Hepburn, secured their screenwriting success.

A proud career woman, Phoebe Ephron disliked being portrayed as a housewife and mother who wrote plays in her spare time. "We have a cook for the cooking

"Always be successful enough to pay for your own psychoanalysis," was just one of the witty bits of wisdom that Phoebe Ephron offered to her four daughters. Taking her own advice, she and her husband Henry collaborated on successful Broadway plays and Hollywood films for forty years. [New York Public Library]

and a nurse for the children. I've been a full-time screenwriter and I put in a full day at the office."

Even at the dinner table, the Ephrons were busy collecting potential screen dialogue. Similar to the legendary Algonquin Round Table, their dinner table was enlivened by clever witticisms, which undoubtedly helped three of the four daughters to pursue careers in literary humor.

Ephron's influence on her daughters' lives, however, had its less light moments. Delia, the second born, observed that her mother was "powerful and opinionated," controlling the lives of her daughters, including choosing their courses in high school. She also expected her children to avoid sororities and organized religion.

Still, a refreshing lightness persisted. For example, while looking out over the Paramount Studio set for *The Ten Commandments*, Ephron wrote to one of her daughters that the Red Sea was made of blue Jell-O. "Never marry a man with fat ankles," she advised her children, "and always be successful enough to pay for your own psychoanalysis." In the screenplay for *This Is My Life*, Delia and Nora Ephron wrote about Dottie Ingel—a character loosely based on their mother—who offered similar witty "life lessons" to her daughters.

Nora Ephron once said that her mother understood that the "tragedies of your life one day have the potential to be comic stories the next." Indeed, when Nora Ephron was visiting her dying mother at Doctors Hospital in New York City, Phoebe Ephron told her, "Take notes, Nora, take notes. Everything is copy." Phoebe Ephron died on October 13, 1971.

BIBLIOGRAPHY

Ephron, Henry. *We Thought We Could Do Anything* (1977).

DONALD ALTSCHILLER

EPSTEIN, CHARLOTTE (1884–1938)

The year 1996 marked the centennial of the modern Olympic Games, and the anticipation of American women's gold medal triumphs in swimming and diving continued a legacy of athletic excellence linked to the efforts of Jewish American Charlotte Epstein. Referred to as the "Mother of Women's Swimming in America," Charlotte Epstein was born to Morris and Sara (Rosenau) Epstein in New York City in September 1884. She demonstrated her love of swimming by influencing U.S. women's swimming to reach prominence in the 1920s and 1930s. Known as "Eppie" by

friends, colleagues, and swimming champions, Epstein started the renowned Women's Swimming Association of New York, launching the national and international fame of American women swimmers in the early twentieth century.

Founded in 1917 by Charlotte Epstein and a few other women charter members who wanted to teach and participate in swimming, the Women's Swimming Association (WSA) promoted the health benefits of swimming. Epstein enjoyed swimming, although she herself did not become a champion swimmer. As a court stenographer, she and a few other businesswomen wanted to swim after work for exercise. In 1914, Epstein started the National Women's Life Saving League to foster swimming for women and girls. She also appealed to the Amateur Athletic Union to allow women to register as athletes in swimming events.

At the WSA, Epstein demonstrated outstanding administrative ability as the swimming club team manager, and then as president in 1929. Epstein attracted young female swimmers who desired to participate and compete in the sport. Louis deB. Handley became the swimming coach of the WSA and taught the girls the American crawl stroke. Under Handley's teaching and Epstein's management, WSA members proved successful in competition, producing outstanding champions like Gertrude Ederle, Aileen Riggin, and Eleanor Holm. Girls pursued both swimming and diving at the WSA and exhibited excellent results in swimming competitions.

Charlotte Epstein played a crucial role in enabling American women to participate in the Olympic Games and compete for medals. In fact, Epstein served as the team manager-chaperon on the 1920 U.S. Women's Olympic Swimming Team, the first time females were allowed to compete in the Olympic Games. One of Epstein's WSA club members, the 1920 and 1924 Olympic diving champion Aileen Riggin, recalled Epstein's importance in providing her and other WSA members with the opportunity to compete in the 1920 Olympics. "We were the three youngest members competing, 14 and 15 years old, and this seemed to cause great commotions with the officials. "They said," Riggin remembers, "there was absolutely no way they were going to take children to the Olympics." Epstein battled the Olympic officials. According to Riggin, "Our manager, Charlotte Epstein, and other women went to the committee and lodged a complaint. They had a bitter session but finally we won and the committee members said they would allow us to go." WSA swimmers dominated the tryouts for the Olympic team. Helen Wainwright won

Founder of the extraordinary Women's Swimming Association, Charlotte Epstein was also team manager of the American women's swim team at the 1920 Olympics, the first in which women were allowed to compete, and at two other Olympics. She is shown here (back row, second from right) with the 1924 American Olympic team. [International Swimming Hall of Fame]

the tryouts for the springboard, and Aileen Riggin placed second and third in high diving, while Helen Meaney won for high diving.

The WSA team members achieved victory at the Antwerp Olympic Games in 1920 with Epstein serving as team manager and chaperon. Aileen Riggin won the gold medal in Olympic fancy diving at age fourteen, and Ethelda Bleibtrey won gold medals in swimming. WSA members broke records and won races, dominating the sport for American swimmers.

During Epstein's leadership at the WSA from 1920 to 1936, WSA members continued their swimming and diving dominance in competitions. Aileen Riggin in the 1924 Paris Olympic Games became the first U.S. Olympian to win medals in different events, diving and the swimming relay. Also in 1924, WSA swimmer Gertrude Ederle won the gold medal in the 400-meter relay and bronze medals in the 100- and 400-meter freestyle events. Then, in 1926, Ederle became the first woman to swim the English Channel, and she accomplished this feat in a faster time than the men's time.

Charlotte Epstein achieved the official position of Olympic team manager of the U.S. Women's Swimming Team in the 1920, 1924, and 1932 Games. She attended the 1928 Games, but not as an Olympic official. She was appointed chair of the U.S. Olympic Women's Swimming Committee, as well as chair of the national women's swimming committee of the Amateur Athletic Union. Epstein's swimmers at the WSA, although holding national and world records, maintained their commitment to their team manager and the swimming club. Epstein's swimmers held fifty-one world records and won thirty national champion team relays during her twenty-two years with the WSA. She fostered adherence to the WSA team slogan,

"Good Sportsmanship Is Greater Than Victory." Individual swimmers desired to participate in championships for their WSA team. Swimming champion Aileen Riggin explains that Eppie "was a great influence," and she told the team members, "'Get points for the club, get in there and dive and never quit, never show off.'"

Epstein, determined to help the WSA prosper, was relentless in locating pools for the WSA members to swim in, arranging trips for swimming meets, and fund-raising for nationals in which her WSA swimmers could compete. Until her death, Epstein maintained her position in the WSA and in other important swimming organizations, promoting competitive swimming for women.

In 1936, she refused to attend the Olympic Games in Berlin because she was opposed to American participation. She withdrew from the American Olympic Committee in protest against Nazi policies. In 1935, Epstein chaired the swimming committee in charge of the trials and selection of the teams for the second Maccabiah Games at Tel Aviv, often called the Jewish Olympics.

In recognition of Epstein's distinguished services, on June 26, 1939, the American Olympic Committee issued a "Resolution on the Death of Miss Charlotte Epstein." The resolution expressed that Epstein "received national and international recognition for the part she played in the development of many swimmers and divers, as well as for her outstanding executive ability." In 1974, to honor her achievement in the development of women's swimming, the International Swimming Hall of Fame inducted Charlotte Epstein as a Contributor. She also is a member of the Jewish Sports Hall of Fame in Israel, inducted in 1982. Moreover, in 1994, Epstein became one of the first women inducted into the B'nai B'rith/Klutznick National Jewish Museum, Jewish Sports Hall of Fame in Washington, D.C. She died in New York in 1938. Epstein provided a significant contribution to the history of American women's swimming and the history of the Olympic Games.

BIBLIOGRAPHY

AJYB 41:421; Epstein, Charlotte. Archives. Charlotte Epstein Collection, Women's Swimming Association Archives, Henning Library, International Swimming Hall of Fame, Ft. Lauderdale, Fla., and Young Women's Hebrew Association Records, 92nd Street Young Men's/Young Women's Hebrew Association Archives, NYC; "Indoor Swims for Girls." *NYTimes*, November 12, 1916, 4:5; "Miss Epstein Dead; Olympics Official." *NYTimes*, August 27, 1938, 13:4; "Passed On." *American Hebrew* 143 (September 9, 1938): 16; Postal, Bernard, Jesse Silver, and Roy Silver. *Encyclopedia of Jews in Sports* (1965); Simons, John, ed. *Living Jews of the U.S. and Canada*. Vol. 13 (1938–1939); Slater, Robert. *Great Jews in Sports* (rev. ed. 1992); Soule, Aileen Riggin. Interview with author, Department of History, Western Michigan University, Kalamazoo, Mich., June 16, 1995; Welch, Paula D., and Harold A. Lerch. "The Women's Swimming Association Launches America into Swimming Supremacy." *The Olympian* (March 1979): 14–16; *WWIAJ* (1938).

LINDA J. BORISH

EPSTEIN, JUDITH G. (1895–1988)

Deeply committed to the establishment and development of the State of Israel, Judith G. Epstein dedicated her career as a social and political activist to HADASSAH, the Women's Zionist Organization of America. She served Hadassah in many leadership roles, including two terms as president. She also attended several meetings of the Zionist World Congress as a delegate, served as a representative to the United Nations, and was largely responsible for funding the Rothschild–Hadassah–University Hospital in Jerusalem.

Judith Epstein was born in Worcester, Massachusetts, on November 2, 1895, to Sarah (Baum) and Edward Epstein, both of Eastern European descent. Her father was a wholesaler of upscale men's sportswear, and her mother, like herself, was active in Hadassah and other charitable organizations. The Epsteins had three children, Judith, the eldest, and two sons, Joshua and Abbe. She graduated from HUNTER COLLEGE in 1916 and went on to teach English at the Julia Richman High School in New York City. She married Moses P. Epstein, a textile manufacturer, in 1917. Epstein's mother was one of the earliest members of Hadassah, and Epstein herself was a member by 1917. By age twenty-four, she had been named president of the West End chapter of Hadassah, and in 1928 she was elected national secretary. In 1934 she was chairman of the building fund for the Rothschild–Hadassah–University Hospital, and then served two terms as president (1937–1939, 1943–1947).

Epstein's early years in Hadassah were marked by great changes for international Jewry. Hadassah's initial mission was to bring much-needed health care, research, and teaching to Palestine. Yet under Epstein's leadership during World War II, the desire for a Jewish homeland became more relevant. As Hadassah's representative, she was involved firsthand in the political battles to establish the State of Israel, attending Zionist World Congress meetings, visiting

A political activist whose primary concern was for the establishment of a Jewish state,
Judith G. Epstein was active in HADASSAH *for many years and served two terms as president.*
She is shown here (on the left) in a 1944 photograph, with another of the organization's
presidents, Rebecca Shulman. [Hadassah Archives]

the displaced persons camps in Europe, and traveling to Israel often.

As Hadassah's representative, Epstein headed delegations to the 1937 and 1939 World Zionist Congresses. The 1939 Congress in Geneva was particularly difficult, as war was declared only twenty-four hours after Epstein boarded a ship home. At the request of her husband, she left the presidency after the Geneva Congress, but returned to the organization four years later. At the time of her leadership, Hadassah's membership grew so rapidly that it became the largest Zionist organization in the world.

Judith Epstein's dedication to Hadassah, however, did not wane after her presidency. She continued to serve the organization by chairing numerous committees and assisting in daily operations. In addition to her Hadassah activities, Epstein served as chairman of the Public Relations Committee of the American Zionist Council and spent several years as Hadassah's representative to the United Nations.

Epstein was recognized for her commitment to Israel and Hadassah when the organization established an endowment and memorial award in her name. She was also named a Distinguished Alumna of Hunter College.

Judith Epstein was the mother of two children, Naomi Cohen and David Epstein, grandmother of five, and great-grandmother of nine. She died of a heart attack on October 27, 1988, in New York City.

BIBLIOGRAPHY

EJ; Epstein, Judith G. Papers. Hadassah Archives, New York; Obituary. *NYTimes*, October 28, 1988; "Old Age: A Case of Spirit Not Chronology." *NYTimes*, January 23, 1974; *UJE*; *WWIAJ* (1938, addenda).

SUSAN FOX

EPSTEIN, SPIRA *see* HADASSAH, SPIRA EPSTEIN

ETRA, BLANCHE GOLDMAN (1915–1995)

Born on March 8, 1915, in Brooklyn, New York, Blanche Goldman Etra was the daughter of Anna (Simon) and Jacob Goldman. Her father was a textile and women's wear executive. The second of three children, she had an older sister, Helen, and a younger brother, Morton.

A graduate of Erasmus High School, she attended Barnard College over the protests of her family. It was considered a *shande* [humiliation] for an observant Jewish family to permit a young woman eighteen years old to attend college. Blanche's sights, however, were set even higher than completing her bachelor of arts degree. She gained entrance into the combined program Barnard had with Columbia University Law School and, in 1938, was one of six women students in a class of three hundred receiving her J.D. from Columbia. That same year, she was admitted to the New York bar.

Married in 1939 to Henry Etra, also a lawyer, Blanche Etra sought a professional position in the male-dominated world of New York law firms. Hired by Hartman, Sheridan, and Tekulsky, she grew tired of being sent out for coffee and resigned in 1941. Although she then joined her husband and brother-in-law's firm of Etra and Etra, it was to be forty years before she returned to full-time legal work.

In Etra's view, while society required that men have jobs, women had unused brain power that could be galvanized in roles outside the home for the good of society. Thus, while raising four sons (Aaron, Marshall, Donald, and Jonathan), working part-time for Etra and Etra, and contributing substantially to the development of her brother's business, Blanche Etra founded the Women's Division of the Albert Einstein School of Medicine in New York in 1950. She involved Rose Kennedy and Eleanor Roosevelt in the task of raising millions of dollars in funds and establishing chapters of the Women's Division around the country. Thus, major financial resources for the newly formed medical school were created.

The Etras were members of Kehilith Jeshurun Synagogue on the Upper East Side of Manhattan, where Blanche Etra served as the first sisterhood president. In 1947, when her grandmother died, she formed a synagogue at the family's summer residence in Atlantic Beach. It became what is now known as the Atlantic Beach Jewish Center.

Blanche Etra's confidence in the ability of women to take important roles in society outside the home was further demonstrated in her work for the United Jewish Appeal and the Jewish Federation. For both organizations she created women's seminars for estate planning, involving New York State surrogate judges, journalists, and other lawyers. As a lawyer, she knew that women's understanding of finances, financial planning, and managing funds was essential to the increasing liberation of women within American society.

In 1977, when her husband died, Blanche Etra became a full partner in the law firm she had served for so many decades in a part-time capacity. Her legal specialties were labor law, litigation, trusts, and estates.

A woman of high intelligence and great energy, characterized by a strong sense of integrity and morality, Blanche Etra set out to use her considerable talents for the betterment of the Jewish and general communities. In recognition, in 1988, Etra became the second woman to receive an honorary doctorate from Yeshiva University. Upon the awarding of the degree, she was given a standing ovation by the graduates of Stern College for Women. Blanche Etra represented that combination of commitment to modern Orthodoxy and professional accomplishment that these young women admired—and that many would emulate in their own lives.

Blanche Goldman Etra died on January 4, 1995.

BIBLIOGRAPHY

Etra, Donald. Telephone interview with author, January 1997; Etra, Marshall. Correspondence with author, February 4, 1997; *Martindale-Hubbell Law Directory*. Vol. 10; *Who's Who of American Women*.

ROCHELLE L. MILLEN

ETTENBERG, SYLVIA (b. 1917)

Sylvia Ettenberg has dedicated her life to the advancement of Jewish education. Her concern for building strong leaders to represent the Conservative Movement prompted her to develop ways to search for and inspire promising teenagers and young adults to further their studies at the Jewish Theological Seminary. Many of today's rabbis, teachers, school administrators, and scholars entered their fields because they were either personally influenced by Sylvia Ettenberg or influenced by the programs she helped to create.

Sylvia Cutler Ettenberg was born on July 27, 1917, in Brooklyn to immigrant parents, Max and Rachel (Amster) Cutler. She was the elder of two daughters. While completing her B.A. in government at Brooklyn College, she chose to prepare for a teaching career by entering the Teachers Institute at the Jewish Theological Seminary. In 1937, she received a B.A. from Brooklyn College and a bachelor's of Jewish pedagogy (B.J.P.) from the Jewish Theological Seminary. At the request of the president of the Jewish Theological Seminary, Louis Finkelstein, she joined the administrative staff of the Jewish Teachers Institute and the Seminary College in 1946 as the registrar. In this role, she managed the day-to-day affairs of the Teachers Institute and Seminary College and imagined, planned, and implemented some of the twentieth century's most successful programs in Jewish education.

As soon as she arrived at the seminary to assume her position as registrar, she began to take action by convincing the president that the Conservative Movement needed to develop Hebrew-language camps committed to providing a religious environment for Jewish youth. In 1947, together with Dean Moshe Davis, she founded the Jewish Theological Seminary's Ramah camps. She remembers long, hot train rides to Ramah's first location in the Midwest, hoping only to ensure the success of her idea. She took responsibility for recruiting staff and campers. She helped to establish the educational agenda, wishing to see a camp committed to providing its campers with a Jewish education. Due to the efforts of Sylvia Ettenberg, Dean Davis, and a devoted staff, Camp Ramah became an indispensable institution that continues to enhance the Jewish education of Conservative youth throughout the United States. In the years since, a network of Ramah camps have opened across North America, attesting to its continued success.

She married Moshe Ettenberg on April 14, 1940. In November 1947, she traveled to Palestine with her husband, a professor of engineering, who had been appointed to teach at the Weizmann Institute. When the War of Independence broke out and Moshe Ettenberg could not assume his position, the Zionist couple refused to leave Palestine. Moshe Ettenberg was called upon to serve in the newly formed Israeli Air Force and established the first radar unit. In the midst of the excitement, the Ettenbergs' first child was born, Israela (Isa) Ettenberg, now a professor of education at Hebrew Union College in Los Angeles. The Ettenbergs' son David, born after they returned to New York, is a computer operations expert.

Ettenberg resumed her work at the seminary as the registrar in 1949, and for the next forty years

encouraged the seminary to expand its course and program offerings. By 1951, the seminary opened the Prozdor, a Hebrew high school, born from Ettenberg's vision. It was, however, more than a school for Jewish youth. Ettenberg used the Prozdor as a training ground for potential Jewish leaders, recruiting as faculty those she thought might enter the fields of Jewish education, the rabbinate, or academia if only inspired to do so.

When Ettenberg became the first woman to be appointed to the academic administration of the seminary as the associate dean of the undergraduate college, she made time to assist Dean Seymour Fox in the creation of the Melton Research Center, a center committed to the betterment of Jewish supplementary and day school education. As the dean of educational development at the seminary, an appointment that was made in 1976, Ettenberg supervised the Melton Research Center, developed a certification program for Jewish day school principals, enabled the seminary to sustain contact with its alumni, and was responsible for overseeing the growth of all facets of the department of education. Recognized for her contributons to Jewish education, she received the Samuel Rothberg Prize in Jewish Education from Hebrew University (1981), a doctor of humane letters from the Jewish Theological Seminary (1959), and the Behrman House Award presented at the Jewish Educators Assembly (1989).

Sylvia Ettenberg remains a tireless and devoted educator dedicated to her mission of enriching the field of Jewish education. Modest about her accomplishments, she continues to be driven by a passion and love for Judaism.

BIBLIOGRAPHY

Ettenberg, Sylvia. "The Changing Image of the Combined Program." In *The Education of American Jewish Teachers* (1967); Ettenberg, Sylvia. Interviews by author, and with Aryeh Davidson. Director, Melton Center, NYC; Ettenberg, Sylvia, and Moshe Davis. *The Ramah Experience: Community and Commitment* (1989).

MARJORIE LEHMAN

EVANS, SARA N. (1905–1986)

Sara Nachamson Evans, the wife of Mayor Emanuel J. Evans, served as the "first lady" of Durham, North Carolina, from 1951 to 1963. Known affectionately as "Miz Evans" by her friends and family, she was, in her own right, a prominent local, regional, and national leader of HADASSAH, the Women's Zionist

Sara Evans was a dynamic public speaker who was known as
HADASSAH's *"Southern accent." She traveled across the South
in the late 1930s and 1940s organizing local and state chapters.
Her activism was a family tradition. Her mother, Jennie
Nachamson, had founded Hadassah in the South in 1919,
and all seven of her sisters were presidents of their local chapters
across the region. [Eli N. Evans]*

Organization with a national membership of 300,000 Jewish women.

Evans served on every level of the organization during her lifetime. She was president of her local chapter in Durham, president of the Seaboard Region of nine states from 1942 to 1945, national vice president from 1954 to 1957, and a life member of its national board for forty-four years from 1942 until 1986. She was a dynamic public speaker who was known as Hadassah's "Southern accent," and she traveled across the South in the late 1930s and 1940s organizing local and state chapters. During World War II, the Evanses signed fifty-five affidavits for refugees from Hitler's Europe, personally guaranteeing jobs from American citizens in order for them to receive visas. Many worked for the Evanses, and she counted meeting their children as some of her most profound moments. "These are my children," she

once tearfully remarked at the bar mitzvah of a child of one of the survivors. After the creation of the State of Israel in 1948, she worked with her husband for the political support of Israel among North Carolina senators and congressmen, as well as among other political leaders in the South.

Born on July 2, 1905, she inherited her passion for Israel from her parents, Jennie B. and Eli Nachamson. Jennie Nachamson had founded Hadassah in the South in 1919 and devoted time to lead it in eastern North Carolina, even as she raised her nine children. Sara, the oldest of eight consecutive daughters and then a son, accompanied her mother on a memorable trip to Palestine in 1933 that handed her the torch of Jennie's idealism and fired her passion for a Jewish state in the Holy Land. All eight sisters have served as presidents of local chapters of Hadassah across the South, and the family was such a legend in Jewish circles that when the sisters went to Israel in October 1968, for Evans's fortieth wedding anniversary, the *Jerusalem Post* ran a photograph and a headline that read, "Sara and Her Seven Sisters." In the synagogue, famous for its Marc Chagall windows, in the Hadassah Hospital in Jerusalem is a plaque commemorating the occasion.

Sara Nachamson Evans came to Durham as a young girl when the Nachamson family moved from Kinston in 1921 and opened United Dollar Store. She attended Duke University, where she played the flute in the Duke orchestra and worked in the family store. When her father became ill, much of the responsibility for running the store fell upon her.

She met E.J. "Mutt" Evans of Fayetteville while he was attending the University of North Carolina, and the unusual Duke-Carolina marriage in 1928 at the Washington Duke Hotel in Durham, with her sisters as bridesmaids and her brother as ring bearer, was a major social and religious event discussed for years. They had two sons, Robert and Eli.

"Mutt" and Sara Evans built the Durham store, renamed Evans United Department Stores, into a chain of stores in North Carolina and Virginia. She was both a talented business executive and a corporate officer of several corporations. She headed the Women's Division of the United Way campaign in Durham in 1952 and was a member of the North Carolina Board of the American Association for the United Nations from 1961 to 1963, the League of Women Voters, and the United Fund Campaign in 1960.

Beginning in the early 1970s, and for seventeen years thereafter, she and her husband created, supported, and raised funds for the Judaic Studies Program at Duke University and the University of North Carolina, Chapel Hill. The director of the program, Dr. Eric Meyers, spoke at her funeral and paid tribute to her life of service to the Jewish community, observing that she was transformed from a businesswoman with a "painful shyness" into a dynamic and passionate advocate at the speaker's podium when she talked about Jewish causes. "She brought Durham to Jerusalem," he stated, "and Jerusalem to Durham."

Sara Nachamson Evans died on March 23, 1986, in Durham.

BIBLIOGRAPHY

Evans, Eli N. *The Provincials: A Personal History of Jews in the South* (1973), and *The Lonely Days Were Sundays: Reflections of a Jewish Southerner* (1993).

ELI N. EVANS

EYTINGE, ROSE (1835–1911)

Notorious for her fiery temperament, Rose Eytinge became one of the most popular female stars of the 1860s and 1870s. She was reputedly the first on the American stage to command a three-figure salary.

She was born in Philadelphia on November 21, 1835, to Rebecca and David Eytinge, a language teacher and translator. Her brother Samuel, also an actor, died in 1859. The family was likely related to the four Jewish merchant Eytinges, then working in Philadelphia, at least two of whom had emigrated from the Netherlands.

Rose Eytinge was schooled informally at home in Philadelphia and then Brooklyn until, at age seventeen, she embarked on a professional stage career. With the help of agent Charles Parsloe, she secured her first engagements, including one with the Green Street Theater in Albany, New York. She married the manager, David Barnes, in 1855 and bore a daughter, Courtney. By 1862, however, Eytinge and Barnes had divorced.

Eytinge then appeared in New York with legendary performers Edwin Booth, E.L. Davenport, and James Wallack. With the latter two stars, she toured Boston, Philadelphia, Baltimore, and Washington, where President Abraham Lincoln attended several of her performances and invited her to the White House. She distinguished herself in the playing of heroines driven to emotional and physical extremes, like Nancy Sykes in the stage version of Charles Dickens's *Oliver Twist*. In 1867, she created the role of Laura Courtland in Augustin Daly's hugely successful melodrama *Under the Gaslight*, which called

upon her, amid the roar of a speeding train, to ax her way out of a locked toolshed and rescue a Civil War veteran bound to the railroad tracks.

Eytinge's acting career went into hiatus for several years beginning in 1869 when she married and left the country with her second husband, George H. Butler, U.S. consul general to Egypt, with whom she bore two children. Writing about her sojourn in this "heathen land" in her autobiography, she assumed the

Ironically, although she didn't acknowledge her Jewish heritage, Rose Eytinge's dark eyes and hair resulted in her being typecast as a formidable, emotional, exotic woman and made her a star of the nineteenth-century stage. [New York Public Library]

perspective not only of an "American" but also of a "Christian" and an "Anglo-Saxon." Indeed, nowhere in her autobiography, *Memories of Rose Eytinge*, does she refer to her Jewish heritage. Because of her husband's abusive behavior, Eytinge divorced him and returned to New York, where she joined the Union Square Theatre Company in 1873.

Thereafter she played her most famous roles, the eponymous Rose Michel and Shakespeare's Cleopatra, for which she utilized her Egyptian experience and props. In 1880, she married her third husband, actor Cyril Searle, but they separated in 1884. She gave her last performance in 1907 and died on December 20, 1911, in Amityville, New York.

Eytinge masked her Jewishness in her autobiography, and she never specialized in playing Jewish characters. The influential manager Daniel Frohman, himself of Jewish descent, however, referred to her as the "black-eyed, black-haired Jewess." By contemporary social and theatrical standards, these attributes marked her for so-called female heavy roles involving displays of fierce passion, which thrilled audiences by transgressing bourgeois expectations of respectable womanly behavior.

BIBLIOGRAPHY

AJYB 14 (1912–1913):125; Clapp, John Bouve, and Edwin Francis Edgett. *Players of the Present.* Vol. I (1899); *DAB*; Eytinge, Rose. Clipping File. Harvard Theatre Collection, Cambridge, Mass.; Eytinge, Rose. *Memories of Rose Eytinge* (1905); *NAW*; Obituary. *NYTimes*, December 21, 1911, 11:5; Odell, George C.D. *Annals of the New York Stage.* Vols. 7–9 (1936–1937); Robinson, Alice, Vera Mowry Roberts, and Milly S. Barranger, eds. *Notable Women in the American Theatre: A Biographical Dictionary* (1989); Tompkins, Eugene, and Quincy Kilby. *History of the Boston Theatre, 1854–1901* (1908); Young, William C. *Famous Actors and Actresses on the American Stage.* Vol. I (1975); Wolf, Edwin, and Maxwell Whiteman. *The Jews of Philadelphia, from Colonial Times to the Age of Jackson* (1957); *WWWIA* 1.

KIM MARRA

F

FABIAN, MARY JACQUELINE (b. 1900)

After debuting in 1923 as Musetta in Puccini's *La Bohème* at the Century Theater in New York, Mary Jacqueline Fabian added to her soprano repertoire the well-known yet demanding roles of Madame Butterfly, Mimi, Manon, Micaëla, Marguerite, Violetta, and Gretel. Touring the United States as a star performer with the Columbia Opera Company during its 1929–1930 season, she appeared at other times with the famed Chicago Civic Light Opera. She also performed thoughout Europe with several companies, enjoying particular success in France and Italy. At different points during her stage career, Fabian sang with the New York Philharmonic Orchestra, with the Chicago Symphony Orchestra, and at the Hollywood Bowl, and was featured in numerous radio productions. A slight figure at five feet, with auburn hair and blue eyes, she was the first star of the grand opera to appear in talking movies and was awarded a gold medal by the Hollywood Breakfast Club.

Mary Fabian was born on July 7, 1900, in Sioux City, Iowa, to David and Rachel (Silke) Fabian. Both she and her sister Rose received musical training. Rose became an accomplished violinist. Fabian studied at the New England Conservatory of Music, the American Academy of Dramatic Arts in New York, the Milano Conservatory of Music, and the Paris Conservatory. Her private vocal instructors included Whitney, Guillo, and Outland in the United States, and Cadore, Storchio, Conti, and Agininni abroad.

Fabian's primary legacy to the arts lies not in her performances, her versatility on stage, or her popularity behind the microphone, but rather in her organizational skills and her unswerving conviction that opera and music education are not just for the elite. Founding and directing three civic opera companies in three areas—Miami, Birmingham, and Westchester—she worked in collaboration with local school and educational boards, incorporating amateur school dancers into her professional performances. In addition, she was among the first to render foreign operas in English for American audiences.

From 1942 to 1948, Fabian was a captain in the Women's Army Corps and served part-time in Europe. After the war, her career took yet another turn, albeit not one out of keeping with her previous preoccupations. In October 1948, she temporarily relocated to Vienna to become youth director of a welfare and educational program handling approximately 250,000 children, part of the rehabilitation program addressing the acute social disruption in the American zone of Austria.

As founder of the American Civic Opera Productions, which sought to further and support the connections between opera and education, Fabian maintained a business address in New York City, while residing more permanently in Birmingham, Alabama.

Her professional associations included the Business and Professional Women's Club, Delta Omnicon (honorary), and the Federated Women's Club. In her rare quiet hours, she enjoyed bridge, theater, hiking, and collecting stamps and objets d'art.

BIBLIOGRAPHY

American Women 2, 1937–1938 (1937): 210; *International Who Is Who in Music.* 5th ed. (mid-century): 169; *UJE*; *Who's Who in America* 20, 1938–1939 (1938): 861; *WWIAJ* (1938).

DAWN ROBINSON ROSE

FAGIN, CLAIRE (b. 1926)

Claire Fagin, a distinguished nursing educator, scholar, dean, and leader, became the first woman interim president of the University of Pennsylvania (June 1993–July 1994) and the first female to achieve this position in any Ivy League university. Her achievement, as a woman and especially as a nurse, was immortalized for Fagin by a friend who slightly altered an old *New Yorker* magazine cartoon showing a boy and girl playing "hospital." In the version given to Fagin, the girl turned to the boy and said: "You can play doctor and I'll play the president of the University of Pennsylvania."

Fagin's family, however, really expected her to be a doctor. Born in New York City on November 25, 1926, Claire (Mintzer) Fagin was the second daughter (her sister Sylvia was born on October 2, 1919) of lower middle-class immigrant parents, Mae Slatin and Harry Mintzer, from Russia and Austria. Her family called her "sonnygirl" to reflect their expectation that she would achieve without being constrained by gender expectations. They hoped she would become a physician, like her aunt. Instead, Fagin chose nursing and for fifty years has been on the cutting edge in changes in nursing practice, scholarship, and education.

Claire Fagin holds a Ph.D. in nursing as well as nine honorary doctoral degrees, and she has received innumerable awards from alumni, civic, and professional associations including the Kaplan-Landy Award from HADASSAH in 1994; served as president of the American Orthopsychiatric Association and the National League for Nursing; and published eight books and monographs and more than seventy articles. As well, from 1977 to 1992, she was professor and Margaret Bond Simon Dean of the School of Nursing at the University of Pennsylvania.

She entered HUNTER COLLEGE in 1943, at age sixteen, with dreams of becoming a singer, wife, and mother. She transferred a year later to the baccalaureate program in nursing at Wagner College on Staten Island after becoming intrigued by the advertisements for the U.S. Cadet Nurse Corps and recalling childhood experiences with visiting nurses. She was advised to enter a college rather than hospital-based nurses' training and to try either Wagner or Adelphi College because she was Jewish. Wagner, a small, private Lutheran-based college with few Jews, accepted her into its second nursing class. Fagin received her diploma in nursing in January 1947 and a B.S. degree in June 1948. Her work in child and adolescent psychiatric nursing at two New York City hospitals gave her the experience of being on an equal level with women of different racial backgrounds. It also taught her how to argue for her own perspective while seeking out colleagues who supported her efforts.

Recognized early for her intellect, activism, and nursing skills, Fagin went on to work at Bellevue Hospital, with its cutting-edge, but exceedingly challenging, psychiatric units. Her skills needed a more theoretical foundation, so she soon left Bellevue for the new psychiatric nursing master's program at Columbia University Teachers College. In the postwar atmosphere of hospital and research expansion, many of the women at Teachers College were being groomed for leadership in the rapidly changing nursing field. Upon graduation at age twenty-four, she became a nursing consultant to the National League for Nursing (NLN), which defined the functions and qualifications for psychiatric nursing throughout the country.

Her marriage to engineer Sam Fagin in 1952 brought with it a commute from suburban Maryland to New York for the NLN job. In that same year, Gwen Tutor Will, a close friend from graduate school and the chief nurse at the yet unopened clinical center of the National Institutes of Health (NIH), invited Fagin to develop the psychiatric children's unit and become her assistant chief. Fagin leaped at the chance to be involved in a new phase of psychiatric nursing, and working at a national research center where members of the psychiatric community would be reporting on their new work.

Fagin's subsequent career moves were once again in the field of nursing education. She taught in a new psychiatric/mental health nursing program at New York University (NYU). During this period she also worked on a Ph.D. and adopted two children, Joshua and Charles. Her groundbreaking study, built upon work done by British researchers she had met at the NIH, demonstrated the critical importance to patients and nurses of allowing parents of hospitalized children to room together. Her published monograph and articles in the mid-1960s, as well as her television appearances and media visibility, were highly influential in transforming hospital practices across the country.

By 1969, Fagin was restless with some of the theoretical directions the NYU program was taking and wanted a chance to try her ideas. She became professor and chair of the nursing department at Lehman College, a division of the City University of New York, a position she held for the next eight years. During that time Fagin created a program which ably demonstrated that college-educated nurses could do both the theory and practice of nursing. Impressed by her success at Lehman, the University of Pennsylvania lured Fagin in 1977 to be the dean of the nursing school and to rebuild its faculty. Fagin served in this capacity until 1992. In her fifteen years as dean, she transformed the school and established international respect for its faculty, its research, and its students as agents of change in the nursing profession. She became known for her courage and forthrightness, as well as her ability to play institutional politics and to attract the funding needed to build Penn nursing into one of the top schools in the country. Fagin's institutional and administrative skills were again put to good use when she became president of the National League for Nursing (1991–1993) and Penn's interim president (1993–1994).

Claire Fagin's ideas and scholarship shaped the debate over nursing education, hospital economics, and nursing practice. In a field that attracted very few Jewish women of her generation, she stood out for her strength of character, melding of theory and practice, intellectualism, forthrightness, and political skills.

SELECTED WORKS BY CLAIRE FAGIN

Abandonment of the Patient: The Impact of Profit-Driven Health Care on the Public, editor with Ellen D. Baer and Suzanne Gordon (1996); *Charting Nursing's Future: Agenda for the 1990s*, editor with Linda H. Aiken (1992); *Family-Centered Nursing in Community Psychiatry: Treatment in the Home* (1970); *Nursing in Child Psychiatry*, editor (1972); *Nursing Leadership: Global Strategies: International Nursing Development for the 21st Century*, editor (1990); *Readings in Child and Adolescent Psychiatric Nursing*, editor (1974).

BIBLIOGRAPHY

Fagin, Claire. "Claire Fagin." In *Making Choices Taking Chances: Nurse Leaders Tell Their Stories*, edited by Thelma M. Schorr and Anne Zimmerman (1988); Reverby, Susan. "Oral History of Claire Fagin." Center for the Study of Nursing History, School of Nursing, University of Pennsylvania, Philadelphia (1982).

SUSAN M. REVERBY

FALK, MINNA REGINA (1900–1983)

The liberation of the concentration camps at the end of World War II made a lasting impression on historian Minna Regina Falk. Falk was on leave from her teaching position at New York University (NYU) at the time, serving as an administrator in Europe with the American Red Cross. The events of the war heightened her resolve to return to academia and complete her own book about the history of Germany. Falk rejected other offers of work to return to teaching and research, but NYU was slow to grant her both leave to write and the promotions that came more readily to her male colleagues. Her textbook, *The History of Germany: From the Reformation to the Present Day*, was not published until 1957. In 1963, thirty-seven years after joining the history faculty, Minna Falk became the first female historian to become full professor at New York University.

Falk spent her entire academic life at NYU. She began her teaching career at NYU (then called Washington Square College) in 1926. She received an M.A. in history in 1927 and, in 1934, became the first person to receive a Ph.D. in European history from NYU. In addition to a heavy teaching load, she was active in extracurricular affairs. In the early 1940s she was the administrator of the Music Box Canteen on lower Fifth Avenue.

Falk was acutely conscious of religious discrimination in many university departments. While she did not publicly identify herself as a Jew, she noted that the history faculty was unusual because it hired professors of "all faiths." This inclusiveness did not extend to women, however. Both the field and the department were, in her words, "a man's world." Discrimination because of her gender was reflected in Falk's teaching load and salary. She taught day and evening classes with no increase in pay between 1931 and 1943, when she was recruited for the war effort by the American Red Cross. She waited fourteen years for a promotion from instructor to assistant professor, which finally came in 1947, when she returned from Europe. She was promoted to associate professor in 1955. Minna Falk was loyal to the department and devoted to her students, who valued her intelligence, scholarship, and sense of humor.

BIBLIOGRAPHY

Claster, Jill. Telephone interview with author. New York University, July 1996; Falk, Minna Regina. Archives. History Department, New York University, and *The History of Germany: From the Reformation to the Present Day* (1957); Obituary. *NYTimes*, May 5, 1983.

JANET WELLS GREENE

*While editorial writers bemoaned the dissolution of the Jewish family, many families clearly
succeeded both in carrying on the Jewish tradition and in realizing the American dream.
Pictured here in 1923 are Jennie B. and Eli Nachamson of North Carolina, and their nine children.
In addition to the more than full time job of raising her family, Jennie Nachamson founded HADASSAH
in the South in 1919. All eight of her daughters served as presidents of local chapters
of Hadassah across the region. [Eli N. Evans]*

FAMILY, THE MODERN JEWISH

"Happy [are] the children who live in the simple, practical atmosphere of the Jewish Home," rhapsodized ESTHER JANE RUSKAY in her 1902 paean to domestic Judaism, *Hearth and Home Essays*, in which she lavishly extolled the Jewish home's "beautiful ceremonies, healthful restraints, and simple pleasures." Thanks to those *heimisch* attributes, the American Jew lived a "temperate, well-ordered life, with none of the evils and none of the fears of this modern age to puzzle or to threaten him." Sober, hard-working, and idealistic, the Jewish family, Ruskay proudly affirmed, furnished the background from which "every country in the world owes its best Jewish citizenship."

Even as Ruskay penned her encomium to the Jewish family, that erstwhile object of public pride was rapidly becoming the subject of growing anxiety. As thousands of young immigrant families poured into America, swelling the ranks of the urban poor, a chorus of concerned social workers, rabbis, sisterhood presidents, and journalists collectively sounded an alarm. The fate of the Jewish family, they feared, hung in the balance. "One need but visit a few families to see that the word 'home' . . . is but a mockery for the dirty, foul-smelling rooms in which our applicants are forced or choose to live," observed a United Hebrew Charities worker early in the century, a sentiment echoed by the president of the National Conference of Jewish Charities. "The tenement is killing the Jewish home, of which we have all been proud," he related. "It is separating families, driving the boys in the streets and the girls into the [dance] hall." With inhospitable surroundings, economic uncertainty, and new social challenges, it was no wonder, observed *Froyen Velt*, a Yiddish women's magazine of the prewar era, that the "foundation of happy family life, of *sholem bayis*, has been undermined."

Illegitimacy and desertion, twin "blots on the eschutcheon of Judaism," posed even greater threats to the family's much-vaunted inviolability. At first, the Jewish community ignored the small but steadily growing number of unwed immigrant mothers; shame and social convention precluded public discussion, let alone intervention. It was "deemed inadvisable to mention it broadcast," an eyewitness recalled many years later. "Remember this was before the days when sex problems, the social evil, and white slavery made parlor conversation and when the Jewish community objected to having its daughters spoken of as not virtuous." Another added: "It is hard to realize what a bomb was exploded in the Jewish community when the Council wished to erect a home for unwed mothers. Intelligent Jewish men and women, prominent in philanthropy, were outraged that the virtue of Jewish girlhood and womanhood could be publicly assailed."

Eventually, such public resistance was overcome. In 1905, the NATIONAL COUNCIL OF JEWISH WOMEN, buoyed by the unstinting (although anonymous) financial support of the philanthropist THERESE SCHIFF, succeeded in opening a tiny shelter for "wayward women" where, amid the splendid isolation of rural Staten Island, they could escape the "finger of scorn" of hostile neighbors and disgraced relatives. "We take by the hand the young first offender and first offender only, the victim of her own ignorance or stupidity or the machinations of vile men or women," the Council explained. Six years later, as the number of unwed mothers continued to spiral upward, the women's organization opened a much larger facility, known as the Lakeview Home, to accommodate as many as forty "erring sisters."

Designed to resemble a private residence rather than a correctional facility, Lakeview sought to refashion the unwed mother into a self-supporting, independent, and genteel woman through an energetic program of vocational training and "ethical and moral reformation." Unwed mothers, insisted SADIE AMERICAN, one of Lakeview's most stalwart supporters, are not "necessarily bad, fallen girls," but girls who "simply haven't had the opportunity to be good." Lakeview provided that opportunity, training its young

charges to be domestic servants, department store clerks, and "good housewives," all the while holding out the possibility of marriage and the promise of respectability.

An apparent success, Lakeview came under the Jewish Board of Guardians' supervision in the early 1920s and continued, well into the 1950s, to develop new strategies for coping with what Sara Edlin, its long-time director, called an "age-old problem." "The attitude of society toward the unwed mother and her child has been persistently condemnatory," Edlin wrote in *The Unmarried Mother in Our Society*, a 1954 account of her tenure at Lakeview. "If we no longer pin a scarlet letter on her, we nevertheless find other if more subtle ways of punishing her."

For many years, neither scarlet letters nor punishment awaited the many men who abandoned or deserted their wives in what became known as a "poor man's divorce." "My wife has been here for five years and I've wanted to leave her ten times," an unhappy husband admitted. "She is a very undesirable woman. She often insults me in the presence of strangers." Like illegitimacy, desertion darkened the prewar Jewish family's good name, casting "discredit on our people's reputation for domestic virtues." Affecting the lives of 10 to 15 percent of Jewish women on relief in New York and Chicago in the early years of the century, the "desertion evil" provoked both moral outrage and concerted action.

Some Jewish communal institutions, such as the *Jewish Daily Forward*, sought to shame deserters into returning to their wives through its "Gallery of Missing Husbands." Much like the rogues' gallery developed by the police, this domestic Yiddish version contained the faces as well as brief biographies of husbands on the lam, hoping that alert readers would report their whereabouts to the authorities. The National Desertion Bureau went further still by taking systematic steps to apprehend deserters. Working in tandem with the courts and local government, it sought to compel the "errant husband" to support his family; failing that, he was encouraged to grant his wife a legal divorce. Between 1911, when the bureau was first established, and 1922, when social workers no longer considered desertion to be a serious problem, over twelve thousand cases, many of them including repeat offenders, came to its attention.

In accounting for the etiology of desertion, bureau workers identified as many as eighteen different factors, ranging from "money fever" and the interference of relatives to laziness and incompatibility. "Roundly speaking, economic pressure was the cause in about 30 percent of the cases, and self-indulgence the cause in about 70 percent," explained Morris Waldman in an address before the Society of Jewish Social Workers. Elaborating, the veteran social worker pointed out that "the new environment affects the immigrant husband and wife differently; the former is more open to its influence and the gradual development of both along different lines naturally carries them further apart."

With growing acculturation and the "gradual development" of the entire immigrant Jewish community over time, the Jewish family continued to experience difficulties, except that the problems it now faced stemmed more from the consequences of affluence than the travails of immigration. Throughout the interwar years, the Jewish family appeared (once again) to be in crisis, alternately "languishing" or awaiting "disintegration." "Those of us who still recall the Jewish family, its sense of kinship, its feeling of entity and oneness, are filled with a longing, with an overpowering nostalgia for the past," wrote Conservative rabbi William Greenfield in 1940. "What has happened? Why has that unique tower of strength disappeared from our midst? Why has the home disintegrated before our eyes into a house rather than a home? Why has the family become an insignificant factor rather than the bulwark of strength that it once was?"

For many, the answers to these impassioned questions had nothing to do with demography, as one might expect, but with culture. To put it another way, the issue at hand was not so much the literal reproduction of the Jewish family as the social reproduction of *yiddishkeit*, or Jewishness. With few exceptions, Jewish communal leaders of the interwar years did not voice much concern over intermarriage, which, they commonly believed, seldom took place. "A few anthropologists may believe the day will come when Americans will be as little opposed to mixed marriage as were medieval Baghdad and Toledo under the Saracens," prophesied the *Jewish Times* in 1930. "But in the main there is little peril that Americans will take the slogan of the Melting Pot too literally. Historic, long established integers will be preserved with little impairment, and America will be unified through means other than racial fusion."

By the same token, a pattern of steadily declining fertility did not seem to imperil the health of the Jewish community. In this instance, as with intermarriage, hardly anyone voiced concern over the "dwindling" or "undersized" Jewish family. On the wane since the 1900s, the American Jewish birthrate remained consistently lower than that of other Americans. As early as 1905, native-born Rhode Island Jewish families, for example, had an average of 2.3 children, compared with 3.2 for native-born Catholic families and 2.5 for native-born Protestant ones, a pattern that persisted for decades. A 1941 study found that in Indianapolis the Jewish birthrate was 25 percent lower than that of Protestants. Ten years later, at the height of the postwar baby boom, studies in Detroit and Providence showed that while the birthrate in both cities tended to "skyrocket," as historian Elaine Tyler May has put it, Jewish families, as a rule, tended to have only 2.3 children.

Despite these rather grim indices, few Jewish communal leaders paid attention, underscoring the extent to which cultural thresholds of alarm vary from generation to generation. Meanwhile, among those who did express concern, more was said about the immediate emotional and cultural drawbacks of small families than about the long-range statistical consequences of physical attrition. "A very small family is never a very interesting one," Jacob Kohn observed, pointing out that Passover "becomes rather pathetic when but two or three sit down to celebrate the seder. The festive meals and even family prayers lose much of their impressiveness and much of their significance as a social expression of religious life, if so few participate."

If neither intermarriage nor fertility was perceived as problematic, what, then, ailed the Jewish family, inspiring the community's moral authorities to liken it to an embattled fortress or a flimsy Maginot Line? Put simply, what ailed the Jewish family was its failure to act like one. Once a "domestic Temple," the Jewish home "has become little more than a hotel," complained one student of Jewish domestic mores in 1940. The Jewish home was now "a place to eat, a place to sleep, and a place from which to flee the moment that one has made use of its hotel functions," a criticism that extended to its appearance as well. Devoid of Judaica and other tangible marks of Jewishness, the average middle-class Jewish home did not even look Jewish. The once-requisite print of Moses, Theodore Herzl, or the Vilna Gaon had given way to "copies of Van Goghs and Renoirs and the usual standard, highly impersonal 'art' of the department store," while formerly cherished Kiddush cups and Sabbath candlesticks had been banished to the attic or hidden inside an armoire. More conspicuous still, or so it seemed to the community's cultural arbiters, was the absence of Jewish ritual. "In the vast majority of American Jewish homes," complained Newark rabbi Leon S. Lang, "Jewish living languishes progressively by default. In such homes it either disappears altogether or retains only a few vestigeal [sic] practices."

Statistical surveys of ritual behavior, conducted frequently and anxiously all throughout the interwar years by the Reform and Conservative movements, highlighted the degree to which modernity had imperiled domestic rituals or, at the very least, repositioned them. A 1931 study by the Union of American Hebrew Congregations of home rituals practiced by urban American Jews, for example, revealed that a striking 60 percent of respondents did not light Sabbath candles, while 80 percent eschewed the dietary laws altogether. What they now had, Lang observed in a 1939 address entitled "Our Changing Jewish Family," are "families of Jews but not Jewish families."

Time and again, women were held accountable for this sorry state of affairs, accused of turning away from the obligations modern society had "deeded" to them. After all, in the modern, postemancipation family, the Jewish woman's responsibilities encompassed much more than the physical and emotional well-being of her children; the very future of Judaism weighed upon her shoulders. "It is woman alone who can make home life a Paradise for the Jew," insisted Brooklyn rabbi Israel Levinthal. "She alone can save Judaism." Many Jewish women were quick to agree. "The Jewish woman who presides over her home is entrusted with a great and noble responsibility," stated TRUDE WEISS-ROSMARIN. "The Jewish fate, past and present, and the Jewish future are in her keeping."

All too often, though, these high-minded prescriptions seemed to be breached more than honored. "The great mass of our women—where are they, what has become of them," the rabbis wondered. Some women, apparently, were out shopping on Shabbat. Others preferred to spend their time reading Browning rather than the Bible, while still others knew much more about opera than cantorial music. Should you attend a Jewish women's club meeting and ask those present to find a passage in Malachi, don't be surprised if one of the women "ask[ed] whether Malachi was the title of an Italian opera," witheringly observed a member of the National Council of Jewish Women.

The modern Jewish woman stood accused of enfeebling Judaism by her inattention, neglect, and cultural illiteracy. "Unless we constantly cultivate a

The difficulties of Jewish life in the lower East Side of New York City are well known. Immigrants who settled in other parts of the country faced different hardships. Pictured here is North Dakota homesteader Bessie Schwartz (left) and several members of her family outside her sod hut, around 1890. [Jewish Historical Society of the Upper Midwest]

Jewish spirit through an intelligent understanding of our religion, of our history, and of our philosophy, we will cease to be Jewesses through inclination and belief and remain Jewesses only through habit and external pressure," Kate Aronson told an audience of attentive Jewish women.

In their campaign to educate Jewish women, some American Jewish leaders unhesitatingly recommended picking up a copy of Sir Walter Scott's *Ivanhoe*, certain that the modern-day Jewess would be inspired and invigorated by Rebeccah's flawless character and stalwart devotion to her people. "We need today women of Rebeccah's type—women who should feel a close attachment to Israel," said Rabbi Levinthal, referring to the biblical term for the Jewish people. Reading *Ivanhoe* was perhaps one way for the modern Jewish women to feel a sense of kinship with the Jewish people and its culture; others found guidebooks and manuals such as DEBORAH MELAMED's *Three Pillars* (1927) and Miriam Isaacs and Trude Weiss-Rosmarin's *What Every Jewish Women Should Know* (1941) more helpful still. Manifestly concerned with defining and interpreting Jewish holiday and food customs in a sophisticated, twentieth-century idiom, these guidebooks were actually designed to engage the imagination and loyalty of those modern-day Jewish women who could "no longer be satisfied with dear old mother's book of prayers."

Whether consulting modern texts in the privacy of one's home or joining together with the members of Ivriah, a New York City organization formed in 1926 to encourage the study of Hebrew and Jewish culture, Jewish women widely agreed that "the way to make the home Jewish is to make the mother Jewish." The apparent zeal and enthusiasm that Ivriah women brought to their study sessions—these are "feminine Paul Reveres," observed the *American Hebrew*, "knocking on the doors of New York, arousing the people to the urgent need to arm themselves spiritually"—was duplicated elsewhere throughout the country as Jewish women redoubled their efforts to achieve for American Judaism, sponsoring educational symposia in Nebraska and flocking to Bible class in Pennsylvania. "In a generation when women are with newly realized potentialities embarking upon careers as physicians, lawyers, journalists, and merchants," remarked STELLA FREIBERG, a president of the National Federation of Temple Sisterhoods, "many hundreds of women have found joyous self-expression in a very old, yet new career—the profession of being a Jewess."

Periodically, men were exhorted to assume or at least share some of the ritual responsibility for perpet-

All family members of recently arrived immigrants usually had to work to keep the family going. But some jobs were more enjoyable than others. This photograph, taken around 1915, depicts Rachael Freedland being nuzzled by a calf on her family's farm near Osseo, Minnesota. [Jewish Historical Society of the Upper Midwest]

uating Judaism lest it become thoroughly feminized. "If the concerns of Judaism and Jewish life are of little moment to the father, if the synagogue is only the goal of the mother's pilgrimage and the father regularly keeps his distance, the son will draw the conclusion that religion in general and Judaism in particular are feminine accomplishments and Jewish life a feminine indulgence," chided Jacob Kohn. While some fathers were no doubt inspired by Kohn's rhetoric and the "new fatherhood" of the interwar years, which encouraged men to find meaning at home and in religion, still others were perfectly content with the domestic division of labor. "I never interfere in religious matters," one such husband and father proudly informed Rabbi Kohn. "The religious training of my children is entirely in the hands of my wife."

In some respects, little has changed since Esther Jane Ruskay took pen in hand nearly a century ago to celebrate the virtues of the Jewish family and to champion the intimate connection that exists between domesticity and Jewishness. Although attenuated, that intimate connection endures: flickering to life at a Passover seder or a bat mitzvah, Jewishness continues to rest in the family. In other respects, however, the contemporary Jewish family seems to be holding on for dear life. Beset by a staggeringly high number of intermarriages and by fundamental and far-reaching changes in the very definition of family, the Jewish home of today is more likely to inspire a requiem than an encomium of the kind Ruskay published. Still, if Jewish history teaches anything, it is that resilience and change, much like the bonds between family and Jewishness, go hand in hand.

BIBLIOGRAPHY

Annual Report. Jewish Protectory and Aid Society (1919–1920); Cohen, Steven M., and Paula E. Hyman, eds. *The Jewish Family: Images and Reality* (1986); Edlin, Sara. *The Unmarried Mother in Our Society* (1954); Joselit, Jenna Weissman. *The Wonders of America: Reinventing Jewish Culture, 1880–1950* (1995); Kohn, Jacob. *Modern Problems of Jewish Parents: A Study in Parental Attitudes* (1932); Kraemer, David, ed. *The Jewish Family: Myth and Metaphor* (1989); Ruskay, Esther Jane. *Hearth and Home Essays* (1902); *Yearbook.* New York Section, National Council of Jewish Women (1903–1912).

JENNA WEISSMAN JOSELIT

FARKAS, RUTH LEWIS (1906–1996)

The impressive and full life of Ruth Lewis Farkas spanned many occupations: educator, sociologist, businesswoman, philanthropist, inventor, wife, and mother. She was born on December 20, 1906, and raised in Manhattan, the fourth of Samuel Lewis and Jennie Bach's five children. Farkas's parents were in the real estate business, but Jennie Lewis also worked with the poor of Manhattan and occasionally allowed her young daughter to accompany her into tenements. She gave Ruth this advice: "No matter what your station in life, always try to contribute to those less fortunate."

Ruth Lewis married her childhood neighbor George Farkas after a long courtship. George proposed to Ruth in her first year of college, but her mother insisted she complete her studies. A Founder's Day Scholar, Ruth received her bachelor's degree from New York University and married George three weeks later on June 7, 1928. Farkas went on to obtain a master's degree in sociology from Columbia in 1932, and a Ph.D. from New York University in 1958. During these years, the couple raised four sons: Alexander (b. 1930), Robin (b. 1933), Bruce (b. 1938), and Jonathan (b. 1948). Always the innovator, Farkas patented

the "roller muff," which fit around the handlebars of strollers and kept mothers' hands and nursing bottles warm. The muff could also be taken from the handlebars and worn around the hands during cold weather.

The year 1928 brought the founding of Alexander's, a New York retail chain, renowned for its discount merchandise and named for George Farkas's deceased father. The first Alexander's opened in the Bronx, grossing $500,000 in 1929, and expanded to eleven locations by 1992. Farkas was the vice chairman, personnel and community relations director, from 1955 to 1972.

Farkas compiled a long list of accomplishments during her lifetime: psychological tutor with the Federation of Jewish Charities (1941–1945), educational sociology instructor at New York University (1945–1955), and president of the Dolma Realty Corporation of Fort Lauderdale, Florida (1955–1972). In 1962, she became the director of the William Alanson White Institute of Psychiatry, and in 1966 was appointed the chair of the President's Advisory Council of the New York University Graduate School of Social Work. In addition to these chairs, she was Women's Division Chairman of the Albert Einstein Medical College, president of the Beth Abraham Hospital for the Chronic Ill, and vice president of the Child Study Association of America.

Her leadership roles in educational sociology brought her to the attention of Secretary of State Dean Rusk in 1964, who appointed her to a three-year nonpaying position with UNESCO and made her adviser to the American delegation to the International Conference on Eradication of Illiteracy, held in Iran in 1965. As a sociologist, Farkas conducted research in the area of male-female behavior and perceptions at the Role Foundation, which she organized in 1967. In 1965, Farkas became the first alumna and the third woman to be named to the board of trustees of New York University since its establishment in 1831.

The latter part of Farkas's life involved some controversy. A lifelong Republican, Farkas and her family supported President Richard M. Nixon in his reelection campaign, donating more than $300,000. Farkas was then appointed ambassador to Luxembourg in 1973. In July of 1974, Nixon's lawyer and fund-raiser Herbert Kalmbach testified before the House Judiciary Committee that Farkas knew her donation would lead to an ambassadorial posting. Farkas denied the charges, and her Senate confirmation was delayed. Prevailing on the strength of her remarkable background, Farkas used her post for philanthropic pursuits.

Farkas continued her contributions to the less fortunate. An active member of the Jewish community,

Farkas was awarded the Louise Waterman Wise Distinguished Service Award in 1966 for leadership in welfare and educational causes. Upon her death, she was hailed as a determined force in social welfare causes and as a friend, mentor, and counselor to many. Her life demonstrated the possibilities that exist for a woman of determination, intelligence, and education.

After a short stay in a Manhattan hospital for a heart ailment, Ruth Lewis Farkas was released and died at the home of her son Robin on October 18, 1996, at age eighty-nine.

BIBLIOGRAPHY

Cheshire, Maxine. "A Lady for Luxembourg." *New York Daily News*, March 1, 1973, 54; "Cost of Costa Rica." *New Republic* 161 (August 31, 1974): 10; *EJ* (1973–1982); Farkas, Ruth Lewis. Biography File. New York University and New York University Medical School Archives; Knight, Michael. "Sociologist, Trustee, Envoy: Ruth Lewis Farkas." *NYTimes*, February 28, 1973, A15; Leavitt, Judith A. *American Women Managers and Administrators: A Selective Biographical Dictionary of Twentieth-Century Leaders in Business, Education, and Government* (1985); Leibowitz, Ed. "Recalling Alexander's: Discount Store with Million-Dollar Memories." *New York Newsday*, August 20, 1992, 47; Pincus, W. "Case of Peter Flanigan." *New Republic* 171 (October 19, 1984): 12–13; Silverman, Edward R. "Up for Grabs: Alexander's Collapse Creates Opportunity for a Successor, and a Potential Disaster for the Bronx and its Merchants." *New York Newsday*, June 22, 1992, 25; Sloan, Allan. "Looking Closer at the Odd Bankruptcy of Alexander's Inc." *Washington Post*, June 2, 1992, C3; Strom, Stephanie. "Alexander's Shuts All Its Eleven Stores: Plans Liquidation." *NYTimes*, March 16, 1992, sec. 1, p. 1; U.S. Congress, House. *Dr. "Dynamo."* Extension of Remarks of Hon. Jonathan B. Bingham of New York. 90th Cong., 1st sess. *Congressional Record* (November 9, 1967), vol. 113; U.S. Department of State. *Biographic Register* (1974); Van Gelder, Lawrence, "Ruth Farkas, Nixon's Ambassador to Luxembourg, Dies." *NYTimes*, October 18, 1996, D25; *Who's Who in America, 1992–1993*. 47th ed. (1992); *Who's Who in the World: 1978–1979*. 4th ed. (1978).

TANYA ELDER

FEDER-KEYFITZ, SARA RIVKA (1900–1979)

Sara Feder-Keyfitz was a Zionist leader, an accomplished sociologist, an outstanding educator, and an ardent feminist who worked hard on behalf of women's rights in America and Palestine. An important leader in the American Labor Zionist movement, she became a lifelong leader of PIONEER WOMEN (the forerunner of Na'amat USA) in the United States, Canada, and Israel.

A woman who could count Golda Meir among her close friends, Sara Feder-Keyfitz fought for women's rights in America and Israel as a life-long member of PIONEER WOMEN, *the forerunner of Na'amat USA. [Na'amat USA]*

Sara Feder-Keyfitz was born in Poland on October 31, 1900, to Benjamin and Shaine (Kumok) Feder. She grew up in Milwaukee, Wisconsin, where her parents owned a store and restaurant in a Jewish section of town. She attended the Milwaukee Fourth Street School and became close friends with Golda Mabovitch, later GOLDA MEIR. The two remained close throughout their lives. With Meir, Feder-Keyfitz became involved in the Poale Zion movement. Through this association she became the secretary of the Yiddish Folk School and developed a love for Yiddish culture. Feder-Keyfitz also became involved in the woman suffrage movement. She attended the University of Missouri, where she earned a doctorate in sociology, and the University of Chicago, where she earned a doctorate from the School of Social Service Administration. While studying education at Columbia University, she joined the newly formed Pioneer Women. On June 21, 1921, Sara Feder married Professor Isidore Keyfitz in Milwaukee. In 1927, with her husband, she took her first trip to Palestine. Returning in 1929 to the faculty of the University of

Missouri to teach sociology and to lecture on the changing role of the family and the status of women, Feder-Keyfitz spent her summers building young Pioneer Women clubs in Chicago. From 1936 to 1942, she served as a member of the Pioneer Women Secretariat, coeditor of *Pioneer Woman* journal, and national president of Pioneer Women from 1951 to 1955.

In Missouri, Feder-Keyfitz worked at the state level on behalf of women's rights, youth, and the aging. She wrote numerous educational and sociological papers, including the chapter "Aging in the Kibbutz," which appeared in a larger work on gerontology called *Aging and Modernization*. Making aliyah in 1970, Feder-Keyfitz joined the faculty of the American College in Jerusalem. In Jerusalem she opened her home to new immigrants and entertained Pioneer Women tourists. She established the Adult Education Association in Israel and remained active in women's rights causes. Sara Feder-Keyfitz died in Jerusalem on January 8, 1979, survived by her daughter, Lami Halperin, and three grandchildren.

SELECTED WORKS BY SARA FEDER-KEYFITZ

"Aging in the Kibbutz." In *Aging and Modernization*, edited by Donald O. Cogill and Lowell D. Holmes (1972): 211–226; "I Remember Golda . . . (on the Occasion of Her 75th Birthday)." *Pioneer Woman* (May–June 1973): 3–5.

BIBLIOGRAPHY

AJYB 81:365–366; *BEOAJ*; Kaufman, Rose. "A Letter from Israel About Sara Feder-Keyfitz." *Pioneer Woman* (March–April 1979): 18; Meir, Golda. *My Life* (1975): 459; "Mourn Passing of Sara Feder-Keyfitz, Past PW President." *Pioneer Woman* (January–February 1979): 29.

JUDITH FRIEDMAN ROSEN

FEINBERG, BEATRICE CYNTHIA FREEMAN *see* FREEMAN, CYNTHIA

FEINGOLD, JESSICA (b. 1910)

Jessica Feingold was the director of Intergroup Activities at the Jewish Theological Seminary of America from 1959 to 1983 and served in administrative capacities in the seminary's two principal "intergroup relations" programs, the Conference on Science, Philosophy, and Religion and the Institute for Religious and Social Studies.

She was born on December 28, 1910, in New Orleans, Louisiana, the first of three children and only daughter of Jessie (Schwabacher) and Meyer William Feingold. Her mother was born in Chicago of a well-to-do German Jewish family. Her father was born in Romania, immigrated to the United States with his family, and grew up in New Orleans where he studied at Tulane University.

During Jessica Feingold's childhood in New Orleans, her father was a partner in Levy, Loeb and Company, a dry-goods business. In 1917, William Feingold accepted a position as an executive at J. Aron and Company on Wall Street, and the family moved to New York City.

Although she had gone to public school in New Orleans, Feingold and her two brothers went to private schools in New York. Jessica Feingold graduated from the Calhoun School in 1927 (originally the Jacobi School), an academically rigorous girls' school

Jessica Feingold devoted more than forty-five years of her life to carrying out the goals of the Jewish Theological Seminary. She edited fifty books that originated at the institution, while also serving in almost uncountable administrative positions, including the principal assistant of Louis Finkelstein, who was provost, president, and then chancellor of the seminary. [Ratner Center, JTS. Photograph by John H. Popper]

attended by daughters of German Jewish families. She also attended the Hebrew school at Temple Emanu-El, but found little there to interest her. Although the Feingolds were nominally Reform, religion played only a small part in their family life.

After Calhoun, Feingold attended Vassar College, where she experienced the social discomfort of being one among very few Jews. She graduated from Vassar in 1931, then attended Columbia University, where she received an M.A. in history in 1933. Uncertain of her vocation in a period when few professional opportunities were open to women, and in the midst of the Depression, Feingold went on to take a business course at the Collegiate Secretarial Institute.

In 1936, after two brief secretarial stints, Feingold answered a blind advertisement in the *New York Times*. The job was to be secretary to Louis Finkelstein, then assistant to the president of the Jewish Theological Seminary in upper Manhattan. It paid twenty dollars per week, half the amount of the allowance she was receiving at home.

Not long after, in 1938, Louis Finkelstein founded the Institute for Religious and Social Studies, the first of what came to be known as the "intergroup relations" programs at the Jewish Theological Seminary. In 1940, the same year he became president of the seminary, Finkelstein founded the second of these programs, the Conference on Science, Philosophy, and Religion in Their Relation to the Democratic Way of Life. Feingold came to be integrally involved with both of these programs. In 1951, she became the executive director of the institute; she became its director in 1964. In 1956, she was appointed executive vice president of the conference, after serving as its assistant secretary-treasurer (1944–1947) and secretary (1948–1956). From 1959 until her retirement in 1983, she was the director of Intergroup Activities, the department that encompassed both programs.

The Institute for Religious and Social Studies was an interfaith educational program for clergy. The institute's principal forum was a Tuesday lecture series, but it also held conferences and seminars, and programs for theological students and faculty. Branches in Chicago and Boston were founded in 1944 and 1945, respectively.

While the "groups" originally implied by the term "intergroup" were Catholic, Jewish, and Protestant, by the 1950s the definition had expanded to include representatives of Islam, Buddhism, Hinduism, and other religions. The institute also expanded its program to take up questions arising from current affairs, urban problems, the arts, social sciences, and,

most important, ethics in cross-cultural perspective. A separate Institute on Ethics emerged out of the Institute for Religious and Social Studies in 1956, and a World Academy of Ethics was planned during the 1950s and 1960s but was never realized. The institute continues today at the Jewish Theological Seminary as the Louis Finkelstein Institute for Religious and Social Studies.

The Conference on Science, Philosophy, and Religion was founded in 1940 as an answer to the increasing distance of scholars in the sciences and humanities from one another, and from religious thought on morality and ethics. Founders of the conference felt they saw the logical conclusion of such estrangements in European fascism. The portion of the conference's original title referring to "the Democratic Way of Life" (later dropped) reflects their wartime desire to ally their work with democratic values.

The conference's original participants were scholars in the sciences and the humanities. Later, businesspeople, government officials, foundation officers, and others from outside the academic world were added. Topics covered by the conference over the years included ethics, race relations, labor relations, and educational policy. It was centered administratively at the Jewish Theological Seminary, and its annual meetings were held alternately at the seminary, Columbia University, the American Philosophical Society, Harvard University, Loyola University, and the University of Chicago. The conference met for the last time in 1968.

When, in 1969, it was decided that the conference should explore the possibility of involving more international participants and even of meeting abroad, Feingold undertook a four-month trip through Asia in an effort to arouse interest and recruit participants. From December 1969 through April 1970, she traveled on her own through Japan, Taiwan, Hong Kong, Indonesia, Thailand, India, Ceylon, and Iran, meeting with scholars, religious figures, and government officials. But on her return, a budget crisis at the seminary and the approaching retirement in 1972 of Louis Finkelstein doomed the project.

Even after her time was fully occupied with matters relating to the intergroup programs, Feingold remained the principal assistant of Louis Finkelstein, who was, successively, assistant to the president, provost, president, and chancellor of the seminary. In addition to editing the forty-nine volumes produced by the institute and conference, she edited some of Louis Finkelstein's books. Her own article, "Up from Isolation—Intergroup Activities at the Seminary," was published in the journal *Judaism* in 1978.

Feingold also continued to carry out such administrative duties as serving on committees; making logistical arrangements for convocations, meetings, and other events; and entertaining seminary visitors. The pattern of her career was similar to that of a number of other talented, educated women who worked for many years in administrative positions at the seminary. While a few achieved positions of some power by force of ability, most worked behind the scenes, failing to receive appropriate recognition, in terms of titles or remuneration, in an institution that primarily valued the work of rabbis and scholars. Not until the end of Feingold's career was the institution beginning to come to terms with women's changing roles. In 1974, the seminary appointed a woman to the faculty of its rabbinical school for the first time, and in 1984, it admitted its first woman candidates for rabbinic ordination.

One of Feingold's most important administrative duties, outside of her intergroup work, was her service on a committee to plan for the transformation of the Fifth Avenue mansion of Felix and FRIEDA SCHIFF WARBURG into a new home for the seminary's museum collection. In 1947, the Jewish Museum formally opened.

Throughout her career at the Jewish Theological Seminary, Feingold saw herself primarily as a vehicle for Louis Finkelstein's ideas. In a sense, she was. Louis Finkelstein was a visionary, charismatic man, a scholar and rabbi, as well as a leading figure in the movement for interfaith cooperation during the 1940s and 1950s. The institute and conference attracted many prominent figures, and the books of proceedings and papers that came out of the two programs went through several editions and were translated into many languages. Yet it is also true that without Feingold's initiative, trained intelligence, and organizational skills operating, often behind the scenes, the programs would not have been the success they were. The fact that she was a rather anomalous figure at the seminary—the founding and central institution of the Conservative Movement in Judaism—a Jew but nonobservant, a woman, and unmarried, were, in this context, assets rather than handicaps. Part insider, part outsider, she was able to function as a kind of gracious bridge between the seminary and the people from a variety of religious and cultural backgrounds who came to it to participate in the institute and conference.

At the time of her retirement, the seminary awarded Feingold two honorary doctorates, in divinity in 1982, and sacred theology in 1983. These were added to the honorary degrees she received from Fordham University (1979) and the General Theo-

logical Seminary (1982). The conference awarded her its first Conference on Science, Philosophy, and Religion Medal in 1956.

Jessica Feingold's life has been occupied chiefly with her work at the seminary, yet during World War II she also served as the director of the West Side of Manhattan's Air Raid Control Center, 1941 to 1945. She was also the director of the West Side of Manhattan's door-to-door bond drives. In 1948, she was a board member of the West Side Community Centers, Incorporated. In 1976, she served on many bicentennial committees, among them the interreligious "Forward '76." She has also been a member of the Asian American Assembly for Policy Research and the Institute for Religion and Social Change in Honolulu.

BIBLIOGRAPHY

Interviews with author, July 21, 1995, and archival materials at the Ratner Center for the Study of Conservative Judaism, Jewish Theological Seminary, NYC, including oral history interview by Mychal Springer, July–September 1989; Records of the Jewish Theological Seminary, R.G.5, Conference on Science, Philosophy, and Religion; R.G.11, Communications Department; R.G.1 General Files; R.G. 16, Institute for Religious and Social Studies; and Jessica Feingold, "Up from Isolation—Intergroup Activities at the Seminary." *Judaism* 27 (Summer 1978): 283–291.

JULIE MILLER

FEINSTEIN, DIANNE (b. 1933)

Political pioneer, tough leader, crime fighter, reformer: These are some of the words that describe Dianne Feinstein, former mayor of San Francisco and United States senator from California since 1992.

The eldest of three daughters, she was born on June 22, 1933, to Dr. Leon Goldman, a surgeon and professor at the University of California, San Francisco, and Betty (Rosenburg) Goldman. Both of her parents came from Russian immigrant families. The Goldmans were proud of their heritage and could trace their family tree back for generations. Sam Goldman, Dianne's paternal grandfather, helped to found several temples in California, while his son Leon became a prominent donor to San Francisco's Mount Zion Synagogue. Dianne's mother's family, the Rosenburgs, had a more distant relationship with Judaism. Some of them belonged to the Russian Orthodox church.

While growing up, she was greatly influenced by her paternal uncle. Morris Goldman, in contrast to his Republican-minded brother Leon, was a populist who

*As mayor of San Francisco and senator from California, as in her entire public life,
Dianne Feinstein has combined social awareness with social responsibility. She is pictured
here with* BARBARA BOXER, *her California colleague in the Senate. [Reuters/Bettmann]*

worked in the city's garment district and who introduced Dianne to the idea of the working class. He
took her to San Francisco's City Hall to watch a meeting of the Board of Supervisors, sparking her interest
in politics early on. By observing her father and her
uncle, she learned to weigh both sides of an argument
and to think about the complexities of an issue.

She attended a Jewish religious school, but later
enrolled at the Convent of the Sacred Heart, a prestigious private Catholic high school, in accordance with
her mother's wishes. At that time she met California
Attorney General Edmund (Pat) Brown, the father of
a classmate. The teenaged Feinstein impressed Brown
with her interest in political life. After Brown was
elected governor of California, he sought out Dianne
and gave her a job as an advocate for prison reform.

After graduating from Sacred Heart (the first Jew
to do so), she entered Stanford University, where she

excelled academically and became actively involved in
politics. She was vice president of her class and joined
the Young Democrats. She graduated in 1955, and
then worked as an intern in public affairs for the Coro
Foundation. In 1956, she eloped with Jack Berman,
now a San Francisco superior court judge, but the
marriage ended in less than three years. Feinstein and
Berman disagreed fundamentally over the role that a
woman should play. Berman wanted her to be a wife
and a mother to their daughter, Katherine (who was
nine months old at the time of divorce). She saw herself in this role, but also wanted a professional career
in the public sector.

In 1962, she married Bertram Feinstein, a distinguished neurosurgeon who was a colleague of her
father and twenty years her senior. Their marriage,
which lasted until Bertram's death in 1978, gave Feinstein the freedom to pursue her political career. In

1980, she married Richard Blum, a successful investment banker who advises her and helps in her political campaigns.

Governor Brown appointed Feinstein a member of the California Women's Board of Terms and Parole in 1960, where she gained her first experiences in criminal reform. In 1968, she served on the San Francisco mayor's committee on crime and committee on adult detention. A year later, she became the first woman president of the San Francisco Board of Supervisors. Her success and popularity in this capacity won her reelection for two additional terms.

The 1970s saw San Francisco torn apart by political strife. After the assassinations of Mayor George Moscone and board colleague Harvey Milk in 1978,

Feinstein decided to run for mayor. She won the election in 1979 and instituted tough legal and social reforms. In 1983 she was reelected to a second four-year term. *City and State* magazine named her America's Most Effective Mayor in 1987.

Feinstein's top priority during her nine years as mayor was public safety. She fought crime by increasing the strength of San Francisco's police department and by cutting down the response time for major emergencies from eight minutes to two. Fiscal responsibility and boosting the local economy were two other important concerns to her. She made sure that the city's budget was balanced in every year that she held office, and she developed relationships with major trading cities in Asia, Europe, and Africa. During her

The two women members of the Senate Judiciary Committee welcome RUTH BADER GINSBURG *to the committee's hearings on her nomination to be an associate justice of the Supreme Court. All three women have made a specialty of breaking glass ceilings. Carol Moseley-Braun (right) was the first African-American woman elected to the Senate; Dianne Feinstein was one of the first two Jewish women elected; Ginsburg was the first Jewish woman on the Supreme Court. [Reuters/Bettmann]*

tenure, the famous San Francisco cable car system was rebuilt, city streets were repaved, and the sewer system was upgraded.

Her long and distinguished political career has been marked by a series of firsts. In 1984, she was considered by the Democratic Party for nomination for vice president of the United States. In 1990, the Democrats selected her as their first female candidate for California governor, a bid that was unsuccessful.

When California senator Pete Wilson left that office to become governor of the state in 1992, Feinstein was elected to finish his unexpired term in the Senate. As a freshman senator, she wrote the California Desert Protection Act, which protects some three million acres of national park land.

In 1994, she was reelected for a full six-year term. As a senator, she has been as actively engaged in criminal reform as when she was mayor of San Francisco. She introduced and saw the passage of the Gun-Free Schools Act (1994), requiring public schools to expel for one year any student who brings a gun to school. Her Hate Crimes Sentencing Enforcement Act (1993) increased the minimum sentences given to those convicted of hate crimes in a federal court. She also introduced the Comprehensive Methamphetamine Control Act, passed in 1996, which limited access to the precursor chemicals needed to make the drug and increased the penalties for smuggling, drug possession, and possession of specialized equipment for making methamphetamine.

As a member of the Judiciary Subcommittee on Immigration, Feinstein is involved in legislative activities aimed at stopping illegal immigration. She was instrumental in the debate and drafting of the Illegal Immigration Reform and Immigration Responsibility Act and helped to block the controversial Gallegly Amendment that would have expelled more than three hundred thousand children of illegal immigrants from the public school system.

In addition, Feinstein takes an active interest in health and medical issues. Her amendment prohibiting health insurance discrimination on the basis of genetic information is now law as part of the Kassebaum-Kennedy health bill. She also worked to pass and increase the funding for the Ryan White AIDS Care Act. As cochair of the Senate Cancer Coalition, she presided over hearings that helped to win much-needed funds for cancer research at the National Cancer Institute and for a study by the National Institutes of Health on the high incidence of breast cancer rates in the San Francisco area.

Feinstein is a member of the Centrist Coalition, a bipartisan group of twenty-two moderate senators, which has proposed a seven-year balanced-budget plan to preserve Medicare and Medicaid while making fair and sensible reductions to them. The Centrist budget plan was narrowly defeated in the Senate, but the coalition plans to reintroduce its proposal in the near future.

In response to the victims of the 1994 Northridge, California, earthquake, Feinstein secured passage of a bill to provide federal disaster relief funds of approximately $11 billion. Her interest in foreign relations has gained her positions on various Senate subcommittees overseeing the Middle East, African affairs, and East Asian and Pacific affairs.

In recognition of her public service, she has been awarded honorary degrees by the University of San Francisco, Mills College, the University of Santa Clara, and Golden Gate University. In 1984, French president François Mitterrand bestowed upon her the Legion d'Honneur, one of France's highest honors.

Other awards recognize Feinstein's role as a Jewish woman in public office. The American Friends of the Hebrew University of Jerusalem gave her the Scopus Award for outstanding public service in 1981. She received a distinguished public service award from the Los Angeles Anti-Defamation League of B'nai B'rith in 1984, the brotherhood/sisterhood award of the National Conference of Christians and Jews in 1986, and a public service award from the AMERICAN JEWISH CONGRESS in 1987.

BIBLIOGRAPHY

Feinstein, Dianne. Printed material from the office of the senator; Morris, Celia. *Storming the Statehouse* (1992).

SONDRA LEIMAN

FELDMAN, SANDRA (b. 1939)

"Just because kids are poor, and maybe come from uneducated parents, and live in an urban setting, doesn't mean they shouldn't have teachers who are paid as well, and whose lives are as comfortable professionally, as teachers from the richest suburbs." For Sandra Feldman, president of the New York City's United Federation of Teachers and of the national American Federation of Teachers, these are fighting words.

Sandra Feldman's commitment to the New York City public schools grew from her own experience. The daughter of Milton and Frances Abramowitz, a milkman and a bakery worker, granddaughter of immigrants from Hungary and Romania, she was born October 14, 1939, and grew up in Coney Island. Her mother was often ill, so Sandra frequently cared for her two younger siblings, Helen and Larry. School was an intellectual and cultural refuge, and she credits Miss Bezman, her second-grade teacher at Public School 188, with expanding her horizons.

Feldman's political education began at Brooklyn College, where she heard Bayard Rustin, the civil rights activist, who became a mentor, speak about organizing a march to integrate schools. In 1963, she was arrested for working to integrate restaurants in Maryland and was active in organizing for Dr. Martin Luther King Jr.'s March on Washington. She earned a master's degree in English literature from New York University. She taught first and fourth grades on the Lower East Side of Manhattan, was one of only two members of the teachers' union there, and helped organize the entire teaching staff. In 1966, on the recommendation of Rustin, she was hired by United Federation of Teachers president Albert Shanker as a full-time field representative. Working her way through the ranks to executive director, she was elected secretary in 1983 and, in 1986, succeeded Shanker, becoming the first woman president of the union, which was founded in 1960.

Upon Shanker's death, Feldman was immediately considered a leading contender to be his successor once again, this time as president of the national American Federation of Teachers, in which position he had served since 1974. Her supporters believed her experience leading a large union, her expertise on political reform, and her innovative success in forming alliances with community and parent groups made her deserving of and qualified for the position; others questioned whether she could successfully serve as president of the UFT and AFT simultaneously (although Shanker had done so from 1974 to 1986) or quarreled with her stand against vouchers that facilitate parents' sending their children to private schools. She was elected AFT president unanimously by the union's executive council on May 6, 1997.

Her first marriage, to Paul Feldman, ended in divorce. She is married to Arthur Barnes, former president of the New York Urban Coalition. Her organizational affiliations reflect a concern for the community. She is associated with the United States Committee for UNICEF, the Coalition of Labor Union Women, the Executive Committee of Education International, the New York Chapter of the NAACP, the Women's Commission for Refugee Women and Children, the Jewish Labor Committee, and many other groups. Her concern for educators, children, women, and labor and a recognition of her Jewish roots are evident in her work and community commitments. She is a powerful and influential voice in the politics of education, in New York City and nationally.

Sandra Feldman, president of the American Federation of Teachers, has been active in the civil rights movement and the labor movement since the early 1960s. Hers is a strong voice for equality in education. [Suzanne DeChillo/NYT Pictures]

BIBLIOGRAPHY

Davis, Ron. Communication with author; "Feldman Elected Head of National Teachers Union." *NYTimes*, May 7, 1997; "Feldman Ranks High on Federation's List for Shanker's Job." *NYTimes*, March 30, 1997; "In Schools' Crisis, Union's Opportunity." *NYTimes*, September 29, 1995; "New Teachers Leader." *NYTimes*, January 10, 1986.

RONA HOLUB

FELLMAN, MARY ARBITMAN (b. 1917)

A community leader in the Midwest, Mary Arbitman Fellman was president of Beth El Synagogue Sisterhood, of the Midwest branch of the National Women's League, and of the Omaha chapter of HADASSAH. She became the first woman elected president of the Jewish Federation of Omaha in 1978. For five years she and her sister, Annie Arbitman Allen, directed the Midwest Jewish Singles Network to help Jewish singles meet.

Mary Arbitman Fellman was born in Omaha, Nebraska, on March 2, 1917. Her father, Max Arbitman, arrived in United States from Odessa in 1905. Her mother, Dora Freed, came from Minsk in 1912, and with her family made their entry to the United States at Galveston, Texas. Max Arbitman was the proprietor of a grocery store from 1916 until 1959. The Arbitmans had three children, of whom Mary was the eldest; her brother, Morris, died in 1941 while in the U.S. military and the youngest, Annie Allen, now resides in Jerusalem.

Mary graduated from Central High School in 1935 and from the University of Nebraska in 1939 with a degree in sociology and journalism. After jobs with the U.S. Engineers and an insurance company, she began work as a news editor for the *Omaha Jewish Press* in 1943. She served as its first woman editor until her marriage in 1947 to Morris C. Fellman. They had three children: Marsha Zimmerman, a registered nurse in St. Paul, Minnesota; Mark Fellman, an attorney in Mendota Heights, Minnesota; and Ronald Fellman, an attorney in Newton Highlands, Massachusetts.

In 1982 she and Oliver B. Pollak cofounded the Nebraska Jewish Historical Society. She has been instrumental in the publication of *Memories of the Jewish Midwest*, the establishment of the Archival Center, and the Henry and Dorothy Riekes Museum in the Dan and Esther Gordman Center for Jewish Learning.

Her many awards include the B'nai B'rith Citizenship Award, the Jewish Federation of Omaha and the Amit Women's Humanitarian Awards, the KETV Jefferson Award, the NATIONAL COUNCIL OF JEWISH WOMEN's Hannah G. Solomons Award, the Beth El Synagogue Earl Siegal Award, and the Omaha Chapter of Hadassah Lifetime of Service Award.

BIBLIOGRAPHY

Nebraska Jewish Historical Society; *Omaha Jewish Press*; personal interviews.

OLIVER B. POLLAK

FELS, MARY (1863–1953)

Mary Fels, an ardent and philanthropic Zionist, promoted Jewish settlement in Palestine and Israel throughout her life. Born March 10, 1863, in Sembach, Bavaria, she was the daughter of Elias and Fannie (Rothschild) Fels. Fels came with her parents to the United States in 1869 and grew up in Iowa, where her father made his living as a purveyor of dry goods. She graduated from Keokuk High School, and then spent one year at St. Mary's Academy in Notre Dame, Indiana. She continued her formal education with one year at the University of Pennsylvania in Philadelphia and, later, with special courses at Bedford College in London.

It was while Mary Fels was in Philadelphia that she met Joseph Fels, a distant cousin. She was charmed by him, and they married on November 16, 1881. The couple maintained residences in Philadelphia and in London, where Joseph Fels and his brothers operated an extremely successful soap manufacturing company. The couple's only child, Irving S. Fels, died while still an infant.

Joseph Fels, much to the consternation of his brothers and partners, was extraordinarily philanthropic. He and his wife believed that the capitalist system that had made them rich was flawed and unjust and that they could justify their wealth only by using it to reform capitalism. When Joseph Fels died in 1914, Mary Fels moved to New York City and became extremely active in a variety of causes, both charitable and political. She wrote *Joseph Fels, His Life-Work* (1916), which, with an understandable bias, charts her husband's life, extols his virtues, and dwells on his many accomplishments and brilliance.

During World War I, Fels served as the main editor of *The Public, A Journal of Democracy*. During her tenure at *The Public* (1917–1919), she wrote a number of editorials that expressed her political opinions. Fels supported President Woodrow Wilson, encouraged labor unions to assert themselves, bemoaned the treatment of "our colored sisters," and chided the "stupid" and "asinine Republicans" who sought to deny the vote to women. After the British capture of Palestine, she used her editorial position to write about the need to establish a Jewish presence in the land based on what she called "Mosaic principles"—ethical and cultural standards of Judaism.

Mary Fels inherited her husband's interest in the increasingly profitable family business and used both her fortune and time to support a number of causes, Jewish settlement in Palestine among them. After the war, and after resigning from her editorial post, she traveled to Palestine several times to promote Jewish settlement. Joseph Fels, too, had supported the need for a permanent Jewish settlement, and, as a member of the Jewish Territorial Organization, he had traveled to Mexico in 1907 to investigate the possibility of settling Jews there. Mary Fels, however, was convinced by her repeated visits that the history of the Jews in

With her husband, Joseph, and after his death, Mary Fels used his fortune to crusade for many political and philanthropic causes, most notably Jewish settlement in Israel and Palestine. [American Jewish Historical Society]

Palestine demanded that the Jews return to their ancient homeland. Their physical return would not suffice. She believed that the "Jewish problem" would be solved only when Judaism's message of social justice was spread through the Jewish and non-Jewish world. To this end, Mary Fels established the Joseph Fels Foundation, which promoted "the enlightenment of Jews and Gentiles in Israel's history and mission, and for the non-political settlement of Palestine." She also used the foundation to continue the work her husband had begun in the areas of land and tax reform. Together, they had established the Joseph Fels International Commission, which sought to promote the single land tax as well as the revitalization of Jewish life in Palestine. Fels dissolved this commission in 1916 and handpicked individuals from the United States, England, and Palestine to carry out a broader agenda.

Joseph Fels had been a fanatical supporter of the single tax, as promoted by economic philosopher Henry George. Mary Fels had been convinced by her husband's fervor and worked to see that land improved by public works was taxed accordingly. There would be no landed aristocracy in the United States or Palestine. She continued to oversee single-tax collective agricultural settlements at Hollesley Bay and Essex, in England, as well as in Mobile Bay, Alabama, and Arden, Delaware.

Mary Fels approached the question of people's relation to the land through her ongoing commitment to the Vacant Lot Cultivation Society, which promoted the establishment of school gardens. In the mid-1920s, she was the vice president of B'nai Benjamin, an organization of Jewish farmers in Palestine. She brought a similar view of the redemptive value of hard work and attachment to the land to her work in the prison reform movement.

Mary Fels died in New York City on May 16, 1953, at age ninety. She had donated millions of dollars to support Jewish settlement and development in Palestine and Israel. More notable than her large financial contributions was her tireless work in support of her Zionist principles. This was not the only cause to which she devoted her time, money, and effort. Fels fought for woman suffrage, prison reform, and, in her husband's honor, the single tax. In her book *Toward the Light* (1929), Fels's commitment to God and justice are reiterated to the point of redundancy. Her sincerity in this, as in all that she did on behalf of Jews and others, is always clear: "Whatever may or may not come this noble, fervid spirit will not, cannot, be undone."

SELECTED WORKS BY MARY FELS

Joseph Fels, His Life-Work (1916); *The Public, A Journal of Democracy*, vols. 20–22, coeditor (1917–1919); *Toward the Light* (1929).

BIBLIOGRAPHY

AJYB 24:137, 55:455; *Biographical Cyclopaedia of American Women*. Vol. 1. Edited by Mabel Ward Cameron (1924); *EJ*, s.v. "Fels"; Howe, Frederic C. "Personals." *The Survey* 31 (March 28, 1914): 812–813; "Mrs. Joseph Fels Dead at Age of 90." *NYTimes*, May 17, 1953, 88:5; *National Cyclopaedia of American Biography*. Vol. A (1930); *UJE*; *Who's Who in America*. Vol. 3 (1960): 275; *WWIAJ* (1926, 1928); *WWWIA* 1, 3; Zangwill, Israel. "Joseph Fels." *The Fortnightly Review* 57 (1920): 922–928.

ELLIOT WEINBAUM

FEMINISM, AMERICAN

Jewish women have played a significant role in all aspects of the American feminist movement. Whether agitating for the reform of marriage and property laws, woman suffrage, birth control, improved conditions for working women, the Equal Rights Amendment, or a myriad of other causes aimed at fostering equal opportunities for women, they lent their support to and often pioneered campaigns for women's rights.

Yet the relationship between Jewish women and feminism has been complex. Despite the energetic contributions of individual Jewish women and of Jewish women's groups to these movements, not all Jewish women's organizations enthusiastically supported the goals of equality or enhanced political rights for women, at least initially. Nor did American feminists acknowledge the substantial contributions of Jewish women to their cause. Feminists, moreover, only rarely spoke out in defense of Jews when they were under attack in the United States or abroad; women's rights proponents and their allies themselves frequently espoused anti-Semitic, anti-immigrant, or anti-Zionist views. Notwithstanding feminists' failures to publicly support or acknowledge Jewish issues, Jewish women have been among the most passionate supporters of feminist goals throughout the long and continuing struggle for women's rights.

One of the earliest activists on behalf of equal opportunity for women was ERNESTINE ROSE. Born in a shtetl in Poland, Rose, the daughter of a rabbi, came to the United States in 1836. She soon became a leader in the fight to reform the married women's property acts and campaigned on behalf of woman suffrage, first in New York State and then, with Susan B. Anthony, throughout the nation. She attended most national women's rights conventions and at the first, in Worcester, Massachusetts, introduced the controversial resolution calling for "political, legal, and social equality with man." Rose worked with Anthony and Elizabeth Cady Stanton to establish the American Equal Rights Association, formed in 1866 as a successor to earlier women's rights conventions and dedicated to the cause of abolition as well as women's rights. With Stanton and Anthony, she transformed the Equal Rights Association into the National Woman Suffrage Association (NWSA), which continued for many decades to lead the suffrage cause. A fervent pacifist as well as a feminist, Rose believed that women had a special stake in crusades for peace.

While Rose's outspoken rejection of religion troubled pious feminists, she took a "fighting stand" against anti-Semitism, publicly disavowing its pres-

ence in her own circle of freethinkers and vigorously defending her people. In her own view, her work on behalf of abolition and women's rights and against anti-Semitism demonstrated the "interrelationships between Jew and non-Jew, Negro and white, men and women. . . ." Susan B. Anthony named her, along with Mary Wollstonecraft and Frances Wright, as the most important women's rights leaders in history.

In the next generation, MAUD NATHAN, a descendant of one of the leading Sephardi families in the United States, became the suffrage movement's most significant Jewish leader. Nathan came to suffrage through her work as president of the New York Consumers League. Lobbying for better protective legislation for working women, she saw that lawmakers ignored women's point of view because they had no political status. With many close friends who were working for suffrage—particularly Harriet Stanton Blatch, daughter of Elizabeth Cady Stanton—this "society woman in politics," as Nathan was often called, became increasingly active, serving as the first vice president of New York's Equal Suffrage League.

One of the movement's boldest and most original tacticians, Nathan invented open-air automobile campaigns, "24 hour" speeches given from cars stationed at simultaneous locations throughout the city, "silent" speeches using motorized placards, and the idea of throwing out suffrage literature wrapped around coins. Because suffragists were stereotyped as aggressive, "masculine" women, short-haired, short-skirted, and supposedly outfitted in bloomers, Nathan dressed in her finest gowns when she spoke at mass meetings or participated in the suffrage skits and burlesques she frequently performed. After one of Nathan's speeches, President Woodrow Wilson commented to a friend, "When I hear a woman talk so well in the public interest, it almost makes me believe in woman suffrage." Nathan assumed the credit when the president finally came out for suffrage.

Nathan's vigorous support for woman suffrage and her lifelong interest in promoting the welfare of working women was rooted in a prophetic Judaism that emphasized the individual's obligations to the social good. For Nathan, righteousness—the wellspring of all Judaic inspiration—meant the application of spiritual ideals to "social growth." She often quoted biblical texts to show their applicability to contemporary society.

While Jewish immigrant women supported suffrage in greater proportions than either native-born American women or those from other ethnic communities, few women of her own class showed the spirited devotion to the cause that Nathan did. Neither the NATIONAL COUNCIL OF JEWISH WOMEN (NCJW), organized in 1896, or any other Jewish women's group officially supported woman suffrage before the passage of the Nineteenth Amendment in 1920. Jewish male groups, including the Reform Movement's Central Conference of American Rabbis, were also ambivalent about the issue and did not pass a resolution in favor of woman suffrage until relatively late in the campaign for the vote for women. A few Jewish women, like Maud Nathan's sister ANNIE NATHAN MEYER, the founder of Barnard College, even agitated publicly against suffrage. So strong was Meyer's support of antisuffragism, in fact, that she was often considered "vice president" of the movement against votes for women.

The lack of organized Jewish women's support for suffrage led observers to believe, incorrectly, that Jewish women as a whole were uninvolved or uninterested in rights for women. Trade union activist CLARA LEMLICH SHAVELSON, the young woman who in 1909 urged her garment industry coworkers to go out on a general strike, and in so doing changed the course of labor history, was a cofounder of the Wage Earners' League for Woman Suffrage. Other working-class leaders active in the suffrage fight were ROSE SCHNEIDERMAN, PAULINE NEWMAN, and THERESA MALKIEL.

In New York City, Jewish neighborhoods provided the strongest voting support for woman suffrage. In 1915, in fact, the only Manhattan assembly district to vote in favor of suffrage was predominantly Jewish, as were other districts with relatively high suffrage votes. When the Woman Suffrage Party blamed immigrants for the defeat of suffrage in that election, LILLIAN WALD, founder of the Henry Street Settlement (often called the Nurses Settlement), and her nursing colleague Lavinia Dock protested that the prosuffrage votes of immigrant districts had not been recognized. The reluctance to talk explicitly about Jews (even Wald and Dock identified "immigrant" rather than "Jewish" support) hid Jewish support for feminism and underlined feminists' continuing failure to deal with issues of anti-Semitism. In part, feminists feared becoming identified with radical Jews, who were prominently associated in the popular mind with socialism.

Yet the failure to credit Jews for their significant contributions to the women's rights movement, and the glossing over of anti-Semitism within the movement itself, was more than a political tactic. In the late nineteenth century, the women's rights movement was characterized by deeply held anti-Judaic and anti-Semitic attitudes. Elizabeth Cady Stanton, the key theoretician of the woman's movement and longtime

president of the National Woman Suffrage Association, introduced a resolution at the 1885 convention of the association that noted that "dogmas incorporated in the religious creeds derived from Judaism" were "contrary to the law of God as revealed in nature and the precepts of Christ." The measure did not pass, largely because members did not want to address the issues of women's role in religion, but it indicated the lack of concern for Jewish women's sensibilities as well as the social acceptability of anti-Jewish and anti-Semitic perspectives.

Anna Howard Shaw, who followed Stanton as president of the National American Woman Suffrage Association (formed when Stanton's organization merged with the rival American Woman Suffrage Association), also exhibited anti-Jewish attitudes, despite her personal friendship with Jewish suffragists. One of the first ordained female ministers, Shaw contrasted what she considered to be Judaism's negative attitudes toward women with Christianity's positive ones.

The anti-Jewish strain of Christian-based feminist thought emerged most clearly in the first volume of Stanton's *The Woman's Bible*. This 1895 tract is laden with criticism of the Jewish God, the Jewish people ("devious," "petty," and "immoral"), and the Pentateuch itself ("a long painful record of war, corruption, rapine, and lust"). In the work, Stanton identified "contempt for women" as a "Jewish dispensation"—a "serpent all through history" that reproduced itself in all subsequent religions. "As long as the Pentateuch is read and accepted as the Word of God," she wrote, a "proper respect for all womankind" would be impossible. In 1896, NAWSA voted to reject Stanton's *Bible*, declaring itself a "nonsectarian" association. Although the vote signaled a decline in anti-Jewish feeling among second-generation reformers, many of whom feared alienating potential Jewish members, the Christian orientation of the movement continued, as did some members' anti-Semitism.

Carrie Chapman Catt, third president of NAWSA, did not exhibit the anti-Jewish, anti–Old Testament hostility of her predecessors, but she nonetheless alienated some Jewish women with her anti-immigrant rhetoric and the claim that the "ignorant foreign vote" was a grave threat to democracy. Catt's activism on behalf of the international woman suffrage movement also worked against her identification with issues of concern to Jews, whom she viewed as a relatively narrow nationality-based interest group.

While Jewish women leaders worked closely with Christian women in suffrage and reform activities and were proud of their friendships with leading Christian feminists such as Catt, the commitment of women like Maud Nathan and REBEKAH KOHUT to Jewish groups like the National Council of Jewish Women reflected their recognition that the interests of Jewish female reformers were often distinct from those of non-Jewish women. Although Nathan admitted little disjunction between feminist objectives and Jewish concerns, in her autobiography she cites evidences of anti-Semitism among Christian colleagues. Rebekah Kohut, who like Nathan worked within secular women's organizations as well as the NCJW, smarted over the fact that some of her closest gentile friends, including philanthropist Grace Dodge, had attempted to convert immigrant Jews to Christianity. And SADIE AMERICAN, the NCJW's corresponding secretary, became bitter over the fact that gentile friends remained silent after the murder, rape, and torture of Jews during the 1903 Kishinev pogrom.

Other Jewish-born feminists, however, did not acknowledge any specific bonds to Jewish women's groups. Lillian Wald is a case in point. A leader in the campaign for protective legislation for women, Wald helped establish the reform-minded National Women's Trade Union League and became a member of the state's Factory Investigating Commission, appointed to prevent industrial abuses like those which caused the horrific TRIANGLE SHIRTWAIST FIRE of 1911, in which 146 garment workers (125 of them women) lost their lives. Although Wald worked on behalf of the immigrant Jewish community and received much of her funding from Jewish philanthropists, she insisted that her concerns were entirely nonsectarian. At the end of her life, she refused to be included in a book about Jewish women in America because its title suggested "work done by women as Jews," which hers was not. For Wald, the promotion of a more definitive religious purpose at Henry Street would have meant the loss of "something fundamental" in the settlement—the common humanity shared by all creeds rather than a more particularistic faith. Active in many movements for human rights as well as women's causes, Wald helped found the National Association for the Advancement of Colored People, the Federal Children's Bureau, the Women's League for Peace and Freedom, and other groups. But she remained little interested in Jewish issues and slow to recognize the threat that fascism posed to Jewish freedom.

Despite differences between Jewish and Christian feminists, individual Jewish women and Jewish women's organizations participated in many aspects of the women's movement that extended beyond suffrage and political rights for women to such issues as reform of the conditions of women's work, the promulgation of birth control methods and information, and the abolition of the traffic in women. Jewish women helped innovate and lead campaigns in each of these areas.

Eastern European immigrant Jews like Clara Lemlich Shavelson, Pauline Newman, Rose Schneiderman, ROSE PESOTTA, and FANNIA COHN went from laboring in sweatshops to championing the cause of working women; Cohn, Pesotta, and Newman were among the handful of Jewish women who served as officers of the INTERNATIONAL LADIES GARMENT WORKERS UNION. Often in conflict with Jewish male trade union leaders, they spent decades attempting to improve the wages and working conditions of women from the front lines of the industrial work force.

Clara Lemlich Shavelson's base of operations was the Socialist and later, the Communist Party, as well as neighborhood women's groups like the United Council of Working Class Housewives (later called the United Council of Working Class Women), which drew on the power of homemakers in the 1920s and 1930s to agitate around such subsistence issues as the price of food and housing. Union organizer Rose Schneiderman found her way into the Women's Trade Union League (WTUL), an association of working women and their middle-class and upper-class allies. For many decades she worked both for traditional union drives and for the protective legislation supported by the WTUL. She also served as president of the New York Women's Trade Union League for over thirty years and was president of the national organization as well. The efforts of Schneiderman, Newman, and other working-class Jewish women on behalf of protective labor laws for women found ready congruence in the work of Maud Nathan, longtime president of the New York Consumers League, to improve the conditions of women in the workplace.

For some Jewish women, sexual and reproductive freedom took precedence in the pantheon of women's issues. Anarchist leader EMMA GOLDMAN insisted that the denial of sexual freedom, not political or economic inequality, lay at the core of women's problems. For this reason she believed that the drive for suffrage and political rights, which imitated rather than dismantled male models of authority, would do little to alter women's subjugation. Goldman faulted suffragists for failing to attack the evils of marriage, which she saw as incompatible with the true flowering of love, and for doing little to promote the right to birth control, which she considered fundamental to women's liberation. In 1915, she began to offer detailed birth control advice in her popular lectures, given in Yiddish and in English. She was arrested in

1916 for distributing birth control pamphlets—a violation of the federal code—but the conviction was overturned. After Goldman's arrest, ROSE PASTOR STOKES, another well-known Jewish radical, publicly proclaimed her own willingness to break the law in order to help women, particularly immigrants, obtain birth control. Jewish women physicians like HANNAH STONE and LENA LEVINE of New York, Rachelle Yarros of Chicago, Sarah Marcus of Cleveland, Nadine Kavinoky of Los Angeles, and BESSIE MOSES of Baltimore were among the pioneer founders and directors of birth control clinics in the United States.

While suffrage, labor reforms, and reproductive rights were issues pursued by individuals rather than by Jewish women's organizations, the campaign against enforced prostitution ("white slavery") became a major focus of the efforts of the National Council of Jewish Women. NCJW's model programs involved rescue homes, friendly visitors, employment guidance, and a worldwide campaign of prevention. Its success in this work gave the organization an entrée into all levels of the secular women's movement.

After the achievement of woman suffrage in 1920, the NCJW joined other women's groups to form the Women's Joint Congressional Committee, a nonpartisan group that pressed for legislation on women's issues. In the 1920s, the NCJW found itself in disagreement with mainstream feminists about the Cable Act, presented to President Harding for signing in 1922 by Maud Wood Park, who had led the club-women's lobbying effort for the bill. The act declared that foreign-born women could no longer become citizens by marriage to naturalized or American-born men but had to take out citizenship papers in their own right. While American feminists rejoiced at the acknowledgment that every woman was an independent human being, NCJW leaders feared that the Cable Act would separate women from their husbands and children and bar them from receiving mothers' pensions or obtaining public employment, health benefits, and other services. They also had grave misgivings about whether immigrant women would have equal access to citizenship training with immigrant men. Secular feminists' failure to denounce German anti-Semitism in the 1930s, and their minimal support of the NCJW's program of rescuing refugees from fascism, reflected the continuing gap between the Jewish women's groups and the broader feminist movement.

Like many other women's groups, the NCJW opposed the proposed Equal Rights Amendment from its inception in 1923 through the 1960s. The council believed that the vote already guaranteed equality to middle-class women and preferred protective legislation as a means of alleviating the burdens of their working-class sisters. Throughout its existence, the NCJW had been firm in its support of the gendered division of functions, and despite many of its own members' public activism, remained convinced of the primacy of the domestic realm for women. In 1962, the council somewhat reluctantly joined President John F. Kennedy's 1962 Commission on the Status of Women, fearing that the commission's true purpose was to promote the ERA. Yet participation in the commission gave the NCJW broad insights into the pervasive problems of sex discrimination in employment, legal inequalities, and lack of child care, among other issues. By 1970, the NCJW had become an enthusiastic supporter of the ERA and other reforms to promote women's equality.

In addition to the work of the president's Commission on the Status of Women and that of subsequent state commissions and networks of professional women, the 1960s ushered in a series of vigorous protests against barriers to women's advancement and continuing discrimination. BETTY FRIEDAN's *The Feminine Mystique*, published in 1963, the same year as the report of the presidential commission, had an enormous impact. In the book, Friedan exploded the myth of domestic contentment, which she argued had infantilized women, "burying them alive" in their suburban homes as if in a "concentration camp." In Friedan's view, the false consciousness of the feminine "mystique," perpetuated by Freudian psychoanalysts, functionalist sociologists, advertisers, business leaders, educators, and child development experts, stifled women's ambitions and kept them in their place. Although Friedan advocated remedies like education and employment—especially, the adoption of a "new life plan" that would enable women to develop creative work of their own—the power of the book lay in its shattering exposé of the "problem that had no name" as a widespread social rather than individual issue. Readers, especially white middle-class women, responded enthusiastically, and the book, which Friedan initially had difficulty placing because of its negative message about domesticity, sold several million copies. Along with the Civil Rights Act of 1964, it played a major role in sparking second-wave feminism in the 1960s.

A summa cum laude graduate of Smith College, class of 1942, Friedan had gone on to a short-lived career as reporter for the *UE News*, the paper of the United Electrical, Radio and Machine Workers of America—the most radical and probably "the largest communist-led institution of any kind" in the United

States, before she lived the "feminine mystique" as a suburban wife and mother of three. Although Friedan attributed her sudden understanding of her own false consciousness to interviews with Smith alumnae from her own class, her earlier labor radicalism had also exposed her to some awareness of sex discrimination. Another factor in the making of Friedan's feminist consciousness was the anti-Semitism she suffered while growing up in Peoria, Illinois.

Born Bettye Goldstein in 1921, Friedan enjoyed a relatively happy childhood in Peoria, but as a member of one of the few Jewish families in the city, she eventually experienced a great deal of social ostracism. Although her father owned the finest jewelry store in the community—the "Tiffany's of the Midwest," according to Friedan—people who associated with him in business would not associate with him elsewhere. The family was not allowed into the Peoria country club, for which her mother blamed her husband rather than the community. Friedan herself, the only Jewish girl in her high school, was not invited to join the sorority. She grew up feeling "marginal," with "the sense of being an outsider, apart, special, not like the others." "Ever since I was a little girl," she acknowledged, "I remember my father telling me that I had a passion for justice. But I think it was really a passion against injustice which originated from my feelings of the injustice of anti-Semitism." In combination with her later outrage at women's false contentment in their domestic roles, Friedan's experience of childhood "marginality" influenced her to write *The Feminine Mystique.*

Like Friedan, many of the leaders and thinkers of the 1960s feminist movement were Jews, albeit largely secular ones. BELLA ABZUG, PHYLLIS CHESLER, LETTY COTTIN POGREBIN, VIVIAN GORNICK, and GLORIA STEINEM all played prominent roles in spearheading women's rights in the 1960s and early 1970s. SHULAMITH FIRESTONE, ROBIN MORGAN, Meredith Tax, Andrea Dworkin, and Naomi Weisstein were among the Jewish women active in the more radical wing of feminism—the women's liberation movement.

Several reasons have been suggested for the prominence of Jewish women not only within the leadership but in the rank and file of feminism. Friedan suggests that contemporary feminism originated in the United States because it possessed large numbers of highly educated women who were expected to concentrate their energies upon the narrow sphere of the home. She speculates that the disparity between talent, ambition, and role identity was especially severe for Jewish women, who were probably the most highly educated of all American women

ROBIN MORGAN *was a founding member of one of the earliest and most influential consciousness-raising groups, the New York Radical Feminists. Her 1970 collection* Sisterhood Is Powerful: An Anthology of Writings from the Women's Liberation Movement *has been described as the radical feminist "Bible."* [Bettye Lane]

yet whose self-definition sprang almost entirely from the family. According to writer ANNE ROIPHE, the "women's movement was fueled by Jewish energies" because Jewish women felt "pain and anguish" at the way they had been portrayed in the media and by Jewish men. When their anger ignited, it "exploded" into the women's movement.

The feminist movement did not spring full-blown from Friedan's pen. For decades, Jewish women had been among the activists who led campaigns for civil rights, nuclear disarmament, and peace. Such work provided women with a sense of personal power as well as experience in mass demonstrations and community organization. Just as women's participation in abolitionism had created demands for greater autonomy for women a century earlier, so a "proto-feminist" consciousness had been rising from within the civil rights movement of the 1950s and early 1960s. After a decade of militant antiwar struggles, activists like Bella Abzug had also come to connect war with violence against women and to identify war as a feminist issue. These women's organizational know-how and skillful coalition building became essential tools in the development of feminism as a mass movement.

Abzug, a Columbia University Law School graduate who devoted her early career to labor law and civil liberties issues, shifted her focus to the peace effort after the United States and the Soviet Union renewed nuclear testing in the early 1960s. Abzug helped to found Women Strike for Peace, which she served as political action and legislative director, and was elected to Congress in 1970 on a women's rights/ peace platform. Reelected in 1972 and 1974, she led the congressional fight for the Equal Rights Amendment and for reproductive freedom. One of the peak moments of her congressional career was bringing Rabbi SALLY PRIESAND to lead the prayer service at the opening of Congress in 1971, the first Jewish woman to do so. A deeply identified though secular Jew raised as a labor Zionist, Abzug believed that her connections to her Jewish heritage shaped the trajectory of her professional and political life.

While leaders like Friedan and Abzug, who were then in their early forties, stimulated like-minded women to wage war on patriarchy, a group of younger women, mostly in their twenties, joined the civil rights and student movements. As the Vietnam War escalated, they became active in the protest against it. By 1967, many had become outraged at their treatment by male radicals, whose beliefs in freedom and equality apparently applied only to men. After their attempts to introduce women's issues into the movement were met by ridicule, they began to organize groups of their own, identifying their cause as women's liberation. "The personal is political" became their slogan and consciousness raising their primary tool.

Among this group were a number of northern Jewish women activists who had gone south to participate in antiracist work led by the Student Non-violent Coordinating Committee and other black groups. They included such activists as FLORENCE HOWE, who would later found the Feminist Press, Susan Brownmiller, who would write *Against Our Will*, a groundbreaking analysis of rape as a feminist issue, and Rita Schwerner, who accompanied her husband Michael Schwerner, one of the young men murdered in Mississippi during the 1964 Freedom Summer. While most of these women were not Jewishly identified, they acknowledged that their sense of "other-ness" as Jews, along with an inheritance of progressive familial values, stimulated their involvement in the civil rights movement. Their experience as allies of African Americans in turn encouraged them to raise questions about their identities as women. Becoming incensed at their second-class treatment by male radicals, they began to organize women's groups in tandem with other disgruntled student and antiwar activists.

Among the Jewish leaders of the women's liberationists was antiwar New Left activist Robin Morgan, a founding member of one of the earliest and most influential consciousness-raising groups, the New York Radical Feminists. Morgan also founded the Women's International Terrorist Conspiracy from Hell (WITCH) and helped organize the 1968 WITCH demonstration at the Miss America pageant. In 1970,

This National Organization for Women poster from the early 1970s uses the symbolism of the prime minister of Israel being asked the question that even highly trained American women were implicitly asked when they applied for jobs.

National Jewish women's organizations often officially became involved in the issues put forward by the feminist movement, as this prochoice button put out by B'NAI B'RITH WOMEN *demonstrates. [Peter H. Schweitzer]*

she engineered the takeover of the New Left magazine *Rat*, publishing a woman's issue in retaliation for the male staff's "sex and porn special." Her essay "Good-Bye to All That," challenging male chauvinism within the New Left and calling for a women's revolution, became "the shot heard round the left." With other radical women, she published *Rat* as a feminist periodical for two years. Her 1970 collection *Sisterhood Is Powerful: An Anthology of Writings from the Women's Liberation Movement*, containing selections from over seventy individual women and organizations, was proclaimed as the radical feminist "Bible." Morgan became a contributing editor of *Ms.* magazine when it was established in 1972. She identifies herself as an "apostate Jew" and has strongly opposed the Israeli occupation of the West Bank and Gaza while sympathizing with the Palestinian cause.

A closer integration between the energies of radical feminism and Jewish sources was made by Meredith Tax, a founder of another early feminist collective, Boston's Bread and Roses. Tax was the first of the women's liberationists to identify with the radical tradition of American Jewish women and to turn to popular fiction as a means of communicating this history to a mass audience. She wrote *Rivington Street* (1982), a historical romance about several generations

of women radicals in Eastern Europe and the Lower East Side, and its sequel, *Union Square* (1988).

Jewish women in the radical feminist movement were also involved in another group that emerged from Bread and Roses, the Boston Women's Health Collective. Nine of the twelve founding members of the collective were Jewish. The collective pioneered the national and eventually international women's health movement and created the popular self-help manual *Our Bodies, Ourselves*, and later, *Our Children, Ourselves* and *Ourselves Growing Older*.

Despite the contributions of Jewish women to the movement, second-wave feminism, like the earlier women's rights movement, did not specifically acknowledge the contributions of Jewish participants. In certain venues, including the first two United Nations International Women's Decade Conferences, feminism came into painful conflict with anti-Semitism and anti-Zionism. In 1975, at the first International Women's conference in Mexico City, third-world delegates attacked Israeli representatives as "racists" and inserted a plank calling for the elimination of Zionism "along with colonialism and apartheid" into the conference's final declaration. Although Bella Abzug, chairing the United States delegation, organized congresswomen and other women leaders, Jews and non-Jews, to lobby the UN General Assembly to reject the Declaration of Mexico, her efforts proved unavailing. Abzug believed that the resolution of the conference thus helped set the stage for the adoption of the General Assembly resolution the following year declaring that "Zionism is racism."

Although Jewish women hoped that there would not be a repetition of the blatant anti-Zionism at the second UN Women's Conference, which took place five years later in Copenhagen, "Copenhagen was even worse," Letty Cottin Pogrebin wrote, with "Jewish women of every nationality . . . isolated, excoriated, and tyrannized," not only by third-world delegates but by their American co-nationals.

Two years after Copenhagen, Pogrebin wrote an eleven-page article on anti-Semitism in the women's movement for *Ms.* Citing "anti-Semitism and sexism" as the "twin oppressions" of women, the article described the prevalence of anti-Semitism on the radical left as well as the political right, within the black community, and among Christian feminists who blamed Jewish monotheism for the extinction of goddess cults and the death of Jesus.

The experiences of anti-Semitism at the conferences in Mexico and Copenhagen revealed other fissures in the women's movement. The American delegation included not only political feminists but also representatives from Jewish women's groups, who were reluctant to support reproductive freedom, abortion rights, and other main aspects of the feminist agenda for fear of offending more traditional members.

In 1981, Jewish women formed a new group, Feminists Against Anti-Semitism, which defined itself as explicitly feminist and Zionist. The group put anti-Semitism on the agenda of a 1981 Women's Studies Association conference for the first time. Three years, later, spearheaded by Judith Arcana, Rabbi Sue Elwell, and EVELYN TORTON BECK, Jewish women formed a permanent Jewish Women's Caucus within the Women's Studies Association, with the goal of integrating the experience of Jewish women "as Jews" into feminist associations.

Jewish feminists also organized to work for change on the community level. In 1984, the AMERICAN JEWISH CONGRESS focused its annual United States–Israel dialogue in Jerusalem on the topic of "Woman as Jew, Jews as Women." The wide-ranging discussions led to the establishment of a new women's lobby in Israel, the Israel Women's Network, chaired by Alice Shalvi, and to the founding of the National Commission on Women's Equality, under the auspices of the American Jewish Congress, with Betty Friedan and Leona Chanin as cochairs. These were some of the first steps that would gather momentum throughout the 1980s and the 1990s as Jewish feminism coalesced as a religious, political, and intellectual force, uniting secular and religious women. In these decades, Jewish women have gained a distinct identity within secular feminist groups at the same time that the work of Jewish feminists has transformed the American Jewish community and religious life in myriad ways.

BIBLIOGRAPHY

Antler, Joyce. *The Journey Home: Jewish Women and the American Century* (1997); Glenn, Susan A. *Daughters of the Shtetl: Life and Labor in the Immigrant Generation* (1990); Kuzmack, Linda Gordon. *Woman's Cause: The Jewish Woman's Movement in England and the United States, 1881–1933* (1993); Lerner, Elinor. "American Feminism and the Jewish Question, 1890–1940." In *Anti-Semitism in American History*, edited by David A. Gerber (1987): 305–328, and "Jewish Involvement in the New York Woman Suffrage Movement." *American Jewish History* 70 (June 1981): 442–461; Orleck, Annelise. *Common Sense and a Little Fire: Women and Working-Class Politics in the United States, 1900–1965* (1995); Pogrebin, Letty Cottin. "Anti-Semitism in the Women's Movement." *Ms.* (June 1982): 45+, and *Deborah, Golda and Me* (1991); Rogow, Faith. *Gone to Another Meeting: The National Council of Jewish Women, 1893–1993* (1993).

JOYCE ANTLER

FEMINISM, JEWISH *see* JEWISH FEMINISM

FERBER, EDNA (1885–1968)

A dedicated writer for more than fifty years, Edna Ferber was born in Kalamazoo, Michigan, on August 15, 1885. She celebrated America even as she exposed its shortcomings. Her published work includes twelve novels, twelve collections of short stories, two autobiographies, and nine plays—most in collaboration with other playwrights. Ferber's novel *So Big* won a Pulitzer Prize in 1925, while the film *Giant* and the musical *Show Boat*, based on her novels, continue to entertain contemporary audiences. World famous in her time, Ferber was, for her readers at home, a beloved chronicler of American working people whose ethnic variety, linguistic idiosyncrasy, toughness, occasional sweetness, and resilience never ceased to fascinate her.

Edna Ferber's enduring love of America and its workers—as well as the form that this passion gave to her life and work—rose, paradoxically, out of a childhood troubled by frequent moves from one state to another; by the business failures and the early blindness and death of her Hungarian-born father, Jacob Ferber; by the labor of her American-born mother, Julia (Neumann) Ferber, in several family stores; and by a period of seven years in which, Ferber remembered, there was never a day in which she was not called a "sheeny." From age five to twelve, Ferber lived with her parents and older sister, Fannie, in Ottumwa, Iowa—a town so brutal toward Jews that she held it accountable until the end of her life for everything in her that was hostile toward the world. As Ferber carried lunch to her father every day, she had to run a gauntlet of anti-Semitic abuse from adult male loungers, perched on the iron railing at the corner of Main Street, who spat, called her names, and mocked her in Yiddish accents. Ferber's parents suffered as well. Her father lost a lawsuit against an employee accused of theft when witnesses who had sworn to the truth of the accusation suddenly, in the courtroom, reversed their testimony.

Ferber herself described the effects of those seven years in various ways. She believed they were "astringent, strengthening years whose adversity" had toughened her. She understood that her terror of legal complications in the course of her writing career—as well as her profound love of justice—owed much to that early experience of injustice. Ferber's sense of herself as a Jew and her adult responses to anti-Semitism were also shaped by the pain of those years. Like the five-year-old child who "didn't run" but "glared" at her oppressors, Ferber confronted directly and caustically the anti-Semitic comments that occasionally marred her adult professional relationships. Her first autobiography, *A Peculiar Treasure* (1939), rings with contempt and rage against Hitler for making of Europe a world she could not recognize, in which it was no longer possible to love the human race.

Ferber believed that her identity as a Jew owed more to persecution and to her love of her family than to religious observance or historical tradition. She suspected that, as a child, her pride as a Jew might have reflected her pleasure in self-dramatization, in feeling herself "different and set apart," in knowing herself to be superior to her persecutors. That sense of superiority stayed with her. As late as 1934, Ferber celebrated the absence of Jewish names among the "despoilers of America"—"paper mill millionaires" and others who had profited from the destruction of America's forests and rivers. In time Ferber even developed a sense of collective Jewish identity that highlighted the positive compensatory effects of oppression. She believed that the Jew, left in peace, would have lost his "aggressiveness, his tenacity and neurotic ambition." More important, oppression had yielded to Jews the priceless gift of "creative self-expression." Jewishly uneducated, she knew nevertheless of "an old Chassidic book" that "says there are three ways in which a man expresses his deep sorrow: the man on the lowest level cries, the man on the second level is silent, but the man on the highest level knows how to turn his sorrow into song." As a writer, Ferber cherished that knowledge all her life.

At first Ferber sought her own path toward "creative self-expression" in the theater. She called herself "stagestruck," a passion nourished not only by her grandfather's puppet plays, by her grandmother's daily reenactments of encounters with tradesmen and neighbors, and by "playing show" with her sister, but also by the Ferber family's frequent attendance at local performances in Ottumwa. Minstrel shows and shoddy traveling theater companies, as well as the earliest versions of what would become movies, dazzled the child. The adult recognized that they afforded "color, escape, in that dour unlovely town." In time Ferber's collaborations with George Kaufman and Jerome Kern on such plays as *Dinner at Eight, The Royal Family*, and *Show Boat* produced successes that gratified her lifelong love of theater.

At age seventeen, however, Ferber abandoned her plans to become an actor to help support her family. They had left Ottumwa for Appleton, Wisconsin, in 1897. Forbidden to study elocution when she graduated from high school, Ferber stomped out of her house and into the office of the *Appleton Daily Crescent*, where the editor hired her as a reporter. Thus, in a moment of stormy reaction, Ferber ended her formal education and entered the profession that was to engage her for the rest of her life. Although she would come to know very well the drudgery and loneliness of a writer's life, and although she sometimes worried that the "gift of writing" might be taken from her at any moment, she cultivated that gift by habitually transforming every detail of sensory and emotional experience into words. The sounds of hangers striking one another in a moving train, the musings of a lonely teenager feeling sorry for herself, the graceful movement of a young gardener as he turned from his work, all went into storage in her imagination, to be pulled out like the spangles and feathers of an antique costume from a trunk in the attic when her stories required them. In love with the work of reporting, she moved from the Appleton paper at age eighteen to a larger paper in Milwaukee, where she relished the company of other reporters and "worked like a man" to the point of breakdown at age twenty-two.

The lifelong habit of writing, grown partly out of the "sorrow" of Ottumwa and poverty, enriched Ferber immeasurably but developed in her, as well, a perspective that alienated her to some extent from engagement in ordinary life. After she came to New York in 1912, she enjoyed an extraordinarily wide circle of friends, among whom were Katharine Hepburn, Moss Hart, George Kaufman, Robert Sherwood, Louis and Mary Bromfield, and William Allen White. But as a reporter, she had learned early to look on life rather than participate in it. She could project herself into "any age, environment, condition, situation, character or emotion" that interested her. However, she also acquired the writer's ability to feel a sensation and to analyze a feeling while having it—a "gift" that she believed was "deathly hard" on romance. Thus she lived a writer's life, socializing and traveling with other writers, editors, producers, performers, and artists. She took as a companion her widowed mother, whose own unhappy marriage served, perhaps as powerfully as her jealous maternal protectiveness, to guard Ferber from matrimony.

After her breakdown, Ferber began to write and publish the short stories that would lead her to New York. Her most famous early character, the businesswoman Emma McChesney—whose fortunes even Teddy Roosevelt followed with relish—was succeeded in time by a multitude of personae whose misfortunes and triumphs showed America to itself. The habit of loving America and Americans, which distinguishes virtually all of Ferber's work, originates—like her ability to observe without participating and her unfettered contempt for bigotry—in the seven painful years she lived in Ottumwa. On Saturday nights in those years, after the matinee, Ferber's pleasure was to watch the crowds passing on Main Street. She liked to see them without being seen. As she watched, she realized that "the passer-by does not notice you or care about you; they, the people, are intent on getting somewhere, their faces are open to the reader; they betray themselves by their walk, their voices, their hands, clenched or inert; their feet, their clothes, their eyes." In the watching child, reading people as they passed, the reportorial eye that would later describe essentials of human behavior peculiar to Texas (in *Giant*), Alaska (in *Ice Palace*), Oklahoma (in *Cimarron*), and the Mississippi River (in *Show Boat*) was developing.

Ferber's pleasure in the rich multiplicity of American character was also rooted partly in her early experience of Ottumwa. When her father's illness drew her mother more and more deeply into the labor of supporting the family, Edna and her sister were cared for by a series of "hired girls"—farmgirl daughters of immigrant parents or new immigrants themselves. Such women, Ferber realized, "influenced the manners, morals and lives of millions of American-born children," introducing them to Old World cooking and costume, folktale, and song. Unhindered by gender in her own ambitions and aware of ways in which her mother had surmounted the trials of her early life, Ferber had little patience with women who allowed themselves to be limited by the constraints of femininity. Like Jews, she believed, women developed special strengths because of their subjection to social limitations. Thus she often wrote about women whose energy and talent made them successful in business, like Fanny in *Fanny Herself* or Emma McChesney in *Roast Beef, Medium*. The "variety" and "fun" brought to Ferber's early life by the hired girls of her childhood inspired an enduring interest in the "vigor and native tang" of working people's talk. To her the conversation of a truck driver was always "more stimulating, saltier" than that of a man who "drove his own Cadillac." As late as 1933, Ferber believed that working people still retained "a kind of primary American freshness and assertiveness," and her stories attempted to do justice to them and their lives. She was one of them. She felt she understood them and America— "its naivete, its strength, its childishness, its beauty, its reality." Until she died on April 16, 1968, in New York City, Edna Ferber's idea of "the ultimate in exciting luxury" still mimicked the early experience of the parade-watching child on Main Street in Ottumwa. She loved to lie back among pillows in an air-conditioned train compartment, "watching the United States of America slide by." This unabashed love of America seems dated now, for it speaks of a simpler time than our own. Ferber's stories and novels, films, and plays continue to make accessible that moment of our collective national experience.

SELECTED WORKS BY EDNA FERBER

American Beauty (1931); *Buttered Side Down* (1912); *Cimarron* (1930); *Come and Get It* (1935); *Dawn O'Hara, the Girl Who Laughed* (1911); *Dinner at Eight*, with George Kaufman (1932); *Emma McChesney and Co.* (1915); *Fanny Herself* (1917); *Giant* (1952); *The Girls* (1921); *Great Son* (1945); *Ice Palace* (1958); *A Kind of Magic* (1963); *Minick*, with George Kaufman (1924); *Mother Knows Best* (1927); *No Room at the Inn* (1941); *Nobody's in Town* (1938); *Our Mrs. McChesney*, with George V. Hobart (1915); *A Peculiar Treasure* (1939); *Roast Beef, Medium: The Business Adventures of Emma McChesney* (1913); *The Royal Family*, with George Kaufman (1927); *Saratoga Trunk* (1941); *Show Boat* (1926); *So Big* (1924); *Stage Door*, with George Kaufman (1936); *They Brought Their Women* (1933).

BIBLIOGRAPHY

AJYB 24:138; *BEOAJ*; Burstein, Janet Handler. *Writing Mothers, Writing Daughters: Tracing the Maternal in Jewish American Women's Stories* (1996); Cronin, Gloria L., Glaine H. Hall, and Connie Lamb. "Edna Ferber." *Jewish American Fiction Writers: An Annotated Bibliography* (1991); *DAB* 8; Dearborn, Mary V. *Pocahontas's Daughters: Gender and Ethnicity in American Culture* (1986); *EJ*; Horowitz, Steven P., and Miriam J. Landsman. "Edna Ferber." *Twentieth Century American-Jewish Fiction Writers*. In *Dictionary of Literary Biography* 28 (1984): 58–64; Lichtenstein, Diane. *Writing Their Nations: The Tradition of Nineteenth Century American Jewish Women Writers* (1992); Obituary. *NYTimes*, April 17, 1968, 1:2; *NAW* modern; *UJE*; Walden, Daniel. "Edna Ferber." *Jewish American Women Writers: A Bio-Bibliographical and Critical Sourcebook*, edited by Ann R. Shapiro (1994); *WWIAJ* (1926, 1928, 1938); *WWWIA* 5.

JANET BURSTEIN

FICTION

Literature by American Jewish women reflects historical trends in American Jewish life and indicates the changing issues facing writers who worked to position themselves as Americans, Jews, and women. Eighteenth- and nineteenth-century writers descending from affluent Sephardic and German families tended to portray Jews and Judaism though a Judeo-Christian lens, playing up the commonalities between

Judaic and Western/Christian traditions. As Eastern European immigrants exponentially increased the number of Jews in American cities, many first- and second-generation authors depicted the distinctive Jewish immigrant experience and the ways in which women struggled with the competing pulls of American and Jewish civilizations. In contrast, other authors, who identified with socialist or secular, international intellectual circles, wrote from a virtually deracinated vantage point, self-declared citizens of the world, devoting little space to their religious or ethnic heritage; some wrote closeted, encoded stories of the American Jewish minority situation, using their own experiences of Jewish marginality to inform their empathetic depiction of other American ethnic and religious groups. At mid-century, female writers created diverse literary ways to respond to the misogynist stereotypes of Jewish women flourishing in fiction by Jewish men. Most recently, a significant trend in writing by American Jewish women has been a dramatic turn toward more particularistic Jewish subjects, characters, and themes; while some American Jewish women writers are only marginally interested in Judaic materials, during the past few decades an increasingly significant group of female writers have focused directly on the American Jewish experience from the inside, many of them exploring the intersection between gender and ethnic and religious identity.

FINDING COMMONALITIES: LITERARY WOMEN PRIOR TO 1880

Literature that emphasizes the perceived moral and spiritual similarities between Judaism and Christianity is common among Jewish women whose families came to the United States when Jews comprised a gradually increasing but still extremely small American religious minority, prior to the mass immigrations of Jews from 1880 to 1924. Descended from wealthy, aristocratic Sephardic families who had participated in the formative decades of the country or from German Jewish families who had come to the United States and established themselves financially and socially during the eighteenth and nineteenth centuries, these cultivated middle- and upper-class American Jewish women produced primarily poetry, devotional verse, hymns, and memoir-type literature, in addition to personal correspondence. From their gracious homes in well-established Jewish communities, American Jewish women writing in the early to mid-nineteenth century tended especially to conform to what they perceived as a synthesis between Christian and Jewish ideals of feminine behavior. In both religious cultures

they felt they saw women placed firmly in the domestic realm and in the extended domesticity of communal good works.

One important prototype of the issues concerning early literary Jewish women is provided by RE-BECCA GRATZ (1781–1869), the daughter of a wealthy, socially prominent, well-traveled, entrepreneurial Philadelphia German Jewish family, whose words blend American and Jewish family ideals in an expressed devotion to domestic, communal, and religious concerns. Like other acculturated Jewish women of her time, Gratz was much influenced by the reigning cultural Christian Myth of True Womanhood, and she promoted the image of Jewish women as the equals of their Christian sisters in piety, spirituality, and literary sensitivity.

Other nineteenth-century American Jewish women writers who wrote from similar milieus reflect parallel concerns and influences. For example, PENINA MOÏSE (1797–1880), a southern Jewish woman of Sephardic and German ancestry, wrote what is believed to be the first American book of poetry by a Jew, *Fancy's Sketch Book* (1833).

A variation on the literary glorification of maternal qualities is provided by REBEKAH GUMPERT HYNEMAN (1812–1875). Her poetic output, including *The Leper and Other Poems* (1853), presents biblical women such as the matriarchs and female prophets and judges as representatives of the valiant but meek and gentle, angel-of-the-hearth type of woman.

Southern writers added regional patriotism to their other American attributes. Posthumously published verses by Octavia Harby Moses (1823–1904), mother of seventeen children, fourteen of whom survived, deal primarily with feminine responsibilities, family life, and praise of her "native" Confederate "beautiful land" of South Carolina. RACHEL MORDECAI LAZARUS (1788–1838), who began her professional career by teaching in her father's academy for young ladies in Virginia, wrote to non-Jewish novelist Maria Edgeworth complaining that Edgeworth's character Mordecai in the novel *The Absentee* (1812) was based on a negative Jewish stereotype. From her vantage point in North Carolina, Lazarus wrote glowingly about "the spirit of unity and benevolence" that animated the relationship between Jews and non-Jews in antebellum Wilmington, although she did note that some non-Jews seemed to feel some "regret" at her religious persuasion (Lichtenstein, p. 100).

As increasing numbers of Jews began to arrive at America's shores during the second half of the nineteenth century, American Jews—and writing Jewish women—expressed their awareness of seemingly growing levels of conflict between Jews and non-Jews, including overt anti-Semitism. Hostility to Jews evoked two responses in female Jewish authors: (1) to defend the Jewish "race," and/or (2) to rid fellow Jews and Jewesses of "undesirable" qualities, as defined by Christian culture. In essays, poetry, correspondence, and the occasional piece of fiction, Jewish women writing in the later decades of the nineteenth century turned their discomfort with Christian anti-Jewish feeling both inward and outward. Still influenced by societal preferences for the domestic angel, they were less able than the women who preceded them to assume serene harmony between Christian and Jewish persons and value systems.

EMMA LAZARUS (1849–1887), the most talented and renowned of American Jewish female writers emerging from the cocoon of upper-class respectability into creative interaction with a changing world, began her career rather removed intellectually from her Jewish heritage, declaring herself to be a transcendentalist and a humanist. As the years passed, however, several factors contributed to Lazarus's growing intellectual fascination with Jewish history and the fate of Jews worldwide, including some personal interactions with anti-Semites, the much-publicized vulnerability and suffering of Jews in pogrom-afflicted Europe and in new American immigrant communities, and literary catalysts such as Heine's Jewishly conscious writings. For Lazarus, the creative rediscovery of the Jews was a passage into peoplehood and ethnic responsibility, rather than an overtly spiritual journey. This preference marked Lazarus not only as reflective of her own assimilated class, but also powerfully predictive of the secularized Jews who would dominate the American scene half a century later, with their cult of sacred civic survival.

ACCULTURATION THROUGH WRITING DURING THE IMMIGRANT YEARS

A different order of personal reinvention faced the large numbers of European women who immigrated to the United States from 1880 to 1924, and their literature illustrates very different attitudes and concerns. Jewish immigrants and their children found themselves in an environment where few traditional Jewish values were salient. Society was often turned upside down, as formerly middle-class, well-educated families found themselves plunged into abject poverty, while formerly impoverished and ignorant emigrés became entrepreneurial successes. Although immigrant women and men came to the New World hoping for comfort and opportunity, many found confusion, poverty, and exploitation instead. As their stories, novels, and letters indicate, life for immigrant women was especially difficult. Relationships between husbands and wives, and between parents and children, were often disrupted. Despite the American preference for the full-time "true woman" homemaker mother, few families were able to survive on the earnings of the husband alone, and both girls and married women worked long hours. Later immigrants provided the major workforce in the mushrooming garment industry, with girls typically working in the factories and married women doing piecework at home. Many immigrant women felt confused and almost powerless in this strange new society.

While American-born aristocrats writing before the mass immigrations conflated American and Jewish cultures into a comforting hybrid, first- and second-generation American Jewish women writers often made themselves over in their writings, creating personal histories only loosely based on the actual facts of their lives, which dramatized the transformative struggle of the immigrant experience. MARY ANTIN (1881–1949) and ANZIA YEZIERSKA (c. 1885–1970) are especially illustrative of this tendency, but a number of lesser-known women writers of this period also follow the pattern. For such writers, Jewish societies became a literary counterpoint to mainstream American culture; they pictured themselves as heroines negotiating between conflicting demands.

Mary Antin's memoir, *The Promised Land* (1912), was read for years as a factual description of the experiences of a young emigré who traveled from pogroms in Polotsk to higher culture in Boston. Antin tells a mostly happy story, glorifying the process through which immigrants who would have had only narrow scope in their countries of origin are emancipated and joyously encounter the opportunities of America's wide world. Later readers, deconstructing Antin's sanitized description, have noted that her own life demonstrated a far more rocky interaction between Jewish and American traditions.

Anzia Yezierska's memoir, *Red Ribbon on a White Horse* (1950), diverged in different ways from the plain autobiographical facts. Yezierska used her Old World heritage to enhance her persona and to make herself seem more vivid. Yezierska builds on the Hollywood public relations hyperbole that described her as "the Cinderella of the tenements," an impoverished young immigrant whose writing talents catapulted her into Hollywood, only to find that she was by nature too sensitive and principled for the falsehoods of this glamorous but shallow world.

JEWISH WOMEN ARTICULATING AMERICA

American-born Jewish writers were far less likely than immigrants to focus openly on the Jewish experience in their writing. GERTRUDE STEIN (1848–1946), EDNA FERBER (1885–1968), FANNIE HURST (1889–1968), LILLIAN HELLMAN (1906–1984), and others, perhaps regarding the world of Jews and Judaism as too narrow and parochial for their literary concerns, created intellectual realms in which some characters might have distinctive Jewish surnames but their Jewishness had little overt significance.

The image of a minority woman moving across ethnic lines through sexual liaisons and intermarriage is a recurring motif in many of Ferber's works. Ethnic women are presented as doubly marginal, subjected to insider/outsider status; their affection for mainstream males is explored both as transgressive behavior that meets with punishment (*Show Boat*) and as a positive, supremely American melting-pot response to ethnic difference (*Cimarron*). Despite her virtual public silence on the subject of Jewishness during the actual war years, in her notes Ferber privately dedicates the Jewishly silent first portion of her autobiography, *A Peculiar Treasure* (1939): "To Adolph Hitler who made of me a better Jew and a more understanding and tolerant human being, as he has millions of other Jews, this book is dedicated in loathing and contempt." The second half of her memoirs, *A Kind of Magic* (1963), deals more overtly with her Jewish childhood and later trips to Nazi death camps (Walden, pp. 72–79).

An important figure in American literary and dramatic worlds, but only marginally identified as a Jew, Lillian Hellman earned her place in history through the writing of twelve serious dramas and her memoirs, as well as her political presence.

Many second-generation American Jewish literary women of Eastern European family origin seemed to avoid overtly Jewish subjects or references. American Jewish authors writing out of the Depression depicted the social activism that was typical of many immigrant Jewish women and their daughters, but much of the proletarian fiction of such writers as TESS SLESINGER (1905–1945) or JO SINCLAIR has little focus on the Jewish identity of characters or Jewish subject matter.

The author of essays, fiction, and poetry, TILLIE OLSEN (b. c. 1913) writes both of women who have lost their sense of direction and of strong women involved in socialist activities. In the compelling novella *Tell Me a Riddle* (1962), one of Olsen's few works in which the Jewish identity of her characters is salient, Olsen draws on her own familial revolutionary, antireligious background.

WOMEN'S VOICES AT MID-CENTURY

Passionate attention to social problems characterized some Jewish women writers, most successfully GRACE PALEY (b. 1922). Paley's distinctive, elliptical short story style and deft characterizations won her a devoted audience. In Paley's fiction, Jewishness is a moral consciousness, a tone of voice, the Yiddish expressions and urban accents of relatives and friends. While Paley's concerns are universal and she has expressed what many consider to be anti-Zionist sentiments, neither she nor her heroines attempt to suppress their Jewishness, and the stories convey an unselfconscious comfort level with the Jewish aspects of her life.

During the 1950s and 1960s, American Jewish female writers were creating their works of fiction in an extremely hostile environment, in which their male—and far more successful—colleagues were scornfully depicting young women whose parents were grooming them to fit into upper-middle-class American norms, as they saw them.

In the early 1970s, several young female authors emerged on the literary scene whose works provided their own, woman-oriented vantage point on societal pressures. Rejecting the image of the materialistic, libidinously timid Jewish female, Erica Jong (b. 1942) created a Jewish heroine, Isadora Wing, who overcomes her symbolic *Fear of Flying* (1973) by trying to live as lustily and fearlessly as any ribald male hero of picaresque sagas. Alix Kates Shulman's (b. 1932) novel *Memoirs of an Ex-Prom Queen* (1972) and Gail Parent's (b. 1940) satiric *Sheila Levine Is Dead and Living in New York* (1972) depicted the social forces shaping and distorting the self-perceptions and behaviors of one beautiful, popular and one plain, unpopular Jewish young woman, respectively. MARGE PIERCY's (b. 1936) diligent chronicle of the stormy, experimental cultural environment of the late 1960s and early 1970s insists that despite the appearance of enormous external change early in the emergence of the contemporary feminist movement, Jewish women were often deluded and denuded, left with what were in actuality *Small Changes* (1972).

EXPLORATION OF GENDERED RELATIONSHIPS

The impact of external forces on the women portrayed in Jewish fiction has evolved perceptibly from decade to decade. American Jewish women struggled with a plethora of challenges in the shifting landscape of America from the 1970s through the 1990s. The whole world was seemingly open to them—they could pursue education as far as their intellectual capacities and ambitions could take them; they could enter any vocational field; they could follow their sexual inclinations into numerous or monogamous, lesbian or heterosexual liaisons; they could combine childbearing and career, juggle or sequence the two, or avoid having children altogether; they could attain rabbinical ordination or completely estrange themselves from Jewish life. The choices were at times bewildering. American Jewish literature depicted and interpreted the battles undertaken by Jewish women in this extraordinary time of change.

Many American Jewish women writers focused on gender role redefinition, often as part of an interface between Jewish values and mores and contemporary American life-styles and demographics. A gay man's lover and former wife both show up at his son's bar mitzvah in Marian Thurm's short story collection *These Things Happen* (1988). Linda Bayer's (b. 1948) *The Blessing and the Curse* (1988) and Julie Salamon's *White Lies* (1987) depict the special pressures infertility and adoption create for Jews. Jewish peoplehood, in all its permutations, attracted much literary attention. The award-winning fiction of Johanna Kaplan (b. 1948) richly and often humorously captures the flavor of urban Jewish middle-class life. In Kaplan's work, such as *Other People's Lives* (stories, 1975) and *O My America* (novel, 1980), conflict between Jewish-radical ideals, the more traditional historical Jewish heritage, and classical American dreams is played out alongside the conflict between several generations of American Jews. Although her characters and milieus are unselfconsciously Jewish, her fiction functions as a social critique of the 1960s New Age sensibility as well as a parody of assimilationist behavior. Roberta Silman also depicted the volatile relationships between Eastern European Jews and their assimilated offspring in books such as *Somebody Else's Child* (1976), *Blood Relations* (1977), and *Boundaries* (1979).

Other authors showed how negative feelings about womanhood, and specifically Jewish womanhood, could poison the relationship between Jewish mothers and daughters. Explorations of mother-daughter relationships, already an intriguing element in earlier American Jewish fiction, emerged as a major motif in women's mid- and late-twentieth-century novels and short stories. Some female characters were portrayed as no longer content to follow in their mothers' footsteps, yet unsure what they wished to be instead. For some, the exploration of new paths was further complicated by anguished feelings of resentment and guilt toward the mothers they loved and hated and, at least psychologically and often physically as well, were leaving behind. In a society that often vented its dis-like of Jewish women, Jewish daughters feared to be too close to their mothers because they did not wish to become like them, but they felt that in abandoning their mother's life-styles they were adding to the burdens that had already oppressed and diminished the older women.

VIVIAN GORNICK's (b. 1935) memoir, *Fierce Attachments* (1987), focused on thwarted women who turn inward, blighting the lives of subsequent generations of women. In a pattern that recalls some of the immigrant fiction, a daughter's entire life is lived in reaction to her mother. Obsessed by the conviction that she does not want to repeat her mother's mistakes, the daughter never truly achieves independence from the past. Mothers can withdraw from their daughters for other reasons, as editor and novelist Daphne Merkin (b. 1954) illustrated in her novel *Enchantment* (1986). In Merkin's novel, Hannah Lehman grows up in an affluent German Jewish Orthodox home on New York's Upper West Side. In contrast with the more familiar stereotype of the "smothering" Jewish mother, Hannah feels that her mother ignores her. Her mother's emotional withdrawal controls Hannah's life just as surely as another mother's direct manipulation.

Some of the most fascinating literature by American Jewish women in the 1980s and 1990s explored the dialectic of appetite and repulsion that female sexuality evokes in some men. While fascinating as a psychological phenomenon, this love-hate relationship has been the basis of profound discrimination against women at many times and in many cultures. American Jewish women often included male characters who project their own psychological ambivalence onto female physical characteristics and virtually convert normal female physiology into a type of pathology. Not infrequently, a mother internalizes restricted expectations of womanhood and passes them along to her daughter.

Lynne Sharon Schwartz (b. 1939) explored the deadening effect of bourgeois expectations for women in several pieces of fiction, especially *Leaving Brooklyn* (1989), an extraordinary short novel. Schwartz's protagonist, Audrey, is a young adolescent girl with one normal eye, through which she sees the ordinary, proper world of middle class Brooklyn, and one damaged eye, through which she glimpses a sinister world of dark impulses, sexuality, and chaotic, uncharted possibilities. The ophthalmologist hired by Audrey's mother to cure Audrey's wandering eye with a specialized contact lens also enters into a sexual relationship with the child. When the relationship is ended and Audrey reevaluates the Brooklyn world of her parents and their card-playing friends, she discovers that human beings—even middle-class Jewish parents—are far more complex than she had imagined: Memory plays tricks, and everyday realities shift and blur with or without a trick eye. In her parents and their friends she discovers a political liberalism that amounts to heroism in the repressive anticommunist era, and in herself she discovers an ineradicable piece of Brooklyn from which she will be forever departing.

In another response to perceived misogyny and patriarchal oppression, some Jewish authors championed lesbianism as both a physical/social orientation and as a political statement. These authors described the worldview and experiences of those Jewish women who reject male-identified gender behavior and identify primarily with other women. Fiction depicting the lives of identified Jewish lesbians, once difficult to find, began to proliferate. Some titles include Alice Bloch's (b. 1947) *The Law of Return* (novel, 1983), Leslea Newman's (b. 1955) *A Letter to Harvey Milk* (stories, 1988), Jyl Lynn Felman's (b. 1954) *Hot Chicken Wings* (stories, 1992), and Joan Nestle's (b. 1940) *A Restricted Country* (1987). While some works were highly critical of Jewish tradition, which they perceived as hostile, much significant Jewish lesbian writing was deeply committed to Jewish peoplehood and Jewish survival, and several anthologies were largely dedicated to Jewish-content feminist and lesbian writing.

Sephardi women have had their own special relationship with patriarchal family and community systems. Many Sephardi Jewish women have stated that women in Sephardi society today have been far more cloistered and restricted in their activities than women deriving from German or Eastern European Jewish societies. Beyond the boundaries of the Sephardi community, some Sephardi Jewish women write that they endure a double discrimination—they are suspect because they are women and because they are not of Ashkenazi derivation. The characters and milieus treated by contemporary Sephardic women writers diverge from those dealt with by aristocratic women of Sephardi descent in the eighteenth and nineteenth centuries, as well as those of Ashkenazi writers. In literature such as Gloria Kirschheimer's "The Voyager" (1984) or "Nona: A Recollection" (1991), Ruth Knafo Setton's "Songs from My Mother's House" (1993) or "Street of Whores", or Rosaly De Maios Roffman's "Sometimes People Think: Puffin Rhapsody" (1988) or "My Japanese Lady" (1992), the reader encounters Jewish and female visions that differ from those of other Jewish societies.

AN UNEXPECTED TURN TOWARD JEWISH CULTURE

In addition to the increasing consciousness of women's issues produced by the varieties of the women's movement, Jewish consciousness was being raised as well. Starting in the late 1960s and 1970s and continuing through the 1990s, enormous changes occurred in the Jewish literary world, in which Jewish women were full and important participants. A significant group of contemporary American Jewish writers produced an inward-turning genre of fiction that explored the individual Jew's connection to other Jewish people, to the Jewish religion, culture, and tradition, and to the chain of Jewish history. Jewishly literate fiction flourished in the 1970s, 1980s, and 1990s on every level; it attracted a broader reading audience than anyone might have predicted. In women's fiction ranging from highly serious to middlebrow to frankly pulp fiction, aspects of Jewish life that earlier in the century might have seemed to be inaccessible esoterica were transformed into exotica. Contrary to the expectations of assimilationists and the example of Jewish literature during the first half of the twentieth century, particularistic women's Jewish fiction became a commonplace.

Among major themes that emerged in late twentieth-century American Jewish fiction focusing on women, some of the most important included: the role of the Holocaust in the identity of survivors, their children, and the broader Jewish community; Israel as a focal point of American Jewish identity and a setting for the exploration of Jewish identity; a variety of religious and cultural subgroups within Jewish life, such as Sephardi Jewish communities, ultra-Orthodox communities, and feminist groups; sexual subgroups, such as Jewish lesbians and homosexuals; gendered relationships and the tension between intellectual and sensual, personal and professional, or Jewish and humanistic agendas in the lives of contemporary American Jewish women.

ORTHODOX CHARACTERS, SETTINGS, AND CONCERNS

Characteristic of American Jewish women's literature during the last quarter of the twentieth century is a depiction of diverse Orthodox societies and characters. This trend differs markedly from American Jewish literature of earlier periods, in which Orthodox characters tended to be cranky old men or force-feeding mothers and aunts. Orthodox Jewish characters and settings now enjoy an unprecedented and variegated focus in new American Jewish fiction.

Among contemporary younger authors, Nessa Rapoport's (b. 1953) moving first novel, *Preparing for the Sabbath* (1981), portrays a young woman struggling with the conflicting demands of youthful passion and spirituality, and of Orthodoxy and secularism, in both American and Israeli settings. Both the title of Allegra Goodman's (b. 1967) first collection of short stories, *Total Immersion* (1989), and the themes, imagery, and subject matter of many of the stories reflect her childhood in an Orthodox family in Hawaii. Her second collection, *The Family Markowitz* (1996), focuses largely on the tendency of modern/liberal/traditional Jews to merge American and Jewish values and behaviors—sometimes comically—in their everyday lives. Savagely humorous depictions of the idiosyncrasies and foibles of Orthodox environments are found in the pages of Tova Reich's (b. 1942) *Mara: A Novel* (1978), which knowingly depicts wealthy contemporary Orthodox New Yorkers, and *The Master of the Return* (1988), which wickedly satirizes the spiritual searchings of a motley collection of *ba'alei teshuva* [born-again Jews], who have gathered under the aegis of the Bratzlaver Hasidic group in Israel.

The focus on Orthodox Judaism is a reflection of the interest Orthodox societies evoked among some seemingly secularized American Jews. The story of such unlikely Orthophilism is found in ANNE ROIPHE's (b. 1935) popular and much-excerpted *Lovingkindness* (1987), a tale of an ultra-assimilated, intermarried, and widowed feminist whose daughter becomes a devoutly Orthodox Jew, much to her mother's initial astonishment and distress. A journey toward exploration of classical Jewish texts and ideas is found in the works of novelist and essayist NORMA ROSEN (b. 1925). Rosen is perhaps best known for her novel about women's reaction to the Holocaust, *Touching Evil* (1969).

Another version of the trajectory in which an intellectual fascination with Judaica is followed by the writing of fiction that deals with it is found in the work of Rhoda Lerman (1936). Lerman's New York suburban, ritually observant Jewish family sent her to Sunday school only, because she was a girl. Lerman's resulting feelings of alienation from the patriarchalism of traditional Jewish life (Satlof, pp. 197–208) were captured in her irreverent, explicit novel *Call Me Ishtar* (1973). However, later contact with a Hasidic rabbi led her to embark on a course of formal Jewish text study in several settings. Her novel *God's Ear* (1989), based in part on her Hasidic mentor, features a protagonist who is first a Hasidic rabbi, then an affluent insurance salesman, and finally once again a rabbi and spiritualist in unlikely Kansas.

This fascination with Orthodox settings extended to mystery novels and to popular fiction as well. For example, Faye Kellerman's homicide detective hero meets the widow of a *kollel yeshivah* student in her mystery *The Ritual Bath* (1986); their relationship continues, with the detective serendipitously discovering in *Sacred and Profane* (1987) that he has Jewish origins and is thus an appropriate romantic interest for the Orthodox widow. The series proved so popular that this seemingly odd couple went on to numerous adventures in subsequent books. Similarly, Naomi Ragen's popular novel *Jepthe's Daughter* (1989) brought a beautiful young Orthodox woman from affluent America to the extremism of a cloistered Jerusalem neighborhood in a disastrous marriage to a rigid and unpleasant Hasidic Jew; she escapes the nightmare by falling in love with a seemingly gentile gentleman who turns out to have had a Jewish mother. Romances especially have mined the exotic settings offered by biblical, Eastern European, Sephardic, and Orthodox worlds, often in combination with American Jewish settings. In scores of popular romances by authors such as CYNTHIA FREEMAN (c. 1915–1988), Belva Plain, Julie Ellis (b. 1933), and Iris Rainer Dart, landmarks of Jewish history previously relegated to textbooks became plot devices in the pages of glossy-covered novels. As expected, their female protagonists are almost always breathtakingly beautiful and, no matter how agonizing their experiences, almost always achieve the romantic and material successes that are a sine qua non of the genre. However, unlike such heroines in the past, these beautiful protagonists are often identifiably, proudly Jewish and achieve their goals not through the ministrations of a handsome and mysterious gentleman but through their own intelligent, energetic efforts. The image of the Jewish woman in contemporary American Jewish literature was affected even at the most basic, grass-roots level.

Emblematic of the new Jewish American women's literature at its highest level are the novels, short stories, and essays of CYNTHIA OZICK (b. 1928). Ozick's signature preoccupation is the conflict between the Jewish intellectual, spiritual, and cultural tradition, on one hand, and the Hellenistic sweep of artistic creativity and secular Western humanism, on the other hand. The conflict between art and Torah is no mere intellectual game for Ozick; she expresses it in numerous stories and novels as a deep, ongoing struggle.

Like Ozick, Rebecca Goldstein (b. 1950) demonstrates in her short stories and novels a thorough familiarity with diverse issues in Jewish society and in traditional Jewish life. Her work explores topics as different as the respective difficulties experienced by children of Holocaust survivors and by urban New York Jews in preppy suburban Princeton. Goldstein's protagonist in *The Mind-Body Problem* (1983) is a "beautiful, brainy" young woman, Renee Feuer, who grew up in a strictly Othodox home. After leaving home for college and then graduate school, Renee moves incrementally away from her training. When Renee abandons religious ritual for the study of philosophy, there is more than a little religious intensity and spiritual searching in her choice. Much to her surprise, she finds that her graduate school professors and her intellectual but Jewishly ignorant husband are at least as sexist as the Orthodox world she left. Renee comes to see her mind as the enemy that threatens her marriage. Her friend, in contrast, sees her body as the enemy that threatens her intellectual career. Even in the secular world, women are often pathologically divided, according to authors such as Goldstein. After writing several novels and short story collections not so directly focused on Jewish themes, Goldstein returned to the theme of Jewish women's identity as women and as Jews in her multigenerational saga *Mazel* (1995). Goldstein captures both the warmth of the traditional Jewish home and the tragic constrictions traditional Jewish societies often impose on creative women, in prose that is moving and playful in turn.

The quandaries experienced by Goldstein's protagonists are paradigmatic of realities in American Jewish societies, which during the final quarter of the twentieth century have seen simultaneous attenuation and intensification of Jewishness among different segments of the population. Even among those writers and readers with little interest in or knowledge of traditional Jewish texts and life-styles, fierce secularism found few voices. Instead, the hostility of earlier generations often mellowed into nostalgia, leaving Jews who once fled from the sights, sounds, and social pressures of the urban ghetto now anxious to read literature that recaptured for them scenes and experiences from their childhood and youth.

THE HOLOCAUST RECONSIDERED

Both Ozick and Goldstein have written powerful fiction dealing with yet another characteristic preoccupation of American Jewish women's writing—the Holocaust and the lost communities of Eastern Europe. Ozick argues against an attempt to try to explain Jewish suffering in the Holocaust as a Christological activity. In *The Shawl* (1989) and *The Messiah of Stockholm* (1987), Ozick mourns the Holocaust destruction of European Jewish culture and portrays survivors as idiosyncratic, flawed human beings, rather than as bland or mystical symbols, at the same time making their pain and confusion palpable. Goldstein's story "The Legacy of Raizel Kaidish" (1985) portrays a mother who tries to mold her daughter into a selfless, dispassionately altruistic saint—all in an effort to expiate her own profound moral failure within the hell of the concentration camps. Only on her deathbed does she acknowledge that she has been wrong to sacrifice her daughter's autonomy.

The scores of Holocaust-related novels and memoirs, both autobiographical and fictional, published by women in the United States run the gamut from simply told personal tales to philosophical explorations of the meaning of evil to lightly fictionalized historical chronicles to cinematic soap operas. Norma Rosen's *Touching Evil* (1969), mentioned earlier, and Susan Fromberg Schaeffer's (b. 1941) *Anya* (1974) are stirring depictions of the Holocaust and its impact. Among Gloria Goldreich's (1934) best-selling, well-researched popular historical sagas, which harken backward to explore the transformation of Jewish life in American immigrant societies and then trace its progress through contemporary times, one of the most moving is her Holocaust novel, *Four Days* (1980).

FEMINISM AND JEWISH SPIRITUALITY

Some feminist literature was experimental in theme, style, or content, and Jewishly spiritual in its concerns. ESTHER M. BRONER's (b. 1930) mystical fiction, *A Weave of Women* (1978), described a dozen women and three girls who dream of and plan for a feminist vision of utopia in Israel. Broner's experimental style in this novel, which blends Hebrew, Yiddish, and biblical motifs within narrative, drama, and poetic forms, might be termed mythic exploration of feminist issues. A nonfiction book, *The Telling* (1992), deals with the creation of Jewish women's religious rituals in the form of a feminist seder involving Broner, GLORIA STEINEM, LETTY COTTIN POGEBRIN, BELLA ABZUG, PHYLLIS CHESLER, and other Jewish activists.

Another example of Jewish feminist/spiritualist fiction was KIM CHERNIN's (b. 1940) *The Flame Bearers* (1986), a historical novel depicting a sect of Jewish women devoted to a female aspect of godhead called Chochma, the Bride. Other works by the prolific Chernin include feminist-oriented and Jewishly intense essays, such as those found in *Reinventing Eve* (1987), and a memoir, *In My Mother's House* (1983). Chernin was among those Jewish feminists who believed that merely giving women access to male forms of Jewish worship, liturgy, and religious imagery does little for truly woman-oriented spiritual expression. Like other writers, Chernin found Israel a particularly felicitous literary setting to make contact with previous suppressed images of female divinity.

CONCLUSION

The literary passage from Rebecca Gratz to Rebecca Goldstein incorporates nearly two centuries of cultural change. From the pedestal of heroic, restricted, self-consciously Judeo-Christian "true" womanhood, through the dislocating crucible of mass immigration, into the passionate Americanization of the first half of the twentieth century, Jewish women's literature preserved women's voices. Nevertheless, for many years, Jewish female writers, doubly marginal, avoided direct literary encounters with some primary aspects of their identity; indeed, Jewish male writers also catered for decades to the predominantly non-Jewish literary establishment either by ignoring Jewish subject matter or by treating Jewish characters as a species of precocious existential or comical "others," whose value consisted in their standing both inside and outside of and commenting on Christian or secular societies. When Jewish men did write directly about Jews, they often cast Jewish women in satirical stereotypes, deflecting cultural anti-Semitism onto the female of the species. However, American Jewish women's literature of the 1980s and 1990s drew on the full, complex, often contradictory and conflicting particularisms of the female Jewish American experience and vision. The female protagonists of late twentieth-century American Jewish fiction struggled with a multiplicity of identities: They were Jewish, Americans, daughters and wives and lovers and mothers; they were moderns—they were heirs to an ancient tradition. The proliferation of Jewish women writing—and being published—as America nears the turn of the twenty-first century literally speaks volumes about the preservation of women's visions and women's voices for the coming generations.

BIBLIOGRAPHY

Antler, Joyce. *America and I: Short Stories by American Jewish Women* (1990); Batker, Carol. "Fannie Hurst." In *Jewish American Women Writers: A Bio-Bibliographical and Critical Sourcebook* (1994); Calisher, Hortense. *Kissing Cousins: A Memory* (1988), and "No Important Woman Writer." In *Women's Liberation and Literature*, edited by Elaine Showalter (1971); Dearborn, Mary V. *Love in the Promised Land: The Story of Anzia Yezierska* (1988), and *Pocahontas's Daughters: Gender and Ethnicity in American Culture* (1986); Fishman, Sylvia Barack. "American Jewish Fiction Turns Inward." *AJYB* 91 (1991); Henderson, Bruce. "Lillian Hellman." In *Jewish American Women Writers*; Hindus, Milton. "Ethnicity and Sexuality in Gertrude Stein." *Midstream* 20 (January 20, 1974); Lichtenstein, Diane. *Writing Their Nations: The Tradition of Nineteenth-Century Jewish Women Writers* (1992); Matza, Diane. *Writing the Culture: Sephardic American Literature* (1997); Satlof, Claire R. "Rhoda Lerman." In *Jewish American Women Writers*; Shapiro, Ann R., Sara R. Horowitz, Ellen Schiff, and Miriyam Glazer, eds. *Jewish American Women Writers: A Bio-Bibliographical and Critical Sourcebook* (1994); Wald, Alan. *The New York Intellectuals: The Rise and Decline of the Anti-Stalinist Left from the 1930s to the 1980s* (1987); Walden, Daniel. "Edna Ferber." In *Jewish American Women Writers*; Weinberg, Sydney Stahl. "Longing to Learn: The Education of Jewish Immigrant Women in New York City, 1900–1934." *Journal of American Ethnic History* (Spring 1989), and *The World of Our Mothers: The Lives of Jewish Immigrant Women* (1988); Wilentz, Gay. "Jo Sinclair." In *Jewish American Women Writers*.

SYLVIA BARACK FISHMAN

FICTION, POPULAR

The explosion of writing by American Jewish women in the twentieth century has produced not only serious fiction, poetry, essays, and autobiography but also a range of popular literature geared to pleasure reading and light entertainment. Jewish women authors have experimented with many genres: regional novels, sagas, historical novels, romances, mysteries and crime fiction, science fiction, fantasy, and humor. This fiction, with its popular appeal, has often been adapted to the cinema, and a number of these women authors have also written screenplays or television scripts. Works by Jewish women appear on best-seller lists with increasing frequency in the later decades of the twentieth century. Some of the best-selling titles do not deal directly with Jewish content, but attention to overtly Jewish themes becomes more and more widespread through the 1980s and 1990s.

EARLY DECADES

Two of the early figures who achieved exceptional success and influence were EDNA FERBER and FANNIE HURST, who began publishing in the 1910s and whose titles first reached the best-seller lists in the 1920s and 1930s. Each wrote more than a dozen novels, as well as short stories, and their fiction served as the basis for successful motion pictures.

Edna Ferber (1885–1968) was the first Jewish American woman to win the Pulitzer Prize (1925), for the novel *So Big* (1924). Ferber is famous for her regional novels, which stress the history, attitudes, local color, and typical characters of various parts of the United States. Her best-known books include *Show Boat* (1926), which deals with life on the Mississippi

River; *Cimarron* (1930), which focuses on the Oklahoma territory; and *Giant* (1952), which portrays Texas ranchers and oil tycoons. While a number of Jewish characters enter these fictions peripherally, they are central to Ferber's *Fanny Herself* (1917), a semiautobiographical novel about a young girl growing up in the Midwest. Fanny strikes out on her own to make a spectacularly successful career in business. After a period of trying to deny her Jewishness, this character comes to take pride in her identity. Indeed, she becomes convinced that Jews possess special talents and sensibilities because of the suffering they have endured over the ages. Here, as in other novels by Ferber, a strong female character helps to build America as she herself achieves the American dream of success.

Fannie Hurst (1889–1968) expressed more ambivalent feelings about Jewish identity than did Ferber, and she treated the topic less openly in her fiction. Notable exceptions are the novel *Family* (1960), which deals with intermarriage, and *Humoresque* (1919), short vignettes that deal with Jewish characters. Hurst wrote frequently on gender politics, highlighting the constricting roles that women in her day faced in marriage and domestic life, as well as the challenges and inequities they met in the labor force. Though Hurst's own success brought her affluence and connections with high society—Hurst was said to be the highest-paid short-story writer of her time, and she earned considerable income from movie rights—she often wrote about ordinary people and expressed solidarity with the poor. Her best-known novel, *Imitation of Life* (1933), recounts the life of a single mother who makes a fortune by opening a chain of restaurants. Hollywood produced two movie versions of this tale.

REBELLION AGAINST THE STEREOTYPES

During the middle decades of the twentieth century, the image of Jewish women in popular fiction was dominated by negative stereotypes. The most prevalent figures were the Jewish mother, seen as an overly anxious, stifling parent who lives through her children's accomplishments, and the JAP—the Jewish American Princess—a spoiled, self-absorbed, materialistic character who is at once shallow and sexually frigid. The assumption underlying this denigrating image of young women is the idea that their entire goal in life is marriage for the sake of financial security. Consequently, the logic of the stereotype dictates that since these women care only about money, they withhold sexual favors until they obtain the kind of marriage that will bring them affluence. The JAP thereby comes to represent the emptiness of affluent

suburban life and of the Jews as a whole, who are seen to be greedy and ostentatious social climbers.

These stereotypes took on currency in the 1950s in large measure through Herman Wouk's novel *Marjorie Morningstar* (1955) and Philip Roth's *Goodbye, Columbus* (1959). These images became entrenched and flourished throughout the 1970s and 1980s. Beginning in the 1970s, however, Jewish women began to challenge those stereotypes and voice opinions about their own lives and experiences. Women writers rejected the narrow roles conferred on them as Jewish daughters, wives, and mothers. Time and again in fiction, female characters present themselves as individuals with thoughts and feelings of their own who are aware of their sexuality and are unwilling to serve merely as symbols of upward mobility. Gail Parent's *Sheila Levine Is Dead and Living in New York* (1972), Louise Blecher Rose's *The Launching of Barbara Fabrikant* (1974), and Susan Lukas's *Fat Emily* (1974) are notable for presenting protagonists who do not play the marriage game because they are not attractive enough. These novels construct funny, brash female characters who lay bare the destructiveness of social norms that place exaggerated importance on women's appearance and do not take seriously their accomplishments. Alix Kates Shulman's *Memoirs of an Ex-Prom Queen* (1972) features a protagonist who is beautiful and finds suitors easily, but she agonizes constantly that her looks will deteriorate as she moves past the age of twenty-five. These and other writers (Myrna Blythe, *Cousin Suzanne*, 1975; Marie Brenner, *Tell Me Everything*, 1976; Sandra Harmon, *A Girl Like Me*, 1975) highlight norms of behavior for women that were often a prescription for self-hatred. That is, women who were urged to invest all of their self-esteem in their appearance were also adjured not to look Jewish, even to the point of using cosmetic surgery to reshape their noses.

These novels, as they protest against narrowly defined expectations for women, are products of the foment that gave rise to the women's movement in the 1970s. Among the best-known texts of the period are SUE KAUFMAN's *Diary of a Mad Housewife* (1967) and ANNE ROIPHE's *Up the Sandbox* (1970), both of which were turned into popular films. These novels do not explicitly enter into questions of Jewishness or examine the mores and foibles of the Jewish middle class, but they are part of the same phenomenon as they protest against the strictures of domestic life for women and against submissiveness to husbands. Erica Jong's *Fear of Flying* (1973) merits special mention in this regard. This novel met with enormous commercial successes (over six million copies sold) and came to be seen as emblematic of the success of the women's movement. Jong's protagonist-narrator, Isadora Wing, flaunts her sexuality and her enjoyment of it while also expressing clearly her ambitions for a career. She is confused about how to balance her need for men and her love life with her professional aspirations, but she is a far cry from the JAP who seeks only material security through marriage. *Fear of Flying*, with the celebrity it achieved, also helped redefine popular fiction. While Jong's detractors dismissed her fiction as a contemptible phenomenon of mass culture, accusing it of positing a shallow view of life in prose marked by vulgarities and clichés, Jong's supporters have argued that her success allowed a silent, unrecognized female majority to express itself, to question women's roles in marriage, and to transform sexual norms previously defined by men.

In her later novel, *Parachutes and Kisses* (1984), Jong continues the tale of Isadora Wing, again joining a picaresque mode with a female sensibility to recount a series of sexual adventures. This novel, however, pays considerably more attention to the protagonist's Jewishness. A now forty-year-old Isadora seeks to understand her creativity and artistic talent as assets inseparable from her Jewish roots and family heritage. Serious attention to these themes makes for an uneasy combination with the comic sexual escapades, and *Parachutes and Kisses* was not so well received either by critics or by the public.

HISTORICAL NOVELS AND FAMILY SAGAS

Historical novels and family sagas have long been a staple of best-seller lists in the United States, and interest in this kind of fiction increased toward the end of the twentieth century. From the 1960s to the 1990s, judging by sales figures, the historical novel was the most popular of all genres. This trend in reading coincided with another: Whereas at mid-century, American Jewish authors commonly depicted Jews as outsiders or as universal symbols, in later decades, American Jewish fiction increasingly showed an overt interest in Jewish tradition, religion, and history. Not surprisingly, then, during the 1970s and 1980s, historical fiction and family sagas frequently became a forum for the exploration of Jewish identity. As they present a panoramic view of a family over several generations, highlighting births and deaths, love affairs, and the ways family members are swept up in historic events, such novels have shown a fascination for the Jewish past and Jewish milieus.

A most familiar scenario is that of impoverished Eastern European Jews who come to America, adjust to immigrant society, and then move on to middle-class comfort or, frequently, to fabulous wealth (in, for instance, Belva Plain's *Evergreen*, 1978, and Gloria Goldreich's *Leah's Journey*, 1978). The rags-to-riches theme, a perennial favorite in the American novel and particularly prominent in light entertainment reading, here coincides with Jewish perceptions of America as a land of opportunity for immigrants. Another preoccupation of popular fiction, increasingly evident over time, is the Holocaust. Family sagas focusing on this issue often emphasize how families have dispersed— some relatives stay in Europe and meet their doom, while others make their way to America or to Israel. Carolyn Haddad's *A Mother's Secret* (1988), MARGE PIERCY's *Gone to Soldiers* (1987), and CYNTHIA FREEMAN's *No Time for Tears* (1981) suggest a strong feeling of kinship among Jews in different nations and a keen sense that "there but for the grace of God go I." One of the most touching characters in this regard appears in Piercy's *Gone to Soldiers*. A young Parisian who reaches safety and finds refuge in Ohio while her twin sister is interned in a concentration camp, Naomi is wracked by guilt over her own comfortable survival. As if by telepathy, she dreams the experiences and vicariously feels the torments that her sister undergoes far away.

Other novels have explored a variety of more exotic settings or less familiar milieus. Faye Kellerman's historical thriller, *The Quality of Mercy* (1989), features converso characters in Elizabethan England who practice their religion in secret. Belva Plain's *Crescent City* (1984) places its heroine in Louisiana during the Civil War. There she faces the dilemmas of being at once a wealthy Southerner, a Jew who cannot condone slavery, and a woman who must take over the family business and intervene in politics due to personal hardships and the tragedies of the war. Julie Ellis's *East Wind* (1983) takes the reader to a more remote location as it focuses on turn-of-the-century Hong Kong and highlights the small Jewish community of Chinese Jews in Kaifeng. Again, however, the unusual setting provides an opportunity to recount a plot with a familiar pattern. This novel, too, follows the major life events of a protagonist aware of the many strata in her identity, even as the author insists on images of female strength, independence, and ability to transcend stereotyped roles and limitations. The protagonist of *East Wind* is a Jew, a woman, and an American (though living in the Orient). Circumstances bring her to take full responsibility for her finances, for raising a family, and for respecting and defending her Jewish identity, even as she pursues fulfillment in passionate love.

Much of this fiction is formulaic in nature, and part of its appeal for readers is its predictability. One of the standard features of such writing is a beautiful and wealthy heroine who proves brilliant in whatever endeavor she undertakes. Often unhappy in love, she nevertheless remains glamorous and overcomes all manner of adversities. Promising page-turning excitement, romance, scandal, and heartbreak, this genre offers fantasies of opulent living and melodramatic emotional highs and lows. Infused with a steady dose of tragedy, historical fiction and family sagas allow readers to identify with the rich and famous but finally not to envy them too much.

These qualities link this fiction with the romance, a related genre that focuses more closely on the life of a single protagonist and pays less attention to wide family ties or to broad historical sweep. Among the prolific writers who have produced more than a dozen such titles are Cynthia Freeman (born Bea Feinberg) and Julie Ellis. Concerned as they are with love and marriage, romances and family sagas are a natural venue for discussion of intermarriage, an important component of Freeman's *Portraits* (1979), *Come Pour the Wine* (1980), *Illusions of Love* (1984), and *The Last Princess* (1988), as well as Ellis's *Glorious Morning* (1982), *The Velvet Jungle* (1987), *The Only Sin* (1986), *Loyalties* (1989), and *Trespassing Hearts* (1992). These novels express a range of attitudes toward assimilation and anti-Semitic prejudice—sometimes true love prevails despite differences in religious background, sometimes the discovery of Jewish roots and connections becomes paramount in defining who is a worthy object of love—but all of this fiction creates opportunity for exploring Jewish identity through the lens of love and marriage. Tending toward clichés, contrived plots, and melodrama, this kind of writing nevertheless provides a remarkable indication of how Jewish themes and positive Jewish characters have developed wide appeal for the mass market.

More in-depth attention to Judaism and to traditional customs and values animates the novels of Naomi Ragen, such as *Jephthe's Daughter* (1989) and *Sotah* (1992). Falling into a category of its own, this fiction is written by an American-born woman who has lived for many years in Jerusalem, but whose books, written in English, were at first published and distributed primarily in the United States. (Later translated into Hebrew, they achieved best-seller status in Israel.) They are of special interest, as they describe the private lives of ultra-Orthodox women, thus giving the general public entree to a milieu ordinarily inaccessible to outsiders. Drawing on some of the usual elements of the romance genre—heroines of stunning beauty, vast wealth, passionate loves—Ragen also explores young *haredi* women's schooling, their

education about sexuality and the Jewish laws of sexual purity (MIKVAH and *niddah*), and their emotional responses to the intimacies of marriage and to family dynamics. This fiction thereby creates a striking intersection of Jewish values and secular ones. Thematically, the author condemns the emptiness, crass materialism, and selfishness of the secular world. At the same time, this highly secular genre, promising sensationalism or scandal, allows the author to explore the inner workings of a community that discourages secular reading of any sort and shuns commerical popular fiction. The result is entertainment, romance with a new slant, but also a thoughtful contrasting of worlds. Ragen uses fiction as a way to examine which Jews live out a decent and spiritually fulfilling life and which ones merely observe Jewish law without true devotion.

MYSTERIES, DETECTIVE FICTION, AND SPY THRILLERS

A somewhat jarring combination of secular and religious values also characterizes the detective and crime fiction by Jewish women that has come into vogue in the 1980s and 1990s. Preceded by mysteries in which Jewish topics were incidental—for example, novels by Amanda Cross (pen name of CAROLYN HEILBRUN), such as *Death in a Tenured Position* (1981), and whodunits that featured Jewish characters and milieus without a focus on Jewish identity or Judaism, such as Susan Isaacs's *Compromising Positions* (1978)—women mystery writers with distinctly, assertively Jewish topics found an enthusiastic readership and gained national visiblity in the late 1980s. Their commercial success has led to series of novels, appearing more or less annually, centered around Jewish women private investigators or amateur sleuths. A confluence of social and literary forces enabled this development. A boom of crime fiction in all its forms took place in the 1980s, and this was a period in which women became more prominently recognized as mystery writers. In addition, as publishers turned increasingly to specialized interests and subcultures, mysteries by and about Jewish women became a highly sought specialty.

The best known of the writers in this genre is Faye Kellerman. She has produced a series of novels featuring Rina Lazarus, a beautiful, young Orthodox widow, and police detective Pete Decker: *The Ritual Bath* (1986), *Sacred and Profane* (1987), *Day of Atonement* (1991), *Grievous Sin* (1993), *False Prophet* (1992), *Sanctuary* (1994), and *Prayers for the Dead* (1996). Attracted by Lazarus's charms, the gentile Decker is drawn, too, to Judaism. Together, the two solve crimes, and eventually he adopts Orthodoxy and they marry. Attention to Orthodox settings accounts in part for the popularity Kellerman has achieved. This element of local color defines for Kellerman a distinctive angle on crime fiction. Rina Lazarus and Pete Decker, for instance, track down a homicidal kidnapper who has lured a boy away from an ultra-Orthodox family in New York. The boy's sheltered environment has left him unworldly and naive in terms of street smarts but also curious about the allure of the secular world. Consequently, he is unusually vulnerable to kidnapping. Centering on this kind of tension, Kellerman poses the question: Is the world of strict religious practice a prison or a refuge?

While some readers identify with things Jewish and seek light reading that reflects their interests, other readers are curious about a set of mores and a milieu that are unfamiliar. Since Harry Kemelman's hugely successful mystery series featuring Rabbi David Small, beginning with *Friday the Rabbi Slept Late* (1965), the combination of Jewish themes with mystery fiction has included efforts to explain Jewish culture to those who know little about it. While Kemelman emphasizes the sleuthing skills of the rabbi, which derive from his talmudic thinking and his ratiocinations, Kellerman's novels place more emphasis on Judaism as comforting contrast to the violent, crime-ridden world so familiar to contemporary America. If readers take pleasure in seeing criminals brought to justice and order restored, Orthodoxy with its orderliness and clear guidelines for behavior appears as an appealing alternative. At the same time, Kellerman's themes and her chosen genre do create jarring incompatibilities. Her mysteries at once present Jews in a positive way but also allow for a kind of titillating voyeurism. This fiction provides readers a chance to peek into the world of the pious and to see when it has gone awry: when it is most vulnerable, how it has been targeted by hatred, and when that world itself has produced criminals who find its strictures overbearing and so respond in pathological ways.

Kellerman is not alone in her attention to religion. Rochelle Krich, for example, adopts an Orthodox setting in *Till Death Do Us Part* (1992), where she combines a focus on Jewish law with feminist themes. In this novel a young *agunah*, a woman whose husband refuses to give her a writ of divorce, wishes that he were dead. Subsequently, he is murdered, and she becomes the prime suspect. In Krich's *Angel of Death* (1994), a police detective discovers Jewish connections in her own mysterious past, even as she finds that the High Holiday liturgy contains important clues to the murder mystery she must solve. And in *Speak No Evil*

(1995), Krich creates another Orthodox protagonist, a defense attorney who puzzles over ways to reconcile Jewish law and ethical teachings with American civil law in order to pursue justice.

Other writers emphasize Jewish ethnicity more than religious practice. Marissa Piesman, for instance, in her Nina Fischman mysteries (*Unorthodox Practices*, 1989; *Personal Effects*, 1991; *Heading Uptown*, 1993; *Close Quarters*, 1994) creates a very funny protagonist-narrator who flaunts her ethnic background and comments at length on the attitudes, values, and humor of a secular Jewish New York milieu. Israeli author Batya Gur has found great popularity in English translation, thus adding to the trend for Jewish settings and characters. Her novels *The Saturday Morning Murder* (1988), *A Literary Murder* (1991), and *Murder on Kibbutz* (1994) have a subversive edge as they examine what has gone rotten and led to murder in the elite institutions of Israeli society: a psychoanalytic institute, a kibbutz, a university. Serita Stevens and Rayanne Moore offer a spoof of the mystery genre in several novels featuring Fanny Zindel, a grandmother in her sixties who recounts her adventures in a thick, stylized Yiddish accent (*Red Sea, Dead Sea*, 1993; *Bagels for Tea*, 1993). As the stereotype dictates, she kvetches about her arthritis, frets that her granddaughter does not eat enough, plays the busybody, and acts the matchmaker with acquaintances she barely knows. At the same time, she stumbles repeatedly onto murder scenes and bumbles her way successfully through tangled webs of deception and international intrigue. Fanny foils villains right and left, and even outmaneuvers the Mossad on her first visit to Israel.

The Fanny Zindel mysteries overlap generically with the spy thriller. At times, that genre has been approached seriously by women authors. For instance, Susan Isaacs's *Shining Through* (1990) features a female protagonist who spies on Nazi Germany and rediscovers her own Jewish ancestry in the process. Carolyn Haddad has published a number of thrillers with Israeli settings. Haddad also contributes to this genre, however, by spoofing it, much as do Stevens and Moore. In *The Academic Factor* (1980), a professor of sociology travels from Columbus, Ohio, to Europe to attend a conference and inadvertently finds herself embroiled in international espionage. Hunted by an assortment of double agents, she ends up in Israel, confounding a husband, a pretend husband, and a lover—all named Saul. As was the case with Fanny Zindel, this fiction presents a comic rejoinder to the narrow or limited roles often demanded of women. Both the grandmother and the bookish academic break out of their stereotypes in rollicking escapades that allow them to outsmart and outfight the most macho of spies and thugs.

These examples indicate that women have explored a spectrum of possibilities in crime fiction and thrillers: From whodunits (Isaacs and Piesman) to entertainment with a serious side (Kellerman's positive portraits of Orthodoxy and Krich's protest on behalf of *agunahs*), to detective stories that emphasize social observation (Gur), to the comic action-packed escape fantasies of Haddad or Stevens and Moore, all of this fiction envisions new roles and new images of Jewish women.

SCIENCE FICTION AND FANTASY

Jewish themes, once unheard of in science fiction, have emerged in that genre since the end of World War II, and particularly since the 1970s. While Jewish authors once sought pseudonyms to disguise their Jewishness, more and more writers have come to recognize rich potential in Jewish content for science fiction stories and novels. Two anthologies of Jewish science fiction and fantasy, *Wandering Stars* (1974) and *More Wandering Stars* (1982), edited by Jack Dann include a number of stories by women. Carol Carr (in "Look, You Think You've Got Troubles") imagines a Jewish father lamenting that his daughter has married a Martian. "Tauf Aleph" by Canadian author Phyllis Gotlieb raises the question, Who (or what) is a Jew? In this story, the last Jew in the universe lies dying on the planet Tau Ceti IV. He worries that he has no one to say Kaddish for him, except for the walruslike creatures of his planet, whom he has instructed in prayer, plus the robot (Og Hagolem), who has vast information stored in his memory regarding Torah, Talmud, Tosefta, Commentaries, Responsa, and more. Posing the question, Do they qualify to say Kaddish or not? Gotlieb's story plants hope for the continuity of Jewish tradition far into the distant future.

Marge Piercy, well-known for her fiction, essays, and poetry, draws on conventions of science fiction in some of her novels. The best known of these is *Woman on the Edge of Time* (1976), in which the main character lives simultaneously in contemporary America and in the year 2137. In *He, She and It*, Piercy combines elements of science fiction with her interest in Jews and feminism. The Jewish, female protagonist of this dystopia lives in the mid-twenty-first century. She helps create a cyborg, a kind of robot endowed with feeling as well as thought. Deliberately recalling the legends of the golem and the mysticism of the Kabbalah, Piercy raises questions about what constitutes personhood and whether the needs for personal and communal defense justify violence. Depicting a world devastated by war and ecological ruin, the author imagines innovative sexual and family relationships that provide an alternative to oppression as well as hope for a revitalized and nurturing future.

Along with Piercy, Rhoda Lerman has been recognized as an innovative author who combines elements of science fiction and fantasy with Jewish thematics. Though difficult to categorize generically, *Call Me Ishtar* (1973) addresses the exclusion of Jewish women from religious and social power by imagining a return of the goddess Ishtar.

CONCLUSION

Many other Jewish women authors have achieved great popularity and renown in recent decades. Names such as JUDITH KRANTZ and Jacqueline Susann have become synonymous with commercial success in the publishing world. Susann's *Valley of the Dolls* (1966) was the best-seller that had reached the highest sales of all time. It should be noted that some of these writers do not write explicitly on Jewish topics. (Some also have tenuous or complicated connections with their Jewishness. Susann, for example, was born Jewish and was buried as a Jew, but lived much of her adult life as a Catholic.) Other writers have explicitly incorporated Jewish characters and themes of social prejudice into their best-selling fiction, for example, Rona Jaffe, *Class Reunion* (1979).

A notable number of women writers are known for their humor. BEL KAUFMAN, granddaughter of Sholem Aleichem, wrote the well-loved, humorous account of high-school teaching, *Up the Down Staircase* (1965). Comedian JOAN RIVERS hit the best-seller charts in 1984 with *The Life and Times of Heidi Abromowitz*, as did BETTE MIDLER with her madcap illustrated fable in verse, *The Saga of Baby Divine*, in 1983. In *Heartburn* (1984), a witty, bittersweet account of a marriage and its breakup, NORA EPHRON writes of her protagonist's Jewish background with humor and irreverent affection. Iris Rainer Dart offers portraits of Jewishness itself as a heritage of humor. Whether writing on romantic love (*Till The Real Thing Comes Along*, 1987), friendships between women (*Beaches*, 1985), or unusual family issues of the twentieth century, such as surrogate mothering and test-tube pregnancies (*The Stork Club*, 1992), Dart presents warmth, humor, and family closeness as enduring, unpretentious values. Her Jewish characters cherish everyday moments. For them, not losing sight of their heritage or of humble beginnings is at once a source of strength and an antidote to glitz, glamour, and superficial values. The humor of Nora Ephron and Iris Rainer Dart is as well known from their scriptwriting (screenplays and television) as from their fiction.

As Jewish women have come to constitute a strong presence in American popular fiction, their work increasingly features an assertively Jewish component combined with the construction of strong women characters. To be sure, this writing expresses a mix of attitudes. Along with pride in Jewishness, there is ambivalence and at times self-hatred, but the wide variety of books and stories published reveals many ways to be Jewish in the contemporary world and many opportunities open to women. Even a brief survey shows female characters as Orthodox Jews, as ethnic Jews, as indifferent Jews, as Jews concerned with the Holocaust, as JAPs and as women who rebel against the JAP stereotype, as futuristic, visionary Jews, and as Jews intent on rewriting and reconceiving women's place in religion. And, to the extent that popular fiction lets out the reins of the imagination, relying as it does on fantasy and a spectrum of imagined worlds and actions, women characters in this literature can be anything—from royalty to inhabitants of outer space, from heroic figures in the Civil War to high fashion models, not to mention entrepreneurs, writers, actresses, detectives, doting grandmothers, and spies.

To the extent that this kind of writing has mass appeal, these authors have spread an awareness of Jewishness into the mainstream of American popular culture. At the same time, these authors have used the formulas of genre fiction to explore Jewish identity. Regional novels have comfortably accommodated portraits of Jewish immigrants and pioneers and their contributions to the American dream. Historical fiction and romance have lent themselves naturally to themes of assimilation and intermarriage. Mysteries just as naturally have become a forum for examining Jewish law and transgressions of it, highlighting the security and the restrictions that traditional Judaism offers observant Jews. Thrillers focusing on Israel tussle with the twentieth-century redefinition of the Jew as warrior, not as scholar. Science fiction has discovered that it lends itself to Jewish themes in the most imaginative and whimsical ways. Drawing on Jewish legends, it projects age-old Jewish concerns into limitless future worlds.

BIBLIOGRAPHY

Antler, Joyce. "Jewish American Writing: Overview." In *The Oxford Companion to Women's Writing in the United States*, edited by Linda Wagner-Martin (1995); Baum, Charlotte, Paula Hyman, and Sonya Michel, eds. *The Jewish Woman in America* (1976); Burch, Beth. "Jewish American Writing: Fiction." In *The Oxford Companion to Women's Writing in the United States*, edited by Linda Wagner-Martin (1995); Fishman, Sylvia Barack. "American Jewish Fiction Turns Inward, 1960–1990." *AJYB* 91 (1991): 35–69, and "The Faces of Women: An Introductory Essay." In *Follow My Footprints: Changing Images of Women in American Jewish Fiction*, edited by Sylvia Barack Fishman (1992); Forman, Ed, Martin H. Greenberg, and Larry Segriff, eds., with Jon L. Breen. *The Mystery Reader's Indispensable Companion* (1993); Greene, Suzanne Ellery. *Books for Pleasure, 1914–1945* (1974); Hackett, Alice. *Eighty Years of Best Sellers, 1895–1975* (1977); Hinckley, Karen, and Barbara Hinckley. *American Best Sellers: A Reader's Guide to Popular Fiction* (1989); Lichtenstein, Diane. "Fannie Hurst and Her Nineteenth-Century Predecessors." *Studies in American Jewish Literature* 7, no. 1 (1988): 26–39, and *Writing Their Nations: The Tradition of Nineteenth-Century American Jewish Women Writers* (1992); Prell, Riv-Ellen. "Cinderellas Who (Almost) Never Become Princesses: Subversive Representations of Jewish Women in Post-War Popular Novels." In *Developing Images: Representations of Jewish Women in America*, edited by Joyce Antler (forthcoming); Shands, Kerstin W. *The Repair of the World: The Novels of Marge Piercy* (1994); Shapiro, Ann R., ed. *Jewish American Women Writers: A Bio-Bibliographical and Critical Sourcebook* (1994); Templin, Charlotte. *Feminism and the Politics of Literary Reputation: The Example of Erica Jong* (1995); Uffen, Ellen Serlen. "The Novels of Fannie Hurst: Notes Toward a Definition of Popular Fiction." *Journal of American Culture* 1 (1978): 574–83, and "The Orthodox Detective Novels of Faye Kellerman." *Studies in American Jewish Literature* 11, no. 2 (1992): 195–203.

NAOMI SOKOLOFF

FIEDLER, BOBBI (b. 1937)

Retired Congresswoman Bobbi Fiedler of Northridge in Los Angeles considers herself "a very private person" who was "pushed into politics by necessity, not by plan." The year was 1976. Fiedler was a thirty-nine-year-old mother and housewife, dividing her days among the PTA, temple affairs, and a family-owned pharmacy. But her tranquil suburban world was abruptly shattered by news that Los Angeles schools were headed toward a court order to desegregate. Unless someone acted quickly, the city's children—her own two included—would soon be riding buses to schools far away from home.

"I felt I had to stop it," she later explained. In the company of parents who shared her concern, she started a group called BUSTOP, which quickly mushroomed into a citywide antibusing crusade. While she could support voluntary integration, she believed forced busing deprived parents of the right to choose where their children attended school.

Identifying children by race or ethnicity was anathema to her, evoking the historical plight of the Jews in Eastern European ghettos. "Being Jewish had

*Congresswoman Bobbi Fiedler began her political career in an antibusing crusade.
Although she supported voluntary racial integration, she believed that defining children
by race or ethnicity was unconscionable, evoking the historical plight of the Jews in Eastern Europe.
She is shown here with her friend President Ronald Reagan. [Ronald Reagan Presidential Library]*

a very strong impact on my political philosophy—not necessarily in the spiritual or religious sense—but in the sense of being a minority, of being the object of discrimination," she said.

Before the year was out, Fiedler won a seat on the Los Angeles Board of Education and quickly built a political machine that finally put the brakes on busing in Los Angeles. In 1980, after a single term in local office, the scrappy Republican ran for Congress in the Twenty-first District and narrowly defeated James C. Corman, a widely respected ten-term Democrat who favored school busing.

Bobbi Fiedler was born Roberta Frances Horowitz on April 22, 1937, in Santa Monica, California, the second of two daughters born to Jack and Sylvia (Levin) Horowitz. Her Brooklyn-born-and-bred father—middle-weight boxing champion, artist, plumber, a builder of the Empire State Building, laundry owner, and building contractor—shared his broad, eclectic worldview with her. Sylvia, born in Springfield, Massachusetts, passed along her interest in Jewish affairs and devotion to Zionism to her younger daughter. Bobbi and her sister, Esther Horowitz

Michaels, drew close as young children when their mother joined their father in the family laundry.

Fiedler attended Santa Monica Technical School and Santa Monica City College and was an interior designer before starting a family with her first husband, a pharmacist. Her daughter Lisa was born in 1961 and her son Randy Alan in 1964.

Fiedler's deep concern for individual rights and intense distrust of government—the catalysts for her opposition to busing—took root during her childhood as World War II raged in Europe. "I recall very clearly what happened to the Jews—how everything they owned, everything they had, including their lives, was taken from them by a government that had no respect for anyone's needs but its own," she said.

Her combative spirit had a similar genesis. Coming of age in a neighborhood where Jews were a rarity, she became accustomed to being the target of anti-Semitic taunts. "Although that hurt at the time, it also helped [me] build some strength and resiliency against the realities of life," she told the *Los Angeles Times* in 1981. "I was always pretty much a fighter. I don't mean physically fighting, but fighting for your rights."

Elected to Congress in 1980 as the only female member of California's delegation, Fiedler kept on fighting. She quickly became known among her peers as feisty and aggressive. She ignored House tradition, which required new representatives to keep their opinions to themselves and make an effort to learn from senior members. However, she won plaudits from both sides of the aisle for her diligence and thoroughness.

Although she rode into Congress on President Ronald Reagan's conservative coattails, she describes herself as an independent Republican who voted her conscience. Her record bears her out. As a member of the House Budget Committee, she upheld party doctrine by fighting for tax and spending cuts, championing defense spending to save jobs, and salvaging nine B-1 bombers that had been marked for extinction. At the same time, she broke with party leadership over her support of abortion rights and the Equal Rights Amendment.

She was not afraid to clash with the U.S. Navy over the lives of 1,500 goats on San Clemente Island. And at times she took the middle road, as when she sponsored bills providing tax credits for child care and pension reforms. Her unswerving support of Israel won her an A+ rating from the American Israel Public Affairs Committee (AIPAC), the pro-Israel lobby.

Fiedler left the House in 1987 to run for the Senate. She finished fourth in a highly contentious primary and temporarily withdrew from politics to join the private sector as a political commentator and consultant. Earlier that year, Fiedler, who was divorced in 1977, married Paul Clarke, her campaign manager and chief adviser throughout her three terms in Congress.

Since leaving Congress, she has advised New York real estate tycoon Donald Trump on business dealings with the Los Angeles School Board, fought off a vicious case of lymphoma, helped put George Bush in the White House and Pete Wilson in the California governor's mansion, and used her expertise to get several Republican women into local and state office. In 1993, she was appointed by Los Angeles mayor Richard Riordan to the city's embattled Community Redevelopment Agency and by the governor to the California Lottery Commission.

But public life had lost its luster for her. Fiedler retired from both boards after a single term and turned her attention to her family, especially her grandchildren.

Fiedler has received at least one hundred awards and honors for her years of public service. They include the Anita Perlman Award from the B'nai B'rith Youth Organization, Outstanding Legislator from the Los Angeles Jewish Federation Council, Legislator of the Year from the Veterans of Foreign Wars, Bulldog Award from the National Taxpayers Union, and an honorary doctorate of law from the West Coast College of Law.

But far beyond her many successes, she cherished a warm, mutually rewarding friendship with President Reagan. She was thrilled to be asked to make his seconding speech during the 1984 Republican Convention. Writing the speech herself, she applauded the president for his strength, vision, and courage and called on her fellow Republicans to join her in choosing a leader "who will encourage us to dream, to build those dreams and to dream on."

Bobbi Fiedler grew up fighting because she was a Jew in a gentile neighborhood. She developed a distrust of government because she grew up at a time when Jewish people an ocean away were being fed into ovens. She entered politics because she believed the rights of children and parents were endangered. She voted her conscience because she knew no other way. As a woman and a Jew, she has forged her own course.

BIBLIOGRAPHY

Bergholz, Richard. "Who Can Beat Alan Cranston?" *California Journal* (May 1986); Cuniberti, Betty. "Fightin' Fiedler Steps into the Ring on Capitol Hill." *Los Angeles Times*, November 29, 1981; Fiedler, Bobbi. Speech delivered to second the nomination of President Ronald Reagan, Dallas, Texas, August 22, 1984, and telephone interview with author, San Diego, California, August 19, 1996; Neumeyer, Kathleen. "The Fiedler Formula: 'Busing . . . Children . . . Boston.'" *California Journal* (December 1981); U.S. House of Representatives. Office of the Historian. *Women in Congress, 1917–1990* (1991); *Who's Who in American Politics* (1993–1994); *Who's Who in the West*, 25th ed.

SUSAN KAHNWEILER POLLOCK

FIELDS, DOROTHY (1904–1974)

A lyricist and librettist whose work embraces the bouncy optimism of "On the Sunny Side of the Street," the brassy seductiveness of "Hey Big Spender," and the tender musings of "The Way You Look Tonight," Dorothy Fields wrote the words to more than four hundred songs in a career that spanned half a century. In a casual and colloquial voice that spoke to the many moods of the human heart, she set her lyrics to the melodies of some of America's best-known and best-loved composers. When Fred Astaire

It is not unusual for Jews to be great songwriters. What's unusual is finding a woman in that crowd. In her fifty-year career, Dorothy Fields wrote more than four hundred songs—including nineteen Broadway musicals—and won an Oscar with composer Jerome Kern for "The Way You Look Tonight."
[New York Public Library]

wooed Ginger Rogers with "I Won't Dance," when he pouted over her reluctance in "A Fine Romance," when Judy Garland belted out "I Feel a Song Coming On," they sang the words penned by Dorothy Fields. She wrote the book and lyrics to Cy Coleman's music for *Sweet Charity* and *Seesaw*, and spent the last day of her life on March 28, 1974, watching a tour company rehearsal of *Seesaw*, her nineteenth Broadway musical.

One of the four children of comedian-actor-producer-director Lew Fields of the famed Weber

and Fields vaudeville team, Dorothy Fields was born in Allenhurst, New Jersey, on July 15, 1904. Along with her brothers Joseph and Herbert, she followed her father's footsteps into the theater—albeit against his better judgment. After attending public school in New York City, she turned to writing songs for revues at the Cotton Club in New York City. Pairing up with Jimmy McHugh in 1928, she wrote lyrics for "Lew Leslie's Blackbirds," "I Can't Give You Anything But Love," "On the Sunny Side of the Street," "I'm in the Mood for Love," "Exactly Like You," and "Don't Blame Me." In later years, she would collaborate with her brother Herbert on the books for such block-buster musicals as *Annie Get Your Gun, Redhead, Up in Central Park*, and *A Tree Grows in Brooklyn*. Fields's lyrics for the ballads "Close as Pages in a Book" and "I'll Buy You a Star" epitomize the seamless melding of poetic imagery into romantic refrain that marks so many of her songs.

Although she wrote lyrics for songs in at least twenty-five films, Dorothy Fields's most famous Hollywood collaboration was with composer Jerome Kern, to whom she referred as her idol. She was working at RKO Studios when the producer of the movie version of *Roberta* gave her a melody Kern had added to the score. "The words I came up with were 'Lovely to Look At,'" she recalled in 1966. "Jerry was delighted with them and asked me to work with him on his next picture, *Swing Time*." From that union came "The Way You Look Tonight" which won both lyricist and composer Oscars for the best song of 1936. Two years later, Dorothy Fields engaged in a different kind of union, marrying Eli D. Lahm. Their son, David, was born in 1941 and their daughter, Eliza, in 1944.

When in 1971 the Songwriters Hall of Fame held the first of what would become its annual elections, Dorothy Fields was the only woman to be named. A minority by virtue of her gender, she was hardly an anomaly as a Jew. The backstage world was dominated by immigrant, first- and second-generation Jewish Americans who found, in the explosive world of twentieth-century show business, releases for creative energies pent up by centuries of European oppression. In the realm of songwriting, Jewish talent flowed as if from a cornucopia: Irving Berlin, George and Ira Gershwin, Richard Rodgers, Lorenz Hart, Oscar Hammerstein II, Jerome Kern, Leonard Bernstein, Kurt Weill, Stephen Sondheim, Betty Comden, and, not least among them, the lyricist who warned an enticing dancing partner, "For heaven rest us, we're not asbestos"—Dorothy Fields.

SELECTED WORKS BY DOROTHY FIELDS

MUSICALS

Annie Get Your Gun. Lyrics and music by Irving Berlin, book by Herbert and Dorothy Fields (1946); *By the Beautiful Sea.* Music by Arthur Schwartz, lyrics by Dorothy Fields (1954); *Redhead.* Music by Albert Hague, lyrics by Dorothy Fields (1959); *Seesaw.* Book by Cy Coleman, lyrics by Dorothy Fields (1973); *Sweet Charity.* Book by Neil Simon, music and lyrics by Cy Coleman and Dorothy Fields (1966); *Swing Time.* Music by Jerome Kern, lyrics by Dorothy Fields (1936); *A Tree Grows in Brooklyn.* Music by Arthur Schwartz, lyrics by Dorothy Fields (1951); *Up in Central Park.* Book by Herbert and Dorothy Fields (1945).

SONGS

"Close as Pages in a Book"; "Don't Blame Me"; "Exactly Like You"; "A Fine Romance"; "Hey Big Spender"; "I Can't Give You Anything But Love"; "I Feel a Song Coming On"; "I'll Buy You a Star"; "I'm in the Mood for Love"; "I Won't Dance"; "Lew Leslie's Blackbirds," with Jimmy McHugh; "On the Sunny Side of the Street"; "The Way You Look Tonight."

BIBLIOGRAPHY

AJYB 76:513; "Dorothy Fields, Lyricist Dies; Wrote 400 Songs in 50 Years." *NYTimes*, March 29, 1974, 38:1; Fordin, Hugh. *Jerome Kern: The Man and His Music in Story, Picture, and Song* (1975); *The New Grove Dictionary of American Music.* Vol. II. Edited by H. Wiley Hitchcock and Stanley Sadie (1986); *NAW* modern; *WWWIA* 6.

MYRNA KATZ FROMMER

FILM INDUSTRY

The story of Jewish women in film reflects the story of Jewish women in America in this century. Although, like their brethren, a large number of Jewish women have contributed to the development of the film industry, they have had to fight for their place. From the early years of the silent era through today, the struggle of Jewish women to be recognized for their talents has been a difficult one.

Any discussion of Jewish women in film must address several different areas. First, there is employment opportunity. How have they been treated as women at their work? What jobs have they been allowed? Second, there is the communication of the Jewish woman's experience to the screen. How has their Jewishness influenced the way screenwriters wrote, actresses acted, and directors directed? And finally, more broadly, how have Jewish women been represented as characters on film, and have those characters been played by Jewish women?

In the early days of film, the silent era, the majority of women of all ethnicities were limited to acting. However, Jewish women also made their presence profoundly felt in the area of screenwriting, and would continue to do so for the rest of the century.

The teens and 1920s were a time of unusual freedom and discovery for the film industry. The industry was more open than it would be in later decades. It made more films with ethnic story lines and roles, stereotypical and sometimes degrading as they were. In fact, by the 1920s, a distinct genre of films about Jewish life had developed: melodramas about Jewish life in the ghettos of New York. Some were sentimental, others harshly realistic, and still others broadly comic; all illustrated the dilemma of the immigrant Jews. During the teens, the films' sympathies were with the older generation, but by the 1920s it was the children who were heroes and heroines, as those children chose assimilation over Orthodoxy.

Jewish-Irish movies, a subgenre of the ghetto film, also promoted the "melting pot" philosophy, which was very prominent at the time. Story lines about adoption—an Irish child into a Jewish family, never the other way around—or intermarriage were used to create happy, assimilated endings. During the same period, the Yiddish film industry added to the profusion of Jewish roles and stories.

The Jewish roles for Jewish women during this period fall into several categories. Most memorable were the Jewish mothers, matronly women who cooked for their families and provided unqualified love to their children. Such a type was played by VERA GORDON in *Humoresque* (1920). She also played Rosie Potash in the silent comedies *Potash and Perlmutter*; Mrs. Horowitz in *Four Walls* (1928), and later Mrs. Cohen in the popular comic series *The Cohens and the Kellys*, which spans the silent and the early sound years. Rosa Rosanova became identified with Jewish motherhood with *Hungry Hearts* (1922), *His People* (1925), *The Younger Generation* (1929), and *Pleasure Before Business* (1927). Other Jewish mothers included Ida Kramer as Mrs. Cohen in *Abie's Irish Rose* (1928) and ANNA APPEL in *The Heart of New York* (1932).

The younger women played the sweet ingenues of the ghetto. Two examples are Jetta Goudal, who appeared in *Salome of the Tenements* (1925), and CARMEL MYERS, a rabbi's daughter, who starred as Sonya Schonema in *Cheated Love* (1921). Myers also appeared in Jewish roles in *Intolerance* (1916) and *Ben-Hur* (1925), which were *not* films told from a Jewish perspective. (The Anti-Defamation League of B'nai

Silent film sensation CARMEL MYERS *played opposite virtually every leading man of her day.*
In the 1926 version of Ben-Hur, *she played the Jewish vamp Iras, opposite Ramon Novarro's Ben-Hur.*
[Museum of Modern Art Film Archives]

B'rith had to persuade D.W. Griffith to cut scenes from *Intolerance* that showed Jews as Christ killers.) Both actresses also acted in non-Jewish roles, which fell into the third stereotype Jewish women were allowed to play: the vamp. Carmel Myers's career is even summed up in *Halliwell's Filmgoer's Companion* as "in the vamp tradition."

But the woman who defined "vamp" was THEDA BARA (born Theodosia Goodman). Born in Cincinnati, Ohio, she made her first screen appearance in *Carmen* (1915), but is best remembered for her performances in *A Fool There Was* (1915) and *Cleopatra* (1917). She made thirty-eight films between 1915 and 1926, when she retired. Theda Bara's ethnic looks were perfect for the silent era, when there was great popular interest in the so-called exotic. Spanish, Latino, and Jewish actresses found themselves employed as the "Arabs"

or mysterious foreigners in a great number of films. Studio publicists promoted Theda Bara's name as an anagram for "Arab death" and informed the public that she was the daughter of an Eastern potentate. Her image was not too ethnic, and certainly not openly Jewish, but ethnic enough to be considered exotic by the public.

Ethnicity was less a problem for those out of the glare of the limelight, but jobs such as directing and producing were closed to most women. Many women, however, became screenwriters, and Jewish women obtained such work from the beginning. Some of the most influential films with Jewish themes were either written by Jewish women for the screen or adapted from novels and stories they wrote.

ANZIA YEZIERSKA wrote stories of exceptional quality. Two of her works, adapted for the screen, were the aforementioned *Hungry Hearts* and *Salome of the Tenements*. Both films attest to the harsh circumstances of immigrant Jewish existence, much of it drawn from her Orthodox Jewish background. However, the contradictions between her Orthodox background and the make-believe world of Hollywood seem to have been too much for her. She returned to the East after only five years in Hollywood and was never produced again.

Another writer whose novels and stories contributed to silent and later sound films was FANNIE HURST. Among these were *Humoresque* (1920, remade in 1946), *The Good Provider* (1922), *The Younger Generation* (1929), and *Imitation of Life* (1934, remade in 1959). While the stories of Yezierska exposed the harsher side of Jewish life, Hurst tended to treat life in America more sentimentally.

With the advent of sound (corresponding with the 1930s and the Great Depression), films began to focus more and more on "WASP" characters. To a greater degree than in the teens and 1920s, the roles Jewish women played in mainstream Hollywood films did not reflect their ethnic or religious heritage. And after a golden age from 1936 to 1939, the Yiddish film industry began its rapid decline.

By 1939 Jewish representation in film had all but disappeared, for a great many reasons. As the major Jewish film moguls became more assimilated themselves, they reflected the American philosophy of the time: It was un-American to focus on an individual's ethnicity, as opposed to his or her "Americanness." At the same time, movies were becoming the most popular form of entertainment in America, from the large metropolitan areas to small rural communities; the moguls believed that ethnic stories would be unpopular with this broader audience. Finally, in the late 1930s, with anti-Semitism on the rise in America as well as Europe, and attacks against the Jewish influence in Hollywood increasing in the right-wing media, it made sense for Jews not to call attention to themselves. The threat of what openly Jewish stars, characters, and stories would do to the sale of Hollywood films in Europe and to their popularity at home was very real.

This trend continued through the end of the 1950s, with a few notable exceptions. Jewish actresses with successful Hollywood careers during this period included Sylvia Sidney, Paulette Goddard, LUISE RAINER, LAUREN BACALL, June Havoc, Betty Hutton, JOAN BLONDELL, JUDY HOLLIDAY, SHELLEY WINTERS and Lee Grant. Stage stars also made successful forays into film, including FANNY BRICE, SOPHIE TUCKER, STELLA ADLER, and Ethel Merman.

Among the most famous of the thousands of stage performers who "went Hollywood" in the 1930s was Fanny Brice (born Fania Borach), who appeared in several early sound films, including *My Man* (1928), *The Great Ziegfeld* (1936), and *Ziegfeld Follies* (1946).

Sophie Tucker (born Sophia Abuza) was a popular singer and *the* star of vaudeville. During her heyday, she was one of the few women in entertainment to make more than men doing the same job. Her first film role was in *Honky Tonk* (1929). She later appeared in *Broadway Melody of 1937* (1937), *Atlantic City* (1944), and *Follow the Boys* (1944), among others.

Stella Adler, best known as an acting teacher—of Marlon Brando and Robert De Niro, among many others—came to Hollywood for a short period in the late 1930s, and appeared in three films: *Love on Toast* (1937), *Shadow of the Thin Man* (1941), and *My Girl Tisa* (1948).

Like Fanny Brice before her, Ethel Merman had a career mainly on the musical stage, but she did appear

LAUREN BACALL *has always been blunt. "I was brought up that way, except when I didn't tell Howard Hawks I was Jewish, because he was anti-Semitic and scared the hell out of me. He made me so nervous I didn't say anything. . . . I was not proud of myself."*

in a dozen Hollywood productions, including *Anything Goes* (1936) and *Call Me Madam* (1953).

Sylvia Sidney (born Sophia Koscow), on the other hand, was pure Hollywood. Starting her career in the early 1930s, she found her fame and fortune by avoiding any kind of ethnic stereotyping. Neither her name, her looks, nor the parts she chose to play gave any hint of her Jewish identity. But she did portray a huge variety of working-class urban heroines. In a career that spanned eight decades, her most famous roles included *Street Scene* (1931), *You Only Live Once* (1937), *Fury* (1936), and *Sabotage* (1936). She was nominated for a best supporting actress Academy Award for her performance in *Summer Wishes, Winter Dreams* (1973). In 1996, she appeared in *Mars Attacks!* Not until the 1970s did Sidney play any openly Jewish roles, among them a part in *Raid on Entebbe*, a 1977 made for television movie.

Luise Rainer began as a stage actress in Vienna, Austria. After moving to Hollywood, she won two Academy Awards. The first was for her performance as ANNA HELD, the great Jewish musical comedy artist, in *The Great Ziegfeld* (1936). The second was for her role as a Chinese peasant (!) in *The Good Earth* (1937).

Paulette Goddard (born Marion Levy) played few openly Jewish roles, but her role as Hannah in Charlie Chaplin's *The Great Dictator* (1940) proved a powerful exception. Goddard began her career when she was selected by Chaplin for the female lead in *Modern Times* (1936). (She also married Chaplin.) A few of the other films she appeared in include *The Women* (1939), *Reap the Wild Wind* (1942), *Unconquered* (1947), and *The Diary of a Chambermaid* (1946). When Chaplin chose Goddard for Hannah—a spunky Jewish waif who sets an example by her fearless response to Nazi brutality—he broke with Hollywood tradition in two ways: by casting a young, attractive woman in an openly Jewish role, and by dealing with the issue of Jews and Nazism.

One of the greatest Jewish-but-never-known-as-Jewish stars hit the big screen in 1944, when Betty Joan Perske debuted in *To Have and Have Not*. The film not only established her as the star Lauren Bacall but also led to her marriage with leading man Humphrey Bogart. Later films included *The Big Sleep* (1946), *Key Largo* (1948), *How to Marry a Millionaire* (1953), *The Shootist* (1976), *Murder on the Orient Express* (1974), and *Misery* (1990). Her most recent film, *The Mirror Has Two Faces* (1996), garnered her an Academy Award nomination for best supporting actress and is one of her few openly Jewish roles.

Three other performers who started in the 1940s were June Havoc (born Ellen Evangeline Hovick),

Betty Hutton (born Betty Thornberg), and Joan Blondell. At one time or another all three could have been characterized as the blonde of the year. Blondell, however, graduated into character roles as her career progressed, and Hutton always had a wholesome, girl-next-door quality.

Blondell made more than eighty films during her long career, as diverse as *Gold Diggers of 1933* (1933), and *A Tree Grows in Brooklyn* (1944). Her most famous were probably *Nightmare Alley* (1947) and *The Cincinnati Kid* (1965); her last was *The Champ* (1979).

Betty Hutton played in light musical comedies and made more than twenty films in the 1940s and early 1950s. Her two biggest successes were *Annie Get Your Gun* (1950) and *The Greatest Show on Earth* (1952).

June Havoc got her training in vaudeville and on Broadway. She appeared with her older sister, who later became the infamous Gypsy Rose Lee. Her film career began early when, at two, she appeared in several Harold Lloyd film shorts. She is best remembered for her later work in musicals, especially *My Sister Eileen* (1943). In *Gentleman's Agreement* (1948), she played a woman who changed her name from Walovsky to Wales in an effort to hide her ethnic identity.

The enormously talented Judy Holliday never played a Jewish role, but won fame on Broadway as a not-so-dumb blonde in *Born Yesterday* and repeated her comic performance in the 1950 film version. She made other memorable appearances in *Adam's Rib* (1949), *The Solid Gold Cadillac* (1956), and her last film, *Bells Are Ringing* (1960).

Shelley Winters (born Shirley Schrift), who rose to fame in the 1951 version of *A Place in the Sun*, was an attempt on the part of the studios to create another bombshell, but here they failed. While producers succeeded in getting Winters to bleach her hair, she refused the nose job. She also insisted upon taking her acting with great seriousness. As a result, her career has spanned fifty years. In the 1950s, her major films included *The Big Knife* (1955) and *The Night of the Hunter* (1955). Most important, from the perspective of the image of Jewish women on film, she performed the role of Mrs. Van Daan in *The Diary of Anne Frank* (1959), for which she won an Academy Award.

Lee Grant (born Lyova Haskell Rosenthal) was of the same era as Shelley Winters, but her career took a very different turn. She made her first film, *Detective Story*, in 1951, receiving an Oscar nomination for best supporting actress. Shortly thereafter, she was blacklisted for not testifying before the House Un-American Activities Committee (HUAC) against her

JUDY HOLLIDAY *played a not-so-dumb blond in both the Broadway and the film versions of* Born Yesterday. *She is shown here in the 1950 film version, with William Holden (right) and Broderick Crawford.*

husband, playwright Arnold Manoff. Over the next twelve years, she acted in only two films.

Later in their careers, both Shelley Winters and Lee Grant would play the ubiquitous Jewish mother. Indeed, this stereotype never completely disappeared from the screen, even during the relatively arid period from the 1930s through the 1950s. The roles were played by both Jewish and gentile women. Several examples are Tamara Shayne in *The Jolson Story* (1946), Gusti Huber in *The Diary of Anne Frank* (1959), and Claire Trevor in *Marjorie Morningstar* (1958), which was adapted for the screen by a Jewish woman, Frances Goodrich, with her husband, Albert Hackett.

Goodrich and Hackett also created the very popular Thin Man series (beginning in 1934), which was based on Dashiell Hammett's novel but soon took on a life of its own. Subsequently, the pair wrote *The Hitler Gang* (1944), *It's a Wonderful Life* (1946), and *Father of the Bride* (1950). Both *The Hitler Gang* and *The Diary of Anne Frank* dealt with the atrocities of Nazi Germany and were rarities of the period for that reason.

The most prolific Jewish woman writer was one whose name is little known. Over the course of her career, SONYA LEVIEN wrote more than seventy screenplays, ten with humorist S.N. Behrman, at least two with William Ludwig, and at least thirty-one on her own. Among her most famous scripts were *Liliom* (1931), *Daddy Long Legs* (1931), *Rebecca of Sunnybrook Farm* (1932), *Quo Vadis* (1951), *Oklahoma!* (1955), and *Bhowani Junction* (1956). She won an Oscar for *Interrupted Melody* (1955).

DOROTHY PARKER, the Manhattan wit, began her successful Hollywood career in the late 1930s. She wrote the original *A Star Is Born* (1937) with her husband, Alan Campbell. Later Parker worked with other writers on *Saboteur* (1942) and contributed dialogue to several films, including *The Little Foxes* (1941), which was based on the play by LILLIAN HELLMAN. Hellman herself not only wrote original, highly successful theatrical plays but also adapted most of them to the screen and penned some original screenplays.

BETTY COMDEN, who also established her reputation on Broadway, was brought to Hollywood by

MGM in the late 1940s. Together with Adolph Green, she wrote the scenario and songs for three Hollywood musicals released in 1949: *The Barkleys of Broadway*, *On the Town*, and *Take Me Out to the Ballgame*. They went on to write some of Hollywood's greatest musicals, including *Singin' in the Rain* (1952), *The Band Wagon* (1953), *It's Always Fair Weather* (1955), and *Bells Are Ringing* (1960). Comden and Green maintained a working partnership for more than forty years.

One of the most prolific women writers was PHOEBE EPHRON, who worked as a team with her husband, Henry. Together they wrote *What Price Glory* (1952), the remake of *Daddy Long Legs* (1955), dialogue for *Carousel* (1956), and *Desk Set* (1957).

FAY KANIN also worked with her husband, Michael Kanin, on *Rhapsody* (1954), *The Opposite Sex* (1956), and *Teacher's Pet* (1958). Alone she wrote the television movie *Tell Me Where It Hurts* (1974). She also served as president of the Academy of Motion Picture Arts and Sciences, the first woman in history to hold this position.

SYLVIA FINE and Danny Kaye were also a husband-and-wife team. Unknown to many, Fine wrote most of the lyrics for Kaye's screen performances. As Kaye himself said, "I am a wife-made man" (*Halliwell's*).

Adeline Schulberg proved that it was possible, though not common, for women (and Jewish women) to move beyond the actress or screenwriter boundary. Her Ad Schulberg Agency, operating in the 1930s, represented such stars as Marlene Dietrich, Fredric March, and Herbert Marshall. During World War II, Schulberg lived in London, where she set up an "underground railroad" for refugee talent from Nazi Germany. After the war, she worked as a talent scout for Columbia Pictures. She is credited with giving Shelley Winters her start in film.

Many Jewish women working in Hollywood in the 1950s had commitments to liberal and social causes. Some, like Schulberg, had been active in the fight against Nazism. Others were members of socialist or communist groups. Some did little but support these efforts financially. However, along with their male counterparts, many were caught up in the HUAC investigations, cited correctly or incorrectly as Communists.

Among the many Jewish women from Hollywood who were blacklisted during the McCarthy era were Judy Holliday, Lillian Hellman, Lee Grant, and GERTRUDE BERG. In this atmosphere, with anti-Semitism more open, fervent, and frightening than ever before in America, it is amazing that any films that openly represented Jewish actors, characters, and stories were made.

In 1949, Gertrude Berg took her beloved radio character, the irrepressible matriarch Molly Goldberg of *The Goldbergs*, to television, becoming one of the medium's first stars. *Molly*, a film version, was released in 1951. *Molly* was one of the few films since the silent era, outside the Yiddish cinema, to deal with the everyday life of Jews in America. Unfortunately, it failed to find an audience.

By the end of the 1950s, the number of exceptions to the unwritten rule against Jewish themes and stories was increasing. Perhaps as a reaction to the Holocaust, or to the creation of the State of Israel, or to the fact that America, albeit belatedly, had rejected McCarthyism—or all of those things—the Hollywood studios began making more films dealing with themes of anti-Semitism and, more specifically, American anti-Semitism. In 1947, the Motion Picture Project had been created, funded by major American Jewish agencies that wanted to encourage Hollywood to make more films with Jewish themes and depict Jewish characters more positively. The influence of this agency, which somehow survived McCarthyism, can be seen in the films of the late 1950s that explore religious tolerance and ethnic hatred. As positive a step as these films were, most did not have leading female characters or explore in any way what it meant to be a woman and Jewish. But the door that had closed on portrayals of Jewish women in film was opening, if just a crack.

One example was *Marjorie Morningstar* (1958). Like *Molly* before it, this feature film was unusual because its story revolved solely around Jewish issues and characters and many of its main characters were women, including Marjorie herself. A sign that Hollywood hadn't changed all that much was the casting of Natalie Wood in the title role. It was becoming somewhat acceptable to introduce the idea that Jews, including Jewish women, did in fact live in America, but the studios were not ready to cast "real" Jewish women to play them.

Another film that succeeded, hugely and on many levels, was Hollywood's 1959 version of the successful Broadway play *The Diary of Anne Frank*. Again, although Susan Strasberg had played Anne on Broadway, the film role was given to a non-Jew, Millie Perkins. As critic Pauline Kael noted, "In the movies, the unfortunate fact that Anne Frank was Jewish and hence not acceptable as the heroine of an expensive production, was rectified by casting Millie Perkins in the role." The film was important in that it constituted one of Hollywood's first treatments of the Holocaust. Although it did not depict the horrors of the camps, it did introduce the subject to a mass audience.

MAYA DEREN was the exception to all the rules limiting women to the makeup table or typewriter. Considered the "mother of underground film," she operated completely outside the Hollywood system and was therefore not governed by any of its rules. Deren was one of the earliest of the experimental avant-gardists. From 1943, when she made her first film, *Meshes of the Afternoon*, until her death in 1961, she influenced actors, artists, photographers (including DIANE ARBUS), and filmmakers. Her other films include *Ritual in Transfigured Time* (1946), *At Land* (1944), and *The Very Eye of Night* (1959). Twenty years before the largest social revolution in American history, Maya Deren was laying the groundwork.

In the 1960s and 1970s, America experienced huge social and political changes. Reflecting those changes, Jewish women's roles in films and in the film industry began to expand. The movements promoting racial and ethnic pride led to an increase in Jewish stories and characters. Marching through the doors opened by the women's movement, Jewish women moved into previously male jobs such as producing and directing.

For many Jewish actresses who had established careers before the 1960s, the changes of the period gave their careers a new boost. Lee Grant's film career revived in 1963 when she made two films, *An Affair of the Skin* and *The Balcony*. She soon established herself as an actress of substance in such films as *In the Heat of the Night* (1967) and *The Landlord*, for which she received her second Oscar nomination for best supporting actress. Her third and fourth nominations came for *Shampoo* (1975) and *Voyage of the Damned* (1976). For *Shampoo* she won the award itself.

Shelley Winters built the latter part of her career around the role of the Jewish mother. She has appeared as Jewish characters in the following films: *Enter Laughing* (1967), *The Poseidon Adventure* (1972), *Blume in Love* (1973), *Next Stop, Greenwich Village* (1976), *Over the Brooklyn Bridge* (1983), and *The Delta Force* (1989).

Susan Strasberg began her career in Hollywood with *Picnic* (1956). Although she was passed over for the role of Anne in *The Diary of Anne Frank*, she did appear later in two Jewish roles of note—*Maritou* (1978) and *Delta Force* (1989)—in addition to non-Jewish roles in films such as *In Praise of Older Women* (1978).

MOLLY PICON, a veteran of the Yiddish stage and film, took roles in several Hollywood films during the 1960s and 1970s. She appeared in *Come Blow Your Horn* (1963), as a Jewish matchmaker in *Fiddler on the Roof* (1970), and as a Jewish madam in *For Pete's Sake* (1974).

In more than eighty years of performing, MOLLY PICON *was successful in every venue she tried, from Yiddish theater to Hollywood. She is shown here opposite Frank Sinatra in* Come Blow Your Horn *(1963). [American Jewish Archives]*

The actress who changed all the rules on how women, and especially Jewish women, could look and behave was BARBRA STREISAND. She proved that an actress could simultaneously be openly Jewish, attractive, sensual, *and* the romantic heroine. She also proved that an openly Jewish story could be a blockbuster

The immensely talented trailblazer BARBRA STREISAND *has done it all.*
In Yentl *(1983) she starred as the young woman who so loved studying the*
Talmud that she assumed a male identity so she could attend a yeshivah.
She also codirected and coproduced the film.

hit. Her breakthrough performance, appropriately enough, was as Fanny Brice in the Broadway and Hollywood versions of *Funny Girl* (1968). (She also played Brice in the 1975 film sequel, *Funny Lady.*) In subsequent roles, she was either clearly identified as Jewish or her ethnicity was implied in her characterization. Some of her most famous early films include *Hello, Dolly!* (1969), *What's Up, Doc?* (1972) and *The Way We Were* (1973).

It could be argued that without Streisand many, if not all, of the other Jewish actresses of the last few decades would have had very different roles in Hollywood. Dyan Cannon, Carol Kane, Jill Clayburgh, GOLDIE HAWN, Barbara Hershey, GILDA RADNER, Janet Margolin, BETTE MIDLER, and Carrie Fisher have played fuller, more arresting characters because of the ground Streisand broke.

Dyan Cannon (born Samille Diane Friesen) began her film career in 1959. Among her best performances were those in *Bob and Carol and Ted and Alice* (1969) and *The Last of Sheila* (1973). She has particu-

larly distinguished herself in comedy. Jill Clayburgh made her first film in 1969. Since then she has starred in such films as *An Unmarried Woman* (1978) and *Gable and Lombard* (1976). She played a Jewish defense attorney in *Hannah K* (1983).

Carol Kane rose to fame in *Hester Street* (1975), for which she received an Academy Award nomination for best actress. She also played Jewish women in *Annie Hall* (1977) and *Over the Brooklyn Bridge* (1983). Other films of note include *Carnal Knowledge* (1971), *Dog Day Afternoon* (1975), and *The Princess Bride* (1987). She has also had major success on television in such shows as *Taxi* and *Pearl*.

Goldie Hawn became famous on *Rowan and Martin's Laugh-In* and won an Academy Award for best supporting actress for her film debut in *Cactus Flower* (1969). Among her better-known films are *Sugarland Express* (1974), *Shampoo* (1975), and *Swing Shift* (1984). In *The First Wives Club* (1996), with Diane Keaton and Bette Midler, she helped to prove that women in their fifties can score box office successes.

Barbara Hershey (born Barbara Herzstein) started in films in the late 1960s. For a short period in the early 1970s, she also used the name Barbara Seagull. Among her works are *Boxcar Bertha* (1972), *Hannah and Her Sisters* (1986), *Beaches* (1988), and *A World Apart* (1988), which was based on the life of a Jewish activist, although religion went unacknowledged in the film. In 1996, she earned an Oscar nomination for her performance in the film adaptation of *Portrait of a Lady*.

Gilda Radner, best known for her comedy work on television's *Saturday Night Live*, died before her film career had a chance to blossom. However, she did appear in *Hanky Panky* (1982), *The Woman in Red* (1984), and *Haunted Honeymoon* (1986). Janet Margolin started her career with *David and Lisa* (1962), playing a Jewish adolescent with emotional problems. She later appeared in *The Greatest Story Ever Told* (1965), *Enter Laughing* (1967), *Take the Money and Run* (1970), and *Annie Hall* (1977).

Bette Midler, who started her career in gay bathhouses, was already famous as a singer before she made *The Rose* (1979), based on the life and death of Janis Joplin. She has appeared as Jewish characters in *Down and Out in Beverly Hills* (1986), *Beaches* (1988), *Scenes from a Mall* (1991), and *The First Wives Club* (1996). She also took starring roles in *Ruthless People* (1986) and *Stella* (1990). Midler, like Streisand, has a strong celebrity persona and tends to be seen as Jewish, even in roles for which the script does not identify a specific ethnicity.

Carrie Fisher, daughter of Debbie Reynolds and Eddie Fisher, made her first film, *Shampoo*, in 1975. But her real fame came when she was cast as Princess Leia in *Star Wars* (1977). She went on to star in the next two films of the trilogy, *The Empire Strikes Back* (1980) and *Return of the Jedi* (1983). Her other films include *The Blues Brothers* (1980), *Hannah and Her Sisters* (1986), and *When Harry Met Sally* (1989).

The First Wives Club *(1996) starred (in addition to Diane Keaton)*
two of the most enduring box office draws, GOLDIE HAWN *and* BETTE MIDLER.

However, Fisher may be remembered for her work as a writer. She has written three novels: *Postcards from the Edge*, *Surrender the Pink*, and *Delusions of Grandma*; when her *Postcards* was made into a film (1990), she wrote the screenplay. Currently she works in that great uncredited Hollywood profession of script doctor—or, as Fisher calls it, script nurse. To date she has nursed more than fifteen filmscripts, among them *Hook*, *Lethal Weapon 3*, and *Sister Act*.

In the "new Hollywood" of the 1960s and 1970s, Jewish women continued to have major influence as screenwriters. Films by Harriet Frank Jr. and her husband, Irving Ravetch, who began a long and successful career toward the end of the 1950s, include *The Long Hot Summer* (1957), *Hud* (1963), *Hombre* (1967), and *Conrack* (1974). Their *Norma Rae* (1983), based on the real-life experiences of the Jewish labor organizer Eli Zivkovich, who helped to unionize the cotton mills in the South, represented a new approach to Jewish issues on the screen: The Jewish character is portrayed as a liberal activist rather than the ubiquitous doctor or lawyer, and the film avoids the commonplace interreligious romance.

Jay Presson Allen (born Jacqueline Presson) has an impressive list of screen credits, writing or adapting *Marnie* (1964), *The Prime of Miss Jean Brodie* (1969), *Cabaret* (1972), *Travels with My Aunt* (1972), *Funny Lady* (with Arnold Schulman, 1975), *Prince of the City* (1981), and *Never Cry Wolf* (1983). She also wrote the novel *Just Tell Me What You Want*, about Jewish producers in Hollywood. It was made into a film starring Alan King.

Among many other significant writers are Eleanor Perry (born Eleanor Rosenfeld), Gloria Katz, and Vicki Polan. Perry began her career in the burgeoning world of independent filmmaking with *David and Lisa* (1962). Subsequent work included *The Swimmer* (1964), *Diary of a Mad Housewife* (1970), and *The Man Who Loved Cat Dancing* (1973). Katz cowrote *American Graffiti* (1973) and *Indiana Jones and the Temple of Doom* (1984). Polan wrote *Girlfriends* (1978).

Stephanie Rothman began writing and directing low-budget productions in the mid-1960s. Because her output was mainly in exploitation films, her work is less well known. However, films such as *The Student Nurses* (1970), *The Velvet Vampire* (1971), and *Terminal Island* (1973) have become cult classics.

A major trailblazer was the writer, director, and actress ELAINE MAY. After starring in *Enter Laughing* (1967), she turned to writing and directing films at a time when few women had won this opportunity. Her first screenplay was *Such Good Friends* (1971), but she was so dissatisfied with the final product that she

ELAINE MAY, *with Mike Nichols part of one of the most successful American comic teams of the 1950s and 1960s, became one of Hollywood's first important female directors in the 1970s and 1980s.*

insisted she be listed under the pseudonym Esther Dale. This experience led her to move into directing, where she thought she would have more control. Her first production was *The New Leaf* (1971). She next directed *The Heartbreak Kid* (1972), based on a screenplay by Neil Simon. The film depicts a newly married Jewish couple in an extremely negative manner. May's daughter Jeannie Berlin took the role of the unattractive bride. However, May's disappointment with the studio's changes to her films led to problems in Hollywood. Though she continued to write and act, she has directed only two more films to date: *Mickey and Nicky* (1976) and *Ishtar* (1987).

As opportunities continued to open up during the 1970s, many more Jewish women turned to directing. It is interesting to note that among the few films of this period that deal with the Orthodox and religious aspects of Jewish life—a subject the Hollywood studios have always resisted treating—the majority have been brought to the screen by Jewish women, in such films as *Hester Street, Crossing Delancey,* and *Yentl.*

Many Jewish women directors of the 1970s began their careers independently, especially as documentary filmmakers. Such was the case with Claudia Weill, who worked for several years on *Girlfriends* with Vicki Polan before Warner Brothers picked it up for distribution in 1978. Her second film, *It's My Turn* (1980), starred Jill Clayburgh and Michael Douglas. Weill has since appeared as an actress in *Calling the Shots* (1988).

At about the same time, JOAN MICKLIN SILVER, who began in educational filmmaking, struggled to interest a Hollywood studio in doing a film about early Eastern European immigrants to New York, which would incorporate some Yiddish. No one was interested, so she wrote, directed, and produced (with her husband) *Hester Street* (1975) herself. Silver went

on to write and direct *Between the Lines* (1977), *Chilly Scenes of Winter* (1979), and *Crossing Delancey* (1988). *Crossing Delancey* offered a wonderful character role for veteran Yiddish stage and film actress Reizel Bozyk.

And then there are the actresses who turned to directing. For many Jewish women who became stars in the 1960s and early 1970s, the world of acting proved too narrow. They wanted more creative control. Recognizing their own power to draw audiences and backers, they became their own writers, producers, and directors, wielding an influence in Hollywood that was unheard of for women.

Again, Barbra Streisand led the way, producing as well as starring in *A Star Is Born* (1976). On *Yentl* (1983), based on a story by the Yiddish writer I.B. Singer, she produced, starred, and directed for the

JOAN MICKLIN SILVER *couldn't interest a Hollywood studio in doing a film about early Eastern European immigrants to New York, which would incorporate some Yiddish. So she wrote, directed, and coproduced* Hester Street *(1975) herself.*

JOAN MICKLIN SILVER's *film* Crossing Delancey *(1988) offered a wonderful character role for veteran Yiddish stage and film actress Reizel Bozyk, playing the grandmother of the film's lead, Amy Irving.*

first time. She continued doing triple duty with *Prince of Tides* (1991), which was nominated for several Academy Awards, and *The Mirror Has Two Faces* (1996), which won a best supporting actress Oscar nomination for Lauren Bacall. Streisand supports Jewish filmmaking on a broader level as well by underwriting an award for the best independent Jewish film.

In 1980, Goldie Hawn starred in and produced *Private Benjamin*, the comic story of a "Jewish American Princess" who enters the United States Army and emerges as a strong, autonomous woman with feminist ideas. In 1995, she produced *Something to Talk About* and currently runs Cherry Alley Productions with Teri Schwartz.

Among the other actresses turned directors and/or producers are Lee Grant, Dyan Cannon, and Bette Midler. Grant produced her first full-length film, *Tell Me a Riddle*, in 1980. Based on a novella by TILLIE OLSEN, it is about the life and death of an elderly Jewish immigrant woman. She won an Oscar for her documentary *Down and Out in America* (1985). Cannon directed a semiautobiographical film entitled *The End*

of *Innocence* in 1990. And Bette Midler, in addition to acting in *Beaches*, produced the film.

Screenwriters too began to expand their worlds in recent years. NORA EPHRON, born into a Hollywood family, coauthored the scripts for *Silkwood* (1983) and *Sleepless in Seattle* (1993). On her own, she wrote *Heartburn* (1985), which was loosely based on her marriage to Carl Bernstein, and *When Harry Met Sally* (1989). She made her directorial debut with *This Is My Life*, (1992) which starred Julie Kavner as a contemporary Jewish comedienne. This was coauthored with her sister, Delia. Jay Presson Allen began producing with *It's My Turn*, directed by Claudia Weill.

The generation of women directors of the 1980s rose from the ranks of independent filmmakers, like Claudia Weill and Joan Micklin Silver before them. Many attended university film programs. Many also had been active in the women's movement and were well aware of the demeaning and distorted images of women that pervaded the film industry. Singly and as a group, these women set out to provide new images and new narratives.

After attending New York University film school, Susan Seidelman wrote, produced, and directed *Smithereens* (1982). This led to opportunities in Hollywood, where she directed *Desperately Seeking Susan* (1985), as well as *Looking for Mr. Right* (1987) and *She-Devil* (1989), both of which she also produced.

Jill Godmilow began as a documentary filmmaker. She later shifted to fiction features with *Waiting for the Moon* (1987), based on the lives of GERTRUDE STEIN and ALICE B. TOKLAS. Similarly, both Mirra Bank and Donna Deitch were documentary makers. Bank moved into feature filmmaking with *Enormous Changes at the Last Minute* (1983, codirected with Ellen Hovde), while Deitch switched to fiction features with *Desert Hearts* (1987), which attempted to provide a more positive and realistic representation of gay women. Joyce Chopra (1938), who appeared in an early documentary by Claudia Weill, has directed two films in Hollywood: *Smooth Talk* (1985) and *The Lemon Sisters* (1989).

Beeban Kidron is another Jewish director who started in independent filmmaking. Her works include *Antonia and Jane* (1990), which focuses on a friendship between a young Jewish woman in London and her gentile girlfriend, and *Used People* (1992), starring Shirley MacLaine as a Jewish widow who is courted by an older Italian widower. Her latest film is *To Wong Foo: Thanks for Everything, Julie Newmar* (1995).

In the less well known areas behind the scenes, Jewish women have been making their presence felt as editors, costumers, scenic designers, and composers. Composer Marilyn Bergman, who worked with her husband, Alan Bergman, won Oscars for the theme of *The Thomas Crown Affair* (1968) and another for *The Way We Were* (1973). They also composed music for *Brian's Song* (1971) and *Yentl* (1983). Carly Simon wrote music for *Torchlight* (1984) and *Working Girl* (1988). Karyn Rachtman has done the soundtracks for *Pulp Fiction* (1994), *Get Shorty* (1995), and *Clueless* (1995).

Actresses doing film work in the 1980s and 1990s have been able to build upon the breakthroughs of their predecessors and play more varied and interesting roles, many of them Jewish women. Among these actresses are Lainie Kazan, Julie Kavner, Jennifer Grey, Sandra Bernhard, Debra Winger, Alicia Silverstone, and Natalie Portman.

Kazan, previously known as a singer, appeared as a Jewish mother in *My Favorite Year* (1982) and has had supporting roles in half a dozen other films. Kavner played the younger sister on the television program *Rhoda* before moving into film. She has appeared in *Hannah and Her Sisters* (1986), *Radio Days* (1987) and starred in *This Is My Life* (1992), all Jewish roles. Grey became famous with her role as the young Jewish heroine of *Dirty Dancing* (1987). Bernhard has had an impressive career on and off the screen. Among her film work, she appeared in *King of Comedy* (1982).

Debra Winger appeared in *Urban Cowboy* (1980), *An Officer and a Gentleman* (1982), *Terms of Endearment* (1983), *The Sheltering Sky* (1990), and *Shadowlands* (1993). In the latter work, Winger plays Joy Gresham, the American Jewish poet who married the British writer C.S. Lewis.

Alicia Silverstone and Israeli-born Natalie Portman both began working while still in their teens. Silverstone had her breakthrough in *Clueless* (1995). Portman's first role was in *Heat* (1995).

Other new talent includes Gina Gershon, who appeared in *Showgirls* (1995), and actress Julianna Lavin, who wrote and directed *Live Nude Girls* (1995). Screenwriters include Carol Seltzer and Ellen Simon, who coscripted *One Fine Day* (1996) and *Moonlight and Valentino* (1995).

It is mainly in production, however, that Jewish women have made the largest strides. One of the earliest examples is Julia Phillips, who in 1976 became the first woman to win an Academy Award for best picture, for producing *The Sting* with her husband, Michael.

Sherry Lansing became the first woman to run a major studio. She served as president of Twentieth Century–Fox from 1980 to 1982, when she left to work on her own. As a producer, she has been responsible for such blockbusters as *Fatal Attraction* (1987) and *Indecent Proposal* (1993), as well as the critically

acclaimed *The Accused* (1988). She also produced *School Ties* (1992), a film about anti-Semitism at a boys' boarding school. Later she served as head of Paramount Pictures.

Dawn Steel was president of production at Paramount Pictures and later president of Columbia Pictures. She was responsible for such hits as *Flashdance* (1983), *Top Gun* (1986), and *The Untouchables* (1987). In the early 1990s, she became an independent producer.

Since the beginning of the 1990s there seems to be a deluge of Jewish women behind the scenes. The following list, which is by no means complete, attests to the immense energy and talent of Jewish women who are now working in production: Susan Arnold, Bonnie Bruckheimer, Lauren Schuler Donner, Connie Field, Wendy Finerman, Ellen Geiger, Liz Glotzer, Lynn Harris, Susan Hoffman, Gale Ann Hurd, Donna Isaacson, Gail Katz, Nana Levin, Rachel Lyon, Nancy Meyer, Linda Obst, Polly Platt, Mimi Polk, Jane

Alicia Silverstone became an acting sensation overnight with the success of the role she created in Clueless *(1995).*

One of the most powerful women in Hollywood, Sherry Lansing was the first woman to run a major studio. She served as president of Twentieth Century-Fox from 1980 to 1982. She has also been head of Paramount Pictures. [UPI/BETTMANN]

Rosenthal, Midge Sanford, Deborah Schindler, Sondra Schulberg, Arlene Sellers, Shelby Sher, Sandy Stern, Shelby Stone, Roselle Swed, Anthea Sylbert, Paula Wagner, Paula Weinstein, and Laura Ziskin.

The history of Jewish women's contribution to the Hollywood film industry has been one of gradual progression toward ever higher levels of participation. For most of Hollywood's history, the dominant tendency was to achieve a universal image that revealed no traces of ethnic heritage. This trend held until the 1960s and affected all ethnic groups. Only a few dozen Jewish actresses were able to make their way into stardom under these constraints. Since the 1960s, however, Hollywood films have reflected a higher degree of ethnic diversity. The result of this change is that increasing numbers of Jewish actresses have been able to establish careers in Hollywood.

The real change in the past few decades has been the number of Jewish women in positions of power and influence. Jewish women have always worked behind the scenes, most often as writers. More recently, and especially in the exponential leap of the early 1990s, they have moved into directing and producing, both independently and as studio executives.

For many, there is no question that Jewish women have gained higher access because of their connections to Jewish men in the industry. An earlier evidence of this pattern is the large number of Jewish husband-wife teams who coauthored screenplays during the 1940s and 1950s. In this way, they have sometimes had an advantage over other ethnic groups.

The irony is, of course, that despite the fact that there have always been relatively high numbers of Jews working in Hollywood, since the days of the ghetto films there have been very few stories about Jewish life and experience. Even fewer have been about Jewish women; fewer even than that told from a Jewish woman's point of view. This still holds true for the new batch of women initiating and bringing projects to fruition. And while the majority of their films have not highlighted Jewish themes or issues, the "notable exceptions" are constantly increasing.

The new opportunities created by these Jewish pioneers have affected all women who want careers in the film industry, as well as all women who watch their films. These women have used their newfound influence to bring more of women's lives and experiences to the screen. And many have used their creative talents to bring Jewish stories to the screen. Though it is too early to assess what the new breed of Jewish producers will achieve, it is clear that the major contributions by Jewish women to the film industry will lie more in the future than in the past.

BIBLIOGRAPHY

Boxer, Tim. "Film Stars." In *The Jews in American Culture;* Cohen, Sarah Blacher, ed. *From Hester Street to Hollywood: The Jewish-American Stage and Screen* (1983); *The Encyclopedia of Film.* Edited by James Monaco and the editors of *Baseline* (1991); Erens, Patricia. "Film." In *Jewish-American History and Culture: An Encyclopedia,* edited by Jack Fischel and Stanford Pinsker (1992) and *The Jew in American Cinema* (1984); Freidman, Lester D. *Hollywood's Image of the Jew* (1982), and *The Jewish Image in American Film* (1987); *Halliwell's Filmgoer's and Video Viewer's Companion,* 9th ed. (1988); Haskell, Molly. *From Reverence to Rape: The Treatment of Women in the Movies* (1973); Kael, Pauline. "Commitment and the Straightjacket." In *I Lost It at the Movies* (1966); Navasky, Victor S. *Naming Names* (1980); Rosen, Marjorie. *Popcorn Venus: Women, Movies and the American Dream* (1973).

PATRICIA ERENS

FILMMAKERS, INDEPENDENT

More than twenty years have passed since the start of the movement of independent American cinema and video. Aided by the developmental breakthroughs of lightweight synch-sound film equipment, the invention of video, and the creation of federal and state arts funding agencies in the 1970s, artists and political activists translated their vision into images that reflected and defined a generation. Free from the constraints of Hollywood studios or network television, directors produced original, provocative works, albeit on a small scale, that challenged not only the forms of Hollywood "product" but also the industry's thematic conventions.

Originally, an independent work was loosely defined as one where the director has creative control and where financing and distribution are independent of major studios, networks, or similar corporate entities driven by the profit imperative. Ironically, the independent world has become so profitable that Hollywood and television have become significant sources of investment and distribution. As a result, the definition of "independent" has evolved. One new definition says that independents can receive partial studio support and distribution. It is hoped that what remains is what is essential to independent film: uniqueness of vision and creative control by the director.

Since the start of the independent movement, American Jews have contributed their share of self-reflective and identity-based work in film and video, and in genres that have ranged from traditional narrative to the most experimental of documentaries. This search for identity, in particular Jewish identity, can be viewed as a reaction to the postwar generation's assimilation or to the 1960s generation's often oppressive internationalism and self-denial. The new work has broken free of old norms and now reflects the concerns of personal and group identity.

Female Jewish directors have made significant contributions. Along with their male counterparts, they have created mainstream and experimental works, attempted to redefine Jewish identity, integrated the specifically Jewish with the universal, and in some cases reflected a need for self-denial. Gender consciousness permeates their films in varying degrees and might be assessed by a wide range of factors: subject (mother-daughter relations, friendship between women), protagonist or point of view (single women, older women, immigrant women), or filmic style.

In the last twenty years, scores of film and video makers have given voice to enduring Jewish themes of historic oppression, resistance, and exile. Some independent feature films have reached much broader audiences, especially when they situate specifically Jewish characters in romantic and/or comedic stories. But what might characterize independent Jewish cinema most, including those works made by Jewish women, is its lack of unifying discourse. If the major signifiers of Jewish life in the post–World War II era continue to be Judaism as religion, the Holocaust, and Israel, independent American Jewish cinema seems to subvert that triumvirate with images of hybrid identities, interfaith romance, oppositional politics, and jump-cut collective memories.

Even the "classic" directors of the independent Jewish pantheon have not played by established rules. Ignoring the male-dominated Jewish literary and Hollywood traditions, JOAN MICKLIN SILVER made American Jewish women, and the choices they make on their own, the catalysts for action in *Hester Street* (1975) and *Crossing Delancey* (1988). Both movies mirror women's changing roles and subtly suggest the struggles for equality that continue to be waged inside the Jewish community. In *Girlfriends* (1978), one of the first successful commercial films to come out of the feminist movement, Claudia Weill made her female protagonist a sensitive, single, sexually independent Jewish woman in New York.

In both fiction and documentary genres, female Jewish directors have countered established rules by honoring left-wing political traditions, perhaps as a paean to their own outsider status within Judaism or perhaps because they inherited the left-wing tradition of the immigrant period. With her trademark charm and humor, Boston filmmaker Marlene Booth documented the 100-year history of the socialist Yiddish newspaper in *The Forward: From Immigrants to Americans*. With discernment and tenderness, Lee Grant directed Melvyn Douglas and Lila Kedrova as a pair of aging Jewish communists who rekindle their love in the film adaptation of TILLIE OLSEN's book *Tell Me a Riddle* (1980). In *Forever Activists* (1990), Bay-area Oscar nominee Judy Montell told with guts and passion of the "premature antifascists"—the mostly Jewish veterans of the Abraham Lincoln Brigade who, as both Jews and as leftists, fought against Franco in Spain. Michal Goldman gave new life to Eastern European Yiddish culture in her film *A Jumpin' Night in the Garden of Eden* (1988), a celebration of klezmer music and its roots in the traditions of the Balkans, the Gypsies, vaudeville, and American jazz.

A number of independent Jewish directors have used the medium either with the explicit intention of redefining Jewish identity or in order to bend filmmaking genres. In *Leaving Home* (1980), Ilana Bar Din documented the strengths and pressures within an assimilated suburban Jewish family as four strong daughters define themselves. Lilly Rivlin explored lineage and tribal memory, and raised questions about how women are left out of Jewish family histories, in *The Tribe* (1983). Lynn Littman movingly portrayed the work of anthropologist BARBARA MYERHOFF in two Los Angeles neighborhoods: *Number Our Days* (1976) provided a portrait of the impoverished Jewish elderly in Venice, California, and *In Her Own Time* (1985) explored and challenged the traditional rituals of Orthodox Jews in Los Angeles's Fairfax district.

Two directors, MEREDITH MONK and Eleanor Antin, known for their *deconstruction* of both Jewish identity and traditional genres, emerged out of the art world and onto the screen in the 1980s. In Monk's short *Ellis Island* (1982) and in her feature-length story of a Jewish girl in a medieval French village, *Book of Days* (1989), history is remarkably re-created through performance pieces that weave together characters, music, movement, and a feeling for the passing of time even as we are transported into timeless realities. The displacement and loss that accompany emigration and the experiences of plague and doom re-created in these works are not unique Jewish experiences. If Jews are "chosen" for anything, it is to interpret what they have experienced for others who share a similar fate.

Eleanor Antin's work scrupulously subverts sentimentality. Her fabrications of nonexistent silent Soviet masterpieces have become cult items. In *The Man Without a World* (1991), she creates a gothic, comic melodrama set in an imaginary shtetl where a young couple's romance is doomed by Gypsies, dybbuks, and the angel of death. Antin produces an extraordinary period piece that could almost have been made at the turn of the century, except that it is imbued with the knowledge, humor, and angst of our own time.

A number of independent filmmakers integrate questions of Jewish identity in their work, but more as subplot than plot. These works are compelling and noteworthy in terms of their attempts to integrate Jewish and universal subjects. Examples include Jan Oxenberg's critically acclaimed *Thank You and Goodnight* (1991), which documents the filmmaker's tender yet devastating relationship with her dying grandmother, and Deborah Hoffmann's *Complaints of a Dutiful Daughter* (1994), which describes how the filmmaker comes to terms with her mother's Alzheimer's disease. With honesty, compassion, and good doses of humor, both films deal with the specificity of the directors' Jewish backgrounds as well as the universal themes of aging, death, family caregiving, and love.

Several films implicitly raise important questions about the ways Jewish filmmakers choose not to make Jewish films. Many films made by Jewish women fall in this category. Often, these films reflect the self-denial and desire for invisibility that have been key themes in Jewish history and culture. For example, Connie Field (who is Jewish) and Marilyn Mulford (who is not Jewish), in their acclaimed documentary on Mississippi Freedom Summer, *Freedom on My Mind* (1994), showcase interviews with Jews who went south as an expression of their identification with the struggle against racism but fails to mention that these interview subjects are Jewish, that Jews were disproportionately involved in civil rights, or that an entire generation's Jewish identity was itself predicated in part on the idea of black-Jewish alliance. Like their antecedents in the Hollywood studios, there will always be many independent Jewish film and video makers, women included, who do not seem to focus at all on Jewish subjects or identity in their work. What is interesting here are the different ways that these films can be seen as Jewish despite the surface self-denial.

The establishment in 1996 of the first Fund for Jewish Documentary Filmmaking at the National Foundation for Jewish Culture will no doubt have a major impact on the field. Six of the eight films chosen for funding in the Fund's first year are directed by Jewish women: *Blacks and Jews* by Deborah Kaufman and Alan Snitow, *The Commandment Keepers* by Marlaine Glicksman, *A Healthy Baby Girl* by Judith Helfand, *The Life and Times of Hank Greenberg* by Aviva Kempner, *The Return of Sarah's Daughters* by Marcia Jarmel, and *Treyf* by Alisa Lebow and Cynthia Madansky.

Jewish female producers, including Vivian Kleiman, producer of *Routes of Exile: A Moroccan Jewish Odyssey* (1982), and Aviva Kempner, producer of *Partisans of Vilna* (1986), have been active over the last twenty years. As well, Jewish women have been involved in other aspects of film and video production, such as scriptwriting and editing, distribution, promotion, and exhibition, and they have been prominent in the fields of film and media theory and criticism. Jewish women have contributed important scholarly books to the field of Jewish film studies, including *Indelible Shadows: Film and the Holocaust* by Annette Insdorf, *The Jew in American Cinema* by Patricia Erens, and *Israeli Cinema: East/West and the Politics of Representation* by Ella Shohat. A number of enormously successful Jewish film festivals, organized primarily by Jewish women, emerged and spread across the United States in the 1980s, providing a bridge between independent filmmakers and Jewish audiences.

Despite the innovations and achievements of the American Jewish independent filmmakers, there is still much to be explored. A generation of independent artists informed by identity politics has slowed the silent slide toward assimilation and self-denial. Jewish women have given voice to a range of concerns and styles and have achieved success within the field. The groundwork has been laid for a new generation of independent filmmakers who have the opportunity to continue contributing to the field.

BIBLIOGRAPHY

Plotkin, Janis, Caroline Libresco, and Josh Feiger, eds. *Independent Jewish Film: A Resource Guide* (1996).

DEBORAH KAUFMAN

FILM, YIDDISH *see* YIDDISH FILM

FINE, IRENE (b. 1936)

In the field of continuing Jewish education for women, the preeminent pioneer is Irene Fine, the founder in 1977 of the Woman's Institute for Continuing Jewish Education, based in San Diego, California. The institute continues to innovate in Jewish women's education and in the publication of books on Jewish women by Jewish women.

She was born in Wadena, Minnesota, on April 22, 1936, to Herman and Sadie (Nadel) Fink. Her brother, Justin, was three years older. Her father owned a dry-goods store, where she started to work after school at age eleven. After two years at the University of Minnesota, she moved to San Francisco, where she received a B.A. in 1958 in physical education, with a minor in dance. She married Lawrence Fine, a physician-in-training, on June 23, 1957, and they settled in San Diego.

Fine followed the pattern of many women of her generation who interrupted education and careers when their children were young. After the births of her three children (Joel, b. 1960; Gil, b. 1963; and Sari, b. 1969), she continued her education at San Diego State University, where she earned a B.F.A. in 1973, and at the Hebrew Union College in Los Angeles, where she pursued graduate studies. In 1977 she embarked on an interdisciplinary Ph.D. program at Union Graduate School.

The program combined Jewish studies, women's studies, and adult education. Since an internship was mandatory for each student, and there was no facility in San Diego that would have permitted Fine to teach courses on Jewish women, she set up her own facility, the Woman's Institute for Continuing Jewish Education. There she taught and administered a program that develops and disseminates new material written by Jewish women. Under her energetic guidance, the Woman's Institute pioneered the teaching of Torah, Talmud, and midrash (Bible interpretation) by women, and established a Shabbat lecture series that brings nationally known female scholars to San Diego to present their research on women.

The Woman's Institute has had an impact far beyond southern California. Its seven publications, all short books written by nonscholars in Jewish studies, have served as a resource for Jewish women nationwide and have empowered lay women to reflect on Jewish sources and to create midrash and liturgy. The *San Diego Women's Hagaddah* was the first women's text available for those seeking to hold a feminist seder. Similarly, *Taking the Fruit: Modern Women's Tales of the Bible* was the first collection of women's midrashim. *A Ceremonies Sampler: New Rites, Celebrations, and Observances of Jewish Women* (1991) brought together the new ritual and liturgy created by Jewish feminists to mark the transition moments of their lives, while *On Our Spiritual Journey* (1984) offered a creative Sabbath service. In addition to contributing to these publications, Fine has written two books of her own that draw upon her life experience and professional expertise: *Educating the New Jewish Woman: A Dynamic Approach* (1985) and *Midlife: A Rite of Passage/The Wise Woman, A Celebration* (1988).

Fine is the model of an educational entrepreneur. She continues to work with young teachers interested in Jewish studies for women and to plan new book projects. But she also revels in spending time with her two granddaughters, delighting them with her "fabulous stories."

BIBLIOGRAPHY

Fine, Irene. *Educating the New Jewish Woman: A Dynamic Approach* (1985); Levine, Elizabeth, ed. *A Ceremonies Sampler: New Rites, Celebrations, and Observances of Jewish Women* (1991); *Midlife: A Rite of Passage/The Wise Woman, A Celebration* (1988); *Taking the Fruit: Modern Women's Tales of the Bible.* 2d ed. (1989); Tolley, Jacquelyn, ed. *On Our Spiritual Journey, A Creative Shabbat Service* (1984); Zones, Jane, ed. *San Diego Women's Haggadah.* 2d ed. (1986).

PAULA E. HYMAN

FINE, SYLVIA (1913–1991)

Contemporary commentators often ascribed much of entertainer Danny Kaye's success to his having a "Fine" head on his shoulders. Publicly, his wife Sylvia Fine's coruscating lyrics supported Danny's zaniness in such films as *Up in Arms* (1944), *Wonder Man* (1945), *The Kid from Brooklyn* (1946), *The Secret Life of Walter Mitty* (1947), *The Inspector General* (1949), and *On the Riviera* (1951). Privately, both Kayes endured the tensions resulting from a talented woman's subsuming her ambition to advance her husband's career.

Born on August 29, 1913, in Brooklyn, Sylvia Fine was the youngest child, following Robert (Fine Forrest) and Rhoda (Gamson), of dentist Samuel and his wife Bessie Fine. Author of parodic songs and humor while still at Jefferson High School, she graduated in 1933 from Brooklyn College, a "Former Field in Flatbush," she recalled, where she found new worlds to conquer.

Teaching piano, she also played at rehearsals for producer Max Liebman when Danny Kaye (born David Daniel Kominsky), a Catskill tummler, auditioned for "Sunday Night Varieties" at Tamiment in the Poconos. Though from the same neighborhood, Danny (the school dropout son of Russian immigrants) had never met Sylvia. Their wit meshed, and when the resulting *Straw Hat Review* (1939) closed ten weeks after its Broadway opening, they eloped to Fort Lauderdale in January 1940 and then remarried on February 22 in a synagogue to satisfy her parents.

With Fine's compositions, such as "Anatole of Paris," "Stanislavski Vonschtickfitz Monahan," and "Melody in 4-F," Kaye achieved almost instantaneous success in New York. They went to Hollywood, where Fine wrote approximately one hundred numbers, including "Lullaby in Ragtime," "Five Pennies," "Popo the Puppet," and "Soliloquy for Three Heads." Fine also wrote "All About You," called by Cole Porter "a perfect love song." Often reflecting Kaye's private preferences, Fine's veto power over his shows' participants earned her a reputation for being difficult.

In addition to working for major studios, the Kayes formed Dena Productions in 1956. Twice nominated for Academy Awards (*The Five Pennies* in 1959 and *The Moon Is Blue* in 1953), Fine also produced Kaye's radio series and television specials.

A member of ASCAP, Fine appeared with Kaye as accompanist until the December 17, 1946, birth of their daughter Dena, later a photojournalist, for whom she named Kitty Carlisle godmother. In 1947, the Kayes separated briefly, thereafter seldom inhabiting the same domicile (in New York and Beverly Hills). Nevertheless, they continued their professional partnership until his death in March 1987.

In general, the Kayes' Jewishness was more social than religious, as exemplified in their founding the Palm Springs Tamarisk Country Club after discovering that other clubs were restricted. After the 1967 war, they became active supporters of the State of Israel, where Fine received the "Pillars of Hope" award (1983) from HADASSAH.

Sharing, with Danny Kaye, a UNICEF award for helping children, and a Performance Arts Council Award, Sylvia Fine also received a City of Los Angeles Award and an honorary doctor of arts from Long Island University. Recipient of a Peabody Award for Musical Comedy Tonight I (1979), based on her courses at the University of Southern California and Yale University, she endowed the Sylvia Fine Chair in Musical Theater at Brooklyn College, which granted her an honorary doctorate (1985). Before she died of emphysema on October 28, 1991, Sylvia Fine contributed $4.1 million to refurbish the HUNTER COLLEGE auditorium, which reopened in 1994 as the Sylvia Fine and Danny Kaye Theater.

Like Gilbert and Sullivan, Fine's clever patter still influences today's songwriters. In her partnership with the frenetic Danny Kaye, she created something unique.

SELECTED WORKS BY SYLVIA FINE

MUSIC FOR FILMS

The Court Jester (1956); *The Five Pennies* (1959); *The Inspector General* (1949); *The Kid from Brooklyn* (1946); *Knock on Wood* (1954); *On the Riviera* (1951); *Up in Arms* (1944).

TELEVISION PRODUCTIONS

"Assignment Children"; "Danny Kaye: A Look in at the Met"; "Musical Comedy Tonight" (Parts I, II, III).

BIBLIOGRAPHY

Fine, Sylvia. Archives. Library of Congress Special Collection, Washington, D.C., and Billy Rose Theatre Collection, New York Public Library, Lincoln Center, NYC; Freedland, Michael. *The Secret Life of Danny Kaye* (1985); "Git Gat Gittle." *Time* (March 11, 1946); Gottlieb, Martin. *Nobody's Fool: The Lives of Danny Kaye* (1994); Obituaries. *The Annual Obituary* (1991), and *NYTimes*, October 29, 1991, and *Variety*, November 4, 1991; Richard, Dick. *The Life Story of Danny Kaye* (1949).

AMY LEZBERG

FINKLER, RITA SAPIRO (1888–1968)

Rita (Ricka) Sapiro Finkler, a pioneering endocrinologist in New Jersey, practiced medicine for over half a century. Her career was characterized by hard-won achievements, persistence, professionalism, and a feminist consciousness.

Born Ricka Sapiro in Kherson, Ukraine, on November 1, 1888, she was admitted at age sixteen to St. Petersburg University to study law, a rare achievement for a Jewish girl. After two years of legal studies, she took the advice of an aunt and left Russia, originally headed for New Zealand. After working her way through Europe, Finkler ended up in Philadelphia, where in 1911 she enrolled in the Women's College of Pennsylvania. She married a chemistry student, Samuel J. Finkler, while in medical school and graduated in 1915. They had one daughter, Sylvia, born in 1921. The Finklers were divorced in 1924, leaving Rita Finkler to devote herself to medicine and travel. For a decade, she practiced mainly pediatrics and then obstetrics in the Italian communities of Philadelphia and Newark, New Jersey. In 1928, attracted by the new field of endocrinology, Finkler did postgraduate work at Mount Sinai Hospital in New York City, and in 1929, she went to the University of Vienna. In Europe Finkler worked with developers of the new Ascheim-Zondek Reaction, a reliable laboratory test for early pregnancy detection. The earliest of Finkler's more than sixty published papers were on the results of these trials. Much of her subsequent research, all based on her clinical work, also focused on endocrinology in women's health, with published papers on a range of endocrine disturbances, including ovarian dysfunction and amenorrhea, on infertility, and on the use—and misuse—of synthetic estrogens for the symptoms of menopause. She exhibited and presented at numerous conferences, including the International Congress on Fertility.

Finkler fought for each of her achievements, including her position as first female intern at the Philadelphia Polyclinic Hospital, first female on the senior medical staff at any Newark hospital, first chief of endocrinology (1938–1950), and first female chief of any department at Newark Beth Israel Hospital, where she became chief emeritus and consultant endocrinologist (1950–1968). Finkler was president of the New Jersey branch of the American Medical Women's Association (AMWA) and was honored as Medical Woman of the Year in 1956. She was on the editorial boards of the *Woman's Medical Journal* and the *Journal of the American Medical Women's Association*. In 1965, the Women's College of Pennsylvania awarded her the Gold Certificate for fifty years in practice and, in 1967, the Alumnae Achievement Award. Finkler and her daughter, Sylvia F. Becker, also a physician, organized discussion groups for New Jer-sey women physicians to provide mutual support, net-working, and cross-disciplinary enrichment.

Finkler was a nonobservant Jew who felt her cultural Jewishness deeply. From 1938 to 1948, she chaired the refugee committee of the AMWA and was actively involved with bringing displaced women physicians, as well as a number of her own relatives, over from Europe.

From 1934, when she was a delegate to the International Women's Medical Association Convention in Stockholm, to 1960, when she presented before the Medical Women's Association of India, Finkler used her love of travel and her ability to speak six languages to meet with women physicians around the world. Her hobby was medical and travel photography, and she published articles on her travels. Rita Sapiro Finkler never did get to New Zealand, however. She died in New York City of a coronary occlusion on November 8, 1968.

BIBLIOGRAPHY

Becker, Sylvia F. Interview with author, September 9, 1996; Finkler, Rita Sapiro. Papers. Archives and Special Collections on Women in Medicine, Allegheny University of the Health Sciences (formerly the Medical College of Pennsylvania), Philadelphia, and American Medical Women's Association, Inc., Alexandria, Va., and Special Collections, F.G. Smith Library, College of Medicine and Dentistry of New Jersey, and memoir, *Good Morning, Doctor* (1967); Gillan, Maria. "Rita Sapiro Finkler, 1888–1968." In *Past and Promise: Lives of New Jersey Women*, edited by The Women's Project of New Jersey, Inc. (1990); Knapp, Sally. "Rita Finkler: Endocrinologist." In *Women Doctors Today* (1947): 165–184; "Medical Women of the Year, 1956." *Journal of the American Medical Women's Association* 11, no. 12 (December 1956): 434–441; Obituary. *NYTimes*, November 9, 1968, 33:5; "Personals." *The Medical Women's Journal* 46 (1939): 123; "Rita Sapiro Finkler, M.D." *Medical Woman's Journal* 49, no. 4 (April 1942): 121–122; *WWIAJ* (1928, 1938); *WWWIA 5*.

MARSHA HURST

FIRESTONE, SHULAMITH (b. 1945)

Arguing that "family structure is the *source* of psychological, economic and political oppression," Shulamith Firestone's *The Dialectic of Sex*, published in 1970, was one of the most widely discussed books of the feminist movement. Firestone, a founder of radical feminism, brought together the dialectical materialism of Marx and the psychoanalytic insights of Freud in an effort to develop an analysis of women's oppression that was inclusive of the dimensions of class and race. Although she wrote for a popular audience, her work was broadly grounded in classic texts and raised many questions that have since been taken up and developed by feminist theorists within the academy.

Shulamith Firestone, the second of six children in the Orthodox family of Saul and Kate (Weiss) Firestone, was born in Ottawa, Ontario, on January 13, 1945. She grew up in St. Louis and attended Yavneh of Telshe Yeshivah near Cleveland before receiving a B.A. from Washington University (St. Louis) and a B.F.A. in painting from the Art Institute of Chicago. Active in the civil rights and antiwar movements, Firestone joined with other feminists denied a forum at the National Conference for a New Politics in Chicago in 1967 to found the first independent women's caucus organized around women's issues since the suffrage era. Moving to New York, she cofounded New York Radical Women (the first women's liberation group in New York City), Redstockings, and New York Radical Feminists, and served as editor of *Notes from the First Year* (1968), *Notes from the Second Year* (1970), and, with Anne Koedt, *Notes from the Third Year* (1971). Firestone disappeared from active involvement in the women's movement shortly after the publication of *The Dialectic of Sex*. She lives in New York.

While taking much from Marx and Freud, Firestone insisted that they had not carried their analyses far enough. Marx and Engels had failed to recognize that what she called sex-class—the domination of men over women rooted in biology—both provided the model for, and offered additional support to, domination by economic class as well as by race. She drew on Freud to argue that sexual repression was at the root of sociocultural malaise, and insisted that the true emancipation of women would require both an end to sexual repression and the emancipation of children.

It was only in the last quarter of the twentieth century, she argued, that "material conditions" had progressed to such a point that a truly revolutionary feminism was possible. Pregnancy and childbirth were "barbaric." The development of contraception, the possibility of creating "test-tube babies," and other scientific advancements meant that humanity would soon have the technological means to separate pregnancy and child rearing from sex and, ultimately, free women from childbearing. Only a destruction of the nuclear family, and the consequent elimination of pressures on women (and men) to marry and have children, would make possible the creation of new, more rational, and voluntarily constituted groups of people committed to raising children in ways that would not require either permanent male-female bonding or the identification of two particular adults with "their" particular children.

Firestone's efforts to salvage Marx and Freud were the first of a series of feminist efforts to use these theorists and their methods both to understand the subordination of women and to articulate strategies to overcome it. On the other hand, her insistence that the subordination of women was fundamentally linked to that of children is an insight that has not been taken up as ardently by later feminists. Finally, what is perhaps most striking to later twentieth-century readers is Firestone's extraordinary faith in technology, and her belief that a truly revolutionary ecology would "attempt to establish an artificial (man-made) balance in place of the 'natural' one, thus realizing the original goal of empirical science: total mastery over nature."

SELECTED WORKS BY SHULAMITH FIRESTONE

The Dialectic of Sex: The Case for Feminist Revolution (1970); *Notes from the First Year*, editor (1968); *Notes from the Second Year*, editor, (1970); *Notes from the Third Year*, editor, with Anne Koedt (1971).

BIBLIOGRAPHY

Gorman, Robert A., ed. *Biographical Dictionary of Neo-Marxism* (1985); Ireland, Norma Olin. *Index to Women of the World from Ancient to Modern Times: A Supplement* (1988); O'Neill, Lois Decker, ed. *The Women's Book of World Records and Achievements* (1979); Uglow, Jennifer S., comp. and ed. *The Continuum Dictionary of Women's Biography* (1989), and *The International Dictionary of Women's Biography* (1982); *The Writer's Dictionary*.

MARTHA ACKELSBERG

FISCH, EDITH (b. 1923)

With great courage and dogged determination, Edith Lond Fisch became a lawyer, legal writer, and law professor despite severe physical limitations, educational prejudices, and sexual discrimination.

Born on March 3, 1923, in New York City, Edith Lond Fisch was the younger of two daughters born to attorney Hyman Fisch and Clara (Lond) Fisch. She grew up in the substantial, intercultural Flatbush (now Midwood) area of Brooklyn. Highly intelligent, sharp-witted, and verbal, Fisch was encouraged from childhood to speak her mind. On June 26, 1935, at age twelve, she was stricken with poliomyelitis. Three years of treatment failed to restore her ability to walk. Confined to a wheelchair, she proceeded to live her life almost as if the illness never occurred.

For the next twenty-five years, with the support of her family, Fisch breached walls of prejudice and discrimination. She was the first physically disabled person in New York City to obtain a high school "academic" diploma (required for college) while on home instruction. Brooklyn College, built on level ground, was the only college to accept her. Although Fisch was awarded a B.S. in chemistry in 1945, the stairs in available graduate schools proved an insurmountable obstacle to a graduate degree. This defeat led Fisch to her life's work. She was accepted to Columbia University Law School and graduated with an LL.B. (1948), an LL.M. (1949), and a J.S.D. (1949), the first person to earn all the school's degrees and the first woman to earn its J.S.D. When Fisch was admitted to practice law in 1948, it became national news. Her father sponsored her for admission to the New York bar and, in 1957, to the United States Supreme Court. Her areas of expertise are estates and charities.

Fisch's goal was to be a professor of law. In 1962, she became the first female professor of law in New York, teaching evidence, legal writing, and agency in New York Law School.

Fisch's most important books are *The Cy Pres Doctrine in the U.S.* (1951), *Charities and Charitable Foundations* (1974), which she coauthored, and *Fisch on New York Evidence* (1959). *New York Evidence* is one of the few treatises on a basic aspect of law written by a woman. It is routinely cited by the bench and is used by the bar and as a law school text. Fisch has written special studies for judicial conferences and almost forty law review articles. She was editor of the *New York City Charter and Administrative Code* from 1965 to 1983 and is a frequent lecturer before bar associations. Fisch maintains membership and has held office in educational, political, and alumni associations. She has been a member of the National Panel of the American Arbitration Association since 1964; the New York Women's Bar Association, serving as president from 1970 to 1971, as director from 1971 to 1973, and as an advisory board member since 1972; the Association of the Bar of the City of New York, serving on committees since 1975 and chairing the Library Committee from 1991 to 1994; the National Association of Women Lawyers; the Women's Bar Association of the State of New York; the American Association of University Women; the Alumni Association of Columbia University and its Committee on Seminars since 1972; and the Lawyers Group of Brooklyn College Alumni Association since 1957, chairing several committees. In 1964, she was a founder of the Foundation for Continuing Legal Education.

Ardently proud of being a Jew, Fisch is a member of Temple Emanu-El, where on December 14, 1963, she had married Steven Ludwig Werner. He died on April 16, 1972, following an exploratory procedure for a cardiac condition.

Edith Lond Fisch continues to write and practice law. Lawyers and judges who know only her writings and then meet this lively wheelchair-bound woman for the first time are stunned. Invariably, they shake their heads and say, "Remarkable woman!"

SELECTED WORKS BY EDITH LONG FISCH

Charities and Charitable Foundations, with Doris Jones Freed and Esther R. Schachter (1974); *The Cy Pres Doctrine in the U.S.* (1951); *Fisch on New York Evidence* (1959, 1977); *New York City Charter and Administrative Code*, editor (1965–1983).

BIBLIOGRAPHY

Fisch, Edith Lond. Interview with author, June 1996; *NYTimes*, February 25, 1951, 55:1; Thomas, Dorothy. *Women Lawyers in the U.S.* (1957).

DOROTHY THOMAS

FISCHEL, JANE BRASS (1865–1935)

An outstanding communal leader in New York City's Orthodox Jewish community, Jane Brass Fischel was a generous philanthropist and active participant in Jewish communal activities. She was born in the Pale of Settlement in Russia on March 21, 1865. In 1883, she immigrated to New York City, where she earned a living as a dressmaker. She met and married Harry Fischel, also a Russian immigrant. Both were committed Orthodox Jews who shared the twin goals of serving humanity and advancing Orthodox Judaism in the United States.

When they married on November 26, 1887, Jane had saved $250; her husband had saved $47. The Fischels lived frugally, and both worked from dawn to dusk. Jane kept boarders, doing laundry, serving breakfasts, cooking and serving suppers, and packing lunch boxes. Harry worked long hours, and eventually became a successful real estate developer.

Four daughters were born to Jane and Harry Fischel, and Jane became an active volunteer and philanthropist in Orthodox Jewish organizations. She was supportive of her husband, and her charitable activities reflected their common values and ideals. She was active in women's groups affiliated with men's organizations in which her husband was a leader, as well as several important women's organizations.

In 1906 Jane Fischel helped found the Home of the Daughters of Jacob, serving as vice president from that time until 1925. She was a founder of the Women's Organization of Yeshiva College in 1925 and was vice president at the time of her death. She worked for Congregation Kehilath Jeshuran, the Hebrew Sheltering and Immigrant Aid Society, the Ladies Mulbish Arumim Society of the Uptown Talmud Torah, the Federation of Jewish Women's Organizations, Beth Israel Hospital, the Hebrew Children's Home, the Hebrew Day Nursery School of New York, the Relief Committee of the Joint Distribution Committee, the Federation for the Support of Jewish Philanthropic Societies of New York City, and HADASSAH Council.

Jane Brass Fischel died on January 3, 1935. According to her obituary in the *New York Times*, more than a thousand mourners gathered on the streets near her apartment building on the day of her funeral. She was eulogized as "the combination of a perfect wife and mother and a communal worker who inspired others to follow in her footsteps." Jane Fischel, beloved by family and community, devoted her life to *tzedaka* [righteousness].

BIBLIOGRAPHY

AJYB 37:256; Goldstein, Herbert Samuel, *Forty Years of Struggle for a Principle* (1928); "Tribute by Throng Paid Mrs. Fischel." *NYTimes*, January 5, 1935; *WWIAJ* (1928).

CORINNE AZEN KRAUSE

FIZDALE, RUTH E. (1908–1994)

As administrator of the Arthur Lehman Counseling Services in New York City, Ruth Fizdale developed a new kind of social agency—a not-for-profit, fee-for-service agency for a private clientele. That program lifted the aura of charity from social work services. Fizdale is credited for making modern social work a profession. The fees were set at a market rate for counseling services. She developed a fair salary scale along with incentive pay and a contingency fund to cover special program or personnel needs. The three dimensions fostered the professional status of social work in a successful program. The model was adopted by social agencies across the country. Fizdale also set national standards for the quality of services. She was mentor and educator to thousands of social workers.

She was born in Chicago on January 6, 1908, to Jewish immigrant parents. She had an older brother, Tom. Both parents came from czarist Russia. Her father, a grain elevator operator, moved the family to Dauphin, Manitoba, where she spent her early years in a rural community with little companionship with other children except in school. School was hiking distance away.

The family returned to Chicago. She attended the University of Chicago, where she took her bachelor's degree. She claimed she was the only graduate of the university who was excused from learning to swim: she was unusually buoyant and could not put her feet down to touch bottom. She received a master's degree from Smith College School of Social Work and an advanced study certificate from the University of Pennsylvania.

As chief of social services staff development for the Veterans Administration, she consulted with schools of social work and VA hospitals throughout the country, enhancing the schools' curricula and the quality of social work health care services. As part of that effort, she helped create competitive stipends for students who would enter VA and other health care social services.

She also was a psychiatric caseworker at the Mandel Clinic of the Michael Reese Hospital in Chicago, and assistant executive director at the Jewish Family Service in Brooklyn and at the New York Association for New Americans. At NYANA, Fizdale used counseling and job training to help immigrants become self-sustaining within a year after entering the country.

To many, Fizdale perhaps is best known for her nineteen years as executive director of the Arthur Lehman Counseling Service (ALCS), where she helped pioneer and develop the fee-for-services system in not-for-profit agencies, removing the "charitable institution" aura from voluntary organizations. She chronicled ALCS's first decade and a half in the book *Social Agency Structure and Accountability*, which was used in graduate schools, agencies, and private practice to standardize quality fee-paid social work services. ALCS, created to serve middle- and upper-income clients, was noted for charging reasonable fees and paying attractive salaries.

Fizdale was an adjunct associate professor at the Mount Sinai School of Medicine. She was a member of the National Association of Social Workers (NASW) and active on various committees from its inception in 1955, as well as a member of a predecessor organization starting in 1948. She was a founding member of the Competence Certification Board, which oversees the Academy of Certified Social Workers. She was a nine-year executive board member of NASW's New York City chapter and an active member of the Council on Social Work Education, the

National Conference on Social Welfare, and the New York State Conference on Social Welfare.

Fizdale was named the New York Social Worker of the Year in 1970, and received a recognition award in 1983 from the University of Pennsylvania for the advancement of social work practice. She was designated a fellow of the Brookdale Center on Aging of HUNTER COLLEGE for her service to the elderly.

Her major efforts were directed toward achieving quality in social work performance. She believed education was primary and continuing education was essential. In her will she created scholarships at four schools: the University of Chicago, Smith College, the University of Pennsylvania, and Hunter College, where she was a major contributor to both the design and implementation of the Hunter–Mount Sinai Academic-Practice model for the education of social workers in health care.

Ruth E. Fizdale died in New York City on October 25, 1994.

BIBLIOGRAPHY

Obituary. *NYTimes*, November 2, 1994.

HELEN REHR

FLEISCHMAN, DORIS (1891–1980)

A writer and a publicist, Doris Fleischman was guided by two antithetical imperatives—her marked public feminism, in contrast to her domestic submissiveness.

Born on July 18, 1891, to Harriet (Rosenthal) and New York City attorney Samuel Fleischman, Doris Fleischman was the second of four children. She first attended Hunter Normal School, then Horace Mann, from which she graduated in 1909, entering Barnard College that fall. While in college, she won varsity letters in softball, basketball, and tennis. She also studied music and considered a career as a singer.

A self-assured pioneer, it never occurred to Fleischman not to work. A swift, clean writer who was extraordinarily verbal, she landed a job with the *New York Tribune*, writing for the women's page. Promoted to assistant Sunday editor, she was the first woman to cover a prizefight. Her father, fearing for her safety, insisted on going with her to this event. While at the *Tribune*, she interviewed Theodore Roosevelt, Irene Castle, and Jane Addams, among others.

In 1919, fledgling publicist Edward L. Bernays, whom she had known since childhood, hired Fleischman as a writer. She spent the next sixty-one years working for and with Bernays, whom she married at City Hall in 1922. When the newlyweds registered at the Waldorf-Astoria Hotel, the bride wrote "Doris Fleischman," a gesture that made headlines the next day. It is plausible that she did this at the request of her husband, who had a healthy appetite for personal publicity.

Before she went to Europe some years later, Fleischman applied for and received a passport issued under her own name—an American first—by writing to the authorities that since "the purpose of a passport is to establish identity, I assume you will not wish me to travel under a false name."

For twenty-six years, Fleischman was a member of the Lucy Stone League, a group of professional women whose aim was to persuade other American women to keep their names after marriage. At age fifty-seven, she published an article in the *American Mercury*, "Notes of a Retiring Feminist," in which she articulated her ambivalence: "Mrs. stands to the right of me, and Miss stands to the left. Me is a ghost somewhere in this middle." Her conflict over self-identification was never resolved.

Meanwhile, Fleischman had given birth to two daughters, Doris, in 1929, and ANNE [BERNAYS], in 1930. As a public relations consultant, Edward Bernays thrived, and Fleischman worked at his office every day. Nominally his partner, she wrote most of the firm's press releases, speeches, and important letters. She also sold articles to national publications, chiefly about women and their work both in and outside the home. In 1955, she published a memoir, *A Wife Is Many Women*.

Fleischman was a member of Theta Sigma Phi, the national sorority of women in communications, and in 1972, she won its Headliner Award. She considered herself a deist but, while acknowledging her Jewishness, practiced no religion. In 1962, Fleischman and her husband moved to Cambridge, Massachusetts, where their two daughters lived. Doris Fleischman died of a stroke there on July 10, 1980.

ANNE BERNAYS

FLEXNER, JENNIE MAAS (1882–1944)

Jennie Maas Flexner was the New York Public Library's original readers' adviser, an innovator in the use of public libraries for adult education, especially for minorities, immigrants, and refugees during the unsettled years of the Depression and World War II.

Born on November 6, 1882, Jenny Maas Flexner came from a prominent Jewish family in Louisville,

Kentucky, the firstborn of Jacob Aaron Flexner, a pharmacist, and Rosa (Maas) Flexner. Her paternal uncles included the educator Abraham Flexner, founder of the Institute for Advanced Study at Princeton; Bernard Flexner, a distinguished lawyer and Zionist; and Simon Flexner, pathologist and scientific director of the Rockefeller Foundation. Her father, who helped finance his brothers' education, eventually was able to attain his own medical degree, but Jennie, the eldest of four daughters and one son, never attended college. Her sister Hortense published seven volumes of poetry and taught at Bryn Mawr and Sarah Lawrence colleges. Another sister, Caroline, became the aide to New York governor and senator Herbert H. Lehman, and held important positions in the Joint Distribution Committee and the United Nations Relief and Rehabilitation Administration.

Jennie Flexner went to the local public schools and did not take a paying job until age twenty-four, when she became a secretary. After two years, she moved on to more congenial work in the Louisville Public Library. In 1908, she was able to study at the School of Library Service at the Western Reserve University in Cleveland. She returned to Louisville and became head of the circulation department at the Louisville Public Library from 1912 through 1928, publishing *Circulation Work in Libraries* (1927), long a standard text for library students, and devoting her attention to library training issues and community service in Louisville and throughout the country for the American Library Association.

In 1928, Jennie Flexner was hired as the readers' adviser at the New York Public Library, a post she retained until the end of her life. In a *Library Journal* article, "Readers and Books" (1938), she explained her mission: "As the Readers' Adviser, I am especially interested in assisting those readers who voluntarily and for the joy of achievement wish to go ahead with constructive reading as a basis for further education. People come to a realization of gaps in their education, [and] . . . they are aware that they can go farther both in life and in work, if they know more. Some are those who have not had rich opportunities in formal education. Others have had college education or special training, but find themselves at a loss when they wish to read about unfamiliar subjects." As the readers' adviser, she not only compiled individualized lists for readers and taught them how to make the best use of the library themselves, but advised the growing ranks of unemployed Americans and new immigrants about retraining and adult education opportunities beyond the library. When the influx of European refugees from fascism began to arrive in New York in

the 1930s, Jennie Flexner was active in helping them find new resources for their professional and intellectual lives. During World War II, she advised the Council on Books in Wartime and chaired the committee that selected books for the Armed Services Editions.

Her final effort was *Making Books Work: A Guide to the Use of Libraries* (1943), written not for fellow librarians, but for the common reader in all his or her variety. Her colleagues and friends remembered her for her warmth, vivacity, and the breadth and depth of her sympathies. She died in 1944 and was buried in the Adath Israel Cemetery in Louisville.

SELECTED WORKS BY JENNIE MAAS FLEXNER

Making Books Work: A Guide to the Use of Libraries (1943); "Readers and Books." *Library Journal* 63, no. 2 (1938): 55–56.

BIBLIOGRAPHY

Bulletin of Bibliography 17, no. 1 (January–April 1940): frontispiece, 1–2; Danton, Emily Miller. *Pioneering Leaders in Librarianship* (1953); *DAB*, supp. 3; *NAW*; Obituary. *NYTimes*, November 18, 1944, 13; *UJE*.

SUSAN HALPERT

FLEXNER, MAGDALEN (1907–1972)

A distinguished foreign service officer, Magdalen Flexner succeeded in crossing gender barriers to assume professional positions traditionally reserved for men. Living in a time of social restriction and limited opportunity for women, she defined herself as an independent woman, unfazed by the mold society dictated. Her ambition refused to deny her intelligence its full potential.

Born in Watervliet, New York, on July 11, 1907, to Otto Glaser and Anna Munro, Magdalen Glaser was raised in New York. After graduating from the Emma Willard School in Troy in 1924, she left New York to attend Bryn Mawr College in Pennsylvania, where she received her bachelor's degree in 1928. She served as the warden of Bryn Mawr from 1930 to 1932, the year she married William Flexner, the son of Simon Flexner of the Rockefeller Institute. Her education, however, did not end with Bryn Mawr. She received her LL.B from Cornell University in 1947, a year after she divorced her husband.

As a single, childless woman, Flexner focused her energy and talents on her career. From 1947 to 1948, she worked as a law clerk at the U.S. 5th Circuit Court of Appeals and, after passing the New York Bar in 1948, went on to be an attorney at the National

Labor Relations Board (NLRB). She stayed at the NLRB until 1951, when she moved to the State Department. In 1954, she became the assistant public affairs adviser. Then, in 1955, she joined the foreign service and a year later was appointed American consul in Bordeaux, France. By 1959, she had moved to Paris, where she stayed until 1962 to serve as the deputy United States representative to UNESCO. She stayed in Europe but moved on to England to serve as United States consul in Cardiff, Wales, for one year. In 1965, Flexner was appointed American consul general in Bordeaux, France. She stayed in Bordeaux until 1967.

Flexner's independence and success trace a lifetime of extraordinary accomplishment. The magnitude of her success can be measured not only in the range of positions she held throughout her life but also in her ability to define herself as a professional equal to her male peers. Her persistent pursuit of success and her consistent hard work defined her as a woman of remarkable accomplishments.

Throughout her life, Magdalen Flexner did not appear to show any particular interest in her Judaism. She died of cancer on April 21, 1972, while she was living in Washington, D.C.

BIBLIOGRAPHY

Obituary. *NYTimes* (April 21, 1972) 42:2; *WWWIA* 5; *Who's Who of American Women*, 6th ed. (1971).

NOA MEYER

FONAROFF, VERA (1883–1962)

Vera Fonaroff began her career in the early 1900s as a solo violinist and recitalist, and later was a member of the critically acclaimed Olive Mead String Quartet. She taught the violin for many years and was esteemed as a violin pedagogue. A dedicated musician and teacher, she believed in the power of music for social good. In 1930, she wrote, "Music trains the hand, the head, the heart. Music is the great emotional leveller, wherein alone we speak to each other in the esperanto of the soul."

Born in Kiev on June 14, 1883, to Alexander and Sonia Hochstein, Vera immigrated to the United States when she was seven years old. She was the fourth of five children. She studied the violin with Mark Fonaroff, who was also a Russian emigré and whom she later married. She debuted as a violin soloist at age nine with the Metropolitan Opera House Orchestra, and thereafter made frequent solo appearances. She later went to England to study with Adolph Brodsky

at the Royal Manchester College of Music. After five years of study, she was awarded a Diploma with Distinction as both artist and teacher. She remained in England after graduating, touring as a soloist and recitalist with the pianist Richard Epstein. She also participated in lecture-recitals presented by George Bernard Shaw. Eventually she returned to New York to study with Franz Kneisel. It was at this time, in 1905, that she eloped with her former teacher, Mark Fonaroff.

In 1909, Vera Fonaroff joined the Olive Mead Quartet as second violinist. This all-woman string quartet was professionally very active for almost twenty years and was highly esteemed. They set a high standard of performance, rehearsed several hours a day, toured extensively, and presented both world and United States premieres of new works (including the world premiere of the Amy Beach Piano Quintet). If it were not for the women's movement of the early twentieth century, the Olive Mead Quartet could not have existed, but the quartet also contributed to the movement by giving an example of what women could achieve, given the means and the opportunity.

Vera Fonaroff had two daughters, Olga and Nina. Olga, who was born in 1910, was mentally handicapped and died at age twenty-three. Nina, who was born in 1914, became a well-known dancer with the Martha Graham Company and an active choreographer in the 1940s and 1950s.

In 1923, after the Olive Mead Quartet disbanded, Fonaroff became an instructor of the violin at the New York Institute of Musical Art (now the Juilliard School) in the preparatory department. A year later, she was appointed director of violin instruction, a post she held until 1930, the year after her husband died. From 1926 to 1939 and 1948 to 1955, she taught violin at the institute itself. In 1929, the pianist Josef Hofmann, then head of the Curtis Institute of Music in Philadelphia, asked Fonaroff to fill a vacancy left by the death of Leopold Auer. Although she remained in New York, she taught at Curtis until 1933. She also taught at the Damrosch Institute and the Henry Street Settlement Music School. In addition, she taught violin privately at her home. In 1941, she joined the faculty of the Mannes College of Music, where she continued teaching until her death at age seventy-nine on July 23, 1962.

BIBLIOGRAPHY

BEOAJ; Bloch, Adrienne F., and Carol Neuls-Bates. *Women in American Music: A Bibliography of Music and Literature* (1979); Fonaroff, Nina. Telephone interviews with author, September 22, 1966, May 17, 1997; Fonaroff, Vera.

Archives. Juilliard School, NYC, and Curtis Institute of Music, Philadelphia; Obituary. *NYTimes*, July 24, 1962, 27:3; Olive Mead Quartet. Clippings files. New York Public Library of Performing Arts, Lincoln Center, NYC; Rockwell, Donald Shumway. *Women of Achievement: Biographies and Portraits of Outstanding American Women* (1940); *Who Is Who in Music* (1941): 95; *WWIAJ* (1938).

BETTY HAUCK

FOOD

In 1901 in Milwaukee, Wisconsin, LIZZIE BLACK KANDER published a pamphlet entitled *The Settlement Cook Book: A Way to a Man's Heart*. Containing one hundred nonkosher German-Jewish and turn-of-the-century American recipes, *The Settlement Cook Book*, now in its twenty-second edition, soon turned into one of the most successful American cookbooks ever published. The proceeds were used to help the wave of immigrants that swept into the United States at the turn of the century, and, in later years, provided the seed money to build the Milwaukee Jewish Community Center. Coming when it did, the cookbook marked a watershed in assimilation.

Kander, the daughter of German-Jewish pioneer farmers, was known as the Jane Addams of Milwaukee for her work on behalf of Eastern European immigrants. In 1896, she established the Milwaukee Jewish Mission, or settlement house, in quarters borrowed from two synagogues. By 1898, the mission had begun to sponsor cooking classes every Sunday for these immigrants. The mission women taught the girls, who ranged in age from thirteen to fifteen, how to build a fire, cook, and bake. They learned to prepare such dishes as German kuchen, cranberry jelly, and waffles in the only kosher cooking school this side of New York, according to the *Sentinel*, a Milwaukee newspaper. Each girl would prepare her own dish, often with her mother, older sisters, or friends as spectators.

Although they were not schooled in "New World" cooking, the young pupils of the mission kitchen were better versed in the practices of kashrut than their teachers, a problem that led to some uncomfortable moments. In 1901, the *Sentinel* wrote about the kashrut problems of the teacher, Miss Pattee, a graduate of the Boston Cooking School: "The other day the little tea table at which the children were to set the food they had been preparing was all in white except for a red bordered napkin laid on as a centerpiece. It gave a bit of color to the table and added to the decorative effect, but the red bordered napkin was 'fleischig' and it happened to be a 'milchig' lunch so it had to be removed before the meal could

proceed. . . . Sometimes Miss Pattee forgets about the 'kosher' and mixes up the custard and the bouillon spoons, but there is always a small girl with large dark eyes and a wealth of coal black hair to point out the mistake."

These small girls knew how to make gefilte fish and to weave eight braids in their challah. Like more than two-thirds of the millions of Jews in America today, they could trace their roots to greater Poland, including parts of Austria and Hungary (Galicia), the Ukraine, Lithuania, and Russia. "Jewish food" came into its own with the arrival of these immigrants. Many Polish and Russian dishes not considered Jewish in Europe, like herring in sour cream, rye bread, and borscht, became identified here as Jewish.

The first national Jewish women's organization, the NATIONAL COUNCIL OF JEWISH WOMEN, was founded in the fall of 1893 as an outgrowth of a national Jewish Women's Congress. By 1900, the 7,080 members in fifty-five cities helped support the rights of women, mission and industrial schools for poor Jewish children, free baths in Kansas City and Denver, and, of course, cooking classes in the settlement houses, such as Kander's in Milwaukee. Council cookbooks were put out nationwide, with proceeds going toward such projects. Like *The Settlement Cook Book*, these books often had a German slant, included shellfish, especially oysters, and featured many goose recipes as well as other American dishes such as chicken chow mein, often made from leftover chicken soup, and Saratoga chips, a turn-of-the-century potato chip.

Other organizations followed suit. In September 1905, for example, the Montefiore Lodge Ladies Hebrew Benevolent Association of Providence, Rhode Island, published the following in a newsletter: "It was voted that 'this lodge publish and sell a cookbook of favorite recipes.' Two separate committees were appointed, one for the cooking recipes and the other to solicit advertising."

Helping the new wave of Eastern European Jewish immigrants was a major concern for the more assimilated Jewish women from coast to coast. Between 1881 and 1921, the year of the first law restricting Jewish immigration, almost 2,500,000 of these Eastern European Jews arrived in cities throughout the United States. All were looking for a new life; many were also hoping to hold onto their Orthodoxy, which included the dietary laws, while others were radicals who rebelled against such traditions.

They came here carrying with them their brass candlesticks, mortars and pestles, and pots and pans, as well as century-old recipes. In many instances whole Jewish communities were transplanted, including the rabbi and *shokhet*. They crowded into New York's Lower East Side, Chicago's West Side, Boston's North End, South Philadelphia, and neighborhoods in other cities. At one time there were almost four thousand kosher butcher shops in New York City alone. The immigrants were generally successful in finding work and housing and became a part of a network of familiar social and cultural institutions, such as *landsmanshaftn*, the Jewish mutual aid societies that were formed by immigrants originating from the same villages, towns, and cities in Eastern Europe. A square block in an immigrant area in any American city would include overcrowded tenements, sweatshops, basement synagogues, saloons, and cafes. In the typical tenement, tiny apartments burst with large families, boarders, and little air.

As the immigrants adjusted to the new food habits, they quickly forgot some of the foods of their poverty, like *krupnick*, a cereal soup made from oatmeal, sometimes barley, potatoes, and fat. If a family could afford it, milk would be added to the *krupnick*. If not, it was called "*soupr mit nisht*" [supper with nothing]. Bagels, knishes, or herring wrapped in a newspaper would be taken back to the sweatshop, providing a poor substitute for the midday lunch they were used to in Eastern Europe.

To combat all these changes and the rise of Reform Judaism in America, many Orthodox Jews clung to their old traditions, including kashrut. (The first kosher cookbook published in America, *Jewish Cookery Book* by Esther Levy, appeared in 1871). It was not always easy. In 1881 in Denver, for example, Jews were unable to acquire kosher meat, so they either had to practice ritual slaughtering for themselves or eat no meat. Later, many of them would become Conservative Jews.

One Orthodox Jew, Rabbi Hyman Sharfman, went from Kennebunkport, Maine, to Corpus Christi, Texas, in a gearless cycle car, sometimes on horseback, kashering meat and teaching people in the community how to do it themselves. Another, Dov Behr Manischewitz, hearing of the huge center of Reform Judaism in Cincinnati, decided to settle there as a *shokhet* [person officially licensed by rabbinic authority to slaughter meat in accordance with Jewish dietary laws]. He later made his fortune in the matzoh industry.

The diverse Orthodox immigrant groups lacked unified Jewish leadership. In a small town in Russia, for example, the rabbi was the leader, and everyone went to the same *shokhet*. In New York, with millions of people and thousands of kosher butchers, not to mention the importance of the separation between church and state, there was no central authority to whom to turn for validation of the religious laws. In 1888, eighteen Orthodox synagogues in New York, Philadelphia, and Baltimore organized themselves and brought over Jacob Joseph, the chief rabbi of Vilna, as their head. Among his other duties, he was supposed to organize the kosher meat business. Not surprisingly, considering what he was up against, he failed miserably. By 1917, at the height of Orthodoxy in America, there were a million Jews eating 156 million pounds of kosher meat annually—or at least meat they believed to be kosher. With no central authority, individual rabbis were putting *hekhsher* [kosher] stamps on the meat. Some was kosher, some was not. It was not until 1944 that a food inspection bureau to

By 1917, at the height of Orthodoxy in America, there were a million Jews eating 156 million pounds of meat annually. This advertisement from 1931 shows that "Strictly Kosher" butchers were still thriving and competing for customers. [Peter H. Schweitzer]

authenticate kosher meats was formed in New York State. It remains in operation to this day, and its inspectors regularly spot-check all kosher meat markets across the state—yet there are still occasional problems.

Because of escalating prices, kosher meat and bread riots broke out at the turn of the century with women leading the lines. One boycott was dubbed the "war of the women against the butchers." The battle cry became "twelve cents instead of eighteen cents a pound."

Eastern European immigrants, many of them deeply interested in the way food was prepared, found great opportunities in the food business. The butchers, bakers, and pushcart peddlers of herring and pickles soon became small-scale independent grocers, wine merchants, and wholesale meat, produce, and fruit providers. As it was in Europe with the religious, it was often the woman who ran the store as well as the family while the husband studied in the back.

Not only did these immigrants go into the business of food, but they also adapted their Eastern European food ways to the new environment. Sunday, for example, a second day of rest, provided them with new gastronomic opportunities like a dairy brunch, an embellishment of their simple dairy dinners in Europe. Bagels, an afternoon snack food in Europe, became embellished with lox and cream cheese and eventually became an American icon.

While the women's organizations were working to help less fortunate Eastern Europeans, another revolution was taking place—that of food technology and scientific discovery. Pioneer women like Lizzie Kander's mother made their own yeast, corned their own beef, and prepared their own ketchups and pickles. Slowly the kitchen was transformed, liberating women from time-consuming chores. Not only was Heinz producing its bottled ketchups and fledgling companies making kosher canned foods, but companies were manufacturing a white vegetable substance resembling lard—the shortening that would change forever the way Jewish women cooked. Three years after Crisco was invented in 1910, Procter & Gamble was advertising that this totally vegetable shortening was a product for which the "Hebrew Race had been waiting 4,000 years." Other inventions, too, like cream cheese, rennet, gelatin, junket, Jell-O, pasteurized milk, Coca-Cola, nondairy creamer, phyllo dough, and frozen foods would affect Jewish cooking in America.

With the growth of food companies, delicatessens, school lunch programs, and restaurants, American food and American Jewish food became more processed and more innovative. In 1925, the

In the 1920s, major American food companies realized that the market for kosher products could be lucrative. Planters Peanut Oil sponsored programs of liturgical music and reminded readers in their advertisements for them that their product was produced under the strictest supervision. [Peter H. Schweitzer]

average American housewife made all her food at home. By 1965, 75 to 90 percent of the food she had used had undergone some sort of factory processing.

As the latest wave of Eastern European Jews became more Americanized, they began trying new dishes like macaroni and cheese and canned tuna casseroles. Jewish cookbooks included recipes for Creole dishes, for chicken fricassee using canned tomatoes, and shortcut kuchen using baking powder. Many of these Jews cared little about the impact of scientific discoveries on kashrut. Others cared deeply.

At the turn of the century, the Union of Orthodox Jewish Congregations of America, the umbrella organization for Orthodox Jews, was established as a means of bringing cohesion to the fragmented immigrant Jewish populations. In 1923, the year it created its women's branch, and four years after women won the right to vote, the union's official kashrut supervision and certification program was introduced.

At about that time, a New York advertising genius named Joseph Jacobs encouraged big companies to advertise their mainstream packaged products in the Yiddish press. Jacobs's mission was to change the way Americans thought about Jewish dietary practices. The chains and the big food companies did not know how to promote to a Yiddish-speaking population since they employed no Jews. Jacobs encouraged the Maxwell House coffee company to write a Haggadah and helped Crisco and Pillsbury to produce Yiddish-English cookbooks to teach the immigrant women, who would salivate over the illustrations in the *Ladies' Home Journal* but could not read English. Now they could use Crisco to make an "American" apple or lemon meringue pie; better yet, they could serve their children "southern fried" chicken.

When canned products like H.J. Heinz Company's baked beans and pork came on the market, an inventive man named Joshua C. Epstein, an Orthodox Jew, had a thought: What if Heinz made kosher vegetarian baked beans? Company officials liked Epstein's suggestions, but they balked at the idea of writing

"kosher" in Hebrew or English on the package. "Heinz wanted something identifiable, but not too Jewish: they didn't want to antagonize the non-Jewish population," recalls Abraham Butler, the son of Frank Butler, Heinz's first *mashgiakh*. With Jacobs and Rabbi Herbert Goldstein, one of the founders of the Union of Orthodox Hebrew Congregations of America, the three devised the Orthodox Union OU symbol, today the best-recognized trademark of the some 120 symbols of kosher certification.

Jews went into the packaged-food business, too. In this land of opportunity, some food merchants struck it rich. One Chicago baker named Charley Lubin made a luscious cheesecake; it was the beginning of the age of frozen foods, so he tried freezing his cake. It worked, and he named it Sara Lee, after his daughter.

The fast-growing influence of radio and television affected how Americans saw each other and how products were sold. *The Goldbergs*, a program about a fictional Bronx family, reached a radio audience of ten million in the 1930s and at least forty million two decades later on television. Just as *I Remember Mama* taught us about Scandinavians, *The Goldbergs* familiarized non-Jews with a simple, everyday Jewish family. Sometimes Molly Goldberg just cooked throughout the whole program, cutting up a chicken or chopping

Advertising genius Joseph Jacobs convinced Maxwell House Coffee to prepare its own Haggadah to give away with a purchase of coffee. [Peter H. Schweitzer]

herring as the problems of her family paraded through her kitchen.

After World War II another "cooking lady" stepped onto television. Her name was Edith Green, and her popular *Your Home Kitchen* ruled the airwaves in the San Francisco Bay area from 1949 to 1954. Although this "queen of the range" was Jewish, her cooking was American—and it was "gourmet." A week's recipes might include veal scallopini, coffee chocolate icebox cake, coconut pudding, or frozen tuna mold. She also showed her viewers how to use the new gadgets, such as electric mixers and electric can openers, that were the products of the postwar period of affluence.

As Jewish women became more Americanized, notions of "Jewish food" changed with the availability of regional ingredients. Taste buds adjusted to local spices and new dietary guidelines. While Jews in Burlington, Vermont, ate potato latkes with maple syrup, Californians preferred theirs with local goat cheese. Gefilte fish was made with whitefish in the Midwest, salmon in the Far West, and haddock in Maine. The matzoh balls, gefilte fish, and even the Passover desserts American Jews eat today are certainly very different from those eaten in Europe or in this country a century ago.

BIBLIOGRAPHY

Green, Edith. Oral interview, July 1991; Heinze, Andrew R. *Adapting to Abundance* (1990); Jacobs, Richard. Oral interview, 1991; Kander, Lizzie Black. Microfilm material. American Jewish Archives, Cincinnati; Marcus, Jacob Rader. *Memoirs of American Jews, 1775–1865* (1955); Nathan, Joan. *Jewish Cooking in America* (1994), and *The Jewish Holiday Kitchen* (1979); Sachar, Howard M. *A History of the Jews in America* (1992); Sharfman, I. Harold. *Jews on the Frontier* (1977).

JOAN NATHAN

FORREST, HELEN (b. 1918)

When Helen Forrest joined the Harry James band in 1941, she broke new ground for American vocalists. She asked that specific arrangements be written just for her and that the band accompany her lead vocal. Harry James agreed, and Forrest went on to record five gold records: "But Not for Me," "I Don't Want to Walk Without You," "I Cried For You," "I've Heard That Song Before," and "I Had the Craziest Dream."

She was born Helen Fogel on April 12, 1918, in Atlantic City, New Jersey. Her parents, Louis and Rebecca Fogel, were Jewish and kept a kosher home.

Helen Forrest's strength of will—and voice—led to a change in the way vocalists were handled by big-band leaders. In a long, successful career, she recorded with musicians like Dick Haymes, Artie Shaw, Benny Goodman, and Harry James. [New York Public Library]

She was the youngest of four children and the only girl; her three brothers were Harry, Ed, and Sam. The Fogels owned a little grocery store. But when Helen was an infant, her father became ill with influenza and suddenly died. Apparently, Helen's mother became so distraught that she blamed her husband's death on her daughter's birth, believing that God had taken away Louis because she had wished so much for a little girl.

The two oldest brothers, Harry and Ed, were old enough to live on their own when Rebecca Fogel moved to Brooklyn with her two youngest children. There, Helen's mother met and married a house-painter by the name of Feigenbaum. Forrest recalled that her parents often asked her not to come home right away after school. As she got older, she began to realize that during the day her home was a brothel. As Helen physically matured, her stepfather tried to sexually accost her. She told her mother of his attempts, but Rebecca Fogel did not believe her daughter.

When Helen was about fourteen, her stepfather trapped her in the kitchen, and she defended herself with a kitchen knife. Subsequently, she went to live with her piano teacher, Honey Silverman, and Silverman's family. While Helen completed grammar school, she continued to take piano lessons, but when Silverman heard her sing, she suggested that Helen concentrate on singing instead. Although Helen did not complete high school, she sang in the school musicals during her years of attendance.

By the time she was fourteen, her older brother Ed had his own band. During one summer, she sang with her brother's band in Atlantic City. Helen later decided that she wanted to be singer and left for New York City, where she visited song publishers and auditioned for a fifteen-minute air slot for a local radio show. During one of the radio spots, the story goes, a sax player thought that the name Fogel was "too Jewish" and therefore Helen Fogel changed her name to Helen Forrest. In 1934, at seventeen years of age, Forrest got her first job at WNEW, New York, singing commercials. During this time, she sang under anonymous names such as Helen, Hilee, Madlene, and Arlene. When she sang for WCBS, she became "Bonnie Blue" and "The Blue Lady of Song." When her brother Ed, whose band was playing in Washington, D.C., called her to let her know that there was an opening for a vocalist in the Washington Madrillon Club, Forrest auditioned and soon after began singing in the popular supper club.

While performing at the Madrillon, she gained a reputation for her singing, and bandleader Artie Shaw came to see her. Shaw's singer Billie Holiday was planning to leave the band, and in 1958 Shaw asked Forrest to go on tour. During the fifteen months she sang with Artie Shaw, his band recorded forty-one sides for RCA Victor's Bluebird record label. In 1939, while still on the road with Artie Shaw's band, Forrest married drummer Al Spieldock in Baltimore. Her husband remained in Baltimore, and Forrest resumed her tour. When Shaw dissolved his band, she went back to Baltimore but was soon asked to join Benny Goodman's band. During her two-year tenure with Goodman, she recorded fifty-three sides. In 1941, she joined the Harry James band. The musical alliance of featuring Forrest's vocals with the band as accompaniment proved very successful.

Traveling with the band, Forrest was the only woman among eighteen or more band members. She fell in love with Harry James, maintaining a sporadic love affair until James married actress Betty Grable. In 1943, a few months after James's marriage, Forrest left the band and appeared in clubs around the country.

Her husband divorced her about the same time. Forrest's agent teamed her up with vocalist Dick Haymes, and together they appeared on their own very popular radio program, running from 1944 to 1947.

Around 1945, Forrest met Paul Hogan, an aspiring actor, at a party. The two began living together and married in 1947. They later separated and divorced in 1956. In the late 1950s, she met businessman Charlie Feinman and married him in 1959. The couple had a son, Michael, in 1960, but the marriage was dissolved in 1961. She continued to perform in major supper clubs around the country, sometimes singing for movie sound tracks as well as performing in "big band nostalgia" tours. She continued to record, achieving several hits as a soloist and several hits singing duets with Dick Haymes. Forrest recorded approximately seventy-four songs as a solo vocalist—twenty-two for Decca Records, forty for MGM, and twelve for Bell Records. In addition, she recorded for Capitol in 1955–1956, singing the hits she had sung with Harry James. From 1969 to 1974, she rerecorded some of her hits for Reader's Digest and Time-Life as well. During various periods of "big band nostalgia," radio broadcasts and shorts were rereleased of Helen Forrest with Artie Shaw's band, Benny Goodman's band, Harry James's band, and Dick Haymes.

Helen Forrest was one of the first singers in the big band era whose vocals were featured throughout a full band arrangement. Before this time, big band vocalists usually sang in the middle of a song. The band would be featured for a full chorus, the vocalist would sing one chorus, and then the band would play another chorus. This arrangement usually confined the singer, not allowing much improvisation in the rhythmic phrasing or melodic line. As well, the song was usually set in the key that suited the instrumentalists' playing, rather than the vocalist's range. During the early big band era, few women vocalists had the confidence to ask for individualized arrangements. Despite an unhappy childhood, frequent illness, and personal disappointments, Forrest remained dedicated to her musical profession until the 1980s.

BIBLIOGRAPHY

Forrest, Helen, and Bill Libby. *I Had The Craziest Dream* (1982); Friedwald, Will. *Jazz Singing: American's Great Voices from Bessie Smith to BeBop and Beyond* (1990); Gourse, Leslie. *Louis' Children: American Jazz Singers* (1984); Kinkle, Roger D. *Complete Encyclopedia of Popular Music and Jazz, 1900–1950* (1974); *Penguin Encyclopedia of Popular Music.* Edited by Donald Clarke (1987); Schuller, Gunther. *The Swing Era* (1989); Simon, George T., et al. *The Best of the Music Makers* (1979).

JAN SHAPIRO

FRAIBERG, SELMA (1918–1981)

Selma Fraiberg was a psychoanalyst, author, and pioneer in the field of infant psychiatry. A woman and a social worker in a profession dominated by male physicians, Fraiberg rose to prominence because of her brilliance, originality, and dedication. She devoted her life to understanding the developmental needs of infants, to creating programs that promote infant mental health, and to reaching parents and policy-makers through clear, persuasive prose.

Fraiberg accomplished enough in her life to fill three careers. She was a psychoanalyst specializing in the treatment of children. She wrote *The Magic Years*, a luminous account of the child mind that is a classic in its genre. Her early work with blind infants and their mothers produced techniques to promote bonding in the absence of visual cues. This work, culminating in *Insights from the Blind*, had major implications for sighted children as well. Fraiberg's close observation of interactions between these mothers and babies elucidated the normal process of bonding and opened the way to working with babies at risk for neglect, abuse, or "failure to thrive." During this last phase of her career, Fraiberg started the Child Development Project at the University of Michigan, which served troubled families, trained clinicians, and developed a treatment model that has been widely replicated.

Fraiberg was born Selma Horwitz on March 8, 1918, in Detroit, the first of three children of Jack and Dorella (Newman) Horwitz. Her father, the son of Russian Jewish immigrants, took over his father's poultry business. On her mother's side were Newmans, long established in Detroit, and Jacobses, Hungarian Jews who had come to the United States via England in the nineteenth century. The men were prosperous salesmen and retail merchants, active in community and synagogue. The women were house-wives and mothers. The extended family was large and close knit.

Selma was feisty, shy, and intellectual. She had an especially close family relationship with her maternal grandmother, Jennie Jacobs, a strong-minded former suffragist who, like her granddaughter, was not in the family mold.

Selma was an undergraduate at Wayne State University in the class of 1940. She continued her education there at the social work school, where she met Louis Fraiberg, then a teaching assistant. They were married in 1945, the year of her graduation.

The Fraibergs' life together was one of fruitful intellectual collaboration. He became a professor of English, teaching at Louisiana State University. He maintained a lifelong interest in psychoanalysis and social work, and assisted his wife with several of her books.

In 1956, the Fraibergs adopted a baby girl, Lisa. Practicing what she preached, Fraiberg stayed home with Lisa and in her spare time wrote *The Magic Years*, which won the 1959 Book of the Year Award from the Child Study Association of America.

For Selma Fraiberg, the years in Ann Arbor, Michigan, from 1965 to 1979, were the culmination of her life's work. She was professor of psychoanalysis at the University of Michigan Medical School and director of the Child Development Project. She wrote, spoke, and traveled widely. She was known to colleagues and students as brilliant, demanding, fiercely principled, difficult, and inspiring. Those close to her knew that she was shy and self-conscious, and that public exposure caused her strain.

In 1979, the Fraibergs moved to San Francisco, where Selma Fraiberg organized and directed an infant-parent program at San Francisco General Hospital. In 1981, she received the Dolley Madison Award in recognition of her critical role in the field of infant mental health. In August of the same year, she learned that she had a malignant brain tumor.

Selma Fraiberg died on December 19, 1981, at age sixty-three.

SELECTED WORKS BY SELMA FRAIBERG

Clinical Studies in Infant Mental Health: The First Year of Life, edited with Louis Fraiberg (1980); *Every Child's Birthright: In Defense of Mothering* (1977); "Ghosts in the Nursery: A Psychoanalytic Approach to the Problems of Impaired Infant-Mother Relationships," with Edna Adelson and Vivian Shapiro. *Journal of the American Academy of Child Psychiatry* 14 (1975); *Insights from the Blind: Comparative Studies of Blind and Sighted Infants*, with Louis Fraiberg (1977); Introduction to *Assessment and Therapy of Disturbances in Infancy*, editor (1989); "Libidinal Object Constancy and Mental Representation." *Psychoanalytic Study of the Child* 24 (1969); *The Magic Years: Understanding and Handling the Problems of Early Childhood* (1959); "Parallel and Divergent Patterns in Blind and Sighted Infants." *Psychoanalytic Study of the Child* 23 (1968); *Selected Writings of Selma Fraiberg*. Edited by Louis Fraiberg (1987); "Smiling and Stranger Reaction in Blind Infants." In *Exceptional Infant*, vol. 2, edited by J. Hellmuth (1971).

BIBLIOGRAPHY

Anthony, E. James. "In Memoriam—Selma Fraiberg." *Frontiers of Infant Psychiatry*, Vol. 12. Edited by Justin D. Call, Eleanor Galenson, and Robert L. Tyson (1984); Coles, Robert, "Talk With Selma Fraiberg." *NYTimes Book Review*, December 11, 1977; *Contemporary Authors* (1981); "Selma Fraiberg Dies at 63, an Authority on Early Childhood." *NYTimes*, December 22, 1981.

CONSTANCE W. BROWN

FRANK, LEE WEISS (1899–1967)

Community leader, artist, newspaper drama critic, and host of a popular radio program in Philadelphia, Lee Weiss Frank was born in Newton Falls, Ohio, on May 16, 1899, the elder of two daughters born to Adolph and Eugenia (Guttman) Weiss.

She attended Swarthmore College, where she was elected to Phi Beta Kappa and graduated in 1921. She also studied painting and sculpture at the Philadelphia Museum of Art School. Swarthmore College provided a congenial setting for Frank at a time when universities and colleges throughout the nation had established tacit quotas to limit the number of Jewish students. An active member of the Swarthmore community after graduation, she served as a member of the board of the college's alumnae association.

In 1921, she became a feature writer for the Ledger newspaper syndicate. Her cultural affairs column appeared in the *Philadelphia Ledger* and in newspapers in New York City. In 1923, she married Victor H. Frank, a prominent oral surgeon in Philadelphia. The Franks had two children, Victor, Jr. and Patricia, and were members of Philadelphia's Congregation Mikveh Israel.

As the host of the Annenberg Syndicate's WFIL Radio's "Tea with Lee" program, Frank marked her debut as a radio drama critic in the 1930s. Her popular program evolved to include interviews with national celebrities.

A prominent public figure in Philadelphia, Frank served as chair of the Women's Committee of the Philadelphia Forum, a cultural and charitable organization. Frank was also active in the Women's International League for Peace and Freedom, serving as chairman of its Children's Play Committee in the 1930s and 1940s. Frank's interest in the well-being of children also led to her participation as a special writer for the Child Health Association of New York. After World War II, Frank served as radio chairman of the United Nations Council of Philadelphia. In this role, Frank was an ardent proponent of the new State of Israel. An active member of the World Affairs Council and the United World Federalists, Frank's affiliations indicated a commitment to peace, cooperation, and international understanding.

Fine art was an important part of Lee Weiss Frank's life. Her works in oil and watercolor were exhibited throughout the Philadelphia area and were included in over 150 private collections, including purchases by Princess Grace of Monaco and Carlos Pena Romulo, Philippine delegate to the United Nations.

Lee Weiss Frank died in Philadelphia on July 22, 1967. In 1980 an exhibit of her paintings at Swarthmore coincided with the creation of a scholarship fund established by her daughter, Patricia Frank Carey, in her memory.

BIBLIOGRAPHY

Chijioke, Mary Ellen. Telephone interview with author; Frank, Lee Weiss. File. Friends Historical Association Library, Swarthmore College, Swarthmore, Pa.; Obituary. *NYTimes*, July 23, 1967, 60:8; *WWIAJ* (1938).

DAVID REGO

FRANK, RAY (1861–1948)

On the evening of Yom Kippur in 1890, a tall, serious-looking young woman named Ray Frank stood before hundreds of men and women in the Opera House of Spokane Falls, Washington. Invited to deliver the sermon at a religious service that she herself had initiated, she implored those Jews in attendance to "drop all dissension about whether you should take off your hats during the service and other unimportant ceremonials and join hands in one glorious cause." With these words, the twenty-nine-year-old journalist from Oakland, California, helped create the first Jewish congregation in Spokane Falls and began her career as a Jewish religious leader.

Born in San Francisco on April 10, 1861 (some records give 1864 or 1865 as her year of birth), to Bernard Frank, a peddler and fruit vendor, and his wife Leah, Ray Frank and her two sisters were raised in what she later described as a deeply religious home. Her mother was a quiet, pious woman, who was fond of reading the Bible, while her father, an Orthodox Jew, was a great-grandson of Rabbi Elijah ben Solomon, the renowned Gaon of Vilna. Primarily raised in San Francisco, where she attended public school, Frank graduated in 1879 from Sacramento High School and moved to Ruby Hill, Nevada, where she taught for six years. In 1885, she rejoined her family, which by then had moved to Oakland, California. To support herself, she offered private literature and elocution lessons and began to write for several periodicals. She also taught Sabbath school classes at First Hebrew Congregation and subsequently become superintendent of its religious school.

During the 1890s, she earned additional income as correspondent for several Oakland and San Francisco newspapers. Based in Oakland, she traveled throughout the Pacific Northwest. In September 1890, she arrived in Spokane, Washington (then known as Spokane Falls) on the evening of Rosh Hashanah. Inquiring where she might find a local

Journalist Ray Frank made her name as a "latter-day Rebecca." She was the first Jewish woman to preach from a pulpit in America and was known for her ability to bring feuding Jewish religious factions together. [American Jewish Historical Society]

together and create a congregation, a Christian man in attendance stood up and offered to donate a site on which the synagogue might be built.

After she preached the next morning and again on Yom Kippur, Frank's call for communal cooperation was so successful that she repeated these efforts elsewhere. While continuing to support herself as a journalist, she preached and lectured widely throughout the western and northwestern United States, healing congregational squabbles and helping to create both Orthodox and Reform congregations. Hailed by local newspapers as a "latter-day Deborah," referring to the biblical judge and religious leader, and erroneously labeled a "Lady Rabbi," she came to the attention of Reform rabbi Isaac Mayer Wise, president of Hebrew Union College (HUC), the rabbinical seminary that he had founded a decade earlier in Cincinnati. Enrolling at HUC in January of 1893, for what proved to be only one semester, Frank told the press that her intention was to study Jewish philosophy, not to become a rabbi. Yet less than two months earlier, in his own *American Israelite*, Wise wrote that "we glory in her zeal and moral courage to break down the last remains of the barriers erected in the synagogue against women and wish her the best of success." Subsequently, in February of 1893, the *American Israelite* identified Frank as the "young lady who has gained much prestige on the Pacific Coast and whose avowed purpose of entering the Jewish ministry has aroused much attention."

Her reputation as a preacher grew, and in September 1893 she delivered the opening prayer and a formal address on "Woman in the Synagogue" at the first Jewish Women's Congress held in conjunction with the Parliament of World Religions at the Chicago World's Fair. After speaking at synagogues and churches throughout North America, even officiating in 1895 for High Holy Day services at an Orthodox synagogue in Victoria, British Columbia, she declined the invitation of a Reform congregation in Chicago to become its full-time spiritual leader, believing that she could do her best work "unfettered by boards of trustees and salary stipulations." Frank's dual career as journalist and preacher ended after her marriage to Dr. Simon Litman in August 1901. He taught economics for the next seven years at the University of California, Berkeley, and then accepted a teaching position at the University of Illinois, Champaign-Urbana. As early as 1915, Frank organized and led at her home an ongoing student study circle on postbiblical Jewish history. Actively involved in local Jewish organizations and institutions, including the Reform congregation to which she belonged, she occasionally

synagogue, she discovered that there was neither a synagogue nor planned religious services, as the Jewish community was small and torn apart by religious dissension. Procuring the help of a local man to whom she had a letter of introduction, Frank offered to deliver the sermon that evening if a minyan [prayer quorum] could be gathered. By five o'clock, a special edition of the *Spokane Falls Gazette* announced that a young woman would be preaching to the Jews of the community at the Opera House that night. According to local newspaper reports, one thousand Jews and Christians were in attendance when Ray Frank spoke about the obligations of Jews as Jews and as citizens. Moved by her plea that her coreligionists come lectured in the community and throughout the Midwest. Ray Frank died in a private sanatorium in Peoria, Illinois, in October of 1948 and was buried in Urbana.

While her career was short-lived, Ray Frank remains significant as the first Jewish woman to preach from a pulpit in the United States, and the first to be seen as a Jewish religious leader.

BIBLIOGRAPHY

Clar, Reva, and William M. Kramer. "The Girl Rabbi of the Golden West." *Western States Jewish History* 18 (1986): 91–111, 223–236, 336–351; Frank, Ray. Papers, correspondence and scrapbooks highlighting her preaching career, American Jewish Historical Society, Waltham, Mass.; Litman, Simon. *Ray Frank Litman: A Memoir* (1957).

ELLEN M. UMANSKY

FRANKEN, ROSE (1895–1988)

Rose Dorothy Lewin Franken was a celebrated Broadway playwright, director, and producer, a popular novelist, and a screenwriter.

Shortly after her birth on December 28, 1895, in Gainesville, Texas, her parents, Hannah (Younker) and Michael Lewin, a businessman, separated. She and her three older siblings were reared by her mother in the Younker family brownstone in New York City. In 1913, after leaving Ethical Culture High School, she married Sigmund Walter Anthony Franken, an oral surgeon, instead of entering Barnard College, to which she had been accepted.

A misdelivered typewriter spurred her long, productive writing career. Despite her disclaimers, her dedication to writing was immediately apparent in her persistent, systematic search for a publisher for her first novel, *Patterns* (1925). Encouraged by her husband, she experimented with short stories and drama while rearing her three sons, Paul, John, and Peter. *Another Language*, her second play, opened at the Booth Theatre on April 25, 1932, and continued for 453 performances. The central conflict in the play was the growing attraction between an older woman and her husband's bohemian nephew. The ending established her signature theme: the primacy of family above a woman's career, social life, or extramarital temptation.

After the death of her husband from tuberculosis in December 1932, she relocated to Hollywood. Her successes on the legitimate stage and her popularity as a writer of fiction made her a sought-after screenwriter, earning $2,000 a week. She was a workaholic who placed only her children's well-being before cur-

rent projects. In the next five years, she produced scripts (*Thirsty Soil, Beloved Enemy*), novels (*Golden Pennies, Of Great Riches*), and short stories, which were published primarily by *Redbook* magazine. On April 27, 1937, she married William Brown Meloney, a lawyer and journalist. They relocated to Longmeadow, a working farm in Lyme, Connecticut, and collaborated on film scripts and serial fiction, usually under the pseudonym Franken Meloney. Their novels included *Woman in White, Call Back Love, Strange Victory*, and *American Bred*.

The war years inspired her to try new directions. In 1939, she wrote the first of many "Claudia" narratives, which she collected in eight novels and transformed into a popular stage comedy in February 1941. This story of a young wife, which Franken also directed, ran for 722 performances. Still experimenting, she wrote and directed two more plays on Broadway in the 1943–1944 seasons: *Doctors Disagree* and *Outrageous Fortune*. Both were produced by her husband when the initial producer backed out. In *Doctors Disagree*, the female physician not only wins the right to a career and marriage but also competes successfully with a male colleague. Critics panned it as sentimental.

Although Franken was an assimilated Jew, many of her works included references to anti-Semitism. In *Outrageous Fortune*, anti-Semitism and discrimination against homosexuals took center stage. Critic Burns Mantle included this and three other Franken dramas in his ten best plays of the season series, but other critics, like Louis Kronenberger, advised her to return to a "more housefrauish direction." The play ran only seventy-seven performances.

When she retreated to the popular formula in *Soldier's Wife* (1945), she scored a hit that ran 253 performances. Although the war bride who became a celebrity when her letters to her husband were published prefers family to fame, Franken inserted sympathetic cameos of career women. *The Hallams*, her last produced play, opened March 4, 1948, but was unsuccessful. Her first and last plays, *Fortnight* and *The Wing*, remain unproduced. *Mr. Dooley Jr.* (1931), a play for children, was published by Samuel French. Her autobiography, *When All Is Said and Done*, appeared in 1963.

Rose Franken relocated from New York to Tucson, Arizona, where she died on June 22, 1988.

SELECTED WORKS BY ROSE FRANKEN

Another Language: A Comedy Drama in Three Acts (1932); *Claudia and David* (1940); *The Hallams: A Drama in Three Acts* (1948); *Outrageous Fortune* (1944); *Soldier's Wife*

(1945); *When All Is Said and Done* (1963); "The Wing." Manuscript. Rare Book and Manuscript Collection, Butler Library, Columbia University, NYC.

BIBLIOGRAPHY

Abramson, Doris E. "Franken, Rose Dorothy Lewin." In *Notable Women in American Theatre: A Biographical Dictionary*, edited by Alice M. Robinson, Vera Mowry Roberts, and Milly S. Barranger (1989); Bordman, Gerald. *The Oxford Companion to American Literature* (1984); Franken, Rose. Clipping file, photograph file, and manuscript collection. Billy Rose Theatre Collection, New York City Public Library for the Performing Arts, Lincoln Center; Rare Book and Manuscript Collection, Butler Library, Columbia University; McGill, Raymond D., ed. *Notable Names in the American Theatre* (1976); Rigdon, Walter, ed. *The Biographical Encyclopedia and Who's Who of the American Theatre* (1966); *UJE; Variety Obituaries, 1987–1988.* Vol. 12. Edited by Barbara Bergeron and Chuck Bartelt (1989); *Who Was Who in Theatre 1912–1976.* Vol. 2 (1978).

GLENDA FRANK

FRANKENTHALER, HELEN (b. 1928)

"The only rule is that there are no rules. Anything is possible. . . . It's all about risks, deliberate risks." This is how visual artist Helen Frankenthaler describes the enterprise she has pursued for five decades. Her constant high achievement ranks her as one of the most important contributors to the history of postwar American painting. More broadly, her work has consistently embodied and illuminated our understanding of modern experience generally; that is, the experience whereby we necessarily confront the risk of determining our relation to the world from within ourselves, without sanction by any external institutional structures and the rules by which they are defined. That Frankenthaler's achievement has been forged and sustained in an era characterized by constant shifts of stylistic taste and fashion, in which artists and art movements seem regularly to appear and vanish overnight, marks at once the strength of the work and the exceptional character of its maker.

Helen Frankenthaler was born in New York City on December 12, 1928. Her father was Alfred Frankenthaler, a respected New York State Supreme Court judge. Her mother, Martha (Lowenstein), had emigrated with her family from Germany to the United States shortly after she was born. Her two sisters, Marjorie and Gloria, were six and five years older, respectively. Growing up on New York's Upper East Side, Frankenthaler absorbed the privileged background of a cultured and progressive Jewish family

that encouraged all three daughters to prepare themselves for professional careers. She attended Horace Mann and Brearley schools, and in 1945, graduated from Dalton School, where she studied with the Mexican painter Rufino Tamayo.

Determined to pursue a career in the arts, she entered Bennington College, Vermont, in the spring of 1946 and commenced study with Paul Feeley. Under his guidance she learned the pictorial language of cubism, while also absorbing a formalist method of analyzing pictorial structure and evolving a deep and abiding respect for the old and modern masters of the history of art. She graduated from Bennington in July 1949. On her twenty-first birthday she received an inheritance from her father (he had died in 1940) that enabled her to secure her own New York apartment while also maintaining a separate studio. She commenced painting full-time, though she also took noncredit graduate courses in the history of art at Columbia University, one of them with the distinguished scholar Meyer Schapiro. A year later, she studied painting in Provincetown, Massachusetts, with Hans Hofmann.

In the spring of 1950, Frankenthaler organized an exhibition of Bennington College alumnae painters for the Jacques Seligmann Gallery in New York. There she met Clement Greenberg, one of the foremost art critics of the day and a recognized spokesman for the then-emerging New York School. She and Greenberg began a close relationship that continued until 1955. They traveled together extensively, to Madrid, Rome, Venice, and London, to look at old master paintings. Through him, she met Willem and Elaine de Kooning, Friedel Dzubas (with whom she shared a studio in 1952), Adolph Gottlieb, Franz Kline, Lee Krasner, Barnett Newman, Jackson Pollock, David Smith, and other leading members of the generation of artists who, as the 1950s unfolded, became nationally and internationally acclaimed as abstract expressionists. After separating from Greenberg, she met painter Robert Motherwell, whom she married in 1958 (they divorced in 1971).

Thrust into this heady milieu—New York was rapidly being acclaimed the new center of the international art world—the precocious Frankenthaler responded by producing a series of audacious paintings, among them *Mountains and Sea*, which she completed in October 1952, shortly before her twenty-fourth birthday.

Measuring more than nine feet wide and seven feet high, *Mountains and Sea* subscribed to the ambitious scale already associated with abstract expressionism, and it also featured the loose, gestural paint handling that was becoming a trademark of the New York School. New and indeed remarkable was Frankenthaler's application of her oil medium, which she thinned to the consistency of watercolor so that it would soak into and stain the canvas rather than accumulate on its surface. Inspired by Pollock's pouring and dripping of paint, as well as by the watercolors she herself had produced the previous summer, Frankenthaler's soak-stain technique enabled an entirely new experience of pictorial color: fresh, breathing, disembodied, exhilarating in its unfettered appeal to eyesight alone.

Its significance was immediately grasped by a number of artists who were searching for alternatives to abstract expressionism's (and especially de Kooning's) more physical approach to paint. Among them were the Washington, D.C.–based painters Morris Louis and Kenneth Noland, whom Greenberg took to Frankenthaler's studio in the spring of 1953. There they saw *Mountains and Sea* and were deeply impressed by it, and they returned to Washington determined to explore its technical implications. The color field painting that came to prominence during the later 1950s and 1960s, by Frankenthaler, Louis, Noland, Dzubas, and Jules Olitski, among many others, can be said to have had its origin at that moment. Referring to it, Louis later said of Frankenthaler, "She was a bridge between Pollock and what was possible." She made history before she was thirty years old.

Frankenthaler's first solo exhibition took place at the Tibor de Nagy Gallery, New York, in the fall of 1951. Since then she has enjoyed virtually countless exhibitions in this country and around the globe, and she has been honored by a series of retrospectives at some of America's most distinguished institutions: the Jewish Museum, New York, in 1960; the Whitney Museum of American Art, New York, 1969; the Sterling and Francine Clark Art Institute, Williamstown, Massachusetts, 1980 (prints); the Solomon R. Guggenheim Museum, New York, 1985 (works on paper); and the Museum of Modern Art, New York, 1989.

Her awards include First Prize for Painting, Premiere Biennale de Paris, 1959; Joseph E. Temple Gold Medal Award, Pennsylvania Academy of Fine Arts, 1968; Annual Creative Artist Laureate Award of American Jewish Congress, 1974; Extraordinary Woman of Achievement Award, National Conference of Christians and Jews, New York, 1978; New York City Mayor's Award of Honor for Arts and Culture, 1986; and Distinguished Artist Award for Lifetime Achievement, College Art Association, 1994.

She has received honorary degrees from Skidmore College (1969), Smith College (1973), Moore College of Art and Design (1974), Bard College (1976), Radcliffe College (1978), Amherst College (1979), New York University (1979), Harvard University (1980), Philadelphia College of Art (1980), Williams College (1980), Yale University (1981), Brandeis University (1982), University of Hartford (1983), and Syracuse University (1985).

She has served the following appointments: Fulbright Selection Committee, 1963 to 1965; trustee, Bennington College, 1967 to 1982; member of the American Academy and National Institute of Arts and Letters, 1974; and member of the Council on the Arts, 1985 to 1991. And she has lectured and conducted seminars at the School of Fine Arts, University of Pennsylvania (1967), Princeton University (1971), Bennington College (1972), Carpenter Center for the Visual Arts, Harvard University (1976), and the Skowhegan School of Painting and Sculpture, Maine (1986).

This is a remarkable record of personal and professional accomplishment as well as institutional recognition. That it extends unbroken from the moment Frankenthaler graduated from college to the present day is equally remarkable, maybe even unique among artists of her generation. Even more impressive, however, is the fact of its accomplishment by a woman, and particularly a woman of her generation. The New York art world of the 1950s and 1960s, the period when she evolved to maturity, was decidedly a man's world in which women occupied a marginal status at best. Few in number and virtually invisible when compared to their male counterparts, they exhibited less frequently, and they were generally excluded from the critical discourse of the day, for none was regarded as working on the "cutting edge." That was male territory, and that was the rule of the day. More specifically, the rule in the 1950s was articulated by critic Harold Rosenberg, a champion of de Kooning, who called for a muscular encounter between artist and medium and a no-holds-barred gestural painting. With the arrival of the 1960s, the rule had shifted, and Greenberg's voice was in ascendancy, calling for a more detached, cool, formal, and objective art—that is, not a battleground, but a sanctuary of contemplation.

Frankenthaler was exceptional in this setting. She showed regularly throughout both decades; in the 1950s with the highly respected Tibor de Nagy Gallery, and in the 1960s with the equally respected, but even more highly visible, Andre Emmerich Gallery. The reviews of her exhibitions were both regular and favorable. She enjoyed two New York retrospective exhibitions before the 1960s ended, at the Jewish

Museum and the Whitney Museum. Based on her talent and the personal resolve that her parents had encouraged, yet clearly within the terms of the male-dominated, institutional rules of the day, she had established for herself a career as an artist. Compared to the women artists around her, she was enormously successful, an exception to the rule that only men could occupy center stage in the New York art world. She demonstrated what was possible in a way Morris Louis never imagined.

More problematically, but at the same time more revealingly, she was also an exception in terms of the critical discourse of the day. Commenting on Frankenthaler's gesturalism in his review of her Whitney Museum retrospective, Rosenberg accused her of having never grasped "the moral and metaphysical basis of action painting," adding that "her compositions fail to develop resistances against which a creative act can take place." Commenting on Frankenthaler's soak-stain technique in his review of her Jewish Museum retrospective, Donald Judd, a follower of Greenberg's formalism, compared her to Pollock, in whom "the result is cool, tough and rigorous. It has implications of objectivity and, as alien as that is, Frankenthaler may eventually need a form of it to continue." These are astonishing conclusions. Frankenthaler did not grasp the basis on which the creative act could take place, and without objectivity she might be unable even to continue. Not physical enough on the one hand, not objective enough on the other, just like a woman—a woman, that is, defined stereotypically by the sexist male perspective of the 1950s and 1960s. Determined to define herself on her own terms and make art dictated from within that self, Frankenthaler risked being an exception to that rule. In doing so, she can be said to have proved it while also helping to bring it to its knees.

The rules and risks and possibilities mentioned by Frankenthaler were meant by the artist in reference to her art, to the traditions and conventions that are acknowledged or altered or discarded by it, to the unknown territory it opens before us and explores, to the deep significance of its creativity. Frankenthaler's art embodies all of this, but it could not do so in the absence of the exceptional human being behind it.

BIBLIOGRAPHY

O'Hara, Frank. *Helen Frankenthaler: Paintings.* Exhibition catalog, Jewish Museum, New York (1960); Rose, Barbara. *Frankenthaler,* 3d ed. (1979); Wilkin, Karen. *Frankenthaler: Works on Paper 1949–1984* (1984).

CARL BELZ

FRANKO, JEANNE (1855–1940)

Jeanne Franko, the distinguished violinist, pianist, and music teacher, was born in New Orleans, the second oldest of at least eight children of Hamman and Helene (Bergman) Franko, German Jews who had immigrated there before their marriage. Hamman's family name originally was Holländer—a distinguished German Jewish family of musicians that included the violinist Gustav and the composer Victor Hollander. Hamman was a successful jeweler in New Orleans. However, when the Union Army occupied the city in 1862, he was forced to flee and moved to Breslau, Germany, with his young family. He immediately provided for the musical education of his children. Franko studied violin with the greatest master of the time, Henri Vieuxtemps, who had played numerous concerts in New Orleans in the 1840s and 1850s; she also studied with Heinrich De Ahna, soon to become concertmaster of the Berlin Royal Orchestra. She made her debut in Paris before the age of fourteen. Upon returning to America in 1869, Jeanne, Selma (1853–1932), Sam (1857–1937), Rachel (b. 1860), and Nahan Franko (1861–1930) caused a sensation by performing as a family in New York's Steinway Hall on September 17—a concert repeated on October 24 at Terrace Garden in New York and in other cities including Washington, D.C., where the child Sousa heard them and later recalled his amazement at their feat. While all five children played the violin, Jeanne, Selma, and Sam also played the piano. During the ensuing seventeen years the siblings frequently performed together, usually with Jeanne as pianist and Rachel as soprano vocalist. The biggest event for Jeanne came on March 22, 1884, when she performed a concert at Steinway Hall in which she played virtuoso piano works by Liszt and Chopin and difficult violin works by Wieniawski and Vieuxtemps. Sam was highly regarded not only as a violinist but as conductor and composer. Nahan was concertmaster and conductor of the Metropolitan Opera Orchestra, and he played viola in the New York String Quartet, whose other members were Sam Franko and Charles P. Schmidt, violins, and Victor Herbert, cello. Selma married David Goldman, her first cousin and a fine amateur violinist, and their second son, Edwin, was the famous American bandmaster; later Selma was Jerome Kern's teacher. In 1888 another sister, Rose (Franko) Burden, accompanied Jeanne on the piano and in 1895 performed with Sam Franko.

After 1886 Jeanne rarely performed with her family. She appeared as violin soloist with orchestras led by Theodore Thomas, Anton Seidl, John Philip Sousa, and others, and in 1895 she founded the Jeanne

Franko Trio with Celia Schiller (piano) and Hans Kronold (cello), which played many public concerts during the next few years. During her professional career she toured to California, Texas, Chicago, St. Louis, and New Orleans, as well as Baltimore and Washington, D.C. She was a member (perhaps leader) of the Woman's String Orchestra of New York (founded in 1896 by Carl V. Lachmund), and she probably was also a member of the all-women's orchestra of the Women's Philharmonic Society of New York (founded in 1899 by Amy Fay's sister). But many of Jeanne's concerts were private musicales in homes or hotels, usually to raise money for charity, including Jewish causes. She spent the summer of 1907 in Germany, where she and Sam performed privately together for a noble family and where Sam discovered baroque music for his New York early music ensemble.

Meanwhile Jeanne was recognized as an important teacher of music in New York. As early as April 24, 1888, eleven of her pupils gave a concert in Steinway Hall, and similar events occurred during the next thirty years.

Franko was married to Hugo Kraemer, who predeceased her. They had no children. She died in New York City on December 3, 1940.

BIBLIOGRAPHY

AJYB (1904–1905): 95; Ammer, Christine. *Unsung: A History of Women in American Music* (1980); Franko, Jeanne. Clippings file. Music Division, New York Public Library; Franko, Nahan. Clippings file. Music Division, New York Public Library; Franko, Sam. *Chords and Discords* (1938); Jolly, Kirby Reid. "Edwin Franko Goldman and the Goldman Band." Ph.D. diss., New York University, 1971; *Musical America* 9 (July 27, 1907); 9 (October 5, 1907): 5; 13, no. 19 (March 18, 1911): 37; 13 (April 29, 1911): 26; 35, no. 13 (1940): 47; *Musical Courier* 24, no. 9 (March 2, 1892): 15; 24, no. 11 (March 16, 1892): 10; 24, no. 13 (March 30, 1892): 9; 30 (January 9, 1895): 34; 34 (January 13, 1897): 27; 34 (January 27, 1897): 23+; 34, no. 9 (March 3, 1897): 35; 34, no. 12 (March 24, 1897): 17; 35, no. 13 (September 29, 1897): 39; 84, no. 3 (1940): 32; Obituary. *NYTimes*, December 4, 1940, A27: 3.

JOHN BARON

FRANKS, BILHAH ABIGAIL LEVY (1688–1746)

No colonial American woman left a more engaging portrait of contemporary family, political, and social life than Bilhah "Abigail" Franks. Her letters to her son Naphtali in England, covering the years 1733–1748, discuss the lives of his growing siblings, political and social life in early eighteenth-century New York City, her extensive reading, and her love of good Scottish snuff. The letters also shed extraordinary insight into the efforts of colonial American Jews to establish a functional equilibrium between being Jewish and being part of the larger colonial Christian society.

Abigail Levy was born in London, the eldest of five children of German-Jewish immigrant Moses Raphael Levy and his first wife, Richea Asher. The family moved to New York City by 1695, and in 1712, Abigail Levy married London-born Jacob Franks, son of a German-Jewish merchant and broker in England. The Frankses had nine children, born between 1715 and 1742. The family was active in New York's Jewish life—they belonged to congregation Shearith Israel, where Jacob Franks was one of four men to lay the cornerstone of the new Mill Street synagogue in 1729 and where he served as *syndic* [president] in 1730—and they were active in broader Christian society, among whose women Franks counted her best friends. Franks reveled in the openness of New York society, rejoicing in the "Faire Charecter" the family enjoyed among both Christians and Jews. But the family never achieved the financial stability the Franks and Levy families had in England, and one by one, beginning around 1732, Jacob and Abigail sent their children to England in order to prosper. Abigail Franks probably never saw her adult children again after their departure, or any of her English grandchildren. For the remainder of her life, the exchange of letters, painted portraits, and small gifts were the only contacts she had with them.

Thirty-seven letters of the Franks family are known to survive, dating from May 7, 1733, to October 30, 1748. All are addressed to Naphtali Franks in England. Thirty-four are from Abigail, one is from Jacob, and two are written by his brother David. They discuss local politics, family and community activities, and aspects of the Franks family's trans-Atlantic business. But Abigail Franks's letters are most significant as an early American Jewish woman's extended thoughts on the fit and fate of Judaism in colonial New York.

Franks worked diligently to raise her children as practicing Jews. Daughters and sons received instruction in Hebrew, and the family practiced traditional Judaism, honoring the Sabbath, keeping kosher, and keeping the Jewish holidays. Franks urged Naphtali in England to keep up with his morning devotions and cautioned him to avoid nonkosher food, warning him off even his uncle's table. But Franks was also critical of much in Judaism. In the open air of colonial America, and likely under the influence of the broad range of philosophers and novelists she read—among her favorite authors were Pope, Fielding, Smollett, Dryden, Montesquieu, Addison, and *Gentleman's Magazine*, all supplied to her by Naphtali—she yearned for a Calvin or a Luther to reform what she deemed Judaism's worst superstitions. She was scathing in her critique of the New York Jewish community, calling its ladies a "Stupid Set of people" and despairing about the pool of Jewish suitors available for her daughters.

But the costs of such ambiguities were high. With a limited pool of Jewish marriage prospects, Franks's disdain for most of them, and the entire Franks family's desire to be part of the larger New York community, it was perhaps inevitable that two of her children would take non-Jewish spouses. Oldest daughter Phila was the first. In the fall of 1742, Phila secretly married Oliver de Lancey, son of a prominent and successful Huguenot New York merchant family. For six months they kept the match secret, but in the spring of 1743, Phila announced the deed and went to live with her husband. Abigail's letters to Naphtali spoke of her sense of betrayal and her pain, and she never spoke to Phila again. And Abigail's daughter Richa, tutored in secular and Jewish studies like all her sisters and brothers, bears the brunt of Phila's defection. She will remain in her parents' house through her middle age, moving to England and marrying only after her father's death.

This was not the last hurt Abigail would feel. Son David married Margaret Evans, a Christian daughter of one of Abigail's close friends. Her younger children seem never to have married at all. Even sons Naphtali and Moses, who married their English first cousins, watched as all of their own grandchildren left the Jewish faith. Of Jacob and Abigail Franks's more than two dozen grandchildren, not one of them appears to have passed on Judaism to his or her descendants.

Other family connections were complex as well. Franks's father, widowed in 1716, married Grace Mears in 1718, with whom he had seven children. Franks despised her stepmother and spared no insult in her prose. But when Grace Levy, left a widow with many young children in 1728, made a bad remarriage in 1735, Franks's assessments of her shifted. Through Franks's letters a rare portrait of a widowed colonial Jewish woman emerges—of Grace Mears Levy Hays as female shopkeeper who singlehandedly supported and raised her young family, survived a deeply unhappy second marriage, and died brokenhearted, too young, and finally admired by her oldest stepdaughter.

Franks's letters also draw a portrait of another early Jewish woman: Grace Levy's oldest daughter, Rachel Levy. Beloved by all members of the extended Levy-Franks family, Rachel married Isaac Mendes Seixas in 1740, a decidedly mixed marriage between New York's leading Ashkenazi and Sephardi families. Franks described the Seixas clan as being in an uproar over the match, and many of them avoided the wedding. Rachel and Isaac removed themselves to New Jersey, where they ran a small country store, and Franks eventually relented in their favor, too. Rachel and Isaac Seixas had eight children; the fourth, Gershom Mendes Seixas, became the eighteenth century's most prominent hazan [religious leader] of Shearith Israel, in his person—and in part through the Levy-Franks family—unifying the many vying strains within the colonial New York community.

Women in the Franks-Levy Family Portrait Series

The Franks-Levy family portraits, oil paintings still in their original frames, are the oldest surviving portraits of colonial American Jews and the oldest family-series portraits to survive in all of American painting. The series consists of seven paintings: Moses Raphael Levy (1665–1728); his second wife Grace Mears Levy (1694–1740); Bilhah Abigail Levy Franks (1688–1746), Moses's oldest child by his first wife Richea Asher Levy; and Abigail's husband Jacob Franks (1688–1769). Three portraits of five of the nine children of Abigail and Jacob Franks complete the series.

Probably executed in the late 1720s and mid-1730s, and attributed by present scholars to Gerardus Duyckinck (1695–1746), the paintings look to English aristocratic models for their costume, background, and pose. The portraits convey signs of a well-established, mercantile family consciously placing itself within the conventions of English portraiture and colonial British society. No symbol, no gesture, no prop identifies these people as Jews.

The four portraits reproduced here are:

1. Bilhah Abigail Levy Franks [American Jewish Historical Society]
2. Grace Mears Levy [Museum of the City of New York. Bequest of Alphonse H. Kursheedt.]
3. Phila Franks [American Jewish Historical Society]
4. Probably David and Richa Franks [American Jewish Historical Society]

1.

2.

3.

4.

Abigail Franks portrays herself primarily as a parent. She doted on her children, referring to Naphtali as "Heartsey," a play on the symbol for the Hebrew tribe of Naphtali [hart], and on "heart"/love itself. She adored her daughters and thrilled to the youngest ones born when she was in her forties. Her letters are full of the pain of her children's departures from her, and she struggles throughout her long correspondence between rejoicing in her offsprings' successes and the ache of never seeing them again. Her correspondence ends where it begins, concluding that a good name, upright behavior, and harmony within the family are the greatest achievements any family can attain.

Abigail Franks's letters are rare testimony to the lived efforts to sustain and adapt Judaism within the realities of Christian New York. Franks's deeply intelligent prose provides a rare example of the first-person views and experiences of an early American Jewish woman, as described in intimate conversation with her son.

BIBLIOGRAPHY

Franks Family. Papers. American Jewish Historical Society, Waltham, Mass.; Hershkowitz, Leo, and Isidore S. Meyer, eds. *Letters of the Franks Family (1733–1748)* (1968); Smith, Ellen. "Portraits of a Community: The Image and Experience of Early American Jews." In *Facing the New World: Portraits of Jews in Colonial and Federal America* (1997).

ELLEN SMITH

FRANKS, REBECCA (1760–1823)

This admired, beautiful, vivacious, intelligent member of the affluent and influential Franks family is a noted figure in Jewish colonial history. She is remembered as one of the young women who warmly greeted British officers of General William Howe's army during their occupation of Philadelphia in 1776. Probably few of these officers realized that her father, David Franks, was Jewish, though married to Margaret Evans, a member of an established Philadelphia Quaker family, or that her grandfather, Jacob Franks, was a prominent merchant who had been *parnas* [president] of New York's Congregation Shearith Israel.

Rebecca Franks was born in 1760 in Philadelphia and raised as a Christian, as was her elder sister, Abigail, named after her father's mother. Abigail married Andrew Hamilton, an attorney general and acting governor of Pennsylvania. Her first cousin was Phila Franks, wife of General Oliver de Lancey, a Loyalist and representative of New York's Anglican aristocracy.

Perhaps due to the openness of colonial society, Rebecca Franks's Jewish background seemingly mattered little to those who knew her. In 1775, Major John André painted a portrait of her in miniature accompanied by lines of poetry. On May 14, 1778, just before the British departed, Philadelphia's grand ball, "the Meschianza," was held, full of color and pageantry. There, in all her radiance, was Miss Rebecca Franks, one of the "Queens of Beauty," in her polonaise dress of white silk lace, her hair adorned with shimmering jewels. It was a scene indelibly etched in the city's history.

Society, manners, and dress were always of great interest to her. On a visit with her father to New York, then also under British rule, she compared the virtues of New York women to those of her own city. The former have more of a "sweet countenance and an agreeable smile," but were duller, if not more stupid, and too eager to throw themselves at men, she wrote in a letter dated August 10, 1781, from Flatbush, Long Island. Her own education was informal; there were few public schools, and she likely had a private tutor.

Her father was a member of the Pennsylvania Assembly in 1748, and a commissary agent for the British army before and during the Revolution and for Congress during the war. Apparently, he remained loyal to the British cause, and found himself accused of aiding the British. Eventually, in 1780, he was ordered out of the state. Rebecca seemed little affected by these events. Though she might have written a Loyalist poem, she was also a good friend of American General Charles Lee, who subtly at times reminded her of her Jewishness.

Attention was paid to her by another English officer, and on January 17, 1782, she married a noted lieutenant colonel who later became General Sir Henry Johnson. He had been in the command of the British garrison at Stony Point, New York, but was forced to surrender the post in 1779. The couple soon left for England. Her father followed at almost the same time. A number of years later, Lady Rebecca Johnson recalled what might have been, "I have gloried in my rebel countrymen . . . Would to God I, too, had been a patriot." She said nothing about her Jewish heritage.

In fact, by the end of the eighteenth century, the Franks family ceased any such connection. One reason might be found in the skepticism, if not open hostility, to institutional religion expressed by her grandmother, ABIGAIL FRANKS, a daughter of the Enlightenment, who found organized religions, especially Judaism and Catholicism, in great need of reform. Her secularism probably influenced her son

David, her other children, and possibly grandchildren. Of David Frank's five children, four married non-Jews and one did not marry. Two of his children were baptized. Rebecca Franks, though not baptized, was surely more at home in the non-Jewish world than that of her grandfather.

She died on February 13, 1823, in Bath, England. Her husband, Sir Henry, died in 1835. They had two children, Sir Henry Allen and George Pigot. Henry Allen married Charlotte Philipse, a member of the prominent New York family. They had thirteen children. Five became generals, two were colonels, and one a captain—all in the British army.

Was Rebecca Franks Jewish? Her mother was not; her grandmother was. Franks herself seems never to have raised the question and moved easily among British officers and in Christian society. Yet there remained a tradition, a memory, and, despite herself, she has always been considered one of the daughters of Israel.

BIBLIOGRAPHY

BDEAJ; Friedman, Lee M. *Jewish Pioneers and Patriots* (1943); Griswold, Rufus W. *The Republican Court* (1856); Hershkowitz, Leo, and Isidore S. Meyer, eds. *The Letters of the Franks Family, 1733–1748* (1968); *JE*; Johnson, Henry P. *The Storming of Stony Point, July 15, 1779* (1900); Marcus, Jacob R. *The Colonial American Jew, 1492–1776* (1970); *NAW*; *PAJHS* 11:184–186; Stern, Malcolm H. *Americans of Jewish Descent* (1960); *UJE*; Wolfe, Edwin, and Maxwell Whiteman. *The History of the Jews of Philadelphia from Colonial Times to the Age of Jackson* (1957).

LEO HERSHKOWITZ

FREEMAN, CYNTHIA (c. 1915–1988)

Cynthia Freeman (Beatrice Cynthia Freeman Feinberg) began her writing career at age fifty-five, publishing her first book, *A World Full of Strangers*, in 1975. The book became an instant best-seller and sold over one million copies. Quite an accomplishment for a woman who quit school in the sixth grade, married at age eighteen, had two children, and worked as an interior decorator for twenty-five years.

She was born around 1915 in New York City to Albert C. and Sylvia Jeannette (Hack) Freeman. The family moved to San Francisco when she was six months old. After Freeman dropped out of school, her well-educated English mother became her tutor. At age fifteen, Freeman attended the University of California at Berkeley, auditing the courses that interested her. Three years later, she married Herbert Feinberg, her grandmother's doctor, who was fifteen years her senior. The couple had two children, Sheldon and Arlene.

Although Freeman always had a love of writing, she never seriously considered it as a career until she suffered a debilitating five-year illness beginning when she was fifty years old. To keep herself occupied, she wrote *A World Full of Strangers*, a multigenerational saga centered around a Jew from New York's Lower East Side who not only concealed his ethnic identity from his son, but also engaged in acts of anti-Semitism. Despite negative reviews, the reading public responded enthusiastically to the novel.

Freeman's subsequent novels were equally successful. By 1980, she had completed *Fairytales* (1977), *The Days of Winter* (1978), *Portraits* (1979), and *Come Pour the Wine* (1980). These novels were also criticized as being simpleminded romances with one-dimensional characters and overly dramatic and unbelievable plots. Still, one critic gave Freeman credit for her compulsively readable writing style and for creating characters that her readers really cared about.

A central theme running through most of Freeman's novels is the struggle of Jewish immigrants to assimilate to American life while at the same time maintaining Jewish traditions. Freeman's work was influenced by her family's closeness and by her concern for the continuation of Jewish life and culture.

Her life was not all fame and good fortune; she also experienced personal tragedies. Her husband developed Alzheimer's disease. In 1985, her daughter died in an automobile accident, followed by her mother's death a few months later. The following year, her husband died. For Freeman, writing became a way to escape the pain.

Her novel *No Time for Tears* (1981) is considered her most ambitious work. Critics agreed that the book was not only a generational saga, but also a portrayal of the quest for a Jewish state in Palestine through the lives of the characters.

In the 1980s, Freeman also wrote *Catch the Gentle Dawn* (1983), *Illusions of Love* (1984), *Seasons of the Heart* (1986), and *The Last Princess* (1987).

On October 22, 1988, she died of cancer. She is remembered as a best-selling author of popular romances during the 1970s and 1980s. Assertive, upbeat, intelligent, and ambitious, Freeman had these inspiring words to say in an interview with *Parade* magazine in 1985: "All of us are gifted in some unique way. . . . Imagination is forever young, dreams don't turn gray. And remember, a royalty check never hurt either."

SELECTED WORKS BY CYNTHIA FREEMAN

Catch the Gentle Dawn (1983); *Come Pour the Wine* (1980); *The Days of Winter* (1978); *Fairytales* (1977); *Illusions of Love* (1984); *The Last Princess* (1987); *No Time for Tears* (1981); *Portraits* (1979); *Seasons of the Heart* (1986); *A World Full of Strangers* (1975).

BIBLIOGRAPHY

Collins, Glenn. "Cynthia Freeman Is Dead at 73: Writer of Best-Selling Romances." *NYTimes*, October 26, 1988, B12; *Contemporary Authors*. Vols. 81–84 (1962–): 165; *Contemporary Authors*, New Revision Series. Vol. 29 (1981–): 137–138; Lawson, Carol. "Behind the Bestsellers: Cynthia Freeman." *Washington Post*, April 3, 1980; *Los Angeles Times Book Review*, December 20, 1981, and February 21, 1988; *NYTimes Book Review*, November 22, 1981; Obituaries. *Chicago Tribune*, October 27, 1988, and *Los Angeles Times*, October 27, 1988; *Publishers Weekly*, May 30, 1977; Ramsdell, Kristin. *Happily Ever After: A Guide to Reading Interests in Romance Fiction* (1987); Stix, Harriet. "Novelist Cynthia Freeman: It's Never Too Late." *Los Angeles Times*, June 12, 1986, sec. 5, pp. 6–7; *Washington Post Book World*, November 28, 1980.

ILENE COHEN

FREIBERG, STELLA HEINSHEIMER (1862–1962)

A memorial in the *American Israelite* newspaper remembered Stella Heinsheimer Freiberg as a woman whose "piety was never stuffy, and revealed itself in endless good deeds." Two causes absorbed most of Freiberg's energy: helping the arts flourish in her hometown of Cincinnati, Ohio, and furthering the growth of Reform Judaism—and the role of women in it—in the United States and Western Europe.

Freiberg was born in Cincinnati on November 29, 1862, to Louis and Emma (Goodhart) Heinsheimer. Louis Heinsheimer, born in Germany, was a partner in a prosperous Cincinnati cotton brokerage firm with J.H. Goodhart, whose daughter Emma would become his wife. The Heinsheimer family had a long history of involvement in the institutions of Reform Judaism. Louis Heinsheimer had been a member of the executive board of the Union of American Hebrew Congregations (UAHC) since its inception in 1873. One of Stella's older brothers, Edward, enrolled in the first class of students at the Reform Hebrew Union College in 1875, and later became the second president of the college's board of governors.

Stella was the second-youngest of six children. Like her siblings, she received her education from Cincinnati's public schools. After high school, she attended the College of Music at the University of Cincinnati. A member of the college's first graduating class, she was certified as a music teacher in 1880.

In 1894, at age twenty-three, she married J. Walter Freiberg, who was a partner in Freiberg and Workum, Distillers. He was the son of a prominent German Jewish Cincinnati businessman who cofounded the distillery. The Freibergs, like the Heinsheimers, had a long history of involvement with the Cincinnati-based Reform Movement. Stella and J. Walter Freiberg had one child, Julius, who became a manufacturer of machinery and a member of the executive board of the UAHC. From 1911 until his death in 1921, J. Walter Freiberg served as president of the UAHC, an office that both his father and father-in-law had held. During her husband's tenure as president, Stella helped to found the NATIONAL FEDERATION OF TEMPLE SISTERHOODS (NFTS), a women's agency within the UAHC. She served as national vice president of the NFTS from its founding in 1913 until 1923, and worked on numerous national committees, including the Committee on Sabbath Schools and the National War Emergency Committee.

Freiberg was also one of the ten women who founded the Cincinnati Symphony Orchestra in 1894 (another was Mrs. Charles P. Taft, sister-in-law of the president), and served as the first vice president of its board of directors. Because of her affiliation with the symphony, her home became a salon for great musicians of the era. She hosted, among others, George Gershwin, Arthur Rubinstein, and Leonard Bernstein. Freiberg herself "scribbled" music for the piano, but she never published it.

After her husband's death, Stella Freiberg became even more active in civic and Jewish life. In 1923, she became president of the NFTS, a position she held until 1929. One of her most significant acts as president was to strongly endorse the proposal that the UAHC and NFTS join the World Union for Progressive Judaism (WUPJ). She especially advocated the presence of women at WUPJ conferences and urged that women be given a voice in the proceedings. She was also instrumental in securing scholarships for European students who wished to study for the Reform rabbinate at Hebrew Union College.

On a local level, Freiberg was a member of the board of directors of both the Cincinnati Section of the NATIONAL COUNCIL OF JEWISH WOMEN and of the Jewish Social Agencies of Cincinnati. In 1923, she donated a gymnasium to Hebrew Union College and helped raise funds for its dormitory. In 1945, she received an honorary doctorate from the college in recognition of her numerous contributions to the school and to the Reform Movement at large.

In 1956, Freund-Rosenthal was elected national president of Hadassah. During her four-year tenure, Hadassah built and dedicated its new medical center at Ein Karem, in Jerusalem, Israel. Freund-Rosenthal was instrumental in persuading Marc Chagall to design and execute the twelve stained-glass windows symbolizing the twelve tribes of Israel for the hospital synagogue, which have come to be known as the "Chagall Windows." After leaving the presidency, she held other board posts, including the chair of Education, Zionist Affairs, *Hadassah Magazine*, two Youth Survey committees, and nongovernmental representative to the United Nations.

She continued her scholarly pursuits as well, becoming a founding member of the World Bible Society and delivering a paper, "Medicine and the Hebraic Tradition," at the twenty-fifth International Orientalist Congress in Moscow in 1960.

In 1968, her husband, Milton Freund, died of a heart attack. In 1974, she married Harry Rosenthal and moved to his home in St. Paul, Minnesota. Together they created an educational endowment fund for National Hadassah, which has sponsored educational seminars. Even in her upper eighties, she spearheaded the compilation and editing of *A Tapestry of Hadassah Memories*, a collection of interviews and memoirs of Hadassah leaders.

**SELECTED WORKS BY
MIRIAM FREUND-ROSENTHAL**

In My Lifetime: Family, Community, Zion (1989); *Jewish Merchants of Colonial New York* (1939); *A Tapestry of Hadassah Memories*, editor with Lonye Rasch (1989).

BIBLIOGRAPHY

EJ.

ROSELYN BELL

A lifelong HADASSAH *leader and a scholar, Miriam Freund-Rosenthal credits her mother Rebecca Kottler,
Hadassah founder* HENRIETTA SZOLD, *and first lady Eleanor Roosevelt with influencing her life.
She is shown here receiving the "Mother of Israel" citation from Roosevelt. From left to right are*
BERTHA SCHOOLMAN, *Freund-Rosenthal, ER, and Moshe Kol. The presentation took place
at the Youth Aliyah Conference in New York City in 1960. [Hadassah Archives]*

FRIEDAN, BETTY (b. 1921)

Activist and writer Betty Friedan is one of the most influential feminist leaders of the second half of the twentieth century, having founded the National Organization for Women (NOW) and presided as its first president. She is considered by many to be the "mother" of the second wave of modern feminism. She has been on the boards of leading women's organizations, fought for legislation to ensure women's equality, and written books analyzing women's role in society and the women's movement.

Bettye Naomi Goldstein was born on February 4, 1921, in Peoria, Illinois. Her father owned a jewelry store, and her mother had given up her position at the local paper to raise her family. She attended Smith College, majoring in psychology and editing the college newspaper. Under her stewardship, the paper became a forum for the fight against fascism abroad and in favor of union organizing at home. She graduated summa cum laude in 1942.

She became a psychology research fellow at the University of California in Berkeley for a year after graduation, before moving to New York to work as a reporter. There, she became involved in labor union activity, working for union publications as a labor journalist and pamphlet writer and showing a keen interest in working women's issues. In 1947, she married Carl Friedan, who would later become an advertising executive. She continued working after her first child was born, but was forced to leave her job during her second pregnancy in 1953. She thus spent the next decade raising her two sons and a daughter. She continued to be a writer, this time for middle-class women's magazines.

In 1957, she surveyed two hundred of her Smith College classmates and found that many of them suffered from "the problem that has no name." They were supposed to be happy in their suburban paradises, with working husband and smiling children, but many were bored, depressed, and anxious. She delved further, not satisfied by the women's explanation that their unhappiness was their own fault. She received widespread response to an article she published in *Good Housekeeping* (September 1960) entitled "Women Are People Too!" and realized that the malaise she found was not limited to women from prestigious eastern colleges.

The result of her inquiries was her book *The Feminine Mystique*, which both labeled the resurgent domestic ideology of the postwar era and exposed those who perpetuated it: women's magazines, advertising experts, Freudian psychologists, social scientists, and educators. Her critique of the romanticization of

When The Feminine Mystique *was published in 1963, it shattered popular beliefs about the roles of men and women in American society and was an instant best-seller. Betty Friedan has spent much of her subsequent life dealing with the fallout, good and bad, of that groundbreaking book. [Bettye Lane]*

domesticity led to a feminist explosion, launching the sex-role revolution. Published in 1963, it was an immediate best-seller, making Friedan a celebrity. It has sold over two million copies, was translated into a dozen languages, and still sells thousands of copies a year. In 1976, a New York literary club included it, along with works by Galileo, Marx, and Mao Zedong, in its exhibit "Books as Troublemakers," about books that stirred millions of people and changed their lives. Despite its popularity, the book caused her personal troubles. Her children were ostracized from car pools, and she and her husband were no longer invited to their friends' dinner party circle. She realized that she was too threatening to other mothers who had not yet come to terms with their own lives.

In *The Feminine Mystique*, Friedan described a depression that afflicted many middle-aged, college-educated women, and she suggested its cause. She argued that the media and educators had created an image of women's proper role as appendages of their husbands and children: "as Tom's wife or Mary's mother." The effect of this "feminine mystique" was that women denied their own desires for the sake of familial harmony. Their lack of excitement about their own lives made them smother their children and cling to their husbands. Thus, on a familial level, they were bored and ineffectual.

On a societal level, the result was to stifle women's growth, waste massive human potential, and cause immense dissatisfaction among women, as well as among their families. At a time when more and more women were entering the workplace as working mothers, Friedan argued that women should not accept their inferior status at home or in the work force. By accepting limitations in their public roles, they would also fail in their private roles. She called for women's self-assertion, for women's equality in the workplace and in the home. By defining women's problems as broad and structural rather than personal, she has been credited with getting women to understand their position in society.

Friedan went on to found NOW, originally a gathering of three hundred women and men, mainly professionals, in 1966 and to become its first president until 1970. NOW's statement of purpose attacked "the traditional assumption that a woman has to choose between marriage and motherhood on the one hand and serious participation in industry or the professions on the other." NOW sought an end to job discrimination through legislation, education, and court action. It also lobbied for paid maternity leaves, the establishment of child care facilities, the legalization of abortion, and the Equal Rights Amendment to the Constitution that would prohibit discrimination on the basis of sex. Friedan declined to run for president of NOW in 1970 due to her feeling that the organization's rejection of men as members and its insistence on equal rights for lesbians was too radical.

Friedan continued to write and lecture on the subject of women's equality while she taught at New York University and the New School for Social Research. She divorced in 1969, the year she helped found the National Abortion Rights Action League. In 1970, she organized a nationwide Women's Strike

for Equality in which forty to fifty thousand women marched down Fifth Avenue in New York City to show that the women's movement had a broad and powerful base. A year later, she convened the National Women's Political Caucus (NWPC), along with BELLA ABZUG and Shirley Chisholm. With the motto, "Make policy, not coffee," she hoped to galvanize women into running for office, to get women elected to office, and to get them seated as delegates in the national conventions. Moreover, the NWPC rallied support for the Equal Rights Amendment. Friedan insisted that women should have a voice in the political process. All along, she advocated women's rights within the Democratic Party and played a role in getting the Democratic Party to reserve half of its delegate slots for women in 1976.

In 1975, Friedan was named Humanist of the Year by the American Humanist Association, and she received an honorary doctorate of humane letters from her alma mater, Smith College. She also was elected to the national board of the Girl Scouts. Since then she has received numerous honorary doctorates of humane letters and law. In 1976, she published *It Changed My Life*. By that time, her message had appeared in such diverse publications as the *New York Times Magazine*, *Woman's Day*, *Redbook*, *The New Republic*, *Ladies' Home Journal*, *Harper's*, *Social Policy*, *Cosmopolitan*, *Family Circle*, and *McCall's*, where she had a regular column in the early 1970s entitled "Betty Friedan's Notebook."

It Changed My Life: Writings on the Women's Movement was a collection of her previous essays, talks, and some of her *McCall's* columns, with comments to bring them up to date. Here she voiced her concerns with the direction that the women's movement seemed to be taking, and described some of the disputes within its leadership. She worried that sexual politics, including issues of sexuality, lesbianism, and "random hatred of men," was "highly dangerous and diversionary," and that "no serious meaningful action emerges from a sexual emphasis. There is simply talk, anger, and wallowing." She feared such an emphasis would alienate "everywoman," and would detract from real action in offices, classrooms, and political arenas. Although she admitted to the validity of the statement "If they succeed in scaring us with words like 'dyke'. . . they'll have won. AGAIN. They'll have divided us. AGAIN," she responded: "Lesbian rights as one issue among many on the agenda of the women's movement is one thing—lesbian rights as the main issue, the hallmark is something else. . . . As an expression of sexual preference, to each her own. But as a political statement, it's a copout."

Her book *The Second Stage* was developed while teaching as a visiting professor of sociology at Temple University, Yale University, the New School, and Queens College of the City University of New York. In this book, Friedan recognized the powerful forces aligned against feminism, but she focused on how the movement itself had gone astray. She defined the "first stage" of feminism as women's "full participation" or "power and voice in the mainstream" (inside the party, the political process, the professions, and the business world); recognition of women's personhood; and women's control over their own bodies (what she called a "woman's right to choose motherhood in dignified, supportive circumstances"). It was time, she argued, for the women's movement to enter its "second stage," a coming to "new terms with the family—new terms with love and with work." She maintained that women, "helped by men," needed to transcend the battle for equal power within institutions. They needed to restructure the institutions themselves, while simultaneously transforming the nature of power. She demanded child care programs, parental leaves, and flexible work hours, and insisted that she was not *for* abortion, but for the choice to have children.

She voiced her ongoing discomfort with new feminist ideologies, argued for more balance within the women's movement itself, and blamed radical elements in the movement who, she worried, being distracted by sexual politics (whether around issues of pornography or lesbian rights), were ignoring the real needs of most women for family and nurturing. She insisted that for the founding mothers of the women's movement "equality and the personhood of women never meant destruction of the family, repudiation of marriage and motherhood, or implacable sexual war with men." She wrote that the women's movement did "not fail in the battle for equality. Our failure was our blind spot about the family." In fact, she worried that a new "feminist mystique" would keep women out of the home, repudiating the family and alienating young women who hoped to balance public lives with domesticity and motherhood.

She was criticized by many feminists for this book, which some felt erased race issues and sexual complexities while blaming the victims, women. Although Friedan had made more public, supportive statements about lesbians since 1977, the book failed to see, wrote Catherine Stimpson in a 1981 *Ms.* article, "how queer bashing is the Red baiting of this decade." Friedan wanted lesbianism in a private, not public place, "brushing it all back into the closet." Friedan stuck to her guns, however: "The recent lead-

ership [of NOW] did not like my book," she said in an interview. "I was right. And I was addressing it at them."

In 1975, 1980, and 1985, Friedan attended the International Women's Conferences sponsored by the United Nations. In 1988, she became a distinguished visiting professor at the University of Southern California's journalism school and its Institute for the Study of Women and Men. She was also a visiting professor at New York University and did research for her next book on aging at the Center for Social Science at Columbia University, the Center for Population Research at Harvard University, and the Andrus Gerontology Center at the University of Southern California.

Friedan's *Fountain of Age*, published in 1993, defined and decried the "age mystique," much as Friedan's first book had attacked the feminine mystique. The age mystique is one in which age "is perceived only as decline or deterioration from youth," and its victims are "rendered helpless, childlike and deprived of human identity or activities," so that they "don't remind us of ourselves." In her book, she admitted to her own denial and fear of age as she attempted to overturn the tendency of experts to treat age only in terms of pathology. Instead, she saw aging as yet another stage for growth, a time for "new qualities and strengths" to emerge. She used her feminist analysis to ask whether, as women's definition of themselves changed from their biological role (as mothers and sexual partners to men) to asserting their full personhood (via feminism), their aging changed too. Simultaneously, she worried about younger women "dressed for success," living and dying "like men." She wondered whether the larger perspectives of women could "change the very biology of the aging process."

She noticed that the polarization between men and women, between the "masculine" and "feminine" sides of personalities, softened in aging. Women, however, made the transition more easily, which may explain, in part, why they live longer. For herself, aging meant her "liberation from the power politics of the women's movement." She "recognized my own compelling need now to transcend the war between the sexes, the no-win battles of women as a whole sex, oppressed victims, against men as a whole sex, the oppressors. . . . The unexpectedness of this new quest has been my adventure into age."

Friedan continues to write and fight. She worries that, with recession and sexual backlash, there will be increasing polarization and a new feminine mystique, a new attempt to send women home again. She sees the portents of this in short skirts and high heels; in the 1986 Yale-Harvard study interpreted to imply that if women did not marry before age thirty they would have a better chance of being killed by a terrorist than of finding a mate; in the "self-help" books showing women how to "get their man"; and in the many films in which women are put in "their place." In fact, she argues that women's image in the media is more and more divergent from the truth, a "blind spot—a symbolic annihilation" of the gains women have really made. Moreover, she fears that economic bad times will scapegoat women, that "downsizing" industries may send women back home "where they belong" to raise children. Her prescription for the future is for the women's movement to fight for a whole "domestic agenda": child care, health care, housing, jobs. Finally, she continues to insist that women should fight next to men. It should not be feminism against men or feminism against the family. "We need a new political movement of women and men toward a new society."

SELECTED WORKS BY BETTY FRIEDAN

The Feminine Mystique (1963); *The Fountain of Age* (1993); *It Changed My Life* (1976); *The Second Stage* (1981).

BIBLIOGRAPHY

American Social Leaders; DAB; Eisenstein, Zillah. "Friedan's Liberal 'Feminist Mystique' and the Changing Politics of NOW." In Eisenstein, *The Radical Future of Liberal Feminism* (1981); *EJ* (1983–1985); *Encyclopedia of American Biography;* Horowitz, Daniel. "Rethinking Betty Friedan and *The Feminine Mystique*: Labor Union Radicalism and Feminism in Cold War America." *American Quarterly* 48, no. 1 (March 1996): 1–42; *Life* 11 (February 1988): 96–98; *Los Angeles Times,* February 24, 1992, E, 2:2.

MARION KAPLAN

FRIEDENWALD, JANE (1847–1923)

Jane Friedenwald, the daughter of German Jews and connected through marriage to one of the most prominent German Jewish families in Baltimore, was a valuable member of the new American Jewish aristocracy. She dispensed charity, created and supported American Jewish institutions, bettered herself intellectually and culturally, and raised her children to honor the family name and legacy.

She was born in Manchester, England, in 1847, to German Jewish immigrants Fannie and Julius Ahlborn. Several years later, the family moved to Dublin, where Jane received her education, and in 1863, the family moved to St. Louis, Missouri. Shortly after coming to the United States, the seventeen-year-old Jane Ahlborn met Moses Friedenwald, twelve years her senior, who was the first American-born son of Merle and Jonas Friedenwald of Baltimore. The following year, Jane and Moses were married. Several years later, they moved to Baltimore, where they spent the remainder of their lives.

Early on, the Friedenwald family had established itself as a pillar of Baltimore Jewry. Emigrating from Germany in 1831 with his wife and five children, Jonas Friedenwald began a business as an umbrella merchant, and in time became a successful hardware merchant. He was one of the founders of the Hebrew Assistance Society, the Hebrew Orphan Asylum, the Hebrew Free Burial Society, and the Orthodox Congregation Chizuk Emmunah. His son Aaron and three of Aaron's five sons became prominent Baltimore physicians. All of Jonas and Merle's children, and many of their grandchildren, were active in Jewish and general philanthropic causes and institutions.

Jane Friedenwald, who was variously described by those who knew her as brilliant, a true critic and splendid conversationalist, dainty, and slightly haughty, became a respected member of the Baltimore Friedenwalds. Her husband, with his brother Joseph and two brothers-in-law, established one of the largest wholesale clothing businesses in the country, Moses Weisenfeld and Company. Jane Friedenwald channeled her wealth and social standing into Jewish communal activities, serving as a charter member of the American Jewish Historical Society, the Jewish Publication Society, and the Jewish Theological Seminary. She was an active philanthropist, giving money and works of art to Jewish and cultural institutions, such as the National Museum in Washington, D.C., to which she donated forty items from her African art collection. She also devoted considerable time and effort to helping indigent and sick Jews in Baltimore.

The Friedenwalds were politically active during the Civil War, all except Aaron supporting the Confederate cause. Physically broken by his efforts during the war, Moses became an invalid and remained sickly for the remaining twenty-four years of his life. After he died in 1889, Jane Friedenwald continued as the family matriarch, engaging in philanthropic activities, serving on the boards of Jewish institutions, and socializing with prominent Jewish lay leaders and professionals. Among her acquaintances were the Szolds of Lombard Street and the social and medical elite of Baltimore. Her daughter, RACIE ADLER, married the eminent scholar Cyrus Adler in 1905. Friedenwald's other two daughters also married notable Jewish

Baltimoreans: the eldest daughter, Belle, married a Belmont, while Merle married Henry Hamburger.

Friedenwald's son Herbert earned a Ph.D. from the University of Pennsylvania and became the first superintendent of the manuscript department at the Library of Congress in Washington. He devoted himself to the study of early American history and to Jewish communal work, serving as the editor of *The American Jewish Year Book* and the first secretary of the American Jewish Historical Society. He also established the Friedenwald Foundation for the Promotion of Higher Learning in memory of his parents.

Jane Friedenwald died in Baltimore on April 13, 1923, at age seventy-six.

BIBLIOGRAPHY

Adler, Cyrus. *I Have Considered the Days* (1941); Berney, Albert. "Obituary." *Papers of the American Jewish Historical Society* 29: 165–167; Blum, Isador. *The Jews of Baltimore* (1910); *EJ*, s.v. "Adler, Cyrus"; Fein, Isaac M. "Baltimore Jews During the Civil War." *American Jewish Historical Quarterly* 60, no. 2 (December 1961): 84–91; Friedenwald, Harry. *Life, Letters and Addresses of Aaron Friedenwald* (1906); Glushakow, Abraham D. *A Pictorial History of Maryland Jewry* (1955); *JE*, s.v. "Adler, Cyrus," and s.v. "Friedenwald"; Levin, Alexandra Lee. *Vision: The Story of Dr. Harry Friedenwald of Baltimore* (1964); Marcus, Jacob Rader. *Memoirs of American Jews, 1775–1865.* Vol. 1 (1956): 303; National Museum. Report (1906): 16. Papers of the Jewish Historical Society of Maryland; *PAJHS* 29: 165–167; Sarna, Jonathan. *JPS: The Americanization of Jewish Culture, 1888–1988* (1990); Schneiderman, Harry. "Herbert Friedenwald." *Papers of the American Jewish Historical Society* 37: 463–466; *WWIAJ* (1938).

ELLEN FRANKEL

FRIEDMAN, PAULINE and ESTHER PAULINE *see* VAN BUREN, ABIGAIL and LANDERS, ANN

FRIEND, CHARLOTTE (1921–1987)

Cell biologist and immunologist Charlotte Friend made major contributions to our understanding of cancer and its causes. In the 1950s, she isolated a virus that produced leukemia in mice and could be transmitted experimentally from mouse to mouse. This virus became known as the Friend leukemia virus (FLV) and was one of the most widely used model systems for studying tumor-inducing viruses and cancer progression. Later, using cells derived from FLV-induced leukemia, Friend demonstrated that cancer cells such as these can be stimulated to differentiate along their normal pathway and thereby lose their unlimited growth potential. Friend's erythroleukemia cells then became an important tool for those studying the regulation and control of cell proliferation and differentiation.

Charlotte Friend was born on March 3, 1921, in New York City, the daughter of Russian Jewish immigrants Morris Friend, a businessman, and Cecilia (Wolpin) Friend, a pharmacist. She had two older sisters and a younger brother, born after her father died when she was three years old. Her mother was left with four young children to raise during the Depression. Friend always admired her mother for never letting the children doubt that, although they were on "home relief," they would complete their education. Friend, a true Renaissance woman, took advantage of all the opportunities and wonders New York offered. She graduated from HUNTER COLLEGE in New York City in 1943 and enlisted in the United States Navy, where she served as an officer in hematology laboratories. After the war, she enrolled as a graduate student at Yale University and received a Ph.D. in immunology in 1950. She returned to New York and joined the staff of the newly founded Sloan-Kettering Institute for Cancer Research. She remained there until 1966, when she became director of the Center for Experimental Cell Biology at the new medical school established by Mount Sinai Hospital.

Friend received national and international recognition for her achievements and contributions. Among her many honorary awards were the Alfred P. Sloan Award for Cancer Research (1962), the Prix Griffuel (1979), and the Papanicolaou Award (1982). In the 1970s, she was elected a member of the National Academy of Sciences and president of three major scientific societies: the New York Academy of Sciences, the American Association for Cancer Research, and the Harvey Society. She was a strong supporter of the women's movement and, throughout her career, was a role model and advocate for other women in science. Though not very religious, she was a strong supporter of Israel and its causes and was one of the original organizers of the Israel Cancer Research Fund, set up in 1975 to support the research efforts of young Israeli scientists at home and abroad. From its inception, Friend insisted that the award process be fair and objective and, to this end, was instrumental in recruiting the cream of the cancer research community to serve on the fund's Scientific Advisory Board. When she was asked why she was working so hard for the organization, she replied, "Because I want to send my talents on Aliyah."

Friend paved the way for a great many avenues of research on viruses, cell differentiation, and cancer. She was renowned for her generosity in distributing Friend virus and Friend cells to those who wanted to work with them and for providing the necessary guidance and assistance. Her demonstration of inducible differentiation of leukemic cells has served most recently as the inspiration and prototype for evaluating the potential therapeutic effects of differentiation-inducing agents in human cancer. Charlotte Friend died of lymphoma on January 7, 1987, shortly after receiving an honorary doctor of science degree from Brandeis University.

SELECTED WORKS BY CHARLOTTE FRIEND

"Cell-Free Transmission in Adult Swiss Mice of a Disease Having the Character of a Leukemia." *Journal of Experimental Medicine* 105 (1957): 307–318; "The Coming of Age of Tumor Virology." *Cancer Research* 37 (1977): 1255–1263; "Hemoglobin Synthesis in Murine Virus-induced Leukemic Cells in Vitro: Stimulation of Erythroid Differentiation by Dimethyl Aulfoxide," with W. Scher, J.G. Holland, and T. Sato. *Proceedings of the National Academy of Sciences* 68 (1971): 378–382.

BIBLIOGRAPHY

Biographical Memoirs 63 (1994): 126–148; "Viral Oncogenesis and Cell Differentiation: The Contributions of Charlotte Friend." Edited by L. Diamond and S.R. Wolman. *Annals of the New York Academy of Sciences* 567 (1989): 5–13.

LEILA DIAMOND

FRIEND, IDA WEIS (1868–1963)

Ida Weis Friend's life of activism began when, at age fifteen, she raised money for a hospital fountain. It ended when she died, at age ninety-five, still serving as president of the board of directors of the Home for the Incurables, a post she had held for over forty years. Her community service, representative of women's club work during the Progressive Era and beyond, encompassed religious organizations, the woman suffrage movement, mainstream politics, public health, child welfare, and cultural philanthropy.

Ida Weis Friend was born on June 30, 1868, in Natchez, Mississippi. Her father, Julius Weis, had migrated there from Bavaria in 1845. He began peddling in the nearby countryside and eventually operated dry-goods stores in various Mississippi towns. In 1864, he married Caroline Mayer, the daughter of the family with whom he first boarded upon his arrival in Natchez. The Weises moved to New Orleans, where

Julius Weis became a successful cotton factor. A prominent member of the Jewish community, he helped found and was president of Temple Sinai, the first Reform congregation in New Orleans. In 1899, he donated $25,000 for a home for elderly Jews that was named in his honor.

Caroline Weis returned to Natchez for the birth of four of her seven children. Ida was the third child, following firstborn Henrietta and oldest son Simon. Her remaining siblings, all brothers, were Sam, Marion, Joseph, and Fred.

Ida began her education at a small private school run by Flora Gayle. In 1882, her family moved to Europe for eighteen months so that the children could be educated there. She studied at Fräulein Singer's school in Frankfurt and Mesdames Yeatman's school in Neuilly, France, and became fluent in both German and French.

She met her future husband, Joseph E. Friend, a Milwaukee native and Yale graduate, during a Colorado vacation. They married on March 19, 1890. After a brief residence in Chicago, the couple returned to New Orleans, and Joseph Friend began work in Julius Weis's firm. The Friends had four children: Henry, Lillian, Caroline, and Julius Weis, who founded and edited the New Orleans–based literary magazine the *Double Dealer.*

Following her father's lead, Friend, a lifelong member of Temple Sinai, devoted herself to Jewish organizations. As a teenager, her first charitable act was raising money for a fountain for Touro Infirmary, a Jewish hospital over whose board her father presided. She founded the New Orleans HADASSAH and served as its first president from 1917 to 1920. She also led the New Orleans women's chapter of B'nai B'rith, which was named after her. From 1926 to 1932, she was president of the NATIONAL COUNCIL OF JEWISH WOMEN.

Friend was a member of the Era Club, a New Orleans woman suffrage organization. In 1920, she was the first Louisiana woman to serve at the Democratic National Convention and the following year was one of two female delegates to Louisiana's constitutional convention. In 1946, she participated in a women's campaign effort to help elect deLesseps "Chep" Morrison, a reform candidate for mayor in New Orleans.

Friend served as president of local, district, and state chapters of the Federation of Women's Clubs, the New Orleans Travelers Aid Society, and the New Orleans Consumer League. An advocate of the playground movement, she donated land to the city for a playground named as a memorial to her son Henry, who died from postsurgery complications at age eighteen. Friend also became involved in interracial work. She was a member of the Commission on Interracial Cooperation in 1932 and helped found the New Orleans chapter of the Urban League in 1938.

For her lifetime of leadership and volunteer work, Ida Weis Friend was awarded the *New Orleans Times-Picayune* Loving Cup in 1946, a prestigious local honor. She continued to serve the community until her death on September 22, 1963, in New Orleans.

BIBLIOGRAPHY

Friend, Ida Weis. Papers. Manuscripts Collection 287, Department of Manuscripts, Howard-Tilton Memorial Library, Tulane University, New Orleans; *The Israelites of Louisiana: Their Religious, Civic, Charitable, and Patriotic Life* [1905]; Kahn, Catherine C. "Ida Weis Friend." In *A Dictionary of Louisiana Biography*, edited by Glenn R. Conrad. Vol. 1 (1988); *New Orleans Item*, March 4, 1946, and January 28, 1953; *New Orleans Times-Picayune*, September 23, 1963; *UJE*; Weis, Julius. *Autobiography of Julius Weis* (n.d.); *WWIAJ* (1938).

KAREN TRAHAN LEATHEM

FRILING, MANIA *see* SHOSHANA, ROSE

FROMENSON, RUTH BERNARD (1880–1953)

Ruth Bernard Fromenson, a Zionist and Jewish communal worker, initiated the system by which vital supplies were sent to Palestine under the auspices of HADASSAH, the Women's Zionist Organization of America.

Born in 1880 in Rochester, New York, she moved to New York City with her parents and five brothers and sisters at an early age. In 1904, she married Abraham H. Fromenson, editor of the English section of the *Yidishes Tageblat*, who was later the public relations director of the Zionist Organization of America. Also in 1904, Fromenson joined the Daughters of Zion, a Zionist women's study group that served as the nucleus for Hadassah, which was founded in 1912. Under the tutelage of HENRIETTA SZOLD, Hadassah's first national president, Fromenson organized sewing groups during World War I to make clothing and dolls for the war orphans of Palestine, who knew her as their "American mother."

Beginning in 1917, these activities were formalized with the establishment of Hadassah's Palestine Supplies Bureau and were expanded to include shipments of medical supplies and hospital equipment. As chair of the bureau, Fromenson demonstrated concern not only for the material welfare of the Jewish settlers in Palestine but for their psychological needs as well. She instructed volunteers to sew clothing with a variety of designs, so that the recipients would not feel like they were wearing "charity clothes." In 1920, she began including toys in the shipments to Palestine, hoping they would ease the stress of children living under difficult circumstances. During Fromenson's twenty-five-year tenure, over four million items were shipped to Palestine. When she retired from her post, she had served on Hadassah's national board longer than any other member.

Ruth Bernard Fromenson died in New York on January 26, 1953.

BIBLIOGRAPHY

AJYB 55:455; Fromenson, Ruth Bernard. "Comments on Miss Seligsberg's Data." Typescript, and Papers, Hadassah Archives, NYC. *New Palestine* (March 5, 1920); Obituary. *NYTimes*, January 27, 1953, 25:5.

ERIC L. GOLDSTEIN

FROMM-REICHMANN, FRIEDA (1889–1957)

Frieda Fromm-Reichmann is best remembered as the compassionate European psychiatrist depicted in *I Never Promised You a Rose Garden*, the autobiographical novel written by her ex-patient Joanne Greenberg. A brilliant and gifted therapist, she emphasized communicating understanding in her innovative treatment of schizophrenics during her twenty-two years at Chestnut Lodge in Rockville, Maryland.

Frieda Reichmann was born in Karlsruhe, Germany, on October 23, 1889. Her father, Adolf Reichmann, was a modern Orthodox merchant who became a bank director after the family moved to Königsberg in 1894. Her mother, Klara (Simon) Reichmann, had trained as a teacher and strongly supported higher education for women. The eldest of three daughters, Frieda was among the first women to study medicine at the University of Königsberg, where she received her degree in 1913.

Petite and lacking physical strength, she decided to specialize in psychiatry rather than obstetrics. During World War I, she worked with brain-injured soldiers at the university's psychiatric hospital. After the war, she continued her research with Kurt Goldstein in Frankfurt, and then worked in a sanitarium near

Dresden. After undergoing a training analysis with Hanns Sachs in Berlin, she served as a visiting physician at Emil Kraepelin's psychiatric clinic in Munich in 1923. A Zionist as well as an observant Jew, she established a small private psychoanalytic sanitarium in Heidelberg in 1924. It was jokingly described as "Torah-peutic," because it combined therapy with Jewish dietary laws and Sabbath observance. In 1926, she married one of her analysands, Erich Fromm, the social philosopher, and together they helped found the Frankfurt chapter of the German Psychoanalytic Society, and then the Psychoanalytic Institute of Southwestern Germany. By 1928, the sanitarium had closed, and the couple had abandoned Orthodox practices for socialist principles. They soon separated, but they did not divorce until 1942.

After the Nazi takeover in 1933, Fromm-Reichmann left Germany for Strassburg in Alsace-Lorraine. After brief stays in France and Palestine, she immigrated to the United States in 1935. She quickly found a position as resident psychiatrist at Chestnut Lodge, a private sanitarium near Washington, D.C. She developed a very productive working relationship with Harry Stack Sullivan and served as training analyst of the Washington Psychoanalytic Society and the Washington School of Psychiatry, as well as the William Alanson White Institute and the Academy of Psychoanalysis in New York. In 1955, she received a fellowship to study the role of nonverbal communication in therapy at the Center for Advanced Study in the Behavioral Sciences at Stanford University.

Fromm-Reichmann succeeded in using intensive psychotherapy to treat schizophrenic and manic-depressive patients who had previously been considered unsuitable for psychoanalysis. She fostered their creative talents and developed fresh insights into the relationship between art and mental illness. A highly gifted clinician and outstanding teacher, she shared her discoveries with large audiences through her popular lectures.

Toward the end of her life, she received international recognition for her contributions to psychotherapy. Her honors and awards include president of the Washington Psychoanalytic Association (1939–1941); Adolf Meyer Award, Association for the Improvement of Mental Hospitals (1952); academic lecture, American Psychiatric Association (1955); and keynote speaker, Second International Congress of Psychiatry, Zurich (1957, posthumous). Suffering from deafness, she kept her unhappiness to herself, while always attempting to cheer and comfort others. She died of a heart attack at Chestnut Lodge on April 28, 1957, deeply mourned by all who knew her.

SELECTED WRITINGS BY FRIEDA FROMM-REICHMANN

An Intensive Study Study of Twelve Cases of Manic Depressive Psychosis (1954); *The Philosophy of Insanity* (1947); *Principles of Intensive Psychotherapy* (1950); *Progress in Psychotherapy*, with J.L. Moreno (1956); *Psychoanalysis and Psychotherapy: Selected papers of Frieda Fromm-Reichmann*. Edited by Dexter M. Bullard (1959).

BIBLIOGRAPHY

Bruch, Hilde. "Personal Reminiscences of Frieda Fromm-Reichmann." *Psychiatry* 45 (1982); *DAB* 6; Dick, Jutta, and Marina Sassenberg, eds. *Jüdische Frauen Is 19. und 20. Jahrhundert: Lexikon zu Leben und Werk* (1993): 132–134; Dickstein, Leah J., and Carol C. Nadelson. *Women Physicians in Leadership Roles* (1986): 73–77; *EJ*; Green, Hannah (pseud. Joanne Greenberg). I *Never Promised You a Rose Garden* (1964), and "In Praise of My Doctor." *Contemporary Psychoanalysis* (Fall 1967); Grinstein, Alexander, ed. *The Index of Psychoanalytic Writings* (1956, 1967); *International Biographical Dictionary of Central European Emigres*. Vol. 2, part 1 (1980): 346; Klotschke, Angelika. "Frieda Fromm-Reichmann. Leben und Werk." Medical diss., University of Mainz (1979); *NAW* modern; Obituary. *NYTimes*, April 30, 1957, 29:2; Peters, Uwe Henrik. *Psychiatrie im Exil* (1992): 173–188; *PSA-Info* 30 (March 1988): 1–29; Rattner, Josef. *Klassifer der Tiefen-Psychologie* (1990): 441–463; Scholem, Gershom. *From Berlin to Jerusalem* (1980): 156; Stevens, Gwendolyn, and Sheldon Gardner. *The Women of Psychology*. Vol. 1 (1982): 205–208; Weigert, Edith. "In Memoriam: Frieda Fromm-Reichmann, 1889–1957." *Psychiatry* 21 (February 1958): 91–95; *Who's Who in World Jewry* (1955).

HARRIET PASS FREIDENRIECH

FUCHS, LILLIAN (1902–1995)

Lillian Fuchs is a legend among musicians and chamber music lovers throughout the world. She was a violist, teacher, and composer. Her musicianship and concept of the viola's glorious, dark, rich, human sonority continue to enhance and inspire the lives of musicians who studied with her, or played her compositions, or had the privilege of hearing her wondrous, soulful playing.

Born in New York City on November 18, 1902, into a family destined to bear luminaries in the classical music world, Lillian Fuchs began her musical life as a pianist. Her parents, Kate and Phillip Fuchs, loved music. Her father, a self-taught amateur violinist, taught violin to neighborhood children. Her parents' inspiration led her brother Harry Fuchs, a longtime member of the Cleveland Orchestra, to the cello, and her brother Joseph Fuchs, a well-known concert violinist and teacher, to the violin.

In a family of brilliant musicians, Lillian Fuchs may have been the brightest light,
eventually achieving legendary status as a violist, teacher, and composer. [New York Public Library]

Already an accomplished pianist who used to accompany her brother Joseph, Lillian Fuchs had always wanted to study the violin. She became a violinist, studying with Louis Svecenski and Franz Kneisel at the New York Institute of Musical Art (now the Juilliard School), where she also studied composition with Percy Goetschius, graduating and winning accolades and awards in violin as well as composition.

Lillian Fuchs made her debut in 1926 as a violinist, but soon after she began playing viola and joined the Perolé String Quartet, with which she performed until the mid-1940s. She toured as a solo violist in Europe and the United States, and often performed chamber music with her brothers. In the 1940s, Joseph Fuchs cofounded the Musicians Guild in New York City, of which he, Lillian Fuchs, Leo Smit, Leonard Rose, Frank Sheridan, and the Kroll Quartet were members. They performed extensively at New York's Town Hall and were a great presence in the musical life of New York for many seasons.

In 1953, Lillian Fuchs appeared as soloist at the Casals Festival in Prades, France. Over the decades, she appeared and taught at the summer festivals in Aspen, Colorado, Banff Center, Canada, and Kneisel Hall in Blue Hill, Maine. Teaching was always a great love and inspiration for Fuchs. She has helped to shape many of today's preeminent musicians, passing on her knowledge to violists and chamber musicians at several of the finest conservatories in the country. In 1962, she started teaching at the Manhattan School of Music; in 1971, at the Juilliard School; and in the 1980s, at Mannes College of Music.

Less familiar to the general public are the compositions of Lillian Fuchs. Staples of the technical studies of violists are three sets of works for unaccompanied viola: *Fifteen Characteristic Studies* (1965), *Twelve Caprices* (1950), and *Sixteen Fantasy Etudes* (1961). In 1956, she composed the *Sonata Pastorale* for unaccompanied viola. Other published works include *Jota* and *Caprice Fantastique* for violin and piano. She also composed unique piano accompaniments to several of the Paganini caprices for violin that she wrote for her brother Joseph.

Lillian Fuchs was the inspiration for some of the greatest composers of the twentieth century. In 1947, Bohuslav Martinu was so inspired by a performance of the Mozart duos by Lillian and Joseph Fuchs that he composed and dedicated to them a set of madrigals for violin and viola, which the brother-and-sister team received several weeks later. For Lillian Fuchs, Martinu also composed *Sonata for Viola and Piano* in 1955. In 1955, Jacques de Menasce wrote *Sonata for Viola and Piano*; in 1957, Quincy Porter wrote *Duo for Viola and Harp* and, in 1962, *Duo for Violin and Viola*; and in 1973, Vittorio Rieti wrote *Triple Concerto for Violin, Viola, Piano and Orchestra*. All of these works were written for Lillian Fuchs.

During her early years of playing the viola, Lillian Fuchs met a young man at one of many musical gatherings at the home of the well-known New York musical patrons, the Leventritts of New York City. Ludwig Stein, a businessman involved in men's haberdashery and a wonderful amateur violinist, violist, and pianist, was to become her husband for over sixty years, until his death in 1992.

The musical tradition has been carried on by the twin daughters of Ludwig Stein and Lillian Fuchs. Barbara Stein Mallow, an accomplished cellist, has an active career, performing solo and chamber music as well as teaching at Queens College, and at Kneisel Hall during the summer. Twin sister Carol Stein Amado is first violinist of the Amado String Quartet in the Philadelphia area and carries on the family traditions of teaching and performing as a soloist. The sisters played with their mother for many years in the Lillian Fuchs Trio.

Lillian Fuchs died on October 5, 1995, at the Actors Fund Nursing Home in Englewood, New Jersey, at age ninety-two.

BIBLIOGRAPHY

Grove's Dictionary of Music; Mallow, Barbara Stein. Interview with author, 1996; Author's personal knowledge as a student of Lillian Fuchs, 1964–1973.

SANDRA ROBBINS

FULD, CARRIE BAMBERGER FRANK (1864–1944)

The daughter of German Jewish immigrant parents, Carrie Bamberger Frank Fuld was a philanthropist who, in partnership with her brother, department store magnate Louis Bamberger, founded the internationally acclaimed Institute for Advanced Study in Princeton, New Jersey. The institute became an important center for scholarship and counted among its first professors Albert Einstein and other refugees from Hitler's Germany. In a quiet and effective manner, Fuld worked with Abraham Flexner, founding director of the institute, to help craft an institution that would become a model for scholarly endeavor, largely unfettered by worldly concerns. They hoped to create a forum for the kind of disinterested scholarship that was almost absent from American higher education in 1930 and that was about to disappear completely from Germany, where Flexner looked for the model of this tradition. In their lengthy correspondence about the nature of this new institution, Fuld and Flexner explored the possibilities of scholarship in a world that was coming apart. In her concern for the success of her most active philanthropic endeavor, Fuld involved herself in the well-being of the permanent members of the institute.

Born in Baltimore, Maryland, on March 16, 1864, Caroline Bamberger was the fifth of the six children born to Theresa Hutzler, who emigrated with her family from Bavaria to America in 1838, and Elkan Bamberger, who also came from Bavaria, in 1840. Both families owned dry-goods stores, and Carrie, with her older brother Louis, followed in that tradition. In 1883, she moved to Philadelphia and married Louis Meyer Frank. A decade later, her husband, her brother, and her brother's friend Felix Fuld started

L. Bamberger and Company in Newark, New Jersey. The store was very successful and was similar in size and influence in its community to stores developed by other German Jewish merchant families like Neiman-Marcus, Filene, Macy, Straus, Rosenwald, and Rich.

Louis Frank died in 1910, and Carrie married Felix Fuld in 1913. Carrie and Felix Fuld and Louis Bamberger were then virtually inseparable. They lived together on a jointly owned thirty-three-acre estate that straddled Newark and its suburbs, South Orange, and East Orange. There they enjoyed the benefits of lush gardens and a small working farm.

While Felix Fuld was alive (he died on January 20, 1929), the family philanthropies had a decidedly community-oriented and Jewish thrust, investing in such institutions as the Newark Beth Israel Hospital and the YM-YWHA. Carrie Fuld associated herself closely with the Jewish Day Nursery and with Neighborhood House, which catered to the needs of Russian Jewish immigrants. The Fulds were members of Newark's B'nai Jeshurun Reform Congregation, the oldest synagogue in the state of New Jersey. She belonged to the local chapter of HADASSAH and was a member of the board of directors of the NATIONAL COUNCIL OF JEWISH WOMEN from 1930 to 1935.

After Felix Fuld's death, Louis Bamberger decided in 1929 to sell the family business to R. H. Macy so that he and his sister could devote themselves to philanthropy. Louis and Carrie were intent upon founding a Jewish medical college in the Newark area, but Abraham Flexner helped change their minds, planting the seed that created the Institute for Advanced Study within a few months of the sale of Bamberger's. Originally planned to be housed on the Bamberger-Fuld estate as a last great gift to the Newark community, Flexner convinced the brother and sister that the institute, for which they provided an initial endowment of $5 million and made subsequent large gifts throughout the rest of their days, needed to be near a great university and library. Carrie Bamberger Frank Fuld made the institute the chief occupation of her last years. She died in Lake Placid, New York, on July 18, 1944.

BIBLIOGRAPHY

AJYB 47:522; Fuld, Carrie Bamberger Frank. Archives. Institute for Advanced Study, Princeton, N.J.; *NAW*; Obituary. *NYTimes*, July 19, 1944, 19:1; Porter, Laura Smith. "From Intelllectual Sanctuary to Social Responsibiltiy: The Founding of the Institute for Advanced Study, 1930–1933." Ph.D. diss., Princeton University, 1988; *UJE*, s.v. "Fuld, Felix."

ELLIOTT SHORE

FURST, NORMA FIELDS (1931–1995)

Norma Fields Furst's family believes that she was happiest when she served as president of Baltimore Hebrew University because the post allowed her to combine her talents as an educator with her commitment to Judaism.

Norma Fields was born in Brooklyn, New York, on February 26, 1931, the only child of Nathan B. and Anne (Cooper) Fields. Her parents divorced in 1941, and her mother later married Jerry Platzer. Norma's maternal grandparents, Menachem Mendel and Jenny (Shayndl) Cooper, were Polish emigrés who came to the United States to secure a better education for their children. Growing up in the Coopers' Orthodox Brooklyn home, Norma inherited their commitment to higher education, the Jewish people, and Jewish values. However, she rejected halakah [Jewish law] until her daughter wanted an observant home.

She graduated from public high school at age sixteen, and graduated Phi Beta Kappa from Brooklyn College in 1951, with a B.A. cum laude in English. On September 9, 1951, she married M. Lawrence Furst. She worked as a research librarian at the New York Public Library (1950–1952) and as registrar to the Pakistan Mission to the United Nations (1952–1955). She pursued graduate studies at New York University, the University of Bridgeport, and Temple University. In 1963, Furst and her husband received master's degrees from Temple, and in 1967, they earned their doctorate degrees, she in education and he in psychology. The Fursts had a son and a daughter: Merrick Lee.

Higher education was not merely a family priority; it also became Furst's professional focus. She worked her way up from English teacher and guidance counselor at Harcum Junior College in Bryn Mawr, Pennsylvania (1962–1963), to professor of psychoeducational processes at Temple University's College of Education (1973–1983). In addition to her teaching duties and extensive research, Furst served as Temple's dean of students from 1974 to 1983. At Temple, Furst's commitment to civil rights and equal opportunity was evident in her advocacy for and personal relationships with her students.

In 1983, Furst became president of Harcum Junior College. During her nine-year tenure she demonstrated her dedication to women's colleges and to Jewish values regarding issues such as minority education and the environment. From 1992 to 1994, Furst served as president of Baltimore Hebrew University. Furst wrote several articles on education and served as editor for two educational journals. She devoted her time and energy to Soviet Jewry, the International B'nai B'rith Hillel Commission, the Jewish Publication Society, and dozens of other educational, Jewish, and community organizations. She received numerous awards for her teaching and humanitarian commitments, including the 1990 LOUISE WATERMAN WISE Award of the AMERICAN JEWISH CONGRESS.

Norma Fields Furst died of lung cancer at her home in Wynnewood, Pennsylvania, on March 7, 1995. The Philadelphia educational and Jewish communities benefited from her untiring commitment to furthering education and freedom, and from her ability to forge a human connection with everyone she encountered.

SELECTED WORKS BY NORMA FIELDS FURST

"Interaction Analysis in Teacher Education: A Review of Studies." In *Interaction Analysis: Selected Papers* (1971); "The Multiple Languages of the Classroom: A Further Analysis and a Synthesis of Meanings Communicated in High School Teaching." Ph.D. diss., Temple University (1967).

BIBLIOGRAPHY

Jewish Exponent (April 26, 1974, April 9, 1976, July 2, 1976, March 21, 1980, August 14, 1981, March 4, 1983, April 1, 1983, November 11, 1983, November 25, 1988, November 30, 1990); Obituary. *NYTimes*, March 14, 1995, B8: 1; *Who's Who in the East* (1992); *Who's Who in World Jewry* (1978); *Who's Who of American Women* (1993); *WWIAJ* (1980).

ADINAH S. MILLER

G

GAMORAN, MAMIE (1900–1984)

When Mamie Goldsmith Gamoran graduated from the Teachers Institute Extension Course of the Jewish Theological Seminary in 1922, she was acutely aware of how much needed to be accomplished in the field of Jewish education. She was saddened that the youth of her generation had "forged new chains and ties," thereby dismissing their heritage. As a proud American and ardent Zionist, Gamoran believed that one could synthesize American culture with one's commitment to Judaism. Although born to parents who were not strongly affiliated Jews, Mamie Gamoran dedicated her life to the Jewish community.

She was born on January 17, 1900, in Long Island City, New York, to Mamie Aronson and Nathan Israel Goldsmith. Named after her mother, who died one week after her birth, Mamie had three older siblings, Joseph, Minnie, and Laurette, and also a half-brother, Edwin, born to her father and his second wife, Mathilde Bauer.

Mamie received her formative education in the New York City public school system. She continued her education at Columbia University and the University of Cincinnati but never matriculated at these institutions. Instead, she chose to receive a degree from the Teachers Institute of the Jewish Theological Seminary of America, a decision that best reflects her lifelong commitment to strengthening Jewish life.

Mamie's interest in the Jewish community and love of Judaism developed in the Association of Jewish High School Girls, led by Leah Konowitz and later DEBORAH MARCUS MELAMED. When the association merged with the Association of Jewish High School Boys and became the League of Jewish Youth, Mamie Goldsmith met Emanuel Gamoran, originally from Belz, Russia. Their paths crossed for a second time at the Jewish Theological Seminary, where Emanuel Gamaron was a member of the faculty extension department of the Teachers Institute and Mamie Goldsmith was a student in the first graduating class. They were married on December 17, 1922. The Gamorans shared a commitment to Jewish education: Both were members of the Bureau of Jewish Education, the first organization in the United States committed to the betterment of Jewish education, under the directorship of Samson Benderly. In 1923, when Emanuel Gamoran was appointed educational director of the Commission on Jewish Education of the Union of American Hebrew Congregations, the Gamorans moved to Cincinnati, Ohio. Although her husband was credited with having revolutionized the curricula and techniques of Jewish religious education, Mamie Gamoran made enormous contributions in this area as well.

Like her husband, Gamoran wrote many textbooks for Jewish schools, including a thoughtful three-volume work, *The New Jewish History* (1953, 1956, 1957). Its goal was to make Jewish children feel that their history was an unending story, dramatic and challenging, in which they would be future participants. This work reflects her theological leanings as well as her beliefs about how children should be inspired intellectually and emotionally. Her most popular book was *Fun Ways to Holidays: A Book of Puzzles Based on American and Jewish Holidays* (1951).

Concerned that her husband's books were not readily accessible to the public, Gamoran prepared a bibliography of his writings and following his death coedited his biography, *Emanuel Gamoran: His Life and His Work* (1979). In addition, Mamie Gamoran wrote a confirmation service for girls, recognizing that they needed a ceremony to mark the completion of the first stage of their Jewish education. She intended this ceremony to be performed on the holiday of Shavuot. Her personal files, containing much unpublished material, testify to her love of and talent for writing. She preferred, however, to spend most of her time writing materials for an audience of Jewish children.

In addition to her writing and synagogue involvement, Gamoran traveled abroad with her husband to carry messages of Jewish education to liberal congregations in England, Ireland, Holland, Rhodesia, and South Africa; and performed volunteer work for HADASSAH as a national board member and for Histadrut Ivrith of America, becoming its vice president. She was also a loving mother to three children: Abraham Carmi, Rabbi Nathaniel Hillel, and Judith Chernin. She taught them at home and spoke to them in Hebrew, hoping to infuse them with a strong sense of Jewish tradition. She also instilled ardent Jewish feelings in her daughters-in-law, treating them as if they were her own daughters. The desire to preserve memories of her family prompted Gamoran to write a memoir to leave for her children, although this extraordinarily modest woman chose not to describe her own accomplishments in it. After her death, her son Nathaniel Hillel ensured that *A Family History* was published.

Mamie Gamoran died in New York City on July 26, 1984.

SELECTED WORKS BY MAMIE GAMORAN

Confirmation Service (1948); *Emanuel Gamoran: His Life and His Work*, editor with Samuel Grand (1979); *A Family History*. Edited by Hillel Gamoran (1985); *Fun Ways to Holidays: A Book of Puzzles Based on American and Jewish Holidays* (1951); *Hadassah Handbook*, editor with Minnie W. Halpern. 6th ed. (1960); *The Hebrew Spirit in America*. Microfilm (1975); *Hillel's Calendar* (1960); *Hillel's Happy Holidays* (1939); *The Jewish Times* (1975); *The New Jewish History*

(1953–1957); *Shimshon Benderly*, translator (1963); *The Voice of the Prophets* (1929).

BIBLIOGRAPHY

AJYB 86:439; *EJ* 4:479, s.v. "Samson Benderly," and 7:308, s.v. "Emanuel Gamoran"; Gamoran, Mamie. Biographical material. Hadassah Archives, NYC; *WWIAJ* (1928, 1938).

MARJORIE LEHMAN

GAMSON, ANNABELLE (b. 1928)

More than any other artist in the mid-1970s, Annabelle Gamson initiated unprecedented attention to the history of American modern dance. Her musically inspired, passionate performances of dances, choreographed by Isadora Duncan and others in the early twentieth century, brought about a resurgence of interest in Duncan's work and her legacy, modern dance. Although Gamson was in her forties when she began performing Duncan's dances, the dynamic strength and maturity of her physical presence, crowned by a mane of long white hair, distinguished her as singularly original.

Annabelle, the second child and first daughter of Russian Jewish immigrants Rose Loonin and Solomon Gold, was born in the Bronx on August 6, 1928, one year after Duncan's death. From ages five to twelve, she studied dance with a family friend, Julia Levien, who had danced in the companies of two of Duncan's adopted daughters, Anna and Irma Duncan. Gamson attended the High School of Music and Art in New York, but by age sixteen she was earning her living as a dancer and continued her education at the Professional Children's School. She also studied dance with May O'Donnell, Helene Platova, and at the Katherine Dunham School, performing with Dunham at Café Society.

In 1950, she went to Paris to study with Etienne Decroux. On her return to New York in 1953, she performed with ANNA SOKOLOW on Broadway and on television. She danced the cowgirl in Agnes DeMille's *Rodeo* with the American Ballet Theatre. On November 21, 1958, she married musician Arnold Gamson. In 1961, her marriage took her to Europe again, this time directing operas. When the couple returned to New York, they settled in Westchester County, where Gamson devoted herself to raising their children, Rosanna and David.

In the early 1970s, Gamson resumed her studies with Levien, for there was something in Duncan's work she had not found in any other kind of dancing. In 1974, at the American Theater Laboratory in New

York City, she performed Duncan's *Water Study* (Schubert), *Five Waltzes* (Brahms), *Dance of the Furies* (Gluck), and *Étude* (Scriabin), as well as her own work. The Duncan pieces made an enormous impression. Through her extraordinary performances, Gamson gave audiences the opportunity to understand and appreciate the craftsmanship of Duncan's choreography, forever doing away with the rumor that Duncan's dances were improvised. To generations of dance lovers, for whom Duncan was a legend previously accessible only through writings and artistic representation, Gamson imbued the dances with a musicality and dynamic spirit that, while never intending to mimic Duncan, gave some sense of what was essential in Duncan's choreography and the apparent spontaneity of her performance.

Following this success, Gamson began work on the solos of another pioneer of modern dance, German expressionist Mary Wigman. Her performances of *Summer Dance*, *Pastorale*, and the *Witch Dance* brought her additional critical acclaim. Later, she added the solos of Eleanor King, an American modern dancer who had performed with the Humphrey-Weidman Company. She celebrated the twentieth anniversary of her solo career in 1994.

Gamson's own choreography revealed the dynamic influence of her predecessors, and she passed on her knowledge of their work to younger performers. While still occasionally coaching younger dancers, in 1996 Gamson returned to painting, an earlier interest.

BIBLIOGRAPHY

Dunning, Jennifer. "Annabelle Gamson: Gamson Dances Isadora." *Dance Magazine* (February 1977): 47–50; Gamson, Annabelle. *On Dancing Isadora's Dances.* Conceived, written, and produced by Annabelle Gamson. 23 min. 1988. Videocassette; Gamson, Annabelle. Interview by author. July 11, 16, 1996; Laine, Barry. "In Her Footsteps." *Ballet News* (February 1982): 22; Tobias, Tobi. "She Brings Duncan's Artistry Back to Life." *NYTimes*, November 11, 1974; *Trailblazers of Modern Dance*. Dance in America. Produced by Merrill Brockway and Judy Kinberg. Directed by Emile Ardolino. 60 min. WNET, January 1978.

ROSE ANNE THOM

GANS, BIRD STEIN (1868–1944)

As a young woman of twenty, Bird Stein joined several married women interested in the new field of parent education. This small group formed the Society for the Study of Child Nature in the autumn of 1888, at the suggestion of Professor Felix Adler, founder of the Ethical Culture Society. These women viewed parenthood as a vocation, believing that parenting was a learned talent rather than an instinctual one. They hoped to cull from scientific sources the knowledge necessary for rearing their children, studying child nature from the psychological, ethical, and physical viewpoints. Gans spent the remainder of her years dedicated to the welfare of parents and their children, not only by promoting the expansion of the society, but by involving herself in many other organizations devoted to enhancing family life.

Bird Stein was born on May 29, 1868, in Allegheny, Pennsylvania, the eldest child of Pauline (Bernhard) and Solomon Stein. Her father was a prosperous woolen merchant who moved his family to New York in 1871. She received her education at Columbia University, the New School for Social Research, and New York University. Her first marriage, to Louis Sternberger, ended in divorce, and she married lawyer Howard S. Gans on July 2 1908. Bird and Howard Gans had two children, Marian and Robert.

Gans was elected president of the Society for the Study of Child Nature in 1897. During the course of her presidency she not only saved the organization from disbanding but also was able to expand its activities as well as its membership. This organization, the first of its kind, was renamed the Federation for Child Study in 1898 to distinguish it from similar organizations that had begun to develop in other cities. In 1924, the name of the organization was changed again, to the Child Study Association of America. The organization's goal was to help parents improve their relationships with their children. Gans traveled throughout the United States and abroad to further parent education, establishing parent education associations in Japan in 1924, and in England in 1929. She remained president of the Child Study Association until 1933 and honorary president until 1939, maintaining her ties to the organization until her death.

From 1893 to 1913, Gans was affiliated with the NATIONAL COUNCIL OF JEWISH WOMEN, which she served as vice president. This umbrella organization, created by HANNAH SOLOMON in 1893, strove to unite Jewish women working for worthy causes. In its early decades, women planned and attended study groups primarily on Jewish topics but also on such subjects as law and psychology. These women also committed themselves to the social welfare of Jewish immigrants whom they helped to settle, Judaize, and Americanize. That Gans chose to be an officer in this organization indicates that she identified herself as a Jew and enjoyed being in the company of Jewish women who shared her concern for the welfare of families.

Bird Stein Gans died on December 29, 1944, in Tuckahoe, New York.

BIBLIOGRAPHY

AJYB 44:522; Child Study Association. Archival materials. Special Collections, Columbia University Teachers College, NYC; *EJ* 7:309–310; National Council of Jewish Women. National office and NYC chapter; Obituary. *NYTimes*, December 31, 1944, 26:1; Rogow, Faith. *Gone to Another Meeting: The National Council of Jewish Women, 1883–1993* (1993); Society for the Study of Child Nature. Chap. 1. Summary, 1896–1906, and Reports, 1890–1895; *UJE*; *WWIAJ* (1926, 1928, 1938).

MARJORIE LEHMAN

GANS, HELENE (1893–1980)

Active throughout her life in labor movements and consumer rights, Helene Gans devoted herself to improving the lives of working Americans.

She was born on December 27, 1893. A native of the South Side of Chicago, she graduated from the University of Chicago in 1914. She spent her first two years after college working with the Chicago Little Theater while attending secretarial school. In 1916, she left home and moved to New York City. The move upset her mother so greatly that she refused to speak with her daughter for two years. Helene was determined to make it on her own. She rented a small one-bedroom apartment in Greenwich Village with a friend, and found work. She met Leonard S. Gans at the home of a relative, and the two were married not long after. During the 1920s, she raised her two daughters, Nancy and Barbara. By the early 1930s, her interests were focused on the impact of the Depression on unemployment and the high cost of living.

Engaged in a study for the National Women's Trade Union League, Gans wrote a paper called "Cut-Rate Wages" in 1932. The paper helped to influence the New York State legislature to enact its first minimum-wage law in October 1938. Gans also wrote about unemployment for the League of Women Voters. To pay for her daughter Barbara's braces, she took a job as the executive secretary of the Consumers League of New York from 1938 to 1941. There, she urged financial support for WNYC, the municipally funded radio station, and supported city legislation that would increase regulation of food, drugs, cosmetics, and health devices.

From 1942 to 1943, Gans was the eastern regional director of the women's division of the United States Treasury's war bond drive. In 1945–1946, she was the director of the women's division of the United Nations Relief and Rehabilitation Administration. Her activist spirit, however, did not include any Jewish causes. She and Leonard had agreed early in their marriage that religion would not play a role in their lives.

Helene Gans died in New York City on May 7, 1980, at age eighty-six.

BIBLIOGRAPHY

Gallant, Barbara. Oral history interview with the author, Gainesville, Fla., January 1997. *NYTimes*, May 7, 1980.

NOA MEYER

GARFIEL, EVELYN (1900–1987)

A successful psychologist who also devoted her life to religious education and leadership, Evelyn Garfiel offered generations of women a model for balancing academic pursuits and religious commitment.

Born in New York on June 10, 1900, Garfiel received a B.A. from Barnard College and a Ph.D. in psychology from Columbia University. In 1923, she married Rabbi Max Kadushin, a Russian-born graduate of the Jewish Theological Seminary of America (JTS). During the 1920s and 1930s, while her husband held posts in the Midwest, Garfiel pursued her own career, teaching psychology at the Universities of Chicago and Wisconsin (at Madison). She also had two sons, Charles and Phineas.

Upon the family's return to New York in 1942, Garfiel turned increasingly to Jewish education and community work. She eventually served on the boards of both HADASSAH and the United Synagogue's Women's League. In 1954, Garfiel introduced the first annual Torah study session at the Women's League Biennial National Convention and subsequently authored a number of educational pamphlets and lectures for the league. Her considerable Judaic knowledge led Garfiel to JTS, where she became involved in the Women's Institute, a program of adult education for women who wished to study Judaica. In addition to teaching her own courses in Hebrew language, Bible, liturgy, and Jewish thought, Garfiel encouraged other prominent scholars to teach for the program.

Garfiel's editorial involvement with some of her husband's publications reflected her own interest in liturgy and Jewish thought. In 1958, she published *The Service of the Heart*, a detailed and passionate exploration of the Jewish prayer book. She also published *Handbook of Hebrew Grammar*, affording her students access to the great Jewish texts that formed such a central part of her own identity.

By the end of her life, Evelyn Garfiel enjoyed the respect of her peers in Hadassah, the Women's League, and JTS, and the admiration of many students. Though she was not an outspoken advocate of organized feminism, Garfiel was a model of women's ability to balance professional and personal commitments. In an article published in *Outlook* magazine, written only three years before her death in New York City on September 6, 1987, Evelyn Garfiel declared that Jewish women should assume traditionally male ritual obligations such as daily prayer and the wearing of a tallith and tefillin. She concluded her article with the question that had inspired her own life: "[C]an we really find the time and the energy in our new, frantically busy lives for marriage and children and career and sheer human responsibilities, not to speak of occasional time for relaxation? . . . [And] can we Jewish women add to these enormous demands the obligation to fulfill *all* the obligations of Jewish law and ritual? Only time will tell."

BIBLIOGRAPHY

EJ, s.v. "Kadushin, Max"; Kadushin, Max. Archives. Jewish Theological Seminary of America, NYC.

LAUREN B. STRAUSS

GAY, RUTH (b. 1922)

"The West Bronx is located in time midway between the lower East Side (or the East Bronx) and West Side Manhattan. It is a community whose residents seem occupied full time in discovering the wonderful things produced by the world that can be had for even the moderate amount of money at their disposal" (Glazer, 1949). With a few strokes Ruth Glazer (later Gay) painted a vivid portrait of the culture of second-generation Jews in New York. As a free-lance writer and editor for the past fifty years, she has explored the Jewish experience of both America and Germany.

The oldest of three daughters of Harry and Mary Pfeffer Slotkin, Ruth was born on October 19, 1922, in New York City and was educated in local schools. When her family moved from the Bronx to Queens so that her milkman father could open a delicatessen—the subject of her first article—Ruth transferred from HUNTER COLLEGE to Queens College, from which she graduated in 1943. At college she was member of Avukah, a leftist student Zionist organization. Shortly after graduation, in September 1943, she married

Nathan Glazer, then a graduate student and later an editor at *Commentary*. They had three daughters, Sarah (b. 1950), Sophie (b. 1952), and Elizabeth (b. 1955). In 1958, they divorced, and the following year she married the historian Peter Gay.

In the early years of her first marriage, Ruth Glazer pursued employment in the fields of education and editing. Working first with the labor movement, she served in 1943–1944 as assistant to the director of the education department of the Amalgamated Clothing Workers and from 1944 to 1946 as education director of the leisure wear joint board of the same union. She then became assistant editor and staff writer at the magazine *Labor and Nation* (1946–1948) and researcher and editor on the American Joint Distribution Committee's *JDC Review*.

Like many educated and talented women of her generation, Ruth Gay combined motherhood with part-time work. Free-lance writing and editing meshed well with her domestic responsibilities. Beginning in 1946, she published human interest articles about contemporary Jewish culture, with such titles as "The Jewish Delicatessen" and "The World of Station WEVD" in the "American Scene" department of *Commentary*. In the late 1960s, she also contributed occasional pieces about American life to *Amerika*, a magazine published in Eastern European languages by the United States Information Agency. In 1965, she published her first book, *Jews in America: A Short History*.

Gay received an M.L.S. from Columbia University's School of Library Service in 1969. From 1972 until 1985, she combined writing with a position as archivist/cataloguer at the Yale University Library. In 1984, she spent three months in Berlin, funded by a grant from the library, to organize the archives of the West Berlin Jewish community.

Since 1985, Gay has devoted herself to her research and writing. Her wide-ranging essays on cooking, Germany, and German Jewry have appeared in such journals as *The American Scholar, Midstream*, and *Conservative Judaism*. She also has published an additional two books, *The Jews of Germany: A Historical Portrait* (1992) and *Unfinished People: Jewish Immigrants to the United States: 1880–1914* (1996). Her current book in progress is "The Diaspora as an Art Form: Jews in Berlin since 1945."

Ruth Gay's life demonstrates how it was possible for an intellectually vibrant woman who became an adult in the mid-twentieth century to build a career that accommodated both marriage and motherhood. She lives in Hamden, Connecticut, with her husband.

SELECTED WORKS BY RUTH GAY

"Baroque Judaism." *Midstream* (April 1972); "Baroque Judaism II." *Conservative Judaism* (Summer 1974); "Berlin and Its Counterworlds." *American Scholar* (Autumn 1992); "Counting Jews." *Commentary* (November 1971); "Danke Schön, Herr Doktor: German Jews in Palestine." *American Scholar* (Autumn 1989); "Fear of Food." *American Scholar* (Summer 1976); "Floors: The Bronx in the 1930s." *American Scholar* (Winter 1995); "How We Used to Laugh." *Commentary* (October 1949); "Inventing the Shtetl." *American Scholar* (Summer 1984); "The Jewish Delicatessen." *Commentary* (March 1946); "The Jewish Object." *Commentary* (January 1951); *Jews in America: A Short History* (1965); *The Jews of Germany: A Historical Portrait* (1992); "Reichenbachstrasse 27: The Jews of Munich Today." *Midstream* (October 1975); "A Spa in Germany." *American Scholar* (Autumn 1987); "The Tainted Fork." *American Scholar* (Winter 1978–1979); *Unfinished People: Jewish Immigrants to the United States: 1880–1914* (1996); "The West Bronx: Food, Shelter, Clothing." *Commentary* (June 1949); "What I Learned about German Jews." *American Scholar* (Autumn 1985); "The World of Station WEVD." *Commentary* (February 1955).

PAULA E. HYMAN

GEIRINGER, HILDA (1893–1973)

Hilda Geiringer's life epitomizes both the successes and frustrations of women in academia in the early twentieth century. A pioneering applied mathematician, she was the first woman to receive an academic appointment in mathematics at the University of Berlin. Despite her distinguished publications, after immigrating to the United States, she could find jobs only at women's colleges.

The second of four children and the only daughter, Hilda Geiringer was born in Vienna on September 28, 1893, to a middle-class Jewish family. Her mother, Martha Wertheimer Geiringer, was from Vienna; her father, Ludwig Geiringer, was a textile manufacturer from Slovakia. A brilliant student with a prodigious memory, she studied mathematics and physics at the University of Vienna from 1913 to 1917 and wrote a groundbreaking doctoral dissertation on double trigonometric (Fourier) series.

In 1921, after teaching adult education and working as an associate editor for a mathematics journal, Geiringer received a research position as the assistant to Richard von Mises, the director of the Institute of Applied Mathematics in Berlin. Von Mises, a Catholic of Jewish origin, became her mentor, collaborator, and eventually her second husband. Also in 1921, Geiringer married another Jewish mathematician from Vienna, Felix Pollaczek, and in 1922 gave birth

to a daughter, Magda. After the couple separated in 1925, Geiringer raised her daughter alone. The divorce was not finalized until 1932.

In 1927, Geiringer became a privatdocent in applied mathematics at the University of Berlin and continued to conduct research on probability and the mathematical theory of plasticity. In 1933, instead of an anticipated promotion to untenured associate professor (Extraordinarius), a rank attained by very few women in Germany, she was dismissed from her job as a result of Nazi anti-Jewish legislation. She left Germany with her daughter and, after spending a year as a research associate at the Institute of Mechanics in Brussels, became professor of mathematics at the University of Istanbul in 1934. Together with von Mises, she remained in Turkey for five years, lecturing first in French and then in Turkish.

In 1939, Geiringer was offered a temporary position as a lecturer at Bryn Mawr College, which enabled her to immigrate to the United States with her daughter on a nonquota visa. During World War II, she did classified research for the National Defense Research Council. In 1944, she married von Mises, who was a professor at Harvard, and received an appointment as professor of mathematics and department chair at Wheaton, a women's college in Norton, Massachusetts, a position she held until her retirement in 1959.

Hilda Geiringer became an American citizen in 1945 and no longer identified herself as a Jew but as a Unitarian. Although she was a dedicated teacher, a prolific researcher, and a Protestant, as a woman already in her fifties, Geiringer found it impossible to obtain an academic appointment in Boston and thus could not live together with her husband except on weekends and vacations. After von Mises's death in 1953, she completed and edited his unpublished works on probability and statistics while continuing to do research in this field herself.

Hilda Geiringer died of pneumonia on March 22, 1973, while on a visit to California.

BIBLIOGRAPHY

American Men of Science (1944): 635; Biermann, K.-R. *Die Mathematik und ihre Dozenten an der Berliner Universität 1810–1933* (1988); Binder, Christa. "Hilda Geiringer: ihre ersten Jahre in Amerika." In *Amphora*, edited by Sergei S. Demidov et al. (1992): 25–53; Boedeker, Elisabeth, and Maria Meyer-Plath, eds. *50 Jahre Habilitation von Frauen in Deutschland* (1974); Dresden, A. "The Migration of Mathematicians." *American Mathematical Monthly* 49 (1942): 415–429; Duren, P., ed. *A Century of Mathematics in America* (1988); Frank, Wilhelm. "Richard von Mises und Hilda Geiringer-Mises." *Vertriebene Vernunft* 2 (1987): 753–757;

Geiringer, Hilda, and Richard von Mises. Papers. Harvard University Archives, Cambridge, Mass; Humboldt University Archives, Berlin, Habilitationen #1242 (1925); *International Biographical Dictionary of Central European Emigres*. Vol. 2, part 2 (1980): 821; *Mathematical Reviews*. Cumulative Author Indexes (1940–1979); *NAW* modern; Obituary. *NYTimes*, March 24, 1973; Pinl, M., and L. Fürtmüller. "Mathematicians under Hitler." *Leo Baeck Institute Year Book* 18 (1979): 131–182; Poggendorff, J.C. *Biographisch-literarisches Handworterbuch der exakten Naturwissenschaften* (1923–1931 and 1932–1953); Richards, Joan L. "Hilda Geiringer von Mises (1893–1973)." In *Women of Mathematics. A Bibliographic Sourcebook*, edited by L.S. Grinstein and P.J. Campbell (1989): 41–46; Rossiter, Margaret W. *Women Scientists in America Before Affirmative Action 1940–1972* (1995); Tisza, Magda. Conversation with author, 1993; *Zentralblatt der Mathmatik und ihre Grenzgebiete*. Cumulative Author Index to Vols. 1–25 (1930–1940).

HARRIET PASS FREIDENREICH

GELEERD, ELISABETH ROZETTA (1909–1969)

It is noteworthy that many early women psychoanalysts from Jewish backgrounds were strongly encouraged by their fathers to pursue their professional aspirations. Elisabeth Rozetta Geleerd, who became a supervisor of several generations of child and adolescent analysts, is a case in point.

Elisabeth R. Geleerd was born on March 20, 1909, in the Netherlands to Moses and Bertha (Haas) Geleerd. The eldest of three children, she and her two younger brothers, Yap and Benedictus, grew up in comfortable circumstances in Rotterdam, where her father's business was outfitting ships. When she was nine or ten years old, her mother died of tuberculosis and she was sent to live with an aunt and uncle. This was not a positive experience, so she returned to live with her father in her early teens. Several years later, Yap died of tuberculosis. The deaths of her mother and brother influenced Geleerd's decision to study medicine at the University of Leyden. Her father supported her ambition to become a physician.

After receiving her M.D. in 1936, she moved to Vienna in order to undertake psychoanalytic training at the Vienna Psychoanalytic Institute, where her analyst was Anna Freud. In 1938, the deteriorating political situation led her to move to London, where she completed her analytic training at the Institute for Psychoanalysis, the training school of the British Psychoanalytic Society. In 1940, she arrived in the United States and worked for several years at the Menninger Clinic in Topeka, Kansas, before finally settling in

New York in 1946. That same year she married the prominent psychoanalyst Rudolph M. Loewenstein. They had one son, Richard, who became a psychiatrist.

In 1947, Geleerd was appointed a training analyst at the New York Psychoanalytic Institute and, as a member of the educational committee, played a formative role in the development of the child and adolescent analysis program at the institute. Recollections of Geleerd invariably note her sensitive and searching temperament. She was by all accounts an empathic therapist, but her approach to patients was based on a thorough grasp of psychoanalytic theory and technique. In a series of papers on the psychodynamics of childhood schizophrenia, the developmental vicissitudes of adolescence, and the psychological states of fugue and amnesia, she delineated the defenses the ego utilizes in its attempt to deal with early, often overwhelming trauma originating in the mother-child relationship. She also sought to suggest new techniques for treating seriously disturbed children and adolescents.

Geleerd's father was an atheist, and her own relationship to Judaism as a religion and cultural tradition is unknown. Certainly the outward course of her life was deeply influenced by her Jewishness, because it is doubtful she would have immigrated to the United States without the Nazi persecution of the European Jewish community. Her adopted country was immeasurably enriched by her contributions as a teacher, writer, and supervisor of other analysts.

Elisabeth Rozetta Geleerd died on May 25, 1969, in New York City.

SELECTED WORKS BY ELISABETH ROZETTA GELEERD

"Borderline States in Childhood and Adolescence." *Psychoanalytic Study of the Child* 13 (1958): 279–295; "Child Analysis: Research, Treatment and Prophylaxis." *Journal of the American Psychoanalytic Association* 12 (1964): 242–258; *The Child Analyst at Work* (1967); "Contribution to the Study of Amnesia and Allied Conditions," with F.J. Hacker and D. Rapaport. The *Psychoanalytic Quarterly* 14 (1945): 199–220; "Evaluation of Melanie Klein's 'Narrative of a Child Analysis.'" *International Journal of Psychoanalysis* 44 (1963): 493–506; "The Psychoanalysis of a Psychotic Child." *Psychoanalytic Study of the Child* 3/4 (1949): 311–332; "Some Aspects of Ego Vicissitudes in Adolescence." *Journal of the American Psychoanalytic Association* 9 (1961): 394–405.

BIBLIOGRAPHY

Kabcenell, Robert. "Eulogy for Elisabeth Geleerd." Unpublished. A.A. Brill Library, New York Psychoanalytic Institute, NYC; Loewenstein, Richard J. Personal communication, 1996; Stein, Martin. "Tribute to Elisabeth Geleerd

Loewenstein." Unpublished. A.A. Brill Library, New York Psychoanalytic Institute, NYC; Tartakoff, Helen. "Obituary—Elisabeth Geleerd Loewenstein." *International Journal of Psychoanalysis* 51 (1970): 71–73; *Who's Who of American Women* (1968–1969); *WWWIA* 5.

NELLIE L. THOMPSON

GERMAN IMMIGRANT PERIOD

The period 1820–1880 has generally been considered the era of German Jewish immigration to the United States. In these sixty years, the bulk of the 150,000 Jewish immigrants who came to the United States hailed from either areas that, in 1871, would become part of a unified Germany, or from a range of other places in Central and Eastern Europe that later in the century adopted either the German language or various aspects of German culture. In these years, Jews came to America from Alsace, Lithuania, Galicia, Moravia, Bohemia, Hungary, Poland, and parts of czarist Russia. Given the fluidity of European political boundaries in the nineteenth century, the volatility of language loyalties, and the absence of accurate immigration and census figures for this period in the United States, for women in particular, the term "German" may still be the most convenient, although not particularly precise, term by which to refer to this era in the history of Jewish immigration. Historical and popular writing consistently employ this term despite the misleading generalization implied in it.

Issues of gender and family shaped this migration from the Germanic regions, and from other parts of Central and Eastern Europe from 1820 to 1880. First, marriage became an increasingly remote option for both Jewish women and men from the poorer classes. In the 1820s and 1830s, a number of jurisdictions in the Germanic regions instituted limitations on Jewish marriage. Young Jews could marry only when a place became available on the community's roster, known as the *matrikel*. These restrictions affected not just the absolute number of Jews who could marry, but it had implications for issues of economic class. Jews who could prove that they had a reasonable chance of earning a decent living could marry, while those whose prospects seemed dimmer were denied the right. This latter group was growing larger at precisely this point in time.

Secondly, the modernization of the economies of much of Central Europe severely undermined the basis of the traditional Jewish economy, particularly that of the poorer classes. Industrialization and improvements in production and transportation wiped out much of the need for the classic Jewish occupations of peddling and eliminated the businesses of other Jews who served as intermediaries between the rural peasantry and the rest of society. As such, the daughters and sons of the less-well-off Jews had to find other options for themselves. Thousands of young Jewish women and men migrated to America because they could not make a living in Europe or marry.

The migration to America began with young, single men, although unmarried women came in relatively large numbers as well, and in some cases, entire families joined the immigrant stream. The first phase of the move to America from any town or region began first with the young men. As a consequence, in the 1820s and 1830s in Germany, for example, Jewish communities saw female majorities developing, particularly in the rural districts.

This imbalance in the earliest years of the exodus from any particular German or other Central European town was only temporary. After achieving some economic stability in America, men frequently returned to their hometowns to find a bride. Other Jewish men in America relied upon the mails to propose marriage to a young woman from the home village, or they relied upon friends or male relatives who were journeying back to Europe, asking them to contract a match for them in absentia. Thus the years that saw the towns in Germany developing Jewish female majorities found the early American Jewish communities characterized in their formative years by male majorities. In most American Jewish communities, the majority of the women arrived later than their husbands, and communities endured some period of time in which a male—and bachelor—society characterized community life.

Despite the seeming masculinity of the early migration, a surprisingly large number of single women joined the migration, even in its earliest years. Women made up 45 percent among those who left the Bavarian town of Kissingen for America in the 1830s and 1840s, for example, whereas from all of Bavaria over the course of the 1830s, men and women emigrated in roughly equal number, 12,806 and 11,701, respectively. Such figures obviously cannot tell the entire story, since some kind of time lag could have occurred between when the majority of the men and the majority of the women migrated to the United States. But importantly, Jewish women who emigrated came from the same classes and for the same reasons as the men. As daughters of the poor, they not only left to follow or meet potential spouses, but they too were victims of economic change.

ECONOMIC PATTERNS

Jewish women in Central Europe in the decades before and during the migration played a key role in the family economy. As the daughters and wives of craftsmen, they participated actively in producing and selling goods. Some women, among the somewhat more well-off, actually owned their own businesses independent of their husbands. Poor Jewish women in Europe had traditionally worked as domestic servants, while others sewed for a living with their families or on their own. Just as the economy had dried up for the men, in the more marginal rungs of the Jewish class structure, so it did for the women. These women had the same incentive to come to America as did their brothers.

The history of Jewish women in the period of the German immigration cannot be understood without an analysis of the particular economic niche that Jews came to occupy in the United States. Because so many of these immigrants were unmarried and arrived unencumbered by parents or children, they could take advantage of economic opportunities wherever they arose. While the small pockets of Jewish settlement that greeted them as of 1820 were limited to a few Atlantic coastal cities, the German Jews fanned out into almost every state and territory of the United States. They made their way through New England, the Midwest, the Great Plains, the South, and even the Far West, although they also settled in New York and Philadelphia and the other cities that already had well-established Jewish communities.

Although primarily going to agricultural areas, the male German Jews who "pioneered" and the women who joined them somewhat later did not do so as farmers, but as small-scale entrepreneurs ready to serve the needs of the rural population. Americans in the hinterlands had little access to finished goods of all sorts, since few retail establishments existed outside the large cities. Jewish men overwhelmingly came to these remote areas as peddlers, an occupation that required little capital for start-up and that fit the life of the single man. In the large regional cities, Jewish immigrant men would load themselves up with a pack of goods, weighing sometimes as much as one hundred pounds, and then embark on a journey by foot, or eventually, if a peddler succeeded, by horse and wagon. So widespread was Jewish peddling that in 1840, 46 percent of all Jewish men made a living this way, and by 1845, the number climbed to 70 percent. Of the 125 Jewish residents of Iowa in the 1850s, 100 were peddlers. Memoir literature and biographical details of Jewish men who began their lives in America as peddlers indicate that most plied their trade during the week and on the Sabbath they gathered together in the larger communities, in Jewish-operated boardinghouses, sometimes managed by the rare Jewish woman resident. In 1854, for example, a Mrs. Weinshank, ran a boardinghouse in Portland, Oregon—five years before statehood—which catered to the Jewish peddlers of the Pacific Northwest.

The concentration of Jewish men in peddling had implications for women and for the process of family and community formation. First, peddling as an occupation sustained the singleness of the migration and the process by which young men migrated first, followed by women later, depending upon the speed with which the peddler could amass the requisite capital to become a shopkeeper. Typically these immigrant peddlers decided to marry at the point at which they had graduated from peddling to owning a small store, either in the hinterlands itself or in a larger city with a more substantial Jewish community already in place. The Jewish man who returned to his Bavarian or Bohemian hometown to contract a marriage frequently made arrangements to find willing women, often the sisters or cousins or friends of his bride, to come back to America as the fiancées of the many eligible Jewish bachelors there. Since the migration of this period flowed continuously, Jewish communities, particularly the smaller ones, tended to experience a dynamic in which single men predominated, followed by the arrival of women, often to be followed by a new influx of single men, who would shortly thereafter be joined by women.

The Jewish women who came to America in the years 1820 to 1880 came from the exact places and classes as did the men. Despite the absence of any kind of statistical evidence, it is possible to say, however, that these women came to America not only to marry but to work. Their exact number cannot be ascertained, however, because most of these women labored in family stores and shops. Numerous contemporary commentators described women in these roles. The smaller the store, the more likely wives, and then daughters, worked. Indeed, men may have timed their marriage with getting off the road and into a shop precisely in order to have the services of a wife to operate the business jointly with them. Some memoirs describe men in a family, the husband and his brothers, continuing to do some peddling, while the wife and other female family members sold from behind the counter, offering the family the possibility of a diversified operation. Jews predominated in the sale of dry goods in small and large communities. These dry-goods stores emphasized the sale of clothing, and many of the Jewish men and women who owned and operated these stores also manufactured the clothes. The success of stores in which clothing was both made and sold along with other kinds of miscellaneous goods depended equally upon the labors of men and women, adults and children. A man could not really envision such a store without a family.

Jewish women in this period worked not only as the wives and daughters of petty shopkeepers, but in other ways as well. When husbands died, wives often carried on family businesses on their own. This widespread phenomenon was particularly significant, because given the nature of the migration process, men tended to marry women significantly younger than themselves, thus making the probability of widowhood higher and accentuating the need for women to be self-supporting.

Married women and widows appeared in many community and family histories as operators of boardinghouses. Recognizing the need for feeding and lodging the stream of single men migrating to America, Jewish women turned their homes into businesses. Boarding operations supplemented income from other family enterprises, or provided the family's sole support. These Jewish women combined their domestic activities of cooking and cleaning with the imperative for making a living.

Jewish immigrant women, married and single, also sometimes created their own businesses, in essence keeping alive what seemed to have been a long-standing European Jewish tradition. Generally these women ventured into the same kinds of small businesses that Jewish men did. A few examples from a number of communities demonstrate this pattern. Amelia Dannenberg came to San Francisco with her husband in the 1850s from the Rhineland, and she launched a children's clothing business. By the 1870s, she branched out to manufacture men's and women's clothing as well. The mother of Judah David Eisenstein, a Hebraist, opened a dry-goods store on New York's Lower East Side in 1872 so that her son could engage in full-time study. As late as 1879, it became clear to the Lissner family in Oakland, California, that the family could not survive on husband Louis's income as a pawnbroker. So the wife, Matilda, decided to raise chickens, and she peddled the eggs on the city streets. Bella Block had learned millinery work in Bavaria before immigrating, and in Newark, New Jersey, she opened her own shop prior to marriage and continued to operate it afterward. She and her husband also jointly ran a grocery store. These and other examples from almost every Jewish community in the United States make it clear that women played a crucial role in the family economy, and indeed such an economy could not have existed without their input.

PHILANTHROPIC AND COMMUNAL ORGANIZATION

Not all Jews, men or women, did well economically, and Jewish women in particular suffered from financial distress and insecurity. Their high rates of widowhood caused a good deal of that distress. Indeed, in most communities, widows made up a disproportionate share of the Jewish indigent. These included both those with and without children to raise. Jewish children turned up in orphanages more often if they had lost fathers than if they had lost mothers, since men could make do, but women had a difficult time supporting children on their own. The development of philanthropic organizations for poor Jewish women indicated the extent of the problem, and asylums in a number of cities pointed to the feminine nature of poverty. Port cities like New York, Philadelphia, Baltimore, and New Orleans had the highest rates of Jewish female poverty, although inland and secondary communities had them as well. In almost every Jewish community special charitable events and organizations turned their attention to alleviating the special suffering of Jewish women.

The specific problems of the Jewish female poor pointed to another aspect of Jewish women's lives in America in the mid-nineteenth century: the creation of philanthropic and communal organizations by women, usually, although not exclusively, for women. The creation of these organizations, which in many communities called themselves Ladies' Hebrew Benevolent Associations, actually represented the fairly simple transplantation to America of traditional Jewish women's organizations from Europe, the *khevrot nashim*. Ritually, the women had responsibility for performing the responsibilities associated with the burial of other women. The women in these associations, in Europe and in America, adhered to a tradition that required Jews to visit the sick (*bikkur holim*) and to prepare the dead for burial. Strict sex segregation had to be maintained: Men took care of the men; women ministered to the women. The women of the association purified the corpse, sat with it, read aloud from the Psalms, and accompanied the body to the cemetery. A women's benevolent association of New Haven, Connecticut, in the 1850s was typical. Named Ahavas Achos [the love of sisters], it operated according to a formal constitution, which mandated a "sick committee" to sit at the bedside of the dying. Between death and burial, two women remained with the deceased at all times. A specially trained group of ten women washed the body, and all members had to contribute six cents toward the "death cloth"—sewed by the women themselves—of any impoverished sister.

Dues collected also went to various charitable purposes, determined by the members. By and large, funds amassed by the women supported the relief of female poverty and distress. Additionally, the women sponsored various fund-raising events, many of them quite American in format, like "dime parties," theatricals, and "strawberry socials."

These *khevrot nashim* functioned as complementary associations to the male, *khevre kadisha*. They served the same religious and communal needs, and members and leaders tended to come from the same families. For example, Sarah Zlottwitz of Swerenz in Posen and Jacob Rich, who had migrated from the same town, married in 1853 at San Francisco's Sherith Israel Congregation. At the time that they married, she served as treasurer of the Ladies' United Hebrew Benevolent Society and he as secretary of the First Hebrew Benevolent Society, the men's association.

In two ways, however, the women's societies differed from the men's, and these differences provide some important insights into the status and vision of Jewish women in the period of the German immigration. First, unlike the male associations, women's groups did not hold title to the cemetery. Since these organizations were structured around issues of death and burial, this amounted to an important difference. Thus, some of the women's associations installed men as their chief officers, and the men, who did own the cemetery, represented the women to the outside society. Secondly, the men's associations tended to break down along congregational lines, according to place of origin in Europe, and even sometimes by occupation or neighborhood in an American city. Women tended to form more inclusive organizations, ones that served a broader swathe of the Jewish female population and which transcended the divisions that split the men.

The women may have opted for the more general type of organization because they did not belong to the congregations, which represented the most crucial and common division for the men. As women who had been excluded from discussions and debates about citizenship and emancipation in Europe, they may not have been especially identified with place of origin in Europe. Or it may be that because many of the Jewish communities in America had experienced periods of time in which women constituted a minority, the women gravitated toward each other, ignoring all sorts of other divisions, in search of female companionship.

Scattered evidence from many individual communities indicates that the women's benevolent organizations did quite well at fund-raising and amassed solid treasuries. Although women did not belong to congregations, their benevolent associations often provided funding for congregations that wanted to rent space, as opposed to worshipping in homes and stores, or that wanted to move out of rented rooms into their own building. Rabbi Liebman Adler of Detroit's Temple Beth El lavishly praised the women of Ahavas Achos on the pages of *DIE DEBORAH*, a German-language supplement to Isaac Mayer Wise's *Israelite*. He noted that in 1859 these women had donated $250 "with the proviso that steps will be taken speedily towards the earnest realization of the long-discussed building of the synagogue." In Baton Rouge, Louisiana, in 1874, the Ladies' Hebrew Association had been asked by the men of the congregation for money. The women agreed to give, but only if "the Gentlemen's congregation . . . not use the money collected for rent of lot Cor[ner] North and Church . . . and that the said money only be used for purposes of the Building Fund."

These Jewish women's associations, and others not necessarily connected to burial, maintained a strong presence in providing charitable relief to the Jewish poor. The widespread involvement of Jewish women in charitable work in America may have been a characteristic way in which Jewish women in America differed from their European counterparts. American Jewish women in this period, immigrants from various parts of Central Europe, created a wide range of charitable enterprises, and funded and operated them as well. In America, Jewish women in various communities created orphanages, day nurseries, maternity hospitals, soup kitchens, shelters for widows, and the like. Groups such as the Montefiore Lodge Ladies' Hebrew Benevolent Association in Providence, Rhode Island, engaged in friendly visiting to the needy and distressed, and gave out coal, clothing, food, eyeglasses, and medicine. The Johanna Lodge in Chicago helped newly arrived single immigrant girls set up businesses. Some of these organizations, such as the Deborah Society in Hartford, Connecticut, grew out of female burial societies. Others, such as the Detroit Ladies' Society for the Support of Hebrew Widows and Orphans, started specifically as female philanthropic organizations. Some of the women's charitable societies at some point had male boards of directors or a male president of the board; others operated with female-only leadership. The organizational activities of Jewish women in America may have been inspired by the activities of charitable activism of Protestant women in their communities. Or it may have been in part modeled on the activities of the upper-class Jewish women and others from the Sephardic congregations like Mikveh Israel, epitomized by REBECCA GRATZ of Philadelphia, who pioneered in the creation of Jewish women's organizations. The origins of the wide range of associational activities of Jewish immigrant women in mid-nineteenth-century America may actually have grown out of the migration experience itself. Young women and men came to America and had to create communities from the ground up. Without the support of parents and other family members, they were forced to create new kinds of institutions to deal with the problems engendered by their move.

Most of Jewish women's associational life existed on the local level. Yet at least one attempt was made by some of them to create a nationally based organization in this period. The Unabhaengiger Treue Schwestern, the United Order of True Sisters, was founded in 1846 in New York, and by 1851 branches had spread to Philadelphia, Albany, and New Haven. Its lodges provided various forms of self-help to members, and like the men who at the same time in American Jewish history founded the B'nai B'rith, Kesher shel Barzel, and other fraternal orders, the True Sisters embellished its meetings with secret rituals, distinctive ceremonial garb, and other kinds of specific paraphernalia. Similar to B'nai B'rith, the True Sisters in some places operated as a kind of female counterpart or, indeed, as a ladies' auxiliary to the larger all-male B'nai B'rith.

RELIGIOUS OBSERVANCE

The period of the German Jewish immigration also changed women's relationship to Judaism as a religious system. Traditionally much of Jewish women's crucial involvement in the maintenance of halakah, the vast body of Jewish law and practice, took place in the home, as women performed their domestic chores. Those tasks had either direct or indirect connection to the fulfillment of ritual obligation, be it in preparing for the Sabbath, guarding the kashrut of the family's food, or monitoring the strict observance of laws of family purity. With a few limited exceptions, such as the *khevrot nashim* and the supervision of the ritual bath, used primarily by women to purify themselves before marriage, after childbirth, and upon the completion of their monthly menstruation, public Judaism in Europe functioned as an all-male preserve.

Migration to America challenged the dichotomization of Judaism into a public and private sphere, which roughly corresponded to the male and female. The migration made the observance of private Jewish ritual life, which is most closely tied to women's activities, more difficult and less often observed. Communities struggled with the problem of securing kosher food, and even in communities where kosher meat was available, high levels of community conflict ensued over the punctiliousness of slaughterers and butchers. Evidence points to a steady decline in the observance of kashrut in America. The shopkeepers and petty merchants who made up the vast majority of American Jews did not adhere strictly to restrictions of Sabbath activities either. Instead, under the pressures of the American marketplace, where, for example, stores were usually closed on Sundays, they worked on the halakically mandated day of rest. It is harder to know how many communities maintained *mikvahs*, the ritual baths, and how many women used them on a regular basis. Minutes of various congregational meetings in the mid-nineteenth century across the United States referred to the construction and maintenance of a ritual bath or to some controversy over its supervision. While the traditionalists among the immigrants of this period denounced Jewish women in America for their failure to fulfill the commandment of *niddah* [ritual impurity], communities did indeed build, according to sacred specifications, these facilities. There is, however, no reason to believe that this ritual proved to be any hardier than the others, and it too probably fell into disuse.

But, over the course of the period 1820 to 1880, Jewish women came to assume a more public presence in the observance of Judaism. This assumption did not come as part of any kind of challenge to the reality that membership in congregations and participation in congregational affairs continued to be limited to men. Women had to be expressly invited to attend congregational events, and no evidence exists that Jewish women sought to challenge overtly this status quo.

But American Jewish women began attending synagogue on a regular basis much more often than they would have had they remained in Europe, and indeed many commentators decried the fact that women worshippers often outnumbered men on any given Sabbath morning. Although they continued to sit in the women's section, mothers often were the ones who brought their children to the synagogue, while husbands may have been standing behind the counters of the family store. The preponderance of women present at synagogue was confirmed by many of the rabbis of the time, who viewed the move toward a feminized congregation as a problem. Isaac Mayer Wise, for example, who was a major advocate of mixed male-female seating, criticized this tendency in American Judaism. In 1877, for example, he reported in the *Israelite*, the newspaper he edited, about a recent trip to the West Coast. "All over California," he lamented, "as a general thing the ladies must maintain Judaism. They are three-fourths of the congregations in the temple every Sabbath and send their children to the Sabbath schools. With a very few exceptions, the men keep no Sabbath."

Jewish women did not seek to participate more fully in the affairs of the synagogues in this era. But the fact that in the years of the German Jewish immigration Jewish women came to predominate as worshippers may have laid the groundwork for a challenge that did take place in future decades. It may also be that the emerging female majority at Sabbath services influenced leaders of the Reform Movement like Isaac Mayer Wise, David Einhorn, and others to begin to call for mixed seating. They may have hoped that moving toward family pews, as opposed to retention of sex-segregated service, would bring the men back to services.

Additionally rabbis, particularly the Reform-oriented, were aware of a public discourse in Christian magazines and among gentile Americans about the supposed backwardness of Judaism, exemplified by the segregation of women during religious services. Some Americans wrote about this practice as an "oriental" atavism, a "mistreatment" of women, and a "great error of the Jews," in which "she is separated and huddled into a gallery like beautiful crockery ware, while the men perform the ceremonies below." Indeed, Christian writers at this time of militant evangelicalism held up the separation of Jewish women in the synagogue as evidence of the rightness of Christianity. "It was the author of Christianity," noted one writer, "that brought her [the woman] out of this Egyptian bondage and put her on an equality with the other sex in civil and religious rites."

Whatever the motivation of the leaders of Reform, Jewish women in the middle decades of the nineteenth century began to make themselves more publicly visible as Jews and as the defenders of Judaism. Jewish women, for example, began to produce religiously inspired literature in almost all of the Jewish publications, including *Die Deborah* and the *Israelite*, which represented the Reform-oriented tendency in American Judaism, and *The Occident* and *Jewish Messenger*, which stood on the more traditional end of the spectrum. Their poems, short stories, and nonfiction emphasized the importance of loyalty to Judaism and to family. They depicted women as the bearers of the Jewish tradition through their families, and they encouraged young Jews, both women and men, to steadfastly resist assimilation into Protestant American culture and to withstand the aggressive efforts of evangelical Christian organizations. The entrance of Jewish women into the world of print journalism represented a significant departure for them. They had no models for women engaging in this kind of activity. Indeed, one woman writing as "Miriam" for the *Jewish Messenger* begged her readers' pardon, for "it may appear presumptuous in a female to enter into comments upon scriptural themes, but the daughters of Israel have always felt that allegiance to Zion was paramount to every other sentiment."

By their behavior, Jewish women in America in the period 1820 to 1880 shared much with other American women. Both Jewish and Christian women responded to the same social and cultural contexts of industrializing America, in which men came increasingly to define their worth and identity in terms of the acquisition of wealth and less in the realm of the sacred. As men moved away from a commitment to community through religion, women filled the vacuum. American women in general participated actively in nineteenth-century public religious life in a way that overtly jarred with traditional European Jewish practice. The "cult of true womanhood" of mid-nineteenth-century America assigned to women the proper zone of morality and goodness and defined religion increasingly as falling under women's sphere of influence. As religion faded in significance to men in Victorian America, women, powerless in the political arena, turned to religion as an institution in which over time they could function comfortably. Jewish women's behavior followed along these lines, although they did not directly challenge the policies and procedures of synagogue life.

The era of the German Jewish immigration brought approximately 150,000 Jews to the United States from Central and Eastern Europe. Women accounted for half of the immigrants, and they played a key role in the functioning of a family economy that allowed for steady and modest economic mobility, for the formation of communities from the ground up, which in turn provided services for the needy and for the emergence of a modern, American Judaism.

BIBLIOGRAPHY

Cohen, Naomi. *Encounter with Emancipation: The German Jews in the United States, 1830–1914* (1984); Diner, Hasia R. *A Time for Gathering: The Second Migration, 1820–1880* (1992); Strauss, Herbert A. "The Immigration and Acculturation of the German Jew in the United States of America." In *Year Book XVI of the Leo Baeck Institute* (1971).

HASIA R. DINER

GERSTEN, BERTA (c. 1896–1972)

Berta Gersten, a tall, regal, soft-spoken actress, was a highly acclaimed leading lady in the Yiddish art theater movement for fifty years. Her career on the English-language stage, though shorter, was also distinguished.

Gersten was born in Cracow, Poland, probably in 1896, the older child and only daughter of Avrom and Meshe (Kopps) Gerstenman. She grew up in an Orthodox family; her father was a religious teacher at a Jewish school. In 1899, the family immigrated to New York, where her mother became a dressmaker, and her father worked as a courthouse translator. Gersten's acting career began when one of her mother's clients, many of whom were Yiddish actresses, needed a child for a performance.

After finishing elementary school, Gersten worked in a box factory to help support her family. Her interest, however, was the theater. In 1908, she played her first formal role as Shloymele in Jacob Gordin's *Mirele Efros*, and subsequently appeared in various Yiddish music halls, including nine months with Kappelman's Vaudeville House.

In 1915, she enjoyed her first success with a leading role in Leon Kobrin's *Yisroel's Hofnung* [Israel's hope] at the Thomashefsky Theater. A highly respected actress on the Yiddish stage by 1918, she was invited by Maurice Schwartz, along with CELIA ADLER, ANNA APPEL, Jacob Ben-Ami, and Ludwig Satz, to be one of the original members in his Yiddish Art Theater. She remained affiliated with the troupe on an irregular basis until its demise in 1950, playing leading roles in a wide repertoire of Yiddish and European plays in New York, as well as on tours in prewar Poland, South America, and the United States. She also played with other Yiddish companies. Most important, however, was her lifelong affiliation with Jacob Ben-Ami. As his leading lady, she toured South America and the United States regularly, always playing to critical and popular acclaim.

Gersten appeared in two Yiddish films. Best known for her performance of Mirele in *Mirele Efros* (1939), she also played Pesenyu in *Got, Mentsh un Tayvl* [God, man, and the devil] (1949).

Her debut on the English-language stage came late in life, at a time when the Yiddish theater had declined significantly. In 1954, she played with Ben-Ami in *The World of Sholom Aleichem*. That same year she made her Broadway debut in Clifford Odets's *The Flowering Peach*, opposite Menasha Skulnik. She also toured with *A Majority of One* (1959). The role of Benny's mother in *The Benny Goodman Story* (1956)

One of the original members of Maurice Schwartz's Yiddish Art Theater, Berta Gersten had a lifelong affiliation with actor Jacob Ben-Ami, often playing his leading lady. [New York Public Library]

remained her only Hollywood film credit. She appeared last opposite Ben-Ami in *My Father's Court* at the Folksbiene Playhouse in New York in 1971.

In 1911, she married Isaac Hershel Finkel (he later changed his name to Irwin H. Fenn), son of Yiddish actors Morris and Anetta Finkel. Fenn, a professor of mathematics and physics for over forty years at Brooklyn Polytechnic Institute, died in 1960. Their son, Albert Fenn, born in 1912, became a photojournalist and was affiliated with *Time* magazine for several decades. During the last few years of her life, Gersten lived with Ben-Ami. On September 10, 1972, she died of cancer in New York City.

BIBLIOGRAPHY

AJYB 24:144; *American Jewish Biography* (1994); "Berta Gerstin: A Hays-Pulsirendik Yidish Harts Hot Zikh Opgeshtelt" [Berta Gersten: A warm Jewish heart stopped beating]. *Forverts* (September 15, 1972): 8; *European Immigrant*

Women in the United States: A Biographical Dictionary. Edited by Judy Barrett Litoff and Judith McDonnell (1994); Gersten, Berta. Press clippings, reviews, and photographs. Billy Rose Theatre Collection, New York Public Library, Lincoln Center, NYC, YIVO Institute for Jewish Research, NYC, and Museum of the City of New York; Gerstin, Berta. "Ikh un Dos Publikum" [The audience and I]. *Der Tog* (February 3, 1928): 3; Kobrin, Leon. *Erinerungen fun a Yidishen Dramaturg* [Memories of a Yiddish playwright]. Vol. 2 (1925); *Leksikon fun Yidishn Teater* [Lexicon of the Yiddish theater]. Vol. 1. Edited by Zalmen Zylbercwaig (1931); *NAW* modern; *NYTimes Biographical Edition*, 1972, and Obituary. September 11, 1972, 40:4; Perlov, Yitskhak. "Dos Mayestetishe Geshtalt fun Berta Gersten" [The majestic figure of Berta Gersten]. *Forverts* (September 15, 1972): 8; *Who's Who in Hollywood, 1900–1976* (1976); *Who Was Who on Screen*, 2d ed. (1977); *WWIAJ* (1926, 1928).

NINA WARNKE

GEZARI, TEMIMA (b. 1905)

Artist and innovator in Jewish art education, Temima Gezari was born Fruma Nimtzowitz in Pinsk, Russia, on December 21, 1905. She immigrated to the United States with her family as an infant and grew up in Brownsville, Brooklyn, where her father, Yisroel, and her mother, Bella (Cohen) Nimtzowitz, raised Temima along with her sister, Etta, and brother, Ruby.

Gezari discovered her interest in both Jewish education and art at an early age. She graduated from the Brooklyn Girls High School in 1921, from the Teachers Institute of the Jewish Theological Seminary of America in 1925, and from the Master Institute of United Arts in 1930. She also studied at Parsons New York School of Fine and Applied Art, the Art Students League, Columbia University, the New School for Social Research, and the Taos School of Art in New Mexico. In March 1995, she received an honorary doctorate of letters from the Jewish Theological Seminary of America.

While serving as artist-in-residence on Kibbutz Mishmar Ha'emek in Palestine, she met Zvi Gezari, an industrial engineer, whom she married in Tel Aviv in 1938. They had two sons, Daniel (b. 1942) and Walter (b. 1944).

Gezari became director of the department of art education at the Board of Jewish Education (BJE) in New York in 1940, when she was hired by Dr. Alexander Dushkin. As a resource to New York–area teachers in Jewish afternoon and day schools, the department provides programming and workshops for art teachers. Each year, the department sponsors citywide exhibitions of children's art, which have been shown in the American Museum of Natural History, the Museum of the City of New York, the Brooklyn Museum, and the Jewish Museum in New York. The BJE also publishes *Brush and Color*, a bulletin for art teachers.

In addition to BJE work, Gezari has taught in a variety of settings. Mordecai Kaplan, then dean of the Teachers Institute, appointed her to the institute's faculty in 1935, and she taught art education and art history there for forty-two years. Gezari also taught in the Clinic for Gifted Children at New York University and lectured across the United States on the philosophy of art.

Gezari has painted and sculpted worldwide and has had solo shows in New York, Philadelphia, Cleveland, Washington, D.C., and Jerusalem. Her murals have adorned the Society for the Advancement of Judaism in New York, and a 1938 mural, originally done for Camp Cejwin in Port Jervis, New York, was restored and reinstalled in the library of Yemin Ord, the children's village on Mount Carmel in Israel. *Lament*, a bronze sculpture, was commissioned by Yad Vashem. Much of Gezari's art work is done at her studio and home in Rocky Point, Long Island.

A gifted artist as well as educator, Gezari has combined her talents in a number of publications. She illustrated several books, including *Gateway to Jewish Song, Children of the Emek, Hillel's Happy Holidays*, and *Dovid'll*. She is the coauthor of *The Jewish Kindergarten* and the author of *Footprints and New Worlds: Experiences in Art with Child and Adult*. She has also produced numerous filmstrips. *Art and the Growing Child* won the Silver Reel Award from the Film Council of America (1957) and the Scholastic Award (1957). Her articles on art and education have appeared in magazines such as *Art in Childhood, The Reconstructionist*, and *Jewish Education Magazine*.

A trailblazer, Temima Gezari has had a profound influence on the course of American Jewish education. Her philosophy of using art to teach about Jewish holidays and customs has left an indelible mark on countless schoolchildren. After more than fifty years in the field, she is a legendary presence in Jewish education.

BIBLIOGRAPHY

Gezari, Daniel, ed. *The Art of Temima Gezari* (1985); Gezari, Temima. *Footprints and New Worlds: Experiences in Art with Child and Adult* (1964); Josephs, Susan. "Where Life and Art Meet." *The Jewish Week*, February 16, 1996, 16–17.

SUZANNE KLING

GIDEON, MIRIAM (1906–1996)

Miriam Gideon had a notable career as a musical educator and as a prolific composer whose works have been widely performed and published.

She was born in Greeley, Colorado, on October 23, 1906. She displayed early musical talents, which were encouraged with piano studies. She continued her studies in Boston, with Hans Barth, and with her uncle Henry Gideon, a composer and conductor. After settling in New York City, she continued studies with Lazare Saminsky and Roger Sessions. She also earned a B.A. degree from Boston University, an M.A. from Columbia University, and, in 1970, a Doctor of Sacred Music degree from the Jewish Theological Seminary of America (JTSA). She joined the faculties of Brooklyn College and CUNY, the Manhattan School of Music, and then in 1955 the newly formed Cantors Institute of JTSA.

In 1949, Gideon married writer-educator Frederic Ewen, a colleague at Brooklyn College. He died in 1989.

Her roster of over fifty compositions includes selections for full and chamber orchestras, instrumental solos and ensembles, piano music, vocal solos, choral works, cantatas, and a chamber opera. Among Gideon's honors are the Ernest Bloch Choral Prize and awards from the American Society of Composers, Authors and Publishers (ASCAP), the National Federation of Music Clubs, and the American Academy of Arts and Letters. She received commissions from the New York Camerata, the Da Capo Chamber Players, the Elizabeth Sprague Coolidge Foundation in the Library of Congress, and Park Avenue Synagogue in New York City, as well as a composer's grant from the National Endowment for the Arts. A strong interest in literature guided her settings of poetry by Robert Burns, Cyril Connolly, Heinrich Heine, Robert Herrick, Friedrich Hölderlin, James Joyce, John Keats, Amy Lowell, Archibald MacLeish, Edna St. Vincent Millay, Christina Rossetti, and William Shakespeare.

Gideon's compositions include several of particular Judaic inspiration: *Sacred Service*, for soloists, mixed choir, flute, oboe, trumpet, bassoon, viola, cello, and organ; a Sabbath evening service entitled *Shirat Miriam L'Shabbat* [Song of Miriam for Sabbath], for cantor-tenor, mixed choir, flute, oboe, trumpet, bassoon, viola, cello, and organ; *Spiritual Madrigals*, for male voices, with viola, cello, and bassoon; a song cycle based upon biblical texts from Psalms and Proverbs called *Eishet Chayil* [A woman of valor], for soprano and piano; *Adon Olam* [Lord God of all], an anthem for chorus, oboe, trumpet, and strings; a cantata based upon the Book of Proverbs, entitled *The Habitable Earth*, for solos, chorus, oboe, and piano or organ; Psalm 84, *How Goodly Are Thy Tents*, for women's voices, with piano or organ; and a wordless spiritual, *Biblical Masks*, for violin and piano or solo organ. Her compositions are profoundly introspective and skillful. Crafted in the genre of what she preferred to describe as "free atonality," they are highly concentrated and of strong impact. She said of her *Shirat Miriam L'Shabbat*, "It is as much an expression of the meaning of Sabbath as it is of what I feel to be my place among the Jewish people."

Miriam Gideon died in New York City on June 18, 1996.

BIBLIOGRAPHY
WWIAJ (1938).

IRENE HESKES

GIKOW, RUTH (1915–1982)

Ruth Gikow reached maturity as an artist during the heyday of abstract expressionism, yet she remained committed to a figurative art that, she believed, reflected the humanity of her subjects and was both politically and socially relevant.

Ruth Gikow was born in Ukraine on January 16, 1915. As a child, Gikow immigrated to the United States with her father, Boris Gikow, a photographer, and her mother, Lena. They settled on the Lower East Side of New York City, where Gikow grew up in poverty. She intended to pursue a career as a fashion artist after graduating from high school in 1932. Instead, unable to find a job, she enrolled at Cooper Union, where she was a pupil of the American regionalist painter John Steuart Curry and Austin Purvis, Jr., director of the school. As she had throughout high school, Gikow continued to support herself and contribute to the family income by working evenings at Woolworth's.

During her studies at Cooper Union, Gikow abandoned her aspiration to do commercial work and chose painting instead. A fellowship during her second year allowed her to study privately with idealistic young Raphael Soyer. Soon an informal exhibition of her work, painted in a social realist style, was held at the Eighth Street Playhouse in Greenwich Village. From then on, her subjects remained the urban environment and the vast multiplicity of its inhabitants.

After finishing her art studies, Gikow worked on the Federal Art Project of the WPA, associating with many other idealistic young artists who believed that art could change the world. Inspired by the Mexican muralists José Clemente Orozco and Diego Rivera, Gikow sought work on the mural section of the FAP. Her first commission was in 1939 for the children's ward of the Bronx Hospital. During World War II, there was little market for Gikow's paintings and she turned instead to free-lance commercial art and textile design. By 1945, she stopped painting and became art director at an advertising agency.

In 1946, Gikow resumed painting and married artist Jack Levine. Her first solo show, held at Weyhe Gallery in New York in November of that year, included experimental and stylized compositions. The couple began traveling to Europe in 1947. Their frequent sojourns thereafter included Italy, France, Spain, Greece, Holland, Belgium, and Japan. Gikow's paintings, particularly those made after a visit to Italy, reflect the country's devastation during the war.

The dominance of abstract expressionism during the 1950s influenced Gikow. However, her figural compositions remained grounded in reality, although she continued to work from memory rather than from models. Surrealism seems also to have influenced her montagelike canvases. Her paintings are characterized by a sensitive rendering of mood and psychology, often revealing the loneliness and pathos of her subjects. Compared to her earlier flat and linear easel paintings, Gikow's paintings from the mid-1950s are bold, simplified, thinly painted compositions that use larger canvases and show figures seemingly in motion. In 1959, Gikow was awarded a grant from the National Institute of Arts and Letters.

During the 1960s and 1970s, Gikow continued to portray subjects taken from her observations of the social and political life around her, including incidents from the civil rights and anti–Vietnam War movements. A rare Jewish subject, *The Burial* (1964), was one of the largest canvases she ever painted. Gikow's work is included in the permanent collections of major American museums, including the Metropolitan Museum of Art, the Museum of Modern Art, and the Philadelphia Museum of Art.

Ruth Gikow died in 1982.

BIBLIOGRAPHY

Cochrane, Diane. "Ruth Gikow Chronicler of our Times." *American Artist* (January 1973): 44–50, 73; Fleischman, Lawrence A. Introduction to *Ruth Gikow: Recent Work* (1976); Josephson, Matthew. Introduction to *Ruth Gikow* (1970); Rubinstein, Charlotte Streifer. *American Women Artists from Early Indian Times to the Present* (1982); "Ruth Gikow Dead: Painter of People." *NYTimes*, April 3, 1982; Weller, Allen. *Art USA Now* (1963).

SUSAN CHEVLOWE

GILBERT, SUSAN BRANDEIS
(1893–1975)

On June 5, 1916, Susan Brandeis, a University of Chicago Law School student, watched her father, Louis Dembitz Brandeis—a Harvard Law School graduate, millionaire, socially conscious Boston lawyer—take the oath of office as an associate justice of the United States Supreme Court. He was the first Jewish associate justice of the Court, and Susan would soon be the first woman lawyer whose parent sat on that bench.

Louis Brandeis and his wife, ALICE GOLDMARK BRANDEIS, were second cousins born to German Jewish emigrés. The Brandeises were nonobservant Jews. Louis's only connection with Jewish life in his youth was through his maternal uncle, Louis Dembitz. Alice Brandeis gave birth to Susan in Boston on February 27, 1893, and to her sister Elizabeth on April 25, 1896. Her mother never fully recovered her physical and psychic energy after Elizabeth's birth. For a while, her maternal aunt, JOSEPHINE GOLDMARK, came to help the family. Her father directed the household and the raising of his daughters. They took their mother's place as his companions during his regular outdoor activities. His intellectual influence was also profound: Susan became a lawyer, while Elizabeth became an economics professor at the University of Wisconsin.

In looks, inner drive, vigor, and political and social skills, Gilbert took after her father. In her lifelong lack of interest in cooking and clothes, she resembled her mother. Her social consciousness, morals, and social values were a legacy of both her parents. To her, literature, law, and causes for human equality were always more important than material possessions.

She was educated at Boston's Winsor School, Bryn Mawr College (B.A., 1915), and the University of Chicago Law School (LL.B., 1919). In 1916, she worked for woman suffrage in Boston.

New York City became her home in 1921. The Brandeis family spent their summers together at the family home in Chatham, Massachusetts, where they boated and swam daily. Although Louis and Alice Brandeis lived frugally, they were important philanthropists supporting HADASSAH, Zionism, and the University of Kentucky.

Admitted to the New York bar in 1921, no law firm would hire her because she was a woman, an event Susan Gilbert remembered all her life. That her father sat on the United States Supreme Court made no difference. Gilbert was appointed special assistant to the United States attorney in New York City. She prosecuted the Trenton Pottery antitrust suit. Shortly thereafter, she went into private practice with Samuel Rosenman. When she came before the Supreme Court to argue a case, Louis Brandeis removed himself from the bench to avoid a conflict of interest. Gilbert lost the case.

She met Jacob Gilbert, who was the opposing attorney in a minor landlord-tenant case. The couple married on December 22, 1925, at the New York Ethical Culture Society, and had three children: Louis (b. 1926), Alice (b. 1928), and Frank (b. 1930). Some traditional Jewish practices now became a part of Susan Gilbert's life. In 1939, she and her husband established the law firm of Gilbert and Brandeis.

A very private woman, Gilbert compartmentalized her life. Many people knew some of her activities, but few people knew all of them. She was the second woman member of the New York State Board of Regents appointed by Governor Herbert Lehman, serving in that post from 1935 to 1949. She was also an active member of the Bar Association of New York City, HADASSAH, the Women's City Club, and the Democratic Party.

When Brandeis University was founded in Waltham, Massachusetts, in 1949, Susan and Jacob Gilbert were deeply involved in its development. She became the honorary national president of its National Women's Committee, was made fellow of the university in 1952, and was awarded a doctor of humane letters in 1963.

Her husband, Jacob, died on April 8, 1966. Susan Gilbert suffered a stroke several years before her death on October 8, 1975. After funeral services in Temple Rodolph Shalom she was buried in Union Fields Cemetery, Queens, New York. Their three children survived them. Alice Popkins is a third-generation lawyer, Frank is with the National Trust for Historical Preservation, and Louis is a researcher.

BIBLIOGRAPHY

AJYB 77:594; Gilbert, Frank Brandeis, and Alice Brandeis Gilbert Popkins. Interviews by author, May 1996; *NYTimes*, October 9, 1975, 44:1; Strum, Philippa. *Louis Brandeis* (1984); Thomas, Dorothy. *Women Lawyers in the United States* (1957).

DOROTHY THOMAS

GILLIGAN, CAROL (b. 1936)

Carol Gilligan has broken new ground in psychology, challenging mainstream psychologists with her theory that accepted benchmarks of moral and personal developments were drawn to a male bias and do not apply to women. Gilligan proposed that women have different moral criteria and follow a different path in maturation. A psychologist who taught at Harvard and Cambridge, Gilligan brought a feminist perspective to challenge Freud and new life to the statement "The personal is political."

Carol Gilligan was born on November 28, 1936, in New York City, the daughter of William E. Friedman and Mabel (Caminez) Friedman. Her father was a lawyer and her mother a teacher. Self-described as a Jewish child of the Holocaust era, she grew up with firm moral and political convictions. As a child she studied language and music. At Swarthmore, she studied literature and graduated with highest honors in 1958.

She went to Radcliffe for her master's in clinical psychology, graduating with distinction in 1960. She got her Ph.D. from Harvard in 1964. Then, disillusioned with mainstream psychology, she left the field.

The 1960s were alive with new ideas and challenges to the establishment, and Gilligan caught the spirit. Having married James Frederick Gilligan—a medical student at Case Western Reserve—she also had the first of her three children. That did not keep her home, however. She became involved with the arts, joining a modern dance troupe. She also became active in the civil rights movement. She was part of a sort of international women's community on campus, in dialogue with one another and keeping an eye on each other's children.

In 1965 and 1966, Gilligan taught psychology at the University of Chicago, where she joined the other junior faculty in protesting the war in Vietnam by refusing to turn in grades that could jeopardize a student's draft status. At the time, Gilligan wondered why members of the junior faculty were leading the protest, while the securely tenured professors—who would have risked little or nothing—held back.

Gilligan returned to teach at Harvard in 1968, working with Erik Erikson and Lawrence Kohlberg, two of the leading theorists in mainstream psychology. She observed that Erikson's theory of identity reflected his own life, and Kohlberg's ideas about moral dilemmas echoed his own experience. But she found that neither truly spoke to women's identity and experience.

Gilligan noticed that approximately fifteen of the twenty-five women who signed up for Kohlberg's class on moral development dropped it, even though

Feminist psychologist Carol Gilligan radically changed the way Americans think about gender and values by challenging traditional theories of maturation. [Harvard University Press. Photo by M.K. Kelly]

it took considerable effort to get into the class. Only about five out of fifty men left. Gilligan found that women in the class proposed difficult questions of human suffering that could not be adequately addressed by moral theories of abstract rights. It was absurd to disregard these women as morally defective, yet they did not seem to fit the mold. Was there, then, a different perspective that women held in common?

Gilligan tracked down the women who left the class and interviewed them for their moral perspective. In 1975, she began writing to clarify these ideas for herself. Her first paper in this area was "In a Different Voice—Women's Conceptions of Self and Morality." She showed it to some students, who took it to the *Harvard Educational Review.* After some debate, the *Review* agreed to publish it.

As Gilligan pursued her idea that women held a different moral voice, she found herself moving further and further away from her colleagues. Her first

book, which triggered nationwide debate, was *In a Different Voice: Psychological Theory and Women's Development,* published in 1982. It argued that the standards of maturity and moral development that were generally used in psychological testing did not hold true for women. Gilligan held that women's development was set within the context of caring and relationships, rather than in compliance with an abstract set of rights or rules. At a time when men and women across the nation were reexamining gender assumptions, Gilligan became a powerful voice.

Gilligan made a number of other contributions to the field of women's moral and identity development. In 1989, she coedited *Mapping the Moral Domain: A Contribution of Women's Thinking to Psychological Theory* with Janie Victoria Ward, Jill McLean Taylor, and Betty Bardige. In 1991, she published *Making Connections: The Relational World of Adolescent Girls at Emma Willard School,* coauthored with Nona P. Lyons and Trudy J. Hammer; *Meeting at the Crossroads: Women's*

Psychology and Girls' Development; and *Women, Girls and Psychotherapy: Reframing Resistance,* coauthored with Annie Rogers and Deborah Tolman.

With the work came recognition. Gilligan became a full professor at Harvard in 1986, a post she continues to hold. She was named Woman of the Year by *Ms.* magazine in 1984 and won the Grawemayer Award in Education in 1992. She held the Laurie Chair in Women's Studies at Rutgers University in 1986–1987 and was Pitt Professor at the University of Cambridge in 1992–1993. Gilligan was named faculty fellow at the Bunting Institute in 1982–1983 and was a senior research fellow at the Spencer Foundation from 1989 to 1993.

While some of her documentation and conclusions remain controversial, it is indisputable that Gilligan changed the nature of debate in psychology. No longer was it casually acceptable to do studies excluding women and then draw conclusions about human behavior. Indeed, Gilligan altered the mainstream.

BIBLIOGRAPHY

Contemporary Authors; Farnsworth, Lori, and Carol Gilligan. "A New Voice for Psychology." *Feminist Foremothers* (1995); Gilligan, Carol. *In a Different Voice* (1982); "Special Report: The *Time* 25." *Time* (June 17, 1996); Tavris, Carol. *The Mismeasure of Woman* (1992).

ANDRA MEDEA

GILMAN, BLANCHE (1886–1976)

A native New Yorker, Blanche Pearl Gilman contributed her energy and resources to a variety of religious, health, social, and activist organizations. She was born January 30, 1886, to Frederick and Matilda (Ottenreuter) Gutter. After graduating from HUNTER COLLEGE in 1905 (she was the president of her class) she married David E. Goldfarb, the son of Julius and Jane (Wilner) Goldfarb, in 1905. The couple had one son, Stanley Sidney Goldfarb.

She began teaching Jewish history in the Mount Neboh Religious School in New York in 1906. As a member of that Reform congregation, she was drawn to synagogue life and became an organizer of the sisterhood. That early volunteer work in the Mount Neboh community led her to take a leadership role in the congregation's chapter of the American Red Cross. The chapter sponsored one of five reclamation centers in New York City, comprising nine hundred

workers and providing medical and social services during World War I. She also did interreligious work as a member of the executive and women's advisory committees of the National Conference of Christians and Jews.

In 1927, she became president of the Federation of Jewish Women's Organizations of Greater New York. During the 1930s, she also held a number of positions at the state and national levels. She became the president of the New York State Federation of Temple Sisterhoods in 1932, and was a member of the NATIONAL FEDERATION OF TEMPLE SISTERHOODS. In recognition of her interest in world Jewry, she was chair of the women's division of the American Pro-Falasha Committee (1930–1931), the women's division of the United Jewish Appeal (1934–1935), the United Palestine Appeal (1936), and the Joint Distribution Committee (1936). She had come a long way from her modest beginnings in the Mount Neboh congregation. Her activity in the Jewish community continued right up until her death in the 1970s.

In the 1930s, she began to participate actively in city and state politics. New York mayor Fiorello La Guardia appointed her in 1934 to serve on a committee to promote increased milk consumption in the state. Later, she worked with the Division of the Blind of the New York State Department of Social Welfare. In 1945, she served as the volunteer chair of the New York State Commission for the Blind. Her tenure continued under governors Thomas E. Dewey, W. Averell Harriman, and Nelson Rockefeller until her retirement from the post in 1969.

It is not known how her first marriage ended. In 1937, she married Isaac Gilman, a paper manufacturer and philanthropist. Isaac Gilman shared some of his wife's interreligious inclinations, and built Protestant and Catholic churches in Gilman, Vermont. The town was named after him, commemorating the site of his first paper mill. Isaac Gilman died there in August 1944. Blanche Gilman died more than thirty years later in New York, on July 8, 1976. Memorial notices issued by Congregation Emanu-El in New York and the Federation of Jewish Women's Organizations acknowledged her substantial contributions to American Jewish life and to society at large.

BIBLIOGRAPHY

AJYB 47:522–523, s.v. "Isaac Gilman"; *NYTimes,* July 10, 1976, 26, and July 11, 1976, 45, and July 12, 1976, B2; *WWIAJ* (1938).

JUDD KRUGER LEVINGSTON

A passionate advocate of women's rights in her years as a lawyer, Supreme Court Justice Ruth Bader Ginsburg has become a cautious jurist, respectful of precedent and reluctant to involve the court in political battles. [Supreme Court]

GINSBURG, RUTH BADER (b. 1933)

I am . . . a first generation American on my father's side, barely second generation on my mother's. Neither of my parents had the means to attend college, but both taught me to love learning, to care about people, and to work hard for whatever I wanted or believed in. Their parents had the foresight to leave the old country,

where Jewish ancestry and faith meant exposure to pogroms and denigration of one's human worth. (U.S. Congress, p. 49)

Ruth Bader Ginsburg is the first Jewish woman (and only the second woman) appointed to the United States Supreme Court. Although not a religiously observant Jew, she is very conscious of her Jewish roots, as evidenced by the statement quoted above and by her reply to Senator Edward Kennedy at the confirmation hearings. When he suggested that her personal experience and pioneering work with gender discrimination would also sensitize her to racial discrimination, she said:

> Senator Kennedy, I am alert to discrimination. I grew up during World War II in a Jewish family. I have memories as a child, even before the war, of being in a car with my parents and passing a place in [Pennsylvania], a resort with a sign out in front that read: "No dogs or Jews allowed." Signs of that kind existed in this country during my childhood. One couldn't help but be sensitive to discrimination living as a Jew in America at the time of World War II. (U.S. Congress, p. 139)

I first heard about Ruth Ginsburg in my third year at Columbia Law School, when Professor Gerald Gunther invited me to his office to discuss the possibility of a judicial clerkship. Professor Gunther told me that based on my record he would recommend me to Justice Felix Frankfurter of the United States Supreme Court, but added that when Ginsburg was recommended to Justice Frankfurter two years earlier, Justice Frankfurter had replied that he would not be the one to break the tradition of male clerks only.

I met Ginsburg about a year later, as I was starting and she was completing a clerkship with Judge Edmund L. Palmieri of the U.S. District Court for the Southern District of New York, one of the few federal judges who hired female law clerks at that time. Her ability and tact became evident very quickly. It was motion day, and Judge Palmieri was about to rule on a motion that had just been argued. Ruth sent him a note, asking whether he could reserve decision, because she thought there was a Supreme Court case on point. She was, of course, right. There was a U.S. Supreme Court decision that was dispositive and that, amazingly, neither lawyer had mentioned.

Years later, I learned from Professor Gunther that even though Judge Palmieri was impressed by Ginsburg's record, he was very reluctant to appoint her and did so only after a great deal of urging by Gunther, who knew him personally, and a written promise by a male student that if the appointment of Ginsburg did not work out he would leave his law firm job to take over the clerkship. That, of course, was not necessary. Palmieri was delighted with her work, and they remained lifelong friends.

Ruth Bader Ginsburg was born on March 15, 1933, in Brooklyn, New York, the child of a Jewish immigrant father and a native-born Jewish mother. Her father, Nathan, came to the United States from Russia when he was thirteen. Her mother, Celia (Amster), was born in the United States, her parents having emigrated from a small town near Cracow, Poland, four months before she was born. Neither of her parents had the financial means to go to college. Her father worked as a furrier and later in a men's clothing store.

Some of Ruth's earliest memories are of going to the public library with her mother, trips that imbued her with a desire to read and a love of learning. She also remembers her mother shopping for bargains to save money for Ruth's college education. Although her mother did not work outside the home, she impressed upon Ruth the need to be independent and to develop her own ideas to the fullest. It was her mother who most influenced her life. "I think of her often when I am in challenging situations that compel a top performance" (Swiger, p. 55). She wore her mother's pin and earrings when arguing cases before the Supreme Court because, she thought, her mother would have liked that. Her mother, she said in her acceptance speech in the Rose Garden, was "the bravest and strongest person I have known, who was taken from me much too soon. I pray that I may be all that she would have been had she lived in an age when women could aspire and achieve and daughters are cherished as much as sons" (*NYTimes*).

Ruth attended P.S. 238 and Madison High School in Brooklyn and edited the school newspaper, the *Highway Herald*, for which she wrote articles on the Magna Carta and on the Bill of Rights. In high school, she was also an active member and officer of the Go-Getters, a pep club for sporting and social events; she wore its black satin jacket, sold tickets to football games and other functions, and chipped her tooth twirling a baton when Madison played Lincoln High School (Ayer, p. 16).

Upon graduation from high school, she received various awards and a New York State scholarship. Cornell University, which she chose, provided additional financial assistance, and she also worked at part-time clerical jobs to earn extra money (Swiger, p. 56).

Ruth Bader is shown here at age fifteen in 1948, speaking to a congregation at Camp Che-Na-Wah, where she was the camp "rabbi." [Collection of the Supreme Court of the United States]

She majored in government and credits Professor Robert E. Cushman, with whom she studied and for whom she worked as a research assistant, with arousing her interest in a career in law. It was, she said, "[the] heyday of McCarthyism [and Cushman defended] our deep-seated national values—freedom of thought, speech and press. . . . The McCarthy era was a time when courageous lawyers were using their legal training in support of the right to think and speak freely. . . . That a lawyer could do something that was personally satisfying and at the same time work to preserve the values that have made this country great was an exciting prospect for me" (Gilbert and Moore, p. 156).

She credits another professor at Cornell, Vladimir Nabokov, with influencing her reading habits and writing style. "He loved words . . . the sound of words. . . . Even when I write an opinion, I will often read a sentence aloud and [ask,] 'Can I say this in fewer words—can I write it so the meaning will come across with greater clarity?'" (Swiger, p. 55).

Ruth graduated from Cornell with high honors in government and distinction in all subjects and was elected to Phi Beta Kappa. In her freshman year at Cornell, she met Martin David Ginsburg, whom she married in June 1954, shortly after her graduation. Martin, who had been a year ahead of her at Cornell, had just completed his first year at Harvard Law School when they married. Although she, too, was accepted by Harvard Law School, they moved to Fort Sill, Oklahoma, where Martin was sent by the army.

Ginsburg took a job with the Social Security Office in Lawton, Oklahoma. When she disclosed that she was pregnant, her superior decided that she could not travel to a training session required for the position for which she had qualified and gave her a lower position at less pay. On July 21, 1955, she gave birth to a daughter, Jane, now a professor of law at Columbia Law School and a leading authority on copyright and trademark law.

The following year, Ginsburg started Harvard Law School. There were only nine women in a class of five hundred. At a dinner he hosted for the women students, Dean Erwin Griswold asked each to explain how she justified taking a place in the class that would otherwise have gone to a man. A room in the Lamont Library was closed to women, making it impossible for Ginsburg to get a periodical she needed to do a cite-checking assignment for the law review. Professors sometimes called on women students "for comic relief" (Gilbert and Moore, p. 158). Even though she was married, had a small child, and gathered notes for her husband's classes as well as her own (while he was seriously ill), she succeeded in getting elected to and carrying on her work for the Harvard Law Review.

In 1958, Martin graduated from Harvard Law School and accepted a position with a prominent New York law firm. Ruth transferred to Columbia Law School, where she was also invited to join the Columbia Law Review and tied for first in the class.

Harvard Law School refused to give her a degree, as is routinely done nowadays for a student who transfers after the second year. However, Columbia Law School gave her a degree, even though she had studied at Columbia only her last year. Years later, when she had become prominent, Harvard offered to give her a degree, on condition that she give up her Columbia degree. She declined to do so.

Based on her outstanding record, Professor (later Dean) Albert Sacks of Harvard Law School recommended her as a law clerk to Justice Felix Frankfurter, but he was not willing to take a woman. Indeed, notwithstanding her impressive credentials, she had great difficulty getting any job. "Not a single law firm in the entire city of New York," she said, offered her a position (Carlson, p. 38). As she explained in a 1993 interview, "In the fifties, the traditional law firms were just beginning to turn around on hiring Jews. . . . But to be a woman, a Jew, and a mother to boot, that combination was a bit much" (Gilbert and Moore, p. 158). Finally, through the efforts of Professor Gerald Gunther, she was hired as a law clerk by Judge Edmund L. Palmieri.

Following her clerkship with Palmieri, Ginsburg did have offers from law firms, but decided to join the Columbia Project on International Civil Procedure. The purpose of the project, financed by the Carnegie Foundation, was to do basic research on foreign systems of civil procedure and to study and propose improvements of U.S. rules on transnational litigation. Professor Hans Smit, originally from Holland, with law degrees both from Amsterdam University and Columbia, joined the Columbia Law School faculty to direct the project. Truly egalitarian, he not only appointed women (Ginsburg and the writer of this article) to work on the project, but paid them and the men the salary that men were being paid by the major law firms at the time. Ginsburg learned Swedish and worked in Sweden with a Swedish judge on a book on Swedish civil procedure, for which she was later awarded an honorary doctorate by the University of Lund.

When she completed work on the project and indicated her interest in pursuing an academic career, Smit urged her appointment to the Columbia Law School faculty, but to no avail. On the recommendation of Professor Walter Gellhorn, a member of the Columbia faculty and at the time the president of the American Association of Law Schools, Ginsburg accepted a position at Rutgers, one of the few law schools willing to accept women on its faculty at that time. She taught at Rutgers from 1963 to 1972.

While at Rutgers, Ginsburg became pregnant with her second child. Afraid that if the pregnancy were discovered she might lose her position, she concealed it by wearing loose-fitting clothes borrowed from her mother-in-law. The Ginsburgs' second child, a son, whom they named James, was born in

September 1965, shortly before the fall semester began.

It was at Rutgers that Ruth Ginsburg first became involved in women's rights. In the late 1960s, sex discrimination complaints began "trickling" into the New Jersey affiliate of the American Civil Liberties Union (ACLU). They were referred to her, Ginsburg said, "because, well, sex discrimination was regarded as a woman's job." Her students prodded her "to take an active part in the effort to eliminate senseless gender lines in the law" (Gilbert and Moore, p. 153), and she was inspired to do so by the women referred to her by the ACLU. In 1971 the U.S. Supreme Court decided *Reed* v. *Reed*, unanimously overturning a state law that gave men preference over women for appointments as administrators of decedents' estates. Although Ginsburg did not argue the case, she was the principal author of the brief. Following the *Reed* victory, the ACLU voted to establish a Women's Rights Project, and Ginsburg became its codirector. Columbia finally offered her a position, and in 1972 she became the first tenured woman on the Columbia Law School faculty.

Ruth Ginsburg divided her time between Columbia and the Women's Rights Project. From the numerous sex discrimination cases brought to the project, she carefully selected those that raised issues she considered "ripe for change through litigation." These were mainly employment-related cases that, in her words, "lent themselves to the strategy of sequential presentations leading to incremental advances" (Cowan, pp. 390–393).

In determining whether a statute violates the equal protection clause of the Fourteenth Amendment, the U.S. Supreme Court has applied three tests: (1) the "rational basis" test, i.e., whether there is a rational basis for the law; (2) "intermediate scrutiny," whether the law is "substantially related" to the achievement of an "important government purpose"; and (3) "strict scrutiny," applied to laws that draw a distinction based on race, which is considered a "suspect" classification. Ginsburg argued that laws that draw a distinction based on gender should also be subjected to strict scrutiny. The problem, as she explained at her confirmation hearings, was that while "race discrimination was immediately perceived as evil, odious, and intolerable," laws discriminating against women were often justified as protecting women (U.S. Congress, p. 122). She therefore chose cases that would show that using gender as a basis for different treatment was harmful not only to women but also to men.

Weinberger v. *Wiesenfeld* (1975) was perfect for that, "a gem of a case" (Cowan, pp. 396–397). Wiesen-

feld's wife had died in childbirth, and he wanted to care personally for their infant son but was denied Social Security benefits. The Social Security Act provided survivor's benefits to women with children, but not to men with children, even though men and women paid Social Security taxes at the same rate. Ginsburg argued that while this regulation appeared to protect women, its effect was to deny women workers and their families the protection provided to male workers. A unanimous Supreme Court held the regulation unconstitutional. The Court did so, however, without holding that gender-based distinctions were, like race-based distinctions, suspect and subject to strict scrutiny. A majority of the Court has still never held gender a suspect classification subject to strict scrutiny.

In 1996 the United States Supreme Court decided another gender discrimination case, *United States* v. *Virginia*. Ruth Bader Ginsburg wrote the opinion for the Court, which held that the exclusion of women from the Virginia Military Institute violated the equal protection clause of the Fourteenth Amendment. Those "who seek to defend gender-based government action," she wrote, "must demonstrate an 'exceedingly persuasive justification' for that action."

Ginsburg was on the Columbia Law School faculty from 1972 to 1980. During that period she directed the ACLU Women's Project, taught courses and seminars in civil procedure, conflict of laws, constitutional law, and sex discrimination, wrote a number of articles, and prepared the first casebook on gender-based discrimination. In 1980 she was appointed by President Carter to the Court of Appeals for the District of Columbia Circuit, a court that hears some of the most interesting federal cases. Two of the cases on which she sat while on the D.C. Circuit Court of Appeals are of particular Jewish interest: *Goldman* v. *Secretary of Defense* and *U.S.* v. *Pollard*. One concerned a Jewish captain in the U.S. Air Force who insisted on the right to wear a yarmulke (head covering) in the military, the other a Jewish man who had been charged with passing classified information to Israel, pleaded guilty, and later sought to withdraw his plea.

On June 14, 1993, Ruth Bader Ginsburg was nominated by President Clinton to be an associate justice of the United States Supreme Court. Some women's groups opposed her appointment because she had spoken and written critically of the Court's rationale in *Roe* v. *Wade*, the Supreme Court decision that there is a constitutional right to abortion, but most women's groups and numerous scholars and academics strongly supported the nomination. She was confirmed by the Senate as an associate justice of the Supreme Court on August 3, 1993.

Justice Ginsburg has made it a point to keep in touch with her Brooklyn roots.
She is shown here in June of 1994 visiting the grade school she attended, P.S. 238,
in the Midwood section. She is seated next to twelve-year-old Antonia Arano. [Mark Bonifacio]

Ginsburg has experienced great adversity in her life. Her only sister died when she was very young. Her mother became ill with cancer just as Ruth was starting high school and died one day before her graduation, at which Ruth was to speak. During his third year at Harvard, her husband was in a car accident and later was diagnosed with a rare form of cancer that few had ever survived and underwent massive surgery and radical radiation while in law school.

She has also had great good fortune: first, in her remarkable intellect, which manifested itself at every stage of her life; second, but perhaps equally important in making it possible for her to reach the pinnacle of her profession, a husband and family who have been wonderfully supportive in every way, as she often notes. At Harvard, Martin assured his friends that she would make law review and later it was he who organized support for her appointments to the U.S. Court of Appeals and to the U.S.

Supreme Court. In her own words, he has been her "best friend and biggest booster" (*NYTimes*). "A supportive husband who is willing to share duties and responsibilities is a must . . . ," she says, "for any woman who hopes to combine marriage and a career." (Ayer, 28).

The extent of her family's belief in and support for her is perhaps best symbolized by an entry in her daughter's high school yearbook. Under "ambition," it stated, "to see my mother appointed to the Supreme Court" (*NYTimes*).

In an address to the American Jewish Committee after her appointment to the Supreme Court she said, "I am a judge born, raised, and proud of being a Jew. The demand for justice runs through the entirety of the Jewish tradition. I hope, in my years on the bench of the Supreme Court of the United States, I will have the strength and the courage to remain constant in the service of that demand."

Although she is the first Jewish woman on the Court, she follows such outstanding Jewish jurists as Brandeis, Cardozo, and Frankfurter, and will no doubt continue their tradition of greatness.

BIBLIOGRAPHY

Ayer, Eleanor. *Ruth Bader Ginsburg: Fire and Steel on the Supreme Court* (1994); Carlson, Margaret. "The Law According to Ruth." *Time* (June 28, 1993): 38; Cowan, Ruth. "Women's Rights Through Litigation: An Examination of the American Civil Liberties Union Women's Rights Project, 1971–1976." 8 *Colum. Hum. Rts. L. Rev.* 373, 390–393 (1976); Gilbert, Lynn, and Gaylen Moore. *Particular Passions: Talks with Women Who Have Shaped Our Times* (1981); Ginsburg, Ruth Bader. Address to the Annual Meeting of the American Jewish Committee, May 1995. Reprinted in "See What Being Jewish Means to Me." Advertisement by the American Jewish Committee. *NYTimes*, January 14, 1996, 13, and "Biographical Data." Public Affairs Office, U.S. Supreme Court, 1993; *NYTimes*, June 15, 1993, A1, A22–24; Swiger, Elinor Porter. *Women Lawyers at Work* (1978); U.S. Congress. Senate. Committee on the Judiciary. *Nomination of Ruth Ginsburg to be Associate Justice of the Supreme Court of the United States.* Hearings. 103d Cong., 1st sess., July 20–23, 1993.

CASES CITED

Goldman v. Secretary of Defense, 739 F.2d 657 (1984); *Goldman v. Weinberger*, 475 U.S. 503 (1986); *Kahn v. Shevin*, 416 U.S. 351 (1974); *Reed v. Reed*, 404 U.S. 71, 92 S.Ct. 251 (1971); *Roe v. Wade*, 410 U.S. 113, 93 S.Ct. 705 (1973); *United States v. Pollard*, 959 F.2d 1011 (D.C. Cir. 1991); *United States v. Virginia*, 116 S.Ct. 2264 (1996); *Weinberger v. Wiesenfeld*, 420 U.S. 636 (1975).

MALVINA HALBERSTAM

GINZBERG, ADELE (1886–1980)

Known as "Mama G." by generations of admirers, Adele Ginzberg was an influential figure in the Conservative Movement as wife of the famed Louis Ginzberg, professor of Talmud at the Jewish Theological Seminary, and was an active member of National Women's League. Ginzberg was a role model and inspiration to rabbinical students and women leaders and an early supporter of equal rights for women in synagogue rituals.

Born on May 11, 1886, in Frankfurt-am-Main, Germany, daughter of Michael and Sophie Katzenstein and older sister of Max and Martha, Adele (Katzenstein) Ginzberg moved to Berlin at age eight after her mother's sudden death. She received basic schooling and then, unable to study nursing as she wanted, she instead worked briefly in her father's real estate office. She married Louis Ginzberg in 1909 and moved to New York. They had two children, Sophie (Ginz-

berg) Gould and Eli Ginzberg, professor of economics and director of the Eisenhower Center for Conservation of Human Resources at Columbia University.

Ginzberg first became involved in community affairs with the Liberty Bond Campaign during World War I. From 1920 on, she was closely associated with National Women's League. Serving as its representative on several national and international organizations, she also wrote a monthly column in its magazine, *Outlook*. She was instrumental in initiating the Girl Scout project in 1946, which led to the establishment of the Menorah Award for Jewish Girl Scouts. Ginzberg was also devoted to aiding the blind through the Jewish Braille Institute.

Ginzberg, together with her husband, unofficially took over the Schechters' role as "Mr. and Mrs. Seminary." A fearless woman with an irreverent personality and colossal energy, Ginzberg brought great vitality to the seminary community. She hosted open houses on Shabbat and holidays and invited each member of the seminary's senior rabbinical school class for Shabbat lunch. After her husband's death in 1953, Ginzberg continued to invite students for Shabbat meals. Ginzberg was also long noted for decorating the Jewish Theological Seminary's sukkah, which is named in her memory. Finally, Ginzberg was one of the few of her generation to join the struggle for equal rights for women in synagogue ritual life.

In recognition of her varied talents and influence, Ginzberg was honored as New York State Mother of the Year in 1966, was inducted in the seminary's Honorary Society of Fellows in 1976, and was awarded the Mathilde Schechter Award posthumously in 1980. Ginzberg died in New York City on May 10, 1980.

Ginzberg exemplified those women whose status and influence derive initially from their illustrious husbands, but who used their position to educate and enrich Jewish life on their own terms. She conveyed the vitality of Jewish life to generations of Conservative Jews and inspired many to adopt a forward-thinking stance.

BIBLIOGRAPHY

AJYB 82:365–366; Ginzberg, Eli. *Keeper of the Law* (1966); "Irrepressible, Unforgettable, 'Mama G.'" *Outlook* 21 (Fall 1980): 4, 20–21; "Presentation of Mathilde Schechter Award." *Women's League Biennial Convention Proceedings* (1980): 74–77; "Quotable Quotes." *Scope* (February 1964): 2; Shenker, Israel. "Adele Ginzberg, at 90, Says, 'So What?'" *NYTimes*, May 16, 1976; United Synagogue of America. National Women's League. *They Dared to Dream: A History of National Women's League, 1918–68* (1967).

SHULY RUBIN SCHWARTZ

GLASER, ELIZABETH (1947–1994)

Elizabeth Glaser made a significant contribution to the littlest AIDS victims. Mobilized to save her own HIV-infected children, Glaser founded the Pediatric AIDS Foundation (PAF) in 1988, which to date has raised more than $50 million.

Glaser contracted HIV in a blood transfusion during pregnancy and then passed the disease through her breast milk to her daughter, Ariel, born on August 4, 1981. Ariel later succumbed to AIDS on August 12, 1988. Her son Jake, born on October 25, 1984, became infected in utero but remains asymptomatic, and her husband Paul Glaser is uninfected.

Elizabeth Ann (Meyer) Glaser was born on November 11, 1947, to Max and Edith Meyer. Max was vice president of the General Cigar Company, and Edith became director of urban renewal for the Town of Hempstead after Elizabeth and her younger brother Peter were in school. She was raised in Hewlett Harbor, New York. She attended the University of Wisconsin and received a master's degree in early childhood education from Boston University. After a brief marriage in the early 1970s and then a move to California, she began teaching in West Hollywood. Soon thereafter, she married the actor and director Paul Glaser on August 24, 1980.

Glaser was not raised as a practicing Jew; in fact, the family had a Christmas tree each year. However, as an adult, she visited Israel with her husband on that country's thirtieth birthday and felt a deep spiritual connection and quiet sense of belonging there. She took up Judaism when she had children. She felt it was important to give her daughter a Hebrew name, and she and Ariel would bake challah and light candles on Friday nights. Glaser joined a temple and went to classes to learn more about Judaism, and after her death, notebooks were found filled with recipes and short stories about the Jewish holidays.

Glaser's efforts with PAF cofounders Susan De Laurentis and Susie Zeegan led to numerous public appearances, including a profile for *60 Minutes* (aired February 4, 1990) and her moving testimony at the 1992 Democratic National Convention. She received the UCLA medal, the humanitarian award from the City University of New York, and the Women in Film Foundation's Crystal Award. She was active until her death on December 4, 1994.

"HIV made Elizabeth more of who she already was," De Laurentis recalled. "She was smart, funny, athletic, and had great energy. I think what she chose to do when her family was diagnosed showed how courageous she was; instead of giving up, she turned it into an amazing, amazing fight."

BIBLIOGRAPHY

AJYB 84:333; Brozan, Nadine. "Chronicle." *NYTimes*, November 13, 1992, B2, and "Commencements." May 28, 1993, B6; De Laurentis, Susan, cofounder, Pediatric AIDS Foundation. Interview with author. April 24, 1996; Glaser, Elizabeth. Photographs and tapes. Pediatric AIDS Foundation, NYC; Glaser, Elizabeth, and Laura Palmer. *In the Absence of Angels* (1991); Kennedy, Randy. "Elizabeth Glaser Dies at 47." *NYTimes*, December 5, 1994, B10; Rich, Frank. "Mary Fisher Now." *NYTimes*, May 4, 1995, A25; "U.C.L.A. Presents 4 Medals at Graduation." *NYTimes*, June 21, 1993, A15; *WWWIA* 8.

NANCY ROSEN

GLAZER, RUTH *see* GAY, RUTH

GLUCK, ALMA (1884–1938)

Alma Gluck, the soprano whose recording of "Carry Me Back to Ol' Virginny" sold almost two million copies, was born Reba Fiersohn on May 11, 1884, in Romania (variously reported as either Iasi or Bucharest). From an impoverished childhood, she rose to become not only one of the finest concert artists of the twentieth century but also one of the most popular.

Alma was the youngest of seven children, born when her mother (whose name is reported as Anna, Zara, and Edith Sarah) was nearly fifty. Of the six other children, three girls survived infancy. The eldest, Cecile (eighteen years older than Alma), ran the household and reared the others. Her father (reported as Israel, Leon, and Louis Saul), who died when Alma was two, was an opera buff: His older daughters told stories of his attending a performance after hauling produce all day and returning home to sing the entire score for his family.

By 1890, Cecile Fiersohn, who had paid her own passage to the United States, had saved enough from her sweatshop earnings to send for her mother and sisters. Alma attended public school through eighth grade on New York's Lower East Side and subsequently worked as an office clerk. Although some accounts indicate that she attended the Normal School (later HUNTER COLLEGE) and Union College, an inspection of school records appears to show that this was not the case. On May 25, 1902, she married Bernard Gluck, an insurance agent (some sources record his name as Glick). They divorced in 1912. Their daughter, Abigail, became the writer Marcia Davenport.

With a physical beauty that rivaled her vocal ability, Alma Gluck was this country's most popular concert singer for a decade in the early part of the twentieth century. Though trained as a classical singer, she is probably best remembered for her recordings of American folk tunes. [New York Public Library]

Although she had a beautiful voice as a girl and learned to play piano, Gluck began vocal training only as an adult. In 1906, a business associate of her husband's who had heard her sing arranged for her to take voice lessons. She also studied in Europe accompanied only by her daughter. An anecdote tells of Gluck's serendipitous encounter with Arturo Toscanini. The conductor heard her sing when she arrived for a lesson at her teacher's house while he and the manager of New York's Metropolitan Opera were dining there. Both men were skeptical of the teacher's motives—Gluck was a beautiful woman—until they heard the soprano warming up. Toscanini then insisted on accompanying her himself. (Marcia Davenport writes that the meeting was no accident: Gluck's teacher engineered it, and Gluck was aware of her listener's identity.) After a formal audition, Gluck was hired. Toscanini conducted the performance in which she made her debut (under the name Alma Gluck), Massenet's *Werther*. It was presented by the Metropolitan Opera but took place at the New Theatre on November 16, 1909. During Gluck's first season with the company, she sang eleven minor roles in three languages.

Gluck, however, was not fond of opera's theatrical nature. Less than a year after her operatic debut, she sang her first recital. By 1911, she had found her niche as a concert artist, a venue in which her charm and elegance were more readily apparent. After leaving the Metropolitan in 1913, she studied in Berlin and Paris. By the following year, Gluck was the most popular concert singer in the United States. She performed in all forty-eight states (traveling later in a private railway car) as a recitalist and orchestral soloist. Until 1921, she gave almost 100 recitals a season, and she continued to perform until 1925. Between 1911 and 1919, Gluck made 124 recordings. Although many were classical, she was famous for her renditions of American folk songs. She was a best-selling artist: Between 1914 and 1918 alone her recording royalties totaled $600,000.

On June 15, 1914, Gluck was married in London to violinist Efrem Zimbalist. They had two children, Maria Virginia Goelet (b. 1915), and Efrem, Jr. (b. 1918), the actor, writer, and director. Husband and wife often appeared together in concert, and several of Gluck's recordings feature Zimbalist's violin obbligatos. In her retirement, Gluck devoted herself to her family and to the artistic world: She was a founder of the American Guild of Musical Artists and was famous for her support of musical causes as well as for her soirées. In 1930, Alma Gluck was diagnosed with an incurable liver ailment. She died in New York on October 27, 1938.

If Gluck identified herself with the Jewish community as an adult, there appears to be no record of it, and she developed strong ties to the Episcopal church. She left bequests to Union Chapel on Fishers Island, New York, where she had a summer home, and to St. Thomas Church in New York City. In addition, all three of her children were baptized: Maria Virginia and Efrem, Jr. at St. Thomas (in 1921), and Marcia Davenport (in 1922) at the boarding school run by Episcopal nuns to which she had been sent, with her mother as one of her sponsors. Gluck herself, Davenport writes, "drifted on the agnostic sea-of-consent where so many barks float or founder or merely keep on circling, but she did not think that right for her children."

BIBLIOGRAPHY

AJYB 24:146; *BEOAJ*; *DAB*; Davenport, Marcia. *Too Strong for Fantasy* (1967); *EJ*; Eke, Bernard T. "Alma Gluck." *The Record Collector* (February 1951): 33–45; Herman, Kali. *Women in Particular: An Index to American Women* (1984); Hitchcock, H. Wiley, and Stanley Sadie, eds. *The New Grove Dictionary of American Music* (1986); Ireland, Norma Glin. *Index to Women of the World from Ancient to Modern Times: Biographies and Portraits* (1970), and *Index to Women of the World from Ancient to Modern Times: A Supplement* (1988); *National Cyclopaedia of American Biography* (1961); *NAW*; Obituary. *NYTimes*, October 28, 1938, 1:23; Sadie, Stanley, ed. *The New Grove Dictionary of Music and Musicians* (1980), and *The New Grove Dictionary of Opera* (1992); Saleski, Gdal. *Famous Musicians of Jewish Origin* (1949); Slonimsky, Nicolas, ed. *Baker's Biographical Dictionary of Musicians*. 8th ed. (1992); *UJE*; *Who's Who in America*; *WWIAJ*; *WWWIA* 1.

PAULA EISENSTEIN BAKER

GLUECK, ELEANOR (1898–1972)

For half a century, Eleanor Glueck worked with her husband, Sheldon, professor of criminology at Harvard Law School, producing basic longitudinal studies of juvenile delinquency and adult crime. Influenced by Dr. Richard Cabot to use follow-up studies as part of medical therapy, the Gluecks applied this concept for the first time to the study of criminals sentenced to reformatories, investigating the etiology, patterns, development, and unfolding of criminal careers. The results were more than twelve books and some thirty thousand items in joint papers. Unusual in size and extensive follow-up and coverage, the studies were also characterized by an interdisciplinary perspective rare and unappreciated at the time.

Eleanor (Leonia) Touroff Glueck, the first of two children, was born on April 12, 1898, to Anna (Wodzislawska) and Bernard Leo Touroff, Jewish immigrants from Poland and Russia, respectively. Both her parents were well-read and financially comfortable, as her father, trained in the law, had a real estate business. Eleanor attended Hunter High School, took a degree in English at Barnard College in 1920, and went to the New York School of Social Work, studying with Bernard Glueck, a psychiatrist at Sing Sing Penitentiary in Ossining, New York, who was interested in criminology. Bernard Glueck recommended her for the post of head social worker in

Boston at the Dorchester Community Center. He also introduced her to his law student brother, Sheldon, whom she married on April 16, 1922. Eleanor Glueck was research assistant (1929–1953) and later research associate (1953–1972) of the Harvard Law School Research Project into the Causes, Treatment, and Prevention of Juvenile Delinquency. From 1966 until her death in 1972, she was, with Sheldon Glueck, codirector of the program. Harvard awarded the Gluecks honorary Sc.D. degrees in 1958, and Barnard College bestowed its Distinguished Alumna Award on Eleanor Glueck in 1969.

Commentators on the Gluecks' work have emphasized the meticulous gathering of data and the precision of the follow-up procedures, wherein the same group of subjects was examined at intervals over a span of years to test the validity and continuing applicability of the original findings. Such long-term studies of criminal careers were unique, and in the division of labor, it was Eleanor Glueck who dealt primarily with the organization of the data.

Their first joint effort was *Five Hundred Criminal Careers* (1930), based on the study of offenders in the Massachusetts Reformatory between 1911 and 1922 for five years after completion of parole. A follow-up study resulted in two more books: *Later Criminal Careers* (1937) and *Criminal Careers in Retrospect* (1943). Their second project addressed women imprisoned in the Framingham, Massachusetts, Women's Reformatory, resulting in *Five Hundred Delinquent Women* (1934). The third concerned juveniles referred by the Boston Juvenile Court to the Judge Baker Foundation (of which Eleanor Glueck was a trustee). This, *One Thousand Juvenile Delinquents* (1934) and its sequel *Juvenile Delinquents Grown Up* (1966), revealed continuing high levels of criminal activity.

After this productive decade came *Unraveling Juvenile Delinquency* (1950), their best-known work and one of the bases for their continuing importance for criminology. This ten-year study looked at the criminal careers of five hundred delinquent and five hundred nondelinquent white boys from disadvantaged backgrounds in Boston and reassessed them at ages seventeen, twenty-five, and thirty-one. Matched for intelligence, ethnicity, and residence, the two sets of boys were examined through their peer groups, teachers, projective tests, and body types. Extensive personal interviews with peers, teachers, families, and friends comprised the data. The results pointed sharply to the crucial role of the family in generating or preventing juvenile delinquency. Family cohesion and parental affection, supervision, and consistent discipline were central to the issue. They tracked these boys for fifteen years, and the results appeared in *Delinquents and Non-Delinquents in Perspective* (1968). The "Social Prediction Tables," an effort to identify potential delinquents from age six, based on what had been learned about older offenders, came from this research (and have been much criticized).

Even this sketchy report reveals the unparalleled body of materials the Gluecks produced for the study of delinquency and crime. Their extensive, carefully organized studies came to have extraordinary significance even for the present. Their work was not always well-received, and they were criticized for various methodological questions and interpretations. Their research, though supported by the Harvard Law School, was not central to the institution's focus.

As well, the climate for women professionals was not welcoming. Eleanor Glueck, though a full partner in the joint work and the sole author of other books, occupied a position offered to Ph.D. candidates. No possibility existed for tenure or anything faintly commensurate with her work or its value. In addition, the very breadth of their work, embracing law, social work, education, economics, psychology, and physiology, was unusual in more narrowly constructed academic environments.

Their own tight-knit family life (they had one child, Anitra Joyce, a poet, who died in 1956 at age thirty-two) contributed to a certain isolation from the mainstream.

Eleanor Glueck died in a drowning accident in Cambridge, Massachusetts, on September 25, 1972.

SELECTED WORKS BY ELEANOR GLUECK
Adventure in Japan (1962).

WITH SHELDON GLUECK
Criminal Careers in Retrospect (1943); *Five Hundred Criminal Careers* (1930); *Five Hundred Delinquent Women* (1934); *One Thousand Juvenile Delinquents* (1934); *Unraveling Juvenile Delinquency* (1950).

BIBLIOGRAPHY
BEOAJ; EJ, s.v. "Glueck, Sheldon"; Glueck, Eleanor, and Sheldon T. Glueck. Papers. Harvard Law School Library, Cambridge, Mass; Kaplan, Benjamin, and Felicia Kaplan, and John Laub. Personal interviews with author; Laub, John H., and Robert J. Sampson. "The Sutherland-Glueck Debate: On the Sociology of Criminological Knowledge." *American Journal of Sociology* 96, no. 6: 1402–1440, and "Unraveling Families and Delinquency: A Reanalysis of the Gluecks' Data." *Criminology* 26, no. 3 (1988): 355–379; *NAW* modern; Obituary. *NYTimes*, September 26, 1972, 50:1; *UJE*, s.v. "Glueck, Sheldon"; *WWIAJ* (1938); *WWWIA* 5.

MIRIAM H. BERLIN

GLUECKSOHN-SCHOENHEIMER, SALOME *see* WAELSCH, SALOME GLUECKSOHN

GOLD, DORIS BAUMAN (b. 1919)

Doris Bauman Gold was motivated by her long participation in Jewish organizational life to found Biblio Press, dedicated to educating Jewish women about their own history and accomplishments.

Doris Bauman Gold was born on November 21, 1919, in New York City, the daughter of Saul Bauman, a tailor and businessman from Felstyn in Austro-Hungarian Galicia, and Gertrude Reiss Bauman, a native New Yorker and designer of infant wear. Doris, who had one older brother, Seymour, married Bernard Gold in 1952. Now retired, Bernard Gold worked as a baker and in banking. Their sons are Albert, a molecular biologist, and Michael, an electrical engineer.

After earning a B.A. in English from Brooklyn College in 1946, where she received the English Department Prize in Poetry, Gold completed an M.A. in English at Washington University in St. Louis, Missouri, in 1955. She also undertook postgraduate work at the City University of New York Graduate Center in women's studies, as well as graduate work in business administration and astronomy education. Her employment experience included directing programs for Jewish teenagers; teaching English, writing, and astronomy at the high school, adult education, and college levels; and working in fund-raising for the women's division of the New York Federation of Jewish Philanthropies and in public relations for the Associated YM-YWHAs of New York. From 1963 to 1972, she edited *The Young Judaean Magazine* for the HADASSAH Youth Commission and wrote *Stories for Jewish Juniors* (1967). Gold served as a volunteer in a number of Jewish and feminist organizations. She was a member of the advisory board of *LILITH* magazine from 1976 to 1982.

Gold began studying Jewish women's volunteer activities in the late 1960s. Her 1970 article, "Jewish Women's Groups: Separate—But Equal?" is reprinted in Jacob Marcus's *The Jewish Woman: A Documentary History* (1981). As a result of her article "Women and Volunteerism" in Vivian Gornick and Barbara Moran's *Woman in Sexist Society* (1971), Gold was invited to join NOW's Volunteerism Task Force, where she became a spokesperson on women and volunteer service (1973–1976). Her experience with NOW strengthened her commitment to educating Jewish women about their own heritage. She founded

Biblio Press in 1979 particularly to inform Jewish professionals, such as social workers, and Jewish volunteers who served Jewish institutions about the backgrounds, experiences, and needs of Jewish women.

A recipient of the Susan B. Anthony Award from the New York City National Organization for Women in 1992, Gold is also the author of *Opposition to Volunteerism: An Annotated Bibliography* (1979); *Honey in the Lion: Collected Poems* (1979); and coeditor with Lisa Stein of *From the Wise Women of Israel: Folklore & Memoirs* (1993). Through Biblio Press, Gold has published more than twenty-seven general audience books that address and illuminate the culture, history, experiences, and spiritual yearnings of Jewish women.

BIBLIOGRAPHY

Gold, Doris Bauman. Interview with author. December 1995; *Who's Who in the East* (1983–1984).

JUDITH R. BASKIN

GOLDBERG, LENORA *see* BAYES, NORA

GOLDBERG, MOLLY *see* BERG, GERTRUDE

GOLDFRANK, ESTHER SCHIFF (1896–1997)

Although she never received a degree in anthropology, Esther Schiff Goldfrank made significant contributions to Pueblo studies.

Born in New York City on May 5, 1896, Esther Schiff was the daughter of middle-class parents, Matilda (Metzger) and Dr. Herman J. Schiff. Her parents and her only sibling, Jack, died before she was twenty. She attended the School for Ethical Culture and graduated from Barnard College in 1918 with an A.B. in economics. Accompanied by Franz Boas and the anthropologist Elsie Clews Parsons, who financed her salary and trips to the Southwest, Esther began her fieldwork collecting recipes from a Laguna Pueblo woman in June 1920. In 1921 and 1922, she accompanied Boas to Cochiti Pueblo, where she wrote that, again, her "helpers were a group of women—by and large it was a woman's party." She wrote "The Social and Ceremonial Organization of Cochiti" (1927) based on her collaborative efforts with Carolyn Quintana, mother of now-famous potter Helen Cordero.

Goldfrank coined the name "Papa Franz" for Boas on the trip to Laguna in 1920, and the term gradually caught on among insiders, both men and women, in the anthropology department. Margaret Mead wrote that Goldfrank and RUTH BUNZEL shared a "German Jewish ethos" with Boas that did much to transform the austere, intimidating "Herr Professor" into "Papa Franz" for all of his students. But in her autobiographical *Notes on an Undirected Life: As One Anthropologist Tells It*, Goldfrank remarks that although she was the first to use the name "Papa Franz," it had nothing to do with a shared "German Jewish ethos" but with an experience in Laguna when Boas shed his employer role to become a "father-protector."

Esther interrupted her career as an anthropologist in 1922 to marry Walter S. Goldfrank, a widower with three sons. She moved to White Plains, had a daughter in May 1924, and did not resume taking courses at Columbia until thirteen years later, after the sudden death of her husband in 1935.

On her return to anthropology, she first studied New York City adolescents for the General Education Board of the Rockefeller Foundation. This work included an unpublished study of the influence of the Ethical Culture Society on the predominantly Jewish Fieldston School in Riverdale, New York, which her daughter attended. The study looked at how the population of Fieldston was divided between two groups: older Jewish "bluestocking," socialist-minded, secularized adherents of Felix Adler's philosophy of Ethical Culture, and "newer" nouveau riche families who observed Jewish holidays. The study also emphasized ("before black identity was part of our social vocabulary") that black students who had begun to attend Fieldston should keep a foothold in the black community in order to maintain their identity and forestall racial traumas.

After this research, Goldfrank participated in Abraham Kardiner's and Ralph Linton's culture-and-personality seminars at Columbia. In 1939, she went to study the Blood Indians in Alberta with a group of Columbia students under Ruth Benedict's direction. She later used her Pueblo research and study of Blood kinship to challenge Ruth Benedict's views on the Pueblo personality.

Influenced by the research of her second husband, world-renowned historian and sinologist Karl Wittfogel, whom she married in 1940, she wrote several essays on the importance of irrigation for Pueblo organization and ceremonial life. These essays opposed Benedict's Apollonian image of Pueblo society. Benedict, inspired by Nietzsche, developed her

Apollonian and Dionysian classification of cultures and labeled the Pueblos as Apollonian in contrast to the rest of aboriginal America. From her "realist" perspective, Goldfrank questioned the validity of the configurational approach and emphasized disharmony in Pueblo society. She argued that Wittfogel's ideas on waterwork societies were equally relevant for an understanding of the miniature water-deficient societies of the Pueblos as for the great nation-states of China, Egypt, and Peru. Goldfrank stressed the importance of irrigation for social and political organization, gender relations, and ceremonial patterns.

Wittfogel was ostracized by the intellectual community after he appeared before the Senate Internal Security Subcommittee in the 1950s and named some of his former students and colleagues as members of the Communist Party. Goldfrank's role in this matter has not been established.

Goldfrank participated in the Columbia University Chinese History Project, which Wittfogel directed in the 1940s. She also completed and published Elsie Clews Parsons's work on Iseleta paintings in The Artist of 'Iseleta Paintings' in Pueblo Society, published in 1967. She became president of the American Ethnological Society in 1948 and was editor of its monograph series from 1952 to 1956.

Esther Schiff Goldfrank never taught and, altogether, spent only six months in the field. Her career was limited by her vision of her role as a mother and wife, and the real demands of running a large suburban household. But despite these constraints, she influenced anthropological study by opposing culture-and-personality theory and focusing attention on the contingent nature of history and politics.

Esther Schiff Goldfrank died on April 23, 1997, in Mamaroneck, New York, at age 100.

**SELECTED WORKS BY
ESTHER SCHIFF GOLDFRANK**

"Another View: Margaret and Me." Ethnohistory 30, no. 1 (1983): 1–14; The Artist of 'Iseleta Paintings' in Pueblo Society. Smithsonian Contributions to Anthropology 5 (1967); Changing Configurations in the Social Organization of a Blackfoot Tribe During the Reserve Period. American Ethnological Society, Monograph 8 (1945); "The Different Patterns of Blackfoot and Pueblo Adaptation to White Authority." In Acculturation in the Americas, edited by Sol Tax (1952); "Historic Change and Social Character: A Study of the Teton Dakota." American Anthropologist 45 (1945): 67–83; "The Impact of Situation and Personality on Four Hopi Emergence Myths." Southwestern Journal of Anthropology 4, no. 3 (1948): 241–262; "Irrigation Agriculture and Navaho Community Leadership: Case Material on Environment and Culture." American Anthropologist 47, no. 2 (1945): 262–277;

Iseleta Paintings, editor, with introduction and commentary written by Elsie Clews Parsons (1962. 2d ed. 1970); "More About Irrigation Agriculture and Navaho Community Leadership." American Anthropologist 48, no. 3 (1946): 473–482; Notes on an Undirected Life: As One Anthropologist Tells It (1978); "Observations on Sexuality Among the Blood Indians of Alberta, Canada." In Psychoanalysis and the Social Sciences, Vol. 3, edited by Geza Roheim (1951); "The Social and Ceremonial Organization of Cochiti." American Anthropological Association, Memoir 33 (1927); "Socialization, Personality, and the Structure of Pueblo Society." American Anthropologist 47, no. 4 (1945): 516–537; "Some Aspects of Pueblo Mythology and Society," with Karl Wittfogel. Journal of American Folklore 56, no. 219 (1943): 17–30; "Two Anthropologists, the Same Informant: Some Differences in Their Recorded Data." Journal of the Anthropological Society of Oxford 16, no. 1 (May 1945): 42–52.

BIBLIOGRAPHY

Babcock, Barbara A., and Nancy J. Parezo. "Esther Goldfrank, 1896–." In Daughters of the Desert: Women Anthropologists and the Native American Southwest, 1880–1980. An Illustrated Catalogue (1988); Caffrey, Margaret M. Ruth Benedict: Stranger in this Land (1989); Goldfrank, Esther. Taped interviews. Wenner-Gren Foundation, NYC; Herskovits, Melville J., ed., and Barbara Ames. "Goldfrank, Esther S." International Directory of Anthropologists. 3d ed. (1950); Lange, Charles H. "The Contributions of Esther S. Goldfrank." In Hidden Scholars: Women Anthropologists and the Native American Southwest, edited by Nancy J. Parezo (1993); Levitas, Gloria. "Esther Schiff Goldfrank." In Women Anthropologists: A Biographical Dictionary, edited by Ute Gacs et al. (1988); Mead, Margaret. An Anthropologist At Work: Writings of Ruth Benedict (1959); Narvaez, Alfonso A. "Karl A. Wittfogel, Social Scientist Who Turned on Communists, 91." NYTimes, May 26, 1988, B14; Obituary. NYTimes, May 25, 1997, p. 38; Theoharis, Athan G. "Authors, Publishers, and the McCarthy Era: A Hidden History; Senator Joseph McCarthy." USA Today 122, no. 2580 (September 1993): 90; Woodbury, Nathalie F.S. "Goldfrank, Esther Schiff." In International Dictionary of Anthropologists, edited by Christopher Winters (1991); WWIAJ (1938).

CYNTHIA SALTZMAN

GOLDMAN, EMMA (1869–1940)

When I was in America, I did not believe in the Jewish question removed from the whole social question. But since we visited some of the pogrom regions I have come to see that there is a Jewish question, especially in the Ukraine. . . . It is almost certain that the entire Jewish race will be wiped out should many more changes take place.

—Emma Goldman

Emma Goldman was born on June 27, 1869, in the Jewish quarter of Kovno, Lithuania, to Abraham and Taube (Bienowitch) Goldman. She had two half-sisters, Helena and Lena, and two younger brothers, Herman and Morris. The anti-Semitism of czarist Russia propelled Goldman's family to move to Königsberg, Prussia, and then to St. Petersburg in search of economic stability. These experiences of displacement, coupled with an aversion to the domesticity of women's lives in the traditional Jewish family, drove Goldman to immigrate to New York at age sixteen. There she countered her father's edict that "girls do not have to learn much! All a Jewish daughter needs to know is how to prepare gefilte fish, cut noodles fine and give the man plenty of children," as she described in her autobiography, *Living My Life*. Inspired by the vision of political and personal freedom shared by the nihilist protagonists of Nikolay Chernyshevsky's Russian novel *What Is to Be Done?*, Goldman hoped to find in America a new world of justice, freedom, and love.

Briefly swept up by the lure of self-chosen marriage and of secure work in the garment industry in Rochester, New York, Goldman soon realized the real promise of the New World was yet to be won. Her husband Jacob Kersner's love of adventure proved illusory, and her own job paid too little for even the occasional luxury of a book or a flower. This personally discouraging early period of Goldman's life in America coincided with an unusually dramatic series of events in the history of American labor. On May 1, 1886, 300,000 workers throughout the country went on strike for the eight-hour workday. On May 4, a bomb was thrown into a meeting in Chicago's Haymarket Square, where laborers had gathered peacefully to protest recent police shootings of striking workers. Then, without conclusive evidence, anarchist organizers were blamed. In a trial that was a mockery of justice, the jury found the eight defendants guilty and sentenced seven to death. Inspired by the final words spoken by August Spies, Albert Parsons, George Engel, and Adolph Fischer, who ultimately were executed on November 11, 1887, Goldman was catapulted into action, certain that death could not silence the free voice of labor. She experienced this moment of transformation as her "spiritual birth."

Consciously drawing inspiration from her childhood heroine, the biblical Judith who cut off the head of Holofernes to avenge the wrongs committed against the Jewish people, the twenty-year-old Goldman armed herself with a resolve to obliterate injustice. Infused with the desire to find expression for the messianic side of her nature, she left the year-long turmoil of her marriage and the provincial constraints of the small city of Rochester. On a hot summer day in 1889, sewing machine in hand, Goldman entered the vibrant culture of New York City's Lower East Side to work and love in freedom.

Various cafés and saloons served as evening meeting places for informal education and lively debate. Under the tutelage of Johann Most, the editor of the anarchist newspaper *Die Freiheit* [Freedom], the young Emma Goldman emerged as a precocious and impressive speaker. She lectured in German and Yiddish to immigrants anxious to improve the miserable working conditions and long hours that choked their lives. Gradually she shifted from the singular focus on hardship and toil to what she articulated in her autobiography as "freedom, the right to self-expression, everybody's right to beautiful radiant things." She dared to advocate sexual and reproductive freedom when the dissemination of birth control information was punishable as obscene publication. As her range of concerns and notoriety grew, her audience swelled. Her ideas and flamboyant style, coupled with the fact that she was a woman in the spotlight, distinguished her from her more cautious male counterparts in the relatively exclusive circle of Yiddish lecturers.

Crossing the language barrier that had previously confined her influence to immigrant labor militants, her versatile command of English attracted receptive listeners among a growing liberal, bohemian, American-born constituency—in direct proportion to government and police attempts to suppress Goldman's voice. Sentenced to a year in prison in 1893 for a speech at a demonstration of the unemployed, Goldman emerged proclaiming that government authorities "can never stop women from talking." Undeterred by the threat of harsh consequences, she was determined to devote her life to teaching the principles of anarchism, and in the process to affirm the right to question authority. Perhaps her roots in the Jewish tradition that encouraged argument, debate, and refining the meaning of the weekly Torah reading fortified Goldman's belief in the centrality of free expression.

And yet during this period, federal anti-anarchist laws made it increasingly impossible even to mention the word. Goldman was linked to a general fear of anarchists as provokers of violence. This fear was based primarily on the 1892 assassination attempt on steel magnate Henry Clay Frick by Goldman's closest comrade, Alexander Berkman, and on the subsequent death of President William McKinley in 1901, shot by self-proclaimed anarchist Leon Czolgosz. The latter professed to having been inspired by Goldman. In part

Jail sentences and threats against her life could not stop Emma Goldman from speaking out against social injustice for more than fifty years. Repulsed by orthodox religion, the values of her Jewish heritage nevertheless infused Goldman with an understanding of the struggles of the working class against political oppression. [Schlesinger Library]

to counter the public's distorted perception of anarchism as a philosophy of disorder rather than of harmony, Goldman helped found the 1903 Free Speech League.

Never knowing whether a locked door or an arrest by the police would greet her at a lecture hall, Goldman dauntlessly continued to speak on the variants of freedom encompassed in her anarchist vision. Attracted by her quick wit and celebrity status, curious crowds rallied to support Goldman's right of free expression, whether or not they believed in the specifics of her message. Roger Baldwin, civil libertarian and cofounder of the American Civil Liberties Union, attributed his political awakening to Emma Goldman and identified her courage as the primary inspiration for his work.

The ultimate gag order on Goldman's ideas came when the United States entered World War I, and her anticonscription lectures and organizing were considered a threat to national security. Eighteen months in federal prison was followed by a dramatic deportation in 1919 with Berkman and a boatload of other such undesirable immigrant radicals. Goldman returned to Russia and eventually to a protracted exile in Europe and Canada. Ironically, she could not escape the restrictions of political expression in Bolshevik Russia—especially for an anarchist. When the Kronstadt Rebellion was violently suppressed, Emma Goldman and Alexander Berkman left Russia in despair. She felt rejected by the public, not only by those to the left and right of her politics, but also by those who could not see beyond her Jewish ethnicity. Her relative freedom in Russia had been marred by lingering traces of anti-Semitism that persisted in England, France, and Canada, her most stable bases in exile. Only in Spain, where she worked as the English-language propagandist for the anarchist labor federation during the civil war, was she received as an international political figure commensurate with her self-image. Later, as the gloom of the Spanish defeat doused all optimism, the storm of Nazism grew, and Stalinism brutally entrenched itself, Goldman began to lecture on the interconnections between what she considered to be variant forms of totalitarianism.

She wrote that her "life was linked with that of the race. Its spiritual heritage was mine, and its values were transmuted into my being. The eternal struggle of man was rooted within me" (*Living My Life*). She also noted that "social injustice is not confined to my own race, I had decided that there were too many heads for one Judith to cut off." Goldman experienced political repression as systematic and not culture specific, and throughout her life, her complex and conflicted identity as a Jew remained a point of creative tension. Never escaping the public's perception of her as a Jewish woman, with the ambivalent overlay the culture placed on the term, Goldman nonetheless preferred to think of herself as a woman who could transcend the boundaries imposed by the stereotypical social constructions of religion.

She distinguished cultural continuity from religious superstition and lectured widely on the "failure of Christianity"—false moralism and self-delusion. Goldman's disbelief in God linked to her strong belief in anarchism and free love made her a vulnerable target in the fearful imagination of the religious mainstream of Christian and Jewish America. Concurrently, the liberal wings of both communities often offered Goldman their pulpit. To Rabbi Harry J. Stern of Temple Emanuel in Montreal, whom she admired for showing her that "one may serve his god and yet be true to man," she wrote with the hope that her work would show him that "one can serve humanity without a god" (Goldman to Rabbi Harry J. Stern, March 1934).

Goldman had a strong Jewish cultural identity, but was repelled by religious orthodoxy. In her circles, not a Yom Kippur went by without an organized picnic or ball sponsored by one of a number of "agitator groups," including those involved with Goldman's own publication, *Mother Earth* (1906–1917). On this holiest day of fasting and repentance, a newspaper reported that Goldman came dressed as a nun and cleared the dance floor for her rendition of "the anarchist slide." Perhaps such yearly extravaganzas served as an atheist form of observance rather than as a dismissal of the Day of Atonement—a vehicle for solidifying a community of rebels against the rituals of their Jewish ancestors.

Another atypical form of cultural continuity may lie in Goldman's affinity to anarchism as a philosophy of social organization antithetical to state politics, consistent with the popular pre-Holocaust conception of the Jewish people held together not by a Jewish state but by a shared belief system. The first volume of Goldman's *Mother Earth* magazine (1906) included a critique of national atavism and asserted that "owing to a lack of a country of their own, [Jews have] developed, crystallized and idealized their cosmopolitan reasoning faculty . . . working for the great moment when the earth will become the home for all, without distinction of ancestry or race" (*Mother Earth*, March 1906, 5). Later in life, Goldman was more defensive about her earlier dismissal of the movement for a Jewish homeland. In 1937, alarmed by the rise of Hitler, she wrote to a friend, "While I am neither a Zionist nor a Nationalist, I have worked for the rights of the Jews and [against] every attempt to hinder their life and development" (Emma Goldman to S. Gleiser, February 2, 1937). She wrote extensively on the rise of Nazism and on the ways in which Jewish culture had contributed to the richness of the Weimar Republic. Foreseeing the dangers that loomed over 1930s Europe, she began reluctantly to acknowledge that, if it were possible to respect the rights of the people of the host country, the need for a Jewish refuge was urgent.

Cast out for playing such a powerful role in the politics and culture of the periphery, Emma Goldman was forced to live the life of a wandering Jew—"A Woman Without a Country," the title of one of her essays. Her longtime friend and attorney, Harry Weinberger, captured the essence of her life while lamenting her death in his funeral oration: "She spoke out in this country against war and conscription, and went to jail. She spoke out for political prisoners, and was deported. She spoke out in Russia against the despotism of Communism, and there was hardly a

Emma Goldman was only twenty years old when she decided to take as her inspiration the biblical Judith and fight against the deplorable working conditions of Jewish immigrants like herself. Broadening her message, she became a spellbinding speaker in the cause of political freedom, though she was eventually deported and died in exile. This picture was taken during her last visit to the United States in 1934, at age sixty-five. [YIVO Institute]

place where she could live" (Harry Weinberger, Funeral Oration, May 16, 1940). Through it all, the Jewish community was her hammock of support and formed the base of her first audiences in America and the core of her audience and support in later years. Sometimes spurned by the men who monopolized the Yiddish lecture circuit, it is Goldman's voice that lives on and that ripples beyond her community of origin.

Emma Goldman died on May 14, 1940, in Toronto.

SELECTED WORKS BY EMMA GOLDMAN

Anarchism and Other Essays (1911); *Living My Life.* 2 vols. (1931. Reprint 1970); *My Disillusionment in Russia* (1923); *Social Significance of Modern Drama* (1914).

BIBLIOGRAPHY

AJYB 42:479; *DAB* 2; *EJ*; Falk, Candace, Stephen Cole, and Sally Thomas, eds. *Emma Goldman: A Guide to Her Life and Documentary Sources* (1995); Falk, Candace, with Lyn Reese and Mary Agnes Dougherty. *The Life and Times of Emma Goldman: A Curriculum for Middle and High School Students* (1992); Falk, Candace, Ronald J. Zboray, et al., eds. *The Emma Goldman Papers: A Microfilm Edition* (1990); *NAW*; Obituary. *NYTimes*, May 14, 1940, 23:1; *UJE*; *WWWIA* 4.

CANDACE FALK

GOLDMAN, HETTY (1881–1972)

As one of the most distinguished archaeologists of this century, Hetty Goldman was the first woman appointed to direct an archaeological excavation by the Archaeological Institute of America. She was born on December 19, 1881, to a Jewish family in New York City. Her parents were Julius and Sarah (Adler). After graduating from college with a major in English, Hetty Goldman decided to forgo a career in writing because she "had nothing to say." Instead, she had a great deal to find.

Goldman graduated from Bryn Mawr College in 1903 and received her M.A. in 1910 from Columbia University and Ph.D. in 1916 from Radcliffe College. She excavated a number of sites in Greece and Turkey, including Halae, Colophon, Eutresis, and Tarsus. In her numerous publications, she illuminated the continuity of culture within the Mediterranean between the Semitic and the Greek cultures.

In 1936, Goldman became one of the first professors at the Institute for Advanced Study in Princeton, New Jersey. When she retired twenty years later, her students and colleagues honored her with a festchrift, *The Aegean and the Near East*. She was also named professor emeritus. In 1966, the Archaeological Institute of America awarded her a gold medal for distinction. At the time of her death on May 5, 1972, she remained the only woman professor at the Institute for Advanced Study.

SELECTED WORKS BY HETTY GOLDMAN

"The Acropolis at Halae." *Hesperia* 9 (1940): 381–514; *Excavations at Eutresis in Boetia* (1931); *Excavations at Gozlu Kule Tarsus* (1962).

BIBLIOGRAPHY

EJ; *NAW* modern; Obituary. *NYTimes*, May 6, 1972, 38:4; *Symposium in Memory of Hetty Goldman*, Princeton University, May 4th, 1973; Weinberg, S.S., ed. *The Aegean and the Near East* (1956); *WWWIA* 5.

PAMELA BARMASH

GOLDMARK, JOSEPHINE CLARA (1877–1950)

Josephine Goldmark's work as a reformer in the Progressive Era did much to redesign the American social contract. Between 1903 and 1930, she shaped laws regulating child labor, the legal length of the working day, and minimum wage. At the National Consumers' League (NCL) headquarters in New York City, she worked with executive director of the NCL Florence Kelley as chair of the publications committee. In that capacity, she compiled data demonstrating the need for legislation, wrote compelling articles using those data, and helped organize legislative campaigns.

Josephine Clara Goldmark was born in Brooklyn, New York, the youngest of ten children and the seventh daughter born to Joseph and Regina (Wehle) Goldmark. Her father, born in Poland and educated in Vienna, was a scientist, member of the Austrian Parliament, and a supporter of the failed liberal revolution of 1848 who immigrated to the United States when the revolution was repressed. Her mother's well-to-do family emigrated from Prague to Madison, Indiana, in 1849. In 1930, Goldmark wrote a tribute to her parents' Jewish heritage, their liberal political beliefs, and the close relationship among the Goldmark, Wehle, and Brandeis families—*Pilgrims of '48: One Man's Part in the Austrian Revolution of 1848 and a Family Migration to America.*

After Joseph Goldmark's death in 1881, two brothers-in-law became important father figures: Felix Adler, founder of the Society for Ethical Culture, who married her eldest sister, HELEN GOLDMARK ADLER, in 1880; and Louis D. Brandeis, who married sister ALICE GOLDMARK BRANDEIS in 1891. Brandeis, a Boston lawyer who in 1916 became the first Jewish justice of the United States Supreme Court, was descended from a family that had migrated from Prague with the Wehle family. His mother was a first cousin of Regina Wehle Goldmark, and he and Josephine Goldmark were descended from the same great-grandfather. Despite their rationalist and assimilationist bent, the Goldmark-Brandeis family retained a strong Jewish identity.

After graduating from Bryn Mawr College in 1898, Goldmark studied and taught at Barnard College. Her sister PAULINE GOLDMARK, a staff member of the New York Consumers' League, introduced her to Florence Kelley. A powerful figure in the burgeoning reform movement sweeping through New York City and the nation, Kelley worked closely with two well-known German Jewish women. She lived at LILLIAN WALD's Henry Street Settlement on Manhattan's

As Florence Kelley's indispensable chief assistant at the National Consumers' League, Josephine Goldmark compiled evidence for many of the organization's most important campaigns on behalf of America's workers. Between 1912 and 1914, she worked with the Factory Investigating Committee of New York that was appointed after the TRIANGLE SHIRTWAIST FIRE. [Schlesinger Library]

Lower East Side and worked with MAUD NATHAN, a founder of the Consumers League movement and head of the New York City league.

Goldmark quickly became Kelley's indispensable chief assistant at the NCL. Especially important was her success in recruiting Louis Brandeis to defend the league's legislative program and her work as the compiler of the Brandeis Brief. In 1908, that brief, a watershed event in American legal history, became the basis of the Supreme Court's acceptance of the constitutionality of an Oregon law that limited the working day of wage-earning women to ten hours. Goldmark's technique in that brief—the gathering and presentation of socially relevant facts—became the main instrument for shaping American law according to social need rather than judicial precedent.

In *Fatigue and Efficiency* (1912), a catalog of evidence that showed how efficiency decreased with fatigue, Goldmark launched her career as the author of penetrating studies of working conditions for women and children. Most of these appeared as articles in leading reform periodicals, such as *Survey*, and were distributed as pamphlets by the NCL. Between 1912 and 1914, Goldmark worked with the Factory Investigating Committee of New York that was appointed after the TRIANGLE SHIRTWAIST FIRE. In 1912, she authored an influential report funded by the Rockefeller Foundation, *Nursing and Nursing Education in the United States*. However, her most important work continued to be the compilation of dramatic facts and figures that went into the briefs that the NCL submitted in support of its legislative agenda.

In the years prior to her death in December 1950 from a heart ailment, she was living with her sister Pauline in Hartsdale, New York, and working on a biography of Florence Kelley, posthumously published as *Impatient Crusader* (1953).

SELECTED WORKS BY JOSEPHINE CLARA GOLDMARK

"An Adirondack Friendship: Letters of William James." *Atlantic Monthly* (September/October 1934); *The Case against Nightwork for Women* (1918); *The Case for the Shorter Work Day* (1916); *Democracy in Denmark* (1936); *Fatigue and Efficiency* (1912); *Imaptient Crusader* (1953); *Nursing and Nursing Education in the United States* (1912); *Pilgrims of '48: One Man's Part in the Austrian Revolution of 1848 and a Family Migration to America* (1930).

BIBLIOGRAPHY

AJYB 53:525; Goldmark family. Papers. Schlesinger Library, Radcliffe College, Cambridge, Mass.; "In Memoriam: Josephine C. Goldmark, 1877–1950." *Social Service Review* 25 (March 1951): 111; National Consumers' League. Records. Library of Congress; *NAW*; Obituary. *NYTimes*, December 16, 1950, 17:3; Reverby, Susan M. *Ordered to Care: The Dilemma of American Nursing, 1850–1945* (1987); Urofsky, Melvin I., and David W. Levy, eds. *Letters of Louis D. Brandeis. Vol. 1 (1870–1907): Urban Reformer* (1971).

KATHRYN KISH SKLAR

GOLDMARK, PAULINE (1874–1962)

Pauline Goldmark was a social worker and activist, part of a group of women seeking the vote and reforms of the urban and industrial excesses of the early twentieth century. A major method of social reformers was to investigate, accumulate facts, present

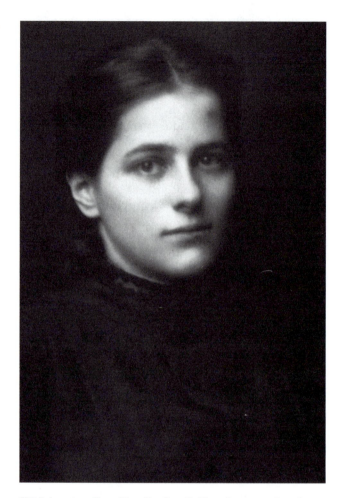

With her sister Josephine, Pauline Goldmark put together the famous Brandeis Brief when Louis Brandeis and the National Consumers' League tested the constitutionality of the Oregon law on maximum hours of work for women. Throughout her career, she was a tireless worker on behalf of women in the labor force. [Schlesinger Library]

these to the public and lawmakers, and assume that, once educated, the public and legislators would enact the desired changes. Goldmark pioneered in methods of social research central to these reform efforts.

Born February 21, 1874, Pauline was the ninth of ten children of Polish and Czech Jewish immigrants, Joseph and Regina (Wehle) Goldmark. She graduated from Bryn Mawr in 1896 and studied two more years at Columbia. First a volunteer, she became assistant, then executive, of the New York State chapter of the National Consumers League (1896–1909). She served for forty years on its national board. The league mobilized the purchasing power and social power of middle-class consumers, mainly women, to buy only goods produced under decent working conditions. They supported legislation regulating child labor, maximum working hours, and minimum working conditions.

Goldmark was appointed associate director of the New York School of Philanthropy, now the Columbia University School of Social Work, and its Bureau of Social Research, while serving on the New York State Department of Labor's Industrial Board, which studied workforce conditions and monitored enforcement (1913–1915), and the New York State Factory Investigating Commission, created to investigate the infamous TRIANGLE SHIRTWAIST FIRE, where 125 women workers died. Two commission reports were written by Goldmark. During World War I, she served as executive secretary of the United States Department of Labor's Commission on Women in Industry. From 1918 to 1920, she managed the Women's Service Section of the U.S. Railroad Administration, supervising the work of over a hundred thousand women workers. She worked closely with many associated with LILLIAN WALD and the Henry Street Settlement, including Florence Kelley, Frances Perkins, MAUD NATHAN, Grace and Edith Abbott, her sister, JOSEPHINE GOLD-MARK, and others active in the Progressive movement.

She wrote or oversaw many publications on the conditions that women faced entering in ever-larger numbers the unregulated workplaces of the time. When Florence Kelley sought the help of Goldmark's brother-in-law, Louis Brandeis, to test the constitutionality of the Oregon law on maximum hours of work for women, the famous Brandeis Brief was born. He described it as three pages of law and one hundred pages of facts—social, economic, and medical. In a period of two weeks, Pauline, her sister Josephine, Florence Kelley, and a number of volunteers assembled those one hundred pages to build a powerful indictment of the harmful effects of long hours and bad working conditions upon women, their families, health, and efficacy as workers. In *Muller* v. *Oregon*, the Supreme Court abandoned its prior policy of the primacy of private property rights and declared that the state had a supervening right to protect citizens from harmful conditions.

Goldmark served as assistant director of research, under Mary Van Kleek, for the Russell Sage Foundation and then for twenty years, from 1919, was a consultant to the American Telephone and Telegraph Company on employment and health issues of their women workers. She died on October 18, 1962, in Hartsdale, New York.

SELECTED WORKS BY PAULINE GOLDMARK

"Art Work in Tenements." *Survey* 26 (April 15, 1911): 114–115; "Child at Work." *Survey* 45 (January 22, 1921):

604–605; "Child Labor in Canneries." *Annals of the American Academy of Political Science* 35, Supp. (March 1910): 152–154; "Facts as to Women in War Industries." *New Republic* 13 (December 29, 1917): 251–252; *The Longshoremen*, with Charles Brinton Barnes (1915); "Preliminary Report of the Factory Investigating Commission" (1912; second report, 1913); "Waste of Overwork." *Independent* 90 (April 28, 1917): 210; *West Side Studies* (1914); "Women Conductors." *Survey* 40 (June 29, 1918): 369–370; "Women in the Railroad World." *Annals of the American Academy of Political Science* 86 (November 1919): 214–221.

BIBLIOGRAPHY

American Women in 1935–1940. Edited by Durwood Howes (1981); *Biographical Dictionary of Social Welfare in America.* Edited by Walter Trattner (1986); Goldmark, Josephine. *The Impatient Crusader* (1953); Obituary. *NYTimes*, October 20, 1962, p. 25.

MIRIAM DINERMAN

GOLDSMITH, EDNA (1874–1945)

Edna Goldsmith was a driving force in the establishment of the Ohio Federation of Temple Sisterhoods. A founder of the federation, she served as its first president from 1918 to 1923 and then served as honorary president until her death. From 1923 to 1929, she was a member of the executive board of the NATIONAL FEDERATION OF TEMPLE SISTERHOODS. Goldsmith also served on the executive board of the Cleveland Council of Jewish Women and as president of the Temple's Women's Association. In her time outside of these commitments, she authored a book of Bible stories for children, *Great Stories of the Bible (Old Testament)* (1924).

Edna Goldsmith was born in Springfield, Ohio, on December 14, 1874. Her paternal grandfather, Theodore Goldsmith, was among the pioneers of Cleveland, settling there in 1849. Her maternal grandfather, Dr. Marcus Ahlenfeld, was a surgeon at the University of Maryland. Edna was the daughter of Herman and Hinda N. (Ahlenfeld) Goldsmith and had a brother, Marcus A. Goldsmith of New York, and three sisters, Mrs. Philip S. Goldberg and Mrs. Louis Bloch of Cleveland, and Mrs. James Lowenstein of Highland Park, Illinois.

Throughout her life, Goldsmith was active in welfare organizations, concentrating particularly in the educational field. She served on the Board of Governors of the National Education League, and in recognition of her work in education, a Hebrew Union College Scholarship was established in her name in the early 1940s. As a member of the Consumers'

League, Goldsmith was also a leader in the campaign for the minimum wage. From 1914 to 1918, she was a member of the National Speakers Bureau for the U.S. Government.

Edna Goldsmith died on November 15, 1945, in Cleveland, Ohio, after a long illness.

BIBLIOGRAPHY

AJYB 48:490; Goldsmith, Edna. *Great Stories of the Bible (Old Testament)* (1924); *Jewish Review and Observer* 17, no. 47 (November 23, 1945), 6:1; *WWIAJ* (1938).

LORI A. FERGUSON

GOLDSMITH, LUBA ROBIN
(1879–1931)

In 1902, Luba Robin was the first woman to graduate from the school of medicine at the Western University of Pittsburgh (later the University of Pittsburgh). The board of directors of the medical school had met several times before they acted affirmatively on her application for admission, the first ever received from a woman. Luba Robin's career combined private medical practice, teaching, writing, lecturing, and active participation in educational, social, and public health work.

Luba Robin was born on January 17, 1879, in Uman, Ukraine. She immigrated to the United States with her parents, Nathaniel and Beatrice Robin, when she was fifteen years old. The family settled in Pittsburgh, where Luba graduated from high school and the medical school of Western University of Pittsburgh. She paid her own way through school, working as a bookkeeper, doing entomological work at the Carnegie Museum, and acting as part-time secretary to a local merchant. After graduation, she did postgraduate work at the University of Pennsylvania. She returned to Pittsburgh, where she married Dr. Milton Goldsmith on March 25, 1905. The Goldsmiths left Pittsburgh for Vienna and Berlin, where they studied for eight months. Luba Goldsmith entered general practice soon after her return to Pittsburgh.

"Dr. Luba," as she was affectionately known, worked on civic and health problems in the community from the earliest days of her career. She was the first chief tenement house inspector in the city and advocated for the purification of city water. From 1915 to 1919, she was medical adviser to women students at the University of Pittsburgh. Goldsmith was the author of a scientific paper, "The Aberhalden Test for Pregnancy."

Goldsmith taught physiology at the University Dental School for four years as an assistant professor; she later taught in the School of Education. She gave courses in medical and social problems at the Margaret Morrison School of the Carnegie Institute of Technology (Carnegie-Mellon University).

A popular lecturer on health topics in schools, clubs, and churches, she remained active in public health movements in Pittsburgh and other cities throughout the Northeast. She served as national chair of the United States Public Health Advisory Committee. She chaired the public health committee of the NATIONAL COUNCIL OF JEWISH WOMEN.

Goldsmith's avocation was the theater. She wrote several plays on health themes, including *Who Cares?* (a copy of which survives at the Brown University Libary), a health fantasy, and *What Next?*, described as "a picture from life." She wrote articles called "The Art of Jewish Living" and "Jewish Legends," and authored a play entitled *East and West*.

Luba Goldsmith was a founding member of the Alpha Epsilon Phi sorority chapter at the University of Pittsburgh and was a member of the National Council of Jewish Women, HADASSAH, College Club, Civic Club of Allegheny County, American Association of University Women, Women's International League for Peace and Freedom, American Medical Association, Women's National Medical Society, Allegheny County Medical Society, and Rodef Shalom Congregation.

She died in October 1931 at age fifty-two. She was survived by her husband and two sons, Norman and Albert.

A medical scholarship was established at the University of Pittsburgh as a permanent memorial to her. The money for the scholarship fund was raised by a committee of women who believed that "the influence of this woman whose life service was so far reaching, will always be alive." Luba Robin Goldsmith achieved in her life the goals to which many contemporary Jewish women aspire—combining family and social service.

BIBLIOGRAPHY

"Civic and Health Problems Sponsored by Dr. Goldsmith." *Pittsburgh Post-Gazette*, February 17, 1931; "Dr. Luba Goldsmith Dies." *Pittsburgh Press*, October 17, 1931; "Medical Scholarship Planned as Tribute to Woman Physician." *Pittsburgh Press*, January 10, 1932; "Pitt Jewish Medical Student with Highest Record to Get Fund." *Pittsburgh Sun-Telegraph*, May 29, 1932; "Who's Who in Pittsburgh Jewry." *Jewish Criterion*, September 19, 1927; *WWIAJ* (1926, 1928).

Interviews with anonymous women for study, "Ethnicity and Mental Health," sponsored by the American Jewish Committee, 1976; interview with Esther Morrow, Pittsburgh, January 2, 1997.

CORINNE AZEN KRAUSE

GOLDSTEIN, FANNY (1895–1961)

Librarian, social activist, and founder of National Jewish Book Week, Fanny Goldstein helped institutionalize national pride in ethnic and immigrant backgrounds through her work in libraries, and settlement houses, and in her lectures and writing.

Born in Kamenets-Podolsk, Russia, on May 15, 1895, Goldstein immigrated to Boston's North End with her family in 1900. After attending Hancock Grammar School and taking classes at Simmons College, Boston University, and Harvard University, she became a librarian in the Boston Public Library's (BPL) North End branch in 1913. Her experience there among the broad mix of immigrant children convinced her that knowledge of one's own ethnic background—and that of one's neighbors—was as important for successful acculturation as was knowledge of American language, job skills, and social customs. In 1914, she helped organize the Saturday Evening Girls Club for immigrant girls and edited the group's magazine. The club provided recreation, socialization, and job skills, but most important to Goldstein, it motivated the immigrant girls to learn about their own ethnic backgrounds and to respect one another's cultural backgrounds.

In 1922, Goldstein transferred to the BPL's West End branch in Boston's other major immigrant neighborhood, where she served until her retirement in 1957. There she refined her focus on teaching Americans about themselves and one another. Goldstein built and published collections of books with specific ethnic concentrations, ran weekly book clubs for children and adults, pioneered library exhibitions on immigrant cultures, and created, among other specialty programs, Negro History Week, Jewish Music Month, Catholic Book Week, and Brotherhood Week. Goldstein founded Jewish Book Week in 1925, which grew to become National Jewish Book Week and the Jewish Book Council of America, of which Goldstein served as lifetime honorary president.

Goldstein was the first Jewish woman to direct a branch library in Massachusetts. Her work developing the BPL's Judaica collection created the state's second-largest Judaica holdings after Harvard University's and culminated in Goldstein's 1954 appointment as the first Jewish woman curator of Judaica in the BPL. She retired from the BPL in 1957, after forty-four years of service to Boston booklovers. She contributed articles to the *Encyclopedia of Jewish Knowledge*, the *American Jewish Year Book*, and the *Universal Jewish Encyclopedia*, and lectured widely on Jewish literature, Americanization, and library administration. After retiring, she served as literary editor of Boston's *The Jewish Advocate*.

Fanny Goldstein died in Boston on December 26, 1961.

SELECTED WORKS BY FANNY GOLDSTEIN

"A Bibliography of Foreign Books and Authors in English Translations as Library Aids in Work with Foreign Born." Boston Public Library (n.d., probably 1940s); "Judaica: A Selected Reading List of Books in the Public Library of the City of Boston." The Trustees [of the Boston Public Library] (1931–1940).

BIBLIOGRAPHY

AJYB 64 (1963): 493; Goldstein, Fanny. Papers. Boston Public Library, Boston, Mass.; Sarna, Jonathan D., and Ellen Smith, eds. *The Jews of Boston* (1995); *Saturday Evening Girls' News*. Boston, 1914–1917; reunion issues 1952 and 1954.

ELLEN SMITH

GOLDSTEIN, JENNIE (c. 1895/1897–1960)

Jennie Goldstein was one of the foremost Yiddish theater tragediennes, beloved by the public and acclaimed by critics for her ability to make audiences cry and for her outstanding voice.

Jennie Goldstein was born in New York City on May 8 in 1895 or 1897, the daughter of Samuel and Beckie (Schaffer) Goldstein. She attended the local public schools and Hebrew school, and studied music privately. Although not from a theatrical family—her father was a butcher—she debuted at age six in the role of the child in *Hanele di Neytorin* [Hanele the dressmaker]. At age thirteen, she left school and began to play adult roles and to perform in vaudeville, where she met Max Gabel, whom she married when she was sixteen years old. Gabel wrote melodramas with titles such as *Alts far Libe* [Everything for love], in which the couple starred. These plays were very successful and enjoyed extended runs.

Goldstein was divorced from Gabel in 1930 and embarked on a new period in her career. She managed

Yiddish melodramas were the mainstay of actress Jennie Goldstein, whose reputation was partially built on her ability to make audiences cry. [American Jewish Historical Society]

the Prospect Theater in the Bronx in 1932–1933 and starred in the Yiddish film *Two Sisters* (1939), her sole movie performance. She married Charles W. Groll, a lawyer, in May 1936. During the 1940s, as opportunities in the Yiddish theater waned, Goldstein transformed herself into a comedienne. She became a popular entertainer at Jewish organizational functions, performed in two Broadway shows in the 1950s, and appeared on television. Interested in Jewish communal life, she was a member of the board of the Bikur Cholim Convalescent Home and a member of the Daughters of Israel Day Nursery and the Hebrew Actors Union.

Jennie Goldstein died in New York City on February 9, 1960. During her lengthy career, she demonstrated great versatility in her acting styles and remarkable resilience.

BIBLIOGRAPHY

AJYB 62:450; *EJ*, s.v. "Theater"; Ehrenreich, Chaim. *Jewish Daily Forward*, February 10–11, 1960; Obituary. *NYTimes*, February 10, 1960, 37:1; *UJE*; *WWIAJ* (1926, 1928, 1938); Zylbercwaig, Zalman. *Leksikon fun Yidishn Teater* [Lexicon of the Yiddish theater], Vol. 1 (1931–1969), s.v. "Goldshteyn, Dzsheni."

SHULAMITH Z. BERGER

GOLDSTEIN, REBECCA FISCHEL (1891–1961)

The heading of the *New York Times* obituary of June 5, 1961, for Rebecca Fischel Goldstein read, "Mrs. H.S. Goldstein, Rabbi's Wife." This truly reflected who Mrs. Rebecca Goldstein was. The quintessential *rebbetzin* [rabbi's wife], she was a prime mover in her husband's drive to build the Institutional Synagogue and make it a center of Jewish life in Harlem. As a consummate volunteer leader, she strove to make women a dominant force in organized Jewish life, helping to found the Women's Branch of the Union of Orthodox Jewish Congregations of America, the Women's League of the Institutional Synagogue, the Hebrew Teachers Training School for Girls, and the Yeshiva University Women's Organization.

Rebecca Fischel was born in 1891 in New York City, the second of four daughters born to philanthropist Harry and Jane (Braz) Fischel. A real estate developer who had emigrated penniless from Russia as a young man, Harry Fischel was determined to provide his children with the finest education. His unyielding devotion to the Orthodox Jewish tradition, to which he attributed his material prosperity, led him to provide home-based Jewish schooling for his daughters. To ensure their success in the secular world, Harry Fischel sent all four girls to college.

While attending Barnard College, Rebecca met Herbert Goldstein, then studying at Columbia University. After graduating in 1912, she continued her studies at the Teachers Institute of the Jewish Theological Seminary. The two married on March 1, 1915, brought together by their immersion in the study of Jewish texts and their determination to teach others and spread the word of Torah. To illustrate the ideal they had set for themselves before their marriage, they decided to produce an ethical work as a wedding souvenir. They chose to translate and publish the *La-Yesharim Tehillah* [Praise to the Righteous], written in Amsterdam by Moses Hayyim Luzzatto in 1743.

When her husband founded the Institutional Synagogue in 1917, Goldstein was by his side, supporting his Jewish revival movement and his dream of an institution that would serve as synagogue, Hebrew school, and community center for the Jews of Upper

Manhattan. While he nurtured the spiritual needs, Goldstein used her community skills to reach out to the young, emphasizing education. Even while raising their own four children—Simeon, Gabriel, Josephine, and Naomi—she founded the Daughters of the Institutional Synagogue, and became a mother figure to countless young women.

Outreach and education were central themes in Goldstein's life. As the first president of the Women's Branch of the Orthodox Union she established the Collegiate Branch to spread Torah to college students. She was a vice chair of the Women's Committee of the Rabbi Isaac Elchanan Theological Seminary, which achieved its goal of raising $250,000 for the building of the first student dormitory at Yeshiva University in 1927.

Rebecca Fischel Goldstein's greatest gift was her ability to inspire leadership and Jewish commitment in others. Even after severe arthritis forced her into a wheelchair in 1947, she continued speaking and motivating women to become involved in a meaningful Jewish life. Her legacy of courage and passion are reflected in these words: "To believe we must feel, to feel we must understand, to understand we must study . . . [there is] no royal road to instilling religion without study."

BIBLIOGRAPHY

AJYB 63:559; *NYTimes*, June 5, 1961, 31:2; Reichel, Aaron I. *The Maverick Rabbi* (1984); Reichel, Josephine Goldstein. Private collection; *WWIAJ* (1926, 1928).

AMY L. KATZ

GOLDSTEIN, ROSE (d. 1984)

An early advocate of increased rights and responsibilities for women in Jewish life, Rose Goldstein was a prominent leader in the National Women's League of the United Synagogue of America (now known as WOMEN'S LEAGUE FOR CONSERVATIVE JUDAISM), which awarded her its coveted *Yovayl* [Jubilee] Award in 1968.

Rose Berman was born in Minneapolis to Sarah and Alexander Berman, the only girl in a family of four children that had emigrated from Lithuania in 1892. After graduating summa cum laude from the University of Minnesota, where she was elected to Phi Beta Kappa, she embarked on graduate study at Columbia University. There, her master's thesis dealt with the newer Sephardi community of New York. She married Rabbi David Goldstein, a noted graduate of the Jewish Theological Seminary of America.

As national chair of program and education for the National Women's League, Goldstein chaired many events and often led prayer services at Women's League conventions. These responsibilities eventually led to her writing, in 1972, *A Time to Pray: A Personal Approach to the Jewish Prayer Book*. In an informal yet scholarly style, Goldstein shared with her readers many of the exciting lessons that delighted and informed those who joined her for study and worship over the years. In the book, she refers to experiences in her own life and to ways in which the ancient words helped her to achieve self-understanding. According to the Women's League *Outlook* magazine (Spring 1973), "She has confronted the daily prayer book for many years with an open mind and with a seeking soul."

An early advocate of increased rights and responsibilities for women in Jewish life, Rose Goldstein was a prominent leader in the National Women's League of the United Synagogue of America (now known as WOMEN'S LEAGUE FOR CONSERVATIVE JUDAISM). *[Women's League for Conservative Judaism]*

Goldstein was widely known as an author and educator, and lectured extensively on Jewish worship. Her appearances before young people and adults were marked by lively discussion and searching inquiry. Over the years, as the busy mother of four sons, she held a variety of national and local Jewish posts that reflected her deep concern for Jewish education.

Rose Goldstein died in December 1984.

BIBLIOGRAPHY

Goldstein, Rose. National Women's League of the United Synagogue of America. *Proceedings of Biennial Conventions*, New York (1950, 1954, 1956); National Women's League of the United Synagogue of America. *Program*, Biennial Convention, New York (1952); *Outlook* (Spring 1973); *Seventy-Five Years of Vision and Voluntarism* (1992); *The Sixth Decade, 1968–1978* (1978); *A Time to Pray* (1972); *WWIAJ* (1938).

SELMA WEINTRAUB

GORDON, DOROTHY LERNER
(1889–1970)

Dorothy Lerner Gordon—musician, broadcaster, author—dedicated her talents to the entertainment and education of children and young people. Born in Russia on April 4, 1889, she was the daughter of Rosa (Schwartz) and American diplomat Leo Lerner. The youngest of four sisters, she spent much of her childhood in Europe as the family followed her father to Italy, various Balkan countries, France, and Germany. Gordon credits her early experiences in Europe with her interest in stories, songs, and folktales of various cultures—an interest that helped to bring her to the stage and then into broadcasting. During these childhood years, her family also recognized her musical talents and offered her training in voice and piano.

The Lerner family returned to the United States, and in 1910 Dorothy Lerner married Bernard Gordon, whom she described as "a very prominent, busy lawyer." Her responsibilities as a wife and a mother to two sons occupied the early years of her marriage, but by the 1920s she had begun her stage career. Spurred by her interest in music and her disappointment in the lack of suitable entertainment for children, Gordon began to mount stage shows for young people. Her repertoire included folk songs, which she sang in the costume of the appropriate country. She toured the country giving concerts to enthusiastic audiences.

In 1923, she began her broadcasting career when the Women's League of the United Synagogue of America invited her to do a recital of folk songs on the radio. During the 1920s, however, Gordon saw radio primarily as a means of advertising. As she traveled around the country performing, she would stop at local radio stations for an interview and perhaps sing a few songs. At first, she disliked the medium because she felt that performers needed contact with their audience. But by the 1930s, as she witnessed the potential reach and educational benefits of radio, she became a strong advocate.

During the 1930s, she moved more directly into commercial radio. She became the musical director of the *American School of the Air*, a five-day-a-week program that examined a different topic each day—history, geography, science, current events, and music. She was the "Song and Story Lady" on the *Children's Corner*, where she narrated and dramatized folk stories. As well, in 1939 she produced *Yesterday's Children*, a program that featured the favorite childhood books

When, as a performer, she recognized a need for suitable children's entertainment, Dorothy Lerner Gordon filled the void, singing and narrating folk stories, first on stage, then on radio and television and in print. [New York Public Library]

of a famous person. After telling or dramatizing the story, Gordon would have that week's guest explain why he or she had loved that story as a child. Throughout this period, Gordon continued to tour the country doing live performances. It was on these tours that she discovered the breadth of the radio audience. Radio, she learned, was bringing literature and music to rural Americans.

In 1941, she turned her attention in a somewhat different direction. She felt that radio could also bring news and current events to children. She became the director of children's programs for the radio division of the Office of War Information. Her work there made her realize the enormous possibilities of radio for bringing information to both children and adults. Two years later, she initiated the Youth Forum, which brought young people together to discuss current events. Not initially designed for radio, the first Youth Forums were sponsored by the *New York Times* and held at Times Hall in New York City. In 1945, however, the *Times* bought WQXR and began broadcasting these programs weekly. Gordon always insisted that the Youth Forum include children from all racial, religious, and social backgrounds. After a few years, she began to include an adult "expert" on each program who could serve as a resource and answer questions for the young people. Among the illustrious guests were Averell Harriman, Dwight D. Eisenhower, GOLDA MEIR, Norman Thomas, William O. Douglas, and Ralph Bunche. The Youth Forum moved to television in 1952 and continued to broadcast for seventeen years. When she died on May 11, 1970, Gordon was still serving as moderator of the weekly television program.

In addition to her careers in music and broadcasting, Dorothy Lerner Gordon was the author of numerous books. *All Children Listen* (1941) discusses her views on the impact of radio on children. Many of her other books were written specifically for children, for example, *You and Democracy* (1951) and *Who Knows the Answer?* (1965).

**SELECTED WORKS BY
DOROTHY LERNER GORDON**

All Children Listen (1941); *Who Knows the Answer?* (1965); *You and Democracy* (1951).

BIBLIOGRAPHY

Gordon, Dorothy Lerner. *The Reminiscences of Dorothy Gordon.* Oral History Collection, Columbia University (1951); *NAW* modern; Obituary. *NYTimes*, May 12, 1970, 39:1; *UJE*; *Who's Who of American Women* (1968); *WWWIA* 5.

CINDY ARON

Her sharp business sense allowed Jean Gordon to succeed as publisher of Dance Magazine *when she came to that publication after her retirement from a completely unrelated—though quite successful—enterprise, the Advance Pattern Company. She is shown here (on the left) in conversation with Alicia Markova, presumably at the intermission of a performance. [*Dance Magazine*]*

GORDON, JEAN (1903–1985)

Jean Gordon had two successful careers in her lifetime, as a founder of the Advance Pattern Company and as the owner and publisher of *Dance Magazine*.

Born Sadie Jean Gordon in New York City on November 1, 1903, to Sarah (Goldstein) and Hyman Gordon, she was one of seven children, three boys and four girls, though one sister died young. Her mother, who was born in the United States, died in 1910, when Jean was seven years old. Her father, who had come to the United States from Vilna in 1888, utilized his entrepreneurial skill to acquire and train horses. He maintained stables in the Bronx and provided horses for street peddlers as well as the New York City Police Department. Gordon was brought up in a fairly observant Jewish household; as an adult she continued to celebrate Jewish holidays but led a cosmopolitan life that was not compatible with active observance.

After graduating from high school, Jean Gordon began her first job at *Pictorial Review*. At that time the magazine was independent, though it later was bought by the Hearst Corporation and became the Sunday supplement to the Hearst newspapers. Jean Gordon married Morris Stern in 1927; he died in 1931, leaving her with an infant son, Robert. Using her husband's life insurance as capital, Jean Gordon (as she continued to be known professionally, though within her family she was Syd or Sadie Stern) cofounded the Advance Pattern Company in 1932 with her former boss, Samuel R. Cohn. By 1940, the company had 350 employees, with offices in Chicago, Atlanta, Dallas, and New York. J.C. Penney was their largest customer. When she left the company in 1950, she was executive vice president.

Jean Gordon's retirement was short-lived; within weeks her second career was launched. Her close friend Rudolf Orthwine, who had recently acquired the ailing *Dance Magazine*, invited her to be associate publisher. Although she was not experienced with dance, her business acumen and high standards helped her lead *Dance Magazine* to financial stability and a prominent place in the dance world. Under her guidance, the magazine developed a broad and devoted dance following. After Orthwine's death in 1970, Gordon owned and published the magazine and continued to be active there until her death on October 22, 1985, at age eighty-one.

During her tenure as publisher of *Dance Magazine*, Gordon established the Dance Magazine Awards, which annually recognize outstanding accomplishments in dance. She was responsible for creating two valuable references, *The Dance Magazine College Guide* and *Stern's Performing Arts Directory*. Under her ownership, the magazine contributed to many scholarships, which led to the establishment of Dance Magazine Foundation's Jean Gordon Stern Scholarship Fund.

Coming to dance as a businessperson, she nonetheless endeared herself to dancers through her generosity and advocacy. She was recognized in 1972 and 1979 by awards from Dance Masters of America (an organization of dance instructors) "in recognition of her outstanding contributions to the dance profession" and in 1975 from the City of New York, which cited her "keen judgment and knowledge of the myriad complexities of publishing."

BIBLIOGRAPHY

Contemporary Authors 117 (1986): 414; "Jean Gordon Stern, 81, Dance Magazine Head." *NYTimes*, October 25, 1985, B14; "Obituaries." *Ballet News* 7, no. 7 (January 1986): 27; Philp, Richard. "Jean Gordon Stern (1903–1985)." *Dance Magazine* (December 1985): 20; Stern, Robert. Telephone interviews with author, May and June 1996.

JOYCE MORGENROTH

GORDON, VERA (1886–1948)

After her star-making turn in the 1920 film *Humoresque*, actor Vera Gordon came to represent the archetypical Jewish mother, both on-screen and off. She played mother roles in almost thirty films, including *The Millionaires* (1926), *Four Walls* (1928), and the successful *The Cohens and the Kellys* series. At the same time, she often gave advice on marriage and children to newspapers and magazines, and furthered her nurturing image by supporting children in Jewish orphanages.

Vera Gordon was born Vera Pogorelsky to Boris and Teigan (Nemirovsky) Pogorelsky on June 11, 1886, in Ekaterinoslav, Russia. She began appearing on the Russian stage before age eleven, although at one point the directors of the Shevchenko Imperial Company fired her after learning of her Jewish heritage. In 1904, she married Nathan A. Gordon, a producer and writer at the Ostoffersk Acting Company, with which she was performing. The next year, the couple had a child, William, and immigrated to the United States.

When the Gordons arrived on New York's Lower East Side with their three-month-old son, neither could speak English. Vera Gordon refused to join the Yiddish Theater Union, believing that her years of experience should count for as much as a union card. This decision cost her the chance to play larger venues, and she appeared instead at smaller houses such as the Liberty and the Lyric Theatres. During her struggle to begin her American career, Gordon bore another child, Nadje, in 1907. In 1916, she performed in Britain, appearing first in vaudeville and then in legitimate theater.

In 1919, during her London run in the play *Potash and Perlmutter*, Paramount Pictures recruited Gordon to star in *Humoresque*. The film, directed by Frank Borzage, opened the next year to rave reviews. Gordon drew especially good notices for her role as a mother raising her family on the Lower East Side. By age thirty-five, she was a successful movie star, and she averaged almost a film a year for the next three decades. Into that busy schedule she also fit regular stage appearances, often with her daughter. In almost all these roles, Gordon played a mother, although in interviews she always stressed her versatility. The Yiddish theater, she explained, prepared an actor to play any part. She often commented, ironically, that the woman whose name was synonymous with the word "mother" once played an old man, complete with beard.

Gordon moved with her family to Beverly Hills, California, in 1928. Although her heyday was in the

The lines between movie star Vera Gordon's on- and off-screen personas eventually blurred, creating a stock but real-life Jewish mother who dispensed nuggets of family wisdom and supported children in Jewish orphanages. [New York Public Library]

1920s and early 1930s, she continued acting until almost the end of her life, making her last film, *Abie's Irish Rose*, in 1946. She died on May 8, 1948, in her Beverly Hills home.

Through her life and work, Vera Gordon put a positive and loving face on the stereotype of the Jewish mother. Despite her rejection of the Yiddish Theater Union, she provided outspoken support of the training the theater itself provided and, during her lifetime, served as an ambassador for both Jewish theater and Jewish culture.

FILMOGRAPHY

Abie's Irish Rose (1946); *The Big Street* (1942); *The Cohens and the Kellys*, (1926); *The Cohens and the Kellys in Africa* (1930); *The Cohens and the Kellys in Atlantic City* (1928); *The Cohens and the Kellys in Paris* (1928); *The Cohens and the Kellys in Scotland* (1930); *Fifty Million Frenchmen* (1931); *Four Walls* (1928); *Good Provider* (1922); *Humoresque* (1920); *In Hollywood with Potash and Perlmutter* (1924); *Kosher Kitty Kelly* (1926); *Living Ghost* (1942); *Madame Satan* (1930); *Michael O'Halloran* (1937); *The Millionaires* (1926); *North Wind's Malice* (1921); *Potash and Perlmutter* (1923); *Private Izzy Murphy* (1926); *Sweet Daddies* (1926); *When Strangers Meet* (1934); *You and Me* (1938); *Your Best Friend* (1922).

BIBLIOGRAPHY

AJYB 24:149, 50:612; *BEOAJ*; Gordon, Vera. Scrapbook. Performing Arts Collection, New York Public Library for the Performing Arts at Lincoln Center; Katz, Ephraim. *Film Encyclopedia* (1979); Stewart, John. *Filmrama*. Vol. 2, *The Flaming Years, 1920–1929* (1977); Truitt, Evelyn Mack. *Who Was Who on Screen* (1974); "Vera Gordon, 61, Screen Actress." *NYTimes*, May 10, 1948, 21:4; Weaver, John T. *Forty Years of Screen Credits, 1929–1969* (1970); *WWIAJ* (1926, 1928).

KATE CULKIN

GORME, EYDIE (b. 1932)

One of the great stylists of the American popular song, Eydie Gorme has had a loyal following from the 1950s to the present. She achieved national prominence with her appearances on Steve Allen's *Tonight!* show, where she met and performed with her husband Steve Lawrence. Gorme's dynamic nightclub act, frequently as a duo with Lawrence, has continued to draw sell-out crowds while resisting passing trends and keeping true to the best traditions of the American "standard"—traditions she herself helped to establish.

She was born Edith Gorme on August 16, 1932 (some sources say 1931), in New York City, the daughter of Nessim Gorme, an immigrant tailor, and Fortune Gorme. Both parents were Turkish-born Jews of Spanish descent, so she and her older siblings, Corene and Robert, grew up speaking fluent Spanish. Ironically, she was the only one of the three not to be given music lessons, since the others had not made much use of theirs.

Gorme made her singing debut at age three, when she toddled away from her parents in a department store and got on line to perform in a children's radio show being broadcast there. At William Howard Taft High School in the Bronx, New York, she was voted "the prettiest, peppiest cheerleader," starred in

It's hard to imagine her without Steve Lawrence, but Eydie Gorme enjoyed much solo success before and after hooking up with her husband and singing partner. [New York Public Library]

most of the school musicals, and sang with her friend Ken Greengrass's band on weekends.

After high school, Gorme briefly worked as an interpreter for a theatrical supply export company and later as its manager, while taking night classes in foreign trade and economics at the City College of New York. But she continued performing with Greengrass on weekends and soon took the plunge, leaving her job to try to make it as a singer. Greengrass disbanded his orchestra to become her manager, a role he retained for many years.

Gorme's first break came when bandleader Tommy Tucker hired her as vocalist for a two-month road tour. She then toured for a year with Tex Benecke's orchestra and also sang with the Ray Eberle orchestra before deciding she was ready to try performing on her own. As a single act, Gorme toured the nightclub and theater circuit and made guest appearances on top radio and television programs. She signed her first recording contract with Coral

Records in 1952 and soon made the Top Twenty. Through the Voice of America, she hosted her own radio show, *Cita con Eydie* [A date with Eydie], which was transmitted to Spanish-speaking countries around the world.

In the fall of 1953, Gorme joined the permanent cast of *Tonight!*, where for the next four years she sang and also wrote and performed in sketches with Steve Lawrence. They had much in common, and friendship gradually blossomed into romance. The son of Eastern European Jewish immigrants, Lawrence was born Sidney Liebowitz in Brooklyn, New York, on July 8, 1935. He had started singing in the synagogue choir where his father served as cantor while supporting the family as a housepainter. Gorme and Lawrence were married in Las Vegas on December 29, 1957. They later had two sons, David Nessim and Michael.

Meanwhile, in February 1956, Gorme made her New York nightclub debut as a last-minute replacement at the Copacabana and was such a hit that she was booked as a headliner for July. The following January brought her first Broadway appearance, as singing star of the *Jerry Lewis Stage Show* at the Palace Theatre. In the summer of 1958, the husband-and-wife team had their own weekly musical variety show on television as summer replacements for Steve Allen. Gorme then embarked on a two-year solo nightclub tour while her husband served in the Army. Reunited in 1960, the pair won a Grammy Award for their first complete duet album, *We Got Us*, which was followed by several others over the next few years. 1968 found them on Broadway in *Golden Rainbow*, and the following year they recorded their first musical, *What It Was, Was Love*.

Gorme has continued to perform both solo and with Lawrence, recording albums and singles, and appearing on television and in nightclubs. Her best-known hits include the singles "Too Close for Comfort," "Mama, Teach Me to Dance" (both 1956), "Love Me Forever" (1957), "You Need Hands" (1958), "Blame It on the Bossa Nova" (1963 Grammy nominee), and "If He Walked into My Life" (1966 Grammy Award), and the albums *Eydie in Love* (1958 Grammy nominee), *We Got Us* with Steve Lawrence (1960 Grammy Award), *La Gorme* (1976 Grammy nominee), and *Muy Amigos/Close Friends* with Danny Rivers (1977 Grammy nominee). Her TV appearances with Lawrence have also won recognition, with a 1976 Emmy nomination for *Steve and Eydie: Our Love Is Here to Stay*, and seven Emmys in 1979 for *Steve and Eydie Celebrate Irving Berlin*.

Throughout the 1980s, Gorme and Lawrence appeared on many well-known stages, including

Carnegie Hall, the Universal Amphitheater in Los Angeles, Harrah's in Lake Tahoe, Nevada, and Bally's in Las Vegas. In 1991, they joined Frank Sinatra on his year-long Diamond Jubilee Tour, in celebration of his seventy-fifth birthday.

In her long career, Eydie Gorme has delighted countless audiences and has helped create a classic style of American popular singing whose appeal and vitality are eternal.

SELECTED WORKS BY EYDIE GORME

ALBUMS

Amor (1964); *Blame It on the Bossa Nova* (1963); *Come in from the Rain* (1985); *Come Sing with Me* (1961); *Don't Go to Strangers* (1966); *Eydie Gorme* (1957); *Eydie Gorme on Stage* (1959); *Eydie Gorme Vamps the Roaring 20s* (1958); *Eydie Gorme's Greatest Hits* (1967); *Eydie in Dixie-Land* (1960); *Eydie in Love . . .* (1958); *Eydie Sings Showstoppers* (1959); *Eydie Swings the Blues* (1957); *Gorme Country Style* (1964); *I Feel So Spanish* (1962); *Let the Good Times Roll* (1963); *More Amor* (1965); *Navidad Means Christmas*, with the Trio Los Panchos (1966); *Sings/Canta* (1987); *Softly, As I Love You* (1967); *Tomame o Dejame* (1985); *Tonight I'll Say a Prayer* (1970); *The Very Best of Eydie Gorme* (1961).

WITH STEVE LAWRENCE

Alone Together (1989); *The Best of Steve and Eydie* (1977); *Cozy* (1961); *The Golden Hits* (1960); *I Still Believe in Love* (1985); *On Broadway* (1967); *Our Best to You* (1977); *Our Love Is Here to Stay* (1977); *Real True Lovin'* (1969); *Since I Fell for You* (1993); *Twenty Golden Performances* (1977); *We Can Make It Together* (1975); *We Got Us* (1960); *What It Was, Was Love* (1969).

BIBLIOGRAPHY

Current Biography (February 1965): 17–18; *The Guinness Encyclopedia of Popular Music*. Edited by Colin Larkin. Vol. 3 (1992): 1706–1707; *Who's Who* (1996).

GWEN NEFSKY FRANKFELDT

GORNICK, VIVIAN (b. 1935)

For Vivian Gornick, self-narrative is a form of cultural criticism: The personal is decidedly political. As a staff writer for the *Village Voice* during the early 1970s, Gornick reported on the explosion of American feminist consciousness through the prism of her own experience, and her willingness to use her own life experiences to tell a larger social story has become the hallmark of her writing. While she acknowledges her Jewish background in much of her work, Gornick marks the urgency of her feminist struggle for "possession of the self" as the force that drives her creative endeavors (*Essays* 169). "It is here, on the issue of being a woman, not a Jew, that I must make my stand and hold my ground," she explains in *Tikkun* (1989).

Vivian Gornick was born on June 14, 1935, in the Bronx, the youngest of Louis and Bess Gornick's two children. Her Ukrainian-born parents, whom Gornick describes as "harried, working-class immigrants," were committed socialists who met and married in New York. Her father worked as a presser in a dress factory for thirty years, and her mother was a bookkeeper and office clerk. When Gornick was thirteen years old, her father died suddenly of a heart attack. Her memoir, *Fierce Attachments* (1987), paints a vivid picture of growing up in "a building full of women" with a mother immersed in her own mourning.

Vivian Gornick's groundbreaking anthology Woman in Sexist Society: Studies in Power and Powerlessness, *coedited in 1971 with Barbara K. Moran, compares women with the Wandering Jew and Noble Savage, symbolically "beyond the pale of ordinary human existence." As a staff writer for the* Village Voice *during the early 1970s, she used her own life experiences to tell the larger story of feminism. [Schlesinger Library]*

Gornick received her B.A. from City College of New York in 1957 and completed her M.A. at New York University in 1960. After teaching English at the State University of New York at Stony Brook in 1966–1967 and at HUNTER COLLEGE in 1967–1968, she worked as a reporter for the *Village Voice* from 1969 to 1977 while also writing for publications such as *The Nation*, the *New York Times*, and the *Atlantic*. Many of Gornick's articles from this period are collected in *Essays in Feminism* (1978) and reflect the revolutionary excitement of the growing women's movement. Since leaving the *Village Voice*, she has divided her time between free-lance writing and teaching in creative writing programs. Gornick has been married and divorced twice.

Whether she is writing impressionistic journalism or memoir, Vivian Gornick explores the actual and metaphoric significance of being an outsider—perpetually "half in, half out." Her groundbreaking anthology, *Woman in Sexist Society: Studies in Power and Powerlessness*, coedited in 1971 with Barbara K. Moran, places women alongside the prototypical Wandering Jew and Noble Savage, symbolically "beyond the pale of ordinary human existence" (71). Such a vantage point not only provides valuable perspective for critiquing society, it also encourages "the camaraderie of the outsider" that allows her to write sympathetically about all marginalized groups (*In Search of Ali Mahmoud* 7). For *In Search of Ali Mahmoud: An American Woman in Egypt* (1973), Gornick traveled to Egypt to explore the culture of a former lover, which she depicts as simultaneously exotic and familiar. Her impression that American women and Egyptian men experience similar kinds of powerlessness is heightened by her perception of herself as "the original stranger" (94)—a Jew in an Arab land. Interviewing one hundred former communists for *The Romance of American Communism* (1977), Gornick examined how their politics enabled them to live "at a level of intense expressiveness" (Perry 118). This passion for understanding what allows the outsider to become an "experiencing self" is echoed in *Women in Science: Portraits from a World in Transition* (1983), where science—like feminism—becomes a means of "demystifying the self and the environment" (162). *Fierce Attachments: A Memoir* (1987) portrays Gornick's own determination to lead a life of the mind and to transcend "the daily infliction of social invisibility" that women experience as outsiders ("Twice an Outsider" 123). Weaving together past and present through a series of conversations and encounters with her mother, Gornick uses their complex relationship as the frame for her exploration of the meaning of success, freedom, and love. Her collection of essays, *Approaching Eye Level* (1996), depicts Gornick's ongoing effort to attain "the dense and original quality of life on the margin" by experiencing the action and rhythm of the streets of New York.

Gornick's work powerfully evokes the urban Jewish American milieu of her childhood and reflects unflinchingly on the parallel humiliations of anti-Semitism and sexism. Despite her claim that "feminism absolutely ended" her emotional attachment to Judaism (Swenson, 16), the experience of being "twice an outsider"—both Jewish and a woman—serves for Gornick as a powerful lesson in marginality. "Being Jewish . . . lives in me as a vital subculture," she explains, "enriching my life as a writer, as an American, and certainly as a woman." ("Twice an Outsider" 125).

SELECTED WORKS BY VIVIAN GORNICK

Approaching Eye Level (1996); *Essays in Feminism* (1978); *Fierce Attachments: A Memoir* (1987); *In Search of Ali Mahmoud: An American Woman in Egypt* (1973); Introduction to *How I Found America: Collected Stories of Anzia Yezierska* (1991); Introduction to *Wasteland*, by Jo Sinclair (1987); "The Reliable Reporter and the Untrustworthy Narrator." *Soundings: An Interdisciplinary Journal* 76, no. 2–3 (Summer/Fall 1993): 267–280; *The Romance of American Communism* (1977); "Twice an Outsider: On Being Jewish and a Woman." *Tikkun: A Bimonthly Jewish Critique of Politics, Culture & Society* 4, no. 2 (March/April 1989): 29+; *Woman in Sexist Society: Studies in Power and Powerlessness*, coedited with Barbara K. Moran (1971); *Women in Science: Portraits from a World in Transition* (1983).

BIBLIOGRAPHY

Burstein, Janet H. "A Response to Vivian Gornick." *Soundings: An Interdisciplinary Journal* 76, no. 2–3 (Summer/Fall 1993): 285–288; Cousineau, Diane. "Women and Autobiography: Is There Life Beyond the Looking Glass?" *Caliban* 31 (1994): 97–105; Laufer, Pearl David. "Powerful and Powerless: Paradox in Vivian Gornick's *Fierce Attachments*." In *Mother Puzzles: Daughters and Mothers in Contemporary American Literature*, edited by Mickey Pearlman (1989); Perry, Donna Marie. "Interview with Vivian Gornick." *Backtalk: Women Writers Speak Out* (1993); Porter, Dale H. "A Response to Gornick." *Soundings: An Interdisciplinary Journal* 76, no. 2–3 (Summer/Fall 1993): 281–284; Swenson, Linda Fader. "Facing Down Secret Fears and Unbearable Wisdoms: An Interview with Vivian Gornick." *Hayden's Ferry Review* 12 (Spring/Summer 1993): 7–19; "Vivian Gornick." *Contemporary Authors: A Bio-Bibliographical Guide to Current Writers in Fiction, General Nonfiction, Poetry, Journalism, Drama, Motion Pictures, Television, and Other Fields*, edited by Frances C. Locher. Vol. 101 (1981).

TRESA GRAUER

GOTSFELD, BESSIE GOLDSTEIN (1888–1962)

Bessie Goldstein Gotsfeld's name is synonymous with American Mizrachi Women, the religious organization she helped to form. For thirty years, Gotsfeld was the Palestine (later Israel) representative for the organization. She supervised the establishment of vocational schools, children's villages, and farms for religious youth, and forged a connection between women in the United States and children in Israel.

The first child of Raisel and Leon Goldstein, Bessie was born in 1888 during Sukkoth, in Przemysl, Poland. When Raisel Goldstein died, Bessie became a mother for her two sisters and three brothers. Her father, a Talmudic scholar, welcomed Zionist travelers in their Hasidic home. Receiving a religious education at home and a secular education in a Catholic school, Bessie graduated as class valedictorian. In 1905, after her father remarried, the family immigrated to New York. There, Bessie married her English tutor, Mendel Gotsfeld, an Australian, in 1909. Mendel Gotsfeld played an integral role in his wife's life, supporting her as a businessman and property owner, and often helping her to entertain leaders of the Mizrachi organization.

In 1911, the couple moved to Seattle, where Gotsfeld helped Jewish refugees fleeing Russia. After seven years, they returned to New York, and Gotsfeld began working for Jewish women's organizations, including a New York group associated with the Mizrachi Organization of America. Gotsfeld believed that religious women needed their own association, and in 1925, at the men's American Mizrachi Convention, she encouraged regional women's groups to form their own national association, the Mizrachi Women's Organization of America (later American Mizrachi Women). The organization set a goal of supporting and administrating its own projects—an extremely bold step for the women to take because, in the past, all organizational money had been administered by men.

In 1926, Gotsfeld traveled to Palestine to find a project for the new organization. Soon, she became its Palestine representative, making Tel Aviv the Gotsfelds' home and the American Mizrachi Women the primary interest in her life. She served as on-site planner and overseer for vocational schools and children's villages for Jewish girls, Youth Aliyah children, Holocaust survivors, and new immigrants. She kept the membership informed about life in Israel through a column in the association's magazine.

Gotsfeld received many honors for her work. In particular, the Bessie Gotsfeld Children's Village and Farm School, Kfar Batya (1947), and the Bessie Gotsfeld Forest (1955) were named for her. When she died in Tel Aviv on July 29, 1962, she was honorary national president of the Mizrachi Women's Organization of America and head of its Israel executive council.

In spite of having diabetes, Bessie Goldstein Gotsfeld was a ceaseless worker, known for her political and diplomatic skills. She was a career woman in an Orthodox society where traditionally only men held positions of leadership and an observant person in a society whose early heroes tended to be secular. In her outlook and in her actions, Gotsfeld was a product of both American and Jewish cultures. She helped to build a bridge between America and Israel, where American democracy, practical knowledge, and funds could flow to Israel, and Jewish tradition, spirituality and culture could travel to America.

SELECTED WORKS BY BESSIE GOLDSTEIN GOTSFELD

"Letter from Mrs. Gotsfeld." *Bulletin of the Mizrachi Women's Organization of America* 1 (January 1933): 5; "The Mizrachi Vocational Institution." In *Mizrachi*, edited by P. Churgin (1936); "Palestine Report." *Mizrachi Women's News* (December 1942): 12; "Palestine Report, 1940–1941." *Mizrachi Women's News* 10 (1941): 3–4.

BIBLIOGRAPHY

Abramov, S. Zalman. *Perpetual Dilemma: Jewish Religion in the Jewish State* (1976); *EJ*; Goldfeld, Leona M. *Bessie* (1982); Goldstein, Belle J. "Twenty Years of Mizrachi Women." *The Mizrachi Women* (January 1946): 5; Golman, Eliezer [nephew]. Interview by author, 1990; Golub, Mollie F. "The American Role of the Mizrachi Women in the Upbuilding of Our Homeland." *Mizrachi Women's News* (September 1942): 7; Gotsfeld, Bessie. Correspondence. AMIT Women Archives, NYC; Halpern, Ben. *The Idea of the Jewish State* (1969); Obituary. *NYTimes*, July 31, 1962, 30:1; "Palestine Correspondence." *Bulletin of the Mizrachi Organization of America* 2–3 (January 1933): 1+; Vital, David. *Zionism: The Formative Years* (1982).

AVA F. KAHN

GOTTESMAN, JEANE HERSKOVITS (c. 1893–1942)

Jeane Herskovits Gottesman, a philanthropist noted for her spiritual devotion to her work, and a member of the national board of HADASSAH, the Women's Zionist Organization of America, assumed a major leadership and fund-raising role as chair of the New York Youth Aliyah Committee in the 1930s. When the threat of Nazism to world Jewry, especially to children, was first recognized, Youth Aliyah, a rescue project, set itself the goal of saving Jewish children from Hitler and bringing them to Palestine. There, in youth villages, they would combine educational labor with the pioneering needs and ideals of the Jewish state. Publicity and information about the program needed to be disseminated, and large sums of money needed to be raised immediately. Working with HENRIETTA SZOLD, the founder and first president of Hadassah, Gottesman brought to bear her extensive volunteer experience in fund-raising and her sense of responsibility to the community and to Judaism.

Jeane Herskovits Gottesman was born in New York City, circa 1893, the daughter of Mr. and Mrs. Albert Herskovits. She married D. Samuel Gottesman, who was born in 1884 in Munkács, Hungary, and they had three daughters, Mrs. J.J. Altman, Mrs. Ira Wallach, and JOY UNGERLEIDER-MAYERSON. She and her husband were part of a wealthy philanthropic extended family. Her father-in-law, Mendel Gottesman, and her brothers-in-law, David, Samuel, and Benjamin, had businesses in the pulp and paper industry and in investment banking. They each established philanthropic foundations to support Jewish education. The family was associated with the establishment and development of Yeshiva University—the major Orthodox Jewish institution of higher education in the United States—as well as several Talmud Torahs on the Lower East Side. In 1941, Gottesman and her husband established the D.S. and J.H. Gottesman Foundation to donate funds for Jewish education, Jewish studies, local welfare, and other causes.

Gottesman focused her attention on health and welfare work, especially for young people, raising money for organizations such as the Federation of Jewish Charities, the Henry Street Visiting Nurse Service, the Jewish Education Committee, Juvenile House, the Women's Zionist Organization of America, Ivriah, Yeshiva College, the American Committee for Christian Refugees, Beth Israel Hospital, and the National Home for Jewish Children at Denver. Her work with Youth Aliyah resulted in thirty thousand Jewish children from Europe, Africa, and Asia reaching safety in Palestine before the establishment of the State of Israel.

Jeane Herskovits Gottesman died in New York City on July 28, 1942.

BIBLIOGRAPHY

AJYB 45:386; *EJ*; Geller, L.D. *The Archives of Youth Aliyah, 1933–1960. Part 1: The Years of the Holocaust and Ingathering* (1983); Kol, Moshe. *Youth Aliyah Jerusalem* Federation Internationale des Communautes d'Enfants. Document no. 1a (1966); "Mrs. D.S. Gottesman, a Welfare Leader." *NYTimes*, July 29, 1942, 17:4; *Women of Valor: The Story of Hadassah, 1912–1987* (1987).

HELENE L. TUCHMAN

GOTTHEIL, EMMA LEON (1862–1947)

When Emma Leon Gottheil sailed from New York to France in the summer of 1897 to visit her family, her husband Richard Gottheil, professor of semitics at Columbia University, remained behind to care for his ailing father, Gustav Gottheil, rabbi of New York's Temple Emanu-El. Both father and son were part of a small group of pro-Zionist Reform Jews excited by the news of the First Zionist Congress to be convened in August in Basel. Richard asked Emma to attend the Congress. She did not go. As a young student, immersed in the study of the French Revolution, she had been convinced that the time had come when differences of creed could make no difference between people. Later, after reading the accounts of the congress she had not attended, she resolved to study Zionism. When she fully appreciated the implications of Theodore Herzl's vision, she vowed to dedicate herself to hastening its fulfillment.

Emma was born in Beirut in 1862. Her father, Rachamim Yehudah, a writer and scholar, had come to Palestine from Russia as a small child. Her mother, Hadassah, born in Hebron, was a member of a prominent Sephardi family. The couple had two other children, Eva and Albert.

When she was twelve, her father brought her to Paris to continue her education. Later, he moved the entire family to France. Emma was a brilliant student, fluent in several languages and drawn to the literature of nineteenth-century French writers. She later came to know many of them personally through the literary salon she held in her home.

Emma married early and had three sons, Maurice, Rene, and Fernand, the latter dying as a young child. Widowed while still in her twenties, she returned to her parents' home with her children. It was here, in 1888, that she met Richard Gottheil. They were married in Paris on September 18, 1891, and embarked for New York.

Before long, Gottheil was lecturing on French literature at Columbia University, translating French works into English, and making the acquaintance of prominent New York writers. At the same time, she

She rejected the idea of the First Zionist Congress, but the brilliant and multilingual Emma Leon Gottheil would have a change of heart and become instrumental in the founding of HADASSAH. *[American Jewish Historical Society]*

immersed herself in Jewish affairs. Among her many projects were the Sisterhood of Temple Emanu-El, the YOUNG WOMEN'S HEBREW ASSOCIATION, and the NATIONAL COUNCIL OF JEWISH WOMEN. On Shabbat afternoons the observant Gottheil drew a diverse group of Jewish and non-Jewish academics and writers to her home.

At the Second Zionist Congress in 1898, Gottheil and her husband were official delegates of the Federation of American Zionists. Along with her father-in-law, she had convinced her husband to assume the presidency of this newly formed federation. Thoroughly charmed by Emma Gottheil, Theodor Herzl invited her to sit on the platform with him and translate his message into French, Italian, and English. Before she returned home, Herzl asked the "Frau Professor" to interest American women in Zionism.

The women of Temple Emanu-El did not respond to Gottheil's message. Undaunted, she invited a young women's club from the Lower East Side, the Daughters of Zion, to study with her. Within a few years, several Daughters of Zion groups were meeting throughout the city. When HENRIETTA SZOLD returned from Palestine in 1910, determined to form a national organization that could carry out practical work there, she asked Gottheil and five other members of the study groups to become the nucleus of a new organization, which came to be known as HADASSAH. Gottheil stubbornly fought alongside Szold to convince the others that they could indeed manage their first project, sending nurses to Palestine.

Though her husband had left the ranks of Zionist leadership by 1914, Gottheil continued to take an active role, lecturing, writing, and organizing. When the American Zionists split ideologically in 1921 over the manner of fund-raising, Gottheil organized the Keren Hayesod Women's League, Keren Hayesod being the fund-raising arm of the Zionist Organization of America. Ultimately, under Gottheil's guidance, the Women's League became a separate organization, the Women's League for Palestine, dedicated to maintaining shelters for single women coming to Palestine as pioneers and, later, as refugees from Germany.

The French government awarded the Cross of the Legion of Honor to Emma Gottheil in 1940, in recognition of her services to the cause of Franco-American friendship.

Emma Leon Gottheil died in New York City on June 11, 1947.

BIBLIOGRAPHY

AJYB, 50:612; Cohen, Naomi W. *Encounter with Emancipation* (1984); Dash, Joan. *Summoned to Jerusalem* (1979); Feinstein, Marnin. *American Zionism, 1884–1904* (1965); Gottheil, Emma Leon. Papers. AJA, Hebrew Union College, Cincinnati; Hadassah. Central and Historical Files. Hadassah Organization, NYC; Leon, Eva. Papers. AJA; Levin, Marlin. *Balm in Gilead* (1973); Lipsky, Louis. *Memoirs in Profile* (1975); Obituary. *NYTimes*, June 13, 1947, 23:5; *WWIAJ* (1926, 1928, 1938).

NORMA SPUNGEN

GRATZ, REBECCA (1781–1869)

Rebecca Gratz believed that with an "unsubdued spirit" she could overcome all of life's difficulties. A pioneer Jewish charitable worker and religious educator, Gratz established and led America's first independent Jewish women's charitable society, the first Jewish Sunday school, the Philadelphia Orphan

Asylum, and the first Jewish Foster Home in Philadelphia. She surmounted the grief caused her by the deaths of many family members and loved ones, confronted Christian evangelism, and became a civic leader. Gratz's accomplishments grew out of her own indomitable spirit and her commitments to both Judaism and America.

Born in Philadelphia, Pennsylvania, on March 4, 1781, a middle child among twelve children born to Michael Gratz of Silesia and Miriam Simon of Lancaster, Pennsylvania, Gratz grew up in Philadelphia's wealthy society. Her father, her uncle Barnard Gratz, and her grandfather Joseph Simon engaged in trading with Indians, land speculation, and coastal shipping. Her brothers Simon, Hyman, Joseph, Jacob, and Benjamin expanded the family financial interest in the American West. Accustomed from youth to the highly charged political atmosphere of postrevolutionary Philadelphia, Gratz became and remained a fervent patriot throughout her life.

In her youth, Gratz attended assembly balls and was part of a circle of writers, including Washington Irving and James Kirk Paulding, who contributed to the *Port Folio* literary magazine, although she herself never published. After abandoning her early poetry, Gratz confined her literary talent to an extensive correspondence. Her correspondents included British educator and novelist Maria Edgeworth, American author Catherine Sedgwick, renowned British actress Fanny Kemble, Jewish British theologian and educator Grace Aguilar, and other less notable friends and family. The children of Alexander Hamilton, publisher John Fenno, and Rev. John Ewing, president of the University of Pennsylvania, were among her closest friends. Gratz was so well known in elite Philadelphia circles that Irving asked Gratz to introduce Thomas Sully to Philadelphia patrons when the artist moved there. The collected Gratz family portraits include many by Sully as well as by Edward Malbone and Gilbert Stuart. In addition to prominent synagogue responsibilities and Gratz's own organizations, the Gratz siblings together promoted the city's Athenaeum, Deaf and Dumb Home, the Academy of Fine Arts, and various libraries.

Well-educated for her day, Gratz attended women's academies and read her father's extensive library stocked with literature, histories, and popular science. To that collection Gratz herself added Judaica, seeking original new works in English, works recently translated into English, as well as requesting new books and early readings of works-in-progress from knowledgeable American Jews like hazan Isaac Leeser and educator Jacob Mordecai.

Born into privilege in Philadelphia shortly after American independence, Rebecca Gratz was responsible for establishing and running a number of Jewish benevolent organizations. A strong believer in American religious freedom, she nonetheless felt that Jews also had a responsibility to be knowledgeable about their own faith. [American Jewish Historical Society]

At age nineteen, Gratz was recruited as a family nurse to help her mother care for her father, who had suffered a stroke. Although Gratz at first found nursing "agonizing," she remained the family nurse throughout her life, sharing duties with her unmarried older sister Sarah, who herself died in 1817. While nursing her father, Gratz joined her mother, sister, and twenty other women, Jewish and gentile, to found Philadelphia's nonsectarian Female Association for the Relief of Women and Children in Reduced Circumstances (c. 1801). Gratz was its first secretary and held that office for many years. In 1815, Gratz helped establish the Philadelphia Orphan Asylum, and served as secretary for its first forty years. In the 1830s, Gratz advised her sister-in-law Maria Gist Gratz on creating and running the first orphan asylum in Lexington, Kentucky.

Gratz sought the post of executive secretary in each of the institutions she founded. As secretary, she not only maintained organizational records, but also annually addressed the managing boards on policy in each year-end secretary's report. The institutions regularly published her reports as pamphlets or in the popular press in order to raise public support for their work. The secretary's role enhanced Gratz's authority and provided her a public forum from which to advance her own ideas about the ways in which organizations could promote both women's roles and Judaism in Philadelphia and in America. The Jewish institutions with which she was involved especially reflected her own strong leadership.

Noting that Christian charitable women evangelized while aiding the poor, Gratz became convinced that Philadelphia's Jewish women and children needed their own charitable institution. In 1819, she gathered women of her congregation to found the country's first nonsynagogal Jewish charity, the Female Hebrew Benevolent Society (FHBS). The FHBS provided food, fuel, shelter, and later an employment bureau and traveler's aid service. The FHBS served only Jewish women and their children, and later coordinated its efforts with those of sewing and fuel societies serving needy local Jews. Gratz offered significant advice and aid to these societies as well. The FHBS remained an independent society until the late twentieth century.

Gratz's religious beliefs reflected her membership in Mikveh Israel as well as her own readings and lively discussions with Christian friends. Although Gratz, like most Jewish women and some men, knew no Hebrew, her congregation's early use of prayer books imported from England, with English translations on facing pages, allowed her a satisfying and devoted synagogue experience throughout her life. Gratz also found religious insight in Shakespeare's dramas and sonnets and gleaned moral guidance from writers like Thomas Carlyle. She insisted that her Christian friends respect her own understandings of biblical texts and frequently argued Judaism's truth. She also insisted on Jews' right to be treated as equals, both as citizens and as pious individuals, under the United States Constitution. These lifelong religious discussions shaped her religious ideas and deepened her convictions. While Gratz believed that American religious freedom presaged a new epoch in Jewish history, she also believed that if Jews were to be respected by the Christian majority they must become religiously knowledgeable and observant. Consequently, she was appalled by Judaism's nascent Reform Movement,

which renounced Zion and diminished ritual. Around 1818, after her sister Sarah's death, Gratz organized an informal Hebrew school in her home for the children of her extended family, instructed by a young rabbi.

An outspoken woman who found few men likely to be an "agreeable domestic companion" for herself, Gratz remained unmarried. She lived with her three bachelor brothers, Hyman, Joseph, and Jacob, and her sister Sarah throughout her life. Despite her skepticism about marriage, Gratz adored children. When Gratz's sister Rachel died in 1823, leaving six children, Gratz brought the children to her home and raised them. Their father soon purchased the home directly across the street from Gratz.

Gratz was the first to apply the Sunday school format to Jewish education. The FHBS women hoped to provide religious education soon after the organization's founding, but they were unable to do so until 1838, when Gratz established the Hebrew Sunday School (HSS), a coeducational institution, with herself as superintendent. She also served as secretary of the managing society and held both offices until she was in her eighties. Her sister congregants, Simha Peixotto and Rachel Peixotto Pyke, who ran a private school in their home, joined her as teachers, and the Peixotto sisters wrote many of the textbooks initially used by the school. Students ranged in age from early childhood to early teens. The HSS soon attracted students and faculty throughout Philadelphia, and it remained an independent, citywide institution until the close of the twentieth century.

The HSS offered Jewish women their first public role in teaching religion and determining curriculum in a Jewish school. Only female graduates were invited to join the faculty, and the HSS's teacher training program furthered the women's religious education. Gratz advised Jewish women in Charleston, Savannah, and Baltimore on establishing similar schools there. Their efforts prompted the country's leading Jewish educators, especially Isaac Leeser, who wrote and translated Jewish catechisms for the school, to provide materials for their use. Leeser publicized the HSS and encouraged Jewish women around the country to take similar action.

By the 1840s, Gratz happily noted that Jewish women were "becoming quite literary." She touted books by British educator Grace Aguilar, who extolled Judaism and argued its importance to women, and used Aguilar's books in the HSS. Gratz hoped the school would demonstrate that Jewish women equaled Christian women in religious piety, then considered a mark of civility. The school flourished, opened several branches, and had served over four thousand students by the end of the nineteenth century.

By the 1850s, the plight of an increasing number of Jewish immigrants convinced Gratz of the need for the Jewish Foster Home (JFH). Jewish orphan associations in New York and New Orleans, which relied on foster families, became inadequate as immigration increased. Gratz, who had served forty years on the board of the Philadelphia Orphan Asylum, became vice president of the JFH managing society. The JFH later merged with several other institutions to form Philadelphia's Association for Jewish Children.

Gratz outlived all but her youngest sibling, Benjamin, and many of her nieces and nephews. Despite her grief in her last years, she was relieved that what she believed to be the American experiment in freedom had not ended with the Civil War. She was sure that her lasting monument would be the Hebrew Sunday School, a highly successful institution that most reflected her own unique blend of Judaism and American culture. Gratz died on August 27, 1869, and was buried in Mikveh Israel's historic cemetery in Philadelphia. By the end of her life, a legend claimed Gratz as the prototype for the character of Rebecca of York in Sir Walter Scott's novel *Ivanhoe*, the first favorable depiction of a Jew in English fiction. Jews pointed to Gratz, an Americanized Jewish woman who retained her Jewish loyalty, to argue the truth of the popular tale. Gratz's own life epitomized the "unsubdued spirit" she admired.

BIBLIOGRAPHY

Ashton, Dianne. *Rebecca Gratz: Women's Judaism in Antebellum America* (1997), and "Souls Have No Sex: Philadelphia Jewish Women and the American Challenge." In *When Philadelphia Was the Capital of Jewish America*, edited by Murray Friedman (1993); *BDEAJ*; Beerman, Leonard I. "An Analysis of the Foremost Jewess of the Nineteenth Century as Reflected in Hitherto Unpublished Source Materials." Ord. thesis, Hebrew Union College (1949); Bodek, Evelyn. "Making Do: Jewish Women and Philanthropy." In *Jewish Life in Philadelphia, 1830–1940*, edited by Murray Friedman (1983); Braude, Ann. "The Jewish Woman's Encounter with American Culture." In *Women and Religion in America*, Vol. 1 (1981); Byars, William V., ed. *B. and M. Gratz, Merchants in Philadelphia, 1754–1798* (1916); Cohen, Mary M. *An Old Philadelphia Cemetery: The Resting Place of Rebecca Gratz* (1920); Cohen, Miriam Moses. Papers. Southern History Collection, University of North Carolina, Chapel Hill, North Carolina; Crockett, W.S. *The Scott Originals* (1912); *DAB*; *EJ*, s.v. "Gratz"; Gratz, Rebecca. Papers. American Jewish Historical Society, Brandeis University, Waltham, Mass.; Gratz Family Papers. Collection 72. American Philosophical Society, Philadelphia, Pa.; Gratz Family Papers. Manuscript Collection 236. Henry Joseph Collection, American Jewish Archives, Hebrew Union College, Cincinnati, Ohio; Jacobs, Joseph. "The Original of Scott's Rebecca." *Publications of the American Jewish Historical Society* 22 (1914): 53–60; *JE*, s.v. "Gratz"; Mordecai, Sarah. *Recollections of My Aunt* (1893); *NAW*; Osterweiss, Rollin G. *Rebecca Gratz: A Study in Charm* (1935); *PAJHS* 11:89–90, 29:53–60; 31:241; 48:71–77; Philipson, David, ed. *The Letters of Rebecca Gratz* (1929); Rosenbloom, Joseph, "And She Had Compassion: The Life and Times of Rebecca Gratz." Ph.D. diss., Hebrew Union College (1957), and "Rebecca Gratz and the Jewish Sunday School Movement in Philadelphia." *Publications of the American Jewish Historical Society* 47, no. 2 (1958): 71–75, and "Some Conclusions About Rebecca Gratz." In *Essays in American Jewish History* (1958); *UJE*, s.v. "Gratz"; Van Renssalaer, Gratz. "The Original of Rebecca in *Ivanhoe*." *Century Magazine* (September 1882).

DIANNE ASHTON

GRATZ, RICHEA (1774–1858)

In 1787, at the age of thirteen, Richea Gratz became the first Jewish woman to attend college in America when she matriculated with the first class at Franklin College (later Franklin and Marshall College of Lancaster, Pennsylvania).

Richea was born on October 1, 1774, to Miriam (Simon) Gratz, the daughter of a prominent Lancaster fur trader, and Michael Gratz, a leading Philadelphia merchant who hailed from Langendorf, Germany. Her family status granted her the educational opportunity very few women in her day enjoyed, and she made the most of it, studying English as well as classical languages while attending college. She was the second of four daughters and the third of ten children. Throughout her life she remained close with her large family, seeing sisters, brothers, aunts, and uncles daily and writing weekly to those who had moved away.

When she married Samuel Hays of New York, on January 8, 1794, she took her place as one of the leading Jewish women of Philadelphia, balancing her strict religious background with her affluent middle-class one. Gratz was very active in Congregation Mikveh Israel, where Hays was a trustee and the Gratz family had been founding members. As a member of one of the city's prominent families, Gratz was able to use her liberal arts education to the benefit of the community by supporting the cultural and educational life of Philadelphia. During the first three decades of the nineteenth century, the Hays family contributed to the Philadelphia Library and the Chestnut Street Theater, and also patronized local artists. Cultural events did not take all of Gratz's time, however, as she made her presence felt in the area of reform and relief work. With her mother and two of her sisters, Gratz was one of eight original members in the Female Association for the Relief of Women and Children in Reduced Circumstances. The organization, founded in 1801, grew to include twenty-three members, about a third of whom were Jewish. Among their efforts, they raised money to provide for a soup kitchen.

As important as her outside activities were, Gratz cherished her close ties with her siblings and invested much time in her own family. She and Hays had five children between 1794 and 1805: Fannie, Isaac, Miriam (Maria), Ellen, and SARA ANN [HAYS MORDE-CAI]. They were brought up under the same strict religious tradition she herself had been raised in. Isaac's career exemplified the fact that Gratz, recalling her early days in college, stressed the importance of education to her children. He received an M.D. from the University of Pennsylvania in 1820 and became a famous scientist, writer, and humanitarian.

Richea Gratz died on November 22, 1858, in Philadelphia. She was laid to rest, according to her wishes, next to her husband on the west side of Philadelphia's Spruce Street Cemetery in an area known as the Gratz Reservation.

BIBLIOGRAPHY

BDEAJ; Dubbs, Joseph Henry. *History of Franklin and Marshall College* (1903); *EJ*; Gratz, Rebecca. *The Letters of Rebecca Gratz.* Edited by Dawn Philipson (1975); Marcus, Jacob. *American Jewry, Documents; Eighteenth Century* (1959); *PAJHS* 19:123; Wolf, Edwin. *The History of the Jews in Philadelphia from Colonial Times to the Age of Jackson* (1957).

JOSHUA GREENBERG

GREENBAUM, SELINA (1866–1925)

The life of the turn-of-the-century working girls of New York City's Lower East Side was often one of austerity and exhausting drudgery. Alarmed by the horrific conditions of the tenement houses and sweatshops, the Board of Jewish Ministers issued an urgent call in 1898 for the provision of healthful recreational facilities for Jewish working girls. Selina Greenbaum was among those influential East Side women who responded to the call, devoting time and energy to the organization of much-needed educational and recreational activities for women.

Selina (Ullman) Greenbaum was born on April 6, 1866, in New York City, the sixth of seven children and third of four daughters of Israel and Julia (Blumenthal) Ullman, emigrés from Bavaria who had made their home on Manhattan's Upper East Side. Israel Ullman's dry-goods dealership provided a comfortable living for the family, and Selina was educated in the New York public schools and at Normal College (now HUNTER COLLEGE). On March 13, 1888, she married Samuel Greenbaum, who was supreme court justice for New York from 1900 until 1929.

Like her husband, whose prominent communal leadership included the presidency of the Educational Alliance, Greenbaum was notable for Jewish charity work. One of the early members of the board of directors of the NATIONAL COUNCIL OF JEWISH WOMEN, she also became involved with the nascent YOUNG WOMEN'S HEBREW ASSOCIATION (YWHA), organized in 1888 under the leadership of JULIA RICHMAN as an auxiliary to the YMHA. Greenbaum was a president of this first downtown auxiliary, as well as an active member of the board of directors of the first recreation rooms on the Lower East Side, which opened in May 1898.

It was in 1890, however, that Greenbaum made her most important contribution to public service. She was instrumental in forming the Jewish Working Girls Vacation Society and took office as its first president, a position she held for many years. Incorporated in 1892, the society maintained homes in Bellport and Arverne on Long Island and at Big Indian and Margaretville in the Adirondacks (New York), where, for a nominal fee, Jewish girls of working age enjoyed a fortnight of vacation from the city. By 1917, the society was assisting over eight hundred girls annually and was also able to provide midweek holidays for mothers.

The Greenbaums raised a family of four children at their home on East 94th Street in Manhattan. Their two sons, Lawrence and Edward, pursued successful careers as attorneys, while both daughters were active in community service. Grace Greenbaum Epstein founded a women's job bureau during the Depression, while Isabel Greenbaum Spone established the Windward School in Harrison, New York.

Selina Greenbaum died at the Greenbaum summer home in Larchmont, New York, on July 15, 1925. The activities of the Jewish Working Girls' Vacation Society continue today under the auspices of Camp Isabella Friedman, the direct descendant of Greenbaum's original project.

BIBLIOGRAPHY

AJYB 1, s.v. "Jewish Working Girls' Vacation Society," and 7 (1905–1906): 64; Bellport-Brookhaven Historical

Society, New York. Collection of photograhic postcards of the Bay House, Bellport, Long Island; Kehillah (Jewish Community) of New York City. *The Jewish Communal Register of New York City, 1917–1918*, s.v. "Jewish Working Girls' Vacation Society," and "Recreation Rooms and Settlements"; Lubitz, Bertha. "Preventive Work for Girls." *Jewish Charity* 3 (1904): 217–220; Obituary. *NYTimes*, July 16, 1925, 19:6; Rabinowitz, Benjamin. *The Young Men's Hebrew Associations and the Jewish Community Center Movement* (1937?); Straus, Mrs. Isidor. "The Recreation Room for Girls." *Jewish Charity* 4 (1905): 117–119; Straus, Sara. "Working Girls' Clubs." *Jewish Charity* 3 (1904): 153–161; Wald, Lillian D., et al. "Summer Outings for the Jewish Poor." *Jewish Charity* 3 (1904): 190–192; Young Men's Hebrew Association of New York. Scrapbook papers. Ninety-second Street YMCA, NYC.

ESTELLE C. WILLIAMS

GREENBERG, BLU (b. 1936)

Blu Greenberg is a traditional Jewish woman who has become a prime voice for feminism as applied to ORTHODOX JUDAISM.

She is the mother of five children and the wife of Yitz Greenberg, an Orthodox rabbi recently retired from the leadership of Clal, an organization devoted to the Jewish education of leaders in the American Jewish community.

Greenberg was raised in a loving traditional home and grew up content with her role as a "good Jewish daughter." As she states in her book *On Women and Judaism* (1981), she "had a fine Jewish education, the best a girl could have" (24). This meant that she was exposed to all Jewish learning, with the exception of Talmud studies. Greenberg's father took even more interest in her Jewish studies than in her secular studies. The personal dignity his study sessions afforded her may have contributed to her later development as a seminal Jewish feminist.

Growing up, Greenberg did not particularly question the male-preferential context of her Orthodox affiliation. The surprise is that she came to question it at all. It was only as a young college woman that an uncomfortable dissatisfaction began to brew in her soul. Studying with Nechama Liebowitz in Israel during her junior year in college, Greenberg knew that she wanted to extend her stay to study further with Liebowitz. But when her parents (and most of her friends) protested, she knew "that it wasn't the sort of thing a nice orthodox Jewish girl would do" (*On Women* 26) and came home, all the time knowing

that had she been a young man wanting to do the same kind of thing, every encouragement would have been forthcoming.

Other incidents began accumulating in her consciousness. When a beloved uncle died, only the male grandchildren were allowed to accompany the casket out of the synagogue. When a grandfather gave her sons a reward for special parts they had taken in a service, her daughter, age eight, said it wasn't fair, and Greenberg's ten-year-old son retorted, "Well, so what—you can't do anything in the synagogue!"

The turning point came in 1973. Greenberg was invited to give the opening address at the First National Jewish Women's Conference. With a unique point of view that respects tradition and recognizes the inequalities for women in that tradition, she addressed five hundred women at the conference.

Since that time, Greenberg has done a great deal of learning, teaching, and developing her special connection with Jewish women. Her theoretical position stems from a belief in women having the same potential as men "whether in the realm of spirit, word, or deed" (*On Women* 39); a belief that the tradition which she respects and upholds is too strong to be in danger from the experimentation of women on their religious responsibilities, rights, and rituals; a belief that women must take charge of their own destinies in this as in other areas rather than waiting for men to do it for them; and a belief that self-realization for a woman underlies all her roles—loving, nurturing, parenting, and career—each to be chosen with respect for her womanhood, selfhood, and Jewish identity.

SELECTED WORKS BY BLU GREENBERG

Black Bread: Poems After the Holocaust (1994); *How to Run a Traditional Jewish Household* (1983); *On Women and Judaism* (1981).

SHULAMIT PECK

GREENBLATT, ALIZA (1885–1975)

Deep love for the Jewish people informed the life of Aliza Greenblatt, an American Yiddish poet and an early, committed leader in Zionist and Jewish women's organizations. Greenblatt was among the first to organize the American Jewish community and raise funds toward the establishment of a Jewish national home. Many of her poems, which were widely published in the Yiddish press, were also set to music and recorded.

Born Aliza Waitzman in September 1885 in Azarenits, Bessarabia, Aliza and her two sisters were sent to heder until their father's death in 1893, because they had no brothers. Their mother remarried five years later. In 1900, Aliza, her stepfather, and three stepbrothers came to the United States. They settled in Philadelphia, where Aliza worked in the garment industry. Four years later, when they could afford to send for her mother, Aliza stopped working and received tutoring in English at home. In 1907, she married Isidor Greenblatt, a fellow Bessarabian immigrant, and they had five children: Herbert, David, Gertrude, MARJORIE [GUTHRIE], and Bernard.

Shortly after the birth of her first child, Greenblatt began her charitable and organizational work. The family moved from Philadelphia to Atlantic City, where Greenblatt served as president of the local chapter of the True Sisters and organized the Atlantic City branch of the *farband*, a Yiddish socialist charitable organization. After the 1917 Balfour Declaration, Greenblatt, finding no local Zionist group, established the Atlantic City branch of the Zionist Organization of America. In time, she became a successful fund-raiser for the Jewish National Fund, an active HADASSAH member, and national president of PIONEER WOMEN.

In 1919, Greenblatt and her husband considered moving to Palestine. To prepare, Isidor spent several months there in the spring of 1920, trying to establish a fruit-canning factory. His absence, however, led to the failure of their business at home and the postponement of their dream of emigrating. Thirty years later, their fortunes improved, and they were able to try again. However, Aliza was so unhappy with the material conditions under which they lived that, after struggling for a year, they returned to the United States for good. They moved to New York to be closer to its Yiddish literary community. Until his death in 1960, Isidor devoted himself to promoting investment in Israel.

In her later years, Greenblatt focused on writing. She published five volumes of poetry and an autobiography, *Baym Fentster fun a Lebn* [At the window of a life], all in Yiddish. Her poems and songs appeared in Yiddish newspapers in the United States and Israel, and were recorded by Theodore Bikel, among others. Fellow poets Jacob Glatshteyn and Avram Reisen praised her work. For many years, Jewish women's organizations sponsored readings of her poetry across the United States. She died in New York on September 21, 1975.

In the American Jewish community, Aliza Greenblatt was a pioneer in her activism for a Jewish national home. As an organizer and fund-raiser, she mobilized

A writer who was praised later in life for her poetry, Aliza Greenblatt spent much of her time as an organizer and fund-raiser, working for the establishment of a Jewish homeland. [YIVO Institute]

support in the United States for the establishment of the State of Israel and fought to involve Jewish women in that cause. Her poetry and autobiography chronicle her life, from its origins in an impoverished shtetl in Eastern Europe to a position in the middle-class Jewish community of New York. Her work adds an important Yiddish voice to the history of twentieth-century American Jewry, and her life provides an exemplar of the activism of American Jewish women.

SELECTED WORKS BY ALIZA GREENBLATT

Baym Fentster fun a Lebn [At the window of a life] (1966); *Ikh un Du* [You and I] (1951); *Ikh Zing* [I sing] (1947); *In Sigate baym Yam* [In Seagate by the ocean] (1957); *Lebn Mayns* [My life] (1935); *Tsen Lider mit Musik* [Ten poems with music] (1939).

SUSANNE A. SHAVELSON

GREENWALD, AMELIA (1881–1966)

As an international public health nurse during World War I and between the wars, Amelia Greenwald was a leader in the field of public health.

She was born in Gainesville, Alabama, on March 1, 1881, to Joseph Greenwald (a grain dealer and mayor) and Elisha (Elise Haas) Greenwald, German Jewish immigrants who married in Memphis, Tennessee. She was the youngest of eight children: Isaac, Carrie, Jake, Morris, Sylvester, Julian, and Isadore. On her father's knee, Greenwald listened to stories of the Confederate nurses during the Civil War and knew that she wanted to became a trained nurse.

After her debut into society, Greenwald entered Touro Infirmary Training School for Nurses in New Orleans, Louisiana, and graduated in 1908. In 1909, she helped to organize Pensacola Sanitarium in Pensacola, Florida. After working in a hospital in North Carolina, she moved to Baltimore in 1913 to attend a postgraduate course in psychiatric nursing at Phipps Clinic at Johns Hopkins University.

In 1914, Greenwald came to New York, where she met HENRIETTA SZOLD, who introduced her to Zionist ideas. Deciding that she would prefer to work among her own people, she took private tutoring in Hebrew, Yiddish, and Jewish history while attending the nursing program at Columbia University Teachers College. After her graduation from Columbia, she worked for Metropolitan Life Insurance Company and then directed the New Jersey Public Health Association in Long Branch, New Jersey, from 1916 until she accepted overseas service with the American Expeditionary Forces (American Red Cross pin number 5532) during World War I. Stationed in France, Greenwald served as acting chief nurse of a hospital in Verdun and as night superintendent of a hospital in Savoy. She assisted German war brides and helped establish the first American hospital, at Coblenz, Germany. For her service at Meuse-Argonne Defensive Sector, she applied for and received the Victory Medal. She maintained her membership in the American Legion throughout her life.

In October 1919, the NATIONAL COUNCIL OF JEWISH WOMEN asked Greenwald to head its farm women program. In 1923, she established the Jewish Nurses' Training School at the Jewish Hospital in Warsaw, using the New York State university nursing curriculum. For four years, she trained leadership staff. The school received international accolades, and Greenwald was decorated with the Polish Golden Cross of Merit. She is remembered in Warsaw not only as a leader in public health but also as the first woman driver in Poland.

After returning to the United States, Greenwald worked in Miami and again in New York with the National Council's Department of Farm and Rural Work. In 1932, she was the director of the Nurse's Training School at Rothschild Hospital (HADASSAH).

Although unmarried, Greenwald adopted her fifteen-year-old cousin Liselotte Levy to save the girl from Nazism. She called Liselotte her "greatest blessing."

Amelia Greenwald died on January 1, 1966, and was interred in Beth Israel Cemetery, Meridian, Louisiana.

BIBLIOGRAPHY

Greenwald, Amelia. *Nursing Education in Poland: International Aspects of Nursing Education* (1925); Kahn, Catherine. "From the Archives." *Tourovues* (Fall 1992): 24–27; Mayer, Susan L. "Amelia Greenwald: Pioneer in International Public Health." *Nursing and Health Care* 15 (1994): 74–78, and "The Jewish Experience in Nursing in America: 1881 to 1955." Ed.D. diss., Columbia University Teachers College, 1996; Sokoloff, Leon. "Amelia Greenwald (1881–1966): Pioneer American-Jewish Nurse." *Korot* (1993–1994): 92–101; Turitz, Leo. "Amelia Greenwald (1881–1966)." *American Jewish Archives* 37 (November 1985): 291–292.

SUSAN MAYER

GROSMAN, TATYANA (1904–1982)

Tatyana Grosman nurtured an entire generation of printmakers and raised printmaking in the United States to the status of a major fine art. Universal Limited Art Editions, which she founded in 1957 at her home in Long Island, New York, published prints by many of the major American artists of her generation and launched collaborative endeavors between artists and writers. Her home became a uniquely fertile environment providing both the tools and the critical encouragement for virtually every type of printmaking.

She was born Tatyana Auguschewitsch in Ekaterinburg (now Sverdlovsk) in Siberia on June 30, 1904 (June 17 according to the Russian calendar), to Jewish parents who had officially converted to Christianity because of the implacable anti-Semitism of Russian laws. The government had sent her father, Semion Michailovitch Auguschewitsch, as a typographer to start a newspaper in Siberia at age twenty-one. Such was his success that the family was able to live in luxury and elegance in the midst of their rough frontier town. While her father never observed any Christian rituals, her mother, Anna de Chochor, who came from a family of Russian Jews that had emigrated to Bavaria in the nineteenth century, made Tatyana wear a cross and go to church. She grew up introverted and shy, a great reader of Russian classics, who studied art and loved to act as well.

In 1918, as the Russian Revolution gathered force, the family left for Japan. There, Tatyana attended the Sacre Coeur Convent in Tokyo, and was captivated by the country's serene, meditative esthetic. The next year they traveled via Venice to Dresden, where her mother's sister lived. Tatyana graduated from the Dalcrose boarding school in nearby Hellerau, and went on to study drawing and fashion design at Dresden's Academy of Applied Arts. Drawing upon Japanese inspiration, she created an Oriental costume that won the school's highest design prize in 1928.

The following year she met and fell in love with Maurice Grosman, a struggling artist who at twenty-nine was already divorced with a son. A Jew from Poland with its Yiddish traditions, he was flamboyant, bohemian, poor, and contemptuous of worldly success, a combination irresistible to Tatyana and anathema to her mother. As Tatyana once said, she had never been in a synagogue but she had always wanted to be Jewish. Her mother banished her, but she willingly left her luxuries behind to live with Maurice in an attic. They were married on June 27, 1931.

In 1932, she insisted they leave an increasingly dangerous Germany for Paris. In Montmartre, Maurice painted and they shared in an artists' community and cafe life with Jacques Lipchitz, Chaim Soutine, and Ossip Zadkine. It was in France that their only child, Larissa, was born on January 31, 1933, only to die sixteen months later. Then in 1938, Tatyana's beloved father, under the strains of a difficult marriage and the hell that Germany was becoming, committed suicide.

In November 1940, two days before the Nazis took Paris, the Grosmans fled. They survived three years of danger and flight, crossing the Pyrenees on foot, and finally reaching friends in Barcelona. With the help of the Hebrew Immigrant Aid Society, they arrived in New York on May 23, 1943, and settled in a one-room, fifth-floor walk-up on 8th Street.

For the next twelve years, Tatyana Grosman played the role of artist's wife as Maurice Grosman eked out a living for them with his painting and teaching. Then, in 1955, he had a heart attack. They left the now insurmountable walk-up for a six-room gardener's cottage they owned in West Islip, Long Island, and Tatyana Grosman assumed new responsibilities as breadwinner.

At first, she promoted Maurice's silk-screen reproductions of famous and contemporary paintings. But museum curators were interested only in original works; a change of direction was needed. The Grosmans found some lithographic stones and bought an old press for fifteen dollars. Tatyana Grosman conceived a vision: She would bring together American artists and poets to produce works equal to the classic French artists' books, and then act as their publisher. With a growing sense of mission and her lifelong passion for art, literature, and the printed page, she began what was to become her lifework: to initiate collaborations between artists and writers, to foster rising artists' use of the tools of printmaking, and then to bring their works to collectors, galleries, and museums. Universal Limited Art Editions (ULAE) was formed in 1957 to pursue these goals.

The first project was a series of prints entitled *Stones*, by two of the Grosmans' friends, painter Larry Rivers and poet Frank O'Hara. A collaboration between Robert Rauschenberg and the French novelist and film writer Alain Robbe-Grillet followed, along with many others. Grosman would urge artists to come to West Islip to work, use printmaking equipment at any hour of the day or night, and enjoy lavish food and lively conversation. She created a nurturing artistic environment in which, despite lack of money, she catered unstintingly to her artists' whims and creature comforts, and provided the finest materials and the most meticulous printers, as well as an unfailing source of personal attention and provocative comment on their work. Painter Robert Motherwell said, "Her integrity, tenacity, endless patience, extravagance with time and materials are as rare as is the ambiance of her workshops, where it is simply assumed that the world of the spirit exists as concretely as lemon yellow or women's hair, but transcends everyday life." As the poet Edwin Schlossberg put it, she "seemed to reach and recognize exactly the you that you always wanted someone to know . . . to give it full range to be what it was and could be . . . Tatyana was in love with the people with whom she worked."

Over the quarter century from the founding of ULAE until her death, Grosman expanded the studio's range of media from silk-screen and lithography to etching and aquatint, woodcuts, offset lithography, and photolithography. Among the many rising artists brought to ULAE through Maurice Grosman's excellent instincts and the recommendations of other artists were HELEN FRANKENTHALER, Grace Hartigan, Jasper Johns, Barnett Newman, Robert Motherwell, Jim Dine, Jacques Lipschitz, Max Weber, Sam Francis,

Lee Bontecue, Marisol, Buckminster Fuller, James Rosenquist, Claes Oldenburg, Cy Twombly, and Saul Steinberg. Gradually, ULAE prints came to be regarded as modern classics. They were exhibited around the world, and many were acquired by the New York Metropolitan Museum of Art and the Art Institute of Chicago. An offshoot enterprise, Telamon Editions, founded in 1969, used offset printing to produce moderate-cost, high-quality posters and books to subsidize and publicize the work of ULAE.

Maurice Grosman died in 1976. After months of depression, Tatyana Grosman was persuaded to resume her work, but was frequently ill. During her last years, she was honored with a doctor of fine arts degree from Smith College in 1973, a doctor of letters from Dowling College in 1977, and a Brandeis University award for outstanding achievement in the arts in 1981. She died on July 24, 1982.

Tatyana Grosman was a pioneer and a risk-taker. Born of a Jewish family that passed as Christian, and raised in Russia and Germany where to be a Jew meant hardship and danger, she chose to embrace Jewishness in her adult life. Brought up in bourgeois luxury and expected to marry well, she chose the life of a struggling artist. In New York, when her husband became ill, she turned hardship into creative opportunity. Here, strands from her early travels and passions flowed together: a love of the printer's craft and the printed page from her childhood as a typographer's daughter in Siberia, an elegant sense of design influenced by her stay in Japan, a feeling for the European traditions of printmaking and the artist's book, and perhaps a Parisian sense of woman as muse, presiding over her salon. With her determination and charisma, she established an extraordinary creative greenhouse in which artists could range freely and flourish, and she tirelessly brought their produce to market. Under Tatyana Grosman's energetic cultivation, contemporary American printmaking came into its own as a major fine art form.

BIBLIOGRAPHY

Mitgang, Herbert. "Tatyana Grosman: 'The Inner Light of 5 Skidmore Place.'" *Art News.* Special prints issue (March 1974): 28–32; Rivers, Larry. "Tatyana Grosman." *Art News* 81, no. 8 (October 1982): 101–102; Russell, John. "Tatyana Grosman, Print Publisher, 78." *NYTimes*, July 26, 1982; Sparks, Esther. *Universal Limited Art Editions: A History and Catalogue: The First Twenty-Five Years* (1989); Tomkins, Calvin. "The Art World: Tatyana Grosman." *New Yorker* (August 9, 1982): 83.

GWEN NEFSKY FRANKFELDT
CELIA GILBERT

GROSSINGER, JENNIE (1892–1972)

It was a rags-to-riches story of the first order. Jennie Grossinger, born to a poor family in a village in Austria, came to the New World, where she became not just successful, but reigning royalty of the Catskill circuit. Warm, kind, and generous, she was doyenne to an opulent resort affectionately known as Waldorf-on-the-Hudson. She was friend to governors, cardinals, and stars, and a philanthropist who enriched the world.

Jennie Grossinger was born on June 16, 1892, in Baligrod, a small village in Galacia, at that time a district of the Austrio-Hungarian Empire. Her father's family included landowners reduced by hard times, and her father, Asher Selig Grossinger, was an estate overseer. Her mother, Malka Grossinger, was the daughter of an innkeeper.

Times were hard, and prejudice against Jews was common. One of her father's cousins had already immigrated to New York, and Selig decided to join him. There wasn't enough money for the family to go with him, so Malka, Jennie, and her sister Lottie stayed behind. Finally, after three years, Selig was able to send for his family to join him in New York. Jennie was eight years old.

The family moved to the Lower East Side, which was in its Yiddish heyday. Jennie enrolled in a Hebrew school, as well as P.S. 174. She was old enough for the third grade, but couldn't speak a word of English. She was demoted to first grade and still couldn't manage. It was a humiliating time.

While Jennie was in elementary school, her mother gave birth to a son who proved to be deaf and mute. When no American doctors were able to help him, Jennie's mother decided to go back to Austria and consult with doctors and rabbis there. Since Lottie was so young, Jennie's mother took her as well. The family had to borrow from friends and neighbors, but the money was found for tickets. Jennie stayed in New York with her father.

This put a strain on the family finances, and when Jennie and her father moved to a new apartment, she took her chance and quietly disappeared from school. At age thirteen she got a job to help out. She started sewing buttonholes piecework at a factory, earning $1.50 her first week. If a single stitch was out of place, the foreman rejected it and she had to start over. But she became proficient, and her wages rose to ten to twelve dollars per week.

Jennie put up her hair in a bun and wore a long coat in an attempt to look older, but she still had to hide when the inspectors came around looking for underaged workers. Her family needed the money, however, so she would not leave. Her father worked in the same factory, and at length the hard work began to wear on him, so he started to look for other work. He tried his hand at several businesses in New York, each of which failed. Finally, in 1914, he decided to buy a farm in the Catskills. He would be a farmer again, and the family would prosper.

However, the farm he bought was a run-down place, a likely prospect for another financial failure. Jennie had helped her father in his previous businesses, and she came to the Catskills to help with the farm. Her husband, Harry Grossinger, a cousin whom she had married two years before, stayed in New York and saw her on the weekends. It was soon apparent that the farm would never pay, so, like many other Jewish families in the Catskills, they took in paying guests from New York.

The guest house wasn't promising, but Jennie Grossinger's naturally warm and welcoming personality helped to make it a success. The house was without electricity, heat, or indoor plumbing. However, Malka was a good kosher cook, and the place became popular with guests. Harry helped by sending customers from New York. By 1919, they had done well enough to sell the original farmhouse and buy a hotel nearby, which had a proper building and extensive grounds.

There was an economic boom soon after World War I, and the resort thrived throughout the 1920s. The family developed the place into an opulent compound with tennis courts, a bridle path, a children's camp, and a seventeen-hundred-seat auditorium with first-rate entertainers. This was the beginning of Grossinger's as an institution. For East Coast Jews, it was the place to be. It still had kosher cooking, but now patrons could dine under crystal chandeliers. Jennie provided world-class service, and hardworking Jews from New York gravitated to it, enjoying their new prosperity.

Grossinger's was hit hard by the Depression, but it managed to stay open. Always innovative, the family not only provided entertainers but brought in well-known boxers to train in their compound before their

Jennie Grossinger is shown here at a $100-a-plate dinner at the Hotel Astor on January 10, 1960.
The proceeds of the dinner went toward the $250,000 Jennie Grossinger Medical Center in Tel Aviv, Israel.
She is being kissed on the cheek by singer Eddie Fisher as his wife, actress Elizabeth Taylor, looks on. [UPI Photo]

big fights. Grossinger's was a place where you might rub shoulders with Rocky Marciano, the boxer, or Nelson Rockefeller, the governor. Eddie Fisher got his start at Grossinger's when he was spotted by Eddie Cantor, who was a guest. By the 1940s, Grossinger's fame had spread so that it began to attract a non-Jewish clientele as well. Its palatial grounds and splendid service brought celebrities from all over. It was very nearly a social experiment: Jews had long been banned from the most prestigious resorts; now Grossinger's had become so prestigious that gentiles flocked to it. In the years that followed, such prominent people as Eleanor Roosevelt, Bobby Fischer, and Senator Robert Kennedy came to visit. All were made at home by that outgoing democrat, Jennie Grossinger.

When Jennie's husband, Harry, died in 1964, she turned over her role in administration to her children, Paul and Elaine. Grossinger's had grown to thirty-five buildings covering twelve hundred acres. The resort hosted as many as 150,000 guests a year. Jennie stayed on in a cottage on the grounds.

For several decades Jennie Grossinger was very active in charitable work. This part of her life began during the Depression. Grossinger's wasn't prospering, but so many other people were suffering worse fates that she felt compelled to do what she could. In time she became a noted philanthropist to both Jewish and non-Jewish causes, garnering a number of awards and two honorary degrees.

On November 20, 1972, Jennie Grossinger died of a stroke, in the heart of the family empire she had helped to create. She was, in the words of *Notable American Women*, "the best-known hotelkeeper in America."

BIBLIOGRAPHY

AJYB 74:556; *EJ*; "Jennie Grossinger Dies at Resort Home." *NYTimes*, November 21, 1972, 1:1; *NAW* modern; Reynolds, Quentin. "Jennie." *Look* (July 13, 1965); *WWWIA*, 5.

ANDRA MEDEA

GROSSMAN, MARY BELLE
(1879–1977)

In 1918, Mary Belle Grossman was one of the first two women admitted to membership in the American Bar Association. After the passage of the Nineteenth Amendment in 1920, she became one of Cleveland's most successful political activists.

One of nine children of Louis and Fannie (Engle) Grossman, she was born in Cleveland on June 10, 1879, and attended local public schools and business college. She determined to become a lawyer while working as a stenographer in a cousin's law firm: "I studied law in self-defense because all the young men were getting promotions faster than I." In 1912, she graduated from the law school at Baldwin-Wallace College and was admitted to the Ohio bar.

Cleveland's suffrage movement launched Grossman's public career. The treasurer of the Woman Suffrage Party of Greater Cleveland, she also led its Wage Earners League and served on its Labor Committee. She later received the political endorsement of Cleveland labor organizations. From suffragists, Grossman learned about meticulous house-by-house, ward-by-ward canvassing, a strategy she successfully employed in her own campaigns. She also learned perseverance, for Ohio suffragists lost three campaigns to get a suffrage amendment to the state constitution.

In 1921, Grossman lost her own first bid for political office—a race for a municipal judgeship. "A woman to succeed in law must have courage and keep a stiff upper lip even in the midst of much that is at first disheartening," she later remarked. In 1923, she became Cleveland's first female municipal judge and Cleveland's second female judge (the first was fellow suffragist Florence E. Allen, later on the Ohio Supreme Court and the U.S. Sixth Circuit Court). Grossman never lost another election, consistently winning endorsements from the major newspapers, organized labor, the Cleveland Bar Association, and women's organizations such as the NATIONAL COUNCIL OF JEWISH WOMEN and the Women's City Club. Although she was a charter member of the League of Women Voters of Cuyahoga County, the league has never endorsed candidates.

In 1926, Grossman was appointed to the new Morals Court, which handled cases involving prostitution, drunkenness, domestic violence, and sex crimes. Grossman often referred to her court as a "social agency" and used her position to protect women and families, publicly urging that abandonment be treated as a felony and that grounds for divorce be made tougher. In 1947, the *Cleveland Press* described her as a "militant feminist [who] has been bad news to wife beaters, gamblers, and persons charged with morals offenses." Associates referred to her as "Hard Boiled Mary." Grossman retired in 1959 after thirty-six uninterrupted years on the bench. She remained involved in a wide range of community activities, including African-American and Jewish women's organizations.

On the fiftieth anniversary of the passage of the Nineteenth Amendment, Grossman, then ninety-one, remembered the victory with enthusiasm: "It was a great day for women. We all went right down to register." Praising the women's liberation movement, she urged women to enter politics and public life as she had.

Mary Belle Grossman died on January 27, 1977.

BIBLIOGRAPHY

Abbott, Virginia Clark. *The History of Woman Suffrage and the League of Women Voters in Cuyahoga County, 1911–1945* (n.d.); Grossman, Mary B. Papers. Ms. collection 3660, Western Reserve Historical Society, Cleveland, Ohio.

MARIAN J. MORTON

GRUBER, RUTH (b. 1911)

Ruth Gruber has moved across most of the twentieth century as a compassionate writer, eloquent speaker, humanitarian, and rescuer of Jews.

She was born on September 30, 1911, in Brooklyn, the fourth of five children of David and Gussie (Rockower) Gruber, Russian Jewish immigrants who owned a wholesale and retail liquor store and later went into real estate. She graduated from New York University at age eighteen and in 1930 won a fellowship to the University of Wisconsin, where she received her M.A. in German and English literature. In 1931, Gruber received a fellowship from the Institute of International Education for study in Cologne, Germany. Her parents pleaded with her not to go: Hitler was coming to power. Nevertheless, she went to Cologne and took courses in German philosophy, modern English literature, and art history. She also attended Nazi rallies, her American passport in her purse, a tiny American flag on her lapel. She listened, appalled, as Hitler ranted hysterically against Americans and even more hysterically against Jews.

Gruber's professors asked her to stay in Cologne and study for a Ph.D. Analyzing the writings of Virginia Woolf, she received her doctorate magna cum laude in one year. The *New York Times* reported that, at age twenty, she was the youngest Ph.D. in the world.

She returned home in the midst of the Great Depression and, like most of her peers, was unable to find a job, so she began writing. After many rejections of her work, she wrote an article about Brooklyn, describing its colorful neighborhoods as a microcosm

An eyewitness to the rise of Hitler and the brutality of the Soviet gulags, Ruth Gruber was a reporter who was recruited by the U.S. Government to escort a thousand refugees from war-torn Europe to America. That was just the beginning of a lifelong calling to aid Jews in trouble by documenting their struggles. She is shown here in her war correspondent's uniform. [Ruth Gruber]

of Europe, which the *New York Times* bought for the Sunday paper. Then Gruber began sending stories to the *New York Herald Tribune*, and with their acceptance felt she had found her home.

In 1935, she won another fellowship, given at the recommendation of the Guggenheim Foundation, to write a study of women under fascism, communism, and democracy. The *Herald Tribune* gave her press credentials, and she became the first foreign correspondent, male or female, allowed to fly through Siberia into the Soviet arctic. She lived among pioneers and prisoners, many of them Jews, in the gulag in Stalin's iron age.

In 1941, Secretary of the Interior Harold L. Ickes, after reading her book *I Went to the Soviet Arctic,* sent Gruber as his field representative to make a social and economic study of Alaska in connection with opening it for GIs and homesteaders. For over nineteen months she covered the vast territory by plane, train, truck, paddle-wheel steamer, and dogsled. On Gruber's return to Washington, Ickes appointed her his special assistant. She worked for him five years.

In 1944, while war and the Holocaust raged, President Roosevelt decided to bring a thousand refugees from Europe to Fort Ontario, a former army camp in Oswego, a small town in upper New York State. Gruber was selected by Ickes to fly to Europe on a secret mission to escort the refugees to America. Ickes told her, "You're going to be given the rank of simulated general." He explained. "If you're shot down and the Nazis capture you as a civilian, they can kill you as a spy. But as a general, according to the Geneva Convention, they have to give you food and shelter and keep you alive."

Escorting the refugees by ship from Naples, Italy, Gruber recorded their stories of how they had survived. Often she had to stop writing because tears were wiping out the words in her notebook. Soon the refugees began calling her "Mother Ruth." The voyage became the defining Jewish moment of her life. She knew that from then on, her life would be inextricably bound with rescuing Jews in danger.

Gruber's book about the experience, *Haven: The Unknown Story of 1,000 World War II Refugees*, became the basis for the permanent Holocaust exhibit in the State Museum in Albany called "From Holocaust to Haven." In 1993, it was made into a musical play, *Oswego: An American Haven.*

In 1946, the war over, she left the government and returned to journalism. The *New York Post* asked her to cover the Anglo-American Committee of Inquiry on Palestine. For four months, she traveled with the committee to the death camps and the displaced persons camps in Germany, then she went on to Palestine, where she became a trusted friend of the founding fathers and mothers of the State of Israel. Her profiles of David Ben-Gurion, who was then almost unknown in the United States, made American readers aware of his prophetic character and unswerving Lincoln-like determination to build a Jewish state.

The next year, she returned to the *New York Herald Tribune* as a foreign correspondent and traveled with the United Nations Special Committee on Palestine through Europe and the Middle East. In Jerusalem, she learned that a ship called *Exodus 1947*, with forty-five hundred survivors of the Holocaust aboard, was battling the British in the Mediterranean. Gruber decided to cover the *Exodus*.

In Haifa, surrounded by tanks and barbed wire, she watched as British soldiers carried down the bodies of Bill Bernstein, the American first mate, and two sixteen-year-old orphans. Some of the refugees came down dejectedly; those who refused were pulled down. All were transferred to three prison ships and returned to Port de Bouc, near Marseilles, the port from which they had sailed. After three weeks, the British announced they were sending the Jews of the *Exodus* back to Germany. They selected Gruber as the pool correspondent to represent the American press. Her photos of the agony inside the prison ship were sent by the *Herald Tribune* around the world, and her photo of the swastika painted on the British Union Jack became *Life* magazine's Picture of the Week. Her book, *Destination Palestine: The Story of the Haganah Ship* Exodus 1947, provided source material for the book and movie *Exodus* and for numerous TV documentaries.

In 1951, Gruber married Philip H. Michaels, a lawyer, vice president of the Sachs Quality Stores, and a member of the New York City Youth Board. In 1952, at age forty-one, she gave birth to her first child, Celia; her son, David, was born in 1954. Gruber continued working as a special foreign correspondent for the *Herald Tribune*, covering every major wave of immigrants into Israel until the paper's death in 1966. At the same time, she also wrote a popular column for *Hadassah Magazine*, "Diary of an American Housewife," and, as a volunteer, served as associate chair of the Greater New York Women's Division of United Jewish Appeal, where she wrote and directed the scripts for their many performances. In 1991, she became honorary chair of the Israel Bonds Golda Meir Club.

Michaels died in 1968, and six years later Gruber married Henry Rosner, then deputy commissioner of the New York City Department of Human Resources. He accompanied her to Israel, where she spent nearly a year writing her best-known biography, *Raquela: A Woman of Israel*, which won the National Jewish Book Award for Best Book on Israel in 1979. In 1982, Henry Rosner died.

In 1985, Gruber traveled to the isolated Jewish villages in the highlands of Ethiopia to aid in the rescue of the Ethiopian Jews. Her book *Rescue: The Exodus of the Ethiopian Jews* was acclaimed by such critics and leaders as Menachem Begin, Abba Eban, and Elie Wiesel. The recipient of many awards, in 1995 Gruber was given Na'amat USA's Golda Meir Human Rights Award for her life's work. That same year, for *Na'mat Woman* magazine, she covered the United Nations Fourth World Conference on Women in

Beijing. In 1997, she won several prestigious awards from the Simon Wiesenthal Center's Museum of Tolerance for her lifelong work rescuing Jews.

SELECTED WORKS BY RUTH GRUBER

Ahead of Time: My Early Years as a Foreign Correspondent (1991); *Destination Palestine: The Story of the Haganah Ship* Exodus 1947 (1948); *Felisa Rincon de Gautier: The Mayor of San Juan* (1972); *Haven: The Unknown Story of 1,000 World War II Refugees* (1983); *I Can Tell It Now: Members of the Overseas Press Club* (1960); *Israel on the Seventh Day* (1968); *Israel Today: Land of Many Nations* (1958); *Israel Without Tears* (1950); *Puerto Rico: Island of Promise* (1960); *Raquela: A Woman of Israel* (1978); *Rescue: The Exodus of the Ethiopian Jews* (1987); *Science and the New Nations* (1961); *They Came to Stay* (1976); *Virginia Woolf: A Study* (1934); *I Went to the Soviet Arctic* (1939).

BIBLIOGRAPHY

Sources for this biography include Ruth Gruber's books, magazine articles, lectures, and appearances in films and documentaries, including *The Great Depression* for PBS, *Truman* for PBS, *Exiles and Emigrants* for Los Angeles County Museum of Art, *Exodus 1947*, and *The Long Way Home*, produced by the Simon Wiesenthal Center, Los Angeles, 1997, as well as interviews and conversations with the author.

BARBARA SEAMAN

GRUENBERG, SIDONIE MATZNER (1881–1974)

In 1973, in her nineties, Sidonie Matzner Gruenberg declared that her eighties had been the best decade of her life. She had published the revised edition of her monumental four-volume *The New Illustrated Encyclopedia of Child Care and Guidance* (1967) and had earned more money than in any previous decade.

Writer and director of the Child Study Association of America from 1923 to 1950, Sidonie Matzner Gruenberg is best known as a leader and publicist in the parent education movement and as an authority in the larger field of child study. She was born on June 10, 1881, near Vienna, Austria, the oldest of four daughters and two sons of Idore and Augusta Olivia (Besseches) Matzner. Her mother was the daughter of a wealthy German Jewish grain exporter. Her father, the son of an Austrian town mayor, was educated at the University of Crakow. The Matzners immigrated to New York in 1895, where they became involved with Felix Adler's Ethical Culture Society. Augusta and Idore Matzner had been involved in reform Jewish activities before leaving Europe, and they transferred their reform impulses to the charismatic vision of Felix Adler's secular humanism.

Sidonie grew up within the decidedly reform atmosphere of the Ethical Culture Workingman's School and later the Ethical Culture Normal School. She married Benjamin Gruenberg, a biology teacher, in 1903. Her husband also came from an educated Jewish background, and as he was attracted by Adler's reformist and egalitarian ideas, they both became active in Ethical Culture activities. In 1907, with the birth of her first child, Gruenberg joined the Federation of Child Study, a study club of Ethical Culture mothers, and made it her life's work. The Gruenbergs had four children: Herbert (b. 1907), Richard (b. 1910), Hilda (b. 1913), and Ernest (b. 1915).

In her first book, *Your Child Today and Tomorrow* (1913), Gruenberg exhibited her talent for synthesizing the best sources of child development information and translating them into language that parents could understand and trust. The combination of conventional wisdom and new ideas that characterizes this book is found in all her work. *We, the Parents* (1939), written in the shadow of World War II, won the *Parents Magazine* award in 1940. Gruenberg recognized the complex needs of modern women and warned mothers to prepare for a number of life stages. "We have to choose not once, but many times and at each stage with the same degree of uncertainty." Her writing for parents includes twenty-six books, numerous pamphlets, and many articles that appeared in *Child Study Magazine* and elsewhere.

Before it received substantial financial support from the prestigious Laura Spelman Rockefeller Foundation in 1923, the Federation for Child Study was subjected to an undercover investigation of its "Jewish leadership." While the organization had a religiously mixed membership and remained affiliated with its secularized parent organization, the Ethical Culture Society, the Rockefeller Foundation nevertheless perceived it as a Jewish organization and made changing its public image a condition of funding. Gruenberg did not step down, as was suggested, but the newly named Child Study Association of America did hire a non-Jew to be its field representative outside New York City. Gruenberg continued as director until her retirement in 1950.

The Gruenbergs neither denied their Jewish background nor experienced conflict with their Ethical Culture affiliations. Benjamin Gruenberg was involved with various Jewish organizations throughout his life, and during World War II both he and his wife worked to bring German and Austrian relatives out of Europe. Professionally and personally, Gruenberg was largely driven by her beliefs in assimilation, in the era's progressive views of the behavioral and natural sciences, and in the power of education to improve the lives of parents and children.

Sidonie Matzner Gruenberg died on March 11, 1974, in her home in New York City.

SELECTED WORKS BY
SIDONIE MATZNER GRUENBERG

The New Illustrated Encyclopedia of Child Care and Guidance. 4 vols. (1954. Rev. ed. 1967); *Sons and Daughters* (1916); *We, the Parents* (1939); *The Wonderful Story of How You Were Born*, with Benjamin Gruenberg (1952. Rev. ed. 1970); *Your Child and You* (1950); *Your Child Today and Tomorrow* (1913).

BIBLIOGRAPHY

AJYB 24:151; *BEOAJ*; Gruenberg, Sidonie Matzner. Papers. Benjamin and Sidonie Gruenberg Collection, Library of Congress, Washington, D.C., and Professional collection. Social Welfare Archive, University of Minnesota, St. Paul; Mainiero, Linda, ed. *American Women Writers* (1980); *NAW* modern; Obituary. *NYTimes*, March 13, 1974, 44:1; *UJE*; *WWIAJ* (1938); *WWWIA* 6.

ROBERTA WOLLONS

GRUENING, ROSE (1876–1934)

Known during her lifetime as the "Angel of Grand Street," Rose Gruening was head worker and founder of the Grand Street Settlement in New York City. Although Gruening never liked this title, it attests to her significance in the eyes of many people. Like Jane Addams, LILLIAN WALD, and other women settlement workers of the early twentieth century, Gruening helped to create a social "safety net" through voluntary civic activism, before the concept of public responsibility for poor and disadvantaged Americans was enacted by the U.S. Government. Once the Depression and the New Deal transformed the workings of social welfare in the United States, the social service concept as practiced by Gruening and her contemporaries changed dramatically. Before it did so, however, thousands of immigrant families from the Lower East Side of New York experienced Gruening's settlement house activism in personal and profound ways.

By the time Gruening established the Grand Street Settlement in 1916, she was intimately familiar with both the urban environment of New York and social service work. Rose Gruening was born in New York City in 1876 to Rose (Fridenberg) and Emil Gruening, a well-known eye and ear specialist. The elder Rose Gruening died of typhoid fever when giving birth to her daughter. Four years later, young Rose's father married his late wife's sister Phebe and with her raised four more children: Clara, Marie, Martha, and Ernest. Both Clara and Martha became writers, and their brother became a well-known journalist and editor for such newspapers as the *New York Evening Post* and the *New York Tribune*. Growing up in New York City near Gramercy Park, Rose Gruening attended the Ethical Culture School and later graduated from Vassar College. While the Gruenings subsequently moved their family home uptown to 57th Street, Rose Gruening began to focus her professional interests even farther downtown, on Manhattan's Lower East Side.

Gruening began her philanthropic career as a volunteer social worker in Madison House, the Ethical Culture Society's settlement on the Lower East Side. Accounts of Gruening's early career suggest that she first became interested in social work after college, when she visited an Ethical Culture School summer camp for poor children. In 1907, after having joined the staff of Madison House, Gruening persuaded its trustees to establish a summer recreation spot in Mountainville, New York, for the settlement's urban dwellers. She called it Camp Moodna. Housing at Camp Moodna originally consisted of twenty converted horse cars, which Gruening obtained inexpensively from a transit company that was about to replace its older, horsedrawn cars with trolley and cable cars.

Over the next few decades, Camp Moodna changed hands as Gruening expanded her settlement house work. By 1916, Madison House was serving more people on the Lower East Side than it could easily accommodate. Rather than build an even larger Madison House, though, Gruening and some of her colleagues wanted to establish a smaller settlement in an underserved neighborhood. Gruening founded the new settlement on Division Street and named it the Arnold Toynbee House after the famous British social reformer. After three years, the settlement moved to larger quarters on the corner of Grand Street and East Broadway, aiming to improve the living and working conditions of people in the community by addressing the underlying causes of their poverty. During the 1920s and 1930s, the settlement organized children's social clubs, offered child care for working parents, and provided showers for community residents whose homes had no running water. In 1925, its name was changed to the Grand Street Settlement, and during the Depression years, Camp Moodna was donated to the Grand Street Settlement in honor of Gruening.

Rose Gruening died at Camp Moodna on July 31, 1934, but the legacy of the "Angel of Grand Street" continues at the Grand Street Settlement even today.

BIBLIOGRAPHY

AJYB 37:257; *EJ*; Gruening, Ernest. *Many Battles: The Autobiography of Ernest Gruening* (1973); Obituary. *NYTimes*, August 1, 1934, 17:4.

ERIN ELIZABETH CLUNE

GUGGENHEIM, FLORENCE SHLOSS (1863–1944)

When Florence Guggenheim died at age eighty, she was recalled in newspapers across the country for her generous support of many causes and her active political and philanthropic contributions to the institutions she had supported.

Florence Shloss Guggenheim was born on September 3, 1863, in Philadelphia, the daughter of Lazarus and Barbara (Kahnweiler) Shloss. She married Daniel Guggenheim on July 22, 1884. As part of the Guggenheim family, Daniel was on the board of directors of the American Smelting and Refining Company. The Guggenheims had two sons, Robert and Harry, and a daughter, Gladys Guggenheim, who would later marry Roger W. Straus of New York, who cofounded the publishing house Farrar, Straus, and Giroux.

In her younger years, Florence Guggenheim was fond of sports, particularly horseback riding and golf, which she played near their Long Island home. Her interests included art and especially music, which later became the focus of much of her philanthropic work. Together she and her husband shared philanthropic interests that became a trademark of the Guggenheim family.

Florence Guggenheim played an active role in Jewish affairs as well as in women's civic endeavors. During World War I, she was involved in the sale of Liberty Bonds and in the area of aviation, which was a particular avocation of her husband's. She was a director of the National League for Women's Service and held what was reputed to be the record for individual sales of Liberty Bonds. Florence Guggenheim was a long-standing member of Congregation Emanu-El and for twenty years served as the treasurer and trustee of the Emanu-El Sisterhood of Personal Services.

As a Republican, Guggenheim was the treasurer of the Women's National Republican Club from 1921, when it was first founded, to 1938. She later served on its board of governors. As philanthropists,

Florence and Daniel Guggenheim were best known for sponsoring the free outdoor concerts in Central Park and at Columbia and New York universities. They were joined in providing the funds for these endeavors by family members Mr. and Mrs. Murray Guggenheim. After the death of her husband in 1930, as a memorial, Florence Guggenheim continued to support the concerts.

In 1924, the Guggenheim Foundation was formed by the family to make their participation in charities more efficient. Florence Guggenheim served as president and a director of the foundation, which supported a variety of artistic causes and institutions.

Philanthropists Florence Guggenheim and her husband, Daniel, were best known for sponsoring free outdoor concerts in Central Park in New York City. Today the family name lives on through the Guggenheim Foundation, which Florence served as president and director. [Library of Congress]

In 1937, she was honored by being elected to a life associate membership in the American Bandmasters Association. She continued to pay homage to her husband's deep interest in aviation, and in June 1942, she donated her 162-acre estate to the Institute of the Aeronautical Sciences for aeronautical research and study.

Florence Guggenheim died in New York City on May 13, 1944.

BIBLIOGRAPHY

AJYB 46:338; Obituary. *NYTimes*, May 14, 1944, 45:1; *UJE*; *WWIAJ* (1938).

CLAUDIA LOGAN

GUGGENHEIM, IRENE ROTHSCHILD (1868–1954)

Irene Rothschild Guggenheim, child welfare advocate and art collector, was born in New York City on December 16, 1868, daughter of Victor Henry and Josephine (Wolf) Rothschild. Her father had come to the United States from the German state of Würtemberg in 1852. During the Civil War, he settled in New York City and opened a manufactory for men's shirts that later expanded into a thriving men's and women's ready-made clothing business. The Rothschilds had five children, three daughters and two sons; Irene was the second daughter.

Irene attended public school and Normal College (later HUNTER COLLEGE). She also studied in Germany at Miss Lindner's School in Frankfurt-am-Main between 1882 and 1884, and at a private school run by Madame da Silva in New York City. In the early 1890s, she began to perform charitable work with poor and afflicted children in New York City. In 1894, Ida Clemons, a social worker, asked Irene to help establish a day nursery for the children of working women. This institution, the Brightside Day Nursery, and its offshoot, the Cannon Street Health Center, became Guggenheim's life work. Elected its first president, she held that office for fifty-four years. Her marriage in 1895 to Solomon Guggenheim, mining magnate, and the birth of three daughters—Eleanor (1896), Gertrude (1898), and Barbara (1904)—did not diminish her involvement.

The Brightside Day Nursery was located on the Lower East Side, where the preponderance of working-class Jewish immigrants lived. The nursery consisted of a crèche for infants as young as ten days old, and a kindergarten for children up to six years old that,

within a year of its inception, was serving more than fifty children a day. The program was designed with the help of LILLIAN WALD and Mary Brewster, who had established a public health nursing service in the same neighborhood the previous year. It reflected the growing interest in early childhood programs spurred by the model day nursery at the Chicago World's Fair in 1893, and the establishment of kindergartens in other immigrant neighborhoods. Open from seven A.M. to seven P.M. six days a week, the program made it possible for single Jewish mothers to earn a living while their children were bathed, fed, clothed, and instructed by competent caretakers.

Like other such institutions, the Brightside Day Nursery was a means of social reform as well as a charitable organization, and as the managers began to perceive the need for other social services they added programs. By 1904, the institution not only provided a day nursery for 150 children, but also served as an after-school facility for graduates. In addition, one hundred girls per day attended industrial classes in sewing, millinery, embroidering, raffia work, and kitchen gardening, while 250 boys and girls came to Saturday morning religious school. The board established a savings fund and circulating library for neighborhood children, sponsored seventeen clubs for older children and a monthly "mothers' club," and opened a summer home where children could stay in the country for two weeks or longer.

While mothers who could afford to pay contributed five cents a day toward each child's support, the institution was primarily funded by charitable contributions. To this end, the almost unlimited resources of the Guggenheim family were particularly helpful. Various members of the Guggenheim and Rothschild families also served as directors of the organization, which continued to grow and diversify. In the late 1920s, the Brightside Day Nursery spawned the Cannon Street Health Center, which provided a range of services including nutrition classes, medical and dental services for children and their mothers, and intelligence testing. The Brightside Day Nursery continued its work until 1948.

Guggenheim became a director of the Association of Day Nurseries of New York City, which set standards for and attempted to improve and coordinate the work of many of the city's child care institutions. In addition, she served as a trustee of the Federation of Jewish Philanthropies and was active in other New York City organizations. Like other members of the Guggenheim family, she and her husband belonged to Congregation Emanu-El in New York City.

Guggenheim was also interested in art. After her marriage, she and her husband collected old masters that ranged from Italian Renaissance panels to nineteenth-century Barbizon oils. She was particularly fond of the works of Antoine Watteau, an early eighteenth-century French rococo painter. When Solomon became interested in nonobjective contemporary paintings in the late 1920s, Guggenheim remained involved in his collecting and his foundation, and even proposed Frank Lloyd Wright as the architect for what later became the Solomon R. Guggenheim Museum.

Irene Rothschild Guggenheim died on November 25, 1954, five years after the death of her husband. She gave meaning to her life of comfort and privilege through her philanthropic efforts to assist poor Jewish women and their children.

BIBLIOGRAPHY

Brightside Day Nursery. Annual reports; Davis, John H. *The Guggenheims: An American Epic* (1978); Guggenheim Family Papers. Archives of the Guggenheim Brothers and the Solomon R. Guggenheim Foundation, NYC; *National Cyclopedia of American Biography* 44:174; *New York Charities Directory*; Obituary. *NYTimes*, November 29, 1954, 25:1; *WWIAJ* (1938).

SUSAN PORTER

GUGGENHEIM, PEGGY (1898–1979)

Born Marguerite Guggenheim in New York City to Florence (Seligman) and Benjamin Guggenheim, Peggy Guggenheim amassed what is now considered to be Italy's most important modern art collection. Her collecting ability was certainly the result of her exposure, at an early age, to the German Jewish emphasis on *Kultur*. The Seligmans were members of the academic and artistic world. As wealthy German Jewish Americans, opera boxes, grand tours of Europe, and the purchase of priceless paintings characterized their life-style, which certainly influenced Peggy.

She was also influenced by her family's financial successes. Both the Seligman and Guggenheim families were very wealthy, and Peggy Guggenheim received a share of this wealth at age twenty-one, when she came into her inheritance. Her father, who lost his life on board the *Titanic*, left his daughter with a trust fund of $450,000, which provided her with a yearly income of $22,000 a year. These resources allowed her to begin her collecting career.

Before she could make a name for herself, Guggenheim decided to escape what she considered her banal New York life and traveled to Europe. She began to adopt a less conventional life-style, wearing outrageous sunglasses and leopard-print handbags, and walking two small dogs.

In 1922, she married writer Lawrence Vail, the "King of Bohemia," hoping that he would bring some excitement into her life. The couple had two children, Sinbad and Peegan, but the marriage ended in divorce in 1930.

Remaining in Europe, Guggenheim discovered the art world, and was intrigued by the notion that she could both help artists and make a profit through sales. Attracted to modern art, Guggenheim learned as much as she could about this movement with the help of Marcel Duchamp. On January 24, 1938, she opened her own gallery in London, called the Guggenheim Jeune. It was her hope that this gallery would become a London version of New York's Museum of Modern Art. However, given the dangerous conditions developing in Europe at this time, she decided to abandon the Guggenheim Jeune, but without abandoning her career in the art world. Residing in France, she was determined to use the money she had set aside for the London gallery to purchase one picture a day. Refusing to let the political chaos stop her completely, she walked into Fernand Léger's studio the day before Hitler conquered Norway and bought *Men in the City* for $1,000. By 1940, Guggenheim had collected fifty works. However, her last name had begun to draw many questions from authorities, and she knew it was time to leave Europe. Three days before the Germans entered Paris, she left for America.

In America, Guggenheim's career in the art world continued at full force. In 1941, she married the artist Max Ernst, whom she would divorce five years later. After her wedding, she worked to establish Art of the Century, a gallery in which she displayed works by both prominent and unknown artists.

By the end of World War II, Guggenheim was eager to return to Europe. In the spring of 1949, she moved into the unfinished eighteenth-century Palazzo Venier dei Leoni on Venice's Grand Canal. It was here that she displayed part of her collection to the public. She had amassed works by the pioneers of the twentieth century, including Pablo Picasso, Salvador Dali, Léger, Max Ernst, and Jackson Pollock. In 1974, she gave her collection and the Palazzo to the Solomon Guggenheim Foundation, established in 1937 by her uncle, who was also an art collector. Peggy Guggenheim died in 1979, leaving the Solomon Guggenheim Museum in charge of her legacy.

For the most part, being Jewish was something Guggenheim tried to hide. She admitted feeling more comfortable around non-Jews and was sometimes accused of being anti-Semitic. However, in her memoirs, Guggenheim does not deny her faith. She discusses her family's Jewish heritage and how she found solace in saying the kaddish upon her father's death.

SELECTED WORKS BY PEGGY GUGGENHEIM

Out of This Century: Confessions of an Art Addict (1979). [Combines two memoirs: *Out of This Century* (1946) and *Confessions of an Art Addict* (1960).]

BIBLIOGRAPHY

Smithsonian (July 1986): 58; *Town and Country* 150, no. 5190 (March 1996): 30; Weld, Jacqueline Bograd. *Peggy: The Wayward Guggenheim* (1986); *WWWIA* 7.

ANDREW JACOBS

GUGGENHEIMER, ELINOR (b. 1912)

Elinor Guggenheimer first toured New York City day nurseries as a member of the Federation of Jewish Philanthropies during the 1930s. Horrified by what she saw, Guggenheimer began a lifelong crusade for improved and standardized child care facilities across the country. A veteran of New York City politics, Guggenheimer has also worked to promote women in public office and was one of the founding members of the Women's Political Caucus in 1971.

Elinor (Coleman) Guggenheimer was born on April 11, 1912, the only child of Nathan Coleman, a commercial banker, and Lillian (Fox) Coleman. After growing up in New York City, she attended Vassar College until 1931. The following year, she married Randolph Guggenheimer, with whom she later had two sons. Guggenheimer earned her B.A. from Barnard in 1934 and worked for a short time as a documentary filmmaker. During the late 1930s and 1940s, she was active in numerous Jewish organizations, including the YOUNG WOMEN'S HEBREW ASSOCIATION, the Jewish Association of Neighborhood Centers, and the Educational Alliance.

Following World War II, Guggenheimer spearheaded a successful effort to save over ninety public day nurseries that had opened during the war. She worked to keep public attention focused on child care issues and, in 1948, founded the Day Care Council of New York, serving as its executive director throughout the 1950s. In 1958, she also established the Intercity Day Care Council, a national child care advocacy organization

Guggenheimer entered city politics in 1960 when she became the first woman elected to the New York City Planning Commission. Work with the Planning Commission occupied Guggenheimer until 1968. The following year, she ran as a Democratic candidate for city council president. The only female candidate in a field with twenty-one men, Guggenheimer campaigned to prove that women could run for political office. By 1974, she was appointed commissioner of New York City consumer affairs, a post that she held until 1978.

Frustrated by the scant representation of women in politics during the 1960s and 1970s, Guggenheimer cofounded the Women's Political Caucus in 1971. With such leaders as BELLA ABZUG and Shirley Chisholm, the organization sought to provide nonpartisan support for women running for elected office. In 1973, Guggenheimer founded the Women's Forum. A local initiative designed to provide a support network for elite women in various professions, the Women's Forum went national in 1980. It is now an international organization based in Washington, D.C.

During the 1980s, Guggenheimer returned to the issue of child care and established the Child Care Action Campaign to lobby for the creation of a national day care program that would provide standardized and adequate child care for all children, despite economic status. She remained interested in building coalitions of professional women and, in 1992, founded the New York Women's Agenda. Each year, the organization holds a large breakfast honoring women of achievement.

Guggenheimer has been involved with numerous other political and social service organizations, including the Council of Senior Centers and Services. She lectured at the Center for New York City Affairs at the New School for Social Research from 1965 to 1976 and comoderated *Straight Talk*, a daily one-hour public affairs television program, in the early 1970s. Her musical *Potholes*, a political satire, was produced in 1979 in an Off-Broadway theater.

One of a handful of women in elected office during the mid-twentieth century, Elinor Guggenheimer forged new paths for women in politics. She has led the fight for a national system of day care in the United States and continues to work to increase the number of women in politics and the professions.

BIBLIOGRAPHY

Berry, Mary Frances. *The Politics of Parenthood: Child Care, Women's Rights, and the Myth of the Good Mother* (1993); Guggenheimer, Elinor C. *Planning for Parks and Recreation Needs in Urban Areas* (1969); Hartmann, Susan. *From Margin to Mainstream: American Women and Politics Since 1960* (1989); *Who's Who in America* (1996).

MICHELLE SPINELLI

GUGGENHEIMER, IDA ESPEN (1866–1959)

Ida Espen Guggenheimer, a woman with a deeply ingrained sense of social awareness, was an early Zionist, a feminist, and a civil rights activist.

Born on December 8, 1866, in Philadelphia, Pennsylvania, she was the oldest child of Jacob and Fannie (Bachman) Espen. She had one brother, Frank, and two sisters, Hannah and Sophie. Her father and his brother were importers of lace. She was educated at the Friends School in Philadelphia and attended school in Dresden, Germany, when her family traveled in Europe.

In 1895, she married Jay Caesar Guggenheimer, an attorney just starting a New York law practice. He died in 1932. Their only child, Clara, was born in 1897.

Although there are no indications of Jewish observance in her family, Guggenheimer was a close friend of HENRIETTA SZOLD and was for some years active in the Zionist movement. She organized and raised funds to establish medical units and, subsequently, the Hadassah Hospital in what was then Palestine. At one time, around 1915, she was the president of HADASSAH's New York chapter.

She became increasingly radical in her views as time went on, and was involved in the suffrage and trade union movements. She marched frequently in suffrage parades and on picket lines in support of such strikers as the employees of May's Department Store and laundry workers. She was active in the Women's Trade Union League, of which she was a board member in the late 1930s and early 1940s, the League of Women Voters, the League of Women Shoppers, the Women's International League for Peace and Freedom, the Southern Conference for Educational Welfare (a group committed to establishing racial equality), Consumers Union, and the American Civil Liberties Union.

In connection with her work with Roger Baldwin of the Civil Liberties Union and Eleanor Roosevelt, Guggenheimer held many meetings at her home to raise money to establish the Bail Fund for Political Prisoners. She also hosted gatherings with Margaret Sanger to promote the cause of birth control.

Her interest in furthering the rights of blacks and other minorities was apparent in the support she gave to the trial of the Scottsboro boys, to Angelo Herndon, Sacco and Vanzetti, Tom Mooney, and numerous others. The author Ralph Ellison was her protégé, and his book *The Invisible Man* is dedicated to her. In her later years she took an active role in the American Labor Party.

During the period of Hitler's oppression of German Jewry, Guggenheimer sponsored countless refugees. Her summer home in Canada served as a halfway house for many who had to leave the United States in order to secure a visa for reentry.

A person of boundless energy and intellectual curiosity, she read widely and attended the theater, concerts, and films. She and her husband were instrumental in furthering the education of many young musicians and assisting struggling artists. She was a friend of the French artist Jacques Villon and owned an extensive collection of his works.

Ida Espen Guggenheimer died in New York, on August 29, 1959, at age ninety-three.

BIBLIOGRAPHY

AJYB 62:450; Baum, Judith. "Bio-Bibliography of Ida Espen Guggenheimer." Research project, May 1976; Bernard, Martha Binswanger [granddaughter]. Telephone interview with author, August 28, 1996; Binswanger, Clara G. Biographical notes on Ida Espen Guggenheimer, c. 1959; Guggenheimer, Ida Espen. Papers. Hadassah Archives, NYC; Hadassah. New York Chapter Questionnaire for Annual Report (May 1918), and *Hadassah Bulletin* (May 1915, August 1917), and *Hadassah Newsletter* (May 1921); Meyer, Charles H. Memorial of Jay Caesar Guggenheimer, c. 1932; Obituary. *NYTimes*, August 30, 1959, 82:4.

ESTHER FARBER

GUTHRIE, MARJORIE (1917–1983)

Marjorie Guthrie is remembered for her several careers. She was first a dancer and then a teacher. She founded the Woody Guthrie Children's Fund and Archive (in 1956) to preserve her husband's works for future audiences. Finally, during the last fifteen years of her life, she became a national advocate for basic biomedical research on the diseases of the chronically ill.

She grew up in an intellectual atmosphere, influenced by her parents' commitment to Zionism, socialism, and Jewish welfare. Her mother, ALIZA WAITZMAN GREENBLATT, was a Russian-born Yiddish poet, later known to the Guthrie family and their friends as "Bubbe." Aliza Waitzman had been an adventurous young woman. In 1900, she "stole the border" (fled illegally) from the shtetl Azarenits, Bessarabia, and made her way to Philadelphia, where she met her future husband. Aliza Waitzman and Isidor Greenblatt courted at the Radical Library, attending lectures on atheism, anarchism and philosophy.

Marjorie Greenblatt was born in Atlantic City, New Jersey, on October 6, 1917, the fourth of five

"If you are over thirty, I am Woody's wife. If you are younger, I am Arlo's mother."
With that introduction, the indefatigable Marjorie Guthrie was able to get the ear of legislators
in her fight for a cure for genetic disorders like Huntington's Disease, which killed her husband.
She is shown here at the National Yiddish Book Center, in the reading room honoring her mother,
the Yiddish poet ALIZA GREENBLATT. *Guthrie donated her mother's books to the center. [Irma Commanday]*

siblings: Herbert, a merchant marine; Gertrude, an artist; David, a mechanical engineer; and Bernard, a psychiatrist. She graduated from Overbrook High School in Philadelphia. While attending a concert by Mary Wigman, a pioneer in modern dance, Marjorie realized that she had to become a dancer. At eighteen, she won a scholarship to study with Martha Graham at the Neighborhood Playhouse in New York. Under her professional name, Marjorie Mazia, she was featured in Graham's first company, appearing in "Primitive Mysteries," "Every Soul Is a Circus," and "American Document," three of Graham's early classics. As Graham's assistant for fifteen years, she was the first member of the group to teach Graham's technique. Two of her early pupils were Merce Cunning-

ham and Erick Hawkins. By 1950, she had established her own dance school in Sheepshead Bay, Brooklyn.

Marjorie Mazia met Woody Guthrie at the Almanac House in Greenwich Village, where hootenannies (folk music sing-alongs) were held. In their small physical size, they resembled each other. They married in 1945 and combined their musical talents and political idealism, calling themselves "World Shakers and World Changers." Woody was Marjorie's second husband; she was his second wife and the main support of the family. In between dancing and teaching, she had four children with Woody Guthrie: Cathy (b. 1943), Arlo (b. 1947), Joady (b. 1948), and Nora (b. 1950). Cathy died in an accident at age four on February 9, 1947.

In 1952, Woody's erratic behavior was diagnosed as symptomatic of Huntington's Disease, inherited from his mother. It was impossible for Marjorie Guthrie to give him the full-time care his condition required. She had to divorce him so that the state would be responsible for supporting his fifteen-year-long hospitalization. She married three more times: to Alfred Addeo (1954), Lou Cooper (1964), and Martin Stein (1974). Her first marriage and those to Addeo and Cooper ended in divorce. Only Stein, who died in 1980, gave her financial security.

After Woody died in 1967, Guthrie dedicated her life to educating the medical community and the public about Huntington's disease. In an effort to help those at risk, she established the Committee to Combat Huntington's Disease, now called the Huntington's Disease Society of America. Through reading and intensive study, she gained a profound knowledge of the problems of genetic and neurologic diseases. She earned many honors. She was appointed a lay member of the Advisory Council of the National Institute of General Medical Sciences from 1973 to 1977 and elected to the Society for Neuroscience. She was also made a member of the American Association for the Advancement of Science and appointed to the Research Commission on Huntington's Chorea of the World Federation of Neurology. Further recognition came with her membership in the New York State Commission on Health Education and Illness Prevention, and in the state's Genetic Advisory Committee.

Guthrie traveled tirelessly around the world, speaking to Huntington families, medical students, congressional committees in Washington, and legislative assemblies in many states. "It's a long way from the world of dance to the world of health care," she said. "And yet, in another way, both depend primarily on communication." Whenever she called for an appointment with a legislator, she introduced herself by asking, "How old are you?" Relying on the popularity of "This Land Is Your Land" and her son Arlo's ballad "Alice's Restaurant," she would add: "If you are over thirty, I am Woody's wife. If you are younger, I am Arlo's mother."

With a grant from the Robert Wood Johnson Foundation, Guthrie held meetings in fifteen cities with self-help organizations that were seeking ways they might better share their resources. She acted as consultant to many of those groups, including Alzheimer's and Tourette Syndrome Associations. Her efforts laid the groundwork for the discovery of the marker for the Huntington gene. After her death on March 13, 1983, a series of lectures by leading scientists was established in her honor at the National Institutes of Health in Bethesda, Maryland.

As a board member and one of the first supporters of the National Yiddish Book Center, in Amherst, Massachusetts, Marjorie Guthrie donated her mother's collection of first-edition books in Yiddish to the center. The reading room was dedicated to Aliza Greenblatt's memory. With this commitment, Guthrie reaffirmed her identification with Yiddish culture.

BIBLIOGRAPHY

Cohen, Joan Z., Karen Levin Coburn, and Joan Perlman. *Hitting Our Stride: Good News About Women in Their Middle Years* (1980); Greenblatt, Aliza. *Baym Fenster fun a Lebn* [A window on a life] (1966); Guthrie, Marjorie. Papers. Woody Guthrie Archives, Woody Guthrie Foundation, NYC, and Committee to Combat Huntington's Disease (CCHD) Newsletters, 1967 to 1983. Huntington's Disease Society of America, NYC; Guthrie, Woody. *Pastures of Plenty: A Self-Portrait* (1989); Klein, Joe. *Woody Guthrie: A Life* (1980).

IRMA COMMANDAY

H

HADASSAH

When seven women concluded on February 14, 1912, "that the time is ripe for a large organization of women Zionists" and issued an invitation to interested friends "to attend a meeting for the purpose of discussing the feasibility of forming an organization" to promote Jewish institutions in Palestine and foster Jewish ideals, they scarcely anticipated that their resolve would lead to the creation of American Jews' largest mass-membership organization. Yet Hadassah, the Women's Zionist Organization of America, became not only the most popular American Jewish organization within a short span of years, maintaining that preeminence to this day, but also the most successful American women's volunteer organization, enrolling more women and raising more funds than any other national women's volunteer organization.

From the beginning, ideals found expression in a language of specific tasks whose rationale reflected Hadassah's emerging sense of mission. "You are going to learn by doing," HENRIETTA SZOLD, Hadassah's founder and first president, told a meeting of collegial Zionist women. "It amazed all who knew her," recalled Margaret Doniger, a member of Hadassah's National Board (1925–1977), "that this scholar, this woman who had been an editor up to that time . . . had unusual genius for leadership, for organization." Szold demanded that Hadassah be exclusively a women's organization: "Women will work better when there are only women in the group." She insisted that "the group must . . . not begin until it has a project." Doniger's recollections highlight critical aspects of Hadassah's approach to Zionism and its organizational philosophy.

The first meeting drew over thirty female Zionists to the vestry rooms of New York City's Temple Emanu-El on February 24, 1912. At the meeting's conclusion, almost two-thirds of those in attendance were elected officers or directors, suggesting the leadership opportunities Hadassah would offer women. The women involved included the seven signers of the invitation: Henrietta Szold, at age fifty-two, was the senior leader, deeply committed to Zionism as a political and moral movement of Jewish renewal; MATHILDE SCHECHTER was married to Solomon Schechter, the distinguished scholar, religious thinker, and president of the Jewish Theological Seminary (JTS); EMMA LEON GOTTHEIL traveled in elite Jewish and gentile social circles and was the wife of the Zionist leader Richard Gottheil; ROSALIE SOLOMONS PHILLIPS, a wealthy and respected member of New York City's oldest Sephardic congregation and a descendant of Revolutionary War hero Haym Salomon, participated in various Jewish and gentile societies and was married to N. Taylor Phillips; Sophia Berger led the Harlem Daughters of Zion study group; LOTTA LEVENSOHN, graduate of the Teachers Institute of JTS, worked as secretary to Rabbi Judah Magnes of the New York Kehillah and belonged to one of the three Daughters of Zion study groups that became a nucleus of Hadassah; and Gloria Goldsmith, at age twenty-one the youngest of the seven, had already helped found Young Judaea and enthusiastically supported Zionism as an expression of Jewish idealism.

The cooperation of these seven women indicates how the idea of Hadassah inspired support from a broad spectrum of American Jewish women. Despite differences in age, background, marital status, and wealth, Hadassah's early leaders shared, in addition to their Zionism, strong Jewish educations and an eagerness to act in concert with other women at a time when women could not vote and were denied many of the perquisites of citizenship and independent action.

FORMATIVE YEARS, 1912–1933

Hadassah recruited a leadership cadre from women of Eastern European, German, and Sephardic backgrounds. The older women "gave Hadassah the high prestige of their moral support at a time when Zionism was neither fashionable nor popular, and individual Zionists were often regarded as crackpots," Levensohn recalled. Many of the women, both young and middle-aged, were native-born college-educated American Jews. Their level of formal learning was unusual for women in this period and signified their cultural aspirations. Often mavericks in their social class, Hadassah leaders were attracted to Eastern European Jews not as objects of assimilation or as inferiors needing help but as "real" Jews: practical idealists. The first board of directors reflected the amalgamation of three groups: young women of the Daughters of Zion study circles, older prominent Zionists, and members of ALICE SELIGSBERG's ethics study group.

In its first year, Hadassah adapted aspects of women's public activities to create a flexible Zionist organization. Aspiring to national stature, it modeled its structure on the NATIONAL COUNCIL OF JEWISH WOMEN. Local chapters linked women irrespective of class, marital status, age, or immigrant background. Although an area contained only one chapter, different groups reflected members' particular interests, including study and sewing circles, English- and Yiddish-language groups, and daytime and evening meetings. Hadassah recruited women from varied socioeconomic and ethnic backgrounds, but many were working women—teachers, stenographers, shopgirls, and garment workers.

Seligsberg recalled that "for reasons of economy, we decided to hold parlor meetings only in houses provided with electric current since acetylene needed for lantern pictures would be an extra expense." Lantern pictures conveyed Jewish women's plight in Palestine and their need for adequate maternity care. Hadassah focused on women's health issues, reflecting the social feminism of settlement house work. Especially influential was LILLIAN WALD's Henry Street Settlement Visiting Nurse Service. In January 1913, with 122 members and $542 in dues collected, Hadassah agreed to support a nurse in Palestine for two years. Emma Gottheil's sister, Eva Leon, who had worked with Jerusalem midwives, raised $5,000 from wealthy Chicago non-Zionists for a second nurse. Two weeks later, ROSE KAPLAN and RACHEL [RAE] LANDY sailed for Jerusalem, where they established Hadassah's Nurses Settlement, a first step to "bring order to that land of chaos."

The decision signaled organization growth. After Leon reported that the nurses needed guidance, Hadassah created a Palestine Advisory Committee in New York City to supervise them, setting an important precedent that policy decisions were to be made in America. In 1914, this committee evolved into the Central Committee, later becoming the National Board. By July 1913, Hadassah had chapters in Philadelphia, Boston, Baltimore, and New York. SARAH KUSSY, who founded Hadassah in Newark in 1914, described it as "composed not of swells, nor of the very poorest class of people," but of "women who have regard for the meaning of a dollar." In 1917, when Hadassah had fifty-three sewing circles, fourteen asked for Zionist literature to be read aloud as the women sewed. Of these circles, ten requested English literature and four Yiddish. From the outset, self-education was a central feature of Hadassah's social activities. JESSIE SAMPTER initiated its modest education program in 1913. "A song is not enough," Sampter declared. In the fall of 1914, the Hadassah School of Zionism opened to provide "intellectual substance," to counteract Christian missionaries, and to prepare Hadassah women to speak in public. Hadassah also started *Hadassah Bulletin*. On June 19, 1914, Hadassah held its first national convention in Rochester, New York, where it officially adopted the name Hadassah and its purpose: "to promote Jewish institutions and enterprises in Palestine and to foster Zionist ideals in America." Hadassah had already chosen a motto, suggested by Israel Friedlaender, from Jer. 8: 19–23, *Aruchat Bat Ami*, translated as "The Healing of the Daughter of My People," and a seal, designed by Victor Brenner, of myrtle [*hadas*] branches around a Jewish star. It affiliated with the Federation of American Zionists (FAZ).

Hadassah introduced many innovations to Zionist organization and ideology. Male leaders of FAZ criticized Hadassah, its women's division, for not engaging in Zionist work designed to change Jews into a self-conscious political entity. Hadassah, they claimed, merely did Palestinian work or charitable endeavors meant to improve Jewish living conditions. In fact, Hadassah's decision to establish an urban nurses' settlement ran counter to Zionist emphasis on cooperative rural settlements and European methods of colonization. Hadassah stressed women-to-women work on humanitarian and religious grounds, as well as American social feminism. Hadassah's Zionism was distinctly nonideological, a form of practical idealism that Szold considered characteristically Jewish. "Zionism as we dreamed it in America," Sampter wrote in 1921, "was the dream of a regenerate humanity." Hadassah also avoided religious controversy: The only two holidays it celebrated were Purim and Hanukkah. Hadassah urged its members to express their Jewish identification through work for Palestine. As Hadassah's first president from 1912 to 1921, Szold wanted to mold "a compact, self-reliant organization . . . to foster solidarity, to weld thousands of women scattered all over the country into a homogeneous group." Hadassah actively recruited non-Zionists. It resisted efforts to decentralize and established an administration fund—a novelty in Jewish organizational circles—to cover costs of its central administration.

World War I challenged Hadassah, which had 34 chapters and 2,100 members when the United States entered the war. Turkish repression of Zionist activities in Palestine forced Hadassah to close its Nurses Settlement in 1915. At home, domestic politics strained Hadassah's unity. Many leaders, including Szold, Seligsberg, Levensohn, Sampter, Nellie Straus, and GERTRUDE GOLDSMITH ROSENBLATT (who married the Zionist activist Bernard Rosenblatt), identified themselves as progressives and advocated socialism, racial equality, and, most important, pacifism. Other leaders, including Gottheil, Berger, and RUTH BERNARD FROMENSON, ardently supported the Allies. At a protracted meeting on the issues in October 1917, Szold agreed to resign from the antiwar People's Council for Peace and Democracy for the sake of Hadassah. JUDITH EPSTEIN, whose mother was part of the group that organized Hadassah, remembered that controversial meeting: "I returned to my new home at one A.M. to find that my husband had called the police!" The Gottheil faction withdrew from Hadassah in 1921, although both groups worked together to raise the thousands of dollars required to fund the American Zionist Medical Unit (AZMU), consisting of forty-five physicians, dentists, and nurses, as well as tons of supplies.

This is the first American Zionist Medical Unit on the eve of its departure for Palestine.
In the front row are members of the Central Committee of Hadassah, from right to left: HENRIETTA SZOLD,
ALICE L. SELIGSBERG, *Dora Lefkowitz (Dorothy Leffert),* RUTH FROMENSON, EMMA GOTTHEIL,
Bertha Weinheim, Ida Danziger, and Libby Oppenheimer. The two top rows are the nurses. [Hadassah Archives]

Seligsberg headed AZMU, which arrived in Palestine in 1918 and established hospitals in six cities: Jerusalem, Haifa, Jaffa, Tiberias, Tel Aviv, and Safed. The hospitals followed Hadassah's policy of providing services to all regardless of race, color, or creed. This reflected the progressive commitments of Hadassah's leaders and set an important precedent, initially established by the Nurses Settlement, of treating equally Arabs and Jews. "What we have sent to Palestine," Hadassah reported, "is not a relief expedition, but rather an embryonic Department of Health, the nucleus of a permanent institution." As soon as municipal authorities were prepared to run the hospitals, Hadassah turned them over. Hadassah rejected Zionist policy of creating institutions only for Jews in Palestine and refused to join the *yishuv*'s political structure.

In 1918, Hadassah joined the restructured Zionist Organization of America (ZOA), despite doubts about its district plan of organization. During the war, Hadassah had moved into separate office space—thus removing its administration from its leaders' homes—and cooperated with Zionist men in organizing AZMU. Yet Hadassah soon discovered its loss of autonomy. As part of the ZOA, it surrendered its practical program and authority, two key elements of its organizational identity. Nevertheless, its membership kept on increasing—by 1922 Hadassah had over twelve thousand enrolled—while the membership of ZOA declined. In 1920, after seven members of Hadassah's Central Committee were expelled from the building and told they had to resign because the committee refused to raise money for the Zionist fund Keren Hayesod, Hadassah began to reassert its autonomy. It started the *Hadassah Newsletter* nineteen months after it had discontinued the *Bulletin*. ROSE GELL JACOBS, a charter member of Hadassah, became editor. The Central Committee also authorized the creation of Junior Hadassah, for girls eighteen and older, despite competition with Young Judaea, the Zionist youth movement. The young women immediately adopted the care of war orphans, a project started by AZMU that lacked adequate funds. Szold suggested their motto: "A joyful mother of children."

The Drop of Milk [Tipat Halav] station was set up by Hadassah nurse Bertha Landsman in 1921 to provide pasteurized milk to parents. The program was such a success that she established the Donkey Milk Express to deliver bottles, each labeled with a baby's name and packed in ice. Notice that the sign on the container is in both Hebrew and English. [Hadassah Archives]

Zip Falk Szold, a Bryn Mawr graduate and wife of HENRIETTA SZOLD's *cousin, Robert, became the fourth president of Hadassah in 1928. She loved keeping tabs on Hadassah's growth and activities throughout the country. By 1928, membership had reached thirty-seven thousand. [Hadassah Archives]*

In 1920, Hadassah's Central Committee created Junior Hadassah, for younger women.
They immediately created a project to care for war orphans.
HENRIETTA SZOLD *suggested their motto: "A joyful mother of children."*
A group of Junior Hadassah members is shown here helping Szold celebrate her seventieth birthday
in New York City in 1930. [Hadassah Archives]

By 1923, Junior Hadassah had its own leaders. Frieda Silbert of Boston served as its first chair, and Mignon Levin Rubenovitz, a graduate of Columbia University's Teachers College and early Hadassah member, was senior adviser.

By 1921, Hadassah began its steady rise to prominence. Seligsberg, who had returned from two years in Palestine, was elected president as Szold departed for Palestine. Although she returned and served again as president for three years beginning in mid-1923, Szold effectively passed on the leadership to younger women. By mid-1926, when Hadassah almost achieved autonomy in its program, IRMA LEVY LINDHEIM became president. Under her leadership, Hadassah initiated its first partnership with the Jewish National Fund. When Lindheim could not continue in a second term because of family problems, Zip Falk Szold, a Bryn Mawr graduate and wife of Henrietta Szold's cousin Robert Szold, accepted the position in 1928. The presidency was "mostly hard, hard work. It was

something that I could not put down." She had loved being organization chair, keeping tabs on Hadassah's growth and activities throughout the country. Growth registered in numbers—by 1928 membership reached a peak of over thirty-seven thousand—while activities demonstrated a commitment for practical work in Palestine, infused with Zionist idealism. Each project's specificity enabled members to identify with the individual undertakings. These included the Hadassah School of Nursing (1919), an urban recreation program (1928), a school lunch program (1923), as well as health and day care centers and a children's village. Each project reflected and reinforced Hadassah's initial social feminism. As Seligsberg explained about the nursing school: "The idea was (1) as soon as possible to turn over the work of nursing to the people of Palestine so that the supply of nurses would be indigenous and normal; (2) to give useful work to the unemployed; (3) to educate the young Jewish girls of Palestine and their parents to respect women's

*Although most of Hadassah's activities were, in the words of Zip Szold, "hard work,"
this photograph from the 1927 convention in Atlantic City shows that the members weren't above having fun.
[Hadassah Archives]*

work. . . ." Many Jewish parents considered nursing an immodest profession, inappropriate for women.

Patterns established during the formative years were subsequently strengthened and reinforced. Hadassah maintained its social feminism, Progressive political commitments, and understanding of Zionism as a movement to renew Jewish practical idealism. It also remained staunchly protective of its autonomy, its focus on specific projects helping women and children, and its openness to women of all backgrounds. Its leaders continued to include an elite of educated women, who drew young women into their ranks. The latter testified to the formative influence of Szold and Epstein. Hadassah fostered close personal ties with the land of Israel, and many early leaders spent years living in Palestine, while a significant number of Hadassah's presidents settled there.

CONSOLIDATION AND GROWTH, 1933–1953

Only in 1933 did Hadassah achieve complete independence from the ZOA, although it remained affiliated with the World Zionist Organization (WZO). Hadassah's organizational, political, and ide-

ological autonomy allowed it to chart its own distinctive course as a women's organization, to consolidate its achievements, to initiate new projects, and to expand its membership.

Hadassah entered the family lives of many American Jewish women: Its leaders often were daughters of mothers who had been Hadassah activists. These mothers transmitted a love of Zionism and Palestine to their daughters who, if they were lucky, actually visited the land of Israel as did MIRIAM FREUND-ROSENTHAL in 1935 and SARA NACHAMSON EVANS in 1933. The eldest of eight daughters, Evans accompanied her mother, Jennie Nachamson, who founded Hadassah in North Carolina in 1919 after an inspiring meeting with Szold in Baltimore. Evans subsequently organized for Hadassah throughout the South in the 1940s and 1950s, gaining a reputation as Hadassah's "Southern accent." All eight Nachamson daughters served as presidents of local chapters.

Such family connections contributed to Hadassah's impressive growth. From 1935 to 1945, Hadassah's membership increased from over 38,000 to over 142,000, and in 1952 Hadassah reached a new peak of almost 275,000 members. The pace did not slacken until 1953. Critical to its broad appeal was the increase in the numbers of native-born American Jews who found its brand of American Zionism compelling, as well as Hadassah's decision to adopt Youth Aliyah in 1934. "One of the most effective movements in human rehabilitation to emerge from an era of unprecedented cruelty and destruction" in ETTA ROSENSOHN's opinion, Youth Aliyah was perhaps Hadassah's most popular practical project.

TAMAR DE SOLA POOL, Hadassah's president from 1939 to 1943, recalled suggesting the idea to the National Board in 1934 when she was president of the New York chapter. Jacobs, then in her second term as Hadassah's president (1934–1937), went to Palestine to investigate the nascent program of Youth Aliyah initiated by Recha Freier from Berlin, in response to Adolf Hitler's rise to power. The choice lay between Youth Aliyah or vocational education. "Jacobs, the pragmatist and superb organizer, came back with a contract, making Hadassah sole representative of Youth Aliyah in America and guaranteeing a contribu-

tion of sixty thousand a year." In fact, Hadassah raised $125,000 in the first year under Marian Greenberg's chairmanship. In 1933, however, Hadassah's total collections had plummeted to $161,697 from $365,000 in 1932, and only $45,860 was collected in 1934 for Youth Aliyah.

Szold agreed to direct the program of rescuing young people from Germany and bringing them to Palestine to settle on kibbutzim and in youth villages. Taking young people from their parents, who it was hoped would follow them to Palestine, Hadassah became their foster parents, nurturing and educating them. Szold dedicated the last twelve years of her life to Youth Aliyah and definitively shaped it into an educational movement and national organization of rescue. Hadassah's practical idealism put it in the forefront of American Jewish organizations: It began to rescue Jews from Nazism before any other Zionist group by choosing a project that continued its social feminist orientation as a women's organization. By 1967, every tenth Israeli under fifty was a Youth Aliyah graduate.

HENRIETTA SZOLD, *the first director of Youth Aliyah, greets the first arrivals from Nazi Europe in 1934. These teenagers were from middle-class German homes and had prepared for aliyah through a pioneer program.* [Hadassah Archives]

Jacobs not only secured Hadassah's sponsorship of Youth Aliyah but also initiated construction of the Rothshild-Hadassah Hospital on Mount Scopus in Jerusalem, designed by architect Eric Mendelsohn. ROSE HALPRIN, who settled in Palestine after finishing her first term as Hadassah president (1932–1934), served on the building committee. "Sometimes, we were penny-wise and pound-foolish," she recalled. "I remember we had to decide whether to put an insignia on the floor in marble." The cost was perhaps $250, but "the vote was against it because it was too much money. Now I always giggle every time I think back on that period." Yet a beautiful hospital emerged, opening in 1939. In 1936, Hadassah and the Hebrew University, also located on Mount Scopus, agreed to establish a joint graduate school of medicine, inaugurated in 1938. World War II transformed the new hospital into a medical center for the entire region. In 1942, Hadassah opened its vocational school for girls, named in honor of Alice Seligsberg.

Despite its focus on Palestine projects, Hadassah also experimented with new ways to foster Zionist ideals in America. In 1934, it continued its early work in adult education by sponsoring the School for the Jewish Woman under the direction of TRUDE WEISS-ROSMARIN. The school conducted afternoon and evening classes for married and single women: Its curriculum included Hebrew, Bible, Talmud, Jewish history, and ethics. But turbulent relations between Hadassah and the school's strong-willed director soon led to the school's dissolution. Hadassah also helped establish the American Zionist Youth Commission in 1940, directed by Shlomo Bardin. The programs of leadership training it sponsored proved quite successful both for Young Judaea and Junior Hadassah, and paved the way for Hadassah supervision of the former. The Speaker's Bureau, which had initially enlisted the aid of Miss Manners, became well established and helped spread Hadassah's message throughout the country. It continued to provide lessons in public speaking for women, so critical to their assumption of leadership positions within Hadassah. The *Newsletter* changed its format to include articles on contemporary issues by well-known public figures. In America, Hadassah leaders often cooperated with individuals associated with the newly established Reconstructionist Movement. Both shared a common attachment to American democratic progressive traditions as well as a deep dedication to Zionism as an international Jewish movement of renewal.

Hadassah forged an independent political path in the Zionist movement. In 1937, it ran its own slate of eighteen delegates to the WZO Congress. It supported the Biltmore Platform of 1942 calling for a Jewish state, even though it had abstained from the prewar debate on the partition of Palestine. Epstein, president of Hadassah for a second term (1943–1947) during the years immediately preceding the establishment of a state, later articulated Hadassah's expectation: "We wanted a Jewish state and a Jewish society. And it was self-evident among Hadassah members that Jewish society would be constituted on the elements of equality, justice, and humanism." Representing Hadassah, Epstein testified before the Anglo-American Board of Inquiry in 1946 to get the British to open Palestine to Jewish refugees. Halprin, whose second term as president (1947–1952) followed Epstein's, explicitly rejected any glorification of the State of Israel: "The State is merely a vessel. It is not a purpose in itself. A State is a means to an end. The end is the content of the state."

Hadassah worked actively on the American political scene to support the establishment of a Jewish state. Women spread the word in their local communities in favor of partition. The personal cost of founding the State of Israel hit Hadassah on April 13, 1948. That night, Arabs ambushed and murdered seventy-five nurses, physicians, and technicians, including Dr. Hayim Yassky, head of the Hadassah Medical Organization, in a convoy on its way to Mount Scopus. Faced with the inability to protect its staff, Hadassah evacuated the medical center it had worked so hard to build, leaving it under Israeli army guard. In 1952, during Rosensohn's presidency, Hadassah broke ground at Ein Kerem to build for the second time a medical center in Jerusalem.

Hadassah's efforts to recruit new members after the establishment of Israel on May 14, 1948, emphasized the relationship of Zionist ideals and American democratic values. "Ever greater numbers of Jewish women should be drawn into Hadassah where they have the opportunity to work on two fronts: as Zionists, for the welfare of the Jewish people in Israel, and as Americans, for a democratic America and a democratic world to help bring peace and security to peoples everywhere." New chapters organized that year reflected the suburbanization of American Jews. Hadassah appeared on Long Island from Levittown to Hollis Hills, in New Jersey from Princeton to Deal, and in Maryland from Silver Spring to Chevy Chase. Irene Ruza joined Young Judaea, but instead of going to Palestine as a pioneer, she went to HUNTER COLLEGE in New York and married. "When I joined the great 'exodus' to Queens suburbia, Hadassah found me—to my eternal gratitude." Ruza gradually moved up from president of the Hollis Hills Chapter to the National Board.

Hadassah effectively negotiated the transition from a "small, compact organization" to a large, national one during years of world war and the destruction of European Jews. It adapted its Zionist practical idealism to the political reality of the State of Israel by becoming one of the founding constituents of the World Confederation of General Zionists. Hadassah has a seat on the executive of the Jewish Agency for Israel and the Zionist General Council. It is also accredited with the United Nations as a nongovernmental organization. Hadassah integrated its democratic American commitments into its social feminism.

MASS-MEMBERSHIP ORGANIZATION, 1953–1976

"Those were the days when if you sat next to a woman, your first question was, 'Are you a member of Hadassah?' If the answer was 'No,' you signed her up on the spot," Rose Dorfman recalled of the 1950s. Hadassah membership drives reached all sections of the country, all states in the union. Young women, mostly married with children and barred from working outside the home by strong social conventions, joined Hadassah for its sociability, its idealism, and the opportunities it offered to learn and to acquire new skills, including those of leadership. As in previous decades, Hadassah recruited women from varied backgrounds. "When I came to the United States thirty and some years ago, Hadassah became my ticket to the New World," Sara Rosen recalled. "In a way, I received an introduction to the idea of women's lib many years before it became a household word. . . . I never imagined, nor had I ever seen, so many independent, accomplished women working together for a cause that did not in any way benefit them personally," she marveled. "Physically remote from the land of Israel, oftentimes removed from Jewish tradition by generations, they nevertheless basked in their Jewishness, and were eager to learn. Hadassah was the '*shaliakh*,' the messenger, which inspired them." The constant recruitment offset normal attrition: Only after the Six Day War of 1967 did membership increase steadily to a new high of 360,000 by 1977.

A successful mass-membership organization, Hadassah's presence registered forcefully on the American scene. Its decision to upgrade its monthly *Newletter* into *Hadassah Magazine* made visible its substantial achievements. Because of its wide circulation to all members, the *Magazine* quickly became self-supporting through advertising. Hadassah continued to sponsor publications to further educate its members. Among its most notable were two anthologies that became classics: *The American Jew: A Composite Portrait* (1942), edited by Oscar I. Janowsky, and *Great Ages and Ideas of the Jewish People* (1956), edited by Leo W. Schwarz. When the Conference of Presidents of Major American Organizations was organized in 1956, Hadassah became a constituent member. In 1970, Hadassah was a founding member of the reorganized American Zionist Federation. In 1967, when the ZOA withdrew financial support from Young Judaea, Hadassah merged Junior Hadassah with Young Judaea into Ha-Shahar [The dawn] and restructured the summer camp activities, leadership training, and study scholarships in Israel that it had sponsored since 1940. As well, Hadassah assumed financial responsibility for all youth programs. "Unfortunately, the merger basically destroyed Junior Hadassah," Barbara Goldstein concluded, and with it "a movement that identified with and loved its parent, Hadassah. Our National Board officers used as their role models National Presidents of Hadassah. I am no exception." The issue of an aging membership would not be felt, however, until the 1980s.

Although Hadassah continued to turn over many of its health centers and programs to municipalities or the Israeli government, it also initiated new projects in both health and education, such as a model family and community health program in a poor Jerusalem neighborhood, Kiryat ha-Yovel, in 1953 and the Rural Vocational Guidance Center at K'far Vitkin in 1952. The latter offered education and training for Arab as well as Jewish youth, maintaining Hadassah's well-established policy of providing equal treatment. In 1968, Hadassah designated the nonmedical aspects of its Israel program as "Hadassah-Israel Education Services."

Perhaps Hadassah's biggest postwar achievement was the rapid construction of the Hadassah Medical Center in Ein Kerem. In cooperation with the Hebrew University, Hadassah established a teaching and research hospital with over fifteen medical departments, as well as a school of dentistry and pharmacy. Freund-Rosenthal dedicated the new buildings in 1960, the last year of her presidency. She also convinced the famous Jewish artist, Marc Chagall, to design twelve stained-glass windows for the hospital's chapel at a modest cost of $100,000 by making her request "not only on behalf of Hadassah, but on behalf of the Jewish people." The windows received widespread critical acclaim. Then, in 1967, Israel's stunning victory in the Six Day War reunited the divided city of Jerusalem, and Hadassah discovered itself once more in possession of its hospital on Mount Scopus. "For Hadassah—rejoicing in the greatest gift in 19 years—the return of our buildings on Mt. Scopus is tempered by the knowledge that the ground on which we shall build is soaked with the blood of precious youth," Charlotte Jacobson wrote in her president's column that year. In 1975, Hadassah rededicated its restored and rebuilt hospital on Mt. Scopus.

In 1968, Hadassah subscribed to the Jerusalem Platform of the World Zionist Congress, including the unity of the Jewish people and centrality of Israel, the ingathering of Jews in their historic homeland, strengthening the State of Israel, preserving Jewish identity through education, and protection of Jewish rights everywhere. Hadassah previously had joined the struggle to free Soviet Jewry, and many of its presidents had made aliyah to Israel. In 1969, it sent the first group aliyah, graduates of Young Judaea, to settle in Neve Ilan near Jerusalem. Four years later, on Thanksgiving Day, graduates of Ha-Shahar founded Kibbutz Ketura in the Arava Valley.

Hadassah continued to draw women from diverse backgrounds into its top ranks of leadership. Lola Kramarsky, president from 1960 to 1964, left Holland with her husband and three children just before the Nazis invaded. FAYE SCHENK, president from 1968 to 1972, was the daughter of an Orthodox rabbi. She married a rabbi and spent ten years in Australia before returning to the United States. Rose Matzkin, president from 1972 to 1976, was born on Ellis Island, the day her mother arrived in the United States. She joined Hadassah immediately after she married. Like many Hadassah leaders, she also joined other organizations, like the League of Women Voters and the Red Cross. "For those of us who came to maturity—real maturity—during the years of the Holocaust, the opportunity to try to do something for Jews outweighed almost everything else. . . ." Hadassah offered that opportunity. Others, like Rebecca Shulman,

SARA N. EVANS (*shown here on the far right, with her siblings in 1957) is one of many Hadassah leaders who received their love of Zionism from their mothers, the "first generation" of Hadassah activists. Her mother, Jennie Nachamson, founded Hadassah in North Carolina in 1919 after an inspiring meeting with* HENRIETTA SZOLD *in Baltimore. Evans and all seven of her sisters served as presidents of local Hadassah chapters throughout the South.* [Eli N. Evans]

Rebecca Shulman spent a lifetime building Hadassah and nurturing the creation of the State of Israel.
She is shown here at the groundbreaking for the Hadassah Medical Center at Ein Kerem, Israel, in 1952.
[Hadassah Archives]

president from 1953 to 1956, grew up in a Zionist family and continued the Zionist tradition through Hadassah. The tradition of leadership, social feminism, and Zionism, passed on from mothers to daughters, carried Hadassah to new heights during the 1970s, making it the preeminent American Jewish women's organization.

THE CHALLENGE OF CONTEMPORARY FEMINISM, 1976–PRESENT

In 1980, Hadassah commissioned a survey, sensing that its blend of Zionism, social feminism, and practical idealism was not reaching a new generation of Jewish women eager to pursue careers and unwilling to join an organization identified with their mothers and grandmothers. The survey revealed the gradual graying of Hadassah members, a decline in the percent of younger members who considered themselves Zionists, a wide diversity of religious affiliation, and increasing levels of education among younger members. Hadassah remained predominantly an organization of married women, attracting only a minority of single or divorced women. Half of the women polled who worked full time had never been members of Hadassah. Feminist feelings were widespread among all women surveyed, while Zionist sentiment was not.

The survey did not document that, along with its success, Hadassah had acquired a host of negative stereotypes. "Hadassah ladies" appeared to young feminists to be the antithesis of the new Jewish woman they hoped to create through the feminist movement and Jewish feminism. New magazines like *LILITH* challenged Hadassah's priorities, the character of its meetings, even its existence as a women's organization that seemed to acquiesce in separate and

The largest women's organization in the country, Hadassah continues to thrive, building on its past success.
Pictured above is the executive committee in February 1997.
Seated, left to right: Maureen Schulman, vice-president; June Walker, vice-president;
Bernice Tannenbaum, honorary vice-president; Marlene Post, president; Charlotte Jacobson, honorary vice-president;
Sue Mizrahi, secretary; Annette Meskin, recording secretary; Judith Saxe, vice-president.
Standing, left to right: Renee Albert, Karen Venezky, Marcie Natan, Bonnie Lipton, Jane Zolot, Mona Wood, Helene Karpa,
Belle Simon, Beth Wohlgelernter (executive director), Joyce Rabin, Ruth B. Hurwitz. [Jennifer Weisbrod]

unequal representation of women in American Jewish communal life. Hadassah's historic role mattered less to these critics than its current agenda. In fact, Hadassah admitted men as associate members in 1966, and men always attended national conventions, albeit as observers (and often critics). But Hadassah's feminism never involved a critique of patriarchy, though it supported the Equal Rights Amendment. Hadassah responded to contemporary feminism by increasing its identification with Israel, becoming active in international women's conferences, and initiating a new series of educational programs.

In 1978, Hadassah held its first national convention in Israel, letting Israelis glimpse the women behind the health institutions. Hadassah had started tours to Israel in the 1960s, including some that focused on the Bible, but these drew small numbers. The Jerusalem convention attracted a record 2,800 members from 45 states. In the 1980s, Hadassah also began to organize throughout the world under the auspices of the Hadassah Medical Organization because the Women's International Zionist Organization (WIZO) broke an unwritten agreement made with Szold that America would be the exclusive province of Hadassah. When WIZO began to organize in the United States, Hadassah created the Hadassah Medical Relief Association, later Hadassah International, in 1983. Hadassah in Israel, made up of former members who had settled there, became its first incorporated chapter. Bernice S. Tannenbaum, president from 1976 to 1980, instigated these initiatives.

When Carmela Efros Kalmanson became Hadassah's nineteenth president in 1988, she recalled: "The first plank in my platform involved returning to the basics that launched us as a distinct movement in the Zionist dream. Hadassah was founded as a study group. . . . I wanted to see us studying together again." In 1989, Hadassah published *Jewish Marital Status*, its first step in programming to reach unaffiliated families. "More than an educational tool, it was to serve as a catalyst for informed action," reported Carol Diament, Hadassah's director of National Jewish Education. Over sixty seminars on Jewish family issues were conducted throughout the United States. In 1991, Hadassah held a three-day symposium devoted to "Israeli and American Jews: Understanding and Misunderstanding." The event, and subsequent one-day symposia on university campuses, involved collaboration with scholars and activists, including feminist women who previously had rejected Hadassah.

Such initiatives did not stop the aging of Hadassah's membership, but they did reflect creative engagement with issues important to Jewish women at the close of the twentieth century, as well as continuity with Hadassah's own history. Innovations accompanied regular Hadassah programs of medical research and care, Youth Aliyah, education, and reclamation of the land through cooperation with the Jewish National Fund. In 1991, Deborah Kaplan assumed the presidency of Hadassah's 385,000 members who raised $74,432,000 that year. The seven signers of that first invitation eighty years earlier would have been impressed. With a dedication to practical idealism, they built a large organization of women Zionists.

National Hadassah Presidents 1912–1997: Henrietta Szold 1912–1920, 1923–1926; Alice L. Seligsberg 1921–1923; Irma Lindheim 1926–1928; Zip Szold 1928–1930; Rose Jacobs 1930–1932, 1934–1937; Rose L. Halprin 1932–1934, 1947–1952; Judith Epstein 1937–1939, 1943–1947; Tamar de Sola Pool 1939–1943; Etta Rosensohn 1952–1953; Rebecca Shulman 1953–1956; Miriam Freund-Rosenthal 1956–1960; Lola Kramarsky 1960–1964; Charlotte Jacobson 1964–1968; Faye L. Schenk 1968–1972, Rose E. Matzkin 1972–1976; Bernice S. Tannenbaum 1976–1980; Frieda S. Lewis 1980–1984; Ruth W. Popkin 1984–1988; Carmela E. Kalmanson 1988–1991; Deborah B. Kaplan 1991–1995; Marlene Post, 1996–.

BIBLIOGRAPHY

Evans, Eli. *The Lonely Days Were Sundays: Reflections of a Jewish Southerner* (1993); Freund-Rosenthal, Miriam, ed. *A Tapestry of Hadassah Memories* (1994); Gal, Allon. "Hadassah and the American Jewish Political Tradition." In *An Inventory of Promises: Essays in Honor of Moses Rischin*, edited by Jeffrey S. Gurock and Marc Lee Raphael (1995); Hadassah. Archives, NYC; *Hadassah Annual Report* (1929–1930, 1947–1948, 1966–1967); Kutscher, Carol Bosworth. "The Early Years of Hadassah: 1912–1921." Ph.D. diss., Brandeis University (1976); Levin, Marlin. *Balm in Gilead: The Story of Hadassah* (1973); Miller, Donald H. "A History of Hadassah 1912–1935." Ph.D. diss., New York University (1968); Weisburgh, Aileen. Hadassah chronology (October 1993).

DEBORAH DASH MOORE

HADASSAH (SPIRA EPSTEIN)
(1909–1992)

"One of the finest artist gifts to come out of Israel is Hadassah," proclaimed the Dance Congress of 1953. Hadassah was a major dance artist of the twentieth century, a dance innovator, a performer of Jewish, Hindu, and other ethnic dance forms, a leading force in presenting the dance of other cultures to the American public, a pioneer in bringing Jewish dance to the United States, and a developer of a method for greater cultural understanding.

Hadassah was descended from a long line of rabbis on both her maternal and paternal sides and was granddaughter of Rabbi Landau, a founder of a famous school of mysticism in Jerusalem. The eldest child of Rabbi Isaac Spira and Menuha (Mina) Landau, Hadassah was born on December 30, 1909, in

Jerusalem. Her siblings were Simon, Israel, Harriet, and Abraham. Palestine was then under Turkish rule, and this prominent family was forced into exile when Hadassah was nine. For two years the family moved from place to place, including stays in Vienna and Constantinople, suffering malnutrition and poor living conditions. Throughout her career, Hadassah danced in pain from physical disabilities incurred from these deficiencies. Nevertheless, these experiences provided Hadassah contact with many diverse cultures.

Hadassah immigrated to the United States with her family in 1924. On October 28, 1933, in New York, Hadassah married Milton Epstein, a painter who also owned a scholarly bookstore. She studied and performed with the renowned pioneer and first lady of modern dance, Ruth St. Denis, and with Jack Cole, famous dancer of early Hollywood cinema—both of whom had been attracted to the dance of India. In her autobiography, St. Denis wrote, "Of those who composed that first little choir, Hadassah springs first to mind. A fine sensitive soul. . . ." Simultaneously, she studied with Mme. LaMeri, founder of the Ethnologic Dance Center in New York, and Nala Najan, a master of the Tanjore Temple style and the leading Hindu dance scholar in the United States. She studied Javanese dance under Radem Mas Kodrat and Radem Mas Wiradat, learning the court dances of Soerakarta, and was the only recipient of a Teacher's Diploma granted an American. Her name first appeared in the New York newspapers as a member of the Kenji Hinoke Japanese Dance Company. She used her given name, Hadassah, as her stage name.

Hadassah's art was deeply rooted in her spiritual beliefs. Her dance was a spiritual expression, not a secular form. She became famous as a Hindu dancer, her affinity with this dance form stemming from her lifelong belief that if the Hebraic chants and cantillations resemble the Hindu chants, then the ancient Hebrew dances, had they been preserved, would have resembled the Indian dances. ". . . on my trip to India, I met the great Sanskrit scholar, Professor Raghavan of the University of Madras, who told me that the Vedic chant and the Hebrew chanting he had heard sound very similar."

Through her interest in traditional dances, Hadassah made a unique contribution to the understanding of other cultures. She observed at age ten that people in deep religious devotion had similar facial expressions. "How could I forget my grandfather's face dancing with the torah in his arms. How his white beard and the torah seemed like a pillar of fire and the ecstasy on his face! When I saw other exotic dancers from other races,

*Her search for the ancient Hebrew dances led Hadassah to India,
where she became a foremost interpreter of traditional Hindu dances.
She was brilliantly innovative, melding folk and modern forms with compassion, humor,
and a sense of spiritual universality. [High Frequency Wavelengths, Inc.]*

colors and beliefs, that ecstatic expression was always similar." She approached the study of ethnic dance by first studying the culture as a whole, the need for the human spirit to honor its creator. She believed this motivation was universal. Thus, all cultures' traditions can be seen as having a common base.

Hadassah created an innovative dance form that is best exemplified by her signature work, *Shuvi Nafshi* (1947), based on an excerpt from Psalm 116, "Return, O my soul." She put gestures common to different cultures in her dances, as well as repeated her message with culturally specific gestures so that the common meaning was given in each cultural dance language. In addition, she went beyond traditional form by fusing it with modern dance and using traditional movements, not only with their literal meaning but also as metaphor.

In 1962, for the Centennial Celebration of Rabindranath Tagore, India's Nobel laureate, Hadassah choreographed the *Tagore Suite* to Tagore's poetry, narrated by Saeed Jaffrey, Broadway and Hollywood Indian actor. She was commissioned by the Tagore Centenary Committee, of which Prime Minister Nehru was honorary chairman.

Hadassah, like Tagore, believed in universal brotherhood of man. In memory of Gandhi, she choreographed *Chant* (1964) to Gandhi's favorite song, a song of love for all people. In the same vein, she choreographed *I Have a Dream* (1969), a dance/theater work depicting the life and message of Gandhi and their influence on Dr. Martin Luther King, Jr., created in honor of the Gandhi Centenary Celebration.

Hadassah's dances were not all spiritually motivated. Her personality was a magnificent blend of warmth, compassion, gentleness, and a tremendous sense of humor. Witnessing Hindu dance popularized in nightclubs to jazz music, Hadassah responded, "In a moment when my sense of humor took the best of me, I made a satire," *Broadway Hindu* (1949), which became a classic. She also choreographed and performed in traditional dance forms of Java, Bali, and Korea. John Martin, dance critic for the *New York Times*, credited Hadassah as an "exceptionally gifted artist . . . one of the best!"

Hadassah debuted her own choreography at Times Hall on January 11, 1945, sharing the bill with her lifelong friend Pearl Primus, already established as a dynamic dancer combining African dance and modern dance, and Josephine Premice, a Haitian singer. Hadassah soon danced on the stages of Carnegie Hall, the Ziegfeld Theatre, the Brooklyn Academy of Music, many Broadway theaters, every major dance series in New York, the Habibi nightclub, and Jacob's Pillow in New England. Previously a solo artist, Hadassah created her own company in 1950, debuting at the YM-YWHA (92nd Street Y) in New York.

Hadassah was recipient of a Rockefeller Brothers Fund grant award to further her knowledge of Indian classical dance and to research the Bene Israel Jews and the Cochin Jews who have lived in India for more than three thousand years. She toured Israel and India in 1959–1960 to sold-out houses. She was recognized in India for her remarkable artistry and her rare ability, as a foreigner, to perform classical Indian dance.

Many, including the famous Inbal Theatre, sought to have Hadassah remain in Israel as their teacher. Noted in the United States as a master teacher, Hadassah was faculty member, board member, and chair of the Ethnic Division of the New Dance Group, the largest school of dance in New York. She taught in many other venues, including Dance Masters of America, the Dance Congress, Pennsylvania Association of Dance Teachers, Columbia University Teachers College, Jacob's Pillow, Henry Street Playhouse, many Jewish Community Centers, and the Menorah Home for the Aged.

She died on November 18, 1992, in New York.

BIBLIOGRAPHY

Chujoy, Anatole, and P.W. Manchester, eds. *The Dance Encyclopedia* (1967); Hadassah. "Dance Themes of Hassidism and Hinduism." *Dance Observer* (March 1963): 37–39; Hering, Doris, ed. *Twenty-Five Years of American Dance* (1954); Lahm, Adam. "Hadassah, A Career Kissed by the Gods." *Arabesque* 9, no. 3 (September–October 1983): 6+; Lloyd, Margaret. *The Borzoi Book of Modern Dance* (1949); Martin, John. "The Dance: Award." *NYTimes*, March 7, 1954; *The Dance: The Story of the Dance Told in Pictures and Text* (1946); Najan, Nala. "Encounters with Dance Immortals." *Arabesque* 9, no. 4 (November–December 1983); Sorell, Walter. "Dance and Israel." In *The Hebrew Impact on Western Civilization*, edited by Dagobert D. Runes (1951).

MARILYNN DANITZ

HAGY, RUTH GERI *see* BROD, RUTH HAGY

HALPERIN, NAN (1898–1963)

Nan Halperin rose to fame as a star of the vaudeville stage. Her comedic musical numbers and her ability to change quickly into many elaborate costumes during a single act earned her the appellation "The Wonder Girl."

Nan Halperin was born in Odessa, Russia, in 1898 and moved to the United States in 1900. She was the daughter of Samuel Halperin, a confectioner, and Rebeka Rose Halperin. She had two brothers—Hal Halperin, manager of the Chicago office of *Variety*, and Max Halperin, a Chicago agent—and two sisters—Sophie Halperin, who sometimes accompanied Nan on her tours, and Clara Halperin.

Halperin grew up in Minneapolis and began her stage career during summer vacations. Her first acting part was at age six in *Little Black Me*. As a child she also appeared in local productions as Little Lord Fauntleroy, as Sir Joseph Porter in *HMS Pinafore*, and in the starring role in *Alice in Wonderland*. Following her graduation from Holy Angels Academy, a Catholic school in Minneapolis, Halperin performed in stock companies throughout the western United States and Mexico. Her most notable performance was in the vaudeville number "Nan Halperin and her Suffragettes."

Halperin first appeared on Broadway with Emma Carus in *A Broadway Honeymoon*. Between 1914 and 1915, she gained increasing attention as a vaudeville star. Her big break came in early 1915 when she headlined at New York's Palace Theatre. Halperin credited her fame to her talents as an actor and to her business acumen. "Many really talented performers do not get ahead because they do not know how to push themselves ahead," explained Halperin in a 1915 magazine interview. "On the other hand," she added, "too much temperament means too little business opportunity."

Coinciding with Halperin's vaudeville success in 1915 and 1916, newspapers publicized the story that her family was less persecuted than other Russian

A big-time vaudeville star sometimes called "The Wonder Girl," Nan Halperin was famous for her humorous song cycles, during which she would delight her audiences with quick, elaborate costume changes. [New York Public Library]

Jews. Her grandfather was a baron and member of the czar's court who gained his title because a relative had offered money to aid the Russian emperor during a war. The veracity of this story is uncertain. Its circulation was possibly a publicity stunt to heighten the allure of Halperin, then a rising celebrity.

Among the most famous of Halperin's musical numbers were her two burlesque "song cycles." The first of these, which she began to perform in 1916, depicted five stages of girlhood. Halperin would grow before her audience from the youngest child in a family to a mischievous high school valedictorian, a comical bridesmaid at a friend's wedding, a bride and, finally, a "blasé divorcée." In her second song cycle, originally performed in 1919, Halperin played an amusing young girl who becomes an indignant debutante and complains that her parents force her to wear "too many swell clothes . . . all to catch just one lone man."

In 1916, Halperin became the first performer to secure a three-year contract with the United Booking

Offices, the central agency of B.F. Keith and E.F. Albee's vaudeville monopoly. By 1919, at age twenty-one, she commanded a salary on a par with vaudeville's highest-paid female performers. This secured her place in what was then called vaudeville's "Big Time." That same year, Halperin also acted in productions outside of vaudeville: She was the female lead in the musical comedy *The Frivolities of 1919*, and she starred in the drama *The Girl in the Stage Box*.

Other notable shows in which Halperin appeared were *Make it Snappy* (1917) and the musical *Little Jesse James* (1923). Halperin continued her acting career into the 1930s. In 1932, she headlined at Los Angeles's Orpheum Theater. The next year, she appeared in a variety performance at the Fox Theater in Brooklyn. Around the same time, she also starred in a Works Progress Administration production of *Personal Appearance*, which toured several theaters in Long Island, New York.

Behind the scenes of Halperin's theatrical success was the talent of her husband, William Barr Friedlander, a Chicago composer who wrote the songs for her acts. Halperin later wed Ben Thomson, on December 21, 1927, and after Thomson's death married Edward D. Gould on January 4, 1934, who died in 1945.

Halperin ended her professional acting career in 1934. She subsequently turned increasing attention to local Jewish and nondenominational charities in Kew Gardens, New York, where she had been residing since at least 1920. Nan Halperin died in 1963.

BIBLIOGRAPHY

AJYB 24:152; Halperin, Nan. Clippings file. Billy Rose Theatre Collection, New York Public Library for the Performing Arts; Locke, Robinson. Collection. Billy Rose Theatre Collection, New York Public Library for the Performing Arts; *Notable Names in the American Theatre* (1976); Slide, Anthony. *The Encyclopedia of Vaudeville* (1994); *WWIAJ* (1928, 1938).

LORI FINKELSTEIN

HALPERT, EDITH GREGOR (1900–1970)

Art dealer, collector, and influential businesswoman, Edith Halpert changed the way Americans feel about their art. Born in Odessa, Russia, on April 25, 1900, she was the daughter of Gregor and Frances (Lucom) Fivoosiovitch. Her father died when she was very young, and, when she was six years old, her mother brought her and her sister to New York City. While in high school, at age fourteen, Edith joined the National Academy of Design after convincing the instructors she was really sixteen.

During this period, Halpert haunted the galleries of Newman Montrose and Alfred Stieglitz, where she discovered a love for modern art, a taste that was frowned on by the academy. In 1918, she married Samuel Halpert, another artist. After her marriage, Halpert gave up painting in favor of earning a living for herself and her husband. Halpert was remarkably successful, becoming an efficiency expert and eventually a member of the board of an investment banking firm.

In 1925, Halpert went to Lille, France, to reorganize a department store. While there she realized that French artists had better opportunities to exhibit and sell new works than did Americans. When she returned to New York, she decided that she would open a gallery to showcase modern American artists. No one else believed the project was possible. Against advice, in 1926, Halpert opened the Downtown Gallery of Contemporary Art in Greenwich Village—the first commercial art gallery in the district.

At that time, Halpert summered in New England, where she learned to love American folk art. Again ahead of her time, she prowled New England barns and junkyards for beautiful pieces. In 1931, she opened the American Folk Art Gallery as part of the Downtown Gallery. The folk art was so successful that it helped support the rest of the gallery during the Depression. Later, Halpert assembled the pieces for the colonial restoration of Williamsburg, Virginia.

Halpert also spearheaded the move for cities to sponsor art exhibits, an idea more common in Europe than in America. Her first municipal exhibit was in Atlantic City in 1929, followed by an exhibit in New York City sponsored by Mayor Fiorello LaGuardia in 1934. In 1941 her gallery held the first commercial showcase of African-American artists in America.

By 1945, Halpert had expanded to an entire building uptown on East Fifty-first Street. By 1965, the gallery found its final home at the Ritz Tower on Park Avenue.

In 1952 she formed the Edith Gregor Halpert Foundation, which sought to guarantee the rights of artists. The foundation promoted codes to help protect artists and help them maintain control over the sale of their works. In 1959, at the height of the Cold War, Halpert was asked by the State Department to organize the National Art Exhibition to go to the Soviet Union.

Halpert began to experience poor health by the late 1960s and developed increasingly strained relations with her artists toward the end. She died of cancer on October 6, 1970.

BIBLIOGRAPHY

NAW; Obituary. *NYTimes*, October 7, 1970.

KATHLEEN THOMPSON

HALPRIN, ANNA (b. 1920)

Anna Halprin is one of the founders of the American avant-garde in modern dance. Beginning with her work in the late 1950s and early 1960s, she radically expanded the ideas of what could constitute a dance, what kind of personal material was permissible as content in a dance work, and how to give voice to forgotten segments of the population—people of color, the aged, the terminally ill.

Anna (Schuman) Halprin was born July 13, 1920, in Wilmette, Illinois, to Ida (Schiff), daughter of Lithuanian immigrants, and Isadore Schuman, a native of Odessa, Russia. She was the youngest of three, with two older brothers. As her father, who had no education beyond elementary school, went from wholesaling women's clothing to being a successful real estate entrepreneur, the family rose rapidly into upper-middle-class comfort. Anna's mother, a housewife with a high school education, indulged her daughter in interpretive dance lessons as a child. Anna also enjoyed exposure to the arts through the model progressive education she received in elementary, middle, and high school in Winnetka, Illinois. By the time she entered the University of Wisconsin at Madison in 1937, she knew she wanted to be a dancer. At university, the fiery redheaded performer became the protégée of the chair of the dance program, the distinguished dance educator Margaret H'Doubler, and received her B.A. in 1941. It was at the University of Wisconsin that she met Lawrence Halprin, a distinguished landscape architect and environmental designer, who was then a graduate student in biology. They were married on September 19, 1940.

After a brief stint performing on Broadway with Doris Humphrey's company, Halprin and her husband moved to San Francisco in 1945, where their daughters Daria (1948) and Rana (1951) were born. (Today Daria Halprin Khalighi is an expressive arts therapist and Rana Halprin is a marriage counselor.) In San Francisco, Halprin, who created several of her early solos based on Jewish themes, founded first a dance studio with Welland Lathrop and then her own company, the San Francisco Dancers Workshop, with which she toured Europe to great acclaim in 1963 and 1965. Starting in 1982, Halprin began her annual performances of *Circle the Earth: A Planetary Dance for Peace*. As an outgrowth of her work with individuals with AIDS, she also founded two ongoing workshop groups for people diagnosed HIV-positive, one for men called Positive Motion, and one for women called Women with Wings.

A recipient of Guggenheim and National Educational Association fellowships, an honorary degree from the University of Wisconsin in 1994, and many other honors and awards, Halprin is also noted for her teaching. She served as a mentor to the leading postmodern dancers, including MEREDITH MONK, Trisha Brown, Yvonne Rainer, and Simone Forti. Through her performing and teaching—which she continues today, leading movement workshops around the world—Anna Halprin helped to redefine American modern dance as a contemporary ritual and a forum for the artist as a morally and socially engaged individual.

BIBLIOGRAPHY

Banes, Sally. *Terpsichore in Sneakers: Post Modern Dance* (1980); Halprin, Anna. *Movement Ritual* (1975), and *Moving Towards Life* (1996); Koegler, Horst. *The Concise Oxford Dictionary of Ballet* (1982).

JANICE ROSS

HALPRIN, ROSE LURIA (1896–1978)

Rose Luria Halprin was one of the foremost American Zionist leaders of the twentieth century, serving twice as the national president of HADASSAH, the Women's Zionist Organization of America, and holding key posts within the Jewish Agency at critical periods in the history of the *yishuv* and the subsequent State of Israel.

Born on April 11, 1896, in New York, Rose Luria Halprin was the daughter of Pesach (Philip) Luria, a dealer in silverware, and Rebecca (Isaacson) Luria. Her parents were ardent Zionists and gave her a Hebrew education. Even as a young girl, she was active in Zionist causes, serving as the leader of the Stars of Zion, a youth division of the Austro-Hungarian Zionist Society, to which her parents belonged. When the society nearly lost its meeting rooms on the Lower East Side because of a lack of funds, Halprin and two friends staged a benefit concert that raised the money necessary to pay the rent. In her later Zionist activities, she would often be called upon to muster vital resources in times of crisis and need.

She completed a course of study at the Teachers Training School of the Jewish Theological Seminary between 1912 and 1913, attended HUNTER COLLEGE briefly in 1914, and later took classes at Columbia University from 1929 to 1931. In 1914, she married Samuel W. Halprin, a businessman, and the couple and their two children made their home in Brooklyn.

From 1932 to 1934, Halprin served as national president of Hadassah. At the end of her term, she moved to Jerusalem with her family while serving as a liaison to the Hadassah Medical Organization during the construction of its new hospital complex on Mount Scopus. A member of the building committee, she was present at the hospital's opening in 1939. Under the leadership of chair Judah L. Magnes, the building committee engaged German Jewish architect Erich Mendelsohn, who built a structure acclaimed for its beauty as well as its suitability for the Middle Eastern setting.

Halprin's Jerusalem years made a deep impression on her. She perfected her Hebrew and came to know the people of the *yishuv* on a more intimate level. She often spoke to friends of the long walks she took with her children through the Old City of Jerusalem and of the view of the Mount of Olives from her door. During her career, she would return more than sixty times to Palestine and, later, Israel.

Her time in Palestine also coincided with a wave of anti-Jewish rioting by Arabs in Hebron and other areas. She helped provide relief for Jewish settlers who came to Jerusalem from outlying areas to escape the violence. It was also a period of increased emigration from Germany, where the Nazi regime was beginning to implement anti-Jewish policies. Halprin became acquainted with HENRIETTA SZOLD, Hadassah's founder, and assisted her in her work on behalf of Youth Aliyah. She traveled to Berlin in 1935 and 1938 on Youth Aliyah missions.

Halprin returned to the United States in 1938 on a speaking tour, reporting to Americans on the conditions of Jewish life in Palestine. Despite the seriousness of tensions between Jews and Arabs, she argued that cooperation between the groups was vital and would help to rid Palestine of its economic problems. Halprin blamed the British mandatory government for the Arab riots, citing its failure to live up to promises made in the Balfour Declaration, and for alternately favoring Arab and Jewish interests according to political expediency.

Halprin returned permanently to the United States in 1939, but her experience in Palestine led to her increasing involvement in international Zionist affairs. From 1939 to 1946, and occasionally thereafter, she was a member of the Zionist General Council, the supreme advisory and supervising institution of the Zionist movement. In 1942, she became treasurer of

A forceful and resourceful American Zionist leader, Rose Halprin played pivotal roles in the establishment of a Jewish state, most notably as a two-term president of HADASSAH *and as a member of the Jewish Agency. She is shown here in the early 1950s, during her second term as president, as part of a delegation presenting an award to Abba Eban. From left to right are: Esther Gottesman,* MIRIAM FREUND-ROSENTHAL, *Eban, and Rose Halprin.*
[Hadassah Archives]

the American Zionist Emergency Council and served as its vice-chair from 1945 to 1947. She was one of the original members of the secretariat of the American Jewish Conference, which was founded in 1943 to coordinate American efforts on behalf of Palestine. In 1946, she was elected to the executive of the Jewish Agency, a post she held for over twenty years.

She faced her most dramatic leadership challenges, however, during her second term as Hadassah president between 1947 and 1952. A tremendous blow came to Hadassah's efforts in Palestine when more than seventy-five doctors, nurses, and students were killed in an ambush as their convoy passed through the Arab neighborhood of Sheikh Jarrah on its way to Mount Scopus. The attack underscored the hospital's vulnerable position surrounded by Arab-held territory, and the complex was evacuated. Under Halprin's leadership, five temporary facilities were set up in

Jerusalem to deal with the urgent medical needs resulting from the War for Independence. Meanwhile, the Medical Organization continued to grow during her presidency, with the establishment of the Hebrew University–Hadassah Medical School in 1949, and the breaking of ground for a new permanent Hadassah Hospital at Ein Karem in 1952.

In addition to her involvement with Hadassah, Halprin played a pivotal role during the struggle for Israel's independence as a member of the American Section of the Jewish Agency, which was charged with arguing for the establishment of the State of Israel before the United Nations. She participated in negotiations that led to the acceptance of the Partition Plan in 1947. Later, when fear of bloodshed caused the United States to recommend a delay of statehood and a temporary "trusteeship" over Palestine, Halprin was one of four members of the Zionist General

Council who brought word from Jerusalem that Jewish officials were determined to bring the new state into existence as planned. After independence, she continued to serve on the Jewish Agency executive, and was asked by Finance Minister Eliezer Kaplan to head an international effort to raise the funds necessary for Israel to absorb the streams of new immigrants entering the country. From 1956 to 1963, and intermittently until 1968, she headed the American Section, first as acting chair and, after 1960, as chair.

In her work for the Jewish Agency and its parent body, the Zionist General Council, Halprin always stressed the mutual reliance of Israel and American Jewry. Much in line with the founding principles of Hadassah, she saw the State of Israel as embodying American ideals of justice and equality, while serving as a source of spiritual and cultural renewal for American Jews. Thus Halprin insisted on an involvement for American Jews in Israel that went beyond philanthropy, and demanded recognition for such a role from the Israelis. As she admonished the Zionist General Council in 1953, "As long as you look on America only as a potential something or other for Israel, you will not help us, and if you do not help us, you will lose Jewish life in its strength and its numbers."

Known for her wit and public-speaking skills, she was at home in the often fierce world of Zionist politics. "She never gave up the right to be heard," recalled Bernice Tannenbaum, one of Halprin's successors in the Hadassah presidency, "and such was her power of persuasion that she usually carried you along *her* road whether you willed it or not." In her later years, an incident that drew strong comment from Halprin was the United Nations 1975 resolution equating Zionism with racism. Although a seasoned international negotiator, she instructed Hadassah members that the most appropriate response was not to protest through diplomatic channels, but to articulate their own definition of Zionism more forcefully through the work they did. Her strong personal qualities and organizational abilities made her perhaps the most revered Hadassah leader since Henrietta Szold.

Rose Luria Halprin died on January 8, 1978.

BIBLIOGRAPHY

AJYB 80:366; Cohen, Naomi W. *American Jews and the Zionist Idea* (1975); *EJ*; Freund-Rosenthal, Miriam, ed. *A Tapestry of Hadassah Memories* (1994); *UJE*; *WWWIA* 7; Haber, Julius. *The Odyssey of an American Zionist* (1956); *Hadassah Magazine* (February 1978): 9; Halprin, Rose. Oral history interview with Judith Epstein, and Papers. Hadassah Archives, NYC; Obituary. *NYTimes*, January 9, 1978, IV 7:3.

ERIC L. GOLDSTEIN

HAMBURGER, JULIA HORN
(1883–1961)

During her nearly lifelong career in social work, Julia Horn Hamburger focused on health and children. She founded and helped run a wide range of Jewish charities primarily servicing the new Jewish immigrants.

Julia Horn was born to affluent German Jewish parents, Jacob Meyer and Hannah Horn, in New York on October 19, 1883, during the early years of the Eastern European Jewish immigration. Like many middle-class women in the Progressive Era, she was able to attain a high level of education, earning a B.A. in 1903. Also like so many women of her class, she turned to teaching. She was a New York public school teacher from 1903 to 1905, and in 1905 she became a teacher of "mental defectives." Since teaching was a career for unmarried women, her paid career ended with her marriage to Gabriel Max Hamburger in 1910. The Hamburgers had two children, son Bernard and daughter Maxsina.

Even before her marriage, she became involved in volunteer social work as the vice president of the Maternity Aid Society from 1906 until 1910. Much of her early charity work focused on providing health and basic care, especially for children. Between 1916 and 1920, Hamburger was the secretary of the Hebrew National Orphan Home. She was the founder and, until her death, the president of the Children's Welfare League, affiliated with the Educational Alliance, an umbrella organization on the Lower East Side funded and run by German Jews. Its purpose was to provide health, social, and educational services for Eastern European immigrants and to Americanize them. In 1921, Hamburger helped start the first free nursery school and kindergarten on the Lower East Side. She also helped found and was the vice president of the Jewish Theater for Children, affiliated with the Jewish Education Association.

Hamburger was deeply involved in Jewish women's organizations. She founded and was for eighteen years the president of Ivriah, the women's division of the Jewish Education Association. She also served as the director of the Federation of Jewish Women's Organizations from 1933 to 1936.

With the rise of anti-Semitism in Europe, Hamburger joined the American Jewish Committee and the Anti-Nazi League. After World War II, she devoted much of her time to speaking for charitable, civic, and religious organizations.

Julia Horn Hamburger died on September 16, 1961, in New York City.

BIBLIOGRAPHY

AJYB 64 (1963): 494; Obituary. *NYTimes,* September 16, 1961, 19:4; *WWIAJ* (1938).

DANIEL BENDER

HANDLER, RUTH MOSKO (b. 1916)

Best known as the inventor of the Barbie doll, Ruth Mosko Handler combined her marketing genius with her husband Elliot Handler's creative designs to form the toy company Mattel, Inc. Starting in their garage in 1939, the Handlers produced Lucite gifts, wooden picture frames, and dollhouse furniture before developing their first toy, the Uke-A-Doodle, in 1947. The success of the Uke-A-Doodle was followed by a series of rubber-belt-driven musical toys, including the Jack-in-the-Box, as well as toy guns such as a Winchester rifle replica. Yet it was the Barbie doll, created in 1959, that "ran off the counter." Thirty years later, sales of the doll that Handler named after her daughter exceeded one billion dollars.

Ruth Mosko Handler, the youngest of ten children, was born in 1916 in Denver, Colorado, to Polish-born parents. Her father, Jacob Mosko, arrived at Ellis Island in 1907. Informing immigration officials that he was a blacksmith, he was sent to Denver, the center of the railroad industry. In 1908, Ida Mosko arrived in America with their six children and joined her husband in Colorado.

Ida Mosko was forty when her youngest child was born, and she became ill soon after. At the age of six months, Ruth was sent to live with her older sister Sarah and Sarah's husband and stayed with them until she was nineteen. It was in Sarah's drugstore/soda fountain that she first developed her enthusiasm for business. Ruth preferred work to play, and grew up in a family where the idea of women working outside of the home was not unusual. In Poland, where anti-Semitism had fueled impoverished conditions, everyone had had to participate in earning a living. She attributes her family's entrepreneurial spirit partly to such circumstances.

In 1932, she fell in love with a poor art student named Izzy Handler. Her family was terrified the teenagers would marry. During her sophomore year at the University of Denver, Handler vacationed in Los Angeles and landed a job at Paramount Studios. Izzy soon joined Ruth in California, and in 1938 the two married in Denver, with her family's reluctant blessing. Returning to California, Handler encouraged her husband to drop the stereotypical "Izzy" in favor of his middle name, Elliot.

Handler returned to her job at Paramount, and her husband enrolled in the Art Center College of Design while working as a lighting fixture designer. He also began to sketch designs for Lucite accessories. Handler encouraged him to produce the pieces and agreed to do the selling. She also negotiated a very large order with Douglas Aircraft: die-cast models of the Douglas DC-3 airplane to be given to corporate customers for Christmas. At the age of twenty-two, the Handlers were in business.

During World War II, President Roosevelt announced that plastics would be restricted to military use. The Handlers had produced a line of plastic picture frames and were in the process of filling a large order. Desperate, they changed the materials to a low-grade wood. The wooden frames were a success, and the order was doubled. That night the Handlers and their colleague Harold "Matt" Matson (whom they had hired as the production expert) celebrated. A name was chosen for the company: "Matt" plus "El" (from Elliot) became Mattel. Although it was Ruth Handler's idea to make picture frames and her selling was critical in landing the accounts, it never occurred to them that her name should be part of the company name.

In search of a new product, the company decided to follow up on entertainer Arthur Godfrey's new popularity and the public's interest in the ukulele. The Handlers created the Uke-A-Doodle and sold eleven million by 1957.

The Handlers were also successful in producing toy guns based on popular television shows. Capitalizing on the western craze, Mattel became a sponsor of a soon-to-debut television show. The *Mickey Mouse Club* became a hit series, and the fifty-two-week, half-million-dollar investment paid off. By 1958, Mattel sales climbed to fourteen million dollars.

In 1956, while vacationing in Switzerland, Handler and her fifteen-year-old daughter Barbara became transfixed by a window display of six eleven-inch dolls in different ski outfits. They looked very similar to an idea that Handler had envisioned five years earlier—a child's doll with an adult body and multiple outfits.

Handler pushed the idea for three years, and in 1959 the Barbie dolls were put on the market. The Ken doll, named for her son, who had been born in 1944, soon followed. By late 1964, the *Saturday Evening Post* reported that Barbie products supported five thousand workers in Japan, eight hundred workers in California, and numerous press agents and advertising executives. Barbie had a secretary to answer twenty thousand fan letters a week. By 1968, the Barbie Fan Club grew to 1.5 million members in the United States. In 1993, a "second issue" Barbie in

Ruth and Elliot Handler, who introduced the Barbie doll in 1959, are shown here holding Ken and Barbie.
This photo was taken in 1987 as they prepared to receive the Lifetime Achievement Award from Doll Reader *magazine.*
After twenty-eight years on the market, Barbie was still on the top-ten list of Toy and Hobby World,
the toy industry's biggest magazine. [UPI/Corbis-Bettmann]

its original box was sold at auction for over five thousand dollars.

In 1970, Handler lost a breast to cancer. Because of her illness, she spent less time at Mattel. Her loss of self-esteem affected her leadership, and she lost control of the business. Major decisions had been made without her consent, and by 1973 Mattel was under investigation by the Securities and Exchange Commission. Although Handler and her colleagues pleaded innocent, they were fined, and by 1975 Handler was forced out of the company she had started.

During her unhappy search for an adequate breast prosthesis, she realized that she should be making them for other women. Through her company Nearly Me, she has helped thousands of women. As she explained to a reporter in the early 1980s, "When I conceived Barbie, I believed it was important to a little girl's self-esteem to play with a doll that has breasts. Now I find it even more important to return that self-esteem to women who have lost theirs."

Ruth Mosko Handler has received numerous awards for her accomplishments in business and philanthropy. Among her honors, she has been named Woman of the Year in Business (*Los Angeles Times*), been inducted into the Toy Industry Hall of Fame (Toy Manufacturers of America), received the Volunteer Achievement Award (American Cancer Society), and was the first "Woman of Distinction" of the United Jewish Appeal.

BIBLIOGRAPHY

Handler, Ruth Mosko. *Dream Doll: The Ruth Handler Story* (1994); Lord, M.G. *Forever Barbie: The Unauthorized Biography of a Real Doll* (1994).

JULIE ALTMAN

HARBY, LEAH COHEN
(1849–1918)

Leah Cohen Harby wore her heritage proudly, practicing fidelity to country, faith, and family in her writing and everyday living. Born to a distinguished family in Charleston, South Carolina, on September 7, 1849, she grew up in an environment that encouraged intellectual development and prized patriotism.

Isaac Harby, her grandfather, was a noted early nineteenth-century dramatist as well as a founding member of the Reform Society of Israelites. Members of the Harby family served in both the Revolutionary War and the War of 1812. Levi Myers Harby, Isaac's brother and Leah Cohen's father-in-law, rose to the rank of captain in the United States Navy before resigning his commission to serve in the Confederacy. At war's end, he had successfully defended and continued to command Galveston harbor.

Loyalty to country was matched by the value accorded education in the family. Armida Harby, daughter of Isaac, married Marx E. Cohen, who had been educated at the University of Glasgow. He seems to have taken an active role in the education of his six children, of whom Leah was the fifth. In addition, the women of the Harby family provided ample literary models for the young Leah. Her aunts Octavia Harby Moses and Caroline de Litchfield Harby wrote poetry. Her sister Caroline Cohen Joachimsen wrote for contemporary newspapers, magazines, and Jewish periodicals.

Upon her marriage to her second cousin John De LaMotta Harby, the couple made their home in Galveston, where Leah Cohen Harby found in Texas the subject matter for her historical works. During the 1870s and 1880s, her contributions of verse and essays to both local and national publications increased. Accolades included first prize for her lyrics to a Texas flag song and recognition by the American Historical Association (AHA) in the form of membership and publication of her articles "The Earliest Texas" and "The Tejas: Their Habits, Government, and Superstitions" in the *AHA Annual Report* for 1891 and 1894. She had attracted the attention of the organization through her article "City of a Prince," an account of the founding of the German community of New Braunfels, Texas, that appeared in the *Magazine of American History* in 1888.

While best known as an author, Leah Cohen Harby's active participation in a variety of organizations establishes her as a role model for her generation and for feminists to come. As a member of the Daughters of the American Revolution and the Daughters of the Confederacy, she acknowledged her American and southern roots. Her devotion to the historical societies of Texas, New York, and South Carolina, as well as to the AHA, affirms her commitment to education through understanding the past. Sorosis, the first women's club in New York City, became a venue for her promotion of intellectual freedom for women. Her many contributions to the *Jewish Messenger* and other Jewish journals testify that she pursued her goals firmly grounded in a context of what it means to be a woman in the light of Jewish religious and family teaching. As the title of one of her articles suggests, she saw and lived the "possibilities."

Leah Cohen Harby died in October 1918.

SELECTED WORKS BY LEAH COHEN HARBY

"City of a Prince." *Magazine of American History* (1888); "The Earliest Texas." *American Historical Association (AHA) Annual Report* (1891); "Our Women and Their Possibilities." In *The American Jewish Woman: A Documentary History*, edited by Jacob Rader Marcus (1981); "The Tejas: Their Habits, Government, and Superstitions." *AHA Annual Report* (1894).

BIBLIOGRAPHY

Adams, Oscar Fay. *A Dictionary of American Authors*, 5th ed., s.v. "Harby, Lee Cohen" (1904. Reprint 1969); *AJYB* 6 (1904–1905): 110, 21:205, 24:153; Herman, Kali. *Women in Particular: An Index to American Women*, s.v. "Harbee, Lee Cohen" (1984); *JE*; Knight, Lucien Lamar. *Biographical Dictionary of Southern Authors*, s.v. "Harby, Mrs. Lee [Cohen]" (1929. Reprint 1978); Lichtenstein, Diane. *Writing Their Nations: The Tradition of Nineteenth-Century American Jewish Women Writers* (1992); Marcus, Jacob Rader. *The American Jewish Woman, 1654–1980* (1981); "Mrs. Lee Cohen Harby, Author." *NYTimes*, October 22, 1918, 13:1; *UJE* (1942), s.v. "Harby, Mrs. Lee C."; *A Woman of the Century: 1470 Biographical Sketches Accompanied by Portraits of Leading American Women in All Walks of Life*. Edited by Frances E. Willard and Mary A. Livermore (1967) ; *WWWIA* 4 (1968), s.v. "Harby, Lee Cohen."

MARY ELLEN HENRY

Her espousal of progressive politics—a woman's right to choose and opposition to school prayer among them—has made Jane Harman's California congressional seat the site of fierce ideological battles. [Office of Congresswoman Jane Harman]

HARMAN, JANE (b. 1945)

Entering elective politics with the theme "This woman will clean House," Democratic congresswoman Jane Harman has managed to establish an increasingly secure seat for herself as representative of the Los Angeles South Bay's 36th District. She was born on June 28, 1945, in New York City, the eldest child of Adolph N. and Lucille (Geier) Lakes. Her father, a physician, fled Nazi Germany in 1935. Jane grew up with her brother David in Los Angeles, where they attended public schools.

A Phi Beta Kappa graduate of Smith College in 1966, she graduated from Harvard Law School in 1969 and became a member of the bar in the District of Columbia. She has two children, Brian Frank and Hilary Frank, from her nine-year first marriage to Richard Frank. She also has two younger children, Daniel Geier Harman and Justine Leigh Harman, with her husband Sidney Harman, an audio equipment manufacturer, whom she married in 1980.

During the 1970s, she worked in a variety of public service roles in Washington, D.C., including chief legislative assistant to California senator John Tunney, chief counsel and staff director on two congressional subcommittees, and deputy secretary to the cabinet during the administration of President Jimmy Carter. Through the 1980s, she held significant positions with the Democratic National Committee (DNC), acting as counsel for the 1984 platform committee and chairing the DNC's National Lawyer's Council (1986–1992) while she practiced law with several Washington firms.

Harman first ran for elective office in 1992, winning the seat in the 36th Congressional District, whose composition became substantially more conservative following redistricting after the 1990 census. Only 41 percent of registered voters in the new district were Democrats at the start of her campaign. Harman's win was unique and costly (at $2.3 million, the third highest of any House candidate that year). That and subsequent political victories have been made possible in part by her family's wealth. In 1994, she was returned to office by such a narrow edge that her opponent, Susan Brooks, ahead by ninety-three votes before absentees were tallied, flew to Washington to join in the celebration for the "Republican Revolution" and undergo orientation for new representatives. Brooks did not concede until the following July, when the House Oversight Committee conducted local hearings on alleged voter fraud. In a 1996 rematch, Harman began the campaign as a "most endangered member," but won by a 9 percent margin of victory.

As a congressional freshman, Harman was appointed to the coveted House National Security Committee through the intervention of Les Aspin, a friend who had chaired the panel and had just become secretary of defense. She was also appointed to the Science, Space and Technology Committee and the Intelligence Committee. She has used these positions effectively to influence political decisions that support the economic well-being of the large defense and aerospace corporations that heavily populate her district. Her advocacy for these industries, including funding of the stealth bomber, has made Harman one of the major recipients of Political Action Committee donations in Congress.

From these committee posts, Harman has also worked for cooperative United States–Israel defense projects and intelligence exchange. She is one of only two Jewish women in the House of Representatives, and she is a member of the Congressional Caucus on Anti-Semitism. Harman has consistently supported pro-Israel policies, including foreign aid, and is one of the few House members opposing school prayer.

Representative Harman's conquest of the 36th District was accomplished with the support of feminists, including Emily's List, which raises money for progressive feminist candidates. Her first opponent, Joan Milke Flores, espoused a strong antiabortion stance, and Harman made abortion rights the central issue of her campaign: "Pro-choice and pro-change" was the slogan. Harman has led efforts to enact pro-female and pro-child policies, cosponsoring legislation that would write abortion rights into federal law, securing rights of women in the military, and increasing financing of public education. She is on the executive committee of the Congressional Caucus on Women's Issues.

Harman has also been a courageous advocate for homosexuals, casting the only audible no vote on the Military Personnel Subcommittee during a voice vote that called for immediate discharge of HIV-positive personnel and an outright ban on gay soldiers. Jane Harman has shown her mettle as a political contender, treading a narrow path between electoral survival and progressive social views.

BIBLIOGRAPHY

Alicea, Ines Pinto. "Flores Has Inside Track in Coastal Thirty-Sixth District." *Congressional Quarterly* 50, no. 40 (October 10, 1992): 3200; Barone, Michael, and Grant Ujifusa, with Richard E. Cohen. "Thirty-Sixth District." In *The Almanac of American Politics, 1996* (1995); Bornemeier, James, and Tom Jennings. "Losing Candidate in Thirty-Sixth District Congress Race Drops Challenge." *Los Angeles Times*, July 7, 1995, B3; Boyarsky, Bill. "Voters Have Democrats Where They Want Them." *Los Angeles Times*, November 7, 1996, B1+; Cassata, Donna. "Social Issues Front-and-Center." *Congressional Quarterly* 53, no. 21 (May 27, 1995): 1522; Donovan, Beth, and Thomas H. Moore. "House Incumbents Raise Money at Record Rate for 1994." *Congressional Quarterly* 52, no. 7 (February 19, 1994): 417; Donovan, Beth, with Ilyse J. Veron. "Freshmen Got to Washington with Help of PAC Funds." *Congressional Quarterly* 51, no. 13 (March 27, 1993): 723; Duncan, Philip D., and Christine C. Lawrence. "Jane Harman (D)." In *Congressional Quarterly's Politics in America 1996: The 104th Congress* (1995); Geffen, Daniel. Personal communication with author. Washington, D.C., January 1997, "Jane Harman, Democrat: California; 36th District." *Congressional Quarterly* 51, no. 3, supplement (January 16, 1993): 54; Oliphant, Thomas. "A Battle of Ideology in California." *Boston Globe*, October 22, 1996, A23; Pike, John. "The Force Is with Her." *Mother Jones* (September/October 1996): 58–59; Ponessa, Jeanne. "House Addresses Challenges to '94 Votes, Settles One." *Congressional Quarterly* 53, no. 19 (May 13, 1995): 1291; Towell, Pat. "Military HIV Policy Debate Rekindled in House." *Congressional Quarterly* 54 (April 27, 1996): 1180–1181; *Who's Who in America, 1996* (1995): 1759; *Who's Who of American Women, 1995–96* (1995): 449.

JANE SPRAGUE ZONES

HARRIS, JANET (1869–1955)

Janet Simons Harris was a community leader and champion of women's organizations. She was born on November 19, 1869, in Titusville, Pennsylvania. Her parents, Abraham Hirsch and Helen Esther (Katz) Simons, were wealthy Reform Jews who were well established in the American Jewish community. Janet's brother Lester Simons was an attorney and an officer in the Spanish-American War.

On April 14, 1896, Janet Simons married Nathaniel E. Harris in Bradford, Pennsylvania, an oil-rich city not far from Buffalo, New York. Nathaniel worked in the oil industry while Janet taught in the Bradford public schools. They had three sons, Lawrence, Howard, and Nathaniel, Jr.

In the 1920s, the Jewish community in Bradford was thriving. It was home to two synagogues, the Reform German Temple and Temple Beth Zion, and numerous Jewish organizations. Janet Harris devoted her time to teaching in the Temple Beth Zion Sunday school and serving as president of the NATIONAL COUNCIL OF JEWISH WOMEN (NCJW). During her term as president, from 1913 to 1920, the organization nearly split during a controversy about its mission. The membership was divided over whether the NCJW would function as a social service and welfare organization or dedicate itself to the education of Jewish women. Although some local sections broke away from the national organization during this period, the NCJW continued to grow during Harris's presidency, and has remained one of the foremost Jewish women's organizations in the United States. Harris's picture still hangs in the boardroom at the national headquarters of the NCJW in New York City.

After completing her term as president, Harris served as the chair of its Foreign Relations Committee, which called an international meeting in Vienna of Jewish women in May 1924. She was also active in the National Council of Women of the United States, chairing the Quinquennial Committee, which in 1925 convened women from fifty-two countries in Washington, D.C. Harris also served in the State Federation of Pennsylvania Women and was chair of the Northwest Pennsylvania District. Influenced by her brother's experiences in the military, Harris joined the American Legion Auxiliary, Veterans of Foreign Wars Auxiliary, Spanish-American War Veterans Auxiliary, Women's Committee for National Defense, and the International League for Peace and Freedom. A loyal citizen and civics worker, Harris was also a member of the League of Women Voters.

In the middle of the 1920s, Nathaniel and Janet Harris relocated to New York City, returning to Bradford for the summers. Their sons attended Ivy League schools and pursued careers in academia and business. After her husband's death in 1932, Janet Harris retired to Florida. However, she traveled extensively, and lived in Spain with one of her sons for some time. It is reported that even many years after she left Bradford, whenever Jews from Bradford traveled to other cities, they would be asked if they knew Janet Simons Harris.

Janet Harris died in January 1955 and was cremated in Florida. Her remains were interred, along with the remains of her husband, in the Jewish section of the Willowdale Cemetery in Bradford.

BIBLIOGRAPHY
WWIAJ (1926, 1928).

R. PAMELA JAY GOTTFRIED

HARRIS, RENEE (1876–1969)

Renee Harris's career as New York's first woman theatrical producer began as a direct result of one of the twentieth century's most renowned tragedies, the

She lost her producer husband on the Titanic *and later her inherited theatrical empire to the Depression, but Renee Harris never lost her sense of moral responsibility to the theatergoing public. [New York Public Library]*

sinking of the *Titanic*. As she watched the "unsinkable" vessel go down in the icy waters off Newfoundland, the handful of survivors on her lifeboat braced against the fierce cold and the shouts of the fifteen hundred passengers still on board. Among these victims was her husband, successful theatrical manager and producer Henry B. Harris, who had stepped out of the lifeboat at the last minute to make room for women and children.

"I feel as though I had died and that my dear husband's spirit was in me and I was here to try to do what he would have done." In these words, taken from her first interview following the disaster, Harris plotted the course of her life in theater.

Renee Harris had assisted her husband in theatrical matters, such as approving scripts, so she had been somewhat prepared for what was to come. She stepped out of his shadow and became a noted producer in her own right. Indeed, "what he would have done" was what she did. She quickly learned that successful producing meant combining the artistic with the commercial. In her own words, "The successful play must tie up somewhere to the general ideas of the public."

Harris's first and most famous production was *Damaged Goods*, starring Richard Benett. This play dealt with syphilis, a taboo subject in the early twentieth century. It was a huge success, at the same time dispelling myths about the disease and enlightening the general public. Her sense of social responsibility continued throughout her career. During World War I, she sent a troupe of legitimate performers to Paris, becoming the pioneer in what is now a common wartime practice.

But despite a foundation of early fortune, Harris's life took a turn for the worse. Late in the 1920s, she refused an offer of $1.2 million for the Hudson Theater, claiming the historic landmark would have been razed for an office building. The Hudson was eventually shut during the Depression, reportedly foreclosed by a panic-stricken bank while the proprietor was in Europe. Returning at once, she sold her residences in Palm Beach, on Park Avenue, and on Long Island, as well as the family yacht, but was unable to save the theater. "When I'm on 44th Street, I turn my back on the Hudson," she said in later years. "It's a movie house with sex pictures."

Harris spent her last years in a West Side hotel, sustained largely by the Actors' Fund, where she died in 1969 at age ninety-three. According to friends, she was full of vigor until the very end, relishing a martini every afternoon. This is not surprising, given that she had always been a survivor, from her harrowing experience on the *Titanic* to the loss of a theatrical empire. Her resolve in the face of adversity, her dedication to the preservation of the theater and of artistic integrity, and her championship of social causes reflect the virtues of the Jewish people as a whole and serve as an inspiration to all people.

BIBLIOGRAPHY

Cleveland Leader (April 18, 1912); *Dramatic Mirror* (November 18, 1912); Morehouse, Rebecca. "The Theatregoer's Notebook," *Showbill* (November 1985); *Newark Star-Eagle* (August 6, 1919); *New York Telegraph* (October 17, 1917); Obituary. *NYTimes*, September 3, 1969, 47:1; *Variety Obituaries: 1905–1986*, vol. 7, 1969–1974 (1988); *WWIAJ* (1928).

BRIAN TRESS

HARTMANN, REINA (1880–1953)

Reina Kate Goldstein, the daughter of Simon and Kate (Mayer) Goldstein, was born in Chicago on February 2, 1880, and lived in the Chicago area her entire life. She became an integral member of the community by devoting her life to organizations that served Chicago's women.

On September 29, 1902, she married Hugo Hartmann, an employee of the Hartmann Trunk Company. He went on to become a successful businessman and executive of the company. The Hartmanns had three children, Dorothy, James, and Hugo, Jr. Members of the wealthy Reform Jewish community in Chicago, the Hartmanns were active in many Jewish welfare organizations.

In 1917, once Hugo, Jr. was in school, Hartmann became the president of the Mothers Aid of the Chicago Lying-In Hospital and Dispensary organization. Her commitment to Mothers Aid can be traced to her own mother's involvement in this organization; Kate Goldstein was one of nine charter members when Mothers Aid incorporated in 1906. The organization was dedicated to improving the conditions of women in the obstetrics ward of the Chicago Lying-In Hospital, and succeeded in raising enough funds for lectures, supplies, and an $85,000 annex to the hospital, which was named the Mothers Aid Pavilion. Hartmann remained president from 1917 to 1921, and under her leadership Mothers Aid became one of the largest Jewish women's organizations in Chicago. After her term as president, Hartmann remained an active member of Mothers Aid and served as its director from 1929 to 1931.

The Chicago Jewish Community Blue Book of 1917–1918 lists Hartmann's additional affiliations with the Chicago Hebrew Institute Women's Auxiliary, Ruth Club, Jochannal Lodge, Sinai Temple Sisterhood, the NATIONAL COUNCIL OF JEWISH WOMEN, as well as the Chicago Women's Aid and Mothers Aid, in which she was most extensively involved. In 1925–1926, Hartmann served in the civics and philanthropy department of Chicago Women's Aid, and occupied a number of leadership positions until 1938. Hartmann was also active in the women's division of Jewish Charities of Chicago.

In the 1930s and 1940s, Hartmann redirected her energy to synagogue organizations and Jewish education, but maintained her dedication to women's concerns, serving several terms as the president of the NATIONAL FEDERATION OF TEMPLE SISTERHOODS. In addition, she was a member of the Department of Synagogue and School Extension Board of the Union of American Hebrew Congregations, the umbrella organization for Reform congregations. In the 1930s, Hartmann was also involved in Chicago's Board of Jewish Education.

On May 8, 1953, at age seventy-three, Reina Hartmann died in her home, in Highland Park, Illinois. Most of her adult life was devoted to improving the lives of Jewish women in the Chicago area. The greatest evidence of her enduring work is that women continue to give birth at the Mothers Aid Pavilion, and Jewish voluntarism continues to thrive in Chicago eighty years after she began her service to the community.

BIBLIOGRAPHY

Hartman, Reina. Archives. Chicago Jewish Historical Society; Meites, Hyman L. *History of the Jews of Chicago* (1924); Obituary. *Chicago Tribune*, May 11, 1953; *Who's Who in Chicago* (1931): 426; *WWIAJ* (1938): 420; *WWWIA* 6.

R. PAMELA JAY GOTTFRIED

HASIDIC WOMEN

Hasidic women represent a unique face of American Judaism. As Hasidim—ultra-Orthodox Jews belonging to sectarian communities, worshiping and working as followers of specific rebbes—they are set apart from assimilated, mainstream American Jews. But as women in a subculture primarily defined by male religious studies, rituals, and legal obligations, they are also set apart from Hasidic men, whose recognizable styles of dress and yeshivah ingatherings have long presented a masculine standard for outsiders' understanding of Hasidism.

Hasidism, as a radical movement of Judaism, emerged from the teachings of Israel ben Eliezer (the Besht) in eighteenth-century Poland, spreading throughout Eastern Europe and giving rise to a variety of regional sects. These Hasidim, or "pious ones," in Russia, Poland, Hungary, and Romania fused meticulous devotion to Jewish practice with a joyful and mystical expression of faith, often expressed through male *farbrengens* [ritual gatherings of a rebbe and his followers for an inspiring evening of speeches, eating, song, and dance]. Hasidic teachings suggest that even the most routine aspects of daily life can reveal a spiritual essence if approached fervently. By concentrating religious intentions toward all acts, some Hasidic followers hope to hasten the coming of Moshiach [the Messiah] and thus end the earthly persecution and suffering of all Jews.

The emphasis on a religious education for Hasidic boys developed into a network of distinctive Eastern European yeshivahs, producing more Hasidic scholars and rabbis to serve far-flung communities. Yet throughout the nineteenth century, women and girls were never expected to move past a basic literacy in daily and holiday prayers. That certain women functioned as respected scholars or mystical *rebbetzins* [female spiritual leaders or teachers], in the movement's early decades, is hotly contested by Jewish his-

torians today. Only in the early twentieth century, when it became clear that young Hasidic women hungry for literacy were pursuing education through secular state schools (or the forbidden movements of Zionism and socialism), did Hasidic education for girls develop in Eastern Europe, for example, in the BAIS YA'ACOV school system, founded by Sarah Schenirer in Poland. This educational awakening of Hasidic women not incidentally paralleled feminist movements in prewar Western Europe. Tragically, the new Hasidic girls' academies served only one generation before their destruction in the Holocaust. By the time that agents of the Nazi Holocaust swept entire Hasidic villages into death camps, many Hasidim had already fled to transplanted communities in North America and Israel. From the 1920s to 1950s, a steady stream of displaced Hasidic leaders, followers, activists, and refugees flowed into low-income Jewish neighborhoods in Brooklyn and Jerusalem. Postwar Hasidism quickly flourished, rebuilding each devastated community of separate and scholarly lineage. Today, descendants of the Lubavitcher, Satmar, Belzer, Ger, Bobover, and other sects populate Hasidic communities on several continents.

Women have served as important agents of faith and family life in the transmission of Hasidic belief to new generations of followers, their public roles increasing with educational experience. Although Hasidic sects in America continue to differ in the work and educational opportunities permitted to women, without question one of the most profound postwar changes overall has been schooling for girls. The rapid expansion of Hasidic parochial schools and girls' yeshivahs, however, has not meant that women have joined the ranks of scholarly men as religious authority figures rendering interpretation of Jewish law. Girls' schools primarily serve to protect Hasidic daughters from the secular influences of the "outside" society, rather than introducing them to the advanced Talmudic curriculum typical of boys' education.

In the United States today, the Hasidic male, in black coat, black hat, *zizit* fringes, beard, and side-curls, is easily recognized today as a symbol of ultra-Orthodox Judaism and Talmud scholarship. Visually, he summarizes an ongoing commitment to religious practices once confined to the Jewish shtetls of Eastern Europe. His yeshivah training and devotion to daily piety make him a "holy man" in our secular society, although some more assimilated Jews find the Hasidic life-style anachronistic or embarrassing. Far less visible is the contemporary Hasidic woman, though no less devout. While her secular education is limited to high school and perhaps some vocational training, she is often a family breadwinner, working outside the home—and this is considered perfectly appropriate, *if* such work frees a scholarly husband for study or pays for children's yeshivah tuition. Economic roles for Hasidic women include shopkeeping, teaching in girls' religious schools, secretarial and computer jobs, and work with a specific Jewish purpose: for instance, matchmaking, and catering *simkhahs* [weddings and other celebrations].

Outside their own communities, Hasidic women are not as identifiable as their male counterparts. Their dress is modest, one truly distinguishing feature being the *sheytl*, a wig or scarf worn by all married women. Indeed, in styled wigs some Hasidic women look far more glamorous than their assimilated Jewish counterparts. But the laws of *zniut* [modesty] are strictly observed, including monthly visits to the *mikvah* [the ritual immersion bath required after menstruation]. Hasidic customs of modesty also prohibit mixed social events, mixed swimming at summer vacation retreats, coeducation, or women performing in front of men. A strong women's culture results from such constant segregation by gender, and in the Lubavitcher movement, women have published articulate explanations of their roles in the separate women's sphere.

Most Hasidic communities are in fact closed to outsiders—meaning that even other Jews cannot join the specific sect if they were not born into its lineage. This clannishness has been a public relations nightmare for some groups. In the mid-1990s, several outstanding court challenges by the Satmar Hasidic communities of Monsey and Kiryas Joel in upstate New York called for greater religious autonomy and separation from outside control. One Hasidic sect, however—the Lubavitcher movement, also known as Chabad—has gained enormous power and visibility by deliberately recruiting assimilated, nonobservant Jews to its ranks. Here, Hasidic women have been highly influential as educated, multilingual outreach activists, speakers, and writers.

Based in Crown Heights, supported by the late Rebbe Menachem M. Schneerson (1902–1994), Lubavitcher women in America have enjoyed fantastic gains in educational and work opportunities. As activists, they represent the face of Hasidic women to other Jews, undertaking campaigns to popularize laws incumbent upon observant Jewish women (such as Sabbath candle-lighting and laws surrounding menstruation). From the moment he assumed leadership in 1950, the Lubavitcher Rebbe brought radical change to a movement that had always been symbolized by male activists. Within one eight-year period—1951 to 1959—the rebbe and his assistants approved the founding of a girls' school system, an organization for all Lubavitcher women (Neshei Ubnos Chabad), two community publications by and for women (*Di yiddishe heym* and the *Neshei Chabad Newsletter*), and annual conventions for Lubavitcher women activists from all over North America. These institutions grew to provide a vast range of roles for women hungry for intellectual and religious challenge. By the early 1970s, when feminist criticism of ultra-Orthodox Judaism's role for women placed the Lubavitcher movement on the defensive, a spectrum of skilled women writers were ready to answer in kind. A variety of books on the Hasidic woman's role and belief system appeared to confront feminist calls for change. These texts included *The Modern Jewish Woman* and *AURA: A Reader on Jewish Womanhood*, both prepared by the Lubavitch Women's Organization.

As outreach missionaries, or *shluchim*, Lubavitcher women as well as men now travel to remote locations or to turbulent college campuses—wherever Jews live—providing, through what is known as the "Chabad House," a lively forum for dialogue and Jewish learning. This aggressive interaction has attracted many young and adult Jews to become Lubavitcher followers. The close-knit Lubavitcher community holds considerable appeal for displaced women in postmodern society, and several books in the 1980s and 1990s explored this appeal. Lis Harris's *Holy Days*, Debra Kaufman's *Rachel's Daughters*, and Lynn Davidman's *Tradition in a Rootless World* are examples of feminist investigators' growing interest in *ba'alot teshuva* [Jewish women who have embraced ultra-Orthodoxy]. Because Harris, Kaufman, and Davidman let Hasidic women speak for themselves, the reading public has now met many a strong-minded Lubavitcher activist, and misconceptions about Hasidic practices are lessening.

However, for real insight into Lubavitcher women's concerns, there is no substitute for the quarterly Yiddish/English journal *Di Yiddishe Heim*, a Lubavitch publication which offers a mixture of Jewish history and legal interpretations, humorous anecdotes about Hasidic family life, and articles on developments in the Lubavitcher girls' school system (Bais Rivka). Moreover, most cities in the United States now feature a Chabad House where interested Jews may attend introductory talks or workshops on women's role in Hasidic Judaism. While other Hasidic sects scorn the Lubavitchers as opportunistic or too willing to compromise on issues of modernity, the Lubavitch movement has enabled Hasidic women to study, advocate, and publish—in short, to gain an American voice.

BIBLIOGRAPHY

Davidman, Lynn. *Tradition in a Rootless World* (1991); El-Or, Tamar. *Educated and Ignorant* (1994); Handelman, Susan. "The Jewish Woman: Three Steps Behind?" *Di Yiddishe Heim* 18 (1977): 8–11; Harris, Lis. *Holy Days: The World of a Hasidic Family* (1985); Hertzman, Chuna, and Shmuel Elchonen Brog. *One: The Essence of a Jewish Home* (1978); Jacobsen, Israel. "Chassidus Study for Girls." *Di Yiddishe Heim* 15 (1967): 11–13; Kamen, Robert. *Growing Up Hasidic: Education and Socialization in the Bobover Hasidic Community* (1985); Kaufman, Debra. *Rachel's Daughters* (1991); Koskoff, Ellen. *Women and Music in Cross-Cultural Perspective* (1987); Lubavitch Educational Foundation for Jewish Marriage Enrichment. *The Modern Jewish Woman* (1981); Lubavitch Educational Foundation of Great Britain. *A Woman of Valor: Anthology for the Thinking Jewess* (1976); Lubavitch Women's Organization. *AURA: A Reader on Jewish Womanhood* (1984); Miller, Yisroel. *In Search of the Jewish Woman* (1984); Morris, Bonnie. "Agents or Victims of Religious Ideology?" In *New World Hasidim*, edited by Janet Belcove-Shalin (1994), and "Female Education in the Hasidic Community." In *Women in Spiritual and Communitarian Societies*, edited by Wendy Chmielewski, Louis Kern, and Marlyn Klee-Hartzell (1993), and "The Tzivos Hashem Movement as an Aspect of Hasidic Identity." *Judaism* 40 (1991): 333–343; Poll, Solomon. *The Hasidic Community of Williamsburg* (1962); Rivkin, Meyer, ed. *The Rebbe: Changing the Tide of Education* (1982); Rosengarten, Sudy. "The Girls' Yeshiva." *Di Yiddishe Heim* 14 (1973): 21–24; Rubin, Israel. *Satmar: An Island in the City* (1972); Schneerson, Menachem Mendel [the Lubavitcher Rebbe]. *Letters by the Lubavitcher Rebbe to Neshei Ubnos Chabad 1956–1980* (1981), and *Letters by the Lubavitcher Rebbe to Neshei Ubnos Chabad Midwinter Conventions. 1963–1987* (1987).

BONNIE J. MORRIS

HASSENFELD, SYLVIA

One of the most significant leaders in the American Jewish community in the twentieth century, Sylvia Hassenfeld has devoted her life to working on behalf of Israel and to easing the plight of Jews around the world. Born in Philadelphia, the only child of Sophie and Joseph Kay, she has been an international leader in business, philanthropy, and non-governmental organizations.

Her activities have been focused primarily in public service involving endangered Jewish populations throughout the world. In addition, because of her concern for and dedication to children, she has provided leadership services to children in need.

Sylvia Hassenfeld has held a variety of national and international leadership positions in over forty years of devotion to the Jewish community. From 1988 to 1992, she was the first female president of the American Jewish Joint Distribution Committee (also known as the JDC or "the Joint"). She served as national vice-chairman of the United Jewish Appeal and chair of its National Women's Division, a member of the Board of Governors of the Jewish Agency for Israel and chair of its Rural Settlement Committee, and as a member of the Boards of the United Israel Appeal, the Jerusalem Foundation, the Council of Jewish Federations, the Memorial Foundation for Jewish Culture, UJA-Federation of Greater New York and Brandeis University.

Mrs. Hassenfeld's involvement in Jewish communal affairs began when she married the late Merrill Hassenfeld and moved to his hometown, Providence, Rhode Island. Sylvia was strongly influenced by the Hassenfeld family's traditional involvement in the Jewish religious and community life in Providence, as well as in Zionism. New England was a center of American Zionism and Providence was very much a part of the early American movement for a Jewish homeland in Palestine. Merrill's parents played a major role in Jewish affairs that Merrill and Sylvia continued, along with Merrill's brother and his wife. Merrill and Sylvia served as role models for their children and today their daughter, Ellen Block, and their son, Alan Hassenfeld, are deeply involved in Jewish as well as general philanthropy, especially that concerned with the needs of children.

The Hassenfeld family business grew from pencil manufacturing to one of the world's largest toy manufacturing businesses—the Hasbro Corporation. While serving on the board of directors of Hasbro Inc. and rearing her family, which also included her late son, Stephen, Sylvia grew increasingly involved in the Providence, Rhode Island, Jewish Federation, eventually rising to the position of president. That involvement led to a role in the Council of Jewish Federations and Welfare Funds and other national and international Jewish organizations.

Sylvia Hassenfeld's most significant contribution to world Jewry to date was her term as President of the Joint Distribution Committee. The liberalization process in the former Soviet Union and Eastern Europe coincided with her presidency and her skillful diplomacy with the heads of state, government officials, and leaders of non-governmental organizations contributed to the protection of Jewish civil and religious affairs. During her tenure at JDC, Mrs. Hassenfeld oversaw the development of social services, health, religious, and educational programs in nations, such as the Czech Republic, Armenia, Hungary, Romania, Russia, Poland, Austria and Bulgaria, among others. In Africa and the Middle East, she represented the

Shown here when she was president of the American Jewish Joint Distribution Committee (JDC),
Sylvia Hassenfeld receives a copy of the first Amharic-Hebrew-English dictionary from authors Edna Lauden, left, and
Mati Elias, right. JDC and Tel Aviv University assisted in publishing the dictionary to bridge the language barrier
for Ethiopian immigrants. It was specifically designed to provide definitions and at the same time teach about Israeli culture.
[Joint Distribution Committee]

Joint Distribution Committee in those countries which had a Jewish population.

Also during her tenure, the Joint Distribution Committee and the Israeli government coordinated a dramatic airlift that relocated thousands of Ethiopian Jews to Israel. Working closely with the Executive Director of JDC, Michael Schneider, and his staff, she was able to mobilize significant financial resources as well as the cooperation of El Al Airlines to carry Ethiopian Jews to Eretz Yisrael. In recognition of her efforts to improve the human condition, especially in regard to world Jewry, the American Jewish Historical Society in 1994 awarded Sylvia Hassenfeld its Emma Lazarus Statue of Liberty Award.

Sylvia Hassenfeld's dedication to improving the lives of people extends beyond the Jewish world to the lives of children around the globe. One of the charitable foundations she and her family helped establish— the Hasbro Children's Foundation—is committed to improving the lives of children by providing funds for direct service programs where the need is greatest.

Another philanthropic endeavor linked to the family interests provides significant gifts of holiday toys to thousands of children each year. The Hasbro Children's Hospital in Providence, Rhode Island, was built as a result of the vision and leadership of the Hassenfeld family and their determination to see that this institution would be a model for children's hospitals nationally and internationally.

The Hasbro commitment to children arises naturally from its involvement in the toy industry, but it also stems from a deep personal commitment from her son Stephen. She traces their focus on improving the lot of children around the world to a conversation they had with the late Dr. Lee Salk, the renowned child psychologist. He described America's children as being without any advocates. She sees her role and that of the Hasbro Children's Foundation as trying to fill that gap with programs which make a difference. Through her daughter, Ellen Block, who is the Foundation Chairman, this goal is being accomplished by funding innovative, direct service programs.

Additionally, the Hasbro company has a corporate philosophy, carefully maintained by its Hassenfeld family leadership, to manufacture toys which promote healthy values in children.

Beyond her involvement in Jewish communal life, Sylvia Hassenfeld serves on the Board of Trustees of the New York University Medical Center, the Paul Nitze School of Advanced International Studies at John Hopkins University, and was appointed by President Clinton as a member of the United States Holocaust Memorial Council. In the business world, Sylvia Hassenfeld serves on the Board of Directors of the Hasbro Corporation and for many years served as its Vice President for Community Affairs.

When asked to reflect on the changing role of women in Jewish communal life since her days as a young leader of the Providence, Rhode Island, Jewish Federation, Sylvia Hassenfeld observed that—"today, many more women are active on governing boards than in the past. Before they spoke only as individuals, now they speak as true partners of the men who once ran the organizations."

According to Sylvia Hassenfeld, "women have risen to prominence in Jewish organizations because it is apparent that the issues that face the public, private and social sectors are increasingly complex and to be dealt with successfully require new partnerships of all the parties."

MICHAEL FELDBERG

HAUSER, RITA ELEANOR (b. 1934)

Rita E. Hauser is a woman of many accomplishments. She was a trailblazer for women in law, politics, and foreign affairs at a time when few women entered the legal profession or achieved top-level positions in business and politics. She was instrumental in persuading Yasir Arafat and the Palestine Liberation Organization publicly to renounce terrorism and to recognize Israel. She has been involved in Republican presidential politics since Richard Nixon's presidential campaign, and she was invited to join a major Wall Street law firm as its first woman partner.

Born in New York City on July 12, 1934, to Nathan and Frieda (Litt) Abrams, Rita Eleanor (Abrams) Hauser was the first of two daughters. She received her B.A. from HUNTER COLLEGE (1954). After college, she won a Fulbright scholarship for graduate work in France. She attended the University of Strasbourg and was awarded a doctorate in political

economy. At a time when women represented only 1 percent of those graduating from law school, she attended Harvard Law School (1955–1956), received her LL.B. from New York University Law School (1959), and became one of the few Americans to obtain a *License en droit* [French LL.B.] from the University of Paris (1958). She is licensed to practice law in New York and the District of Columbia.

Hauser's first job as an attorney took her to Washington, D.C., to serve as counsel in the Justice Department's Appellate Tax Division under the Attorney General's Honors Program. While in Washington, she was invited to join Richard Nixon's first presidential campaign and distinguished herself as a speechwriter and campaign strategist. Raised in a Republican family, Hauser subscribes to the party's approach in governance. After Nixon lost the 1960 election to John F. Kennedy, she moved to New York and worked in the international law department of a New York law firm while continuing her association with Republican politics.

In Nixon's successful 1968 presidential campaign, Hauser served as cochair of New Yorkers for Nixon. She was next appointed the United States representative to the United Nations Commission on Human Rights, a position she held from 1969 to 1972. As well, she served as a member of the United States delegation to the twenty-fourth UN General Assembly. It was during her tenure at the UN that she met the key players in Middle East politics and became committed to her pursuit of conflict resolution in the Middle East, human rights, and humanitarian law. During her term at the UN, she helped Jewish immigrants leave Russia and visited Palestinian refugee camps throughout the Middle East.

Hauser identified GOLDA MEIR, whom she met during her tenure at the UN, as her mentor and role model. Meir inspired Hauser's involvement in Middle East politics and encouraged her, a secular Jew, to learn more about Jewish history and her own Jewishness.

In 1972, Hauser was invited to join a major Wall Street law firm, Stroock, Stroock and Lavan, as a senior partner and the firm's first female partner. In that capacity, she was instrumental in developing its international law department, became mentor to a number of its female associates, and advocated an increase in the number of women partners in the firm.

Throughout her career, Hauser has served the United States in numerous high-level public service assignments. Of particular note, in her capacity as head of the American branch of the International Center for Peace in the Middle East (1984–1991), she participated in secret diplomatic negotiations,

In a career that took her from presidential campaigns to United Nations representative to law partner, Rita Eleanor Hauser's shining moment was her work as a key player in the PLO's 1988 recognition of Israel and renunciation of terrorism.

coordinated by the Swedish foreign minister, which culminated in Yasir Arafat's 1988 public recognition of the State of Israel and the Palestine Liberation Organization's renunciation of terrorism. As chair of the International Peace Academy, Hauser was invited by the head of the Palestine Elections Commission to be an official observer of the 1996 Palestinian elections.

In 1988, Rita Hauser and her husband, Gustave M. Hauser, created the Hauser Foundation, a private philanthropic organization, to "meet the challenge of bringing about the peaceful resolution of conflict and promote democracy"—particularly in the Middle East. In 1996, the Hausers donated thirteen million dollars to Harvard Law School, the largest gift ever donated to a law school, to fund the building of Hauser Hall. Previously, they gave five million dollars to New York University Law School to establish the Global Law School Program, which will support the Hauser Scholar Program for postgraduate foreign students and advance the integration of foreign law into the law school curriculum.

In 1992, Hauser left the full-time practice of law to manage the work of the Hauser Foundation, of which she is president. In her current capacity of counsel to the Stroock law firm, she continues practicing international law, with a client base in Europe, the Middle East, and Latin America.

Over the years, Hauser has been the recipient of numerous awards and honors and currently serves on diverse boards of directors.

Hauser credits the "enormous support" she has received from her husband during their forty-year marriage in helping her to handle her overlapping careers as wife, mother, attorney, United States representative to the UN, and world traveler. Gustave Hauser, an attorney, business executive, and pioneer of the modern cable television industry, is the chairman and CEO of Hauser Communications, Incorporated. They have two adult children, Ana Patricia (b. 1962) and Glenvil (b. 1963).

BIBLIOGRAPHY

Hauser, Rita. Curriculum vitae, and interview by author, December 20, 1995; Waring, Nancy. "Gus and Rita Hauser's Lifetime Legal Merger." *Harvard Law Bulletin* (Summer 1995): 3–7.

RUTH GURSKY

HAWN, GOLDIE (b. 1945)

Goldie Hawn was born in Silver Spring, Maryland, on November 21, 1945, to Laura (Stienhoff) Hawn, a dance school owner and jewelry wholesaler, and Edward Rutledge Hawn, a professional musician. Hawn was raised Jewish although, she notes, "not in a strictly religious atmosphere," and describes a happy home life. She began dancing at age three, and danced in the Ballet Russe de Monte Carlo's *Nutcracker* chorus at age ten. Hawn recalls being asked to dance on point for a friend's bar mitzvah. The music started, and she slipped and fell—twice. Succeeding on her third attempt, "I realized I was probably the little girl who was going to make it."

After graduating high school, Hawn attended American University while running her own ballet school. Two years later, she moved to New York City to pursue acting and dance seriously. To support herself, she danced in the Texas Pavilion at the 1964 World's Fair, at numerous clubs, and in the chorus of touring Broadway musicals. Producers from *Rowan and Martin's Laugh-In* spotted her dancing on an Andy Griffith television special in 1967 and hired her as a regular. Hawn's endearing giggles and improvisational ability on *Laugh-In* (1968–1970) earned her an Emmy and, less welcome, comments about her "dumb-blonde

"Women have to be very, very tough," says actor-producer Goldie Hawn, who practices what she preaches. Despite the difficulties of working in a male-dominated industry, she has become a force to be reckoned with in front of and behind the camera.

routine." Her character, Hawn clarifies, "was a deeply joyful blonde. I never thought of her as dumb."

In 1969, Hawn won a Best Supporting Actress Oscar and a Golden Globe Award for the film *Cactus Flower.* She went on to a critically acclaimed dramatic role in Steven Spielberg's first film, *Sugarland Express.* With 1980's highly successful comedy *Private Benjamin,* she added the role of executive producer to that of star. In perhaps her most accomplished performance, Hawn shows Benjamin's metamorphosis from selfish, stereotypical Jewish American Princess to self-aware, empowered woman in charge. Behind the camera, Hawn faced the challenges common to women filmmakers in the traditionally male-dominated industry. "Women's power in Hollywood is not an easy thing to come by," she says. "A woman is constantly tempering her own point of view, her own passion."

But, Hawn remembers, "I just stuck to my guns . . . and this was hard because I didn't want people to see me as a bitch."

Hawn values her independence, although she believes "it's hard for any woman. Women run households, they raise children, they have to be very, very tough. I always saw my mother working, so I never grew up thinking that a man would take care of me, ever." She also stresses the importance of family and states that her main goal in life has been "to be a good mother." Her 1969 marriage to dancer Gus Trikonis ended in 1974. Hawn had two children, Oliver (b. 1976) and Kate (b. 1977), with musician Bill Hudson, whom she married in 1976 and divorced in 1980. Since 1983 Hawn has lived with actor Kurt Russell, whom she met on the set of the film *Swing Shift.* Hawn and Russell's family includes Kate, Oliver, Boston (b. 1980, Russell's son from a former marriage), and Wyatt (b. 1986).

Hawn is one of the most successful women in Hollywood. She has acted in over thirty films; in 1996 she was seen in *The First Wives Club,* which quickly made over $100 million at the box office, and in Woody Allen's musical film *Everybody Says I Love You.* She continues to produce, including the 1995 blockbuster *Something to Talk About,* and runs Cherry Alley Productions with Teri Schwartz. Hawn has made eight trips to India since her first in 1980, most recently to film *In the Wild,* a 1996 PBS documentary on saving the elephants.

BIBLIOGRAPHY

Bachrach, Judy. "Goldie's Big Splash." *Vanity Fair* (January 1997); "Mirror Mirror on the Wall, Who's the Fairest of Them All: Goldie." *Tatler* (December 1996); Ellerbee, Linda. "The Goldie Years." *Live* (October 1996); Fuller, Graham. "The Goldie Rush." *Interview* (September 1996); James, Ryan. "Hawn in Her Golden Years: Forever Blond, Forever Smart." *NYTimes,* December 1, 1996, sec. 2, p. 13; Marshall, Leslie. "Goldie Hawn: At Home with Her Family in Los Angeles." *In Style* 3, no. 8 (August 1996); Michaelson, Judith. "Goldie Hawn: Just a Homebody After All?" *Los Angeles Times,* December 24, 1987, pt. 6, p. 1.

ANNE S. BORDEN

HAWTHORNE SCHOOL *see* CEDAR KNOLLS SCHOOL FOR GIRLS

HAYDEN, MELISSA (b. 1923)

A ballet dancer possessing technical virtuosity and dramatic brilliance, Melissa Hayden thrilled her audiences with consistently excellent performances in a career that spanned four decades. Although her association with the New York City Ballet dominated her career, she performed with other ballet companies, in film, and on Broadway. Critics recognized, early in her career, that she possessed uncommon strength and energy. As her dancing matured, Hayden was able to modulate both qualities into a lyrical mode when appropriate, so that she danced an extraordinary range of roles in the course of her long career.

Hayden was born Mildred Herman, April 23, 1923, in Toronto, Canada. Neither of her parents, Kate Weinberg and Jacob Herman, who had immigrated from the region surrounding Kiev in Russia, had any artistic talents. Her father operated a successful wholesale fruit and vegetable business. Her sister Leola was eight years her senior; her sister Annette was three years younger. Hayden started her ballet training fairly late, at age fifteen, with Boris Volkoff, an influential Toronto teacher. After five years of study with Volkoff, for which, when she was out of

Her technique and versatility made dancer Melissa Hayden a favorite of legendary choreographer George Balanchine. In a brilliant four-decade career, she worked with companies like the American Ballet Theatre and the New York City Ballet. [New York Public Library]

high school, she paid by working as a bookkeeper, she decided it was necessary to continue her training in New York.

She found a job with the Radio City Music Hall Ballet Company, and spent every spare moment taking class. In 1945, she joined the American Ballet Theatre (ABT) and spent two and a half years touring with that company, dancing in its first production of Jerome Robbins's *Interplay* (1945) as well as other important ballets. While she was with ABT, the choreographer Antony Tudor advised her to change her name. When she asked for suggestions, he chose the name Melissa Hayden. To family, close friends, and devoted fans, however, she remained Millie.

When ABT disbanded temporarily, in 1948, Hayden joined the company of Cuban ballet dancer Alicia Alonso for a season. In 1949, George Balanchine and Lincoln Kirstein invited Hayden to join their fledgling company, the New York City Ballet (NYCB). She remained there until her retirement in 1973, excluding a brief return to ABT in 1954. Early in the history of the NYCB, Hayden was one of a select group of dancers chosen by Balanchine, ballet master and chief choreographer, to work on technique on a daily basis for an intense six-week period. Balanchine created a number of significant roles for Hayden. That he recognized the versatility of her dancing is apparent. The stark, rhythmic precision of her dancing in *Agon* (1957) contrasted with the lush romanticism of *Liebeslieder Walzer* (1960), her unabashed bravura as Miss Liberty Bell in *Stars and Stripes* (1958), and her mercurial delicacy as Titania in *A Midsummer Night's Dream* (1962). She also danced key roles in Jerome Robbins's *Age of Anxiety* (1950) and *In the Night* (1970), Frederick Ashton's *Illuminations* (1950), and John Taras's *Jeux* (1966). Of equal importance, as one of the company's most dependable and resilient performers, she danced a vast number of roles within the repertory, very often paired with a favorite partner, Jacques D'Amboise. For her retirement gala on May 16, 1973, Balanchine created *Cortège Hongrois* in her honor.

Following her retirement from the New York City Ballet in 1973, Hayden became artist-in-residence at Skidmore College, in Saratoga Springs, New York. In 1976, she went to Seattle to assume the directorship of the Pacific Northwest Ballet. A year later, she returned to New York to start her own school on Manhattan's Upper West Side. In 1983, she joined the faculty of the North Carolina School of the Arts in Winston-Salem.

Hayden has also maintained a very full family life. She and her husband, lawyer-businessman Don

Coleman, whom she married January 29, 1954, have a son, Stuart (b. 1954), and a daughter, Jennifer (b. 1961).

Hayden has been the recipient of numerous honors and awards.

SELECTED WORKS BY MELISSA HAYDEN
Dancer to Dancer (1981); *Offstage and On* (1963).

BIBLIOGRAPHY
Chujoy, Anatole, and P.W. Manchester. *The Dance Encyclopedia* (1967); *EJ*; Gruen, John. *The Private World of Ballet* (1970); Gustaitis, Rasa. *Melissa Hayden Ballerina* (1967); Hayden, Melissa. Clippings file, and Interview by Jocklyn Armstrong, tape recording. January 11, 1975. New York Public Library for the Performing Arts at Lincoln Center; Koegler, Horst. *The Concise Oxford Dictionary of Ballet* (1977).

ROSE ANNE THOM

HEBREW TEACHERS COLLEGES

During the early waves of immigration to the United States, Sephardi and German Jews established full-time schools in large population centers. Rabbis, clergy, and predominantly European-trained male teachers provided religious instruction in private-school settings, often sponsored by and housed in synagogues.

When REBECCA GRATZ established the Hebrew Sunday School Society in Philadelphia (1838), teachers were "appointed from among the young ladies" of the Mikveh Israel Congregation. Similarly, in Baltimore, the "teaching ladies" were unwed, well-meaning, untrained women who provided instruction in the local Reform Sunday schools. There was no profession of Jewish education in nineteenth-century America.

While experienced teachers came to the United States with each immigrant group, among the Russians who came in the early years of the *haskalah* [enlightenment] were *melamdim* [teachers] well-suited to the task of training children in traditional Eastern European ways. As Diane A. King wrote in "A History of Gratz College 1893–1928," "Even the well-educated East Europeans who were engaged in teaching could not be spoken of as trained teachers."

At the beginning of the twentieth century, there were few paid religious school teachers. Most were volunteers, and many of those were public school teachers—trained for assignments in general education but woefully lacking in knowledge of Judaism.

It became apparent that the new country and the new young American Jew could not be educated in the same manner and by the same teachers as before.

While parents sought an education that would keep their children "traditional," the children found little appeal in an educational system that prepared them to live their parents' lives.

The founders of Boston Hebrew College felt the need for American scholars and cultured laypeople. They wanted "a spiritual elite for New England . . . who would be able to mold a creative and vigorous generation with a sense of belonging to a revitalized Jewish community." A difficult goal such as this would be unattainable unless the elite had "a profound knowledge of Jewish sources and general erudition."

The growth of the large American public school system in the nineteenth century, with its predominant goal of assimilating immigrant children into American life and culture, influenced the course of Jewish education in the United States. The after-school communal Talmud Torah became the predominant mode of Jewish education and remained so until the synagogue school replaced it as the most popular form of American Jewish education in the mid-twentieth century. Congregational or synagogue schools promoted denominational Judaism, and by the mid-1980s, 90 percent of school-age children who were enrolled in Jewish schools were in this setting.

The formal Jewish education of girls was generally neglected in the early decades of the twentieth century. Boys were educated in the Talmud Torah system, at heder, or with private or visiting teachers. Most formally concluded this education at age thirteen with bar mitzvah. In America, sons would achieve status through higher secular education; daughters would not necessarily follow this route.

Institutions for the training of Jewish teachers developed in major American cities, primarily in the eastern part of the United States where there was the largest concentration of Jewish population. The preparation of teachers and their availability in areas beyond the large urban centers was, and remains, a challenge.

Women were attracted to Jewish teaching. It combined a love of and commitment to Judaism, interest in children, and the opportunity to earn wages in a highly acceptable and honorable profession. While literature about early female students is limited, it is clear that they were raised in mainly Orthodox and traditional homes by parents who encouraged them to be teachers. In later years, schools, camps and youth groups, and Israel would be as strong influences as the home and family.

Two teacher training institutions were established prior to World War I: Gratz College (1897) and the Teachers Institute of the Jewish Theological Seminary (1909).

There were eight women and five men in Gratz's first afternoon class, and twelve women and nine men in Gratz's first evening class. The list of twenty-one scholarship recipients for the years 1901 to 1908 includes only three women. Because Gratz's early emphasis was the training of Sunday school teachers, some do not consider Gratz College to be the first Jewish teacher's training school. In 1910, according to Alexander Dushkin, "There was not a single Jewish teacher's training school in the country for the training of professional teachers."

The 1886 charter of the Jewish Theological Seminary includes as one of its objects "the establishment and maintenance of a Jewish Theological Seminary for the training of Rabbis and teachers." From its inception, the Teachers Institute welcomed able female students: "Any Jewish man or women of good character above the age of fifteen who in the opinion of the President of the Faculty is capable of profiting by the course may be admitted as a student." By 1919, there were fifty-seven women and sixty-eight men enrolled: The significant number of women included the "girl graduates of the first class of the Hebrew High School of the Bureau," a group of students with thorough Hebrew training.

According to King, "The large number of women who were prepared to undertake advanced Jewish education particularly in the 1920s probably reflected the growth in the number of Talmud Torah schools during this period . . . a system which attracted girls as well as boys." The growth of Hebrew teachers colleges would in time depend on the enrollment and education of girls and young women in the Talmud Torah system.

Seven additional schools were established in the decade following World War I: the Teachers Institute of Mizrachi Zionist Organization (1917), later affiliated with Yeshiva University (1921); the Jewish People's Seminary (1918); Baltimore Hebrew Teachers College (1919); the Hebrew Teachers College of Boston (1921); Herzliah Hebrew Teachers Institute (1923); the College of Jewish Studies of Chicago (1926); and the Hebrew Teachers Training School for Girls (1928), later affiliated with Yeshiva University.

The Hebrew Union College School for teachers was founded in 1920 and reorganized in 1947 as the Hebrew Union College–Jewish Institute of Religion School of Sacred Music and School of Education. An earlier Reform Teachers College established in 1909 was closed: In 1923, it became the Union of American Hebrew Congregations Teachers College, independent of the Hebrew Union College.

After World War I, the Tarbut movement—a cultural and educational movement begun in Russia after the Revolution—helped bring about a revitalization of the Hebrew language. Teacher-training institutions were influenced by the Hebrew language societies founded in the early years of the century: The first *Ivrit b' Ivrit* [Hebrew in Hebrew] classes were in Boston and New York schools. The curricular emphasis was on the study of classical texts, Hebrew language and literature, and cultural Zionism. In time, all Hebrew teachers colleges would go beyond training classroom teachers and prepare students for work in adult education, Sunday schools, youth groups, and advanced studies leading to the rabbinate (for men only) or academic careers.

The schools varied in their orientation. Each was unique in some way, yet there were shared characteristics among some. Community-sponsored schools were established to meet predominantly local needs. They were, and remain, supported locally as a responsibility of the community and as an indication of the community's commitment to Jewish education. These schools drew the majority of their students from the local area, and they tended to remain in the community after graduation.

The seven types of schools included: the Hebrew teachers training school with a two- to three-year or four-year course leading to teacher certification; the college as a distinct school within a larger institution; the college of Jewish studies, with a department for the training of teachers; the teachers institute within a rabbinical seminary; a branch or department of a university; the pedagogic institute of a *yeshivah gedolah* (not open to women); and normal secondary schools (primarily in South America and Europe). Most teacher-training institutions began as secondary schools or as special institutes at the precollege level.

According to the 1921–1922 registry of Baltimore Hebrew College, male or female applicants from sixteen years of age and upward were encouraged to apply for admission. Nine students—six women and three men—enrolled in Herzliah when it opened in 1927. Its aim was to train young women to become teachers in Hebrew schools, where male teachers were predominant. There were no female faculty members at Herzliah for many years. Early students recall that the only female presence was the school secretary.

The early Hebrew teachers colleges were male-dominated institutions. Women's participation in governance was limited to the activities of the women's auxiliaries, with the notable exception of FRIEDA WARBURG, who served as a director of the Jewish Theological Seminary of America (JTSA).

Few women served on the faculties of the Hebrew colleges in the first decades of their existence.

In describing the accomplishments of the Teachers Institute, Mordecai M. Kaplan wrote in 1939: "All this that the Teachers Institute and its affiliated departments have achieved would not have been possible without the men of the faculty." Part-time and adjunct faculty positions were occupied by specialists such as JUDITH KAPLAN EISENSTEIN (music at JTSA), TEMIMA NIMTZOWITZ GEZARI (arts and crafts at JTSA), and Shulamith Scharfstein Chernoff (nursery education at JTSA). Instructors of Hebrew within the college programs at JTSA included Rebecca Aaronson Brickman (1911–1914) and Rose Abramson Maximon (1912–1914). Current estimates of female faculty members at schools that train for careers in Jewish education are as high as 75 percent.

Women were camp directors, teaching supervisors, librarians, and assistant librarians (Jeanette Newman Bloom, Helen Sarna, and later Ann Lapidus Lerner at Boston Hebrew College). No women are included in the list of the leadership of the profession of Jewish education in the 1920s and 1930s "in the United States and their writings that represent the professional literature" of the period.

From 1929 to 1954, the following community-based colleges were established: the Hebrew Teachers Seminary in Cleveland; the School of Jewish Studies in Pittsburgh; and the Midrasha/College of Jewish Studies in Detroit. As well, community-based colleges were established in Alabama; in Essex County, New Jersey; in Denver; in St. Louis; and in Washington, D.C. The Teachers Institute of the University of Judaism (1947), Brandeis University (1948), the Teachers Institute for Women of Yeshiva University (1952), and Stern College for Women of Yeshiva University (1952) were established following World War II.

Gratz College and the University of Pennsylvania were the first to propose a joint degree program with local colleges, but it was never developed. In 1930, arrangements were made by the Jewish Theological Seminary with Teachers College of Columbia University for students to complete a combined course and receive the degrees of bachelor of science in education from Columbia and bachelor of Jewish pedagogy from the Teachers Institute. Herzliah urged its graduates to attend a secular school and, following graduation, implemented a plan for students to enroll in New York University's School of Education. Hebrew Union College and the University of Southern California also developed joint programs, as did the College of Jewish Studies in Chicago and Roosevelt University.

By 1950, the colleges, partly because of their encouragement of secular studies for their students and graduates, were meeting only 25 percent of the need for classroom teachers in Jewish schools. They expanded beyond teacher training to undergraduate and graduate programs in Jewish studies, and by 1981 the term "Hebrew" had been dropped from the official name of all but a few schools. Hebrew was the language of instruction for only about 20 percent of the courses offered.

In 1951, the Iggud Betey Midrash: Association of Hebrew Teachers Colleges was established to bring together accredited Jewish teachers training institutions. The Association of Institutions of Higher Learning in Jewish Education currently brings together the eleven accredited North American institutions that provide graduate training for careers in Jewish education. The degrees offered by the teachers colleges over the years have included Hebrew teachers diploma, bachelor of religious education, bachelor of Jewish education, bachelor of Jewish pedagogy, master of Jewish pedagogy, and master of arts in Jewish education. Doctoral degrees granted include doctor of philosophy, doctor of Jewish pedagogy, doctor of Hebrew letters, and doctor of education.

Major curriculum revisions occurred in the mid-1950s to meet the changing needs of schools. For many years, the schools had been subject to criticism by professional educators. Teachers were still being prepared for traditional approaches in traditional self-contained classrooms. Courses of study did not reflect the changing nature of American Jewish life and developments in general education. Israel programs were added, as were specialized tracks to prepare experienced teachers for administrative positions. Now, the colleges as a group often recruit from similar applicant pools and offer training for the full range of careers in Jewish education. Most concentrate their efforts on graduate training.

Students who now enter preparatory programs for teaching are often lacking in fundamental knowledge of Hebrew, come from unobservant homes, and are strongly influenced by experiences in Jewish camps, Israel programs, day schools, and youth groups. Many prepare for careers in education that take them beyond traditional classroom settings to programs in informal settings, family and adult education, camping, and retreats. There is a broader range of career options available to the granddaughters and great-granddaughters of the early female graduates of Hebrew teachers colleges. Yet the profession is still challenged to attract women to the field and to meet both "qualitatively and quantitatively" the demand for Jewish teachers.

SYLVIA CUTLER ETTENBERG (JTSA) and Elsie Chomsky (Gratz) were the first to hold full-time and administrative positions in teachers colleges. NORMA FIELDS FURST served as president of Baltimore Hebrew University (1993–1995). Women occupy and have held leadership positions as directors of programs in institutions where more women than men are enrolled: SARA S. LEE at the Rhea Hirsch School of Education of Hebrew Union College, Lifsa B. Schachter at the Cleveland College of Jewish Studies, Gail Z. Dorph at the Fingerhut School of the University of Judaism, and SHULAMITH REICH ELSTER at the Baltimore Hebrew University. Full- and part-time faculty appointments in schools that provide teachers and educators for the American Jewish community are still held primarily by men.

In *The Education of American Jewish Teachers*, Oscar J. Janowsky wrote: "The most important single factor in Jewish education is the training of teachers. . . . The teacher has a responsibility far more difficult to fulfill than in other periods when Jews clung together for protection. The teacher must be well-informed, imaginative, incandescent. He [sic] is now the final defense in depth for precious sanctions that are the core of Jewish life." Today the vast majority (80 percent) of those training for careers in Jewish education are women twenty-one years of age or older. The Jewish teaching profession remains, like its public elementary school counterpart, a largely "feminine preserve."

BIBLIOGRAPHY

Davidson, Aryeh. *The Preparation of Jewish Educators in North America: A Status Report to the Commission on Jewish Education in North America* (1990); Dushkin, Alexander M., with Nathan Greenbaum. *Comparative Study of the Jewish Teachers Training Schools in the Diaspora* (1970); Janowsky, Oscar J., ed. *The Education of American Jewish Teachers* (1967); King, Diane A. "A History of Gratz College 1893–1928." Ph.D. diss., Dropsie College, 1979; Margolis, Isidor. *Jewish Teacher Training Schools in the United States* (1964); Reimer, Joseph, ed. *To Build a Profession: Careers in Jewish Education* (1987); Schiff, Alvin. "New Models in Preparing Personnel for Jewish Education: Overview of Programs." *Jewish Education* 43, no. 3 (Fall 1974); Steiner, M.J. "Hebrew Teachers College of Boston: 1921–1951." *Jewish Education* 23, no. 1 (Winter 1952).

SHULAMITH REICH ELSTER

HECHT, LINA FRANK
(1848–1921)

Called "Mrs. Hecht" by her colleagues and "Aunt Lina" by three generations of immigrant children in Boston, Lina Frank Hecht was Boston's premiere Jewish female philanthropist of the late nineteenth and early twentieth centuries.

Born in 1848 in Baltimore to wealthy Bavarian immigrants, Lina received a private education and moved in Baltimore's elite Jewish circles. In 1867, she married Jacob Hecht (born 1834), who had immigrated to America in 1848, established a wholesale shoe business with his family in California, Baltimore, and Boston, and who, by the time he met Lina, was already a wealthy man. The couple moved to Boston and became leading members of the German Jewish philanthropic community. Uniquely in her time and society, Lina Hecht established her independent identity as a female philanthropist and social reformer.

Hecht began her career in the 1870s, funding small educational and health services programs for Boston's newly arriving Eastern European immigrants. In 1878, she revived, as its president, the Hebrew Ladies Sewing Circle (founded 1869). The group bought cloth that they paid immigrant women to sew into blankets, clothing, and undergarments; the results were then distributed free to needy Jewish immigrants. Hecht initiated fund-raising "Calico Balls" to support the circle's Hanukkah parties for the poor. Throughout the late 1870s and 1880s, she worked with her husband to professionalize Boston's major Jewish charitable organization, the United Hebrew Benevolent Association (UHBA), ensuring uniform and rationalized services to the city's Jewish poor. When the UHBA merged with four other Boston Jewish charities in April 1895 to form the first federated Jewish charitable organization in the nation—the Federation of Jewish Charities—Lina Hecht organized the fund-raisers to help make the merger financially possible and was one of only three women appointed to its founding board. "We must be as one family," she told the major donors, encapsulating her lifelong vision for the Jewish community. Childless, Hecht often commented that she viewed all of Boston's Jewish children as her own.

In the late 1880s, Hecht started a Jewish Sunday school for immigrant children, hoping to teach them the basics of Judaism and an American way of life. With advice from social activist GOLDE BAMBER, Hecht expanded those efforts in 1890 and founded the Hebrew Industrial School for Girls (HIS), a pioneering settlement house in Boston's North End. A partner HIS for boys opened in Boston's West End in 1892, and for four decades the schools taught good citizenship, Jewish history and culture, and economic self-sufficiency to immigrant children and their families. Following her death in 1921, the school purchased new headquarters in Boston's West End with monies left in Hecht's bequest, and the school was renamed the Hecht Neighborhood House in her honor. The name followed the community center to Boston's Dorchester neighborhood in 1936 and bore her name through the 1970s.

Jacob Hecht died in 1902. Rare for a woman of her time, Lina Hecht continued her philanthropic leadership alone for the next two decades. In 1908, she was the first female named to the vice presidency of the Federated Jewish Charities. It was not the first time she was so honored and acknowledged. Rabbi Solomon Schindler's 1889 publication, *Israelites in Boston*, had featured short biographies of Boston's leading Jewish citizens. All his biographies were of men. But the frontispiece to the volume featured a photograph of Boston's premiere Jewish charitable leader and citizen: Lina Frank Hecht.

BIBLIOGRAPHY

Combined Jewish Philanthropies of Greater Boston. Papers. American Jewish Historical Society, Waltham, Mass.; Hecht Neighborhood House. Papers. American Jewish Historical Society, Waltham, Mass.; Schindler, Solomon. *Israelites in Boston* (1889); Solomon, Barbara Miller. *Pioneers in Service: The History of the Associated Jewish Philanthropies of Boston* (1956).

ELLEN SMITH

HEILBRUN, CAROLYN G. (b. 1926)

Throughout her life, Carolyn G. Heilbrun has successfully managed to sustain a triple career. As wife and mother, literary academic, and mystery writer, her ultimate goal has been to encourage women to strive for intellectual and professional independence.

Carolyn (Gold) Heilbrun was born on January 13, 1926, in East Orange, New Jersey, the only child of Archibald and Estelle (Roemer) Gold. Her father, who came to America from Russia around 1900 as a destitute, Yiddish-speaking child, became a certified public accountant and rose to riches as a partner in a brokerage firm. He lost his wealth in the Depression, and in 1932 the family moved to Manhattan on borrowed money. Although Carolyn's father gradually rebuilt his fortune, her mother remained deeply traumatized by the family's sudden loss of security and social status. Born in America to religious Austrian-Jewish parents as the first of seven children, Estelle Roemer cut her ties to the Jewish world as a young woman. According to Heilbrun, she "identified all that limited her life as Judaism." Archibald Gold, whom she married in 1919 when both were twenty-

three years old, had also distanced himself from his Jewish past.

Not surprisingly, the family turned to a consoling form of American Protestantism in times of spiritual need. Socially and financially still fragile, the Golds began to attend the Divine Science Church of the Healing Christ in the mid-1930s and sent their daughter to its Sunday school. She was educated at an all-girls private preparatory school in Manhattan. She went on to Wellesley College, where she earned her B.A. in 1947. On February 20, 1945, she married James Heilbrun, with whom she had three children. Her marriage, which she called probably the single most fortunate factor in her life, offered her some of the resilience and strength she needed to pursue a career as an English literary scholar in the still male-dominated world of Ivy League academe. Having earned her M.A. in 1951 and her Ph.D.—with a biography of *The Garnett Family* (1961)—in 1959 from Columbia University, she was appointed, after a brief teaching stint at Brooklyn College, to an instructorship in English at Columbia's School of General Studies, the university's adult extension program. Throughout the 1950s and 1960s, the School of General Studies served as the only gateway to academic careers for women scholars at Columbia. Heilbrun was tenured in 1971, appointed to a full professorship in 1972, and given an endowed chair in 1986. In 1993, she took early retirement to protest the university's continued discrimination against women.

Heilbrun has received many honors and awards. She was a Guggenheim Fellow (1966, 1970), a Bunting Institute Fellow at Radcliffe College (1976), a Rockefeller Fellow (1976–1977), and a National Endowment for the Humanities Senior Research Fellow (1983). She served as a member of the executive council of the Modern Language Association (1976–1979) and as MLA president in 1984.

Although Heilbrun claimed that she "had been born a feminist and never wavered from that position," men rather than women dominated her early career. Her father was her acknowledged role model, Lionel Trilling (Columbia's éminence grise) was her academic idol, and her second book was a study of the poet Christopher Isherwood (1970). But as the women's movement gathered momentum, Heilbrun began to write some of its most widely read texts. In 1973, she published *Toward a Recognition of Androgyny*, in which she pleaded for a modification of conventional notions of masculinity in the direction of feminine traits, in order to stem the self-brutalization and destructiveness experienced by an American society unable to extricate itself from the Vietnam War. Six years later, Heilbrun sharpened her plea by urging women to reinvent their role in society. Her book *Reinventing Womanhood* (1979) was not only an analysis of women's contribution to English literature and culture, but a manifesto of independence, containing suggestions on "how a woman might convert the materials of her male-centered education into a guide for female accomplishment."

Heilbrun's next book, *Writing a Woman's Life* (1988), provided examples of independent women intellectuals. Its six chapters were devoted to George Sand, Dorothy Sayers, women poets and their fathers, women novelists and marriage, and women writers and friendship. The last chapter explained the invention of Amanda Cross in 1963, Heilbrun's persona as a mystery writer, and Cross's creation of professorial sleuth Kate Fansler. Heilbrun rounded off her academic work with the publication in 1990 of *Hamlet's Mother and Other Women*, a collection of her essays on women in fiction and culture written during the 1970s and 1980s. In 1995, Heilbrun ventured into new territory with her biography of a living person, *The Education of a Woman: The Life of Gloria Steinem*. With this book, Heilbrun intellectual life came full circle. As a young girl, she had been an avid reader of biographies because they allowed her, as she explained, "to enter the world of daring and achievement." As a seasoned cultural critic, she put her pen to the service of future readers by chronicling the daring and achievement of one of America's most prominent feminist activists.

The mysteries that Heilbrun began publishing in 1964 under the pen name Amanda Cross (eleven to date) offer occasional glimpses of life in academe. Her amateur detective, Kate Fansler—a gutsy, childless, elegant literature professor of WASP descent and upper-class upbringing, who in ripe middle age marries a man younger than herself—has charmed a large audience and allowed her author to familiarize, in an entertaining way, a readership outside the university with issues alien to their everyday world. A number of the books deal with the precarious situation of women (and minorities) in academe (*Poetic Justice*, 1970; *Death in a Tenured Position*, 1981; *Sweet Death, Kind Death*, 1984; *A Trap for Fools*, 1989; *An Imperfect Spy*, 1995). Others portray the eccentric lives of women writers and their ambitious biographers (*The Question of Max*, 1976; *No Word from Winifred*, 1986; *The Players Come Again*, 1990).

Like many American Jewish women who grew up materially privileged but estranged from their Jewish roots, Carolyn G. Heilbrun worked hard to create a significant identity for herself. The women's movement provided her with a framework within which she could rethink not only her field (modern British literature), but also herself. In the process, she wrote inspiring critical studies that reconsidered the stature of European women writers, encouraged her readers to reconceive the role of women in society, and propelled her to the forefront of American feminism.

SELECTED WORKS BY CAROLYN G. HEILBRUN

Christopher Isherwood (1970); *The Education of a Woman: The Life of Gloria Steinem* (1995); *The Garnett Family* (1961); *Hamlet's Mother and Other Women* (1990); *Lady Ottoline's Album: Snapshots and Portraits of her Famous Contemporaries (and of Herself)*, editor (1976); *The Last Gift of Time: Life Beyond Sixty* (1997); *Reinventing Womanhood* (1979); *The Representation of Women in Fiction*, editor, with Margaret R. Higonnet (1983); *Toward a Recognition of Androgyny* (1973); *Writing a Woman's Life* (1988).

MYSTERIES WRITTEN AS AMANDA CROSS

Death in a Tenured Position (1981); *An Imperfect Spy* (1995); *In the Last Analysis* (1964); *The James Joyce Murders* (1967); *No Word from Winifred* (1986); *The Players Come Again* (1990); *Poetic Justice* (1970); *The Question of Max* (1976); *Sweet Death, Kind Death* (1984); *The Theban Mysteries* (1971); *A Trap for Fools* (1989).

BIBLIOGRAPHY

Directory of American Scholars. Vol. 2, *English, Speech and Drama* (1982); *The International Who's Who of Women* (1992); Klingenstein, Susanne. "'But My Daughters Can Read the Torah': Careers of Jewish Women in Literary Academe." *American Jewish History* 83 (1995): 247–286, and *Enlarging America: The Cultural Work of Jewish Literary Scholars, 1930–1990* (1998); *Who's Who in America* (1996).

SUSANNE KLINGENSTEIN

HEIMAN, ADELE BLUTHENTHAL (1900–1979)

Adele (Bluthenthal) Heiman's exuberance for life and dedication to Judaism permeated all that she was or did as a communal leader. Her lifelong concern for others and her indefatigable spirit, evident in her participation in many community organizations, was inherited from her forebears.

She was born on August 22, 1900, the eldest child of Adolph and Rachel (Rae Solmson) Bluthenthal. Her siblings were Henriette, Madeline, and David. Adolph Bluthenthal, born in 1865 in Germany, had come to Pine Bluff, Arkansas, as a teenager. Family members had settled there before the Civil War. Adolph established a leading men's clothing store and was active in civic and religious life. In December 1895, he married Rae Solmson, daughter of prominent Pine Bluff settler Solomon Solmson. Rae's mother was German-born Henrietta Berlin, whose family settled in Baltimore, Maryland, when she was fourteen.

In 1921, Adele graduated Phi Beta Kappa from Goucher College, a women's school in Baltimore. On September 29 of that year, she married Jesse Heiman of Little Rock. Jesse was the son of Max Heiman, who helped develop the Gus Blass Company into the state's largest department store. Jesse, a graduate of Columbia University, was with the Blass company from 1906 to 1945, serving as vice president and treasurer. Adele and Jesse Heiman had three children: Rose (b. 1923), Max Adolph (b. 1925), and Robert Jesse (b. 1930).

Judaism was important to the Heiman family. They were members of Congregation B'nai Israel, the state's largest Reform Jewish congregation, and faithfully attended services. Heiman served on the temple board and twice as sisterhood president. She was president of the Arkansas-Oklahoma Federation of Temple Sisterhoods. She served simultaneously as a member of the national board of the NATIONAL COUNCIL OF JEWISH WOMEN and the national board of the NATIONAL FEDERATION OF TEMPLE SISTERHOODS and was a board member of the Little Rock Boys Club Auxiliary. As well, she served on the city board for the United Service Organizations during World War II.

During the 1930s and 1940s, the Arkansas Jewish Assembly was an umbrella organization that brought together the Jewish congregations and served the needs of the Jews throughout the state. Heiman was elected its first vice president in 1932 and served as its first woman president in 1935. In 1938, she headed the assembly's work in cooperating with national efforts to resettle German Jewish immigrants in America.

Three years after Jesse Heiman died on December 27, 1952, Adele Heiman married Ernest E. Ellman, a retired department store executive. The latter died on January 17, 1974.

Heiman was an intelligent woman, determined to become well educated and pursue a life of service to her community and her religion. While expending limitless energy in her efforts for others, she also exuded an aura of graciousness and warmth that made her all the more appreciated by those she helped or who knew her. She gave exemplary credit to her Jewish heritage.

Adele Bluthenthal Heiman died on April 3, 1979.

BIBLIOGRAPHY

Arkansas Democrat, April 4, 1979, 8d; *Arkansas Gazette*, November 7, 1917, 1; Firestone, Bill. "The Pine Bluff Connection," Bluthenthal Family Tree; Heiman, Robert. Interview with author, Blytheville, Arkansas, November 25, 1982; LeMaster, Carolyn Gray. *A Corner of the Tapestry: A History of the Jewish Experience in Arkansas, 1820s–1990s* (1994); Loeb, Rose Heiman. Telephone interview with author, September 3, 1996; *WWIAJ* (1938).

CAROLYN GRAY LEMASTER

HELBURN, THERESA (1887–1959)

Named "'Top Man' on Broadway" in 1936 by the *New York Woman*, Theresa Helburn, the intrepid administrative director of the Theatre Guild for almost forty years, dedicated herself to raising the artistic standards of the American theater. She played a major role in creating the modern American musical.

Helburn was born on January 12, 1887, in New York City, the younger of two children of Hannah (Peyser) and Julius Helburn. Her father was a leather merchant; her mother, who became Helburn's role model, established her own experimental elementary school. An assimilated Jew, Helburn attended Horace Mann, the fashionable Windsor School in Boston, and Bryn Mawr College. She graduated in 1908 with many senior prizes, having organized, directed, and acted in all the school plays. She continued her education at Radcliffe College, in George Pierce Baker's celebrated playwriting workshop, English 47, and at the Sorbonne. She joined the Poetry Society of America, created a course in Shakespearean acting at Miss Merrill's Finishing School, Mamaroneck, New York, and wrote drama criticism for *The Nation*.

Helburn's varied interests coalesced when she volunteered to head the nascent Theatre Guild, a position no one else wanted. She learned on the job. The Guild, formally organized in 1919, grew out of the recently disbanded Washington Square Players, founded in 1914 by patent attorney and playwright Lawrence Langner, actor Helen Westley, director Philip Moeller, and Rollo Peters. In 1921, the Guild's governing board of managers consisted of Helburn, banker Maurice Wertheim, and four of its founders: set designer Lee Simonson, Langner, Westley, and Moeller. Helburn credited the Guild's high rate of successful productions to this mixture of diverse backgrounds and tastes. Her title changed from executive director (1919–1932) to administrative director in 1933 after a reorganization that left Helburn, Langner, and his wife, the actor Armina Marshall, at the helm.

The Guild was established to prove that a theater devoted to art could attract talent and a broad-based audience. During the first four years, the Guild staged primarily modern European drama. After producing

*She was possessed with impressive managerial skills, but Theresa Helburn's
uncanny sense of theatrical innovation resulted in productions like* Oklahoma! *and*
Carousel *that virtually redefined the American musical. As this photo demonstrates,
she was "intrepid" in more than just administrative situations. [New York Public Library]*

Sidney Howard's *They Knew What They Wanted*, which won the 1924 Pulitzer Prize, the Guild began to concentrate on producing the works of native talent, such as Eugene O'Neill, S.N. Behrman, and Maxwell Anderson, as well as European innovators such as George Bernard Shaw. Under Helburn's guidance, New York subscriptions grew from 135 to six thousand in five years. By 1940, the Guild had developed ten subscription cities for their road shows.

Helburn's individual theater contributions were equally impressive. Envisioning a new musical theater, she tried for years to bring song teams and dramatists together. Her first success was in uniting Lynn Riggs, who wrote *Green Grow the Lilacs*, with Richard Rodgers, Oscar Hammerstein II, and Agnes de Mille to create *Oklahoma!* (1943), the musical based on that book, which ran for 2,212 performances. *Carousel*, the Rodgers and Hammerstein adaptation of *Liliom* by Ferenc Molnár, followed in 1945. She cast actors Alfred Lunt and Lynn Fontanne together for the first time in *The Guardsman* (1924). Always scouting for new voices, she established the Bureau of New Plays with John Gassner and, although not an ideological feminist, publicly lamented the small percentage of women dramatists. When Lee Strasberg, Cheryl Crawford, and Harold Clurman rebelled against

Guild policy, Helburn secured funds for their experiments, facilitating the birth of the Group Theatre.

In 1922, Helburn married John Baker Opdycke, a prolific scholar. Helburn's plays include *A Hero Is Born* (1937, a two-act extravaganza based on her play *Enter the Hero*, 1916), *Allison Makes Hay* (1919, formerly titled *Crops and Croppers*), *Other Lives* (1921, with Edward Goodman), and *Denbigh* (1927).

Theresa Helburn died on August 18, 1959, in Norwalk, Connecticut. *A Wayward Quest*, her autobiography, was published posthumously.

SELECTED WORKS BY THERESA HELBURN

Allison Makes Hay (1919); *Denbigh* (1927); *A Hero Is Born* (1937); *Other Lives*, with Edward Goodman (1921); *A Wayward Quest* (1960).

BIBLIOGRAPHY

AJYB 24:154; Atkinson, Brooks. *Broadway* (1974); *BEOAJ*; Bordman, Gerald. *The Oxford Companion to American Theatre* (1984); Brockett, Oscar G., and Robert R. Findley. *Century of Innovation* (1973); *Current Biography 1944* (1945), s.v. "Helburn, Theresa," and "Langner, Lawrence"; *DAB* 6; Helburn, Theresa. Clipping file, photograph file, and manuscript collection. Billy Rose Theatre Collection, New York City Public Library for the Performing Arts at Lincoln Center, and Papers. The Theatre Guild Archive, Collection of American Literature, Beinecke Library, Yale University, New Haven, Conn., and Play manuscripts. Archives. Bryn Mawr College, Bryn Mawr, Pa.; Langner, Lawrence. *The Magic Curtain* (1951); "In Memoriam: Theresa Helburn: The First Lady of Broadway Producers." *Theatre* (October 1959): 28, 46; Menken, Harriet. "A Woman and Her Career." *Jewish Tribune* (February 1, 1929), 18; *NAW* modern; Obituary. *NYTimes*, August 19, 1959, 29:3, correction August 20, 1959, 25:4; Stock, Jennifer. "Helburn, Theresa." *Notable Women in the American Theatre: A Biographical Dictionary*. Edited by Alice M. Robinson, Vera Mowry Roberts, and Milly S. Barranger (1989): 314–316; "'Top Man' on Broadway." *New York Woman* (September 30, 1936); *UJE*; Waldau, Roy S. *Vintage Years of the Theatre Guild, 1928–1939* (1972); Webster, Margaret. *Don't Put Your Daughter on the Stage* (1972); *Who Was Who in Theatre 1912–1976*. Vol. 2 (1978); *WWIAJ* (1926, 1928, 1938); *WWWIA* 3.

GLENDA FRANK

HELD, ANNA (c. 1873–1918)

Anna Held was a performer with a flamboyant reputation for bathing in milk and champagne. An actor in numerous farces, comedies, and musical comedies, her life was a story of showmanship that prevents bibliographical certainty.

The date and place of Anna Held's birth are shrouded in mystery, confusion, or vanity. They range from March 18, 1865, in Warsaw, Poland, to 1878 in Paris, France, a thirteen-year difference. That she was born in Warsaw on March 18, 1873, may be most accurate. Held was the youngest and only survivor of eleven children. Her parents were Maurice (or Shimmle), a glovemaker, and Yvonne (or Helene) Pierre. Some sources suggest that both her parents were Jewish, while one source states that her mother was Catholic.

The Helds moved from Warsaw to Paris as early as 1871, but most probably in 1876. Anna Held sang in the streets at age eight. After her father died in 1884 or 1885, she and her mother moved to England, where they were befriended by an actor in Jacob Adler's Yiddish Theatre. Shortly thereafter, her mother died.

Upon leaving the Adler company, Held capitalized on her tiny five-foot-tall, 115-pound body. With her corseted eighteen-inch waist, she played the precocious gamin with a come-hither look. Returning to Paris, she quickly became a star of light comedy. Around 1894, in France, she secretly married Maximo Carrera, a fifty-year-old South American. They had one daughter, Liane Carrera (b. 1896), who also became a stage performer.

In 1896, Held was courted with rare orchids and a diamond bracelet by twenty-five-year-old Florenz Ziegfeld. That year, she divorced Carrera and moved to the United States. Again mystery shrouds the union of Held and Ziegfeld. They had a common-law ceremony and lived together from 1896 or 1897 to 1908 or 1909. A divorce was granted in 1913. Ziegfeld's second wife, Billie Burke, described Held as "frugal, domestic, and maternal."

From 1896 to 1918, Held acted in numerous farces, comedies, and musical comedies and promoted the Ziegfeld Follies. She made her American debut at the Herald Square Theater in New York on September 21, 1896, in *A Parlor Match*, Ziegfeld's revival of a farce. In New York, she performed in the Lyric Theatre, New York Casino, Knickerbocker Theater, and Broadway Theater. Her style was suggestive, mocking, and playful.

Held's mythical exploits included capturing a runaway horse, daring American women to drive fast, and bathing in gallons of milk. She wore flamboyant costumes and Parisian gowns. She became an early product endorser: There were Anna Held corsets, face powder, pomade, and cigars. She made one movie in 1915, *Madame la Presidente*.

Held was ill for the last six months of her life. The initial diagnosis, multiple myeloma, was changed to pernicious anemia complicated by acute bronchial pneumonia. A publicity diagnosis was "lacing too tight with corsets." Anna Held died on August 12, 1918.

About the only things that are certain about Anna Held's life is that she was flamboyant and very successful. A comedian of international status, she playfully toyed with her public both on- and offstage, employing outrageous stunts and gimmicks to garner publicity. [Library of Congress]

BIBLIOGRAPHY

AJYB 6 (1904–1905): 113; Burke, Billie. *With a Feather on My Nose* (1949); Farnsworth, Marjorie. *The Ziegfeld Follies* (1956); Held, Anna. *Memoires* (1954); Hoffman, Michael Owen. "Anna Held: A Biography." Master's thesis, Portland State University, 1982; *NAW*; Obituary. *NYTimes*, August 13, 1918, 9:3; Sandrow, Nahma. *Vagabond Stars* (1977); *WWWIA* 1.

OLIVER B. POLLAK

HELDMAN, GLADYS (b. 1922)

Gladys Heldman, born in New York City on May 13, 1922, to scholarly Jewish parents, was an unlikely person to become a leader in women's tennis. Yet women tennis players today owe their equal status in the sport to her important efforts.

Her father, George Z. Medalie, a famous lawyer and jurist, and her mother, Carrie, a Latin and Greek scholar, raised their daughter in New York and then sent her to Stanford University in 1939, where she earned a bachelor's degree and a Phi Beta Kappa key in three years. Two days after graduation, she married Julius Heldman, an avid tennis player with a Ph.D. in physical chemistry, who became a chemistry professor at the University of California, Berkeley. Heldman studied medical history there, received a master's degree in the subject, and planned to pursue a doctorate. She also had a daughter, Carrie.

In 1949, however, her husband's career took him to Shell Oil Company and Texas. Julius Heldman, who had played tennis for UCLA as a teenager, encouraged his wife to take up tennis after their second daughter, Julie, was born. Heldman became proficient, earning a number-one ranking in Texas in the early 1950s. In 1954, she got a berth in the Wimbledon draw, although she lost in the first round.

When she stopped playing competitive tennis, Heldman channeled her love for the game in a different direction. In 1953, she created, edited, and published *World Tennis Magazine* and became the sole voice for women's tennis coverage. Indeed, in the early 1950s, tennis was what longtime commentator Bud Collins called the "secret sport"—newspapers, magazines, and radio never reported on the game. In 1959, when the United States Lawn Tennis Association (USLTA) decided not to hold the National Indoor Championship because the competition had lost money the previous year, Heldman agreed to underwrite the losses. She ended up realizing a profit for the event. This contribution was the beginning of her active sponsorship of women's tennis events.

In 1962, she sponsored eighty-five women players from overseas to participate in the U.S. Open at Forest Hills. During the winter of 1969, Heldman staged three tournaments for women. In 1970, Billie Jean King and her longtime friend and doubles partner Rosie Casals were so upset by the disparity in prize money between the men and the women that they threatened to boycott the upcoming U.S. Open. Heldman, their friend and adviser, suggested an alternative: She planned a women's tournament to occur the same week as the Pacific Grove Open, the event preceding Forest Hills. Gaining financial support from her friend Joe Cullman, the president of Philip Morris, she formed the Virginia Slims tour.

At first, the male tennis establishment, headed by Jack Kramer, punished the women who dared to play in the Heldman-sponsored events. But after a three-year power struggle that included lawsuits initiated by Heldman and King against the USLTA, a reconciliation was reached. Purses were brought into line, and the men and women professionals played at the same events. Part of the 1973 agreement, however, was for Heldman to give up her leadership role in the women's organization. "I was out," she was quoted as saying, "but the war was over, and that was the most important thing." Shortly thereafter, Heldman sold *World Tennis Magazine*, which had become the most popular and influential magazine in the field.

When Heldman began her crusade for equal purse money and equal recognition for women tennis players, men's prize money was fifteen times greater than women's. By the time she retired, women tennis players were treated equally. The current generation of women tennis players owe their equal status to the important efforts of Gladys Heldman.

Gladys Heldman lives with her husband in Santa Fe, New Mexico.

BIBLIOGRAPHY

Collins, Bud. *Modern Encyclopedia of Tennis* (1980), and *My Life with the Pros* (1989); King, Billie Jean, with Cynthia Starr. *We Have Come a Long Way* (1988); LaFontaine, B. "Busiest Voice in a Busy, Busy Clan." *Sports Illustrated* 20 (June 22, 1964): 38–40+.

JUNE SOCHEN

HELLER, FLORENCE (1897–1966)

Florence Grunsfeld Heller, who became a social worker, volunteer leader in Chicago, and benefactor of Brandeis University, was born in Albuquerque, New Mexico, on March 2, 1897, the daughter of Ivan and Hannah (Nusbaum) Grunsfeld and the grand-daughter of Albert and Heldegarde (David) Grunsfeld. Her parents and grandparents were German immigrants who came to the United States in 1873, settling in the territory of New Mexico. Her father was a wholesale merchant. Her initial years of schooling in Albuquerque were followed by years at Bradford Academy in Boston, Massachusetts, and the Faulkner School for Girls in Chicago, Illinois. In Chicago, at age sixteen or seventeen, Florence Grunsfeld lived with her maternal uncle, Julius Rosenwald—the founder of Sears Roebuck and Company—and his wife. Florence

Heller's son Peter credits the Rosenwalds with instilling in her a strong devotion and sense of obligation to society.

According to a family legend, Florence met her future husband, Walter E. Heller, at a formal dance when he was wearing a purple tuxedo. Walter Heller was chairman of the board of Walter E. Heller and Company, a firm in the financial industry. They were married in Chicago on February 22, 1917, just before Florence turned twenty. They had three sons: John Andrew, Peter Eugene, and Paul Walter. Their marriage ended in divorce in 1953.

Heller's primary activities as a philanthropist and organizational leader were in Chicago. As a volunteer in the 1920s, she served individuals in need of relief at the United Jewish Charities in Chicago. Not long afterward, she became involved with settlement work, serving new immigrants to the United States through the Jewish Peoples Institute. From 1923 to 1941, she served as president of its women's auxiliary.

During World War II, her activities extended beyond the Jewish community, leading her to work with the United Service Organizations (USO) in helping to provide ancillary services to American servicemen both in the United States and overseas. As chair of the management committee of the Central USO Club of Greater Chicago, she led one of the most active branches of that organization.

The *National Cyclopaedia of American Biography* links Heller's "intense interest in social welfare work" with her involvement with the national Jewish Welfare Board (JWB). From 1948 to 1964, she was vice president; from 1964 to 1966, she was the president. She represented the JWB to the United Nations Conference Group of Non-Governmental Organizations. Her *New York Times* obituary recognizes her as the first female president of a general national Jewish organization.

The JWB offered a forum for Heller's growing interest in the training of aspiring social workers. She helped to establish a research center for the JWB in conjunction with Brandeis University and served as a trustee there. In 1959, she concretized her commitment to the training of social workers in the gift of a million-dollar endowment to found the Florence Heller Graduate School for Advanced Studies in Social Welfare at Brandeis. She also served as a trustee of Brandeis University.

In Chicago, her philanthropic inclinations also found a home in an endowment for the Florence Heller Isotope Laboratory and the Florence G. Heller Blood Bank at the Louis A. Weiss Memorial Hospital. She was also a member of Chicago Women's Aid,

Mothers Aid to Chicago Lying-In Hospital, Infant Welfare of Chicago, the Art Institute of Chicago, and the Field Museum of Natural History.

She contributed to the international Jewish community through her membership on the board of the World Federation of Young Men's Hebrew Associations and Jewish Community Centers. As an early supporter of the Jerusalem YM-YWHA, she attended the groundbreaking ceremonies there in 1964. She served as treasurer and board member of Sinai Temple in Chicago.

Florence Heller died in Chicago, on January 5, 1966.

BIBLIOGRAPHY

AJYB 68 (1967): 528; Heller, Peter E. Correspondence with the author, September 26, 1995; *National Cyclopaedia of American Biography* (1969); *NYTimes*, January 6, 1966, 27:4; July 10, 1976, 26; July 11, 1976, 45; and July 12, 1976, B2; *WWIAJ* (1928, 1938); *WWIA* 5.

JUDD KRUGER LEVINGSTON

HELLMAN, CLARISSE DORIS (1910–1973)

C. Doris Hellman was one of the first professional historians of science in the United States. She devoted a considerable part of her life to the study of Johannes Kepler and to the history of exact science in the Renaissance. As a scholar and writer, she was adept at working in foreign languages, especially German. Her most lasting contribution is her translation of Max Caspar's monumental biography, *Johannes Kepler* (1959).

Clarisse Doris Hellman was born on August 28, 1910, in New York City. The daughter of obstetrician Alfred M. and Clarisse (Bloom) Hellman, she was raised in a Jewish family that had a special appreciation for the sciences. After graduating from the Horace Mann School, she attended Vassar College, where she studied mathematics and astronomy with such distinction that she was elected to Phi Beta Kappa and graduated with honors in 1930. She then went on to Radcliffe College as a Vassar College Fellow and received one of the country's earliest advanced degrees in history of science, a master's degree, in 1931. From Radcliffe, she returned to New York, where she received a prestigious Columbia University Fellowship and went on to complete her Ph.D. at Columbia in 1943.

In the interim, she managed to balance the demands of her graduate study with the responsibilities of marriage and parenthood. In 1933, she married a prominent New York attorney, Morton Pepper, and together they raised two daughters, Alice (b. 1937) and Carol (b. 1940).

In 1951, Doris Hellman accepted a position at the Pratt Institute, where she taught until 1966. She also taught briefly as an adjunct professor of history of science at New York University (1964–1966) before accepting an appointment in 1966 at Queens College of the City University of New York, where she also served on the faculty of the university's graduate school until 1973.

Doris Hellman's doctoral thesis at Columbia, *The Comet of 1577: Its Place in the History of Astronomy*, was published in 1944 (reprinted 1971). She contributed three articles to *The Dictionary of Scientific Biography*, a major undertaking sponsored by the National Science Foundation (NSF) and the American Council of Learned Societies: on Brahe, Dörffel, and Peuerbach (the last of which she coauthored with Noel Swerdlow). She also wrote a broad survey of "Science in the Renaissance" for *Renaissance News*.

Hellman was a member of the Columbia University Seminar on the Renaissance (1956–1973). Her scholarship was recognized by an NSF Senior Postdoctoral Fellowship in 1959–1960. Additionally, she was a Fellow of the Royal Astronomical Society and of the American Association for the Advancement of Science, which she served as secretary of its section for history and philosophy of science in 1957.

Hellman was prominent among the women who helped support the history of science in its earliest years in the United States. She served as an elected member of the Council of the History of Science Society from 1949 to 1959, and again from 1964 to 1966. She was also a member of the Advisory Council of the Renaissance Society of America. While serving as secretary of the U.S. National Committee of the International Union of History and Philosophy of Science (1958–1960), she was a delegate representing the National Academy of Sciences and the National Research Council to the Ninth International Congress of the History of Science that met in Barcelona, Spain, in 1959. Later she also served as secretary of the Tenth Congress, held in Ithaca, New York, and Philadelphia in 1962. Hellman was elected to the International Academy for the History of Science as a corresponding member in 1963 and was elected a *membre effectif* six years later. In addition to her work as a historian of science, she was active in supporting the Jewish Foundation for Education of Girls (1942–1973).

Clarisse Doris Hellman died in New York City, on March 28, 1973.

SELECTED WORKS BY
CLARISSE DORIS HELLMAN

"Brahe," "Dörffel," and, with Noel Swerdlow, "Peuerbach." In *The Dictionary of Scientific Biography* (1970–1980); *The Comet of 1577: Its Place in the History of Astronomy* (1944. Reprint, 1971); Caspar, Max. *Johannes Kepler.* Translated by C. Doris Hellman (1959. Reprint, 1962); "Science in the Renaissance." *Renaissance News* 8 (1955): 186–200.

BIBLIOGRAPHY

Obituary. *NYTimes*, March 29, 1973, 50:4; Rosen, Edward. *Archives internationales d'histoire des sciences* 25 (1975): 94–95, and "Éloge." *Isis* 66 (1975): 561–562; *WWWIA* 6 (1974–1976): 188.

JOSEPH W. DAUBEN

HELLMAN, LILLIAN (1905–1984)

Lillian Hellman's father once referred to her as the "Jewish nun of Prytania Street," a description that aptly suggests the complexity of her life and of her relationship to Judaism and Jewish culture. Both as a writer and in her private life, Hellman lived out many contradictory roles, some of which, the historical record and her contemporaries suggest, may well have been self-invented, blurring the lines between biography and art in her own presentation of self. Controversial both during and after her life, Lillian Hellman is one of the leading women of letters of mid-century America and a pioneer in the area of women as playwrights. Some corners of her life will probably always remain clouded and impossible to verify, an irony in a woman for whom questions of ethics and truth-telling were recurrent themes in her plays and memoirs.

Lillian Hellman was born on June 20, 1905, in New Orleans, Louisiana. Her parents, Max and Julia (Newhouse) Hellman, were both German-American Jews. Her mother's family was wealthy and later became the models (though stripped of Jewish identity) for Hellman's most famous creations, the Hubbards, in her two plays *The Little Foxes* and *Another Part of the Forest*. Max Hellman's sisters Hannah and Jenny were similarly the basis for the central characters in one of Hellman's last plays, *Toys in the Attic*.

In 1911, when Max's shoe business failed, the Hellmans left New Orleans and moved to New York City. From the time Lillian Hellman was eleven until she was sixteen, the family divided its time between New Orleans and New York City, giving the young girl a sense of always belonging to multiple cultures. She attended New York University for a time and in 1924 went to work for the prestigious publishing house Boni and Liveright. The following year, she

married the writer Arthur Kober. Five years later, they moved to Hollywood, where Kober was employed as a screenwriter. Hellman also found work in the fledgling sound film industry, working first as a reader and later as a writer for the legendary mogul Sam Goldwyn. The marriage between Kober and Hellman, her only legal marriage, ended in divorce.

During the 1930s, Hellman began to write plays. Her first produced play, *The Children's Hour* (1934), would also prove to be her most controversial. In it, Hellman explored the effects of a lie, spread as gossip, in a small New England town. What produced controversy was the nature of the lie: a little girl taking revenge on two teachers at a private school by telling her grandmother that they were lesbians. Though the rumor is groundless, it causes financial ruin for the women and results in one of them, Martha, questioning her own sexuality and killing herself in the last act of the play. Discussion, let alone representation, of homosexuality onstage and in film was then close to taboo (indeed, the play was banned in many cities) and was, according to critics of the time, the primary reason the play was denied the Pulitzer Prize for best drama of the year. Interestingly, in 1936, Sam Goldwyn filmed the play as *These Three*, omitting all references to lesbianism and turning the lie into one suggesting a romantic triangle between the two women and the doctor who is engaged to one of them. While some felt that such an alteration removed the play's power, others (Hellman included) felt that it maintained the central focus of the play: the power of a lie to destroy lives.

Hellman continued to write and produce plays throughout the next three decades, including some of the greatest critical and popular successes of the Broadway stage. Virtually all of the plays were "well made," following in the realistic and naturalistic traditions of such dramatists as Henrik Ibsen and Anton Chekhov. Hellman shares with Ibsen a concern for the drama as a representation of social problems and as a keen insight into the psyche and power of women in societies that restrict their political and economic power. With Chekhov, she shares the craft of dramatizing the complex orchestrations of families and small towns. Her most important plays, in addition to *The Children's Hour*, include *The Little Foxes* and *Another Part of the Forest*, which follow the machinations of the Hubbard family in the antebellum South. In these two plays, she creates her most memorable and lasting character, Regina Hubbard Giddens, a virago descended from such prototypes as Medea and Lady Macbeth, played by such disparate actors as Tallulah Bankhead (who originated the role in *Foxes* on

Broadway), Bette Davis (who transferred the role to film), and Elizabeth Taylor. Of such epic proportions were the Hubbards that *The Little Foxes* was translated into opera form by Marc Blitzstein, as *Regina*.

Other plays include her World War II dramas *Watch on the Rhine* (1941) and the less memorable *The Searching Wind* (1944). *The Autumn Garden* (1951), which Hellman and many critics believed to be her finest play; and *Toys in the Attic* (1960), in which she returned to family material. Hellman won the New York Drama Critics Award for both *Watch on the Rhine* and *Toys in the Attic*. Hellman also adapted foreign plays as well as novels for the stage.

Throughout Hellman's career as a playwright, her "offstage" life was lively and dramatic as well. During the 1920s and 1930s, she took a number of trips to Europe—trips which raised her political awareness. What actually occurred on these trips is the source of much debate. In her memoirs, particularly in the section of *Pentimento* called "Julia," Hellman depicted herself as a participant in anti-Nazi work. Recent biographers have called into question the identity of "Julia" (a pseudonym in Hellman's writings) and Hellman's actual participation in underground activities. The questions remain unanswered, and perhaps will always remain unanswered as presumably most of the principals involved have died.

Though Hellman never remarried after her divorce from Kober, she sustained a complex, passionate, and tempestuous relationship with the mystery writer Dashiell Hammett from 1930 until his death in 1961. The two of them, individually and together, became important figures in left-wing literary and intellectual circles, with Hellman in particular becoming a noted pro-Stalinist. Indeed, their left-wing activities led to Hellman's being blacklisted from Hollywood in 1948, during the first years of the witchhunts led by Senator Joseph McCarthy. She was called to testify before the House Un-American Activities Committee (HUAC) in 1952. In a letter that has now become famous as one of the most articulate and eloquent responses to McCarthyism, Hellman declined to testify, not out of fear for her own safety or her own unwillingness to speak of her beliefs or activities, but because she could not name her friends and coworkers and still keep her self-respect. In an era when many other writers and actors did name "fellow travelers" in order to exculpate themselves, Hellman's stand was considered a brave one at the time, though it came under considerable revision in later years, particularly after Hellman's presentation of it in her third memoir, *Scoundrel Time*. Contemporaries of Hellman's, such as Diana Trilling, Irving Howe, and Mary McCarthy,

Like her art and her politics, Lillian Hellman's Jewishness and its place in her work have been subjected to intense scrutiny and, in some cases, intense criticism. There is no doubt, however, about her impact on twentieth-century literature.
[New York Public Library]

questioned what they saw as Hellman's revision of her actual participation in pro-Stalinist work and of her self-congratulatory stance toward her actions during the HUAC hearings.

Despite such revisionism, Hellman was lionized in later years, particularly after the publication of her memoirs. Her first memoir, *An Unfinished Woman* (1969), won the National Book Award. She subtitled her later memoir, *Maybe* (1980), "A Story," but it seems clearly autobiographical, at least in part.

The importance of Judaism and Jewish culture in Hellman's life is ambiguous. She rarely wrote about Jewish themes in her plays and certainly never from the stance of an observant Jew. To the extent that leftist intellectual liberalism has been marked by a Jewish presence, Hellman fits into that tradition comfortably. In her memoirs, she addresses her Jewish heritage as part of a cultural background. Even here, she notes that the fact of her Jewishness didn't fully hit her until she was confronted with anti-Semitism in the national socialism of Germany during a trip there in 1929. Being a woman and being a southerner seemed more important texts of identity for Hellman than being Jewish. In interviews, she remarked that southern Jews tended to downplay their Jewishness. If one only read Hellman's plays, one would not necessarily guess that she was Jewish. And, while her memoirs do address this part of her identity, it is clear that Jewish life was not central to her sense of self, at least the self that was an artist and the self that she constructed in her memoirs. Indeed, Meyer Levin felt that Hellman was instrumental in blocking the production of his dramatization of *Anne Frank: The Diary of a Young Girl* because Levin's play was "too Jewish" in its depiction of Jewish religious practices and in its articulation of Anne Frank's Zionist sympathies.

Lillian Hellman remains a complicated figure in the history of Jewish American women. Her contributions to the arts of drama and memoir are significant and lasting. Her successes as a professional playwright at a time when that arena was dominated almost exclusively by men were considerable. However controversial, her presence in the world of ideas and politics of the times is undeniable. But the degree to which she brought her identity as a Jew to bear on either her art or her life must remain a question open to debate.

Lillian Hellman died on Martha's Vineyard, on June 30, 1984.

SELECTED WORKS BY LILLIAN HELLMAN

PLAYS

Another Part of the Forest (1947); *The Autumn Garden* (1951); *Candide* [adaptation] (1956); *The Children's Hour* (1934); *Days to Come* (1936); *The Lark* [adaptation] (1956); *The Little Foxes* (1939); *Montserrat* (1950); *My Mother, My Father, and Me* [adaptation] (1963); *The Searching Wind* (1944); *Toys in the Attic* (1960); *Watch on the Rhine* (1941).

BOOKS

The Collected Plays (1972); *Conversations with Lillian Hellman*. Edited by Jackson R. Bryer (1986); *Eating Together*, with Peter Feibleman (1984); *Maybe: A Story* (1980); *Pentimento* (1973); *Scoundrel Time* (1976); *An Unfinished Woman* (1969).

BIBLIOGRAPHY

Adams, Timothy Dow. *Telling Lies in Modern American Autobiography* (1990); *AJYB* 86:440; Bills, Steven. *Lillian Hellman: An Annotated Bibliography* (1979); Chinoy, Helen Kritch, and Linda Walsh Jenkins, eds. *Women in American Theatre*. Rev. ed. (1987); *EJ*; Estrin, Mark W., ed. *Critical Essays on Lillian Hellman* (1989); Falk, Doris V. *Lillian Hellman* (1978); Feibleman, Peter S. *Lilly: Reminiscences of Lillian Hellman* (1988); Gillin, Edward. "'Julia' and Julia's Son." *Modern Language Studies* 19, no. 2 (1989): 3–11; Graver, Lawrence. *An Obsession with Anne Frank: Meyer Levin and the Diary* (1995); Grossman, Anita Susan. "Art Versus Truth in Autobiography: The Case of Lillian Hellman." *CLIO* 14 (1985): 289–308; Henderson, Bruce. "Lillian Hellman." In *Jewish American Women Writers*, edited by Ann R. Shapiro (1994); Lederer, Katherine. *Lillian Hellman* (1979); Lyons, Bonnie. "Lillian Hellman: 'The First Jewish Nun of Prytania Street.'" In *From Hester Street to Hollywood: The Jewish-American Stage and Screen*, edited by Sarah Blacher Cohen (1983); Riordan, Mary Marguerite. *Lillian Hellman: A Bibliography, 1926–1978* (1980); Rollyson, Carl E. *Lillian Hellman: Her Legend and Her Legacy* (1988); *UJE*; Wright, William. *Lillian Hellman: The Image, the Woman* (1986); *WWIAJ* (1938); *WWWIA* 8.

BRUCE HENDERSON

HENENBERG, HATTIE LEAH (1893–1974)

In 1925, a Texas governor reluctantly appointed the first all-female supreme court to hear an appeal involving Woodmen of the World, a fraternal group whose members included virtually every male lawyer in the state. Hattie Leah Henenberg, a lawyer since 1916, was among the trio of special associate justices. A pioneering jurist who launched her legal career as a stenographer, Henenberg set other precedents. In 1924, she was founding director of the Dallas Free Legal Aid Bureau and, in the 1940s, she created a unit in the Dallas district attorney's office that jailed fathers who failed to pay child support.

Born on a farm in Ennis, Texas, on February 16, 1893, Hattie Henenberg was the second child of Hungarian-born Rosa (Trebitsch) and Samuel Henenberg, parents of four daughters and two sons. The family moved to nearby Dallas in 1904 to help her ailing paternal grandfather, Lazar, owner of Dallas's oldest pawn and jewelry shop. Henenberg took night classes from 1913 to 1916 at Dallas Law School, part of Southern Methodist University. She was assistant Texas attorney general from 1929 to 1930; special assistant U.S. attorney general in Washington in 1934, and an assistant district attorney in Dallas from 1941 to 1947. In addition, Henenberg was a delegate to the 1932 Democratic National Convention in Chicago, a member of the Order of Eastern Star, Business and Professional Women's Club, Temple

In 1925, the governor of Texas appointed the state's first all-female supreme court to hear an appeal involving Woodmen of the World, a fraternal group whose members included virtually every male lawyer in the state. Pioneering in other ways as well, Hattie Henenberg was a member of this court. In this photo, she is in the center, with her fellow justices Hortense Ward on the left and Ruth Brazzil on the right. [Texas State Library]

Emanu-El, and Dallas president of Zonta International. The ideals of social justice that permeated her quest for legal aid to the poor reflected the principles of Judaism. Judaism also manifested itself through her decision not to marry a non-Jew and through religious observances such as not eating pork.

Hattie Leah Henenberg died in November 1974.

BIBLIOGRAPHY

BEOAJ; Henenberg, Sam [nephew]. Telephone interview by author, May 2, 1996; Stayton, John William. "The First All-Woman Supreme Court in the World." *Holland's Magazine* (March 1925): 5+, and "Miss Henenberg, Law Pioneer, Dies." *Dallas Morning News*, November 29, 1974, 11-B; *UJE*; *Who's Who of American Women* (1958, 1961, 1964); *WWIAJ* (1926, 1928, 1938).

HOLLACE AVA WEINER

HENNOCK, FRIEDA BARKIN
(1904–1960)

Frieda Barkin Hennock was the first woman to serve on the Federal Communications Commission (FCC), where she became the champion of noncommercial

An ambitious and brilliant lawyer, Frieda Barkin Hennock was at one time the youngest woman practicing law in New York City. She was also the first woman appointed to the Federal Communications Commission, where she championed the cause of educational television. [Library of Congress]

educational television. As a Jewish female of foreign birth, she endured a lifetime of undeserved—largely sexist—attacks for everything from excessive aggressiveness to innuendoes of immoral personal conduct. At the same time, she did not hesitate to take advantage of her sparkling feminine charm, sense of high fashion, and occasional flood of tears to manipulate a male-dominated society. As a committed Jew, Hennock also used her contacts with the Jewish community for professional advancement. She said daily prayers and was fluent in Yiddish. She was a devoted and supportive member of her extended family.

Born in Kovel (formerly Russia and Poland), now Ukraine, on September 27, 1904, to Boris and Sarah (Barkin) Hennock, Frieda Hennock was the youngest of six girls and two boys. After immigrating to the United States in 1910, she became a United States citizen in 1916 when her father, a real estate broker and banker in New York City, was naturalized.

Before graduating from Morris High School in the Bronx, Hennock displayed promise as a pianist, and her parents wanted her to be a professional musician. When she insisted on becoming a lawyer, they refused to pay her law school tuition. Thereupon, she proceeded to work during the day as a clerk at several law firms to pay for her evening classes at the Brooklyn Law School. In 1924, at age nineteen, she graduated with an LL.B. but had to wait until she was twenty-one before being admitted to the New York bar. At twenty-two, Hennock was the youngest woman lawyer practicing in New York City.

Stating that, as a female lawyer, she "had to work twice as hard" to win a case, Hennock formed a partnership in 1927 with Julius Silver, a mentor of Edwin Land, founder of Polaroid Company. She won seven acquittals in celebrated murder trials in 1928 and 1929. The partnership dissolved in 1934 after litigation over disputed ownership of some Polaroid stock held by the firm.

In 1941, Frieda Hennock became the first woman and the first Democrat to join the prestigious law firm of Choate, Mitchell and Ely. At the same time, she was a prominent fund-raiser in support of President Franklin D. Roosevelt, Mayor William O'Dwyer, liberal Democrat causes, and women's rights.

President Harry S. Truman named Hennock to the FCC in 1948. During the confirmation hearing, in the Republican-controlled Senate, she gained the support of powerful Republicans including Senator Robert A. Taft and Owen Brewster. After Hennock was sworn in as the first woman commissioner on July 6, she stated that "it seems fundamental that in this field, so peculiarly affecting women, the viewpoint of their sex should be presented." While in office, Hennock emerged as the major spokesperson for the fledgling educational television movement, pressing for permanent reservation of frequencies for this purpose, in opposition to her fellow commissioners and the commercial broadcasting industry lobby.

In 1951, Hennock was appointed a federal district judge in New York. But owing to sexist accusations of incompetence and personal misconduct, she withdrew. This humiliation turned out to be a great blessing in disguise, because as a result of it, she served out her FCC term. In recognition of her efforts, Hennock was invited to inaugurate the first educational television station, KUHT, Houston, Texas, in 1953. She also became noted for her landmark dissenting opinions against the powerful telecommunications special interests, thus influencing the shape of every aspect of television in its formative years.

In 1955, at the end of her term on the FCC, she was disappointed when President Dwight D. Eisenhower failed to reappoint her to the slot requiring a Democrat. Thereafter she returned to the practice of law, first as a partner at Davies, Richberg, Tydings, Beebe and Landa, and then on her own. She also acquired a commercial television station in Arkansas. In 1956, she married William H. Simons, a prosperous Washington realtor.

During her short but brilliant public career, Frieda Hennock became noted as the liberal gadfly on the FCC. Her style was confrontational, often abrasive. Her greatest triumph was the establishment of educational—now known as public—television. Fundamentally an idealist, she held that "television channels represent one of America's most valuable resources" to be preserved in the public interest. On June 20, 1960, at age fifty-five, Frieda Barkin Hennock succumbed to a brain tumor.

BIBLIOGRAPHY

AJYB 62:450; *Current Biography* (1948); Hennock, Frieda. Papers. Harry S. Truman Library, Independence, Mo., and Frieda Hennock Collection. Schlesinger Library, Radcliffe College, Cambridge, Mass.; Morgenthau, Henry. "Dona Quixote: The Adventures of Frieda Hennock." *Television Quarterly* 26, no. 2 (1992); *NAW* modern; Obituary. *NYTimes*, June 21, 1960, 33:4; Neustadt, Stanley, and Arthur Stambler, and Nicholas Zapple. Interviews with author.

HENRY MORGENTHAU

HERRMAN, ESTHER (1823–1911)

"Israel is proud of her Queen Esther to-night," concluded Rabbi Samuel Schulman at the 1902 testimonial dinner at the Waldorf-Astoria honoring philanthropist Esther Herrman, who supported numerous organizations publicly and untold individuals and causes in private.

Esther Herrman was born on August 7, 1823, in Utrecht, the Netherlands, to Sophia (Van Ysen) and Emanuel Mendels. She had three sisters, Gamma (b. 1821), Jette (b. 1821), and Adelaide (b. 1825), and came to the United States as a child following her mother's death in 1827. In 1843, she married Henry Herrman, a native of Baden who was born October 13, 1822. By 1847, Esther and Henry had moved from New York City to New Bedford, Massachusetts, where he started a business supplying sailing vessels. Their first children were born there: Sophia (1847) and Henrietta (1848). They moved to Boston, where Henry operated a clothing business and their son Abraham was born (1850).

By 1852, they returned to New York City, where Caroline (1854), Lillie (1855), and Daniel Webster (1861) were born. They purchased a residence in a well-to-do neighborhood in 1871, by which time Henry had become a successful importer of worsteds and woolens, operating as H. Herrman, Sternbach & Co. Henry died on February 14, 1889, and left his family with a significant fortune.

In 1876, Esther Herrman joined Sorosis, the city's pioneer women's club, and in 1881, she became chairman of its philanthropic committee. This marked her entrance into club life and was the starting point for thirty-five years of membership in, and financial support of, dozens of educational, philanthropic, and patriotic organizations. Through Sorosis she became friendly with such socially prominent women as suffragist Lillie Deveraux Blake. Esther Herrman believed in suffrage, attended suffrage meetings, and supported women's and suffrage organizations.

Her largest gifts, each ten thousand dollars or more, were directed to five local beneficiaries. Her support of Barnard College in the early 1890s, shortly after its establishment as the city's first secular institution to grant the B.A. degree to women, earned her the honorific of "founder." A granddaughter, Laura Levy Jackson, was a member of the first graduating class in 1893. Her gift in 1897 of an educational endowment fund for the Young Men's Hebrew Association (now the 92nd Street YM-YWHA) immediately followed Jacob Schiff's gift of a building for the Y. The positive educational experience of one of her sons many years earlier at the Young Men's Christian Association, she said, induced her to provide for classes specifically for Jewish young men. For similar reasons she supported the Hebrew Technical Institute, a training school in the mechanical trades for teenaged boys. As donor of the school's first large gift, she was named an honorary vice president in 1897. After donating a herbarium to the New York Botanical Garden in the Bronx in 1896, she endowed a fund there to give teachers the opportunity to study botany from nature. In 1901, she provided a major gift to the New York Academy of Sciences, initially for a new building but later designated for scientific research.

At the 1902 testimonial she told her admirers, "You have rewarded me not only for the things I have done, but also for all the dear and happy things I would like to do." She continued "doing" until her death on July 4, 1911, at her home in New York City.

BIBLIOGRAPHY

Obituaries. *NYTimes*, July 6, 1911, and *Tribune*, July 5, 1911, and *Hebrew Standard*, July 7, 1911; *A Testimonial and Dinner Given to Mrs. Esther Herrman by Her Many Friends in Recognition of Her Good Deeds at the Waldorf-Astoria April 19, 1902* (1902). Smith College, Sophia Smith Collection, New York Public Library, Jewish Division.

STEVEN SIEGEL

HERSCHER, SYLVIA (b. 1913)

Sylvia Herscher's career in the theater encompasses several occupations and spans decades. Since the 1950s she has been general manager, producer, publisher, agent, and board member, as well as friend and guide to countless writers and composers finding their way into the business. Her own word for what she has done in the theater is "matchmaker." The composer Jerry Herman (*Hello, Dolly!*, *La Cage aux Folles*) once referred to her as the embodiment of all his leading ladies: "a woman who arranges things." Herscher has matched writers with composers, producers with writers, and musical scores with publishers.

Herscher was born Sylvia Kossovsky to Louis and Anna (Spar) Kossovsky on December 10, 1913, in New York City. Her brother, Morris, two years older, died in the Battle of the Bulge in 1944. She graduated from the University of Arizona in 1934, and in 1935 married Seymour Herscher, who for eighteen years was company manager to the producer Alexander Cohen. Seymour Herscher, whom John Gielgud called "a man of grace in the theater," died in 1994. The Herschers were members of B'nai Jeshurun in New York. Their two children are David (b. 1943), a public relations executive much involved in promoting the New York City Marathon, and Miriam (b. 1945), a banking executive.

Sylvia Herscher began her career in the theater as a production assistant for *Make a Wish* in 1951, and then for Jule Styne's *Pal Joey* in 1952. She was general manager for Styne's *Hazel Flagg* (1953) and associate producer for *Will Success Spoil Rock Hunter?* (1955). Over the next four years, she was general manager for several shows, including *Mr. Wonderful, Visit to a Small Planet,* and *Say, Darling.*

In 1960, Herscher joined the William Morris Agency as a writers' and artists' representative, and was involved in *Tchin-Tchin* (1962) and *Dylan* (1964), both by Sidney Michaels, *Any Wednesday* by Muriel Resnick (1964), *The Blood Knot* by Athol Fugard (1964), *Oh, What a Lovely War!* by Ted Allan (1964), and *Golden Boy* by William Gibson, Lee Adams, and Charles Strouse (1964), among other shows.

From 1966 to 1975, Herscher was head of the theater department of the Edwin H. Morris Company, music publishers. In this capacity, she matched composers with writers, and properties for the musical stage with producers, and also arranged for the publication of these works with the Edwin H. Morris Company.

As a music publisher she was instrumental in the publication of such shows as *Mame* (1966), *Superman* (1966), *Applause* (1970), *Grease* (1972), *Mack and Mabel* (1974), *Shenandoah* (1975), and *A Chorus Line* (1977). She was subsequently the head of the theater department of G. Schirmer, a division of Macmillan Performing Arts, where she continued to put together people and properties, including *The Robber Bridegroom* by Alfred Uhry and Robert Waldman (1976), until her "retirement" in 1982. For Herscher, the theater is "the most collaborative art of all."

Herscher has also worked with the Jewish Repertory Theater. "Judaism has informed my entire life," she says. Her lifelong dedication to the theater has been the expression of her humanity and her religion.

Sylvia Herscher's career in theater bridged the great transition from the 1950s to the 1980s, through the era of expansion in post–World War II America, when the Ford Foundation made the arts a national priority. As a member of the board of trustees of the Goodspeed Opera Company in Connecticut and a board member of Musical Theatre Works in Manhattan, she is still deeply involved in "matchmaking" in the 1990s.

BIBLIOGRAPHY

Notable Names in the American Theatre (1976).

ANGELA WIGAN MARVIN

HERSTEIN, LILLIAN (1886–1983)

The history of Jewish women in the American labor movement tends to focus on those whose careers unfolded in the needle trades. Such was not the case with Lillian Herstein, who was a teacher and a nationally known labor leader.

Ethel Lillian Herstein, the youngest of six children, was born on April 12, 1886, in Chicago. Her parents, Wolf and Cipe Belle, emigrated from Vilkovishk, Lithuania, shortly after the U.S. Civil War, not only for economic reasons but because of Wolf's admiration for Abraham Lincoln and his ideals.

Wolf Herstein worked as the sextant of a synagogue, while his wife operated the C.B. Herstein Hebrew Book Store. When Wolf died, Cipe struggled to keep the store open, sending the older children out to work. Only twelve-year-old Lillian remained in school. With family help and a job, she went on to graduate from Northwestern University in 1907.

Convinced that teaching was "the most wonderful thing in the world," Lillian found positions in small rural schools. In 1912, she became a Chicago high school teacher and joined a union, the Federation of Women High School Teachers. Within a short time, she became the federation's delegate to the Chicago Federation of Labor (CFL). When the various teachers' organizations consolidated into the Chicago Teachers Union in 1937, Herstein represented the union in the CFL, serving as the only woman on its executive board for twenty-five years. She used her position to gain the CFL's support for school issues, often expressing her views on radio.

Herstein's career as a union organizer was launched when she was asked by Agnes Nestor of the Women's Trade Union League (WTUL) to speak to the CFL about the league's educational program for workers. Impressed with her speaking skills, the CFL asked her to go on its speakers' circuit. Herstein went on to organize couture seamstresses, steel workers, packing house workers, newspaper reporters, coal miners, and sleeping-car porters.

Through her work with the WTUL, Herstein became an advocate of workers' education. She taught classes in English and public speaking at the Chicago Labor College, a project of the WTUL and CFL. As the workers' education movement spread in the 1920s and 1930s, she taught summer courses at Bryn Mawr College and the University of Wisconsin. During the 1920s, Herstein also taught at Chicago's Crane Junior College. One of her pupils, Supreme Court Justice Arthur Goldberg, credited her with inspiring him to become a labor lawyer. An advocate of free junior colleges, Herstein successfully fought to keep them open during the Depression years.

Between 1922 and 1932, Herstein entered politics, running unsuccessfully for state and federal offices. In 1937, she was asked to become the adviser on child labor legislation at a meeting of the International Labor Organization in Geneva.

Returning to this country, she became involved in a fight between the American Federation of Labor and its Committee on Industrial Organization (CIO). Convinced that industrial organization was the only way for unskilled minorities to come into the labor movement, she feared the feuding that might arise from the CIO forming its own national organization. A passionate believer in arbitration, she unsuccessfully tried to heal the breach.

During World War II, Herstein was sent by the War Production Board to the West Coast, where she plunged into the tasks of providing housing, decent working conditions, and day care centers for defense workers.

Herstein retired from the city college system in 1952. During her retirement years, she worked with the Jewish Labor Committee to improve race relations, receiving an award from the Chicago Commission on Human Relations in 1953 for her work in integrating building trades. Herstein was an active member of HADASSAH, Histadrut, the NATIONAL COUNCIL OF JEWISH WOMEN, and the American Civil Liberties Union.

She died on August 9, 1983, at age ninety-seven.

Born into an Eastern European intellectual family, Herstein grew to adulthood with a passion for social justice and an enduring belief in the value of education. She came to maturity in fin-de-siècle Chicago, when its intellectual atmosphere was enhanced by such great social reformers as Jane Addams, John Dewey, and Thorstein Veblen. Educated young people could not help but be influenced by these thinkers. Thus Herstein's life represents a blending of the particular and the universal, a paradigm of the American Jewish experience.

BIBLIOGRAPHY

Ginger, Ray. *Altgeld's America* (1986); Herstein, Lillian. Interviews by Elizabeth Balanoff (1970–1971), Oral History Project in Labor History, Roosevelt University Archives, Chicago, and Papers. Chicago Historical Society, and Chicago Jewish Archives, Spertus Institute of Jewish Studies, Chicago; Kornbluh, Joyce L. *A New Deal for Workers' Education* (1987); Payne, Elizabeth Ann. *Reform, Labor, and Feminism* (1988); Reid, Robert L., ed. *Battleground: The Autobiography of Margaret A. Haley* (1982); Wrigley, Julia. *Class Politics and Public Schools: Chicago, 1900–1950* (1982); Zieger, Robert H. *American Workers, American Unions, 1920–1985* (1986).

NORMA SPUNGEN

HERZOG, BERTHA BEITMAN (1874–1958)

Bertha Beitman Herzog was an active participant in local and national women's associations in Cleveland, Ohio. From 1928 to 1930, Herzog served as the first woman president of the Jewish Welfare Federation (later the Jewish Community Federation) in Cleveland and received the Charles Eisenmann Award for outstanding community service in 1941. She helped create several local organizations for Jewish women, including the Cooperative League of Jewish Women's Organizations of Cleveland (later the Cleveland Federation of Jewish Women's Organizations), which she chaired in 1926. Herzog presided over the local Council of Jewish Women (CJW), later the NATIONAL COUNCIL OF JEWISH WOMEN (NCJW), Cleveland Section, from 1920 to 1924, and served as women's cochair for the National Conference of Christians and Jews.

Bertha Beitman Herzog was born in Washington, Indiana, to Emanuel and Molly Beitman. She moved to Cleveland Heights, Ohio, after her marriage to Siegmund Herzog on March 1, 1900. Her husband later became vice president and treasurer of H. Black, a local clothier. He died in 1943.

A member of Suburban Temple, Herzog was among the earliest participants in prominent local cultural and civic groups such as the Women's City Club of Cleveland and the Women's Committee of the Cleveland Orchestra. During her tenure as president of CJW, the council grew to three thousand members and rejoined the NCJW after a thirteen-year hiatus of independence. Under Herzog's leadership, the CJW initiated its *Monthly Bulletin* and developed efforts such as Martha House (inc. 1919) and the Jewish Big Sister Association to help single Jewish women and girls. After leaving the helm of the Cleveland section, Herzog assumed the chair of the NCJW's committee on communal and civic affairs. From 1928 to 1929, she served the local group on the executive board and was designated an honorary trustee in 1930.

Well-traveled in Europe, Herzog promoted the study of world affairs among Cleveland women of all faiths and ethnic backgrounds. She headed the immigration department of the CJW from 1908 to 1909, chaired the League of Women Voters of Cleveland's international relations committee, participated in a women's discussion group on world affairs in the 1920s (one predecessor of the Cleveland Council on World Affairs), and, in 1923, served as vice president of the Council for the Prevention of War (later the Women's Council for the Promotion of Peace), a combined effort of local women's organizations.

Health and education, especially for women, also occupied Bertha Herzog's reform energies. She served on the board of trustees of Cleveland's pioneer birth control clinic, the Maternal Health Association (later Planned Parenthood of Greater Cleveland), from its founding in 1928 until the 1940s. Herzog nourished parochial education as a member of the board of trustees of the Bureau of Jewish Education. She promoted professional training for women, serving on various committees at the School of Social Sciences at Western Reserve University (now Case Western Reserve University) from its founding until the late 1940s. Herzog also supported the fledgling Cleveland College in its efforts to attract nontraditional students through night classes.

Bertha Beitman Herzog died at her home in Cleveland on July 9, 1958. She was cremated and her remains are located at the Cleveland Temple Memorial.

BIBLIOGRAPHY

Abbott, Virginia Clark. *The History of Woman Suffrage and the League of Women Voters in Cuyahoga County 1911–1945* (1949); Gartner, Lloyd. *History of the Jews of Cleveland* (1978); Herzog, Bertha Beitman. "Civic and Communal Affairs." *Jewish Woman* (April 1924). Reprinted in National Council of Jewish Women, Cleveland Section, *Monthly Bulletin*, no. 5 (1924): 16; Meyer, Jimmy E.W. "Birth Control Policy, Practice, and Prohibition in the 1930s: The Maternal Health Association of Cleveland, Ohio." Ph.D. diss., Case Western Reserve University (1993); Council of Jewish Women. *Monthly Bulletin* 1, no. 1 (January 1924): 2, and 1, no. 5 (May 1924), and 3, no. 6 (March 1926), 2; Neely, Ruth J. *Women of Ohio*. Vol. 3 (n.d.); Obituaries. *Cleveland Plain Dealer*, July 10, 1958, 34, and *Jewish Independent*, July 11, 1958, 1+; Obituary of Siegmund Herzog. *NYTimes*, January 14, 1943; Rose, William Ganson. *Cleveland: The Making of a City* (1950); Van Tassel, David, and John Grabowski, eds. *Dictionary of Cleveland Biography* (1996), and *Encyclopedia of Cleveland History* (1987), and *Encyclopedia of Cleveland History*. 2d ed. (1996); *WWIAJ* (1926, 1938).

JIMMY E. WILKINSON MEYER

HESSE, EVA (1936–1970)

Eva Hesse is recognized as one of the most innovative and potent artists to emerge in New York in the fertile 1960s. She created new sculptural forms in such eccentric materials as latex and fiberglass, and has become known for giving minimal art organic, emotional, and kinetic aspects. Her material and formal inventions, with their sensuous and emotional extremes, were balanced by an active verbal intelligence that won her the respect of the art community—as her warmth and wry humor won her many friends.

Both her life and her art were fraught with extreme contradictions. Almost impossibly demanding of herself, she was nevertheless completely open to the unknown. She scorned good taste and the decorative, and believed the authentic was never reached through subject matter, messages, or programs. The dynamic of her work was not expression, but discovery. She wrote, "It is my main concern to go beyond what I know and what I can know." She pulled new meanings from deep in her psyche and gave them new formal structures that related to order yet resisted it. Usually these structures involved repeated units—the same but not exactly the same—that embodied opposite extremes: order/chaos, hardness/softness, directness/irony, horror/humor, mechanical/organic. The absurd is as inescapable in her work as it is in Samuel Beckett's. Her subject, not merely her expression, is abstract. Her central theme is existence itself, the possibility of identity in a deranged world.

Eva Hesse was born in Hamburg, Germany, on January 11, 1936, to educated Jewish parents, Wilhelm Hesse, a criminal lawyer, and the artistic Ruth Marcus House. In 1938, to escape the Nazis, she and her sister Helen (later Helen Charash), who was three years older, were separated from their parents. The next year the family made it to New York. There her mother, severely depressed, took her own life in 1946, a year after her divorce from Wilhelm Hesse and his subsequent remarriage to Eva Nathanson.

The legacies of the Holocaust and of her disastrous family history were the horrible fears and anxieties that Hesse battled throughout her life. Creative and "difficult" in her youth, she found much of her artistic identity outside her formal education. She graduated from the High School of Industrial Arts in 1952. She then attended Pratt Institute of Design for one and a half years and Cooper Union for three years, graduating in 1957. In 1959, she received her B.F.A. from the Yale School of Art and Architecture and immediately moved back to New York. There she continued an intense regimen of drawing and painting, attending exhibitions, and reading art history and twentieth-century literature. She also began to establish herself among her peers, including Sol LeWitt and Mel Bochner. In 1961, Hesse married the well-known American sculptor Tom Doyle.

In an extraordinary group of small ink and gouache works on paper she produced in 1960–1961, forms emerged that uncannily predicted her great late sculptures. Translucent and dark, fragile and potent, abstract or all-but-abstract—these images of boxes, circles, and strings claimed her ambiguous structural and emotional territory.

Over the next few years, Hesse worked urgently to extract her artistic identity from painting, but it resisted her needs. It was in the drawings from 1962 to mid-decade that she made the strange linear and spatial discoveries that she later developed in grids and serial treatments.

From early adulthood to the end of her life, Hesse kept diaries in which she examined her struggle for authentic psychological and artistic identity. Her analytic intelligence, constantly judging, worked uphill against her debilitating terrors to achieve the high aesthetic ground her standards and ambition required. The encouragement of her peers and friends, particularly Sol LeWitt, helped—both in New York and when she accompanied Doyle to Germany on a sponsored work stay in 1964–1965.

There, it was Doyle's suggestion to forget painting and work with plaster and string, to make things with her hands, which provided the connection Hesse had sought so desperately. It sparked her breakthrough into the bright wound string reliefs with found objects and jazzy titles. These in turn led, after she was back in New York, to the monochromatic or gradated black and gray sculptures with more wound string, wrapped forms, and such nonart materials as net bags, rubber tubing, and dangling cords.

The year 1966 was disruptive: Her father died and her marriage came to an end. Yet in terms of her art, it was excellent. Major new works by Hesse were featured both in "Abstract Inflationism and Stuffed Expressionism" at the Graham Gallery and in Lucy Lippard's "Eccentric Abstraction" at the Fischbach Gallery, and new drawings were shown at the Visual Arts Gallery.

By 1967, though still haunted by fear and panic, Hesse had arrived at a period of high accomplishment and recognition. Black or gray grids of circular forms, often with strings dangling from their centers, and rows of rectangular boxes were her dominant motifs. These evolved eccentrically into, for example, raw latex floor pieces with the round units jumbled, out of order. This sort of idiosyncratic placement was one of Hesse's contributions to sculptural structure: similar but not identical units placed neither too close nor too distant, neither too ordered nor too disordered. Such placements in relation to wall or floor grids or to rows—yet unchartable—characterized the sculpture in her major exhibition, "Eva Hesse: Chain Polymers" at the Fischbach Gallery, and in the historic "9 at Leo Castelli" show at the end of the year. Her large fiberglass and latex works have been recognized by museums and writers worldwide as major works of the era.

Despite being diagnosed with a brain tumor and undergoing operations in April and August of 1969 and in March of 1970, she overcame her physical weakness by a tremendous appetite for both art and life. She continued to think and work energetically to the end.

Eva Hesse died on May 29, 1970, in New York City.

BIBLIOGRAPHY

Barrette, Bill. *Eva Hesse Sculpture* (1989); Cooper, Helen A., with Maurice Berger et al. *Eva Hesse: A Retrospective.* Exhibition catalog (1992); David, Catherine, and Corinne Diserens. *Eva Hesse.* Exhibition catalog (1993); Frank, Elizabeth. *Eva Hesse Gouaches 1960–1961.* Exhibition catalog (1991); Johnson, Ellen H. *Eva Hesse: A Retrospective of the Drawings.* Exhibition catalog 1982); Kozloff, Max. *Eva Hesse Paintings.* Exhibition catalog (1992); Lippard, Lucy R. *Eva Hesse* (1976); *NAW* modern; Nemser, Cindy. *Art Talk: Conversations with Twelve Women Artists* (1975); Obituary. *NYTimes*, May 30, 1970, 23:5; Reinhardt, Brigitte, with Naomi Spector et al. *Eva Hesse: Drawing in Space—Paintings and Reliefs* (1994); Shearer, Linda, with Robert Pincus Whitten. *Eva Hesse.* Exhibition catalog (1972).

NAOMI SPECTOR

HIGHER EDUCATION ADMINISTRATION

The academy and Judaism share a tender core of values. At both their roots lies a passion for knowledge—the love of learning, the necessity for debate and discussion, an appreciation for the challenge of scholarship. This would suggest no mystery in the number of Jews in universities. However, it is women's space in these intellectual settings—historically unwelcomed by the academy and unsupported by Jewish scholarly institutions—that poses the wonder.

HISTORICAL CONTEXT

Higher education began as an enterprise by and for men. In the United States, women's formal entry into higher education came less than two hundred years ago, in the 1830s. Many colleges established before the Civil War were single-sex institutions and were backed by Christian denominations; some state colleges and universities, established before and after the Civil War, began as single-sex (male) institutions also, but soon became coeducational. Women's colleges always needed some women administrators, especially to assist with student housing. However, the pattern was established early, even in most women's colleges, that men, not women, should be the guardians of academic standards and the presidents of institutions.

As the twentieth century progressed, the route to becoming a senior university administrator became more formal. Entry into the professoriate with a doctoral degree (usually in arts and sciences) was followed sequentially by experience as chair of a department or director of a program, dean, provost or vice president for academic affairs, and finally a presidency. Since the proportion of doctorates awarded to women has hovered around 20 percent throughout the twentieth century, the likelihood of a woman becoming a university administrator has always been small, even without taking into account the traditional pattern of male leadership in higher education. The first women in university administration were in women's colleges, or as dean of women, or in fields such as nursing and home economics. Overall, however, there were very few women in positions of senior administration in four-year colleges and universities in the first half of the twentieth century.

Despite the immigration of Jews from Eastern Europe, Jewish women formed only a small proportion of the female undergraduate population until the 1920s. Before this time, Jewish students were marginalized in university culture—attendance at prayers was often compulsory, at least at private colleges and universities, and sororities and fraternities refused admission to Jews. Admissions practices also discriminated against Jews in less overt ways. The elite women's colleges, in particular, grew as "socioeconomically and ethnically homogeneous communities," building thriving centers of intellectual stimulation and opportunity for white upper-middle-class women. But schools such as Barnard (with a more recent history of Jewish women leaders), Vassar, Bryn Mawr, and Wellesley maintained subtle policies such as "geographic diversity" or more blatant quotas to control the "Jewish problem." Growing interest in higher education at women's colleges by Jewish women prompted fears that a large Jewish population would endanger the "Christian missionary spirit" of a college, or simply devalue the prestige of these growing elite institutions. The tides of change brought a gradual shift away from the overt discrimination against Jews in admissions policies, as well as a relaxing of rules for religious practice, particularly in public institutions, which enabled Jews to enter colleges and universities with greater comfort in the second and third decades of the twentieth century (Gordon 1990). "The Jewish immigrants, few though they were, played their part, directly and indirectly, in the reform of higher education" (Gorelick 1981, p. 59).

Not until the end of the Second World War, however, when the demand for university teachers expanded, did many Jewish women (and men) stay in academia to become professors in colleges and universities. Jewish women were prominent in the development of feminist scholarship. As they matured as scholars, some chose or were chosen to become department chairs, deans, and senior university administrators. For instance, in 1963, historian BARBARA MILLER

In 1963, BARBARA MILLER SOLOMON *was named associate dean of Radcliffe College, and in 1970,
she became the first woman dean of Harvard College. The importance of higher education for women
was a central theme in her prize-winning book* In the Company of Educated Women:
A History of Women and Higher Education in America, *published in 1985,
the year she retired from Harvard. [Schlesinger Library]*

SOLOMON was named associate dean of Radcliffe College, and in 1970, she became the first woman dean at Harvard College. From 1977 to 1992, CLAIRE M. FAGIN served as dean of the School of Nursing at the University of Pennsylvania; during the academic year 1993–1994 she served as the university's interim president. In 1978, Frances Degen Horowitz became vice chancellor for research, graduate studies, and public service and dean of the Graduate School at the University of Kansas; in 1991, she became president of the Graduate School and University Center of the City University of New York. In the 1980s, more Jewish women gained deanships at universities, such as Elaine L. Cohen at Notre Dame University, June T. Fox at Lesley College, and Joan N. Burstyn at Syracuse University, while Daryl Goldgraben Smith became vice president at Scripps College, Judith Shapiro, provost at Bryn Mawr College, Judith Walzer, provost at the New School for Social Research, and Ellen Futter, president of Barnard College.

During the 1990s, Jewish women served as administrators in all levels of higher education across the country. Some younger women with degrees in business and management became financial officers or deans of schools of business; others became student affairs administrators, or academic deans like Rochelle Robbins at Boston University. Several were appointed to presidencies, including Hannah Friedman Goldberg (Wheaton College), Shirley Strum Kenny (SUNY–Stony Brook), and Judith Rodin, who became dean of the Graduate School at Yale University in 1991 and provost in 1992 then, in 1994, president of the University of Pennsylvania.

In the last decades of the twentieth century, women also gained senior administrative positions in Jewish institutions, such as Anne Lapidus Lerner (vice chancellor, Jewish Theological Seminary), Rena Spicehandler (dean of students, Reconstructionist Rabbinical College), and Marsha Edelman (dean, Gratz College). While these women faced some different

"Jewish women bring into their academic experience consciousness about difference, being female and being Jewish," says Frances Degen Horowitz, president of the Graduate School and University Center, City University of New York.
[Don Hamerman]

problems from those in secular institutions, they also experience the need to negotiate multiple roles.

UNDERSTANDING JEWISH IDENTITY

To ascertain how their being Jewish influenced their work, we interviewed nine Jewish women administrators and focused on the aspects of their work that they attributed to their Jewish roots and identity. As these women attested, many Jews struggle with naming their connection to Judaism, which they perceive as more than just a system of faith parallel to other faith communities in the world. When Jews first came to America, Orthodox traditions of belief and practice were the only form of Jewish observance. As the demands of American life-styles made Jewish observance more difficult, the Reform Movement, with its less rigid interpretations of Torah and halakah [Jewish law], became increasingly attractive to those

who wished to maintain their Jewish identity in a non-Jewish world. As of 1990, almost two hundred years later, the Jewish population in America identified itself in a survey conducted by the Council of Jewish Federations as 42 percent Reform, 38 percent Conservative, 7 percent Orthodox, and the remaining 13 percent Reconstructionist or Other.

Individuals vary in the ways they define their Jewish identity even within these formal movements. Immigration, the Holocaust, the creation of the State of Israel, and assimilation into American culture have all contributed to shifting identities for the Jewish community, which has been called a "religion," a "race," a "nation," and a "culture" (Borowitz 1979, pp. 72–73). Several of the women we interviewed live their Judaism as a cultural commitment—a shared context of family and values, celebration and ritual, history and tradition. Most live their professional lives in secular spheres, where their Jewish identity (belief and practice) has to be negotiated.

Several women we interviewed had no religious affiliation and no involvement with Jewish organizations; others belonged to synagogues, where they were active in their children's Jewish education. Their involvement in Jewish community activities was also influenced by their geographical location, the size of the Jewish population there, and the general ethos of the college and university communities to which these women belonged. Those with young children, particularly, commented on the difficulty of juggling university administration, family, and Jewish community activities. Community activities were often what they curtailed. One woman saw this curtailment as a reason why, now that her children were adults, she had only a minor role in the Jewish community compared to her Jewish male counterparts. A woman administrator in a Jewish institution regretted her lack of time to further her own Jewish learning even while she fostered others' learning daily. Some women, particularly those in their fifties or older, had held office in Jewish organizations, such as board member of the university Hillel, youth advisor to B'nai Brith, and officer in Jewish community organizations such as HADASSAH and community councils. Some had become speakers for Jewish organizations such as the Anti-Defamation League. One had taught a college course in Jewish studies; another had incorporated her interest in Judaism and Israel into her research.

Some women commented on the relationship between their Jewish community involvements and their university lives as another space where a Jewish woman administrator's identities become intertwined. One woman suggested that her dual roles in Jewish community and university community "feed off one another," a leadership role and prestige in one realm leading to leadership and prestige in the other. Another woman wished that at times she could separate the two roles, desiring to go to Jewish holiday services as a synagogue congregant, but often being addressed by others in her university title even in that context.

GEOGRAPHIC LOCATION OF JEWISH WOMEN ADMINISTRATORS

The percentage of Jewish women administrators at four-year colleges is greatest in the region where the largest number of Jews lives. This is not the region where there are the most four-year colleges and universities, even though that region might suggest more opportunities in administration. As of 1990, the Jewish population in the United States consisted of approximately 8,100,000 people, with 39.8 percent residing in the Northeast, 24.4 percent in the West, 23.5 percent in the South, and 12.5 percent in the Midwest (Council of Jewish Federations survey). Four-year colleges and universities across the country fall into a slightly different distribution, most heavily weighted to the southern part of the United States, where 30 percent of the 2,200 institutions exist. Another 27 percent fall in the Midwest, 26 percent in the Northeast, and 16 percent in the West (Digest of Education Statistics 1996). In our sample of eighty-two Jewish women administrators, 55 percent held positions in the northeastern part of the United States. (These data represent a sample of Jewish women—80 percent self-identified Jewish, 20 percent identified by other means—in senior administrative positions at four-year colleges and universities obtained through interviews, listserve requests, and Dialog and Lexis/Nexis searches.) Another 17 percent held positions in the Midwest, 15 percent in the South, and 13 percent in the West.

INFLUENCE OF BEING JEWISH ON ADMINISTRATIVE STYLE

Not all the women we interviewed could articulate why their attitudes toward their work were Jewish. For instance, having a liberal approach to education, one that valued intellectual creativity over rote learning, "felt Jewish" to one person. Many of the things that these women spoke about could be attributed to other sources: to family influence, to social and cultural norms, to university ethos, or to their personal work ethic. But we took very seriously the ways that these women attributed their attitudes and behaviors to their identities as Jews.

Several women said they drew upon metaphors from Judaism to explain situations to themselves and others. One described her job as "that of the Rashi of the rules and regulations." Because she was Jewish, she said, she did not feel, as her colleagues did, that her job as a university administrator was to "remove occasions for sin." Some considered the Jewish metaphors they used to be cultural; they commented that other minorities might use different ones. Others considered their Jewish metaphors as religious, bound to Jewish morality and Jewish observance. One woman described her concern for life at the university in the here-and-now, as opposed to primary concern for shaping its future, as the "Fiddler on the Roof syndrome," inherited from the need for Jews to be ready to move at any time.

Jewish women administrators mentor Jewish students, particularly women. On campuses with few Jewish administrators, they serve also as authorities on Jewish issues, consulted by presidents on issues of sensitivity to Jews, particularly those affecting the academic calendar. One person described herself as "the Jewish One," a position she held with pride, having always been considered an encyclopedia of Jewish knowledge. Another had addressed the issue of hate speech on campuses, condemning hate but defending free speech. Many others work on behalf of other minorities as well as Jews, claiming that their experience as Jews provides them with an understanding of what it means to be "the Other" in society.

INTERTWINED ALLEGIANCES

Some women we interviewed found it "hard to say" how their being Jewish influenced their administrative style. Frances Degen Horowitz (1988, p. 12) wrote that "Jewish women bring into their academic experience a double consciousness about difference being female and being Jewish." Most women we interviewed had difficulty disentangling the influence on their work of their being a Jew and being a woman. Several expressed their concern for the well-being of faculty and administrative colleagues, which might as well have grown out of their socialization as women as out of their upbringing as Jews. However, some distinguished between them as they told their stories. One woman drew upon having "rakhmones" [compassion] for others as the source of her concern for the well-being of faculty, while several others attributed their concern to their parents' commitment to helping others. Still others felt they brought to their work a profound understanding of the role of diversity in society from their experience as Jews. Such double consciousness about difference apparently is not shared by all Jewish women academics, however. A few of the women we interviewed, who live and work in cities with large, active Jewish populations, claimed never to have experienced, as a Jew, being an outsider.

Some women felt a sense of purpose that came from being a Jew in a non-Jewish setting such as the academy. One named her "passion" as arising from her Jewish past. For some this passion was visible in the value they placed on education, in their love of learning, in their intensity for rigorous scholarship and debate in the tradition of Talmud and midrash. Others connected this passion to a general sense of personal ambition and drive, handed down from grandmothers, in the "tradition of strong, Jewish women." One woman noted that she finds herself encouraging students to take a stand on issues, often posing to them the question, "Is this something you believe in?"

Regardless of synagogue affiliation, involvement with Jewish activities, or commitments to Jewish belief or to Jewish practice, women who identify themselves as Jewish in the academy share something—a spirit of inquiry, community, perseverance, and a passion for equity—that shapes how they live. While these things are not unique to Judaism, they were expressed by those we interviewed as integral to their lives as Jewish women administrators.

BIBLIOGRAPHY

Borowitz, Eugene. *Understanding Judaism* (1979); Council of Jewish Federations. 1990 National Jewish Population Survey. Alta Vista Archives, accessed April 8, 1997. web.gc.cuny.edu/dept/cjstu/highint.htm; Digest of Education Statistics (1996); Gordon, Lynn. *Gender and Higher Education in the Progressive Era* (1990); Gorelick, Sherry. *City College and the Jewish Poor* (1981); Horowitz, Frances Degen. "A Jewish Woman in Academic America." In *Seeing Female: Social Roles, and Personal Lives,* edited by S. Brehm (1988), and "Jewish Women, Jewish Life and the Academic World." Unpublished invited address, Jewish Lecture Series, Queens College (1993); Kaufman, Polly Welts, ed. *The Search For Equity* (1991).

JOAN N. BURSTYN
LESLEY BOGAD

In 1910, around the time this photograph was taken, Bessie Abramowitz led a walkout of sixteen young women button sewers at the Chicago factory where they worked, protesting a cut in wages. Her rebellion was greeted with amusement by most other workers, but within a matter of months thousands of workers from other factories were also out on strike.
[Photograph courtesy of Philoine Fried]

HILLMAN, BESSIE ABRAMOWITZ (1889–1970)

"I was Bessie Abramowitz before he was Sidney Hillman." While no feminist in the late twentieth-century sense of the word, Bessie Abramowitz Hillman, wife of famed labor leader Sidney Hillman (1887–1946), simply reflected facts when she spoke these words. She was a militant labor movement leader before her husband became involved and remained a union stalwart her entire life.

Bas Sheva Abramowitz ("Bessie" was created by an Ellis Island immigration officer) was born on May 15, 1889, in Linoveh, a village near Grodno in Russia. She was one of ten children born to Emanuel

Abramowitz, a commission agent, and Sarah Rabinowitz. In 1905, Bessie, who spoke only Yiddish and some Russian, joined an older cousin in immigrating to America. Most 1905 immigrants fled czarist oppression and anti-Jewish violence, but Bessie reported that her aim in leaving home was to escape the services of the local marriage broker.

Arriving in Chicago, where she had some distant relatives, the fifteen-year-old found a job as a button sewer in a garment factory and enrolled in night school at Hull House. When she organized a shop committee to protest working conditions and pay of three dollars for a sixty-hour week, she was fired. Looking for other work, she found herself on an employers' blacklist and finally took a job, under an assumed name, at the Hart, Shaffner, and Marx clothing firm.

In September 1910, the twenty-year-old rebel again fought back, now against a cut of a quarter of a cent in the four-cent piece rate for sewing buttons on pants. She led a walkout of sixteen young women, an outburst at first viewed with amusement by most other workers in the plant, including Sidney Hillman, a twenty-four-year-old Lithuanian-born cutter. As the young women persisted, however, they gained adherents, and by mid-October most of the eight thousand workers at Hart, Shaffner, and Marx were out, soon joined by thousands in other plants. Sidney Hillman, too, followed the lead of the young women, joining the strike three weeks after its initiation and soon emerging as a strike leader. The strike won the support of Jane Addams of Hull House and its Women's Trade Union League, which hired Bessie Abramowitz as an organizer.

On the union barricades, Bessie and Sidney's friendship blossomed into a romance, and they were secretly engaged in 1914. Since both were sending money back to their families, an immediate marriage seemed impossible in that time of nonworking wives. In late 1914, garment workers in Chicago, New York, and other clothing centers split from the conservative United Garment Workers to form the Amalgamated Clothing Workers of America, and Bessie Abramowitz, then a business agent for a vestmakers' local, was elected to its general executive board. She became a leader in the campaign to draft Sidney Hillman, who, a few months earlier, had taken a job in New York City with the INTERNATIONAL LADIES GARMENT WORKERS UNION, to be president of the new union. He accepted and, during 1915, the young couple again fought together in an industrywide strike for the union shop.

The two lovers announced their engagement publicly by heading, arm-in-arm, the clothing work-

ers' contingent in the Chicago May Day parade of 1916. They were married on May 3, 1916. They moved to New York City, headquarters of the new union, and from then until 1946, when Sidney Hillman died, all of Bessie Hillman's considerable union work was performed as an unpaid volunteer.

A daughter, Philoine, was born in 1917 and another, Selma, in 1921. Hillman continued to do Women's Trade Union League volunteer work at

She bragged, "I was Bessie Abramowitz before he was Sidney Hillman," but her early union activism did not keep her from marrying the soon-to-be-famous labor leader in 1916. They announced their engagement by publicly heading the clothing workers' contingent in the Chicago May Day parade. They are shown here in 1922, with their daughters Selma, left, and Philoine, right. [Photograph courtesy of Philoine Fried]

home, and in 1924 she returned to active union work. She organized workers in Pennsylvania, Ohio, upstate New York, Connecticut, and elsewhere. Her Yiddish accent presented no real barrier in organizing nonimmigrant workers, who saw her devotion to the cause and her signal role in creating the union.

In 1937, Bessie Hillman became education director of the Laundry Workers Joint Board, an affiliate of the Amalgamated. She emphasized cultural programs, as well as union leadership education, and gave early performing opportunities to, among others, Zero Mostel, JUDY HOLLIDAY, and Sam Jaffe, continuing to back these artists when some of them were blacklisted for political reasons. In the Laundry Workers, a union with many nonwhite workers, Bessie Hillman became strongly involved in civil rights work, a dominant concern for the rest of her life.

During World War II, while her husband forged strong political bonds between labor and the Roosevelt administration, Bessie Hillman helped lead the union's war efforts. She was named by Governor Herbert H. Lehman to the advisory board of the New York Office of Price Administration.

The Hillmans' home life was determinedly secular. While Sidney Hillman became a close friend of Rabbi Stephen Wise, the noted Zionist and leader of Reform Judaism, the rabbi's influence was limited to moral and political issues. Yet the Hillmans were firm in identifying as Jews. They spoke Yiddish at home and, while their daughters received no religious training, Jewish holidays were observed as family celebrations. When Jews, including some of Bessie Hillman's brothers and sisters, fell victim to the Holocaust, the Hillmans protested vigorously. Their strong support of the war effort in the 1940s was, in large measure, part of their fight against the Nazi campaign to wipe out Jews. In 1947, Bessie Hillman traveled to Europe on a union-sponsored mission to examine the problems of displaced persons.

When Sidney Hillman, who insisted on a standard of living no better than that of a cutter in his union, died in 1946, he left virtually no estate. The Amalgamated hired Bessie Hillman as a paid vice president in charge of the union's education programs. She spoke at union conferences, helped organize summer schools for rank-and-file leaders, and played a significant role at the union's conventions, both as an inspirational link with the past and as a gadfly urging the union to greater efforts for civil rights, peace, and economic justice.

Over the years, Bessie Hillman served with the CIO and AFL-CIO Civil Rights Committees, the CIO Community Services Committee, the National Consumers League, the American Labor Education Service, Inc., the Committee on Protective Labor Legislation, the American Association for the United Nations, the Child Welfare Committee of New York, and the Defense Advisory Commission on Women in the Services, and she was appointed by President John F. Kennedy to the President's Commission on the Status of Women.

Bessie Abramowitz Hillman remained active in union activities until her death in New York City, on December 23, 1970, at age eighty-one.

BIBLIOGRAPHY
Amalgamated Clothing Workers of America. Archives. Cornell University School of Industrial and Labor Relations, Ithaca, N.Y.; Fraser, Steven. *Labor Will Rule: Sidney Hillman and the Rise of American Labor* (1991); Josephson, Matthew. *Sidney Hillman: Statesman of American Labor* (1952).

ANTONIO RAMIREZ

HIMMELFARB, GERTRUDE (b. 1922)

Gertrude Himmelfarb has dedicated her long and noted career as a historian of ideas to the study of nineteenth-century Britain, an intellectual commitment that has been guided by a profound identification with the moral atmosphere of the Victorian era. Since earning her Ph.D. from the University of Chicago in 1950, Himmelfarb has maintained that the Victorian experience offers unique insights and lessons, immediate and even imperative, for the problems that haunt the modern world. In the 1950s, it was the specter of totalitarianism; in the 1990s, the plight of American inner cities.

A professor emeritus at the Graduate Center of the City University of New York, Himmelfarb has become one of the most eloquent advocates, albeit increasingly controversial, for the reintroduction of traditional values (she prefers the term "virtues"), such as shame, responsibility, chastity, and self-reliance, into American political life and policy-making. Consequently, the ideological battles in the wake of the Republican victory in the 1994 congressional elections conferred a new poignancy to Gertrude Himmelfarb's blend of historical scholarship and conservative political criticism.

Gertrude Himmelfarb was born in Brooklyn, New York, on August 8, 1922, second child of Bertha and manufacturer Max Himmelfarb. She attended New Utrecht High School in Brooklyn and then earned a B.A. from Brooklyn College, while also taking courses in history, scripture, and Judaic literature at the Jewish Theological Seminary.

The years that Himmelfarb spent at the University of Chicago, where she embarked on doctoral studies in 1942, had the most profound influence on her political approach, style of scholarship, and, no less important, her belief in the usefulness of historical research. The University of Chicago was then a breeding ground for innovative reformulation of Western political thought as a counterweight to the threats of fascism and communism that ravaged Europe. This effort, high-minded and deeply informed by classical and modern philosophy, was led by European, mostly Jewish, thinkers. It also had a decidedly conservative bent. Under the supervision of Louis Gottschalk, Himmelfarb wrote her Ph.D. dissertation on the British parliamentarian and historian Lord Acton, which she later published as *Lord Acton: A Study in Conscience and Politics* (1952). Himmelfarb found Lord Acton's ambivalent blend of liberalism and pessimism, ideas of progress, and notions of human sinfulness, as well as his advocacy of a "judicious mix of authority, tradition, and experience, to be highly relevant for the post World War II world." Even in this early work, she discerned a connection between the modern neglect of personal moral character and the political catastrophes of the twentieth century, including the rise of fascism and totalitarianism.

In the following decades she continued her exploration of politics, morality, and history in books and articles on leading intellectuals of the Victorian period, most notably John Stuart Mill, whose works she also edited, and Charles Darwin. *The Idea of Poverty: England in the Early Industrial Age* (1984) examined the rise of poverty as a social problem and was her first direct attempt to exonerate the early Victorian treatment of the poor. This was followed by the anthology *Marriage and Morals Among the Victorians* (1986) and her exploration of late Victorian attitudes toward social issues in *Poverty and Compassion: The Moral Imagination of the Late Victorians* (1991). In both books, she seems to lament the replacement of Victorian moral nerve with Edwardian aestheticism and "value-free" relativism.

Himmelfarb's husband, Irving Kristol, and her brother, Milton Himmelfarb, are also well-known conservative essayists. She has two children, William and Elizabeth. William Kristol was Vice President Dan Quayle's chief of staff and is now editor of the Washington, D.C.–based *Weekly Standard*..

Despite the prestigious awards that she has received during her prolific career (among them, fellowships from the Rockefeller, Guggenheim, and Wilson foundations) and ten honorary degrees (from institutions such as Yale, Williams College, Jewish Theological Seminary, and Smith College), Gertrude Himmelfarb has always been somewhat of an outsider in the historical profession. She had engaged in independent research for fifteen years before joining the City University of New York in 1965. By then, history departments were increasingly influenced by methodologies and insights borrowed from the social sciences. Himmelfarb criticized harshly the departure from traditional models of historical scholarship and argued that the dominance of the new social history "belittles the will, ideas, actions, and freedom of individuals." *The New History and the Old* (1987) was an outright attack on Marxist determinism, quantohistory, and psychohistory as well as other types of narrativeless "history with the politics left out." As in her political critique, she reproached academic historians for their alleged moral relativism, for their disregard for human achievements ("greatness"), and their refusal to identify heroes and villains in their writings. When postmodernism became the academic vogue, its manifestations in historiography (especially in feminist history) did not escape Himmelfarb's ire. Postmodernist history, she wrote, "recognizes no reality principle, only the pleasure principle—history at the pleasure of the historian." She also argued against multiculturalism in history, asserting that such an approach trivializes history and renders it meaningless and that it "demeans and dehumanizes the people who are the subjects of history" by denying the "common (generic) humanity of all people, whatever their sex, race, class, religion and the like."

In *The De-Moralization of Society* (1995), Himmelfarb compared Victorian societies on both sides of the Atlantic to modern America and found the latter lacking. The Victorians were highly successful in curbing social ills such as crime, illegitimacy, poverty, and illiteracy by making morality "a conscious part of social policy." Conversely, the constant deterioration of the American social condition, argued Himmelfarb, is rooted in a climate of moral relativism, skepticism, and "de-moralization." Following the nineteenth-century British writer Thomas Carlyle, she maintained that social problems cannot be reduced to economical calculations and material gains. As important is the insistence on the moral disposition of the weakest echelons of society, their sense of right and wrong. The re-moralization of society would necessitate assigning social stigmas to practices such as illegitimacy, as well as reshaming dependency on public welfare. Thus Himmelfarb found the Victorian distinction (derided by generations of historians) between the "deserving" and "undeserving" poor to be particularly inspiring, as she did the idea of "less eligibility" institutionalized in the first Victorian welfare reform (the Poor Law Act of 1834) to discourage the condition of "able bodied paupers." She also found merit in House of Representatives Speaker Newt Gingrich's proposal to resurrect old, discredited Victorian institutions such as orphanages. In her view, these institutions were highly effective and certainly more humane than one may gather from Dickensian "exaggerations." *The De-Moralization of Society* and much of her writing in the preceding decade met with controversy, both political and scholarly. The dispute over her work, which in the past was praised for its prodigious scholarship and lucidity, grew as Himmelfarb's writings increasingly focused on the present rather than on the past and as her tone became more "bellicose." One critic even accused her of writing a "revisionist history" for the Republican party.

Himmelfarb has been greatly involved in Jewish conservative intellectual circles. In *De-Moralization of Society*, she dedicates a chapter to the "Jew as a Victorian." The assimilation of Jews, she maintained, was one of the clearest indications of the openness and social advancement of the Victorian era. Moreover, she argued that the Jewish community perhaps more than any other segment of the British population epitomized a host of Victorian values: self-reliance, free-market meritocracy, philanthropy. In a symposium on "Liberals and the Jews," published by *Commentary* in January 1980, Himmelfarb contended that the traditional Jewish affiliation with liberalism has been maintained by a "nostalgic commitment" to the old nineteenth-century liberalism that accepted Jews as individuals and as a group. But "latter-day liberalism," with its support of discriminating quotas, rejection of individualism, and hostility to Israel, is, according to Himmelfarb, inhospitable to Jews. "We may conclude," she said, "that a quite different philosophy is required if we are to survive in the modern world, survive as individuals and Jews."

SELECTED WORKS BY GERTRUDE HIMMELFARB

Darwin and the Darwinian Revolution (1959); *The De-Moralization of Society* (1995); "A Demoralized Society—The British American Experience," *Public Interest* 117 (Fall 1994): 57–80; "George Eliot for Grown-Ups (*Middlemarch* and Morality)," *American Scholar* 63, no. 4 (Fall 1994): 577–581; *The Idea of Poverty: England in the Early Industrial Age* (1984); *Lord Acton: A Study in Conscience and Politics* (1952); *Marriage and Morals Among the Victorians* (1986); *The New History and the Old* (1987); "Of Heroes, Villains, and Valets," *Commentary* 91, no. 12 (June 1991): 20–26; *On Liberty and Liberalism: The Case of John Stuart Mill* (1974); *On*

Looking into the Abyss: Untimely Thoughts on Culture and Society (1994); "The Politics of Dissent," *Commentary* 98, no. 1 (July 1994): 32–37; *Poverty and Compassion: The Moral Imagination of the Late Victorians* (1991); "Supposing History Is a Woman—What Then?" *American Scholar* (Autumn 1984); "Telling it as You Like it—Post-Modernist History and the Flight from Fact," *Times Literary Supplement* 16 (October 1992): 12–15; *Victorian Minds* (1968); "Where Have All the Footnotes Gone," *NYTimes Book Review* (June 16, 1991).

SELECTED WORKS EDITED BY GERTRUDE HIMMELFARB

Acton, Lord. *Essays on Freedom and Power* (1948. Reprints, 1955, 1984); Malthus, Thomas Robert. *Essays on Population* (1960); Mill, John Stuart. *Essays on Politics and Culture* (1962. Reprints, 1963, 1971); Mill, John Stuart. *On Liberty* (1974).

BIBLIOGRAPHY

Contemporary Authors (1975); *Current Biography* (1985); *World Authors 1980-1985* (1991); *The Writers Directory* (1988–1990, 1988).

OZ FRANKEL

HIMMELSTEIN, LENA *see* MALSIN, LANE BRYANT

HIRSCHLER, GERTRUDE (1929–1994)

Not prepared to compromise her ideals by accepting work that did not meet her ideological approval, Gertrude Hirschler rejected the offer of a well-recognized publisher, who submitted a book by an Israeli leftist writer to her for translation. True to her principles, she removed her name from *The Hirsch Siddur* that she had translated, due to changes to the finished product that did not meet her standards. A brilliant perfectionist, Hirschler's literary contributions as a translator, editor, and writer are highly regarded in the areas of Jewish history, accounts of the Holocaust, religious literature, and Zionism.

Gertrude (Raizel) Hirschler was born in Vienna, Austria, on August 11, 1929, and was the elder of the two daughters of Alice Dukes and Bernard Hirschler. Her mother attended gymnasium. Her father ran a successful household goods business in Austria, and the family led an aristocratic, well-to-do life there. After fleeing Nazi Europe, the family arrived in Baltimore, Maryland, in 1939. As refugees, the economic situation was difficult.

Valuing Jewish studies, Hirschler attended Baltimore Hebrew College and Teachers Training School from 1942 to 1945. She graduated from Johns Hopkins University night school with a B.S. with honors in 1952.

Her positions of employment were of Jewish significance: staff member of the Baltimore Jewish Council (1948–1955), free-lance translator (1955–1994), assistant editor for the *Encyclopedia of Zionism and Israel* (1965–1971), assistant editor for Herzl Press (1965–1976), lecturer at Theodor Herzl Institute (1972 to the late 1980s), and free-lance author and editor (1971–1994).

Orthodox and observant, she lectured at numerous organizations and synagogues. Her writing abilities were respected by some of the foremost Orthodox scholars of the century. She took pride in being a descendant of Rabbi Akiva Eger. She was a member of Emunah Women and Bar-Ilan Women's Organization.

The scope of her publications is diverse. In the realm of Jewish history, they include translator of Selma Stern's *Josel of Rosheim* (1965); editor of Solomon Zeitlin's *The Rise and Fall of the Judaean State*, Vol. 3 (1978), Esra Shereshevsky's *Rashi: The Man and His World* (1982), and Yeshiva University museum's catalog *Ashkenaz: The German Jewish Heritage* (1988); author of articles in the *Encyclopedia Judaica* and *Lexicon des Judentums*. Some of her works in the area of Holocaust literature are translator and editor of Simon Zucker's *The Unconquerable Spirit* (1980); editor of Rabbi Alter Pekier's *From Kletzk to Siberia* (1985), and Adam Starkopf's *There Is Always Time to Die* (1981). In the field of religious literature, her writings are widely acclaimed, especially her translations of Rabbi Samson Raphael Hirsch. Her works include translator of Rabbi Hirsch's *T'rumath Tzvi: The Pentateuch* (1986), *The Psalms* (1978), *Chapters of the Fathers* (1979), and Rabbi Alexander Z. Friedman's *Wellsprings of Torah* (1969); author of *To Love Mercy* (1972). Hirschler's publications on the study of Zionism include assistant editor and contributor of over fifty articles to the *Encyclopedia of Zionism and Israel* (1971); coauthor of *Menahem Begin: From Freedom Fighter to Statesman* (1979).

Hirschler's lucid translations were true to the authors' original ideas. When editing, she researched and rewrote, insisting upon accuracy. As an author, her words were precise. Her interests in Jewish history and literature were wide and varied. Through her editorial and translation works and her own writings, she left a significant legacy.

Gertrude Hirschler died in 1994.

BIBLIOGRAPHY

Birnbaum, Jacob. "Gertrude Hirschler: Jewish Scholar Dies." *The Jewish Press*, February 18, 1994; Eckman, Lester. Telephone conversations with author, November 9 and December 14, 1996; Hecht, Ida. Telephone conversation with author, November 24, 1996; Kestenberg, Vera. Telephone conversation with author, December 8, 1996; Preschel, Tovia. "Gertrude Hirschler, Author, Translator and Editor." Parts 1–3. *The Jewish Press*, March 4, 11, and 18, 1994; Weinberg, Chana. Conversation with author, November 14, 1996; *WWIAJ* (1980); *Who's Who in World Jewry* (1987).

SUSAN J. (LIEF) ROTENBERG

HIRSH, MARILYN (1944–1988)

"K'tonton existed only on the pages of a book, but I saw him clearly—more clearly—than I saw the teacher." These are the words written by FRANCINE KLAGSBRUN, the well-known author, in her introduction to the book *The Best of K'tonton*, one of the thirty children's books, primarily of Jewish interest, illustrated by Marilyn Hirsh.

Writer and illustrator of children's books, Marilyn Hirsh was born in Chicago, Illinois, on January 1, 1944, to Eugene and Rose (Warshell) Hirsh. Her father owned a meat market. Hirsh was married on November 18, 1973, to James H. Harris.

Hirsh's educational background consisted of Chicago's Art Institute, the Carnegie Mellon Institute, and the New York University Institute of Fine Arts. She then used this education to transmit to children her views of the world and her love of Judaism. Her views of the world are reflected in the four books on India that she illustrated while serving in the Peace Corps. As historian of Indian and Buddist art, she taught at Cooper Union and the New York University Institute of Fine Arts.

However, the primary focus of her books was on Jewish subjects. She researched each subject and era intensively to remain true to texts of Jewish life and times. For instance, *Tower of Babel* depicts races in many different costumes to show the existence of harmony before the Tower of Babel story takes place. Ancient Near Eastern and Babylonian life is also accurately portrayed.

The illustrations in *Butchers and Bakers, Rabbis and Kings* reflect the costumes and life of Tudela and Spain around the year 1114, from the details of the castle and the medieval village to the turbans of the townspeople and the helmets of the guards. The costumes and buildings in *The Hanukkah Story* are true to

637

Hellenistic times, from the robes and the headgear to the Greek and Roman architecture.

In 1979, Marilyn Hirsh received the first SYDNEY TAYLOR Award for Jewish Children's Literature, given by the Association of Jewish Libraries, for her book *Potato Pancakes All Around*, written in 1978. A true-to-life representation of shtetl life, along with a delightful Hanukkah story line, earned her the award. Hirsh also visited Jewish day schools in Nassau County, New York, drawing for the children and explaining her books—transmitting her enthusiasm for Judaism to them. Her other books include *Rabbi and the Twenty-nine Witches*, *Joseph Who Loved the Sabbath*, and *I Love Hanukkah*. *Zaydeh*, which she illustrated with comforting black-and-white pictures for Moshe Halevi Spero in 1983, discusses mourning and death. *Sidduri*, which was illustrated for the United Synagogue Commission on Jewish Education in 1983, is in full-blown color with feelings of joy emanating throughout. Finally, *Best of K'tonton* and others in the series, such as *K'tonton in the Circus*, written by Sadie Rose Weilerstein, all show that lovable little fellow and his adventures.

Marilyn Hirsh died in New York City of cancer, on October 17, 1988.

SELECTED WORKS BY MARILYN HIRSH

Best of K'tonton (1980); *Butchers and Bakers, Rabbis and Kings* (1984); *The Hanukkah Story* (1977); *I Love Hanukkah* (1984); *K'tonton in the Circus* (1981); *Potato Pancakes All Around* (1978); *Rabbi and the Twenty-nine Witches* (1976); *Sidduri* (1983); *Tower of Babel* (1981); *Zaydeh* (1983).

BIBLIOGRAPHY

AJYB 90:610–611; Obiturary. *NYTimes*, October 22, 1988; *Something About the Author* 7 (1975): 126.

ANNETTE MUFFS BOTNICK

HISTORIANS

American Jewish women have been prominent within the historical profession. Indeed, many have been on the cutting edge of historical scholarship since the 1960s. In particular, Jewish women were at the forefront of developments within social history and in the creation of women's history. While women generally, and Jewish women in particular, rarely made careers as historians in the first half of the twentieth century, Jewish women represented a significant proportion of academic historians both in American and European history as discrimination against Jews and prejudice against women lessened in the decades after World War II. Perhaps because of their sensitiv-

ity to the situation of powerless groups, most of them focused their attention not on traditional power elites but rather on those social groups traditionally ignored by academic historians: ordinary people, workers, peasants, minority groups, Jews, and especially women. They helped create, and were influenced by, new trends in historical scholarship that favored the study of such groups.

Many Jewish women became leading social historians as that field developed in the 1960s and 1970s. European historians like NATALIE ZEMON DAVIS and Joan Wallach Scott and American historians like Tamara Hareven greatly influenced how historians came to view the lives and relationships of peasants and workers. In a series of groundbreaking articles, published by Stanford University Press in 1975 as *Society and Culture in Early Modern France: Eight Essays*, Davis presented a breathtaking view of family relationships, daily life, and religion among peasants in sixteenth- and seventeenth-century France. Her ability to use archival material about ordinary people and to tease out of the records the details of everyday life has influenced students during her long and distinguished academic career at Brown University (1959–1963), the University of Toronto (1963–1971), the University of California at Berkeley (1971–1977), and Princeton University from 1978 until her retirement in 1996. Her collaboration as historical adviser to the successful popular film *The Return of Martin Guerre* brought her insights about peasant life in sixteenth-century France to the general public. She shared the results of her investigation into this court case, and her understanding of sixteenth-century family life, marital relations, and religious views in a 1983 book *The Return of Martin Guerre* (Harvard University Press).

Both Joan Wallach Scott and Tamara Hareven devoted themselves to understanding the lives of industrial workers. Scott's first work, *The Glassworkers of Carmaux: French Craftsmen and Political Action in a Nineteenth-Century City* (Harvard University Press, 1974), studied the lives of the workers themselves and their relationship to those who exercised power over them. Eschewing traditional labor history's focus on union activities, Scott was more concerned with the role of work and the community of workers. Hareven focused on American workers, in particular mill workers in New England, and on such demographic issues as marriage and family in the nineteenth century. She wrote (with Randolph Langenbach) *Amoskeag: Life and Work in an American Factory-City* (Pantheon, 1978) and *Family Time and Industrial Time: The Relationship between the Family and Work in a New England*

Industrial Community (Cambridge University Press, 1982). In addition, she edited a large number of books on American social history, most of them about the development of the family, including *Anonymous Americans: Explorations in Nineteenth-Century Social History* (Prentice-Hall, 1971), *Family and Kin in Urban Communities, 1700–1930* (New Viewpoints, 1977), *Family and Population in Nineteenth-Century America* (with Maris Vinovskis; Princeton University Press, 1978), and *Family History at the Crossroads: A Journal of Family History Reader* (with Andrejs Plakans; Princeton University Press, 1987).

By the 1970s, many of these social historians helped develop the newly emerging field of women's history. They were all utterly honest in admitting that their involvement as feminists in the women's movement had influenced their intellectual focus. Joan Wallach Scott best exemplifies this trend among European historians. Born in Brooklyn in 1941, educated at Brandeis and the University of Wisconsin, Scott began her career studying French workers, but all of her subsequent work, which continues to deal with power relations and hierarchies, has been on women and gender. She began, naturally enough, with a concern for women workers, publishing in 1978 a book with fellow social historian Louise Tilly, titled *Women, Work, and Family* (Holt, Rinehart and Winston; Routledge, 1987). In the preface to the second edition, the authors declared that feminist debates about women had made them wonder about the impact of the Industrial Revolution and the new forms of women's work that it created on the role of women within the family. After much research, they concluded that industrial wage work did not change that role, nor did it liberate women from traditional power relations within the family. They called on historians to think of women, work, and family as inseparable and interdependent categories. In other books and articles, Scott continued to deal with women workers, their lives, relationships, and struggles. In a teaching career at the University of Illinois, Chicago Circle (1970–1972), Northwestern (1972–1974), the University of North Carolina (1974–1980), Brown University (1980–1985), and the Institute for Advanced Study, Princeton, Scott has trained two generations of European women's historians.

Like Scott, other European women's historians also understood that their scholarly concerns derived from and could make a contribution to their political interests. That is, they chose to write women's history because they were active feminists, committed to the struggle for equality for women. In a book edited with Claudia Koonz, *Becoming Visible: Women in European History* (Houghton Mifflin, 1977), Renate Bridenthal, for example, indicated that her work was born out of the women's movement. Like other women's historians, she sought to abandon male models of history and explore the experience of women from a feminist perspective. Similarly, in the introduction to their volume *When Biology Became Destiny: Women in Weimar and Nazi Germany* (Monthly Review Press, 1984), Renate Bridenthal, Atina Grossmann, and Marion Kaplan made it clear that as activists from the 1960s, they intended their book to be a contribution to the feminist movement. Seeking a usable past and concerned with women as agents and victims of history, they wanted to understand how women's experience interacted with class and ethnic identity. Unlike most women's historians with Jewish backgrounds, however, Bridenthal, Grossmann, and Kaplan admitted that their backgrounds as women whose families had to flee Nazi Germany because they were Jews also influenced their choice of scholarly subject. Although the book did not focus on German Jewish women, these historians wanted to understand the world of their parents. Other European historians who focus on women include Judith Walkowitz, the author of books on prostitution and sexual danger in Victorian England, and Claire Goldberg Moses, who has written on feminism in France.

Among historians of the United States, Jewish women like Alice Kessler-Harris, Nancy Cott, GERDA LERNER, Linda Kerber, and Kathryn Kish Sklar took the lead in developing the new field of women's history in the 1960s and 1970s. Most of these women have devoted all of their scholarly efforts to understanding the role and status of women in American life. Nancy Cott, for example, wrote an influential book on women in the early American republic, *The Bonds of Womanhood: "Women's Sphere" in New England, 1780–1835* (Yale University Press, 1977), which explored how the "cult of domesticity" and the "cult of true womanhood" related to the actual circumstances and experiences of women. In addition, she has published an important collection of documents, *Roots of Bitterness: Documents of the Social History of American Women* (Dutton, 1972; Northeastern University Press, 1986, 1996), and edited a great many volumes of significant articles on American women, including *A Heritage of Her Own: Toward a New Social History of American Women* (Simon and Schuster, 1979) and the multivolume *History of Women in the United States: Historical Articles on Women's Lives and Activities*, published by K.G. Saur in New York and Munich, twenty volumes of which have appeared since 1992. These volumes cover a wide range of issues, including industrial, agricultural, white-collar, and professional work; household and family; health, law, education, organizational life, religion, sexuality, politics, and war. Cott has also written a history of feminism, *The Grounding of Modern Feminism* (Yale University Press, 1987), and edited the letters of Mary Ritter Beard (Yale, 1991).

Like Nancy Cott, Kathryn Kish Sklar's first work dealt with the "cult of domesticity," which dominated the lives of middle-class American women in the nineteenth century. Her *Catharine Beecher: A Study in American Domesticity* (Yale University Press, 1973) greatly influenced the first generation of women's historians. Sklar has used biography most effectively to explore the lives of individual women and women generally. She has edited the autobiography of American reformer Florence Kelley (1986) and written a biography of the same woman, *Florence Kelley and the Nation's Work: The Rise of Women's Political Culture, 1830–1900* (Yale University Press, 1995). Like most of her colleagues in women's history, Sklar has published collections of articles and readers, including (with Thomas Dublin) *Women and Power in American History: A Reader* (Prentice-Hall, 1991).

Unlike Cott and Sklar, Linda Kerber did not begin her academic career by writing about women. Her first book was a study of the ideology of the federalists, *Federalists in Dissent: Imagery and Ideology in Jeffersonian America* (Cornell University Press, 1970). Only later did Kerber, a professor at the University of Iowa since 1971, change her focus to deal with women. Her *Women of the Republic: Intellect and Ideology in Revolutionary America* (University of North Carolina Press, 1980) was an important analysis of the role of women in the devolopment of revolutionary and republican America. Primarily an intellectual historian, she has also edited a collection of articles and documents with Jane DeHart Matthews, *Women's America: Refocusing the Past* (Oxford University Press, 1982) and with Alice Kessler-Harris and Kathryn Kish Sklar, *United States History as Women's History: New Feminist Essays* (University of North Carolina Press, 1995). Blanche Wiesen Cook also began her career as a traditional political historian, but then turned her attention to women. In 1981, she published *The Declassified Eisenhower: A Divided Legacy* (Doubleday), and in 1992, *Eleanor Roosevelt* (Viking).

In contrast to Cott, Kerber, and Sklar, who have focused primarily on middle-class women, Alice Kessler-Harris has devoted her scholarship to women workers. A professor at Hofstra University from 1968 to 1988, and at Rutgers since 1989, Kessler-Harris is the author of *Women Have Always Worked: A Historical*

Overview (McGraw-Hill, 1981); *Out to Work: A History of Wage-Earning Women in the United States* (Oxford University Press, 1982); and *A Woman's Wage: Historical Meanings and Social Consequences* (University Press of Kentucky, 1990). She has also edited several collections of essays and a collections of stories by the Jewish immigrant writer ANZIA YEZIERSKA.

Cott, Sklar, Kerber, and Kessler-Harris were all born around 1940 and educated in the 1960s. Gerda Lerner's life experiences stand in marked contrast to those of these women. Born in Vienna in 1920, she had just completed high school at the time of the anschluss with Nazi Germany. Although she and her family had the good fortune to be able to immigrate to America, she resumed her education only in the 1960s, obtaining her Ph.D. from Columbia in 1966. Her experiences doubly sensitized her to the experiences of marginalized groups. Her early work focused on black and white women who fought against injustice, in particular against slavery. Her first study, *The Grimké Sisters from South Carolina: Rebels Against Slavery* (Houghton Mifflin, 1967), dealt with abolitionist women. She then went on to publish *Black Women in White America: A Documentary History* (Pantheon, 1972). A professor at Long Island University (1965–1968), Sarah Lawrence College (1968–1980), and the University of Wisconsin (1980–1991), she has also devoted her prodigious scholarly energy to the study of feminism and gender relations, publishing *The Majority Finds Its Past: Placing Women in History* (Oxford University Press, 1979), *The Creation of Patriarchy* (Oxford University Press, 1986), *The Creation of Feminist Consciousness: From the Middle Ages to the Eighteenth Century* (Oxford University Press, 1993), and several collections of documents.

In the 1970s and early 1980s, most women's historians concerned themselves with uncovering the experiences of women, both famous and ordinary. By the late 1980s, many of these historians had turned instead to a concern with gender, that is, with the social construction of female (or male) identity. Influenced by developments in literary criticism such as deconstructionism and postmodernism, some women's historians increasingly turned to theoretical issues. Once again, Joan Wallach Scott was at the forefront of this development. In her *Gender and the Politics of History* (Columbia University Press, 1988), Scott argued that poststructural theory as developed by Jacques Derrida and Michel Foucault offered feminism a powerful analytic tool to explore how gender hierarchies are constructed and legitimized. In a series of articles, she explored the varied and inherently unstable meanings attached to gender. Always interested in power relations, Scott insisted that studying gender as a category provided an excellent way to analyze all hierarchies of difference in society. Scott hoped that her studies of gender would alert people to inequalities, which could then be rectified. Other volumes of essays, *Learning about Women: Gender, Politics and Power*, edited with Jill Conway and Susan Bourque (University of Michigan Press, 1989), and *Feminists Theorize the Political*, edited with Judith Butler (Routledge, 1992), continued these theoretical concerns.

Not all Jewish women in the historical profession are women's historians, of course. Many have pursued traditional fields of scholarship. GERTRUDE HIMMELFARB, an active scholar since the 1950s who taught for decades at Brooklyn College, has written over ten books on intellectual developments in England in the nineteenth century. Her first book, *Lord Acton: A Study in Conscience and Politics* (Routledge, 1952), was followed by *Darwin and the Darwinian Revolution* (Doubleday, 1959) and *Victorian Minds* (Knopf, 1968). Himmelfarb also wrote a major study of the liberal thinker John Stuart Mill, *On Liberty and Liberalism: The Case of John Stuart Mill* (Knopf, 1974), edited volumes of works by Mill and Thomas Malthus, and wrote books on Victorian attitudes, including *The Idea of Poverty: England in the Early Industrial Age* (Knopf, 1984), *Marriage and Morals Among the Victorians: Essays* (Knopf, 1986), and *Poverty and Compassion: The Moral Imagination of the Late Victorians* (Knopf, 1991). Increasingly upset with new trends in historiography, Himmelfarb has evaluated them in *The New History and the Old* (Harvard University Press, 1987). Like her husband, neoconservative Irving Kristol, Himmelfarb has herself become a social critic upset with current values and has written two books of such criticism, *On Looking into the Abyss: Untimely Thoughts on Culture and Society* (Knopf, 1984) and *The De-Moralization of Society: From Victorian Virtues to Modern Values* (Knopf, 1995).

Adrienne Koch (1912–1971), who served as professor at the University of California at Berkeley and at the University of Maryland, also was a prominent intellectual historian. She wrote many books on the American Enlightenment, including *Power, Morals, and the Founding Fathers: Essays on the Interpretation of the American Enlightenment* (Cornell University Press, 1961) and *The American Enlightenment: The Shaping of the American Experiment* (Braziller, 1971), and on the ideologies of the Founding Fathers, including *The Philosophy of Thomas Jefferson* (Columbia University Press, 1943) and *Jefferson and Madison: The Great Collaboration* (Oxford University Press, 1950). She also published editions of the writings of Thomas Jefferson and John Adams and John Quincy Adams. Pauline

Maier has worked primarily as a political historian. A professor at the Massachusetts Institute of Technology, she has authored *From Resistance to Revolution: Colonial Radicals and the Development of American Opposition to Britain, 1765–1776* (Knopf, 1972) and *The Old Revolutionaries: Political Lives in the Age of Samuel Adams* (Knopf, 1980).

Other historians have continued to write social history. Elaine Tyler May, for example, has written several books on the family in America: *Great Expectations: Marriage and Divorce in Post-Victorian America* (University of Chicago Press, 1980); *Homeward Bound: American Families in the Cold War Era* (Basic Books, 1988), and *Barren in the Promised Land: Childless Americans* (Basic Books, 1995). Mary Flug Handlin coauthored with her husband, Harvard professor Oscar Handlin, several books in American political and social history, including studies of the role of government in the economy of Massachusetts before the Civil War, of youth and the family in American history, and of American affluence. Other American social historians include Paula S. Fass, author of *The Damned and the Beautiful: American Youth in the 1920s* (Oxford University Press, 1977) and *Outside In: Minorities and the Transformation of American Education* (Oxford University Press, 1989); Regina Morantz-Sanchez, author of *Sympathy and Science* (Oxford University Press, 1985) and coeditor of *In Her Own Words: Oral Histories of Women Physicians* (Greenwood Press, 1982); and Sheila Rothman, who has published several volumes on illness, hospitals, and the poor, including *Woman's Proper Place* (Basic Books, 1978), and *Living in the Shadow of Death: Tuberculosis and the Social Experience of Illness in American History* (Basic Books, 1994).

There are also European historians who have not focused primarily on women. Jan Goldstein at the University of Chicago has worked in intellectual history, writing *Console and Classify: The French Psychiatric Profession in the Nineteenth Century* (Cambridge University Press, 1987) and editing *Foucault and the Writing of History* (Blackwell, 1994). Jane Caplan has focused on the nature of government administration in Nazi Germany. The author of *Government Without Administration: State and Civil Service in Weimar and Nazi Germany* (Oxford University Press, 1988), she has also edited (with Thomas Childers) an important collection of essays on the Third Reich. Temma Kaplan has published two books on anarchists and other radicals in Spain. In medieval history, Gabrielle Spiegel of the University of Maryland and Johns Hopkins University has worked on the creation of French vernacular historiography in the twelfth century, and Brigitte Bedos-Rezak of the University of Maryland has authored books on how medieval seals illustrate the social and cultural worlds of eleventh- and twelfth-century France.

Despite the fact that Jewish women have placed themselves on the leading edge of much of historical scholarship in the past three decades, most of them have not chosen to deal with Jews. Natalie Zemon Davis, however, after a long career dealing with French men and women, is an exception, exploring the life of a German Jewish woman in *Women on the Margins: Three Seventeenth-Century Lives* (Harvard University Press, 1995). Davis included Glikl bas Judah Leib, generally known as Glikl of Hameln, a prosperous Jewish woman who spent most of her life in Hamburg and Metz, the wife of Jewish merchants and herself a merchant, who wrote a long autobiography to console herself after the death of her first husband. Davis, who mastered the difficult Yiddish text, has placed Glikl squarely within her seventeenth-century milieu, astutely describing the sources of her piety and inner religious life. Davis well understands how Glikl viewed the hostile Christian world around her. Despite the fact that she was on the margins of the dominant society, both as a Jew and as a woman, Glikl, and the Jews generally, created a Jewish world that sustained them and in turn marginalized the Christians.

Jewish women have also been prominent in developing the field of modern Jewish history, many of them in social history and women's history. Within Jewish history, few women have become prominent in ancient or medieval history, but many have played a leading role in American and modern European Jewish history. Among the earliest women to pursue careers as professional Jewish historians were NAOMI W. COHEN, LUCY S. DAWIDOWICZ, and NORA LEVIN. Cohen studied Jewish history with Salo Baron at Columbia University in the late 1940s, obtaining her Ph.D. there in American and Jewish history. The author of six books, Cohen concerned herself with traditional historiographic concerns: Jewish politics, Jewish/non-Jewish relations, and the status of Jews in American society. Her first book, *A Dual Heritage: The Public Career of Oscar S. Strauss* (Jewish Publication Society, 1969), was a study of the first Jew to hold a prominent position in the American government. Cohen, who taught for decades at HUNTER COLLEGE, also wrote monographs on the American Jewish Committee (*Not Free to Desist: The American Jewish Committee, 1906–1966*, Jewish Publication Society, 1972), American Jews and Zionism (*American Jews and the Zionist Idea*, Ktav, 1975), the American response to the

riots in Palestine in 1929–1930 (*The Year After the Riots: American Responses to the Palestine Crisis of 1929–1930*, Wayne State University Press, 1988), and the Jewish struggle for religious equality (*Jews in Christian America*, Oxford University Press, 1992). In addition, she published *Encounter with Emancipation: The German Jews in the United States, 1830–1914* (Jewish Publication Society, 1984).

Lucy Dawidowicz worked on Eastern European Jews and on the Holocaust. Born in 1915 and educated at Hunter College and Columbia, she spent a year as a fellow in Jewish history at the YIVO Institute for Jewish Research in Vilna in 1938–1939, a year she movingly describes in her memoir *From That Time and Place* (Norton, 1989). Like most women of her generation, she did not pursue a straightforward academic career. Instead, during World War II, she worked for the YIVO in New York as Max Weinreich's scholarly assistant, returning to Columbia at the end of the war to study Jewish history with Salo Baron, and then working for the Joint Distribution Committee with Jewish Holocaust survivors in Europe. While there, she became involved in 1946–1947 in arranging for the transfer of YIVO's Vilna library, which had been captured by the Nazis but was then in the possession of the American army, to YIVO in New York.

Dawidowicz assumed an academic career path only in the late 1960s, when she began to publish books and teach at Yeshiva University. Her first scholarly book was *The Golden Tradition: Jewish Life and Thought in Eastern Europe* (Holt, Rinehart and Winston, 1967), a collection of translated documents depicting the literary, religious, and political history of Eastern European Jewry in the nineteenth and twentieth centuries. Most of Dawidowicz's scholarship was devoted to the Holocaust. In 1975, she published *The War Against the Jews, 1933–1945* (Holt, Rinehart and Winston), which dealt both with the Nazi policy of annihilation and the Jewish response to the Nazis. A year later, she published a collection of documents on the Holocaust, *A Holocaust Reader* (Behrmann House), and in 1981, *The Holocaust and the Historians* (Harvard University Press), an attempt to understand how different historians, including those in Germany and those who played down its significance, have treated the Holocaust. Dawidowicz also published on American Jewry (*On Equal Terms: Jews in America, 1881–1981*, Holt, Rinehart and Winston, 1982), and several collections of essays on various issues in modern Jewish life.

Like Dawidowicz, Nora Levin did not pursue a standard academic career path. Her work also focused on Eastern Europe and the Holocaust. The author of *The Holocaust: The Destruction of European Jewry, 1933–1945* (Crowell, 1968), *While Messiah Tarried: Jewish Socialist Movements, 1871–1917* (Schocken, 1977), and *The Jews in the Soviet Union Since 1917: Paradox of Survival* (New York University Press, 1989), she taught at Gratz College after years as a research librarian.

As modern Jewish history grew as a field in the 1970s, women came to play an increasingly prominent role within its ranks, publishing pathbreaking works in Jewish social history, including Jewish women's history, and occupying prominent positions at leading American universities. Many of these women were trained in Jewish history at Columbia University or Brandeis, while others received their original training in related fields of history but chose to work primarily on Jewish life in modern Europe or America.

The career of Paula Hyman most typifies this new generation of Jewish historians. Born in 1946 in Boston, Hyman was educated at Radcliffe and Columbia, receiving her Ph.D. in 1975. She has taught at Columbia University (1974–1981) and the Jewish Theological Seminary of America (1981–1986), where she also served as dean of the Seminary College of Jewish Studies, and has been the Lucy Moses Professor of Modern Jewish History at Yale University since 1986. A social historian of great distinction, Hyman has written two important books on the Jews in France: *From Dreyfus to Vichy: The Remaking of French Jewry, 1906–1939* (Columbia University Press, 1979), a study of how the immigration of Eastern European Jews to France in the early twentieth century transformed the Jewish community there; and *The Emancipation of the Jews of Alsace: Acculturation and Tradition in the Nineteenth Century* (Yale University Press, 1991), a work that both revealed the persistence of traditional Jewish economic, social, and religious behavior patterns in Eastern France, despite early legal emancipation, and demonstrated how the economic and social forces of modernity ultimately undercut Jewish traditionalism in the late nineteenth century. An activist in the women's movement since the 1960s, Hyman has also devoted much scholarly attention to Jewish women, coauthoring with Charlotte Baum and Sonya Michel *The Jewish Woman in America* (Dial Press, 1976), writing many articles, and also producing a recent book, *Gender and Assimilation in Modern Jewish History: The Roles and Representation of Women* (University of Washington Press, 1995), a study of the role of gender in Jewish assimilation in Western Europe, Eastern Europe, and the United States. In all of her books and articles, Hyman displays a sensitivity to the unique situation of Jewish women and the role of gender in modern Jewish history.

Within the field of European Jewish history, other Jewish women have also made significant contributions. Marion Kaplan, for example, professor at Queens College in New York (Ph.D. Columbia), is the leading historian of German Jewish women. She is the author of *The Jewish Feminist Movement in Germany: The Campaigns of the Jüdischer Frauenbund, 1904–1938* (Greenwood Press, 1979) and *The Making of the Jewish Middle Class: Women, Family, and Identity in Imperial Germany* (Oxford University Press, 1991), which showed the crucial role played by women in the development of the bourgeois German Jewish family, a family that facilitated Jewish acculturation to the social mores of the gentile middle classes and also served as the vehicle through which Jews maintained Jewish religious traditions, Jewish social life, and a sense of Jewish ethnic solidarity in Germany. Indeed, after Kaplan's work, no serious study of Jewish assimilation anywhere could be made without taking gender issues into account. Kaplan has also edited works on women and dowries in European history and on women in Weimar and Nazi Germany. Other important historians of European Jewry include Frances Malino, professor at Wellesley College (Ph.D. Brandeis), the author of *The Sephardic Jews of Bordeaux: Assimilation and Emancipation in Revolutionary and Napoleonic France* (University of Alabama Press, 1978) and *A Jew in the French Revolution: The Life of Zalkind Hourwitz* (Blackwell, 1996); Phyllis Cohen Albert (Ph.D. Brandeis), author of *The Modernization of French Jewry: Consistory and Community in the Nineteenth Century* (Brandeis University Press, 1977); Harriet Freidenreich (Ph.D. Columbia, 1973), professor at Temple University, who has written on the Jews of Yugoslavia in the interwar period (*The Jews of Yugoslavia: A Quest for Community*, Jewish Publication Society, 1979), the Jews of Vienna (*Jewish Politics in Vienna, 1918–1938*, Indiana University Press, 1991), and is now working on Jewish "new women" in Germany and Austria in the early twentieth century; Marsha Rozenblit (Ph.D. Columbia, 1980), professor at the University of Maryland, who has written on Jewish assimilation in late Habsburg Vienna: *The Jews of Vienna, 1867–1918: Assimilation and Identity* (State University of New York Press, 1983); Vicki Caron (Ph.D. Columbia), professor at Brown University, who has written *Between France and Germany: The Jews of Alsace-Lorraine, 1871–1918* (Stanford University Press, 1988); Deborah Hertz, professor at the State University of New York at Binghamton, who has published *Jewish High Society in Old Regime Berlin* (Yale

University Press, 1988) and a volume of correspondence between Rahel Varnhagen and Rebecca Friedländer; and Judith Baskin, professor at the State University of New York at Albany, the author of *Jewish Women in Historical Perspective* (Wayne State University Press, 1991).

Within American Jewish history, Jewish women have been equally prominent since the 1970s. Deborah Dash Moore (Ph.D. Columbia, 1975), for example, professor at Vassar College, has written such major works as *At Home in America: Second Generation New York Jews* (Columbia University Press, 1981), a study of the process by which the children of Eastern European Jewish immigrants Americanized and yet still maintained a strong Jewish ethnic identity in New York in the 1920s and 1930s; *B'nai B'rith and the Challenge of Ethnic Leadership* (State University of New York Press, 1981); and *To the Golden Cities: Pursuing the American Jewish Dream in Miami and L.A.* (Free Press, 1994). Jenna Weissman Joselit (Ph.D. Columbia), is likewise the author of several important books in American Jewish social history, beginning with *Our Gang: Jewish Crime and the New York Jewish Community, 1900–1940* (Indiana University Press, 1983), a study of how both Jewish criminal activity and the response of the organized Jewish community to Jewish crime reflected the successful Americanization of the Eastern European immigrants in the early twentieth century. Joselit has also written a study of modern Orthodoxy, *New York's Jewish Jews: The Orthodox Community in the Interwar Years* (Indiana University Press, 1990), and *The Wonders of America: Reinventing Jewish Culture 1880–1950* (Hill and Wang, 1994). Deborah Lipstadt (Ph.D. Brandeis), a professor at Emory University, has focused on the reception of the Holocaust in America in two books: *Beyond Belief: The American Press and the Coming of the Holocaust, 1933–1945* (Free Press, 1986) and *Denying the Holocaust: The Growing Assault on Truth and Memory* (Free Press, 1993).

Among historians of American Jewish life, Hasia Diner (Ph.D. Illinois), who has taught at the University of Maryland and New York University, has simultaneously made major contributions to the fields of immigrant history, women's history, and Jewish history. Her first book, *In the Almost Promised Land: American Jews and Blacks, 1915–1935* (Greenwood Press, 1977), was a study of how the Yiddish press viewed the struggle for civil rights of American blacks in the early twentieth century. She then went on to write a pathbreaking study of Irish women in the United States, *Erin's Daughters in America: Irish Immigrant Women in the Nineteenth Century* (Johns Hopkins University Press, 1983). Returning to Jewish history, Diner provided a completely new understanding of the nineteenth-century Jewish immigrants to America from German-speaking Central Europe in *A Time for Gathering: The Second Migration, 1820–1880* (Johns Hopkins University Press, 1992). Here, Diner argued that although these Jews acculturated and Americanized, they also forged new forms of Jewish identity as a means of preserving Jewish community in America. Diner is now working on a study of how the foodways of different immigrant groups in America, including the Jews, Italians, and the Irish, reveal the dynamic tension between Americanization and the preservation of ethnic community. Other historians of Jewish immigrant women include Susan Glenn, *Daughters of the Shtetl: Life and Labor in the Immigrant Community* (Cornell University Press, 1990); Sydney Stahl Weinberg, *The World of Our Mothers: The Lives of Jewish Immigrant Women* (University of North Carolina Press, 1988); and Judith E. Smith, *Family Lives: A History of Italian and Jewish Immigrant Lives in Providence 1900–1940* (State University of New York Press, 1985).

Jewish women, uniquely sensitive to the position of minority groups, have thus been in the forefront of new developments within academic history in social history, women's history, Jewish history, and minority history generally. Products of America in the 1960s and 1970s, they have made a major contribution to many fields of historical inquiry.

MARSHA L. ROZENBLIT

HOBSON, LAURA Z. (1900–1986)

Laura Z. Hobson was passionate about many things: people, ideas, word puzzles, politics, her family, her daily bicycle rides through Central Park that she began at age sixty-seven, and, most of all, her writing. The author of nine novels, two children's books, numerous short stories, and articles, she also wrote promotions for *Time* and *Life* magazines and edited the Double Crostics puzzles in the *Saturday Review* for twenty-seven years. Before she became a full-time novelist with the 1947 publication of *Gentleman's Agreement*, she had been a successful writer of advertising copy.

When she was eighty-three years old, she published *Laura Z.: A Life*, the first volume of her autobiography. She explained her name and the book's title in this way: "The Z is for Zametkin, my maiden name, and I have clung to it through all my years because it held my identity intact before that Anglo-Saxon married name of Hobson."

She and her twin sister, Alice, were born on June 19, 1900, in New York City. The twins had an older brother, Fred, and an older half-brother, Joel. Their parents, Michael and Adella (Khean) Zametkin, were refugees from czarist Russia. Michael was a mathematician who had been imprisoned and tortured in Russia for his socialist beliefs. In the United States, he became a labor organizer and the editor of the *Forverts*, then the most powerful Yiddish paper in the country. Adella wrote for *Der Yidisher Tog*, attended dental school, lectured on American life, and taught English to women newly arrived from Eastern Europe.

Laura studied at Cornell University. In 1930, she married publishing executive Thayer Hobson, with whom she coauthored two westerns. The couple divorced in 1935.

In 1937, she adopted a son, Michael Z. Hobson. This was an unusual action for an unmarried woman at that time. In 1941, still single, she gave birth to Christopher Z. Hobson. Because she did not want Michael to feel stigmatized as her only adopted child, she kept her pregnancy secret, giving birth under an assumed name. She then adopted Christopher using her own name. She did not tell her children the truth about Christopher's birth until they were grown.

Hobson said that her novels were partly autobiographical. *First Papers* (1964) was based upon her childhood. *The Tenth Month* (1970) tells of an unmarried woman giving birth. *Consenting Adult* (1975), about a mother's growing understanding of her son's homosexuality, was based upon Hobson's own experiences with Christopher. *Untold Millions* (1982) portrays an advertising copywriter who supports a man she loves, just as Hobson had done.

Three of her novels refer to Jews and Jewishness. *The Trespassers* (1943) describes the flight of refugees from nazism. *Gentleman's Agreement* (1947) depicts "polite" anti-Semitism, yet it also decries nationalism, including that of Jews. The Jewish Book Council named *Gentleman's Agreement* the best Jewish novel of 1947, but Hobson refused the award, saying that her book was an American novel about issues important to Jews. (Later, she reconsidered, describing her refusal as "doctrinaire.") In *Over and Above* (1979), she reexamined attitudes toward Jewishness and Israel.

Although Hobson did not call herself a feminist, her life provides an important, positive model for contemporary women. From the 1930s onward, she supported herself and her sons through her writing. She defied convention by becoming an unmarried mother long before it was socially acceptable. Her works demonstrate that she was constantly thinking about and assessing, but never retreating from, the world.

Hobson died on February 28, 1986, of cancer.

SELECTED WORKS BY LAURA Z. HOBSON

The Celebrity (1951); *Consenting Adult* (1975); *First Papers* (1964); *Gentleman's Agreement* (1947); *Laura Z.: A Life* (1983); *Laura Z.: A Life: Years of Fulfillment* (1986); *The Other Father* (1950); *Over and Above* (1979); *The Tenth Month* (1970); *The Trespassers* (1943); *Untold Millions* (1982).

BIBLIOGRAPHY

Allen, Suzanne. "Laura Keane Zametkin Hobson." *American Women Writers*, edited by Lina Mainiero (1980); Giffuni, Cathe. "Laura Z. Hobson: A Bibliography." *Bulletin of Bibliography* 45, no. 4 (December 1988): 261–270; Gitenstein, R. Barbara. "Laura Z. Hobson." in *Dictionary of Literary Biography*. Vol. 28 (1984): 107–110; "Laura Z. Hobson, Author, Dies at 85." *NYTimes*, March 2, 1986, sec. 1, p. 40; Leon, Masha. "An Interview: Laura Z(ametkin) Hobson." *Forward*, September 14, 1984, p. 5+, and September 21, 1984, p. 9+; Mazow, Julia Wolf. "Remembering Laura Z. Hobson." *Lilith* 15 (1986): 6–7; Steinberg, Sybil S. "PW Interviews: Laura Z. Hobson." *Publishers Weekly* (September 2, 1983): 82–83.

JULIA MAZOW

HOCHFELDER, ANNA WEINER (1883–1968)

To make a successful career move from New York to California, a married woman needs flexibility and an unusual spouse. Julius Hochfelder, whom Anna Weiner married on June 17, 1906, was a rare, adoring, helping husband and, with their two sons Julian (b. 1908) and Richard (b. 1910), they were a close-knit, devoted family. Individualists, the Hochfelder sons called themselves Julian Harmon and Richard Elder.

Anna Weiner Hochfelder, daughter of Herman and Henrietta (LaFrantz) Weiner, was born in Lask, Poland, on May 1, 1883, and came to the United States in 1885. She had at least three sisters and one brother. Educated in New York public schools, she earned a B.A. from HUNTER COLLEGE (1903) and an LL.B. (1908) and J.D. (1915) from New York University.

Her husband, Julius Hochfelder, was born in Hungary and came to the United States in 1888. A large, sturdy man, considered a genius, he was a highly educated (LL.B., Ph.D.) patent lawyer, author, organizer of the Seaman's Evening College, director of the Homework Protective League and, in World War I, member of the Jewish Welfare Board.

From 1903 to 1914, Anna Hochfelder taught in public and Hebrew schools; while she studied law, she was a probation officer in the New York City Children's Court from 1914 to 1919. Admitted to the bar, Julius and Anna practiced together until 1923, when she was appointed assistant corporation counsel in New York City. In 1933, she left that post and became executive secretary of the New York United Parents Association, serving until 1935. She was legal adviser to the New York City Federation of Women's Clubs from 1922 to 1938

Anna Hochfelder, a founder of the American Alliance of Civil Service Women in 1912, was its president from 1912 until 1938. Active in Democratic politics, she was vice president of the Sixteenth Assembly District Democratic Club from 1923 to 1938.

In 1940, at fifty-seven, she and her family moved to Hollywood, California, where some of Anna's family lived. Julius Hochfelder retired and, ignoring the then-traditional role of men in marriage, ran the household while Anna started a second career.

Admitted to the California bar in 1940, she practiced with Nadia Williams for two years. From 1944 to 1946, she was a civil service personnel technician, and from 1946 to 1953 a deputy public defender in Los Angeles. After her son Julian was admitted to the bar in 1954, she practiced with him until 1966. She was a family law consultant to the American Institute of Family Relations. Her son Richard was a lieutenant colonel in the United States Army until sometime in the 1960s.

A conservative Jew, Anna Hochfelder was a member of the AMERICAN JEWISH CONGRESS and HADASSAH. She joined the National Association of Women Lawyers and the New York County and Southern California Lawyers Associations.

Hochfelder, a small, dynamic woman, was a spirited and gifted leader with an easy, friendly smile and gracious manner. She exuded a confidence that came from experience and a supportive family. However, in the 1960s, disaster ravaged the family. Julius Hochfelder died, and Julian Harmon, her son and law partner, died at fifty-eight in 1966. Two years later, seventy-eight-year-old Anna Hochfelder died on November 16, 1968. After funeral services at Mt. Sinai Memorial Park Chapel, she was buried in the Memorial Park, Los Angeles, California.

BIBLIOGRAPHY

Los Angeles Times, November 18, 1968; Nathan, Marilyn Kemeny, and Joan Kemeny Weitzman. Interviews by author, October 1996; Thomas, Dorothy. *Women Lawyers in the U.S.* (1957); *WWIAJ* (1938); *Who's Who of American Women*. 3d ed. (1964–1965).

DOROTHY THOMAS

HOFFMAN, ANNA ROSENBERG
see ROSENBERG, ANNA LEDERER

HOFFMAN, FANNY BINSWANGER (1862–1949)

Fanny Binswanger Hoffman belonged to a distinguished American family with roots deep in American history. Her father, Rabbi Isidor Binswanger, was head of the Maimonides School in Philadelphia, the first Jewish institution of higher learning in the United States. Hoffman followed in her father's footsteps, dedicating her life to Jewish education for children.

Fanny Binswanger Hoffman was born in Philadelphia in 1862 to Rabbi Binswanger and Elizabeth Sophie (Polock). As a young woman, she knew the advantages that culture could offer. Her own schooling in the United States and in Europe, her wide travels, and her deep appreciation of the best in American Jewish life helped prepare her for responsible leadership in her adult years.

While still a young woman, Fanny became the first principal of the Sunday school of the Mikveh Israel Congregation in Philadelphia. Later she helped to found, and became the first president of, the Philadelphia branch of the NATIONAL COUNCIL OF JEWISH WOMEN. Her chief interest lay in working with children. A pioneer in teaching at a period when young girls were not accustomed to leaving their homes to study or work, she became one of the first Jewish female kindergarten teachers in the United States. Her love of children led her to found the Young Women's Union of Philadelphia, later called the Jewish Neighborhood Center.

In Philadelphia, she met and married Charles I. Hoffman, a lawyer who later gave up the law to study for the rabbinate in England. When they returned to Philadelphia, they raised their five children in the full tradition of Judaism and gave them the finest that American educational facilities could offer.

As the second president of the National Women's League (later, WOMEN'S LEAGUE FOR CONSERVATIVE JUDAISM), Fanny Hoffman was personally selected by MATHILDE SCHECHTER, whom she had first met in England, and served from 1919 to 1928. Hoffman's

*The second president of the National Women's League
(now the* WOMEN'S LEAGUE FOR CONSERVATIVE JUDAISM*),
Fanny Hoffman dedicated her life to making a Jewish
education possible for all Jewish children. [Women's League
for Conservative Judaism]*

great contribution to the National Women's League
was to carry forward and expand the work begun by
Mathilde Schechter and to reinforce the league's program of Jewish education for children. By personal
example, in the practice of Judaism and in her love for
Jewish tradition, this "aristocrat of the spirit, whose
innate fineness expressed itself in simplicity and
humility," won the allegiance of thousands of synagogue women to the National Women's League's aims
and goals.

Fanny Binswanger Hoffman died on August 15,
1949.

BIBLIOGRAPHY

National Women's League of the United Synagogue of
America. *They Dared to Dream* (1968); *NYTimes*, April 16,

1948, 19:3; Women's League for Conservative Judaism.
Seventy-five Years of Vision and Voluntarism (1992); *WWIAJ*
(1926).

SELMA WEINTRAUB

HOLLIDAY, JUDY (1921–1965)

"Your name is Judy Holliday as a stage name, is
it?" "Yes." "A professional name?" "Yes." "What other
name have you used in the course of your life?" "Judy
Tuvim, T-u-v-i-m." "Do you have a married name?"
"Yes." "What is your married name?" "Mrs. David
Oppenheim." So began the interrogation of Judy
Holliday on March 26, 1952, by the United States
Senate Subcommittee to Investigate the Administration of the Internal Security Act and Other Internal
Security Laws of the Committee on the Judiciary. Just
one year earlier (March 29, 1951), she had won the
Academy of Motion Picture Arts and Sciences award—
the Oscar—for the best screen actress of 1950 for her
portrayal of Billie Dawn in *Born Yesterday*. In many
ways, winning the Oscar was the culmination of her
career, although she later played other screen and
stage roles.

Born on June 21, 1921, at Lying In Hospital in
Manhattan, the only child of Helen Gollomb and Abe
Tuvim, Holliday was the only child in a family of
childless uncles and aunts, particularly on her
mother's side. Her parents, who met at the Rand
School in New York, married on June 17, 1917, and
often frequented the Café Royale, a meeting place on
New York's Lower East Side for people in the Yiddish
theater. After they separated when Holliday was about
six, she was brought up by her mother's extended family, although later she reestablished relations with her
father. President of the American Federation of Musicians from 1929 to 1937, a member of the American
Zionist Strategy Council in 1944, and executive director of the Jewish National Fund of America from
1951 to 1958, Abe Tuvim, who died of cancer at sixty-
four, was also a journalist for the Jewish-language
press. Judy's mother, whose parents emigrated from
Russia—her father had made epaulets for the czar and
died shortly after arriving in this country—grew up
under the tutelage of a strong socialist mother and
amid several brothers. After separating from her husband, Helen Tuvim gave piano lessons during the
hard times of the Depression.

Educated in New York City public schools, Holliday graduated from Julia Richman High School at the
top of her class in January 1938, having already scored
172 on an IQ test when she was ten. Refused entrance

to drama school, probably because of her age, she briefly worked the switchboard at Orson Welles's Mercury Theatre, hoping to enter the theater world from the periphery. Unfortunately, she kept disconnecting telephone calls. Her life as a performer began, instead, after a vacation in the mountains where she met Adolph Green, the camp's "social director." With him, she was responsible for the formation of the Revuers, a successful group that performed at Max Gordon's Village Vanguard and included BETTY COMDEN, Alvin Hammer, and John Frank. Apocryphal stories of the group's beginnings exist. Young and optimistic, the Revuers eventually accepted an invitation to Hollywood, then watched the opportunity evaporate for everyone but Holliday. Loyal to her friends—for they were friends by then—she refused to split from them. Finally, however, in 1943 they persuaded her to sign a contract with Twentieth Century-Fox. At the studio's insistence, she changed her name, choosing "Holliday" because it related to the Hebrew word *tuvim*, meaning holiday. But the roles were minuscule, and eventually she was released from her contract, returning East in 1945.

The theater was more receptive. She opened in *Kiss Them for Me* in March 1945 and won the Clarence Derwent Award of $500 as best supporting actress. Next came her major role, Billie Dawn, the tough ex–chorus girl in *Born Yesterday*. Her voice, her walk, her manner on stage all captured the essence of this dumb blonde who somehow fools the gangster she accompanies. Given the role in its pre-Broadway tryout in Philadelphia in January 1946, she made it her own. And yet, despite 1,643 performances and great applause, she was long refused the screen role by Harry Cohn, head of Columbia Pictures. She was too Jewish, thought this Jewish movie mogul, who screen-tested others for two years. Not until Katharine Hepburn and Spencer Tracy, the stars of *Adam's Rib*, turned Holliday's short role in that film into a screen test and then invited Cohn to see it, was he convinced. After making the film, she returned to Broadway in *Bells Are Ringing*, for which she won the New York Drama Desk Award and the Tony in 1957.

Her brief life included marriage on January 4, 1948, to David Oppenheim—whom she divorced in March 1957—and a son, Jonathan Lewis, born in 1952 at Doctors Hospital in New York City. She died of cancer on June 7, 1965, at Mount Sinai Hospital. Her funeral services, conducted by the president of the Ethical Culture Society, were followed by a small private Jewish service at the Westchester Hills Cemetery, reflecting her mother's wishes.

Judy Holliday was at first thought to be "too Jewish" for the film role that would eventually win her an Oscar—Billie Dawn in Born Yesterday *(1950). A brilliant comedian on stage and screen, her short career was marred by her investigation by Senator Joseph McCarthy's witch-hunts in the 1950s. [New York Public Library]*

A brilliant comedian, Judy Holliday epitomized the duality of her American-Jewish heritage. She achieved the American dream of success on stage and film; she also felt the pressures of anti-Semitism as she became part of that large sweep of theater people being investigated for subversive activities in the McCarthy years of the 1950s. Her life offers a glimpse of the emergence of Jews in the theater and film communities.

BIBLIOGRAPHY

"Abe Tuvim." *NYTimes*, January 16, 1958; *AJYB* 67:537; Carey, Gary. *Judy Holliday: An Intimate Life* (1982); *Current Biography* (1951, 1965); *DAB* 7; Holliday, Judy.

Clipping file. Billy Rose Theatre Collection, New York Public Library; Holtzman, Will. *Judy Holliday* (1982); *NAW* modern; Obituaries. *New York Post*, June 8, 1965, and *NYTimes*, June 8, 1965, 1:7; Rickey, Carrie. "Hollidays High and Low." *Village Voice*, October 26, 1982, 64; U.S. Senate. Subcommittee to Investigate the Administration of the Internal Security Act and Other Internal Security Laws of the Committee on the Judiciary. *Subversive Infiltration of Radio, Television, and the Entertainment Industry: Hearings.* 82d Congress. (82) S1026-4-B. March 26, 1952: 141–186; *WWWIA* 4.

IRENE G. DASH

HOLMAN, LIBBY (1904–1971)

"I always have to break a song over my back. . . . I just can't sing a song; it has to be part of my marrow and bones and everything," Libby Holman explained in a 1966 interview. Daring, dark, and impetuous, Holman led a rich public life that touched a dizzying array of people, from Martin Luther King, Jr. to Montgomery Clift, from ALICE B. TOKLAS to JANE BOWLES. A musical and sexual revolutionary from the 1920s to the 1960s, Holman succeeded at two different musical careers. Known as the "Statue of Libby," she carried one of the smokiest torches of American music hall society in the 1920s and 1930s, and was the inventor of the strapless evening dress. From a deep sense of personal commitment, she later made significant contributions to the civil rights movement as both an artist and a wealthy benefactor. However, murder, millionaires, death, and suicide were morbid recurring themes in Libby Holman's life, reaching tabloid proportions.

She was born Elizabeth Lloyd Holzman at home in Cincinnati, Ohio, on May 23, 1904, to middle-class parents of German Jewish descent. Libby, younger brother Alfred, and older sister Marion were not raised in the Jewish faith. Alfred Holzman, a lawyer/ stockbroker and Rachel (Workum) Holzman, a schoolteacher, had converted to the Christian Science church.

In 1923, after completing a major in French in three years, Libby Holman was the youngest woman to graduate from the University of Cincinnati. At nineteen, still too young to attend law school as she planned, she moved to New York with dreams of Broadway.

In 1925, she landed her first significant role in the play *The Sapphire Ring* and soon after joined the road company of *The Greenwich Village Follies*. Her big break came in Richard Rodgers and Lorenz Hart's musical revue, *The Garrick Gaieties* (1925), which ran over 211 performances. Her nearsightedness provided an unexpectedly alluring stage persona, while her palate, an eighth of an inch askew, helped produce her strangely throaty sustained laments and a grunting style she liked to call her "vomit." Holman, now a minor celebrity, landed roles in *Merry-Go-Round* (1927), *Rainbow* (1928), and *Gambols* (1929). Entrenched in New York's bohemian, Prohibition dance-and-bathtub-gin culture, Holman swore, drank, and made regular late-night excursions to Harlem's Cotton Club and Inferno.

In 1929, she sang her trademark torch song, "Moanin' Low," in Clifton Webb's *The Little Show*. Framed by a theatrical sketch in which Holman played a two-timing "mulatto" lover, "Moanin' Low" made her a legend. Her unusual basso contralto, Betty Boop lips, and untraditional beauty created what *Times* critic Brooks Atkinson labeled a "dark purple

A throaty torch singer whose nickname was the "Statue of Libby," Libby Holman was a sexual and social revolutionary who cultivated racial ambiguity in her act. Though always a magnet for scandal and tragedy, in her later life she embraced her Jewish heritage and, through her art and philanthropy, became a champion of the civil rights movement.
[New York Public Library]

menace." Many people believed that Holman was a "Negro" who passed as white, because of her rich black hair, dark skin, and "racial" style of singing. She always insisted, "Nothing could have pleased me more." Inspired by her musical admiration for singers such as Ethel Waters, Holman cultivated racial ambiguity in her art.

During this period, Clifton Webb introduced Holman to Louisa Carpenter, a millionaire member of the du Pont family. By the time Howard Dietz and Arthur Schwartz's *Three's a Crowd* opened at the Selwyn Theater on October 15, 1930, Carpenter and Holman had become inseparable lovers. Her bisexuality became the talk of Broadway, only the first of many tabloid scandals she inspired in the thirties. Costarring with Fred Allen, Holman sang "Give Me Something to Remember You By" and "Body and Soul." The latter was banned from the radio for obscenity but became one of the best-selling records of the time and the song most identified with Holman throughout her career.

Zachary Smith Reynolds, heir to the R.J. Reynolds tobacco fortune, began, literally, to follow Holman's career. An aviator, he flew from city to city courting her attentions until November 16, 1931, when, just a few days after his divorce from Anne Cannon was finalized, the two were married by a justice of the peace in Monroe, Michigan. The famously ill-fated marriage ended tragically at the Reynolds estate, "Reynolda," near Winston-Salem, North Carolina. On July 5, 1932, Reynolds was shot in his bedroom; he died the next morning in the hospital and the coroner declared the death a suicide. Even after being presented with accusations of tampered evidence, two anti-Semitic grand juries approved murder charges against Holman, who had been with Reynolds at the time of the shooting, and against Ab Walker, Reynolds's best friend.

Holman went into hiding with Louisa Carpenter, and eventually the case was dropped through the influence of the Reynolds family. When Holman gave birth on January 9, 1933, to Christopher "Topper" Reynolds, it brought a new heir to the R.J. Reynolds tobacco fortune and became one of the biggest news stories of the year, later inspiring two Hollywood scandal films, *Reckless*, starring Jean Harlow (1935) and *Written on the Wind* (1956).

Although she returned briefly to Broadway in 1934, in *Revenge with Music*, singing Arthur Schwartz and Howard Dietz's "You and the Night and the Music," Holman was becoming vehemently anti–Tin Pan Alley. Cole Porter's *You Never Know* in 1938 was the last musical in which she appeared. Unfortunately,

Reynolds's death was only the first in a series of tragic events. In 1939, Holman married a second time, to Ralph de Rimer Holmes, an actor who spent most of the marriage at war and committed suicide soon after his return. On her own, Holman adopted two sons at birth: Tim (b. 1945) and Tony (b. 1947). Soon after, in August 1950, her first son, Topper, died climbing a mountain.

In 1941, Holman met Leadbelly and Josh White at a Greenwich Village nightclub. For the next four years, as Holman's guitar accompanist, White interested her in adapting songs previously sung only by black performers. Building on her earlier cross-over career, Holman researched American folk and blues songs at the Library of Congress, making use of the Lomax field recordings.

In 1947, Gerald Cook became her primary mentor and co-artist in this enterprise, composing and rearranging songs she referred to as "Earth Songs." Their highly theatrical collaborative performance, *Blues, Ballads and Sin Songs*, included lyrics by Tennessee Williams and Paul Bowles, and made three continental tours. Mainbocher designed her trademark floor-length skirt, which served as a prop. She also used a small chair dramatically to suggest prison bars at one moment and an executioner's block the next. Among their last appearances were a UNICEF Concert (1965), a Georgetown University benefit concert for civil rights (1966), and a World Federation of United Nations Association Benefit (1968). Embracing a Jewishness she had at times denied, Holman also made a point of accepting the invitation of the mayor of Jerusalem to perform at the first anniversary of the city's new museum.

Libby Holman adopted and practiced Zen at the end of her life, and when, on June 18, 1971, she apparently committed suicide at her Connecticut estate "Treetops," a Quaker service was held in her memory. She was survived by her third husband, New York sculptor Louis Schanker, as well as her two adopted sons. The latter half of her life had been devoted to social and philanthropic activities. In Topper's memory, Holman founded the Christopher Reynolds Foundation, which financed her friend Martin Luther King, Jr.'s visit to India to meet Mahatma Gandhi, and is still devoted to civil rights, peace, and disarmament programs.

SELECTED WORKS BY LIBBY HOLMAN

Blues Till Dawn, with Josh White. Decca (1942); *Body and Soul*. From *Three's a Crowd*. Brunswick 4910 (1930); *The Legendary Libby Holman*, with Gerald Cook. Evergreen MRS 6501 (1965); *Libby Holman: Moanin' Low (Early Recordings*

1927–1934). Take Two Records (1995); *Libby Holman Sings,* with Gerald Cook. MB 101 (1953); *Libby Holman Sings Blues, Ballads and Sin Songs,* with Gerald Cook. MB 102 (1954); *Moanin' Low.* From *The Little Show.* Brunswick 4445 (1929); *Original Cast! 100 Years of the American Musical Theater. The Thirties.* MET 802 (1995); *Something to Remember Her By,* with Gerald Cook. Monmouth Evergreen MES/ 7067 (1954); *You're the Top: Cole Porter in the 1930's.* Indiana Historical Society (1992).

BIBLIOGRAPHY

Bradshaw, Jon. *Dreams That Money Can Buy: The Tragic Life of Libby Holman* (1985); Holman, Libby. Interview by Arlene Francis. *Radio Broadcast WOR NY,* January 26, 1966, and Interview by Richard Lamparski, "Whatever Became of . . . Libby Holman," *Radio Broadcast WBAI,* January 31, 1966, and interview by Duncan McDonald. *Radio Broadcast WQXR,* November 10, 1965; "Libby Holman Goes into New Seclusion." *NYTimes,* August 10, 1932, 3:1; Machlin, Milt. *Libby* (1980); "Open Verdict Given in Reynolds Death: Widow Is Released." *NYTimes,* July 12, 1932, 1:3; Perry, Hamilton Darby. *Libby Holman: Body and Soul* (1983); "Says Libby Holman Asks 'Modest Sum.'" *NYTimes,* January 14, 1933, 30:8; "Seek Libby Holman in Delaware Home." *NYTimes,* August 6, 1932, 1:4; Wilson, John S. "Libby Holman Sings at U.N. Next Week: Her First Time Here in 11 Years." *NYTimes,* October 30, 1965, 38:2.

JEANNE SCHEPER

HOLOCAUST STUDIES

Holocaust studies is a dynamic and diverse field of research that embraces various approaches toward the study of the Holocaust. Jewish American women have made critical contributions to this field in a variety of areas, including general history, women and gender, children, literary criticism, autobiography and biography, curriculum development, religious studies, sociology, psychoanalytic theory, biomedical ethics, and archive and museum curatorship. Jewish American women have contributed original research and have reshaped the way the Holocaust is studied through innovative theoretical and methodological approaches. They come to the study of the Holocaust as Jews, as women, and as Americans. With each of these roles and experiences they bring different concerns and questions. Some of these scholars are survivors or refugees or are the daughters of survivors or refugees. Some were born in the United States, some came to the United States during or after the war. Many have focused exclusively on the study of women.

The earliest historical treatments were general overviews that put the Holocaust in its political and social historical context. LUCY DAWIDOWICZ (1915–

1990) is the best-known American Holocaust historian and also one of the earliest female historians of the Holocaust. She was a professor of history at Yeshiva University in the area of Holocaust studies and wrote extensively on the subject. Her *The War Against the Jews: 1933–1945* (1975) examines the Holocaust in terms of its historical context, investigates the Jewish response to the Nazis' Final Solution, and ultimately explores why the world did not prevent this systematic slaughter.

NORA LEVIN (1916–1989) is another early contributor to Holocaust studies. Levin was an instructor at Gratz College and is best known for *The Holocaust: The Destruction of European Jewry, 1933–1945* (1968), a general history of the Holocaust. Although more recent scholarship has critiqued much of Dawidowicz's and Levin's work, these scholars are important because they are Jewish American women who made early and significant contributions to a field that previously had been male-dominated.

Since Dawidowicz and Levin, female American scholars have consistently expanded Holocaust studies by bringing new questions and evidence to the field. Historian Sybil Milton (b. 1941) is a prolific scholar who has expanded the boundaries of the historical study of the Holocaust. Milton studies the Holocaust as a major event of the twentieth century within the context of Central European and German history. As such, the Holocaust includes but is not limited to the Nazi genocide of European Jews. Milton continues to explore new dimensions of the Holocaust through her historical consideration of gender issues, non-Jewish children, the fate of Gypsies, postwar trials, and the problem of memorials in Germany and Austria. Milton has also critically evaluated the role of visual images as historical evidence and analyzed art and photography as tools of interpretation. She has explored this topic in numerous articles and books, including *The Camera as Weapon and Voyeur: Photography of the Holocaust as Historical Evidence,* where she fully develops her analysis of the role of photography as historical evidence and the problems that visual images pose for interpretation of the Holocaust. Milton is senior historian at the United States Holocaust Museum Research Institute. She has worked extensively as an archival and exhibit consultant for museums, archives, and memorials in the United States, Europe, and Canada.

Holocaust studies also include responses to the Holocaust. Deborah E. Lipstadt (b. 1946) is the foremost scholar working in the area of Holocaust denial and has done extensive research into American responses to the Holocaust by examining the public discourses during and after the event. Lipstadt is Dorot Professor of Modern Jewish Studies at Emory University and serves on the United States Holocaust Memorial Council's executive committee. Lipstadt designed the section of the United States Holocaust Memorial Museum that is devoted to the American response to the Holocaust. She is also chair of the museum's education committee. Lipstadt's *Beyond Belief: The American Press and the Coming of the Holocaust, 1933–1945* (1986) examines how the American press reported on the Nazi persecutions of Jews in Eastern Europe and provocatively explores what the American public knew about the persecution of European Jewry between 1933 and 1945. Lipstadt's more recent book, *Denying the Holocaust: The Growing Assault on Truth and Memory* (1993), contains the most comprehensive examination of Holocaust denial and deniers. Lipstadt's work has expanded and reformulated the historical study of the Holocaust by positioning the problem of denial and deniers as a central issue.

Sociological approaches to the study of the Holocaust have become increasingly important to our understanding of the social phenomenon that occurred prior to, during, and after the Holocaust. Helen Fein (b. 1934) has contributed original research and analysis to both Holocaust studies and genocide studies, combining historical and sociological methods of analysis and interpretation. She is executive director of the Institute for the Study of Genocide and the first president of the Association of Genocide Scholars, an international organization that she helped to found in 1995. Fein's *Accounting for Genocide: National Responses and Jewish Victimization During the Holocaust* (1979) challenges the questions that have been asked about the Holocaust. Rather than focusing on the success of the Nazi destruction of European Jewry, Fein analyzes the rate of survival of Jews according to nation-states and proposes understanding the differences of survival rates in terms of national responses. As part of this innovative analysis, Fein examines the empiric responsibility and moral accountability of churches, Jewish leadership, and the Allies in the destruction of European Jewry. Fein extends her analysis of the Holocaust to account for other racial victims such as Gypsies and begins to develop a theoretical account of ideological genocide in the twentieth century. Since then, Fein has continued her work in the area of genocide, connecting it to violation of human rights.

NECHAMA TEC (b. 1931) is professor of sociology at University of Connecticut, Stamford, and is a scholar at the International Institute for Holocaust Research at Yad Vashem, Jerusalem. She is a member of the advisory boards of the Braun Center's Foundation to Sustain Righteous Christians and the Braun Center for Holocaust Studies. In *Defiance: The Bielski Partisans* (1993), using original research, Tec challenges the historical paradigm of Jew as victim during the Holocaust by examining the phenomenon of Jews as rescuers—Jews who rescued others even while they were themselves in danger of being killed. By focusing on the Bielski partisans, Tec critically demonstrates that not all Jews were passive victims. Although her early interest was in Christian rescuers, Tec became interested in Jews who rescued other Jews. Tec makes clear that her own experiences of being a hidden child in Poland (where she lived under an assumed name, pretending to be a Catholic) prompted her interest in the wartime relationships between the rescuers and the rescued. Tec's and Fein's reputations testify to the growing centrality of sociological analysis in the historical study of the Holocaust.

The study of women and the Holocaust is one of the fastest growing areas of research within Holocaust studies. Although not all female scholars are working specifically in the area of women, there is a consensus among them that women do need to be accounted for in the study of the Holocaust. Including women is, Sybil Milton argues, simply a matter of good scholarship. After all, women represented half of the population and half of those who perished. Women also ask questions about the Holocaust that have not been posed by male scholars. Early male scholars often focused on the history of the Holocaust as if it were only the history of men in the Holocaust. Female scholars have opened up the study of the Holocaust to include accounts of women's roles and experiences and have made the consideration of gender a basic category of analysis. Joan Ringelheim (b. 1939), director of the Department of Oral History at the Research Institute of the United States Holocaust Memorial Museum, pioneered in the study of women and the Holocaust, convening the first conference on the subject in 1983. Her interest in the study of the Holocaust was also influenced by her family's experience of the Holocaust. Ringelheim's paternal grandparents and eighty-eight paternal relatives lost their lives in Poland during the Holocaust. Growing up, she had long discussions with her father about prejudice, racism, and the Holocaust. Ringelheim underlines the significance of gender as a category of analysis. However, Ringelheim also is concerned about the assumptions we use when we assert the importance of gender when we study the Holocaust. In her article "Women and the Holocaust: A Reconsideration of the Research" (1985), she demonstrates that the assumptions we make about gender color the questions we ask and influence the conclusions we draw about women and the Holocaust. Ringelheim is concerned that feminist questions about women, intended to challenge traditional understandings of women as passive and oppressed, have a tendency to interpret women's responses to the Holocaust in the best possible light. For example, if we look at women's responses to the murder of their children in terms of their ability to "mother" other persons, this positive interpretation obscures the reality of the victimization of women by the Nazis.

Marion Kaplan (b. 1946) is professor of history at Queens College and the Graduate Center of the City University of New York as well as a consultant to the Museum of Jewish Heritage in New York City. Kaplan's interest in Holocaust studies was shaped by being the daughter of German Jewish refugees. She describes her own work as an attempt to enrich both Jewish history and German history with evidence and questions from both areas. By studying Jewish and non-Jewish German women, Kaplan demonstrates in *The Jewish Feminist Movement in Germany: The Campaigns of the Jüdischer Frauenbund, 1904–1938* (1979) that women shared common experiences. At the same time, in *Jewish Life in Nazi Germany* (1997) Kaplan highlights the distinctive experiences of women as Jews under Nazism. Kaplan argues that Jewish women were doubly stigmatized by anti-Semitism and sexism.

Many scholars combine their interest in the area of women and the Holocaust with other areas of study. Judith Tydor Baumel (b. 1959) is an Israeli-American scholar who works in the area of women and the Holocaust but is also interested in collective memory. Baumel has raised important questions about the role of women during and after the Holocaust through her work on Jewish refugee children and on survivors. She is lecturer in the department of Jewish History at the University of Haifa. She describes her focus on the Holocaust as stemming from a natural response to her family's history, with her work on refugee children and postwar Jewish experiences being prompted by her family's experience of the Holocaust. Together with Walter Laqueur, Baumel is associate editor of the *Yale Encyclopedia of the Holocaust* (1998). Ringelheim, Kaplan, and Baumel are exemplary representatives of a growing number of Jewish American female scholars who are not only challenging the way we understand women and the Holocaust but also are transforming the ways we study and think about the Holocaust.

Deborah Dwork (b. 1954) has contributed important research into the history of the children of the Holocaust. Dwork's mother was born in the United States, but her mother's adopted sister was born in Poland and was a survivor of the Holocaust. Dwork grew up with an awareness of how the Holocaust had affected her family. Although there has been tremendous research into the Holocaust, there had been no historical study of children. In her classic, *Children with a Star: Jewish Youth in Nazi Europe* (1991), Dwork argues that it is the history of the children that particularly and painfully underlines the horror of the Holocaust: It is the children who show that there can be *no* excuse for the Nazi Judeocide. Dwork has organized her research into patterns of children's experience during and after the war. By studying the lives of the children during the Holocaust, Dwork also explores how adults, particularly women, were active in trying to hide and protect children. Dwork is Rose Professor of Holocaust Studies at Clark University. She also works with the Jewish Foundation for the Righteous, where she has developed an educational resource for teachers of the Holocaust. She is a consultant for the Anti-Defamation League, is on the national advisory board for Facing History and Ourselves, and works with the United States Holocaust Memorial Museum and other organizations centrally concerned with the future disposition of Auschwitz-Birkenau.

In addition to the historical study of the Holocaust, Holocaust studies includes literary criticism and biography and autobiography. Austrian-born Ruth Kluger (b. 1931; formerly known by her married name, Ruth Angress) has made contributions to Holocaust studies through her award-winning autobiography and her literary criticism. Her autobiography begins with her earliest memories of being a child before the war, describes her experiences in the camps, and ends after the war when she was twenty-one. Kluger became an American citizen in 1952. Kluger's experiences during the Holocaust in Theresienstadt, Auschwitz, and Gross-Rosen have had a major impact on her scholarship. She explains that her experiences have led her to be more critical and less empathetic about German literature, creating a tension that she sees as essential to her analysis of the literature. The literature must be analyzed in light of the historical reality of the Holocaust. Kluger was the first chair of German at both Princeton University and the University of Virginia. She recently retired as professor of German at the University of California at Riverside and is currently on the council of the Fritz Bauer Institute of Holocaust Studies in Germany.

Sidra DeKoven Ezrahi (b. 1942), is associate professor of comparative Jewish literature in the Institute of Contemporary Jewry and the Rothberg School at the Hebrew University and lectures regularly at Yad Vashem. Born and educated in the United States, Ezrahi was among the first scholars to investigate and critically analyze Holocaust literature. Her powerful analysis has had important implications for both Holocaust studies and literary analysis. Her *By Words Alone: The Holocaust in Literature* (1980) interprets Holocaust literature by examining cross-cultural types of imaginative responses to the Holocaust. Since then, Ezrahi's most recent work examines the problems of representation in Holocaust literature.

Sara R. Horowitz (b. 1951) is associate professor of English and comparative literature and director of the Jewish Studies program at the University of Delaware. Horowitz's work focuses on issues of gender, genocide, and Jewish memory. She describes her work as examining Holocaust literature as a form of deep meditation. In terms of gender, Horowitz perceives significant difference in the ways men and women are represented in Holocaust literature. Horowitz argues persuasively that these differences often correspond to differing gendered experiences of the Holocaust. In her recent *Voicing the Void: Muteness and Memory in Holocaust Fiction* (1997), Horowitz examines a wide variety of Holocaust fiction by authors of different nationalities, genders, and styles in terms of muteness—the painful inability to account meaningfully for and respond to the horrors of the Holocaust.

Jewish American women come to the study of the Holocaust with diverse experiences, questions, and concerns. However, they all come to the subject with compassion and a profound sense of responsibility to the victims.

BIBLIOGRAPHY

Baumel, Judith Tydor. *Kibbutz Buchenvald: Survivors and Pioneers* (1997), and *Unfulfilled Promise: The Jewish Refugee Children in the United States 1934–1945* (1990), and *A Voice of Lament: The Holocaust and Prayer.* (Heb.) (1992); Dawidowicz, Lucy S. *From That Time and Place: A Memoir, 1938–1947* (1989), and *The War Against the Jews: 1933–1945* (1975); Dwork, Deborah. *Children With a Star: Jewish Youth in Nazi Europe* (1991); Dwork, Deborah, and Robert Jan van Pelt. *Auschwitz, 1270 to the Present* (1996); Ezrahi, Sidra Dekoven. *By Words Alone: The Holocaust in Literature* (1980), and "The Grave in the Air." In *Probing the Limits of Representation: Nazism and the Final Solution*, edited by Saul Friedlander (1992), and *The Holocaust and the Limits of Representations* (1994), and "Representing Auschwitz." *History and Memory* 7, no. 2 (Winter 1996); Fein, Helen. *Accounting for Genocide: National Responses and Jewish Victimization During the Holocaust* (1979), and *The Persisting Question: Social Contexts and Sociological Perspectives of Modern Antisemitism* (1987), and "Reading the Second Text: Meanings and Misuses of the Holocaust." In *The Challenge of Shalom: The Jewish Tradition of Peace and Justice*, edited by Murray Polner and Naomi Goodman (1994); Grossmann, Atina. *Reforming Sex: The German Movement for Birth Control and Abortion Reform, 1920–1950* (1995); Horowitz, Sara. "Memory and Testimony in Women Survivors of Nazi Genocide." In *Women of the Word: Jewish Women and Jewish Writing*, edited by Judith Baskin (1994), and "Mengele, the Gynecologist, and Other Stories of Women's Survival." In *Judaism Since Gender*, edited by Miram Peskowitz and Laura Levitt (1997), and *Voicing the Void: Muteness and Memory in Holocaust Fiction* (1997); Kaplan, Marion. *The Jewish Feminist Movement in Germany: The Campaigns of the Jüdischer Frauenbund, 1904–1938* (1979), and *Jewish Life in Nazi Germany* (1997); Kluger, Ruth. *Katastrophen: Uber Deutsche Literatur* (1994), and *Weiter Leben: Eine Jugend* (1992); Kremer, Lillian S. *Witness Through the Imagination: Jewish-American Holocaust Literature* (1989); Levin, Nora. *The Holocaust: The Destruction of European Jewry, 1933–1945* (1968); Lipstadt, Deborah. *Beyond Belief: The American Press and the Coming of the Holocaust, 1933–1945* (1986), and *Denying the Holocaust: The Growing Assault on Truth and Memory* (1993); Milton, Sybil. *The Camera as Weapon and Voyeur: Photography of the Holocaust as Historical Evidence* (forthcoming); *The Holocaust: Ideology, Bureaucracy, and Genocide: The San Jose Papers.* Edited with Henry Friedlander (1980), and *In Fitting Memory: The Art and Politics of Holocaust Memorials* (1991), and "Women and the Holocaust: The Case of German and German-Jewish Women." In *When Biology Became Destiny: Women in Weimar and Nazi Germany*, edited by Renate Bridenthal, Marion Kaplan, and Atina Grossmann (1984); Ringelheim, Joan. "The Unethical and the Unspeakable: Women and the Holocaust." *The Simon Wiesenthal Annual* 1 (1984): 69–87, and "Women and the Holocaust: A Reconsideration of the Research." *Signs* 10, no. 41 (1985): 741–761, reprinted in *Jewish Women in Historical Perspectives*, edited by Judith Baskin (1991); Tec, Nechama. *Defiance: The Bielski Partisans* (1993), and *Dry Tears: The Story of a Lost Childhood* (1984), and *In the Lion's Den: The Life of Oswald Rufeisen* (1990), and *When Light Pierced the Darkness: Christian Rescue of Jews in Nazi-Occupied Poland* (1990).

DEIDRE BUTLER

HOLOCAUST SURVIVORS: RESCUE AND RESETTLEMENT

They had made it through World War II and now they were coming to America, 140,000 strong. The women, along with the men, had survived the rigors of the ghettos, the horrors of the concentration camps, the final agony of the death marches. They had been in hiding, or fighting with the partisans. They had escaped to the Soviet Union, some to Shanghai. And even after the war, they had been penned into displaced persons camps, in a holding pattern, waiting for a place to live, determined to get out of Europe. Now America was finally opening its doors, the doors that had been so tightly guarded during the war and, before, in the 1930s. And the American Jewish community was about to shoulder a responsibility that would sorely test its resources, commitment, and understanding.

The newcomers were refugees, but refugees extraordinaire. Unlike even their Jewish predecessors who had fled Nazism in the 1930s and early 1940s, these people were virtually the only survivors of their entire families and had been victims of and witnesses to unimaginable crimes. Yet they had kept moving, going about the business of living, jump-starting their lives with a remarkable determination. While the men were bent on earning a living, the women were equally determined to raise a family and make a life for themselves and their husbands. In looking over their experience, many of these women today argue that their task was actually more difficult than that of the men. "The men were responsible for work, for a job, but women had to find schools, organizations, care for children, run the household." "While he was in the store all day, I had to take care of everything else!" "We had to be more flexible and strong." This was no mean feat considering the fact that they did this not only in an alien culture but, in most cases, without any close family members who could lend guidance and emotional support.

In studies that were conducted both in the early 1950s and then forty years later, researchers concluded that Holocaust survivors did indeed adjust to a new life in America with an "amazing resiliency" that was most impressive, perhaps even heroic. The data on immigrants, however, are not broken down or explored, by and large, with gender in mind. This is particularly surprising given the fact that the majority of professional social workers and volunteers who interacted with the refugees were themselves women. Women's issues, if were defined at all, were merely subsumed under the men or ignored. And yet, while there appears to be no variation in the long-term, overall adjustment of men and women, there does appear to be a clear difference in the nature of the struggle that each group fought. Men and women had divergent responsibilities and priorities. They saw life and measured their achievements differently.

The women who came to America after the war were distinct from the majority of women refugees who had escaped in the 1930s. They were generally younger (many in their early twenties), from Eastern Europe versus Germany and Austria, and were less educated or set upon a career path. After the war, despite all the adversity they had suffered, their number one priority was to marry and raise a family. While most women admitted that they had married so quickly after the war out of loneliness and the need for security, the decision to have children was different: It was a positive step of hope and affirmation that the women were making.

The business of marrying and having children had begun in the displaced persons camp immediately after the war. By the end of 1946, nearly a thousand Jewish children were being born each month in the DP camps. In looking back over their experiences, most of the women interviewed in a Pittsburgh study of survivors recalled their great joy at being pregnant. They pointed out that not only were they eager to start a family but they were relieved that they could indeed get pregnant, since most of the women in the concentration camps had not menstruated while they had been there, due to their near-starvation diets. They also had been concerned that, perhaps because of what they had gone through, they would not be able to carry a healthy baby to term. Several women did admit, however, that either they never realized how difficult the job of raising their children would be or that they were scared.

When the women came to America, they knew they would have to work. Very few of the refugees expected the streets to be paved with gold as perhaps an earlier immigration had fantasized. But the work they expected to do generally revolved around the home or, if it involved pay, was to add a little extra to the family income. In a study of survivors that was conducted in Detroit in 1953, the women who were employed, or had at one time been employed, saw their jobs primarily as a way to supplement their husbands' income. They had no interest in being "career women." (Neither did most American-born women of that time, for that matter.) Moreover, their occupation range was narrow—nurses' aides, seamstresses, salespeople, and office workers. In a Cleveland study that included several single women who were heads of households (usually widows with children), none apparently was striving to better herself vocationally. They were "marking time" mostly as factory laborers or seamstresses until they would marry again. In Pittsburgh, the majority of women who did work were either seamstresses working out of their homes or they helped their husbands in small businesses such as cleaning or roofing. But their career or lack thereof was not how they judged their success in America. They, much more than the men, tended to measure their success in America by their family—their children's character, education, success, happiness, Jewishness. That had been their goal and the source of so much satisfaction and pride.

But there was frustration. Most of the women did not continue the education the war had interrupted, and for some this was a source of dissatisfaction as they looked back over their lives. They felt that they had just been too busy and never had the time. Some women indicated that they did not know that free high school classes, for example, would have been available to them and they bemoaned the fact that nobody really had told them. One woman speculated that perhaps her social worker wanted to make sure that she stayed home and took care of the children. Others noted that no agency or organization (even a woman's organization) ever offered child care, something that would have been very much appreciated in the absence of family members. There was also no possibility that the women could pay for a baby-sitter to allow them to go to school.

Yet while women often did not pursue educational opportunities in this country, they did adjust rapidly to American life, which in large measure was tied to their ability to learn English. While many women had indicated that upon arrival their toughest problem was the language, they still felt they learned the language faster than the men. And they did this without the help of classes, which the men, but not the women, were encouraged by social workers to take before obtaining a job. Unlike an earlier wave of immigrants at the turn of the century, being housebound was not nearly as stifling and isolating as it had been, for much could be learned from the radio as well as from children. A number of women interviewed in Pittsburgh felt that women tended to talk more to Americans for a variety of reasons as they went about their daily household business and/or they had a greater natural facility for languages than the men.

The program that assisted the refugees after the war was a far-reaching one that depended on national and local community organization and cooperation. Communities around the country were given quotas of new immigrants that they were asked to resettle so that the financial burden would be distributed. The United Service for New Americans (USNA), which was formed in 1946 from a merger of the National Refugee Service and the Service to Foreign Born Department of the NATIONAL COUNCIL OF JEWISH WOMEN (NCJW), coordinated the resettlement of the postwar refugees in America. KATHARINE ENGEL of the NCJW became the first chair of the USNA board. Indeed, since the turn of the century, NCJW women had offered an array of services to assist immigrants, from location of relatives to Americanization programs. In the 1930s, CECILIA RAZOVSKY of NCJW had become the first head of the newly formed National Coordinating Committee to aid refugees.

By 1950, more than two hundred local sections of the NCJW were carrying on a wide program of services, and in communities where there was no Jewish family agency, the women volunteers were the heart of the immigrant resettlement program. In Pittsburgh, for example, NCJW women met newcomers at the train station, took them to appointments, offered English and naturalization classes, and helped them find housing (a particularly difficult task given the postwar housing shortage and the fact that landlords often chose not to rent to couples with a child). NCJW women also established a special thrift shop which, at the height of the refugee crunch in 1949 and 1950, relieved some of the financial strain on the Pittsburgh Jewish community and provided clothing and household goods to the refugees.

Yet, despite the efforts of NCJW women, there was still a distance between them and the newcomers that was keenly felt by the refugee women. NCJW volunteers did not provide the friendship and warmth that many of the survivors of the Holocaust needed. Americans, both men and women, did not understand or appreciate what these "greeners" had been through, and the survivors soon learned, if they had been so inclined, not to talk about their experiences except among themselves. Ethel Landerman, a young social work intern for Montefiore Hospital where the refugees were treated free of charge, remarked: "We had no sense of the Holocaust as we know now, with a capital H. We really didn't understand what people were telling us. The stories sounded too horrible. We simply did not believe them." The women survivors associated with one another. They met in the park with their children. If they joined American organizations (which they did do at a greater rate than the men), they tended to join organizations (at least in the Pittsburgh sample) that were dedicated to Israel. This, of course, is not surprising, since so many of the women had wanted to go to Palestine immediately after the war but for a variety of reasons, including pregnancy, could not. Not one woman in Pittsburgh mentioned joining the National Council of Jewish Women, which had provided them with early assistance. Hospitality was extended to the Pittsburgh survivors through the women of the Friendship Club, a group of German Jewish refugees formed in the early

1930s. However, while many postwar refugees appreciated their outreach and went occasionally to Hanukkah parties and the like, many of these Eastern European women were uncomfortable with the older German women.

The women survivors who came after the war were driven to re-create a world of family. This was their priority and the task to which they dedicated themselves, but they were on their own, often citing Dr. Spock as their only adviser. They had to maneuver in a culture that offered exciting possibilities and opportunities, which they appreciated, but that also was not beyond criticism. While they applauded the freedom children had in America, for example, they deplored the numbers of "sassy and fresh" kids it produced. In inventing a family and running the household, these women acted as the bridge between the despair and destruction of the past and the hope of the future. They were the ones who communicated to the next generation the sense of possibility to which their children so readily responded. The very fact that women chose to have children was itself an act of faith and courage.

These were traditional women, but they were faced with anything but traditional challenges. The fact that they succeeded so well in raising children and making a life for themselves and their husbands can be seen as more than their defiant response to Hitler. It is a testament to the strength of these women and to the human spirit.

BIBLIOGRAPHY

Research included interviews with fifteen women Holocaust survivors, Pittsburgh, Pennsylvania, summer 1996.

Burstin, Barbara S. *After the Holocaust* (1989); Davie, Maurice. *Refugees in America* (1947); Glassman, Helen L. *Adjustment in Freedom* (1956); Heimreich, William B. *Against All Odds* (1992); Kirschmann, Doris, and Sylvia Savin. "Refugee Adjustment—Five Years Later." *The Jewish Social Service Quarterly* 30, no. 2 (Winter 1953): 197–201; Smith, Lyman Cromwell. *Three Hundred Thousand New Americans* (1957).

BARBARA BURSTIN

HOLTZMAN, ELIZABETH (b. 1941)

A member of the generation that came of age in the 1960s, Elizabeth Holtzman has pursued a public career epitomizing some of the most important trends in postwar American and Jewish life. In her successive roles as a congresswoman, Brooklyn district attorney, and comptroller of New York City, she emerged as an effective and activist public servant, a forceful campaigner, and a champion of liberal and feminist causes. Her career illustrates the recent empowerment of ambitious, highly motivated, professional young women and the increasing role of Jewish figures in electoral politics. In addition, she has been a dedicated Jew, with a highly regarded record of communal commitment and achievement.

Elizabeth Holtzman was born in Brooklyn on August 11, 1941, one of twin children, to Sidney Holtzman, a criminal lawyer, and Filia (Ravitz) Holtzman, a professor and former chair of the Russian department at HUNTER COLLEGE. Holtzman attended Abraham Lincoln High School in Brooklyn and then earned her B.A. at Radcliffe College. She entered Harvard University Law School, receiving her degree in 1965. While a law student, she engaged in civil rights work in Georgia and was an organizing member of the Law Students Civil Rights Research Council, a national group.

Following a stint at the private New York law firm of Wachtell, Lipton, Rosen, Katz and Kern, Holtzman served in Mayor John V. Lindsay's administration as liaison to the New York Department of Parks, Recreation, and Cultural Affairs from 1968 to 1970. She then joined the law firm of Paul, Weiss, Rifkind, Wharton and Garrison, and became active in local Democratic Party affairs.

In a dramatic political upset in 1972, she won the Democratic nomination as candidate representing Brooklyn's Sixteenth Congressional District, beating the fifty-year incumbent, Emanuel Celler. Holtzman went on to defeat Celler, running as a Liberal candidate, at the polls that November, becoming at age thirty-two the youngest woman ever elected to the House of Representatives. For Brooklynites and New Yorkers, her victory signaled a changing of the guard, while at the same time symbolizing the ties that bound her to her heavily liberal, Jewish, and Democratic constituency.

As a member of the House Judiciary Committee, Holtzman took part in the famous Watergate hearings that investigated the links between the Nixon White House and the coverup of illegal activities. As chair of the House Subcommittee on Immigration, Refugees and International Law, she challenged the dismal record of the Immigration Service and the Justice Department in relation to former Nazi war criminals admitted to the United States after the war. She wrote and pushed through Congress the Holtzman Amendment, which authorized the deportation of such war criminals and which led to the establishment of a

The youngest woman ever elected to the House of Representatives, Elizabeth Holtzman went on to prove herself an effective public servant and a champion of liberal and feminist causes. She wrote and pushed through Congress the Holtzman Amendment, authorizing the deportation of Nazi war criminals and establishing a special investigation unit at the Justice Department. She is shown here silhouetted against the icon of the New York borough where she was born and raised—the Brooklyn Bridge. [Schlesinger Library]

special investigation unit at the Justice Department. She also authored a rape privacy act, helped to extend the deadline for ratification of the then-proposed Equal Rights Amendment, and coauthored what became the country's first refugee law. The provisions under this law helped thousands of Jews from the Soviet Union to enter the United States as refugees in the late 1970s and 1980s.

In other spheres, Holtzman worked to increase public benefits for the aged and the poor, and to bar sex discrimination in federally funded employment programs.

In 1980, she ran for the United States Senate in a new bid to unseat another veteran liberal Jewish politician, New York Republican senator Jacob Javits. She won the Democratic nomination, but both she and Liberal candidate Javits lost in a controversial three-way contest against Alphonse D'Amato, the Republi-

can candidate. In 1981, Holtzman won election as the district attorney for Kings County (Brooklyn), becoming the first woman D.A. in New York City. She left that office in 1990 to become comptroller of New York City, one of the three most important municipal offices (the other two being the mayor and the presidency of the city council). Her record in public administration included substantial savings and increases in the city's pension funds, which were used to build low-cost housing and to expand employment opportunities. In addition, she improved women's access to breast cancer screening and children's immunization programs, and took pro-choice positions in the fierce political controversies that raged over abortion.

In 1982, she made another unsuccessful bid for the Senate in a rancorous campaign that pitted her against Geraldine Ferraro (the former Democratic vice presidential candidate on the Walter Mondale ticket). The following year, Holtzman failed to gain reelection to the comptroller's office. She returned to private practice, joining the real estate firm of Herrick, Feinstein. She remained a member of the Helsinki Watch Committee and of the advisory board of the National Women's Political Caucus.

As an eminent public figure, with both investigatory credentials and a proven commitment to Jewish affairs, Holtzman was named to the American Jewish Commission on the Holocaust. Chaired by former Supreme Court justice Arthur J. Goldberg, this group of dignitaries was convened under the initiative of Seymour Finger, a retired Foreign Service official. The commission's task was to review a set of specially commissioned reports by historians and to evaluate American Jewish leadership during the Holocaust. The final report of the commission, called *American Jewry During the Holocaust* (1984), was sharply critical of the American Jewish leaders of that period. But Holtzman, in a thoughtful and perceptive dissenting statement, disputed the notion that the commission had succeeded in reaching a definitive evaluation of the American Jewish political response to the Holocaust. She preferred to draw an activist's conclusion, calling for Jewish unity and "outspoken activism" in the face of threats to Jewish survival.

For her work as a public servant and as an attorney, Holtzman has been honored by the NATIONAL COUNCIL OF JEWISH WOMEN; the Civil Liberties Unions of New York, New Jersey, and Los Angeles; the Young Women's Christian Association; the Warsaw Ghetto Resistance Organization; the Brooklyn Coalition for Soviet Jewry; Radcliffe College; and many other organizations.

BIBLIOGRAPHY

Finger, Seymour, ed. *American Jewry During the Holocaust* (1984); Polner, Murray, ed. *American Jewish Biographies* (1982); *Who's Who in America; Who's Who in American Politics, 1979–1980*.

ELI LEDERHENDLER

HOLTZMANN, FANNY E. (1903–1980)

"I don't follow precedent. I establish it," Fanny E. Holtzmann was quoted as saying. And she did. As a lawyer for some of the most famous artistic and political personalities of her day, she traveled the globe and lived what seemed to be a fantasy life.

She was a middle child in a family of seven children. Born in Brooklyn to Henry and Theresa Holtz-

mann, she grew up ignored by her busy family. Her close relationship with her maternal grandfather was crucial in encouraging Fanny, once labeled the "class dunce," to complete three years of high school and enroll in night classes at Fordham University's law school. During the day, she worked as a clerk for a theatrical law firm. The only woman to graduate in her law class of 1922, she opened her office half an hour after passing the bar.

Her clients included Gertrude Lawrence, Noel Coward, Fred Astaire, George Bernard Shaw, and the Russian Romanoffs, whom she successfully defended in a libel suit against MGM Studios in 1934. She was the official counsel to Chiang Kai-shek, the Republic of China's representative, at the founding of the United Nations.

Before World War II, Holtzmann was active in the effort to help Jews escape from Hitler. After the war, she turned her attention to the newly established State of Israel, contributing both time and money.

She was always close to her siblings and their children. A few years before her death, her nephew, Edward Berkman, wrote a biography of her entitled *The Lady and the Law: The Remarkable Story of Fanny Holtzmann* (1976). She died of cancer on February 6, 1980. A few weeks earlier, in a bedside ceremony on January 18, Hebrew Union College awarded her an honorary doctorate in humane letters.

BIBLIOGRAPHY

Berkman, Edward O. *The Lady and the Law: The Remarkable Story of Fanny Holtzmann* (1976); Obituary. *NYTimes*, February 7, 1980, D1; *NYTimes Biographical Series* 11 (February 1980): 222; *WWIAJ* (1938).

EMILY TAITZ

HOMOSEXUALITY *see* LESBIANISM

HOWE, FLORENCE (b. 1929)

"The chief editor, fund raiser, cheerleader and occasional staff photographer" is the way the *Chronicle of Higher Education* described Florence Howe's work at the Feminist Press. She has made the publishing company her life's work.

Florence Howe was born on March 17, 1929, in New York City to Samuel and Frances (Stilly) Rosenfeld. Her father was a taxi driver and her mother a bookkeeper. She received her B.A. from HUNTER COLLEGE in 1950 and her M.A. from Smith College in

1951. She then did graduate study at the University of Wisconsin from 1951 to 1954.

From 1954 until 1957, Howe was an instructor in English at Hofstra College (now University) in Hempstead, New York. During part of that time she was also a lecturer in English at Queens College. From 1960 until 1971, Howe was assistant professor of English at Goucher College in Towson, Maryland. It was during that time that she founded the Feminist Press.

Dedicated to making available the works of women writers, the Feminist Press quickly became a valuable resource and a voice of change. Its first publication was a children's book about a little girl who wanted to be a doctor, but its specialty soon became reprints of the works of little-known women writers. In 1973, Howe edited, with Ellen Bass, the landmark anthology of women's poetry *No More Masks*. Its influence on the literary world and on women was immediate and profound. The press has also published a number of "readers" focused on various women's issues or groups of women. One of the most important of these is *All the Women Are White, All the Blacks Are Men, But Some of Us Are Brave: Black Women's Studies* (1982), edited by Gloria T. Hull, Patricia Bell-Scott, and Barbara Smith.

Howe has written several books, including *The Conspiracy of the Young* (1970) and *The Impact of Women's Studies on the Curriculum and the Disciplines* (1980), both coauthored by her then husband, Paul Lauter. Her essays were collected in a book entitled *Myths of Coeducation: Selected Essays, 1964–1983* (1984). She has edited a number of anthologies in addition to *No More Masks* and has herself been included in several others.

In 1993, a second edition of *No More Masks* was published by HarperCollins. Again, Howe edited the volume and wrote the introduction. For many who had long awaited the book, it was somewhat disappointing. One reviewer noted that Howe's selection of poems was "surprisingly narrow" and that those poems which were chosen did not usually demand much of the reader. Still, even this critic conceded that "Howe's material is so rich that she can't help but hit the nail on the head some or even much of the time."

Writing in the *Chronicle of Higher Education*, Ellen Coughlin quoted Howe's own summation of her work at the Feminist Press. "I don't think there's a lot of magic in it. What matters is finding someone who thinks about publishing in a somewhat different way from traditional publishers, and I think I do that. I don't think of publishing either as money making for the moment or as noise making for the moment. I really think about publishing in relation to learning and consciousness over the long haul, and what is needed to make something that represents more accurately the world we live in."

BIBLIOGRAPHY

Bekker, Karen. "25 Years of Celebrating Women Authors." *Lilith* (September 30, 1995); *Contemporary Authors*; Coughlin, Ellen. "The Chief Editor, Fund Raiser, and Cheerleader of the Feminist Press." *Chronicle of Higher Education*; Oktenberg, Adrian. "Smashing the Mold Straight Off: Feminist Poetry Now." *Kenyon Review* (June 1, 1994); *Who's Who of American Women* (1996).

KATHLEEN THOMPSON

HUNTER COLLEGE

Long known as the "Jewish Girls' Radcliffe," Hunter College of the City University of New York was founded in 1870 as the Normal College of the City of New York. It was a public, tuition-free secondary and teacher-training school that admitted students solely on the basis of academic merit, determined by competitive examination, and by residency in the city. Over the years, it became a haven for academically advanced students unable to afford more costly schools or to gain admission to institutions with more restrictive admissions criteria. Women who were considered "socially undesirable"—African Americans, Catholics, and Jews, especially those from Eastern Europe—attended Hunter in disproportionate numbers. Hunter's student body, therefore, differed significantly from that of other women's colleges in America. From 1900 to the end of World War II, decades when many institutions of higher education implemented policies of selective admissions specifically designed to deflect minority students, Hunter gladly welcomed these same women. Hunter educated scores of intellectually gifted and professionally talented women whose skills and achievements amply repaid the city's largesse.

With the founding of Hunter College as the female counterpart to all-male City College, New York City offered all of its citizens a system of public schools from kindergarten through college. For nearly a century, all students who resided in New York and who passed the highly competitive academic entrance examinations were assured a superb free education. An integral part of the public school system, the college used no selective criteria—social, financial or racial—other than competitive examination to determine admission.

The student body rapidly grew to reflect the ethnic composition of the city. Jewish students, as well as a small number of African Americans, attended from the beginning. Their steadily increasing numbers, claimed William Wood, president of the board of education, demonstrated that Jewish parents knew how to avail themselves of the magnificent training they had the right to obtain for their daughters.

Thus, in 1878, approximately 200 of a total student body of 1,542 were Jewish. By 1889, 50 of 300 graduates were Jewish, including the valedictorian. That year, Jewish students read four of six prize essays at commencement, won four of nine prizes, and received at least eighteen honorable mentions. The students of 1889 also unanimously selected a Jewish senior to deliver the address welcoming President Benjamin Harrison to New York City for the centennial of the Constitution.

Despite a nondenominational Christianity that pervaded the school in its early years, President Thomas Hunter ensured that the college respected the rights and feelings of all students. Hunter devised a system of discretionary absences to allow students to celebrate religious holidays without penalty and demanded that student societies and debating clubs exclude theological issues as topics of discussion or debate. He also insisted that competitive examinations remain in force as the only impartial, democratic means of determining admission to the college.

Until the great immigration of the 1880s brought large numbers of Eastern European and Russian Jews to New York, Hunter's Jewish students came primarily from old German and Spanish families. As the only public high school and eventually the only college for girls, the school attracted daughters of families able to spare their children's contribution to the household economy. By the first decades of the new century, however, both Jewish and gentile middle-class families began to desert the public colleges in favor of private, selective schools. As these colleges began imposing selective admissions criteria based on ethnic and social factors, the free and nonselective public colleges of New York absorbed the highly intelligent but "socially undesirable" students unable to find acceptance elsewhere. Normal College, renamed Hunter College in 1914, and City College became the symbols of educational opportunity for generations of Jewish immigrants.

By the 1920s, Hunter's students were overwhelmingly first-generation Americans: Although 80 percent of the students were American-born, only 28 percent of their fathers had been born in the United States. Estimates of the number of Jewish women at Hunter

Long known as the "Jewish Girls' Radcliffe," Hunter College provided New York City residents with a superb free education for nearly a century. Shown here is the long-time executive director of HADASSAH, ALINE KAPLAN, receiving Hunter College Hall of Fame recognition in 1983 from the institution's president, Donna Shalala. [Hadassah Archives]

range from 40 percent of the student body in the 1920s to 75 percent in the 1930s when restrictive quotas at most private colleges and universities barred Jewish women from admission. The Depression effectively barred others, who could not afford the tuition of private colleges and universities. Hunter absorbed all who qualified and was soon the largest college for women in the world. Jewish life in the college flourished, and Jewish sororities and clubs, such as the Menorah Society, Avukah, and Hillel, proliferated. Students found both comfort and strength in belonging to a community of their own.

Although immigrant families placed less emphasis on education for girls than for boys, Jewish parents generally supported their daughters' desire to attend Hunter College and fostered their efforts to become teachers. Increasingly viewed as a means of upward social mobility, financial security, and intellectual gratification, teaching became the profession of choice for thousands of Jewish women. For many, Hunter provided the only choice of professional training: It was free, and its graduates dominated the eligibility lists for coveted teaching positions. Inevitably, as Jewish women graduated from Hunter in ever larger numbers, they came to dominate the ranks of New York's teaching force and the city's public schools.

Although a significant number of Hunter students through the 1960s were Jewish, most alumnae remember an equally large Catholic presence in the college. In recognition of this diversity, Hunter College acquired, through a special act of the New York State legislature, the Sara Delano Roosevelt Memorial House in 1940 for use as the first collegiate interfaith center. Traditionally, the president of the college was a Catholic and, acceding to the wishes of the church, the main campus on Park Avenue remained single-sex long after the heavily Jewish Bronx Campus—now Herbert H. Lehman College—became coeducational in 1951. Hunter College has had many Jewish acting presidents and subsidiary administrators but never a permanent Jewish president.

In recent years, Hunter's student population has continued to reflect the demographics of New York City. Now a senior college of the City University of New York, offering a vast array of undergraduate, graduate, and certificate programs, Hunter is coeducational, charges tuition, and attracts an extraordinarily diverse student body. After a decline in Jewish enrollments in the 1970s and 1980s, the college is again witnessing an upsurge as recent immigrants and refugees from the former Soviet bloc countries apply for admission. By becoming Hunter students, they are joining a long list of distinguished alumni, including Nobel Prize winners ROSALYN SUSSMAN YALOW and GERTRUDE BELLE ELION, author BEL KAUFMAN, politician BELLA ABZUG, consumer advocate and former Miss America BESS MYERSON, and several presidents of HADASSAH. These alumni demonstrate the tradition that placed Jewish students in the forefront of the drive for education.

BIBLIOGRAPHY

Grunfeld, Katherina Kroo. "Purpose and Ambiguity: The Feminine World of Hunter College, 1869–1945." Ed.D. diss., Teachers College, Columbia University (1991); Hunter, Thomas. *The Autobiography of Dr. Thomas Hunter.* Edited by his daughters (1931); Markowitz, Ruth Jacknow. "Subway Scholars at Concrete Campuses: Daughters of Jewish Immigrants Prepare for the Teaching Profession, New York City, 1920–1940." *History of Higher Education Annual* 10 (1990): 31–50; "The Normal College of New York City." *Harper's New Monthly Magazine* (April 1878): 680–682; Patterson, Samuel White. *Hunter College: Eighty-Five Years of Service* (1955); Shuster, George N. *The Ground I Walked On: Reflections by the Former President of Hunter College* (1961); Synnott, Marcia Graham. *The Half-Opened Door: Discrimination and Admissions at Harvard, Yale, and Princeton, 1900–1970* (1979); Wechsler, Harold S. *The Qualified Student: A History of Selective College Admission in America* (1977).

KATHERINA KROO GRUNFELD

HURST, FANNIE (1889–1968)

Fannie Hurst was among the most popular and sought-after writers of the post–World War I era. In her heydey, Hurst was a contributor to the *Saturday Evening Post*, the *Century* magazine, and *Cosmopolitan* magazine, and was featured in annual editions of *The Best American Short Story.* Her novels and stories were translated into a dozen languages. Hurst commanded huge sums from the motion picture magnates who acquired the rights to her works, thirty of which have been made into movies. *Back Street* (1932, 1941, 1961), *Imitation of Life* (1934, 1959), and *Humoresque* (1920, 1946) are among the best known. Tagged with the sobriquet "highest-priced short-story writer in America," Hurst was rumored to have received a million dollars for *Great Laughter* from Metro-Goldwyn-Mayer.

Born on October 18, 1889, in Hamilton, Ohio, and raised in comfortable circumstances in St. Louis, Missouri, Fannie Hurst was the only surviving child of Rose (Koppel) Hurst and Samuel Hurst, American-born Jews of German descent. The Hursts did not practice their religion and referred their daughter to the library when she inquired about her heritage. However, they were not entirely without race consciousness. They complained of prejudice, knew a little Yiddish, and enjoyed traditional foods. Hurst's father deplored the absence of Jews in their community and threatened to send her to temple and Sunday school over the objections of his wife. Yet when Hurst's younger sister, Edna, died of diphtheria at three years of age, it was her father who counseled Hurst to say the Lord's Prayer before going to bed. Distraught over Edna's death, Rose and Samuel Hurst indulged Fannie in countless ways, providing piano and dancing lessons, extravagant clothing, a brief stint at private school, and eventually a college education at Washington University.

Hurst's mother frequently came into conflict with her husband, formerly a salesman from Memphis,

Known as "the highest-paid short-story writer in America," Fannie Hurst penned such works as Back Street, Imitation of Life, *and* Humoresque, *which became Hollywood films. Her family's ambivalence toward Judaism is reflected in her work, which nonetheless reveals her empathy for minorities and working people in general. This stunning photograph was taken on May 28, 1914. [Library of Congress]*

Tennessee, who had risen to the position of president of a shoe manufacturing concern. Her derisive comments about her husband's "leather bellies" (that is, cheap shoes) and parsimony often ended in humiliating public invectives against him. Rose Hurst was fiercely sensitive to slights and patronage from her husband's rich relatives, whom she virtually barred from contact with Fannie. Consequently, Fannie Hurst was shut out of an exclusive literary club, the Pioneers, which would have afforded her highbrow Jewish contacts. Her mother preferred her own interfaith kaffeeklatsch where she was the reigning luminary, with her brilliant sense of humor. Rose complained volubly about her daughter's solitary scribbling, which deprived her of help with the housework. But she wanted Fannie to have the best of everything and endowed her with a sense of self-worth and entitlement. Hurst claims to have loved her gay and temperamental mother ardently, only hinting at resentments.

Although she was less attached to her elegant and remote father, whose watchword was "knowledge is power," Hurst derived a glimmering of refinement and culture from him. When Hurst's first published story, "Ain't Life Wonderful," appeared in *Reedy's Mirror* in 1908, she was a junior in college. Her father was ecstatic, but her mother was concerned that a brilliant daughter might prove unmarriageable. When Fannie fell in love with the Russian émigré pianist Jacques Danielson, whom she married in May 1915, she predicted that her parents would disapprove. To the Hursts, all Eastern European Jews were "kikes" (*Anatomy* 90). Their childless marriage ended with Danielson's death in 1952.

Hurst sublimated the ethnic and class tensions of her home environment into a concern for African Americans, immigrants, and working people in general. When she dealt with Jewish subjects directly, such as the violin prodigy Paul Boray of "Humoresque" (1919), she concentrated on the trials of the upwardly mobile saddled with the baggage of traditional values. In *Lummox* (1923), the reader's sympathies are with old lady Wallenstein, who keeps kosher in spite of her daughter-in-law, a "blonde shixsa" who calls her own husband a "Sheenie!" Yet the novel's heroine, a Scandinavian-Slav maid-of-all-work, undermines the affirmation of religious identity because it is an obstacle to peace and tolerance. In her autobiography, Hurst echoes the refrain that her heart belongs to the people. It took the rise of Hitler to force her to acknowledge anti-Semitism, and the creation of Israel to forge a sense of Jewishness. Hurst's interest in the poor, sparked by a downturn in her family's fortunes that occasioned a move from reputable Cates Avenue to a boardinghouse, emerged as a leading theme in her early writings.

In 1909, following graduation, Hurst secured a job in a shoe factory. Once in New York City, she worked as a restaurant server, salesperson, and actor. In her spare time, she combed the city and Ellis Island picking up local color. Hurst, this prolific and determined writer, received thirty-four letters of rejection from the *Saturday Evening Post* before publishing "Power and Horse Power" in 1912. After breaking that barrier, success came swiftly, and Hurst never again knew a dry spell.

Fannie Hurst sensed that mass appeal somehow precluded artistic greatness—"If I did not write 'down,' I was myself down"—but Hurst's fans continue to enjoy her purple prose and sentimentality. Best loved for the tearjerker *Back Street* (1931), Hurst favored her most self-consciously social novel, *Lummox*, which earned the praise of Vladimir Ilyich Lenin and Leon Trotsky. In fact, Trotsky entertained her with an impromptu recitation of the chapter "The

Cathedral Under the Sea" when she visited him in the Soviet Union. Hurst's best-seller *Imitation of Life* (1933) was well received in Harlem, though one critic, in an article in *Opportunity* magazine, pilloried the novel's depiction of the loving mammy and tragic mulatto.

A prominent member of the Urban League, Hurst was friends with leading figures of the Harlem Renaissance, such as Zora Neale Hurston, whom she met in 1925. Hurston, who served as Hurst's chauffeur, secretary, and confidante while studying anthropology at Barnard, classed Hurst with the "Negrotarians," a mildly derisive term for whites dedicated to Negro uplift. Though Hurston was sincerely fond of her patron, she could not have liked Hurst's penchant for dressing her up as an Asian princess and parading her around deluxe resorts. Hurst was well intentioned, and she should be commended for her eagerness to combat injustice through a popular medium. Unfortunately, her work often reinforced ethnic stereotypes.

Hurst played an active role in New Deal politics. She was perplexed by the cynicism of the more glamorous writers of the fabulous twenties and was confident that people would go on saving to put their children through college and striving to better themselves. As chair of the National Housing Commission (1936–1937) and Committee on Workman's Compensation (1940), among many related activities, Hurst labored so that others might share in the American dream of which her own success was exemplary.

Hurst also firmly allied herself with Jewish causes. In the 1920s she was the keynote speaker in the campaign for the relief of Jews in Eastern Europe; in the 1940s she was active in raising funds for refugees from Nazi Germany; and in the 1950s she was a staunch promoter of the State of Israel.

Fannie Hurst died on February 23, 1968, in New York City.

BIBLIOGRAPHY

For a complete bibliography of Hurst's work, except for *Fool Be Still* (1964), and for her various activities, see *Who's Who of American Women* (1969).

AJYB 24:157, 70:521; *DAB* 8; Douglas, Ann. *Terrible Honesty: Mongrel Manhattan in the 1920s* (1995); *EJ*; Flitterman-Lewis, Sandy. "Imitation(s) of Life: The Black Woman's Double Determination as Troubling 'Other.'" *Literature and Psychology* 34 (1988): 44–57; Hurston, Zora Neale. "Two Women in Particular." *Dust Tracks on a Road: An Autobiography* (1984); Koppelman, Susan. "The Educations of Fannie Hurst." *Women's Studies International Forum* 10 (1987): 503–516; Lewis, David Levering. *When Harlem Was in Vogue* (1989); *NAW* modern; Obituaries. *NYTimes*, February 24, 1968, 1:3, and *St. Louis Globe Democrat*, Febru- ary 25, 1968; Uffen, Ellen Serlen. "Fannie Hurst." *American Women Writers*. Vol. 2 (1982); *UJE*; WWIAJ (1926, 1928, 1938); *WWWIA* 4.

WENDY GRAHAM

HYDE, IDA HENRIETTA (1857–1945)

Physiologist Ida Henrietta Hyde's proudest accomplishment wasn't her pioneering research—it was her work on behalf of other women scientists. In 1896, she conducted research at the Zoological Station in Naples, Italy, after completing her Ph.D. in Heidelberg, Germany. The next year, she persuaded America's foremost women educators and philanthropists to make this opportunity available to other American women scientists. The group she founded was known as the Naples Table Association for Promoting Scientific Research by Women. Using a subscription system, the group raised five hundred dollars annually to fund a research "table," actually a small laboratory, where thirty-six American women in all benefited from Hyde's vision.

Ida Hyde was born on September 8, 1857. Her parents, Meyer H. and Babette (Loewenthal) Heidenheimer, had emigrated from Germany before she was born, anglicizing the family name to Hyde. Hyde's mother ran a prosperous store until it burned in the Chicago fire of 1871. This abrupt change in the family finances forced Hyde to leave school. At age sixteen, when she apprenticed at the millinery establishment, she was living in a female-headed household consisting of her mother, a younger brother Ben, and two sisters, Clara and Sophie. Her sister Tillie had already married. While working six days a week, Hyde attended evening classes at the Chicago Athenaeum.

Hyde's family valued education for sons but not for daughters. At twenty-four, Hyde used all her savings for one year of college. She took and passed the county teachers' exam and, three years later, the Chicago teachers' exam. One year she attended a summer school for teachers at Martha's Vineyard, an experience that provided the catalyst she needed to become a scientist. Although she taught several more years, her entire attention was riveted on attaining a college degree in science.

In 1889, Hyde left Chicago to attend Cornell University, graduating in 1891. Giving up her initial plan to attend medical school, she instead accepted a graduate fellowship at Bryn Mawr, where she worked with such major scientists as T.H. Morgan and Jacques Loeb. Her summers were spent at Woods Hole Marine Biological Laboratory in Massachusetts. In 1893, she received an Association of Collegiate

Alumnae fellowship to study in Europe. This organization of women college graduates is known today as the American Association of University Women (AAUW).

Hyde's doctorate was problematic because she chose to combine a zoological thesis with physiology, a discipline in medical school where women were not welcome. She finally received her doctorate in 1894, at age thirty-seven. But the difficulties she overcame led to invitations—to do research first at the Zoological Station in Italy and later at the Harvard Medical School, while she supported herself by teaching science at private girls' schools and took a few medical courses. During this time in Boston, Hyde founded the Naples Table Association and served as its first secretary for several years.

In 1899, Hyde was hired to found a physiology department at the University of Kansas in Lawrence—a remarkable accomplishment, because it was a very rare occurrence for a woman to be hired as a professor at a coeducational college. A popular teacher, Hyde drew on her European and Harvard experiences to have state-of-the-art facilities constructed. During summer vacations, she continued her medical education, spending three summers at Rush Medical School in Chicago. Her request for a leave of absence to complete her residency was denied. In 1916, the leadership of her department changed to a committee form, and she was eventually forced out. Her religion (Society for Ethical Culture) and lack of an M.D. may have been factors, but mainly her colleagues wanted a man in her position. Finally, in 1918, she took a leave of absence for wartime duties and never returned to the University of Kansas. For three years, she traveled around the world, studying women's education as a representative of the AAUW. She retired in California and continued to do research.

On August 22, 1945, at age eighty-eight, Ida Henrietta Hyde died of a cerebral hemorrhage. She is buried in the cemetery at Woods Hole, Massachusetts.

Hyde's research spanned work on the nervous, circulatory, and respiratory systems. She also invented a microelectrode. Her research on the effects of alcohol, caffeine, and narcotics was decades ahead of its time. The merit of her research is evident: In 1902, the American Society of Physiologists elected her its first woman member.

SELECTED WORKS BY IDA HENRIETTA HYDE

"Before Women Were Human Beings . . ." *AAUW Journal* 31, 4 (1938): 226–236; "The Kaiser and the Devilfish." *The New York Evening Post Magazine*, May 25, 1918.

BIBLIOGRAPHY

Hyde, Ida Henrietta. Papers. American Association of University Women Archives, Washington, D.C., and University Archives. University of Kansas, Lawrence; Johnson, Elsie Ernest. "Ida Henrietta Hyde: Early Experiments." *The Physiologist* 24, no. 6 (1981): 10–11; Jones, T. Sydney. "Ida H. Hyde." *Notable Twentieth-Century Scientists* (1995): 988–990; *NAW*; Sloan, Jan Butin. "The Founding of the Naples Table Association for Promoting Scientific Research by Women, 1897." *SIGNS: Journal of Women in Culture and Society* (1978): 208–216; Tucker, Gail S. "Ida Henrietta Hyde: The First Woman Member of the Society." *The Physiologist* 24, no. 6 (1981): 1–9; Wittig, Gertraude. "Hyde's 1896 German Doctorate: Opening Science to Women" (Unpublished paper).

JAN BUTIN

HYMAN, LIBBIE HENRIETTA (1888–1969)

In 1960, zoologist Libbie Hyman explained her work: "I like invertebrates. I don't mean worms particularly, although a worm can be almost anything, including the larva of a beautiful butterfly. But I do like the soft delicate ones, the jellyfishes and corals and the beautiful microscopic organisms." Hyman transformed her love of the soft creatures to writings that brought her international recognition as an expert on invertebrates and as the world authority on flatworms.

Libbie Henrietta Hyman was born December 6, 1888, in Des Moines, Iowa, to Jewish immigrant parents, Joseph and Sabina (Neumann) Hyman. She had one younger and two older brothers. Her father was born in Russian Poland, while her mother came from Stettin, Germany. Joseph Hyman was an unsuccessful clothing retailer, and the family was poor.

Hyman grew up in Fort Dodge, Iowa, where she was valedictorian of her high school graduating class in 1905. She entered the University of Chicago in 1906 and began her studies in botany, but left that department when she encountered anti-Semitism. She moved into zoology, her lifetime field of work.

After receiving a B.A. in 1910 and a Ph.D. in 1915, she became research assistant to Professor Charles Manning Child, under whom she had studied. For the next sixteen years, she worked with Child on his studies of lower invertebrates and published more than forty research articles. Hyman also wrote two laboratory manuals that made a major impact on her career path. The *Laboratory Manual for Elementary Zoology* was published in 1919 and revised in 1929, while the *Laboratory Manual for Comparative Vertebrate Anatomy* also went through two editions, in 1922 and 1942.

"I like invertebrates . . . [especially] the soft delicate ones, the jellyfishes, and corals and the beautiful microscopic organisms." Libbie Hyman devoted her life and her considerable intellect to studying and writing about invertebrates, publishing a six-volume work and more than ninety articles. [American Museum of Natural History]

Hyman found that she could live on the income from royalties on the two manuals and left Chicago in 1931, when Child was nearing retirement. She decided to devote herself full time to preparing a treatise on invertebrates and moved to New York City to use the library at the American Museum of Natural History. In 1937, she became an honorary research associate at the museum, an unpaid position that provided office and laboratory space. She devoted most of her time to study, with little socializing or leisure activity. Between 1940 and 1967, Hyman published the six-volume work *The Invertebrates*, as well as some ninety articles.

Hyman's work was recognized from the start as outstanding. In 1941, the University of Chicago gave her an honorary Sc.D.; in 1960, the Linnaean Society of London awarded her its Gold Medal in Zoology.

Hyman developed Parkinson's disease during the 1950s but continued her long work days. She was in a wheelchair, under the care of a nurse, when she com-

pleted the sixth volume of *The Invertebrates*. The museum honored her with a Gold Medal Award for Distinguished Achievement in Science in April 1969, just four months before her death on August 3. Although Hyman had no ties with the Jewish community, she bequeathed one thousand dollars to the Federation of Jewish Philanthropies of New York.

Libbie Henrietta Hyman was a major contributor to the field of zoology. Her publications have continued to be cited and used. *The Invertebrates* is still considered a masterly source.

SELECTED WORKS BY LIBBIE HENRIETTA HYMAN

The Invertebrates. 6 vols. (1940–1967); *Laboratory Manual for Comparative Vertebrate Anatomy* (1922). Revised as *Comparative Vertebrate Anatomy* (1942); *Laboratory Manual for Elementary Zoology* (1919. Revised 1929).

BIBLIOGRAPHY

BEOAJ; Blackwelder, Richard E. "Libbie H. Hyman Memorial Issue: Her Life." *Journal of Biological Psychology* 12 (1970): 4–12; *Division of Invertebrate Zoologists Newsletter* (Fall 1991); Emerson, William K. "Bibliography of Libbie H. Hyman." In *Biology of the Turbellaria*, edited by Nathan W. Riser and M. Patricia Morse (1974); Hast, Adele. "Hyman, Libbie Henrietta." In *Historical Encyclopedia of Chicago Women* (forthcoming); Linnaean Society of London. *Proceedings of the Linnaean Society of London* 172 (1961): 162–163; *NAW* modern; *NYTimes*, August 5, 1969, 37:1; Stunkard, Horace W. "In Memoriam Libbie Henrietta Hyman, 1888–1969." In *Biology of the Turbellaria*, edited by Nathan W. Riser and M. Patricia Morse (1974); *UJE*; *WWIAJ* (1928, 1938); *WWWIA* 4; Yost, Edna. *American Women of Science* (1943).

ADELE HAST

HYNEMAN, REBEKAH GUMPERT (1812–1875)

Rebekah Gumpert Hyneman was best known to mid-nineteenth-century American Jews as the author of *The Leper and Other Poems* (1853). However, she also published stories, poems, and essays in the *Occident and American Jewish Advocate*, the *Masonic Keystone and Mirror*, and other periodicals.

Born on September 8, 1812, to a Jewish father and a non-Jewish mother, Rebekah (Gumpert) Hyneman led a sheltered life in and around Philadelphia. Her marriage to Jewish businessman Benjamin Hyneman intensified her feelings about Judaism. Her husband disappeared on a business journey after only five years of marriage, yet for the rest of her life Rebekah remained committed to "the faith of [her] adoption."

Rebekah and Benjamin Hyneman had two sons, Elias and Barton. Elias, the elder, born in 1837, was a Union cavalry soldier who died in 1865 in Georgia's Andersonville Prison. Hyneman was close to her sister Sarah, who married Benjamin Hyneman's brother Leon. Leon Hyneman was an active Mason who founded the *Masonic Keystone and Mirror* in 1852.

Hyneman's devotion to Judaism is evident in much of her writing. "The Chosen," for example, published in *Leper*, articulates concern for Jews who forsake Judaism because of "temptations" and an "oppressor's hand." "The Lost Diamond," a story published in *Occident* in 1862, makes those temptations concrete, in the form of material well-being. The characters resist: They are unwilling to pay the price, conversion to Christianity. Ultimately, these faithful Jews are rewarded with wealth and love.

In a significant number of her works, Hyneman promoted ideals of Jewish women's behavior. "Female Scriptural Characters," a series of poems that appeared in *Occident* between 1846 and 1850 (subsequently included in *Leper*), pays homage to fourteen women including Sarah, Rebekah, Ruth, Esther, Deborah, and Judith. Repeatedly, Hyneman emphasized the womanliness of these faithful Jews, particularly by noting their piety and valor as well as their adherence to white middle-class American codes of female behavior. In "Miriam's Song," Miriam loudly proclaims, "Shout ye his name—the Lord our God is one!" but the speaker of the poem concludes with, "Oh, woman! weak and powerless, yet unto thee is given / The task to prune the budding branch, and bid it bloom for heaven." Such rhetoric reinforced, more than it challenged, cultural ideals of womanhood.

Hyneman herself rarely defied expectations in her adherence to mid-nineteenth-century conventions of Jewish and American womanly propriety, in either her personal conduct or her writing. Yet she was one of a small number of American Jewish women of the time who published their work. She took that bold step into the public arena in order to share with other American Jews her belief in the significance of Judaism, as well as to educate uninformed, and even anti-Semitic, non-Jews.

Rebekah Gumpert Hyneman died on September 10, 1875.

SELECTED WORKS BY
REBEKAH GUMPERT HYNEMAN

"Female Scriptural Characters." *Occident and American Jewish Advocate.* Series (1846–1850); *The Leper and Other Poems* (1853); "The Lost Diamond." *Occident and American Jewish Advocate* 19 (March 1862): 551–555, and 20 (April): 10–15, and 21 (May): 71–75, and 22 (June): 117–123, and 23 (July): 163–171.

BIBLIOGRAPHY

Cohen, Nina Morais. "Rebekah Hyneman." *American Jews Annual 5646* (1885); *JE*; Lichtenstein, Diane. *Writing Their Nations: The Tradition of Nineteenth-Century American Jewish Women Writers* (1992); Marcus, Jacob Rader, ed. *The American Jewish Woman 1654–1980: A Documentary History* (1981); Morais, Henry Samuel. *The Jews of Philadelphia: Their History from the Earliest Settlements to the Present Time* (1894); Umansky, Ellen, and Dianne Ashton, eds. *Four Centuries of Jewish Women's Spirituality: A Sourcebook* (1992); *UJE*.

DIANE LICHTENSTEIN

I

ICAR *see* **INTERNATIONAL COALITION FOR AGUNAH RIGHTS**

ILGWU *see* **INTERNATIONAL LADIES GARMENT WORKERS UNION**

IMMIGRATION *see* **CONTEMPORARY JEWISH MIGRATIONS; EASTERN EUROPEAN IMMIGRATION; GERMAN IMMIGRANT PERIOD**

INTERMARRIAGE AND CONVERSION

INTRODUCTION AND HISTORICAL BACKGROUND

In this article "intermarriage" refers to the marriage of a Jew to a non-Jew who does not convert to Judaism. The terms "interfaith marriage" and "mixed marriage" will be used interchangeably with "intermarriage." In sociological terms, marrying within one's ethnic or religious group is called endogamy, while marrying outside is exogamy.

Although it was known that there were large numbers of mixed marriages among the third and fourth generations of the Spanish and Portuguese Jewish immigrants of the 1700s and 1800s and the German Jewish immigrants to America in the mid- to late nineteenth century, within the American Jewish community intermarriage was by and large not the subject of research or analysis until the 1960s. Until then, it was the consensus of social scientists that with the large influx of Eastern European Jewish immigrants between 1880 and 1920 mixed marriage had become a null category. In fact, in a chart drawn by Milton Gordon in his book *Assimilation in American Life* (1964), Jews are listed along with "Negroes" as having virtually no "marital assimilation," as he called it. The leadership and the masses of American Jews were preoccupied with breaking down any barriers to complete assimilation. Fighting discrimination and prejudice was the order of the day. Benjamin Ringer's volume of the paradigmatic Lakeville Studies of the mid-1950s was entitled *The Edge of Friendliness: Relationships Between Jews and Their Non-Jewish Neighbors.* It would have been difficult at that time to convince social scientists that just three decades later a similar community study might be entitled "Intermarriage: Intimate Relationships Between Jews and Their Non-Jewish Neighbors"! Even in 1990s America, however, mate selection is not solely a matter of romantic love. As noted in a popular text for courses in marriage and the family: "Although we use the system of marital choice by mutual selection in our society, the belief that the selection is completely free is an illusion" (Saxton, p. 138).

The first voice noting a growing rate of mixed marriage was heard in an article written by Eric Rosenthal for the 1963 *American Jewish Yearbook*. Rosenthal analyzed the mixed-marriage rates of Jews in Iowa and later (in 1967) of those in Indiana, the only two states that recorded the religion of future bride and groom when they registered for a marriage license. He found that the out-marriage rate of Jews was over 20 percent in these states. However, his findings were largely ignored because the Jewish populations of Iowa and Indiana were so small that it was hard to imagine that what Rosenthal found there could be generalized to the whole United States.

So, interfaith marriage as a whole was only given cursory notice. The differential rate of men and women in the cases that were known was noted but not emphasized. There was data to indicate that in most ethnic, racial, and religious groups women were more likely than men to marry out. In the market or economic model of marriage utilized by analysts, women were seen as marrying out of their ethnic groups in order to rise in the stratification system or to "marry up" by trading beauty for social position. Men, the theory held, could rise in the social system through achievement in the worlds of the intellect, business, or finance, while women could only do so by trading one ascribed status for another. Marriage to highly achieving men from older American backgrounds was seen as the primary way for women to climb the ladder of success. In a recent textbook, the resulting shortage of eligible men for high-status women is described for American society in general as follows:

The phenomenon of the dating differential also helps explain why unmarried women are often from relatively higher-status populations than are unmarried men of the same age. Overall, there are about equal numbers of young men and young women. But because men tend to date and marry women with lower statuses with respect to age, physical size, education, intelligence, and social class, the women who get left out ("undating women") are those with high status with respect to those factors. (For the same reason, men of low status become "undating men.") (Saxton, pp. 141–142)

Jewish women, however, were anomalous in this regard. They did not define marrying out as marrying up. They were raised to believe that there was nothing superior to a Jewish man. And, despite the social class advantages that might have accrued to them through

marrying non-Jews, the rate of interfaith marriage for Jewish women was, until the decade of the 1970s, always considerably lower than that of Jewish men. In the Council of Jewish Federations 1970 National Jewish Population Survey (NJPS, 1970) this differential persisted, though by the time a comprehensive reanalysis was undertaken of intermarriage patterns as reflected in eight Jewish community studies conducted between 1985 and 1988, the authors uncovered a trend toward equalization of the rates of outmarriage for Jewish men and women. They wrote that

in the past, Jewish men were much more likely than Jewish women to intermarry. Although rates of intermarriage and mixed marriage for both men and women have risen steadily over time, Jewish men are still more likely than Jewish women to intermarry. . . . The proportion of inmarriages declines by 35 percent in three decades, from 90 percent before 1960 to 55 percent in the decade of the 1980s. For Jewish women, the proportion of inmarriages declines by 28 percent during the same period, from 98 percent to 70 percent. . . . Apart from the fact that both groups are subject to the same societal influences, the two rates are also integrally connected to each other: as increasing proportions of Jewish men intermarry, there will be fewer available Jewish males for Jewish women. (Medding et al., pp. 8–9)

THE RELUCTANT EXOGAMISTS

Until the mid-1970s, the issue of gender differentials in exogamy was often noted in passing in articles describing mixed marriage. However, the reluctance of Jewish women to marry out was never emphasized. If there was any analysis of the phenomenon, it took the form of blaming Jewish women for the outmarriage of Jewish men. Several analysts theorized that some Jewish men felt that marrying Jewish women would be like "marrying their mothers." Other social scientists explained away the greater penchant for interfaith marriage on the part of Jewish males by citing characteristics that were "wrong" with Jewish females, implying that if only Jewish women were different there would be considerably fewer Jewish males marrying out of the group. Needless to say, these authors (who were all male) never praised Jewish women for refraining from exogamy nor did they seek to interpret the gender discrepancy from the perspective of Jewish women.

At least two factors would lead the naive observer to suppose that Jewish women would, in fact, have been more prone to interfaith marriage than Jewish men. First, according to the sex-ratio data derived from the 1970 NJPS, there were more Jewish women than men available for marriage in the middle decades of the twentieth century. Since women have traditionally been more dependent upon marriage than men, both for their identity and their economic survival, we would expect that, faced with the probability of spinsterhood, they would choose intermarriage over the single life.

A second reason to suppose that Jewish women might have married out more than Jewish men is that, according to traditional Jewish law, a child's religion is determined by the religion of the mother. Thus the fact that a woman married out did not affect the official Jewish affiliation of her children. An exogamous Jewish man, however, must either have had his spouse convert prior to the birth of their children or have seen to it that the children themselves were formally converted for them to be considered Jewish by the overwhelming majority of Jews. One would therefore expect stronger sanctions against out-marriage for men than for women, whose exogamy would not appear to threaten group survival to the same degree.

Why is it, then, that, until the last two decades or so, Jewish women were so reluctant to intermarry? First, there was the structure of the Jewish family together with the prevalence of traditional gender-role distinctions. Sons could fulfill their parents' expectations through educational and occupational success. The legend of "my son the doctor" and the sacrifices parents made to ensure the actualization of this dream are well known. Sons were also expected to provide future *nakhes* [satisfaction] in the form of Jewish grandchildren, but parents found it difficult to abandon "my son the intermarried doctor," since he was still fulfilling parental expectations in other ways. On the other hand, daughters were not necessarily expected to "make it" in the occupational world. Until the 1970s, "success" for a nice Jewish girl was defined as marriage to an educated Jewish man who could support her in the proper style, and close oversight of daughters in the courting years effectively limited the possibility of their forming intimate relationships with non-Jewish men.

Second, further reinforcing daughters' early and suitable marriage was the fact that while it was and is still generally difficult to function in the Jewish community as a single person, it is even harder for women. Finally, the general closeness of daughters to their families was expected to carry over to married life. Intermarriage would not only be a "failure" for the Jewish daughter but would also cut her off from anticipated and accepted future warm ties with her nuclear family. These ties were not projected as strongly for sons, who have been shown to extend their loyalty to the nuclear family into the broader community of all Jews and to move toward a closer relationship with their wives' kinfolk. As late as the 1970 NJPS, Massarik and Chenkin reported that twice as many Jewish men as women were contracting interfaith marriages.

By the 1990 NJPS, all of this had broken down. Daughters had the same occupational expectations as sons, and they were as likely to go away to university and interact with non-Jews as their brothers; the median age of first marriage for Jewish women was twenty-four. The gender differential was largely the product of two factors: structural differentials in the circumstances of Jewish women and men, and a methodological anomaly. The structural props minimizing the rate of interfaith marriage among Jewish women were radically altered or disappeared entirely between 1965 and 1990.

The methodological anomaly was also done away with by 1990 through the random-digit-dialing method of sampling employed in the later National Jewish Population Survey. Until that survey there was always a sampling bias leading to an underenumeration of the percentage of Jewish women who married non-Jews. As a result of the normative practice of women changing their names when they married, Jewish women who married non-Jews were more likely than men to disappear from lists from which, until the most recent surveys, respondents were drawn. A man named David Cohen retained that name even after mixed marriage, and thus was more likely to be found on a list of known Jews than a woman named Susan Cohen who became, after her marriage to a non-Jew, Susan McDevitt or Susan Smith. Since women who married out of the faith were undercounted on the lists, they were undersampled, and it appeared that fewer Jewish women married out than was actually the case.

THE RISE OF INTERFAITH MARRIAGE SINCE 1965

Perspectives on the rates of interfaith marriage changed in the late 1960s due to a multiplicity of intersecting factors. Along with the civil rights movement, the antiwar movement and the budding feminist movement came enhanced self-awareness and pride in ethnic and racial identity. Predictions of the demise of ethnic consciousness in favor of religious identity—for example, those made by Will Herberg in his book *Protestant, Catholic, Jew* (1955)—turned out to be decidedly premature. It might have been thought that greater adherence to cultural pluralism would lead to endogamy. However, the opposite was true. Pride in one's own identity went hand-in-hand with a revitalized sense of equality, which meant that all available singles were potential mates. Moreover, particularly on the university campuses in the late 1960s and early 1970s, young people from different ethnic, racial, and religious origins met each other face-to-face and worked together in the antiwar, civil rights, and feminist movements. Young men and women were physically, intellectually, and ideologically available to each other. For the first time in Jewish history, both physical propinquity and psychological availability—the necessary conditions for mate selection between men and women of differing ethnic and religious backgrounds—were present.

By 1990, the rate of interfaith marriage among Jews had risen to 52 percent and, although the rates were still higher for men than for women, the gap was getting smaller every year. The democratic ethic and welcoming arms of the open society that raised the interfaith marriage rates of Jewish men reached out as well to Jewish women. The only differential remaining was in the area of conversion, with more women than men converting both out of and into Judaism as a result of interfaith marriage.

CONVERSION

All of the studies to date show that converts to Judaism make steadfast and loyal members of the community. At the time of the 1970 NJPS, the conversion rate to Judaism in husband Jewish/wife non-Jewish mixed marriages was as high as 25 percent, though in the wife Jewish/husband non-Jewish cases it was less than 10 percent. By 1990, conversion to Judaism took place in less than 5 percent of interfaith marriages, though still more often in cases where the husband was the Jewish partner. (The reasons for this decline are largely unexplored. It is thought that the patrilineal descent decision of the Reform movement together with the rise of an American norm that it was unethical to ask one's spouse to convert if one was not willing to convert oneself had some effect on the rates.)

One reason offered for the higher propensity of women to convert has been that men still have more power in marital relationships. Therefore, if the husband feels strongly about religion, the wife is more likely to convert to his religion than he is to hers. As societal norms concerning spousal roles become more egalitarian, it is likely that this differential will narrow, as has the general gender gap in interfaith marriage.

BIBLIOGRAPHY

AJYB (1963, 1967); Council of Jewish Federations National Jewish Population Survey (1970, 1990); Gordon, Milton. *Assimilation in American Life* (1964); Herberg, Will.

Protestant, Catholic, Jew (1955); Medding, Peter Y., et al. *Jewish Identity in Conversionary and Mixed Marriages* (1992); Saxton, Lloyd. *The Individual, Marriage, and the Family* (1993).

RELA MINTZ GEFFEN

INTERNATIONAL COALITION FOR AGUNAH RIGHTS (ICAR)

An *agunah* (plural, *agunot*) is a woman "chained" to a husband who is either unwilling or unable to grant her a Jewish divorce. Because halakah [Jewish law] requires that the *get* [divorce document] be granted by the husband, an *agunah* cannot remarry, and any subsequent children she bears are considered *mamzerim* [illegitimate children] who can never marry legitimate Jews. Legal loopholes exist to allow nondivorced husbands to remarry; none exists to help wives. The plight of *agunot* has become an increasing problem in contemporary times, with Jewish communities unable to pressure recalcitrant husbands into granting divorces to their wives. In addition, in the State of Israel, both marriage and divorce fall within the realm of religious law; there is no civil alternative. Some husbands have taken advantage of the situation, either blackmailing their wives before granting a divorce or leaving their wives to suffer while they move on.

Organizations exist in various countries to help individual women caught in this situation. Activists recognize the additional need to address the source of the problem and to implement a solution that would prevent it from occurring at all. This solution must be international, because the domain of Jewish law does not coincide with national borders. Norma Joseph (Canada), Alice Shalvi (Israel), and Rivka Haut (United States) met to discuss the problem, and on October 26, 1992, founded the International Coalition for Agunah Rights (ICAR) together with representatives from many women's groups.

The coalition's two goals are education and activism. Educational activities include conferences, vigils, press releases, interviews, and raising awareness about particular cases. An international ICAR conference was held in 1994 in Jerusalem. Annual vigils are held in various countries to commemorate the *agunot* victims. The first United States vigil was held in 1995. In Canada, an annual vigil is held on the Fast of Esther (the day before Purim). In Israel, an annual vigil or demonstration is held around the time of Rosh Hashanah, the New Year. Several vigils have also been held in England. ICAR held sessions at the General Assembly of Councils of Jewish Federations of North

An agunah *is a woman "chained" to a husband who is either unwilling or unable to grant her a Jewish divorce.*
The ICAR is dedicated to working toward a solution to this very serious problem. Their prayer on behalf of these women
contains the following: "Creator of heaven and earth. / May it be your will to free the captive wives of Israel /
Soften the hearts of their misguided captors. / Liberate your faithful daughters from their anguish."
[Joan Roth]

America for three years (1993, 1994, and 1995), to increase awareness of the problem and to exhort members of the federations to pressure rabbinical authorities to find a solution. The Canadian group has also held an educational retreat and is in the process of creating a documentary film on *agunot*.

ICAR's activism includes attempts to convince the rabbinical authorities to find a solution to the problem. Their halakic recommendations are prenuptial agreements that address the issue of divorce, convincing

recalcitrant husbands to grant a divorce, annulment of the marriage by rabbinic court, obligating the husband to grant the divorce, and conditional divorce that creates a document at an earlier time to be enacted if it becomes necessary. ICAR has met twice with Rabbi Lau, the Ashkenazi chief rabbi of Israel. So far, no global solution has been reached. ICAR also campaigns for solutions that originate in the non-Jewish legal world. Canada, at the federal level, and New York, at the state level, have both enacted laws that make a civil divorce difficult if there are obstacles to a religious remarriage. This has helped, but not alleviated, the problem.

ICAR's prayer for *agunot* is:

Creator of heaven and earth. / May it be your will to free the captive wives of Israel / When love and sanctity have fled the home, / But their husbands bind them in the tatters of ketubot. / Remove the bitter burden from these agunot and / Soften the hearts of their misguided captors. / Liberate your faithful daughters from their anguish. / Enable them to establish new homes and raise up children in peace. / Grant wisdom to the judges of Israel. / Teach them to recognize oppression and rule against it. / Infuse our rabbis with courage to use their power for good alone. / Blessed are you, creator of heaven and earth, who frees the captives. / *Baruch mateir asurim.*

BIBLIOGRAPHY

Alter, Susan D. "The Anchored Woman—A Cry for Help." *Bat Kol* (Fall 1987): 30–34; Biale, Rachel. *Women and Jewish Law: An Exploration of Women's Issues in Halakhic Sources* (1984); Breitowitz, Irving. *Between Civil and Religious Law: The Plight of the Agunah in American Society* (1993); Cwik, Marc S. "The Jewish Domestic Abuse and *Agunah* Problem Web Page." Available from http://users.aol.com/agunah; Greenberg, Blu. "Jewish Divorce Law: If We Must Part Let's Part as Equals." In *Jewish Marital Status*, edited by Carol Diament (1989); Haut, Irwin. *Divorce in Jewish Law and Life* (1983).

SONIA ZYLBERBERG

INTERNATIONAL LADIES GARMENT WORKERS UNION

The International Ladies Garment Workers Union was founded in 1900. The eleven Jewish men who founded the union represented seven local unions from East Coast cities with heavy Jewish immigrant populations. This all-male convention was made up exclusively of cloak makers and one skirt maker, highly skilled Old World tailors who had been trying to organize in a well-established industry for a couple of decades. White goods workers, including skilled corset makers, were not invited to the first meeting. Nor were they or the largely young immigrant Jewish workers in the newly developing shirtwaist industry recruited for the union in the early years of its existence. But these women workers still tried to organize.

The shirtwaist was a woman's garment with a mannish touch: a buttoned front. Charles Dana Gibson, an illustrious illustrator of the time, popularized this daring design by featuring his handsome Gibson girl wearing a shirtwaist.

The introduction of the shirtwaist lent itself to a system of inside contracting where the work done by women was moved into factories and workshops, still under the control of a contractor but not within the household. As a result, women workers faced different kinds of control, regulation, and, ultimately, sexual harassment. However, the new system also provided larger work sites where numbers of women could gather together to talk about their grievances, among other things. Thus the possibility for unionizing increased. A handful of these women workers, goaded on by the intolerable sweatshop conditions in which they toiled, joined the shirtwaist makers' Local 25 of the International Ladies Garment Workers Union.

The struggling local had few members, fewer finances, and virtually no bargaining power until the historic UPRISING OF THE 20,000 in 1909. This was partly due to the men's insistence that only "skilled" workers could effectively organize, partly to the sex-segregated nature of the industry, which kept women in relatively less skilled jobs, and partly to the rapid turnover of women garment workers who moved from job to job in search of better wages. Nonetheless, small strikes and work protests by women pockmarked the first decade of the century. Most of them were quickly lost. Then came the 1909 uprising, itself preceded by a two-month strike at the soon-to-be-infamous Triangle Shirtwaist Company.

The uprising was more than a "strike." It was the revolt of a community of "greenhorn" teenagers against a common oppression. The uprising set off shock waves in multiple directions: in the labor movement, which discovered women could be warriors; in American society, which found out that young "girls"—immigrants, no less—out of the disputatious Jewish community could organize; in the suffragist movement, which saw in the plight of these women a good reason why women should have the right to vote; and among feminists, who recognized this massive upheaval as a protest against sexual harassment. This strike and subsequent ones in the apparel industry stemmed from long days, low wages, manipulations of pay, and the denial of work in the absence of sexual favors, distinctive aspects of the garment trades.

The uprising had its Joan of Arc, a wisp of a "girl" arising out of nowhere, or so it seemed to the men who ran the union. Her name was CLARA LEMLICH

[SHAVELSON]. She was not one of the scheduled speakers, although she had proved herself an outspoken activist and daring organizer in previous strikes. But she spoke the words that sparked the conflagration. The overflow meeting in the Great Hall at New York's Cooper Union, the site of Abraham Lincoln's historic speech on Union and Liberty, was to be addressed by Samuel Gompers, president of the American Federation of Labor; Benjamin Feigenbaum, later elected as a socialist to the New York State Assembly; Jacob Panken, later elected a judge; Bernard Weinstein, head of the United Hebrew Trades; Meyer London, a labor attorney and the first socialist to be elected to Congress from the Lower East Side; and Mary Dreier, a prominent progressive socialite who had been walking the picket line with the strikers and was head of the Women's Trade Union League.

When Jacob Panken was introduced, he was interrupted by a high-pitched voice from the audience. "I want to say a few words," she said. From the audience came a clamor of voices, "Get up on the platform." Chairman Feigenbaum sensed the mood of the moment. He ruled that since this girl was a striker and had been beaten up on the picket line, she should be heard. Panken acquiesced.

In what one press report called a "philippic in Yiddish," Clara Lemlich concluded, "I offer that a general strike be declared now." Although not everyone in the audience was conversant in Yiddish—there were many Italian immigrant workers in the garment industry—they all understood.

Feigenbaum reached into the Jewish past to endow the moment with a touch of tradition. He called upon all those present to raise their hand and to "take the old Jewish oath. If I turn traitor to the cause I now pledge, may this hand wither from the arm I now raise."

The strike, directed against employer tyranny in the sweatshop, served many purposes, one of which was to draw the attention of suffragists to the plight of working women. Up to that time, those at the forefront of the fight for women's right to vote came almost exclusively from the economic and educated elite in the United States. To these women, the conditions of the shirtwaist makers were evidence of what happens when women are denied a voice in the governance of their communities and country. The active resistance to economic exploitation of these young Jewish women indicated that they should, and could, add new legions to the ranks of the suffragists. Indeed, Jewish immigrants subsequently became outspoken supporters of suffrage, helping to pass the New York State law in 1917. As a consequence of the uprising, the crusades for the rights of working people as workers and of women as women and as citizens were coming together.

The lasting meaning of the uprising was summarized by Samuel Gompers at the American Federation of Labor convention after the shirtwaist strike. It "brought to the consciousness of the nation," he declaimed, "a recognition of certain features looming up on its social development. These are the extent to which women are taking up with industrial life, their consequent tendency to stand together in the struggle to protect their common interests as wage-earners, the readiness of people in all classes to approve of trade-union methods on behalf of working women, and the capacity of women as strikers to suffer, to do, and to dare in support of their rights."

Inspiring as the uprising was, its immediate consequence in terms of working conditions was limited. This was especially true in the case of the Triangle Shirtwaist Company, whose brutal mistreatment of its employees was the original cause célèbre that set off the uprising and which remained unorganized. The Jewish employers of Triangle had been cited several times for violation of the city's fire safety code; the company paid the fine and then went about doing its business as usual.

On March 25, 1911, a fire broke out in the Triangle factory. It claimed 146 lives, mainly Jewish women. These victims became the martyred dead in a cause that, in time, revolutionized labor conditions and labor relations in America. It led to more effective fire and safety regulations in New York State, and it inspired women like ROSE SCHNEIDERMAN of the Women's Trade Union League to argue forcefully that legislation was less important than organization.

The large numbers of women garment workers in the ILGWU shaped its labor philosophy, despite the conspicuous absence of women among the union's top leadership. The ILGWU looked upon the union not only as a means to protect and promote the immediate interests of garment workers but also as part of a greater international movement to convert a dog-eat-dog economic system into a global cooperative commonwealth. Its leaders viewed the class struggle as a classroom where working men and women would learn about the whys and hows of improving their personal lives and remolding the social order. For members to pay dues was vital, but it was equally important for them to pay attention to their own development and to their role in the reshaping of

FANNIA COHN, *in her position as the executive secretary of the ILGWU's education department,*
created one of the most remarkable worker education programs in America.
Which is what you would expect from someone who can come up with a slogan like
"Stick to Your Union Bunch or You'll get Skinned!"
[Fannia Cohn Papers, New York Public Library]

society. Through education, working people would become their own messiah.

Women, especially activists in Local 25, championed this mission. In 1916, spurred by Local 25, the union convention voted to establish an education department to be headed by Juliet S. Poyntz, a former history teacher at Barnard College. To supplement the teaching skills of this outsider, the union chose FANNIA COHN, for many years the only woman on the union's general executive board, to apply her organizing skills as an insider to enroll members en masse in this novel grass-roots educational program. When Poyntz

Picket lines were often a way of life for ILGWU activists.
The demonstration shown here is against the W.H. Woodard Company in Los Angeles.
ROSE PESOTTA *is in the front of the photo on the far left.* [Rose Pesotta Papers, New York Public Library]

The ILGWU's enormously successful review Pins and Needles *ran for 1,108 performances in 1937 to consistently enthusiastic audiences who appreciated its humor, its political message, and its sharp social commentary. One "special" fan of the review was President Franklin Roosevelt. He is shown here with cast members, and (far left) David Dubinsky, the president of the union. [Kheel Center, Cornell University]*

resigned in 1918 under pressure from the general executive board, Cohn, named as executive secretary of the education department, carried on under a male education director, and she generated one of the most remarkable worker education programs in America.

Under Cohn's guidance, the ILGWU instituted a Workers University in New York City's Washington Irving High School where union members attended lectures by such distinguished college professors as Charles Beard, Harry Carmen, and Paul Brissenden. The U.S. Bureau of Labor Statistics noted in a 1920 report that "the first systematic scheme of education undertaken by organized [labor] in the United States was put in practice by the ILGWU." It further reported that "up to the spring of 1919 eight hundred [members] had either completed one or more courses or were engaged in the study of various subjects." Cohn greatly expanded the union's educational offerings, setting up programs in Cleveland, Boston, and Philadelphia.

While the university was the jewel in the diadem of the union's educational work, there were, in addition, eight Unity Centers that offered basic courses in literacy. Union leaders were trained in public speaking and parliamentary procedure. There were also classes in health—how to stay well. As the union grew, many of these activities proliferated. Members took classes on college campuses during the summer, and there was a formal Officers Training Institute, as well as intensive pretraining for citizenship and extensive education in health care.

Many of these, which became models for the entire American labor movement, derived from the early initiatives of Fannia Cohn. Women in Local 25, where the membership was more than 75 percent female in 1919, wanted the union to perform a social role that would create community and comradeship as well as loyalty to the union. So, for example, the ILGWU created vacation houses and developed a pioneer medical institution—the ILGWU Health

Center. It was a unique and influential conception of unionization.

By 1919, drawing on their confidence gained from classes and discussion groups, women in Local 25 began to question why they had not a single woman officer. The demand for union democracy took hold. But soon women's issues were taken over by male insurgents, many of them Communist Party organizers. Trusted women leaders like Fannia Cohn and PAULINE NEWMAN were caught in the middle between a battle of the "lefts and rights." The political infighting seriously weakened the union; women declined as members from 75 percent to a mere 39 percent by 1924, and male union leaders were reluctant to start new organizing drives to unionize women.

In the 1930s, rejuvenated by the New Deal's support of labor organizing, women once again came to dominate the membership of the ILGWU. And once again the issue of women's leadership arose. ROSE PESOTTA was the only woman on the union's executive board. When Miriam Speishandler of Local 22 was

Evelyn Dubrow served as the ILGWU legislative voice in the halls of Congress for almost half a century. She is shown here with President Lyndon Baines Johnson (and old friend from when he was a senator) and Lady Bird Johnson. "After signing the education bill," recalls Dubrow, "LBJ pulled me up from my seat and said, 'This little lady is responsible for this bill.' I don't think that was entirely true, but it sure was nice to hear." [UNITE magazine]

nominated as a delegate to the national convention, she took the opportunity to ask ILGWU president David Dubinsky why there were not more women on the executive board of a union that was 85 percent female. Pesotta's visibility in California led to her election in 1934 as a vice president of the ILGWU, serving on the general executive board. Pesotta was conflicted about her ten years of service in that position. Sexism and a loss of personal independence continually troubled her, until she finally resigned from the position in 1942.

The heady days of the 1930s also led to such unusual innovations as the musical revue *Pins and Needles*. Written by Harold Rome, the successful musical ran for an impressive 1,108 performances in 1937 to consistently enthusiastic audiences who appreciated its humor, its political message, and its sharp social commentary. The show's cast were all union members who effectively propagandized the trade union movement through song and dance.

More recently, as the ILGWU's membership has shifted from Jewish and Italian women to Latino, African-American, and Asian women, one Jewish woman has served as the union's legislative voice in the halls of Congress for almost half a century. Unlike the other Jewish women of prominence in the union, Evelyn Dubrow was not an immigrant. She grew up in New Jersey and was educated at the New York University School of Journalism. When American labor, through the Congress of Industrial Organizations, began to reach into mass manufacture in the 1930s, Dubrow served as education director for the New Jersey Textile Workers of America. As a writer, she worked as secretary of the New Jersey Newspaper Guild from 1943 to 1946.

Subsequently she became national director of organization of the Americans for Democratic Action and a founder of the Consumer Federation of America. By her performance on the Hill, Dubrow has won recognition and admiration from those who know how the wheels of government run. In 1982 the *Washington Business Review* named her as one of D.C.'s top ten lobbyists, and in 1994 *Washingtonian Magazine* listed her as one of America's top 100 women.

Although Evelyn Dubrow is distinguished for her political work, she was exceptional among the Jewish women in the union only in her official assignment to that mission. All of the women leaders mentioned were intensely political, as were many of the rank and file. For them it was never enough to have a union to ease and enrich the lives of those in the apparel industry. They dreamed of and worked for a movement that would someday transform the world into a place where the ideals of equality and justice for all would be a reality.

BIBLIOGRAPHY

Glenn, Susan A. *Daughters of the Shtetl: Life and Labor in the Immigrant Generation* (1990); Howe, Irving. *World of Our Fathers: The Journey of East European Jews to America and the Life They Found and Made* (1976); ILGWU. *Pauline Newman* (1986); Kessler-Harris, Alice. "Organizing the Unorganizable: Three Jewish Women and Their Union." *Labor History* 17 (Winter 1976): 5–23, and "Rose Schneiderman and the Limits of Women's Trade Unionism." In *Labor Leaders in America*, edited by Melvyn Dubofsky and Warren Van Tine (1987); Leeder, Elaine. *The Gentle General: Rose Pesotta, Anarchist and Labor Organizer* (1993); Levine, Louis. *The Women's Garment Workers* (1924); Orleck, Annelise. *Common Sense and a Little Fire: Women and Working-Class Politics in the United States, 1900–1965* (1995); Pesotta, Rose. *Bread upon the Waters* (1945); Seidman, Joel. *The Needle Trades* (1942); Stein, Leon. *Out of the Sweat Shop* (1977), and *The Triangle Fire* (1962); Stolberg, Benjamin. *Tailor's Progress* (1944); Tyler, Gus. *Look for the Union Label* (1995).

THE EDITORS

ISAACS, EDITH SOMBORN (1884–1978)

Edith Somborn Isaacs was a volunteer in New York City's political, philanthropic, and cultural life.

She was born in New York City on June 18, 1884. After graduating from Barnard College, in 1910 she married Stanley M. Isaacs, with whom she had two children, Myron (b. 1911) and Helen (nicknamed Casey, b. 1913). When Stanley Isaacs ran for office (he served as Manhattan borough president from 1938 through 1941, and later as Republican minority leader on the City Council), Edith Isaacs ran his campaigns. She described her work as writing clever jingles for him, "corralling and instructing volunteers, drafting letters to constituents, working with experts on newspaper articles and advertising, and after the election, writing letters of thanks to all who helped."

Barnard College produced one of her plays, and in 1954 she chaired the college's annual alumnae campaign. She was the author of *Love Affair with a City: The Story of Stanley M. Isaacs* (1967). An active member of the Women's City Club of New York, she served on its board for thirty years and as a president. She was also a board member of the New York Service for the Handicapped, the Barnard Committee on Development, and the Phi Beta Kappa Alumnae

Campaign manager for and biographer of her politician husband, Edith Isaacs was also extremely active in community activities, serving on the board of the Women's City Club of New York for thirty years. [New York Public Library]

Association, and a trustee of the Bank Street College of Education.

Edith Somborn Isaacs died on May 7, 1978.

BIBLIOGRAPHY

Herrick, Casey Isaacs. Interview with author; Isaacs, Edith S. *Love Affair with a City: The Story of Stanley M. Isaacs* (1967); *NYTimes, passim,* 1944–1978.

ELISABETH ISRAELS PERRY

ITTLESON, BLANCHE FRANK
(1875–1975)

Blanche Frank Ittleson was a philanthropist and a pioneer in social work intervention for retarded and mentally and emotionally disturbed children.

She was born September 27, 1875, into the third generation of a prominent German Jewish family in St. Louis. She was the oldest of four siblings, all brothers. After completing high school, she trained as a kindergarten teacher. In 1898, she married Henry J. Ittleson. They had two sons, Henry, Jr., and Lee, who was retarded. Moved by Lee's needs, Ittleson continued her interest in child development and studied social work at Washington University's School of Social Economics. The Ittleson family moved to New York City in 1915, where Henry Ittleson founded Credit and Investment Company, the first time-payment company in the United States. (It is now the CIT Financial Corporation, a broadly diversified financial company.)

To meet the needs of "maladjusted" women in the city, Ittleson organized the Vocational Adjustment Bureau for Girls in 1919. This introduced a new program in social work administration and rehabilitation. The bureau tested, treated, and trained emotionally disturbed and retarded girls. As well as obtaining employment for them, it provided a sheltered workshop where the young women could work while they were being treated and vocationally trained. The organization represented a new concept in specialized and integrated care for "maladjusted" girls. The bureau continued to run until 1950, when its functions were absorbed into other agencies.

In 1932, Ittleson and her husband used their wealth to found the Ittleson Family Foundation (now the Ittleson Foundation) as a general philanthropic organization. With the death of Henry Ittleson in 1948, Henry Ittleson, Jr., assumed control of CIT Financial Corporation, and Blanche Ittleson redirected the foundation to focus on the fields of health, welfare, and public education for mental health, with special emphasis on children. In 1953, she funded and organized the Henry Ittleson Center for Child Research in New York for the modern care of emotionally disturbed children. The center, which still operates, provides therapy and schooling for children with psychotic disorders or autism and for victims of abuse. Ittleson also endowed the Blanche F. Ittleson Chair of Child Psychiatry at the Washington University School of Medicine in 1955, the first endowed chair in child psychiatry in the United States.

Later in life, Ittleson continued to be active in the fields of social work, mental health, and philanthropy. She was director and officer of the National Association for Mental Health, a board member for the Board of Jewish Guardians, an honorary president of the U.S. Committee for the World Federation of Mental Health, and a trustee for the Federation of Jewish Philanthropies. She was the recipient of many awards and honors. In 1962, for example, the Social Work Recruiting Committee for Greater New York established the Blanche F. Ittleson Award for outstanding community service. True to her legacy, the Ittleson Foundation remains active today in promoting intercultural relations, and in supporting and developing innovative programs that aid the mental, medical, and social well-being of disadvantaged women and children.

Blanche Frank Ittleson remained active and vital well into her nineties. She died on August 16, 1975, six weeks short of her hundredth birthday.

BIBLIOGRAPHY

AJYB 77:595; Ittleson, Anthony [head of Ittleson Foundation]. Interview with author, May 1996; Ittleson, Blanche Frank. Archives. Ittleson Foundation, NYC; Obituary. *NYTimes*, August 17, 1975, 45:1.

SETH ALOE COHEN

J

JACKSON, LAURA RIDING
see **RIDING, LAURA**

JACOBI, LOTTE (1896–1990)

In 1935, Lotte Jacobi rejected the Nazis' offer to grant her honorary Aryan status and fled first to London and then to the United States, where she became one of America's foremost portrait photographers.

Born Johanna Alexandre Jacobi on August 17, 1896, in Thorn, West Prussia, Germany, to Maria and Sigismund Jacobi, she was called Lotte by her family and thereafter by all others. Jacobi began taking pictures as a young child, using a pinhole camera that her father constructed for her as a birthday present. The oldest of three children (her sister was also a photographer; her brother died following an accident at age twenty), she grew up in a family of photographers. Her great-grandfather Samuel Jacobi learned his craft in 1839 from Louis Daguerre, the inventor of modern photography. Samuel Jacobi founded a studio in West Prussia that was carried on by his son Alexander; his grandson Sigismund, who moved the studio to Berlin; and in 1927 by his great-granddaughter Lotte. Jacobi studied cinematography at the University of Munich and photography at the Bavarian State Academy of Photography. Jacobi married Fritz Honig in 1916. They had a son, John, in 1917, and the couple sepa-

rated the same year. They were divorced in 1924. She tried her hand at acting and cinematography before returning to Berlin in 1927 to run her father's studio.

During the Weimar period, artists, political leaders, scientists, and authors moved in and out of the Jacobi studio to be photographed and to engage in stimulating conversation. The family was active in the leftist social and political movements of the time. Among her satisfied customers were high-ranking German officials. Unaware that she was Jewish, they praised her work as "good examples of Aryan photography." While some of these photographs from the 1930s remain (among them photographs of Lotte Lenya, Kurt Weill, Peter Lorre, and Kathe Kollwitz), many more negatives and photographic plates were left behind and lost when Jacobi and her son fled Nazi Germany in 1935, shortly after her father died. Her mother later joined them in New York.

While Jacobi's Jewish heritage as well as her moral and political stance determined the course of her immigration to America, she did not speak much about her past, and many of her friends did not even know that she was Jewish.

In 1940, Jacobi married Erich Reiss, a respected German book publisher who had survived the concentration camps and immigrated to the United States. They enjoyed a happy marriage until his death in 1951.

Jacobi opened a studio in New York and soon was photographing the artists, scientists, political leaders, and literary figures of the day. Among the people she photographed were Albert Einstein, who was a family friend, and prominent Americans such as Robert Frost, Eleanor Roosevelt, and Paul Robeson. She not only photographed the cultural elite, many of them European emigrés, but was one of them.

In 1955, Jacobi moved to rural Deering, New Hampshire, with her son and his wife, Beatrice Trum Hunter. There, with John's help in 1960, she rebuilt a cabin in the woods, adding on a studio and room to display the work of other photographers. She continued to have many visitors and was a mentor to young photographers.

Her photographs are notable for their intimacy and for the personal qualities that she reveals in the faces of her subjects. Jacobi intended the photograph to reveal the personality of the subject, not of the photographer. While capturing the right angle and light, she engaged her subjects in topics that interested them until they felt at ease and forgot about the camera. While she enjoyed taking pictures of the great men and women of her time, she was not awed by them ("Don't they get dressed in the morning like the rest of us?"), and took equal pleasure in photographing children in city streets and, later, her neighbors in rural New Hampshire. She experimented with photogenics, a cameraless photography in which she exposed photosensitive paper to light to create abstract images.

In Deering, Jacobi returned to her lifelong political interests, both locally and nationally. She was a delegate to the Democratic National Convention in 1976, and when she forgot to register in time for the 1980 convention, she bartered a press pass from the *Concord Monitor*. At age eighty-four, she was celebrated as the oldest working press photographer at the convention.

Jacobi was awarded an honorary doctorate of fine arts by the University of New Hampshire in 1973, and later an honorary doctorate of humane letters from New England College.

Lotte Jacobi died on May 6, 1990, at age ninety-three in the Havenwood Nursing Home in New Hampshire. She bequeathed forty-seven thousand negatives to the Lotte Jacobi Archives established at the University of New Hampshire, her record of mid-twentieth-century history revealed in the faces of the artists, world leaders, intelligentsia, and ordinary people of America and Europe.

BIBLIOGRAPHY

Bacon, Richard M. "Lotte Jacobi." *Yankee* (August 1976): 60–91; Beck, Tom. "'I Remember Einstein' A Photographer's Recollections." *University of Maryland Magazine* 7:2 (1979): 6–11; Carlson, Martha. "Lotte Jacobi: Still Unpredictable at 89." *Business NH* (November 1985): 77–83; Hunter, Beatrice Trum. Interview with author, March 23, 1996; Karanikas, Alexander. "Lotte Jacobi's Place." *New Hampshire Profiles* 21, no. 4 (April 1972): 32–78; Savio, Joanne. "A Visit with Lotte Jacobi." *Women Artists News* 2, no. 3 (June 1986): 26–27; Slade, Marilyn Myers. "Lotte Jacobi." *New Hampshire Profiles* 36, no. 1 (January 1987): 38–45; Vesperi, Maria D. "Lotte Jacobi." *St. Petersburg Times*, June 24, 1990; Warnock, Phyllis K. "Home of the Month." *New Hampshire Profiles* 12, no. 10 (October 1963): 35–40; *WWIAJ* (1938).

MARION LEVENSON ROSS

JACOBS, FRANCES WISEBART (1843–1892)

There are sixteen stained-glass windows in the dome of Colorado's state capitol, each one illustrating a pioneer who was an important influence on Colorado's development. Among them is one woman, Frances Wisebart Jacobs.

Frances Wisebart Jacobs was born in Harrodsburg, Kentucky, on March 29, 1843, the first daughter and second child of Leon and Rosetta Wisebart, who had emigrated from Bavaria. During Jacobs's early childhood, the family moved to Cincinnati, Ohio, where Leon Wisebart worked as a tailor. Frances, with her six siblings, attended public schools. There she met Abraham Jacobs, a friend of her brother Benjamin.

Abraham Jacobs and Benjamin Wisebart traveled to the West in 1859 and settled in the area that would soon become the frontier town of Denver. Both men were active in the political and Jewish life of the community. Abraham Jacobs started a general store and operated a stagecoach that rode to Santa Fe, New Mexico. In 1863, he returned to Cincinnati, where he and Frances Wisebart were married on February 18. The couple had three children: Benjamin, who became a lawyer; Evelyn, later a schoolteacher; and another child who died young.

The Jacobses' first home was in Central City, Colorado, a thriving mining town about thirty miles west of Denver. In 1870, they moved to Denver, and Frances Jacobs's contributions as a volunteer social worker were first recorded.

In 1872, Jacobs organized and became president of the Hebrew Ladies' Relief Society. However, she soon realized that the problems of poverty, sickness, malnutrition, and unsanitary living conditions were not limited to the Jewish community. Accordingly, she broadened the scope of her work, and through her leadership, the Denver Ladies' Relief Society was established in 1874. Jacobs was vice president and acted as the group's public speaker.

In 1880, Jacobs was instrumental in setting up Denver's first free kindergarten for children of poor parents. In 1887, Reverend Myron Reed of Denver's First Congregational Church, Monsignor William O'Ryan of the Catholic archdiocese, and Frances Jacobs formed the Charity Organization Society, the forerunner of the community chest. Jacobs became known as Denver's "mother of charities." She was a magnetic and compelling speaker and addressed many national conferences of the Association of Charities and Corrections.

Because Colorado's dry air and sunshine were considered to be a cure for tuberculosis, hundreds of sufferers, among them many Jews, came to Denver. As part of her work, Jacobs regularly visited impoverished homes to bring food, coal, clothing, and soap. She was not afraid to touch an emaciated body, and she did not flinch at the sight of blood. She often stopped to give aid to someone who had fallen on the street from a hemorrhage. A woman of great compassion, Jacobs began intense work to establish a sanatorium.

On April 8, 1890, articles of incorporation of the Jewish Hospital Association of Colorado were filed. The association bought land east of the city, and on October 9, 1892, the cornerstone of the hospital was laid. Less than one month later, on November 3, Frances Wisebart Jacobs died in her Denver home. The sanatorium for which she had worked so diligently was named after her: the Frances Jacobs Hospital. In 1900, under the sponsorship of B'nai B'rith, it became the National Jewish Hospital.

BIBLIOGRAPHY

Anfenger, Milton L. *Birth of a Hospital* (1942); Breck, Allen D. *Centennial History of the Jews of Colorado 1859–1959* (1960); Hornbein, Marjorie. "Frances Jacobs: Denver's Mother of Charities." *Western States Jewish Historical Quarterly* (January 1983); *NAW*; Smiley, Jerome, ed. *History of Denver* (1901); Smith, Joseph Emerson. "Jewish Pioneers of Colorado." *Denver Jewish News*, September 15, 1939; Uchill, Ida. *Pioneers, Peddlers and Tsadikim: The Story of Jewish Colorado* (1957).

MARJORIE HORNBEIN

Called "mother of charities" by her neighbors, Frances Wisebart Jacobs's compassion extended to all of Denver. She set up the city's first free kindergarten and established a tuberculosis sanatorium which, after her death, was named in her honor. There are sixteen stained-glass windows in the dome of Colorado's state capitol, each illustrating an important pioneer in the state. The one window honoring a woman, Frances Jacobs, is reproduced above.

JACOBS, ROSE GELL (1888–1975)

A member of the original circle of women who established HADASSAH, the Women's Zionist Organization, in 1912, Rose Jacobs epitomized the spirit of American Zionist voluntarism. She gradually rose from a grass-roots organizer to the leadership of the organization, and came to play a central role in Zionist affairs worldwide.

Rose Gell Jacobs was born in September 1888 and, along with a brother and two sisters, was raised in New York City. She graduated from Columbia University and taught in the city's public schools before marrying Atlanta attorney Edward Jacobs.

While raising their two children, Joshua and Ruth, Rose Jacobs helped create Hadassah chapters in Georgia, Tennessee, and Washington, D.C. In the process she gained recognition as an articulate and effective Zionist speaker. She was named editor of the national *Hadassah News Bulletin* in 1920, vice president of Hadassah shortly afterward, and acting president of the organization from 1920 to 1923, while Hadassah's president and founder, HENRIETTA SZOLD, was in Palestine. Later Jacobs served two terms as president, from 1930 to 1932 and from 1934 to 1937.

During Jacobs's second term, the Hadassah membership urged the organization to move away from its

Rose Gell Jacobs was a lifelong supporter of Zionist causes who contributed to the founding of HADASSAH *and a number of its chapters. She served two terms as president and convinced the organization to adopt the Youth Aliyah program, which helped young German Jews flee Nazi persecution and immigrate to Palestine. [Hadassah Archives]*

exclusive focus on medical projects in Palestine and take a more active role in assisting the Jews in Nazi Germany. Jacobs was dispatched to Palestine in 1935 to explore possible new directions for Hadassah activity there. She became enamored of the Youth Aliyah program, led by Szold, which facilitated the immigration of young German Jews to the Holy Land. Hadassah soon adopted Youth Aliyah, a decision that proved both a boon for fund-raising and a source of inspiration for Hadassah activists during the Nazi era. Brushing aside her colleagues' fears for her safety, Jacobs traveled to Nazi Germany in the summer of 1936 to examine the plight of German Jewry firsthand and solidify Hadassah's relationship with the Youth Aliyah program.

An active participant in international Zionist affairs, Jacobs was named to the Jewish Agency Executive in 1937. Under her leadership, Hadassah opposed the British Peel Commission's 1937 Palestine partition plan, protesting the small size of the territory allotted to the proposed Jewish state. Jacobs was the only woman delegate to the St. James Conference in 1939, at which British, Arab, and Zionist leaders sought, unsuccessfully, to resolve the Palestine conflict.

Maintaining a prominent role in Hadassah affairs even after her terms as president, Jacobs was responsible for initiating the establishment of the Hadassah Hospital in 1939 on Mount Scopus, in Jerusalem. In 1940, she organized the Hadassah Emergency Committee in Palestine, which supervised the group's Palestine affairs during the war years.

Jacobs, like many of her colleagues in the Hadassah leadership, was keenly interested in the subject of Arab-Jewish relations in Palestine. In the wake of Palestinian-Arab rioting and British restrictions on Jewish immigration in the late 1930s, Hadassah established the Committee for the Study of Arab-Jewish Relations, with Jacobs as its chair. It marked the first time that an American Zionist organization had taken an official interest in the problem of Arab-Jewish relations in Palestine. The committee, which operated until 1943, held private discussions on the subject and met with American experts on the Middle East and Zionist leaders from Palestine to discuss ways to alleviate Arab-Jewish tension.

After World War II, Jacobs assumed a senior role in the ESCO Foundation, which raised funds for industrial development in Palestine (later Israel).

Rose Gell Jacobs died in New York City on August 14, 1975.

BIBLIOGRAPHY

AJYB 77:595; *BEDAJ*; *EJ*; Jacobs, Rose G. "The Beginnings of Hadassah." In *Early History of Zionism in America*, edited by Isidore S. Meyer (1958), and Papers. Hadassah Archives, NYC; Miller, Donald H. "A History of Hadassah, 1912–1935." Ph.D. diss., New York University (1968); Obituary. *NYTimes*, August 16, 1975, 22:5; *UJE*; *WWIAJ* (1938).

RAFAEL MEDOFF

JACOBSON, ANNA (1888–1972)

As a member of the faculty in the German department at HUNTER COLLEGE, Anna Jacobson fought to preserve the study of German language and literature during the 1930s and 1940s, when many felt that it was inappropriate for American students to study the language of the Nazis. During her tenure as chair of the German department from 1947 to her retirement in 1956, she worked to present the richness of German thought and writing to Hunter students and to the American public.

Anna Jacobson was born on January 10, 1888, in Lüneburg, Germany, to Arnold and Clara (Heinemann) Jacobson. She was a cousin of the philosopher Fritz Heinemann. She received diplomas from the University of Nancy in 1908 and a Ph.D. from the University of Bonn in 1917.

She came to the United States in 1922, and joined the faculty of the German department at Hunter College as instructor in 1924. Her publications included books and articles on Hermann Hesse, Charles Kingsley, Walt Whitman, Franz Werfel, Thomas Mann, Heinrich Heine, and Richard Wagner in both German and English. By 1941, she was a respected scholar and an expert on Thomas Mann.

Jacobson earned the rank of assistant professor in 1927, associate professor in 1934, and full professor in 1950. She was active in the Modern Language Association, served as president of the Hunter College chapter of the American Association of University Professors, from 1936 to 1938, and president of the New York City chapter of the American Association of Teachers of German, from 1949 to 1951.

In 1938, Jacobson found herself caught in the controversy over whether Hunter College—an institution with a student body of predominantly Jewish women—should continue to teach what critics increasingly referred to as the "language of Hitler." The college administration, responding to anti-German sentiment, threatened several times to dissolve the department, and in the fall of 1941 assigned an instructor in Hebrew to the department. Jacobson, who served as acting chair during 1941 and 1942, pressed her colleagues to defend the importance of German literature and culture and its distinction from the Nazi regime. To this end, she was active with the National Conference of Christians and Jews beginning in 1940, and led her colleagues and students at Hunter to organize fund-raising events to aid refugees from Germany.

Jacobson worked to integrate the study of German literature into new humanities offerings in the college curriculum at Hunter, including a course on world literature that began in the fall of 1943. She lectured widely to nonacademic audiences ranging from women's clubs to the listeners of Voice of America radio broadcasts. She organized many important events in celebration of German authors at Hunter College, including four lectures by Thomas Mann

during the 1940s, a commemorative concert for Heinrich Heine in 1947, and a Goethe exhibit in 1949.

Although Anna Jacobson had become an American citizen by 1937, after her retirement in 1956 she lived for many years in Switzerland, where she died on June 26, 1972.

SELECTED WORKS BY ANNA JACOBSON

Hermann Hesse: Der Novalis, Der Zwerg, editor (1948); *Kingsley's Beziehungen zu Deutschland* (1917); *Nachklange Richard Wagners im Roman* (1932).

BIBLIOGRAPHY

Jacobson, Anna. Archives, and Minutes of departmental meetings, 1914–1962. Department of German, Hunter College, NYC; *WWIAJ* (1928, 1938).

JANET WELLS GREENE

JACOBSON, JANIE (c. 1860–1915)

Combining her Jewish background with her skill and penchant for writing, Janie Jacobson succeeded as a biblical playwright. The children's plays she authored were performed nationally. Among them were *For Liberty* (1903), a play about Jewish patriotism for the Jewish holiday of Hanukkah; *Joseph and His Brethren* (1905), a play based on scripture in four acts; *Ruth, the Moabitess* (1910), a scriptural play in three acts; and *Esther* (1912), a scriptural play in five acts. In addition to being an accomplished writer, she was a talented musician.

Janie Jacobson was born in London, England, in about 1860, and lived there for thirty years. She was the niece of former mayor Nathan Barnert of Paterson, New Jersey. After she and her husband, Selly Jacobson, settled in New York City, she became a dynamic member of the growing Jewish community there. Jacobson participated actively as a Jewish settlement worker, founded the Bible School of Temple Beth El in New York, and served as secretary of the NATIONAL COUNCIL OF JEWISH WOMEN of New York City.

While Jacobson's Jewish social activism was fairly representative of educated Jewish women in the United States during the early twentieth century, her literary career was unique for that period. She arrived in this country during the first wave of immigration from Eastern Europe, but as a cultured person from England whose native tongue accommodated her relatively quick adaptation to American society, she possessed great advantages over her contemporaneous immigrants. Because little is known of her Jewish orientation, one can only assume from her plays that she was familiar with and interested in Jewish religious culture. Janie Jacobson made her mark as one of the few Jewish women in America at that time who were both knowledgeable in Judaic subjects and successful at wielding the pen creatively in those realms.

Janie Jacobson died in New York on July 2, 1915. She was survived by her husband and sister.

SELECTED WORKS BY JANIE JACOBSON

Esther (1912); *Joseph and His Brethren* (1905); *For Liberty* (1903); *Ruth, the Moabitess* (1910).

BIBLIOGRAPHY

AJYB 18 (1916–1917): 108; Bzowski, Frances Diodato. *American Women Playwrights, 1900–1930* (1992); Obituary. *NYTimes*, July 3, 1915, 7:6.

TAMAR KAPLAN

JAFFE, JEAN (1900–1958)

From the 1920s until her death, Jean Jaffe distinguished herself as one of the leading journalists in the Yiddish press. Jaffe roamed the globe as a reporter—the very best in her field according to some colleagues. A lifelong Labor Zionist, Jaffe spent several lengthy periods in Palestine and Israel.

Born on April 20, 1900, in a Lithuanian shtetl (sources differ on the exact place), Jean Jaffe immigrated to New York City with her parents in 1910. Along with six brothers and sisters, Jaffe grew up on Henry Street, in the heart of the Lower East Side. She attended both public school and a Labor Zionist *natsyonaler arbeter farband* [national workers organization] school, where she mastered Yiddish and Hebrew. She later studied at HUNTER COLLEGE and Columbia University. Jaffe embarked on a literary career writing short stories in Hebrew but soon thereafter took up Yiddish as her primary medium. In 1916, Jaffe began writing for the daily *Der Yidishes Tageblat*, where she quickly gained popularity as a journalist. She also contributed to several other newspapers, including *Der Amerikaner, Di Fraye Arbeter Shtime* [The free voice of labor] (an anarchist weekly regarded for its high literary standards), and the satirical weekly *Der Groyser Kundes* [The big stick]. In 1920, Jaffe joined the staff of the liberal daily *Der Tog* [The day] (after 1928, *Der Tog-Morgn Zhurnal*), where she remained employed until her death. Throughout her career, Jaffe's work appeared in Canadian, South American, Israeli, and (until World War II) Polish Yiddish publications. Jaffe also published articles in English-language publications in New York, such as the *New York Herald Tribune*, and sat on the editorial board of *Pioneer Woman*, a Labor Zionist monthly to which she regularly contributed.

Jaffe's work encompassed a range of areas including art, music, theater, political affairs, and human interest stories. Primarily, though, Jaffe earned a reputation as an outstanding reporter blessed with a keen eye for a story and extraordinary empathy for her subjects. Known as a restless spirit and inveterate explorer, Jaffe traveled internationally as a correspondent for *Der Morgen Zhurnal*. She sent dispatches from Poland on the eve of World War II and from the displaced persons camps, where Jaffe was one of the first American reporters to arrive on the scene after the war. In the early 1950s, Jaffe accompanied Yemenite Jews on their journey to Israel, and in 1956, she covered the Hungarian uprising, interviewing refugees as they crossed into Austria.

Jaffe was a rare figure in the history of the Yiddish press. She achieved distinction in a field that claimed few women beyond the confines of the so-called women's pages (though Jaffe did contribute to *Der Morgen Zhurnal*'s women's section under the pseudonym Helen Blum). Perhaps more remarkable, Jaffe chose a journalistic career primarily in Yiddish at a time when most of her Jewish contemporaries in the United States sought a wider audience in English or did not know Yiddish at all.

Jean Jaffe died of a heart attack on November 20, 1958, while aboard a freighter en route from Hong Kong to India.

BIBLIOGRAPHY

AJYB 61 (1960): 417; Chaikin, Joseph. *Yidishe Bleter in Amerike* (1946); Glants, A. "Faktn un Perushim." *Der Morgen Zhurnal*, December 10, 1958; Glatshteyn, Yankev, Sh. Niger, and Hilel Rogof, eds. *75 Yor Yidishe Prese in Amerike* (1945); Howe, Irving. *The World of Our Fathers* (1976); "Khyene Yafe, Bavuste Shrayberin, Shtarbt Plutsim." *Der Morgen Zhurnal*, May 23, 1958; *Leksikon fun der Nayer Yidisher Literatur*, s.v. "Khyene Yofe"; Margoshes, S. "News and Views [English]." *Der Morgen Zhurnal*, December 6, 1958; Obituary. *NYTimes*, November 23, 1958; Raskin, R. "Di Tsaytungs-froy." *Der Morgen Zhurnal*, November 2, 1957; Rotbard, Dvoyre. "Jean Jaffe z"l [Yiddish]." *Pioneer Woman* (February 1959): 10; "Shrayberin Kh. Yafe Toyt Afn Veg fun Hong Kong keyn India." *Forverts*, November 23, 1958; Syrkin, Marie. "Jean Jaffe." *Pioneer Woman* (January 1959): 9; *WWIAJ* (1938).

TONY MICHELS

JAHODA, MARIE (b. 1907)

Marie Jahoda is an important figure in psychology in England as well as the United States. Her biography by Stuart Cook, himself a major figure in American social psychology, begins with the following words:

While most women who entered psychology before the gender enlightenment of recent years encountered major obstacles in their professional careers, few have faced less promising circumstances than did Marie Jahoda. She was born into a Jewish family in a country and at a time when anti-Semitic discrimination was widespread. Most of the copies of the book reporting her first major research were burned because its authors were Jewish. She lived through World War II under the Nazi aerial bombardment of London. (Cook 1990, p. 207)

Despite these circumstances, Cook noted, Jahoda built a distinguished scientific career. She authored or coauthored eight books and coedited five more. Jahoda received an award for distinguished contributions to the public interest from the American Psychological Association in 1979. The citation for the award read: "The inspiring model that Marie Jahoda has set for many—of socially concerned, empirically competent, responsible, and psychoanalytically enriched psychology brought to bear on the important issues of freedom, justice, and equality in the contemporary world, as they touch the lives of real people— continues to serve psychology and the public interest."

Jahoda received honorary awards from the British Psychological Society as well as the Commander of the British Empire medal, personally bestowed by Queen Elizabeth. She became internationally famous for her pioneering work on the psychological consequences of unemployment, the psychodynamics of racial and ethnic prejudice, and the psychology of positive mental health.

Jahoda was born on January 26, 1907, in Vienna, Austria. During her undergraduate and doctoral work at the University of Vienna, she worked with Karl and Charlotte Bühler (born Jewish, but baptized by her parents to protect her from German anti-Semitism), who had founded the Psychological Institute there. Jahoda was also secretly analyzed by one of Freud's students during this period and retained a lifelong interest in psychoanalysis. During this time she married Paul Lazarsfeld, a young instructor at the institute. Their daughter, Lotte Bailyn, born in 1930, is a professor of organizational psychology and management at the Massachusetts Institute of Technology.

After the end of World War II, Jahoda came to the United States—partly to be reunited with her daughter, who had spent the war years here. In the years between 1945 and 1958 (when she returned to England), Jahoda became one of the best-known social psychologists in the United States. She worked with the American Jewish Committee on efforts to reduce prejudice through persuasive communications and on the identification of a personality type, the authoritarian personality, that was predisposed to prejudice. Later, while a professor at New York University, she coauthored a widely used book on research methodology (*Research Methods in Social Relations*, with Morton Deutsch and Stuart W. Cook, 1951), which focused on the needs of the rapidly developing field of social psychology. Still later, during the McCarthy period, Jahoda investigated the psychological effects of the suppression of political opinion by loyalty oaths and employment blacklisting.

In 1953, only eight years after she had come to the United States, Marie Jahoda was elected the first woman president of the Society for the Psychological Study of Social Issues; in 1980 that organization awarded her its Kurt Lewin Memorial Award "for furthering in her work, as did Kurt Lewin, the development and integration of psychological research and social action."

BIBLIOGRAPHY

American Psychologist 35 (1980): 74–76; Cook, Stuart W. "Marie Jahoda." In *Women in Psychology: A Bio-Bibliographic Sourcebook*, edited by Agnes N. O'Connell and Nancy F. Russo (1990): 207–219; Stevens, Gwendolyn, and Sheldon Gardner. *The Women of Psychology*. Vol. 2 (1982).

RHODA K. UNGER

JASTROW, MARIE GRUNFELD (1898–1991)

Chronicler of two critically acclaimed books on immigrant life, Marie Grunfeld Jastrow was born on June 10, 1898, in the Prussian city of Danzig, present-day Gdansk, Poland. The elder of two daughters of Julius and Johanna (Deutsch) Grunfeld, she was educated in a German school, and lived in Serbia before moving to the United States with her family at age ten. They settled in the Yorkville section of Manhattan, which Jastrow recalled in a 1979 interview with the *New York Times*: "We enjoyed Yorkville when it was a melting pot for immigrants from all over Europe. It was a wonderful time. People were poor in money, but no one felt poor otherwise."

In 1921, she married Abraham Jastrow, an automobile salesman. They had two children, Dorothy and Robert, an astrophysicist, author, professor of earth sciences at Dartmouth College, and director of the Mount Wilson Institute. Robert Jastrow comments on the Jewish aspects of his parents' home: "We had an heirloom menorah, my maternal grandfather's tallith, and not much else. I did however attend Hebrew school and was a bar mitzvah."

Jastrow began writing when she was a young girl, but had always received rejection slips. She was eighty-two when her first book, *A Time to Remember: Growing Up in New York Before the Great War*, was published in 1979. It was followed in 1986 by a sequel, *Looking Back: The American Dream Through Immigrant Eyes, 1907–1918*.

A Time to Remember is a memoir of Jastrow's early days in New York. It tells of her father's arrival in America, from Austria, in the immigration wave of the 1900s. He was barely skilled and ignorant of the English language. With thirty dollars in his pocket, he came in search of the legendary gold that would provide for his wife and daughter left behind in Serbia. After a beginning that seemed directed to inevitable failure, he survived against impossible odds and sent for his family.

Jastrow potently describes the terrible ordeals of future Americans on the decrepit, less-than-seaworthy ships, and the family's fears of being turned back upon arrival at Ellis Island. She focuses on the bleakness of the strange new world and on the gap—so much more than geographical—between the Old Country and the New. Jastrow details the perils of the reunited family through portraits of the incredible efforts and teamwork required to survive in the new homeland. Too proud to ask for help, her father collapsed from hunger one day, but the American dream eventually prevailed and better fortune followed. Nonetheless, family conflicts surfaced as her father tried to maintain tradition in the face of her mother's enthusiasm for the new. Women's liberation surfaced when Papa pressed Mama to do more ironing in his laundry business. She put her foot down: "No, I will not iron another thing for you in the evening. I have found work in the bakery. For this I will get paid at least, and a thank you once in a while. From you what do I get? Nothing!"

One short chapter in *A Time to Remember* serves as an example of how Jastrow's Jewish voice is sublimated to the acculturation experience she chooses to relate. "A Mitzvah" tells the story of the good deed done by the landlord of the Hester Street tenement where her father roomed, when he assisted her father to gain employment.

Looking Back is a series of vignettes of some of the people and places Jastrow knew best in the turbulent years between the Panic of 1907 and the end of the Great War in 1918. This book, like *A Time to Remember*, is a loving tribute to Jastrow's parents and a nostalgic salute to the fortitude of countless Europeans who, like them, had forsaken their homelands and sailed to America—that mythic place where dreams could become realities.

Jastrow relates the importance of politics to the immigrants and tells of the families divided by sentiments concerning the war in Europe. Although Jastrow makes no claim to anything more than a personal documentary, *Looking Back* reads like engrossing fiction. The smallest accomplishments are pridefully depicted. The public school system was a precious gift, teachers a special race. The most telling feature of the book is the implied juxtaposition with Abraham Jastrow's mother's visit to Serbia—marking Abraham and Marie's fiftieth wedding anniversary. There the once successful family had been reduced to poverty, while in America the poor who had fled in desperation were enjoying the beginning of success.

Marie Jastrow died at age ninety-three on March 30, 1991, at her home in Tucson, Arizona.

SELECTED WORKS BY MARIE JASTROW
Looking Back: The American Dream Through Immigrant Eyes, 1907–1918 (1986); *A Time to Remember: Growing Up in New York Before the Great War* (1979).

BIBLIOGRAPHY
Jastrow, Robert. Telephone conversation with author, April 17, 1996; Obituary. *NYTimes*, April 7, 1991, 32; Rose, Peter I. "A Tribute to Latter Day Pioneers." *Christian Science Monitor*, June 2, 1986, 30; Seebohm, Carolyn. "Non-Fiction in Brief." *NYTimes Book Review*, July 29, 1979, 13.

HARRIET L. PARMET

JEWISH EDUCATION

Among the traditions that Jews brought to America, one may include the diligent study of the Torah and honor to those distinguished in its study. Torah study and its public recognition, however, were restricted to men and, obviously, to those among them who had the means and talent to devote themselves to it. Traditional Jewish communities neither wanted nor expected women to take part in intellectual life. There were occasional exceptions, such as talented daughters taught privately by learned fathers.

This sharp gender division began to be blunted with the coming of the Jewish Enlightenment, starting in Germany in the mid-eighteenth century and gradually moving eastward through Bohemia and Galicia to Poland and Russia. The new schools that were founded by the Jewish Enlightenment's advocates were sometimes for girls only, but in most cases

This photograph of the graduating class of Talmud Torah Tiferet Yisrael in Brooklyn, New York, was taken in 1925 (5685, as the reproduction indicates). [Peter H. Schweitzer]

for both sexes. The new curriculum not only included general subjects such as arithmetic, reading, writing, German, and music, but it also revised the Jewish curriculum. Bible study, the principles of the Jewish religion, and the correct use of Hebrew were emphasized at the expense of Talmud study. Religion, as such a new subject, was also inculcated usually by means of a catechism. The new education swept German Jewry, including in time the Orthodox, and came to America with German Jewish immigrants.

However, the Jewish immigrants from Eastern Europe who were the dominant immigrant group after the 1870s generally came from small towns and villages where the new educational movement was slow to reach. For them the one-room schoolhouse (heder) in the teacher's dwelling remained the basic form of education for boys. There were some part-time heders for girls taught by women, but in general, women's education beyond the rudiments of reading and piety was quite exceptional.

As with the other traditions that Jewish newcomers brought, American views and practices in education exerted their influence. For example, girls and boys attended public school together and received almost identical education there. Immigrant leaders

soon perceived that a requirement for perpetuating Judaism on American soil was Jewish education for girls equal to that for boys.

Jewish schools had been few and short-lived in colonial America, and were attended by girls as well as boys. Most teaching, it appears, was the work of private tutors. For several generations, the early Spanish and Portuguese Jewish immigrants had desired their children to learn these ancestral languages, to which the parents still felt attached. So far as is known, the Jewish curriculum for both sexes was the same, except that boys were prepared for the bar mitzvah while girls, at least in some places, learned needlework and embroidery and sometimes music. Where there were no Jewish schools, girls acquired Jewish educational rudiments from the surroundings of family and synagogue. Like the boys, they learned the elements of Hebrew reading and the prayer book, and Bible stories in English. Altogether, colonial American Jews aspired to transmit simple traditional Judaism to their sons and daughters, and they achieved this. Scholarship and deep piety were not considered, especially for girls.

The best-known Jewish educational enterprise of antebellum American Jews was the Hebrew Sunday School Society of Philadelphia. To a large extent,

Christian Sunday schools provided a model. It was founded in 1838 and long directed voluntarily by REBECCA GRATZ, the descendant of an old and wealthy Jewish family. As its name indicates, this school, which in time produced several branches, existed for transmitting basic Judaism on Sunday mornings to girls and boys, mainly from poor families.

Until the closing years of the nineteenth century, American Judaism was influenced by predominantly German immigrants of that century. Educational philosophy and practice were strongly influenced by German culture. Parents ardently desired that their offspring master German, the native tongue that continued in use for many decades. Girls and boys attended German American Jewish schools, where the German language held a central position. Since German Jews in America largely followed Reform Judaism and conceived of Judaism as a moral code, they dispensed with most of its ritual content, whose performance was largely a function of men. As a consequence, girls' education was not overshadowed by any special requirements for boys such as bar mitzvah. Instead, both sexes participated in an annual group confirmation rite. Although the teaching was often carried on in separate classrooms as was done in the public schools, Jewish education itself showed little difference between boys and girls. There were numerous women teachers, but it is not clear whether they taught only their own gender. On the other hand, young Jewish women, notwithstanding the equal education they had received with boys, were unequivocally expected to adopt the role of wife and mother. As was the case with the American middle classes to which the majority of German American Jews belonged, careers with the exception of teaching were frowned upon. Volunteer social and charitable work was commended.

Jewish education for girls during the peak generation of Eastern European immigration and its aftermath, from approximately 1890 to 1940, faced particular obstacles. Pupils in all the types of Jewish schools went eight or ten hours a week after some thirty hours in public school. If one reason for the long Jewish school hours was the desire to cover an ambitious curriculum, another potent reason was keeping off the teeming streets boys and girls who could not spend their time in crowded homes.

The burden of Eastern European Jewish tradition favored education for boys far more than for girls, and the mass of parents cared for their boys' Jewish education mainly in order to prepare them for their bar mitzvah or to recite basic prayers. This teaching was done primarily by private tutors and in the heder, and girls had no part in it. During the first decades of Eastern European immigration, perhaps until 1900, girls' Jewish education was almost disregarded, although a few girls from culturally elite immigrant families had private Hebrew tutors.

Modern Jewish education began at the turn of the twentieth century, when a new type of Jewish school appeared. The Talmud Torahs that had preceded the new schools were little more than several heders under one roof, usually without girls. The new Hebrew school, however, emphasized the study of the Hebrew language and the Bible, along with modern songs and religious practices described as "customs and ceremonies." Plays and pageants were prominent in the curriculum. The influence of cultural Zionism permeated these schools.

The new Hebrew schools spread throughout the United States, and girls attended them equally with boys. In numerous places, they were in the majority because many boys still went to a heder or an old-fashioned Talmud Torah. Girls did not come for bar mitzvah preparation, as boys, often unwillingly, did, and girls were often the more diligent pupils. A list of Talmud Torahs in the immigrant working-class neighborhood of Brownsville in Brooklyn shows all varieties of enrollment: a large majority of boys, or boys only, or a majority of girls. Most of the schools were for boys and girls, with boys in the majority. Yet, many schools, especially those conducted by Orthodox immigrant congregations, still made no provision for girls.

By about 1920, the Jewish education of girls was generally accepted, with women furnishing an increasing proportion of the modern Hebrew schools' teaching staff. The seminaries for training teachers for the Hebrew schools, three of them in New York City, had a substantial majority of female students. The rationale of girls' Jewish education was not simply the intellectual equality of the sexes or religion fused with ethnic loyalty. It also laid heavy emphasis on the likelihood that these young girls would one day be mothers and would need the knowledge and assurance to bring up their own children as Jews. Their responsibility as mothers would be even greater, because under the economic conditions of the time fathers had to work too hard and long to pay close attention to their children's schooling.

Beginning around 1910, several networks of Yiddish secular schools developed whose teaching emphasized the Yiddish language that was spoken in most of the pupils' homes. These schools' ideological underpinnings were Yiddish, as the language of the masses of the people, and a socialist philosophy; Labor Zionism was the philosophy in one school network. Girls studied equally with boys in all the Yiddish schools. In fact, they were probably a majority of the pupils, since some parents sought a more religious bar mitzvah–oriented school for their sons. By 1960, however, Yiddish had faded as the popular language and Yiddish secular schools were nearly extinct.

American Jews were strongly attached to the public schools, not only for their sons' and daughters' general education but also as the means of assuring their acceptance into American society. Private day schools were very few on account of public school loyalty, as well as the expense of maintaining a school without government support. With two known exceptions, both in Brooklyn, Jewish day schools were for boys only. During the 1930s, a day school for girls, Shulamith, was established in a spirit of Orthodoxy and modern Hebraism. Its curriculum did not differ in any basic respect from that of boys' day schools. The Center Academy of the Brooklyn Jewish Center was Zionist, emphasized Hebrew, was Conservative in religion, and was for boys and girls.

The Jewish educational constellation after World War II is quite different from what it had been two decades earlier. Social and economic changes underlay most of these changes. Talmud Torahs dwindled and disappeared as dense urban Jewish neighborhoods broke up and suburbs blossomed. The new afternoon school was the congregational school, three times weekly instead of the Talmud Torah's five. On the other hand, many Sunday schools broadened beyond one day weekly. There was a vast growth of day schools, especially in the cities, as Jews became prosperous enough to maintain them. Jewish secondary day schools became significant. The equalization of boys' and girls' Jewish education also found expression in the near universality of the bat mitzvah for girls at age twelve or thirteen, even among the modern Orthodox. The observance itself was varied, with the Conservatives marking it in synagogue services like a boy's bar mitzvah and the Orthodox conducting the event largely outside the synagogue.

Only in Orthodox day schools was girls' education an issue of sorts. The general trend of the past

By the mid-twentieth century, the education of girls and boys together in Hebrew schools was not an issue for much of American Judaism. The above photo is a class from the early 1950s in a Massachusetts synagogue.
[American Jewish Historical Society]

three decades has shown a movement among the Orthodox toward greater religious rigor that has included stricter separation between the sexes. Orthodox schools where boys and girls study together now establish separate classes, and many other schools are for boys or for girls only. The curricula for the sexes also differ. In ultra-Orthodox schools this is apparent from the exclusion of girls from Talmud study, the central subject in boys' curriculum. A large network of ultra-Orthodox girls' schools, called BAIS YA'ACOV, provides Jewish and general education from kindergarten through a teachers' seminary. Girls in Bais Ya'acov study Bible and manuals of Jewish law, emphasizing the strictest ritual conformity, particularly in matters such as kashrut and relations between the sexes. Premarital association between the sexes is frowned upon or prohibited. Girls from the Bais Ya'acov seminary are of marriageable age, and their families arrange matches for them, often with yeshivah students. The ultra-Orthodox schools prepare young women for their role not only as mothers but also as breadwinners, while their husbands devote themselves to Talmud study in a yeshivah.

Near the close of the twentieth century, Jewish education for women has long ceased to be an issue. The large majority of American Jews tacitly endorses equal education for both sexes, including vocational education for a career as a rabbi. Among the most Orthodox, women's education is likewise accepted, but there are basic differences between what boys and girls received in school.

BIBLIOGRAPHY

For the most comprehensive bibliography on this topic, see *A Bibliography of Jewish Education in the United States*, compiled and edited by Norman Drachler (1996).

Gartner, Lloyd P. *Jewish Education in the United States: A Documentary History* (1969); Goren, Arthur A. *New York Jews and the Quest for Community: The Kehillah Experiment 1908–1922* (1970): 86–133; *The Jewish Communal Register* (1917); Marcus, Jacob R. *The Colonial American Jew 1492–1776*. 3 vols. Vol. 2 (1970): 86–133; Moore, Deborah Dash. *At Home in America: Second Generation New York Jews* (1981).

LLOYD P. GARTNER

JEWISH FEMINISM

Challenging all varieties of American Judaism, feminism has been a powerful force for popular Jewish religious revival. Of America's four Jewish denominations, all but the Orthodox have accepted women as rabbis and cantors. In contrast to the past, girls are now welcomed into the Jewish community with impressive ceremonies that celebrate their birth, and they are being educated Jewishly at virtually the same rate as boys. Feminist scholarship has begun to recover the previously ignored experience of Jewish women and has offered new perspectives for the interpretation of classical Jewish texts. Although men still predominate in positions of power within the organized Jewish community, the presence of Jewish feminists in communal institutions ensures that issues of gender equality are discussed rather than suppressed.

The movement toward gender equality in the American Jewish community in the past generation was spurred on by a grass-roots movement of Jewish feminism. Well-educated and liberal in their political and cultural orientation, many Jewish women participated in what has been called the second wave of American feminism that began in the 1960s. Most did not link their feminism to their religious or ethnic identification. But some women, whose Jewishness was central to their self-definition, naturally applied their newly acquired feminist insights to their condition as American Jews. Looking at the all-male *bimah* [stage] in the synagogue, they experienced the feminist "click"—the epiphany that things could be different—in a Jewish context. Two articles pioneered in feminist analysis of the status of Jewish women. In the fall of 1970, TRUDE WEISS-ROSMARIN criticized the liabilities of women in Jewish law in her "The Unfreedom of Jewish Women," which appeared in the *Jewish Spectator*, the journal she edited. Several months later, Rachel Adler, then an Orthodox Jew, published a blistering indictment of the status of women in Jewish tradition in *Davka*, a countercultural journal. Adler's piece was particularly influential for young women active in the Jewish counterculture of the time.

In the early 1970s, Jewish feminism moved beyond the small, private consciousness-raising discussion groups that characterized the American women's movement to become a public phenomenon. Calling themselves Ezrat Nashim, a small study group of young feminists associated with the New York *Havurah*, a countercultural fellowship designed to create an intimate community for study, prayer, and social action, took the issue of equality of women to the 1972 convention of the Conservative Rabbinical Assembly. The founding members of Ezrat Nashim represented the highly educated elite of, primarily, Conservative Jewish youth. (Several of them, such as Paula Hyman, Elizabeth Koltun, Arlene Agus, and Martha Ackelsberg have contributed to the development of Jewish feminist writing for more than two decades. Other founding members were Dina Rosenfeld, Maureen McCleod, Leora

Fishman, and Betty Braun. Joining Ezrat Nashim in its early activist years were Toby Reifman and feminist scholars Judith Hauptman and Judith Plaskow.)

In separate meetings with rabbis and their wives, the women of Ezrat Nashim issued a "Call for Change" that put forward the early agenda of Jewish feminism. That agenda stressed the "equal access" of women and men to public roles of status and honor within the Jewish community. It focused on eliminating the subordination of women in Judaism by equalizing their rights in marriage and divorce laws, counting them in the minyan [the quorum necessary for communal prayer], and enabling them to assume positions of leadership in the synagogue as rabbis and cantors. In recognition of the fact that the secondary status of women in Jewish law rested on their exemption from certain mitzvot [commandments], the statement called for women to be obligated to perform all mitzvot, as were men. Ezrat Nashim caught the eye of the New York press, which widely disseminated the demands of Jewish feminism.

Jewish feminism found a receptive audience. In 1973, secular and religious Jewish feminists, under the auspices of the North American Jewish Students' Network, convened a national conference in New York City that attracted more than five hundred participants. A similarly vibrant conference the following year led to the formation of a short-lived Jewish feminist organization. Although Jewish feminists did not succeed in establishing a comprehensive organization, they were confident that they spoke for large numbers of women (and some men) within the American Jewish community.

Feminists used a number of strategies to bring the issue of gender equality before the Jewish community. Feminist speakers presented their arguments from the pulpit in countless synagogues and participated in lively debates in Jewish community centers and local and national meetings of Jewish women's organizations. Jewish feminists also brought their message to a wider public through the written word. Activists from Ezrat Nashim and the North American Jewish Students' Network published a special issue of *Response* magazine, devoted to Jewish feminism, in 1973. With Elizabeth Koltun as editor, a revised and expanded version, entitled *The Jewish Woman: New Perspectives*, appeared in 1976. That year, LILITH, a Jewish feminist magazine, was established by Susan Weidman Schneider and Aviva Cantor; Susan Weidman Schneider has served as its editor since that time. *Lilith* has combined news of interest to Jewish women with articles bringing the latest Jewish feminist research in a popular form to a lay audience along with reviews of new publications.

Under the aegis of Ezrat Nashim, Toby Reifman, one of *Lilith*'s members, edited and distributed a pamphlet containing baby-naming ceremonies for girls. The very lack of formal Jewish feminist organizational structures allowed for grass-roots efforts across the country. In 1977, for example, IRENE FINE of San Diego, California, established the Woman's Institute for Continuing Jewish Education. Not only does it regularly bring speakers and artists to southern California, it has also published collections of Jewish women's interpretations of Jewish texts as well as women's rituals.

Through their publications and speaking engagements, Jewish feminists gained support. Their innovations—such as baby-naming ceremonies, feminist Passover seders, and ritual celebrations of *rosh hodesh* [the new month, traditionally deemed a woman's holiday] were introduced into communal settings, whether through informal gatherings in a home or in the synagogue. In a snowball process, participants in the celebration of new rituals spread them through word of mouth. Aimed at the community rather than the individual, new feminist celebrations designed to enhance women's religious roles were legitimated in settings that became egalitarian through the repeated performance of these new rituals. Indeed, one of the major accomplishments of Jewish feminism was the creation of communities that modeled egalitarianism for children and youth.

The concept of egalitarianism resonated with American Jews, who recognized that their own acceptance as citizens was rooted in Enlightenment views of the fundamental equality of all human beings. With growing acceptance of women in all the professions, the Reform Movement, which rejected the authority of halakah [Jewish law], acted on earlier resolutions that had found no obstacles to women serving as rabbis. Hebrew Union College, the seminary of the Reform Movement, ordained the first female rabbi in America, SALLY PRIESAND, in 1972, and graduated its first female cantor in 1975. The Reconstructionist Movement followed suit, ordaining Sandy Eisenberg Sasso as rabbi in 1974. Although the issue of women's ordination was fraught with conflict for the Conservative Movement, it, too, responded to some feminist demands. In 1973, the Committee on Jewish Law and Standards of the Conservative Rabbinical Assembly ruled that women could be counted in a minyan as long as the local rabbi consented. And the 1955 minority decision on *aliyot* for women was widely disseminated, leading to a rapid increase in the number of congregations willing to call women to the Torah.

The most striking achievement of Jewish feminism was the acceptance of women as rabbis and cantors in the Conservative Movement, then the largest denomination within American Judaism. Because the Conservative Movement considers halakah binding, but also acknowledges that Jewish law is responsive to changing social conditions and concepts, the decision to ordain women as rabbis and invest them as cantors had to be justified in halakic terms. The combined impact of American and Jewish feminism on Conservative congregations and their rabbis led to a decision by the movement in 1977 to establish a national commission to investigate the sentiment of Conservative Jews on the issue. Holding meetings throughout the country, the commission members heard the anguished testimony of women who felt ignored in public Jewish life, as well as statements of men offering their support. Although it took note of the arguments against ordination, in its report submitted early in 1979, the commission recommended the ordination of women.

The divisions within the Conservative Movement and among the faculty of the Jewish Theological Seminary, the educational institution of the movement responsible for the training of rabbis, led to the tabling of the issue, but it would not disappear. With strong support from the Rabbinical Assembly and ultimately from Chancellor Gerson Cohen, and after consideration of faculty position papers supporting and opposing women as rabbis, the faculty of the seminary voted in October 1983 to accept women into the rabbinical school as candidates for ordination. Amy Eilberg, who had completed most of the requirements for ordination as a student in the seminary's graduate school, became the first female Conservative rabbi in 1985. Women were welcomed into the Conservative cantorate in 1987. As of 1996, there were almost 400 women rabbis, including 78 female members of the Conservative Rabbinical Assembly, 73 female graduates of the Reconstructionist Rabbinical College (which has accepted women since its founding), and between 250 and 300 women in the Reform Central Conference of American Rabbis (they claim not to distinguish between female and male rabbis). The Academy for Judaism, a nonsectarian seminary located in New York City, has also ordained women rabbis.

Although the Conservative Movement was the center of Jewish feminist activism in the 1970s and 1980s, Jewish feminism has always been diverse in its constituency and its concerns. The case for Orthodox feminism was made most eloquently by BLU GREENBERG in her 1981 book *On Being a Jewish Feminist*. Small groups of courageous Orthodox women established women's *tefilla* [prayer] groups that respected all the halakic constraints on women's public prayers, and persisted in their activity in the face of rabbinic opposition. Despite the fact that most Orthodox spokesmen deny feminist claims of the secondary status of women within traditional Judaism and disavow feminist influence, Jewish feminism has had an impact on American Orthodoxy, however unacknowledged. Girls are now provided with a more comprehensive Jewish education in Orthodox schools than was ever the case in the past. In altered forms that conform to Jewish law, feminist rituals such as celebrations of the birth of a daughter and bat mitzvah rites have found their place within modern Orthodox communities. And Orthodox leaders have felt constrained to issue apologetic defenses of the "separate but equal" status of women in Judaism.

Judaism as a religious tradition has animated Jewish feminism. But secular or "cultural" Jews have also contributed to Jewish feminist ranks. Some feminist Jews rediscovered their Jewishness as they encountered anti-Semitism within the women's movement. Jewish women who participated in the 1975 United Nations Conference on Women were stunned by the prevalence of anti-Semitic statements, and were angered in the 1980s that some feminists articulated anti-Zionist statements that incorporated anti-Semitic assumptions and stereotypes. As LETTY COTTIN POGREBIN and the theologians Judith Plaskow and Susannah Heschel have pointed out, feminists often blamed Judaism for the "death of the goddess" and for the theological legitimation of patriarchy. More generally, feminists refused to acknowledge the validity of Jewish identity. Some feminists who were Jews responded to this erasure and critique of Jewishness by exploring the meaning of a Jewish secular identity. Particularly sensitive to "otherness," lesbians were active in combating anti-Semitism within the women's movement and in asserting the validity and cultural value of Jewishness. They have also articulated the importance of diversity within the Jewish community. *Nice Jewish Girls* (1982), edited by EVELYN BECK, became a classic statement of lesbian issues within the Jewish feminist movement and a powerful assertion of lesbian feminist identity.

Beginning in the 1980s, Jewish feminists raised issues that went beyond the acceptance of women into male-defined positions of visibility and power. The emergence of women as religious leaders and as equal participants in the non-Orthodox synagogue allowed women to see themselves in public Jewish ritual, but feminists were increasingly concerned that women's sensibility and experience be reflected in Jewish life.

They hoped that women would be allowed to reshape the rabbinate and the cantorate, rather than simply follow traditional male models. Most importantly, they sought to incorporate women's voices and insights into Jewish liturgy and into the interpretation of classical Jewish texts. Arguing that Jewish liturgy and culture should reflect the understanding of women as well as men, Jewish feminists called for a revision of the siddur, the prayer book, and the Passover Haggadah and for the creation of feminist midrash, interpretation of biblical and talmudic texts. Scholar-activists such as Judith Plaskow and Ellen Umansky challenged the male-dominated concepts of Jewish theology and God-language that drew primarily upon masculine imagery. The poet and Hebrew scholar Marcia Falk created blessings that supplant traditional liturgy with innovative forms that introduce feminist concepts: a subversion of hierarchy and naturalistic images of God gendered in Hebrew in the female.

The issue of God-language raised by feminists has, to one extent or another, influenced the prayer books and other ritual texts, particularly in the Reform and Reconstructionist movements. In 1975, the Reform Movement introduced some gender-inclusive language in English sections of its new prayer book, *Gates of Prayer* and published fully gender-sensitive versions for Sabbath and weekdays in 1992. The Reconstructionists also created a fully gender-sensitive siddur, *Kol Haneshama*, with the Sabbath edition published in 1994 and the weekday edition in 1996. Although the Conservative Movement has been reluctant to introduce feminist-inspired changes in liturgy, the revised version of its *Sim Shalom* prayer book offers the option of including the names of the matriarchs along with those of the patriarchs in a central section of the prayers. Its most recent (1982) version of the Passover Haggadah, the first to be edited by a woman, Rachel Anne Rabinowicz, includes several stories of women in its sidebar interpretations. All denominations, however, have refrained from altering the Hebrew liturgy, and reconceptualizing images of God in light of feminist critiques has made only modest inroads.

Much of the continuing impact of Jewish feminism stems from the informal "old girls" network that professionally successful Jewish feminists have created. The establishment in 1991 of the Jewish Feminist Center in Los Angeles was made possible by a gift from the Nathan Cummings Foundation at the direction of Rabbi Rachel Cowan, its Jewish life officer. The funds were donated to the regional office of the AMERICAN JEWISH CONGRESS, whose director was

Rabbi Laura Geller. Geller conveyed this financial support to Rabbi Sue Levi Elwell, who became the founding director of the center. The center became the headquarters for a range of adult education courses on Judaism from a feminist perspective. Its classes and spirituality workshops elicited an enthusiastic response. Its feminist seders, in particular, led by the composer and singer Debbie Friedman, drew large numbers of women seeking Jewish feminist spiritual expression.

Because it succeeded in acquiring accreditation for its courses from the Los Angeles Bureau of Jewish Education, which supervises the continuing professional education of teachers in Jewish schools, the Jewish Feminist Center was able to affect the Jewish education of children and youth. In 1994, Elwell was hired to serve as rabbinic director for Ma'ayan, the Jewish Women's Project in New York City, founded by the philanthropist Barbara Dobkin, who serves as its executive director. Like the Jewish Feminist Center, Ma'ayan, which declares its "commitment to an inclusive feminist vision," sponsors a range of educational and spiritual events for Jewish women that include "study, ritual and celebration, research, advocacy, community building, and *tzedakah*" (Ma'ayan 1996). Similarly, Jewish feminist scholars not only provide a feminist perspective in their courses but model a feminist Jewish identity for their students, and Jewish feminists who work in communal institutions promote feminist programming.

Despite the fact that Jewish feminism has greatly influenced the American Jewish community, it has not achieved all its goals. Women who remain under the jurisdiction of Jewish law are still victimized in divorce proceedings. Some Orthodox men use their privilege in Jewish divorce law to extort large sums from their wives or leave them *agunah* [deserted wives], unable to remarry according to Jewish law.

Although women are more visible and wield more power in the institutions of the Jewish community than a generation ago, they have not yet attained parity. Only a handful of the women ordained as rabbis have secured positions as senior rabbis in large and prestigious congregations. To some extent this fact reflects the choices of women rabbis themselves. As one woman rabbi put it, "Climbing up the ladder is not necessarily what we want" (*Lilith* 1990: 25). Those who have chosen to define their careers in nontraditional ways, avoiding positions in large and impersonal synagogues, have realized that they have also limited their influence within their denominations. They offer a different model of success. Yet, the "glass ceiling" that continues to exist in the corporate boardroom operates as well within the American Jewish community. Many prosperous congregations refrain from considering female candidates when they search for a rabbi.

The failure of women to reach the top is even more blatant in the secular organized Jewish community than in its religious denominations, perhaps because more power and money are at stake in this sphere. In 1972, at the General Assembly of the Council of Jewish Federations, the umbrella organization of Jewish communal life, JACQUELINE LEVINE, a vice president of the council, spoke passionately to the assembled delegates of the need to include women in the decision-making of the Jewish community: "We are asking . . . to be treated only as human beings, so that we may be . . . participants in the exciting challenge of creating a new and open and total Jewish community" (*Response* 1973: 65). Twenty years later she concluded sadly that "tokenism is and will continue to be the name of the game" (Fishman 219). Although there are more women board members of Jewish communal institutions than ever before, and some women have advanced into executive positions, men predominate in the top positions, especially in the largest communities.

Jewish feminism faces particular challenges in the contemporary American Jewish community. Many communal leaders consider feminist issues secondary to more pressing concerns, such as assimilation or communal unity. Often they present feminism as a danger to "Jewish continuity," the current buzzword for Jewish survival. Yet Jewish feminists persist in their activism, animated by the vision of a diverse and inclusive Jewish community, created and sustained by women and men sharing responsibility and power.

BIBLIOGRAPHY

There is a collection of Jewish feminist sources in the Jewish Women's Resource Center, located at the New York Section of the National Council of Jewish Women, NYC.

Beck, Evelyn Torton, ed. *Nice Jewish Girls: A Lesbian Anthology* (1984); Falk, Marcia. *The Book of Blessings: A Feminist-Jewish Reconstruction of Prayer* (1993); Fishman, Sylvia Barack. *A Breath of Life: Feminism in the American Jewish Community* (1993); Greenberg, Blu. *On Women and Judaism* (1979); Heschel, Susannah, ed. *On Being a Jewish Feminist* (1983); Hyman, Paula E. "Ezrat Nashim and the Emergence of a New Jewish Feminism." In *The Americanization of the Jews*, edited by Robert M. Seltzer and Norman J. Cohen (1995); Koltun, Elizabeth, ed. *The Jewish Woman: New Perspectives* (1976); Lerner, Anne Lapidus. "Who Hast Not Made Me a Man: The Movement for Equal Rights for Women in American Jewry." *AJYB* (1977): 3–38; *Lilith* (Fall 1990); Ma'ayan. Spring Program (1996); Plaskow, Judith.

Standing Again at Sinai (1990); *Response* (Summer 1973); Schneider, Susan Weidman. *Jewish and Female* (1984); Umansky, Ellen. "Creating a Jewish Feminist Theology." In *Weaving the Visions: New Patterns in Feminist Spirituality*, edited by Judith Plaskow and Carol P. Christ (1989), and "(Re)Imaging the Divine." *Response* 13, 1–2 (Fall–Winter 1982): 110–119; Wertheimer, Jack. *A People Divided: Judaism in Contemporary America* (1993).

PAULA E. HYMAN

JEWISH WOMAN, THE

The Jewish Woman, a quarterly magazine published under the auspices of the NATIONAL COUNCIL OF JEWISH WOMEN (NCJW) between 1921 and 1931, was created to give the world "its first organized record of Jewish womanhood's aspirations and successes." The distinctly Jewish feminist message that the magazine's editors strove for was evident on the cover of its first issue. It featured a Rosh Hashannah message that displayed the NJCW's motto and seal alongside twin pillars indicating the council's work in civics, philanthropy, religion, and education. Publication of *The Jewish Woman* also coincided with the council's objective of expanding its membership and influencing various social issues of its day.

The Jewish Woman was a precursor to the *Council Woman*, a magazine that NCJW published in the 1940s and 1950s, and also to its successor, the current *Council Journal*. During its eleven-year history, *The Jewish Woman* was edited by ESTELLE STERNBERGER, a national board member from Cincinnati. A 1926 editorial by Sternberger crystallized the goals of *The Jewish Woman*: The magazine "was launched to meet a two-fold purpose; first to give the members of the National Council of Jewish Women, and the public, information on all phases of the Council's work, international, national and local; and secondly to provide a medium that would voice the ideals and aspirations of Jewish womanhood in every field of endeavor."

Both of these expectations were realized in the magazine's feature articles, the message from the NCJW president, editorials, book reviews, and reports from the "eighteen fields": NCJW's various committees that focused on a variety of subjects including education, religion, and civic life. One such committee, Purity of Press, tracked anti-Semitism in the media by performing the watchdog role later taken up by groups such as the Anti-Defamation League. However, the first issues of *The Jewish Woman* were targeted to council members, a cross section of middle-class women. Some of them thought of the council primarily as a social outlet; others wanted their council participation to be more political and civic minded. It was also directed to the newly arrived immigrant who sought help from the first two groups.

A 1922 article on Jewish women in civic life provided insight into this varied audience. The author scolded council members for being too impatient and therefore unable to meet the challenges of civic life. "We [Jews] are not a particularly patient people. We are willing to do things, but want them done quickly. We want to see results. Hence philanthropic work appeals to us keenly, and club work has its prompt and pleasant returns for time expended."

Another article in 1926 was more prescient in its evaluation by suggesting that women's lack of political experience might be "counterbalanced by a certain freshness and hopefulness that [they] bring to the adventure of participating in their government and their distinctly feminine point of view as to human values in government."

The magazine also broadened the focus of the council's influential and award-winning monthly newsletter, *The Immigrant*. Early issues reflected NCJW's self-appointed role as "The Great Interpreter." The council, renowned for its work with immigrants, spoke out against the harsh immigration laws then recently enacted in Congress. A 1924 editorial entitled "Sane Americanism" decried the "unfortunate tendency [that] has recently appeared among some of our legislators and citizens to challenge this distinctive feature [the melting-pot idea] of America's history."

In her April 1922 "President's Message," ROSE BRENNER wrote that when the council "assumed as its chief obligation, the care and protection of the immigrant woman and girl, it became the interpreter of America to the foreign-born Jewess." To that end a 1925 editorial lauded the opening of a Jewish School of Social Work as filling a great void in American society. NCJW took pride in its social work activity and thought of it as a valuable scientific discipline. The creation of a professional school gave credence to that view.

However, Brenner was unequivocal about NCJW's goal to "re-interpret the Jew and Judaism back to America. . . . It is neither just nor fitting that the greater American public should see in the foreign-born its only exemplar of Judaism and the Jew." Balancing assimilation into American society with Judaic practice was continuously reflected upon and redefined in the magazine. The February 1923 issue highlighted the tension

between the social and religious demands of the old and new worlds. "The organization woman realizes that she is a new type in the History of Women, and lives in a new world which her grandmothers did not know—the world of conflicting ideas."

Many of those contradictory ideas, examined in the pages of *The Jewish Woman*, were extrapolated from the current events of the day. Women's equality through suffrage and economic freedom was the subject of a 1922 editorial that cautioned that women "will have to determine whether the proposed 'freedom' and 'rights' would be to the hurt rather than to the benefit of women." The recent memory of World War I also inspired pacifism in the NCJW ranks. *The Jewish Woman* often reported on NCJW resolutions that called for the elimination of war as a means of settling any dispute.

In keeping with the council's efforts to boost membership as well as the expanding editorial focus of *The Jewish Woman*, the editors attempted to establish a paid circulation. At the end of 1924, a plan was proposed to "increase the scope and influence of the magazine" by instituting a fifty-cent subscription rate and soliciting advertisers. Subsequent issues demonstrated that the plan was ineffective or never implemented. The only advertisements that appeared in those issues were for council publications and pamphlets. No published record of circulation appeared in any of the issues.

By 1925, the magazine had made the transition from an in-house organ to a more nationally oriented publication. The tensions between modernity and assimilation were investigated in articles such as "Is the Modern Girl Different?" and "Has Suffrage Caught Our Women Unprepared?" The status of Jews in America was explored in articles concerning the importance of Jewish education, unifying Judaism's branches, and opposing Bible instruction in public schools. That same year, *The Jewish Woman* also reported that the pendulum had swung back in favor of reinvigorating American Jewish practice with more tradition and "ceremony."

Although the articles continued to keep pace with current events, in 1927 the magazine began to shrink in size—pared down to three or four articles from the usual six to eight. The editorials from those years summarized the achievements of the council rather than commenting on international and national issues. The last issue of *The Jewish Woman* appeared in October of 1931, without comment on cessation of publication. However, the legacy of *The Jewish Woman* is the example it set by continuously aiming to serve as "a platform that would unite all Jewish women in the interests that they share in common."

BIBLIOGRAPHY

The Jewish Woman 1–11 (1921–1931); Rogow, Faith. *Gone to Another Meeting: The National Council of Jewish Women, 1893–1993* (1993).

JUDITH BOLTON-FASMAN

JEWISH WOMEN INTERNATIONAL
see B'NAI B'RITH WOMEN

JEWISH WOMEN'S RESOURCE CENTER (JWRC)

The Jewish Women's Resource Center (JWRC) of the NATIONAL COUNCIL OF JEWISH WOMEN, New York Section, maintains an extensive collection of materials by and about Jewish women and creates Jewish programming with a feminist focus. The JWRC was founded in 1976 to document and advance the modern Jewish women's movement. In addition to a library and archival repository about Jewish women, the JWRC has sponsored workshops, formed study and self-help groups, and held various events revolving around personal, religious, cultural, and political concerns of Jewish women. The JWRC was established by women who were active in the Jewish feminist movement and who wanted to document the emergence of feminism in the context of Judaism.

The JWRC originated as the New York Women's Center, which was founded by students affiliated with the Jewish Feminist Organization (JFO) who were interested in exploring what it means to be both Jewish and female. They envisioned a center that would appeal to as many college women as possible, "women who are certain of their identity as Jews but not as feminists, as well as feminists who are coming to terms with their identity as Jews." In so doing, they changed the name of the JFO College Project to the New York Women's Center and officially opened in October 1976.

The Women's Center aimed to "enhance the education and self-growth of Jewish women and to become an educational, social, and resource center which would bring together Jewish women of different ages, backgrounds, and beliefs." Toward this end, the Women's Center offered a wide range of seminars and workshops, including such topics as the impact of Jewish feminism on daily living and zero population growth versus Jewish survival. A Jewish "woman-school" held classes on Jewish law, women in the midrash, heroines in Jewish folklore, and a practicum on ritual skills. In addition, a women's prayer group met regularly.

The Women's Center shared information and offered assistance to Jewish women who had specific requests or needs pertaining to their feminism and/or Judaism. Its growing collection of books by and about Jewish women was housed in volunteers' apartments. By the end of 1977, the library had become an integral part of the Women's Center, and programs were planned in conjunction with the development of its resources. At about this time, a decision was made to change the name of the Women's Center to the Jewish Women's Resource Center.

The JWRC received some financial support from grants, donations, and membership fees but lacked a centralized location. Its two directors, Rabbi Nina Beth Cardin (a founder of the original library) and Rabbi Carol Glass, approached the 92nd Street YM-YWHA for space, and subsequently the library was moved there. A publicity brochure described the scope of the collection and noted that the JWRC's main focus would be "customary and innovative rituals, as well as programming on aspects of history, sociology, art, and folklore of Jewish women." Ongoing self-help groups included one for female rabbinic and cantorial students and another for women who had miscarried.

In 1982, the National Council of Jewish Women offered a permanent home to the JWRC, and it became one of New York Section's community services. Over 100 years old, New York Section is a multifaceted membership organization. Through education, advocacy, and outreach, it provides direct services to those in need and offers educational and enrichment programs for children and adults. Both organizations were greatly enriched when the JWRC became a project of NCJW.

Reporters, parents, professors, students, scholars, rabbis, and laypeople contact the JWRC for information on all aspects of Jewish women's lives. It is a clearinghouse for books, dissertations, journals, prayers, ceremonies, liturgies, midrashim, study guides, and conference proceedings. Also included are the archival materials containing the official records of the JWRC, which document the correspondence and programs from the 1970s to the present.

As part of its ongoing programs, the JWRC sponsors lectures, author receptions, and conferences, and publishes a poetry annual by Jewish women. The first biennial conference, held in 1983, marked the dedication of the JWRC as a project of NCJW New York Section and celebrated the tenth anniversary of the first National Jewish Women's Conference. Subsequent conference topics have included "Sarah the Matriarch," "Jewish Women in the Arts," and "*Di Froyen*: Women and Yiddish." Other innovative programs have included an annual celebration of the biblical character of Ruth, a Jewish lesbian support group, and an annual feminist Tu B'Shevat seder.

Constantly growing, the library currently has over ten thousand items and is a national and international resource for browsers and scholars. In addition to being the only repository for materials by and about Jewish women, it is catalogued in such a way as to allow research on hundreds of topics pertaining to Jewish women. The Jewish Women's Resource Center has always maintained that there is no monolithic female Jewish community, but that there is strength in the process of learning, sharing, and studying together as women.

BIBLIOGRAPHY

Cardin, Nina Beth. "Presentation to the Board of Directors of the National Council of Jewish Women New York Section." Papers, Jewish Women's Resource Center, September 1982; Eisner, Rosalyn T. "Application for Recognition of Exemption." Papers, National Council of Jewish Women Archives, NYC, Jewish Women's Resource Center, 1977; Hyman, Paula. "The Rise and Continuing Impact of Jewish Feminism." Conference at Hebrew Union College–Jewish Institute of Religion, NYC, April 1991; Rogow, Faith. *Gone to Another Meeting: The National Council of Jewish Women, 1893–1993* (1993).

RUTH ANN BINDER
CATHERINE GROSS

JOCHSBERGER, TZIPORAH H.
(b. 1920)

In March 1939, Tziporah Jochsberger's musical talents won her acceptance to the Palestine Academy of Music in Jerusalem, good fortune that ultimately saved her life. Since then, Jochsberger has used her music to stir the Jewish soul.

Tziporah H. Jochsberger was born in Leutershausen, in southern Germany, on December 27, 1920, the only child of Sophie (Enslein) and cattle dealer Nathan Jochsberger. Their middle-class status enabled her mother to buy the first piano in their small village and start her seven-year-old daughter on the music lessons she herself had been denied.

Tziporah attended Wurzburg High School and the Jewish Teachers Seminary, the only school of higher learning still open for Jewish students in Germany in 1934. Her love for Judaism and for music stem from this period during which she taught herself to play the recorder and cello. In 1939, she entered the Palestine Academy of Music in Jerusalem, graduating in 1942 as a piano and school music teacher. Jochsberger was later elected one of five directors of the school, which would become the renowned Rubin Academy for Music and Dance.

Reeling from the death of her parents in Auschwitz and the loss of millions like them, Jochsberger resolved to use music and Jewish melodies to waken the dormant Jewish soul of American Jewry. A 1947 summer of study at the Juilliard School in New York introduced Jochsberger to an American Jewish community scarcely acquainted with its heritage. With a grant from the Jewish Agency, Jochsberger returned to New York in 1950 and started what would become her life's work by using Israeli folk melodies as the basis for teaching recorder to college students at Hillel Foundations throughout the New York metropolitan region.

In 1952, Jochsberger was invited to help establish the Hebrew Arts School. The school developed a strong Jewish profile, using Jewish values, holiday celebrations, and the music of the Jewish people to attract students and faculty eager to explore Jewish culture. An invitation to teach at the Seminary College of the Jewish Theological Seminary of America forced her to deepen her limited knowledge of Jewish music. In 1956, she began her own studies at the seminary, counting Hugo Weisgal, Max Wohlberg, and Johanna Spector among her teachers as she earned master's (1959) and doctoral (1972) degrees in Jewish music.

During her years in New York, Jochsberger also used radio and television to reach a wider audience of students. She served as host and producer of three thirteen-part half-hour television series produced by the Tarbuth Foundation: *Music of the Jewish People* (1976), *Experiences in Jewish Music* (1977), and *A Kaleidoscope of Jewish Music* (1978).

In addition to her teaching and administrative responsibilities, Jochsberger has found time for an active career as a composer. She has combined her love for the songs of the Jewish people with her desire to reach children through music. In much of her work, she gathers, edits, and arranges traditional folk melodies for recorder or piano in settings appropriate for young players. A member of the American Society of Composers, Authors and Publishers (ASCAP) since

1965, she has also published a variety of choral compositions. Her numerous unpublished compositions include works for voice and various instrumental combinations. Jochsberger's compositions have been performed in major concert halls throughout the United States and Israel. *Four Hebrew Madrigals*, commissioned and recorded by the Western Wind Vocal Ensemble, was broadcast by Voice of America as part of Bicentennial celebrations in 1987. Jochsberger herself conducted the Hebrew Arts Chamber Singers in a recording of her *A Call to Remember: Sacred Songs of the High Holidays. Jewish Choral Music*, the first of a set of three compact discs of her choral and instrumental music, has recently been released.

Jochsberger "retired" to Israel in 1986 but has remained active, now providing opportunities for Israel's people to understand their own culture. She founded the Israel Music Heritage Project (IMHP) to preserve, foster, and disseminate knowledge of the varied musical traditions of the Jewish people. Jochsberger was executive producer of the IMHP's eleven-part documentary video series *A People and Its Music*, which captures the authentic musical expressions of Jewish communities in Israel whose roots are in Eastern Europe, North Africa, and the Middle East. Jochsberger remains an active composer and is a member of Israel's Composer's League and of ACUM, Limited, Israel's affiliate of ASCAP. She is also busy as a member of the governing boards of some of Israel's most prominent music institutions, including Zimriyah: The International Assembly of Choirs in Israel, the Jerusalem Institute of Contemporary Music, and the Jerusalem School for Music and Arts. When she rejoined the board of governors of the Jerusalem Rubin Academy for Music and Dance in 1990, Tziporah H. Jochsberger completed her own life's circle of devotion to the Jewish people and its music. She remains a seminal figure in the teaching and expression of Jewish music throughout the United States and Israel.

SELECTED WORKS BY TZIPORAH H. JOCHSBERGER

Bekol Zimra: A Collection of Jewish Choral Music (1966); *A Call to Remember: Sacred Songs of the High Holidays* (1978); "Ein Keloheinu" (1992); *Experiences in Jewish Music* (1977); *Four Hebrew Madrigals* (1971); *A Harvest of Jewish Song* (1980); *Hallel: Psalms of Praise* (1958); *Hava N'halela: A Method for the Recorder Based on Israeli Folk Melodies* (1987); *A Kaleidoscope of Jewish Music* (1978); *Music of the Jewish People* (1976). Television series, host and producer; *A People and Its Music* (1991–). Video series, executive producer; "Tzur Mishelo" (1992); "Yom Zeh Mekhubad" (1992).

BIBLIOGRAPHY
Jochsberger, Tziporah H. Interviews with author.

MARSHA BRYAN EDELMAN

JOEL, LYDIA (1914–1992)

Lydia Joel's career in dance involved many different roles: performer, editor, writer, and educator. To all her enterprises she brought a quick mind, buoyant vitality, and unbounded curiosity. Born in New York City on July 27, 1914, to Abraham and Helen (Mandel) Tarnower, she was the oldest child and grew up with three brothers. Her father was a manufacturer of millinery, and her mother was a housewife and part-time singer.

While growing up in New York City, she attended many dance performances. After her graduation at eighteen from New York University with a B.S. in English and journalism, she studied dance with Hanya Holm and Harald Kreutzberg, and at the School of American Ballet. She spent her summers at the Bennington School of the Dance, which attracted the most important choreographers and teachers of the time. Her first performance was as a soloist in the Max Reinhardt spectacle *The Eternal Road*. She also performed in Hanya Holm's monumental work *Trend* in the Bennington premiere and later in the New York season.

She taught dance at Southern Methodist University in Dallas from 1938 to 1944, where she also led her own dance group, which toured throughout the Southwest. Her first husband, German conductor Gerhard Joel, whose name she retained for professional use, died in 1946. In 1947, she started working for *Dance Magazine* as the advertising manager, then took on the position of young dance editor, and then associate editor. She was married in 1953 to Edwin Miller, entertainment editor of *Seventeen* magazine, with whom she had two children: a daughter, Diana, who died at age sixteen, and a son, Eric.

In 1952, Joel had become the editor-in-chief of *Dance Magazine*. Under Joel's direction, the magazine adopted a new interest in visuals, adding more photographs and creating striking covers. She expanded the magazine's coverage to include reports on companies around the United States, correspondents abroad, and writings on a wide variety of dance forms, ranging from ballet and modern dance to Asian, jazz, folk, and television dance. Her emphasis on essays, criticism, and photographic features, and her ability to attract contributions from prominent dance writers, such as Edwin Denby, increased the magazine's audience.

Throughout her life as a performer, teacher, writer, and editor, Lydia Joel was dedicated to dance.
She used her leadership skills and vision to transform Dance Magazine *into a publication of international stature*
during her tenure as editor-in-chief. [New York Public Library]

During Joel's tenure, the magazine grew from 24 to 120 pages per issue, and the staff increased from three to fifteen.

Among Joel's frequent contributions to *Dance Magazine* was coverage of major dance festivals in the United States and abroad, including the Royal Swedish Ballet in Stockholm, Bèjart at Avignon, and the Royal Ballet in London. Her writings were published in *Vogue*, *Parents Magazine*, the *New York Times* arts section, and various encyclopedias. She was regularly invited to lecture for clubs and colleges and to lead symposia. In addition, she was called upon to adjudicate dances by the National Association of Regional Ballet and the American College Dance Festival Association.

After leaving *Dance Magazine* in 1970, Joel served as a consultant to the United States Department of Education. In 1973, the School of Performing Arts in New York City, dedicated to training young professionals, invited Joel to head its dance program. In that capacity, she oversaw the curriculum, taught dance history, produced annual concerts, and, in 1982, arranged for the students to perform in a festival at Spoleto, Italy. After her retirement in 1984, Joel continued to write, publishing four articles on Catherine de Medici in *Dance Magazine* in 1990. She also was a founding member and served on the boards of the American College Dance Festival, the Association of American Dance Companies, and the National Association for Regional Ballet. Lydia Joel remained active in the dance world until her death on May 24, 1992.

BIBLIOGRAPHY

Anderson, Jack. "Lydia Joel, Former Chief Editor of *Dance Magazine*, Dies at 77." *NYTimes*, May 26, 1992, D16;

Joel, Lydia. "Edwin Denby Remembered." *Ballet Review* 12 (Spring 1984): 37–39; Miller, Edwin. Telephone interview with author, June 1996; Moseley, Monica. Obituaries. *Dance Magazine* (August 1992): 26; Obituary. *Dancing Times* (July 1992): 959+; Tarnower, Helen, and Irving Tarnower. Telephone interview with author, June 1996; Wasserman, Paul, ed. *Who's Who in Consulting* (1973).

JOYCE MORGENROTH

JOSEPH, HELEN (1888–1978)

An internationally renowned puppeteer and author on marionettes, Helen Haiman Joseph made a career entertaining and educating audiences of all ages with the performance of puppetry.

Helen Joseph was born in 1888, in Atlanta, Georgia, to Elias and Frances (Lowenthan) Haiman. Her father's factory in Georgia produced farm tools and

Author of the first history of puppetry ever written in English, Helen Joseph modeled, carved, painted, and dressed her wooden creatures—and even wrote the plays in which they performed. At the height of her career, she performed for as many as fifty thousand children a year. [New York Public Library]

made Confederate swords during the Civil War. The family moved to Cleveland when he became the manager of the Empire Plow Company there. Helen graduated from Cleveland's Central High School and attended both Vassar College and the College for Women of Western Reserve University (now Case Western Reserve University). She received bachelor's degrees from both.

After her 1910 graduation, she joined the Cleveland Play House, where she made and manipulated puppets for her first production, "The Death of Tintagiles." From 1914 to 1920, she directed Marionette Productions at the Play House. In 1918, she married Ernest A. Joseph. He died the next year, leaving her with their daughter Anne and pregnant with daughter Ernestine. Despite the tragedy, Joseph continued with her passion, puppetry.

In 1920, her *Book of Marionettes*, the first definitive history on puppetry written in English, was published. The next year, Joseph took her daughters on a three-year tour through Europe, where her book gained her entry into the most inaccessible marionette studios. In 1924, she returned to the United States, struggled financially, and turned to full-time puppetry as her profession. That same year in Cleveland, she started the Pinnochio Players and, with her staff, wrote and produced puppet plays performed in clubs, schools, and hospitals. "I became a puppet showman in earnest," she wrote in the *Vassar Quarterly* (1935) of this time in her life, "writing plays, modeling, carving, painting and dressing the marionettes, selecting and training puppeteers, rehearsing and promoting the plays."

In the 1930s, Joseph toured the country with her marionette troupe, performing for as many as fifty thousand children a year. She also established a traveling puppet show business, performing shows in factories to express different ideas of management. Her popular puppet engagements at the outdoor playhouse in Cleveland's Cain Park stopped at the outbreak of World War II because many of her puppeteers and crew were drafted into the military. During the war, she worked in such disparate jobs as writing copy for the Fuller, Smith, and Ross advertising firm and making bullet shells in a factory. After the war, she resumed her marionette performances, still charming audiences with her puppet wizardry.

In addition to *A Book of Marionettes*, Joseph wrote *Ali Baba and Other Plays for Puppets* (1927) and *Little Mr. Clown* (1932), a children's book based on the marionette Joseph often used in her puppet plays. A series of marionettes sold with the *Mr. Clown* books were extremely successful in toy stores all over the country.

In Cleveland, she served on the boards of the Women's City Club, the League of Women Voters, and the Consumers League.

In a 1935 article she wrote for the *Vassar Quarterly*, Joseph reflected on the satisfactions of puppetry. "It seemed an almost too delicate, too poignant power," she wrote of the contact with hundreds of children, "playing upon the hearts and imaginations of those great groups of boys and girls, evoking their laughter, their sorrow, their fears, their loyalties by the twitch of a finger inside of a wooden doll."

Helen Joseph died just two weeks before her ninetieth birthday in August 1978.

BIBLIOGRAPHY
Joseph, Helen. Clippings file in New York Public Library, Lincoln Center, NYC; *UJE*; *Vassar Quarterly* (July 1935); *WWIAJ* (1938).

MICHELE SIEGEL

JUDAIC STUDIES

When the Association for Jewish Studies (AJS) was established in 1969 as the professional organization of scholars in the interdisciplinary field of Judaic studies, there were no women among its founders. In 1997 the AJS membership of some fourteen hundred includes about 35 percent females. Within the past generation a field that was traditionally dominated by men has gradually witnessed the emergence of a significant number of women scholars. Although those scholars are clustered in modern Jewish history, literature, and the social sciences, for the first time in Jewish history the study of Jewish texts and culture is no longer virtually a male preserve.

Both traditional Jewish culture, which held the study of Bible and rabbinic texts as an ideal, and the modern Western university excluded women from their ranks. It is no surprise, then, that in America there were no women in the nascent field of Judaic studies. Most of the earliest professors of Semitics and later of Jewish history acquired their expertise through their study for the rabbinate, a profession closed to women in America until 1972.

The expansion of the field of Judaic studies in American universities beginning in the 1960s coincided with the entry of women in substantial numbers into Ph.D. programs. Under the impact of feminist consciousness, increasing numbers of women have specialized in Judaic studies over the course of the past generation, assuming positions in American colleges and universities, and have led the way in introducing considerations of gender into the study of both Jewish history and literature.

Even before the expansion of Judaic studies a few women carved out for themselves scholarly careers in the field in America, though generally without receiving as much recognition as they merited. NAOMI COHEN (b. 1927) worked in the area of American Jewish history as a professor of American history at HUNTER COLLEGE, until her retirement in 1996. LUCY DAWIDOWICZ (1915–1990) held positions at the YIVO Institute and Yeshiva University and wrote widely for Jewish publications, but became well known as a scholar only after the publication of her *The War Against the Jews* in 1975. Two refugee scholars from Europe, RACHEL WISCHNITZER (1885–1989) in the field of the history of Jewish art and architecture and SELMA STERN TAÜBLER (1890–1981) in early modern European Jewish history, concluded their careers in the United States but had little impact on the American academy.

In the 1980s and 1990s, however, these pioneer historians have been joined by a host of others. Modern Jewish history has proven especially appealing to women in Judaic studies, initially because it required less specialized knowledge of religious texts but increasingly because it offered opportunities for original work in social and women's history. Paula Hyman (b. 1946), the Lucy Moses Professor of Modern Jewish History at Yale University, has specialized in modern French Jewish history of the nineteenth and twentieth centuries and has contributed to the growth of the area of Jewish women's history. Columbia University produced not only Hyman but also the historians Esther Feldblum (1933–1974) and Deborah Dash Moore (b. 1946), whose scholarship on American Jewry, particularly of the twentieth century, has contributed significantly to our understanding of American Jewish ethnicity and of Jewish life in the United States. Harriet Freidenreich (b. 1947), who has published on Jews in east central Europe, and Marion Kaplan (b. 1946), who trained as a German historian but all of whose work has been on German Jewry, also received their doctorates from Columbia. Working with Hyman at Columbia University, Vicki Caron (b. 1951), Marsha Rozenblit (b. 1950), and Shulamit Magnus (b. 1950) have also published important studies on the history of Jews in modern Europe, while Jenna Weissman Joselit has illuminated a broad swath of American Jewish culture. Ellen Umansky, a specialist in Jewish women's spirituality and religious leadership, also received her Ph.D. from Columbia, in her case from the Department of Religion. Columbia thus provided an opportunity for women scholars in Judaic studies to establish an informal network.

Other female scholars received their graduate education elsewhere. Frances Malino (b. 1940) and Phyllis Cohen Albert, both of whom specialize in modern French Jewish history, trained at Brandeis University, as did Deborah Lipstadt (b. 1947), whose work focuses on the Holocaust, particularly on Holocaust denial. Hasia Diner (b. 1946) and Pamela Nadell, both specialists in American Jewish history, received their doctorates, Diner in American history at Illinois and Nadell at Ohio State University.

The social sciences have also proven supportive of female scholars. Shulamit Reinharz (b. 1946) has applied her sociological tools and interest in women's studies not only to research on women in the *yishuv*, the prestate Jewish settlement of Palestine, but also to the creation of a Jewish Women's Studies Program at Brandeis University. Like Reinharz, Ewa Morawska, who was educated in Poland, and Shelly Tenenbaum (b. 1955) have also recently published significant works of historical sociology, both of American Jews. As a sociologist whose focus is quantified and contemporary, Rela Geffen has conducted a number of important studies, most recently on American Jewish women. Similarly, Sylvia Barack Fishman (b. 1942) has explored contemporary American Jewry, and particularly American Jewish feminism. Women have also conducted ethnographic studies as sociologists, anthropologists, and folklorists. Both Lynn Davidman (b. 1955) and Debra Kaufman (b. 1941) have produced ethnographic studies of women *ba'alot teshuva* [newly Orthodox]. Barbara Kirshenblatt-Gimblett (b. 1942) has written not only on Eastern European and immigrant American Jewish folklore but also on the representation of Jewish culture in a variety of different venues. As a specialist in American studies, Riv-Ellen Prell (b. 1947) began her career with an ethnographic study of a *havurah* [religious fellowship] and has recently explored stereotypes of American Jewish women. Yael Zerubavel, whose graduate training in folklore and academic career have taken place in the United States, has written on the construction of Israeli collective memory.

In the social sciences and in history some scholars have specialized in the study of the Jews although they did not receive their training in programs of Judaic studies and are not formally attached to Judaic studies programs. As "outsiders" to the field they have often promoted a sensitivity to gender lacking in the graduate education of those who received their doctorates in Judaic studies. Deborah Hertz, for example, has focused on German Jewish history as a historian of modern Germany. Joyce Antler (b. 1942), trained in the interdisciplinary field of American studies, has written widely on American Jewish women's experience and literature.

Literature has often been depicted as the field most appropriate for female scholars, and this has been the case in Hebrew and Yiddish literature and in American Jewish literature as well (although I will not deal with the latter subject). Women teach both Hebrew language and (generally modern) literature in Judaic studies programs throughout America. Anne Lapidus Lerner (b. 1942) teaches Hebrew literature at the Jewish Theological Seminary of America, where she is currently the first female vice-chancellor in that institution's history; Naomi Sokoloff (b. 1953) teaches Hebrew literature at the University of Washington. Esther Fuchs (b. 1953), whose position is at the University of Arizona, has focused on gender issues in her study of Israeli literature, while Yael Feldman (b. 1941), a professor at New York University, has provided a psychological analysis of that literature. Focusing on the Bible and its impact on modern literature, Nehama Aschkenasy teaches at the University of Connecticut. Jewish literature of the Holocaust has been the primary subject of Sidra DeKoven Ezrahi (b. 1942), who teaches at the Hebrew University of Jerusalem, and of Sara Horowitz (b. 1951).

Ruth Wisse (b. 1936) was one of the first professors of Yiddish literature in North America and has contributed to the dissemination of knowledge about Yiddish culture through her monographs and edited books of literature in translation. Anita Norich (b. 1952), who has combined her interests in English and Yiddish literature in her teaching, has focused on twentieth-century Yiddish prose in her writing. Chana Bloch (b. 1940), Marcia Falk (b. 1946), and Katheryn Hellerstein have combined scholarship with translation, Bloch in Hebrew poetry, Falk in both Hebrew and Yiddish poetry, and Hellerstein in Yiddish poetry. All three have also published their own poetry.

Although female scholars in Judaic studies have worked primarily on the modern period, a handful of women have pioneered in the study of classical Jewish texts and premodern history. Adele Berlin, Tikva Frymer-Kensky, and Carol Meyers (b. 1942) have contributed to the area of biblical studies. Judith Hauptman became the first woman to teach Talmud at the Jewish Theological Seminary, the educational center of the Conservative movement. Judith Romney Wegner, who trained first as a lawyer, received her Ph.D. and has published in the field of rabbinics. Judith Baskin (b. 1950) specializes in both rabbinic

Judaism and medieval Jewish history. The two books she has edited, *Jewish Women in Historical Perspective* and *Women of the Word: Jewish Women and Jewish Writing*, have become important resources for the teaching of courses on Jewish women's history and for incorporating gender perspectives into general courses. In her innovative work on *tkhines*, Jewish women's liturgy of the early modern period, Chava Weissler has opened up the area of women's spirituality and popular culture. Jane Gerber (b. 1938), who focuses on Sephardi Jewry both in Spain and in its diaspora, has expanded her interests from the medieval to the modern period. Among younger scholars Elisheva Carlebach has produced innovative work on early modern Jewish history. In the field of Jewish philosophy two scholars, Hava Tirosh-Rothschild (b. 1950) and Tamar Rudavsky (b. 1951), have both published work on the medieval period.

Despite their shared sociological characteristics, women in the variegated field of Jewish studies have explored a wide range of subjects from many disciplinary perspectives. They have had their greatest impact as a group, however, in their introduction into Jewish studies of issues of gender and women's experience, which are currently yielding many academic presentations and monographs and as subjects of research are no longer limited to female scholars. As prejudice against female scholars has decreased, as the field of Judaic studies has expanded, and as opportunities for women to receive a traditional Jewish education have grown, younger women are distributed more evenly across the field than were their predecessors. This process is likely to continue. With the entry of large numbers of women into the field and under the impact of women's studies, the construction of "Jewish learning" as well as the image of the "learned Jew" has been transformed.

BIBLIOGRAPHY

HISTORY

Albert, Phyllis Cohen. *The Modernization of French Jewry* (1977); Antler, Joyce. *The Journey Home: Jewish Women and the American Century* (1997); Baskin, Judith, ed. *Jewish Women in Historical Perspective* (1991); Carlebach, Elisheva. *The Pursuit of Heresy: Rabbi Moses Hagiz and the Sabbatian Controversies* (1990); Caron, Vicki. *Between France and Germany: The Jews of Alsace-Lorraine, 1871–1918* (1988); Diner, Hasia. *In the Almost Promised Land: American Jews and Blacks, 1915–1935* (1977), and *A Time for Gathering* (1992); Feldblum, Esther. *The American Catholic Press and the Jewish State, 1917–1959* (1977); Freidenreich, Harriet. *Jewish Politics in Vienna, 1918–1938* (1991), and *The Jews of Yugoslavia* (1979); Gerber, Jane. *Jewish Society in Fez, 1450–1700*

(1980), and *The Jews of Spain* (1992); Gerber, Jane, ed., *Sephardic Studies in the University* (1995); Hertz, Deborah. *Jewish High Society in Old Regime Berlin* (1988); Hyman, Paula. *The Emancipation of the Jews of Alsace: Acculturation and Tradition in the Nineteenth Century* (1991), and *From Dreyfus to Vichy* (1979), and *Gender and Assimilation in Modern Jewish History* (1995); Hyman, Paula E., Charlotte Baum, and Sonya Michel. *The Jewish Woman in America* (1976); Hyman, Paula E., and Steven M. Cohen, eds. *The Jewish Family: Image and Reality* (1986); Joselit, Jenna. *New York's Jewish Jews* (1990), and *Our Gang* (1983), and *The Wonders of America* (1994); Joselit, Jenna Weissman, and Susan L. Braunstein, eds. *Getting Comfortable in New York* (1990); Kaplan, Marion. *Jewish Feminism in Germany: The Campaigns of the Jüdischer Frauenbund* (1979), and *The Making of the Jewish Middle Class: Women, Family and Identity in Imperial Germany* (1991); Kaplan, Marion, ed. *The Marriage Bargain: Women and Dowries in European History* (1985); Kaplan, Marion, Renate Bridenthal, and Atina Grossmann, eds. *When Biology Became Destiny: Women in Weimar and Nazi Germany* (1984); Magnus, Shulamit. *Jewish Emancipation in a German City* (1997); Malino, Frances. *A Jew in the Revolution* (1996), and *The Sephardic Jews of Bordeaux* (1977); Moore, Deborah Dash. *At Home in America* (1980), and *B'nai B'rith and the Challenge of Ethnic Leadership* (1981), and *To the Golden Cities: Pursuing the American Jewish Dream in Miami and L.A.* (1996); Nadell, Pamela. *Conservative Judaism in America* (1988); Rozenblit, Marsha. *The Jews of Vienna, 1867-1914* (1981); Stillman, Yedida K., and Norman A. Stillman, eds. and trans. *Travail in an Arab Land* (1989); Stillman, Yedida K., and George K. Zucker, eds. and trans. *New Horizons in Sephardic Studies* (1993); Umansky, Ellen. *Lily Montagu and the Advancement of Liberal Judaism* (1983); Umansky, Ellen, and Dianne Ashton, eds. *Four Centuries of Jewish Women's Spirituality* (1992).

SOCIAL SCIENCE

Davidson, Lynn. *Tradition in a Rootless World* (1991); Fishman, Sylvia Barack. *A Breath of Life: Feminism in the American Jewish Community* (1993); Geffen, Rela, ed., *Celebration and Renewal: Rites of Passage in Judaism* (1993); Kaufman, Debra. *Rachel's Daughters* (1991); Kirshenblatt-Gimblett, Barbara, and Luczan Dobroszycki. *Image Before My Eyes* (1977); Prell, Riv-Ellen. *Prayer and Community: The Havurah in American Judaism* (1989); Reinharz, Shulamit. "Toward a Model of Female Political Action: The Case of Manya Shohat, Founder of the First Kibbutz." *Women's Studies International Forum* 7 (1984); Tenenbaum, Shelly. *A Credit to Their Community: Jewish Loan Societies in the United States, 1880–1945* (1993); Weissler, Chava. *Making Judaism Meaningful: Ambivalence and Tradition in a Havurah Community* (1989); Zerubavel, Yael. *Recovered Roots: Collective Memory and the Making of Israeli National Tradition* (1995).

LITERATURE

Aschkenasy, Nehama. *Biblical Patterns in Modern Literature* (1984), and *Eve's Journey* (1986); Baskin, Judith, ed. *Women of the Word: Jewish Women and Jewish Writing* (1994); Bloch, Chana, and Ariel Bloch, eds. and trans. *The Window:*

New and Selected Poems/Dahlia Ravikovitch (1982); Bloch, Chana, and Stephen Mitchell, eds. and trans. *The Selected Poetry of Yehuda Amichai* (1996); Ezrahi, Sidra DeKoven. *By Words Alone: The Holocaust in Literature* (1980); Falk, Marcia. *The Book of Blessings* (1996); Falk, Marcia, ed. and trans. *Song of Songs: A New Translation and Interpretation* (1990), and *With Teeth in the Earth: Selected Poems of Malka Heifetz Tussman* (1992); Feldman, Yael. *Approaches to Teaching the Hebrew Bible as Literature* (1989), and *Modernism and Cultural Transfer: Gabriel Preil and the Tradition of Jewish Literary Bilingualism* (1985); Fuchs, Esther. *Encounters with Israeli Authors* (1982), and *Israeli Mythogynies* (1987); Horowitz, Sara. *Voicing the Void* (1997); Lerner, Anne Lapidus, Anita Norich, and Naomi Sokoloff, eds. *Gender and Text in Modern Hebrew and Yiddish Literature* (1993); Norich, Anita. *Homeless Imagination in the Fiction of Israel Joshua Singer* (1991); Sokoloff, Naomi. *Imagining the Child in Modern Jewish Fiction* (1992); Wisse, Ruth. See bibliography of her entry.

BIBLE, RABBINICS, AND PHILOSOPHY

Berlin, Adele. *Biblical Poetry Through Medieval Eyes* (1991), and *Poetics and Interpretation of Biblical Narrative* (1983); Frymer-Kensky, Tikva. *In the Wake of the Goddesses: Women, Culture and the Biblical Transformation of Pagan Myth* (1992); Hauptman, Judith. *Development of the Talmudic Sugya* (1988); Meyers, Carol. *Discovering Eve* (1988); Rudavsky, Tamar, ed. *Divine Omniscience and Omnipotence in Medieval Philosophy: Islamic, Jewish, and Christian Perspectives* (1985); Tirosh-Rothschild, Hava. *Between Worlds: The Life and Thought of Rabbi David ben Judah Messer Leon* (1991); Wegner, Judith Romney. *Chattel or Person: The Status of Women in the Mishnah* (1988).

GENDER AND WOMEN'S STUDIES

Antler, Joyce. *The Journey Home: Jewish Women and the American Century* (1997); Aschkenasy, Nehama. *Eve's Journey* (1986); Baskin, Judith, ed. *Jewish Women in Historical Perspective* (1991), and *Women of the Word: Jewish Women and Jewish Writing* (1994); Biale, David. *Eros and the Jews* (1992); Biale, Rachel. *Women and Jewish Law* (1984); Boyarin, Daniel. *Carnal Israel* (1993); Davidman, Lynn. *Tradition in a Rootless World* (1991); Davidman, Lynn, and Shelly Tenenbaum, eds. *Feminist Perspectives on Jewish Studies* (1994); Falk, Marcia. *The Book of Blessings* (1996); Fishman, Sylvia Barack. *A Breath of Life: Feminism in the American Jewish Community* (1993); Frymer-Kensky, Tikva. *In the Wake of the Goddesses: Women, Culture and the Biblical Transformation of Pagan Myth* (1992); Fuchs, Esther. *Israeli Mythogynies* (1987); Glenn, Susan. *Daughters of the Shtetl* (1990); Hertz, Deborah. *Jewish High Society in Old Regime Berlin* (1988); Hyman, Paula. *Gender and Assimilation in Modern Jewish History* (1995); Hyman, Paula, Charlotte Baum, and Sonya Michel. *The Jewish Woman in America* (1976); Kaplan, Marion. *Jewish Feminism in Germany: The Campaigns of the Jüdischer Frauenbund* (1979), and *The Making of the Jewish Middle Class: Women, Family and Identity in Imperial Germany* (1991); Kaplan, Marion, ed. *The Marriage Bargain: Women and Dowries in European History* (1985); Kaplan, Marion, Renate Bridenthal, and Atina Grossmann, eds. *When Biology*

Became Destiny: Women in Weimar and Nazi Germany (1984); Kuzmack, Linda Gordon. *Woman's Cause* (1990); Meyers, Carol. *Discovering Eve* (1988); Orleck, Annelise. *Common Sense and a Little Fire* (1995); Peskowitz, Miriam, and Laura Levitt, eds. *Judaism Since Gender* (1997); Plaskow, Judith. *Standing Again at Sinai* (1990); Reinharz, Shulamith. "Toward a Model of Female Political Action: The Case of Manya Shohat, Founder of the First Kibbutz." *Women's Studies International Forum* 7 (1984); Rogow, Faith. *Gone to Another Meeting: The National Council of Jewish Women, 1893–1993* (1993); Rudavsky, Tamar, ed. *Gender and Judaism* (1995); Sacks, Maurie, ed. *Active Voices: Women in Jewish Culture* (1995); Sokoloff, Naomi, Anne Lapidus Lerner, and Anita Norich. *Gender and Text in Modern Hebrew and Yiddish Literature* (1993); Umansky, Ellen. *Lily Montagu and the Advancement of Liberal Judaism* (1983); Umansky, Ellen, and Dianne Ashton, eds. *Four Centuries of Jewish Women's Spirituality* (1992); Wegner, Judith Romney. *Chattel or Person: The Status of Women in the Mishnah* (1988); Weinberg, Sydney Stahl. *The World of Our Mothers* (1988); Weissler, Chava. "The Traditional Piety of Ashkenazic Women." In *Jewish Spirituality*, Vol. 2, edited by Arthur Green (1987).

PAULA E. HYMAN

JUDEO-SPANISH *see* LADINO PRESS; LADINO THEATER

JUNG, IRMA ROTHSCHILD
(1897–1993)

Irma Rothschild Jung, a native of Randegg, Baden, Germany, was born on July 1, 1897, and until her death close to a century later, dedicated her substantial energies to pioneering Jewish communal programs in aid of the needy. Her maternal family, the Langs, had a written code of ethics, based upon observance and practice of Judaism, which served as a blueprint for family behavior in the public and private sectors. This code would guide Jung's service to others for her entire life.

One of twelve children, Jung was educated in Switzerland, attending the University of Zurich from 1917 to 1919. In response to the needs of the Jewish communities after World War I, Jung served as the director of the Bureau of the World Congress of Orthodox Jewry in 1919, and of the Central Bureau of the Agudat Israel World Organization from 1919 to 1921. She organized free camps for refugee children in Stansstad, Switzerland, from 1920 to 1921.

On February 28, 1922, she married Leo Jung, a Moravian-born and London-educated rabbi in Germany. That same year, the couple came to New York, where Rabbi Jung would further a blossoming career as a charismatic Orthodox spiritual leader, activist, thinker, and writer. Going beyond her considerable duties as the *rebbetzin* [rabbi's wife] of the Jewish Center, a fast-growing and increasingly influential modern Orthodox congregation, Jung continued her communal activism and charitable work on new shores.

Her concern and provision for the feeding and clothing of students at New York's Yeshiva University during the Great Depression is legendary. She served as chair of the Yeshiva Dormitory on East Broadway from 1926 to 1928, and as vice president and acting chair of the Yeshiva College Women's Organization in 1934–1935. With funds collected by fellow committee

Rebbetzin Irma Rothschild Jung dedicated her energies to pioneering Jewish community programs in aid of the needy. During the Great Depression, she ministered to both body and soul when she appeared at Yeshiva University before Passover every year with bolts of cloth, offering students a choice of a new brown or a new gray suit. [Debbie Kram]

members, Jung would provide stipends to needy students every Sunday. Before Passover, she would appear with bolts of cloth, offering students a choice of a new brown suit or a new gray suit.

Together with her husband, Jung labored for many years on behalf of the Rabbonim Aid Society, whose center of operations was located at the Jewish Center. Some of Rabbi Jung's associates—particularly victims of the Holocaust—as well as rabbinical widows were impoverished. The Jungs raised much-needed funds in order to send monthly checks to numerous rabbis and widows from the 1950s onward.

Jung was a founder of the women's branch of the Union of Orthodox Jewish Congregations of America, spearheading the effort to involve women in the union's activities promoting Jewish life.

The Jungs also devoted their energy to at least a dozen causes in Palestine and Israel. They championed schools and social services, and were recognized by rabbinical colleagues and friends with the July 1983 dedication of the Rabbi Leo and Irma Jung Forest in Safed, Israel.

Jung and her husband raised four daughters: Erna Villa, Rosalie Rosenfeld, Julie Etra, and Marcella (Micki) Rosen. Long after her arrival in America, Jung retained a bit of her Swiss background. As a young girl, she had enjoyed mountain climbing, and in her later years would yodel at the request of her grandchildren. After her husband's death in 1987, she continued to be a formidable presence at the Jewish Center. Her leadership and influence were deeply felt in the broader Jewish community by the countless individuals, young and old, who benefited from her generous spirit.

Irma Jung died in New York on May 22, 1993.

BIBLIOGRAPHY

Jung, Leo. *The Path of a Pioneer: The Autobiography of Leo Jung* (1980); Miller, Rabbi Israel, and Rosen, Micki. Telephone conversations with author, summer 1996; Rosenfeld, Ezra [grandson]. Correspondence with author, Alon Shvut, Israel, summer 1996; Schacter, Jacob J. Telephone conversation with author, summer 1996; Schacter, Jacob J., ed. *Reverence, Righteousness, and Rahamanut: Essays in Memory of Rabbi Dr. Leo Jung* (1992); Sherman, Moshe D. *Orthodox Judaism in America: A Biographical Dictionary and Sourcebook* (1996); *WWIAJ* (1938): 496.

DEBBIE KRAM

JUNGREIS, ESTHER (b. 1936)

A dynamic orator, Esther Jungreis played a significant role in the back-to-Judaism movement in the United States during the 1970s. Born in Szeged, Hungary, Esther was the only daughter of Rabbi Avraham and Miriam Jungreisz. Her two brothers, Jacob and Binyamin, both became rabbis. She married Rabbi Theodore Jungreis, and they had four children: Chaya Sara (b. 1958), Yisrael (b. 1960), Slava Chana (b. 1964), and Osher Anshil (b. 1967). A Holocaust survivor and an Orthodox *rebbetzin*, Jungreis established in 1973 Hineni (Hebrew for "Here I Am"), an organization that sought to discourage intermarriage and Jewish participation in cults. In its heyday, Hineni had considerable success on college campuses, and Jungreis spoke to large audiences across the country, including a full house at Madison Square Garden's Felt Forum. Her lectures invoked stirring images of traditional Jewish life and the Holocaust, and culminated in dramatic pleas to assimilated Jews to explore their heritage. Jungreis remains active in outreach efforts through her cable television program, newspaper column, and classes at the Hineni Heritage Center in New York City.

BIBLIOGRAPHY

Jungreis, Esther. *The Jewish Soul on Fire* (1990); "'The Jewish Soul on Fire.'" *Time*, June 15, 1981; "Reaching the Heart." *The Jewish Homemaker*, April 1995; "The Revivalist Rebbetzin." *Jerusalem Post*, July 12, 1974; "Spirit." *People*, May 23, 1977.

RAFAEL MEDOFF

K

KADUSHIN, EVELYN GARFIEL
see **GARFIEL, EVELYN**

KAHAN, SHOSHANA
see **SHOSHANA, ROSE**

KAHN, DOROTHY C. (1893–1955)

Dorothy C. Kahn, an outstanding social worker, lived through the Depression and World War II, major crises of her generation and this century. Through her innovative administrative capacity, she developed, implemented, and advocated for social welfare programs and policies whose underlying principles upheld her deepest beliefs about what social welfare could mean in a democracy.

Dorothy Kahn was the eldest of three children born to Julius and Viola (Cohen) Kahn of Seattle, Washington. Her mother was the daughter of a famous rabbi, and her father was an innovative and successful businessman. When Kahn was a young girl, the family moved to Chicago. She returned to Chicago after graduating from Wellesley College in 1915. Inspired by her family friend Frances Tausig, executive head of the Jewish Family Agency, she decided to pursue a career in social work. She became

a case worker at that agency from 1915 to 1918, attended the University of Chicago School of Social Work, and then was civic director of Chicago Women's Aid from 1918 to 1919.

Kahn demonstrated both talent and interest in administrative work and, at twenty-six, was offered the job of superintendent of the Hebrew Benevolent Association of Baltimore. In this position (1919–1928) and then as director of the Jewish Welfare Society of Philadelphia (1928–1932), Kahn developed innovative programs that challenged the traditional view of social work. She thought that social work, like education, should be publicly supported, universal, and available to all citizens.

The 1930s brought the Depression and widespread unemployment. When it became apparent that only public agencies could deal with the vast economic problems, the responsibility for the transfer of relief shifted from private to public organizations. In 1932, Kahn became the first executive director of the Philadelphia County Relief Board. In developing and administering programs for relief, Kahn upheld democratic principles. She believed that people were in need through no fault of their own, and that every citizen had the right to a minimum standard of living as a matter of human rights and social justice, not charity. Kahn urged social workers and the social work profession to take leadership roles in developing and building an adequate national system for social welfare. From

1934 to 1936, she was president of the American Association of Social Workers. In 1936, she convened and gave a keynote address at the national conference that focused on relief, and the same year she reported on relief practices in America at the International Conference of Social Workers. Kahn chaired the subcommittee on employment and relief of President Roosevelt's Commission on Economic Security.

During these years in Philadelphia (1930–1945), she had close associations with the University of Pennsylvania School of Social Work. She filled students with her social philosophy as she taught courses in administration and trained students to implement social welfare programs and policies. Citizens in Philadelphia and across the country protested in 1938 when, amid controversy, Dorothy Kahn was fired as executive officer by the local board. Her dismissal was a tremendous loss for Philadelphia, but it gave impetus to a movement to clarify standards for civil service employment and provide protection for workers.

Kahn left Philadelphia to become staff executive secretary and then staff president of the American Association of Social Workers. In these positions, she developed professional standards for public welfare workers and helped the social work profession define its role in the development of social policy and social welfare programs access the country.

From 1941 to 1943, she focused on the relief of refugees. She served as director of Economic Adjustment and Family Services at the National Refugee Service in New York. After World War II, she became the executive director of the Health and Welfare Council of New York City from 1945 to 1950 and concentrated on issues of adoption, the needs of the elderly, and the plight of recently immigrated Puerto Ricans.

From 1951 to 1954, Kahn was chief of the Social Welfare Division of the Department of Social Affairs of the United Nations. She directed her energies to meeting the challenge of worldwide social needs and raising the general level of human rights and welfare on a global level. She represented the UN at conferences on social work and child welfare in India, and advised the Israeli government of social welfare legislation.

After retiring from the UN in 1954, she returned to Hickory Farm, her summer home in New Hope, Pennsylvania. When Hurricane Diana hit the region in August 1955, bringing floods and dislocation, she organized emergency relief for the community. A few days later, on August 26, 1955, Dorothy C. Kahn died at home of a heart attack.

Kahn, an extraordinary woman, grappled with the major social problems of her day. Through social work programs and policies, she responded to the unmet human needs of her time. Underlying her life's work and articulated in her writings was a core of deeply held values that guided her. She viewed human need as part of the human condition and thought—as a matter of social justice—that society should find ways through its democratic institutions to meet those needs. She also believed that society should inculcate in all its citizens a sense of social responsibility and offer them the freedom to live productive and autonomous lives.

SELECTED WORKS BY DOROTHY C. KAHN

"The Challenge of World Wide Need." *Journal of Social Work Process* 6 (1955): 1–14; "Democratic Principles in Public Assistance." *Proceedings in the National Conference of Social Work: Selected Papers of the Sixty-Sixth Annual Conference of Social Work* (June 1939): 18–24; "Experiment in Selective Intake in a Family Society." *The Family* 13, no. 1 (March 1932): 3–8; "The Future of Family Social Work." *The Family* 9 (1928): 185–188; "The International Aspects of the Problem of the Unemployed in Relation to the Community." *Proceedings from the Third International Conference of Social Work* (1936): 537–545; "Problems in the Administration of Relief." *The Annals of the American Academy of Political and Social Science* 176 (November 1934): 40–48; "This Business of Relief: The Occasion for the Conference." *Proceedings from the 1936 Conference of the American Association of Social Workers* (1936): 7–14; "The Use of Cash, Orders for Goods, or Relief in Kind in a Mass Program." *The Family* 14 (October 1933): 198–202; "What is Worth Saving in 'This Business of Relief.'" *Survey Journal of Social Work* 73 (February 1937): 38–39.

BIBLIOGRAPHY

AJYB 58:477; *EJ*; Guler, Alvin. "She Failed to 'Cooperate.'" *The Compass* (October 1938) 3–23; Obituaries. *The Journal of Social Work Process* 6 (1955): 5–8, and *NYTimes*, August 27, 1955, 15:6, and *Social Sciences Review* (1955): 405; Trattnor, Walter. *Bibliographical Dictionary of Social Welfare in America* (1986); West, Walter, ed. "Dorothy Kahn Joins the Staff." *The Compass* (July 1939): 20; *WWIAJ* (1928, 1938).

JOAN DITZION

KAHN, FLORENCE PRAG (1866–1948)

"There is no sex in citizenship and there should be none in politics." So believed Florence Prag Kahn, the first Jewish woman to serve in the United States Congress. Though she arrived in the House of Representatives via a special election after the death of her Republican congressman husband, Julius Kahn, in

"There is no sex in citizenship and there should be none in politics."
So believed Florence Prag Kahn, the first Jewish woman to serve in Congress.
She is shown here in 1926, when she was acting speaker of the House of Representatives.
[Western Jewish History Center]

1924, she went on to win reelection in her own right five times (1925–1937) and to play a major role in shaping the economy and the geography of the San Francisco Bay Area.

Born in Salt Lake City, on November 9, 1866, but raised in San Francisco, Florence Prag Kahn was the first child of Mary (Goldsmith) Prag and Conrad Prag. Her only brother, Jessie, died at age ten in 1879. Conrad Prag, a Jewish merchant born in Warsaw, Poland, traveled to gold rush country in 1849, and in 1851 he helped found San Francisco's Congregation Sherith Israel. Kahn's mother came to San Francisco as a child of five and was raised in the city's young Jewish community. Mary Prag was a religious school (Congregation Emanu-El) and high school teacher who went on to become a vice principal and serve on the San Francisco Board of Education from 1921 until her death in 1935 at age eighty-nine. Florence was raised in a home that emphasized both Jewish and secular education.

That she graduated from the University of California in 1887 as one of only seven women in a class of forty gives some idea of her intense drive for education and achievement. Following in her mother's footsteps, she made teaching her profession, and taught high school English and history. On March 19, 1899, she married Julius Kahn, and the couple had two sons, Julius Jr. (b. 1902) and Conrad Prag (b. 1906). While her mother set an example for Kahn in public service, her husband brought her to national attention. Born in Germany, Julius Kahn came to San Francisco as a child.

Kahn and her husband arrived in Washington, D.C., as newlyweds in 1899. With Florence as his secretary, Julius Kahn would serve continuously in the House, except for the term 1902–1904, until his death in 1924. While very responsive to the needs of his constituents in California's Fourth Congressional District, Julius Kahn was especially concerned, as a member of the Military Affairs Committee, with the issue of preparedness. It was he, for example, who introduced the bill authorizing a draft following America's entry into World War I in 1917. When Florence Kahn succeeded him, she would follow his lead in her devotion to her district and to preparedness—but not out of blind allegiance to her late husband's memory. Rather, she had formulated her own ideas about public policy over the course of the decades.

Thanks to the columns she wrote for the *San Francisco Chronicle* in 1919 and 1920 while a congressional wife needing to supplement the family income, a great deal is known about Kahn's views before she became a politician in her own right. Indeed, Kahn's subsequent claim, when running to succeed her husband, that she had spent many hours haunting the House gallery is borne out by her close analyses of public issues.

Kahn had the conceptual and strategic capacities to envision sweeping changes for the Bay Area, and the political skills to implement them—at a time when only a tiny handful of women sat in Congress. For example, in her annual report to her constituents in 1930, shortly after she became the first woman to serve on the Military Affairs Committee, she discussed the military installations that she saw as good for her region and for the country. During her tenure in office, she introduced legislation that led to the creation of Moffett Field in Sunnyvale, Alameda Naval Air Station, and Hamilton Field, and to the building of the Bay Bridge linking Oakland and San Francisco. Newspaper accounts describe her as successfully maneuvering to get her bills passed. That she had a close relationship with her party no doubt helped her to be effective.

A deeply conservative woman, Kahn had opposed woman suffrage before California adopted it in 1911. As a member of Congress, she was a party loyalist. Yet she was also the first Republican member to dine in the Roosevelt White House in the 1930s. Said the frequently acerbic Alice Roosevelt Longworth, daughter of Theodore Roosevelt, in 1934: "Mrs. Kahn, shrewd, resourceful, and witty, is an all-around first-rate legislator, the equal of any man in Congress and the superior of most." In her years in Congress, Kahn was noteworthy for her opposition to Prohibition and to movie censorship.

Belonging to many Jewish and secular organizations, in both San Francisco and Washington, Kahn supported the NATIONAL COUNCIL OF JEWISH WOMEN, HADASSAH, the Association of University Women, and the Congressional Club. She was also a member of Congregation Emanu-El in San Francisco. Kahn possessed a sparkling wit, often bringing her Jewishness to the forefront. As the daughter and granddaughter of founders of San Francisco and its Jewish community, Kahn was especially qualified to represent its diverse population.

When Florence Prag Kahn died on November 16, 1948, she left a legacy of women's and Jewish leadership for generations to follow. Truly, she was a female politician ahead of her time.

BIBLIOGRAPHY

AJYB 44:413, 47:629, 51:522; *BEDAJ*; *DAB* 4; Dalin, David G. "Jewish and Non-Partisan Republicansim in San Francisco, 1911–1963." *American Jewish History* 68 (June 1979): 492–516; *EJ*, s.v. "Kahn, Julius"; Gelfand, Duff. "Gentlewomen of the House." *American Mercury* 18 (October 1929): 151–160; Hansen, Harriet. "Woman Enters Politics: San Francisco's Pioneer Congresswoman, Florence Prag Kahn." Master's thesis, San Francisco State University (1969); Kahn, Florence Prag. Papers. Western Jewish Center, Judah Magnes Museum, Berkeley, Calif.; Keyes, Frances Parkinson. "The Lady from California." *Delineator* 118 (February 1931); Longworth, Alice Roosevelt. "What Are the Women Up To?" *Ladies' Home Journal* 51 (March 1934); *NAW*; Obituary. *NYTimes*, November 17, 1948, 27:5; Prag, Mary Goldsmith. "Early Days." Typescript, Kahn Papers. Western Jewish History Center, Berkeley, Calif.; Stern, Norton B. "The Prags in Brief." *Western States Jewish History* 17 (January 1985): 163–169; *UJE*, s.v. "Kahn, Julius"; *WWIAJ* (1926, 1928, 1938); *WWWIA* 2.

AVA F. KAHN
GLENNA MATTHEWS

KAHN, JOAN (1914–1994)

In 1947, Harper Brothers launched Harper Novels of Suspense under the leadership of a new editor named Joan Kahn. Several years later, in an interview with John Winterich, Kahn spoke about the inception of this extremely successful publishing venture: "At first, every agent cleaned out the bottom drawer. We got something like 200 manuscripts that had been everywhere and seen everybody. I was discouraged and decided I was in the wrong business. But I went through the manuscripts and we took several." When one of those books, *The Horizontal Man* by Helen Eustis, won the annual Edgar Allan Poe Award from the Mystery Writers of America as the best first mystery novel of 1946, Kahn decided she "was in the right business."

After a few more books selected by Kahn won Edgars, Harper added the phrase "A Joan Kahn Book" to its mystery imprint. Kahn edited the work of hundreds of writers, including Tony Hillerman, Dick Francis, John Creasey, Nicholas Blake, John Dickson Carr, and Nicholas Freeling. She introduced American readers to many British writers, including Dorothy Sayers, whose books were out of print until Harper republished her complete works in the 1950s.

In 1985, Kahn received the Ellery Queen Award from the Mystery Writers of America for lifetime service to the industry. When she retired in 1989, she received a special Edgar—she is the only editor who has ever received one—in recognition of her distinguished career.

A native New Yorker, Joan Kahn was born on April 13, 1914, the oldest child of Ely Jacques Kahn, an architect renowned for his mastery of the art deco style, and Elsie (Plaut) Kahn. Her brother, E.J. Kahn Jr., was a writer; her sister, Olivia, is a painter. Kahn attended the Horace Mann School, the Yale School of Art, Barnard College, and the Art Students League. She wrote two novels—*To Meet Miss Long* (1943) and *Open House* (1946)—and four children's books, and edited eleven mystery anthologies.

In 1980, she left Harper to join Ticknor & Fields. She also worked at E.P. Dutton and St. Martin's Press, where she stayed until she retired. Joan Kahn died on October 12, 1994.

SELECTED WORKS BY JOAN KAHN

Chilling and Killing (1978); *The Edge of the Chair* (1967); *Hanging by a Thread* (1969); *Hi, Jock, Run Around the Block* (1978); *Ladies and Gentlemen, Said the Ringmaster* (1938); *Open at Your Own Risk* (1975); *Open House* (1946); *Ready or Not, Here Come Fourteen Frightening Stories!* (1987); *Seesaw* (1964); *Some Things Dark and Dangerous* (1970); *Some Things Fierce and Fatal* (1971); *Some Things Strange and Sinister* (1973); *Some Things Weird and Wicked: Twelve Stories to Chill Your Bones* (1976); *To Meet Miss Long* (1943); *Trial and Terror* (1973); *You Can't Catch Me* (1976).

BIBLIOGRAPHY

Bannon, Barbara A. "Authors & Editors." *Publishers Weekly* 196 (December 29, 1969): 21–22; Kahn, Joan. Papers and book collection. Sterling Library. Yale University; Rule, Sheila. "Joan Kahn, 80, Respected Editor of Mysteries, Dies." *NYTimes*, October 13, 1994, B15; *Who's Who in America*. Vol. 1 (1984–1985): 1704; Winterich, John T. "Joan Kahn and Harper Mysteries." *Publishers Weekly* 166 (July 21, 1954): 450–453.

ANNE GLICKMAN

KALICH, BERTHA (1874–1939)

Known for her majestic bearing, great beauty, and fine diction, Bertha Kalich was the first actress to make the transition from the Yiddish to the English stage. Critics called her the "Jewish Bernhardt" and she herself later estimated that she had played some 125 roles in seven languages during her long theatrical career. Kalich was one of the great stars of the golden age of the American Yiddish theater and, for a time, a leading light of mainstream American drama as well.

Born Beylke Kalakh on May 17, 1874 (according to some sources, 1872 or 1875), in Lemberg, then Austria-Hungary, she was the only child of Solomon

Known as the "Jewish Bernhardt," Bertha Kalich was one of the great stars of the golden age of the American Yiddish theater and, for a time, a leading light of mainstream American drama as well. [American Jewish Historical Society]

Kalakh, a brush manufacturer of modest means and an amateur violinist, and Babette (Halber) Kalakh, a dressmaker who made costumes for local theaters. A devotee of the opera, Babette Kalakh often took her daughter to performances, where the child fell in love with the stage.

Kalich studied music and drama in private schools and attended the Lemberg Conservatory. At age thirteen, she joined the chorus of the local Polish theater. She later performed in German as well. As a prima donna with the pioneering Yiddish theater group of Yankev Ber Gimpel, she played the title role in Avrom Goldfaden's *Shulamis*. It was at that time that she adopted the name Bertha Kalich. (Other variations of her name include Kalisch and Kalish.) After performing in Budapest, Kalich returned to Lemberg to become a member of Goldfaden's troupe, with which she traveled to Romania. There she learned Romanian in a matter of months and appeared in major roles with the state theater. She was such a success that anti-Semitic theatergoers, who had come with the intention of pelting her with onions, threw flowers instead.

In 1890, Kalich married Leopold Spachner. The couple had two children, Arthur, who died young, and Lillian.

Fearing a rumored assassination plot by jealous rivals, Kalich accepted an offer by Joseph Edelstein to come to New York to perform in his Thalia Theater. She arrived in the United States in 1894 (according to some sources, 1895 or 1896), appearing in *Di Vilde Kenigin* [The wild queen] and a Yiddish production of *La Belle Hélène*. She also took the roles of Shulamis, Juliette, and Desdemona.

In America, Kalich sought to emphasize her dramatic skills over her musical talents. She became known as a proponent of the movement for a Yiddish theater of higher artistic quality than was common at the time. Kalich's performance in Leon Kobrin's *The East Side Ghetto* won critical and popular acclaim. She distinguished herself especially in the works of playwright Jacob Gordin, whose didactic plays brought serious subjects to the Yiddish stage. In 1900, she starred as Freydenyu in the first production of Gordin's *God, Man, and Devil*. Gordin wrote the role of Etty in *The Kreutzer Sonata* and the title role of his *Sappho* especially for Kalich. Over the years, Kalich played in many other Gordin roles. She also appeared in plays by Z. Libin, Dovid Pinsky, I.L. Peretz, and others.

For a time, Kalich was a partner with her husband and several others in the Thalia Theater. In addition to the Thalia, she appeared in the Rumania Opera House, the Grand Theater, and elsewhere. For at least one season, Spachner rented the Windsor Theater and renamed it the Kalich Theater.

Kalich's work on the Yiddish stage attracted the attention of prominent English-language theatrical producers. Her first English part was in the title role of *Fédora*, by Victorien Sardou, at the American Theater in 1905. Later that year, she signed with Harrison Grey Fiske and appeared in his production of Maurice Maeterlinck's *Monna Vanna* at the Manhattan Theater. She labored for months with Minnie Maddern Fiske to correct her foreign accent, an effort in which she was largely successful. Over the next several years, Kalich acted in a number of plays for Fiske, both original works and adaptations of roles that she had created in Yiddish. By 1910, however, she was having trouble finding suitable roles in the light American theater for her more emotional and tragic style. She and Fiske parted company, and her career receded. Over the next decade, Kalich worked with Lee Shubert and Arthur Hopkins, and appeared in several early films. In 1923, she performed in *Jitta's Atonement*, adapted by George Bernard Shaw from the work of Siegfried Trebitsch. Her other English roles in the 1920s included revivals of her earlier successes such as *The Kreutzer Sonata*.

Beginning in 1915, Kalich returned frequently to the Yiddish stage. There her success in the broader American theatrical world enhanced her prestige. Kalich appeared at the Second Avenue Theatre with Dovid Kessler, at Boris Thomashefsky's National Theater, at the Irving Place Theatre, and at other New York theaters, as well as in Philadelphia and Chicago. She acted in plays by Rose Shomer and MIRIAM SHOMER ZUNSER, Esther Steinberg, Peretz Hirschbein, Moyshe Shor, and others.

By the late 1920s, Kalich's health began to fail, and she gradually lost her sight. She announced her retirement in 1931, but took the stage occasionally thereafter, especially at several evenings mounted by the theatrical community especially for her benefit. She also played scenes from Goldfaden's historical plays on *The Forward Hour* on radio station WEVD, rehearsing strenuously even for short parts. Her last appearance came on February 23, 1939, at a benefit for her at the Jolson Theater, when she recited the final scene of Louis Untermeyer's poem "Heine's Death."

Bertha Kalich died on April 18, 1939. Only fifteen hundred people attended her funeral, considered a disappointing turnout. By that time, she seemed to be a relic of the theatrical past, with a manner too romantic and grand even for the Yiddish stage. Nevertheless, in the prime of her career at the beginning of the twentieth century, Kalich played an important role in efforts to improve the artistic standards of the Yiddish theater, whose status she also helped to raise with her success with English-speaking audiences.

BIBLIOGRAPHY

AJYB 6 (1904–1905):192, 41:425; Brynner, Witter. "Bertha Kalich: The Yiddish Actress." *Critic* 47 (1905): 26; Danziger, Adolph. "The Hebrew Theater." *Metropolitan Magazine* 27 (December 1907): 348–359; *EJ*; Lifson, David S. *The Yiddish Theater in America* (1965); *NAW*; Obituaries. *Jewish Daily Forward*, April 19, 1939, 1 and *NYTimes*, April 19, 1939, 23; *Tog*, April 19, 1939, 1; Zylbercweig, Zalmen. *Leksikon fun Yidishn Teater* (1963), 4:2425–2458.

DANIEL SOYER

KANDER, LIZZIE BLACK
(1858–1940)

"The way to a man's heart is through his stomach." In 1901, Lizzie Kander and Mrs. Henry Schoenfeld used this adage in the title of a cookbook produced for the benefit of the first settlement house in Milwaukee, Wisconsin. By 1984, nearly two million copies of *The Settlement Cook Book: The Way to a Man's Heart* had been sold. Its success can be attributed to the determination and ingenuity of a woman known as the "Jane Addams of Milwaukee."

Lizzie Black Kander, born in Milwaukee on May 28, 1858, was the third of John and Mary (Pereles) Black's five children. Siblings included Annie Wetzler, Flora Gottachalk, and Herman, a newspaper publisher. She graduated in 1878 from Milwaukee High School and married Simon Kander, a salesman from Baltimore, on May 17, 1881. They were married for fifty years.

Kander began her service to the Jewish community in 1878 as a volunteer in the Ladies Relief Sewing Society, an organization that evolved into the Milwaukee Jewish Mission formed in 1896 under her leadership. As president of "The Settlement" (1900–1918), Kander took a pragmatic and practical approach to problems and programs. In one project, excess steam from a local brewery was utillized to heat water for community bathing facilities. Along with other volunteers, Kander developed popular cooking classes for young immigrants and supervised educational, social, and recreational programs for neighborhood residents.

In 1901, the Settlement's board denied Kander's request to underwrite the cost of printing recipe booklets for her classes. Undaunted, Kander approached the Milwaukee business community, secured outside funding, and had one thousand copies printed. Excess copies were sold through a local department store for fifty cents each. An expanded 1903 edition, supported by sixty-five local sponsors, included 180 pages of household hints, kitchen-tested recipes, and reliable instructions for preparing traditional and German Jewish foods. Kander became head of the Settlement Cook Book Company in 1914 and subsequently supervised the publication of twenty-three editions. Profits from this successful business venture funded newer and larger facilities, the Abraham Lincoln House, built in 1911, and the Jewish Community Center, opened in 1931.

Kander utilized her leadership skills in a voluntary association and carved out a unique career as a female activist and entrepreneur. She identified issues, devised creative strategies, and sought out alternative funding

Lizzie Kander used the adage "The way to a man's heart is through his stomach" on the cover of the first edition of her Settlement Cook Book *in 1901. She was right. By 1984, nearly two million copies had been sold. The above photo of Kander is the frontispiece of the twenty-fourth edition (1941). [Collection of Barbara Kirshenblatt-Gimblett, New York. Jewish Museum/Art Resource, NY]*

solutions in order to shape and support a vital community institution. *The Settlement Cook Book* tapped into and capitalized on emerging local services and pioneering national trends: the organization and development of settlement houses, the interests of American women in nutritious meal planning and scientific home management, and the growth of autonomous funding mechanisms for nonprofit charitable associations.

Kander was an advocate of vocational education for women. She served on the Milwaukee school board from 1907 to 1919, helping to establish the Girls Technical High School as well as the nursery school at Milwaukee Teachers College. In 1939, Wisconsin honored Kander as one of the state's outstanding women. She belonged to the Social Science Club, the NATIONAL COUNCIL OF JEWISH WOMEN, the Southside Women's Club, and Congregation Emanuel B'ne Jeshurun. She died at age eighty-two on July 24, 1940.

BIBLIOGRAPHY

Crocker, Ruth Hutchinson. *Social Work and Social Order: The Settlement Movement in Two Industrial Cities, 1889–1930* (1992); Obituary. *NYTimes*, July 26, 1940, 17:6; *NAW*; Scott, Anne Firor. *Natural Allies: Women's Associations in American History* (1991); Trolander, Judith A. *Professionalism and Social Change: From the Settlement House Movement to Neighborhood Centers, 1886 to the Present* (1987).

BETH DiNATALE JOHNSON

KANIN, FAY (b. c. 1917)

Fay Kanin, first female president of the Motion Picture Academy, served an unprecedented four terms (1983–1988). Over a sixty-year career as a writer, actor, coproducer, and activist, she was awarded several Emmys and Peabodys, the ACLU Bill of Rights Award, the Crystal Award from Women in Film, the Burning Bush Award from the University of Judaism, and nominations for Oscar and Tony awards.

Born Fay Mitchell in New York City in a year she never disclosed, her parents, American-born Reform Jews, were Bessie Kaiser Mitchell, a housewife and activist, and David Mitchell, whose work managing small department stores took the family to Elmira, New York.

Resourceful and fearless, Fay was enchanted by films and performers. An only child, she benefited from her parents' encouragement but "grew up fast," mediating in their unhappy marriage.

At age twelve, she won a state spelling contest and met New York governor Franklin D. Roosevelt. She was "smitten" with both Roosevelts, who maintained a connection with her. Although too young to vote, Kanin was a speaker for FDR in the 1932 presidential campaign and afterward visited the Roosevelts at the White House.

At Elmira College, Fay "joined any activity involving words" (including radio). After her father took a job in Los Angeles, she completed her B.A. at the University of Southern California (1937).

Soon she became a script reader at RKO studios, where she "stayed on at night to do my own writing. I walked on sets, invaded editing rooms, snooped, made friends. Hollywood was like all your childhood fantasies come true, full of beautiful people having a simply marvelous time."

At RKO, Fay and Michael Kanin met. They married in 1940 and spent their honeymoon writing a screenplay. Aided by a vogue for husband-and-wife teams (among them Michael Kanin's brother Garson Kanin and his wife, Ruth Gordon), they became

The first female president of the Academy of Motion Picture Arts and Sciences, Fay Kanin served an unprecedented four terms. As a veteran in the highly competitive field of screenwriting, Kanin speaks through the journalist in her TV movie Hustling, *who tells a prostitute, "Everybody hustles. Some of us just don't get arrested for it." She is shown above with her husband, Michael, with whom she has written a number of screenplays. [New York Public Library]*

established screenwriters. They had two sons, Joshua and David, who were sent to the Brandeis Camp Institute for a Jewish education.

During World War II, with Roosevelt's support, Kanin produced a radio series encouraging women to contribute to the war effort. After the war, she wrote *Goodbye, My Fancy*, a play whose congresswoman heroine was modeled on Eleanor Roosevelt. By 1949, Kanin had a Broadway hit.

The Kanin screenwriting team went on to earn an Academy Award nomination for *Teacher's Pet* (1957). A frothy romantic comedy, the film also expressed Fay Kanin's valuation of women's worth and of civil liberties. Doris Day's feisty journalism professor character upholds the allure of brains in an era when "sexy" and "smart" were considered incompatible. She treasures free speech at a time when left-leaning Americans were blacklisted from employment. When the Kanins themselves had appeared on "red" lists, they turned for work to Broadway. *Rashomon* (1957), their version of the Japanese film, became a staple of theater repertory. After some twenty years, the professional Kanin team broke up. "We decided we would have to keep the working collaboration or the marriage. We decided on the marriage," Fay Kanin explained.

Kanin took on responsibilities for the Writers Guild and, as president of the Screen Branch, sat on the Motion Picture Academy board. With director Martin Scorsese, she led the American Film Institute's effort to preserve films. Because prevalent Hollywood wisdom deemed women fit to write only "women's pictures," "small" stories of character and relationships supposedly unsuited to the big screen, Kanin turned to the new TV movie genre, where a writer (especially if she coproduced) could see her conception realized. She wrote (or adapted) and coproduced *Tell Me Where It Hurts* (1974), *Hustling* (1975), *Friendly Fire* (1979), and *Heartsounds* (1984), movies featuring women's lives and issues.

Kanin rightly calls her television films "the blossoming of my own personal statements." As a veteran of a high-risk field, Kanin speaks through the journalist in *Hustling*, who tells a prostitute, "Everybody hustles. Some of us just don't get arrested for it." Kanin, the socially entrenched daughter-wife-mother-partner, is heard in the prostitute's declaration of interdependence: "It's okay to owe somebody. It's good." In *Friendly Fire*, Lieutenant Schindler uses the words of the Talmud to speak for Fay Kanin, liberal Jewish-American: "If you save a single person, you save the world."

Fay Kanin has combined a journalist's curiosity, a dramatist's appreciation for points of view, and a rabbi's

gift for teaching through the word to interpret her times for a mass audience. Embraced by women as a model and trailblazer, she responded, "I don't think you think of yourself as a pioneer. I just felt very fortunate."

SELECTED WORKS BY FAY KANIN

The Gay Life. Katharine Cornell Collection, New York Public Library of the Performing Arts; *Goodbye, My Fancy* (1949); *Grind*; *Rashomon*, with Michael Kanin (1957).

FILM AND TELEVISION

Friendly Fire (1979); *Heartsounds* (1984); *Hustling* (1975); *The Opposite Sex* (1956); *Teacher's Pet*, with Michael Kanin (1957).

BIBLIOGRAPHY

Atkins, Irene Kahn. *Fay Kanin*. Oral history for American Jewish Committee, July 15, 1980, August 20, 1980, July 31, 1981. Jewish Collection, New York Public Library; *Contemporary Theatre, Film, and Television*. Vol. 4 (1987); *Fay Kanin: An American Film Institute Seminar on Her Work* (1977). Microfilm, New York Public Library of the Performing Arts; Froug, William. *A Screenwriter Looks at the Screenwriter* (1972); *International Motion Picture Almanac* (1966); Kanin, Fay. Interview with Ally Acker. Transcript, Museum of Modern Art Film Study Collection, NYC; Kanin, Fay. Telephone interview by author, August 21, 1996; *Notable Names in the American Theatre* (1976); *Notable Women in the American Theatre*. Edited by Alice M. Robinson, Vera Mowry Roberts, and Milly S. Barranger (1989); Reilly, Sue. "Fay Kanin Throws a Party for Tout Hollywood and the World: She's Oscar Night's First Lady," *People Weekly* (April 21, 1980): 45; Smith, Sharon. *Women Who Make Movies* (1975).

HARRIET REISEN

KAPLAN, ALINE (1923–1983)

Aline Kaplan was one of the most dynamic Jewish leaders of the twentieth century. As executive director of HADASSAH, the Women's Zionist Organization, Kaplan touched thousands of lives both in the United States and abroad. She credited Hadassah's success to "the level of creative leadership and commitment of its volunteers," which numbered 370,000 worldwide under her leadership.

Kaplan was born to Morris and Dora (Zeresky) Kaplan in New York in June 1923, one of three daughters. Her family was committed to Jewish culture and Jewish values, which Kaplan incorporated into her adult life. She devoted herself to strengthening Judaism and Zionism.

Kaplan practiced law from 1946 to 1952, with expertise in estate planning and real estate matters. The practice of law, however, did not fulfill her intellectual

One of the most dynamic Jewish leaders of the twentieth century, Aline Kaplan, when she was executive director of HADASSAH, pushed the membership of the organization to an unprecedented 370,000 women worldwide. [Hadassah Archives]

or spiritual needs. In 1952, she left her law practice to become the director of Junior Hadassah (now Hashachar). She found creating educational programs for Jewish youth a better way of living out her Jewish values than the practice of law. In order to better serve the Jewish community she undertook graduate studies at Yeshiva University, earning a doctorate in Jewish history.

Kaplan held a succession of important posts within Hadassah: in 1964, assistant to the executive director; in 1970, assistant executive director; and in 1971, executive director, a post she held until her death. Fluent in Hebrew, Kaplan made yearly trips to Israel, both to oversee Hadassah's work there and for her own pleasure.

Kaplan was a delegate to the World Zionist Congress beginning in 1956. She was a member of the board of directors of the American Zionist Federation, the United Israel Appeal, and the National Council of the American-Israel Public Affairs Committee. She

wrote articles for the *Zionist Encyclopedia* and other publications.

Aline Kaplan died of heart failure on September 29, 1983.

BIBLIOGRAPHY

AJYB 85:416; Hunter College Hall of Fame, Alumni Association, 1983; Obituary. *NYTimes*, October 2, 1983; "Tribute to Aline Kaplan" (October 6, 1984). Hadassah Archives, NYC; *WWWIA* 8.

DEBRA NEWMAN KAMIN

KAPLAN, REGINA (1887–1957)

"Woman of valor" and "a tiny dynamo"—these phrases describe Regina Kaplan (nicknamed Kappy), nurse, teacher, hospital administrator, and health care innovator.

She was born to Gershon and Adella (Hannah Traube) Kaplan, German-born immigrants, in Memphis, Tennessee, on May 12, 1887. Her father had taught school in Germany. Kaplan was the third of five children: Sally, Belle, Regina, Louis G., and Dora. She always said that she learned *chesed* [loving-kindness] from her parents.

In 1908, Kaplan graduated first in a class of twelve from Mercy Hospital Training School for Nurses, in Denver, Colorado, and worked as a private duty nurse. Although rejected as too short for military service during World War I, she enrolled with the American Red Cross on January 14, 1915 (badge number 5482).

For thirty-five years, Kaplan was superintendent and administrator of the Leo N. Levi Hospital in Hot Springs, Arkansas. Beginning in 1916, she developed its School of Nursing, the first school in the South to admit males. The school closed in September 1952.

In 1917, Kaplan organized and directed its outpatient dispensary. She set up a local Red Cross chapter and taught classes in nurse's aide preparation, home nursing, and first aid to adults and high school students. She hired the first school nurse for Hot Springs and encouraged the establishment of a free public health nursing program.

Kaplan belonged to the American Nurses Association from 1918 on, the Arkansas Nurses Association, and the Colorado State Nurses Association. She chaired the National Rehabilitation Association in the State Hospitals (1928) and was a member of the American College of Hospital Administrators. She attended two hospital administrators institutes: Purdue

University in 1940 and Colorado University in 1945. She belonged to the American Hospital Association (vice president, 1945–1946) and urged Levi Hospital's participation in Blue Cross. Kaplan felt so positively about Blue Cross that she became a member of the board of trustees of the Arkansas Blue Cross, Blue Shield. She continued serving the Garland County Red Cross as executive secretary (1917–1945). In 1944, she was honored with brunch at the White House.

Kaplan founded the Lakewood Convalescent Home for "old age indigents" of Garland County and served as its president from 1946 to 1953. During this time, she also served as president of the Arkansas Hospital Association (1947–1948), was a member of the Mid-West Hospital Association (1948–1949), and was on the advisory consultant board of hospitals for Arkansas, State Board of Health (1949–1953). From 1942 to 1951, she listed herself as organizer and director of the National Arthritis Research Foundation (NARF), an organization that competed with the American Rheumatism Association. NARF funded several projects at the University of Arkansas, then folded. Kaplan contributed to professional journals and read papers before sectional meetings of the American College of Surgeons.

Kaplan served as director and chair of the Temple Beth Israel choir, in which she sang soprano. She also served on Beth Israel's board of directors. She was a member of the board of directors of the Community Concert Association, president of the Federation of Church Women (1943–1945), secretary of the Hot Springs Community Council, and a member of Eastern Star, HADASSAH, and B'nai B'rith. Her club associations included Dale Carnegie, Business and Professional Women, and Explorers.

Kaplan retired on January 16, 1951, but remained a consultant to Levi Hospital. In 1953, she began a second career as director of central supply, St. Joseph's Hospital, Hot Springs, and was a charter member of the St. Joseph's Hospital Guild.

Diagnosed with cancer, she left Hot Springs to return to Denver. Regina Kaplan died at the Jewish Hospital in Denver on October 8, 1957, her adopted daughter Betty Uzick at her side.

BIBLIOGRAPHY

De Kruif, Paul. "The Ace of Hearts." In *Life among the Doctors* (1949); LeMaster, C. *Regina Kaplan: Arkansas's 'Lady with the Lamp.'* (1987); Mayer, Susan L. "The Jewish Experience in Nursing in America: 1881 to 1955." Ed.D. diss., Teachers College, Columbia University (1996); *WWIAJ* (1938).

SUSAN MAYER

KAPLAN, ROSE (1867–1917)

Rose Kaplan was a pioneer in health care in Palestine and helped to initiate the medical work funded by HADASSAH, the Women's Zionist Organization of America, in the years after its founding in 1912.

Born on September 4, 1867, in Petrograd (St. Petersburg), Russia, Kaplan immigrated to the United States in 1892. After graduating from Mount Sinai Hospital Training School for Nurses, she served as a nurse in the Spanish-American War. Although not a Zionist, she was hired by Hadassah in 1913 to travel to Palestine and set up its district visiting nursing program, along with RAE LANDY. Together, with financial assistance from Nathan and Ida Straus, Kaplan and Landy set up the Hadassah Nurses Settlement in the Mea Shearim section of Jerusalem. While the aim of the nurses was to provide health care to patients in Jerusalem and other settlements, they received almost no cooperation from local doctors, who were unaccustomed to visiting nurses and viewed them as little more than assistants. Eventually, Kaplan and Landy established working relationships with a few doctors, doing maternity work and trachoma prevention in Jewish schools.

With the outbreak of World War I, when shipments of supplies and communication with the West became difficult, Hadassah offered to release the two nurses from their contracts, although they decided to continue their work in Jerusalem. As conditions deteriorated, however, both Kaplan and Landy returned to the United States, leaving the settlement in the hands of Dr. Helena Kagan, who had established a medical practice there.

Arriving back in New York in January 1915, Kaplan expressed to Hadassah officials her desire to be sent to work as a nurse in the refugee camp set up by the British in Alexandria, Egypt, for Jews expelled from Palestine. While in the United States, she underwent surgery for cancer, but chose to return to work despite a poor prognosis. In November, she sailed for the Middle East, but her ship, the SS *Athenai*, caught on fire after two days at sea. The passengers were rescued, and Kaplan was returned to New York, where she resolutely demanded to be sent again to Alexandria.

In Alexandria, she carried on trachoma work, treated children with skin diseases, fought malnutrition, and taught hygiene to children. She distributed clothing and linens sewn by Hadassah women and sent cheerful descriptions of her activities back to the American organization. From both Jerusalem and Alexandria, her detailed and optimistic reports to Hadassah,

This 1913 photograph includes the first two American nurses sent by HADASSAH to Jerusalem, Rose Kaplan (on the left) and RACHEL LANDY, on the right, with a visitor in between. They are posing outside the original Hadassah welfare station, which provided maternity care and treatment of trachoma. [Hadassah Archives]

many of which were published in the *Hadassah Newsletter*, promoted the Zionist cause among American Jewish women, allowing them to see the tangible results of their organizational efforts.

Although failing in health and constantly losing weight, Kaplan determined to continue her work and never revealed her condition to her American sponsors. She died in Alexandria on August 3, 1917, and was buried there among the Jewish soldiers of the Zion Mule Corps. Several years later, her remains were moved to Jerusalem under Hadassah auspices and reburied on the Mount of Olives. In the months after Kaplan's death, HENRIETTA SZOLD, the founder of Hadassah, wrote that if the organization's medical work was to resume in Palestine after the war, it could do so only by emulating the selflessness and dedication to public service that Kaplan had exemplified.

BIBLIOGRAPHY

AJYB 20 (1918–1919): 229; Brownstone, Mina. "Rose S. Kaplan, 1867–1917." Typescript, Hadassah Archives, NYC; Dash, Joan. *Summoned to Jerusalem: The Life of Henrietta Szold* (1979); Obituary. *NYTimes*, August 8, 1917, 7:4; Szold, Henrietta. "Rose Kaplan." *Maccabaean* 31 (1918): 37–39.

ERIC L. GOLDSTEIN

KARFF, N. MAY (b. 1914)

May Karff, the "queen of American chess," was a dominant force in American women's chess for over forty years. She was born in Europe (exact place unknown) in 1914 and immigrated to America with her father sometime between 1927 and 1933. Her training in chess came both from her father and from experts in Palestine, with whom she played in her early years. Karff made her debut on the international chess scene at a tournament in Stockholm in 1937. Playing for Palestine, she placed an impressive sixth out of a field of twenty-six opponents.

Her first American appearance was even more striking. The United States Women's Championship of 1938 was the site of two firsts for Karff. It was not only her first American tournament, it was the first tournament held under national auspices for the women's title. The awarding of that title, "woman champion of the United States," was heralded as an indicator of the great strides women were making in chess. Karff made the title hers by besting seven other players without a single loss. When the results of Karff's dramatic victory were announced, it was to a prolonged burst of applause. The queen of American chess had arrived.

Demonstrating a champion's mettle, Karff fought to a triple tie in her next tournament and won in the playoff. She lost her title to A. Rivero in 1939, but did not play her again until 1941 because the championship was changed to a biennial basis. The champion was forced to give up her title when Karff raced to a five-to-one lead in the best of eight series. Her monetary reward for this authoritative comeback, in which she won the second game in only twenty-five moves, was, at the time, a staggering $197. During the next United States Women's Open Championship, May Karff demolished eight formidable opponents in a row, having a close call in only one of the matches.

The United States Women's Open was unmistakably Karff's personal domain. As late as 1974, she won the championship with a score of six wins and four losses. She played in the tournament eighteen times. She was first or tied for first seven times, was second four times, and was third or tied for third seven times.

At a contest held in Moscow in late 1949, Karff was one of two players representing the United States. She tied for fourteenth place out of sixteen. Although in 1939 she had placed fifth among twenty, Karff never achieved as well outside the United States as she did at home. Her prowess on the American scene and her solid play, if not yielding satisfying results, earned her the title of International Female Master in 1950 from the Fédération Internationale des Echecs. May Karff lives in New York City.

BIBLIOGRAPHY

American Chess Bulletin 34 (July/August 1937): 66, and 35 (March/April 1938): 27, and 38 (September/October 1941): 104, and 38 (November/December 1941): 122, and 39 (March/April 1942): 26; *UJE*; Weygant, Heather. Communication with author, December 6, 1996.

MARK OEHLERT

KARMEL, ILONA (b. 1925)

Ilona Karmel has transformed details of her experiences as a Polish-Jewish prisoner in Nazi work camps and as a patient undergoing a prolonged convalescence into two compelling and memorable novels.

Born in Cracow to Hirsch and Mita (Rosenbaum) Karmel on August 19, 1925, Ilona joined her older sister, Henryka (later Henia), in a middle-class branch of a Jewish family that embraced both nonobservant and Orthodox members. Her comfortable childhood ended when the Nazis occupied Poland. Along with her mother and sister, Ilona was interned in three successive labor camps; she credits their mother with ensuring the girls' survival.

Karmel followed her sister to the United States in 1948 after spending two years recuperating in German and Swedish hospitals from leg injuries she sustained during the last days of the war. Within four years, Karmel had earned her B.A. in English from Radcliffe (and a Phi Beta Kappa key), won the 1950 *Mademoiselle* College Fiction Contest, and prepared the manuscript of her first novel, *Stephania*. Her prize-winning short story was not her first published material, however. Poems that Ilona and Henryka had secretly written in the camps were published in New York, in their original Polish, before Ilona's arrival in the United States.

The protagonist of *Stephania* is a young Polish-Jewish woman seeking treatment in a Swedish hospital for her spinal curvature, worsened by Nazi abuses. By the novel's end, she understands her blamelessness in the death of her parents and realizes that she can have a meaningful life despite her loss. Reviewers praised Karmel's perceptiveness and skillful prose. Most also acknowledged her own recent hospitalization and emigration, but few directly addressed her Jewishness or the extent of her persecution by the Nazis.

Published in 1969, *An Estate of Memory* describes the struggle for survival of four unrelated Jewish women imprisoned in a Nazi labor camp in Poland. The women's commitment to one another and to themselves undergoes its greatest test in response to the pregnancy of one of them. As with actual camp inmates, even the most valiant efforts could not guarantee their return to life "in the freedom" beyond the war, and only the precious and incomplete legacy of remembrance would remain to those who survived the war's immeasurable damage. Early reviews of *An Estate of Memory* were mixed, though in her front-page appraisal in the *New York Times Book Review* Elizabeth Janeway compared Karmel to Hemingway and Solzhenitsyn. Perhaps the daunting subject, represented moreover in a technically challenging prose, accounts for the book's indifferent reception. Until the Feminist Press reissued it in 1986, it had been out of print for several years.

Karmel has played an important role in the lives of many students. From 1979 to 1995, she was a senior lecturer in creative writing at the Massachusetts Institute of Technology, which recognized her exceptional success as a teacher with two significant awards. In May 1994, Karmel received the rare Dean's Award for Distinguished Service; upon her retirement in 1995, the annual Writing Prize (a competition she had organized for many years) was renamed in her honor.

Even without additional publications, Karmel's reputation has grown. Both of her novels have been translated into several languages. The development of feminist and Holocaust studies has renewed interest in *An Estate of Memory*, which now is considered one of the most significant novels in English to address the particular experiences of Jewish women during World War II. Yet Karmel herself avoids using labels like "feminist" or even "Holocaust" to categorize her work—or to classify people. She has traveled to Germany several times, often accompanying her husband, physicist Francis Zucker, on his lectures abroad. In a 1953 interview, she said, "People are not evil, [just] weak. . . .You can't hate everyone if you are to go on living."

SELECTED WORKS BY ILONA KARMEL

An Estate of Memory (1969. Reprint 1986); "Fru Holm." *Mademoiselle* (August 1950): 203; "Ivan Karamazov." *Ironwood* 15 (Fall 1987): 211–226; *Spiew za Drutami* [Song behind the wire], with Henryka Karmel-Wolfe (1947); *Stephania* (1953).

BIBLIOGRAPHY

Angress, Ruth K. Afterword to *An Estate of Memory*, by Ilona Karmel (1986); "Camp Consolations." *Times Literary Supplement*, August 14, 1970, 893; Ezrahi, Sidra Dekoven. *By Words Alone: The Holocaust in Literature* (1980); Gaither, Frances. "The Three in Hospital Room Five." *NYTimes Book Review*, March 29, 1953, 4; Heinemann, Marlene. *Gender and Destiny: Women Writers and the Holocaust* (1986); [Hollowood, A.B.] Review of *Stephania*, by Ilona Karmel. *Punch*, May 5, 1954, 562; Holzhauer, Jean. "Little People." *Commonweal*, April 24, 1953, 81–82; [Hook, Stuart.] "Poor Girls." *Listener*, August 6, 1970, 187; Horowitz, Sara R. "Ilona Karmel." In *Jewish-American Women Writers: A Bio-bibliographical and Critical Sourcebook*, edited by Ann R. Shapiro (1994), and "Linguistic Displacement in Fictional Responses to the Holocaust." Ph.D. diss., Brandeis University, 1985, and "Memory and Testimony of Women Survivors of Nazi Genocide." In *Women of the Word: Jewish Women and Jewish Writing*, edited by Judith R. Baskin (1994); Hutchens, John K. "On an Author." *New York Herald Tribune*, April 12, 1953, 2; "Ilona Karmel." *NYTimes Book Review*, September 21, 1969, 38; Janeway, Elizabeth. Review of *An Estate of Memory*, by Ilona Karmel. *NYTimes Book Review*, September 21, 1969, 1; Kremer, S. Lillian. "Holocaust-Wrought Women: Portraits by Four American Writers." *Studies in American Jewish Literature* 11 (Fall 1992): 150–161; "Literature: Ilona Karmel." *Mademoiselle*, January 1954, 83; Nichols, Lewis. "Talk with Ilona Karmel." *NYTimes Book Review*, March 29, 1953, 25; Peterson, Virgilia. Review of *Stephania*, by Ilona Karmel. *New York Herald Tribune Book Review*, 29 March 1953, 1; Pickrel, Paul. "Outstanding Novels." *Yale Review* 42 (Summer 1953): vi; Pomerantz, Gayle. "An Exploration of the Literature by Women Survivors of the Holocaust." Senior thesis, Brandeis University, 1983; Poore, Charles. "Books of the Times: Review of *Stephania*, by Ilona Karmel." *NYTimes*, March 28, 1953, 15; Raleigh, John Henry. Review of *Stephania*, by Ilona Karmel. *New Republic*, May 4, 1953, 19; Rice, Martin. "Universe of a Bed." *Saturday Review*, May 9, 1953, 21; Ross, Robert E. "Read It." *Prairie Schooner* 47 (Summer 1973): 171.

CATHERINE DALIGGA

KARPF, FAY BERGER (1891–1964)

Fay Berger Karpf made important contributions to Jewish American intellectual and social history. Both she and her husband, Maurice Joseph Karpf, were key figures in the Jewish welfare movement in New York, Chicago, and Los Angeles from the 1920s through the 1950s. But Karpf was also a significant social scientist and teacher, as well as an ardent supporter and interpreter of Otto Rank, the eminent psychoanalyst who studied with Sigmund Freud and later broke with Freud's teachings. For most of her professional career, Karpf lectured, taught, and wrote about the profound influence of Rankian theories on American psychoanalytic practice.

Fay Berger Karpf was born in Austria on April 17, 1891, to Barnett and Ethel Berger, who immigrated to Chicago in 1899. In June 1915, she married Maurice Karpf in Gary, Indiana. Karpf earned her teacher's certificate at Chicago's Normal College in 1918, taught in the Chicago public school system for a year, and then earned a bachelor of science degree from Northwestern. In 1925, she was awarded a Ph.D. in psychology from the University of Chicago. Karpf and her husband moved to New York City, where she lectured on social theory and methods in social investigation at the Graduate School for Jewish Social Work. In 1928, she accepted the directorship of the school's department of social research.

Karpf's first book, *American Social Psychology* (1932), traced the historical and professional development of social-psychological thought, from its European roots among nineteenth-century philosophers and sociologists through its use among American educators such as John Dewey. Although it was heralded in the early 1930s, *American Social Psychology* was rescued from obscurity when it was rereleased in 1970. In 1987, it was translated into Japanese. Karpf's second study, *Dynamic Relationship Therapy* (1937), was a compilation of essays she had published in the professional journal *Social Work Technique*. In this book, she combined Otto Rank's contributions to psychoanalysis with the kinds of clinical case studies with which she and her husband were both familiar.

While her husband was a major proponent for Jewish social workers during the 1930s and 1940s, Fay Karpf remained primarily a vigilant teacher, lecturer, and author in the academic realm. Therefore, it would be hard to say whether Karpf was drawn to Rank, or to the social psychology movement in general, because of the movement's prominent position among Jewish intellectuals and activists or because of its increasing popularity among her professional cohort. For the remainder of her career, a good deal of which was spent as a researcher in Los Angeles, Karpf worked hard to disseminate Rank's ideas and writings as widely as possible. During the late 1940s, she published several academic pamphlets, which were later collected, expanded, and published in her full-length study, *The Psychology and Psychotherapy of Otto Rank* (1953).

After decades of teaching and lecturing, Fay Berger Karpf died in Los Angeles on April 7, 1964.

SELECTED WORKS BY FAY BERGER KARPF

American Social Psychology: Its Origins, Development, and European Background (1932); *Dynamic Relationship Therapy: The Psychology of Otto Rank as Related to Other Schools of Psychotherapy* (1937); *The Psychology and Psychotherapy of Otto Rank: An Historical and Comparative Introduction* (1953).

BIBLIOGRAPHY

BEOAJ; *UJE*, s.v. "Karpf, Maurice J."; *WWIAJ* (1938).

DAVID SERLIN

KARPILOVE, MIRIAM (1888–1956)

Miriam Karpilove was one of the most prolific and widely published women writers of Yiddish prose. Her short stories and novels explore issues important

One of the most prolific and widely published women writers of Yiddish prose, Miriam Karpilove often addressed the central anxiety of the young immigrant woman: how to negotiate emotionally satisfying relationships in a new, sexually liberated culture. [YIVO Institute]

in the lives of Jewish women of her generation. Frequent themes are the upbringing of girls and women in Eastern Europe, the barriers they encounter when they seek secular education, and the conflicts they experience upon immigration to North America. For instance, one of Karpilove's best-known works, *Dos Tagebukh fun an Elender Meydl, oder der Kamf Gegn Fraye Libe* [The diary of a lonely girl, or the battle against free love] addresses the central anxiety of the young immigrant woman: how to negotiate emotionally satisfying relationships in a new, sexually liberated culture.

Born in a small town near Minsk in 1888, to Elijah and Hannah Karpilov, Miriam Karpilove and her nine siblings were raised in an observant home. Her father was a lumber merchant and builder. Karpilove was given a traditional Jewish and secular education, and was trained as a photographer and retoucher. After immigrating to the United States in 1905, she became active in the Labor Zionist movement and spent the latter part of the 1920s in Palestine. She resided in New York City and in Bridgeport, Connecticut, where several of her brothers had settled.

One of a handful of women who made their living as Yiddish writers, Karpilove debuted in 1906, publishing dramas, *feuilletons*, criticism, sketches, short stories, and novellas in a variety of important Yiddish periodicals during her fifty-year career. Her work appeared in *Fraye Arbeter Shtime, Tog, Groyser Kundes, Tsukunft, Forverts, Haynt, Yidisher Kemfer*, and *Yidishes Tageblat*, among others. She is best known, however, as a writer of serialized novels. More than twenty of these appeared in leading American Yiddish daily newspapers such as *Forverts, Morgen-Zhurnal*, and *Tog*. During the 1930s, Karpilove was a member of the *Forverts* staff, publishing seven novels and numerous works of short fiction in that paper between 1929 and 1937. Only five of Karpilove's works were published in book form. None has been translated into English.

Miriam Karpilove died in Bridgeport in 1956.

SELECTED WORKS BY MIRIAM KARPILOVE

Brokhe, a Kleyn-Shtetldike [Brokhe, a small-town girl] (1923); *In di Shturem Teg* [In stormy days] (1909); *A Provints-Tsaytung* [A provincial newspaper] (1926); *Tagebukh fun an Elender Meydl oder der Kamf Gegn Fraye Libe* [Diary of a lonely girl, or the battle against free love] (1918); *Yudis* [Judith] (1911).

BIBLIOGRAPHY

AJYB 58:477; Glatshteyn, Yankev. "Ershte Trit—Mit Fuftsik Yor Tsurik" [First steps—fifty years ago]. *Yidisher Kemfer*, March 23, 1956: 5; Karpilov family tree and personal scrapbook of Miriam Karpilov. Courtesy of Miriam Whaples, Northampton, Mass.; Karpilov, Miriam. Papers. YIVO Archives, NYC; *Leksikon fun der Nayer Yidisher Literatur* 8 (1981): 147; Marmor, Kalmen. "Der Pruv tsu Antviklen Froyen-Shrayberins" [The attempt to develop women writers]. In *Mayn Lebns-Geshikhte* (1959); Muselevitsh, Iser [Talush]. "Miriam Karpilov" [Miriam Karpilove]. In *Yidishe Shraybe* (1953); Reyzen, Zalmen. *Leksikon fun der Yidisher Literatur, Prese un Filologye* 3 (1929): 575–576.

ELLEN KELLMAN

KAUFMAN, BEATRICE (1895–1945)

Regarded as one of the wittiest women in New York during the 1930s and 1940s, Beatrice Kaufman edited important works of modernist poetry and fiction, published short stories of her own in the *New Yorker*, and saw several of her plays produced on Broadway.

She was born Beatrice Bakrow in Rochester, New York, on January 20, 1895, to businessman Julius and Sarah (Adler) Bakrow. She had two brothers, Leonard and Julian. Although few direct references to her Jewishness found their way into Kaufman's later editorial work and writings, her early life fits the description of upper-middle-class German Jews who thought of themselves as liberal, modern, and forward-looking.

She was one of only a few Jewish women admitted to Wellesley College in 1913. Perhaps she disliked it, for she transferred to her hometown's University of Rochester, where she studied in 1914 and 1915. On March 15, 1917, she married George S. Kaufman, who was just getting his start as a journalist. The couple moved to Manhattan, where George Kaufman's plays secured them a place at the famous Algonquin Round Table (along with Alexander Woollcott, EDNA FERBER, Harold Ross, and DOROTHY PARKER, among others). The Kaufmans developed a reputation for their sophistication and their tempestuous relationship.

In 1918, Beatrice Kaufman began what was to be a long and successful career in editing when she became assistant to the press agent for the Talmadge sisters. A short time later, she was hired as a reader by the publisher Al Woods. She earned her most influential post in 1920, when she became the head of the editorial department for the maverick publishing company Boni & Liveright, which introduced to the publishing world the practices of giving authors large advances and using direct advertising to increase book sales. During her five years at Boni & Liveright, Kaufman solicited and edited works by many of the most important modernist poets, novelists, and playwrights, including T.S. Eliot, Djuna Barnes, William Faulkner, e.e. cummings, John Steinbeck, George S. Kaufman, and Eugene O'Neill. Her enthusiasm for Ernest Hemingway's first book, *In Our Time*, helped to overcome publisher Horace Liveright's initial objections to it. In the 1930s, Kaufman went on to other editorial positions, serving as eastern story editor for Samuel Goldwyn and as fiction editor for *Harper's Bazaar* and the Viking Press. When the bombastic theater critic and Kaufman's close friend Alexander Woollcott died in 1943, Kaufman and Joseph Hennessey brought out an edition of his letters for the Viking Press.

While she made her name as an editor, Kaufman also wrote and published short stories in the *New Yorker* and plays that were produced on Broadway. In the guise of light, descriptive sketches, her short stories describe the frustration of middle-class women at their husbands' condescension and at the drudgery of their child-rearing responsibilities. Kaufman also wrote two plays, *Divided by Three* (with Margaret Leech) and *The White-Haired Boy*, both of which were produced. The former, about a woman whose ties to her husband, son, and lover result in her splitting herself into three, was called "gaily sophisticated" but "overdrawn" by the *New Yorker*.

As her wry observations in her story "The Social Bridge Game" attest, Kaufman was an avid bridge player, as well as an occasional member of the Thanatopsis Inside Straight and Literary Club, a group of mainly men in the Algonquin circle who gathered to play a weekly poker game. She was also a member of the Dramatists Guild and the Seeing Eye, an organization for training dogs to lead the blind.

Kaufman died at age fifty-one on October 6, 1945, at her Park Avenue home. She was survived by her husband and their daughter, Anne Kaufman Booth. Her life demonstrated that a perceptive, ironic, and acculturated Jewish woman could become a valuable contributor to New York's literary subculture. She was influential in shaping American taste and culture in the early twentieth century.

SELECTED WORKS BY BEATRICE KAUFMAN

Divided by Three, with Margaret Leech (1928); "Every Twenty-Four Hours." *New Yorker* (July 14, 1928): 59–62; *The Letters of Alexander Woollcott*, edited with Joseph Hennessey (1944); "The Phone Call." *New Yorker* (June 1, 1929): 48–49; "The Social Bridge Game." *New Yorker* (November 24, 1928): 60–64; "Tea with the Grownups." *New Yorker* (April 27, 1929): 83–85.

BIBLIOGRAPHY

AJYB 48:492; Dardis, Thomas. *Firebrand: The Life of Horace Liveright* (1995); Review of *Divided by Three*, by Beatrice Kaufman with Margaret Leech. *New Yorker* (October 20, 1934): 30–34; "Beatrice Kaufman, Story Editor, Dies." *NYTimes*, October 7, 1945, 44:3; Wilson, Edmund. "The Letters of Alexander Woollcott." *New Yorker* (July 29, 1944): 61–62; *WWIAJ* 38:525.

MICHAEL GALCHINSKY

KAUFMAN, BEL (b. 1911)

Bel Kaufman, best known for her novel *Up the Down Staircase* and its subsequent film, was born in Berlin, Germany, on May 10, 1911. She is the granddaughter of the great Yiddish writer Sholem Aleichem (on whose work the musical *Fiddler on the Roof* is based). Having spent her early childhood in Odessa and Moscow, she considers Russia to be her true home and Russian her native language. Her parents,

Bel Kaufman became famous when she published her best-selling novel Up the Down Staircase, *but she comes from a family of writers. She is pictured here as a child, sitting on the knee of her grandfather, the great Yiddish writer Sholem Aleichem. Her mother,* LYALA KAUFMAN, *was also a successful writer.*

Born with the given name of "Belle," Bel Kaufman became the first woman to publish in Esquire *magazine with a byline by changing the spelling of her name on the assumption that the editors would think she was a man. The strategy worked, and she has gone by the name Bel ever since.*

Michael J. Kaufman, a physician, and LYALYA KAUFMAN, a writer and Sholem Aleichem's daughter, were both native Russians. In December 1923, they immigrated to the United States with their twelve-year-old daughter to escape the hardships of postrevolutionary Russia.

When the family arrived in New York City, the young Kaufman did not speak a word of English. She was taken to the local public school by her mother, who knew no more English than she did. Kaufman was enrolled in a first-grade class with children half her age and felt immensely awkward. Her uneasiness was appeased by the kindness of her teacher, which had a profound effect upon the twelve-year-old: She decided that she too wanted to be a teacher.

Kaufman's education progressed quickly, graduating magna cum laude from HUNTER COLLEGE in January 1934. That same year she married Sidney Goldstine, from whom she was divorced in the 1960s. They had two children, Jonathan and Thea. Kaufman went on to complete her master's degree in literature at Columbia University, graduating in 1936 with highest honors. At Columbia, she was offered a doctoral fellowship, which she had to decline because she intended to support her husband in medical school. After her graduation, Kaufman began a teaching career in New York City public schools, which spanned three decades and inspired *Up the Down Staircase.*

Kaufman began writing and publishing her short stories in the late 1930s and early 1940s. In its early life, *Esquire* was considered a gentlemen's magazine exclusively; it did not publish writing by women. When Kaufman wrote a short story in the early 1940s entitled "La Tigresse" about a *femme fatale,* her agent suggested that it would be perfect for *Esquire* if not for the unfortunate fact that she was a female writer. They decided to submit the story anyway, but not before shortening her real first name, Belle, to the more androgynous Bel. The short story was published in *Esquire,* and Kaufman has used the name ever since.

Up the Down Staircase was originally a short story—only three and a half pages long—published in *The Saturday Review* on November 17, 1962. Gladys Justin Carr, then an editor at Prentice-Hall, contacted Kaufman after reading it and encouraged her to extend her fledgling story into a full-length novel. Kaufman's efforts resulted in what *Time* magazine would call "easily the most popular novel about U.S. public schools in history."

The novel offers a portrait of a young teacher who shares much of Kaufman's iconoclastic spirit. It chronicles the career of Sylvia Barrett, a new teacher in the public school system, and offers an incisive and humorous portrait of the interaction between teachers and students in public school. It is also a satirical look at the administrative bureaucracy teachers must overcome in order to perform their jobs. The novel was released in 1964 and spent sixty-four weeks as a bestseller, of which five months were spent in the number-one position. *Up the Down Staircase* was translated into sixteen languages and has sold over six million copies.

Up the Down Staircase became such a success that in 1967 a film was made based on the novel, starring Sandy Dennis and directed by Robert Mulligan. Kaufman, who served as a consultant on the film, was given a brief cameo as one of the teachers punching in with Sylvia Barrett. The film opened at Radio City Music Hall in New York City and was chosen to represent the United States at the Moscow Film Festival (where its title translated into *Up the Staircase Leading Down*). In June 1977, *Up the Down Staircase* became a play and a popular choice for many public school drama productions.

Kaufman's contributions to social awareness continued well beyond the reach of her famous book. On

December 7, 1987, Kaufman accepted an invitation from the Soviet embassy to join Russian leader Mikhail Gorbachev as his guest at a reception held for prominent Americans. During this same year, she participated in the Moscow International Forum for a Nuclear-Free World at the invitation of the Soviet Union. There she delivered a speech on "The Role of Culture in Protecting Civilization and Universal Human Values."

In her later career, Kaufman has been involved in theatrical writing and lecturing, and is a popular public speaker. In the 1970s, she married Sidney Gluck, who heads the Sholem Aleichem Memorial Foundation, where she is an honorary chair. The foundation was created to commemorate her grandfather and the world of Yiddish literature.

Bel Kaufman is the recipient of many awards, including UJA, ADL, and Bonds for Israel plaques, the Paperback of the Year Award, and the National School Bell Award. Bel Kaufman's great legacy is in the literature about education in America and in the propagation of Jewish culture. Her life's work is a poignant reminder of the struggles and dedication necessary in the search for knowledge.

SELECTED WORKS BY BEL KAUFMAN

Abroad in America (1976); *Love, etc.* (1979); *Up the Down Staircase* (1964).

RUTH ANDREW ELLENSON

KAUFMAN, JOYCE JACOBSON
(b. 1929)

Inspired as a little girl by Marie Curie, Joyce Jacobson Kaufman has herself become one of the most distinguished international scientists in the fields of chemistry, physics, biomedicine, and supercomputers.

Born on June 21, 1929, in the Bronx to Robert and Sarah (Seldin) Jacobson, she was raised in Baltimore, Maryland, after her parents separated in 1935, living with her mother and immigrant maternal grandparents. She grew up in a traditional Jewish family. In 1940, her mother married Abraham Deutch, a successful roofer. Deutch, who was born in Riga, immigrated to the United States in 1924 after having spent seven years as a *halutz* [pioneer] in Palestine. He raised Joyce as his daughter.

Inspired as a little girl by Marie Curie, Joyce Jacobson Kaufman has done groundbreaking work in the fields of pharmacology, drug design, quantum chemistry, and chemical physics of energetic compounds such as explosives and rocket fuels. When this 1963 photograph of her working at a computer was taken, the idea of such a machine fitting in one's lap would have been taken as a joke. [Jan Kaufman]

At the age of eight, Joyce was picked to attend a summer course at Johns Hopkins University for gifted children in math and science. In 1945, she was admitted as a special student to Johns Hopkins, which did not grant women regular student status until 1970, and earned her B.S. in 1949. It was there that she met Stanley Kaufman, a returning veteran from World War II and an engineering student. They were married on December 26, 1948, and divorced in 1982. Their daughter, Jan Caryl Kaufman (b. 1955), was ordained in 1979—one of the first female rabbis in the United States and one of the first three women admitted to the Conservative rabbinate.

After graduating from Johns Hopkins, Kaufman worked as a librarian and then as a research chemist at the Army Chemical Center (Edgewood, Maryland). Encouraged by her undergraduate professor of chemistry Dr. Walter Koski, Kaufman returned to Johns Hopkins in 1952 and enrolled formally in a Ph.D. program there in 1958. In 1960, she earned her doctorate and a long-overdue Phi Beta Kappa key (as a special student, she could not receive this award when she graduated with her bachelor's degree). In 1962, she was appointed visiting scientist at the Centre de Mécanique Ondulatoire Appliquée at the Sorbonne, and moved to Paris with both her mother and daughter. In 1963, she received a D.E.S. *très honorable* in theoretical physics from the university.

Kaufman went to the Research Institute for Advanced Studies of the Martin Marietta Company, first as a scientist in the quantum chemistry group and finally as leader of the group. In 1969, Kaufman joined Koski's research group at Johns Hopkins as principal research scientist and was also appointed associate professor of anesthesiology at the Johns Hopkins School of Medicine. In 1976, she was appointed associate professor of plastic surgery. Recipient of numerous awards, Kaufman was named *une dame chevalière* of France in 1969 and received the Garvan Medical Award of the American Chemical Society in 1973, in recognition of her exceptional research accomplishments in the application of theoretical and quantum chemistry. The following year, the Jewish National Fund honored her as one of the ten outstanding women in Maryland. In 1981, she was elected *membre correspondant* of the Académie Européenne des Sciences, des Arts, et des Lettres.

Kaufman's research has yielded groundbreaking work in the fields of pharmacology, drug design, quantum chemistry, and chemical physics of energetic compounds such as explosives and rocket fuels. Among her most distinguished contributions are a novel strategy for computer prediction of toxicology and drug reactions, and chemical calculations on carcinogens.

She has served on the editorial advisory board for John Wiley Interscience Publishers and as editor of the Benchmark Book series. She has also edited the journals *Molecular Pharmacology, International Journal of Quantum Chemistry, Journal of Computational Chemistry,* and *Journal of Explosives.* She has been a consultant to the National Institutes of Health, a member of the National Academy of Sciences Committee on Nuclear Science, and a member of the National Science Foundation Evaluation Committee on the evaluation of supercomputers. Joyce Jacobson Kaufman is the author of over three hundred publications.

BIBLIOGRAPHY

Koski, Walter S. "Joyce Jacobson Kaufman." In *Women in Chemistry and Physics: A Biobibliographic Sourcebook,* edited by Louise S. Grinstein, Rose K. Rose, and Miriam H. Rafailovich (1993): 299–313. This article includes an extensive bibliography of Kaufman's publications.

JAN CARYL KAUFMAN

KAUFMAN, LYALYA (1887–1964)

Although her earliest writings for the *Forverts* were translated from Russian to Yiddish by Dina Blond-Mikhelovitch, Lyalya Kaufman wrote most of her over two thousand sketches and short stories in Yiddish herself. Up until her death in 1964, Kaufman, the eldest daughter of Sholem Aleichem, was the only one of his six children who pursued a literary career.

Lyalya Kaufman was born Sarah Rabinowitz in Belaya Tserkov, near Kiev, in 1887. She studied at the gymnasium in Kiev and attended university in Geneva. In 1909, she married Michael Kaufman. The young couple moved to Berlin, Germany, where Michael studied medicine. In 1922, the family went to America and lived in Newark, New Jersey, where Kaufman practiced medicine and Lyalya Kaufman continued to write and translate. In 1926, she published a poignant memoir of her father in *The Sholom Aleichem Book.*

She wrote for the *Tsukunft* and other Yiddish literary journals. However, it was her charming, intimate, "minimalist" vignettes that appeared in the *Forverts* every Monday for well over thirty years that gained her thousands of loyal readers. She translated some of her father's works into Russian and English. According to her daughter, novelist BEL KAUFMAN, Sholem Aleichem urged his daughter to become a writer since she wrote such wonderful letters and stories. In later years, Abraham Cahan, editor of the *Forverts*, and others encouraged her to develop her narratives more fully. More specifically, she was asked to write a more extended memoir of her illustrious father but, in Bel Kaufman's words, her mother wrote "on one foot."

In 1968, several years after Lyalya Kaufman's death, her younger sister, Marie Waife-Goldberg, wrote the long-awaited memoir of their father.

Lyalya Kaufman died on December 24, 1964, in New York City.

BIBLIOGRAPHY

AJYB 66:577; Fogelman, L. *Forverts*, February 15, 1964, 9; Kaufman, Bel. Telephone interview with author, February 7, 1996; Obituary. *NYTimes*, December 25, 1964. 29:3; Raskin, Saul, ed. *Leksikon fun der Nayer Yidisher Literatur* [Biographical dictionary of modern Yiddish literature]. Vol. 8 (1965): 161; "Vi Ikh Ze Im." [How I see him]. *Dos Sholem Aleykhem Bukh* [The Sholem Aleichem book], edited by Y.D. Berkowitz (1926); Waife-Goldberg, Marie. *My Father, Sholom Aleichem* (1968).

DOROTHY BILIK

KAUFMAN, RHODA (1888–1956)

A preeminent player in the establishment of Georgia's social welfare network, Rhoda Kaufman was one of the most highly regarded southern reformers in the country. Despite being a Jewish woman in a society that marginalized her identity, Kaufman became a respected professional within the confines of a male-dominated profession. While her primary goal was to apply the precepts of objectivity and "professionalism" to the field of social work, Kaufman's Jewish beliefs played a central role in her work.

Born on October 26, 1888, in Columbus, Georgia, to middle-class German immigrants, Kaufman earned a B.S. in physics, logic, and psychology from Vanderbilt University in 1909. After moving to Atlanta, she became involved in both charity work and women's voluntary organizations, including the NATIONAL COUNCIL OF JEWISH WOMEN. As president of the local American Association of College Women (1913–1915), she successfully lobbied for state funding of a girls' reform school, the Georgia Children's Code Commission, and the School for the Feeble-Minded.

Kaufman served in most city and state welfare organizations, including the State Council of Social Agencies (1921–1923) and the Department of Public Welfare (1920–1923). She was appointed executive secretary of Georgia's Department of Public Welfare (1923–1929), one of only three women in the country to hold so high an office.

Kaufman belonged to the major national welfare organizations, including the National Conference of Social Work and the American Association of Social Workers, and she administered the U.S. Children's Bureau Statistics Project in Georgia. She also served on President Herbert Hoover's White House Conference on Child Welfare (1930–1931). In 1943, she was named Georgia's Social Welfare Woman of the Year. After her retirement in 1945, she joined the United Nations Women's Organization, the League of Women Voters, and the Institute for Citizenship, a world affairs organization. She maintained strong ties with her local Jewish community by joining both the Atlanta Council of Jewish Women and the Atlanta Temple. She died on March 4, 1956, in Atlanta.

BIBLIOGRAPHY

Gordon, Linda. *Heroes of Their Own Lives: The Politics and History of Family Violence, Boston, 1880–1930* (1988); Kaufman, Rhoda. Manuscript collection. Georgia Department of Archives and History, Atlanta, and Papers. Association of American University Women Collection. Georgia Department of Archives and History, Atlanta; Rogow, Faith. *Gone to Another Meeting: The National Council of Jewish Women, 1893–1993* (1993); Smith, Patricia E. "Rhoda Kaufman, a Southern Progressive's Career, 1913–1956." *Atlanta Historical Bulletin* 17–18: 43–50; Wenger, Beth. "Jewish Women of the Club: The Changing Role of Atlanta's Jewish Women, 1870–1930." *American Jewish History* 76, no. 3: 311–333; *WWIAJ* (1938).

LEE S. POLANSKY

KAUFMAN, SUE (1926–1977)

Sue Kaufman railed against "having my work held up against a yardstick, measuring whether I am or am not writing about women's issues." Her resentment is well founded, for Sue Kaufman wrote about *people's* issues, most specifically modern urbanites who struggled with the stresses of city life which, like ancient water torture, relentlessly wore them down.

Born on August 7, 1926, on Long Island, New York, the daughter of Marcus and Anna (Low) Kaufman, Sue Kaufman had one older brother. In the same year that she earned a B.A. degree from Vassar College (1947), Kaufman published her first short story, in *Junior Bazaar*. From 1947 to 1949, she worked as a part-time assistant fiction editor for *Mademoiselle*; in 1949, she became a free-lance fiction writer.

An apt observer of the upwardly mobile urban middle class in which she lived, Kaufman sketched characters with delicate strokes of a pen dipped in mild acid. Her best-known work is *Diary of a Mad Housewife*, published in 1967 and made into a movie by Universal Studios in 1970 with Carrie Snodgress in the title role. Her other books are *The Happy Summer Days* (1959), *Green Holly* (1962), *The Headshrinker's Test* (1969), *Life with Prudence: A Chilling Tale* (1970), *Falling Bodies* (1974), and *The Master and Other Stories* (1976).

In 1953, Kaufman married Dr. Jeremiah A. Barondess. The couple had one son, James. Sue Kaufman was a member of the Authors League and a two-time recipient of an honorable mention in the Martha Foley collection of short stories.

She died on June 25, 1977, in New York City, after a long illness.

SELECTED WORKS BY SUE KAUFMAN

Diary of a Mad Housewife (1967. Movie, 1970); *Falling Bodies* (1974); *Green Holly* (1962); *The Happy Summer Days* (1959); *The Headshrinker's Test* (1969); *Life with Prudence: A Chilling Tale* (1970); *The Master and Other Stories* (1976); "Memoirs of a Vassar Gel." *NYTimes Magazine* (December 22, 1968): 12+.

BIBLIOGRAPHY

Bryfonski, Dedria, and Phyllis Carmel Mendelson, eds. *Contemporary Literary Criticism* (1978); Dickstein, Lore. *NYTimes Book Review*, February 3, 1974, p. 7; *Contemporary Authors* (1967, 1981); Garrett, George. *Sewanee Review* (Winter 1977); Obituaries. *NYTimes*, June 26, 1977, 26:3, and *Newsweek* (July 11, 1977); Skow, John. "Fun City." *Time* (January 21, 1974): 74+; Todd, Richard. *Atlantic Monthly* (May 1974); Tyler, Ann. *NYTimes Book Review*, July 11, 1976, p. 7; *WWWIA 7*.

ANN KNEAVEL

KAVEY, LILLIAN KASINDORF
(1889–1986)

Lillian Kasindorf Kavey was a banker, a community activist, and an advocate for Conservative Judaism and Ethiopian Jewry. She was born in New York City on July 19, 1889, and married Abraham H. Kavovitz, an itinerant clothing merchant and shoe salesman, in 1908. They settled in Port Chester, New York. Ambitious, intelligent, and indomitably energetic, Lillian Kavovitz, as she was called at that time, opened a pawnshop and loan office that served the European immigrants who worked in the town's factories. After learning that many immigrants hoarded money in lumpy mattresses to bring over their next of

Businesswoman Lillian Kasindorf Kavey devoted more than fifty years to helping Ethiopian Jews.

kin, she decided to help overcome the bureaucracy at both ends and transformed her business into a loan company and a travel agency. Customers left money with her to gather interest. When sufficient funds accumulated, Kavey prepared the tickets and arranged passage with the steamship companies for her clients' relatives. When newcomers had difficulties with immigration authorities, she would travel on their behalf to Ellis Island, where she soon became a familiar figure.

Port Chesterites trusted Kavey, whose linguistic talents matched her business acumen. She conversed with her clients in Russian, Polish, German, and Czech. To accommodate Italians, her largest group of clients, a local Catholic priest, Father Meyerhoffer, tutored her in several Italian dialects.

In 1913, Kavey became the first woman to be granted a banking license in New York State. Encouraged by his wife's success, Abraham Kavovitz sold his dry-goods business in 1916 and helped found a private bank that bore both of their names: The A.H. and L. Kavovitz Bank. When two sons joined their parents in business in 1940, they changed the name of the family as well as the business. Kavey and Sons remained a private bank handling loans, savings accounts, and transfers of funds to foreign countries. The bank survived until 1955, when it merged with a larger local institution and, ultimately, Barclays Bank.

Kavey was very active in Jewish and general local communal affairs. First as advocate for youth, then as the paramount founder of the Jewish Community Center of Port Chester, she personally sponsored two clubs for teenaged boys in the interwar period. During World War II, she corresponded with the young men and extended moral and material support. At the same time, she convinced local Italians and African-Americans to establish centers for their youth based on the Jewish model.

An early champion of Conservative Judaism in the suburbs, Kavey convinced the sisterhood of Congregation Kenesses Tifereth Israel to affiliate with the WOMEN'S LEAGUE FOR CONSERVATIVE JUDAISM and the congregation to sponsor late Friday evening services on a Conservative model, even as Saturday morning services retained their immigrant ambiance. Beyond Port Chester, she raised funds for the Jewish Theological Seminary and convinced sisterhoods throughout metropolitan New York to join the Women's League.

During Baltic and Mediterranean vacations in the late 1930s, Lillian and Abraham Kavey urged Jewish businesspeople to leave their lands of residence. They filed affidavits for 125 families from Egypt, Morocco, Italy, Poland, and Scandinavia.

After meeting the Orientalist Jacques Faïtlovitch in 1923, Kavey devoted more than fifty years to helping Ethiopian Jews. With Rabbi Israel Goldstein, she was a vocal advocate of their cause before the Italian invasion of 1936. During the 1960s and early 1970s, she visited Gundar, Ethiopia, three times, succeeded in getting some black Jews moved to more arable land, and then contributed money for three tractors. Efforts to transfer large numbers of Ethiopian Jews to Israel, however, ran into opposition from the Israeli rabbinate. In this endeavor, as in her commercial, philanthropic, and communal activities, Kavey was a herald of future trends.

Lillian Kasindorf Kavey died on May 10, 1986, in Port Chester, New York.

BIBLIOGRAPHY

Kavey, Lillian Kasendorf. "The Falashas Revisited." *Woman's League Outlook* 39 (Fall 1968): 18–19; Shargel, Baila R., and H.L. Drimmer. *The Jews of Westchester: A Social History* (1994).

BAILA R. SHARGEL

KAYE, JUDITH S. (b. 1938)

Judith S. Kaye was the first woman to serve as chief judge of the state of New York and chief judge of the Court of Appeals of the state of New York.

The daughter of Lena and Benjamin Smith, Judith Smith Kaye was born on August 4, 1938, in Monticello, New York, where she lived until she attended Barnard College (B.A., 1958) and New York University Law School (LL.B., 1962). Married to Stephen Rackow Kaye, partner at Proskauer Rose Goetz and Mendelsohn, she takes great pride in her three successful children, Luisa Kaye Hagemeier, Jonathan Kaye, and Gordon Kaye.

She began her illustrious career as a litigation associate at the distinguished New York law firm of Olwine, Connelly, Chase, O'Donnell, and Weyher

Judith S. Kaye is the first woman to serve as chief judge of the state of New York. She previously had served as chief justice of the New York State Court of Appeals, a position once held by one of her idols, Benjamin Cardozo. [Chambers of Judge Kaye]

(1969–1983), later becoming the firm's first woman partner. Her experience and accomplishments as a trial lawyer and her efforts on behalf of the bar association distinguished her from other lawyers. Recognizing her talents and looking to diversify the court system, Governor Mario Cuomo appointed her as the first female justice of the New York State Court of Appeals in its 150-year history. On September 12, 1983, she began as associate judge and then became chief justice of the Court of Appeals. On February 22, 1993, she was also appointed by Governor Cuomo as the first female chief judge of the state of New York.

Kaye believes that although the Court of Appeals is an outstanding court and has maintained its tradition of excellence, the court system of the state of New York has been bogged down in an overabundance of cases. Her goal as chief justice is to make the court system work better and become "more responsive to the needs of modern society."

As an attorney and as a chief justice, Kaye has worked diligently to improve the status of women and children and to address domestic violence. Championing women's health issues, she was a founding member and honorary chair of the Judges and Lawyers Breast Cancer Alert. She cochairs the Permanent Judicial Commission on Justice for Children and is a member of the American Bar Association Commission on Domestic Violence. She has written many articles concerning domestic issues.

Kaye has been a trustee and vice president of the Legal Aid Society, a trustee and vice-chair of the Clients Security Fund (now the Lawyers Fund for Client Protection), and a trustee of the American Judicature Society. She is active on various committees of several bar associations. She was appointed by President Jimmy Carter to the United States Nominating Commission for Judges of the Second Circuit.

She serves as a trustee of the New York University Law Center Foundation and of Barnard College. She sits on the board of directors of the Institute of Judicial Administration, the board of editors of *New York State Bar Journal*, and the board of directors of the Conference of Chief Justices.

Kaye has been awarded many honorary doctor of laws degrees at several universities and law schools. She has also been the recipient of many special awards and medals.

A frequent speaker on issues involving gender, the legal profession, and state and constitutional law, she delivered the 1996 commencement address, "Enduring Values in a Changing World," at the Jewish Theological Seminary and a special lecture, "An Appreciation of Justice Benjamin Nathan Cardozo," at the Sephardic

Congregation Shearith Israel in 1995. Both speeches referred to the life and the values of Benjamin Cardozo, one of the greatest jurists of all time.

Taking great pride in her role as first female chief judge, Kaye compares and contrasts her role to that of Cardozo, a Jewish justice of the United States Supreme Court, who, like herself, served as chief judge of the Court of Appeals of New York (for eighteen years). Kaye and her family are long-standing members of the Sephardic Congregation Shearith Israel in New York City, as was Cardozo. On one point, however, the two justices did not agree. When the synagogue moved to new quarters, the board voted to retain separate seating in accordance with Cardozo's eloquent arguments against the elimination of separate seating for men and women. As a result, Judith Kaye, chief justice of the state of New York, may not pray in the main sanctuary, but must sit upstairs in the women's gallery.

SELECTED WORKS BY JUDITH S. KAYE

"The Changing World of Children: The Responsibility of the Law and the Courts." 65 *New York State Bar Journal* 7 (November 1993); "Children Centers in the Courts: A Service to Children, Families and the Judicial System." 76 *New York State Bar Journal* 6 (September/October 1995); "The Status of Women in Law Firms and the Need for More Woman Judges." 28 *Trial Magazine* 20 (August 1992); "Women and the Law: The Law Can Change People." 66 *NYU Law Review* 1929 (December 1991).

JUDITH FRIEDMAN ROSEN

KAYE, SYLVIA FINE *see* FINE, SYLVIA

KENIN, LENA (1897–1968)

Popular myth suggests that during the height of her practice, Dr. Lena Kenin delivered at least half of the Jewish babies in Portland, Oregon. This joyful responsibility was not without challenges. As was more customary in the mid-twentieth century than now, expecting a child was a private affair. Most of Kenin's patients wanted to keep their pregnancies a secret, but risked running into a friend or an acquaintance in the waiting room. Kenin designed her office so that patients could exit through another door.

Born to David and Naomi (Swartz) Nemerovsky in Portland, on November 5, 1897, Lena Nemerovsky Kenin attended Reed College and graduated with a B.S. from the University of Washington in 1921. Her first career, as a schoolteacher, lasted three years. In

1924, she enrolled at the University of Oregon Medical School, from which she graduated with an M.D. in 1929. After interning at Good Samaritan Hospital, she set up a practice in obstetrics and gynecology in Portland that would flourish for over twenty-five years.

Despite her success as an obstetrician, Kenin felt ill-equipped to offer the emotional support needed by new mothers. As a result, in 1958 she enrolled in a psychiatric program at the University of Pennsylvania Graduate School. After residencies at Johns Hopkins and the Philadelphia Hospital for Mental and Nerve Disorders, she returned to Portland in 1961 to establish a practice in psychiatry. Her dual interest in obstetrics and psychiatry is demonstrated in a 1962 article, "Mental Illness Associated with the Postpartum State," which she coauthored with Norman Blass. Besides having a private practice, Kenin was an associate professor of psychiatry at the University of Oregon Medical School and the chief consultant for the school's health service, which served medical, dental, and nursing students. She belonged to numerous professional organizations, including the Oregon Medical Association, the American Medical Association, the American Psychiatric Association, the Multnomah County Medical Society, the American Women's Medical Association, the American Association of University Professors, and the League of Professional Women.

Kenin married a Philadelphian, Harry Marvin Kenin, in Seattle, on November 21, 1921. Trained as a lawyer, Harry Kenin served in the Oregon state senate, on the Portland school board, and on the state's Welfare Commission. Both Kenins were life-long Democrats. In 1947, Lena Kenin registered with the Americans for Democratic Action.

Although Lena Kenin was a secular thinker who did not involve herself with synagogue life, her husband served a term as president of the B'nai B'rith Lodge and was affiliated with Temple Beth Israel in Portland. He died in 1954.

By all accounts, Lena Kenin's intelligence and compassion were legendary. When she died in Portland on March 24, 1968, at age seventy, she had distinguished herself in two separate fields of medicine: obstetrics and gynecology and psychiatry.

BIBLIOGRAPHY

Bulletin of the Multnomah County Medical Society 23 (1968): 37; *Journal of the American Medical Association* 204 (1968): 182; Kenin, Esther. Telephone interview with author, July 1996; Kenin, L., and N. Blass. "Mental Illness Associated with the Postpartum State." *Clinical Obstetrics and Gynecology* 5 (1962): 716–728; Obituaries. Oregon *Journal*, March 26, 1968, 10, and *The Oregonian*, March 26, 1968, 5; University of Oregon. *Medical School Catalogue* (1929): 40; *WWIAJ* (1938).

JUDITH MARGLES

KENT, ALLEGRA (b. 1938)

The beloved American ballerina Allegra Kent created and danced in nearly all principal roles in George Balanchine's celebrated ouevre during her thirty years as a dancer with the renowned New York City Ballet.

Born Iris Margo Cohen on August 11, 1938, to Harry Cohen of Texas and Shirley Weissman of Wisznice, Poland, she spent her childhood being shuttled back and forth from Florida to California while her father pursued various means of supporting the family. During a period of relative stability, she settled with her mother and older brother Gary in Los Angeles. Through her own initiative, she began studying dance with Bronislava Nijinska, sister of Vaslav Nijinsky, and Spanish dancer Carmelita Maracci.

With her father traversing the country as a traveling salesman, Kent's mother took control of the family, exerting a tremendous influence, both positive and negative, on her daughter's life and career. In her autobiography, *Once a Dancer . . .* , Kent describes her mother's aversion to Jewishness, beginning with changing their last name, adopting Christian Science, and later coercing her daughter to undergo reconstructive facial surgery. Following her older sister Wendy's example, Kent chose a new name.

Allegra Kent and her mother joined Wendy, an actress, in New York in 1951. Kent immediately received a scholarship to the School of American Ballet and was admitted to the New York City Ballet (NYCB) one year later, at age fifteen, four years after beginning her dance training. Balanchine reportedly said of Kent when he first saw her, "I have never seen such raw talent."

His interest in Kent was evident when he choreographed *Ivesiana* for her in 1954. Following a brief withdrawal from the company under pressure from her mother, Kent rejoined for another European tour. Upon her return to the United States, she was promoted directly from the corps to principal dancer. She was immediately cast in leading roles in *Swan Lake* with Jacques D'Amboise, *The Seven Deadly Sins*, and the new *Stars and Stripes*.

Kent caught the attention of the famous photographer Bert Stern during a Broadway stint in *Shinbone Alley*. Their troubled marriage lasted ten years, until Stern's addiction to drugs drove Kent to sever the relationship.

George Balanchine reportedly said of Allegra Kent when he first saw her, "I have never seen such raw talent."
She danced in nearly all the principal roles in his ballets during her thirty years as a dancer
with the renowned New York City Ballet. [New York Public Library]

Kent suspended her career three times during their union to have children. Trista's birth followed Kent's performances in Balanchine's landmark *Episodes* (1959) and a revival of *La Sonnambula* with Erik Bruhn. Kent became the darling of Russian audiences during a 1962 tour of the U.S.S.R. At the height of the cold war, Kent brought down the house of the Maryinsky Theatre with Arthur Mitchell in *Agon* and danced in the Kremlin. In the United States, the openly erotic, Japanese-style *Bugaku* (1963) featured Kent and Edward Villela. Her daughter Susannah was born in 1964 and her son, Bret, in 1967.

Kent survived as a single mother through her contract with NYCB (although with her declining emotional stability, she danced only once a year), as well as by teaching and making guest appearances, including in *Apollo* with Mikhail Baryshnikov.

The death of her father led to further depression and decline in Kent's career. Her dismissal from New York City Ballet following Balanchine's death coincided with her happy but short-lived marriage to filmmaker Aram Avakian. Following Avakian's death, Kent continued teaching and coaching. In 1992, she met and married her third husband, Bob Gurney.

Despite continued personal, financial, and physical problems, Kent persevered. At age fifty, she came out of retirement to dance in John Clifford's *Notturno*. Critics once again praised her unique expressiveness, humor, refinement, and sensuality. She lives in New York City.

SELECTED WORKS BY ALLEGRA KENT

Allegra Kent's Book of Water Beauty (1976); *The Dancer's Body Book*, with James and Constance Camner (1984); *Once a Dancer . . .* (1997).

BIBLIOGRAPHY

"Dancing for Balanchine: Six Balanchine Ballerinas." Anne Belle, dir. Seahorse Productions in association with WNET/NY (1989); Greskovic, Robert. "Some Artists of the New York City Ballet." *Ballet Review* 4, no. 4 (1973); Kirstein, Lincoln. *What Ballet Is About: An American Glossary* (1970).

NAOMI ABRAHAMI

KESSLER, LILLIAN RUTH
(1908–1993)

In 1982, when she retired from the presidency of Kessler International Corporation, Lillian Kessler prepared a brochure listing the principal export items of the company she had founded in 1946. The list included abrasives, adhesives, locomotive parts, chemicals, navigational and meteorological instruments, tank and jeep bearings, crankshaft and camshaft grinders, and many other automotive parts. A pioneer in a "man's business," Kessler established the first American export business that catered exclusively to buying missions attached to foreign embassies in Washington, D.C. For many years, she was the only female member of the Overseas Automotive Club, a national trade organization.

Lillian Ruth Kessler was born on March 15, 1908, in Cleveland, Ohio. She was the first of three children, followed by Beatrice and Edwin, born to Mary (Galen) and Julius Kessler. Julius, a manufacturer and wholesaler of men's sport clothing, had emigrated from the Ukraine to New York at age fifteen to join his father and siblings. Mary Galen came to New York from Odessa with her parents at age four. Galen's family moved to Philadelphia and then to Cleveland.

A brilliant child, Lillian Kessler excelled academically, developing interests in history and politics. She became president of Glenville High School's competition-winning debate team and was, for a time, its only female member. At age sixteen, she entered the University of Michigan. She transferred to Radcliffe College the following year, but completed her college degree at Western Reserve in 1929. She then became a junior high school history teacher in the Cleveland public school system.

In 1930, she married Joseph Fuchs, the concertmaster of the Cleveland Orchestra. A daughter, Elinor Clare Fuchs, was born in 1933. As a young mother, Kessler returned to graduate school to study American history at Western Reserve, earning an M.A. and embarking on a Ph.D. Her mentor, Professor Robert C. Binkley, who was a consultant in the creation of the Works Projects Administration's Historical Records Survey, recommended Kessler as a prototype developer for the Ohio State program. She accordingly left academic life for the workplace.

Lillian Kessler and Joseph Fuchs separated in 1938, divorcing in 1940. In 1939, Kessler was appointed director of the Historical Records Survey for the state of Ohio. Around this time she also collaborated with Philip D. Jordan on an anthology of old American songs called *Songs of Yesterday* (1941).

In 1943 she moved to Washington, D.C., accepting a position as Library of Congress archivist of the now-discontinued white-collar projects of the WPA. She left that position after only a few months to work as a technical analyst, studying postwar reconstruction for the Foreign Economic Administration, a federal agency. After the war, she briefly worked as a foreign markets consultant to various companies, including

Sinclair Oil. During this period, she wrote the article "The Industrialization of China" for the anthology *Towards World Prosperity* (1947).

In 1945, Lillian Kessler was well positioned to recognize a postwar opportunity. American automotive equipment covered the globe; the foreign governments that owned U.S.-built trucks, jeeps, and tanks would require spare parts to keep these vehicles serviced. By learning the secrets of "parts interchange" (for instance, that General Motors spark plugs might actually be made by another company), Kessler saw that she could supply foreign governments at prices below those offered by the automotive manufacturers. The business that she began in 1946, Kessler International Corporation, specialized in automotive parts, but eventually expanded to the sale of road- and dam-building equipment, electronic and communications components, and military support supplies.

To represent her business, Kessler traveled widely in the 1960s and 1970s, making solo trips to India, Pakistan, Iran, South Korea, and Japan. Health problems forced her to seek a buyer for the business in the late 1970s. Kessler International has continued, in greatly expanded form, under new leadership.

Kessler maintained an active family life with her daughter, her two grandchildren, Claire and Katherine Finkelstein, and the five children of her brother Edwin, a psychoanalyst, who established his practice in Washington, D.C., after the war. She became a collector of modern Latin American artwork, eventually donating twelve paintings by the Panamanian painter Dutary to the Art Museum of the Americas.

Kessler's maternal grandfather broke with Orthodox Jewish tradition, identifying with the socialist thinking then sweeping Jewish circles. Her parents joined Abba Hillel Silver's Reform Jewish temple in Cleveland, where Lillian was confirmed at age fourteen. Later in life, she maintained a nominal attachment to the Reform Washington Hebrew Congregation. However, her Jewish identification was largely cultural, and evinced itself in her racially progressive views and liberal politics.

After a long illness, Lillian Kessler died on September 18, 1993, in Washington, D.C.

ELINOR FUCHS

KING, CAROL WEISS (1895–1952)

Carol Weiss King was one of the outstanding practitioners of immigration law during the period bounded by the Palmer Raids and the McCarthy era. In her thirty-year career, she represented hundreds of foreign-born radicals threatened with deportation in administrative proceedings in the lower courts and in the Supreme Court.

She was born on August 24, 1895, to Samuel and Carrie (Stix) Weiss. Their youngest child, she had two brothers and one sister. Samuel Weiss founded one of New York City's first corporate law firms, Frank and Weiss, and one of his sons, Carol's older brother Louis, was a founding partner of Paul, Weiss, Rifkind and Wharton. The Weiss children were raised in a caring, liberal, intellectual environment. At Barnard College, from which she graduated in 1916, King developed a deep interest in the problems of labor and volunteered to work with Local 25 of the INTERNATIONAL LADIES GARMENT WORKERS UNION. She wed author Gordon King in 1917.

After graduating from New York University Law School in 1920, King spurned her family's affluent life-style and Wall Street legal practice for a loose partnership with radical attorneys Joseph Brodsky, Swinburne Hale, Walter Nelles, and Isaac Shorr. This early experience led to a lifelong association with left-wing activists, including members of the Communist Party of the United States. From 1924 to 1931, King edited the *Law and Freedom Bulletin*, the important digest of the American Civil Liberties Union and one of the country's earliest efforts to record state and federal cases involving significant questions of constitutional law. She became a founder and principal of the International Juridical Association and the National Lawyers Guild. In 1942, she became general counsel to the American Committee for the Foreign Born. Her clients included union leader Harry Bridges, Communist Party leader William Schneiderman, Negro Communist organizer Angelo Herndon, the Scottsboro Boys, and numerous left-wing activists.

When her husband died of pneumonia in 1930, leaving King a widow with one son, she threw herself into her work. Her best-known client was the colorful Bridges, who faced deportation in 1938 for alleged membership in the Communist Party. King guided the Australian-born longshoreman's case through several rounds, until the Supreme Court reversed the deportation order during World War II.

King had an extraordinary record of success in enlisting other attorneys to work for free on key constitutional cases. Her most significant accomplishment in this regard was her recruitment of Wendell Willkie, the 1940 Republican Party presidential nominee, to represent her client William Schneiderman in the Supreme Court. The case, in which the U.S. Government tried to revoke the Communist Party leader's citizenship, was decided favorably in 1943.

As a female attorney in a predominantly male-dominated profession, and unwilling to let her clients' interests be compromised by sexist assumptions about their advocate, King frequently retained men to argue cases that she herself had prepared. Although a number of her cases reached the Supreme Court, she herself made only one appearance there, in *Butterfield* v. *Zydok* (342 U.S. 524, 1952), a case in which her client lost.

Because of her association with controversial clients, King herself was subject to surveillance by the FBI. She took special satisfaction in her battles against the Immigration and Naturalization Service (INS). Her most important legal victory against the INS came in *Sung* v. *McGrath* (339 U.S. 908, 1950), in which the Supreme Court acknowledged her argument that the agency was subject to the same administrative and procedural rules as all other federal departments. This ruling resulted in an immediate freeze on deportation hearings until the INS agreed to comply with the requirements of the Administrative Procedures Act.

After a bout with cancer, Carol Weiss King died on January 22, 1952.

BIBLIOGRAPHY

ACLU Law and Freedom Bulletin (1924–1931); *DAB* 5:389–390; Ginger, Ann Fagan. *Carol Weiss King* (1993); King, Carol Weiss. Papers. Carol Weiss King Collection. Meiklejohn Civil Liberties Institute, Berkeley, Calif; King, Carol Weiss, and Walter Nelles. "Contempt by Publication in the United States." *Columbia Law Review* 28 (1928); *NAW* modern; Obituary. *NYTimes*, January 23, 1952, 27:1.

BERNARD UNTI

KING, CAROLE (b. 1942)

Carole King, a nice Jewish girl from Brooklyn, gave Aretha Franklin reason to croon "A Natural Woman," inspired Little Eva to tell a generation about the latest dance craze in "The Loco-Motion," and let James Taylor warm our hearts with "You've Got a Friend."

Singer-songwriter Carole King was born Carol Klein on February 9, 1942, in Brooklyn to a middle-class Jewish family. She took piano lessons from her mother, starting at age four. At Queens College she met future husband and songwriting partner Gerry Goffin, whom she married in 1958.

King and Goffin were part of the "Brill Building Sound," having written with other predominantly Jewish New York writers for Aldon Music, located around the corner from the famous Brill Building. After writing over a hundred hits, including "Will You

Carole King, a nice Jewish girl from Brooklyn, gave Aretha Franklin reason to croon "A Natural Woman," inspired Little Eva to tell a generation about the latest dance craze in "The Loco-Motion," and let James Taylor warm our hearts with "You've Got a Friend." [New York Public Library]

Love Me Tomorrow?" and "Take Good Care of My Baby," and giving birth to Louise in 1960 and Sherry in 1963, Carole King divorced Goffin in 1968.

Yet the 1970s were an equally, if not more, successful time for King. As a solo artist, she produced the album *Tapestry* (Ode), which won four Grammy Awards in 1972. She was not able to accept the awards in person, having recently delivered daughter Molly in late 1971 with new husband Charles Larkey. The following years brought more gold records, notably *Music* and *Wrap Around Joy* (Ode), and a fourth child, Levi, in 1974.

King and Larkey divorced in 1976. She later married Rick Evers, who died in 1978, and then Rick Sorensen in 1982.

King still tours and records regularly. She and Gerry Goffin were inducted into the Songwriters Hall of Fame in 1987. She received the National Academy of Songwriters Lifetime Achievement Award a year later, and was inducted into the Rock and Roll Hall of Fame in 1990. In 1994 she appeared in the Broadway production of *Blood Brothers* and contributed to *Life's a Lesson*, an album of Jewish liturgies.

BIBLIOGRAPHY

Cohen, Mitchell S. *Carole King: A Biography in Words and Pictures.* Edited by Greg Shaw (1976); Peeples, Stephen. "Carole King, a Natural Woman." Liner notes to *The Ode Collection, 1968-1976* (April 1994); *Rolling Stone Encyclopedia of Rock and Roll.* Edited by Patricia Romanowski and Holly George-Warren; *Who's Who of American Women, 1995–1996.* 19th ed. (1995).

NANCY ROSEN

KISCH-ARENDT, RUTH (b. 1906)

Ruth Kisch-Arendt, an Orthodox Jew who celebrated the musical and cultural traditions of German lieder, performed the songs of Schubert, Mendelssohn, Liszt, and Wagner before small-town German Jewish audiences during some of the most violent outbreaks of anti-Semitism in the 1930s. These performances stand as a poignant and ironic reminder of the inhumanity of the Holocaust.

Born in Goldberg, Silesia, in 1906, Ruth Kisch-Arendt studied music in Germany, Switzerland, and Italy. She specialized in lieder, nineteenth-century German songs characterized by secular themes, derived in part from allegorical poetry.

Kisch-Arendt achieved prominence as one of the foremost lieder singers in Europe. In the late 1920s, she sang at the Niederrheinisch Festival in Cologne, the Beethoven Festival in Bonn, and the Hamburg Centenary Festival. After the rise of the Nazi Party in Germany, Kisch-Arendt joined the Jewish Kulturbund in 1933, presenting her interpretations of lieder to Jewish audiences.

In 1938, Kisch-Arendt and her husband, physician and physiologist Bruno Kisch, immigrated to the United States, entering the country on nonquota visas. Settling in New York City, Kisch-Arendt continued her career as a singer, performing in many American music festivals in the 1940s, including the New York Festival of Jewish Art in 1941. In 1945, she departed from her usual repertoire of lieder, presenting a program of works by Jewish composers that spanned four centuries. In 1948, she sang the debut performances of Frederick Jacobi's *Vocalise* and Irvin Heilner's *The Traveler.*

Regarded by American critics as a sympathetic interpreter of lieder and other songs, Kisch-Arendt was described by one contemporary observer as "lively and touching in a field where there is so much arid professionalism."

BIBLIOGRAPHY

Kisch, Bruno Z. *Wanderungen und Wanderlunger* (1966); *New Grove Dictionary of Music and Musicians.* Edited by Stanley Sadie. Vol. 10, s.v. "Lieder" (1980); *UJE,* s.v. "Kisch, Bruno"; Whitton, Kenneth S. *Lieder: An Introduction to German Song* (1984).

DAVID REGO

KLAGSBRUN, FRANCINE (b. 1931)

Author of more than a dozen books and countless articles in national publications, and a regular columnist in two Jewish publications, Francine Klagsbrun is a writer of protean interests. She has succeeded in making an impact on both American and American Jewish culture.

She was born Francine Lifton in 1931, the daughter of Anna and Benjamin Lifton. From an early age, she displayed an uncanny ability to take the best from each situation in which she found herself. Her elementary education in the all-girls Orthodox Shulamith School of Borough Park, Brooklyn, gave her a sense of what women can accomplish and a wealth of female role models. She also developed there a love of both classical Jewish texts and language, particularly Hebrew. Her love of learning was supported by her parents, who nurtured in her an expectation of excellence. Her mother was responsible for her enrollment at Shulamit and her father, himself quite learned in Jewish texts, would often help her with her studies. She attended public school and then the Jewish Theological Seminary. Many of her professors there, including Abraham Halkin, Judah Goldin, and Gerson D. Cohen, were important influences.

Throughout her education, Klagsbrun maintained her interest in both secular and Jewish subjects. She earned a B.A. degree, magna cum laude, from Brooklyn College, where she was elected to Phi Beta Kappa, a B.H.L. (Bachelor of Hebrew Literature) from the Jewish Theological Seminary, and an M.A. in art history from the Institute of Fine Arts.

Klagsbrun's work has been notable for the careful research that undergirds it and the clarity and elegance of her prose. Although her academic training was in art history, her professional career turned early toward publishing, including executive editorships at both Encyclopedia Americana and World Book Encyclopedia. Her earliest books were written for children, on topics as diverse as psychiatry, Moses, and spices. Her more recent publications have reflected her interest in feminism and Judaism.

Klagsbrun's early involvement in the current feminist movement is reflected in her writing for *Ms.* and her editorship of both *The First Ms. Reader* (1973) and *Free to Be . . . You and Me* (1974). Her interest in personal and interpersonal issues came to the fore in books like *Too Young to Die—Youth and Suicide* (1976), *Married*

Francine Klagsbrun's early involvement in the feminist movement is reflected in her editorship of both The First Ms. Reader *(1973) and* Free to Be . . . You and Me *(1974). She is shown here in 1991 carrying the Torah to the* Kotel *[the Western Wall] to conduct a prayer service. [Joan Roth]*

People: Staying Together in the Age of Divorce (1985), and *Mixed Feelings: Love, Hate, Rivalry and Reconciliation Among Brothers and Sisters* (1992). Her deep commitment to Judaism and Jewish scholarship is most evident in *Voices of Wisdom—Jewish Ideals and Ethics for Everyday Living* (1980) and *Jewish Days: A Book of Jewish Life and Culture Around the Year* (1996). Ultimately, a remarkable aspect of Francine Klagsbrun's work is that each of her interests informs the others, allowing her to intertwine the various strands of her scholarship.

Klagsbrun's communal commitments have included membership on the commission for the Study of Women in the Rabbinate of the Jewish Theological Seminary and chairing its Board of Overseers of the Library, as well as serving as secretary of the board of trustees of the Jewish Museum and cochairing its exhibitions committee. She is a member of the Publication Committee of the Jewish Publication Society of America, the Commission on Equality for Women of the American Jewish Congress, the Professional Advisory Board of the Petschek National Jewish Family Center of the American Jewish Committee, and the Artistic Advisory Committee of the National Foundation for Jewish Culture.

Francine Klagsbrun is married to Samuel Klagsbrun and is the mother of Dr. Sarah Devora Klagsbrun.

ANNE LAPIDUS LERNER

KLAUS, IDA (b. c. 1910)

Known by the press in the 1950s and 1960s as the woman "who thinks with a man's brain," Ida Klaus has distinguished herself in the area of labor law.

She was born around 1910 in the Brownsville section of Brooklyn, New York, where her family ran a grocery store. Her brother, Samuel, died in 1963. She graduated Phi Beta Kappa from HUNTER COLLEGE and from the Teachers Institute of the Jewish Theological Seminary of America. One of six women accepted in 1928 into the first class of Columbia Law School to admit women, she graduated in 1931.

After serving as a research assistant to Columbia law professor Herman Oliphant, Klaus was recruited by him as one of ten of the nation's ten most promising lawyers to work for President Franklin D. Roosevelt's New Deal. The National Labor Relations Act of 1935 served to focus Klaus's interest in labor law, and she went on to become solicitor of the National Labor Relations Board under Harry S. Truman, from 1948 to 1954. At that time, she held the highest-ranking position of a female lawyer in the federal government.

In 1954, Mayor Robert F. Wagner, Jr., appointed Klaus to head the New York Labor Department, and she successfully negotiated the "Little Wagner Act," which gave city employees the right to organize and use collective bargaining. She also served as a consultant to John F. Kennedy on federal employee labor relations. As the executive director (until 1975) of the Labor Relations and Collective Bargaining Office of the New York City Board of Education, she negotiated the first citywide teachers' contract. In 1980, while working as a private arbitrator, she was called in by President Jimmy Carter as one of three mediators in the Long Island Railroad strike.

Klaus was awarded an honorary doctorate from the Jewish Theological Seminary in 1994, and in 1996 was given an award for distinguished achievement from the Columbia Law School.

BIBLIOGRAPHY

Breasted, Mary. "Career Labor Expert." *NYTimes*, January 18, 1974; Klaus, Ida. Program of Commencement Exercises, Jewish Theological Seminary of America, NYC, May 19, 1994; Pomerantz, Sharon. "Ida Klaus: Making History." *Masoret* 3, no. 3 (Spring 1994): 8.

SUZANNE KLING

KLEIN, GERDA WEISSMANN
(b. 1924)

"I pray you never stand at any crossroads in your own lives, but if you do, if the darkness seems so total, if you think there is no way out, remember never ever give up. The darker the night, the brighter the dawn, and when it gets really, really dark, this is when one sees the true brilliance of the stars." These words illustrate the courage and inner strength that made it possible for Gerda Weissmann Klein to endure the horrifying conditions of the Holocaust.

Gerda Weissmann, the second child of Julius Weissmann (fur manufacturing executive) and Helene Mueckenbrunn Weissmann (housewife), was born on May 8, 1924, in Bielsko, Poland. She attended Notre Dame Gymnasium in Bielsko until the Nazis invaded Poland in 1939. Both of her parents, as well as her older brother Arthur (b. 1919), died during the Holocaust. Miraculously, Gerda survived the ghetto, deportation, slave-labor camps, and the infamous three-month death march from the Polish-German border to southern Czechoslovakia. As the sole survivor of her family, she has provided the world a glimpse of her ordeal through her written and oral testimonies.

In 1946, Gerda Weissmann married her liberator, Kurt Klein, an American intelligence officer, in Paris. After their marriage, they traveled to the United States, where Kurt Klein owned a printing business and was an editor. Kurt Klein, a German Jew, had been sent to the United States in 1937 as a safety measure, and later he served in the armed forces. His parents remained in Germany and died in Auschwitz. The Kleins have three children: Vivian E. (b. 1948), Leslie A. (b. 1952), and James Arthur (b. 1957).

In 1957, Klein published her first book, *All But My Life* (now in its thirty-ninth edition). This remarkable autobiography recounts her experiences during the Holocaust and has been used as a primary source for Holocaust studies in this country as well as Great Britain. Her Holocaust experiences were also the subject of an HBO special, *One Survivor Remembers*, which received an Oscar for Best Documentary–Short in 1996, a TV Emmy Award, and two Cable Ace Awards. Gerda Weissmann Klein's story also is presented in the "Testimony" film, which is part of the permanent exhibit at the United States Holocaust Memorial Museum in Washington, D.C. Her other books include *A Passion for Sharing*, which received the Valley Forge Freedom Award. It is a biography that narrates the fascinating life of EDITH ROSENWALD STERN (1895–1980), one of Julius Rosenwald's children and a prominent New Orleans Jewish philanthropist who throughout her life was deeply involved in her community, education, race relations, politics, and the arts. She has written two children's books. *The Blue Rose* (1974) is a poignant story that depicts the life of an autistic child through pictures, poetic verse, and the symbolism of a blue rose. During the International Year for Disabled Persons (1981), *The Blue Rose* was translated into Hebrew by the Begin family, and the term became a synonym for a handicapped child in Israel. *Promise of a New Spring: The Holocaust and Renewal* (1981) is a sensitive and compassionate book designed to teach young children about the Holocaust using the allegory of a forest fire. *Peregrinations, Adventures with the Green Parrot*, published by the Josephine Goodyear Committee, benefits the Children's Hospital of Buffalo. She was also the featured columnist of "Stories for Young Readers," a weekly column in the *Buffalo Sunday News* for more than seventeen years (1978–1996) and is a noted author of television scripts and biographical profiles.

Klein's participation within the Jewish community is best exemplified by her volunteer work for HADASSAH, the United Jewish Appeal, Israel Bonds, and the United States Holocaust Memorial Museum. She received the Hannah Solomon Award from the NATIONAL COUNCIL OF JEWISH WOMEN (1974), the Myrtle Award from Hadassah (1985), the Women of Inspiration Award at the International Lion of Judah Conference in Jerusalem from the Women's Division of the United Jewish Appeal (1996) (she was the only American Jewish woman to receive the latter award).

Due to her charisma and her undeniable abilities as an author, historian, and columnist, Klein has a become an internationally recognized motivational speaker. She has been featured on the *Oprah Winfrey Show*, *CBS Sunday Morning Show*, and *60 Minutes*. In

1997, she received an appointment to the United States Holocaust Commission by President Clinton.

Throughout her life, Klein has been an inspiration. Her response to the Holocaust, her devotion to her family, her work with all types of children, her commitment to the American Jewish community and Israel, her active support for the war against hunger, racism, and intolerance, and her prolific writing and lecturing are all examples of her dynamic role as an American Jewish woman in the twentieth century. Her life exemplifies the ability to overcome adversity by striving to link a fractured past with the future of American Judaism.

**SELECTED WORKS BY
GERDA WEISSMANN KLEIN**

All But My Life (1957); *The Blue Rose* (1974); *A Passion for Sharing* (1984); *Promise of a New Spring: The Holocaust and Renewal* (1981).

BIBLIOGRAPHY

Booklist (October 1, 1996): 362; Commire, Anne, ed. *Something About the Author.* Vol. 44 (1986); "Gerda Does it Again—Latest Book Chronicles Life of New Orleans Woman." *Buffalo News,* October 24, 1984, p. B6; "Gerda Klein Leaves Her Mark on Israel." *Buffalo News,* January 1, 1981, p. 27; "Gerda Klein's Riches—an Oscar, Fame and Family Admiration." *Buffalo News,* April 10, 1996, p. D1; "Journey to Jerusalem: The Search for Peace and Brotherhood." *Buffalo News Magazine,* December 24, 1978, pp. 4–7; *JUF News* (Chicago). October, 1996: 19+; May, Hal, ed. *Contemporary Authors.* Vol. 116 (1986); "New Books are Aimed at Children (Peregrinations)." *Buffalo News,* June 22, 1986, p. 9E; *One Survivor Remembers.* Videotape; "Oscar-Nominated Film Recalls War's Grip on Kenmore Couple." *Buffalo News,* April 8,1984, p. 3E; "An Oscar Speech that was Close to Transcendent." *Buffalo News,* April 7, 1996, TV Topics, p. 2; "Talk Stirs Teachers of Disabled." *Buffalo News,* January 28, 1984. p. 5A; Television Review. *NYTimes,* May 17, 1995; "Tragic Story Ends, A New Life Begins." *Buffalo News,* February 16, 1970, p. 15.

SANDRA K. BORNSTEIN

KNOPF, BLANCHE WOLF
(1893–1966)

Blanche W. Knopf was one of that small group of women who were major book publishers. Married to Alfred A. Knopf in 1916, she became a vice president of the firm in 1921 and president in 1957. During her tenure, the firm was noted for publishing such authors as André Gide, Jean-Paul Sartre, Albert Camus, Elizabeth Bowen, Ilya Ehrenburg, Mikhail Sholokov, Thomas Mann, and Sigmund Freud. Her intellectual interests, flawless French, and sensitivity to emerging literary trends were matched by her personal style and social prowess. Although much less known than her famous husband, she deserves a much larger share of the credit for the success of Alfred A. Knopf, Inc., than usually accorded her.

Born in New York City July 30, 1893, the daughter of Julius Wolf, a successful jeweler, and Bertha (Samuels) Wolf, Blanche grew up in a privileged ambiance, tutored by French and German governesses. She attended New York's Gardner School. One summer, around 1911, she met Alfred Knopf, two years her senior. Married on April 4, 1916, they had one child, Alfred Jr., born June 17, 1919.

Alfred A. Knopf launched his eponymous publishing firm in 1915, with his then-fiancée's encouragement. From the beginning the firm was a shared enterprise. In 1921, five years after their marriage, hiring a full-time nurse allowed Blanche Knopf to assume a larger part of the operations; she became a director and vice president. Because of her acuity and her fluency in European languages, she soon became a traveling publisher's agent as well as office manager. On her first trip to Europe in 1920, she and her husband met most of the major publishers. By the 1930s, she had made arrangements to publish the American editions in translation of Gide, Ehrenburg, Sholokov, and, in 1938, Freud's *Moses and Monotheism.* Two years before, after a voyage to Germany, she had told a reporter for the *New York Times* (July 14, 1936): "There is not a German writer left in Germany who is worth thinking about. . . . Only the Nazi writers and publishers remain."

Although her annual trips abroad resulted in manuscripts and translations for the firm, she was able to develop close relationships with several of the writers, in particular H.L. Mencken, Albert Camus, Robert Nathan, Willa Cather, and Joseph Herbesheimer. At her urging, the firm published both the classics and such popular writers as Dashiell Hammett, Raymond Chandler, James M. Cain, Fannie Hurst, Warwick Deeping, and Kahlil Gibran. Gibran's *Prophet* (1923) was one of Knopf's all-time best-sellers. William L. Shirer's *Berlin Diary* was another runaway best-seller. It was Blanche Knopf who urged Mencken to enlarge his nostalgic, essentially autobiographical *New Yorker* articles into *Happy Days* (1940), *Newspaper Days* (1941), and *Heathen Days* (1943). It is a tribute to the esteem in which he held her that she was the only woman allowed to visit Mencken in his last days. In the same vein, when Camus died in an auto accident in 1960, Blanche Knopf wrote a poignant piece for the *Atlantic,* "Albert Camus in the Sun" (February 1961). Significantly, she was named a chevalier of the Legion of Honor in 1948.

During the World War II years she was successful in obtaining books from Jorge Amado, Gilberto Freyre, Eduardo Mallea, and German Arciniegas. Her "Impressions of British Publishing in Wartime" was published in *Publishers Weekly* (December 18, 1943). "There is a healthy, active, exciting creative spirit," she wrote, "such as I have not seen there in fifteen years." In 1948, as a result of her dynamic relationship with her authors and her personal supervision of the manuscripts and translations, Geoffrey Hellman described her as "aggressive, hunchy, dynamic, social, politically minded, and capable of exerting a very considerable charm" even while "she courts writers the firm would like to publish . . . and keeps those already on the roster happy with celebrity-studded parties, and promises, which she is in a position to implement, of liberal advertising and other promotion."

Blanche Knopf's abilities and what she added to the firm were not without their cost. During the 1950s, she and her husband, two ambitious, talented, and strong-willed people, clashed often. Each, with a stable roster of authors, established areas of control within the firm and in the industry. As Harding Lemay, the firm's publicity director, saw it, their relationship had become one of strained politeness punctuated by outbursts of rage on his part followed by "quick sarcasm" on hers. The offices in Manhattan, he thought, looked like an "intimate royal court of eighteenth-century Germany, with its tyrannical Emperor, devious Empress, and ebullient, if somewhat apprehensive Crown Prince." In 1957, when Alfred became chairman of the board, Blanche became president. Their son, Alfred Jr., left Knopf in 1959 to become one of the founders of Atheneum Publishers. A year later, perhaps as a consequence of Alfred Jr.'s departure, Alfred A. Knopf, Inc., was sold to Random House, although the Knopf imprint continued as an independent entity and Blanche, as president, remained involved.

Throughout her career she preferred to be known as Blanche W. Knopf, not as Mrs. Alfred A. Knopf. A petite woman, frail looking, fond of jewelry and high fashion, she was seen by her friends as witty, loyal, and amusing. Her satisfaction was, she wrote in *House Beautiful* (January 1949), that "the world of books is the world I know. I would not change it for any other, but to pretend that publishing is anything but a constant round of overcoming obstacles and frustrating difficulties would be untrue."

In a profession historically dominated by men, Blanche W. Knopf became known as a respected professional, an editor and publisher in her own right. A bit resentful in her late years that she was still seen as

Blanche Knopf was as ambitious, talented, and strong-willed as her husband, Alfred. Their relationship as they ran their distinguished publishing firm has been described as "one of strained politeness punctuated by outbursts of rage on his part followed by 'quick sarcasm' on hers." She is shown here on September 7, 1928, returning from a European trip, where she had been cultivating their large contingent of continental authors. [Bettmann]

someone in her husband's shadow, thought of as Mrs. Knopf by some, she deserves to be recognized as an almost equal with Alfred A. Knopf in helping establish one of the great publishing firms of the twentieth century; she was certainly the one who was responsible for the firm's receptivity to the newer literary trends. In her late years, plagued by ill health and failing eyesight, she continued to work. She died in New York in her sleep on June 4, 1966.

BIBLIOGRAPHY

Current Biography 1957 (1958); *DAB* 8; Hellman, Geoffrey. "Publishers." *New Yorker* (November 20 and 27, December 4, 1948); Knopf, Blanche. Personal Papers and Library. Harry Ransom Humanities Center, University of Texas, Austin; Lemay, Harding. *Inside, Looking Out* (1971); Madison, Charles A. *Book Publishing in America* (1966); *NAW* modern; Obituaries. *NYTimes*, June 5, 1966, 86:1, and *Newsweek* (June 20, 1966), and *Publishers Weekly* (June 13, 1966); Whitman, Alden. *The Obituary Book* (1971); *WWWIA* 4, 5.

DANIEL WALDEN

KOENIGSBERGER, IRENE CAROLINE DINER (1896–1985)

A distinguished chemist credited with discovering the structure of rubber, Irene Caroline Koenigsberger was also an important figure in the Washington, D.C., Jewish community.

Born in New York City on September 21, 1896, she was the eldest child of Jacob Diner, a professor of chemistry and founder and dean of the Fordham University Pharmacy School, and Jeannette (DëLowe) Diner. While her younger brother, Milton, embarked on a career as a successful businessman in New York City, young Irene's interest in science was encouraged by her parents.

She was educated at HUNTER COLLEGE, Columbia University, and New York University, where she received her doctorate in chemistry in 1921.

While conducting dissertation research on the molecular structure of rubber, Koenigsberger discovered a method for determining the life of rubber products. Companies sought to purchase the rights to her discovery, which was important to the growing automotive tire industry in the United States, but she refused, reasoning that such a sale would keep her discovery secret and would benefit only certain manufacturers.

In the 1920s, Koenigsberger was an associate chemist for the Chemical Warfare Service and a research consultant in rubber and microscopy in Washington, D.C. In the 1930s, she was chief chemist at the National Voice Amplifying Company, and during World War II she was employed by the U.S. War Department. Koenigsberger was also a fellow of the American Institute of Chemists and a member of the American Chemical Society.

In 1922, she married Lawrence Koenigsberger, a Washington, D.C., lawyer. With her husband, she founded Temple Sinai in Washington, serving as honorary vice president. Koenigsberger was active in B'NAI B'RITH WOMEN throughout her life and served as the first president of District Five. She also established the B'nai B'rith Hillel Foundation at George Washington University. Under her guidance, B'nai B'rith Women supported a home for emotionally disturbed children in Jerusalem. A founder of the Jewish Community Council of Greater Washington, Koenigsberger was also a board member of the NATIONAL COUNCIL OF JEWISH WOMEN in Washington.

In 1980, Koenigsberger received the Hunter College Distinguished Alumna Medal in recognition of her achivements in science and civic affairs.

Irene Caroline Diner Koenigsberger died at her home in Chevy Chase, Maryland, on August 12, 1985, at age eighty-seven.

BIBLIOGRAPHY

AJYB 87 (1985): 440; Obituary. *NYTimes*, August 18, 1985; *WWIAJ* (1938).

DAVID REGO

KOHLER, ROSE (1873–1947)

Rose Kohler was a multitalented woman who was known as an accomplished painter and sculptor. She was a teacher in, and later the chair of, the NATIONAL COUNCIL OF JEWISH WOMEN's religious schools in Cincinnati, Ohio, and wrote many articles on art and religion.

Born in Chicago, Illinois, on March 21, 1873, Rose Kohler was the daughter of Johanna (Einhorn) Kohler and Rabbi Kaufmann Kohler. Dr. Kohler was a leader in Reform Judaism, the rabbi of Temple Beth-El on Fifth Avenue in New York, which later merged with Temple Emanu-El. He was also the president of the Hebrew Union College in Cincinnati. Rose Kohler had a sister, Lili, and two brothers, Max and Edgar, both attorneys.

Kohler studied at the training school of the Normal College (now HUNTER COLLEGE), Well's School for Girls, and the Cincinnati Art Academy. She also

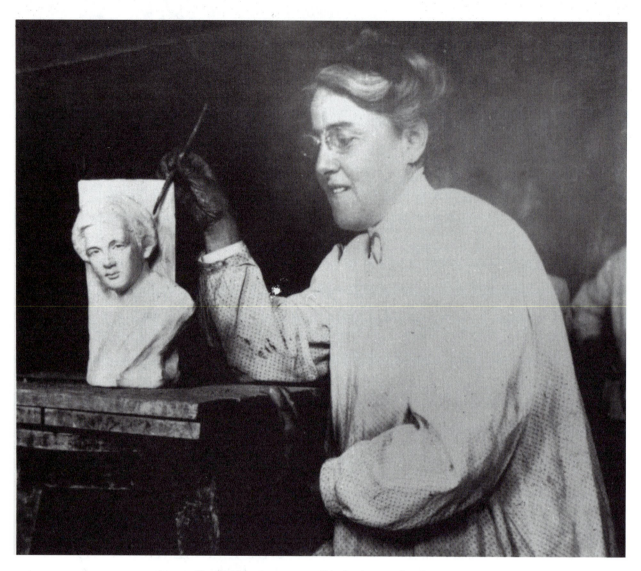

Rose Kohler was an accomplished painter and sculptor.
She also wrote many articles on the origins and development of Jewish art.
[American Jewish Archives]

attended the Art Students League of New York. Kohler had exhibits at the American Art Association, the Art Institute of Chicago, the Pennsylvania Academy of Fine Arts, and the National Academy of Design in New York City. Her works have also been displayed in Temple Emanu-El in New York (where she was once a member of the women's auxiliary) and Temple Beth El in Detroit, as well as the temple of Hebrew Union College in Cincinnati. Kohler's best-known works include a bust of her father, replicas of which are in Detroit, New York, and several other cities, and *The Spirit of the Synagogue*, a detailed medallion with an inscription that reads "My House

shall be called a House of Prayer for all peoples," replicas of which can be found in religious centers throughout the country. Other portrait reliefs and busts are on display in institutions in Chicago, New York, and Washington, D.C.

She wrote many articles on the origins and development of Jewish art. In "Art as Related to Judaism," written for the National Council of Jewish Women, she stated, "Art for Judaism was not an end in itself . . . it was but a means—and could become a powerful one—of illustrating, for Jew and non-Jew, Judaism's religious mission for humanity." Kohler discussed how art reflected hostility toward the Jew and how it was used to arouse hatred and start pogroms in some European countries.

Rose Kohler wrote about the importance of Jewish education in *Religious School Work* and stated there are those who feel "religious faith is like a life-preserver in time of trouble, and in times of health and peace is laid quietly on the shelf." She urged Jewish mothers not to deprive their children of instruction in religion and encouraged them to put "proper stress upon that great educational force which more than any other trains the heart and the soul and ministers to that part of her child's nature which requires nutrition as well as his body, his soul—that spark of the divine within him that molds his character for the good and sanctifies and hallows his entire life."

Rose Kohler died in New York City on October 4, 1947, at age seventy-four. She is remembered not only for her beautiful works of art but also for her firm commitment to Jewish art, as well as her love of the Jewish religious school.

BIBLIOGRAPHY

AJYB, 50:518; *BEOAJ*; Kohler, Rose. Archives. Temple Emanu-El, NYC; Obituary. *NYTimes*, October 6, 1947, 21:1; *UJE*, s.v. "Kohler, Kaufmann"; *Who Was Who in American Art* (1985); *WWIAJ* (1926, 1928, 1938).

SUE LEVINE

KOHN, C. MARIAN (1884–1969)

A product of the Progressive Era and conservative Philadelphia German Jewish society, social worker C. Marian Kohn would not have defined herself as a feminist, yet her efforts on behalf of poor Philadelphia Jewish immigrant women clearly indicated that she was a woman ahead of her time. She was aware that the court system was stacked against women, and her advocacy of pensions that would allow mothers to stay home to care for their children puts her in tune with a concept of radical feminism.

C. Marian Kohn was born on April 2, 1884, into Philadelphia German Jewish "society" through her Bavarian-born maternal grandfather, Charles Bloomingdale. She was the fifth and youngest child of Florence (Bloomingdale) and Morris Kohn, a shirtmaker and later a manufacturer's agent who was born in Marback, Germany.

Kohn was afflicted with congenital cataracts and was considered legally blind. She attended Overbrook School for the Blind in Philadelphia and, upon graduation, the Neff School of Oratory. She had no degree in social work when she began, but took courses and received vocational certification from the Pennsylvania School of Social Work in 1934. Her first job was as house mother at the Industrial Home for Jewish Girls in 1907. Two weeks later, she became superintendent.

In 1911, Kohn was named director of clubs and classes at Neighborhood Centre, an agency established to aid in the social adjustment of Jewish immigrants. In 1917, Kohn became head worker, distinguishing herself and enhancing the agency. She became the first executive director of the Orphans Guardian Society in 1925, where she remained until 1934 when she became supervisor of the Blind Pension Fund. When the Pennsylvania Department of Assistance was created in 1937, Kohn became a consultant on issues regarding the visually disabled. She retired in 1955.

A pioneer in the battle to improve the lot of women and to achieve rights for the disabled, Kohn died on July 1, 1969, at age eighty-five.

BIBLIOGRAPHY

Greifer, Julian L. "Neighborhood Centre—a Study of the Adjustment of a Culture Group in America." Ph.D. diss., School of Education, New York University, 1984; Kohn, C. Marian. Papers, Acc. 214, 1164, and 1309. Philadelphia Jewish Archives Center; Rose, Elizabeth. *World of Our Mothers: Jewish Women, Families and Social Workers* (1988); Schneyer, Mark. "Mothers and Children, Poverty and Morality: A Social Worker's Priorities." *Pennsylvania Magazine of History & Biography* (April 1988); Schwartz, Lily G. "C. Marian Kohn (1884–1969): The Most Caring Person I Ever Met" (1985).

LILY SCHWARTZ

KOHN, ESTHER LOEB (1875–1965)

"The great need today is for social inventions for the prevention of destitution and illness." This statement, made in 1938, illustrates two of the primary interests of Esther Loeb Kohn's life—social reform and medical social work. A thirty-year resident of Hull House, the famous Chicago social settlement founded by Jane Addams, Kohn was also an active volunteer and financial supporter of Jewish charitable organizations in Chicago. A "professional board lady," in addition to her work on behalf of child welfare she devoted great effort to bridging the gap between volunteer and professional social workers.

Esther Loeb Kohn came from the old-line, well-to-do, German Jewish Loeb family. The daughter of Emma (Mannheimer) and William Loeb, a former captain in the Civil War, she was born on Chicago's Near North Side on January 12, 1875. The second-oldest child of seven and the eldest daughter, Kohn left school at age fifteen to help raise her younger siblings. She had a fine singing voice and, while still a youth, was invited by Theodore Thomas, who later established the Chicago Symphony, to sing with his Apollo Club.

In December 1894, at age nineteen, Esther Loeb married Alfred D. Kohn. He possessed a Ph.D. in English but decided to attend medical school, and the couple later went to Germany, where he completed his training. Rather than retiring to her home after marriage, Esther Loeb Kohn took courses at the University of Chicago. While in Europe, she took advantage of the opportunity to further her musical training in Munich and Paris and also attended the University of Vienna. When the couple returned to Chicago, Kohn continued her education, taking courses at the School of Civics and Philanthropy, from which she eventually received a certificate. Later, in 1920, she played an important role in the merger of the school into the School of Social Service Administration at the University of Chicago.

A member of the Chicago Board of Education, Alfred Kohn started the first nutrition program in the Chicago public schools, work that brought him into contact with Jane Addams. When he died suddenly in December 1909 at age thirty-seven, Esther Kohn had never met Addams personally but, nevertheless, decided to devote her energies to social service by becoming a Hull House resident. Realizing her administrative and organizational ability, Addams placed Kohn in charge of Hull House whenever she herself was not in residence, an occurrence that became more frequent with the passing years.

Always a supporter of Jewish causes, Kohn served as director, vice president, and president of the Jewish Social Service Bureau of Jewish Charities from 1921 to 1941. She was on the board of the Jewish Vocational and Employment Service and was instrumental in organizing the Work Shop for Handicapped Persons. She was also a board member and later president of the Board of the Scholarship Association for Jewish Children. In the 1930s, Kohn became a member of various groups engaged in rescuing victims of Nazi tyranny, and later she was active in the Chicago Committee on Displaced Persons and the Jewish-American Joint Distribution Committee, organizations that helped displaced persons admitted to the United States. A confirmed pacifist, Kohn had attended the 1921 peace conference in Vienna under the auspices of the International League for Peace and Freedom. In the 1930s, she backed groups such as the Chicago

Committee Against Rearming Europe, and she opposed peacetime conscription following World War II. Concerned with the fate of children of working mothers, during the war Kohn was active in the Committee on War Problems.

Placed in charge of children's activities and the summer camp at Waukegan, Illinois, upon her arrival at Hull House, Kohn directed the volunteer movement and initiated a trade school for girls forced to leave school and seek employment. Later she persuaded the Chicago Board of Education to adopt the program for the city school system. It developed into the Vocational Guidance program and the Scholarship and Guidance Association, established in 1911. Immediately attracted to the Immigrants Protective League, Kohn became a board member in 1911. She remained a member of the board for fifty years, becoming chair of its finance committee.

Through her husband's profession, Kohn became interested in the medical social work field and was in its vanguard. She recommended that trained laypeople help medical social workers so that the professionals could be freed for large-scale "community planning for health and well-being," and she organized voluntary programs in various Chicago area hospitals.

With the growing professionalization of Hull House, Kohn became a link between volunteer and professional social workers. When a power struggle developed over control of the settlement after Jane Addams's death in 1935, Kohn was one of the committee members whom residents selected to work with the board in choosing a new head resident. When the board failed to consult the residents, however, Kohn disapproved of the changes and left Hull House in 1941. She and a widowed sister moved to a fashionable apartment where Kohn lived until her death and from which she continued to pursue her multiple activities. Always interested in politics, she financially backed liberal candidates, especially Adlai Stevenson, with whom she became friends. In later years, Kohn and Stevenson became the only honorary board members of the Immigrants Protective League.

Kohn was shy in front of large groups and never sought the limelight for herself. Toward the end of her long life, she began to receive recognition for her achievements as honors and awards were showered upon her. The Institute of Medicine of Chicago made her a Citizen Fellow in 1956 and reelected her to their board after her ninetieth birthday. She received the Golden Age Hall of Fame Award from the Jewish Community Centers of Chicago in 1960. Honored by the Immigrants Protective League in 1955 and 1959, she was named Sweetest Woman of the Year in 1960. In the spring of 1961, the Immigrants Service League, as the IPL was called by then, established the annual Esther L. Kohn Award, given each year to a native-born citizen who has helped immigrants. Active until the end, Esther Loeb Kohn died at age ninety on September 1, 1965.

Esther Loeb Kohn devoted her life to helping those less fortunate. Although she was a recognized expert in the child welfare and medical social work fields, financial security allowed Kohn to perform all her service as a volunteer. She was thus in a unique position to act as a link between the professionals and volunteers in Chicago social welfare organizations. Kohn, consequently, was an important figure in both Chicago's secular and Jewish communities.

BIBLIOGRAPHY

Abbott, Edith, and Grace Abbott. Papers. University of Chicago; *BEOAJ*; Kohn, Esther Loeb, and Adela Miller Rich. Papers. Jane Addams Memorial Collection, University of Illinois at Chicago.

PAULA F. PFEFFER

KOHUT, REBEKAH BETTELHEIM (1864–1951)

Rebekah Bettelheim Kohut made her mark on the American Jewish community in the areas of education, social welfare, and the organization of Jewish women. Grounded in her Jewish identity as the daughter and wife of rabbis, Kohut had a public career that paralleled the beginnings of Jewish women's activism in the United States.

Rebekah Bettelheim was born in Kaschau, Hungary on September 9, 1864. Her father, Rabbi Albert Bettelheim, came from a long family tradition of rabbis and doctors. Trained in Hungary as a rabbi, he also took up the study of medicine while serving as a rabbi in Richmond, Virginia. Rebekah's mother, Henrietta A. Weintraub, was widowed with one son at the time of her marriage to Bettelheim. Together, the couple had one more boy and four girls; Kohut was the third child and third daughter.

Albert Bettelheim's outspokenness in the midst of political and religious turmoil in Hungary earned him the enmity of many in the Jewish community, and, in 1867, he immigrated with his family to America. He served briefly as a rabbi in Philadelphia before taking a post in 1869 in Richmond, where the family remained for seven years. While in Richmond, Henrietta

Bettelheim died, and Albert Bettelheim married a second time and had another daughter.

In 1875, the family moved to San Francisco, where Rebekah graduated from high school and normal school and for two years attended classes at the University of California. Her first entry into social welfare work was with the Fruit and Flower Mission of San Francisco, a non-Jewish association of young women that offered flowers and aid to poor residents of the city. She also worked in San Francisco's first kindergarten.

On a trip east in 1886, she met Alexander Kohut. Having arrived from Hungary in 1885 to serve a New York congregation, Rabbi Kohut was a widower who

Rebekah Kohut was an early leader in the NATIONAL COUNCIL OF JEWISH WOMEN. *Despite the sometimes conflicting demands of public and private life, she helped to create frameworks that brought American Jewish women into philanthropic, religious, and educational spheres. [American Jewish Archives]*

had become the champion of Jewish traditionalists in the United States. With their marriage on February 14, 1887, Rebekah Kohut became stepmother to his five sons and three daughters, six of whom were under age thirteen. Apart from caring for her new family and doing some limited public speaking, Kohut put most of her energy into facilitating her husband's scholarly work, maintaining his correspondence, and translating his sermons from German into English. After the death of her younger brother and her father in 1890, Kohut sought distraction in a more active public life. She participated in the New York's Women's Health Protective Association's campaign for better public sanitation and, drawing upon the example of a new women's organization at New York's Temple Emanu-El, she founded the American Jewish community's second sisterhood at Central Synagogue, the congregation served by her husband. Working with the women of Emanu-El and with other sisterhood groups that soon arose, Central Synagogue's Sisterhood of Personal Service tried to relieve the hardships faced by the newly arrived Jewish immigrants of New York's Lower East Side. Alexander Kohut's failing health added to his wife's concerns and responsibilities. Although she was invited to deliver a paper at the Jewish Women's Congress held at the Chicago World's Fair in 1893, at the last moment Kohut was forced to stay home so that she could look after her husband.

After her husband's death in 1894, she entered a wide range of public activities. Although her husband's illness had kept Kohut out of the early planning for the NATIONAL COUNCIL OF JEWISH WOMEN (NCJW), New York's Jewish women leaders hoped that the outspoken widow of the Conservative rabbi could calm the religious tensions prevailing among those involved. She accepted their invitation to become president of the newly formed New York section and spoke widely on behalf of the new national organization. Her council work led to an invitation to be the only Jewish woman to speak before a meeting of the national Mother's Congress in Washington, D.C., presided over by President Grover Cleveland's wife. Forced into the role of breadwinner for the six young Kohut children, Rebekah Kohut offered a series of lectures on English literature, which she had prepared during the long hours of her husband's illness, to a regular group of several hundred that gathered at the home of THERESE LOEB SCHIFF. This lecture series continued for many years. Kohut also turned her attention beyond the Jewish community, working with prominent non-Jewish women on the turn-of-the-century mayoral campaigns of Columbia University president Seth Low.

In 1899, after bad investments wiped out her financial security and that of her sisters and stepmother, Kohut opened the Kohut College Preparatory School for Girls. With the help of her stepson George, she successfully oversaw the school until 1905, when she concluded that the responsibilities of running a boarding school demanded too much of her time and separated her from her stepchildren. Investing the profits made in selling the school, Kohut realized a steady income and freed herself from future financial concerns.

She reimmersed herself in the world of social service and teaching through work with the Temple Emanu-El sisterhood and the Educational Alliance. When George Kohut established a school for boys in Riverdale in 1907, she served as a housemother to his students. She also helped to create and edit a religious school newspaper, *Helpful Thoughts*, sponsored by the National Council of Jewish Women.

With her school closed and her stepchildren increasingly independent, Kohut felt the want of a calling. When invited to become a trustee of the YOUNG WOMEN'S HEBREW ASSOCIATION in 1914, she asked to be put in charge of its employment bureau. Heavy demand for the bureau's services in 1914 and 1915 strengthened Kohut's commitment to employment work both within and beyond the Jewish community. During World War I, she worked with New York's Women's Committee for National Defense to place women in jobs created by the war economy. At the national level, she worked for the Federal Employment Clearing House and served as industrial chair of the National League for Women's Service. She also sold war bonds and raised money for Jewish war relief.

In 1917, Kohut won support from the NCJW for her proposal to send units of Jewish women abroad to help rebuild the devastated Jewish communities of Europe. Although the proposal failed to gain the support of the principal male-led Jewish relief work organizations, the NCJW named Kohut chair of the Reconstruction Committee and after the war sent her to survey what needed to be done abroad. Upon her recommendation, the council sent social workers to rebuild communities and to teach English and useful skills to those awaiting permission to leave for the United States. The NCJW work in Europe inspired women in many European cities to create council organizations of their own. In 1923, two hundred women from nineteen different countries met in Vienna at the World Congress of Jewish Women, where they formed an ongoing organization and elected Rebekah Kohut president.

Kohut's work with the devastated Jewish communities of Europe took its toll upon her health. Forced to take a leave from active life in 1924, Kohut used the opportunity to compose her memoirs, *My Portion.* Once her strength returned, she reentered the public arena, notably in the area of employment work. In 1931, New York governor Franklin D. Roosevelt appointed her to the state's Advisory Council on Employment and, in 1932, to the advisory commission of the New York State Employment Service. From 1932 to 1933, she served as the sole female member of the Joint Legislative Committee on Unemployment and the only member to call for the immediate establishment of state unemployment insurance.

When her stepson George died in 1933, Kohut took his place as executive director of the Columbia Grammar School, guiding the school for two more years. In 1935, she was honored by eight hundred of New York's philanthropic and political elite, who gathered to celebrate her fifty years of service in social and educational work and presented her with $50,000 to distribute to those causes most dear to her. In 1934, she received an honorary doctorate from the Jewish Institute of Religion.

After suffering a broken hip, Kohut was bedridden for the last seven years of her life. During her confinement, she wrote another memoir, *More Yesterdays,* published in 1950, which reflected upon her life and the experience of old age. Rebekah Bettelheim Kohut died on August 11, 1951, in New York City.

As founder of one the first synagogue sisterhoods and as an early leader in the National Council of Jewish Women, Rebekah Kohut emerged as a public figure at the same time that Jewish women's activism took hold in American Jewish life. Despite recurrent tensions between the demands of public and private life, she helped to create frameworks that systematically brought acculturated American Jewish women into the philanthropic, religious, and educational work of the American Jewish community.

SELECTED WORKS BY REBEKAH KOHUT

As I Know Them: Some Jews and a Few Gentiles (1929); *His Father's House: The Story of George Alexander Kohut* (1938); *More Yesterdays* (1950); *My Portion* (1925).

BIBLIOGRAPHY

AJYB 7 (1905–1906): 76, 24:1164, 54:539; Antler, Joyce. *The Journey Home: Jewish Women and the American Century* (1997); *BEOAJ; EJ;* Kohut, Rebekah. Papers. AJA, Cincinnati, Ohio, and American Jewish Historical Society, Waltham, Mass.; Kuzmack, Linda Gordon. *Woman's Cause: The Jewish Woman's Movement in England and the United States, 1881–1935* (1993); *NAW* modern; Obituary. *NYTimes* August 12, 1951, 79:3; Rogow, Faith. *Gone to Another Meeting: The National Council of Jewish Women, 1893–1993* (1993); *UJE; WWIAJ* (1926, 1928, 1938).

KARLA GOLDMAN

KONECKY, EDITH (b. 1922)

Edith Konecky, despite a small body of work, can lay claim to a large literary achievement with *Allegra Maud Goldman* (1976), a coming-of-age novel that chronicles the growth of a young female artist. In brilliantly comic, deceptively simple vignettes, Konecky depicts the world of a nouveau riche Jewish American family in the early part of the twentieth century. In her later novel, *A Place at the Table* (1989), Konecky explores similar territory through the eyes of an older, more experienced heroine, Rachel.

Konecky candidly acknowledges that her insight into the lives she depicts in her novels comes from personal experience. Like her heroines, Konecky was born in Brooklyn in the early 1920s (on August 1, 1922). Like Allegra, she has a brother, Martin Rubin, who is sixteen months older than she. And like both Allegra and Rachel, she is the daughter of a well-to-do dress manufacturer. For the father in the novels, the governing measure of worth—for himself or others—is money. Through this difficult, blunt, often cruel character, Konecky captures the crassness of a life lived in the pursuit of purely materialistic goals. Of her father, "the self-made man," Allegra asks, "If he had to make himself, why couldn't he have made himself nicer?"

Konecky suggests answers to this question in her second book, *A Place at the Table.* A child of immigrants escaping pogroms, an education that came more from the streets of the Lower East Side than the classroom, a shrewd reading of and subsequent internalization of American values provide a context for men like this father. He is the kind of man who scorns those who, unlike him, do not have a thriving business, a chauffeur, a cook, a wife who does not work, and a splendid home. He judges others with the statement, "If [they're] so smart, why [aren't they] rich?"

Not surprisingly, the materialistic emphasis in such a family relegates religious Jewish values to a minor place. Konecky, in fact, shows Jewish observance to be generally perfunctory and prominently gastronomic. She masterfully portrays the resentments and the meanness of this kind of life, the limited choices open to those "weaker souls"—the women and the sensitive children—not willing or not able to share these values, and the crushing family dynamics that leave scars and build strengths.

Konecky has said that Jewish custom made her a feminist before she had a word for it. She frames her work with that feminist perspective, examining ever-shifting Jewish female types and models of success in the twentieth century. First, there is the grandmother who escaped from Eastern Europe to become the *baleboosteh*, the successful American homemaker, offering love, superstition, and nourishment with her *kreplakh*. Then there is the mother, a once-strong woman who is tamed by social expectations to comply with her husband's values and to channel her energies into card games and shopping.

Konecky, as well as her heroines, rejects this inheritance. But the biographical data of her life suggest that the rejection was gradual, keeping pace with the social movements of her day. Like Allegra, she began her writing career while still in high school, winning a short story contest for which she was paid a penny a word. The daughter of Harry and Elizabeth (Smith) Rubin (to whom she dedicates her first novel), she attended New York University from 1939 to 1941, enrolling when she was seventeen. In 1944, she married Murray L. Konecky. They had two children, Michael and Joshua, and lived a suburban life for close to twenty years. Konecky raised her children and wrote occasional short stories. When she was thirty-seven, she returned to college, this time taking classes at Columbia (1959–1960). The women's movement had begun, and many standards for women were changing. She began writing *Allegra Maud Goldman* at the MacDowell Colony in 1962, winning fellowships to work there in succeeding years through 1996. In 1965, she was divorced. She won fellowships to Yaddo from 1969 to 1977, continuing to write and publish short stories.

Konecky dramatizes some of the details of her transformations in her second novel, in which the heroine, Rachel, approaching sixty, reflects on the traumas and triumphs of her life: marriage, divorce, motherhood, grandmotherhood, her love of women, and her relationship to her work. The novelist's own work, writing, occupies a primary place in Konecky's current life. She won a Wurlitzer Foundation Fellowship in 1974 and was a New York Foundation of the Arts Fellow in 1992. *Allegra Maud Goldman* was reissued in 1990, fourteen years after its initial publication, with a new introduction by TILLIE OLSEN and an afterword by Bella Brodzki that pay tribute to the complexity and depth of Konecky's work.

SELECTED WORKS BY EDITH KONECKY

NOVELS

Allegra Maud Goldman (1976. Reprint, with an introduction by Tillie Olsen and afterword by Bella Brodzki, 1990); *A Place at the Table* (1989).

SHORT STORIES

"The Box." *Virgina Quarterly* 46 (1970): 624–628; "The Breakdown." *Story Magazine* (1963); "Charity." *Kenyon Review* 25 (1963): 81–90; "Death in New Rochelle." *Cosmopolitan* (1973); "The Hour." Unpublished; "Lessons." *Virginia Quarterly* 52 (1976): 79–90; "Love and Friendship." *Cosmopolitan* (1971); "The Passion of Magda Wickwire." *Saturday Evening Post*, July 31, 1965: 58–60; "Past Sorrows and Coming Attractions." In *Women on Women II* (June 1993); "The Power." *Massachusetts Review* 4 (1963): 651–670; "Ralph." *Cosmopolitan* (1970); "The Sound of Comedy." *Esquire* (January 1961): 53–56.

POETRY

Selected poems in *Open Places*, Fifteenth Anniversary Issue (1981), and *Open Places*, Humor in America Issue (1985).

NONFICTION

"The Breath of Life." In *The Writer's Handbook* (1991).

BIBLIOGRAPHY

Brodzki, Bella. Afterword to *Allegra Maud Goldman* (1990); D'Erasme, Stacey. *Village Voice* (September 19, 1989), 55; Jacobs, Barbara. *Booklist* 73 (December 1, 1976): 526; Levin, Martin. *NYTimes Book Review*, December 19, 1976, 22; Olsen, Tillie. Introduction to *Allegra Maud Goldman* (1990); Shulman, Alix Kates. "A Me Grows in Brooklyn." *Ms.* (April 1977); Williamson, Barbara Fisher. *NYTimes Book Review*, June 4, 1989, 22.

MERLA WOLK

KRANTZ, JUDITH (b. 1927)

Judith Krantz is the third-largest-selling female novelist in history. She creates plots and subplots as she writes about fascinating women, beauty, fame, money, and sex. Although her goal is for her books to provide escape and entertainment, she does try to make some serious points and has woven such issues as anti-Semitism and the German occupation into her novels. All of her heroines are working women, and she has said that the subtext of all her books is women's opportunities.

Judith Krantz was born on January 9, 1927, in New York City, the eldest child of Jack D. Tarcher, an advertising executive, and Mary (Braeger) Tarcher, an attorney. She is close to her brother, Jeremy Tarcher, a publisher, and to her sister, Mimi Brien, a financial analyst.

She grew up in an affluent world that included exclusive schools, but she was not a happy child. Although she always knew she was smart, she described herself as an unpopular child who grew up thinking there was something wrong with her. Her mother praised her accomplishments, but reportedly never noticed her daughter's insecurity.

She attended Wellesley College and received her B.A. in 1948. She was a fashion publicist in Paris in the late 1940s. She then became the fashion editor for *Good Housekeeping* magazine. She has also been a contributing writer to *McCall's* magazine and *Ladies' Home Journal*, and she was the contributing West Coast editor of *Cosmopolitan* from 1971 to 1979.

In 1953, Judith Tarcher was introduced to Stephen Krantz, her future husband, by BARBARA WALTERS. When they met, Stephen Krantz was head of programming for WNBC in New York. He was later named director of program development for Columbia Pictures Television, had animation studios in New York and Los Angeles, and became a producer, producing television miniseries based on Judith

Krantz's novels. The Krantzes have two sons, Nicholas and Anthony, and live in the Bel-Air section of Los Angeles.

Krantz's first novel, *Scruples*, was published in 1978. She has said that at first she was afraid she did not have enough of an imagination to write a novel, having been a journalist. Perhaps that is why she incorporated what she knew best, fashion and Hollywood, into her writing. She views *Scruples* as a source of entertainment, with no illusions about it being literature. Krantz's quick-paced, romantic plot, her concern for details, and her talent for description paid off and helped *Scruples* remain on the *New York Times* best-seller list for more than a year. On the basis of her first novel's huge success, there was much interest in her second novel, *Princess Daisy*, published in 1980. Even before the hardcover edition was in bookstores, the paperback rights were sold for what was then the highest price ever paid for such a book. Since then, Krantz has written seven other novels, all of them best-sellers.

SELECTED WORKS BY JUDITH KRANTZ

Dazzle (1990); *I'll Take Manhattan* (1986); *Lovers* (1994); *Mistral's Daughter* (1983); *Princess Daisy* (1980); *Scruples* (1978); *Scruples Two* (1992); *Spring Collection* (1996); *Till We Meet Again* (1988).

BIBLIOGRAPHY

"The Booklist Interview." *Booklist* (October 1, 1992): 240–241; Davis, Sally Ogle. "Enter Judith Krantz, Dripping with Cashmere." *Los Angeles Magazine* (June 1992): 90–98; Evory, Ann, and Linda Metzger, eds. *Contemporary Authors*, New Revision Series. Vol. 11 (1984); Locher, Frances Carol, ed. *Contemporary Authors*. Vols. 81–84 (1979); McMurran, Kristin. "A Creature of Habit: Talking with Judith Krantz." *People Weekly* (April 4, 1994): 25.

NANCY BRODY

Judith Krantz is the third-largest-selling female novelist in history. Her novels include fascinating women, beauty, fame, money, and sex. But she has also woven in such issues as anti-Semitism and the German occupation. [Crown Publishing Group]

KRASNER, LEE (1908–1984)

This is so good, you would not know it was done by a woman.

—Painter Hans Hofmann to his student Lee Krasner, in 1937

In 1951, *Life* magazine published a celebrated photograph of the "Irascibles," eighteen artists who protested the Metropolitan Museum of Art's refusal to exhibit modern art. This photograph defined the New York School of artists, a group committed to stretching the boundaries of modern art beyond cubism and surrealism. Despite the fact that Lee Krasner was a staunch supporter of the integrity of modern art, being one of two painters in New York working in completely abstract styles prior to World War II, the artist organizers of the photograph did not invite her to participate. After all, who was she but the wife of Jackson Pollock?

Fleeing anti-Semitism and the Russo-Japanese War, Lee Krasner's father, Joseph Krassner, preceded his wife Anna and his five children in immigrating to the United States from Odessa in 1905. In 1908, he sent passage for his family to join him. Anna Krassner gave birth to her sixth child, Lee Krasner (born Lenore Krassner), on October 27, 1908, nine months after she arrived in New York and reunited with her husband. The first Krassner born on American soil, Lee Krasner would go on to forge other family firsts, female firsts, and artistic firsts.

The Krassner family lived in a traditionally observant Jewish home on Jerome Avenue in Brooklyn. They observed the laws of kashrut and spoke Yiddish among themselves. The children attended Hebrew school as a supplement to public education. As often proved the case in families of Eastern European descent, both father and mother contributed to the family income. They operated a produce store at the Blake Street Market in Brooklyn. Anna Krassner stood at the helm of the family business, directing the daily operation of the store. In her mother, Lee Krasner observed a strong female role model as a child. The elder Krassner sisters rejected their mother's lifestyle, consenting to matrimony and lives as housewives in their teens. Krasner proceeded definitely in another direction—art.

Krasner possessed the most extensive training and education of any of the New York School of artists. She began her odyssey of education in 1922. At age fourteen, she applied to Washington Irving High School in Manhattan, the only high school in New York City that permitted girls to study studio art. Admitted to the program, Krasner traveled daily the short subway ride to Manhattan that made a world of difference. In 1925, she graduated from Washington Irving, but not from Manhattan. Her education continued, via scholarship, at the Women's Art School of Cooper Union. The training that Krasner received at Cooper Union, and later at the National Academy of Design, grounded her in technique from which she skillfully ascended into new artistic territory.

After graduation from Cooper Union, Krasner began her training at the prestigious National Academy. Students attended classes tuition-free, but promotion depended on the unanimous support of a professorial committee. Krasner's individualist style rarely mustered support of a unanimous nature. Thus, when she applied for promotion to the academy's life drawing class, several professors dismissed her self-portrait as a fake, believing that such an inexperienced artist could not produce a plein air self-portrait. Krasner explained her method. She used the woods behind her parents' new home in Huntingdon, Long Island, as her setting. There, she nailed a mirror to a tree and painted what she saw. Krasner saw herself in nature. Surrounded by trees, she stands tall in her 1930s self-portrait, with her red hair pushed behind her ears and paintbrushes held firmly in hand. She appears serious, determined. Art historian Barbara Rose comments on the self-portrait: "The defiant expression was characteristic of her tough minded attitude: She would submit to any discipline deemed necessary to achieve her goals of acquiring the techniques and skills necessary to produce great art, but she would do it in her own way and on her own terms." The Academy of Design accepted these terms, promoting her to the life class, and onward, until she completed her studies in 1932.

Graduating in the midst of the Depression, Krasner worked a series of jobs as a waiter, a hat decorator, and a factory worker before acquiring a job with the Works Projects Administration's Federal Art Project in 1934. The project employed artists to teach art, illustrate textbooks, and create paintings, sculpture, mosaics, and stained glass decorations for public buildings. Krasner held various positions for the project, from illustrating a marine biology textbook to executing murals for public buildings.

In 1937, while employed by the WPA, Krasner sought to continue her artistic training by enrolling in classes with the German expressionist Hans Hofmann. Krasner held a passion for modern art, which she nourished through visits to galleries and museums. Hofmann taught her to feed herself. A virtuoso of Matissian color and Picasso-like planes, Hofmann encouraged Krasner's move toward abstraction more than any previous teacher.

In the 1940s, Krasner left Hofmann's studio, enriched by her experience there and ready to progress. She embarked upon a string of group exhibitions in the early 1940s with the American Abstract Artists group. Her first exhibition season culminated in an invitation from John Graham to participate in "American and French Paintings" at the McMillen Gallery in New York. The exhibit proved a watershed for both the art world and for Krasner's personal world. For the first time in art history, such American "unknowns" as Jackson Pollock, Willem de Kooning, and Lee Krasner hung beside European masters. In addition, for the first time, Krasner met a sober Jackson Pollock. (Technically, Krasner and Pollock had met previously at an Artist Union loft party in 1936, when he made a drunken pass at her.)

Krasner and Pollock maintained a roller-coaster relationship that began with their involvement in "American and French Paintings" and continued for fourteen years until Pollock's death in 1956. They shared an intense passion for, and commitment to, art. They also maintained a lifelong mutual respect for each other's work. However, that is where their similarities end. A fiercely independent and determined woman, Krasner served as the rock that held Pollock, a troubled alcoholic, afloat.

On October 25, 1945, the couple married at the Marble Collegiate Church on Fifth Avenue in New York. By this time, Krasner had ceased to affiliate herself with Judaism. However, she retained an interest in spirituality throughout her life, which manifests itself in her art. Directly after their marriage, despite abject poverty, Krasner and Pollock purchased a farm in East Hampton at Krasner's request. She sought to create a safe, serene environment for Pollock in the country where, she felt, he would be less tempted by the urban bars and parties that invite drunkenness. Thus began a period in her life when Krasner's work and her very being succumbed to the all-encompassing task of managing Jackson Pollock, emotionally and financially. As his friend and companion, Krasner filled Pollock's life with friends and activities in an attempt to divert him from drinking. As his business manager, Krasner promoted Pollock's work ceaselessly. She organized meetings with dealers, dinners with critics, and sales to galleries. In the 1950s, as Pollock's artistic reputation grew, so did his emotional problems. Exhausted by his antics and horrified by his recent public pursuit of adulterous affairs, Krasner decided to travel to Europe in the summer of 1956. For the first time since their marriage, Krasner and Pollock were separated. While she was gone, Pollock, driving drunk, crashed his automobile in the front yard of their farm and died on August 11, 1956.

After Pollock's death, Krasner reclaimed her own life force—painting. As Barbara Rose attests, a Krasner painting defies compartmentalization. Like nature, its essence, color, and rhythm prove organic. Her early work, pre-1956, challenges the perceived physical and mental boundaries of a canvas, using vehicles as varied as mosaic, collage, and image painting. The *Little Image* series emerged from this period. Several of these allover abstract pattern paintings include calligraphic elements that resemble Hebrew. Krasner recalls painting these images from right to left, just as she was taught to read Hebrew as a little girl. Post-1956, Krasner's work grew in size and scope. From floral abstractions to turbulent expressions of rage, Krasner's later canvases breathe color and emotion. In 1965, Krasner received her first retrospective in London at the Whitechapel Gallery. Following an extended illness, Lee Krasner died on June 20, 1984, at age seventy-six. The first New York retrospective of her work opened at the Museum of Modern Art six months after her death—a long overdue tribute to a pioneer of American abstract art.

BIBLIOGRAPHY

Baro, Gene. *Lee Krasner: Collages and Works on Paper 1933–1974* (1975); Campbell, Lawrence. "Of Lilith and Lettuce." *Art News* 67 (March 1968): 42+; Cummings, Paul. *A Dictionary of Contemporary American Artists*. 2d ed. (1972); Freed, Hermine Benheim. "Lee Krasner: East Hampton Studio." Video interview with Lee Krasner [1973?]. Oral History Collection, Pollock-Krasner House and Study Center, East Hampton, N.Y.; Friedman, B.H. *Jackson Pollock: Energy Made Visible* (1972); Friedman, Sanford. *A Haunted Woman* (1968); Gabor, Andrea. *Einstein's Wife: Work and Marriage in the Lives of Five Great Twentieth-Century Women* (1995); Glaser, Bruce. "Jackson Pollock: An Interview with Lee Krasner." *Arts Magazine* 41 (April 1967): 36–39; Guggengheim, Peggy. *Confessions of an Art Addict* (1960); Harrison, Helen A. "Artists Find a Special Light on Lee Krasner." *NYTimes*, February 15, 1981, 17; Hobbs, Robert. *Lee Krasner* (1993); Howard, Richard. *Lee Krasner: Paintings 1959–1962* (1979); Janis, Sidney. *Abstract and Surrealist Art in America* (1944); Kramer, Hilton. "Lee Krasner's Art—A Harvest of Rhythms." *NYTimes*, November 22, 1973, C50; Naifeh, Steven, and Gregory White Smith. *Jackson Pollock: An American Saga* (1989); Nemser, Cindy. "A Conversation with Lee Krasner." *Arts Magazine* 47 (April 1973): 43–48; Obituary. *NYTimes*, June 21, 1984; Robertson, Bryan, and B.H. Friedman. *Lee Krasner: Paintings, Drawings, and Collages* (1965); Rose, Barbara. *Krasner/Pollock: A Working Relationship* (1981), and *Lee Krasner: A Retrospective* (1983), and *The Long View*. Film (1978) ; Slater, Elinor, and Robert Slater. "Lee Krasner." *Great Jewish Women* (1994); Taylor, Robert. "Lee Krasner: Artist in Her Own Right." *Boston Globe*, May 18, 1990, 1; *WWWIA* 8.

JOELLYN WALLEN

KRASNOW, FRANCES (1894–1983)

In 1917, Frances Krasnow graduated from Barnard College with a bachelor of science cum laude, from Columbia University with a master's degree, and from the Teachers Institute of the Jewish Theological Seminary. Krasnow would eventually receive recognition for being a pioneer in both science and Jewish education.

She was born in New York City on October 16, 1894, to Raphael and Sara Rifka (Lubarsky) Krasnow. After receiving her master's, she continued in Columbia's doctoral program and obtained her Ph.D. in bacteriology, chemistry, and biochemistry in 1922. From 1922 to 1928, she was a fellow of the Rhein-Levy Research Fund. Until 1932, she was an instructor at Columbia's College of Physicians and Surgeons.

On December 25, 1930, she married Marcus Thau, an industrial research chemist. They had a daughter named Hudelle, born in 1933.

From 1932 to 1944, Krasnow was assistant director and head of fundamental science at the School for Dental Hygiene at the Guggenheim Dental Clinic. From 1934 to 1960, she was active in the New York chapter of the International Association of Dental Research, acting at various times as president, vice president, and editor of the organization. In 1944, she was appointed director of research at the Guggenheim Clinic, a position she would hold until 1952. From 1952 to 1974, she was research director at Universal Coatings, Inc., a firm based in New Jersey. In 1973, the American Chemical Society bestowed a citation on Krasnow for fifty years of active membership and forty-three years of participation in its *Chemical Abstracts.*

Much of Krasnow's work concerned the chemistry of dental conditions: the effect of diet on teeth, root canal bacteriology, and the chemistry of saliva. She also examined cholesterol and blood chemistry in syphilis and skin diseases, agglutinins, and the correlation between metabolic inorganic and organic levels in blood saliva and urine.

Krasnow was also a leader in the field of Jewish education. She was instrumental in promoting Hebrew language and literature as subjects of study in American high schools and colleges. In 1969, she became a member of the board of overseers for the Jewish Theological Seminary. She was also involved with many American Jewish organizations. In 1974, the Jewish Theological Seminary honored her with the degree of Doctor of Letters in recognition of her lifelong activity on behalf of Jewish education and her endeavors in biochemical research.

According to a 1941 article in *Science* magazine, dental research in the early part of the twentieth century was a relatively undeveloped field, hampered by infighting and lack of academic rigor. Krasnow, with her strong biochemistry background, helped to bring scientific discipline to the field. She also made contributions to biochemistry in medicine.

She studied Jewish education during a time of its reinvigoration—the years around World War I. In particular, the Jewish Theological Seminary and Columbia University Teachers College were centers for exploring new ways to promote Judaism to assimilating Jews. Krasnow's early experiences formed the basis for her lifelong interest in Judaism and her advocacy of Hebrew language and literature.

Frances Krasnow died on October 5, 1983, in New York City.

BIBLIOGRAPHY

American Chemical Society. *Chemical Abstracts* (1930–1973). Edited by Frances Krasnow; *American Men and Women of Science* (1992); Barnard College Alumni Office. Interview with author, June 1996; Cohen, Harry, and Itzhak J. Carmin, eds. *Jews in the World of Science* (1956); Krasnow, Frances. Commencement Program (1974). Jewish Theological Seminary, NYC; Hones, Durwood, ed. *American Women: 1935–1940: A Composite Biographical Dictionary* (1981); Moore, Deborah Dash. *At Home in America: Second-Generation New York Jews* (1981); Rosenburg, Theodore. "Biological Research After a Century of Dentistry." *Science* 92 (1940): 247; *WWIAJ* (1938, 1980); *World Who's Who in Science from Antiquity to Present* (1968).

BETTY BARRER

KRAVITCH, PHYLLIS A. (b. 1920)

Appointed to the United States Court of Appeals by President Jimmy Carter in 1979, Phyllis A. Kravitch was the third woman to become a United States circuit judge. When her alma mater, the University of Pennsylvania Law School, presented her with the James Wilson Award for service to the legal profession in 1992, Kravitch in her acceptance speech attributed her professional accomplishments to her father, attorney Aaron Kravitch. Not only did the daughter follow in the footsteps of her father at the University of Pennsylvania, but after her graduation in 1943, she joined him in a law practice devoted to the protection of individual rights, especially those of poor people and minorities. In her hometown of Savannah, Georgia, Kravitch prevailed against gender and religious discrimination then prevalent in the Deep South.

Phyllis Kravitch was born on August 23, 1920, the second of four daughters of Aaron and Ella (Wiseman) Kravitch. With a blend of American Jewish heritages on both sides of her family, she became a lifelong member of the Mickve Israel Congregation in historic Savannah, where she was confirmed in 1935. From her mother and maternal grandmother, Kravitch learned to appreciate music, dance, and art. Her maternal grandmother, an unusual woman, had been valedictorian of her class and, before her marriage, a schoolteacher.

One of the first woman trial lawyers in the South, Phyllis A. Kravitch was active in establishing a family shelter for battered women and a rape crisis center in Savannah and assisted the Georgia legislature in revising family, juvenile, and child abuse laws. In 1979, she was appointed to the United States Court of Appeals by President Jimmy Carter. [Chambers of Judge Kravitch]

Described as "never one to be strapped by convention," Kravitch was one of the first woman trial lawyers in the South. She was also the first woman president of the Savannah Bar Association (1973), the first woman superior court judge in Georgia, and the first woman judge on the Fifth Circuit (later divided into the Eleventh Circuit) Court of Appeals. In the Senate hearing confirming her appointment, Senator Edward Kennedy called Kravitch "courageous." A poll by the American Association of University Women of Savannah selected her as "Savannah's Most Influential Woman." She has received numerous honors, including an honorary doctor of laws from her undergraduate alma mater, Goucher College, in 1981; the American Bar Association's Margaret Brent Woman Lawyers of Achievement Award in 1991; and the NATIONAL COUNCIL OF JEWISH WOMEN's Hannah G. Solomon Award in 1978.

Kravitch has devoted her life to myriad scholastic, civic, and professional activities. Prior to ascending to the federal bench, she was active in establishing a family shelter for battered women and a rape crisis center in Savannah, and she also assisted the Georgia legislature in revising family, juvenile, and child abuse laws. As a member of the Chatham County Board of Education (1949–1955), she was instrumental in eliminating sex- and race-based salary discrepancies and the use of substandard school buildings.

At present, Kravitch serves on the standing committee on the rules of practice and procedure of the Judicial Conference of the United States (1995–), the law school council of Emory University School of Law (1986–), the Truman Scholars selection committee (southeast region) (1993–), and the Board of Visitors, Georgia State University Law School (1994–). She has also been a member of the visiting committee of the University of Chicago Law School (1989–1992), the selection committee of the Rhodes Scholarships (1980–1984), the White House fellowship committee (1980–1983), the American Bar Association, the American Law Institute, and other organizations.

BIBLIOGRAPHY

"Award of the Margaret Brent Woman Lawyers of Achievement Award." *ABA Journal* (August 11, 1991); "Battler for Civil Rights: 'Miz' Phyllis Kravitch Vows to Be a Fair Judge."*Atlanta Journal*, March 22, 1979; "'Courageous' Attorney Joins U.S. Court." *Times-Picayune*, May 29, 1979, sec. 4, p. 2; *Democratic Women of DeKalb News* 1, no. 2 (June 1979); *Democratic Party of Georgia Newsletter* 2 (June/July 1979); "Judge Kravitch to Take Senior Status." *Fulton County Daily Report* (November 19, 1996); Kravitch, Phyllis A. Oral interview by author, October 12, 1996; "'Little Judge' Again Makes History."*Atlanta Journal-Constitution*, April 1, 1979, 12B; "Noteworthy Rulings." *Almanac of the Federal Judiciary* 2 (1996); *Southern Jewish Weekly*, April 1979, p. 24; "Symposium." *Penn Law Journal* (February 1993); "Tribute to Judge Phyllis A. Kravitch." *Georgia State University Law Review* (February 1997).

BERYL H. WEINER

KREINDLER, DORIS BARSKY
(1901–1974)

Vigorous, rapid, and exciting use of the palette knife is not usually associated with women painters in any era, but Doris Barsky Kreindler's abstract expressionist works in the 1950s, 1960s, and early 1970s, inspired by Hans Hofmann, were exceptional. Abstract expressionism is the art of gesture and movement associated primarily with male artists in the period immediately following World War II. Her 1964 oil painting, *Skyscraper*, in the National Museum of American Art demonstrates her transition from still lifes of vases of flowers to large-scale (48 inches by 38¼ inches) abstractions taken from the landscape of her native New York City.

Doris Barsky was born on August 12, 1901, in Passaic, New Jersey to Jacob Barsky, a furniture maker, and Rebecca (Levitch) Barsky, a homemaker. The Barskys, Jewish immigrants from Russia, arrived in the United States in 1893. Doris had one older sister, Pauline, and two younger sisters, Mildred and Bernice.

She was educated at the New York School of Applied Design for Women, the National Academy of Design, and the Art Students League in New York City. She also studied with Hans Hofmann.

Doris Barsky married Harry E. Kreindler on February 12, 1920, in Brooklyn. Harry Kreindler was an attorney who founded the firm of Kreindler and Kreindler, originally of Brooklyn and later of New York City. The Kreindlers had two children: Lee Stanley (b. 1924), who is a lawyer with Kreindler and Kreindler, and Rosamond Kreindler Koffman born (b. 1928), who is a retired teacher of language arts.

Her first solo exhibition was held at the Brooklyn Museum in 1935. For a period of about fourteen years, none of her works were exhibited in the New York City area and she took the time to travel widely. These travels became the basis for her later exhibitions, which featured abstract landscapes that were inspired by specific locations but contained the universal essence of many outdoor experiences. Her strong, rapid, brightly colored brushstrokes animated the regions that she depicted. Reviews in journals of the time praised her work for its vigor and liveliness—praise usually reserved for male abstract expressionists. She achieved this effect through the thick application of color in diagonal strokes on her atmospheric canvases.

In addition to oils, Kreindler worked in watercolor, lithography, woodblock, engraving, etching, and casein (a sticky, thick paint made from the whey derived from skim milk mixed with color).

She belonged to the American Society of Contemporary Artists, National Association of Women Artists, Artists Equity, National Association of Painters in Casein, Society of American Graphics, Alabama Water-Color Society, and the New York Society of Women Artists. Her work is in many national and regional museums, including the Rose Art Museum of Brandeis University, Metropolitan Museum of Art, Museum of Modern Art, Fogg

Museum of Art, Brooklyn Museum of Art, Philadelphia Museum of Art, the Art Institute of Chicago, and the Tel Aviv Museum of Art.

Doris Barsky Kreindler died in May 1974 in Florida while on vacation.

BIBLIOGRAPHY

Collins, J.L. *Women Artists in America: Eighteenth Century to the Present* (1973); "Exhibition at Esther Robles Gallery, Los Angeles." *Art News* 56 (January 1958): 51; "Exhibition at Pulitzer." *Art News* 58 (March 1959): 57; "Exhibition at Seligmann Gallery." *Art News* 68 (January 1970): 62; "Exhibition at Seligmann's." *Art News* 50 (January 1952): 46; "Exhibition of Abstract Landscapes at Seligmann." *Art Digest* 29 (February 15, 1954): 26; "Exhibition of Paintings: Seligmann Gallery." *Art Digest* 26 (January 15, 1951): 20+; Gilbert, Dorothy B., ed. *Who's Who in American Art* (1973); Havlice, Patricia Pate. *Index to Artistic Biography.* Vol. 2 (1973); McNeil, Barbara, ed. *Artists Biographies: Master Index* (1986); National Museum of American Art. *Descriptive Catalogue of Painting and Sculpture in the National Museum of American Art* (1983); Obituary. *NYTimes*, May 4, 1974, 44:5; "Seligmann Gallery, New York: Exhibition." *Art News* 72 (February 1973): 83; "Show at Seligmann Gallery." *Art News* 65 (February 1967): 16; "Show of Paintings and Drawings at Seligmann." *Art News* 52 (February 1954): 47; "Showing at Pulitzer." *Arts* 33 (April 1959): 48; *WWIAJ* (1938).

JILL WEXLER GREENSTEIN

KREMER, ISA (1887–1956)

Diva, folksinger, and citizen of the world, Isa Kremer was born in Belz, Bessarabia, on October 21, 1887, to Jacob and Anna (Rosenbluth) Kremer. She grew up in bourgeois comfort, because her father had served as provision master in the czar's army. She had a governess and attended a Russian Orthodox school; however, she could not ignore the plight of impoverished Jews in her hometown. As a teenager, she wrote revolutionary poems, which she sent to the *Odessa News*. The editor Israel Heifetz invited her to Odessa and, convinced of her musical talent, underwrote her studies with the famed Professor Ronzi in Milan, Italy. She sang opera for a brief time, debuting as Mimi in *La Bohème* opposite Tito Schipa in Cremona in 1911, and then toured czarist Russia as a star of the Imperial Opera in Petrograd, of operettas, and of the concert hall.

After her marriage to Heifetz (twenty-seven years her senior) around 1912, Kremer became involved in the intellectual life of Odessa and was especially influenced by the circles of Mendele Mocher Seforim, Mark Warshavsky, and Chaim Nachman Bialik. Bialik convinced her to sing Yiddish folk songs, which she started to collect. At that time only men, usually cantors, performed these traditional songs of home and hearth on the stage.

After the Russian Revolution, the Bolsheviks imprisoned Heifetz, garrisoned the couple's Odessa home, and confiscated their other property. Heifetz and Kremer had supported Kerensky. Kremer, at that time singing in Istanbul, remained there until she could arrange to smuggle her daughter Toussia (b. 1917), the governess, and her parents out of Odessa. Like countless Russian emigrés, the family

Isa Kremer faced virulent anti-Semitism while performing in Europe during the 1920s and 1930s before coming to the United States. After making films and records in this country for a number of years, she married psychoanalyst Gregorio Bermann and immigrated to Argentina for the third and final stage of her remarkable career. [New York Public Library]

lived in Poland, Berlin, and Paris. Kremer bribed officials to release her husband from prison. After they settled in Paris, however, the couple separated. During the Nazi occupation of France, Heifetz was taken to a concentration camp in Belgium, where he died.

Kremer's extensive tours throughout Europe in the 1920s and 1930s exposed her to virulent anti-Semitism. She sang at the Warsaw Symphonic Hall in 1922, despite death threats and demonstrations by the Stowarzyszenie Patritow [Patriotic League]. At Berlin's Jüdischer Kulturbund, an institution created after Hitler segregated Jewish performers and audiences from "Aryan" ones, Kremer insisted upon including Yiddish songs although the German Jews preferred the classical art songs in her repertoire.

Represented by Sol Hurok, Kremer gave her first concert in the United States on October 29, 1922, at Carnegie Hall, to critical acclaim. She brought her family to the United States in 1924 and eventually became a citizen. She made talking films for Vitaphone in 1927 and recorded for Brunswick and Columbia. In 1931, Chappell in London published *A Jewish Life in Song*, a book of twenty-four Yiddish folk songs, named after Kremer's popular concert series.

In the 1930s, her tours took her through the United States, Canada, Europe, Africa, Palestine, and Latin America. Alexander Olshanetsky wrote the song "Mayn shtetele Belz" to honor Kremer's hometown, and she starred with Seymour Rexite in her only Second Avenue musical, *The Song of the Ghetto*. In 1938, she went to Argentina, where she married the eminent psychiatrist Gregorio Bermann. In Argentina, she sang at benefits for Nazi victims and for striking workers, often in collaboration with María Teresa León, a Spanish Republican exile. Because Kremer and Bermann were blacklisted by the dictator Juan Perón, the 1940s and 1950s were years of economic hardship and political harassment for the couple. Kremer died of cancer in Córdoba, Argentina, on July 7, 1956. Her archives, including an extensive collection of folk music in the twenty-four languages in which she sang, were donated to the IWO Library in Buenos Aires.

BIBLIOGRAPHY

BEOAJ; Jabotinsky, Vladimir. "Odessa—Isa Kremer's City." *Every Friday* (Cincinnati), February 5, 1932, 5; Kremer, Isa. *A Jewish Life in Song* (record album of Jewish songs) (1931); Obituary. *NYTimes*, July 9, 1956, 23:4; Saleski, Gdal. *Famous Musicians of Jewish Origin* (1949); Schwartz, Marcel M. "Isa Kremer—A Biographical Sketch." *Every Friday* (Cincinnati), February 5, 1932, 3, 5; *WWIAJ* (1926, 1928, 1938).

LOIS BAER BARR

Through her involvement in a wide variety of activities from actor to historian,
Miriam Kressyn left an indelible mark on Yiddish culture of the twentieth century.
She is shown here (center) in a still from Joseph Green's 1937 Polish film, Der Purimshpiler,
where she played opposite Max Bozyk. [The National Center for Jewish Film]

KRESSYN, MIRIAM (1911–1996)

Miriam Kressyn—of the Yiddish theater and film, songwriter, translator, recording star, radio announcer, historian of the Yiddish theater, news analyst, and teacher—left an indelible mark on Yiddish culture of the twentieth century.

She was born on March 4, 1911, in Bialystok, Poland, to Yankev and Mashe Kressyn, who already had two sons and four daughters. The daughters had been taken to the United States by their father several years before Miriam was born. He then returned to Poland to be with his wife and sons. With the outbreak of World War I, Kressyn's mother took her to the town of Orle, near Bialystock, while her father and brothers were recruited to dig ditches for the Polish army. Two of her older sisters also returned to Europe.

In Orle, Kressyn studied with a teacher sent by the secular Yiddish school organization called Tsysho. At age seven or eight, she was caught smuggling leaflets for the socialist Bund to another town. Her experience in the secular classroom proved formative and enlightening, drawing her away from the pious traditions of her father.

In 1923, she immigrated to America with her parents. They settled in Boston, where two of her sisters lived. Kressyn's love of music and beautiful voice won her a scholarship to the New England Conservatory of Music, where she studied for several years, planning eventually to study law.

Boston was frequently visited by touring Yiddish theater troupes. On one occasion, a troupe headed by Julius Nathanson was in town and visited her sister. When Nathanson heard Kressyn sing, he exclaimed, "Who is this girl?" After being thus "discovered," she began playing children's roles in Yiddish theater. Soon, producers and stars in New York City learned of this young talent in Boston. In 1929, she was invited to join the company of the legendary Aaron

Lebedeff in Chicago, where she performed a leading role for the first time.

While performing at the Arch Street Theater in Philadelphia in 1930, Kressyn was informed by the Hebrew Actors Union that she needed to audition for membership. For her audition, she prepared two scenes, one musical and one dramatic. Her performance won her the overwhelming approval of the union at a time when it accepted very few new members.

In 1931, she was invited to Buenos Aires as the leading lady of a touring American company. Her scheduled thirteen-week season was extended to nine months. From Argentina she traveled to Europe, performing in Antwerp, Paris, Bucharest, Kovno, Vilna, and Warsaw. She would return to Warsaw three times. Her success there caused many of the city's Yiddish literati to go to her performances, even though she appeared in so-called *shund* [lowbrow] productions. In 1937, she returned to Warsaw for the last time to star in the Joseph Green film *Der Purimshpiler.*

Miriam Kressyn later joined the Yiddish Art Theater, run by Maurice Schwartz, performing at New York's National Theater on Second Avenue and Houston for several seasons. She appeared with many of the luminaries of the Yiddish theater's heyday. She recorded numerous albums, some with her husband of over fifty years, Seymour Rexite. For over forty years, the couple broadcast their famous *Memories of the Yiddish Theater* program on WEVD radio.

During the last decade of her life, Kressyn wrote and hosted the weekly *News of the Week in Review* on WEVD. She died in New York on October 27, 1996.

BIBLIOGRAPHY

Sandrow, Nahma. *Vagabond Stars: A World History of Yiddish Theater* (1977).

MOISHE ROSENFELD

KRIM, MATHILDE (b. 1926)

Mathilde Krim is unique among philanthropists. She was able to combine her years of experience in medical research with her extraordinary skills as a fund-raiser to create and sustain AmFAR (the American Foundation for AIDS Research), the preeminent national organization supporting research on AIDS and advocating public policies that respond to the needs of people with AIDS.

She was born in Como, Italy, on July 9, 1926, the first of Elizabeth Rosa Krause and Eugene Emmanuel Galland's four children. Eugene Galland was the son of a Swiss Calvinist and an Italian Catholic; Elizabeth

Krause was the daughter of Austrian Catholics who were then living in Czechoslovakia. At the time of his marriage, Eugene Galland had earned a Ph.D. and was working in Italy as an agronomist.

Mathilde (Galland) Krim was thus born into a multinational, multireligious family, with relatives who spoke French, German, and Italian, who lived in Italy, Czechoslovakia, and Switzerland, and who attended both Protestant and Catholic churches. When she was a small child, her parents moved to Geneva, Switzerland, where her father found employment as a municipal public health officer. This was not the kind of work for which his doctorate had prepared him, but Mussolini's Italy had not been kind to him and he had felt obliged to leave.

Mathilde was educated in Geneva. Immediately after completing secondary school at the École Supérieure des Jeunes Filles, she entered the University of Geneva where, over her parents' objections, she enrolled in the faculty of biology.

Early in her university career, she came to the attention of the noted invertebrate embryologist Émile Guyenot, who, impressed with her technical and experimental skill, invited her to be an assistant in his laboratory. In 1948, she was granted the License degree (the equivalent of a bachelor of science degree in the United States). She continued to work as an employee in Guyenot's laboratory but independently undertook exceptionally difficult electron micrographical studies of the chromosomes of some of the organisms that interested Guyenot. For these latter studies she was awarded a Ph.D. in 1953.

Thus she became a member of the very tiny group of women with advanced degrees in science. From her vantage point, however, this accomplishment almost paled by comparison to the other extraordinary turn that her life had taken. During the war years, she had found a job as a part-time clerk in the office of a Jewish lawyer, Maître Jean Heyman. Assigned the task of carrying papers to various government offices, she became dimly aware that, for some reason, large numbers of Jews were trying desperately to get Swiss visas. In the spring of 1945, in a newsreel preceding a film she had gone to see, she found out the reason—a discovery, she says, that changed her life. Her parents did not sympathize with her passionate concern with the Holocaust and its victims. Somewhat apolitical, they had more or less assumed that Europe would be improved when the Axis was successful and were initially unwilling even to believe that the Holocaust had happened.

In the late 1940s, a small group of Palestinian Jews (as they were then called) began attending

Geneva's world-famous medical school, and Mathilde, to her parents' dismay, became friendly with them. She began taking courses in the history of Judaism and also became involved in some of their underground gunrunning enterprises. In the summer of 1948, just a few months after the founding of the State of Israel, she married one of those medical students, David Danon. Danon was a member of the *Irgun;* his medical studies and his residence in Geneva were frequently interrupted by his political and military activities. Nonetheless, the couple managed, during those years, to coauthor several papers on electron micrography. Their daughter, Daphna, was born in Geneva in 1951. When Daphna was eighteen months old, their degrees finally completed, the Danons moved to Israel. Mathilde had converted to Judaism before her marriage, but in Israel it proved necessary for her to undergo the training, examinations, and ceremony again.

The marriage did not flourish in Israel, in part because Mathilde was not enthusiastic about the hard life of desert pioneering to which her husband was attracted. In 1953, because of her unusual skills in electron micrography, she had found a job as a research assistant at the newly founded Weizmann Institute in Rehovot. She was able to work and care for Daphna because, early on, the institute had created a child-care center for its employees. Within a year, Mathilde was promoted to junior scientist (and, subsequently, to research associate) and was living with her daughter in a small apartment on the grounds of the institute, having separated from her husband.

During her years at Weizmann, Mathilde worked in the laboratory headed by Leo Sachs; she coauthored, with Sachs and others, more than a dozen research papers. The very first of these research studies was the one for which Sachs's laboratory is probably most famous: "The Diagnosis of Sex Before Birth Using Cells from the Amniotic Fluid." This paper was rushed into print in order to establish priority for this fundamental discovery, which helped lay the foundation for the prenatal diagnostic technique called amniocentesis and the discipline called medical genetics. As a result of this work, Mathilde became an expert on the then new techniques of cell culturing. She also did some research on the viruses that cause some forms of cancer.

In 1957, she met Arthur Krim, a wealthy American, who was a trustee of the Weizmann Institute. They married a year later. At first, the Krims thought that they could manage to live apart (he in New York, she in Rehovot), but they soon realized that this arrangement was untenable. Mathilde Krim and her daughter moved to New York and to an entirely different world. At the time of their marriage, Arthur Krim was the president of United Artists, a leading film production studio. He was also involved in fundraising for the Democratic Party and in numerous other philanthropic and policy-related activities. His wife fairly quickly became his partner.

These activities were not, however, sufficient to satisfy Krim's restless intellect. Within a few months, she had found a job as part of a research team at Cornell Medical College in New York (and, subsequently, at the Sloan-Kettering Institute for Cancer Research, also in New York), working on various cancer-inducing agents. In part because of her involvement in this research, Krim was appointed to the congressional advisory commission on the war against cancer. She soon became interested not in the agents that cause cancer but in the family of natural substances—the interferons—that were then thought to have great potential as cures for various cancers as well as for other diseases.

For a decade, between 1975 and 1985, Krim served either as the coleader or the leader of Sloan-Kettering's research and clinical evaluation program on interferon. During those years, she published (with many coauthors) more than thirty scientific papers on interferon and also organized a series of international research workshops.

In 1983, Krim and her laboratory staff were asked to assist in the treatment of some Sloan-Kettering patients who were suffering with a rare skin cancer, Kaposi's sarcoma, which was associated with a new immunological disease, AIDS. At that time, her laboratory work was beginning to wind down. Interferon therapies had not proved successful, and many of the young people trained in her laboratory had been hired away by the burgeoning biotechnology industries. Simultaneously, Krim became fascinated by AIDS research, sympathetic to those with the disease, and enraged by the dual difficulties involved in funding the research and aiding the victims.

In 1985, these sentiments—coupled with her extraordinary social and political network—inspired her to create a foundation dedicated to fund-raising for AIDS research and advocacy. Although she now holds an adjunct appointment as professor of public health at the Columbia University School of Public Health, most of Krim's time and energy, since 1985, has been devoted to various fund-raising, supervisory, and lobbying activities, all directed either to finding a cure for the AIDS virus or to creating supportive public programs to help people with the disease. Since 1990, when the American Foundation for AIDS Research merged with a similar organization on the West Coast (created by Elizabeth Taylor), Krim has served as its founding cochair and chairman of the board.

Mathilde Krim has been awarded several honorary degrees and is the recipient of numerous other honors. In addition to serving on the advisory commission on cancer (1970–1971), she was a member of the President's Committee on Mental Retardation (1966–1969) and the President's Commission for the Study of Ethical Problems in Medicine and Biomedical and Behavioral Research (1979–1981). Reflecting her various interests and concerns, she has also been an active member of the boards of the American Committee for the Weizmann Institute, the National Biomedical Research Foundation, the Committee of 100 for National Health Insurance, the Federation of Parents and Friends of Lesbians and Gays, and the African-American Institute.

SELECTED WORKS BY
MATHILDE (DANON) KRIM

"The Diagnosis of Sex before Birth Using Cells from the Amniotic Fluid," with L. Sachs et al. *Bulletin of the Research Council of Israel* 5B (1955): 137–138; "Electron Micrograph of a Chromosome of *Triton*," with E. Guyenot, E. Kellenberger, and J. Weigle. *Nature* 165 (1950): 33; "Prenatal Diagnosis of Sex Using Cells from Amniotic Fluid," with L. Sachs and D.M. Serr. *Science* 123 (1956): 548; "Towards Tumor Therapy with Interferons. Part I. Interferons: Production and Properties," and Part 2. Interferons: *In Vivo* Effects." *Blood* 55 (1980): 711–721, 875–884.

BIBLIOGRAPHY

Friedman, Jeanette. "Dr. Mathilde Krim: Caring Heart." *Lifestyles* (Summer 1995): 6–9; Krim. Mathilde. Interview by author, August 1996, and Typescript of biographical essay on Arthur Krim.

RUTH SCHWARTZ COWAN

KROSS, ANNA MOSCOWITZ
(1891–1979)

Anna Moscowitz Kross—lawyer, judge, public official, and advocate for women and the poor—was born in Neshves, Russia, on July 17, 1891. One of two surviving siblings out of nine, she was brought to New York City at age two by her immigrant parents, Maier and Esther (Drazen) Moscowitz. Her parents were poor but deeply supportive of her ambitions and social goals. While still in high school, she helped to support her family by teaching English and by working in a factory at night.

She studied at Columbia University in 1907 and won a scholarship to New York University's law school, becoming its first woman graduate in 1910 at age nineteen. In 1911, she received an LL.M., but could not take the bar examination until she turned twenty-one years old in 1912. She married Dr. Isidor Kross, a noted surgeon, on April 15, 1917. They had two daughters: Dr. Helen K. Golden and Dr. Alice K. Frankel.

Kross became a lawyer so that she could help others and create better opportunities for the disadvantaged. Her first related activities were volunteering assistance to women brought into New York's night court and crusading for woman suffrage. In 1918, she was appointed the first female assistant corporation council for New York City and was assigned to the Family Court from 1918 to 1923. In the Family Court, she insisted that not only prostitutes but also their

Graduating from law school at nineteen, Anna Moscowitz Kross quickly became involved in working for women and the poor. She became the first woman judge in New York's city magistrates court in 1933, establishing special court facilities for minors and the home term court for domestic cases. In 1954, she was appointed the first woman commissioner of corrections for New York City. [YIVO Institute]

clients be booked. She resigned in 1923 and developed a legal practice in labor relations, in which she worked until she was appointed the first woman judge in the city magistrates court in 1933, a position she held for twenty years. As a judge, Kross attained national prominence for her sociological approach to cases. For example, in 1946, she established special court facilities for minors and the home term court for domestic cases, which had previously been assigned to the night court. The home term court facilities included one of the first day care centers for the children of parents in court, equipped privately through Kross's efforts.

In 1954, she was appointed the first woman commissioner of corrections for New York City. Her "contributions to the administration of justice and to the conservation of youth through juvenile crime prevention" were commended in the citation accompanying an honorary LL.D. she received from New York University in 1956. As commissioner, Kross was responsible for making the city's prison system less dungeonlike and more humane. She installed new shower rooms and mess halls, established token wages for some prison jobs, and built separate facilities for adolescents. She also introduced programs for rehabilitating prisoners through training in trades such as baking, stenography, and woodworking. Program graduates received certificates of proficiency and help in placement. During her tenure as commissioner, Kross received a great deal of publicity for her outspoken manner and criticism of government policies discriminating against poor people. She served with the corrections department until her retirement (after several extensions) in 1966 at age seventy-five.

Kross received numerous citations, awards, and honorary degrees, including a doctorate in Hebrew literature from Hebrew Union College in 1965. She belonged to numerous organizations, including American and international law associations, groups concerned with law enforcement and correction, the Lucy Stone League, the national board of HADASSAH (1930–1933), and the United Jewish Philanthropies. She died on August 27, 1979, at age eighty-eight.

BIBLIOGRAPHY

EJ; Frankel, Alice K., and Helen K. Golden. Interviews with author, April–May 1996; Kross, Anna Moscowitz. Papers. Russell Sage College, Troy, N.Y.; *Mamaroneck Daily Times*, August 29, 1979; *NYTimes*, June 7, 1956, and August 29, 1979, and December 21, 1980; *WWIAJ* (1928, 1938); *Who's Who of American Women* (1966–1967).

NAOMI GOODMAN

KRUGER, BARBARA (b. 1945)

An image like a 1950s advertising poster of a girl looking admiringly at a boy making a muscle is captioned "We don't need another hero" in red. A woman looking into a shattered mirror is underscored by the jagged headline "You are not yourself." These works, by artist Barbara Kruger, are not only among the most easily recognizable in American art of the last twenty years, but are also—through their relentless questioning of gender roles, consumer society, and the power of the media—among the most provocative.

Barbara Kruger was born in Newark, New Jersey, on January 26, 1945, into a lower-middle-class Jewish family. Her father was a chemical technician, her mother a legal secretary. Kruger studied at Syracuse University, the School of Visual Arts, and the Parsons School of Design. At Parsons, she took courses with photographer DIANE ARBUS and graphic designer and art director Marvin Israel. Although she never completed a degree in her chosen field, fine arts, Kruger's association with Israel landed her a job with Condé Nast Publications. Within a year, at age twenty-two, she was chief designer at *Mademoiselle*.

Her graphic design background is evident in her art, as is the influence of John Heartfield and Hannah Höch, two artists who used photomontage and collage techniques to create politically charged art in Germany in the 1920s. A kind of propaganda in reverse, Kruger's works grab one's attention much as an effective advertisement does, with one significant difference. Where advertising conceals its methods of persuasion, Kruger draws attention to them, asking us to scrutinize these methods, so as to better educate ourselves about the power of the media. The artist uses advertising's techniques—enticement, shock, provocation, and a direct address to the viewer—in order to teach us how the two languages of persuasion, photographs and words, influence us. Believing that no message is neutral, Kruger would have us be critical interpreters, rather than passive consumers, of the media.

Entering the New York art scene of the late 1960s, she found a largely male world not welcoming of women artists. But she was inspired by the efforts of another woman artist, Magdalena Abakanowicz, and began to make art under Abakanowicz's influence. The 1970s were a time of steady intellectual and artistic growth for Kruger. Her art was exhibited in the prestigious Whitney Biennial and several other group and solo exhibitions. Beginning in the mid-1970s, her reading and participation in a group called Artists Meeting for Social Change introduced her to feminist film criticism and structuralist literary theory, which were to shape her work as a mature artist. These influences drew her away from her previous artistic efforts, which she came to consider as lacking in intellectual challenge and political content. Inspired by new ideas and her own graphic design experience, Kruger began developing a signature style and subject matter. She also started to teach, to write criticism about television and cinema, and to curate exhibitions, which centered on her interests in advertising and media.

Kruger has exhibited in galleries and museums in the United States and Europe. Perhaps more significantly, she has brought her art to such urban public spaces as bus stops, subway stations, and billboards, thus appropriating advertising's domain for her own message. She has contributed criticism to the journal *Artforum* and has published anthologies of her writings. She makes her home in New York.

SELECTED WORKS BY BARBARA KRUGER

Beauty and Critique (1983); *No Progress in Pleasure* (1982); *Picture/Readings* (1978); *Remote Control: Power, Cultures and the World of Appearances* (1993); *T.V. Guides: A Collection of Thoughts about Television* (1985).

BIBLIOGRAPHY

Alternative Museum. *Contra Media: Hans Haacke, Barbara Kruger, Michael LeBron, Erika Rothenberg* (1982); Dunford, Penny, ed. *A Biographical Dictionary of Women Artists in Europe and America Since 1850* (1989); Foster, Hal. "Subversive Signs." *Art in America* 70, no. 10 (1982): 88–92; Linker, Kate. *Love for Sale: The Words and Pictures of Barbara Kruger* (1990); Marks, Claude, ed. *World Artists 1980–1990* (1991); Pohlen, Annelie. "The Dignity of the Thorn." *Artforum* 21, no. 1 (1982): 59–61; Squiers, Carol. "Barbara Kruger." *Aperture* 138 (1995): 58–67, and "Diversionary (Syn)tactics: BK Has Her Way with Words." *Artnews* 86, no. 2 (1987): 76–85; *Who's Who in American Art 1993–94* (1993).

MICHAEL DASHKIN

KUBIE, MATILDA STEINAM
(1869–1944)

Born in the Midwest, Matilda Steinam Kubie spent her adult life as a resident of New York City. Although often identified as Mrs. Isaac Kubie, she created a public persona distinct from that of her husband, becoming actively involved in a large array of civic and welfare organizations. A member of the Free Synagogue and Congregation Emanu-El, she dedicated much of her time and energy to strengthening New York's institutional infrastructure of Jewish philanthropies.

Matilda Steinam Kubie, the daughter of Simon and Fannie (Wolff) Steinam, was born on September 13, 1869, in La Crosse, Wisconsin. She attended the Normal College (later known as HUNTER COLLEGE) in New York City, graduating in 1888. She married Isaac Kubie, the son of Albert and Theresa Kubie, on November 12, 1914. The fifty-eight-year-old groom was president of the Kubie Corporation, an exporting and importing business located on Wall Street, and was Matilda's senior by thirteen years. Soon after their marriage, Matilda Kubie undertook charitable work, assisting in various emergency war fund drives, most notably as a chair of the Salvation Army Fund Drive.

In 1917, Kubie became chair of publicity for the newly formed Federation for the Support of Jewish Philanthropic Societies of New York City, an organization dedicated to coordinating and supporing the activities of Jewish charities. During her long association with the federation, she served as associate chair of the women's division, director of the Business Men's Council in 1920, and honorary trustee-at-large for life. Her accomplishments in these roles were manifold: She obtained free advertising space in the newspaper ads of department stores, on outdoor billboards, in the programs of Carnegie Hall and the Metropolitan Opera House, and during the broadcasts of several radio stations, including the municipally owned WNYC. Within five years after joining the federation, Kubie was on the boards of the YOUNG WOMEN'S HEBREW ASSOCIATION, the Beth-El Sisterhood, and the Jewish Big Sisters, and had become the membership secretary of the Jewish Women's Organization. In 1922, Bird S. Coler, commissioner of New York's Department of Public Welfare, recognized Kubie's work by appointing her an honorary deputy to assist in relations between the department and agencies that cared for Jewish dependents. Kubie was the only woman to hold such a post.

On June 1, 1926, Isaac Kubie died at age seventy. Like his wife, he had actively participated in nonprofit organizations, serving as vice president of the Freundschaft Society and as a member of the Home for Aged and Infirm Hebrews. After Isaac's death, Kubie multiplied her activities during the interwar period, engaging in both religious and secular pursuits. During her tenures as vice president, chair of membership and publicity, and chair of the committee on employment and vocational problems of the Federation of Jewish Women's Organizations of Greater New York, membership of the federation increased from 35 to 280 affiliates. Kubie also assisted in the publicity and fund-raising campaigns of the Henry Street Settlement, helped to publicize several United Jewish campaigns, and was a member of such organizations as the American Birth Control League and the League of Women Voters.

With the coming of World War II, she offered her talents to British, French, Greek, Chinese, and Russian relief organizations. In 1942, she served as chair of the local Red Cross War Fund's committee on foreign press relations, praising the foreign-language media for their support of the fund. She did not live to see the end of the war, passing away at her Central Park West home on February 19, 1944, at age seventy-four.

Wife of a prosperous businessman, resident of a fashionable New York City district, Matilda Kubie, like other society women of her era, chose to direct her energies toward the support and growth of charitable institutions that sought to better the lives of those in the Jewish community.

BIBLIOGRAPHY

AJYB 46:340; *BEOAJ;* "Isaac Kubie Dead at 70." *NYTimes,* June 2, 1926: 25; Obituary. *NYTimes,* February 19, 1944: 13:4; "Red Cross Plans Plea to City Aides." *NYTimes,* January 23, 1942: 23; *UJE;* "Walker Asks All to Aid Jewish Drive." *NYTimes,* May 5, 1926: 22; "Woman a Welfare Deputy." *NYTimes,* May 7, 1922: 20; *WWIAJ* (1938).

JOE KOMLJENOVICH

KUMIN, MAXINE (b. 1925)

"Writers are all secret Jews," declared poet and writer Maxine Kumin in a *Massachusetts Review* interview in 1975, two years after receiving the Pulitzer Prize for *Up Country: Poems of New England.* This statement is particularly significant for what it implies about Kumin's Jewish background and the role it has played in her work—a role frequently overlooked by readers and critics. Because much of her subtle, elegantly crafted poetry focuses on the details of country living—gardening, mushrooming, horse raising, coping with wild animals, experiencing the change of seasons—it is frequently classified as pastoral. Kumin has been compared to Robert Frost, an association that pleases her. She has also been considered a confessional poet, in the manner of her friend and colleague Anne Sexton. These descriptions, though not inaccurate, are limited. For Kumin is also a Jewish American woman poet whose writing closely examines what it means to negotiate the demands of two different cultures. Her work constantly questions and expands the concept of Jewishness in contemporary, culturally divided America.

Born Maxine Winokur on June 6, 1925, in Germantown, a well-to-do suburb of Philadelphia, Pennsylvania, she was the youngest of four children and the only girl. Her father, Peter Winokur, was a successful pawnbroker whose family had emigrated from Eastern Europe. Her mother, Doll (Simon), whose family emigrated from Bohemia to Virginia in the nineteenth century, had wanted to become a professional musician, an ambition thwarted by her father. Similarly, Maxine, an excellent swimmer, was prevented from joining Bill Rose's Aquacade by *her* father. Peter Winokur, however, did approve of her writing. As a "Jewish patriarch," he respected the written word.

As a child, she attended the convent school run by the Sisters of St. Joseph next door to her home for three years; later, she attended secular Philadelphia schools. She received her B.A. in history and literature from Radcliffe College in 1946. Soon after graduation, she married Victor Montwid Kumin, an engineer, with whom she had three children: Jane Simon, Judith Montwid, and Daniel David. She returned to Radcliffe for a master's degree in 1948. Participating in a workshop conducted by the poet John Holmes at the Boston Center for Adult Education proved to be extremely beneficial in Kumin's own development as a poet. Since 1961, she has published thirteen books of poetry; taught poetry writing at Tufts, Washington, Columbia, Brandeis, and Princeton Universities; received the Pulitzer Prize (1973) and the American Academy and Institute of Arts and Letters Award (1980); served as a consultant in poetry to the Library of Congress (1981–1982); and was elected chancellor in the Academy of American Poets (1996). She has also published four novels, three collections of essays, two books of short stories, and numerous children's books (four with Anne Sexton). She now lives on a farm in Warner, New Hampshire, where she writes and raises horses.

While her fiction reflects Jewish concerns, it is in her poetry that such themes are most thoroughly explored. Kumin's earliest relationships with gentiles initiated a dialogue between cultures that recurs throughout her poetry. In an early poem, "Mother Rosarine," the poet expresses both the attractions of the convent world, from which the child-speaker steals a rosary, and a sense of alienation from it: "Wrong, born wrong for the convent games." In "The Spell," Kumin's Jewish mother has apparent power in the garden that borders the convent's yard. Perhaps the most powerful expression of Kumin's ambivalence toward both cultures occurs in "Sisyphus." In terse couplets, another child-speaker tells of helping a man in a wheelchair. When he praises her as "a perfect Christian child," she wishes to contradict him, to assert her Jewishness, but cannot do so. This failure becomes her burden.

In a series of "tribal poems," Kumin explores her family, its history, and its stories. "The Pawnbroker" is a moving tribute to her father, written after his death. "The Chain" evokes her mother's life as a Jew in a small Virginia town and connects her parent to a "chain" of mothers and daughters. "Sperm" wittily traces the histories of seventeen cousins. "For My Great-Grandfather: A Message Long Overdue" describes her mother's ancestor, a tailor from Bohemia, who has moved to Newport News, Virginia. In his new surroundings, he writes letters to his family, ending in blessings, on the backs of bills-of-sale.

Kumin moves from the personal sphere to a wider historical context in another group of poems. In "The Order of History," the speaker dreams of a pogrom in which her Polish lover would be her enemy, not her ally. The subject of one's role, whether chosen or not, in the horrifying events of the twentieth century is raised in "The Amsterdam Poem": The speaker visits Anne Frank's house, expresses guilt at having been safe in Pennsylvania while other Jews were murdered, and concludes, "for suffering there is no quantum." In "Woodchucks," the speaker compares her own escalating determination to exterminate the garden pests to the Nazis' mad social Darwinism. Violence against a demonized enemy, the poet implies, is regrettably a universal human trait.

In two later poems, the cultural dialogue takes another turn. "Living Alone with Jesus," written while Kumin was teaching in Danville, Kentucky, begins in a state of alienation and ends with a whimsical act of cross-religious communication. At first, the speaker appears overwhelmed by the "thirty-seven churches" and the hymns flooding her room. Then she imagines Jesus as a guest to whom she offers grapefruit with honey. Kumin shows that in the realm of imagination, religious and cultural differences can be bridged. In "For a Young Nun at Breadloaf," the religious-cultural divide is resolved in human terms. The engaging Sister Elizabeth asserts that the speaker is, like herself, doing "Christ's work," but the speaker calls herself an "Old Jew." In this poem, the tongue-tied, confused girl of "Sisyphus" has become an adult, well able to manage complicated issues of identity.

In her work, Kumin affirms her Jewish past in "a nation losing its memory," and extends that past forward to encompass a wider cultural family. In doing so, she leaves her mark, deftly and sensitively, as an important contemporary Jewish American poet.

SELECTED WORKS BY MAXINE KUMIN

Connecting the Dots: Poems (1996); *The Designated Heir* (1974); *The Eggs of Things*, with Anne Sexton (1963); *Halfway* (1961); *House, Bridge, Fountain, Gate* (1975); *In Deep: Country Essays* (1987); *The Long Approach* (1985); *Looking for Luck: Poems* (1992); *The Microscope* (1984); *More Eggs of Things*, with Anne Sexton (1964); *The Nightmare Factory* (1970); *Our Ground Time Here Will Be Brief* (1982); *The Passions of Uxport* (1968); *The Privilege* (1965); *The Retrieval System* (1978); *Selected Poems: 1961–1990* (1997); *To Make a Prairie: Essays on Poets, Poetry and Country Living* (1979); *Up Country: Poems of New England* (1972); *What Color is Caesar?* (1978); *Why Can't We Live Together Like Civilized Human Beings?* (1982); *Women, Animals and Vegetables* (1996).

BIBLIOGRAPHY

Contemporary Authors. New Revision Series. Vol. 21 (1987); *Contemporary Literary Criticism.* Vol. 5 (1976).

ENID DAME

KUNIN, MADELEINE MAY (b. 1933)

The specifics of Madeleine May Kunin's life, as she herself states in her autobiography, *Living a Political Life* (1994), hardly suggest a typical governor of Vermont: "As a feminist, an immigrant, and a Jew, I was perhaps too different from the average Vermont voter, yet it was this identity that inspired me to enter public life and shaped my values." Yet her public career as that state's first woman governor—and the first (and, to date, only) woman elected to three terms as governor of any state—has been shaped in large measure by distinctive aspects of her identity.

Born in Zurich, Switzerland, on September 28, 1933, Madeleine May Kunin was the second child of a German father and Swiss mother, Ferdinand and Renée (Bloch) May. Her father died when she was almost three years old; not until she was in college did she learn that his death had been a suicide. Her mother moved the family several times, finally settling in a small town, Hergiswil, where she thought they might be safer in case of a Nazi invasion. As the German threat grew, Renée May sought a visa to enter the United States. In June 1940, the family arrived in New York City.

Members of Madeleine's parents' families became scattered throughout Europe, Palestine, and the United States during the period between the two world wars. Several relatives died in concentration camps. These events left a deep impression on her, as she wrote in her autobiography:

On some level that I do not yet fully understand, I believe I transformed my sense of the Holocaust into personal political activism. This was the source of my political courage. I could do what the victims could not: oppose evil whenever I recognized it. The United States of America would protect me. I lived in a time and place when it was safe for a Jew to be a political person, to speak, to oppose, to stand up.

She graduated from the University of Massachusetts in 1956, with a B.A. in history. She earned an M.S. from the Columbia School of Journalism. As a fledgling journalist, she first encountered career barriers based on her sex. Potential employers unabashedly stated that they would not hire her because she was a woman, while others offered her work only for the "women's page." She obtained her first job as a journalist with the *Burlington Free Press* in Burlington, Vermont, where she became a general assignment reporter. She left the newspaper in 1958 to serve as a guide in the American Pavilion at the Brussels World's Fair, returning to her native Europe for the first time since fleeing in 1940.

In Burlington, she met Dr. Arthur S. Kunin, whom she married on June 21, 1959. Four children—Julia, Peter, Adam, and Daniel—followed between 1961 and 1969, and for a decade, Kunin devoted her attention largely to domestic concerns. Yet, during those years, living in Burlington, in Cambridge, Massachusetts, and in Bern, Switzerland, when her husband was on sabbatical, Kunin was developing skills, contacts, and attitudes that would shape her political career in the years ahead.

Although not employed outside the home, she became, in effect, a community organizer. She and other doctors' wives challenged the Vermont State Medical Society, arranging a public forum to educate Vermonters about health care legislation that the society opposed but which Kunin and her friends favored. Kunin also organized a program of live music and theater for children in her community. She sought to convince the local board of aldermen to build sidewalks in her neighborhood, losing the immediate battle but gaining fresh awareness of political strategies and networks. These lessons were successfully applied when, having moved to a different neighborhood, she discovered an unmarked railroad crossing on a route used by children walking to school. With a group of neighbors, she petitioned the public service board for—and won—a flashing warning light. With victory came a new recognition of her own political efficacy and the power of the groups of women who had taken part in each of her ventures.

After an unsuccessful bid to become a member of the Burlington board of aldermen in early 1972—a post for which she had not intended to run but for which she was nominated after she made a speech decrying the absence of women on the board—Kunin won her first office, a seat in the state legislature, later that same year. The women's movement was on the rise, the campaign for the Equal Rights Amendment was in full swing, and Kunin was one of a growing number of women who saw running for public office as a way to translate their blossoming feminist awareness into action. As a Democratic member of the Vermont House of Representatives, she continued her interest in such "traditional" women's issues as education and the welfare of children and families, but also pursued such concerns as the environment, lobbying reform, and transportation. As a member of the Government Operations Committee, she was heavily involved in the process of reapportionment. She learned the processes, strategies, and traditions of the legislature well, winning, in her second term, the post of minority whip and, with it, membership on the Appropriations Committee. In so doing she became the first woman elected to a legislative leadership position in Vermont. In her third term, she was named chair of appropriations, a position in which she became an expert on the state budgeting process.

Kunin was elected lieutenant governor in 1978. Although it was not a powerful position, it gave her experience in running for statewide office and an opportunity to learn more about the executive branch, positioning her in her later bid for governor. Serving under Republican governor Richard Snelling, she was given little formal responsibility beyond the statutory duty of presiding over the state senate, but she was able to work on issues close to her heart, such as child care, energy, and highway safety. In 1980, she was reelected in the midst of a Republican sweep. As the only statewide elected Democratic official in Vermont, she became the nominal leader of her party.

In 1984, she was elected governor of Vermont in a race for which she had laid the groundwork in an unsuccessful bid two years earlier. In her three terms as governor, Kunin amassed an impressive record of achievements in such areas as education, the environment, the establishment of a family court, and the implementation of a new land-use planning law. She enacted budget cuts and tax increases aimed at stabilizing the economy. She spoke out on women's reproductive rights.

But perhaps more impressive than any of her specific policy achievements was Kunin's distinctive stamp on Vermont government as a woman. She staffed her administration with large numbers of women in both traditional and nontraditional roles, repeatedly establishing "firsts" for the state in the

Vermont's first woman governor—and the first (and, to date, only) woman elected to three terms as governor of any state—Madeleine May Kunin opened doors for other women in her administration and through her influence on schools and industry. [Schlesinger Library]

executive and judicial branches. She used the symbolic power of her office to promote feminism, bringing portraits of women into the governor's office and speaking to schoolchildren about her role. Her political leadership was an inspiration for women in the state: Female lobbyists gained prominence when their bosses used them to impress the Kunin administration, and women on welfare found the courage to change their lives as they watched the example of their governor.

When her third term ended in early 1991, Kunin returned to private life, lecturing and writing at Radcliffe College, Harvard's Kennedy School of Government, and Dartmouth College. In 1992, she was active in Bill Clinton's presidential campaign, serving on the three-person team that helped select his running mate; later, she was a member of Clinton's presidential transition board of directors. President Clinton

named Kunin deputy secretary of education in 1993, a position she held until 1996, when she became United States ambassador to Switzerland, the country of her birth.

In her life and career, Madeleine May Kunin has epitomized the American experience. As a woman, an immigrant, and a Jew, she has taken advantage of the opportunities American democracy has to offer and, in turn, has contributed substantially to making America a better, more inclusive society.

BIBLIOGRAPHY

Butterfield, Fox. "Besieged Vermont Governor Rules Out Race for Fourth Term." *NYTimes*, April 4, 1990, and "Leahy and Kunin Defeat Challengers." *NYTimes*, November 5, 1986, 27, and "Vermont's New Governor Confronts Development and Budget Problems." *NYTimes*, January 11, 1985, A10; Day, Nancy. "Woman in the News: Madeleine Kunin." *Working Woman* (July 1986); *EJ* (1985–1987); Gold, Allan R. "Governor Offers Vermont a Plan on Controlled Growth." *NYTimes*, January 13, 1988; *Living a Political Life* (1994); *Who's Who of American Women, 1993–1994* (1993).

RUTH MANDEL
KATHERINE KLEEMAN

KUSNITZ, ROSE CHERNIN
see **CHERNIN, ROSE**

KUSSY, SARAH (1869–1956)

Sarah Kussy was a versatile and accomplished leader of American Jewry who devoted her educational training and organizational skills to the community throughout her long life. She was a founder and leader of a constellation of significant Jewish organizations, including HADASSAH and the United Synagogue Women's League, both of which named her an honorary national vice president. Through her many associations, Kussy worked to change the face of Jewish education, Zionist activities, and women's participation in Jewish American communal life. Her energy, erudition, and leadership inspired Jewish women and educators across North America.

Born in Newark, New Jersey, on June 27, 1869, Kussy was the fourth child of six born to one of Newark's most established Jewish families. In later years, Kussy wrote a chronicle, never published, of her parents' history since their mid-nineteenth-century arrival in America. In this evocative memoir, she chronicled not only the fortunes of one immigrant family, but, through their experiences, the rise of an entire Jewish community. Gustav Kussy and Bella (Bloch) Kussy, both born and raised in Germany, managed a successful butcher shop in Newark while maintaining a traditional Jewish home for their six children: Bertha, Meyer, Herman, Sarah, Nathan, and Joseph. Her parents' emphasis on education, both religious and secular, was transmitted to Kussy throughout her formative years. After completing public school and studies at New York University's Extension Department, she attended the Jewish Theological Seminary's Teachers Institute and graduated in its first class, in 1906. She became a teacher in several schools in the Newark area, teaching for thirty-five years at Camden Street Public School, at Congregation Oheb Shalom's religious school, and at several other Hebrew schools in the city.

In 1912, Kussy was one of a small group of women who joined HENRIETTA SZOLD in founding Hadassah, the Women's Zionist Organization. Kussy served for many years on Hadassah's national executive board, and in 1926 founded the Newark chapter. Under her leadership as president of the entire northern New Jersey region, Newark and its surroundings soon ranked among the most active Hadassah branches in the nation. In 1918, Kussy worked with MATHILDE SCHECHTER to found the National Women's League of the United Synagogue of America (the organizational body of Conservative synagogues). She served on the league's national board for decades, chairing its organization and propaganda committee and its education committee, lecturing for its speakers' bureau, and writing numerous articles for *Outlook*, the league's publication.

Not content to limit her Jewish activities to women's organizations, Kussy helped to found the AMERICAN JEWISH CONGRESS and Young Judaea. She served as a delegate to the Jewish Agency for Palestine, the United Synagogue of America, the American Jewish Conference, and the Jewish Welfare Board. She visited and spoke in cities throughout the United States, Europe, and Palestine, and was also a delegate to five World Zionist Congresses in Switzerland and Austria between 1907 and 1939. Responding to widespread missionary efforts among Jews in her native Newark, she organized a campaign against the "Christianization" of Jewish children. In a more secular realm, she was active in the Newark and New Jersey Teachers Associations, and in the League of Women Voters.

Sarah Kussy died in Newark on October 2, 1956. Toward the end of her life, she was honored by a number of organizations. She received a citation for Jewish cultural leadership from the Jewish Education Association of Essex County, New Jersey, and saw the Newark Hadassah chapter renamed after her. Perhaps the most enduring tribute to her tireless work and Zionist commitment came in 1950, when the Northern New Jersey branch of Hadassah donated ten thousand trees to Israel to be planted as the Sarah Kussy Forest. It is this living tribute, as well as the organizations Kussy helped to found, that preserves the memory of this remarkable and gifted leader of American Jewry.

SELECTED WORKS BY SARAH KUSSY

"Reminiscences of Jewish Life in Newark, NJ." *YIVO Annual of Jewish Social Science* 6 (1951): 177–186; *The Story of Gustav and Bella Kussy of Newark, N.J.: A Family Chronicle* (n.d.); *The Women's League Handbook and Guide* (1947).

BIBLIOGRAPHY

AJYB 59:475; Obituary. *NYTimes*, October 3, 1956, 33:3; *WWIAJ* (1938).

LAUREN B. STRAUSS

L

LABOR MOVEMENT

Jewish American women have played a central role in the American labor movement since the beginning of the twentieth century. As women, they brought to trade unions their sensibilities about the organizing process and encouraged labor to support government regulation to protect women in the workforce. As Jews who emerged from a left-wing cultural tradition, they nurtured a commitment to social justice, which would develop into what is often called "social unionism." From their position as an ethnic and religious minority, as well as from their position as women, they helped to shape the direction of the mainstream labor movement.

Jewish mass immigration reached the United States just as the ready-made clothing industry hit its stride at the turn of the century—a circumstance that provided men and women with unprecedented incentives to unionize. In the Old Country, where jobs were scarce, daughters were married off as fast as possible. But many immigrant women had learned to sew in the workshops of Russian and Polish towns, and in America, where families counted on their contributions, they were expected to work. Girls sometimes immigrated as teenagers, seeking out an uncle or older sister who might help them to find a first job so that some part of their wages could be sent back to Europe. The wages of other young women helped to pay the rent, to buy food and clothing, to bring rela-

tives to America, and to keep brothers in school. When they married, young women normally stopped working in the garment shops. But, much as in the Old Country, they were still expected to contribute to family income, sometimes by taking in clothing to sew at home.

In early twentieth-century New York, Philadelphia, Boston, and other large cities, only the exceptional unmarried woman did not operate a sewing machine in a garment factory for part of her young adult life. Factory or sweatshop work before marriage and the expectation of some form of paid labor afterward fostered a continuing set of ties to the garment industry for this first generation of urban Jewish American women, encouraging a community of understanding around its conditions and continuing support for the ever-changing stream of workers who entered it. Women who worked long hours at extraordinarily low wages, in unsanitary and unsafe working conditions, and faced continual harassment to boot, found succor in their communities and benefited from a class-conscious background.

To be sure, competitive individualism and the desire to make it in America could hinder unionization efforts. But a well-developed ethic of social justice played an equally important role, producing perhaps the most politically aware of all immigrant groups. Socialist newspapers predominated in New York's Yiddish-speaking Lower East Side. Jews were well represented in the Socialist Party after 1901. Though their unions were weak, Jews were among the best organized of semiskilled immigrants. In the immigrant enclaves of America's large cities, as in Europe, women benefited from the shared sense that women worked for their families, as they absorbed much of their community's concern for social justice. This did not deflect the desire of working women to get out of the shops, but it did contribute to the urge to make life in them better.

Still, even under these circumstances, it could not have been easy for a woman to become politically active. A number of small unions dotted New York's Lower East Side at the turn of the century. There, where the boss was almost always an immigrant like oneself and sometimes a relative, and where shops were small and vulnerable, unions sprang up and flowered, or withered, as trade picked up and declined. Organized largely by the INTERNATIONAL LADIES GARMENT WORKERS UNION (ILGWU) and members of a socialist umbrella organization called the United Hebrew Trades, they reflected the weakness of a labor movement rooted in an industry of poorly paid workers and undercapitalized ventures.

The men in these unions did not, at first, welcome the women, placing them in a dilemma. In order to improve their working lives, incipient activists found themselves choosing between a conservative trade union movement hostile to women in the workforce and a women's movement whose members did not work for wages. A young and inexperienced ROSE SCHNEIDERMAN, for example, was turned away from the cap-makers' union to solicit the signatures of twenty-five of her coworkers before the union would acknowledge them or provide aid. Her friend PAULINE NEWMAN recalled that when she and her friends "organized a group, we immediately called the union so that they would take the members in." Despite the early devotion of women—despite the fact that women were often baited, beaten, and arrested on picket lines—the ILGWU insisted that women, destined for marriage, were unorganizable. Even those who managed to enter were badly treated. During the 1905 cap-makers' strike, for example, married men got strike benefits but even women who were supporting widowed mothers and young siblings received nothing.

Discouraged by their union brothers, recognizing their issues as different from those of male workers, women turned to other women for help with their work-related problems. They developed solidarity and loyalty with women workers from other industries and areas, sometimes striking when their sisters were attacked and resisting separation from one another

when they were jailed. They also sought and received help from the Women's Trade Union League, an organization that brought together wealthy upper-middle-class women with women wage earners. To be sure, solidarity was limited by class as well as by ethnic divisions. Jewish women thought they were superior unionists and often treated "American-born" women, as well as Polish and Italian colleagues, as suspiciously as they themselves were treated. But, isolated as they were from the mainstream of the labor movement and divided from other working women who came from less class-conscious backgrounds, Jewish women had little choice but to accept financial help and moral support from wherever it came. There was inevitable tension here. Jewish women had been nurtured in the cradle of socialism. For them, alliances with other women were largely ways of achieving a more just society. Even their middle-class friends viewed labor organization among women as a way of transcendng class lines in the service of feminist interests. Early organizers like Newman, Schneiderman, and CLARA LEMLICH [SHAVELSON] spent enormous amounts of time and energy reconciling the seemingly divergent interests of the male-dominated skilled labor movement, working women, and middle-class allies.

A major strike of shirtwaist makers, in the winter of 1909–1910, dramatically altered the position of women and their role in the trade union movement. Popularly called the UPRISING OF THE 20,000, the strike began when a tiny local, consisting of about 100 Jewish shirtwaist makers, veterans of a series of small but brutal strikes for better working conditions, called a meeting of workers in the industry. Thousands of women turned out for the November 22 meeting, surprising the reluctant leaders of the ILGWU into supporting a general strike. The event and its aftermath turned out to have significance not only for Jewish women but also for the entire trade union movement.

The young—often teenage—garment workers who walked the picket lines in the cold winter months that followed provided their own organizational strategies, solicited funds, and set goals alien to men. They introduced into the movement qualities of idealism, self-sacrifice, and commitment that appeased skeptical male leaders and stirred what they called "spirit" into a revitalized movement. Refusing to settle for small increases in wages, and even for shorter hours (the bread-and-butter issues that traditional craft unions thought crucial), women demanded union recognition. In the end, most settled for less, but in the process they inserted into the negotiations a range of issues that translated into dignity, honor, and justice.

This formal portrait of the executive board of the Amalgamated Clothing Workers was taken in 1914.
BESSIE ABRAMOWITZ [HILLMAN] *is in the front row with her future husband, Sydney Hillman, seated on her left.*
On her right is the up-and-coming lawyer Fiorello LaGuardia. [Photograph Courtesy of Philoine Fried]

The strikers insistently emphasized the discrepancy between the starvation wages and harsh working conditions they endured on the one hand, and their ability to fulfill widespread expectations of future marriage and motherhood on the other. Pressured and unsanitary conditions, they argued, yielded little room for personal needs or safety. Malnourished and exhausted, they could hardly protect their virtue, much less the health and stamina they would require to nurture the next generation. These arguments won the grudging respect of a hostile public and energized young women whose resistance to unionization often came from their expectation of marriage. Moral outrage, not economic pressure, became their trump card, and public support, indignation, and protest was their path to victory.

Relying on moral suasion created bonds among women that courageous and innovative organizers quickly reinforced with new organizing strategies. Women organizers urged individual women who would remain only briefly in the labor force to fight for the women who would follow them. Fired by idealism, women did not hesitate to put themselves in positions where they forced the authorites to violate convention, as when they were beaten by police or thrown into jail with prostitutes. They welcomed the efforts of their more affluent allies to publicize brutal incidents by joining them on picket lines or sponsoring public meetings. By such extreme measures, women dramatized the injustices of their daily treatment in the shop and factory. Addressing a nation committed to the rhetoric of chivalry, motherhood, and the idealization of the weaker sex, they demonstrated the brutal treatment that daily violated ideas about womanhood inside as well as outside the workplace. These tactics worked. In the big New York strike of 1909–1910, and in a wave of garment workers' strikes that followed, women members became the heart of a revivified union movement.

Unionized women introduced into their new unions energy and ideas alien to those of male craft unions that aimed to raise wages by restricting the labor supply. They brought notions of self-sacrifice for the future, a recognition of women's particular needs, and special attention to sanitation and cleanliness, as well as traditional demands for higher wages and shorter hours. They wanted time to attend to family and personal needs: to launder, to cook, to help out at home. They wanted sufficient wages to dress decently and contribute to family support. Above all, they wanted education, opportunities to learn not just about trade union matters but about the world around them. To foster loyalty and solidarity, they pushed for a broader vision of unionism, one that incorporated what union officials called "spirit" but that contemporaries sometimes called "soul." As FANNIA COHN put

the issue, "I do not see how we can get girls to sacrifice themselves unless we discuss something besides trade matters . . . there must be something more than the economic question, there must be idealism."

The "girls local"—Local 25 of the ILGWU—sponsored dances, concerts, lectures, and entertainments. They suffered the derision of male colleagues who asked, "What do the girls know? Instead of a union, they want to dance." But the women persisted. In 1916, Fannia Cohn persuaded the ILGWU to create the first education department in an international union, and soon, it organized a network of "unity centers" in public schools across New York City. These centers offered night-school classes in literature, music, economics, and public policy. Local 25 also

FANNIA COHN *hit the nail on the head when she said that women workers wanted more than just increased wages.*
They wanted education, opportunities to learn not just about trade union matters but about the world around them.
In 1916, she persuaded the ILGWU to create the first education department in an international union.
She is pictured here with George Meany. [Fannia Cohn Papers, New York Public Library]

In 1915, the Amalgamated Clothing Workers went out on strike.
Their objective was the abolition of the sweatshop and home work, and a reduction of the twelve-hour workday.
[American Jewish Archives]

bought an old country house that they turned into a vacation retreat for members, spawning a network of such houses by other locals until the International bought them out in 1921. These innovations, inspired and fought for by women, became the basis of a new social unionism, which garment unions sustained in the threatening atmosphere of the 1920s, which flourished in the 1930s, and which has sparked the imagination of the trade union movement since.

The pattern established by the women of the ILGWU was expanded and developed by women who worked in the men's clothing trades. The history of their union can be traced back to a 1910 protest by a small group of Jewish women who worked at the big Hart, Schaffner, and Marx factory in Chicago. After several years of trying to work effectively with more established unions, this group, led by BESSIE ABRAMOWITZ

[HILLMAN], formed their own union, the Amalgamated Clothing Workers of America (ACWA). Abramowitz later married Sidney Hillman, who became the new union's president. By the 1920s, workers in the men's clothing industry were a heterogeneous group, and women in the Amalgamated faced the challenging task of convincing potential members of the values of social unionism. Under Hillman's leadership, and supported by an active group of Jewish women who turned the union's women's bureau into a lively discussion center, the Amalgamated pioneered such social programs as unemployment insurance for seasonal workers, vacations with pay, and retirement pensions.

What unions could not do, or could do only for their members, Jewish women in the labor movement encouraged others to do for them through protective labor laws. In a period when the labor movement as a whole remained suspicious of government intervention, and the passage of laws on behalf of workers was largely supported by middle-class reformers, Jewish women trade unionists helped to educate the labor movement in the value of legislation. After the devastating TRIANGLE SHIRTWAIST FIRE in 1911, they turned to the state for protective laws that would establish industrial safety standards and regulate sanitary conditions. They joined with middle-class men and women in the National Consumers League to agitate for legislation that would restrict the numbers of hours women could work; place a floor under their wages; establish standards of cleanliness in workrooms and factories; mandate clean drinking water, washrooms, dressing rooms, and toilets; and provide seats and ventilation at work. Insisting that the quality of women's lives was as important as the wages they earned, Jewish women, like Rose Schneiderman, served on state-level investigative commissions and offered testimony that pressured state legislatures into providing new ground rules for women at work. In her capacity as president of the New York Women's Trade Union League (WTUL), Schneiderman not only played an important role in achieving a fifty-four-hour work week for women but also provided an important bridge to help craft unions accept the principle of protective labor legislation for women only. Arguably, at least, these women opened the eyes of male unionists to the positive aspects of government regulation.

By the 1920s, probably 40 percent of all unionized women in the country were garment workers—most of them Jews in the ILGWU and the Amalgamated Clothing Workers of America. The garment industry remained the only place where Jewish women were organized in large numbers. Yet the male leadership persistently discouraged women's efforts to expand their voices within unions. Women were recruited, sometimes reluctantly, as dues-paying members, tolerated as shop-level leaders, and occasionally advanced to become business agents and local officers. Only rarely did women of exceptional promise, like Fannia Cohn, DOROTHY JACOBS BELLANCA, and ROSE PESOTTA, reach the status of international officers. Where they could have fostered harmony, cooperation, and a sense of belonging, the garment unions instead mistrusted their female members, creating friction, resentment, and defensiveness among them, reducing their value, and undermining their ability to do good work. As far as the male leaders were concerned, women remained outsiders who threatened to undermine the wages of men and for whom labor legislation, rather than unionization, increasingly seemed the appropriate strategy. As if this were not enough, the social unionist strategies

that women had initiated and deeply valued became implicated in the strife-filled politics of the early 1920s.

Deeply divided by efforts of the newly formed Communist Party to seek power inside unions, male leaders identified women's demands for education and democratic participation as threats, seeing a fundamental conflict between the search for "soul" in the union and their own restrictive solidarity around wage issues. Rather than risk the possibility that the women might ally with Communist Party supporters, they chose to eliminate or take over most of the women's programs, including their vacation houses, unity centers, and educational initiatives. Women simply dropped out, leaving their unions in droves. A last-ditch effort to restore morale in the ACWA by reestablishing a women's bureau failed to stanch the flow.

Even as the Jewish labor movement was being wracked by political divisions in the early 1920s, Jewish women began to move outside its confines in order to provide benefits for women workers. Schneiderman increasingly turned to the WTUL, which she urged into the movement for protective labor legislation and which she persuaded to found a school for women workers. Cohn, distressed at new union limits on the broad educational opportunities that had so inspired women, turned to a more ambitious program of labor education. In 1921, she borrowed money to establish Brookwood Labor College, where Rose Pesotta was an early student. Brookwood inspired another experiment: the Bryn Mawr Summer School for Women Workers, which became the first of a series of schools to provide residential programs for women, many of them garment workers. Its faculty included economist THERESA WOLFSON. Some of these schools, like Brookwood, were open to workers of both sexes, but in the 1920s, women remained their major clientele. In all these experiments, women in the rank and file of unions, especially Jewish women, remained among the most ardent supporters of workers' education. They kept the flame alive until, in the 1930s, a revivified labor movement once again began to sponsor its own coeducational schools.

The Depression of the 1930s restored union activism, giving voice to women's earlier demands for community within unions and institutionalizing many of their visions in the social programs of the New Deal. Not surprisingly, Sidney Hillman and the Amalgamated Clothing Workers, with its heavily female membership, played a key role in extending social unionism into the national legislative arena. Like the ILGWU, the Amalgamated had developed a health-care program for its own members in the 1920s. The Amalgamated also initiated old-age pensions and unemployment insurance. But these had limited scope and rarely covered any but long-term workers. Under the pressure of the Depression, Hillman, abetted by his wife, Bessie Abramowitz, and vice president Dorothy Jacobs Bellanca, agitated for and helped to draft bills for unemployment compensation and fair labor standards. He also played a key role in the development of the Congress of Industrial Organizations (CIO), which, in the 1930s, promised to harbor the residues of the social unionist tradition. Jewish women unionists reaped some rewards in these days: tied to Frances Perkins and Eleanor Roosevelt through the New York Women's Trade Union League, they entered the federal bureaucracy, where they worked to soften the edges of the new legislative agenda.

Under the impetus of a dramatic upswing in female membership sparked by industrywide strikes in 1933, the trade union movement regained some of its vigorous support for the cultural and recreational programs it had earlier abandoned. Drawing on its earlier tradition, unions sponsored gym classes, athletic teams, dramatic clubs, choral groups, orchestras, and, of course, educational opportunities of all kinds. The ILGWU's long-running Broadway hit, *Pins and Needles*, testifies to the value of these programs, both for developing the morale of members and for reaching out into the community to expand understanding and support.

Still, the union movement remained uncomfortable with the leadership style of women. Neither in the garment industry nor in the other unions that Jewish women now began to join were women welcomed as leaders. As the only female vice president of the ILGWU in the 1930s, Rose Pesotta adapted the unorthodox female style that had started a generation earlier to become perhaps its most successful organizer. She created pleasant headquarters, threw parties for members and potential members, and devised style shows, festivals, and dances to attract women to the

Jewish women traditionally made up a large proportion of the members of teachers' unions.
Pictured here (left to right) is SANDRA FELDMAN, *who became head of the American Federation of Teachers in 1997;*
Albert Shanker, who was the head of the AFT before her; and Ann Kessler, who was the legislative liaison
for the United Federation of Teachers. [United Federation of Teachers]

Union work was not all picketing and organizing. This photo of a square dance
(the woman in the center is BESSIE ABRAMOWITZ HILLMAN*) was taken in the 1950s at a union summer school in the South.*
[Photograph courtesy of Philoine Fried]

union. In Los Angeles, she constructed a picket line of women in gowns to embarrass factory owners attending a charity event. Before Easter, she demanded and got special strike allowances for mothers to buy holiday clothes for their children. Nobody questioned her success: She became the union's most important troubleshooter, traveling far afield, to places like Puerto Rico, Seattle, Akron, Boston, and Montreal to resolve outstanding disputes. But neither the leaders of the ILGWU nor those of other unions understood these tactics. David Dubinsky regularly berated Pesotta for extravagance and mistrusted techniques that appealed to women's interest in human welfare as much as their interest in wages.

These issues emerged in other arenas where women began to organize in the heyday of the Depression. Jews had begun to enter school teaching, social work, retail sales, and office work in the 1920s. Though by no means dominant in any of these arenas, Jewish women played prominent roles in the organizational battles of all of them in the 1930s. Sometimes the daughters of unionists and often the heirs of the Jewish tradition of social justice, these women were

drawn to the humane vision then offered by the Communist Party. Inevitably, this created conflicts with the traditional bread-and-butter image of many male and non-Jewish unionists. Ann Prosten, who in the 1930s organized office staff for the United Office and Professional Workers, spoke for many Jewish union women when she said, "the basic problems of women will not be solved until we have socialism."

The battles among schoolteachers for union control illustrates the point. Although there were ephemeral teachers' unions even before World War I, professional identification prevented large numbers, even of Jewish women, from joining. Nor were Jewish women encouraged by the fact that the largely native-born leadership of the two national unions, the American Federation of Teachers (AFT) and the National Education Association, remained wedded to narrow strategies for improving the status of the teaching profession. Still, by the mid-1920s, in large cities like New York and Chicago, where the administrative and teaching staffs of public schools remained predominantly Irish Catholic, the majority of local union members were Jews, most of them women. By 1925,

Jewish women made up half of the New York Teachers Union executive board. The onset of the Depression coincided with the entry of the children of immigrants into the field, and, inspired by the spirit of the times, more and more teachers sought the protection of unionism. Jewish women rapidly became the majority of union activists in every major city. Like Rebecca Coolman Simonson, who came from a family of trade unionists and socialists, and who presided over the noncommunist Teachers Guild, which split from Teachers Union in 1935, these women carried their traditions with them.

But to be a Jewish unionist in an occupation still largely non-Jewish was to be associated with left-wing policies. From the beginning, unionists refused to hew a narrow line, fighting not only for higher salaries but also for a range of socioeconomic programs. In the schools, they wanted better facilities, relief from overcrowding, and child-welfare provisions like free cooked lunches. But they also advocated policies to aid unemployed teachers, to democratize the schools, and to support progressive education. To pay for these programs, they demanded federal and state aid to schools. Organized teachers opposed efforts to remove married women from the classroom. When fascism became an overriding issue, they attempted to stymie racial and religious bigotry by stepping up a long-standing campaign for academic and religious freedom.

If women's vision of social justice seemed to find a natural ally in the communist vision of the 1930s, the alliance did little to enhance women's voices. The leadership of the teachers' unions remained male. LILLIAN HERSTEIN failed to take over an important Chicago teachers' local in 1937. In New York, women members opted to support the communist leaders of Teachers' Union, Local 5, of the American Federation of Teachers, believing that radical ideas harbored the best hope for opening up the union movement, as well as for social change. But more conservative AFT leaders could not tolerate dissent and retaliated by expelling the communist locals from party leadership. Jewish women would not play a major role in the AFT again until the 1960s, when they slowly reentered union leadership positions. By then, their influence was once again important in the local arena where women like New York's SANDRA FELDMAN rose through the ranks to become president first of New York City's United Federation of Teachers in 1986 and then of its parent body, the AFT, in 1997.

Nor did Jewish women have much influence on the CIO, which in its early days espoused the rhetoric of radical change. Its leadership remained relentlessly male. A tiny proportion of delegates to its first convention were women, and by 1946, it could boast only twenty women among its six hundred convention delegates. Those who did attend reflected the diversity of the two million women who had joined union ranks in the 1930s. They were Jewish and Catholic, white ethnic and African American. Among them was Ruth Young, a member of the executive board of the United Electrical Workers, and daughter-in-law of Clara Lemlich, who had sparked the Uprising of the 20,000.

Women's enhanced loyalty to communism undermined long-standing alliances with women's groups, and particularly with the Women's Trade Union League. Under Rose Schneiderman's leadership, the WTUL straddled a delicate line between its traditional support for the AFL and its sympathy for the goals of the new CIO. But neither Schneiderman nor the WTUL's leaders could tolerate communist influence, and here the WTUL drew a line in the sand. Schneiderman alienated many women (Jews and non-Jews) when she refused to help the militant female members of a United Electrical, Radio and Machine Workers local in a bitter 1937 strike. And many more, like Boston's Rose Norwood, abandoned her as she passively watched the AFL bully local leagues into expelling members from CIO unions. Norwood resigned from the leadership of the Boston WTUL to work for the CIO.

By the end of World War II, three million women workers belonged to trade unions, and half a million more would join union ranks in the two years that followed. Among union members, Jewish women now formed a tiny minority, their presence minimal even in the unions they had once deeply influenced. Most new recruits joined unions out of necessity, not because they chose to do so. And though, on paper, every national union admitted women, a sex-segregated labor market ensured that most would have precious few women members. Under these circumstances, the role of Jewish women became less distinctive.

As leadership remained either firmly tied to men or passed to a second generation of women, many of them organized in the 1930s, the battleground shifted. Both inside and outside unions, women joined together to extend the limited coverage of New Deal legislation beyond traditional manufacturing sectors to the domestic workers, public sector workers, retail clerks, and part-time employees who had been left out. They fought now for equal pay for equal work and to push back the barriers of occupational segregation. Younger women in the labor movement began to protest the restrictions imposed by the protective labor legislation that Schneiderman had supported all her life. They wanted to guarantee equality with an Equal Rights Amendment. Schneiderman vacillated, finally compromising on night work. Her old friend Pauline Newman refused to budge. Newman's partner Frieda Segelke Miller pushed for an equal pay bill.

Within unions, the influence of Jewish women eroded as they were expelled or marginalized for their earlier communist sympathies. Some, like BETTY FRIEDAN, a staff writer for the United Electrical Workers Union, quit to raise a family when their left-leaning unions came under attack. Yet many, like Friedan herself, abandoned union activism only to find other ways of organizing women. A younger generation of women unionists, including many African Americans, replaced them to battle for an equality that Jewish women had only imagined. Their struggle, begun in the 1950s, prefigured the feminist movement of the late 1960s and 1970s. Often, they allied themselves with the incipient civil rights movement in an effort to draw attention to race as well as to sex discrimination. Organizing efforts turned to the public sector: Teachers, nurses, and clerical workers were their new targets. The legacy of Jewish women remained merely an echo.

Labor's most effective representative on Capitol Hill was Evelyn Dubrow, of the ILGWU, who pushed for a progressive agenda in Congress for more than fifty years.
[UNITE magazine]

Two events symbolized the change. The first was the death of the Women's Trade Union League in 1950. The league had been the vehicle of partnership between Jewish immigrant women and the trade union movement. It provided a place where women could develop their skills, draw support and sustenance, and find responses to creative ideas. It served to remind men that women had special needs and interests that the labor movement would need to fill if it were to retain their loyalty. Yet it also maintained the legislative pressure that enabled men to marginalize women in the movement.

The second was the conflict that erupted in 1968 in the Ocean Hill–Brownsville section of New York City. Jewish teachers were faced with a largely African-American school district, which had been authorized to modify its public schools to conform to its own sense of priorities. African-American community representatives decided to replace some of the teachers with new recruits of their own choosing. The teachers, mostly Jewish women led by a Jewish male, found themselves protecting their union rights against the community rights of African Americans. In the bitter struggle that followed, one irony was lost on the participants. The descendants of the Jewish women who had fought to incorporate their vision of justice and dignity in a reluctant union movement half a century earlier were now using a trade union to prevent another disadvantaged group from fostering its own sense of dignity and community.

BIBLIOGRAPHY

Baum, Charlotte, Paula Hyman, and Sonya Michel. *The Jewish Woman in America* (1976); Glenn, Susan A. *Daughters of the Shtetl: Life and Labor in the Immigrant Generation* (1990); Howe, Irving. *World of Our Fathers: The Journey of East European Jews to America and the Life They Found and Made* (1976); Kessler-Harris, Alice. "Organizing the Unorganizable: Three Jewish Women and Their Union." *Labor History* 17 (Winter 1976): 5–23, and "Problems of Coalition Building: Women and Trade Unions in the 1920s." In *Women, Work and Protest: A Century of Women's Labor History*, edited by Ruth Milkman (1985), and "Rose Schneiderman and the Limits of Women's Trade Unionism." In *Labor Leaders in America*, edited by Melvyn Dubofsky and Warren Van Tine (1987); Leeder, Elaine. *The Gentle General: Rose Pesotta, Anarchist and Labor Organizer* (1993); Markowitz, Ruth Jacknow. *My Daughter, the Teacher: Jewish Teachers in the New York City Schools* (1993); Murphy, Marjorie. *Blackboard Unions: The AFT and the NEA, 1900–1980* (1990); Orleck, Annelise. *Common Sense and a Little Fire: Women and Working-Class Politics in the United States, 1900–1965* (1995); Pesotta, Rose. *Bread Upon the Waters* (1944, 1987); Seidman, Joel. *The Needle Trades* (1942); Strom, Sharon Hartman.

"Challenging 'Women's Place': Feminism, the Left, and Industrial Unionism in the 1930s." *Feminist Studies* 9 (Summer 1983): 359–386; Weinberg, Sydney Stahl. *The World of Our Mothers: The Lives of Jewish Immigrant Women* (1988).

ALICE KESSLER-HARRIS

LADINO (JUDEO-SPANISH) PRESS

Ladino-speaking Jews, descendants of the Iberian Jewish exiles of the fourteenth and fifteenth centuries, began to immigrate from the Ottoman Empire (Turkey and the Balkans) to the United States in the 1880s. By 1924, thirty thousand had settled in the United States, with the largest concentration (approximately twenty thousand by the early 1920s) in the city of New York. By the 1930s, the American Judeo-Spanish press estimated the total Ladino-speaking population nationally at roughly fifty thousand. Sephardic historian Joseph Papo has written that in 1916 approximately 10 percent of the twenty thousand Sephardim of New York were women. (This figure seems low. While Papo is most likely correct that female Sephardic immigrants were initially outnumbered by their male contemporaries, as were female immigrants of many other non-Jewish ethnic groups, the ratio probably evened out in later years as Jewish immigration from the Orient increased.)

Sephardic Jews, with their unfamiliar physiognomy and languages, coupled with their ignorance of Yiddish, were often not recognized by their Ashkenazi brethren as Jews. One of the independent mediums Sephardim formed in order to remedy their social isolation and create their own channels of community self-help was the Judeo-Spanish press. The American Ladino press, printed in Hebrew letters, from 1910 through 1948 included nineteen known publications, and, with the exception of one Los Angeles bulletin and one tabloid published in New Brunswick, New Jersey, appeared exclusively in New York. Although Ladino literacy was more prevalent among Sephardic men, Judeo-Spanish publications did assume some female readership. Though its editors were male, and while men comprised the overwhelming majority of its contributors and readers, the American Ladino press is not only an important source of information about the social status and activities of Oriental Sephardic women, but also illuminates the ways in which "Turkinas," as they were internally known, were perceived by their male contemporaries.

The female dimension of the Ladino press can be roughly divided into three categories: daily activities (communal activism and role in the work force), conceptual approaches (discourses on the social and economic status of women in the Sephardic community), and fictional portrayals of women (serialized novels featuring Sephardic female characters and humorous advice columns directed at Sephardic women). This article considers all American Ladino periodicals and bulletins that have been preserved in the major archives in the United States. (Several Judeo-Spanish periodicals, whose existence can be ascertained through references in surviving Ladino newspapers, have been lost.)

DAILY ACTIVITIES

One important publication was that of the Sephardic Brotherhood of America, a New York burial society founded in 1915 by thirty (male) Salonikan immigrants, which by 1923 had expanded to an organization of mutual aid and communal activities offering services to over a thousand members and their families. The brotherhood's bulletins focused on the history and activities of the organization and generally did not consider women in its articles. This is partly because women received membership benefits through their husbands or late husbands, and thus were assumed to have little incentive to become active members themselves. Yet women were active members of the organization from early on, and many of their communal activities are recorded in the brotherhood's publications. In addition, a few of the leading female leaders of the brotherhood published articles pertaining to Sephardic women and the organization's sisterhoods.

Among the early activities of women recorded in the brotherhood's reviews are those of the Committee of Education, which in 1922, under the direction of Fannie Angel, Rebecca Nahoum Amateau, and other women volunteers, organized a series of lectures of "general interest" that succeeded in attracting hundreds of listeners. (These lectures included a discussion given by Angel in 1924 on "love and sex," for which she was congratulated by the serious-humorous Ladino tabloid *La Vara* [The staff] as "the first of our Sephardic women to speak with courage in public.") The Sisterhood of Uptown (Harlem) was founded in 1922 by Rebecca Amateau, who in 1928 served as president with the assistance of Rashel Amariyo (vice president), Suzan Nahoum (secretary), Lina Perahia (treasurer), and Fannie Angel (trustee). The committee of the Uptown Sisterhood was involved in both social and educative endeavors, including organizing lectures and aiding the sick and indigent. Upon the

מיס ראשיל אמאריאו

מאראם לינה פרחיה   מאראם פיני אנג׳יל

Pictured above are three of the most important leaders of the Sisterhood of Uptown (Harlem): Rashel Amariyo, vice president; Fannie Angel, trustee; and Lina Perahia, treasurer. [El Ermanado, 1928, courtesy of Aviva Ben-Ur]

the Ottoman Empire and first wife of the great Sephardic activist Albert Amateau, published an article in the *Sephardic Brotherhood Review* entitled "The Relationship Between the Sephardic Immigrant Mother and Her American Children," in which she urged Ladino-speaking mothers to educate themselves in order to prevent a cultural gulf from developing between themselves and their Americanized children. "Mothers, it is not too late!" she wrote. "We still have the time to repair our life and win the hearts, the friendship and the respect of our children. It is no shame to go night school and to learn enough to be able to read the English papers and to be informed of what is going on around us." Fannie Angel, in her article "Appeal to Our Sephardic Sisters," published in the same issue, counseled Sephardic women to emancipate themselves and organize sisterhoods within their societies.

According to the brotherhood's constitution (revised in 1922), sons and daughters of members could themselves become members from the age of sixteen.

פוסטימאס די מזיר

This is a caricature of "Bula Satula" [Aunt Satula] the fictional author of the column "Postemas de Mujer" [Pet peeves of a woman]. The advice column for Sephardic immigrant women was serialized in the Judeo-Spanish tabloid La Vara *from 1922 to 1934. In fact, the column was written by a man, Moise B. Soulam. [*La Vara, *courtesy of Aviva Ben-Ur]*

dispersal of many of its members, and especially its three most important leaders (Amariyo, Angel, and Perahia), the Uptown Sisterhood discontinued its activities temporarily. In 1929, the Sisterhood of Downtown (Lower East Side) was organized, headed by Mme. Kuenkas, Mme. Elvira Rubi, Mme. Dudun Kohen, and others who "have given all of their time for the success of this Brotherhood institution." The Downtown Sisterhood was especially active in the distribution of clothes among Sephardic orphans. By 1935, the sisterhoods were cited in the brotherhood's reviews as the solution to the problem of waning interest and activism among brotherhood members.

Two women were particularly vociferous regarding the social status of Judeo-Spanish women. In 1931, Rebecca Nahoum Amateau, niece of the chief rabbi of

This by-law helped to encourage female activism among the younger generation. By 1935, six of the eleven members of the Temporary Executive Committee of Juniors were women: Ester Alaluf, Emily L. Bueno, Fannie Esformes, Pearl Eskenazi, Silvia Florentine, and Eta Matatia. The Junior League was in fact seen as "the nucleus of the future Brotherhood." That same year, Silvia Florentine was appointed by the brotherhood's Central Executive Committee to contribute an article in English for *El Ermanado* on how the brotherhood could assist juniors in organizing themselves. Her words, addressing the older members of the brotherhood, epitomize the distinct gender roles adopted by men and women active in the New York Sephardic community: "Amongst your sons you will find your leaders of tomorrow. Amongst your daughters you will find the helping spirit and cooperation that will make possible the realization of your goal, that will surge forward into different fields—social working, sisterhoods, etc."

The only surviving Ladino organ published outside of New York is *El Mesajero* [The messenger], a monthly Los Angeles bulletin reporting community activities and local and international Jewish news, and published by the publicity committee, composed of Sephardic youths. *El Mesajero* addressed itself to both male and female readers. Like the brotherhood's reviews, the female dimension of *El Mesajero* is generally confined to descriptions of the communal activities of Sephardic women. The Komité de las Damas Auxiliar [Auxiliary committee of women], founded in 1919, was identified by *El Mesajero* as one of the most important Sephardic organizations of Los Angeles. The auxiliary organized "card parties" to benefit the secret fund (a society distributing aid anonymously to needy families), sponsored dances to support Jewish hospitals and impoverished Sephardic communities abroad, raised money to benefit the local Sephardic Talmud Torah, and arranged dinner dances to finance a synagogue building for the Los Angeles Sephardic Hebrew Center. In 1933, efforts to organize the community's Baruch Spinoza Library were directed by Matilda Kadranel, who actively sought donations of literature in Hebrew, English, Judeo-Spanish, Italian, and French.

In contrast to community bulletins, Ladino periodicals are much more comprehensive in their coverage of women, providing abundant information not only on female communal activism but also on women in the labor force. While Sephardic society could be very conservative with respect to married women as wage earners, Ladino tabloids constantly published want ads seeking both male and female workers. Certain occupations consistently distinguished along gender lines,

most notably the position of domestic servant to Sephardi families living in the suburbs or Harlem, who specifically sought "Sefaraditas." The garment industry often specifically solicited girls to operate Singer machines at apron factories or to sew children's clothing, kimonos, lace, curtains, or petticoats. Both boys and girls were invited to apply for positions at electric battery factories. Women were almost never cited as owners of their own businesses. A few exceptions were Turkish midwives, who serviced clients both "uptown" (Harlem) and on the Lower East Side (1915, 1924), and Madame Gilda Malky of the Bronx, who in 1938 advertised herself as a European-style seamstress and importer of ladies' brassieres, and who claimed prior working experience in Salonika and Istanbul. The Ladino press encouraged both men and women to attend classes in Castilian, designed for those interested in employment in businesses dealing with Spanish-speaking countries and for those seeking positions as correspondents and secretaries in export houses. In 1924, *La Vara* announced a public lecture, "Mexico and Its Opportunities," on the commercial and political aspects of Mexico and of the Jews of that country, and specified that women were also invited.

CONCEPTUAL APPROACHES

Issues regarding the position of women in Sephardic society were also addressed in the Ladino press. In April of 1911, Moise Gadol, in his paper *La Amérika*, published a series of articles under the pseudonym "a suffragette." These articles dealt with discrimination against women, in particular, the mistreatment of females in Oriental society, and argued for suffrage and cooperation between men and women to work toward betterment of the female condition in America. Gadol also encouraged his female readers in 1913 to hold a strike protesting horrendous working conditions and low pay. He accomplished this in part by citing the efforts of Ashkenazic women, who, he asserted, succeeded in winning their demands by joining unions. The socialist-oriented newspaper *El Progreso* reported in 1915 that attempts undertaken two years previously to unionize the five thousand Sephardic girls of the Lower East Side had failed, since these "Turkinas" had, in the end, allowed themselves to be intimidated by their bosses and returned to work under the original harsh conditions. In 1917, *La Boz del Pueblo* (the new name of *El Progreso* since December of 1915) published a series of articles urging the emancipation of Sephardic women and launched a campaign for the "awakening of our women from the apathy into which a large part of them has sunk."

Some of the most vitriolic debates concerning Sephardic women occurred in response to reports on the Sephardic immigrant community appearing in the Ashkenazic American press. In 1916, an internal debate among Sephardic male leaders was sparked after the journalist Celia Silbert, a librarian at the Educational Alliance who was prominent in the activities of Sephardi women, published an article on the Oriental Jewess in New York in an issue of the *American Jewish Chronicle*. The controversy, the highlight of Ladino newspapers for several weeks, focused on Silbert's preference for the adjective "Turkish," rather than "Sephardic," to describe her subjects, and on the dismal picture she painted of the backward economic status of Oriental Jewish women.

The short-lived monthly magazine *El Luzero Sefaradí* [The Sephardic beacon], described by its editors as a national and apolitical review of science, art and literature, published an occasional women's page, entitled "Para las Damas" [For ladies]. This column, offering advice to mothers concerning maternal duties and the discipline of children, demonstrates the extreme degree to which Sephardic mothers were seen as the determiners of their children's emotional and physical well-being. "The child's health is in the power of its mother," the magazine cautioned. "It is the mother who should receive all credit if her little ones are healthy, and it is the mother who is to blame, in most cases, if her children fall ill" (1927).

FICTIONAL PORTRAYALS OF WOMEN

The serialized novels of *El Luzero Sefaradí* and Ladino periodicals featured female characters, usually in secondary roles. These works of fiction, while of dubious literary value, suggest the development of a "Cult of Sephardic Womanhood," in which women were often portrayed as insightful, self-sacrificing enablers. Of particular interest is the semiautobiographical novel published by Simon (Shimon) S. Nessim, a community leader who graduated from New York University Law School in 1923 and was admitted to the bar the following year, in *La Luz* (1921). In this novel, a young Sephardic idealist of the Lower East Side falls in love with Roza, a Ladino-speaking immigrant who encourages him to organize Sephardic unions and, ultimately, to pursue his calling as a community activist.

One of the most vibrant and socially revealing portrayals of women appearing in the Ladino press was an advice column written by the Salonikan immigrant Moise Soulam (1890–1967), under the pseudonym of "Tía Satula" [Aunt Satula] or "Bula Satula."

Variably entitled "Palavras de Mujer" [Words of a woman] and "Postemas de Mujer" [Pet peeves of a woman], this column appeared sometimes intermittently in the newspapers *La Amérika*, *El Progreso*, and *La Vara* from 1913 until 1934. Written in a popular Ladino idiom and peppered with humor, ironic proverbs, and slang, this column's stated purpose was "to proffer good morals to the people, and to counsel women to take the right path in this blessed city." The column dealt with issues such as gambling, bargaining in public marketplaces, rowdy social gatherings, and ostentatious dress and makeup. Though the column occasionally expressed nostalgia for the ways in which women celebrated Jewish holidays in Turkey, its primary message was to encourage the Americanization of its female readers and to persuade them to abandon the mores and mentality of the Old Country.

The Sephardic Jews in the United States never numerically rivaled the three million Eastern European Ashkenazim who arrived on American shores from 1881 to 1924, nor did the readership of the Ladino press ever remotely match the quarter of a million plus who subscribed to the Yiddish *Forward* during its peak in the 1920s. Nevertheless, the Judeo-Spanish press of the United States, still largely unexplored, is the most vital and fertile source for the multifaceted history of Sephardic women in early twentieth-century America.

[Note: All transliterations and translations from the Ladino are the author's.]

BIBLIOGRAPHY

Note: All publications are in Judeo-Spanish except where noted.

BULLETINS

El Ermanado 8th Annual Review (1928), 16, 20th anniversary issue (1935), and 17 (1938); *El Mesajero: Buletín Mensual Sefaradí*. Edited by Dr. Robert Benveniste (1933–1934); *The Sephardic Brotherhood of America, Inc.*, 6th Annual Review (1923), 7th Annual Review (1927); *The Sephardic Jewish Brotherhood: 75th Anniversary* (1991, English).

MAGAZINES

El Luzero Sefaradí: Revista Mensuala Ilustrada. Edited by Albert J. Levi and Moise Soulam (September 1926–August 1927).

PERIODICALS

La Amérika. Edited by Moise Gadol (1910–1925); *La Boz del Pueblo/El Progreso/La Époka de Nu York*. Edited by Maurice S. Nessim (1915–1920); *La Luz* (1921–1922); *La Vara*. Edited by Moise Soulam, Albert J. Levi, and Albert J. Torres (1922–1948).

SECONDARY SOURCES

Angel, Marc D. *La America: The Sephardic Experience in the United States* (1982); Ben-Ur, Aviva. "The Judeo-Spanish (Ladino) Press in the United States, 1910–1948." In *Multilingual America: Transnationalism, Ethnicity, and the Languages of American Literature*, edited by Werner Sollors (forthcoming), and "Nuestra Kolonia: A Report on the Sephardic Community of the Lower East Side as Conveyed Through the Judeo-Spanish Press, 1910–1925." Unpublished manuscript written under the direction of Dr. Jane S. Gerber for the Komunidad Project of the Lower East Side Tenement Museum (May 1995); Papo, Joseph M. *Sephardim in Twentieth-Century America: In Search of Unity* (1987).

HOLDINGS OF LADINO BULLETINS, MAGAZINES, AND PERIDIOCALS

El Ermanado 8th Annual Review (1928). Harvard College Library, Judaica Division, and Yeshiva University, Sephardic Reading Room; *El Ermanado* 16, 20th anniversary issue (1935). American Jewish Historical Society, Waltham, Mass., and Hebrew Union College; *El Ermanado* 17 (1938). Harvard College Library, Judaica Division; *El Mesajero*. Ben-Zvi Institute, Jerusalem, Israel, and Brandeis University Library, and American Jewish Periodicals Center, Cincinnati; *The Sephardic Brotherhood of America, Inc.*, 6th Annual Review (1923). Yeshiva University, Sephardic Reading Room; *The Sephardic Brotherhood of America, Inc.*, 7th Annual Review (1927). Harvard College Library, Judaica Division; *The Sephardic Jewish Brotherhood: 75th Anniversary* (1991). Sephardic Jewish Brotherhood, archives, Queens, N.Y.; *El Luzero Sefaradí: Revista Mensuala Ilustrada*. Library of Congress, and Ben-Zvi Institute, Jerusalem, Israel, and Harvard College Library, Judaica Division, and Brandeis University Library, and New York Public Library, and Yeshiva University, Sephardic Reading Room, and Hebrew Union College.

AVIVA BEN-UR

LADINO (JUDEO-SPANISH) THEATER

The Judeo-Spanish theater traces its origins to Turkey and the lands of the Balkans, where women participated as actresses, directors, and playwrights. In the Old Country, female Ladino playwrights were sometimes prolific, though uncommon. Spanish scholar Elena Romero has identified three of these dramatists active in the late nineteenth and early twentieth centuries: Elda Moriano of Salonika, Roza Moïse Gabay of Constantinople, and especially Laura (Bohoreta) Papo of Sarajevo, who wrote numerous dramas and comedies enlivened with *romansas* (traditional Judeo-Spanish ballads) and dances. Mirroring their sisters in the Orient, women in the United States were also active in the Ladino theater as both performers and dramatists. The American Judeo-Spanish press, which appeared almost exclusively in New York from 1910 to 1948, is perhaps the best source for documenting the role of women in the Ladino theater. The press is a rich source for both announcements of upcoming performances and critical reviews, often providing the names of individual actresses, a description of their roles, and a commentary on the quality of their performances. While most of these reports were positive, reviewers exhibited little hesitancy to openly criticize poor acting. Generally, drama groups readily cast females in their productions, although occasionally female roles were interpreted by male actors.

On the Lower East Side, where some twenty thousand Ladino-speaking immigrants resided by the early decades of the twentieth century, Ladino drama troupes, formed by Sephardic drama clubs and political and social organizations, served numerous functions. These groups provided social activities for both performers and audience members, and the resulting production was sometimes followed by a lively ball lasting until the early hours of the morning. Judeo-Spanish performances brought every sector of the community together: men and women, adults and children. They were means through which Sephardim could express political and social activism, since many shows donated their proceeds to local Sephardic clubs, to both local and overseas charities, and to the victims of the two world wars. Performances sometimes attracted huge audiences from one to two thousand people. This figure is particularly outstanding considering that the Judeo-Spanish theater of the United States was by definition communal, and never achieved professional status. (The performances of such troupes as the Association of Sephardic Actors, organized in February of 1917, were of such high quality that an editorial in *La Luz* [The light] of 1922 encouraged the association and other Ladino drama groups to form professional theatrical companies, a suggestion that, regrettably, went unheeded.) Perhaps the most important reason for the vibrancy of the Ladino theater in the *kolonia*, as Sephardic immigrants referred to their community, was that it often combined social idealism with lively entertainment.

The earliest dramas performed in the United States in Judeo-Spanish were most likely Purim plays sponsored by communal organizations. In terms of genre, Judeo-Spanish drama ranged widely, encompassing religious, historical, and original themes. Plays such as the Hebrew drama *Love and War*, also known as *Yehuda Makabi* [Judah the Maccabee], were historical in nature, while works such as *Ataliahu*, also known as *El Koronamiento del Rey Yoash* [The crowning of King Yoash], focused on biblical themes. Several plays were original in theme and composition, such as *Margarita*, a three-act love story written by the founder and editor of the socialist Ladino newspaper *El Progreso* [Progress], Maurice S. Nessim, and serialized in his tabloid in 1915. Based on a selective reading of the Ladino press, perhaps the majority of Judeo-Spanish plays performed in America represent Jewish and non-Jewish dramas translated from other languages into Judeo-Spanish, while a minority of performances are original works composed by Ladino playwrights of the Old Country and the United States. Among the translated dramas performed by Ladino theater groups were European literary classics, such as *Romeo and Juliet* (translated by Alberto Halfón, a former actor in the national theater of Sofia, Bulgaria) and the works of Molière. Ladino scripts, translated from the Hebrew and Yiddish, were available for sale to Ladino societies at the editorial offices of *La Amérika*, and that newspaper actively solicited acquisitions of Judeo-Spanish plays in both published and manuscript form.

One of the earliest American Judeo-Spanish productions was *Ahashverosh i Ester* [Ahasuerus and Esther], staged in the spring of 1911 by La Sosietá Hesed VeEmet de Kastorialís [Charity and Truth Society of Kastoria], an undertaking the Judeo-Spanish tabloid *La Amérika* hailed as "a step of progress [deserving] all support." In 1916, the same play was performed by La Sosietá Ahavat Shalom de Monastir [Love of Peace Society of Monastir], with Miss Adelle Confino starring as Esther. Maurice S. Nessim, reviewing the performance in *El Progreso*, found Miss Confino's acting "admirable" and reported that a professional American actor present in the audience declared that if Miss Confino "practiced the art of acting, she would establish a brilliant career." Nessim cited Miss Adela Farash, who "also played marvelously," but complained that "assigning her two parts was a very bad idea," since "many of the audience members were confused by this."

Romeo i Julieta [Romeo and Juliet], the first New York performance of Shakespeare in Judeo-Spanish, was performed by the Young Men Sephardim [sic] Association in 1916. A drama critic for *El Progreso* commented that Miss Ester Assael was outstanding as Juliet, "especially a few minutes before she imbibed the sleep-inducing drug." The reviewer also cited Regina Taragano and Rica Medini for their "tactful" performances.

The Association of Sephardic Actors staged biblical plays and some original plays written by cast members, such as Eli Mushabak's *The Family at War*, a drama "based on the ideas formulated by the great Karl Marx." Miss Katarina Habib was cited for her acting in a 1916 performance, along with Rashel Tsedaka, for her interpretation of Estreya. In 1915, the play *Ataliahu* was performed before an audience of over eight hundred. It was the fourth drama staged by La Sosietá Hesed VeEmet de Kastorialís, and proceeds were sent to indigent Jews of Kastoria. A review published in *La Amérika* praised Sta. Buena M. Kopio, who played Queen Ataliahu "magnificently," and declared that Sta. Sol Yosef Cohen "distinguished herself no less with her ability in the scene playing the role of [the] High Priest's wife . . . [and] savior of Yoash."

"A sensational success," wrote the Ladino newspaper *La Luz* of the 1922 performance of *Amor i Dezespero* [Love and desperation], or *La Arleziana*. The drama, a love tragedy in five acts, was sponsored by the Sosiedad de Karidad de Ozer Dalim [Charity Society of Aid to the Poor]. The play, followed by a lively ball, drew a thousand audience members, "one of the largest audiences in the history of Sephardim of America." Present were "many prominent Sephardim of our colony," such as R. Haim Nahoum, the former chief rabbi of the Ottoman Empire. "Lusi Betón," wrote the reviewer, "played her role as mother with a delicacy, art and ability that attracted the attention of many." "We should rejoice," continued the critic, "that there exists among us girls of this type." "The innocent Perla Gabay," according to the reviewer, "performed very well . . . [and] despite being of a very tender age . . . demonstrated ability in her role." The performance of *Amor i Dezespero* was followed by a "warm reception" in honor of R. Nahoum, in which he addressed the audience from the stage, "criticizing the Sephardim of New York for the spirit of separatism that reigns among us and calling the people to form a tight unity in order to achieve a central and powerful . . . organization."

Perhaps the most extraordinary example of the female role in the American Judeo-Spanish theater is Esther Cohen, who wrote and performed in her own plays in New Lots, Brooklyn, in the 1930s. Cohen's contributions to Ladino drama are chronicled in the longest-lived Judeo-Spanish newspaper of the United States, *La Vara* [The staff], which appeared in New York from 1922 to 1948. A reviewer for *La Vara*, commenting on both Cohen's performing talents and her abilities as a playwright, proclaimed in a 1938 issue that, "if there exists any dramatic talent in our colony, we may assert that Mrs. Cohen is of first rank."

In the 1930s, one of the overriding concerns of the Sephardic colony was the escalating violence against the European Jewish people by the Nazis and their collaborators. *La Vara*, at the time the Nazis rose to power, was the only surviving Ladino newspaper in the United States, and is thus a major source chronicling the involvement of American Sephardic Jews in Holocaust relief efforts. Esther Cohen's community expressed its distress about Nazi persecution of Jews through a performance in June of 1938, sponsored by a number of New Lots Sephardic organizations to benefit the United Palestine Fund. The play, *Baron Lenzer of Germany*, was based on issues of assimilation within German Jewish society and was directed by Cohen's husband, Victor, and R. Albert Nahoum. Esther Cohen played the role of a servant employed in the house of Baron Lenzer, an assimilated German Jew. In one scene, she recited a dirge bemoaning Nazi brutality and pleading for the repatriation of the Jewish people in the land of Israel. Cohen, who composed the lyrics herself, sang the solo to the tune of "Eili, Eili" and, as *La Vara* reported, "moved the audience intensely." The verses, transliterated and translated from the Ladino, read as follows:

> *Diós de los sielos, arekoje tu puevlo,*
> *Aronjados por los Romanos,*
> *Matados por los Jermanos.*
> *Dámos libertad, dámos un lugar para repozar.*
>
> *Diós de los sielos, estamos mucho sufriendo,*
> *Mándamos un regmidor, mándamos la salvasión.*
> *Dámos libertad, damos un lugar para repozar.*
>
> *Diós de los sielos, perdónamos nuestros yeros.*
> *Mira a tus kreados, arastando i yorando,*
> *Mira a Hitler ke se está vengando,*
> *Dámos libertad, dámos un lugar para repozar.*

> God of the heavens, restore life unto Your people,
> Thrown out by the Romans,
> Murdered by the Germans.
> Grant us liberty, grant us a place of respite.
>
> God of the heavens, we suffer greatly!
> Send us a savior, send us salvation!
> Grant us liberty, grant us a place of respite.
>
> God of the heavens, pardon our errors,
> Look upon Your creatures, wandering and wailing,
> Look upon Hitler, who is wreaking his vengeance.
> Grant us liberty, grant us a place of respite.

After the performance, *El Sapatero* [The shoemaker], a comedy also written by Esther Cohen, was performed by the same actors and actresses. The reviewer in *La Vara* noted that the comedy produced "side-splitting" laughter and provided the names of the performing actresses: Ana Behar, Estela Levi, Victoria Ashkenazi, Esther Mokatíl, Rashel Cohen, Esther Cohen, (Zalma) Esther Victor Cohen, Lili Motal, and Sara Crespi.

Though the Judeo-Spanish theater died out as Sephardim began to leave the city and as their language fell into desuetude among the younger generation, vestiges continued. The Sisterhood of Congregation Or VeShalom of Atlanta, Georgia, staged many productions between 1958 and 1973. Though most of these productions were in English, the dialogue and song lyrics were peppered with Judeo-Spanish, Turkish, and Greek. The casts of these semiprofessional shows numbered from thirty to forty actors and actresses, and performances lasted two hours. Representative of the influence Judeo-Spanish language and culture exerted on these plays is the 1960 production *My Fair Mujer*, a spoof on *My Fair Lady*.

Recently, the American Ladino theater has been resurrected in New York by The Ladino Players, an amateur troupe founded in 1994, whose cast is roughly half female. These cast members are of both Ashkenazic and Sephardic (Ladino and non-Ladino) background. Their first production, *Ester A-Malká* [Queen Esther], a Purim play written by the Turkish-Israeli playwright Nissim Danon, was performed twice in the spring of 1995. Their second production, staged during the spring and summer of 1996, was *Merekiyas de Orchard Street* [Orchard Street blues], an original play written and directed by the theater group's founder and director, Professor David Fintz Altabé. The play, set in 1922 on New York's Lower East Side, focuses on the friendship between a melancholy Sephardic widow and her witty Ashkenazic neighbor, and deals with many historical themes including the immigrant experience of Ladino-speaking Jews and the tensions between old and new ideals of courtship and marriage.

Recently, The Ladino Players have increasingly come under the organizational efforts of women. In 1996, the theater group elected Izmir-born Daisy Sadaka Braverman as its director and Egyptian-born Esther (Cazés) Daiell as its president. In the spring of 1997, they performed their third production, *Forsyth Street*, a drama written by David F. Altabe and edited by Daisy Sadaka Braverman. The Ladino Players have received coverage in the New York Jewish press and represent the only Judeo-Spanish theater group in the

United States. This contemporary Ladino theater group, in contrast to its early twentieth-century New York predecessors, seeks to celebrate and revive the Judeo-Spanish heritage, culture, and language.

The role of women in the Ladino theater is an eloquent testimony to the ways in which they have contributed to their communities, responded to national crises, and lent their energies to the continuation of the Judeo-Spanish cultural and linguistic heritage.

[Note: All transliterations and translations from the Ladino are the author's.]

BIBLIOGRAPHY

PERIODICALS

La Amérika. Edited by Moise Gadol (1910–1925); *La Boz del Pueblo/El Progreso/La Époka de Nu York.* Edited by Maurice S. Nessim (1915–1920); *La Luz* (1921–1922); *La Vara.* Edited by Moise Soulam, Albert J. Levi, and Albert J. Torres (1922–1948).

SECONDARY SOURCES

Angel, Marc D. "The Sephardic Theater of Seattle," *American Jewish Archives* 25, no. 2 (November 1973): 156–161; Ben-Ur, Aviva. "The Judeo-Spanish Theater of the Lower East Side." In "Nuestra Kolonia: A Report on the Sephardic Community of the Lower East Side as Conveyed Through the Judeo-Spanish Press, 1910–1925," pp. 136–141. Unpublished manuscript written under the direction of Dr. Jane S. Gerber for the Komunidad Project of the Lower East Side Tenement Museum (May 1995); Maslia, Lenore. "Or VeShalom Was Just 'Off Broadway.'" In *Sephardim and a History of Congregation Or VeShalom.* edited by Sol Beton (1981): 174–177; Papo, Joseph M. *Sephardim in Twentieth-Century America: In Search of Unity* (1987); Romero, Elena. *La Creación Literaria en Lengua Sefardí* (1992), and *Repertorio de Noticias Sobre el Mundo Teatral de los Sefardíes Orientales* (1983).

HOLDINGS OF LADINO TABLOIDS

La Amérika. Ben-Zvi Institute, Jerusalem, Israel, and Hebrew University, Jewish National and University Library, and Harvard College Library, Judaica Division, and Brandeis University Library, and American Jewish Historical Society, Waltham, Mass., and New York Public Library, Judaica Room, and American Jewish Archives; *La Boz del Pueblo.* Library of Congress, and Brandeis University Library, and New York Public Library, Judaica Room; *La Luz.* Library of Congress, and Ben-Zvi Institute, and Brandeis University Library, and New York Public Library, Judaica Room; *La Vara.* Library of Congress, and Hebrew University, Jewish National and University Library, and Harvard College Library, Judaica Division, and Brandeis University Library, and American Jewish Historical Society, and New York Public Library, Judaica Room, and Yeshiva University, Sephardic Reading Room, and American Jewish Periodicals Center, Cincinnati.

AVIVA BEN-UR

LANDAU, SARA (1890–1986)

"I'm determined to amount to more than one row of pins some day," Sara Landau wrote in her diary in 1912, and by the time she died three-quarters of a century later, she had indeed earned a reputation as a talented economist, a devoted teacher, and a tireless community activist.

Sara Landau was born in Philadelphia, Pennsylvania, on November 4, 1890, to Morris (Fred) and Frieda (Shapiro) Landau, who had married in Poland before coming to America in the early 1880s. Sara was the first surviving child of the Landaus, who later had two other daughters, Minnie and Mathilda. She spent part of her early life in Louisiana, graduating from high school in Crowley in 1906, attending Southwest Industrial Institute in Lafayette, and teaching business courses for several years. Around 1914, she and her family moved to Louisville, Kentucky, where her father operated a boys' clothing factory until the Depression of the 1930s.

In Kentucky, Landau continued her formal education. She graduated from the Bowling Green Business University in 1916 and, after interrupting her studies to serve as a Red Cross volunteer in France in 1918–1919, she earned a bachelor's degree from the University of Louisville in 1920 and a master's degree in economics from the same institution in 1921. While still a student, she began teaching at the University of Louisville, and continued on the faculty after earning her master's degree, taking a leave from 1924 to 1926 to pursue doctoral work at the University of Pennsylvania, although she never completed her Ph.D. She was promoted from instructor to assistant professor at the University of Louisville in 1926 and to associate professor in 1927. She also served as the assistant dean of women at the university. In 1928, she resigned from the university in protest against the actions of university president George Colvin, which were perceived by many as anti-Semitic and which prompted the departure of history professor Louis Gottschalk. Throughout the 1920s, Landau was also active in community affairs. She taught English and citizenship to newcomers, worked with young women at the Louisville YMHA, and met immigrants at the New York docks on behalf of the NATIONAL COUNCIL OF JEWISH WOMEN.

After leaving Louisville, Laudau became a teaching fellow at the University of Chicago, and then headed the department of economics and sociology at Wheaton College in Massachusetts. In 1931, she returned to Louisville, where she managed some of her family's affairs, held several government jobs, and again became active in several service organizations. At a time when only about one in five college teachers was a woman, Landau's achievements as a university professor and community volunteer led to her inclusion in *Who's Who in American Jewry* in both 1928 and 1938.

During World War II, Landau held research positions with various government agencies in Washington, D.C., and a number of college teaching posts in Louisiana, Alabama, North Carolina, and Massachusetts. In 1946, she joined the faculty of the newly established Roosevelt University in Chicago, where she remained until 1954. After her retirement, she returned to Louisville for good, although she did accept invitations to offer courses at Berea College in the mountains of eastern Kentucky.

Even in retirement, Landau was a civic activist and a prolific writer. At age eighty-five, she became president of the Women's Overseas Service League, an organization of World War I volunteers. Throughout her life, she wrote articles, book reviews, plays, and hundreds of letters, many to political figures. She also produced a primer on economics for women, which she attempted on several occasions to publish. She traveled widely, visiting Japan, Holland, and Iceland as early as 1913, and embarking on a year-long world tour by freighter and steamer in 1960.

In 1980, she received the Louisville Jewish Community Center's prestigious Ottenheimer Award, a prize named for its donor, Blanche B. Ottenheimer (one of Landau's mentors), and bestowed annually for contributions in the field of human relations. Sara Landau died in Louisville on September 17, 1986, survived by her sister Mathilda. Landau represented a whole category of economically independent middle-class Jewish women in twentieth-century America who both developed their own careers and devoted their energy to volunteer efforts, especially on behalf of their fellow Jews.

BIBLIOGRAPHY

Landau, Herman. *Adath Louisville: The Story of a Jewish Community* (1981); Landau, Sara. Papers. University of Louisville Archives; Schiavone, Colleen, et al. *Sara Landau Papers* (1991); *WWIAJ* (1928, 1938).

LEE SHAI WEISSBACH

LANDERS, ANN (ESTHER PAULINE FRIEDMAN LEDERER) (b. 1918)

In the past forty years, the Ann Landers advice column has helped lovelorn teens, confused parents, couples on the brink of divorce, grieving widows, and a myriad of others who are in need of counsel. Translated into over twenty languages, Esther Pauline

Friedman Lederer, known professionally as Ann Landers, reaches millions of readers with her clear, witty, and sometimes sarcastic column.

Her parents, Abraham and Rebecca Friedman, were Russian Jewish immigrants who arrived in the United States in 1908. They moved to Sioux City, Iowa, in 1910, where two daughters, Helen and Dorothy, were born. Like many Russian Jewish immigrants of that time, the family slowly earned enough money to leave the poorer section of the city, first by peddling chickens from a pushcart and then, by 1911, by amassing enough earnings to buy into a grocery store. When Esther Pauline was born on July 4, 1918,

One of the most popular columnists of all time, Ann Landers reaches millions of readers with her clear, witty, and sometimes sarcastic column. Those who believe that genes determine everything will find confirmation in the fact that her twin, ABIGAIL VAN BUREN, *is also an enormously successful advice columnist. [UPI/CORBIS-BETMANN]*

her parents owned a small house in Sioux City. When she was in her early teens, her father became part owner of a movie and vaudeville theater. Active in the Jewish community of Sioux City, Abraham Friedman's civic stature grew as he acquired other theaters and diversified his business interests.

Nicknamed "Eppie," Esther Pauline was born only seventeen minutes apart from her twin, Pauline Esther (later known as columnist ABIGAIL VAN BUREN). The two girls experienced many important events simultaneously, participated in similar activities, and shared the same interests. The twins attended Central High (during their four years there they were refused admission to an all-girls club because of their religion), graduated in 1936, and matriculated at a small college nearby. After her twin became engaged to Mort Phillips, Esther Pauline met her future husband, Jules Lederer. She and her sister had a double wedding in their Sioux City synagogue on July 2, 1938. The Lederers had one daughter, Margo, and were divorced in 1975. Ann Landers made her impending divorce public to her readership on what would have been her thirty-sixth wedding anniversary.

Because Jules Lederer was a salesman, the family traveled a great deal. They lived in New Orleans until Lederer was offered a job in Eau Claire, Wisconsin. There, Esther Lederer became active in politics, serving as Democratic Party county chair. After moving to Chicago, she contacted family friend Wilbur Munnecke, the executive and business manager of Field Enterprises, in order to inquire whether *Sun Times* columnist Ann Landers needed any assistance. Fortuitously, the *Sun Times* was in the process of searching for Ann Landers's replacement. Esther Lederer offered the *Sun Times* a unique departure from its traditional advice column. Because of her extensive political and volunteer contacts, she was able to request advice from experts in all fields, to which she then referred in her responses. When she became the new Ann Landers, the column had already been in existence for twelve years.

As Ann Landers, Esther Lederer acted as both counsel and advocate for her readership. Openly opposing racism and anti-Semitism, she devoted many columns to fighting injustices in urban, rural, and national settings. Liberal in her politics but conservative in her morality, Lederer's understanding of the public and private roles of women changed over time. While in the 1950s she encouraged women to stay at home and to accept, if necessary, their husbands' infidelities, by the 1970s she was urging women to find worthwhile occupations and was a champion of liberalized abortion laws.

Three months after Lederer assumed her position at the *Sun Times*, her twin began her own advice column, "Dear Abby." While the sisters attempted to curb any acrimony between them, their competition intensified after Esther Lederer signed a one-year contract with the *Sun Times* and appeared on *What's My Line?* In 1956, her sister allegedly offered "Dear Abby" at a reduced rate to the *Sioux City Journal*, as long as it promised not to run "Ann Landers." *Life* magazine informed the public of their acrimony in April 1958. While the sisters publicly reconciled in 1964, their competition continued.

By 1959, "Ann Landers" had already received 1,004 speaking invitations and made 101 appearances in 30 cities, and had visited China. Active in national and local causes, such as the Christmas Seal Campaign of which she was national chair in 1963, Esther Lederer championed the rights of children and women. Because of her professional and volunteer work, and her diverse and loyal readership, she succeeded in publicizing issues that were of concern both to Jewish and non-Jewish women.

BIBLIOGRAPHY

Astor, David. "Ann Landers Departs the Just Sold NAS." *Editor and Publisher. The Fourth Estate* 120 (February 1987): 53+; Drevets, Tricia. "Ann Landers Discusses Her Long Career." *Editor and Publisher. The Fourth Estate* 119 (April 1986): 144+; *EJ*; Hays, Charlotte. "The Evolution of Ann Landers: From Prime to Progressive." *Public Opinion* (December/January 1984): 11–13; McNulty, Henry. "Dear Ann Landers, How You've Changed." *The Quill* 74 (November 1986): 22–23; Pottker, Jan, and Bob Speziale. *Dear Ann, Dear Abby: The Unauthorized Biography of Ann Landers and Abigail Van Buren* (1987); "Queen of Hearts." *Psychology Today* 26 (May/June 1993): 56–60+; Rottenberg, Dan. "Ann and Abby's Lessons for Journalists." *The Quill* 72 (January 1984): 20–24; Sackett, Victoria A. "Everyday Ethics and Ann Landers." *Public Opinion* 9 (November/December 1986): 9; Stein, M.L. "Controversy in California." *Editor and Publisher. The Fourth Estate* 119 (April 1986): 68–69.

ROBIN JUDD

LANDES, RUTH SCHLOSSBERG (1908–1991)

Ruth (Schlossberg) Landes, a social and cultural anthropologist, was born in New York City in 1908 to Joseph and Anna (Grossman) Schlossberg. Her father had emigrated from Russia to the United States as an adolescent. A self-educated man, he was the cofounder and long-term secretary-general of the union of Amalgamated Clothing Workers of America. Her mother was born in Ukraine, educated in Berlin, and immigrated to New York City as a young adult.

In 1928, Ruth received her B.C. from New York University and a master's degree in social work from the same institution a year later. Her 1929 marriage ended shortly thereafter when she chose a career that her husband, a medical student, opposed. She still kept his name, Landes.

Landes belongs to the first generation of professional American female anthropologists. In 1935, she earned a Ph.D. in anthropology from Columbia University. Her dissertation research was based on fieldwork she conducted in 1933 among the Ojibwa of Ontario, Canada. It resulted in five published monographs, including *Ojibwa Sociology* (1937) and *The Ojibwa Woman* (1938). Landes's primary interests in anthropology continued to be the social life and religion of the Ojibwa, the Potawatomi, and the Sioux.

Landes's professional career actually began with the Harlem project, a study of the Garvey Movement as it led to the founding of the black Jews (1929–1932). The story was published as "Negro Jews in Harlem" (1967), but the original manuscript was lost in a book burning in Nazi Germany. (The anthropologist Franz Boas had sent it in 1934 to Richard Thurnwals, the Africanist editor of *Sociologus*.) Landes's continued interest in race relations brought her to conduct research among blacks in the United States, Brazil, and the United Kingdom. She is also known for her pioneer work in the anthropology of women, the anthropology of education, and the interrelations of culture and personality. On focusing on women as one of her chief areas of research, she commented, "For me, the separate treatments of women were the accident of special materials about them that were previously neglected in the literature, and still are."

Landes's academic career was thwarted for more than two decades by a joint letter from the psychological anthropologist Arthur Ramos and the anthropologist Mellville Herskovitz to Gunnar Myrdal, for whom Landes worked in 1939. In the letter, they allegedly slandered her method of fieldwork she conducted in Brazil. As a result, Landes was unable to get any permanent academic position until 1965, when she was offered one at McMaster University, in Hamilton, Ontario, Canada. She continued her association with McMaster University as professor emerita until her death, in 1991.

During World War II, President Roosevelt appointed Landes research director and coordinator of the Inter-American and the President's Fair Employment Practices Commission in Washington (1941–1945). She also served as the study director of the scientific research department of the American Jewish Committee (1948–1951) and director of the Los Angeles City Health Department's geriatric program (1958–1959). From 1953 to 1955, Landes lectured at the New School for Social Research and the William A. White Psychiatric Institute in New York. She also held temporary and summer appointments at Brooklyn College, Fiske University, Claremont University, Los Angeles State, and Tulane University.

Ruth Schlossberg Landes died in 1991.

SELECTED WORKS BY RUTH SCHLOSSBERG LANDES

The City of Women (1947); *Culture in American Education* (1965); "Hypothesis Concerning the Eastern European Jewish Family," with M. Zobrowski. *Psychiatry* 13 (1950): 447–464; "Negro Jews in Harlem." *Jewish Journal of Sociology* 9, no. 2 (1967): 175+; *Ojibwa Sociology* (1937); *The Ojibwa Woman* (1938); "Women Anthropologists in Brazil." In *Women in the Field*, edited by Peggy Goldie (1970).

BIBLIOGRAPHY

EJ; Park, George, and Alice Park. "Ruth Schlossberg Landes." In *Women Anthropologists: Selected Biographies*, edited by Gacs Ute, Aisha Khan, Jerrie McIntrye, and Ruth Weinberg (1989).

SHIFRA EPSTEIN

LANDY, RAE D. (1885–1952)

During a 1937 commemorative broadcast on NBC radio marking the twenty-fifth anniversary of HADASSAH, the Women's Zionist Organization of America, Army Nurse Corps Lieutenant Rae D. Landy spoke to First Lady Eleanor Roosevelt at the White House in a transoceanic hookup. Landy recalled her formative role in establishing Hadassah's first district nursing service for the benefit of Jewish immigrants in Palestine in 1913. This pioneering venture had ignited Landy's interest in public health nursing, administration, and national service, areas she would pursue throughout her career.

Born in Lithuania on June 27, 1885, Rachael (later shortened to Rae) Landy was one of seven children in the family of Rabbi Jacob and Eva (Gross) Landy. The family immigrated to the United States and settled in Cleveland, Ohio, in 1888. Rae had three sisters—Lena, Mae, and Bessie—and three brothers—Reuben, Harry S., and Louis A. Landy's parents helped to found the Hebrew Orthodox Old Age Home in Cleveland.

Landy graduated in the first class of nursing students (1904) sponsored by the Jewish Women's

Hospital Association (later Mount Sinai Hospital) in Cleveland. In 1911, she became an assistant superintendent at Harlem Hospital in New York City. Recruited by Hadassah founder HENRIETTA SZOLD, Landy and ROSE KAPLAN traveled to Palestine in February 1913 to start a district visiting-nurse program among destitute immigrants, many of whom suffered from malaria, typhoid, and dysentery. The two Americans expanded the child and maternal health services begun by Eva Leon, utilizing the services of a university-trained physician and three experienced midwives. Landy initiated a program to combat trachoma, a common eye disease among children. From their home of two rented rooms at the edge of the Old City of Jerusalem, Landy and Kaplan launched a clinic and a nurses' settlement house where young girls received training in nursing, first aid, and hygiene. Landy remained with the project for two and a half years before returning home when Hadassah activities were suspended during World War I.

In 1918, she entered the United States Army Nursing Corps. She served overseas with the American Expeditionary Forces in Germany, Belgium, and France, and in the Philippines during the 1930s. She was on duty at the White House when President Calvin Coolidge's son, Calvin Jr., died there on July 7, 1924. Promoted to captain in 1940, Landy became assistant superintendent at the headquarters of the Second Corps Area at Governors Island in New York. Named chief of nurses at Crile General Hospital in Cleveland in 1944, she retired with the rank of lieutenant colonel, the second highest rank in the Army Nursing Corps. Until her death on March 5, 1952, she worked with the Cleveland Red Cross and recruited nurses for Mount Sinai Hospital. She was buried in Arlington National Cemetery in Washington, D.C.

Within the context of the local, national, and international Jewish community, Landy trained for a profession, developed leadership skills, and dedicated her services to the nursing field. While her role as a pioneering Hadassah nurse is notable in Jewish history, her military career also demonstrates how women in the first half of the twentieth century were able to pursue a career, assume positions of leadership, and create new opportunities for themselves.

BIBLIOGRAPHY

AJYB 33 (1932): 180–184, and 54:540; Arthur, Julietta K. "Child Welfare in the Holy Land." *American Journal of Nursing* 40 (1940): 410–414; Benson, Evelyn R. "Hadassah and the Nursing Connection: Early Days." *American Association for the History of Nursing Bulletin* 26 (Spring 1990): 4–6; *Cleveland Press*, March 7, 1952; Kaplan, Rose. "Letters from Missionary Nurses, II." Proceedings of the 17th Annual Conference of the ANA, St. Louis, Missouri, April 23–29, 1914. *American Journal of Nursing* 14 (1914): 870–872; J.D. Deutsch Funeral Home. Records, MS 4339. Western Reserve Historical Society, Cleveland, Ohio; *Jewish Observer* (Cleveland), July 28, 1916, 21, 23, 5:1, and September 15, 1916, 22, 5, 6:3; *Jewish Review and Observer* (Cleveland), March 14, 1952, 78, 11, 6:5; "News About Nursing: Nursing and the National Defense Program." *American Journal of Nursing* 41 (1941): 223–224; *NYTimes*, February 26, 1937, 16:4; Obituary. *NYTimes*, March 7, 1952, 23:4; Seligsberg, Alice L. "A Modern Training School for Nurses in Jerusalem." *American Journal of Nursing* 21 (1921): 721–723; Van Tassel, D., and J. Grabowski, eds. *Encyclopedia of Cleveland History* (1987).

BETH DiNATALE JOHNSON

LANG, LUCY FOX ROBINS
(1884–1962)

A committed anarchist by age fifteen, Lucy Fox Robins Lang participated actively in the labor and free speech movements of early twentieth-century America. She directed regional and national committees in support of persecuted anarchists, antiwar activists, and labor organizers, while earning her livelihood as a printer, waitress, vegetarian restaurant owner, and real estate broker. Eventually, she moved into the mainstream of the labor movement, becoming an adviser to and confidante of Samuel Gompers, president of the American Federation of Labor (AFL). Although her focus shifted, the impulse behind Lang's work remained constant. She credited her activism to the legacy of her paternal grandfather, Reb Chaim "the Hospitable," who helped members of the Jewish community in Kiev, Russia, deal with personal difficulties and conflicts with the authorities.

The eldest child of Moshe and Surtze Broche Fox, Lucy was born on March 30, 1884, in Kiev, Russia. She grew up in the nearby town of Korostyshev, in a household and a community governed by Jewish tradition. Her family immigrated to the United States when Lucy was nine, settling briefly in New York's Lower East Side and then in Chicago with relatives. A silversmith by trade, Moshe Fox found work applying gold leaf to picture frames. Lucy worked in a cigar factory and, as the eldest child, helped to care for her sister and three brothers. At night, she took English and citizenship courses at Chicago's Hull House, a settlement house.

When Hull House founder Jane Addams asked Lucy to assist a dancing instructor, a crisis erupted in the family. She asked Jane Addams to visit her home to persuade her parents to allow her to participate in the interreligious and coeducational dance class. Lucy was dazzled by what she called Addams's "bright vision of freedom" and soon moved on to even more daring ventures.

Late nineteenth-century Chicago seethed with left-wing political activities, and Lucy was drawn to the most radical group, the anarchists. She began attending lectures, reading political literature, and participating in meetings and demonstrations. Never an advocate of anarchism's direct-action wing, she favored practical and results-oriented political activism to achieve anarchism's aim of maximum freedom for every individual. While still a teenager, she met fellow anarchist Bob Robins and married him in 1904. Adopting the anarchist view that love alone should govern a marriage, Lucy insisted that they sign a legal document limiting the union to five years, allowing her to continue her political activities, requiring the sharing of all household tasks, and stipulating that there would be no children. The couple did separate as specified by their contract, but soon reunited and remained married for twenty years.

The couple moved to New York City, where Lucy met EMMA GOLDMAN and was drawn to her interpretation of anarchism. Goldman's emphasis on the contributions that women could make to social and political causes and her ability to function outside the confines of the immigrant community appealed to Lucy. She began to provide various anonymous and unpaid services to the frequently arrested Goldman and to many other well-known political activists. She arranged speaking tours, rented halls, raised bail money, and directed defense committees to raise public awareness of the activists' beliefs. Due in part to her efforts, two legal cases involving labor leaders gained national attention: that of James and John McNamara, charged with dynamiting the Los Angeles Times building, and that of Tom Mooney, a California AFL leader falsely accused of bombing a parade held to support military preparations for World War I.

For more than a decade, the Robinses moved around the country in order to carry out their political activities. Some of their travels were in a mobile home they called the Adventurer, designed and driven by the mechanically inclined Lucy. An insulated room atop a car chassis, the Adventurer featured running water, bookcases, a birdcage, an aquarium, and a printing press that enabled the couple to print pamphlets and earn money as they traveled.

In 1918, while in Washington, D.C., to urge government officials to grant a new trial in the Mooney case, Lucy met labor leader Samuel Gompers. The brash and articulate woman criticized Gompers for not acting in support of Mooney. When Gompers produced evidence of his behind-the-scenes negotiations with authorities on Mooney's behalf, Lucy realized that pressure from outside the system was not the only way to solve labor conflicts. She became a lifelong partisan of Gompers and his organization, the AFL.

Lucy called Gompers a "philosophical anarchist," whose outrage at oppression sprang from his Jewish heritage, as did her own. Their common Jewish background forged a strong bond beween the two activists. Through Lucy, Gompers gained access to the left wing of the labor movement, including many radical Jewish labor leaders who had openly disdained Gompers's apolitical unionism. Lucy, in turn, acquired influence among major labor and government figures. On three occasions, she addressed the AFL's annual convention, one of very few women to do so.

In 1919, she became executive secretary and organizer of the Central Labor Bodies Conference for the Release of Political Prisoners and the Repeal of War-Time Laws. This group spearheaded a national labor campaign to obtain amnesty for thousands of World War I political prisoners, including conscientious objectors, court-martialed soldiers, and those, such as socialist Eugene Debs, jailed for speaking out against the war. Her book *War Shadows* (1922) documents the successful amnesty campaign.

Later, she became an unpaid, informal assistant to Gompers, and served as executive secretary of the first campaign undertaken jointly by the long-feuding AFL and Socialist Party, raising funds to resist the rise of German fascism. After Gompers's death, she remained a consultant to the AFL, but at a reduced level of influence due to the increasingly bureaucratic structure of the organization and a less personal relationship with the new president, William Green.

As Lucy became more closely aligned with the AFL, her husband and others with whom she had worked moved in the opposite direction, rejecting anarchism for the communism of the new Soviet Union. The Robinses separated over their political differences and divorced in the mid-1920s. Soon after, she married Harry Lang, a long-time acquaintance and labor editor of the *Jewish Daily Forward*.

Between 1928 and 1937, the Langs made three trips abroad: to Europe, the Soviet Union, and the Middle East. In Palestine, Lang's interest in Zionism was stimulated by the efforts of organized labor, women, and young people in national development. Around 1939, she headed a group raising funds to establish Kfar Blum, a cooperative in Palestine for German and Austrian refugees. She continued to conceive of new projects, such as a labor-managed medical center to study, prevent, and cure occupational diseases; but this venture was halted by United States entry into World War II.

Despite her refusal to be a paid employee of any political or labor organization and, like many female activists, often working far from the limelight, Lang made significant contributions to American political and labor history. She kept public attention focused on the legal battles of anarchists and labor leaders, and skillfully bridged party affiliations that divided the labor movement. She described herself as motivated more by the plight of individual victims of injustice than by ideology. Yet she never repudiated her anarchist past; in later years, she still called herself a radical idealist and continued to endorse what she considered the fundamental principle of anarchism—respect for the individual.

In the mid-1940s, Lang settled down for the first time when she and her husband purchased a house in Croton, New York. Here, she worked on her autobiography, *Tomorrow Is Beautiful* (1948). The Langs later moved to Los Angeles, where Lucy Fox Robins Lang died on January 25, 1962.

SELECTED WORKS BY LUCY FOX ROBINS LANG

Tomorrow Is Beautiful (1948); *War Shadows* (1922).

BIBLIOGRAPHY

Avrich, Paul. *Anarchist Portraits* (1988); *DAB* 7; Gentry, Curt. *Frame-Up: The Incredible Case of Tom Mooney and Warren Billings* (1967); Goldman, Emma. *Living My Life* (1931); Gompers, Samuel. *Seventy Years of Life and Labor: An Autobiography* (1925); Kenneally, James J. *Women and American Trade Unions* (1978); Mandel, Bernard. *Samuel Gompers: A Biography* (1963); Marcus, Jacob R. *The American Jewish Woman, 1654–1980* (1981); Obituary. *NYTimes*, January 26, 1962, 31:2; Szajkowski, Zosa. *Jews, Wars, and Communism* (1972).

LINN SHAPIRO

LANG, PEARL (b. 1921)

In the world of modern dance, Pearl Lang holds two distinctions. As one of Martha Graham's most expressive soloists, she was the first dancer to perform some of Graham's own roles. As the "poetess of the diaspora and the Holocaust," Lang was also a choreographer and performer passionately attached to her Jewish heritage.

She was born Pearl Lack, the daughter of Freida (Feder) and Jacob Lack, on May 29, 1921, in Chicago.

Both her parents were Russian Jews, her mother having been born in Pinsk and her father near Vilna. Her father, a tailor, died when she was seven years old. Lang had one brother, who later became a doctor.

In Pearl's socialist, working-class family, music, theater, and poetry were integral to the daily routine. Her father played piano, her mother wrote poetry, and both actively participated in Chicago's Jewish cultural societies. Yiddish was the first language in the household. Pearl would be powerfully influenced not only by her family's Jewish heritage but also by the cultural riches of Chicago. She learned English with

A choreographer and performer passionately attached to her Jewish heritage, Pearl Lang was one of Martha Graham's most expressive soloists. [Pearl Lang]

her mother at night school and at Hibbard Elementary School, which offered classes integrating art, literature, history, and geography. Not surprisingly, her own interest in artistic activities began early. Freida Lack took her children to operas such as *Hansel and Gretel* and *A Midsummer Night's Dream*, to the Chicago Symphony's children's concerts, and to modern dance performances.

If there was a defining moment in Pearl's life, it would have occurred during a performance by the Duncan Dancers, the adopted daughters of Isadora Duncan, which took place at Chicago's Orchestra Hall. Three-year-old Pearl watched as one of the Duncan dancers, dancing to a Russian song, skipped from the back of the stage to the front, opening her arms and appearing to fill the theater with a cascade of light. At that point, Pearl states that she recognized the dancer's rebellious and independent spirit as her own.

At age ten, she choreographed her first dance—about the flooding of the Nile River—for one of her classes. After-school and weekend classes at the Workmen's Circle, a Yiddish school, provided her with additional drama, dance, and music instruction. When she was sixteen, she made her public debut at a Chicago opera house, choreographing and performing a group dance with fellow students to the first movement of Mozart's *Eine Kleine Nachtmusik*.

In high school, while studying with Frances Allis, she started her own dance company. She performed a solo work for the Chicago choreographer Ruth Page as part of the Work Projects Administration program and watched performances by the prominent modern dancers of the time: Martha Graham, Hanya Holm, Doris Humphrey, Harald Kreutzberg, and Charles Weidman. In the summer of 1941, she convinced her mother to let her study with Martha Graham. She went to New York, and within a few months she became a member of Graham's famous company. In her first performance with the company, she danced in *Letter to the World*, based on the poetry of Emily Dickinson. In the same year, she performed a solo and a duet with Erick Hawkins in the premiere of *Punch and Judy*. Soon after, she danced in the Graham classic *Deaths and Entrances*, about the Brontë sisters, and in *Appalachian Spring*. It was also during this time that her last name was changed. Graham and the influential dance critic John Martin felt the young dancer needed a more appropriate stage name. Over her objections, Pearl Lack became Pearl Lang.

To support herself in New York, she performed in Broadway musicals, including *Carousel* and *Finian's Rainbow*, as well as in plays by Kurt Weill and S.J. Perelman. She also played Solveig opposite John Garfield in *Peer Gynt*, directed by Lee Strasberg. To Lang, these were merely jobs; her artistic self belonged to the Martha Graham Company, with whom she performed off and on from 1941 to 1978. She eventually took over many of Graham's leading roles—in *Primitive Mysteries*, *El Penitente*, *Letter to the World*, *Herodiade*, *Night Journey*, *Clytemnestra*, and *Appalachian Spring*—making a name for herself as the premier interpreter of the great artist's work.

In 1953, Lang formed her own company. Martha Graham encouraged her new venture and gave her money to hire a composer when she decided to choreograph the famous Jewish play *The Dybbuk*. The first piece that Lang choreographed for her new troupe was a duet for two women called *Song of Deborah*. She later revised the work and presented it with the New York Philharmonic in 1956 as part of the annual Israel Bonds Hanukkah Festivals, an event she choreographed for and performed in for five years.

Lang's choreography has been praised for its drama and poetry. Its "ecstatic" style of movement and ability to portray passionate feeling are striking. Lang claims that her work comes from a "hasidic" impulse: "Through ecstatic dance, one is lifted nearer to God."

As a performer, Lang has been described as a dancer of "speed and ecstasy" and one of the most lyrical performers in American dance. "Grace and strength are united in her natural dynamic," declared the *New York Times*. A review in the *Village Voice* called Lang "one of the few dancers it is safe to call great." Lily Rosen in *Dance News* and the *Jewish Journal* stated, "The choreography of Lang never fails to touch secret places in our hearts."

Lang has choreographed fifty works. More than half have Jewish themes, ten of which are set to Sephardi songs and prayers with Spanish, Greek, and Moroccan influences. Key works include *The Dybbuk* [Possessed], based on the Yiddish play by Ansky; *I Never Saw Another Butterfly*, based on poems written by children who died at Theresienstadt and on biblical songs, *Tongues of Fire*, inspired by prophetic writing; and three programs of dances based on Yiddish poetry. Moved by the suffering of Jews during World War II, Lang choreographed *And Again a Beginning*, *Kaddish* and *Two Poems of the Holocaust*.

Shira [Song], set to the music of Alan Hovhaness, is Lang's signature piece. It embodies the hasidic parable that inspires the artist. The parable, attributed to Rabbi Nachman of Bratzlav, reads: "At the end of the world stands a high mountain, and from it flows a spring. At the opposite end is the heart of the world. The heart of the world keeps the spring ever in sight.

If, for one moment, it loses sight of the spring, it loses, in the same moment, its life."

Lang remains a busy choreographer and teacher. Dance companies that commission her work include the Netherlands National Ballet, the Batsheva Dance Company of Israel, the Repertory Dance Theater of Utah, and the Boston Ballet. She has choreographed dances for theatrical productions, including *Oedipus Rex* with Seiji Ozawa and the Boston Symphony, and plays at the Shakespeare Festival and the Yale Repertory Theater. Lang also has instructed directors and actors at Yale University and performers at the Juilliard School.

While codirecting a version of *The Dybbuk* for the Canadian Broadcasting Company, she met her future husband, actor Joseph Wiseman. They married in 1964. Both Lang and Wiseman are well-known performers of Yiddish poetry.

Her long list of honors includes two Guggenheim Fellowships, the Martha Graham Award for Performance and Choreography, and six awards from the Jewish community, including the Workmen's Circle Award (an achievement award from Artists and Writers for Peace in the Middle East) and the National Foundation for Jewish Culture Annual Cultural Achievement Award for 1992. In May 1995, she received an honorary Doctor of Fine Arts degree from the Juilliard School. Lang continues to teach modern dance technique and choreography in New York.

BIBLIOGRAPHY

de Mille, Agnes. *The Life and of Work of Martha Graham* (1956); Stodelle, Ernestine. *Deep Song: The Dance Story of Martha Graham* (1984); Tobias, Tobi. Interview with Pearl Lang. Dance Collection Oral History Project, New York Public Library, 1975 and 1979.

JOAN TIMMIS STRASBAUGH

LAREDO, RUTH (b. 1937)

Ruth Meckler, a piano prodigy from Michigan, became Ruth Laredo when she married violinist Jaime Laredo. A petite woman, she yields to no one in the strength of her playing and her dedication to the instrument. "Ruth Laredo is about as big as a hummingbird. Her hands sometimes appear to hover over the keys, a blur to the eyes if not the ears. . . . But what hummingbird ever packed such power?" wrote Donal Henahan in the *New York Times.*

Ruth (Meckler) Laredo was born the older of two daughters in Detroit, on November 20, 1937. Her first teacher was her mother, Miriam (Horowitz)

Meckler, who chose Edward Bredshall as Ruth's instructor when the time came for more formal training. Her mother took Ruth to concerts at a very early age. One was a Vladimir Horowitz recital. "It changed my life irrevocably. I knew then, as an eight-year-old, that I wanted to become a pianist." Her first public appearance was with the Detroit Symphony Orchestra when she was eleven years old, playing two movements of Beethoven's Second Piano Concerto. A turning point was when she met Seymour Lipkin, pianist, and Berl Senofsky, violinist, at Indian Hill, a summer workshop in the arts. They introduced her to Rudolf Serkin, who became the most important influence in her career. Serkin said, "I can see you play like a tiger!"

After graduating from Detroit's Mumford High School, Laredo studied with Serkin at the Curtis Institute in Philadelphia, and spent many summers at the Marlboro Summer Festival in Vermont. She is a charter member of "Music from Marlboro," and joined the first touring group in 1965, which included a visit to Israel. There she played Bach's Concerto for Three Pianos in the Mann Auditorium with Rudolf and Peter Serkin. At Curtis and at the Meadowmount summer music festival, Ivan Galamian and Leonard Rose chose her to play for their students, who included Arnold Steinhardt, Michael Tree, Pinchas Zuckerman, and Itzhak Perlman. And during Marlboro summers, some of her colleagues were Murray Perahia, Richard Goode, Emanuel Ax, and Yo-Yo Ma. At the end of each festival season, the traditional closing work was Beethoven's Choral Fantasy with Rudolf Serkin as soloist and the entire Marlboro community in the chorus.

Ruth Meckler met Jaime Laredo at Curtis. They married in 1960 and performed together until their divorce in 1974. Their daughter Jennifer was born in 1969 and is married to Paul Watkins, principal cellist of the BBC Symphony; they live in England. In the early 1970s, Ruth Laredo began a solo career that developed rapidly after her New York solo debut at Avery Fisher Hall. She made her New York Philharmonic debut, playing the Ravel Concerto with Pierre Boulez conducting. She has traveled extensively in the United States, Europe, and Japan, and has performed as soloist with many major orchestras in this country and abroad. She frequently joins the Tokyo, Shanghai, and Vermeer quartets in chamber music recitals, and appeared with the Guarneri Quartet on Lincoln Center's "Great Performers" series.

In December 1974, she was honored as Musician of the Month by High Fidelity/Musical America, and has been nominated three times for a Grammy Award. She was also honored by the Music Teachers International Association for Distinguished Service to Music in

America, and was given the Music in Humanity award by the Gretna, Pennsylvania, Music Festival in 1994.

Laredo's innovative series "Speaking of Music" is a continuing event at the Metropolitan Museum of Art. She writes the comments, and discusses the lives and works of musicians whose compositions she performs, assisted by guest artists. She has a strong commitment to Jewish tradition. In a lecture about Felix Mendelssohn, she discussed the significance and depth of his Jewish background. His father's decision to convert to Protestantism, said Laredo, was a practical one to ensure his son's acceptance into the music profession of Germany. In addition to Mendelssohn, the series has included the work of composers Clara and Robert Schumann, Scriabin, Rachmaninoff, Chopin, Brahms, Tchaikovsky, Ravel, Fauré, Franck, and Dvorak.

Laredo was commissioned to edit a new edition of Rachmaninoff's piano works, and in 1992 published a guide for aspiring pianists, *The Ruth Laredo Becoming a Musician Book.*

Noted pianist Ruth Laredo created the innovative series "Speaking of Music" at the Metropolitan Museum of Art, in which she discusses the lives and works of musicians whose compositions she performs. [New York Public Library]

Laredo has recorded the complete solo piano music of Rachmaninoff and Scriabin. The Rachmaninoff collection of five CDs was produced under the Sony Classics label; the Scriabin records, originally released by Connoisseur Society, were rereleased by Nonesuch. She has been a member of the faculty of Yale University and the Curtis Institute, and has given master classes at the Eastman School, Indiana University, the New England Conservatory, and the Academy of the West in Santa Barbara, California. She is now on the faculty of the Manhattan School of Music in New York City.

BIBLIOGRAPHY

Current Biography (October 1987); Laredo, Ruth. *The Ruth Laredo Becoming a Musician Book* (1992).

The International Piano Archives at the University of Maryland, College, Park, Md., include Laredo's collection of personal and professional material relative to her career.

IRMA COMMANDAY

LASKER, MARY WOODWARD (1900–1994)

Mary Woodward Lasker often joked, "I am opposed to heart attacks and cancer and strokes the way I am opposed to sin." Indeed, she garnered support for the medical causes she felt strongly about with a crusading spirit. When she died in 1994 at age ninety-three, she was still president of the Albert and Mary Lasker Foundation, honorary president of the American Cancer Society, and a trustee and vice-chair of the United Cerebral Palsy Research and Education Foundation. These positions of responsibility are indicative of her lifelong work as an advocate for health issues. However, beyond her work as a philanthropist and lobbyist, Lasker also made an impact through her urban beautification projects and her collection of French impressionist and modern art. Although she was Jewish, her religion and ethnic heritage were not the focus of her charitable work.

Mary Woodward Lasker was born on November 30, 1900, in Watertown, Wisconsin, to Frank Elwin Woodward, a banker with holdings in lumber, and Sara (Johnson) Woodward, a civic leader and founder of two local parks. Mary's belief in the importance of parks and gardens as a means of urban improvement began during her childhood, and her frequent ear infections as a young girl contributed to her interest in national health. After finishing high school, she studied fine arts at the University of Wisconsin from 1918 to 1920, and then transferred to Radcliffe College from which she graduated cum laude in 1923.

She continued her schooling with a semester of study at Oxford, and then obtained a job with the Reinhardt Galleries in Manhattan, where she was engaged in such activities as arranging benefit loan exhibitions of French artists and selling paintings to collectors and museums. She worked as an art dealer for seven years before leaving the position. In 1926, she married Paul Reinhardt, owner of Reinhardt Galleries. The two divorced in 1934.

During her gallery career, personal art collecting became a passion for Lasker. She traveled abroad and purchased works, including pieces by Renoir and Miró. Although she was no longer involved in art professionally when she married her second husband, Albert Davis Lasker, in 1940, she remained committed to the art world for the rest of her life. She eventually sold most of her collection because she "wanted to be able to give away the money."

Albert Lasker had earned his money and fame through his work as an advertising executive of Lord and Thomas, but he held a long-standing philanthropic interest in medicine and education. Two years after marrying Mary Woodward, he retired from his business and set up the Albert and Mary Lasker Foundation with his wife. The foundation was established to aid and encourage medical research and public health administration. Every year it presents the Albert Lasker Awards for outstanding contributions to clinical and basic medical research. These awards hold international prestige and have often been seen as predecessors to the Nobel Prize in Medicine. The foundation also supports urban beautification and art programming.

After Albert Lasker died in 1952, Mary Lasker continued the work that the couple had started and referred to herself as a "self-employed health lobbyist." Her achievements in this area were tremendous and wide-ranging. Dr. Irvin D. Fleming and Larry K. Fuller, respectively president and chair of the board of the American Cancer Society at the time of her death, called her "our pioneer cofounder" and stated, "She may have contributed more to medical research in the United States than any other citizen."

Lasker's work with the American Cancer Society is a good example of her determined nature. She became interested in the cause of cancer research in 1943 when her housekeeper was diagnosed with untreatable cancer of the uterus. Lasker was dismayed to learn that the Women's Field Army of the then-named American Society to Control Cancer was raising only about $240,000 a year. After she discussed the matter with her husband, he contacted NBC television and convinced the popular shows *Fibber McGee*

and Molly and *The Bob Hope Show* to send out messages about the need to raise funds for cancer research. Lasker herself persuaded *Reader's Digest* to do the same. From this point onward, the Laskers became the driving force behind the society's growing research program. In 1945, Lasker agreed to hire professional fund-raisers for the organization if 25 percent of all funds were used solely for research. Her specification became the rule, and this percentage remains the minimum spent on research by the American Cancer Society. Lasker's work toward a cure for cancer was driven even more by her husband's own death from cancer. Ironically, much of his fortune originated from his advertising campaign for a product now deemed a major cause of cancer, heart disease, and other ills: Lucky Strike cigarettes.

Involvement in a range of health issues was clearly important to Lasker. Besides serving as chair of the board of the American Cancer Society and as a trustee of the Cancer Research Institute, she was a trustee of Research to Prevent Blindness, the founder and director of the National Health Education Committee, vice president of the Planned Parenthood Federation, and director of the National Committee for Mental Hygiene. Her work as a lobbyist in Washington, D.C., was successful in persuading Congress to allocate more money toward research into cancer, heart disease, mental illness, blindness, and other major killing and crippling diseases. Lasker was also largely responsible for increasing the National Institutes of Health's funding from $2.4 million in 1945 to nearly $11 billion in 1994. As she once commented, "Without money, nothing gets done."

For her efforts, Lasker was awarded the Presidential Medal of Freedom in 1969 and a Congressional Gold Medal in 1989. Also in 1989, a health sciences professorship at the Harvard School of Public Health was named for her.

Sometimes called "Annie Appleseed," Lasker embarked on urban beautification projects in New York and Washington, DC. She arranged for flower bulbs and trees to be planted in public spaces, and donated three hundred Japanese cherry trees to the United Nations. In 1985, a new variety of pink tulip was named for her. Her interest in art and urban improvement led to terms of service on several non-health-related boards, including the John F. Kennedy Center for the Performing Arts, the Museum of Modern Art, the Norton Simon Museum, New York University, and Braniff Airways.

She died at her home in Greenwich, Connecticut, on February 21, 1994, leaving two stepchildren, Frances Lasker-Brody and Edward Lasker.

BIBLIOGRAPHY

Altman, Lawrence K. "The Doctor's World; Why Many Trailblazing Scientists Must Wait Many Years for Awards." *NYTimes*, September 26, 1995, C3; *Biography Index* (1980). Cohen, Gary. "A Tobacco Fortune for a Cancer Cure." *U.S. News and World Report* (March 7, 1994): 21; Cohen, Gary, and Shannon Brownlee. "Mary and Her 'Little Lambs' Launch a War." *U.S. News and World Report* (February 5, 1996): 76–77; *Current Biography* (1959); Debakey, Michael E., and Jordan U. Gutterman. "The Lasker Awards at Fifty." *Journal of the American Medical Association* 274 (October 4, 1995): 106; Gelb, Cynthia A. "A Tribute to Mary Woodward Lasker." *Cancer News* 48 (Summer 1994): 2; *Good Housekeeping Women's Almanac*. Edited by Barbara McDowell and Hana Umlauf (1977); *NYTimes Biographical Service*. Pace, Eric. "Mary W. Lasker, Philanthropist for Medical Research, Dies at 93." *NYTimes*, February 23, 1994, A17; *Who's Who of American Women*. 14th ed., 1985–1986 (1984).

SARA COEN

LAUDER, ESTÉE (b. 1908)

Estée Lauder's name connotes beauty and healthy skin through her profitable cosmetics lines: Estée Lauder, Clinique, Aramis, Lauder for Men, and Prescriptives. An astute businesswoman, she made a fortune manufacturing, marketing, and distributing cosmetics to women around the world.

Estée Lauder was born Josephine Esther Mentzer in Queens, New York, to Max and Rose (Schotz Rosenthal) Mentzer, a Hungarian immigrant with a French Catholic mother and Jewish father. Rose, who lived until age eighty-eight, warned Estée about the harmful effects of the sun; she always wore gloves and carried a parasol to guard against its rays. Estée remembered this lesson but also remembered how embarrassed she was by her mother's parasol, her thick accent, and both her parents' immigrant behavior. Estée wanted to be one hundred percent American. She was the youngest of the Mentzer children, who grew up Jewish in a mostly Italian neighborhood. Two children had died by the time Estée was born. Her sister, Grace, whom the family called Renee, was two years older than Estée.

Her father was a custom tailor, but found that he could provide a better living for his family by running a hardware store. Her father's hardware store provided Estée with merchandising experience. It was her uncle John Shotz, however, who influenced her future business. Shotz was a chemist who created face creams in a makeshift laboratory, set up behind her family's house. He discouraged Estée from using detergent soaps on her face and showed her how to make the cream that, years later, she would improve upon and market under her own name. She launched her cosmetics business during the Depression in New York and later in Miami Beach, Florida.

Estée Lauder remembered an influential experience that had occurred years earlier at a Florence Morris salon in New York City where she sold her products. Lauder recalls in her autobiography (1985) how she admired the blouse of an elegant customer in the salon and asked where she had bought it. The woman scoffed, "What difference could it possibly make? . . . You could never afford it." The young Estée walked away humiliated, but vowed that no one would ever say something like that to her again. Some day she would have so much money that she could buy anything she wanted.

Estée was about nineteen when she met Joseph Lauter, son of Lillian and William Lauter, immigrants from Galicia. They married on January 15, 1930, and their son Leonard Allen was born on March 19, 1933. In about 1937, Estée Lauder began to use the Lauder spelling of her name for her products. Years later in her autobiography she lamented that she neglected her husband and family by paying too much attention to building her business. In 1985 she said, "I did not know how to be Mrs. Joseph Lauder and Estée Lauder at the same time."

She divorced her husband in 1939 and married him again in 1942. This time their marriage cemented a lifelong bond and launched a business partnership as well. Joseph quit his business to join hers in order to run the factory and deal with production and the finances, while Estée took charge of the sales staff and marketing. Even their son Leonard ran errands for the business. The couple had a second child, Ronald, born in February 1944.

Estée Lauder was an exceptionally talented and successful promoter. She was a pioneer in giveaway promotions, always including a lipstick in the gift package. Women tried her products, liked them, and told other women about them. Much of her initial success came from this word-of-mouth advertising. She called her strategy "Tell-a-Woman" marketing. Eventually, she invested in larger marketing concepts, using beautiful models to sell her products. Estée Lauder chose carefully the models for advertising her products, selecting the "Estée Lauder kind of woman," rather than a movie star. The photographer Victor Skrebneski published a book of his photographs of women who modeled for Estée Lauder products.

Estée Lauder believed in selling her cosmetics at the best department stores, ignoring the advice of her accountant and lawyer, who urged her to get out of

Estée Lauder is an astute businesswoman and a noted philanthropist.
She made her fortune manufacturing, marketing, and distributing cosmetics to women around the world.
She is shown here at an awards ceremony sponsored by the Commission on the Status of Women held
at the Metropolitan Museum of Art on October 30, 1985. She is sitting between
GERTRUDE G. MICHELSON *and* ELIZABETH HOLTZMAN.
[Bettye Lane]

this particular business. She started at Saks Fifth Avenue in New York City, an upscale store where women could charge their purchases. After succeeding at Saks Fifth Avenue, she expanded to Neiman Marcus in Dallas, and then several department stores around the country. Estée Lauder opened each store herself and trained the saleswomen who were demonstrating her products.

In 1953, she launched another phase of her business with Youth Dew, a bath oil with a scent that could be used as a perfume. In fact, Lauder said that this product influenced the popularity of perfume at this time. Later she brought out many other popular scents such as Azurée, Aliage, Private Collection, White Linen, Cinnabar, and Beautiful. Lauder, always vigilant about competitors, trusted only family members with formulas for the various fragrances.

Estée Lauder decided to venture into the male cosmetic market in 1964, using her son and seven other men in her company to test her products. In 1965, she came out with Aramis and an entire line for men's skin, which she relaunched in 1967. Another of her creative ideas was the fragrance-free Clinique line, which was launched after extensive medical testing.

It took some time, but she was able to create a successful European market after correcting her original mistake of bypassing the buyer at Harrods in London. Finally Englishwomen's demand for Lauder's cosmetics and the enormously successful Youth Dew body oil cracked the British market. Establishing counter space in good stores in France was even more difficult. She persevered and, by 1985, half of Estée Lauder and related product sales took place in seventy-five foreign countries.

At one time, both Leonard and Ronald Lauder, Wharton graduates, contributed to the business, along with their wives, Evelyn and Jo Carole. Leonard Lauder took over as president of Estée Lauder, Inc., in 1973. Ronald Lauder worked as chairman of Lauder International, but later left to use his training in government work.

Lauder has accumulated enormous wealth through her business acumen. She follows her own admonition: "Measure your success in dollars, not degrees."

In addition to numerous awards in the cosmetics and fashion industries, Estée Lauder has received the French government's Insignia of Chevalier of the Legion of Honor in 1978, the Gold Medal award by the City of Paris in 1979, the Crystal Apple from the Association for a Better New York in 1977, the Albert Einstein College of Medicine Spirit of Achievement Award in 1968. In 1970, she was recognized by 575 business and financial editors as one of Ten Outstanding Women in Business. In 1984, she and seven others were chosen as Outstanding Mother of the Year.

A philanthropist, she has contributed to National Cancer Care and to the Manhattan League. The Lauder family is also known for charity work in Jewish and other causes.

BIBLIOGRAPHY

Allen, Margaret. *Selling Dreams: Inside the Beauty Business* (1981); Israel, Lee. *Estée Lauder: Beyond the Magic* (1985); Kennedy, Trevor. "Estée Lauder." In *Top Guns* (1988); Lauder, Estée. *ESTÉE: A Success Story* (1985); Skrebneski, Victor. *Five Beautiful Women* (1987); Slater, Elinor, and Robert Slater. "Estée Lauder." In *Great Jewish Women* (1994).

SARA ALPERN

LAVIN, LINDA (b. 1937)

"The work makes me feel strong. I like to play women who walk through fire and come out standing." Linda Lavin's work as an actress/activist has had a positive influence on many of America's working women. Although her Jewish heritage has not been the central focus of her acting career, she has powerfully portrayed Jewish women on stage and screen.

Linda Lavin was born on October 15, 1937, in Portland, Maine, to David J. Lavin, owner of a flourishing furniture business, and Lucille (Potter)

The response Linda Lavin received to her memorable portrayal of a hardworking single mother on the television series Alice *led her to political activism championing the rights of working women. She is shown here at the "Working Women" conference in New York City in January 1980. [Bettye Lane]*

Lavin, a singer and local radio show host. The Lavins were active participants in the local Jewish community. In 1939, Lavin received her B.A. in theater arts from the College of William and Mary. After struggling to "make it" in Broadway musicals, she became frustrated with the vapid female roles. She switched to drama and was acclaimed for her work in *Little Murders*, *Last of the Red Hot Lovers*, and *Broadway Bound*, which won a Tony Award.

Lavin and Rob Leibman were married in 1969, but they divorced in 1980 because of their divergent interests. Two years later, Lavin married Kip Niven and became a stepmother to his two children, Jim and Kate. Because of his mental and emotional cruelty, Lavin divorced Niven in 1992.

For many, Lavin's most memorable role is that of Alice in the television show of the same name (1976–1985). The emotional truths of life as a hardworking, single mother spoke to women across the country. The positive response Lavin received led her to political activism championing the rights of working women.

Lavin has received many awards for her work. She continues to perform, produce, and direct in theater and television, consistently featuring female role models.

BIBLIOGRAPHY

Brantley, Ben. "New Cast for 'Sisters Rosensweig,'" *NYTimes*, September 24, 1993, C3; Brozan, Nadine. "Linda Lavin Is Happy to Pay $675,000," *NYTimes*, July 3, 1992, B4; Cimons, Marlene. "My Side: Linda Lavin," *Working Woman* (February 1980): 88; *Current Biography Yearbook* (1987); *Notable Names in American Theater*; Rich, Frank. "Linda Lavin Takes Her Turn as Mama Rose," *NYTimes*, September 18, 1990, 11; See, Carolyn. "Linda Lavin Can Take Care of Herself," *McCalls* (October 1978): 114; "When Linda Lavin Meets the First Lady, She'll Speak of Women Like Alice," *NYTimes*, May 4, 1994, 8; *Who's Who in America* (1996); *Who's Who in Theater*.

INGERLENE VOOSEN

LAW

The situation of the Jewish community in the United States is shaped fundamentally by the condition of political equality. This legal status is shared with all other citizens and is assumed as an essential baseline. Where there are violations of that status—when an individual otherwise of full legal capacity is treated as a member of a subordinated racial or religious group, and when group membership defines rights and duties—we discuss the problem under the heading "discrimination."

In Jewish history, political equality has a specific historical dimension. It is a "postemancipation" phenomenon. Count Clermont-Tonnerre's famous words are descriptive: "to the Jews as a people, nothing; to the Jews as citizens, everything." In this modern view, the word "law" itself is related to official behavior. Emancipation assumes that, in relation to the state, members of groups are in general treated equally, regardless of religious background or ethnicity. In such a context, "law" means secular law, the law of the state regulating the status of subjects and citizens. Any other law—religious law or folk law—is considered not really law at all.

We would have a very different picture if we were describing the idea of law in other times and places. The index to *Life Is with People*, a well-known book on the shtetl, has an entry that makes the point: "law, see Torah." Until recently, "law" in relation to the Jewish community meant religious law. The existence of external governmental law was acknowledged, of course, but that external law was seen largely as something to be accommodated, an aspect of the historical situation. This is reflected in the maxim *Dina de-Malkhuta Dina*: the law of the Kingdom is law.

For the women who came as immigrants to the United States, the American approach—built on ideas from the eighteenth-century Enlightenment and nineteenth-century liberalism—often was a new situation. They had come from countries in which religious law was the defining law of their communities, under the system of state law. In such systems of state regulation, certain authority was delegated to the religious leadership. Religious law was, in effect, recognized by the state as the law of an internally regulated autonomous community that operated its own system of sanctions. Both such delegation to religious law and the customs of the Jewish community restricted the roles of women.

This article juxtaposes the idea of "law" with the idea of "Jewish women in America." The result of this juxtaposition is a brief inquiry into three separate subjects: the interaction of legal systems; the impact on women of particular changes in the substance of the law(s); and the contributions to law of individual women.

THE LAW OF THE NATION
AND THE LAW OF THE GROUP

The Old Testament describes an ideal of law, and of church and state, in which religious and secular law are fused in a religious commonwealth. Long after the dispersion of the Jews, the theocracies of ancient

Israel provided a model of such a government for the Western world. The early colonists in North America, for example, attempted to establish a city upon a hill, modeled (particularly in Massachusetts and Connecticut) on the commonwealth of ancient Israel described in the Old Testament.

Law and government in the West were not, however, typically theocratic even in those centuries characterized by the unity of Christendom. Law emanated from a multiplicity of sovereignties, some associated with kings and public officials, others with popes and clerics, still others with smaller units of society operating as self-regulatory bodies. In the medieval situation of pluralist law, any particular religious community's law was one body of law competing with others. The modern state had not yet so clearly triumphed that its law was given the name "Law."

We often assume today that the triumph of the secular government is complete. We talk as though religious authority has been eliminated and state power is all that remains. Yet we might more accurately say that the decline of religious authority is a decline in the public coercive aspects of religious regulation, but that religious authority, in the lives of an observant religious community, is still powerful. Today it operates in what is called the "private" sector, generally as a matter of individual submission to the will of the religious community and its sanctions.

In the modern American situation, secular law and religious law are still interdependent and interacting legal systems. In one model interaction, a rough substantive correspondence is assumed between the law of a religious system and the law of the state. The state considers itself, in more or less structured ways, for example, to be a "Christian Nation" in a world of Christian denominations, with smaller or larger non-Christian communities tolerated by the state. This generally was the situation in what is loosely termed Christendom, and it was equally the situation in the Ottoman Empire. In some contexts, both historically and today, this system involves a kind of official delegation of authority to religious leaders of minority traditions to administer their own law under the auspices of—and within limits set by—the majority system. Appeal to the state from the community was possible. Thus the nineteenth-century feminist Ernestine Rose successfully fought her father, a Polish rabbi, in the Polish civil courts. But such appeals to the state were rare.

A comparison between the situation of a Jewish and a Catholic immigrant to the United States in the late nineteenth century is useful on this point. When newcomers arrived in the United States, they found a law of marriage and divorce that assumed complete state authority. Following Christian approaches, state law restricted divorce—though it was becoming increasingly available—insisted on monogamy, and prohibited incestuous marriages. The illegality of birth control was assumed by the state system—following the Catholic position—until the mid-twentieth century. Jewish law was more open on the issue of contraception—and on divorce—though its availability in practice was restricted in part because of the rules of the surrounding state systems. Other family law issues (relating, for example, to religious matching in the context of adoption) had an impact on both groups.

Problems under the law were different for the two immigrant groups. For Catholics, the possibility of divorce in the secular culture raised the question of whether to divorce and remarry in the outside system without the blessing of the church. (The church typically insisted that the first marriage, unless annulled by the church, remained valid.) For Jews, the question might result in confusion on the issue of which official—religious or secular—had authority to issue a divorce, because both systems recognized divorce and remarriage. Rabbinic authority in the country of origin was sometimes sufficient to effect such a change in legal status. In the United States, it was not. The risk was that mistaken reliance on a religious divorce would result in a bigamous second marriage. This was an issue well into the twentieth century. It was a matter of concern, for example, for the New York City Kehilla—the attempt by Jews in New York to form a modern version of the traditional, quasi-autonomous Polish Jewish community.

Some aspects of tension between rabbinic and secular authority are still visible today. Among the most difficult problems arise in the context of family law. A prime example is the *get*, the Jewish divorce, which must, according to tradition, be issued by the husband to the wife. Because religious sanctions are no longer sufficiently powerful in all cases to pressure a recalcitrant husband to give a *get*, the *agunah* [chained wife] has sought state intervention to pressure husbands to give divorces. Some have focused on state solutions (e.g., the New York get law) to this problem, while others have worked on finding solutions within the religious tradition (e.g., the possible use of conditional divorce).

It may be that, indirectly, ideas of egalitarianism and emancipation have had an impact on religious tradition and modern understandings of its rules. The division of religious authority in the United States makes a variety of religious options available for individuals. Difficulties are most acute for those who want not only to remain within traditional religious structures but also to absorb the egalitarian values of the modern state into their own lives. (Still, it may be noted that the situation is less difficult in the United States than in Israel, where traditional religious authority is given governmental power.)

Emancipation operates to free individuals from the restraints of groups. In modern conceptions of religious liberty, religious group membership is voluntary, at least as understood by the state. Exit from a group is a serious possibility, because, in effect, emancipation simultaneously opened both the doors of the larger society and the doors of the community. A situation in which everyone has to be a member of some community, and exit from one either involves membership in another (conversion) or some sort of outlaw status, is quite different from a situation in which state citizenship is a residual category for everyone and group membership is viewed as a private associative option. Emancipation and assimilation produce exits from communities as well as changes in those communities. It may be noted on this point that groups themselves often adopt different definitions of affiliation. For some groups exit is impossible, at least from the point of view of the group. The state's answer to that question, where it becomes relevant, is often different depending on the legal system of the country in which the question is raised. In some legal systems, (e.g., the United States), the issue turns almost entirely on an idea of voluntary association or personal affiliation and commitment. In others, the matter is decided on the basis of formal religious or racial definitions. Group sanctions continue to exist, but some, such as expulsion and excommunication, operate most effectively on those most strongly identified with traditional structures. Thus the claim of the group to a permanent and irrevocable affiliation is one that in the modern situation can be simply denied by an individual who chooses to reject the group and, in effect, move away into the larger society. The more open the social and practical situation, the more real the possibility of exit.

THE IMPACT OF STATE LAW ON WOMEN

We can speak of the impact of state law on Jewish women in the United States across a time frame of several hundred years, from the time that the first group came to New Amsterdam in 1654. And we can note here that one form of religious freedom could involve a recognition of group authority. (See the Rhode Island statute authorizing the uncle-niece marriage of Jewish law as an exception to the state incest law dating from 1798.)

Yet the early experience must be viewed against two other points. First, we must note the diversity and strength of later Jewish immigration. Most of the Jewish women affected by changes in the law were not the descendants of those original settlers. Rather, the Jewish population was regularly enlarged and changed by waves of immigrants arriving over the next two centuries. Some came from situations in which emancipation had been in place for a century, others from contexts built on the conception of a separate, autonomous Jewish community. If HANNAH ARENDT can represent women of the twentieth-century German refugee tradition, the tradition of the shtetl might be represented by some women of Eastern European communities. The class background of Jewish immigrants generally ranges from those like the Brandeis family (described by JOSEPHINE GOLDMARK), who arrived in the mid-nineteenth century with a grand piano or two, to those who came later in steerage with virtually nothing. Immigrants came (and come) from Eastern Europe and from the Middle East, from backgrounds more or less affluent, Westernized, observant.

Second, the legal context changed substantially with the disestablishment of the Christian churches, a process formalized at the national level through the First Amendment to the Constitution. At the state level, the process was not concluded until 1833, when Massachusetts disestablished its church. Under the theories of separation of church and state formulated in the First Amendment ("Congress shall make no law respecting an establishment of religion, or prohibiting the free exercise thereof"), the state could not act directly against any protected "exercises of religion." The state thus cannot insist, for example, on the ordination of women or the revision of the liturgy.

The diversity of the social and economic situations of Jewish immigrants meant that the particular attributes they brought to the United States were very different. Yet the openness of the American situation had an impact on all of them. The change in the legal status of women in the first part of the twentieth century, for example, relating to suffrage and jury service, touched all women. Attempts to discriminate against women came to be rooted less in law than in social role definitions, which made it difficult if not impossible for women both to maintain public or market positions and to raise families, despite the formal equality marked by full political rights. General societal concern with violence against women also reached the Jewish community.

It is also true, however, that the traditional rules of the Jewish community continued to exclude women from full participation in the synagogue service and from ordination as rabbis, and insisted on separate seating in houses of worship. The assumption that a woman's primary role was as a mother and a supporter of the family—a carrier of cultural values but not religious values institutionally understood—remained unchanged in the less assimilated parts of the community.

But it should also be noted that while women were subordinated in the Jewish tradition, they were in other ways not dependent. In Eastern Europe, for example, it was entirely conventional to say that it was an honor for a wife to support her scholar husband. (The scholarship was assumed to be religious scholarship.) To the extent that women were understood to be responsible for the support of their families by working in the family business (but not for strangers), we see a pattern quite different from the subordination and economic and psychological dependency often associated with the idea of the "separate spheres." The managerial skill, shrewdness, and competence that parts of traditional Jewish culture allowed women made possible a transition to the modern commercial and professional world for Jewish women that was presumably more difficult for women socialized in more stereotypically male-dominated cultures.

PARTICIPATION OF WOMEN IN LAW

As general societal discrimination against women in the professions weakened, women entered the professions for reasons somewhat similar to those that influenced men. To begin with, law has a very special place in America. It is at the center of the culture, a road to middle-class success and status. It is, simultaneously, a way to seek reform and social change, a path for those pursuing justice in the prophetic tradition. Jerold Auerbach suggests that law had a highly particularized role in the minds of the Jewish immigrants to the United States. For many, commitment to American legal forms and American democratic faith replaced the traditional faith. This observation may well hold across genders.

Having said this, however, we should consider the specific contribution of Jewish women to law.

Women lawyers would be a useful addition to the list—largely if not entirely male—offered in the *Encyclopedia Judaica*. In *Women in Law*, Cynthia Epstein describes the careers of Nanette Dembitz Brandeis and JUSTINE WISE POLIER, daughter of the Rabbi Stephen Wise. (Both were judges in New York.) Of course, in addition to Justice RUTH BADER GINSBURG on the Supreme Court, today there are Jewish women who serve as state court judges.

The contribution of women to law need not, however, be limited to those who practice law (with or without their husbands) or become judges. Contributions to law might well be looked at more broadly. To illustrate with a familiar example, the famous Brandeis brief, which brought social science material to the attention of the Supreme Court in *Muller* v. *Oregon* (208 US 412 (1908), upholding the Oregon statute regulating hours of employment for women), was the work of Brandeis's sister-in-law, Josephine Goldmark. She was not a lawyer, but her contribution to the law is plain. We also might look for Jewish women who have been plaintiffs in lawsuits, particularly lawsuits understood as test cases involving significant public propositions. Esta Gluck, president of a parent-teachers association, and active in the AMERICAN JEWISH CONGRESS, for example, was a plaintiff in *Zorach* v. *Clauson* (343 US 306 (1952), upholding the New York released-time program). More broadly, it would be appropriate to see the impact on law of the activity of Jewish women who have been effective members of lobbying groups, consumer groups, or trade unions, directing their efforts to reform. Finally, we might include the Jewish women associated with the process of law in its various institutional forms, for example, the many administrative and welfare agencies that implement governmental programs.

The contribution of Jewish women to law is part of a larger story about legal change. If law is taken to be male, women's law might well be different, as the sociologist Georg Simmel suggested. In the twentieth century, women have become members of political society in a new way. Questions concerning the meaning and the consequences of that change—the question of the significance of a "different voice" of women—are regularly discussed in the legal academic literature under the broad heading "feminist jurisprudence." Some writers are highly self-conscious about the ways Jewish commitment or identity has influenced their understanding of issues of difference and of pluralism in modern societies. Whether, in the end, women's law is basically different from men's law is still not known. That women—including Jewish women—already have altered the legal conversation in the United States seems entirely clear.

BIBLIOGRAPHY

Auerbach, Jerold. *Rabbis and Lawyers: From Torah to Constitution* (1990); Baum, Charlotte, Paula Hyman, and Sonya Michel. *The Jewish Woman in America* (1976); Biale, Rachel. *Women and Jewish Law: An Exploration of Women's Issues in Halakhic Sources* (1984); Borden, Morton. *Jews, Turks and Infidels* (1984); *EJ*, s.v. "Law"; Epstein, Cynthia. *Women* in Law (1981); Goldmark, Josephine. *The Pilgrims of '48* (1930); Goren, Arthur. *New York Jews and the Quest for Community: The Kehillah Experiment (1908–1922)* (1970); Graff, Gil. *Separation of Church and State: Dina de-Malkhuta Dina in Jewish Law (1750–1848)* (1985); Gulak, Asher. "Jewish Law." In *Encyclopedia of the Social Sciences*; Hall, Kermit, ed. *Oxford Companion to the Supreme Court of the United States* (1992); Hertzberg, Arthur. *The French Enlightenment and the Jews* (1968); Meiselman, Moshe. *Jewish Woman in Jewish Law* (1978); Minow, Martha. *Making All the Difference: Inclusion and Exclusion, and American Law* (1990); Pfeffer, Leo. *Church, State, and Freedom* (1967), and *Creeds in Competition* (1958); Shepherd, Naomi. *A Price Below Rubies: Jewish Women as Rebels and Radicals* (1993); Simmel, Georg. *On Women, Sexuality and Love* (1984); Weisbrod, Carol. "Family, Church, and State." *Journal of Family Law* (1987. Reprinted in Meyers, Diana Tietjens, Kenneth Kipnis, and Cornelius F. Murphy, Jr. *Kindred Matters: Rethinking the Philosphy of the Family*, 1993); Zborowski, Mark, and Elizabeth Herzog. *Life Is with People: The Culture of the Shtetl* (1952).

CAROL WEISBROD

LAZARUS, EMMA (1849–1887)

"Give me your tired, your poor, / Your huddled masses yearning to breathe free," proclaims the "Mother of Exiles" in Emma Lazarus's sonnet "The New Colossus." Her best-known contribution to mainstream American literature and culture, the poem has contributed to the belief that America means opportunity and freedom for Jews, as well as for other "huddled masses." Through this celebration of the "other," Lazarus conveyed her deepest loyalty to the best of both America and Judaism.

Born on July 22, 1849, Lazarus was the fourth of Esther (Nathan) and Moses Lazarus's seven children. She grew up in New York and Newport, Rhode Island, and was educated by private tutors with whom she studied mythology, music, American poetry, European literature, German, French, and Italian. Her father, who was a successful sugar merchant, supported her writing financially as well as emotionally. In 1866, when Emma was only seventeen, Moses had *Poems and Translations: Written Between the Ages of Fourteen and Sixteen* printed "for private circulation." Daughter Emma dedicated the volume "To My Father."

Soon after *Poems and Translations* was published, Lazarus met Ralph Waldo Emerson. The two corresponded until Emerson's death in 1882. During the early years of their relationship, Lazarus turned to Emerson as her mentor, and he in turn praised and encouraged her writing. In 1871, when she published *Admetus and Other Poems*, she dedicated the title poem

"To My Friend, Ralph Waldo Emerson." Despite his support, Emerson failed to include any of Lazarus's poetry in his 1874 anthology, *Parnassus*, but he did include authors such as Harriet Prescott Spofford and Julia C.R. Dorr. Lazarus responded with an uncharacteristically angry letter and subsequently modified her idealized image of Emerson. However, student and mentor obviously reconciled; in 1876, Lazarus visited the Emersons in Concord, Massachusetts.

Admetus and Other Poems includes "In the Jewish Synagogue at Newport" and "How Long" as well as translations from the Italian and German (Goethe and Heine). "In the Jewish Synagogue at Newport" echoes in form and meter Henry Wadsworth Longfellow's "The Jewish Cemetery at Newport." Yet where Longfellow's meditation closes with "the dead nations never rise again," Lazarus's reverie concludes by announcing that "the sacred shrine is holy yet." "In the Jewish Synagogue at Newport" is one of Lazarus's earliest creative expressions of a Jewish consciousness. "How Long" is significant because its proclamation of the need for a "yet unheard of strain," one suitable to prairies, plains, wilderness, and snow-peaked mountains, places Lazarus among those mid-nineteenth-century American writers who wanted to create literature that did not depend on British outlines.

Lazarus published her next book, *Alide: An Episode of Goethe's Life*, in 1874. Her only novel, *Alide* is based on Goethe's own autobiographical writings and focuses on a love affair between the young Goethe and a country woman. The lovers part at the end, because the poet must be free to fulfill his "sacred office." Lazarus's only other piece of fiction, a story titled "The Eleventh Hour," was published in 1878 in *Scribner's*. The story raises questions about the needs and rights of the artist, like *Alide*, and about the status of American art, like "How Long."

In 1876, Lazarus privately published *The Spagnoletto*, a tragic verse drama. Throughout the 1870s and early 1880s, Lazarus's poems appeared in American magazines. Among these are "Outside the Church" (1872) in *Index*; "Phantasmagoria" (1876) and "The Christmas Tree" (1877) in *Lippincott's*; "The Taming of the Falcon" (1879) in the *Century*; and "Progress and Poverty" (1881) in the *New York Times*.

Lazarus's most productive period was the early 1880s. In addition to numerous magazine poems, essays, and letters, she published a highly respected volume of translations, *Poems and Ballads of Heinrich Heine*, in 1881, and *Songs of a Semite: The Dance to Death and Other Poems*, in 1882. This was also the period in which Lazarus most obviously spoke out as self-identified Jew and American writer simultaneously.

Russian pogroms in the early 1880s kindled Lazarus's commitment to Judaism. This change in attitude is evident in her writing, as well as in her work with the Hebrew Emigrant Aid Society—meeting Eastern European immigrants on Wards Island—and in her efforts to help establish the Hebrew Technical Institute and agricultural communities for Eastern European Jews in the United States.

Songs of a Semite was published by the *American Hebrew*. The title, as well as many of the poems in the collection, publicly proclaimed Lazarus's identity as a Jewish poet. In that role, Lazarus battled against both anti-Semitic non-Jews and complacent Jews. In "The Banner of the Jew," she urged "Israel" to "Recall today / The glorious Maccabean rage," and she reminded readers that "With Moses's law and David's lyre" Israel's "ancient strength remains unbent." And in *The Dance to Death*, a poetic dramatization of Richard Reinhard's 1877 prose narrative *Der Tanz zum Tode*, Lazarus celebrated the courage and faith of the Jews who were condemned to die in Nordhausen, Germany, in 1349 for allegedly causing the plague. *The Dance to Death* was dedicated to George Eliot, "who did most among the artists of our day towards elevating and ennobling the spirit of Jewish nationality" with her novel *Daniel Deronda*.

Lazarus published *Songs of a Semite* in the same year that she adopted a more public Jewish identity in the realm of American magazines, particularly in the *Century*. Three essays published in that magazine over a ten-month period attest to Lazarus's concerns. In the first, "Was the Earl of Beaconsfield a Representative Jew?" (April 1882), Lazarus offered an ambivalent portrait of Benjamin Disraeli; she defined "representative" as embodying the best as well as the worst of Jewish traits. In the second essay, "Russian Christianity vs. Modern Judaism" (May 1882), Lazarus included a personal plea for informed understanding of Russian Jews and their situation. And in the third essay, "The Jewish Problem" (February 1883), she observed that Jews, who are always in the minority, "seem fated to excite the antagonism of their fellow countrymen." To this problem she offered a solution: the founding of a state by Jews for Jews in Palestine. Lazarus promoted Zionism throughout the 1880s.

Although Lazarus had published occasionally in the Jewish press, she became a regular contributor to the *American Hebrew* in the early 1880s. This weekly, edited by Philip Cowan, printed "Judaism the Connecting Link Between Science and Religion" and "The Schiff Refuge" in 1882, "An Epistle to the Hebrews" in 1882–1883, "Cruel Bigotry" in 1883, and "The Last National Revolt of the Jews" as well as

Few words are more famous or more evocative than these from Emma Lazarus's "The New Colossus": "Give me your tired, your poor, / Your huddled masses yearning to breathe free." Inscribed on the base of the Statue of Liberty, they have come to represent to all the world America's promise.
[American Jewish Historical Society]

Until this period, Lazarus's "interest and sympathies were loyal to [her] race," but, as she explained in 1877, "my religious convictions . . . and the circumstances of my life have led me somewhat apart from my people." Although her family did belong to the Sephardic Shearith Israel synagogue in New York, and she did write "In the Jewish Synagogue in Newport" when she was young, it appears that learning of the

"M. Renan and the Jews"—an essay, which won first prize in a contest sponsored by the Philadelphia Young Men's Hebrew Association—in 1884. In "An Epistle to the Hebrews," a series of fifteen open letters that appeared between November 1882 and February 1883, Lazarus suggested that assimilated American Jews should recognize their privileged status as well as their vulnerability in America, that all Jews should understand their history in order not to be misled by anti-Semitic generalizations, and that Eastern European Jews should emigrate to Palestine.

At the same time that Lazarus was writing more self-consciously as a Jew, she was also writing as an American. Her 1881 essay "American Literature" (*Critic*) defended American literature against the charge that America had no literary tradition and that America's poets had left no mark. "American Literature" was followed by "Henry Wadsworth Longfellow" (*American Hebrew*) and the eulogy "Emerson's Personality," both published in 1882. The latter appeared in the *Century*, three months after "Was the Earl of Beaconsfield a Representative Jew?" and two months after "Russian Christianity vs. Modern Judaism." Lazarus also published the poem "To R.W.E." in 1884 (*Critic*).

Lazarus wrote "The New Colossus" in 1883 "for the occasion" of an auction to raise money for the Statue of Liberty's pedestal. The poem was singled out and printed in the *Catalogue of the Pedestal Fund Art Loan Exhibition at the National Academy of Design* because event organizers hoped it would "awaken to new enthusiasm" those working on behalf of the pedestal.

In the following year, Lazarus published the essay "The Poet Heine" in the *Century*. Lazarus explained her fascination with Heine, born a Jew and later baptized and educated as a Catholic: "A fatal and irreconcilable dualism formed the basis of Heine's nature. . . . He was a Jew, with the mind and eyes of a Greek." Lazarus admired Heine's ability to understand the "internal incongruity" of his mind as well as his Jewish "pathos" and worldly sensibililily.

Lazarus traveled to Europe twice, the first time in 1883. During her stay in England and France, she met Robert Browning, William Morris, and Jewish leaders. Her essay "A Day in Surrey with William Morris" (the *Century*, 1886) paints a positive portrait of the English socialist. Noting that Morris's "extreme socialistic convictions" elicited criticism, Lazarus explained that English inequalities were more "glaring" than American ones and therefore more in need of dramatic reform.

Lazarus's second trip to Europe was a longer one, lasting from May 1885 until September 1887. According to her sister JOSEPHINE LAZARUS's biographical sketch, Emma "decided to go abroad again as the best means of regaining composure and strength" after Moses Lazarus died in March 1885. This journey included visits to England, France, Holland, and Italy. Lazarus returned to New York very ill, probably with cancer. She died two months later, on November 19, 1887. Two of Lazarus's sisters, Mary and Annie, published *The Poems of Emma Lazarus, I and II* posthumously, in 1888. Volume I contains the biographical sketch written by sister Josephine. In the same year, the sketch also appeared in the *Century*. Volume II includes her final work, "By the Waters in Babylon, Little Poems in Prose," which had previously appeared in the *Century* in March 1887. This set of prose-poems suggests that Lazarus was exploring new directions for her art. Volume II also contains translations of "Hebrew poets of mediaeval Spain," Solomon Ben Judah Gabirol, Abul Hassan Judah Ben Ha-Levi, and Moses Ben Esra.

Lazarus's work received consistently positive reviews. By the late 1870s and 1880s, American writers and readers knew Lazarus as a frequent contributor to periodicals such as *Lippincott's*, the *Century*, and the *American Hebrew*. She corresponded with writers and thinkers of the time, including Ivan Turgenev, William James, Robert Browning, and James Russell Lowell. When she died, the *American Hebrew* published the "Emma Lazarus Memorial Number." In it, John Hay, John Jay Whittier, and Cyrus Sulzberger, among others, praised Lazarus for her contributions to American literature as well as to "her own race and kindred."

Lazarus dedicated her life to her work. Yet she still had to contend with American and Jewish middle-class prescriptions for womanly behavior. These gender expectations included limitations on a woman artist's expression. In "Echoes" (probably written in 1880) Lazarus spoke self-consciously about women as poets, describing the boundaries drawn around a woman poet who cannot share with men the common literary subjects of the "dangers, wounds, and triumphs" of war and must therefore transform her own "elf music" and "echoes" into song. Successful at that act of transformation, Lazarus found some space in the American literary world.

More than any other Jewish woman of the nineteenth century, Lazarus identified herself and was recognized by readers and critics as an American writer. She was also an increasingly outspoken Jew, and she was a woman. Lazarus's writing benefited from the complexities of her identity. She would not have been as effective on behalf of Jews if she had not believed deeply in America's freedoms, and she could not have been as passionate a writer if she had not uncovered her own meaningful response to Judaism.

SELECTED WORKS BY EMMA LAZARUS

Admetus and Other Poems (1871); *Alide: An Episode of Goethe's Life* (1874); *Emma Lazarus: Selections from Her Poetry and Prose.* Edited by Morris Schappes (1944); *Poems and Ballads of Heinrich Heine* (1881); *Poems and Translations: Written Between the Ages of Fourteen and Sixteen* (1866); *The Poems of Emma Lazarus.* 2 vols. (1888); *Songs of a Semite: The Dance to Death and Other Poems* (1882); *The Spagnoletto* (1876).

BIBLIOGRAPHY

Blain, Virginia, Patricia Clements, and Isobel Grundy, eds. *The Feminist Companion to Literature in English: Women Writers from the Middle Ages to the Present* (1990); *DAB*; *EJ*; *JE*; Kessner, Carole. "The Emma Lazarus–Henry James Connection: Eight Letters." *American Literary History* 3 (1991): 46–62; Lazarus, Josephine. "Emma Lazarus." In *The Poems of Emma Lazarus.* 2 vols. (1888). Also in the *Century* 36 (1888): 875–884; Lichtenstein, Diane. *Writing Their Nations: The Tradition of Nineteenth-Century American Jewish Women Writers* (1992); Merriam, Eve. *Emma Lazarus: Woman with a Torch* (1956); *NAW*; Obituary. *NYTimes*, November 20, 1887, 16:2; *PAJHS* 37: 17–29; 38: 261–287; 45: 248–257; Rusk, Ralph, ed. *Letters to Emma Lazarus in the Columbia University Library* (1939); Schappes, Morris, ed. *The Letters of Emma Lazarus, 1868–85* (1949); Schoen, Carol. "Emma Lazarus." In *American Women Writers: A Critical Reference Guide from Colonial Times to the Present.* Vol. 2 (1980); *UJE*; Vogel, Dan. *Emma Lazarus* (1980); Young, Bette Roth. *Emma Lazarus in the World: Life and Letters* (1995).

DIANE LICHTENSTEIN

LAZARUS, JOSEPHINE (1846–1910)

Josephine Lazarus was the best known of the poet EMMA LAZARUS's five sisters. Her essays and reviews appeared in several leading journals of the day, and three volumes of her work exploring issues of Jewish destiny and identity were published during her lifetime.

Lazarus, the second of seven children, was raised in a home of wealth, culture, and privilege. Her parents, Moses and Esther (Nathan) Lazarus, were both descended from the first Jews to settle in the United States, refugees from Brazil who landed in New Amsterdam in 1654. Moses Lazarus was a successful sugar merchant who was able to retire young. Both parents were Sephardi Jews who were members of New York's prestigious Spanish and Portuguese synagogue, Shearith Israel, and of the Union and Knickerbocker clubs, which Moses Lazarus helped to found. These affiliations reflected both a proud Jewish heritage and the family's secure position in the most sophisticated social circles of late nineteenth-century New York City.

While little is known about Lazarus's early schooling, like Emma she was fluent in the major European languages and well educated in literature, music, and the arts. The family summered in Newport, and the Lazarus daughters were members of Julia Ward Beecher's exclusive Town and Country Club, where members took turns presenting prepared discourses on a range of scientific and literary topics.

Lazarus's life seems to have centered on her family. For years, she oversaw the management of the family homes, caring for her parents, her sisters, and, after the death of her sister Agnes, her two nieces. She began publishing her writing only after Emma's death, when Lazarus was in her forties. Her first published piece was a memorial essay on Emma, followed by a series of literary biographies of contemporary women writers. In 1893, she was one of the few Jewish women invited to speak at the Congress of Religions at the World Columbian Exposition in Chicago. Like the other Jewish speakers at the Congress, Lazarus emphasized the spiritual identity of Judaism, introducing her vision of combining the truths of Judaism and Christianity in a nonsectarian ethical monotheism. She further refined her ideology in *The Spirit of Judaism*, published in 1895. Lazarus's understanding of Jews and Judaism provides a stark alternative to Emma Lazarus's political and social analysis, which led the latter to found the short-lived Society for the Improvement and Colonization of East European Jews. While the society proposed to educate and then resettle immigrants to America in Palestine, Lazarus saw the challenge of these dispossessed immigrants in very different terms. Revealing the influence of contemporary liberal Christian writers on her thinking, she proposed the embrace of a universal humanism: "Away . . . with all the Ghettos and with spiritual isolation in every form. . . . The Jew must change his [sic] attitude before the world and come into spiritual fellowship with those around him. . . ."

Like many of her contemporaries, Lazarus was profoundly affected by the pervasive anti-Semitism unmasked during the Dreyfus Affair, and she began to consider political Zionism as a viable option for European Jewry. The last essay to be published during her lifetime reflects her struggle to bring together her deep concern for Jewish safety and her strong belief in the power of a transcendent universal faith.

Lazarus's life and work provide important insights into a pattern of Jewish identification and assimilation in late nineteenth-century America. She wanted to identify with Judaism and Jews, but, like her sister and many contemporaries, had little in common with the Eastern European immigrants flooding America's shores. While she decried Jews' ignorance of the rich spiritual heritage of Judaism, she herself was unable to draw upon classical texts or traditional sources for her own spiritual nourishment. She mistakenly understood rabbinic Judaism, which she rejected, to be the only source of spiritual sustenance for Jews, while claiming that contemporary Reform Judaism was spiritually bankrupt. While she was not a systematic thinker, her work reflects her deep sense of obligation to respond to the pressing issues of the day. Josephine Lazarus's legacy is of a woman yearning for a Judaism that satisfies both the intellect and the spirit, a Judaism that can connect the past with the present and the future. Josephine Lazarus died on February 3, 1910.

SELECTED WORKS BY JOSEPHINE LAZARUS

"Emma Lazarus." *Century* 36 (October 1888): 875–884; "From Plotzk to Boston." *Critic* 24 (April 1899): 317–318; "Louisa May Alcott." *Century* 42 (May 1891): 56–67; *Madame Dreyfus: An Appreciation* (1899); "Margaret Fuller." *Century* 45 (April 1893): 923–933; "Marie Bashkirtseff." *Scribner's Magazine* 6, no. 5 (November 1889): 633–640; *Mystery, Prophecy, Service, Freedom* (1910); "The Outlook for Judaism." In *The World's Parliament of Religions*, edited by J.W. Hanson (1894); *The Spirit of Judaism* (1895); "Zionism." *New World* 8 (June 1899): 228–242.

BIBLIOGRAPHY

AJYB 6 (1904–1905): 134, 12 (1910–1911): 110; *JE*; Lazarus, Josephine. Autograph File. Houghton Library, Harvard University, Cambridge, Mass., and Letters. Private collection of Helena Dekay Gilder; Rapport, Joe Rooks. "The Lazarus Sisters: A Family Portrait." Ph.D. diss., Washington University (1988); *UJE*; Young, Bette Roth. *Emma Lazarus in Her World: Life and Letters* (1995).

SUE LEVI ELWELL

LAZARUS, RACHEL MORDECAI (1788–1838)

In 1815, Rachel Mordecai Lazarus, a twenty-six-year-old North Carolina schoolteacher, met a "Shylock." Dishearteningly, he was a character in her favorite writer's latest novel. Even worse, the malicious London coachmaker of Maria Edgeworth's *The Absentee* (1812) was named Mr. Mordicai. The sting festered, and Rachel wrote to Edgeworth, a best-selling Irish writer of fiction and progressive educational guides, requesting an explanation. Rachel's genteel, principled criticism moved and shamed Edgeworth, who not only begged pardon but set out in her next tale to unveil anti-Semitism's irrational roots. So began an epistolary friendship that continued until Rachel Mordecai Lazarus's death, though few knew of it. Adhering closely to social strictures on women—to be widely known was to risk one's virtue—she refused ever to have her name publicly linked to Edgeworth or to the apologetic novel she inspired, *Harrington* (1817).

The eldest girl in a family of thirteen, Rachel Mordecai Lazarus was born July 1, 1788, in Goochland County, Virginia. Both her parents had Ashkenazic roots. Her father, Jacob, grew up in Philadelphia. Her mother, Judith, was the eldest daughter of colonial New York silversmith Myer Myers. When Rachel was three, the family moved to Warrenton, North Carolina, where they were the small town's sole Jews. Following her mother's death, her father married his sister-in-law Rebecca Mears Myers. When the family store failed, the Mordecais opened a girls' boarding school in 1809, with Rachel Lazarus as head instructor. The academy quickly filled up with daughters of the region's Protestant plantation elite, who were joined by a handful of girls from southern Jewish families.

In 1821, Rachel married the widower Aaron Lazarus, a Wilmington, North Carolina, merchant and shipper. After years of teaching strangers, Lazarus saw her new domestic circle as the proving ground for her conviction—based on Enlightenment and early feminist ideas, alongside a strenuous domesticity—that the family itself was the institution where affection and intellectual life, through continual instruction, could best flourish. Religion did not play a large part in this vision, but when Aaron Lazarus's son Gershon nearly converted in 1823, Rachel Lazarus immersed herself in Judaism in order to better understand—and defend—her faith. But she found in the prayers "so much repetition, so many epithets strung together, that the mind cannot fix itself on the sense of each in repeating them, and this in a measure prevents devotion." Five years later, an almost fatal infection contracted in childbirth gave greater urgency to Lazarus's religious search. The baby was named Mary Catherine, after Lazarus's closest female friends, evangelical Christians who nursed her through her darkest hours.

Successive pregnancies frightened and disappointed Lazarus. Each new child required years of education, work Lazarus felt she must manage closely. Her husband was preoccupied with business. Most upsetting, continued religious studies only deepened

Rachel's attraction to Christianity. Her dream of enlightened domesticity was flickering out. An emotional and physical breakdown convinced Lazarus, in 1835, to go where faith led her. She announced her intention to convert, setting off a bitter struggle with her father and husband. Aaron Lazarus threatened to take their children (Marx Edgeworth, Ellen, Mary Catherine, and Julia) away if she left the faith. Lazarus relented, but for the remaining years of her life believed as a Christian in all but name. On her deathbed, at the home of her still-Jewish siblings Samuel Mordecai and Ellen Mordecai in Petersburg, Virginia, Lazarus was baptized into the Episcopal Church.

With almost no formal education, Lazarus defied the view of women as intellectually inferior to men and systematically pursued a life of the mind within the private sphere. Though she grew up far from an organized Jewish community, for most of her life she defended the faith of her fathers as vigorously as any American Jewish woman of the time. Lazarus and her siblings, professionals who always mixed freely with gentiles, regularly faced questions about their belief and strained to fit Judaism to their lives. Only two of Mordecai's thirteen children became practicing Jewish adults. Despite an almost excessively dutiful nature, Lazarus balked at the patriarchal Judaism practiced by her father and husband and called for changes that Reform Judaism brought only after her death. First as an intellectual, later as a Christian, and always as a dutiful woman, Rachel Mordecai Lazarus sought meaning in ideals. Not suprisingly, the world and the people she loved never lived up to her dreams.

Rachel Mordecai Lazarus died on June 23, 1838.

BIBLIOGRAPHY

Berman, Myron. *Richmond's Jewry, 1769–1976: Shabbat in Shockoe* (1979); Bingham, Emily S. "'Mind Torn . . . Spirit Broken': Enlightened Domesticity and Evangelical Piety in the World of Rachel Mordecai Lazarus." Master's thesis, University of North Carolina, 1991; MacDonald, Edgar E., ed. *The Education of the Heart: The Correspondence of Rachel Mordecai Lazarus and Maria Edgeworth* (1977); Mordecai, Alfred. Papers. Library of Congress, Washington, D.C.; Mordecai, Jacob. Papers. Special Collections Library, Duke University, Durham, N.C.; Mordecai Family Papers. Southern Historical Collection, University of North Carolina, Chapel Hill; Myers Family Papers. Virginia Historical Society, Richmond, Va.; Richards, Penny Leigh. "'A Thousand Images, Painfully Pleasing': Complicating Histories of the Mordecai School, Warrenton, North Carolina, 1809–1818." Ph.D. diss., University of North Carolina, 1995; Sarna, Jonathan D. "The American Jewish Response to Nineteenth-Century Christian Missions." *Journal of American History* 68 (June 1981): 35–51.

EMILY BINGHAM

LEBENSBOIM, ROSA *see* MARGOLIN, ANNA

LeBLANG, TILLIE (1881–1945)

Tillie LeBlang is known as a businesswoman, philanthropist, and mother. When her husband, Joseph, died in 1931, she took control of a family business valued at $12 million to $15 million. During their thirty years of marriage, the LeBlangs built a small retail cigar shop into a cultural empire that operated three ticket agencies and controlled five theaters, three in New York City and two in Newark, New Jersey. LeBlang worked with her husband while raising three daughters. She continued to manage the business until just a few months before she died, with the help of her second husband, William Jasie, who had been the LeBlangs' business lawyer.

Tillie LeBlang was born in New York on April 25, 1881, to Ignatz and Adele Richter. One of nine children, she attended public school and married Joseph LeBlang in 1900 when she was nineteen. While operating a cigar store at the corner of Sixth Avenue and 30th Street in Manhattan, Joseph LeBlang would allow a press agent to display posters in the window of his store. In return, the agent gave Joseph free tickets to theatrical productions. Joseph would sell these tickets in his store.

Eventually, he persuaded some theater managers to allow him to sell unsold tickets at a discount. For many years, theatrical producers used the phrase "Let's go see Joe" to help them stay alive during unpopular shows. To keep such productions running, the LeBlangs established ticket agencies that took full responsibility for the sale of all seats. The tickets were sold at a discount, in the hope that the show would eventually become popular.

Tillie LeBlang became as well known in the theatrical world as her husband. After Joseph's death, she guided the ticket and theater businesses through the Depression years and during the wartime boom. She also became a producer of plays, most notably *Tell Her the Truth* and *The DuBarry*, both staged in 1932. When she became ill in 1944, she kept the business in the family by transferring it to her three daughters from her first marriage, Etta Samilson, Dorothy Mark, and Adele Greenbaum.

LeBlang also led several Jewish philanthropic organizations in the New York area. She was a founder and first president of Ivriah, the women's division of the Jewish Educational Alliance, a director of the Children's Welfare League, a branch of the

Jewish Settlement House of the East Side, and a director of Blue Bird Camp for children.

Tillie LeBlang served in the American Red Cross during World War I and supported charities connected with the theatrical profession, including the Stage Relief Association. She was also a member of the League of New York Theaters. She died on March 1, 1945, in a house not far from where she was raised.

BIBLIOGRAPHY
Obituary. *NYTimes*, March 2, 1945, 19; *WWIAJ* 3 (1938).

ELLIOT ASHKENAZI

LEDERER, ESTHER PAULINE FRIEDMAN *see* LANDERS, ANN

LEE, MALKA (1904–1976)

A writer of lyrical and sometimes sentimental poetry, Malka Lee was one of the most beloved female poets writing in Yiddish in America during her lifetime. Her poems had great folk appeal to Yiddish readers as reflections of their own experiences in the Old World and the New. Her work was favorably received by literary critics of the time, such as Shmuel Niger and Melech Ravitch. In 1965, she was awarded the Hayim Greenberg Award of PIONEER WOMEN of America.

Born Malka Leopold on July 4, 1904, in the shtetl of Monastrikh, Galicia, to Frieda (Duhl) and Chaim Leopold, Lee spent part of her youth in Vienna, where she fled with her family during World War I. After the war, she returned to Poland, only to immigrate to New York in 1921. In New York, she attended HUNTER COLLEGE and the Jewish Teachers Seminary.

As a young girl, Lee wrote her first poems in German, but in America she turned to Yiddish, her mother tongue, to write for people of her own background. Her first published poetry appeared in 1922, and she continued to contribute her works to Yiddish literary magazines and anthologies all over the world until her death in 1976.

A short autobiographic article published in July 1927 in the Yiddish newspaper *Frayhayt* was later expanded into a book of memoirs entitled *Durkh Kindershe Oygn* [Through the eyes of childhood] (1955) and dedicated to her family, shot by the Nazis in Monastrikh in 1941. A portion of this work was translated into English in the book *Found Treasures: Stories by Yiddish Women Writers* (1994). Her other volume of

prose, *Mayselekh far Yoselen* [Little stories for Yosel] (1969), is a book of short stories and fables for children.

Lee's body of work, which includes six volumes of published poetry, is representative of an entire generation of Jewish women born and educated in Eastern Europe at the beginning of the twentieth century who found a very different life in America. Her early poetry intertwines the memories of shtetl life in a Hasidic family with the realities of the secular immigrant experience. Her volumes published between 1945 and 1950 reflect the personal pain of observing the Holocaust, with its destruction of family and childhood home, from the safety of distance in America. Her later work expresses a love of nature and her attachment to America, as well as her Zionist devotion to the State of Israel.

Lee and her first husband, writer Aaron Rappaport, owned and managed a bungalow colony in High

Beloved Yiddish writer Malka Lee wrote of the pain of observing the Holocaust, with its destruction of family and childhood home, from the safety of distance in America. She was a passionate American and a devoted Zionist. [YIVO Institute]

Falls, New York, which became a haven for a coterie of Yiddish intellectuals based in New York. There she cultivated friendships with a variety of Yiddish writers and critics. After Rappaport's death, she married Moshe Besser in 1966. Malka Lee, mother of Joseph Rappaport (b. 1924) and Yvette Rappaport (b. 1937), died in New York on March 22, 1976.

SELECTED WORKS BY MALKA LEE

"Am Yisroel Chai." Text to music (1964); *Durkh Kindershe Oygn* (1955); *Durkh Loytere Kvaln* (1950); *Gezangen* (1940); *In Likht fun Doyres* (1961); *Kines fun Undzer Tsayt* (1945); *Lider* (1932); *Mayselekh far Yoselen* (1969); *Untern Nusnboym* (1969).

BIBLIOGRAPHY

EJ (1972); Forman, Frieda, Ethel Raicus, Sarah Silberstein Swartz, and Margie Wolfe, eds. *Found Treasures: Short Stories by Yiddish Women Writers* (1994); Korman, Ezra, ed. *Yidishe Dikhterins Antologye* (1928); *Leksikon fun der Nayer Yidisher Literatur* (1963); Niger, Shmuel. *Tsukunft* (October 1932): 556+; Rappaport, Joseph [son]. Interview by author, NYC, July 30, 1995; Ravitch, Melech. *Meyn Leksikon*. Vol. 2, bk. 4 (1948); *UJE*; *Who's Who in World Jewry* (1965).

SARAH SILBERSTEIN SWARTZ

LEE, SARA (b. 1933)

Sara Lee, a Jewish educator who combines charisma with caring and vision with realism, has become a central figure in the effort to ensure Jewish continuity. In recent years the American Jewish community has recognized both the critical need for and the difficult challenge of providing all Jews with an excellent, compelling Jewish education.

Sara Lee was born on March 10, 1933, in Boston, Massachusetts. She was the oldest, and only female, among three children of her accountant father, Reuben Schwarz, and homemaker mother, Anna (Cohen) Schwarz. Their home was nominally Jewish, but Sara received only a minimal Jewish education as a child. She attended Radcliffe College (graduating cum laude in 1955) and, in 1954, married David A. Lee, a surgeon. They moved to Los Angeles in 1962 and had three children, Joseph (a filmmaker), Aviva Lee-Parritz (a physician), and Joshua (also a physician).

Lee credits her interest in Jewish education to four formative experiences: as a leader in Young Judaea, the Zionist Youth Movement, in her teen years; as a student in the Zionist Youth Leaders Institute in Israel in 1952–1953; as a teacher and educator in congregational life (during the 1960s and early 1970s); and as a volunteer lay leader in HADASSAH, Congregation Ramat Zion, and the Heschel Day School in Northridge, California.

In 1974, David Lee died suddenly, and Sara, who still had three children to support, entered a new phase in her life. She enrolled in the relatively new Rhea Hirsch School of Education at Hebrew Union College, receiving a master of arts in Jewish education in 1977 and a master of science in education at the University of Southern California in 1979. Upon graduation from the Rhea Hirsch School she joined its faculty, becoming director of the school in 1980.

Under her leadership the Rhea Hirsch School of Education has achieved a national reputation for the preparation of leaders in Jewish education. The school's course of study and pioneering work in clinical education have set a standard for other institutions in the field. Believing that the work of the educational leader should extend beyond the classroom and school to the congregation and community, Lee broadened the Rhea Hirsch School's mission to include experimentation and research on the transformation of core institutions of Jewish learning, such as the day school and the congregational school, as well as advocacy for the enhancement of education in Jewish life. Lee has also been a major voice in the increasingly active dialogue among academics and practitioners of religious education of many faith traditions, serving as a board member of the Religious Education Association and codirector of the Lilly Endowment Colloquium for Catholic and Jewish Educators.

Lee's influence in the field of Jewish education extends far beyond the hundreds of students she has nurtured and leaders she has inspired. In recent years, as concerns about Jewish continuity have come to the fore, a number of national commissions have been convened, among them the North American Commission on Jewish Identity and Continuity and the Commission on Jewish Education in North America. Lee has represented the profession of Jewish education on these commissions and at many similar gatherings.

As an increasing number of foundations have become catalysts for the generation of new ideas and experimental efforts in Jewish education, Lee has been involved in many of these efforts, as either a consultant, reviewer, or grantee.

The field of Jewish education owes much to Sara Lee for her vision, skill, and commitment.

BIBLIOGRAPHY

Lee, Sara. Interviews with author, Los Angeles, 1996.

ISA ARON

LEHMAN, ADELE LEWISOHN (1882–1965)

Adele Lehman, a New York City philanthropist, was not only a substantial donor and fund-raiser for a number of organizations and causes, but was also an administrator and served as an officer or board member for many agencies. Although Lehman is primarily recognized as honorary chairperson for the Federation of Jewish Philanthropies, most of her volunteer work centered around secular organizations. She was a board member of the New York Service for the Orthopedically Handicapped and founder and board member of the Arthur Lehman Counseling Service.

Adele Lewisohn Lehman was born in New York on May 17, 1882 to Adolph and Emma (Cahn) Lewisohn. Her father was also active in charitable work and was a leader in prison reform. Adele was educated at the Anne Brown School and attended Barnard College. On November 25, 1901, she married Arthur Lehman, son of Mayer and Babette (Newgass) Lehman. Arthur Lehman had two brothers, Herbert H. Lehman, former governor and senator of New York, and Irving Lehman, former judge of the state court of appeals. A senior member of the investment banking firm Lehman Brothers, Arthur Lehman was also a philanthropist and founded the Federation of Jewish Philanthropies. He died in 1936.

Adele and Arthur Lehman had three daughters, DOROTHY LEHMAN BERNHARD, Frances Lehman Loeb, and HELEN LEHMAN BUTTENWIESER. As her children grew older, Lehman devoted an increasing amount of time to volunteer work and was particularly involved in the Service for the Orthopedically Handicapped. She also served as the president of the East Side Free School for Crippled Children (P.S. 157, Manhattan) and was a volunteer for the Purple Box, an outlet for the sale of goods made by disabled women. Lehman was director of the Adoption Bureau and a board member of the New York Board of Charities, as well as a member of the Crusade for Children, which was part of the Child Welfare League of America. In the 1940s, Lehman was active in the League of Women Voters and served as vice president until 1945.

Some of Lehman's volunteer work was focused around specifically Jewish causes. She was a board member of the Hebrew Sheltering Guardian Society and was active in the Federation for Support of Jewish Philanthropic Societies. Lehman was also a member of the women's auxiliary at her synagogue, Temple Emanu-El of New York City.

Lehman was devoted to both civic and cultural causes, and was elected to the board of directors for the Philharmonic Symphony Society of New York in 1947.

In 1957, she made a gift to Barnard College that established Adele Lehman Hall, which currently houses Barnard's Wollman Library. Until approximately the end of World War I, she was also a championship tennis player and won thirty-eight competitions.

Adele Lehman died on August 11, 1965, in her home in Purchase, New York, of a cerebral hemorrhage. Her involvement in charitable activities and welfare work, both with secular and Jewish organizations, makes her a significant figure in the history of New York City philanthropy.

BIBLIOGRAPHY

AJYB 67 (1966): 539; *DAB* 7; Obituary. *NYTimes*, August 12, 1965, 27:1; *WWIAJ* (1938).

LAURIE SOKOL

LEHMAN, EDITH ALTSCHUL (1889–1974)

Although she preferred to be addressed as Mrs. Herbert H. Lehman, and often insisted that marriage was her career and family was the greatest interest in her life, Edith Altschul Lehman's public persona belied her commitment to social causes. Known to many only as the cultured wife of one of New York's most popular governors and senators, she was in her own right a passionate social activist and philanthropist, although much of her philanthropy was not made public.

Edith Altschul Lehman was born in San Francisco on August 8, 1889, the eldest of three children. Her parents, Charles and Camilla (Mandlebaum) Altschul, were members of the wealthy and cultured Jewish aristocracy of the city. Charles Altschul, born in London to American parents and educated in Germany, had migrated to San Francisco in 1877 and had become a successful banker.

When Edith was eleven, her father moved the family to New York to take a position in the investment firm of Lazard Frères and Company. She attended Dr. Julius Sachs' School for Girls and Miss Jacoby's (later Calhoun School). As a teenager, she accompanied her parents on their frequent trips abroad, where she eagerly absorbed European culture.

At eighteen, she chose not to attend college, but to study nursing instead. Her plans changed, however, when she met Herbert Lehman, the thirty-one-year-old member of a very influential New York family and a partner in the Lehman Brothers investment firm. They were married on April 28, 1910.

The young couple had much in common. They came from families with traditions of giving aid to welfare and religious causes. They shared concerns for decent government, better schools and housing, and strong trade unions, and had great faith in the government's ability to address these social conditions.

Early in their marriage, Herbert Lehman turned his attention to a political career and Edith Lehman to volunteerism. Her success in organizing a lay social service committee to take care of the family needs of hospitalized patients led to the establishment of Mount

Sinai Hospital's first professional social service department and to her many years of association with the hospital. She was involved in two other institutions that would also become lifelong causes: the Henry Street Settlement, founded to improve conditions of life on the Lower East Side, and the Play Schools Association, organized to care for children of working mothers.

The Lehmans became the parents of Peter (b. 1917), John (b. 1920), and Hilda (b. 1921). For

Wife of one of New York's most popular political figures, Edith Lehman was highly active in social and philanthropic activities, supporting the Henry Street Settlement and a wide variety of institutions in health and education. She is shown here with her husband, Herbert Lehman, registering to vote in November 1950. [Library of Congress]

Lehman, who delighted in her roles as mother and activist, there was yet another role to assume in 1928—political wife. Throughout her husband's long public career as lieutenant governor and governor of New York, as a United States senator, and as a leader in Democratic politics, Edith Lehman described herself as an innocent bystander who "tagged along with him." Nevertheless, after Herbert Lehman's death in 1963, Democratic politicians continued to call at the Lehman home for advice and endorsements. It was a testimony to Edith Lehman's keen intelligence and astute political savvy.

While lax in their religiosity, assimilated American Jews of Lehman's generation were faithful to the dictum that "all Israel are responsible for one another." Although she did not attend her first Passover seder until 1959, Lehman was, from a young age, deeply interested in Jewish communal affairs. A staunch supporter of Israel, she made her first trip to the country in 1949, traveling on a refugee ship from Marseilles with her husband.

In recognition of her assiduous work as a fundraiser and as a benefactor to the United Jewish Appeal and the Federation of Jewish Charities of New York, the Edith Lehman High School in Dimona, Israel, was built by the Women's Division and dedicated to her.

The Lehmans balanced their philanthropy between Jewish and non-Jewish causes. They built Pete's House in 1948, an addition to the Henry Street Settlement, as a gift to the children of the neighborhood, and dedicated it in memory of their son Peter, who had been killed in World War II. In 1961, they built the Children's Zoo in Central Park.

After her husband's death, Lehman's larger philanthropic works were dedicated to him: the establishment of the Mount Sinai Hospital Medical School and the Lehman Professorship in Pediatrics; the Lehman Educational Fund for Afro-American college students; the Lehman School of Ethics at the Jewish Theological Seminary; and donations to Williams College, Herbert's alma mater.

Lehman was awarded honorary doctor of humane letters degrees from Williams College and from Mount Sinai School of Medicine and a doctor of laws from Columbia University.

Edith Altschul Lehman died on March 8, 1974, in New York City.

BIBLIOGRAPHY

AJYB 78:543; Cohen, Naomi W. *Encounter with Emancipation* (1984); Diner, Hasia R. *The Jewish People in America.* Vol. 2, *A Time for Gathering* (1992); Lehman, Edith Altschul. Papers. The Herbert H. Lehman Suite and Papers, Columbia University, NYC; Lehman, Herbert H. Papers. The Herbert H. Lehman Suite and and Papers, Columbia University; Marcus, Jacob Rader. *United States Jewry, 1776–1985.* Vol. 2, *The Germanic Period* (1991); Nevins, Allan. *Herbert H. Lehman and His Era* (1963); Obituary. *NYTimes*, March 9, 1974, 36:1; Sochen, June. *Consecrate Every Day* (1981).

NORMA SPUNGEN

LEIBER, JUDITH (b. 1921)

"Hitler put me in the handbag business," Judith Leiber recalled in Enid Nemy's book, *Judith Leiber: The Artful Handbag.* She was born Judith Peto in Budapest, Hungary, on January 11, 1921. Her well-to-do parents, Emil and Helen Peto, originally planned that she make a fortune in skin creams. In 1939, she was accepted at King's College, Cambridge, as a chemistry major, but she was unable to attend because Jews were restricted from traveling in Europe. Instead, she enrolled in the Hungarian Handbag Guild.

Judith, her older sister Eva, and her mother survived the Nazi occupation of Budapest by staying in a building designated for Jews and then in a house set aside for Swiss citizens. Her father, an Austro-Hungarian who managed the grain department of a bank, obtained a pass for himself and forged the words "and family," using the same typewriter used to issue the pass.

During the war, Judith met Gerson (Gus) Leiber, a Brooklyn native, who was a Signal Corps sergeant in the United States Army serving in Eastern Europe. The two married in 1946 and moved to New York City in 1947. Gerson Leiber is an abstract expressionist painter and a member of the National Academy of Design. His paintings hang in the Philadelphia Museum of Art, the Smithsonian Museum in Washington, D.C., the Israel Museum in Jerusalem, and other institutions.

It was Gerson who encouraged Leiber to strike out on her own in 1963 after she had worked for various handbag manufacturers. Her company, situated in midtown Manhattan, began with a handful of employees and has since grown to two hundred strong.

Though she has created scores of different handbag styles in materials ranging from cashmere to fish skin, Leiber is probably best known for her crystal minaudières. These evening bags are constructed of a metal shell encrusted with beads and have taken the form of baby pigs, slices of watermelon, penguins, and snakes. Almost every first lady since Mamie Eisenhower has been the owner of at least one Judith

Leiber original. Jacqueline Kennedy took hers to the Inaugural Ball, while Hillary Clinton carries her Socks the cat pocketbook when dressed in evening gowns.

It is primarily first ladies and the very rich who can afford to own a Leiber handbag, which can carry a price tag of up to $7,500. Collecting these bags has become synonymous with fashion savvy, indulgence and wealth. BEVERLY SILLS, chair of Lincoln Center for the Performing Arts, owns seventy bags; New York socialite Pat Buckley owns eighteen. However, these figures pale in comparison to the Olympic champion of Leiber collecting, Bernice Norman, an arts patron in New Orleans, who owns close to three hundred bags.

Leiber designs are in the permanent collections of museums around the country, including the Smithsonian, the Los Angeles County Museum, and the Dallas Museum of Fine Arts. A retrospective of her collection, was displayed at New York's Fashion Institute of Technology in late 1994.

Time Products purchased Leiber's firm in March 1993 for $18 million, but she is still active in the details of the company, including the operation of her first boutique on Manhattan's Upper East Side. She also has shops at upscale department stores such as Bergdorf Goodman, Saks Fifth Avenue, and Neiman Marcus.

Her jeweled creations make Leiber the "Fabergé of today," as one customer remarked. She has been similarly recognized by professional organizations. After only six years in business, she received the Swarovski Great Designer award for artistic use of the company's rhinestones. She was also the first in her field to win the Coty American Fashion Critics Award (1973). In 1980, she won the Neiman Marcus Winged Statue for Excellence in Design, and in 1991, the Silver Slipper Award from the Costume Institute of the Museum of Fine Arts in Houston. Recently, she accepted the Lifetime Achievement Award from the Council of Fashion Designers of America, wearing a striking blue evening gown and one of her minaudières around her neck as a pendant.

BIBLIOGRAPHY

Goodman, Wendy. "To Have and to Hold." *Harper's Bazaar*, no. 3396 (November 1994): 68; Nemy, Enid. *Judith Leiber: The Artful Handbag* (1995); "Splurge." *The New Yorker* 68, no. 14 (May 25, 1992): 28; Wadyka, Sally. "Small Wonders." *Vogue* 185, no. 3 (March 1995), 232+; Witchel, Alex. "Handbags That Make Headlines." *NYTimes*, May 1, 1996, C1.

NANCY ROSEN

LEIBOVITZ, ANNIE (b. 1949)

For decades, Annie Leibovitz and her camera have exposed to the public eye subtleties of character in rock stars, politicians, actors, and literary figures that lay beneath their celebrity personae. Her work first fueled the American fascination with rock 'n' roll dissidents in the 1970s and then, in the 1980s and 1990s, captured the essence of the day's great cultural icons. Her photographs make plain that, as Leibovitz herself once put it, she was not afraid to fall in love with her subjects.

Anna-Lou Leibovitz was born on October 2, 1949, in Westbury, Connecticut. She was the third of six children to Marilyn Leibovitz, a modern dance instructor, and Sam Leibovitz, an air force lieutenant colonel. As the daughter of a career military officer, Leibovitz moved with her family frequently from town to town. The constant relocation fostered strong ties among the six Leibovitz children.

Leibovitz attended the San Francisco Art Institute from 1967 until 1971. She shifted her focus from painting to photography early in her college career. In 1969, she lived at Kibbutz Amir in Israel. The archaeological team on which she worked during her five months in Israel uncovered the remains of King Solomon's Temple. By the time Leibovitz received her bachelor of fine arts degree in 1971, her photographs of Israel and a picture of the poet Allen Ginsberg at a San Francisco peace march had already landed her a job at the music magazine *Rolling Stone*.

Soon after she was hired, Leibovitz convinced editor Jann Wenner to grant her a breakthrough assignment. Leibovitz flew with Wenner to New York City to interview John Lennon. A photo from that trip adorned the cover of *Rolling Stone*, the first of dozens Leibovitz would shoot over the course of her career with the music magazine. In 1973, she was named chief photographer.

The mid-1970s brought Leibovitz an increasing amount of notoriety and its concomitant tribulations. In 1975, the rock band the Rolling Stones invited Leibovitz to document their six-month concert tour. Living in the world of her subjects, her camera did not shield Leibovitz from the rock 'n' roll life-style. She began using cocaine on tour and struggled for years afterward to recover.

In 1983, Leibovitz put together her first major exhibit, which led to the publication of her book *Annie Leibovitz: Photographs* (1983). Her ability to work with her subjects to get beneath the veneer of superficiality that typically characterizes Hollywood paparazzi has reinforced her reputation as the most prominent celebrity photographer of her generation. The rapport Leibovitz develops with her subjects creates an atmosphere in which celebrities will strike the most unconventional of poses and show emotions that other photographers could not evoke. Among her most famous shots are a naked John Lennon curled around a fully clothed Yoko Ono, BETTE MIDLER in a bed of roses, and the Blues Brothers painted blue.

In 1983, after more than a decade of photographing such rock 'n' roll legends as Lennon, Bob Dylan, Stevie Wonder, and Bruce Springsteen, Leibovitz left *Rolling Stone* for *Vanity Fair.* This move gave her the opportunity to shoot a broader range of subjects, including the Dalai Lama, Vaclav Havel, and Donald Trump. Her art did not suffer from the change. The American Society of Magazine Photographers selected her as the Photographer of the Year in 1984.

In addition to her work for *Vanity Fair,* Leibovitz became active in advertising photography. In 1986, she was the first photographer ever to be commissioned to design and shoot posters for the World Cup. A campaign she designed for American Express brought Leibovitz a storm of critical acclaim. In 1987, she received the Innovation in Photography Award from the American Society of Magazine Photographers, a Clio Award from Clio Enterprises, and a Campaign of the Decade Award from *Advertising Age* for the "Portraits" campaign she produced for American Express. Then, in 1990, the International Center of Photography recognized the same work by giving Leibovitz the Infinity Award for applied photography.

In 1991, Leibovitz became only the second living photographer to be featured in an exhibit at the National Portrait Gallery in Washington, D.C. She published this retrospective in book form under the title *Annie Leibovitz: Photographs, 1970–1990.* In anticipation of the centennial Olympic games, Leibovitz spent two years photographing athletes around the world. Her tour culminated in the 1996 book *Olympic Portraits.* Today, as in 1970, Annie Leibovitz is still shaping public conceptions of the celebrities she photographs.

SELECTED WORKS BY ANNIE LEIBOVITZ

American Ballet Theatre: The First Fifty Years (1989); *Misha and Others: Photographs* (1992); *Olympic Portraits* (1996); *Annie Leibovitz: Photographs* (1983), and *Annie Leibovitz: Photographs, 1970–1990* (1991); *Shooting Stars* (1973); *Visual Aid,* with others (1986).

BIBLIOGRAPHY

Amende, Coral. *Legends in Their Own Time* (1994); *Contemporary Authors.* Vol. 140 (1993): 278–280; *Current Biography Yearbook, 1991* (1991): 360–364; *Dictionary of the Arts* (1994); *ICP (International Center of Photography) Encyclopedia of Photography* (1984); Rood, Gale L. *Dictionary of Twentieth-Century Culture.* Vol. 1: *American Culture After World War II* (1994); *Who's Who in America, 1996.* 50th ed. (1995); *Who's Who of American Women, 1995–1996.* 19th ed. (1995).

GREG CAPLAN

LEISURE AND RECREATION

In the wake of the Civil War, one of the bloodiest wars in the nation's history, Americans discovered pleasure. "Vacation" became a verb as well as a noun and, in some quarters, even a form of moral exhortation. A vacation, insisted reformer Melvil Dewey, is not just a luxury but a "necessity for those who aim to do a large amount of high-grade work." Well-to-do, hardworking German-born Jews of the 1870s heeded Dewey's words. Like other affluent Americans, they vacationed at Saratoga Springs, then one of the country's premier watering holes, had enjoyed the bracing sea air of the New Jersey shore where luxuriously appointed hotels dotted the beach. "Fond of fun and frolic," they spent their mornings and afternoons promenading on the boardwalks and boulevards of America's resort towns; in the evenings they dined, danced, and gambled. America, they believed, was truly God's playground.

Within a few short years, however, their faith was shaken. In 1877, Saratoga hotelier Henry Hilton refused to host leading Jewish financier Joseph Seligman and his family at the world-renowned Grand Union Hotel. An otherwise valued guest, Seligman was banished from this latter-day Eden, Hilton explained, because his presence might attract "colonies of Jewish people," whose behavior was considered "obnoxious" by the "majority" of Grand Union habitués.

At the time, many American Jews believed Hilton's behavior to be little more than the idiosyncrasy of a misguided curmudgeon. But when, two years later, a similar statement was made, this time at the popular middle-class New York resort town of Manhattan Beach, waves of alarm spread across the pages of the country's Jewish newspapers. "We do not like the Jews as a class," declared Austin Corbin, president of the Manhattan Beach Company, in the summer of 1879. "There are some well-behaved people among them; but as a rule they make themselves offensive to the kind of people who principally patronize our [rail]road and hotel. I am satisfied we should be better off without than with their custom."

As the Hilton and Corbin incidents made clear, the pursuit of pleasure for Jews was often fraught with disappointment. Nowhere, it seemed, was the fault line between expectation and reality, between acceptance and social ostracism, more exposed than when Americans were at play. A holiday by the sea or in the country, which promised a respite from daily restrictions, instead often heightened them. "Race prejudice at summer resorts," explained Alice Hyneman Rhine

in an 1887 exposé of the phenomenon, was "sweeping" the country. Rhine reported that like Hilton and Corbin ("Hilton the Second," as he was dubbed in some quarters), many hotel owners were taking a dislike to Jews because of their supposed boisterousness. Others disapproved of the Jews' "disregard of table etiquette and ignorance of the courtesies of the

Well into the twentieth century, Jews found that they were excluded from many vacation possibilities,
as the above flyer from a hotel in Miami Beach indicates.
[Peter H. Schweitzer]

drawing-room." Still others frowned upon their attire: "It is said of [the Jews] that their ill-breeding shows itself in an ignorance of the canons of good taste in dress, which causes them to affect patent leather boots, showy trousers and conspicuous and vulgar jewelry."

Publicly, Jews were quick to defend themselves against such charges and to denounce "race prejudice" as a form of "petulant bigotry" at best and of "unjust, injurious, wicked," and un-American behavior at worst. Privately, though, many Jews conceded that some of the allegations were not without merit, especially those regarding displays of flamboyance. When Jews walk and talk loudly, dress "showily," and use a tooth-pick "profusely" while in public, said one Jewish newspaper, it was no wonder that hotel keepers were justified in "exercising discretion." Columnist HENRI-ETTA SZOLD, or "Sulamith," as she styled herself at the time, was quick to agree. Writing in the *Jewish Messenger* in the aftermath of the "Corbin affair," Szold was as fierce in her condemnation of the behavior of fellow Jews as she was of Corbin's. She roundly took them to task for their all-consuming pursuit of money and their cavalier disregard for spiritual matters.

Szold's was hardly the last word on the subject. Well into the 1890s, German Jewish women were publicly exhorted—often by one another—to keep up their guard on vacation, to comport themselves with "unobtrusive modesty," and to eschew material and emotional excess at all costs. In 1895, for instance, ROSA SONNESCHEIN's newspaper, THE AMERICAN JEW-ESS, featured an editorial, "The Jewess at Summer Resorts," in which, characteristically, denunciation mingled with apologetics:

> Our Jewish ladies will, as usual, form no inconsiderable contingent of the gay throngs on pleasure and recreation intent. . . . Let them continually bear in mind that is it their bounden duty to so comport themselves in public, as to give the lie to those aspersions cast upon the entire race . . . because of the forward, vulgar and pompous demeanor of a few individuals.

If a non-Jewish woman adorned herself with all manner of trinkets and "glittering gewgaws," laughed boisterously, and treated waiters with undisguised contempt, she would have only herself to blame. "Let, however, Mrs. Abrahams indulge in the same offenses against the canons of good breeding and Jewish womanhood, *en masse*, must atone for her sins."

To prevent the further proliferation of women like Mrs. Abrahams, the American Jewish community needed "social missionaries," insisted Sonneschein. "We need Jewish women of wealth, who will make propaganda for a dignified simplicity of dress and speech, who by their example will teach the masses to maintain their dignity at hotels and watering places." Warming to her subject, the magazine publisher asserted that the American Jewish community required "missionaries to teach the world that American Jews are the product of civilization."

In the years following Sonneschein's peroration, the vacation "habit" extended to virtually all segments of the American population, from the well-heeled dowager to the recently arrived working girl. "There are towns in this state, in the Catskill region, and along the seashore whose summer population is made up almost entirely of East Siders," observed a writer for the *American Israelite* in 1903, contemplating the recent democratization of leisure. "A Sunday afternoon spent on the boardwalk at Arverne or on Ocean Avenue, Long Branch or Bath Beach, will attest to the truth of this statement. It would seem that the entire East Side has closed up home and shop and has gone to the seashore."

Preferring to spend vacations in the company of their own kind rather than run a gauntlet of disapproving gentiles, Eastern European Jewish immigrants created a summer world of boardinghouses, bungalows, inns, and "exclusive" hotels populated entirely by Jews. In some instances, would-be farmers played host to guests from the city. An article entitled "A Voice from the Ghetto," in the August 1903 pages of the *American Hebrew*, made this wry observation:

> For eight months in the year [the Jewish farmer] is forgotten . . . but with the oncoming of the summer, a host of friends appear on the scene. . . . These friends are not unlike friends everywhere. They like to visit you at your summer home and dine with you, and some of them bring their baggage along with them for an extended stay.

Soon, quite a number of enterprising farmers began to charge their guests a modest fee for room and board. "In this way," concluded "A Voice from the Ghetto," the farmer "entertains his friends at no loss to himself."

While vacationers fancied farm life, others made do with the *kochalein* [literally, "cook for yourself"], one of the most inventive and affordable of summer institutions. "For about sixty dollars for the season, which could last from Memorial Day to Hanukkah if one wished, each family had had a sleeping room,

You didn't really have a vacation unless you could bring back photos to prove you had a good time.
This posed photo from Atlantic City, New Jersey, is of Louise and Florence Mandel of Chicago.
[Chicago Historical Society]

cooking and food storage privileges in a communal kitchen with half a dozen wood stoves and . . . tomatoes, cucumbers and string beans from the garden," wrote Jack Luria, a veteran of many *kochalein* summers at Schaine's boardinghouse. A delight for children, the shared living arrangements could fray adult nerves and give rise to daily quarrels as too many women fought to use too few stoves. Luria quoted his mother as saying, "If you had cooked a summer in Schaine's kitchen, you need not fear the tortures of *Gehennom* [hell] in the world to come."

For those more concerned with keeping up appearances than with saving money, nothing less than a "first-class" hotel would suffice. Observed one student of immigrant social mores:

> Social climbing demands it. . . . One cannot do without it and still maintain the respect of one's friends. One would fall considerably if it were known that he or she had not gone to Tannersville, or Hunter, or Arverne . . . especially if one happened to belong to the fair sex.

To satisfy the demand for accommmodation, Jewish businessmen purchased or assumed control of existing luxury hotels. "Now Under Jewish Management," announced the Grossmans, the new owners of the luxurious Pavilion Hotel in 1927. Our hotel

> benefit[s] a new American people and a new generation. The ballroom, where the Vanderbilts, Goulds and Astors danced to soft music their dainty minuets and ancient waltzes, will now see Jewish youths and maidens gyrating to jazz. The dining hall that rang to the tune of Yankee Doodle will resound now to the *Hatikvo*. Dark eyes flashing with Oriental fire will gaze from the porch of that aristocratic hotel.

As they sat, gazing, on the veranda or rowed on the lake or dressed for dinner, Eastern European Jews and their children gave themselves over completely to the "gospel of relaxation." "We are all talking and thinking and dreaming of our vacation," they told a reporter for the *Tageblat*. With the first hint of spring, advertisements for the Ocean Spray Hotel, High View Villa, Clinton Farm House, and the Pleasure Lake House filled the pages of the *Tageblatt* and other American Jewish newspapers, fueling readers' dreams. By midsummer, editorials urging vacationers to mind their manners and behave with restraint were just as frequent. Warning against the "indifferent parvenus, the reckless gamesters, the frivolous and the giddy," the communal press urged Jewish pleasure-seekers to cultivate their intellect as well as their sensations. Women often bore the brunt of such public exhortations. Time and again, the prospect of idle Jewish women sporting red lacquered nails and flimsy, though expensive, summer dresses greatly troubled the community's cultural custodians. In 1922, for example, the *Froyen Zhurnal*, a popular Yiddish women's magazine of the period, encouraged its female readers to be "intelligent vacationers." "Think twice before going into any undue expenditures," the paper cautioned, recommending that working women plan carefully for their much awaited vacations, especially in planning their wardrobes. "Girls, remember please . . . that to be rigged out in fine style," one doesn't need much, just one or two skirts, two dress blouses, two "dressy gowns," a wide-brimmed hat, and a sweater. "Rest assured, you girls, who have to rely upon a limited wardrobe during your vacation, that the woman who has gone on vacation with her trunks full of elaborate clothes will not find contentment and pleasure if she will have to rely wholly upon her clothes for that."

Leisure activities were not necessarily limited to extended vacations,
as this group demonstrates on the "High Ride" in Riverview Park, in Chicago, in June 1915.
[Chicago Historical Society]

What you do on your vacation depends on the part of the country where you live. This photo shows Alice and Abraham Rosenberg and friends in Yosemite. [Western Jewish History Center]

In addition to sartorial advice, the community's cultural arbiters dispensed a different kind of wisdom, suggesting that women spend their summers "wisely." Attend lectures, read "good books," and engage in good deeds, they were told. After all, recommended the *Hadassah News Letter* in 1927, "psychologically, a summer resort is a superb setting for disseminating HADASSAH knowledge. The necessarily constant companionship of the resorts and the leisureliness of vacationing create just the right atmosphere for conversation and exchange of ideas."

Despite such entreaties, Jewish daughters seemed to delight in the pursuit of pleasure, much to the disappointment and consternation of communal leaders such as DORA R. SPIEGEL, president of the WOMEN'S LEAGUE FOR CONSERVATIVE JUDAISM. Writing in 1934, Spiegel fulminated against those women who "talked small talk all day long between food, drink, mah jong and golf and judged all others by the clothes they wore." Though these women "eschew all talk of politics and books lest they be thought bores, they like to think of themselves as the cream of Jewish society." "Perhaps they were," Spiegel acidly concluded, "but the cream has turned rancid."

American Jewry's leading literary lights felt much the same way. Taking aim at the apparent ease with which so many Jewish daughters took to the good life, Jewish writers produced some of the harshest critiques of American leisure culture ever published. Take, for example, editor and writer Abraham Cahan's wrenching tale of deracination, *The Rise of David Levinsky*, in which forty pages are given over to depicting the social machinations and sartorial aspirations of largely female vacationers at a fictitious Catskill resort. Saturday dinner "was not merely a meal. It was, in addition, or chiefly, a great social function and a gown contest." Bediamonded and bedecked, young women were "powdered and painted. Prosperity was rapidly breaking the chains of American Puritanism, rapidly 'Frenchifying' the country and the East Side was quick to fall in line." Belletrist Maurice Samuel was equally scathing. In his 1925 poem, "Al Harei Catskill," published in the high-toned *Menorah Journal*, he mocked the mindlessness of Catskill culture.

And here in Catskill what do Jews believe? In Kosher, certainly; in Shabbas, less . . . in charity and in America. But most of all in Pinochle and Poker, in dancing and in Jazz, in risqué stories and everything that's smart and up-to-date.

In the Catskills and other summer retreats, the prospect of romance loomed large, inflaming passions and roiling the search for quiet. "Our seashore pastimes are becoming artificialized and complicated and straining," observed Brooklyn rabbi Alexander Lyons in 1915, referring to such popular resort towns as Arverne and Long Branch. "They are becoming too extensively fashionable parade places and . . . matrimonial marts." Much the same could be said of many of the adult summer camps that sprang up during the interwar period to provide affordable vacations for single men and women in their twenties. While some adult camps like Boiberik, Lakeland, and Unity House, the ILGWU-sponsored facility, stressed their educational programming (and their older, married clientele), others, such as Camp Utopia in the Poconos or the fictitious South Wind popularized in Herman Wouk's novel *Marjorie Morningstar*, seemed entirely given over to personal fulfillment. "Part of that vacation at camp had as its goal sex on the part of the boys and marriage on the part of the girls," reminisced Moss Hart, who in the 1920s served as Camp Utopia's social director. "It was a game of endless variations—a stately minuet of lying and pretense," which often crescendoed into marriage.

Having found a mate, many married people, ironically enough, found themselves without one for much of the summer. By and large, gainfully employed middle-class and working-class men of the prewar era could not afford to take a lengthy vacation. Sending their wives and children off to the country for an entire summer, the men joined their families only on weekends, arriving with great fanfare on the Friday evening or Saturday afternoon train—the so-called husband train—and leaving in a more subdued fashion on Sunday night. In their absence, Jewish leisure society was, de facto, a gendered affair. By the sea or in the mountains, at the grandest hotel or in the most modest *kochalein*, women and children dominated the scene.

Other vacation spots, like those maintained by the Jewish Working Girls Vacation Society, practiced a deliberate form of gender segregation. Established in 1892 by ESTHER JANE RUSKAY and SELINA GREENBAUM on the model of the "unsectarian" Working Girls Vacation Society, the New York organization provided affordable vacations for those least likely to afford them: single, working Jewish women. For three dollars a week, milliners, stenographers, and machine workers—over one thousand women a season—enjoyed a respite from their ordinary routine amid the "cheery hospitality" of the society's two vacation homes, one in Bellport, Long Island, and the other in the Adirondacks. At these facilities, staffed and inhabited entirely by women, the "Jewish working girl enjoys all the advantages of mountain air or seashore.... Here her health and her pleasures are studied, her comfort provided for and her social well-being considered." A proven success, the Jewish Working Girls' Vacation Society inspired the formation of similar societies throughout the country. The Welcome House Vacation Home in Long Branch, New Jersey, for example, catered to the recently arrived immigrant woman. "These girls feel happier among themselves rather than being with English-speaking girls," explained Carrie Wise, its director. In Chicago, the local chapter of the NATIONAL COUNCIL OF JEWISH WOMEN maintained a summer sewing school in which students capped their education with a two-week group vacation. The Philadelphia Vacation Home for Jewish Working Girls sought to acquaint city-bred girls with the beauties of botany, giving them "a glimpse into the wonders of mother nature." Frolicking in the surf or catching butterflies, formerly fatigued, downtrodden young women reemerged as "care-free, merry-hearted sprites." Small wonder, then, that contemporary observers likened the Jewish Working Girls' Vacation Society to a "truly American fairy tale."

Several philanthropic organizations helped the underprivileged find respite from "sultry" city streets by exposing them to the cooling breezes of "marine ozone" or mountain air. "Summer Outings for the Jewish Poor," explained the National Conference of Jewish Charities in 1904, "form an especially valuable branch of what is technically known as 'preventive' charity." Claiming that "Jewish faults and failings can be traced to their being cooped up in towns," conference officials argued for programmatically acquainting tenement residents with the joys of rural life. "You cannot pitch forth the Ghetto dweller into the country. You must lead him there by his own desire, and summer outings are one of the most effective methods of inducement."

The "worn and fragile mother" of the ghettos came in for special consideration. "If preventive charity is to have a chance . . . here is the opportunity," settlement house workers were told. Remove the tired mother, "overburdened with care, with drudgery, with discouragement," together with her children, to restful surroundings, and within a week, one would witness a marked physical and social improvement. "Too tired to take the journey on Monday morning . . . they return home on Saturday night, rested and bright and hopeful." Heartened by such empirically based evidence of success and convinced that there was "probably no means by which so much happiness can be conveyed for so small expenditure," dozens of Jewish welfare organizations such as the Educational Alliance and the Henry Street Settlement sponsored a steady round of harbor excursions, picnics in the park, and week-long trips to the country or the seashore for the urban poor.

Many of these philanthropically inspired facilities, attentive to the ritual requirements of their clientele, made sure a "truly Jewish spirit" reigned at their resorts. The New York Jewish Working Girls' Vacation Society insisted that its strictly kosher meals be opened with a "short Hebrew grace" and closed with a "benediction." Others, like Philadelphia's Vacation Home for Jewish Working Girls, placed a premium on Friday evening services. "The festive air of lighted candles and best gowns," an eyewitness related, "set Friday evening apart as something altogether different from the other evenings." Elsewhere, however, the familiar rhythms of Jewish life were sharply interrupted as many summering Jews appeared to take a vacation from God as well. "Out for a holiday time," Jews have "thrown off all restraints of religion and of Jewish self-respect and deport themselves as though no tie bound them to race or religion," observed one vacationer. On Friday evenings, they danced in the ballroom instead of singing *zmirot* at the dinner table; on Saturday, more people attended tennis matches, lawn parties, swimming contests, and horse shows than Shabbat services. Not one to let this "reckless indifference" go unnoticed, Esther Jane Ruskay angrily denounced her coreligionists for their "summer resort Judaism." Year after year, until her demise in 1911, she filled the pages of the *American Hebrew* with her impassioned, seasonal pleas for ritual constancy and steadfastness.

Still, laments about "summer Judaism" continued to multiply, becoming in their own way as much a summertime ritual as a two-week vacation. "Many Jews and Jewesses who are compelled to pay a considerable charge for excess baggage because of the number of gowns and hats and shoes which they feel called upon to take with them consider it an encumbrance to include also their Judaism when they leave for the summer vacations," wrote Althea O. Silverman in the 1930s. But Judaism, she insisted, should not be discarded like a winter coat. "A garment of the soul," Judaism was appropriate for every season. "It might be thought and felt and lived during the summer also—in the cottage, in the bungalow, in the hotel, as well as in the city home and in the Synagogue. The spirit of Judaism," Silverman ringingly concluded, "suffers no climatic disturbances."

Toward that end, concerned organizations like the Union of American Hebrew Congregations' Bureau of Summer Services expended much effort to provide religious services and rabbis at summer resorts throughout Michigan and Wisconsin where "Jewish people congregate in large numbers." Others urged the vacationing American Jew to follow the lead of his or her "Gentile neighbor," who, spending time at a local chautauqua or a Methodist summer colony

like Ocean Grove, "makes the best possible use of the summer life for religious propaganda. Wherever he goes his church goes along." Resistant at first, Jews eventually developed summer congregations. By the 1920s, according to the *United Synagogue Recorder,* summer synagogues with memberships "equally divided between men and women" began to take root in resort towns everywhere.

For many Jews, camp provided the best solution to the doldrums of "summer Judaism" and, by extension, the anomalies of the American Jewish experience. "American Jewish children ... do not live a natural Jewish life," explained Shlomo Shulsinger, who, with his wife, Rivka, founded Massad Camps in the 1940s. "Radio, movies, newspapers, books, games—all the factors which go towards developing a child's character and mode of living are far removed from Jewish realities." At a Jewish summer camp, however, youngsters could live in an environment where Jewish culture mattered: Buildings and walkways carried the names of legendary Jewish personalities, while lively, contemporized Yiddish or Hebrew could be heard on the baseball diamond and on the outdoor stage.

Initially, Jewish summer camp was inspired more by charitable than cultural concerns. As "armies" of poor, unsupervised Jewish children took to the streets in July and August, many communal leaders such as Rabbi Maurice Lewisohn worried about their physical and moral well-being. "There is no plainer fact than the relation of the lack of recreation to moral breakdown," he observed, adding, "recreation is not only educational, it is a moral force." To Lewisohn's way of thinking, supervised play, especially in the form of a two-week stint at a summer camp, was the perfect antidote to the anomie of the slums. Other likeminded Jews formed, in the early years of this century, a number of "philanthropically correct" summer camps where young boys, "far removed from the temptations and pettiness of city life," learned the gentleman's code of behavior. "Camp should become the Mecca for every young man who enjoys camping and is willing to live up to the rules," stated William Mitchel, the director of Surprise Lake Camp in 1910.

In the years that followed, girls, too, raised their eyes toward these mountain Meccas, and began to enroll in summer camp. "Nowadays even the girls may go to a camp, though they may not live in tents," reported the *American Hebrew* in 1911. Over the next two decades, as camping increasingly became an acceptable middle-class phenomenon, the number of Jewish camps catering to girls grew dramatically. Eager to throw off their previous association with the poor, these

The NATIONAL COUNCIL OF JEWISH WOMEN *was one of a number of Jewish organizations that sponsored summer camps. This 1937 photo shows Meta Goldstein, a camp counselor at the NCJW's camp in Wauconda, Illinois, taking her charges on a hike.*
[Chicago Historical Society]

camps made a point of stressing their affluent clientele and well-equipped campuses. Camp Jo-Lee for Girls in North Belgrade, Maine, for example, was "limited to girls from the finest American Jewish homes throughout the United States." Meanwhile, Jo-Lee's competitor, Camp Dunmore for Girls in Brandon, Vermont, advertised its "atmosphere of refinement" and promised to "develop the mind and body of the growing [Jewish] girl along the lines of recreational play and sports."

Whether single sex or coeducational (increasingly "the thing to do," reported one disgruntled camping professional in the 1930s), Jewish summer camps tended to reflect and promote gendered notions of play. Boys played basketball; girls gardened. "Boys had a lot more sports and girls a lot more culture,"

recalled veteran Cejwin camper and counselor Susan Addleston. Even popular pursuits commonly associated with Native Americans, from council ring to tracking, were experienced differently by the sexes. "Young boys," observed Surprise Lake Camp's longtime director Max Oppenheimer, "like to play at games in which the cunning and swiftness of the Indian is brought out." The girls, by contrast, associated Indians with more sedentary matters. "I have good and bad news," wrote Ruth Braude, a camper at Camp Waziyatah, to her parents in the summer of 1932, informing them that at a recent Indian council ring, green feathers were awarded for good posture, yellow feathers were distributed for fair posture, and red feathers were given out for poor posture. "I got a green feather and Hilda [her sister] got a red one. My feather is good news. Hilda's is bad."

With their emphasis on feathers, fun, and friendship, bygone summers inevitably yielded to new seasonal demands. Little by little, advertisements for school shoes replaced those for sandals, while the sale of seats in synagogues and temples, "the first premonition of the approach of fall," replaced those for summer getaways. But no sooner did worshipers, bedecked in their holiday finery, exit the synagogue, their collars turned up against the autumn chill, than thoughts turned once again to the "vagaries of vacation."

BIBLIOGRAPHY

Cahan, Abraham. *The Rise of David Levinsky* (1917); "The Ghetto and Summer Resorts." *American Israelite* (August 20, 1903): 8; Joselit, Jenna Weissman, and Karen S., Mittelman, eds. *A Worthy Use of Summer: Jewish Summer Camping in America* (1993); Rhine, Alice Hyneman. "Race Prejudice at Summer Resorts." *Forum* (July 1887): 523–525; Ruskay, Esther Jane. "Summer Resort Judaism." *American Hebrew* (August 18, 1905): 351–352; Wouk, Herman. *Marjorie Morningstar* (1955).

JENNA WEISSMAN JOSELIT

LEMLICH, CLARA *see* SHAVELSON, CLARA LEMLICH

LERNER, GERDA (b. 1920)

Entering the field of United States history with a freshly minted Ph.D. in 1966, Gerda Lerner blazed a new professional path that led to the establishment of the field of women's history. The force of her personality and her commitment to the possibilities contained in the historical study of women made her impervious to the ridicule with which the male-dominated historical profession initially responded to the notion of women's history.

Gerda (Kronstein) Lerner was born and educated in Vienna, Austria, the elder of two daughters of Robert and Ilona (Newmann) Kronstein. She grew up in a well-to-do, assimilated family that considered itself liberal and thoroughly Austrian. Sent to a Hebrew school to prepare for her bat mitzvah, she was nevertheless keenly aware that women could not fully participate in Jewish services. In her first feminist action, Gerda decided not to join the ceremony, declaring that she did not believe in God.

Her father, a pharmacist and businessman, fled after the Nazis annexed Austria in 1938. When stormtroopers subsequently raided the family's apartment, young Gerda angrily denounced their search, and the stormstroopers left shortly thereafter. However, to force her father to sign over his property to the Nazis, they imprisoned Gerda for six weeks under conditions that made her believe she would not survive. Facing death in this way became a source of courage for her and enabled her to face with equanimity the dragons of the academic world.

Gerda immigrated to New York in 1939, the only member of her family to obtain a visa. Working as a waitress, salesgirl, office clerk, and X-ray technician to support herself while she learned English, she began to write fiction about Nazi brutality and the capacity to resist it. "The Prisoners" was published in 1941 and "The Russian Campaign" in 1943. She married Carl Lerner, a respected film editor, in 1941. They lived in Hollywood for some years before returning to New York. Their daughter, Stephanie, was born in 1945; their son, Daniel, in 1947.

Undeterred by the ridicule of conservative male historians in the 1960s and 1970s, Gerda Lerner was a trailblazer in the field of women's history with such works as Black Women in White America *and* The Female Experience. *[Schlesinger Library]*

Lerner became politically active in the Congress of American Women, a progressive grassroots women's group concerned with economic and consumer issues. She also participated in events sponsored by the EMMA LAZARUS FEDERATION, worked in support of the United Nations, and actively supported civil rights for African Americans. Continuing to write, she collaborated with EVE MERRIAM on a musical called the *Singing of Women*, which was produced in 1951. Her novel *No Farewell* (1955) focused on Vienna on the eve of Nazi occupation. For Carl Lerner's directorial debut she coauthored the screenplay *Black Like Me* (1964). She later described her husband's death in a moving memoir, *A Death of One's Own* (1978).

In the late 1950s, Lerner began work on a novel about Sarah and Angelina Grimké, the South Carolina sisters who migrated north, became featured speakers of the American antislavery society, and ignited the explosion of women's rights within the abolitionist movement. Seeking more information about her subject, she enrolled in courses at the New School for Social Research. There her fascination with the topic prompted her to teach one of the first courses in women's history. After completing a B.A. in 1963, Lerner went on to complete a Ph.D. at Columbia in 1966. Her dissertation was published as *The Grimké Sisters from South Carolina: Rebels Against Slavery* (1967).

Thereafter, Lerner poured her considerable talents into the development of the field of women's history. Her energies flowed in three directions: As an author she produced important writings, as a teacher she built new curricula, and as a member of the historical profession she demanded equality for women within its ranks.

Lerner's efforts were amplified by the new generation of women who joined the historical profession between 1967 and 1972, many of whom were attracted to women's history. The field began to take shape as the questions posed by the women's movement combined with answers forged through the methodological innovations of social history. During the years that women's history gradually emerged as an academic discipline, Lerner's leadership remained crucial.

As an innovative writer, Lerner expanded the boundaries of women's history. Her 1969 article "The Lady and the Mill Girl" was an early and influential example of class analysis in women's history. Her documentary anthology *Black Women in White America* (1972) demonstrated the importance of African-American women within women's history. In *The Female Experience* (1976), she developed a chronology and periodization that reorganized history around life-cycle categories. Her methodological writings, collected in *The Majority Finds Its Past* (1979), analyzed the field's achievements and predicted its future trajectory.

In 1968, Lerner joined the faculty of Sarah Lawrence College and later became director of its women's history master's degree program. At Sarah Lawrence, Lerner fostered projects that demonstrated the relevance of women's history to women's lives, including the establishment of women's history month and a project for the promotion of African-American women's history. Through summer institutes and a vigorous speaking schedule, she worked tirelessly to advance women and women's history in American culture and the historical profession. Her labors were rewarded in 1981 when she became president of the Organization of American Historians, the first woman to hold that position since 1946. In 1980, Lerner moved to the University of Wisconsin, where she headed a new Ph.D. program in women's history. Her interest in graduate teaching led to a national conference in 1988 at which sixty-three scholars from fifty-five institutions evaluated graduate teaching in United States women's history.

In the late 1970s, Lerner's scholarly interests shifted to European history. Raising some of the same questions that Friedrich Engels had addressed in 1884 in *The Origin of the Family, Private Property, and the State*, she searched for the origins of patriarchy and the subordination of women. In *The Creation of Patriarchy* (1986), she challenged traditional conceptions of the emergence of slavery to construct new definitions of class and to reveal new meanings of customary ideas and metaphors about women. Her work received the Joan Kelly Prize of the American Historical Association for the best book in women's and social theory that year. In *The Creation of Feminist Consciousness* (1993), Lerner exposed the devastating effects on women of their exclusion from the historical record. She persuasively argued that women's struggle to comprehend their own history lies at the heart of their ability to envision a world in which they are full participants.

In 1995, the Austrian Ministry of Women's Affairs awarded Lerner the Kaethe Leichter Prize, which honors exiled Jewish intellectuals who have built lifetimes of distinguished achievement. That year, she was also awarded the Austrian Cross of Honor for Science and Art, the highest honor given by the State of Austria. In 1997, she published two new books, *Why History Matters: Life and Thought* and *The Feminist Thought of Sarah Grimké*.

Although for many years Gerda Lerner felt that her Jewish identity was irrelevant to her achievements, in interviews in the 1990s she spoke of the importance of her experiences as a Jew, a Jewish woman, and a refugee in shaping her commitment to history and to women's history. The Holocaust created in her a need to keep memory alive, and her status as an outsider helped her understand women as an out-group.

BIBLIOGRAPHY

Antler, Joyce. *The Journey Home: Jewish Women and the American Century* (1997); "Gerda Lerner." *Profiles*. History Department, University of Wisconsin, Madison; "Introduction." *U.S. History as Women's History: New Feminist Essays*. Edited by Linda K. Kerber, Alice Kessler-Harris, and Kathryn Kish Sklar (1995); Lerner, Gerda. Interview by author, January 19, 1997.

KATHRYN KISH SKLAR

LESBIANISM

For most of its three-thousand-year history, lesbianism has been a subject of little interest in Jewish texts and societies. Only in the late twentieth century have Jewish scholars and communities faced the issue of erotic love between women.

BIBLICAL TIMES (1000–165 B.C.E.).

Lesbianism is not mentioned in the Hebrew Bible, in contrast to male homosexual behavior, which is expressly forbidden as a capital crime. The absence of discussion of lesbianism in this context has raised scholarly interest. Biblical critics have suggested that this difference exists because female homoerotic behavior would not have been considered sexual behavior, which in ancient times was understood to require the emission of semen. A related theory suggests that nothing women did without men would matter because women were not full persons by biblical standards. More traditional Jewish scholarship suggests that the writers of the Bible knew nothing of erotic attraction between women, and could not prohibit something about which there was no knowledge or awareness. Another traditional interpretation is that the behavior was obviously prohibited because what applied to men applied to women. Feminist interpreters posit that biblical society accepted erotic love between women as a matter of course. Without further evidence, all arguments are inconclusive. We have no information about erotic love between women in this time period in Jewish history.

RABBINIC TIMES (165 B.C.E.–A.D. 900)

The first discussion of female homoeroticism in Jewish texts is found in Sifra, a postbiblical commentary on the book of Leviticus, edited in the second century A.D. The reference is to a passage in Leviticus 18, which prohibits Israelite participation in acts deemed "the doings of Egypt." The commentator in Sifra suggests that lesbian marriage was one of the acts that would be included in this category. What we can infer from this text is that at the time of the writing of Sifra, Jewish communities were cognizant of the Roman practice of women marrying other women.

The Talmud, a compendium of Jewish law and practice compiled in the fifth century A.D., includes passages about *mesolelot* [female homoerotic behavior], not lesbian marriage. The word *mesolelot* is understood by later commentators to refer to the practice of tribadism (women rubbing genitals against each other). A passage in the Talmud (Yevamot 76a) questions whether women who practice *mesolelot* are eligible to marry priests. Virginity is the criterion upon which eligibility for priestly marriage is based: For example, a divorced woman or widow is not allowed to marry a priest. The Mishnah gives two opinions about the eligibility for priestly marriage of one who practices *mesolelot*. The accepted opinion is that such a woman is eligible, although the minority opinion is that she is not. In the majority opinion, lesbian behavior is considered a minor infraction. This passage establishes the existence of female homoeroticism in Jewish communities in ancient times. It also suggests that this behavior was understood by rabbinic authorities as a specific practice, not as a person's sexual orientation, as the question is raised in the context of marriage to a man. Some authorities place it in the category of sexual practice, and as such it disqualifies the practioner from the category of virgin.

MIDDLE AGES (900–1700)

There is one significant discussion of female homoerotic behavior in the medieval era. This is found in a compilation of laws known as the *Mishneh Torah*, written by legal scholar and philosopher Moses Maimonides in the twelfth century. Maimonides reiterates the connection to the Levitical prohibition against the "doings of Egypt," but also suggests that this behavior should not disqualify a woman from marrying a priest because it is still only a minor infraction. Maimonides then goes on to suggest that the courts administer a flogging to a woman who is caught engaging in homoerotic behavior. Finally, Maimonides warns men to keep their wives from visiting with women who are known to practice *mesolelot* with other women. This text views lesbian behavior as threatening to the institution of marriage and worthy of punishment.

MODERN ERA (1700–1945)

During the modern period, female homoeroticism is mentioned infrequently in Jewish sources. Most references are from fictional writings. An early example is found in a Yiddish play written by Sholem Asch entitled *Got fun Nekome* [God of vengeance]. It was translated into English and produced on Broadway in 1923. This play was the first with a lesbian theme to be performed on the American stage. The plot focused on a lesbian relationship between a prostitute and the daughter of a brothel owner, and included several explicit homoerotic scenes. Noted Yiddish author Isaac Bashevis Singer also wrote several short stories about lesbian love.

CONTEMPORARY TIMES (1945–)

The first Jewish novel by a woman that explored lesbian themes was *Wasteland* (1946), written by Ruth Seid under the pseudonym of JO SINCLAIR. The heroine was open about her sexuality to her family. The novel is about her brother's effort to come to terms with her lesbianism. This frank discussion of lesbian themes and the portrayal of lesbianism as a psychologically healthy alternative was unusual for its time.

During the early part of the twentieth century, women began to live openly as lesbians, including Jewish women. GERTRUDE STEIN is perhaps the best-known example. PAULINE NEWMAN, an organizer of the Jewish labor movement, lived openly with her partner in Greenwich Village, where they raised a child together. But for the most part, women who loved women prior to the 1960s neither identified publicly as lesbian nor had the opportunity to live openly in partnerships. The example of LILLIAN WALD, noted Jewish social reformer, was more typical of this period. Wald's relationships were crucial to her social world, yet remained hidden from view. It is still considered controversial to label Wald a lesbian, despite considerable historical evidence.

One result of the feminist and gay liberation movements in the 1960s and 1970s was that large numbers of women began to claim lesbian identity. It was in the context of these movements that lesbians began to explore Jewish identity as well. The early 1980s witnessed an explosion of small groups of lesbians who were beginning to make connections to their Jewish identities. The members of these groups identified their simultaneous rejection as Jews in the

lesbian community and as lesbians in the Jewish community. EVELYN TORTON BECK made these issues visible in her groundbreaking anthology of writings by Jewish lesbians, *Nice Jewish Girls: A Lesbian Anthology* (1982). Many lesbian novels with Jewish themes were published by women's presses. Progressive Jewish organizations like New Jewish Agenda began discussions of how to incorporate the needs of gay men and lesbians in Jewish life.

This exploration of the connections between lesbian and Jewish identities was continued in *Tribe of Dina* (1986). Edited by leading secular Jewish lesbian thinkers Irena Klepfisz and Melanie Kaye/Kantrowitz, *Tribe of Dina* included essays by heterosexual and lesbian feminists exploring Jewish identity. In 1989, Christie Balka and Andy Rose edited *Twice Blessed: On Being Lesbian or Gay and Jewish*, which highlighted the concerns of lesbians and gay men for inclusion in the Jewish community.

Jewish lesbians also made inroads in religious movements. In the 1980s, lesbian women rabbis, among them Stacy Offner and Linda Holtzman, began to disclose their sexual orientation, and many lost their jobs. The Reform and Reconstructionist movements developed policies that sanctioned the ordination of lesbian and gay rabbis and raised the issue of performing commitment ceremonies for lesbian and gay couples. The Conservative and Orthodox movements remained intransigent. The Conservative Movement struggled over permitting lesbians and gay men to teach in religious schools. Orthodox leaders publicly denounced lesbianism as a sin.

The gay and lesbian synagogue movement, which began in the early 1970s, also provided a locus for lesbians to explore religious identity. There are gay and lesbian synagogues in most metropolitan centers in the United States. Several of those synagogues have lesbian rabbis, including Congregation Beth Simchat Torah in New York City, which named Sharon Kleinbaum, a graduate of Reconstructionist Rabbinical College, as their first rabbinic leader in 1992. Reform rabbis Denise Eger and Lisa Edwards both serve gay and lesbian congregations in Los Angeles.

The 1990s have borne witness to a growing interest in lesbian issues in the Jewish community. Articles have been published in the Jewish press. Symposia and conferences have been held by mainstream Jewish organizations. Some synagogues have incorporated discussions of lesbian issues into their agenda and actively welcome lesbian and gay members. These activities have made it possible for lesbian Jews to feel welcome in the Jewish community. Yet lesbian Jews continue to voice concerns that go beyond acceptance and toleration. They seek a reinterpretation of Jewish values, including the assumption that heterosexuality is normative. They desire inclusion of their visions and stories as part of a reconstructed Jewish textual tradition. And they aim to create an environment of complete comfort in which to claim their identity and celebrate the occasions of their lives.

BIBLIOGRAPHY

Alpert, Rebecca. *Like Bread on the Seder Plate: Jewish Lesbians and the Transformation of Tradition* (1997); Balka, Christie, and Andy Rose, eds. *Twice Blessed: On Being Lesbian or Gay and Jewish* (1989); Beck, Evelyn Torton, ed. *Nice Jewish Girls: A Lesbian Anthology* (1982. Rev. and updated 1989); Biale, Rachel. *Women and Jewish Law: An Exploration of Women's Issues in Halakhic Sources* (1984); Kaye/Kantrowitz, Melanie, and Irena Klepfisz, eds. *Tribe of Dina: A Jewish Women's Anthology* (1986); Moore, Tracy, ed. *Lesbiot: Israeli Lesbians Talk About Sexuality, Feminism, Judaism and Their Lives* (1995); Rogow, Faith. "Why Is This Decade Different from All Other Decades? A Look at the Rise of Jewish Lesbian Feminism." *Bridges* 1 (Spring 1990): 67–79; Sarah, Elizabeth. "Judaism and Lesbianism: A Tale of Life on the Margins of the Text." *Jewish Quarterly* 40 (1993): 20–23.

REBECCA T. ALPERT

LEVENSOHN, LOTTA (1882–1972)

A writer, publicist, and Zionist activist, Lotta Levensohn was among the original founders of HADASSAH, the Women's Zionist Organization of America. Born in Syracuse, New York on August 13, 1882, and raised in Titusville, Pennsylvania, she was the daughter of Moshe Gerson Levensohn, a cantor, and Eva F. (Dvoretzky) Levensohn. Moving to New York, she attended the Teachers Institute of the Jewish Theological Seminary of America. Levensohn was one of the leaders of the Harlem chapter of the Daughters of Zion, a women's study group, which in 1912 decided to launch Hadassah as a national movement. Levensohn was for many years a director of the organization, serving as head of its Central Committee (an office equivalent to the presidency) during 1920 and 1921. At that time, Hadassah had briefly ceased to function as a separate organization, and Levensohn was one of two board members who favored the absorption of the group by the Zionist Organization of America. The seven members who opposed the plan prevailed, however, and Hadassah reemerged as an autonomous entity.

Levensohn served as secretary to Jacob de Haas and Judah L. Magnes when each held the office of secretary of the Federation of American Zionists. When Magnes became head of the New York Kehillah, Levensohn followed him there and remained secretary of that organization until 1923. Later that year she settled in Palestine, where she devoted her time to writing and translating Zionist literature. Levensohn also served as a public relations officer for the Hadassah Medical Organization and the Hebrew University of Jerusalem. Among her many publications were *Outline of Zionist History* (1942), *Vision and Fulfillment*, a history of the Hebrew University (1950), and an English translation of Theodor Herzl's *Das Altneuland* (1940). Levensohn returned to the United States during the 1950s and settled in Los Angeles. She died in Santa Monica, California, in September 1972.

BIBLIOGRAPHY

Dushkin, Julia A. "Lotta Levensohn." Typescript. Seligsberg/Jacobs Papers, Hadassah Archives, NYC; Levensohn, Lotta. "The Beginnings of Hadassah." *Hadassah Magazine* (April 1972): 22; Schoolman, Bertha. "Three American Pioneers in Israel." *Hadassah Newsletter* (January 1956): 4+; *UJE*; *Who's Who in World Jewry* (1965, 1972).

ERIC L. GOLDSTEIN

LEVIEN, SONYA (1888–1960)

For forty years, from the silent movie era through 1960, Sonya Levien was one of the busiest screenwriters in Hollywood.

Sara Opesken Levien ("Sonya" is the Russian diminutive, which she used) was born on December 25, 1888, to Julius and Fanny Opesken in Panimunik, formerly Russia, now Lithuania. (She altered the date later to 1898). By the time her father immigrated to the United States in 1891, she had two younger brothers, Arnold and Max. Sonya's father changed his name to Levien, the name of the man who had helped him escape from Siberia, where he had been exiled for political activities, and in 1896 brought his family to New York. By the time Sonya, her parents, and her Russian-born brothers were naturalized in 1905, she had two more brothers, Nathan and Edward.

Levien's brothers worked their way through school and became engineers. When Levien graduated from grammar school, however, she worked in a feather-duster factory and then became a secretary. In that position for four years, she became involved in settlement work and labor union activity.

Levien wanted to be a writer and began contributing minor pieces to *Life* magazine. In 1906, she enrolled at New York University Law School. Although she eventually applied to the New York bar, she practiced law less than six months and instead pursued her career in writing and editing. In 1912, she was hired by Carl Hovey, the coeditor of the *Metropolitan*, a leading liberal literary journal. As a writer, she traveled to London in 1913 and 1914 to cover the activities of the suffragists. Her sympathies and those of the magazine lay with radical and socialist movements, but she was greatly influenced by Theodore Roosevelt, whose work she edited for the magazine.

Levien married Carl Hovey on October 11, 1917, with little protest from either her Jewish family or his "Puritan, Plymouth-Rock, New-England, rock-ribbed" family. She turned her focus to her first love, writing fiction, and in 1918 sold her first story to a motion picture studio. Her earliest pieces were about immigrant daughters. Her first screen credit, in January 1919, was for *Who Will Marry Me?* She helped rewrite *Heart of a Jewess* as *Cheated Love*, a 1921 movie that told the story of a Jewish immigrant named Sonya.

In the mid-1930s, Levien and her husband moved to California so that she could write scenarios while he became a story editor. He was not successful, but she was, and from then on they were primarily dependent on her income. They had two children, Serge (b. 1920), and Tamara (b. 1923).

During the next twenty-five years, Levien became one of Hollywood's highest paid and most highly sought screenwriters. She was known for her ability to adapt any story quickly and to fix an ailing script. She was generous with her time in assisting others and was, simply, a good colleague.

While she claimed to be attracted to the teachings of Orthodox Judaism, Sonya Levien was a secular Jew. Her youthful activism vanished, and in political Hollywood she was known for being apolitical. In the early 1950s, her daughter, Tamara, and son-in-law, Lee Gold, were blacklisted for being members of the Communist Party, but Levien was publicly silent on the situation.

By the time Sonya Levien died on March 19, 1960, she had been credited with the stories and screenplays of more than seventy motion pictures, including some of the most highly acclaimed movies of her day: *A Ship Comes In* (1928), *Daddy Long Legs* (1931), *Rebecca of Sunnybrook Farm* (1932), *State Fair* (1933), *Berkeley Square* (1933), *Kidnapped* (1938), *Drums Along the Mohawk* (1939), *The Hunchback of Notre Dame* (1939), *The Great Caruso* (1951), *The Student Prince* (1954), *Oklahoma!* (1955), and *Pepe* (1960).

SELECTED WORKS BY SONYA LEVIEN

Berkeley Square (1933); *Cheated Love* (1921); *Daddy Long Legs* (1931); *Drums Along the Mohawk* (1939); *The Great Caruso* (1951); *The Hunchback of Notre Dame* (1939); *Kidnapped* (1938); *Oklahoma!* (1955); *Pepe* (1960); *Rebecca of Sunnybrook Farm* (1932); *A Ship Comes In* (1928); *State Fair* (1933); *The Student Prince* (1954); *Who Will Marry Me?* (1919).

BIBLIOGRAPHY

AJYB 24:169; *BEOAJ*; Ceplair, Larry. *A Great Lady: A Life of the Screenwriter Sonya Levien* (1996); Hurwitz, Edith. "Sonya Levien." *Dictionary of Literary Biography: American Screenwriters* (1986), 171–178; Obituary. *NYTimes*, March 20, 1960, 86:8; *WWIAJ* (1928, 1938).

SHERRY LEVY-REINER

LEVI-MONTALCINI, RITA (b. 1909)

In 1986, Rita Levi-Montalcini and Stanley Cohen shared the Nobel Prize in physiology or medicine for their identification of the nerve growth factor, which, as the Nobel Committee said, "held out the prospect of shedding light on many disorders, such as cancers, the delayed healing of wounds, and senile dementia, including Alzheimer's disease."

Rita Levi-Montalcini was born on April 22, 1909, in Turin, the capital of the province of Piedmont in northwestern Italy. Her family consisted of father Adamo Levi, who was an engineer and manager of a factory, mother Adele Montalcini, brother Gino (seven years older), sister Anna (five years older), and fraternal twin sister Paola. They enjoyed a comfortable middle-class life-style and were nonobservant Jews.

Levi-Montalcini soon understood the profoundly patriarchal structure of her household. Largely in reaction to the submissive role of her mother, Levi-Montalcini concluded that a career of creativity for women, whether in science or in art, was incompatible with the demands of marriage. In her best-selling autobiography, *In Praise of Imperfection, My Life and Work*, she emphasized that she never regretted this decision, further suggesting that she never met anyone in whose company she would have liked to spend a lifetime. This decision was a key to her subsequent career in science, as was the death of a former governess from cancer when Levi-Montalcini was twenty. She had received only limited education, because of her family's unequal expectations regarding male and female children, but undertook to close the gap and was admitted to the Turin School of Medicine in 1930, graduating in 1936.

Giuseppe Levi, a professor of anatomy, antifascist activist, and coreligionist, served as an inspiring role model and mentor to Levi-Montalcini. Under his guidance, she began working with cells of the nervous system, which would be the focus of her career. After graduation, she continued working with Levi as his assistant in neurological research. Following the increasingly anti-Semitic fascist Italian government's 1938 banning of Jews from university positions and the practice of medicine, they worked in Belgium for a time, but the Nazi invasion sent them back to Turin, where they continued laboratory work. Eventually hiding in the countryside, and later in the antifascist urban underground, they survived World War II relatively unscathed. The experience forced Levi-Montalcini not only to confront the issue of her ethnic identity but to try to understand the incomprehensible conduct of her countrymen.

Levi-Montalcini's scientific career flourished rapidly after World War II, largely because she was able to work in the new center of world science, the United States. She came to Washington University in St. Louis, Missouri, in 1946 at the invitation of the distinguished experimental embryologist Viktor Hamburger, who had fled Nazi Germany in the 1930s and had read published reports of her experiments in neurobiology. Though a more sustained collaboration may have been thwarted by Hamburger's increasing duties as chairman of the zoology department, his mentorship during the late 1940s and early 1950s shielded Levi-Montalcini from the common fate of women scientists at that time: marginality. She continued to study nerve cell development, and in 1951, repeating Elmer Bueker's experiments grafting cancerous mouse tumors onto chicken embryos, she first hypothesized the existence of the nerve growth factor (NGF). The hypothesis was soon confirmed experimentally, offering scientific proof, as Levi-Montalcini said, "that there is a physical connection between a sound mind and a sound body, namely the NGF." Between 1953 and 1959, she and collaborator Stanley Cohen, whose biochemical specialization complemented her own anatomical focus, developed methods to extract significant amounts of NGF from snake venom and the salivary glands of mice and identified NGF as a protein. It was for this work that they would share the Nobel Prize, as well as the Albert Lasker Medical Research Award, in 1986.

Levi-Montalcini also received the National Medal of Science, America's highest scientific award, in 1987, and was the first woman named to membership in the Pontifical Academy of Sciences in Rome.

Levi-Montalcini's association with Washington University, a leading center in experimental life sciences, would continue for three decades, as research associate (1947–1951), associate (1951–1958), and full professor (1958–1977). In the early 1960s, she began splitting her life between the American Midwest and Rome, where a new National Laboratory for Cell Biology was established, which she eventually came to direct. She became an American citizen, while retaining her Italian citizenship as well, in 1956.

In Levi-Montalcini's remarkable autobiography, factual data become the springboard for the expression of a moral consciousness that combines the historical sensibility of the well-born European, the pragmatism of the successful American immigrant, and the cultural resonance of the Jewish World War II survivor. Her life and work, in their scientific, European, American, Jewish, and female dimensions, will inspire generations to come.

BIBLIOGRAPHY

Abir-Am, Pnina G. "Nobelesse Oblige: Lives of Molecular Biologists." *ISIS* (1991): 323–346; *EJ* (1986–1987); Levi-Montalcini, Rita. *In Praise of Imperfection, My Life and Work* (1988); Slater, Elinor, and Robert Slater. *Great Jewish Women* (1994).

PNINA ABIR-AM

LEVIN, BERTHA SZOLD (1874–1958)

Bertha Szold Levin, a civic leader and Jewish communal activist, was born on December 21, 1874, in Baltimore, Maryland, the youngest daughter of Rabbi Benjamin and Sophie (Schaar) Szold. Along with her sisters, Rachel, Sadie, Adele, and HENRIETTA SZOLD, she grew up in a household infused with a love for both German culture and Jewish learning. Three other sisters died as children. Educated in Baltimore's public schools, she received a B.A. from Bryn Mawr College in 1894 and returned home to work as a teacher. In 1901, she married Louis H. Levin, an attorney who later founded the Associated Jewish Charities in Baltimore. The couple had five children. Levin assisted her husband as a writer and translator for the Baltimore *Jewish Comment*, which he edited. In 1924, she became the first woman appointed to the Baltimore City School Board, a post that she held until 1940.

An ardent Zionist, Levin was active in HADASSAH, the national organization founded by her sister Henrietta Szold in 1912. In 1933 and 1939, Levin traveled to Palestine to assist her sister in refugee work; she was later named an honorary vice president of Hadassah. Bertha Szold Levin died in Baltimore on January 2, 1958.

BIBLIOGRAPHY

Levin, Alexandra Lee. *Dare to Be Different* (1972); Levin, Bertha Szold. Papers. Jewish Historical Society of Maryland, Baltimore; *WWIAJ* (1938); Obituary. *Baltimore Sun*, January 3, 1958.

ERIC L. GOLDSTEIN

LEVIN, NORA (1916–1989)

In the introduction to her 1977 book *While Messiah Tarried*, a history of Jewish socialist movements, Nora Levin wrote that she hoped "young Jews groping for ways to reconcile their own social radicalism with Jewishness . . . will be heartened in their quest by the knowledge that there have been several generations of other young Jews who have made a similar struggle."

Levin was the author of three very readable histories and numerous magazine articles about the last hundred years of Jewish history. Her accounts are personalized with stories of individual Jews—and Jewish organizations—who acted and interacted with the political and social world around them. Levin wrote Jewish history not for scholars and specialists, but for the general reader. Her writing conveys remarkable compassion and sensitivity toward the vicissitudes of Jewish life in Europe, czarist Russia, and the former Soviet Union, highlighting social and political nuances within Jewish communities. She especially focused on activists with a core Jewish identity: Jewish partisans in Hitler's Europe; the Jewish labor movement in America; the socialist Jewish Labor Bund in Russia and Poland; socialist Zionists; and refuseniks and other Jews who struggled to maintain Jewish identity and meaning in the Soviet Union.

Levin lived most of her life in Philadelphia, where she was born September 20, 1916, to Joseph and Bertha (Landberg) Levin. She had an older sister, Dorothy. Levin received her B.S. in education from Temple University and her M.L.S. from Drexel University. Her D.H.Lit was awarded posthumously in 1989 by Philadelphia's Gratz College of Jewish Studies. Early in her career, she worked as a research librarian and public high school instructor in American and European history. At the time of her death on October 26, 1989, she had taught at Gratz College for nearly twenty years, and was the founder and director of the college's Holocaust Oral History Archives. The archives department has recorded hundreds of interviews with Holocaust survivors, liberators, and eyewitnesses.

Levin's research, writing, and teaching were always intertwined with her activism in the Jewish community. From 1948, the year of Israel's founding, to 1953, she was the executive director of the Philadelphia Council of PIONEER WOMEN, the women's labor Zionist organization. She also served on the executive boards of the Soviet Jewry Council, the Philadelphia Jewish Community Relations Council, the National Conference of Christians and Jews, and the Hebrew Immigrant Aid Society.

In the introduction to her first book, *The Holocaust: The Destruction of European Jewry, 1933–1945* (1968), Levin wrote, "The extermination of two-thirds of Europe's Jews was not inevitable." History, she suggested, does not repeat itself, and should not be written to fit anyone's theoretical framework. Though she stressed the influence of ideological and political beliefs on people's actions, her histories are more descriptive than theoretical or analytical. *The Holocaust* focuses on the creation of the terror-state, the struggle of the Jews to understand their fate, and the various forms of Jewish resistance. Reviews of the book were mixed. Historian LUCY DAWIDOWICZ criticized it as amateurish, saying Levin's use of sources was indiscriminate. Other reviewers such as Louis Snyder of the *Saturday Review* hailed the book as first-rate. *The Holocaust* became one of the early standard texts on the topic; it has been through nine printings and has been translated into several languages.

Levin's second book, *While Messiah Tarried* (1977), is a thorough treatment of Jewish-affiliated left-wing radical movements. The author described in detail the Jewish Labor Bund's development of its policy of Jewish national cultural autonomy and its subsequent political battles with Lenin, tensions between Jewish socialists and left-wing Zionists, and the various factions of the Jewish American labor movement. Though the Bund lost its struggle with Lenin, and though there is no longer a specifically Jewish labor movement, Levin's history portrayed "Jewish ways of looking at society and possible Jewish roles as social catalyst."

Her final work, the two-volume *The Jews of the Soviet Union Since 1917*, was published in 1989, the year that Levin died. The work is marred by Levin's use of lengthy quotes from other sources without proper attribution. Still, Zvi Gitleman wrote in *America*, Levin "captures the human drama played out in the often great expectations and equally profound disappointments that have characterized Soviet Jewry."

Nora Levin's books, articles, and activism were inspired by her commitment to the Jewish people and to a living legacy of action and community involvement.

SELECTED WORKS BY NORA LEVIN

"Assaults on Holocaust History." *Midstream* (April 1989); *The Holocaust: The Destruction of European Jewry, 1933–1945* (1968); *The Jews of the Soviet Union Since 1917: Paradox of Survival.* 2 vols. (1989); "Postwar Reflections on the Holocaust from a Jewish Point of View." In *Movements and Issues in World Religions: A Sourcebook and Analysis of Developments Since 1945—Religion, Ideology, and Politics* (1987); *While Messiah Tarried: Jewish Socialist Movements, 1871–1917* (1977).

BIBLIOGRAPHY

Contemporary Authors; Dawidowicz, Lucy. "The Holocaust." *Jewish Social Studies* (April 1970); *Dictionary of International Biography;* Gitleman, Zvi. "The Jew in the Soviet Union Since 1917." *America* (November 25, 1989); Snyder, Louis. "Two Views of Hell." *Saturday Review* (March 9, 1968); *Who's Who Among American Women.* 10th ed.

CLARE KINBERG

LEVINE, JACQUELINE (b. 1926)

Jacqueline Levine is an outstanding example of a new type of female activist leadership in American Jewish life. In over five decades of service to the Jewish community, she has combined her powerfully deep liberal political beliefs and activities, which benefit the poor and disadvantaged, with her concern for the vast needs of specific Jewish communities.

She was born on January 28, 1926, into a highly educated Jewish family. In the 1920s, her mother, Theresa (Shulhin) Koldin, received her M.A. and studied toward her Ph.D. at Columbia University. Her father, Harry Koldin, received his M.A. in history and worked as a dress manufacturer. They were socialist, antireligious, antifascist, deeply committed secular Jews living in Manhattan Beach, New York. Her younger sister is Nina Solarz, wife of former congressman Steven Solarz, who represented Brooklyn for many years.

After completing her studies at Abraham Lincoln High School, Jacqueline attended Bryn Mawr College, graduating in the war class of 1942. She received a B.A. studying psychology and political science. She continues to serve on Bryn Mawr College's board of trustees.

On January 5, 1949, she married Howard Levine. They spent their first year of marriage in Puerto Rico, where Howard Levine was a professor of sociology at the university. During that year, Jacqueline Levine studied various disciplines. In 1950, they moved to New Jersey, where she worked in a department store and he began his business career. They had three children: Ellen (b. 1951), Stephen (b. 1953), and Ned (b. 1958).

In 1954, Levine began her lifelong career of liberal volunteerism. Her first involvement was in 1954, with the AMERICAN JEWISH CONGRESS in its fight to oppose Joseph McCarthy. She picketed Woolworth stores for their refusal to seat African Americans at their lunch counters. In 1963, she participated in the famous March on Washington. In 1965, she joined the celebrated march from Selma to Montgomery, which changed American history and fueled the burgeoning civil rights movement.

At the 1965 New York World's Fair, Levine and eleven others peacefully distributed leaflets in front of the Jordanian pavilion, protesting its anti-Israel mural. Their arrest generated a great deal of publicity, and their vindication proved very significant. It affected Levine's later political involvement in protesting restrictive Soviet Jewish emigration policies.

The Vietnam War deeply affected Levine and her family. From 1964 onward, they participated in many peace marches. Levine's involvement with the American Jewish Congress intensified as she influenced its decision to oppose the Vietnam War. It was the first Jewish organization to take this stance. From 1971 to 1975, she served as the national president of the American Jewish Congress Women's Division.

Levine also began assuming prominent leadership roles in her local Jewish community. In 1965, she became Women's Division campaign chair for what is now known as Metro West, New Jersey, Federation. For over thirty years she has served on the executive committee of Metro West's board of directors. As well, she represented Metro West on the Council of Jewish Federations (CJF) joint budgeting council.

In 1969, Levine became national president of the CJF's Women's Division. She is a talented and powerful speaker who cares deeply about poor people and Jewish communal needs. In what is perhaps her most famous speech, "The Changing Role of Women in the Jewish Community," she raised this essential challenge to CJF leadership: Why were they ignoring women's leadership? At that time, nationally, only three federations welcomed women as president. Levine's words galvanized women to begin to demand Jewish leadership, both as lay and professional leaders.

In 1980, Levine became the first woman to serve as the national chair of the American Jewish Congress's governing council. Her commitments to the

Jewish domestic and international agenda led her to become involved with the National Jewish Community Relations Advisory Council (NJCRAC). Her desire to help Jews in the Soviet Union emigrate led her to become NJCRAC's first woman chair for Soviet Jewry. In 1984, she took a harrowing trip to the Soviet Union where she was harassed and made to remain an extra day. In March 1985, she protested the plight of Soviet Jews on the steps of the Soviet embassy in Washington and was arrested. From 1986 to 1987, she served as national chair of the Mobilization for Soviet Jewry, which brought 250,000 American Jews to Washington to protest Soviet policies. Shortly after that, Soviet Jews began to pour out of the U.S.S.R. Levine has been honored many times by NJCRAC, most recently in February 1995 for her outstanding activities in the fields of civil rights, protection of the First Amendment, Soviet Jewry, and support for the State of Israel.

In 1985, Levine was a founding member of MAZON: A Jewish Response to Hunger, an organization that encourages the Jewish community to donate 3 percent of the costs of family celebrations such as bar and bat mitzvahs or weddings to fight hunger. In the 1980s, Levine also was a founding member of the Jewish Fund for Justice, a cause that remains close to her heart.

From 1989 to 1995, Levine served as chair of U.S. operations and vice chair of the national board of directors to the Hebrew Immigrant Aid Society. In 1996, she became chair of administration and personnel. Levine is also on the board of the American Jewish Joint Distribution Committee.

Jacqueline Levine's life is a distinguished record of service to the Jewish and general communities. She was an early feminist, advocating that Jewish women assume their rightful position as leaders in the Jewish community. She combined liberal political activism with devoted service to many areas within the American and world Jewish communities.

BIBLIOGRAPHY
Levine, Jacqueline. Interview with author.

JULIE K. GORDON

LEVINE, LENA (1903–1965)

Lena Levine was born in Brooklyn, New York, on May 17, 1903, the youngest of seven children of Sophie and Morris Levine, Jewish emigrants from Vilna, Lithuania. Educated at Girls High School in Brooklyn, HUNTER COLLEGE, and Bellevue Hospital Medical College, Levine graduated in 1927, married fellow student Louis Ferber, and established a private practice in obstetrics and gynecology in Brooklyn. A daughter, Ellen Louise, was born in 1939, followed three years later by a son, Michael Allen, who developed viral encephalitis in infancy and was left severely retarded. Tragedy struck again in 1943 when Louis Ferber died of a heart attack.

Unable to accommodate her responsibilities as a single mother to an unpredictable professional schedule, Levine studied psychoanalysis with Sandor Rado at the Columbia Psychoanalytic Institute and converted her practice to psychiatry. With doctors Abraham and HANNAH STONE, she then combined her interests into developing innovative services in birth control, sex education, and marriage counseling at Margaret Sanger's pioneering Birth Control Clinical Research Bureau. Following Hannah Stone's death in 1941, Levine and Abraham Stone ran the clinic together and acquired an international reputation for the treatment of a range of sexual and reproductive problems including female frigidity and infertility.

With Sanger, they helped found the International Planned Parenthood Federation in 1948 and then traveled and lectured extensively. In best-selling advice books, including *The Doctor Talks with the Bride* (1938) and *The Modern Book of Marriage: A Practical Guide to Marital Happiness* (1957), Levine championed equality for women in marriage, along with greater sexual fulfillment. She died of a stroke in New York City, on January 9, 1965.

SELECTED WORKS BY LENA LEVINE
The Doctor Talks with the Bride (1938); *The Modern Book of Marriage: A Practical Guide to Marital Happiness* (1957).

BIBLIOGRAPHY
AJYB 67:539; Chesler, Ellen. *Woman of Valor: Margaret Sanger and the Birth Control Movement in America* (1992); *NAW* modern; Obituary. *NYTimes*, January 11, 1965, 45:3.

ELLEN CHESLER

LEVINGER, ELMA EHRLICH (1887–1958)

Active in an array of Jewish women's and youth organizations, Elma Ehrlich Levinger was also the author of over thirty books for children and several for adults—all of which emphasize the importance of maintaining Jewish identity in America. Levinger used both drama and the short story as a means of educating young people and women about Jewish history and traditions, hoping to encourage them to participate in Jewish social life.

Elma Ehrlich Levinger was born on October 6, 1887, in Chicago to Samuel and Sarah (Fernberg) Ehrlich. At age eighteen, she became a teacher in rural schools in Iowa and Illinois for two years. After attending the University of Chicago (1907–1908) and Radcliffe College (1911–1912), where she studied English and drama, she gradually extended her talents as a teacher to Jewish education. Combining the arts and community service, she worked as the director of a junior drama league in Chicago in 1912, and as director of entertainment for the Bureau of Jewish Education in New York City (1913–1915). On June 15, 1916, she married Lee J. Levinger, who later became a rabbi at the Veterans Administration Hospital in Menlo Park, California. The couple had three children, Samuel Harold, Leah Judith, and Joseph Solomon.

Sharing a belief in the importance of Jewish education for American youth, the Levingers worked collaboratively on a book entitled *The Story of the Jew for Young People* (1929). Through her books and as editor of the magazine *Jewish Child*, Levinger actively sought to build a strong cultural identity among Jewish youth in the process of American assimilation. Her series of tales, *In Many Lands* (1923), emphasizes the role of different traditions in connecting Jews throughout the diaspora. In her book *Great Jewish Women* (1940) and her biography of HENRIETTA SZOLD called *Fighting Angel* (1946), she highlights the importance of women's contributions to Jewish life.

Combining her roles of community leader and writer, Levinger also attempted to cultivate Jewish identity among middle-class women. *The Tower of David* (1924), published for the NATIONAL COUNCIL OF JEWISH WOMEN, is a collection of stories that served a social purpose, especially for Jewish women's organizations. Underscoring the ability of the short story to "amuse, inspire, and instruct," the book offers suggestions on how to plan programs accessible to a variety of women.

A member of the NATIONAL COUNCIL OF JEWISH WOMEN's National Committee on Religion, the National Council for Prevention of War, the Birth Control League, and HADASSAH, Levinger was a vocal participant within the Jewish community, as well as a prolific writer.

Elma Ehrlich Levinger died suddenly on January 28, 1958, in Hawaii, while traveling to her home in Los Altos, California, after a three-month vacation in the South Pacific.

SELECTED WORKS BY ELMA EHRLICH LEVINGER

The Burden: A Play in One Act (1918); *A Child of the Frontier: A One-Act Play About Abraham Lincoln* (1925); *Fighting Angel: The Story of Henrietta Szold* (1946); *Grapes of Canaan: A Novel* (1931); *Great Jewish Women* (1940); *In Many Lands: Stories of How the Scattered Jews Kept Their Festivals* (1923); *Jephthah's Daughter: A Biblical Drama in One Act* (1921); *Jewish Adventures in America* (1954); *Jewish Holyday Stories: Modern Tales of the American Jewish Youth* (1918); *More Stories of the New Land* (1938); *The New Land: Stories of Jews Who Had a Part in the Making of Our Country* (1920); *Pilgrims to Palestine and Other Stories* (1940); *The Story of the Jew for Young People*, with Rabbi Lee J. Levinger (1929); *The Tower of David: A Book of Stories for the Program of Women's Organizations* (1924).

BIBLIOGRAPHY

AJYB 24:170; "Author Elma Levinger Dies in Hawaii." *San Francisco Chronicle*, January 29, 1958, 35; *EJ*, s.v. "Levinger, Lee J."; "Mrs. Lee Levinger Dies." *NYTimes*, January 31, 1958, 21:1; *UJE*; *Who's Who in America*. Vol. 30, 1958–1959 (1958): 1652; *WWIAJ* (1926, 1928, 1938); *WWWIA* 3.

JOAN MOELIS

LEVIN-RUBIN, MELBA (b. 1906)

Melba Levin-Rubin, an accomplished lawyer, was born to Max and Kunia Levin on December 5, 1906, in Slonim, Russia. When her family arrived in the United States in 1914, they settled in Detroit, where she grew up and attended school. She received an LL.B. degree from the Detroit College of Law in 1925 and an LL.M. degree from the Detroit Law School in 1932. In 1933, she earned a B.S. from Wayne State University.

Levin-Rubin began practicing law in 1926. She became the public administrator of Wayne County, Michigan, in 1930, and was made a member of the Welfare and Relief Study Commission for the state in 1936. In that same year, she became the assistant attorney general of Michigan. Active in both professional and Jewish communal organizations, Levin-Rubin was a member of the Women's Lawyers Association of Michigan and the Women's League for Character Building in the NATIONAL COUNCIL OF JEWISH WOMEN.

On September 26, 1926, she married Samuel H. Rubin of Detroit, who already had a son, Harris. They had three children: Gloria, Richard, and Robert.

In her professional career, Levin-Rubin distinguished herself both as a Jew and as a woman. Women in the first half of the twentieth century—and Jewish women in particular—rarely studied or practiced law. An indication of Levin-Rubin's forward-thinking views is her last name, in which she retained her maiden name while adding on her married one.

BIBLIOGRAPHY
WWLAJ (1938).

TAMAR KAPLAN

LEVITT, JENNIE DAVIDSON
(1889–1980)

Jennie Davidson Levitt represented the "finest synthesis of Americanism and Judaism," according to the leaders of the Minneapolis Jewish National Fund at a 1968 dinner in her honor. Deeply aware of her responsibilities as a financially secure Jewish woman, Levitt labored to improve social conditions for diverse groups in the United States and abroad. Her broad approach to social reform, and the particular issues that she addressed, paralleled the changing concerns of the NATIONAL COUNCIL OF JEWISH WOMEN (NCJW), her most beloved organization for more than fifty years.

Born on November 18, 1889, Jennie was the oldest of four children of Lithuanian immigrants, Saul and Mary (Cohen) Davidson. She grew up in a household that valued hard work, education, and charity. Saul Davidson had left Lithuania in 1879 at age seventeen and immigrated to Des Moines, Iowa, to become a peddler for an uncle who owned a peddler-supply business. He opened a secondhand furniture store in Des Moines in 1887, which developed into the Davidson Furniture Company by 1903, the largest retail furniture institution of its kind in Iowa. He married Mary Cohen in 1888, and the young couple took in boarders to supplement their income. Mary Cohen Davidson became an officer of the Hebrew Ladies Aid Society, and regularly donated food, clothing, and money to local poor families and impoverished relatives in Europe.

Jennie Levitt recalled a comfortable childhood with piano and elocution lessons. She and her sister Sarah were the only girls to study Hebrew at the Conservative congregation their parents helped to found. She further developed her leadership and oratorical skills as the only girl on the West High School debating team. She received a degree from the Highland Park Conservatory of Music in 1909 and a B.A. from

Drake University in 1913. She married Thomas I. Levitt, a close childhood friend, in 1914, after which Thomas joined his father-in-law's furniture business.

The Levitts moved to Kansas City, Missouri, in 1918 to open a Davidson Furniture branch and to Minneapolis in 1937 when the company reorganized. The mother of three children, Aaron, Norman, and Sarah, Levitt began volunteering in the 1920s. She explained her activism as carrying on her family's charitable traditions, but her efforts extended beyond direct charity to working with voluntary political organizations focused on domestic and international issues.

Levitt was particularly active in Jewish women's organizations. She served as president of the Kansas City branch of the National Council of Jewish Women from 1931 to 1936 and was a board member of both the Jewish Welfare Association and the Federation of Jewish Charities. In Minneapolis, she chaired the SOS division of the Joint Distribution Committee, was president of the women's division of the Minneapolis Federation for Jewish Services, and served on the board of the national women's division of the United Jewish Appeal. As a uniformed Red Cross Home Service worker during World War II, she helped to rescue Jewish children from Nazi Germany and to process immigrants after the war.

Levitt worked to strengthen the political influence of women as a board member of the League of Women Voters and of the District Federation of Women's Clubs in Kansas City. Representing the NCJW, she became a peace activist in the 1930s and helped to organize Kansas City chapters of the World Peace Council and of Carrie Chapman Catt's National Conference on the Cause and Cure of War. These organizations and the NCJW taught Levitt about the potential power of organized women.

Widowed in 1953, Levitt turned her attention in the 1950s and 1960s to building women's hospital auxiliary organizations. She served as president of Mount Sinai Hospital's Women's Auxiliary in Minneapolis and of the Minnesota State Hospital Auxiliary Association. Distressed by the state's decision to close state mental hospitals, she lobbied for the development of a volunteer program to assist patients in the process of returning to their communities. She also became a philanthropist in this period, donating major gifts to Mount Sinai Hospital, the NCJW, and the Hebrew University High School in Jerusalem. In 1972, she established the Jennie D. Levitt Institute for Research in Education of the Disadvantaged at Jerusalem's Hebrew University.

Still active in her eighties, Levitt offered to march with the Mount Sinai Women's Auxiliary to demand that a woman be appointed to the hospital's board of governors. Remembered for her eloquent speeches, sense of humor, loyalty, and generosity to family and community, she relished taking charge in charity work. The National Council of Jewish Women and the Jewish National Fund honored her with testimonial celebrations. She represented a generation of American-born daughters and wives of successful Jewish businessmen, who devoted their energies to improving the quality of life in their local communities.

Jeanie Davidson Levitt died in 1980.

BIBLIOGRAPHY

Levitt, Jennie Davidson. Papers. In the possession of Thomas W. Levitt, Shawnee Mission, Kansas; Levitt, Thomas W. [grandson]. Interview with author, May 1996; Rosenthal, Frank. *The Jews of Des Moines: The First Century* (1957); Smith, Beth K. [niece]. Interview with author, September 1996; Solomon, Hannah G. *Fabric of My Life* (1946); *Who's Who in American Women* (1968); *WWIAJ* (1938).

SARAH S. MALINO

LEVY, ADELE ROSENWALD (1892–1960)

Adele Rosenwald Levy used her affluence to promote public-spirited philanthropy and Jewish causes. Active in thirty-five charitable, artistic, and community organizations, Levy never failed her father's principle that those of good fortune should assume "the obligations that come with wealth."

Adele Rosenwald Levy was born in Chicago on July 19, 1892, one of five children of Julius Rosenwald, a Chicago merchant and philanthropist who established the Julius Rosenwald Foundation in that city. In 1911, she married Armand Deutsch, a childhood neighbor. They had two sons: Richard Deutsch and Armand Deutsch Jr., a film and stage producer. She and Deutsch divorced sometime before 1927, when she married Dr. David M. Levy, a child psychologist whom she had met at the Institute for Juvenile Research in Chicago.

Upon moving to New York, Levy entered public life in a manner considered acceptable for a woman of her class. Her responsibilities and honors suggest a genuine capacity for leadership. At different times in her career, Levy contributed to the Citizens Committee for Children of New York City, Play Schools Association, and Stadium Concerts, Inc. She sat on the board of trustees of Brandeis University and on the executive committees of the Museum of Modern Art, New York State Youth Commission, New York City Youth Board, and the Wiltwyck School for Boys,

where she served as first vice president. Levy collected awards for her service as well: Woman of the Year from the Federation of Jewish Philanthropies, and Outstanding Jewish Woman of 1946 from the NATIONAL COUNCIL OF JEWISH WOMEN.

During World War II, Levy became the first chair of the National Women's Division of the United Jewish Appeal (UJA). She also served as vice-chair of the Citizens Committee on Displaced Persons and as a member of the executive committee and board of directors of the Jewish Joint Distribution Committee, where she contributed to the monthly bulletin.

Levy's most significant efforts came after the war when she helped to direct the UJA in a time of frantic fund-raising to aid the survivors of the Holocaust. As a member of the UJA's executive committee for the campaign of 1947, Levy faced the problem of asking American Jews to contribute $170 million, more than UJA had asked of its member communities during the war. Levy told the committee that they faced a situation "which not even the most pessimistic of outstanding governmental authorities had foreseen."

Levy demonstrated her commitment to the arts when she and her husband donated their collection of thirty-one fine paintings, including Cézanne's *Château Noir*—her favorite—and works by Renoir and Degas, to the Museum of Modern Art in New York and a number of other museums across the country. Levy came to her opportunities through the possession of her father's wealth, but she understood the power of money to mend the world.

Adele Rosenwald Levy died in New York City at Mount Sinai Hospital after a short illness on March 12, 1960.

BIBLIOGRAPHY

Adele Rosenwald Levy, July 19, 1892–March 12, 1960 (1961); *AJYB* 62:451; Levy, Adele. "Destination Unknown." *The JDC Digest* (October 1942): 1–2; Obituary. *NYTimes*, March 13, 1960, 86:3; Raphael, Marc Lee. *A History of the United Jewish Appeal, 1939–1982* (1982); Urofsky, Melvin I. *We Are One!: American Jewry and Israel* (1978).

STEVEN STOLL

LEVY, BELLE (b. 1898)

Belle Levy was a private detective, an unusual profession for a woman. Crime-solving, however, ran in her family, since her father was a lieutenant with the New York City police force.

Belle Rosenfeld Levy was born in New York City on December 29, 1898, to Ray and Monroe (Wieser)

Rosenfeld. She progressed through the city's public school system and married Charles Levy before her eighteenth birthday. Her first independent job was designer of children's clothes, but at age twenty-five, she began working for a private detective agency. In 1927, she formed her own detective agency, the Colonial Detective Service. She continued as a private investigator at least through 1942; records show that she appeared in court that year as the owner of the detective service.

Levy had one daughter, Madeline. She maintained her detective office at various locations in Manhattan, including West 42nd Street and Columbus Circle.

BIBLIOGRAPHY

NYTimes, May 9, 1942, 28, and May 20, 1942, 16; *WWIAJ* (1938).

ELLIOT ASHKENAZI

LEVY, FLORENCE NIGHTINGALE (1870–1947)

Florence Nightingale Levy's most significant achievement was the founding of the *American Art Annual* in 1898. A comprehensive directory of the American art world, the *Annual* catalogued schools, associations, exhibitions, and artists nationwide. Levy went on to perform invaluable editing, organizing, and educational roles in the American art world for the next fifty years.

An only child, Florence Levy was born on August 13, 1870, in New York City, to Joseph Arthur and Pauline (Goodheim) Levy. She studied art at the National Academy of Design, but turned to art history and criticism. She went on to further study at the Louvre in Paris under curator Gaston Lafenestre (1894–1895), at Columbia University, with leading American artists (including John La Farge), and with art historian John C. Van Dyke.

Known as "Florence the Clipper" for her habit of clipping articles from newspapers, Levy turned her clipping collection into the first volume of the *American Art Annual* in 1898. For the next twenty-one years, she edited the *Annual*. In December 1901, she also began publishing the weekly New York *Art Bulletin*. In six years, it grew to twenty-four pages, became a national newsheet, and was eventually sold to *Art News*. Her other major publication, *Art in New York*, a guide to the New York art scene, went through six editions between 1916 and 1939.

Levy's knowledge of the New York and national art communities led her to art education, museums, and an exploration of the relationship between art and industry. She began teaching private art history classes in 1901. In 1908, she helped edit a guide called *Art Education in the Public Schools of the United States;* other guides followed, including *Professional Art Schools in the United States* (1914) and *Art Education in New York City for Artists and Artisans* (1916). In 1909, Levy was a cofounder of the School Art League of New York, an organization that brought art into public schools. In that same year, she also helped to create the American Federation of the Arts, dedicated to promoting art through means such as traveling exhibitions.

Levy worked on the staff of the Metropolitan Museum of Art (1909–1917), and later became director of the newly founded Baltimore Museum (1922–1926). During the hiatus between museum positions, she began her involvement with art and industry and with vocational guidance, areas that would shape the rest of her career. From 1917 to 1919, she ran the Art Alliance of America, which urged industrial use of American arts and design during World War I. In 1922, she published a survey of the silver industry in *Art in Industry*. From 1927 to 1932, she was director of the Arts Council of New York City (renamed the New York Regional Art Council in 1929). The council was affiliated with the National Alliance of Art and Industry, for which Levy served as the supervisor of vocational service (1932–1934). In 1934, she became director of the Federated Council on Art Education (later renamed the Art Education Council), where she focused on vocational guidance and edited *Occupations Requiring a Knowledge of Art*.

Levy was a member of Congregation Shaara Tefila. She died in New York on November 15, 1947. Known for her dedication, efficiency, and ability, she left a major legacy of national and New York–based arts advocacy and organizing.

BIBLIOGRAPHY

AJYB 6 (1904–1905): 138, 24:171, 50:519; *BEOAJ*; Howes, Durwood, ed. *American Women, 1935–1940: A Composite Dictionary*. Vol. 1 (1981): 524; Leonard, John William, *Woman's Who's Who of America, 1914–1915* (1914); Levy, Florence Nightingale. Papers. Archives of American Art, Smithsonian Institution, Washington, D.C., and Florence Nightingale Levy Collection. New-York Historical Society, NYC; *National Cyclopaedia of American Biography*; *NAW*; Obituary. *NYTimes*, November 17, 1947, 22:2; "Preface." *American Art Annual*. Vol. 1 (1899); *UJE*; *Who's Who in American Art*. Vol. 4 (1940–1947): 284; *WWIAJ* (1926, 1928, 1938).

KIRSTEN SWINTH

LEWINSON, RUTH (1895–1979)

Ruth Lewinson, one of the earliest femaie Jewish lawyers in the United States, was born to Benno and Fanny (Berliner) Lewinson in New York City on July 1, 1895. She received her B.A. degree, graduating Phi Beta Kappa, from HUNTER COLLEGE in 1916, and a law degree from New York University in 1919. She then taught English to immigrants and gave lectures on practical law. In 1920, she was admitted to the New York bar and became a senior member of the firm established by her father. She worked with him until 1953, when she started her own private practice.

Lewinson was the treasurer and director of the New York County Lawyers Association and a member of the Advisory Committee on Surrogate's Court Practice. From 1921 to 1939, she was a trustee of Hunter College and served on the Board of Higher Education.

She was also active in various other organizations, including the Federation for the Support of Jewish Charities, Northrop Memorial Camp, Hunter College Associate Alumnae, the Children's Shelter of Manhattan, Young Democrats, the League of Women Voters, the NATIONAL COUNCIL OF JEWISH WOMEN, and the International Federation of Business and Professional Women.

Ruth Lewinson died in Manhattan, in December 1979.

BIBLIOGRAPHY

Obituary. *NYTimes*, December 3, 1979; *Who's Who of American Women* (1958–1959).

JULIE ALTMAN

LEWIS, SHARI (b. 1934)

Shari Lewis is a ventriloquist, symphony conductor, author, producer, and performer. She and her puppet friends have won numerous awards. She was asked by former first ladies Nancy Reagan and Rosalyn Carter to be the sole performer at the annual White House Christmas party for the children of the

At the age of twenty-six, ventriloquist Shari Lewis had her own television show, with Lamb Chop, Charlie Horse, and Hush Puppy, for three years. Almost three decades later, during which time she acted, conducted, and had a television series on the BBC, she was back on American television to enthrall another generation with her humor, charm, and imagination.
[New York Public Library]

Diplomatic Corps, and she emceed the annual White House Easter festival for the Bushes and the Clintons.

Shari Lewis was born Phyllis Hurwitz to Ann (Ritz) and Abraham Hurwitz on January 17, 1934, in New York City. Abraham Hurwitz was a founding professor of Yeshiva University of New York City. His lifelong specialty was encouraging children in their studies through play, a focus that his daughter has continued. Lewis's mother, a pianist, was one of six music coordinators for the Board of Education for the City of New York. Shari took piano lessons from her mother starting at age two. She married and divorced Stan Lewis, and has been married to television producer and publishing executive Jeremy P. Tarcher since 1958. They have one daughter, Mallory, a writer of children's books. Lewis's imaginative offspring include the hand puppets Lamb Chop, Charlie Horse, and Hush Puppy.

With encouragement from both parents, Shari began performing at the age of thirteen when her father taught her magic acts with Jewish content: one candle multiplying to become eight candles to illustrate Hanukkah and a torn newspaper that, when restored, had the design of a Jewish star. As a youth, she had lessons in acrobatics, juggling, piano, violin, and ventriloquism. She took her lessons in ventriloquism from John Cooper, with whom she would practice on a park bench. When she started performing ventriloquism, she added Old Testament tales to her repertoire. She studied piano and violin at New York's High School of Music and Art, dance at the American School of Ballet, and acting with Sanford Meisner of the Neighborhood Playhouse. She attended Columbia University for one year, then left college to become a performer.

In 1952, Lewis and her puppetry won first prize on Arthur Godfrey's *Talent Scouts* television show. In March 1956, she and Lamb Chop appeared on *Captain Kangaroo*, and by 1960 she had her own television program, with Charlie Horse and Hush Puppy joining the crew. The show ran three years, until animated cartoons replaced live performances.

After 1963, Lewis did television specials, acted in touring companies, and conducted symphony orchestras. She has performed and conducted with more than 100 orchestras, including the national symphonies of the United States, Canada, and Japan. She performed in national and summer stock productions of *Damn Yankees*, *Bye Bye Birdie*, and *Funny Girl*.

From 1968 until 1976, she had her own TV series on BBC-1 in England. During that period, she also did television series and specials in Canada and Australia.

After twenty-seven years' absence from American television, the Public Broadcasting System approached her about reviving her television show. During those twenty-seven years, Lewis says, the nature of children's television became commercial and producers focused on age groups for the purpose of marketing products. *Lamb Chop's Play-Along*, seen on PBS stations and reproduced in video, grew out of PBS interest and Lewis's discontent with commercial television.

"The show stresses the joys of diversity," Lewis said in a *New York Times* interview, with songs in languages other than English and a trio of on-air children chosen to represent an ethnic mix. The program involves physical involvement on the part of the children and is aimed at an audience from two to ten years old. Children from the television audience join in the show. Buster the Bus and Lamb Chop's teddy bear Mr. Bearly debuted during the second PBS season. The shows stress situations that affect children, such as not being invited to a party or feeling lonely. The shows do not preach; they demonstrate.

Lewis's productions include the video *101 Things for Kids to Do*, *One Minute Bedtime Stories* with brief versions of traditional tales, and *Don't Wake Your Mom*, winner of the 1992 Parent's Prize. Videos from *Lamb Chop's Play-Along* television series include *Action Stories* in which children can participate by filling in missing words or mimicking sounds, *Let's Make Music*, teaching children about music and musical instruments, and *Jokes, Riddles, Knock-Knocks and Funny Poems*.

The video *Lamb Chop's Special Chanukah* was released in 1996 and received the Parent's Choice award of that year.

Among her awards are twelve Emmy Awards, the Dor L'Dor award of the B'nai B'rith (1996), three Houston Film Festival awards, the Peabody Award (1960), the Silver Circle Award of the National Academy of Television Arts and Sciences (1996), the Film Advisory Board Award of Excellence (1996), two Charleston Film Festival Gold Awards (1995), the Houston World Festival silver and bronze awards (1995), the New York Film and Video Festival Silver Award (1995), the Monte Carlo Prize for the World's Best Television Variety Show (1963), and the Kennedy Center annual award for excellence (1983).

BIBLIOGRAPHY

"At Forty, Lamb Chop Still Plays Along Successfully." *Los Angeles Times*, March 16, 1996; *Contemporary Authors*. Vol. 19 (1987); *Contemporary Authors*. Vols. 89–92; *Contemporary Theatre, Film and Television*. Vol. 3 (1986); "Dishing Up Lamb Chop." *Washington Post*, April 4, 1994; "Forever Young." *Parent's Magazine*, July 1994; *Legends in Their Own Time* (1994); "Lewis, Lamb Chop Now on CD-ROM."

Chicago Tribune, May 6, 1996; Lewis, Shari. "Conversation." *NYTimes*, December 27, 1992; "Mild and Wooly." *People Magazine*, October 19, 1992; *Who's Who in America; Who's Who of American Women*.

JANET BEYER

LEWISOHN, IRENE (1892–1944)

Irene Lewisohn was a German Jewish philanthropist whose devotion to the arts led to the formation of two important New York City cultural institutions, the Neighborhood Playhouse and the Museum of Costume Art (now part of the Metropolitan Museum of Art). Her involvement in these and other social and philanthropic activities make her an important figure in New York's cultural history.

Irene Lewisohn was born in New York City on September 5, 1892, to Leonard and Rosalie (Jacobs) Lewisohn. She was the fifth daughter and the youngest of ten children. Lewisohn's mother came from a wealthy German Jewish New York banking family, while her father, a native of Hamburg, Germany, worked in his family's export business. The Lewisohns were rich industrialists, and Leonard Lewisohn and his brother Adolph were the principal founders of the American Smelting and Refining Company and the Amalgamated Copper Company. Irene Lewisohn's mother died in 1900, and her father died two years later.

Lewisohn was educated at the Finch School in New York, where she studied theater and dance. She also studied independently with many actors and dancers, including Yvette Guilbert. Lewisohn's love for the arts was balanced by a strong inclination toward social work. Her father had been a longtime supporter of the Henry Street Settlement in New York City, and Lewisohn soon became a teacher, club leader, and vocational counselor at Henry Street. She was frequently associated with LILLIAN WALD, founder and head of the settlement house. Lewisohn and her sister Alice taught acting and dancing at the settlement house, staged amateur productions, and organized a company of "Festival Dancers." In 1912, the dancers called themselves the Neighborhood Players, and in 1914 they moved into the Neighborhood Playhouse, purchased by Irene and Alice Lewisohn.

The Neighborhood Playhouse eventually broke away from the Henry Street Settlement as an independent theater, and by 1920, it housed a professional company of actors and dancers. The playhouse became famous for producing plays by experimental and esoteric writers such as James Joyce and Sholem

Asch. It also produced a number of plays that reflected the various ethnic backgrounds of people who lived in the area. Three of the Neighborhood Playhouse's best-known productions were *The Little Clay Cart* (1924), a Hindu drama; *The Dybbuk* (1925), a classic Yiddish folk play; and Walt Whitman's *Salut Au Monde* (1900). The Neighborhood Playhouse closed in May 1927. In 1928, Lewisohn collaborated with Rita Wallach Morgenthau in founding the Neighborhood Playhouse School of the Theatre. At the school, she conceived and planned "orchestral dramas" where pantomime and dance were used as accompaniment to a full orchestra. The Manhattan Opera House produced the first of these dramas in May 1928.

Although Lewisohn was shy, people who knew her through her work in the theater marveled at her artistic vision and intense dedication. Lewisohn moved away from dance in the 1930s and devoted herself to the Museum of Costume Art. She was also active in a number of social welfare and occupational guidance groups, including the Spanish Welfare Committee for the Loyalist cause during the Spanish Civil War. During World War II, Lewisohn was active in entertaining servicemen in the American Theatre Group's Stage Door Canteen and the Club for Merchant Seamen.

Lewisohn did not affiliate with any Jewish organizations. Jewishness did, however, play a role in her work in the theater. Lewisohn gave voice to people of many cultural, ethnic, and religious groups and embraced ethnic themes in her productions, including those about Eastern European Jews. By incorporating the songs, dances, costumes, and ceremonies of various cultures in her work, she sought to inculcate a general sense of ethnic pride and diversity. Lewisohn died on April 4, 1944, of lung cancer at Doctors' Hospital in New York.

BIBLIOGRAPHY

AJYB 46:341; "Irene Lewisohn, Welfare Aide, Dies." *NYTimes*, April 5, 1944, 19:3; *NAW*.

LAURIE SOKOL

LEWISOHN, MARGARET SELIGMAN (1895–1954)

Margaret Seligman Lewisohn—education advocate, philanthropist, art collector, and college trustee—was born in New York City on February 14, 1895. She was the daughter of Isaac Newton and Greta (Loeb) Seligman. Lewisohn came from a prominent German Jewish family. Her father headed J. & W. Seligman, the bank that served as the fiscal agent for the Union during the Civil War, and her mother's father founded the firm of Kuhn, Loeb & Company.

Margaret Lewisohn graduated from Miss Masters School in Dobbs Ferry, New York, in 1912. An aspiring pianist, she attended the Institute of Musical Art (later known as the Juilliard School of Music), earning a degree in 1914. During her two years of conservatory study, Lewisohn also pursued course work at Teachers College of Columbia University, where she was particularly interested in the progressive education ideas of John Dewey and others. Her interest in education was, in part, an outgrowth of her family's long-standing connection to the Ethical Culture School. At the same time, Lewisohn worked at the Hudson Guild Settlement House, where she also performed as a pianist.

Margaret Lewisohn was married to Sam A. Lewisohn, son of Adolph Lewisohn, benefactor of City College and other major New York cultural institutions, on February 2, 1918. The couple collected major works of art, including a substantial number from the modern period. They resided on East End Avenue in Manhattan and in Harrison, New York.

Calling herself "a citizen interested in education," Lewisohn had a long and illustrious career acting in the interests of public education, including membership in the Public Education Association, which she joined in 1922. In 1941, she became the professional director of the organization, which worked with the city's board of education to improve the quality of teachers, school facilities, and curricula. From 1946 to her death, she served as the chair of the association's board of trustees. She often wrote of her views on education, arguing that "the schools will only be as good as we citizens desire them to be. . . . We must continue to create an aroused public opinion that will demand the best in education and that will be willing to pay for it now."

In addition to her professional work in education, Lewisohn devoted her time and energy to a number of New York City's most prominent educational and cultural institutions. From 1930 to 1936, she served as the chair of the Women's City Club education committee, which devoted its energies to studying the progress of so-called super-normal and sub-normal children in the New York City public schools. She served as chair of the board of trustees of the Little Red School House from 1936 to 1940 and was a member of the Museum of Modern Art's education committee from 1936 to 1944. From 1939 to 1946, Lewisohn was a trustee of Bennington College, which

two of her four daughters attended, and she was a trustee of Vassar College at the time of her death.

Lewisohn was killed in an automobile accident on New York's Taconic State Parkway near the small town of Shenandoah on June 14, 1954. She was on her way home from a visit with Adlai Stevenson, the 1952 Democratic presidential candidate, who had presented the commencement address at Vassar. Lewisohn was fifty-nine years old and was survived by four daughters: Marjorie Lewisohn, Mrs. Sidney Simon, Mrs. Julian Eisenstein, and Mrs. Ernest Kahn. Her memorial service at Temple Emanu-El in New York City drew more than five hundred prominent citizens. In her will, she bequeathed major works to the Metropolitan Museum of Art, the Museum of Modern Art, the National Gallery, the Brooklyn Institute of Arts and Sciences, Vassar College, and the Whitney Museum of American Art.

BIBLIOGRAPHY

AJYB 56:570; *EJ*; Obituary. *NYTimes*, June 15, 1954, 1:7; *WWIAJ* (1938); *WWWIA* 3.

BARBARA L. TISCHLER

LEWITZKY, BELLA (b. 1916)

For more than six decades, Bella Lewitzky, a maverick in the world of modern dance, has distinguished herself as a preeminent performer, choreographer, artistic director, educator, public speaker, and civic activist. With an unshakable preference for living in the West, she defied norms that posit New York City as the center of American dance, maintaining the Lewitzky Dance Company in Los Angeles for over thirty years. She is also known for two highly publicized encounters with the federal government, risking professional ostracism to stand upon principle.

The second of two daughters, Bella Rebecca Lewitzky was born on January 13, 1916, to Joseph and Nina (Ossman) Lewitzky, Russian-Jewish immigrants living in a Southern California socialist utopian colony, Llano del Rio [Plain of the river]. The family relocated to San Bernardino, where Lewitzky attended high school. In 1934, when the family chicken ranch failed, she moved to Los Angeles to help her father find work. Lewitzky had always loved to dance but found ballet too restrictive. In Los Angeles, she was directed to Lester Horton, who introduced her to modern dance, and Lewitzky immediately felt at home. She collaborated with Horton for fifteen years, first as his pupil, but soon as his stellar protégé who could embody his wildly imaginative movement ideas.

On June 22, 1940, Lewitzky married Newell Taylor Reynolds, a Horton dancer who had recently graduated from the University of Chicago. During World War II, he served in the navy and eventually became an architect. He has remained Lewitzky's offstage partner, collaborating frequently as a set designer.

In 1946, Lewitzky and Horton cofounded Dance Theater in Los Angeles, a unique institution, housing both a dance school and theater. They created dances critical of religious fanaticism, bigotry, the violent anti-Semitism of Nazi Germany, and the abuse of women. Notable examples are *The Beloved* (1948) and *Warsaw Ghetto* (1949). In 1950, their partnership was severed.

In 1951, Lewitzky was anonymously accused of being a member of the Communist Party and was subpoenaed to appear before the House Un-American Activities Committee (HUAC). An "uncooperative" witness, refusing on constitutional grounds to answer invasive questions, Lewitzky responded afterward to reporters with an often quoted sound bite, "I am a dancer, not a singer."

From 1951 to 1965, Lewitzky taught modern dance in her school, Dance Associates, throughout Southern California, and at the University of Judaism. When her daughter, Nora, was born in 1955, she took a hiatus from performance.

At age fifty, Lewitzky formed the Lewitzky Dance Company, and in 1971 the company made its first cross-country tour into national prominence, with Lewitzky lauded by New York critics for an ageless and brilliant technique and a passionate performance style, particularly in her solo *On the Brink of Time* (1969).

The Lewitzky Dance Company achieved international status, touring thirty weeks each year, appearing in forty-three states and nineteen countries. It was one of three companies selected for the short-lived but highly successful IMPACT (Interdisciplinary Model Program in the Arts for Children and Teachers) artists in the schools program funded in the early years of the National Endowment for the Arts (NEA) (1970–1972). Lewitzky's daughter, Nora Reynolds, first performed with the company in the premiere of *Kinaesonata* (1971) and was a member of the company from 1973 to 1978.

Lewitzky has created more than fifty major concert works, several commissioned by national and international arts patrons. *Spaces Between* (1975) demonstrates Lewitzky's expansive embrace of space with a translucent, swinging Plexiglas set designed by Reynolds. While producing dance for the Los Angeles Olympic Arts Festival, Lewitzky premiered her acclaimed universal statement of human survival in the gripping *Nos Duraturi* [We who shall survive] (1984).

On June 14, 1990, Lewitzky held a press conference at the Hollywood Roosevelt Hotel, the scene of the 1951 HUAC hearings. In signing the contract for a grant from the National Endowment for the Arts, she had refused on constitutional grounds to agree to the newly legislated policy requiring grantees to pledge not to create obscenity. With her were Los Angeles mayor Tom Bradley and former blacklisted peers from the film industry. Referring to the McCarthy era, she asked, "How many times must history repeat itself? We must act. Having been witness, I must act." Supported by the People for the American Way, Lewitzky filed suit, and on January 9, 1991, Los Angeles U.S. District Judge John G. Davies ruled in her favor, eliminating the pledge.

Lewitzky was chair of the University of Southern California's contemporary dance department at Idyllwild (1956–1972) and founding dean of the School of Dance at the California Institute for the Arts (1969–1972). She has received numerous awards, including five honorary doctorates, the *Dance Magazine* Award (1979), the first California Governor's Award for Lifetime Achievement (1989), the American Society of Journalists and Authors Open Book Award (1990), the University of Judaism Burning Bush Award (1991) and the National Dance Association Heritage Award (1991). An outspoken advocate for government support of the arts, Lewitzky was vice-chair of the NEA's dance advisory panel (1974–1977).

The American Dance Festival premiere of *Greening* (1976) was the last group dance choreographed by Lewitzky in which she included herself. After that, she began a transition from the stage. With consistently strong performances, she quietly retired at age sixty-two.

Lewitzky has remained dedicated to the art of dance, eloquently creating expressive human motion with exquisitely trained dancers. A champion of freedom of expression, she symbolizes courage in her stand for constitutional rights in the public arena and courts. Lewitzky's eightieth birthday and the Lewitzky Company's thirtieth anniversary were celebrated in the 1996–1997 season.

JENIFER CRAIG

LHÉVINNE, ROSINA (1880–1976)

Rosina Lhévinne was one the most noted pianists of the twentieth century and a highly influential teacher. She was a virtuoso performer who delayed a solo career until age seventy-six, twelve years after the death of her husband, pianist Josef Lhévinne. One of the last artists in the nineteenth-century Russian pianistic tradition, Lhévinne taught some of the most famous musicians of the twentieth century, including Van Cliburn, John Browning, Mischa Dichter, Adele Marcus, Ralph Votapek, Martin Canin, David Bar-Ilan, James Levine, and Arthur Gold.

She was born Rosina Bessie, in Kiev, Ukraine, on March 29, 1880, the younger of two daughters of Maria (Katch) and Jacques Bessie, a Dutch diamond merchant. There were violent anti-Semitic riots in Kiev during her first year, and the Bessies moved to Moscow in 1881 or 1882. At age six, she began to study piano privately at home; at age nine, she was accepted into the Moscow Conservatory. Admission to the Conservatory was extremely competitive at that time, especially for Jews, since Czar Alexander III had instituted a quota that limited the number of Jewish students. Although her circumstances were profoundly affected by her Jewish heritage, her parents were not observant and she did not grow up with a strong religious connection.

Rosina studied with Remesov in the lower school of the conservatory, and later with Vasily Safonov in the upper school. She also met Josef Lhévinne at the school; he was six years her senior and one of the conservatory's most accomplished piano students. Rachmaninoff and Scriabin were among their classmates.

She made her public orchestral debut at age fifteen, playing Chopin's Piano Concerto No. 1 in E Minor with the Conservatory Orchestra, conducted by Safonov. In 1898, she graduated from the Moscow Conservatory with a gold medal—the youngest woman ever to receive the school's highest honor. She and Josef Lhévinne were married a week after her graduation.

During the first year of their marriage, the Lhévinnes made their two-piano debut in Moscow. At this time, Rosina Lhévinne decided to abandon her solo career and devote all of her musical energies to support her husband's. They lived in the Russian city of Tiflis from 1899 to 1901, in Berlin during 1901, and returned to Moscow in 1902 when Josef Lhévinne was appointed to the faculty of the Moscow Conservatory.

Josef Lhévinne made his first American tour in 1906. Their first child, Constantine (later called Don), was born in Paris on July 21, 1906. The Lhévinnes made their American two-piano debut in Chicago on February 17, 1907. She firmly refused to play solo works during their two-piano concerts, wanting the spotlight to be primarily on her husband.

Josef Lhévinne continued to tour Europe and the United States from 1907 to 1914. The family made their home in Wannsee, a suburb of Berlin, where he taught a large number of piano students, many of whom were American. Rosina Lhévinne filled in for him while he was away on tour. When World War I broke out, the Lhévinnes were subjected to internment in Wannsee because they were Russian citizens. Their second child, Marianna, was born in a hospital in Berlin, Germany, in July, 1918.

Immediately after the war, the Lhévinnes immigrated to the United States and settled in Kew Gardens, Queens. In 1924, both were invited to join the faculty of the newly established Juilliard Graduate School. They shared the same studio, and she was considered to be the better teacher by many of their students.

Lhévinne was devastated by the sudden death of her husband on December 2, 1944. She also feared that Juilliard would not renew her teaching contract without him. In fact, her teaching and performing careers blossomed after her husband's death. She moved from Queens to Manhattan to be closer to Juilliard and expanded her roster of students. Her fame grew as her students began to win many national and international piano competitions.

Lhévinne did not resume her own solo performing career until 1956. On August 25 of that year, she performed Mozart's Piano Concerto in C Major, K. 467 with the Aspen Festival Orchestra. During the following seasons she performed with orchestras around the country. In January of 1963, a few months before her eighty-third birthday, Lhévinne performed Chopin's Piano Concerto No. 1 in E Minor—the same work she had played at her debut sixty-one years earlier—in four performances with the New York Philharmonic, under the direction of Leonard Bernstein, to great critical acclaim.

Rosina Lhévinne taught at Juilliard through the 1975–1976 academic year. She died on November 9, 1976 at age ninety-six in Glendale, California, at the home of her daughter. In a tribute to Lhévinne after her death, Peter Mennin, then the president of the Juilliard School, said, "She was quite simply one of the greatest teachers of this century. With her passing, a whole concept of teaching and performing goes with her."

BIBLIOGRAPHY

DAB 10; Highstein, Ellen. "Lhévinne, Rosina." *New Grove Dictionary of American Music* (1986); Lhévinne, Rosina. Biographical file. Juilliard School Archives, The

Juilliard School, NYC; Wallace, Robert K. *A Century of Music-Making: The Lives of Josef and Rosina Lhévinne* (1976).

JANE GOTTLIEB

LIBRARIANS

The development of the field of librarianship as a profession for American Jewish women had much to do with Melvil Dewey (founder of the first library training school in 1887 and creator of the classification scheme bearing his name) and little to do with Judaism and Jewish culture. Paralleling the developing opportunities for women in the United States during the twentieth century, American Jewish women found librarianship, like teaching and social work, an attractive career choice. American Jewish women did not find acceptance in professional or even volunteer positions within Jewish communities until the late 1940s and early 1950s. The establishment of Jewish libraries in the United States reflects the tradition of male leadership within the Jewish community; leadership of major Jewish libraries was perceived as a scholar's (in other words, man's) position.

The most prominent and creative of the earliest American Jewish librarians was FANNY GOLDSTEIN. A native of Boston and educated at Boston University and Simmons College, Goldstein entered library work in 1913. She was the first Jewish librarian appointed in the Commonwealth of Massachusetts. Goldstein became librarian of the West End Branch of the Boston Public Library in 1922, then the largest branch. Her creative energies extended to all areas of outreach to the general community as well as the Jewish community where she was known as an outstanding and inspirational speaker and writer. Her endless enthusiasm and commitment to her work brought her honors and awards as well as being called "one of the best liked Jewesses in New England." Goldstein sought to awaken an appreciation and familiarity among American Jews of their own history in the United States as demonstrated in her article "Jewish Women in the Literary World" in *The American Jewish Outlook* and in speaking engagements throughout the Northeast.

In 1925, six years after the inauguration of the first Children's Book Week in America, Goldstein pioneered Jewish Book Week in Boston. Eventually it was expanded across the United States thanks to the efforts of the Jewish Book Council. In 1940, Goldstein became national chairman of the National Committee for Jewish Book Week.

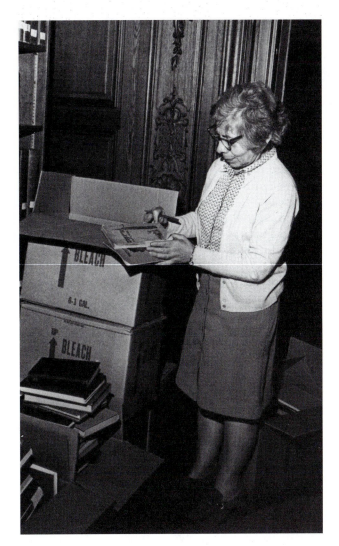

In addition to her responsibilities at the library of the YIVO Institute, DINA ABRAMOWITZ *was one of the compilers of bibliographies for the* Jewish Book Annual. *[YIVO Institute]*

Through Goldstein's initiative, the West End Branch of the Boston Public Library developed a Judaica Collection, which later became known as the Fanny Goldstein Judaica Collection. Goldstein was given the added title of curator of Judaica in 1954.

In the late 1940s, the Jewish Book Council began to encourage the development of Jewish libraries in synagogues, centers, and other institutions throughout the United States as a way of increasing interest in Jewish books and thus Jewish culture. The role of the public libraries in aiding the Americanization of immigrants in the first four decades was significant, a point not lost on the council. The need to develop

Jewish libraries in communities across the United States was clearly articulated by Rabbi Philip Goodman in his annual report of the Jewish Book Council of America in 1947–1948. Under the chairmanship of I. Edward Kiev (librarian of the Jewish Institute of Religion), a Committee on Citations developed a set of minimum requirements for which the Book Council would grant a citation of merit for a Judaica collection. The first citations were presented to twenty libraries. No mention of the librarian, if there was one, was made. During the next five years, there was an accelerated growth of Jewish libraries throughout the United States. Generally these were grass-roots efforts. This was especially true of synagogue libraries, the largest single group type. The initiative to create these libraries did not arise from the educational committee or the synagogue administration, but usually from the sisterhood. Other Jewish organizations that were library conscious included Jewish day schools, Hillel foundations, and Jewish community centers.

With Volume 10 of the *Jewish Book Annual* in 1951–1952, regular bibliographies began to appear primarily compiled by American Jewish women librarians. The bibliographies, most of which remain a regular feature of the annual, serve as recommended lists with brief citations. Regular bibliographic topics include American Jewish Fiction Books, American Jewish Juvenile Literature, *Dos Idishe Bukh in Amerika* later American Yiddish Books, Anglo-Jewish Books, Selected Books on Israel, and American Jewish Non-Fiction Books. The American compilers of these annual bibliographies during the 1950s and 1960s included DINA ABRAMOWICZ, Sophia N. Cedarbaum, Elizabeth E. Eppler, Fanny Goldstein, Ruth C. Kanner, Mary N. Kiev, Dorothy K. Kripke, Miriam Leikind, and Augustra Saretsky; and in the 1970s and 1980s, Deborah Brodie, Fannie Chipman, Nettie Frishman, Adina Kling, Sylvia Landress, Linda P. Lerman, Inabeth Miller, Marcia Posner, Debra Reed (later Reed-Blank), Ina M. Rubin-Cohen, Bertie G. Schwartz, and Hilda B. Wagner.

In the 1950s, individual women librarians began to lay the foundation for cooperation in librarianship in the synagogue, school, and center environments as well as in specialized research libraries.

Miriam Leikind, the first full-time librarian of The Temple in Cleveland, was a creative force and catalyst for collective activity. She organized gatherings and persuasively convinced educators, librarians, rabbis, and others involved in Jewish education of the need to cooperate to improve the quality of library services. With the encouragement of her rabbi, Abba Hillel Silver, Leikind extended her dream of cooperation to institutions throughout North America. Leikind and her colleague and fellow librarian Mae Weine of Philadelphia (now of Detroit) cofounded the Jewish Library Association in Atlantic City in June 1962 after both the American Library Association and the Special Libraries Association did not accept their recommendation for a separate Judaica section in their organizations.

At the instigation of Miriam Leikind in 1962, the Jewish Book Council provided financial support to hold the first exhibit on Jewish libraries at the annual convention of the ALA. The exhibit booth was visited by several thousand people, and its popularity encouraged the council to make the exhibit an annual event. Although the council arranged for the exhibit booth at the ALA convention in a different location each year, it was the librarians of the Jewish community centers, synagogues, and schools who assumed responsibility for local arrangements and appointed a committee to create and staff the exhibit booth. The purpose of these activities was twofold: First, the booth was designed to increase knowledge and awareness of Jewish books; more important, it generated great interest in and support for the new Jewish Library Association.

A 1957 Drexel graduate in library science, Mae Weine took a more pedagogic approach to her efforts. In addition to teaching courses at the Drexel Library School in library administration, acquisitions, cataloging, and reference, Weine wrote several works that became the standard for Judaica librarianship for many decades, among them *Weine Classification Scheme for Judaica Libraries, Standards for Jewish Libraries in Synagogues, Schools, and Centers* and *A Basic Periodical List*. Weine also recommended the inclusion of synagogues in the newly formed Church and Synagogue Library Association started by the former dean of the Library School at Drexel.

Other women librarians wrote significant works for the use of their colleagues. Sophie N. Cedarbaum's *A Manual for Jewish Community Center, School and Congregational Library* (1962) was a standard tool for more than a decade. Diana Bernstein revised her *Paperbound Books of Jewish Interest* (1963). Sheva B. Brun compiled *General Reference Books in English for Jewish Research* (1964). Pearl Berger was the project editor for *Guide to Yiddish Classics on Microfiche* prepared at the YIVO Institute for Jewish Research with Dina Abramowicz as consultant and Chone Shmeruk project editor (1980). Edith Lubetski with Meir Lubetski wrote *Building a Judaica Library Collection: A resource guide* (1983).

Until the 1980s, there were only a few American Jewish women in leadership positions in research Jewish libraries in the United States. SOPHIE A. UDIN established and directed the Zionist Archives and Library in New York from its founding in 1939 until 1949, when she was succeeded by Sylvia Landress. Udin played a crucial role in the formation of the Jewish Librarians Association in October 1946, although she herself never became a member. The association, whose entire membership was male, was the first organization of Judaica research librarians in the United States. Its members represented outstanding scholars and bookmen in the great tradition of bibliographers. Udin left to become the first director of the Israel State Archives and later the librarian of the Knesset.

Only one other woman librarian held a top-level position in a Jewish research library until the mid-1980s. In 1962, Dina Abramowicz became head librarian of the YIVO Institute for Jewish Research in New York, a position she held until 1987. The mid-1980s brought a new generation of American Jewish women librarians to high level positions in Judaica research and special libraries. Pearl Berger, previously a cataloger at the YIVO Institute and head of the main library at Yeshiva University, in 1985 became dean of libraries at Yeshiva University. In 1986, Aviva Astrinsky became librarian of the Annenberg Research Institute, formerly at Dropsie College and now known as the Center for Jewish Studies at the University of Pennsylvania. A year later, Linda P. Lerman became the first woman Judaica bibliographer at Yale University and four years later the first woman Judaica curator in the United States. She was succeeded by Nanette Sthal.

After several years, the Jewish Librarians Association faltered, until the early 1960s when its dynamic leader Herbert C. Zafren (Hebrew Union College–Jewish Institute of Religion) suggested merging with the much larger and more active Jewish Library Association. Meetings in 1965 led a year later to the founding of the Association of Jewish Libraries (AJL) comprising two divisions representing the synagogues, schools, and centers and the research and special libraries. The women who have held the office of AJL president from 1966–1996 are Mae Weine (1969), Anne Kirshenbaum (1972), Margot S. Berman (1976), Barbara Leff (1980), Hazel Karp (1984), Edith Lubetski (1986), Marcia W. Posner (1988), Linda P. Lerman (1990), and Esther Nussbaum (1996).

An entire issue of the award-winning journal *Judaica Librarianship* (Vol. 5, no. 2) is devoted to the history of the Association of Jewish Libraries, 1965–1990. Among AJL's Executive Board members are librarians who made significant contributions to the profession and AJL during that time, including Pearl Berger, Edith Degani, Rita C. Frischer, Mildred Kurland, Miriam Leikind, Dorothy Schroeder, and Bertie Schwartz. The professional journal *Judaica Librarianship*, published by AJL, reflects the creative energies and tireless devotion of its editor-in-chief, Bella Hass Weinberg (professor, Division of Library and Information Science, St. John's University). The journal's coeditor (Posner), associate editors (Berger, Karp, Lerman, and Lubetski), and contributing editors are a virtual who's who in Judaica librarianship. The association's newsletter, coedited by Irene Levin and Karp, provides time-sensitive information and book reviews. In addition to these print methods of communication, the association has its own Web page (http://aleph.lib.ohio-state.edu/www/ajl.html) with the current officers, convention information, publications list, award-winning books, and other information about the association.

BIBLIOGRAPHY

Eve Magazine (June 1936). Box 20, Judaica (West End) Collection, Boston Public Library; *EJ* 3:391, s.v. "Major Israeli Archives"; Fanny Goldstein Judaica Collection bookplate. Box 7, Judaica (West End) Collection, Boston Public Library; Goodman, Philip. "The Jewish Book Council of America in 5708 (1947–1948)." *Jewish Book Annual* 7 (1948/1949): 109–113; Greenblatt, Judith S. "An Interview with Mae Weine, President of the Association of Jewish Libraries, 1969–1970." *Judaica Librarianship* 5, no. 2 (Spring 1990–Winter 1991): 157–158; *Jewish Advocate*, November 25, 1930; *Jewish Book Annual* (1943/1944–1994/1995); *Jewish Book Week Annual* 1 (1942/1943); "Jewish Women in the Literary World." *American Jewish Outlook* September 27, 1935, p. 20; *Judaica Librarianship* (Fall 1983–Winter 1995); Judaica (West End) Collection, Boston Public Library; Landress, Sylvia. "The Zionist Archives and Library." *Jewish Book Annual* 34 (1976/1977): 79–81; Posner, Marcia. "The Association of Jewish Libraries: A Chronicle." *Judaica Librarianship* 5, no. 2 (Spring 1990–Winter 1991): 110–150; Simon, Ralph R. "A Pioneer Remembers: The Activities Miriam Leikind Initiated to Create the Association of Jewish Libraries." *Judaica Librarianship* 5, no. 2 (Spring 1990–Winter 1991): 155–156; Weine, Mae. "Libraries for the Jewish Layman." *Jewish Book Annual* 24 (1966/1967): 50–54; Whiteman, Maxwell. "The Association of Jewish Libraries in its Cultural Milieu." *Judaica Librarianship* 5, no. 2 (Spring 1990–Winter 1991): 151–154; *WWIAJ* (1980): 513, s.v. "Mae Weine"; Zafren, Herbert C. "A Veteran Looks at the Future (and the Past) of the Association of Jewish Libraries." *Judaica Librarianship* 5, no. 2 (Spring 1990–Winter 1991): 177–179.

LINDA P. LERMAN

LICHTENSTEIN, TEHILLA
(1893–1973)

In 1951, the New York–based Society of Jewish Science published a small pamphlet entitled "What to Tell your Friends About Jewish Science." Written by the society's leader, Tehilla Lichtenstein, the pamphlet sought to clarify the differences between the religions of Jewish Science and Christian Science. Portraying Christian Science as the outgrowth of a Christian philosophy of denial, Lichtenstein defined Jewish Science as the positive application of Jewish teachings to everyday life. She elaborated on this idea in over five hundred sermons delivered between 1938 and 1972, becoming the first Jewish American woman to serve as the spiritual leader of an ongoing Jewish congregation. While the society, which continues to exist, never sought formal affiliation with any of American Judaism's major religious movements, it retains strong historical and theological ties to classical Reform Judaism.

Born in Jerusalem on May 16, 1893, to Eva (Chava) Cohen and Rabbi Chaim Hirschenson, Tehilla came to the United States at age eleven and was raised in Hoboken, New Jersey, where her father served as the rabbi of a small Orthodox congregation. One of five children, she retained a close relationship with her siblings, especially her sister TAMAR DE SOLA POOL, who, with her husband, David, a rabbi, provided Lichtenstein with constant encouragement, support, and friendship. While the religious education she received was adequate, her secular education was exceptional. She earned a B.A. in classics from HUNTER COLLEGE in New York City in 1915, an M.A. in literature from Columbia University, and had begun doctoral work in English literature at Columbia when she left school in 1920 to marry Reform rabbi Morris Lichtenstein. She gave birth to a son, Immanuel, in 1922, and to another son, Michael, in 1927, raising her family in New York, where she remained until her death.

Working closely with her husband, Lichtenstein helped to establish the Society of Jewish Science in 1922; it was one of several efforts by a handful of Reform rabbis to stem the tide of Jews attracted to Christian Science. Borrowing from Christian Science and New Thought (a Protestant-based alliance with a similar emphasis on healing) such prayer techniques as affirmation and visualization, the Society of Jewish Science acknowledged, as did New Thought but not Christian Science, the reality of matter, evil, and suffering as well as the benefits of modern medicine. At the same time, it emphasized, as did Christian Science

sects, that God alone is the true source and restorer of health. Thus, to be healed one needs to recognize, and actively affirm, that God's presence and healing power lies within oneself.

While leadership of the society remained firmly in Morris Lichtenstein's hands until his death in 1938, during its early years Tehilla Lichtenstein served as the principal of its religious school and as the editor of its monthly periodical, the *Jewish Science Interpreter*. Upon her husband's death, Lichtenstein became the society's spiritual leader, a position she assumed more by circumstance than by design. In his will, Morris Lichtenstein had specified that leadership of the society should go to one of his sons or, if neither was willing to succeed him, to Tehilla. Since her sons did not aspire to the rabbinate, Lichtenstein took on the position, which she held until shortly before her death in 1973. According to the *New York Times*, over five hundred people came to hear her deliver her first sermon on December 4, 1938. Although the society's membership gradually decreased, Lichtenstein retained a loyal lay following, many of whom remained society members long after her death.

In 1956, the society built a synagogue in Old Bethpage, Long Island, which regularly held Sabbath and holiday services, usually led by a local Reform rabbi or rabbinical student. Lichtenstein continued to preach in New York City at the society's "home center," the hall at which Sunday morning services were held. She also continued to edit the *Jewish Science Interpreter*; taught classes in Jewish Science and occasionally in the Bible, counseled those in need, regularly trained a number of members to become practitioners, or spiritual healers, and, in the 1950s, hosted a weekly radio broadcast offering a combination of practical advice and Jewish Science teachings. While she viewed herself as Morris Lichtenstein's disciple, many of the religious images and ideas that she presented were her own. For example, having spent much of her adult life as a wife and mother, she often drew upon images related to marriage, motherhood, and the home. She also focused, far more than her husband had, on the relationships between human beings, which underscored her conviction that, as God's children, people have a responsibility toward one another. Such human relationships, she believed, serve as a model of the relationship between the individual and God. Lichtenstein frequently described God as a kind and benevolent father, but also suggested that seeking the divine presence was analogous to running toward one's mother. Both images, she believed, were of the same "divine fabric" and expressed the love of God in the "same boundless way."

Lichtenstein also placed great emphasis on divine election as a reminder of shared responsibility and destiny and spoke frequently and passionately about the founding of the Jewish state. After Israel's formation in 1948, she continued to voice her support and to hope that the new country would incorporate Jewish ideals and teachings into its notion of statehood. Both Tehilla and Morris Lichtenstein viewed Judaism as a practical religion. Yet, perhaps because by the late 1930s American Jews were drawn less to the teachings of Christian Science than to those of Norman Vincent Peale, Lichtenstein placed greater emphasis than her husband on the power of positive thinking, which she identified as the power of positive prayer. Many of her sermons focused on specific how-tos: how to achieve inner poise; how to get along with people; how to pray and when to pray. At the same time, however, she attempted to show the applicability of Jewish teachings, as understood by Jewish Science, to national and international problems. To demonstrate her conviction that Judaism could provide an answer to any and all situations, she gave sermons focusing on such issues as Nazi aggression, Soviet foreign policy, and anti-Semitism in postwar America.

Due to illness, Lichtenstein stepped down from the pulpit in 1972, although she remained the society's leader until shortly before her death on February 23, 1973. Today, the Society of Jewish Science identifies both Morris and Tehilla Lichtenstein as its founders and continues to print their sermons in the *Jewish Science Interpreter.* Lichtenstein remains historically significant for her religious leadership, thirty-four years before the ordination of women as rabbis. Her sermons are an important resource for those interested in Jewish Science, American Reform Judaism, and women's spirituality.

BIBLIOGRAPHY

Friedman, Doris. *Applied Judaism: Selected Jewish Science Essays by Tehilla Lichtenstein* (1989); Lichtenstein, Tehilla. Papers. Archives, Society of Jewish Science, NYC, and American Jewish Archives, Cincinnati, Ohio; Umansky, Ellen M. "Piety, Persuasion, and Friendship: Female Jewish Leadership in Modern Times." In *Embodied Love: Sensuality and Relationship as Feminist Values,* edited by Paula M. Cooey et al. (1987).

ELLEN M. UMANSKY

LIEBER, LILLIAN R. (1886–1986)

Lillian R. Lieber devoted her professional life to introducing modern mathematics to young people and to making them aware of the political and ethical implications of science and mathematics. In her books and lectures, she noted that although as much mathematics was created since 1800 as in the period from the origin of mathematics until 1800, students were not taught any of the modern mathematics until they reached college. She believed that in order to get students excited about mathematics, it was essential to teach the revolutionary aspects of such fields as Galois theory of groups, non-Euclidean geometry, and modern logic. In a series of books, each devoted to a single branch of mathematics or physics, she treated these subjects as well as lattice theory, the theory of infinities, and Einstein's theory of relativity.

Her books, illustrated with whimsical drawings by her husband, Hugh Gray Lieber, were characterized by their free verse style. Each phrase began on a new line to facilitate understanding of the mathematics. However, the mathematics was not oversimplified. For example, her book on lattice theory, a branch of abstract algebra, included enough mathematics to allow an explanation of unsolved research problems.

Of equal importance to Lieber was the message or, as she called it, the "moral" of her presentation of mathematics. The postulates of a mathematical field are not self-evident objective truths but are constructions of the human mind that can help us understand different aspects of the world. Non-Euclidean geometry arose when mathematicians questioned the logical necessity of the seemingly obvious postulate that given a line and a point not on that line, one and only one straight line can be drawn through that point parallel to the given line. Lieber argued that questioning old ideas and openness to new ones were central to science and art as well to as mathematics. She believed that science, art, and mathematics (or SAM as she referred to them) are the cornerstones of human culture. She called those intolerant of new ideas in these fields "anti-SAMites." Anti-SAMites were indifferent to "the good, the true, and the beautiful," and there was a clear implication that anti-SAMites were responsible for prejudice and war. To Lieber, war was the greatest danger facing humanity, and SAM our greatest hope against its destructive forces.

Lillian Rosanoff Lieber, the youngest of three children of Abraham H. and Clara (Bercinskaya) Rosanoff, was born in Nicolaiev, Russia, on July 26, 1886, and came to the United States in 1891. She received her B.A. degree from Barnard College in 1908, her M.A. from Columbia University in 1911, and her Ph.D. from Clark University in 1914. From 1917 to 1918, she was the head of the physics department at Wells College in Aurora, New York. She taught at the Connecticut College for Women from 1918 to 1920, and joined the mathematics department of Long Island University in 1934. At the time she was hired, Hugh Gray Lieber, whom she had married on October 27, 1926, was head of the department. In 1945, he became chairman of the art department and she succeeded him as chair of the mathematics department. She became a full professor in 1947 and remained at Long Island University until her retirement in 1954.

Lillian R. Lieber died in Queens, New York, on July 11, 1986, less than a month from her hundredth birthday.

SELECTED WORKS BY LILLIAN R. LIEBER [ALL WITH HUGH GRAY LIEBER]

The Education of T.C. Mits (1944); *The Einstein Theory of Relativity* (1945); *Galois and the Theory of Groups* (1932); *Infinity* (1953); *Lattice Theory: The Atomic Age in Mathematics* (1959); *Mits, Wits, and Logic.* 3d ed. (1960); *Non-Euclidean Geometry; or, Three Moons in Mathesis* (1940); *Take a Number* (1946).

BIBLIOGRAPHY

WWIAJ (1938); *WWWIA* 7.

JOSEPH S. ALPER

LIEBERMAN, JUDITH BERLIN (1903–1978)

In her contribution to the book *Thirteen Americans: Their Spiritual Autobiographies*, Judith Berlin Lieberman wrote that her goal was to "elevate the teaching of Bible and the traditional commentaries to their rightful place in the curriculum for girls," to help them "acquire a knowledge of and love for the Hebrew tongue" and of Eretz Yisrael.

She was born Judith Berlin in Latvia in 1903 into a distinguished rabbinic family. She was strongly influenced by her paternal grandfather, Rabbi Naftali-Zvi Yehuda Berlin (the Natziv), head of the prestigious Volozhin Yeshivah, and by her father, Rabbi Meyer Berlin, head of the world Mizrachi Organization and the person for whom Bar-Ilan University is named.

Another guiding force in her life was her paternal grandmother. She wrote that her grandmother was determined "to live a life that had inner meaning" and was "happy in the role of helpmate to the great man who was her life companion." Her grandmother took "complete charge of the finances of the Yeshiva." Even at age eighty and living in Jerusalem, she "kept

up her interest in men of learning and in the study of the Bible."

Judith lived in Berlin, Germany, shortly before World War I. On the day she was to return to Berlin after visiting her grandmother in Lithuania, war was declared. Unable to cross the border, she spent the war years with her grandmother in Lithuania and Belorussia. There, amid the hardships, she had access to a private library containing the works of Tolstoy, Jack London, Byron, and many other writers. "The morbid characters of Dostoyevski were gleeful topics for discussion by adolescent girls," she wrote in her autobiography. She also sought answers to "how" and "why" in pictorial abridged editions of Darwin and Haeckel.

In 1918, Judith was reunited with her family in the United States. She completed her secondary school education in New York City and received her B.A. from HUNTER COLLEGE. The thesis for her Ph.D., which she received in the early 1930s from the University of Zurich, was "Robert Browning and Hebraism: A Study of the Poems of Browning Which Are Based on Rabbinical Writings and Other Sources in Jewish Literature."

From 1932 to 1940, she lived in Jerusalem with her husband, the world-renowned rabbinic scholar and professor Saul Lieberman. Lieberman herself taught European history and literature at the Mizrachi Teachers Training School for Girls. "In the thirties . . . in an air charged with tension, when shots were heard intermittently, it became imperative to found all-day nurseries to enable mothers to take the place of their husbands on duty elsewhere. I felt that the obligation to establish such institutions in Jerusalem, especially for religious groups, fell on me," she wrote.

In 1940, the Liebermans returned to the United States "after days of flying over the sandy waters of the Middle East, a stop-over at the British oil wells of Bahrein and days spent at Bombay." Shortly afterward, she became the principal of Shulamith, one of the first yeshivahs for girls, in Borough Park, Brooklyn. She would hold that post for almost three decades.

Lieberman considered the Shulamith students to be "her girls." She looked after them, helping them to get scholarships and insisting on a rigorous curriculum. For years after they graduated, former students would visit Lieberman, bringing their babies and studying with her. Rivka Haut, a religious feminist and author and former Shulamith student, described Lieberman as "energetic, extraordinarily learned, with great warmth . . . a role model . . . a powerful and lasting influence."

As she got older and frailer, teachers would accompany Lieberman on the long subway ride from school in Borough Park to her home on Manhattan's Upper West Side. She thought they came with her because they had errands to do in the area.

Judith Lieberman died in December 1978, in New York, and was buried in Jerusalem.

BIBLIOGRAPHY

AJYB 80:369; Haut, Rivka. Interview by author, November 1996; "Lieberman, Judith Berlin." In *Thirteen Americans: Their Spiritual Autobiographies*, edited by Louis Finkelstein (1953); Lieberman, Judith Berlin. *Robert Browning and Hebraism* (1934); Rogoff, Rabbi David. Interview by author, November 1996.

YOCHEVED HERSCHLAG MUFFS

LIEBLING, ESTELLE (1880–1970)

A member of a very musical Jewish family, Estelle Liebling, soprano and one of the most influential teachers of singing in America, was born in New York City on April 21, 1880, to Matilde (de Perkiewicz) and Max Liebling. Her father and her uncles, George, Emil, and Solly Liebling, all studied with Franz Liszt and had significant careers as pianists and composers. She had three brothers, Otto, Leonard, and James; Leonard and James were also professional musicians. At first, Liebling was trained as a pianist but, as she stated, "Fortunately, they found I had a voice." She studied in Berlin with Selma Nicklass-Kempner, serving also as her teacher's accompanist during lessons with other students. She also studied in Paris with Mathilde Marchesi.

Liebling made her operatic debut at the Dresden Royal Opera House at age eighteen, singing the title role in Donizetti's *Lucia di Lammermoor.* Other roles she sang in Dresden were the Queen of the Night in *The Magic Flute* and Rosina in *The Barber of Seville.* She also appeared at the Stuttgart Opera and at the Opéra-Comique in Paris. Back in the United States, her unofficial debut at the Metropolitan Opera House in New York came in 1902, when at a few hours' notice she filled in for an ailing singer in the role of Marguerite in Meyerbeer's *Les Huguenots.* Liebling sang her role in German, the language in which she had learned it for performance in Dresden, while the rest of the cast sang in French. She also appeared at the Metropolitan in the roles of Musetta in *La Bohème* and the First Boy in *The Magic Flute.*

From 1903 to 1905, Liebling was the soprano soloist for John Philip Sousa's band, which toured throughout the United States and Europe. She sang some sixteen hundred times with Sousa, never missing a performance—a testament to her strength of will, strength of constitution, and reliable vocal technique. Critics praised the great facility and flexibility and the extraordinary range and sweetness of her voice.

In 1905, Liebling married Arthur Rembrandt Mosler, an engineer and inventor, the son of the American painter Henry Mosler. The wedding announcements in the newspapers stated that marriage would not mean the end of Liebling's musical activities, and this was true, although in the course of the next two decades Liebling devoted less time to performing and more to teaching. The marriage, which lasted until Mosler's death in 1953, produced one son, Arthur Mosler, Jr.

After a notable career as a concert singer, Estelle Liebling became one of the most influential teachers of singing in America. The Metropolitan Opera singers she trained or coached numbered close to eighty, leading one wit to dub her "the power behind the throat." [New York Public Library]

Liebling taught and coached singers for more than half a century. She was on the faculty of the Curtis Institute for Music in Philadelphia from 1936 to 1938, but for most of her career she taught at her studio in New York. The unusual range and flexibility that marked her singing also characterized her teaching. She prepared singers not only for the concert or operatic stage but also for careers in popular music. Among the singers she taught, coached, or advised were Amelita Galli-Curci, Frieda Hempel, Titta Ruffo, and BEVERLY SILLS in the operatic field and Jessica Dragonette, Adele Astaire, Gertrude Lawrence, and Kitty Carlisle in the popular field. The Metropolitan Opera singers she trained or coached numbered close to eighty, leading one wit to dub her "the power behind the throat." In interviews in the 1930s, she enthusiastically described training singers to make effective use of their voices on the radio. She was also willing to take on students as young as eight years old.

Liebling influenced the art of singing not only through teaching but also through books, including *The Estelle Liebling Vocal Course* and *The Estelle Liebling Coloratura Digest*. She also published a revised edition of vocalises written by her teacher Mathilde Marchesi, and a revised edition, with new piano accompaniments, of a collection of eighteenth-century arias. In addition, she wrote some compositions for piano and for voice.

After suffering a heart attack in her eighties, Liebling reluctantly reduced her teaching load to eight students a day. She died on September 25, 1970, at age ninety, having outlived her brothers, husband, and son.

BIBLIOGRAPHY

DAB 8; Eaton, Quaintance. "First Lady of Voice." *Opera News* 33 (March 1, 1969): 26–28; Fowler, Alandra Dean. "Estelle Liebling: An Exploration of Her Pedagogical Principles as an Extension and Elaboration of the Marchesi Method." D.M.A. diss., University of Arizona, 1994; *International Encyclopedia of Women Composers* (1987); J.V. "Heeding Musical 'Handwriting on the Wall.'" *Musical Courier* (October 1, 1937): 19; Kutsch, K.J., and Leo Riemens. *Grosses Sangerlexikon* (1987); Monson, Karen. "Estelle Liebling." *New Grove Dictionary of American Music* (1986); Obituary. *NYTimes*, September 26, 1970, 33:2.

CHARLOTTE GREENSPAN

LILITH

Founded in 1976 by a small group of women led by Susan Weidman Schneider "to foster discussion of Jewish women's issues and put them on the agenda of the Jewish community, with a view to giving women—who are more than 50 percent of the world's Jews—greater choice in Jewish life," *Lilith: The Independent Jewish Women's Magazine* has remained true to its mission. From its inception, it has intentionally, though not exclusively, emphasized religious and social issues rather than areas such as economics or politics. The contours of the Jewish women's movement and its own consciousness of a role that exceeds that of a magazine can be traced through over two decades of publications.

Although during its initial years publication was sporadic, the magazine has settled into a regular rhythm of quarterly issues. About two-thirds of the ten thousand copies printed go to subscribers; the rest are sold on newsstands or distributed. The readership is estimated to be twenty-five thousand and, according to a 1991 readership survey, is highly educated, between twenty-five and fifty-five years of age, married, and middle class (with average household income of more than $65,000). The readers also read close to a book a week. Advertising, sparse since *Lilith*'s inception, has grown, but it continues to cover a relatively small proportion of the cost of the magazine. Subscriptions, donations, and grants cover the rest.

The character Lilith, whom the magazine honors in its name, was the mythic first partner of Adam. While absent from the biblical text of the creation story, she is assumed by later interpreters to have merited banishment from the Garden of Eden because she refused to do Adam's bidding, particularly in sexual matters. She is the quintessential female rebel, a woman who would not take direction from a man. Her children were, according to some rabbinic versions of this legend, killed, leading her to attempt vengeance by killing infants. By taking her name, *Lilith* attempts a rehabilitation of her reputation and underscores the extent to which it identifies with the voices of insubordinate women.

Lilith attempts both to engage the interest of feminists in Judaism and to heighten the feminist consciousness of Jews, particularly Jewish women. Its proudly proclaimed independence is not to be misconstrued as a lack of position. Rather, its position is precisely that women, specifically Jewish women, ought to be independent.

The range of features *Lilith* has covered over the years is fairly broad, as is the variety of its contributors. In the initial years, it focused on the religious and organizational establishment of the Jewish community. The struggle to ordain women at the Jewish Theological Seminary was, for example, carefully covered with frequent updates and articles. The position of women in Jewish education and culture has also been examined, as has the place of women in Jewish organizational life. *Lilith* has chronicled the development of women's religious rituals and liturgy, reported on the position of women in Israeli life, and regularly addressed women's health issues. Lesbianism is often a particularly difficult issue to deal with in a magazine like *Lilith*, but it is regularly covered and, indeed, the magazine has served as a "safe space" to raise the issue within the community. *Lilith* also publishes fiction and poetry, as well as thought-provoking book reviews.

The issues discussed in *Lilith* have stimulated a great deal of thinking and, indeed, fostered change

Founded in 1976 "to foster discussion of Jewish women's issues and put them on the agenda of the Jewish community," Lilith has succeeded. After twenty years of publication it remains widely influential as "the independent Jewish women's magazine." This photo reproduces the cover of the first issue. [Lilith]

within the Jewish community. For example, CYNTHIA OZICK's article "Notes toward Finding the Right Question: A Vindication of the Rights of Jewish Women" moved the question of women's rights in Judaism from the sacred to the social domain. In so doing, she opened the issue for many who had considered the question in exclusively theological terms. The issue of so-called JAP-baiting on campus was also brought to the attention of a broad public through the pages of *Lilith*. A two-part series by Susan Weidman Schneider explored the differing ways women and men approach philanthropy. This research has had an impact on the United Jewish Appeal–Federation world and on many others seeking to fund Jewish causes. Finally, an issue devoted to hair confronted Jewish women's self-image.

The writers range from professional writers to professors to graduate students, and the articles are intended for a lay rather than an academic audience. The letters to the editor reveal the breadth of the readership: North America and Israel clearly dominate geographically; many more women than men write letters, and they have a wide range of interests.

Lilith is impelled by a vision that is broader than a magazine. Both within its pages and beyond them, it is clearly attempting to effect fundamental change in Judaism and Jewish society. Thus, for example, the "Kol Ishah" [Woman's voice] section presents short news items of particular interest to Jewish women. "Tsena Rena" [Go out, see] is subtitled "where to go for what if you're Jewish and female." It describes products and programs and includes information about contacting the providers. Each of these features draws its name from a piece of the traditional Jewish past and each challenges the original concept. Both of these features, part of the magazine since its inception, help *Lilith* foster change in the Jewish community.

It is the activities fostered by *Lilith* beyond the covers of the magazine that are most distinctive. Its editor-in-chief is, for example, regularly invited to speak at the General Assembly of the Council of Jewish Federations and Welfare Funds. It has also developed a talent bank of more than four hundred Jewish women who can serve as resources in many fields. This partnership between the magazine and activists strengthens *Lilith*'s impact on the community.

ANNE LAPIDUS LERNER

LINDHEIM, IRMA LEVY (1886–1978)

Irma Levy Lindheim was a colorful American Zionist millionaire, fund-raiser, and educator. Born in New York City on December 9, 1886, into a German Jewish assimilated family with roots dating back several generations in the American South, Lindheim discovered Zionism at age twenty-one. In 1926, she succeeded HENRIETTA SZOLD as president of HADASSAH, the Women's Zionist Organization of America. Then, in 1933, as a forty-seven-year-old widow and mother of five, Lindheim joined Kibbutz Mishmar Ha'emek in Israel, where she remained, aside from frequent stays in the United States and elsewhere for Zionist and political activity. To create greater interest in Judaism and Zionism, she designed family-based educational programs, a project on which she worked until her death.

Irma's father, Robert Levy, was a successful importer and avid businessman. Her mother, Mathilda (Morgenstern), dedicated herself to her husband and to her daughters, Amy, Edna, and Irma. Her mother and grandmother felt spiritually attached to Judaism, but lacked any form of Jewish education. Thus the family celebrated no Jewish holidays and had Christmas trees in their home.

As a child, Irma stuttered badly and compensated by voracious reading and mastery of riding, tennis, golf, and swimming. She was educated at Dr. Julius Sachs' School for Girls, which she appreciated for its scholastic excellence and abhorred for its exclusiveness. The family's few friends were her father's business associates. Eastern European Jews were never welcome at home. According to her autobiography, *Parallel Quest* (1962), written at age seventy-six, she felt rootless and lonesome as a child.

Irma defied her father's insistence that he select her husband, and in 1907 she married fledgling attorney Norvin R. Lindheim, a graduate of Johns Hopkins and Columbia University Law School. The couple's five children were Norvin Jr., Donald, Richard, Hortense (Babs), and Stephen (named for Rabbi Stephen S. Wise). Upon her father's death in 1914, Lindheim became independently wealthy.

Because Norvin Lindheim's firm dealt with German companies and he did not serve in World War I, the U.S. Government questioned his loyalty. In 1920, he was charged with conspiring to defraud the United States and, after a very lengthy trial, found guilty. After serving a prison sentence in 1924, he appealed the verdict and was finally declared innocent in 1928, shortly after his death at age forty-seven.

In spring 1917, after the birth of her fourth child, Lindheim enlisted and became one of the few Jewish women officers in the Motor Corps. Later, challenged by an Ethical Culture teacher to learn something about her Jewishness, she visited her husband's cousin, Hortense Guggenheimer Moses, in Baltimore, where she met American Zionists and Palestinian Jews. She was a Zionist from then on.

After six months, Lindheim began lecturing about Zionism. Inspired by the Balfour Declaration of 1917, she also brought Judaism home by celebrating Hanukkah. Henrietta Szold, head of the cultural division of the American Zionist Organization, recognized Lindheim's leadership potential, as did Judge Julian Mack, Sam Rosensohn, Abraham Tulin, and Menahem Ussishkin. Lindheim took up the challenge of chairing New York's nonphilanthropic Seventh Zionist District

In her role as HADASSAH president in the late 1920s, Irma Lindheim presented the case for Palestine in speeches throughout the country. Later, becoming more radical, she withdrew from Hadassah but worked with the group repeatedly in her passionate zeal for Jewish identity. [Hadassah Archives]

by creating a cultural center whose opening was attended by Justice Louis Brandeis. The center initiated an intercollegiate Zionist organization, offered lessons to children, and provided speakers for adults. Although membership and donations soared, the Brandeis/Weizmann dispute at the 1921 Zionist Convention in Cleveland led to the center's closing.

Dismayed by petty politics, Lindheim redirected her energies in 1922 and began studying at Rabbi Stephen S. Wise's new Jewish Institute of Religion. Because women had never been rabbinical candidates, Lindheim wanted to pave the way. For three and a half years, she engaged in religious study at the institute while also exploring child development with Professor John Dewey at Columbia University's Teachers College.

In 1925, Lindheim traveled to Palestine with Bertha Guggenheimer, where, as she described in *The Immortal Adventure* (1928), she attended the opening of Hebrew University and toured the country by horseback on a trip organized by Zionist pioneer Manya Shohat, Lindheim's future lifelong friend. Shohat introduced Lindheim to kibbutz life and to the possibility of Arab-Jewish friendship. In Kibbutz Kfar Giladi, Shohat's daughter Anna dubbed Lindheim "Rama," her name thereafter in Palestine. Lindheim befriended *yishuv* [settlement] leaders, was treated for malaria in the Safed Hadassah Hospital, and toured the Negev with Rachel and Yitzhak Ben Zvi, who urged her to raise money for the Jewish National Fund's project of purchasing the Negev. Lindheim took pride in Hadassah's health services for Arabs and in Judah Magnes's opening Hebrew University to Arab students.

Upon her return to the United States, Lindheim raised funds for Zionist causes and abandoned her studies. Sari Berger and Nadia Stein, emissaries from Palestine, helped her train women volunteers for the Women's Jewish National Fund Council, later integrated into Hadassah. Lindheim then launched an extensive speaking tour and soon became the third national president of the thirty-thousand-member Hadassah in 1926. Concerned that her children did not know their heritage, Lindheim also held her first seder that year.

At that time, Hadassah faced possible absorption into the Zionist Organization of America by detractors such as Louis Lipsky. A well-run group that abided by the "100 percent clause" (that is, sending all money except dues to Palestine), Hadassah fought to preserve its autonomy. In her role as Hadassah president, Lindheim presented the case for Palestine in speeches throughout the country. In addition to health, her concerns were education, land purchase, pioneering work, and Arab-Jewish friendship. Having been director of the Child Study Association, she also tried to create programs for American parents to raise their children in the Jewish tradition. Lindheim was reelected president of Hadassah in 1927 and served as its delegate to the World Zionist Congress in Basel. At the congress's conclusion, she flew to Palestine.

After spending time in Palestine, she planned a short return to the United States, which resulted in a more lengthy stay after the stock market crash. Ironically, the only part of her fortune saved was the money she had invested in Palestine. When Lindheim next joined Labor Zionist Poale Zion, Hadassah's national board demanded her resignation on the grounds of political conflict. From then on, Lindheim was critical of Hadassah, defining herself as further to the left and entitled to political autonomy.

Lindheim next raised funds for Histadrut and Hashomer Hatzair, with friends Mordechai and Zipporah Bentov, members of Kibbutz Mishmar Ha'emek. Some Zionists vilified Hashomer Hatzair as a communist group that abetted Arab against Jew. Shocked by such charges, Lindheim returned to Palestine to investigate the accusations. Back in the United States, satisfied with her findings, she resumed her speaking tour, believing that the spirit of Palestine could help Americans during the Depression.

In March 1933, Lindheim moved to Palestine with her children and tried to create a Histradut-funded clearing house for newcomers. After attending a disillusioning Zionist Congress in Prague, she decided to abandon organizational work and join Kibbutz Mishmar Ha'emek, choosing it for its beauty and respect for individuality and privacy. Despite limited water and food on the kibbutz, Lindheim admired its system of total democracy. She worked half days in the kitchen (which she defined as productive labor) and half days on her writing, Hebrew (which she never mastered), and knitting. At forty-seven, she was an average twenty-five years older than the other kibbutz members.

During World War II, the Keren Kayemet drafted Lindheim to raise funds in England during the blitz. She also petitioned the Lord Chancellor of England to cease home-destroying searches in Palestine, for which she earned Chaim Weizmann's praise. In 1939, her son Norvin died of illness at age thirty-one, in the United States.

In 1943, Lindheim beseeched Hadassah's national board to work with young people to confront anti-Semitism and build a Zionist youth movement. In 1945, she traveled to the United States, after her son

Donald died at age thirty-one in combat when Allied troops invaded Europe. She then sailed to Australia and New Zealand to raise funds for Palestine. After visiting Palestine to witness the end of British rule, she returned to the United States to help Hadassah raise money for Youth Aliyah. In 1948, she ran an unsuccessful campaign for the Queens congressional seat on Henry Wallace's Progressive Party ticket, which advocated civil rights and world government.

Back in Israel, Lindheim helped create Kibbutz Adamit and Kibbutz Ein HaShofet (named for *shofet* [judge] Louis Brandeis). In the mid-1960s, she stayed in the United States, developing educational programs to counteract assimilation among Jewish children. Returning to Israel, she was, at age seventy, lauded in the Israeli press as "the grandmother of the kibbutz" and wrote diverse articles for Zionist publications, including a lengthy appreciation of Manya Shohat, who had died in 1961.

Returning to the United States again, Lindheim tried to establish, through Hadassah, "Operation Jewish Survival," a program to help Jewish mothers and grandmothers instill a Jewish identity in their children. In a *Ha'Aretz* interview at age eighty-six, she expressed enthusiasm for the kibbutz and criticism for Israeli decadence. Lindheim spent her last years near relatives in California. She died in Berkeley on April 10, 1978, at age ninety-two.

SELECTED WORKS BY IRMA LEVY LINDHEIM

The Immortal Adventure (1928); "The Making of Young Pioneers." *Israel Horizons* 10, no. 6 (June-July 1962); *Parallel Quest: A Search of a Person and People* (1962).

BIBLIOGRAPHY

AJYB 80:369; *BEOAJ*; *EJ*; Lindheim, Irma. Correspondence, July 26, 1943–August 1, 1963. Record group 7, Special Collections, Hadassah Presidents Correspondence Series, Hadassah Archives, NYC, and Papers. Bet Hashomer Archives, Kibbutz Kfar Giladi, Israel, and Collection A274. Central Zionist Archives, Jerusalem; Obituary. *NYTimes*, April 11, 1978, 40:1; Szold, Henrietta. Collection. Central Zionist Archives, Jerusalem; *UJE*; *WWIAJ* (1926, 1928, 1938).

SHULAMIT REINHARZ

LIPMAN, CLARA (1869–1952)

As a playwright and actress, Clara Lipman enjoyed a long and accomplished career in show business. A prolific writer with many stage credits, Lipman proved herself worthy of a powerful place in the not-so-woman-friendly New York theater world at the beginning of this century.

Born on December 6, 1869, in Chicago to Abraham and Josephine (Brueckner) Lipman, Clara attended public schools in Chicago and New York, as well as being educated by private tutors. She began acting in ingenue roles and quickly joined A.M. Palmer's venerable New York theater company. After a stint touring Europe with English and German classical companies, Lipman returned to New York and married fellow actor Louis Mann.

She starred with her husband in many plays, often lightweight comedies on Franco-American themes, with titles like *Girl from Paris*, *All on Account of Eliza*, *Julie Bon Bon*, and *Marriage of a Star*. In 1903, one journalist explicitly related Lipman's and Mann's success to their ethnicity. "Mr. Louis Mann is a comedian of a unique sort, who is thoroughly a Jew," the reporter wrote. "His wife Miss Clara Lipman is a Jewess. Miss Lipman, a beautiful woman, is indeed one of the beauties of today's stage, and her features are distinctly Jewish. She is also a comedian . . . she has the rich idea of humor that is innate." Lipman never denied being perceived as Jewish, but the identity was not central to her career or commitments.

Due to an accident in 1902, which left her arm broken, and messy contract disputes with her managers, Lipman was forced to take a long absence from the stage. In 1906, anxious to get back into theater, she single-handedly persuaded the Shuberts to let her produce and perform in *Julie Bon Bon* under their management. A *New York Herald* reviewer wrote that *Julie Bon Bon* "is not great but [Lipman] is quite chic and Mr. Mann is most amusing." *Marriage of a Star*, another play with French flair, was a "most refreshing bit of sane wholesome comedy," affirmed one reviewer. However, another critic panned the play, denouncing it as "the most dreadful example of bad dramatic construction you can imagine." Despite the scathing comments, Lipman continued to attract audiences. Throughout her career she wrote eleven plays herself, including *Marie de Fleury* and *The Wolf at the Door*, and collaborated on fifteen more with playwright Samuel Shipman, including *Flames and Embers* and *The Good-for-Nothing*. She continued to write and perform until 1927.

In 1919, the *New York Star* cited Lipman as a featured hostess at a table for a dinner supporting the Woman Suffrage Party; she was one of only two actresses who attended. Her engagement in a political cause specific to women was no doubt connected to professional struggles she faced because of her gender. In June 1952, Clara Lipman died at her home in New York at age seventy-nine. Forty-six years earlier, in 1906, a Chicago interviewer had asked Lipman if she felt women were really more determined than men, to which she had replied, "In business they will accomplish more in a day than the average man in a week. I believe in woman, and if she is given half a chance, she will succeed."

During a career in which she made a reputation as a charming light comedian, Clara Lipman also wrote eleven plays and collaborated on fifteen more. She was reported to have said that a woman "will accomplish more in a day than the average man in a week. I believe in woman, and if she is given half a chance, she will succeed." [New York Public Library]

BIBLIOGRAPHY

AJYB 6 (1904–1905): 142, 24:173; *BEOAJ*; *JE*; Lipman, Clara. Clippings file. Robinson Locke Collection, vols. 238, 318. New York Public Library Center; Obituary. s.v. "Mann, Clara L." *NYTimes*, June 23, 1952, 19:5; *UJE*, s.v. "Mann, Louis"; *WWIAJ* (1926 addenda and 1938); *WWWIA* 3.

MICHELE SIEGEL

LIPSKY, CHARLOTTE (1879–1959)

Charlotte Schacht Lipsky, interior decorator, was born in Riga, Latvia, in December 1879. The eldest of five children, she was the only girl.

Lipsky immigrated to the United States in 1895, accompanied by her mother, who lived with Lipsky until her death. Upon arriving in the United States, Lipsky immediately involved herself in politics, specifically in the Jewish socialist movement, becoming one of "EMMA GOLDMAN's girls" on the Lower East Side of New York.

In 1905, she married Louis Lipsky, known by some as the "dean of American Zionists," who became a leader of the Zionist movement in America. She had a great sense of loyalty to her husband and took pride in his prominence. On nights when he was not traveling, Louis Lipsky would take tea at the Tiptoe Inn, a cafeteria on 86th Street and Broadway. A group of people who wished to speak with him or to listen to him would join him there. Charlotte Lipsky accompanied him to these teas, for which Louis Lipsky would often pick up the tab for everyone. This habit, in addition to his wish to donate much of his paycheck to the Zionist movement, made it necessary for Charlotte Lipsky to find another source of income to support her family.

Lipsky came from an artistic family. Her brothers Gustav and Henry were both actors; another brother, William, was an art dealer; and all of the brothers painted, even James, who was a businessman. It was this background and her own artistic talents that led Lipsky to her career as an interior decorator. She had no office and no other accoutrements to suggest an official business setting. Her home was her showroom, and business with clients was conducted there. She would accompany these clients on trips to Lower East Side shops to choose fabrics, furniture, or whatever was needed. She would then receive a commission for her help and advice.

In addition to her decorating talents, Lipsky was a sculptor and a singer, giving concerts when she went back to Europe in the summers of 1933 and 1936. She also was a founding member of the Manhattan chapter of WOMEN'S AMERICAN ORT and was active in HADASSAH.

Charlotte Lipsky had three children: Eleazar Lipsky, a historian and head of the Jewish Telegraphic Agency for many years; David Lipsky; and Joel Carmichael, who is a writer and the editor of *Midstream* magazine.

Charlotte Lipsky died on May 15, 1959 at age eighty.

BIBLIOGRAPHY

AJYB 61:418; Carmichael, Joel. Interviews with author, November 14, 1995, and January 1996; Lipsky, Hannah [daughter-in-law]. Interview with author, November 1995; Obituary. *NYTimes*, May 17, 1959, 33:3.

ELANA KANTER

LITERATURE *see* CHILDREN'S LITERATURE; FICTION; FICTION, POPULAR; POETRY; YIDDISH LITERATURE

LITERATURE SCHOLARS

At the close of the twentieth century, women of all classes, races, and ethnicities are so fully integrated into American literary academia that it is astonishing that, as little as a century ago, the idea of a woman professor teaching, for example, the novels of George Eliot or Henry James to a roomful of young men and women was inconceivable. In all highly literate cultures, secular and religious knowledge used to be the domain of men, while women were in charge of the practical side of daily life, and, in the upper classes, of certain social matters.

In this regard, Jewish culture is no exception. Despite the premium Judaism places on literacy and learning, which in some instances persuaded fathers to teach their daughters and husbands to instruct their wives, the motto among observant Jews remained until fairly recently, *a meydl darf nisht lernen* [a girl need not study]. While European gentile culture considered women intellectually inferior to men, Jewish culture argued that God designed woman to be man's "helper" (Gen. 2:18). Women relieved men of domestic chores, and, in Eastern Europe, women often contributed to the family income.

The disturbing attitudes of gentile culture toward both Jews and women, which have only recently begun to change, are responsible for the late entry of Jewish women into colleges and universities. For those Jewish women who sought admission to institutions of higher learning and became the first female Jewish humanities professors, their struggle against Jewish tradition caused many to turn away from Judaism as the source of an intellectually vibrant and spiritually meaningful life.

The first generation of Jewish women professors, especially those in the field of literature, consisted of militantly secular women from a variety of Jewish social backgrounds (labor, socialist, Yiddishist, Zionist, immigrant, and mercantile). They had two things in common: a love of Western literary culture and an ignorance of the Jewish intellectual tradition, its major texts, authors, and debates. While many Jewish women in literary academia were familiar with the most popular ritual and cultural expressions of Judaism, such as the blessing of candles on Shabbat, or the prohibition against pork and shellfish, none had been educated to locate the specific practices of observance within the framework of an intense and ongoing intellectual discussion spanning two millennia, a discussion carried on, until very recently, exclusively by men.

Ignorance of Judaism's intellectual underpinnings, coupled with a vague emotional appreciation of certain Jewish customs, ranging from hamantaschen on Purim to latkes on Hanukkah, is the single unifying feature of an otherwise extraordinarily diverse group of individuals—Jewish women in literary academe—whose history as a group this article, paradoxically, attempts to sketch.

Overall, the integration of Jewish women into literary academia is much more closely linked to the history of women than to the history of Jews in American universities. The sequence of integration runs roughly as follows: White Protestant men of Anglo-Saxon descent grudgingly accepted Catholic men before accepting Jewish men as colleagues and instructors of English literature. Jewish men, in particular, were ready to open academe further by hiring women, who in turn agitated for the integration of other minorities, such as African Americans, Hispanics, and gays. The history of Jews in American academia shows a significant gender bias; whereas Jewish men were discriminated against as Jews, Jewish women had difficulties not as Jews but as women. The reason for the difference is that Jewish men and women entered the field in different generations—men during the 1920s and 1930s, women during the 1950s and 1960s.

Until the early 1930s, white Protestant men dominated the study of literature. Throughout the 1920s and 1930s, a few white Protestant women, often educated at elite women's colleges, struggled into the field. They achieved recognition and full professorships in the early years of World War II, as their male colleagues either volunteered for or were drafted into the army. At the same time, a handful of Jewish men were finishing their dissertations in literature. If these Jewish scholars secured jobs at all at top schools during the late 1930s, their appointments were due to special circumstances. Most of them, however, were hired either in the early 1940s to fill vacancies created by America's entry into the war or right after the war to help satisfy the enormous demand for college teachers created by the GI bill.

Among the soldiers returning from the European and Pacific theaters were Jews who had started college in the late 1930s, became interested in literature, but graduated without much hope of being able to pursue an academic career in the humanities. Drafted into the United States Army or Navy upon graduation, they now returned to American campuses to find that a few Jews had broken through the ethnic barrier to become professors of English and American literature. Encouraged by these appointments and convinced that the equalizing experiences in trenches and on battleships had undermined the prejudices against Jews they had encountered during their college days, they enrolled in graduate English programs. As teachers, they attracted the third generation of male Jewish literary critics entering college in the late 1940s and early 1950s, when the first Jewish women were enrolling in graduate literature programs and the first sizable number of young Jewish women were starting college. While the men of that generation, receiving their doctorates in the late 1950s and early 1960s, secured jobs without too much effort, their female colleagues faced many problems, not only as women in academe, but also in the culture at large as women who did not wish to be homemakers.

This diverse group of women scholars, born in the mid-1920s to mid-1930s, were more often than other women raised in either all-girl families or as the oldest daughter, or they were an only child. One of the most prominent members of this group is CAROLYN HEILBRUN. Born in 1926 as the only child of affluent parents who had cut themselves off from their Jewish past, Heilbrun, early on, wanted to find out the nature of other people's identities. Her resource was the biography section in the local branch of the New York Public Library. Heilbrun received her B.A. from Wellesley College in 1947, and went on to pursue graduate studies in English literature at Columbia University with Lionel Trilling. She received her M.A. in 1951 and completed her Ph.D. in 1959. After a brief teaching stint at Brooklyn College, she joined Columbia's School of General Studies, the university's adult extension school. Throughout the 1960s the

School of General Studies was the only gateway for women scholars to academic careers at Columbia.

Until the beginning of the women's movement in the early 1970s, women did not figure distinctly in Heilbrun's scholarship or detective fiction, which she has been publishing under the pseudonym Amanda Cross since 1964. Feminism enabled Heilbrun to analyze and name the problems she had faced throughout her career at Columbia. Her insights transformed her literary criticism, as well as her mysteries, and Heilbrun became one of the most outspoken early feminists in literary academia. Judaism, however, did not influence Heilbrun's work as an intellectual, cultural, or religious force. Nor does Jewishness have a place in her writing, with the exception of a few remarks about Trilling's descent and her own, and some oblique allusions in her *Theban Mysteries* and *A Trap for Fools.*

For Carole Kessner, however, Heilbrun's junior by six years, Jews had always been as important as women. Born into modest social circumstances in Jewish Brooklyn, Kessner's role models were firmly anchored in Jewish culture. Her American-born, athletic father raised his two daughters like sons in every respect, except in Judaism. As a result, Kessner did not pursue her Jewish education and abandoned observance. "I could not go to an Orthodox shul," she remembers, "because the fact that it was not egalitarian turned me off, and I simply could not deal with my father's 'Don't rip the paper on *shabes*! . . . God will punish you.' Reform was horrendously attenuated, and Conservatism was nothing, neither here nor there." Kessner, who eventually found her home in the Reconstructionist movement, turned into a secular but culturally identified Jew, a decision that her college of choice reenforced. In 1949, Kessner enrolled in the second graduating class at Brandeis University, where she became attached to her English professor MARIE SYRKIN, a writer and secular Zionist.

The ideals and ideology of the 1950s, however, were stronger than Syrkin's example, and in 1953, shortly before graduating, Kessner married and quickly had three children. Confined to her home in a New York suburb, Kessner became increasingly depressed. She resolved to go back to school. Joining the literary vogue of the time, she studied Milton with Miriam Starkman at Queens College. But Kessner did not get excited about her intellectual venture until she met the Yiddishist Joseph Landis, who encouraged her to drop the high art of Milton for the analysis of the down-to-earth Jewish immigrant novel before 1917. This topic allowed her to examine and validate her own cultural history. Gradually, she discovered that

her strong, smart, yet pragmatic immigrant grandmother was one in a long line of independent Jewish women who had created successful lives for themselves. Energized by a gallery of self-reliant, creative Jewish women, from the seventeenth-century memoirist Glikl of Hameln to Marie Syrkin and CYNTHIA OZICK, Kessner pursued an academic career specializing in Jewish American literature.

Kessner's efforts at transforming literary research into cultural rootedness were duplicated by other women born during the 1930s, who published their first books on Jewish American literature during the 1970s. Among them are Evelyn Avery, Dorothy Bilik, Sarah Blacher Cohen, S. Lillian Kremer, Ellen Schiff, and Ann R. Shapiro. Interestingly, none of these scholars was able to get a position at an Ivy League, seven sisters, or similarly prestigious school. If one desired entry into that enclave during the late 1960s and early 1970s, one was not supposed to dabble in "parochial" (i.e., ethnic) research, but was compelled to demonstrate intellectual seriousness by pursuing mainstream scholarship in the Western literary canon.

Barbara Herrnstein Smith, like many other Jewish women, rose to the top of literary academia during the 1980s. Born in 1932 and raised in the Bronx, New York, Smith believed, even as a little girl, that her "destiny was going to be one of autonomy and intellectuality." At the age of fourteen, she enrolled at Hunter High School in Manhattan, which was then still largely Jewish and famous for accepting only the smartest girls. She went on to City College, where she met Richard Herrnstein. Married in 1951, she followed her husband to Harvard a year later. Having then two more years of college to finish, she applied to Radcliffe, but was turned down. "Well, you have an excellent record," she remembers the dean saying, "but I see here that you are married. I am afraid we are only interested in serious students." Smith applied to Brandeis University. The brand-new university, founded in 1948 by secular Jews, represented to her a "ferocious, ambitious, unapologetic intellectuality." Hunter High School and Radcliffe College cultivated the ideal of the mellow, elegant, feminine intellectual. This was a gender ideal at Hunter and a class ideal at Radcliffe. The ideal woman at Brandeis—irreverent, pioneering, exuberant—was the exact opposite. Faculty and students reveled in displays of brilliance to a degree that Radcliffe and Hunter would have considered crude.

At Brandeis, "I could be an intellectual," Smith recalls. "And as a woman I didn't feel I had to apologize for being smart, or hide it. . . . I could be everything I was without worrying." She enjoyed her teachers, among them Irving Howe, Philip Rahv, and J.V. Cunningham, who were contentious, rudely charming, and determinedly plebeian. Jewishness, which Hunter High School and Radcliffe worked hard to ignore in their sizable Jewish student body, stopped being an uncomfortable issue for Smith. She was among Jews whose religion was brilliance; to be brilliant was to be Jewish.

Smith graduated in 1954, earned a master's degree in 1955 specializing in Renaissance poetry, and in 1962, just before finishing her doctorate, got a job at Bennington College, another irreverent, iconoclastic institution that suited her well. Divorced, remarried, and divorced again, Smith developed into one of academia's leading literary theorists. In 1980, she was hired by the University of Pennsylvania, and a few years later, was invited by the academic iconoclast Stanley Fish to join his avant-garde English department at Duke University. Having come of age intellectually before the rise of ethnic particularism in the late 1960s and of feminism in the early 1970s, Smith is one of a handful of prominent Jewish literary women scholars (among them Dorrit Cohn of Harvard University and Marjorie Perloff of Stanford University) whose work has not been influenced by their cultural identities or gender.

Such detachment became virtually impossible for the Jewish women of the next generation, born in the 1940s, who were swept up in the women's movement at important junctures in their lives. They entered academia as energetic assistant professors in the mid-1970s, and with their experimental feminist literary criticism, published in the late 1970s and throughout the 1980s, revitalized and gave direction to a profession that had become exhausted and disorganized in the aggressive scrambling for employment and tenure during the late 1960s. This first generation of feminist literary scholars, specializing in British and American fiction, includes Elizabeth Abel, Nina Auerbach, Nina Baym, Judith Gardiner, Susan Gubar, FLORENCE HOWE, Annette Kolodny, Nancy K. Miller, Naomi Schor, and Elaine Showalter. With books such as *Communities of Women: An Idea in Fiction* (1978), *Women's Fiction: A Guide to Novels by and about Women in America* (1978), *Shakespeare's Sisters: Feminist Essays on Women Poets* (1975), *A Literature of Their Own: British Women Novelists from Brontë to Lessing* (1977), these scholars rewrote literary history by resurrecting neglected women writers and postulating an independent female literary tradition. However, Jewish women did not figure in these works.

As women scholars became more established, smaller groups began to crystallize that were interested in particular aspects of women's identity, such as class, race, ethnicity, and sexual preference. What is remarkable about these subgroups is that the closer their members were to the centers of academic power, the less they identified themselves as Jews or made Jews their topic of study. One group of poets, composed of Jewish women such as ADRIENNE RICH, ALICIA OSTRIKER, and Rachel Blau DuPlessis, who were affiliated with a university but not defined by it, would readily acknowledge the impact their Jewish parents, childhoods, and experiences, however attentuated, had had on their identity formation. Members of a group at the opposite end of the spectrum, the high-powered Jewish women scholars devoted to questions of lesbianism and bisexuality (for instance, Marjorie Garber of Harvard University and Eve Kosofsky Sedgwick of Duke University), find questions of Jewish identity irrelevant to their academic pursuits.

As Bonnie Zimmerman, a specialist in lesbian fiction, wrote, many gay Jewish women find themselves in an antagonistic relationship with Judaism, despite the creative mediations proposed by poets like Adrienne Rich or scholars such as EVELYN TORTON BECK. Zimmerman's description of her own intellectual development is representative of that of many young Jewish feminists. Born in 1943 and raised in Chicago in a secular family hyperconscious of who was and who was not Jewish, Zimmerman confessed that she, too, made note of women who were:

> I am proud that so many of the world's greatest intellectuals and artists have been Jewish. . . . I am pleased that so many of the founders and stars of the women's movement—GLORIA STEINEM, BETTY FRIEDAN, BELLA ABZUG, Andrea Dworkin—are Jewish. . . . I remember when I first began to notice the disproportionate number of Jews in every feminist or lesbian group of which I have ever been part. . . .
>
> But as a feminist and lesbian in the 1970s, it never occurred to me that being Jewish might mean something more than a cultural curiosity, that it might matter to my politics and my scholarly work. (Rubin-Dorsky and Fishkin, pp. 205–206)

While Judaism in the abstract—already insignificant for most assimilated American Jews—was not an issue for the early feminists, its social and cultural remains became the focal point of personal antagonism, as Zimmerman attests:

> To me, brought up in a strongly cultural, but not religious, Jewish family, Judaism represented the

ties that bound me to family, the traditional role of women, compulsory heterosexuality, and the structure of patriarchy. To a certain extent, I had become a feminist and embraced my lesbianism in order to break those ties and establish my own adult identity. Judaism reeked of the past, of childhood, of strangling bonds and expectations. Judaism represented the secondary status of women. (p. 207)

While some feminists identified Judaism with the oppressive, patriarchal social structures in their personal environments, others identified it with the materialism and hypocrisy of their rich 1950s suburbs. Marjorie Garber, for instance, who grew up in an affluent area on Long Island, reacted strongly to the intellectual vacuity of the people in her neighborhood. "I was surrounded by extremely well-dressed, wealthy people," she recalls, "who read the transliterations on the other side of the Reform prayer book. With the passion of a rebellious sixteen-year-old, I declared this to be hypocritical. I was an absolutist and wanted nothing to do with it." She experienced her parents only as "culinary Jews," since the activities that defined her home as Jewish were "Passover and other celebrations that had food attached to them." Hence, Garber thought of the world of the Jews and the world of the intellect as completely dissociated. "It took me a long time," she confesses, "to free myself from the feeling that the world of the Jews was an anti-intellectual world and to realize that the world of culture and scholarship was full of Jews."

For many feminist literary scholars, however, Judaism did not arouse animosity. For straight women, in particular, as Nancy K. Miller explains, Judaism and Jewishness often became a matter of indifference, once gender provided a satisfying answer to the nagging question of identity:

With my conversion to feminism in the early 1970s, the aimless questing about "who I was" and "what I would do" shifted away from the marriage plot and moved into the new categories of "theory." Being "different" stopped being a matter of personal anguish and became a question about gender and sexual politics. Suddenly there was a language for understanding the malaise of identity. . . . At the same time, the Jewish question disappeared from the horizon. To the extent that it had always been tied to the wars with my parents, and that my prolonged adolescence seemed finally at a close, Jewishness no longer figured among my conscious concerns. (Rubin-Dorsky and Fishkin, p. 161)

For some Jewish literary scholars of that generation, on the other hand, questions of gender and social justice could not override or erase a preoccupation with Jewishness and Jewish experience. These scholars were, in some way, touched by the Holocaust. Although issues of the feminist and left-liberal political agenda dominated the foreground of their academic lives during the 1970s and 1980s at the expense of overt Jewish identification, they were nevertheless intensely aware of the upsetting events in recent Jewish history. For reasons of psychic sanity, their direct or indirect experience of the Holocaust was stored in what the physician Lewis Thomas called the attic of the brain. During the 1990s, however, as this generation of scholars was turning fifty and sixty years old, some of them were beginning to retrieve the burden of the past.

Literature professors born in Europe during the 1930s who had made their careers primarily in foreign language and comparative literature departments rather than in English and American studies began to publish memoirs of their experiences. Most notable are the books by Ruth (Angress) Kluger, a professor of German at the University of California at Irvine, and Susan Rubin Suleiman, a professor of French at Harvard University. Kluger's *weiter leben: Eine Jugend* (1992) describes her childhood in Vienna and her deportation first to Theresienstadt and from there to Auschwitz-Birkenau. Suleiman's *Budapest Diaries: In Search of the Motherbook* (1996) reveals her childhood in Budapest and her wartime survival, hidden with Christian farmers in the Hungarian countryside.

For a few Jewish literary scholars, their Jewishness was never in doubt and they managed, in ways even more pronounced than the scholars of Jewish American literature, to combine their intellectual, social, and political commitments as Jews with careers in academia. This is particularly true for professors of Yiddish literature, such as RUTH WISSE and Anita Norich, who began their studies in the English departments of, respectively, McGill University and Columbia University. Their scholarship helped to establish Yiddish studies as an academic discipline.

While Yiddish was spurned by top academics during the 1970s and 1980s as a parochial backwater and the domain of nostalgic amateurs, Israel was even more shunned among progressive literary women scholars, since feminists tended to identify and identify with the Palestinians as the oppressed. Shortly after the Six-Day War of 1967, however, when a young Israel, radiant with victory, was at the apex of its strength, the country was attractive to assimilated

American Jews, shell-shocked by the Vietnam War. Yet few literary scholars actually went there and stayed. Miriyam Glazer did. She recalls:

> In 1968, I left the chaotic rebellion of my generation in the States for Jerusalem, in search of something more. I imagined a brief and romantic expatriation: Jerusalem after the Six-Day War would be my version of Paris in the 1920s. . . . But Israel for me was more than a respite; it was an awakening, a revelation. In the radiant air of Jerusalem, the biblical past felt alive in me as in the stones. Perhaps most important of all, among the vastly varied beauty of the Jewish people . . . my own American-bred internalized stereotype of who Jews are dissolved. I felt I belonged. My very body felt different. (Rubin-Dorsky and Fishkin, p. 440)

When Glazer was offered a job at the fledgling English department of Ben-Gurion University, she accepted. "To me, that offer meant a beckoning to participate in the pioneering national dream of 'building a state': I would help the desert culturally to bloom. I would bridge my world of English literature with the destiny of the Jews. I ceased being an 'American expatriate,' and stayed at Ben Gurion for eleven years" (p. 440). Other American women scholars, such as Hana Wirth-Nesher, one of Lionel Trilling's last doctoral students, and Emily Miller Budick, who married a Zionist, moved to Israel and built distinguished careers at Tel Aviv University and the Hebrew University, respectively.

Budick and Wirth-Nesher are part of the generation of women scholars born in the late 1940s and 1950s who attended college at a time when the first generation of male Jewish critics, like Trilling, was at the zenith of its power and a second generation of Jewish men, who were much less guarded about their Jewish descent than their precursors, was beginning to establish itself in literary academia. Men like Harold Bloom, Geoffrey Hartman, John Hollander, Stanley Fish, and Sacvan Bercovitch became role models for their Jewish students, because they made it possible to talk about Jews in their literature courses. Budick's testimony, summing up her post-1960s college experience, is particulary illuminating:

> One of the first requests made of us by Professor Colacurcio in his undergraduate survey of American literature at Cornell was that we not, please, repeat the error of Sacvan Bercovitch's students at Columbia. Bercovitch's students, Colacurcio reported, were under the strange illusion that the Puritans were Jews. Colacurcio insisted that he himself did not think that they were Roman Catholics. It was not until some years later, after I had heard Bercovitch lecture at Cornell and had read *The Puritan Origins of the American Self* (1975) and *The American Jeremiad* (1978), that I understood just what Colacurcio meant. But by the time we were only a few weeks into Colacurcio's survey, I knew exactly what Colacurcio meant about himself. Colacurcio's Puritans were sacramental symbolists of dazzling incarnationalist powers. They came to inform the whole of my vision of American literature. They weren't, however, to captivate me so completely as Bercovitch's "American Israelites," his "Jewish" Puritans.
>
> The ethnic revivals of the 1960s and 1970s, galvanized by the Civil Rights movement and black power, might themselves have forced me to rethink my Jewish identity. But it was Bercovitch, sensitive to the ways in which ideology constructs the sociopolitical sphere of everyday discourse (let alone literary texts), who returned me to a specifically Jewish American consciousness, a consciousness, that is, of the inseparability of my American and Jewish identities, as if America were, indeed, the only promised land there ever was, or was ever meant to be. (Rubin-Dorsky and Fishkin, pp. 221–22)

In later years, having moved to Israel and thus gained distance from America, Budick explains that she would gradually begin to understand Bercovitch's skepticism about the seductive machinations of American ideology. Skepticism, "mistrust of national authorities," and distrust of established social structures and traditional values certainly characterizes the generation of literary scholars who were born in the postwar era and entered early adulthood during the 1960s. When that generation ascended to professorships and other leadership roles in American colleges and universities, it brought about changes undreamed of by the previous generation. Not only did advocacy for the integration of minority scholars into literary academia become mandatory, but the concept of "minority" itself was expanded to include not only categories such as race, ethnicity, or gender, but also sexual orientation (gay/lesbian, bisexual, and, most recently, transgendered), whereas, tellingly, the category of class was dropped.

The extraordinary diversification of the literary faculty was matched, if not topped, by the astounding diversification of the literary canon during the 1980s and 1990s. Any author and any text (including advertisements and television soap operas) could become the subject of instruction and scholarship, and methods of interpretation ranged from feminism and psychoanalysis to deconstruction and new historicism. It is, perhaps, not surprising that Jewish scholars, both men and women born during the late 1930s and 1940s, were among the most ardent advocates of diversification. According to a survey conducted by Susan Gubar, many of them considered themselves as being "by definition and by blood, on the side of the oppressed," defined Judaism as a "passionate moral outrage at injustice," and thought of being Jewish as being "positioned by . . . heritage already on the left" (Rubin-Dorsky and Fishkin, p. 27).

For the subsequent generation, born in the 1950s and trained as scholars during the late 1970s and 1980s, the opening of academia to all and everything meant great opportunities—the pursuit of whatever one fancied—but also posed great challenges, namely, how to distinguish the fad from the worthwhile, the con artist from the real thing. Today, Jewish women can be found in all niches of traditional literary academia, that is, in departments of English, American studies, and foreign languages. But they have also begun to infiltrate a domain that is as new to secular academia as women scholars themselves are—Jewish studies.

Secularism, feminism, and attrition through assimilation have worked together to open Jewish academia to women. While in the religious institutions of Reform and Conservative Judaism women are becoming cantors and rabbis, in secular academia, women have advanced from reading Jewish American fiction to "engendering Holocaust memoirs" to producing vibrant, often feminist, psychoanalytic, or poststructuralist scholarship, not only on modern Yiddish and Hebrew literature (e.g., Naomi Sokoloff, Janet Hadda, and Naomi Seidman), but also on rabbinic texts as well (e.g., Talya Fishman and Dvora Weisberg). Rabbi Meir's brilliant wife Beruriah, as the writer Cynthia Ozick once put it, "was known to speak satirically of those rabbinic passages which made light of the intellect of women" (Ozick, p. 22). Two millennia later, her daughters are proving that she was right.

BIBLIOGRAPHY

Klingenstein, Susanne. "'But My Daughters Can Read the Torah': Careers of Jewish Women in Literary Academe." *AJH* 83 (June 1995): 247–286, and *Enlarging America: The Cultural Work of Jewish Literary Scholars, 1930–1990* (forthcoming), and *Jews in the American Academy, 1900–1940: The Dynamics of Intellectual Assimilation* (1991); Ozick, Cynthia. "Notes Toward Finding the Right Question (A Vindication of the Rights of Jewish Women)." *Lilith* 6 (1979): 22; Rubin-Dorsky, Jeffrey, and Shelley Fishkin, eds. *People of the Book: Thirty Scholars Reflect on Their Jewish Identity* (1996).

SUSANNE KLINGENSTEIN

LITMAN, RAY FRANK *see* FRANK, RAY

LITZINGER, DOROTHEA (1889–1925)

An artist best known for her paintings of flowers, Dorothea Litzinger also painted landscapes, decorative screens, and panels. It is not apparent that her work reflected any connection with her Jewish background: Her choice of subject matter was completely in concert with acceptable norms for upper-class women who painted. In her art and social milieu, Litzinger appears to have lived a highly assimilated life. In the artist's file at the New York Public Library there is an invitation, dated March 1923, from Messrs. Kennedy and Company at 693 Fifth Avenue to a "special Easter Exhibition of decorative flower and landscape paintings by Dorothea Litzinger." She was also involved in civic and community issues, and served as chair of the executive committee of the Beekman Hill Association. In that capacity, she was credited with organizing neighborhood children in a campaign for "sanitary streets."

Born in Cambria County, Pennsylvania, on January 20, 1889, Dorothea Litzinger studied art at the Margaret Morrison Carnegie School of Pittsburgh and at the Pratt Institute in New York. From 1908 to 1910, she attended the National Academy of Design. She was married to an attorney, John W. Thompson, although she was known solely as Dorothea Litzinger in all reference material, including her obituary in the *New York Times*.

Litzinger served as director of the Art Alliance and belonged to the Allied Artists of America, an organization established in 1914 as an exhibition cooperative that elected its own juries. As a member of the Connecticut Academy of Fine Arts, Litzinger participated in the annual exhibition at the Wadsworth Atheneum. She also belonged to the New Haven Paint and Clay Club. In 1924, Litzinger held a solo exhibit of her work at the Ralston Gallery in New York City.

In an article in *Art News*, "The Career of Dorothea Litzinger" (1925), Litzinger is described as "radiant, young and full of energy, never afraid of hard work." Her paintings of flowers are referred to as "an expression of herself in the generosity of their color and richness of design." Dorothea Litzinger was "an artist of intelligence and promise, always striving for something better, and could she have lived, would no doubt have attained great heights in her decorative painting."

After a brief bout with pneumonia, Dorothea Litzinger died at her home on January 5, 1925.

BIBLIOGRAPHY

AJYB 24:175; *Art News* 23 (November 15, 1924): 6; Litzinger, Dorothea. Clippings. Artist file, New York Public Library; Collins, J.L. *Women Artists in America*; Judson, Alice. "The Career of Dorothea Litzinger." *Art News* (June 1925); Pettey, Chris. *Dictionary of Women Artists*; *NYTimes*, March 2, 1924, 8:10; Obituary. *NYTimes*, January 6, 1925, 25:4; *Who Was Who in American Art*.

BETH HABER

LIVERIGHT, ALICE SPRINGER FLEISHER (1882–1958)

A woman from an affluent background who devoted her life to the underprivileged, Alice Springer Fleisher Liveright was part of a new generation of female professionals who helped to transform reform work from a pastime for middle-class women into a livelihood. This sense of professionalism, combined with left-leaning ideals of social justice and an outspoken manner, led her to work for equal rights for women and African Americans, and social welfare for children and poor adults.

Alice Springer Fleisher Liveright was born on December 18, 1882, in Philadelphia, Pennsylvania. Her parents, Martha (Springer) and Alexander Fleisher, were from prominent German Jewish families in Philadelphia. Her younger brother, Mayer, became a university professor in St. Louis. After her father died in 1888, Alice took on much of the responsibility for running the household. She attended a finishing school and in 1902 enrolled at the Drexel Institute of the University of Pennsylvania. On March 1, 1906, she married I. Albert Liveright, a manufacturer from another important Philadelphia German Jewish family. They had one child, Alexander "Sandy" Albert, and belonged to Reform congregation Keneseth Israel.

After studying at the Pennsylvania School of Social Work from 1912 to 1918, Liveright was involved with a variety of charity and reform groups, first in the Jewish community and then beyond. She served on the board of directors of the Juvenile Aid Society, a Jewish organization for troubled youth, starting in 1916, and later served as president. In 1931, she resigned and was appointed honorary director. She sat on the board of the Federation of Jewish Charities in 1926, and in 1928 aided community welfare organizations.

Devoted to social work as a profession, Liveright presided over the Philadelphia Conference of Social Work, helped found the Community Council, and served on the boards of the Pennsylvania School of Social Work and the Social Work Publicity Council. An advocate for women's issues, she was very involved with the Women's International League for Peace and Freedom, and served as the Philadelphia chair of the Bryn Mawr Summer School for Industrial Workers, which educated and trained working-class women. In addition, she was involved with the National Association for the Advancement of Colored People and sought to expand social services and social work opportunities to African Americans.

The peak of Liveright's professional career was as Pennsylvania's state secretary of welfare under liberal Republican governor Gifford Pinchot from 1931 to 1935. During this time, Pennsylvania had the third highest unemployment rate in the United States and the highest demand for welfare or other forms of state relief. Liveright contributed to the organization and regulation of state welfare delivery systems by shifting relief responsibilities from local private charities to the state and federal governments. She went on to serve on the advisory staff of the Works Progress Administration (WPA) in Washington, D.C., from 1935 to 1936.

Liveright was very active in politics. She was initially a member of the Republican Party, the dominant party in Philadelphia, but she became a socialist in the 1920s. She returned to the Republican Party to serve under Pinchot because of his liberal stance on social issues but shifted to the Democratic Party when working for the WPA. She then chaired the Philadelphia Progressive Party and supported Henry Wallace in his 1948 presidential campaign.

Throughout her career, Liveright demonstrated what is considered a modern understanding of poverty and social welfare. This approach tried to look scientifically at the roots of poverty and antisocial behavior, and it focused on a person's environment rather than just the morality of a person's actions. Liveright knew the cost of preventative welfare programs, but maintained that the cost of eliminating such programs was even greater. She also recognized and used the power of the media to get support for her initiatives. Practical in her approach, Alice Springer Fleisher Liveright was nonetheless passionate in her quest for social justice. She died in Philadelphia on February 18, 1958.

BIBLIOGRAPHY

Coode, Thomas H., and John F. Bauman. *People, Poverty, and Politics: Pennsylvanians During the Great Depression* (1981); Juvenile Aid Society. Annual reports and minutes. Association of Jewish Children Records, series 4, boxes 1–6, Philadelphia Jewish Archives Center; Kiebert, Emma Liveright. Interview by author, July 1996; Liveright, Alice Fleisher. "The Citizen and Public Welfare." *Social Science Review* 8 (September 1934): 415–422; "Mrs. Liveright, 75, A Welfare Aide." *NYTimes*, February 19, 1958, 27:4; State Welfare Commission. *Report on State Aid to Private Charitable Institutions and Agencies* (1935); *WWIAJ* (1938).

MINNA PEARL ZISKIND

LOEB, JOHANNA (1844–1917)

"In the death of Mrs. Johanna Loeb the Jewish Community of Chicago has lost one of its earnest and pioneer workers in the cause of charity. There are few of the Jewish charities of Chicago with which she was not identified in an active and efficient way. She was among the first who understood what personal service meant and she gave of her time and thought and energy willingly and cheerfully to help along those who had fallen by the way." These words were written in 1917, at the time of Johanna Loeb's death, in an editorial in the *Sentinel*, a Chicago Jewish weekly newspaper. Johanna Loeb was truly an outstanding Jewish social welfare worker in Chicago during the latter part of the nineteenth century and the first two decades of the twentieth century.

Johanna Unna was born in Rendsburg, Schleswig-Holstein, Germany, on May 25, 1844. In her early years, she was educated in Europe. She immigrated with her family to the United States in 1856 and eventually settled in Chicago, where she continued her basic education. She married Moritz Loeb, who emigrated from Bechtheim, Germany, and who died on April 10, 1892, at age fifty-two. They had four sons, Jacob M., Albert H., Julius, and Sidney. All of them were prominent in business and continued the family legacy of civic and communal service. Jacob was president of the Chicago Hebrew Institute, the predecessor of the Jewish Community Centers of Chicago, from 1912 to 1932, and was a board member and president for the Chicago Board of Education. Albert was the general manager of Sears, Roebuck and Company. Julius became vice president of George Kraft Company. Sidney was a successful real estate broker.

Johanna Loeb served on many Chicago Jewish charitable organizations. She was a director for the Home for Jewish Friendless, the German Old Peoples Home (*Altenheim*), the Home for the Crippled Children, the Jewish Consumptive Relief Society of Chicago, Resthaven, the Chicago Winfield Tuberculosis Sanitarium, the Josephine Club, and the Miriam Club. She also volunteered her time to the Baron Hirsch Woman's Club, the NATIONAL COUNCIL OF JEWISH WOMEN, and Deborah Verein, and she was a member of Sinai Congregation. Like most of the leading female German Jewish communal workers who lived in Chicago around the turn of the century, she had a strong personal relationship with Dr. Emil Hirsch, the rabbi of Sinai Congregation from 1880 to 1923.

The Jewish Training School (1890–1921), an innovative school founded by the German Jews affiliated with Sinai Congregation, created a philosophy of education that combined vocational, domestic, and general education for the Eastern European Jews of Chicago. Loeb was a founding member of the Industrial School/Jewish Training School, serving on the board of directors for many years and also playing an active role in the selection of a building site.

After the World's Columbian Exposition of 1893, Chicago suffered a period of financial depression. Loeb, as president of a society of ladies affiliated with the Central Unterstützungsverein [support association], opened numerous soup kitchens to care for Chicago's destitute.

At the turn of the century, the Chicago Jewish community recognized the need to help immigrants become accustomed to American life by establishing a Jewish communal institution. Loeb was an active participant in the women's auxiliary of the Chicago Hebrew Institute, which assisted the men in planning, development, and fund-raising. This organization eventually became the Jewish Community Centers.

During her first term as president of the Johanna Lodge No. 9, United Order of True Sisters (UOTS), Loeb led her chapter away from the platform of the national organization. A new focus of helping the Jewish disadvantaged was instituted, and Loeb served three terms as president. She was also instrumental in the founding of two other lodges for the UOTS—the Sarah Greenebaum Lodge No. 16 and the Lincoln Lodge. The Sarah Greenebaum Lodge supported Resthaven, a home for convalescing Jewish women and girls.

The history of the Jewish Federation of Metropolitan Chicago can be traced back to several organizations. One of these institutions, the United Hebrew Charities (1888–1900), was an important part of Loeb's life. She was the first woman appointed to its board of directors. She was also a member of the ladies' auxiliary committee.

Johanna Loeb died in Chicago on October 22, 1917, and was buried next to her husband in Rose Hill

Cemetery. She represents the beginning of an era in which Jewish women in Chicago devoted their time and money exclusively to Jewish communal service. Her charitable work within the Jewish community highlights the limitations that were placed on women and the role that separate women's philanthropic groups and women's auxiliaries played in Jewish American society during her lifetime.

BIBLIOGRAPHY

AJYB 7 (1905–1906): 82, and 20 (1918–1919): 229; Bregstone, Philip P. *Chicago and Its Jews* (1933); *The Chicago Jewish Community Blue Book* (1918); Gutstein, Morris A. *A Priceless Heritage* (1953); Industrial School/Jewish Training School. Minutes. Spertus Institute, Chicago; Jewish Community Center. Archival collection. Chicago Historical Society; Jewish Federation of Metropolitan Chicago. Archival collection. Spertus Institute; Meites, Hyman L., ed. *History of the Jews of Chicago* (1990); "The New Soup Kitchen." *Illinois Staats Zeitung*, December 19, 1893, 5; Obituary. *Sentinel*, October 26, 1917; Obituary of Moritz Loeb. *Reform Advocate*, April 16, 1892, 212; Reis, Nannie. "In the World of Jewish Womankind." *Reform Advocate*, October 27, 1917, 273+; Stein, Oswald. *Leading Women in Social Service* (1914?).

SANDRA K. BORNSTEIN

From Pennsylvania, Loeb had submitted essays to the *New York Evening World* on social discontent in the industrial town of McKeesport. Once in New York, she secured a position as a reporter and feature writer for the *World*. Loeb interviewed widowed women who, unlike her own mother, had been forced to place their children in orphanages. These interviews inspired her to work for the allocation of public funds for "widows' pensions." She publicized the movement to provide widows with such support, adding her voice to those of leaders—many of them Jewish women, children of immigrants—such as HANNAH BACHMAN EINSTEIN.

In 1913, Loeb and Einstein served on the newly created State Commission on Relief for Widowed Mothers. Loeb visited Europe for comparative studies of welfare policies. Her work on the commission report, as well as her campaign in the pages of the *World*, contributed greatly to the 1915 passage of a bill creating child welfare boards in every New York county. These boards distributed public funds to widowed mothers.

Loeb was appointed to New York City's Child Welfare Board in 1915, and for eight years served as the board's president. Under her direction, the board

LOEB, SOPHIE IRENE SIMON
(1876–1929)

"Not charity, but a chance for every child." Sophie Irene Simon Loeb adopted this as the creed of her life work for orphaned children in the United States and throughout the world. During the Progressive Era, Loeb was one of many women to enter the political arena through reform work, calling for government involvement to mitigate the problems of poverty. Loeb brought her life experience and her personalized approach to work for the rights of women and children to quality of life.

Sophie Simon Loeb was born in Rovno, Russia, on July 4, 1876. In 1882, at age six, she and her parents, Samuel and Mary (Carey) Simon, and five younger siblings joined the great wave of Jewish immigration to the United States, settling in McKeesport, Pennsylvania, near Pittsburgh. Sophie's father, a jeweler, died ten years later, leaving the family in dire straits. Still attending high school, she began part-time work in a local store to ease the family's financial burden. She was teaching grade school when she married Ansel Loeb, an older man who owned the store where she had worked, on March 10, 1896. The marriage proved unsuccessful, and in 1910 the couple divorced and Sophie moved to New York City.

"Not charity, but a chance for every child." This motto is on the gravestone of Sophie Irene Loeb, and she lived it throughout a life dedicated to women's rights and a better life for all children. [Hadassah Archives]

increased the city's appropriation from $100,000 to $4.5 million. Loeb worked in many arenas of urban reform and used public schools for civic centers and community forums. Her call for an investigation into corruption within the Public Service Commission resulted in the appointment of a new body. In 1917, she served as the first woman strike mediator, settling a taxi industry strike in seven hours. During these same years, she worked with her friend Governor Alfred E. Smith on a commission to codify child welfare legislation in New York State.

Loeb extended her campaign for child welfare nationally and internationally. Her book *Everyman's Child* (1920) addressed the themes of her campaign, stating that if any child fails to receive proper food and clothing, "the Government must stand in place of his parents." She spoke before state legislatures throughout the country and in 1924 helped to found the Child Welfare Committee of America. She also served as its first president. In 1925, the First International Congress on Child Welfare in Geneva accepted her resolution endorsing family home life as opposed to orphanages. Her report on blind children in the United States was accepted by the League of Nations in 1926. Her travels, speeches, and articles contributed to the passage of widows' aid legislation in forty-two states.

Though her mother had been an Orthodox Jew, Loeb maintained a secular life-style. In 1925, however, when the *Evening World* sent her to Palestine to report on Jewish settlements, Loeb was captivated by the Jewish homeland. She became a passionate Zionist, and her reports to the *World* were both investigative and romantic, full of arguments for welfare measures needed in the "pilgrimage center of all peoples." The following year, she published *Palestine Awake: The Rebirth of a Nation*, a compilation of these articles, and donated all royalties to the Palestine Fund.

Even with her generosity to so many causes, and her refusal to receive a salary for her public service work, Loeb's earnings from speaking and writing engagements—including authorship of several works of life observations, such as *Epigrams of Eve* (1913)—were high enough to afford her quite a comfortable life-style. Many mourned her loss when, on January 18, 1929, at age fifty-two, she died of cancer at New York City's Memorial Hospital. Governor Alfred E. Smith praised her as "one of America's most distinguished public servants, an indefatigable worker." She is buried in Mount Hope Cemetery in Westchester Hills, New York, where her gravestone reads: "Not charity, but a chance for every child." Loeb's work for scores of reform causes, particularly for new public

policies of relief, served as the foundation for more expansive policies of welfare in the United States. She stands as one of the many important American Jewish women involved in social and political reform in the early part of the century.

**SELECTED WORKS BY
SOPHIE IRENE SIMON LOEB**

Epigrams of Eve (1913); *Everyman's Child* (1920); *Fables of Everyday Folks* (1919); *Palestine Awake: The Rebirth of a Nation* (1926).

BIBLIOGRAPHY

AJYB 24:175, 31:93; *DAB*; *Liberty's Women*. Edited by Robert McHenry (1980); *NAW*; Sickels, Eleanor. *Twelve Daughters of Democracy: True Stories of American Women, 1865–1930* (1942); "Sophie Irene Loeb." *NYTimes*, January 21, 1929, 20:4; "Sophie Irene Loeb, Social Worker, Dies." *NYTimes*, January 19, 1929, 17:1; *UJE*; *WWIAJ* (1926, 1928); *WWWIA* 1.

MARJORIE N. FELD

LOEWITH, SADIE (1890–1956)

"Politics makes strange bedfellows," the adage states. Those "bedfellows" were joined by a feisty, strong, opinionated woman in Bridgeport, Connecticut, in the 1920s. She was Sadie Loewith, teacher, businesswoman, active Republican Party worker, chairperson, organizer, and politician of high repute. Her interests were many and varied, and her ability to lead and to elicit respect was unwavering.

Sadie (Rosenthal) Loewith, born July 17, 1890, was the eldest daughter of Philip J. and Jennie (Berman) Rosenthal. She moved with her parents, her brother, Albert, and her sister, Helen, from New York City to Bridgeport in 1894. She excelled academically and graduated first in her class from Bridgeport Normal School. On June 14, 1912, she married Walter Loewith. After teaching for several years and taking private instruction at Yale Art School, she joined her husband in his insurance brokerage firm in 1929. Upon his death in 1952, she took over the operation of the firm.

Loewith's interest in politics began prior to the ratification of the Nineteenth Amendment to the United States Constitution in 1920. She worked ardently in support of woman suffrage. Following the passage of the amendment, Loewith vowed to use her new enfranchisement to effect positive changes for women. From 1920 on, she served in every election—local, state, and national—as an active party worker. She organized, and served as president of, a string of Republican women's groups, including the Bridgeport

Council of Republican Women and the Fairfield County Women's Republican Association. She also served for six years as an active and innovative member of the Bridgeport Board of Education. Under her tenure, and as a result of her backing, new buildings were erected and a single salary schedule for men and women was implemented. In addition, she helped establish a higher minimum wage for teachers. Loewith also served Bridgeport in other areas—as a member of the board of recreation and as a lobbyist working on the Aid to Dependent Children bill, which was passed by the 1939 legislature. In 1947, she was named a Fairfield County commissioner.

Throughout her political career, Loewith was an articulate advocate of women's representation on the policy-making level. She was instrumental in establishing such representation in the police department and on the board of health as well as on the GOP town committee. Among her other civic involvements were the arts and community services.

During World War II, Loewith was chair of the women's division of the Bridgeport War Finance Committee for five bond drives. As a member of the Bridgeport War Council, she chaired the Women's Mobilization Committee to recruit women for war work in industrial, retail, and commercial establishments.

Within the Jewish community, Loewith served as president of the sisterhood of the Park Avenue Temple (now known as Congregation B'nai Israel), as honorary president of the Bridgeport Section of the NATIONAL COUNCIL OF JEWISH WOMEN, which she helped organize and which she headed for eight years, and as director of the Inter-Group Council, which was affiliated with the National Conference of Christians and Jews.

Sadie Loewith died on January 26, 1956, at age sixty-five.

BIBLIOGRAPHY
Obituaries. *Bridgeport (Conn.) Post*, January 26, 1956, and *NYTimes*, January 27, 1956, 23:3; *WWIAJ* (1928, 1938).

HOWARD LOEWITH

LOPEZ, REBECCA TOURO
(c. 1779–1833)

In 1824, Rebecca Touro petitioned the Rhode Island state legislature on behalf of preserving Touro Synagogue in Newport, the oldest synagogue building in North America and one that symbolizes Jewish survival and the American belief in religious freedom. At the time of her petition, no Jews were living in Newport, but her brother had left the state ten thousand dollars to restore and maintain the synagogue. The synagogue, designed by the eminent colonial architect Peter Harrison, was not only a beautiful building, but also represented a history of religious toleration, both in the Rhode Island colony founded by Roger Williams and in the new nation. Today, the synagogue is an active house of worship and, as a National Historic Monument, draws thirty thousand visitors a year from all over the country and around the world.

In the years from 1760 to 1776, when the synagogue was built and first active, Newport was at the pinnacle of colonial wealth. Jews had found refuge there from the Spanish Inquisition. By 1779, when Rebecca was born, Newport had been devastated, hundreds of its buildings burned down (although its synagogue was spared), and its population, for the most part, dispersed. It would never recover its commercial preeminence, although after the Civil War it was reborn as an opulent summer resort.

As an infant and child, and as a dependent single woman, Rebecca moved repeatedly during her life, first because of the effects of the Revolution and then because of deaths in her family. Her family had moved to New York by 1780, and shortly afterward to Kingston, Jamaica, where her father died in 1784, then to her uncle's house in Boston, where her mother died in 1787. When her uncle died, she moved to her brother Abraham's house in Boston, and when he died in 1822, she went to live in New York with the Lopez family.

The Touro name originated in Spain, probably as Toro. In the years after 1492, this family, like many other Sephardi families, moved to Amsterdam, Curaçao, and Brazil. Isaac Touro, Rebecca's father, had emigrated from Holland in 1760 to be the first hazan [minister or reader] of Newport's congregation. Its synagogue Yeshuat Israel [Salvation of Israel], dedicated in 1763, would come to be known as the Touro Synagogue. Isaac Touro and his wife, Reyna Hays Touro, had two sons, Abraham and Judah, in Newport before Rebecca was born. A fourth child, a son, was born in New York and probably died young.

Abraham Touro was a successful Boston merchant known for his bequests for the preservation of the synagogue and the reconstruction of the street on which the synagogue and cemetery are located. He had also arranged for replacing the deteriorating fence around the cemetery with a brick wall. The 1677 deed required maintenance of the fence to prevent the burial ground from reverting to the original owner. Judah Touro, a New Orleans merchant, attained national prominence as a philanthropist. Among his many hundreds of thousands of dollars of gifts all over the United States were ten thousand dollars that made possible the completion of Boston's Bunker Hill Monument and ten thousand dollars to the synagogue.

A successful petition to the Rhode Island General Assembly in 1685 had protected Jews from seizure of their property. In the colonial and early American eras, the right of petition was an important entitlement of disenfranchised individuals.

Living with the Lopez family in New York City after her brother's death, and inspired by Moses Lopez, the last Jew to leave Newport, Rebecca petitioned the Rhode Island General Assembly. The legislature had created a trust fund with her brother's bequest, but two years after his death, the money was sitting idle while the building was deteriorating. Stephen Gould, a Newport resident and a Quaker, was looking after the synagogue and cemetery, and she urged that he be paid out of the fund. She had earlier written on the same subject to the executor of her brother's will. But in late 1824, the issue was still unresolved. Her petition noted that the interest from her brother's "liberal donation was intended to be appropriated for the benefit of the two places in any way conducive to keep them always in a state of complete repair, to be transmitted and conveyed to a succeeding Congregation which he then contemplated might in progress of time settle again at Newport ... if my prayer is finally rejected and both places are to be abandoned and forsaken to save a just recompense to an agent indispensably necessary to have a constant eye on them, they inevitably must go to ruin, contrary to my brother's laudable design."

The assembly responded to Rebecca Touro's petition on January 12, 1825. The two-year restoration of the synagogue was begun in 1827. Putting these dates in context, one may note that the last recorded auto-da-fé of the Spanish Inquisition was in 1826, in Valencia.

The preservation of the synagogue represents one of the first efforts in the United States to restore and maintain an unoccupied historic building. This preservation led the way in Newport's extensive program of maintaining its architectural legacy. However, the Touro preservation was focused on preserving not just an impressive edifice but also the principle of religious freedom and the survival of a people.

Even in 1822, the cemetery and unoccupied synagogue were opened to visitors, but after the restoration, visits took on additional meaning. Two visitors in the second half of the nineteenth century, Henry Wadsworth Longfellow and EMMA LAZARUS, wrote poems after their visits. "The sacred shrine is holy yet," wrote Emma Lazarus in 1867, "With its lone floors where reverent feet once trod. / Take off your shoes, as by the burning bush, / before the mystery of death and God."

Late in life, when she was fifty, and he around sixty, Rebecca married Joshua Lopez, son of one prominent colonial Newport merchant, Aaron Lopez, and grandson of another, Jacob Rodrigues Rivera.

In her will, Rebecca Touro Lopez asked for Newport burial. In December 1833, her body arrived from New York by steamboat, the synagogue was opened for a service, and she was buried with other members of her Newport community.

BIBLIOGRAPHY

Crane, Elaine Forman. *A Dependent People: Newport, Rhode Island in the Revolutionary Era* (1985); "The Gould Family and the Jews of Newport." *PAJHS* 27 (1920): 423–442; Guinness, Desmond, and Julius Trousdale Sadler, Jr. *Newport Preserv'd: Architecture of the 18th Century* (1982); Gutstein, Morris A. *To Bigotry No Sanction: A Jewish Shrine in America, 1658–1958* (1958), and *The Touro Family in Newport* (1935); "Items Relating to the Jews of Newport." *PAJHS* 27 (1920): 207+; "Items Relating to the Newport Cemetery." *PAJHS* 27 (1920): 413–415; "Items Relating to the Newport Synagogue." *PAJHS* 27 (1920): 404–412; "Items Relating to the Touro Family, Newport." *PAJHS* 27 (1920): 417–422; Marcus, Jacob. *The Colonial American Jew, 1492–1776* (1970); Rosenbloom, Joseph. *A Biographical Dictionary of Early American Jews: Colonial Times Through 1900* (1960).

JANE MUSHABAC

LORBER, FANNIE ELLER
(1881–1958)

Fannie Eller Lorber was Denver's twentieth-century "friend of children." The Colorado philanthropist worked on behalf of Jewish children suffering from the devastating effects of lung disease, believing that "the cause of a child is the cause of humanity." Lorber epitomized the volunteer spirit of urban Jewish women in the American West, where established institutions for the poor and infirm were scarce. She founded the Denver Jewish Sheltering Home for the children of tuberculosis patients in 1907, and remained its president and chief fund-raiser for over fifty years. Later renamed the National Home for Jewish Children (NHJC), the institution merged with the National Jewish Hospital in 1978, and it remains a world-class medical and educational facility. Thousands of the NHJC's "alumni" are the living legacy of Fannie Lorber and Jewish female philanthropy during the Progressive Era.

Fannie Eller Lorber was born in Geishen, Russia, in 1881. She and her family immigrated to the American West in the early 1890s, settling in Denver, Colorado, in 1896. There she married Jacob Lorber, a Jewish Hungarian immigrant, on February 4, 1902. The Lorbers established a family retail shoe business in the bustling urban center of the Rocky Mountain region. Known as a mecca for sufferers of lung disease, Denver's sunshine and clear air attracted thousands of "health seekers." Into the Lorbers' neighborhood poured hundreds of indigent Eastern European Jewish immigrants, posing a challenge to Denver's small but growing Jewish community.

The Progressive Reform Movement and the benevolent traditions of the faith motivated Jewish women to serve Denver's poor. The "Mother of Charities," FRANCES WISEBART JACOBS, inspired Lorber to reach out to the "poor kids from New York" who populated her neighborhood in the Jewish district of West Denver. A tragic suicide by a desperate tubercular father of two youngsters spurred Lorber to action. In 1907, she founded the Denver Sheltering Home, housing eight children of TB victims. A larger facility was quickly necessary, and the facility gradually grew into a parklike compound.

Lorber sought innovative approaches to the care of young orphans. She insisted upon spacious living quarters, individual attention, and creative freedom—a dramatic break with the old-style crowding, regimentation, and impersonal character associated with nineteenth-century orphanages and asylums. While elements of white middle-class "social control" were present, the Denver Sheltering Home offered sick children an alternative to poverty and dependence.

When growing numbers taxed the Denver Sheltering Home's resources beyond capacity, Lorber opened a national fund-raising office on New York City's East Side in 1920. She set up a chain of local auxiliaries to support the Home, which became a model strategy for effective fund-raising. Jewish women in cities and towns across the nation formed the backbone of Lorber's auxiliaries, enabling hundreds of young residents to live in the nonsectarian facility free of charge. Innovative medical researchers joined the Denver facility, which now enjoyed national recognition as the leading institution for young respiratory patients.

Lorber was an active member of Temple Emanuel sisterhood, the Town Club, the Denver Section of the NATIONAL COUNCIL OF JEWISH WOMEN, and HADASSAH. However, she found time in her busy schedule as an organizer, a fund-raiser, and a motivational speaker to raise two young sons, Milton and Arthur. Jacob Lorber supported his wife's work by overseeing the family's retail shoe business in Denver.

By the late 1940s, a new TB vaccine virtually killed this dreaded disease. Lorber's work did not end,

however. Under her leadership, the facility began treating patients with chronic, intractable asthma and was renamed the National Jewish Home for Asthmatic Children.

Fannie Eller Lorber died in Denver, June 9, 1958, at age seventy-six. She devoted her entire adult life to a single philanthropic cause. Her legacy thrived in the volunteer network of auxiliaries, which had grown to over 130,000 members nationwide.

Lorber met the challenges of early twentieth-century urbanization by drawing upon networks of women to weave a safety net for indigent, infirm children in the West. Her Jewish heritage and her middle-class goals of Americanization of immigrants, modernization of education, social uplift of the lower classes, and a sense of female mission informed her philosophy of charity work. Above all, Lorber put children first. "With the Jewish people, the cause of the underprivileged child has always been placed at the very head of every charity," she stated. "Children have been the hope of future generations throughout the ages and continue to be the foundation of our people and country."

BIBLIOGRAPHY

Abrams, Jeanne. "'For a Child's Sake': The Denver Sheltering Home for Jewish Children in the Progressive Era." *American Jewish History* 79, no. 2 (Winter 1989–1990): 181–202; *AJYB* 60:356; "Asthmatic Home Dorm Honors Late President." *Rocky Mountain News*, August 11, 1958, 9; *BEOAJ*; Breck, Allen. *A Centennial History of the Jews of Colorado* (1960); Ehler, Dolores. "Asthmatics Treated in Home-like Setting." *Rocky Mountain News*, August 4, 1981, 38; Hodges, Eva. "Friend of Children: Fannie Lorber Wins Fame in Founding of N.H.J.C." *Denver Post*, May 4, 1952, 2AA; McGraw, Pat. "Merger Announced by Hospital, Center." *Denver Post*, September 6, 1978, 43; Obituary. *Denver Post*, June 10, 1958, 3, *NYTimes*, June 10, 1958, 33:4, and *Rocky Mountain News*, June 10, 1958, 5; Uchill, Ida. *Pioneers, Peddlers, and Tsadikim: The Story of Jews in Colorado* (1957); Van Loon, Dirk. "A Tribute to Mrs. Fannie Lorber: CARIH Achievement Award." *Festival Magazine, Rocky Mountain News*, July 23, 1967, 2–7; *WWIAJ* (1928, 1938).

MARCIA TREMMEL GOLDSTEIN

LORBER, FRIEDA (1899–1976)

A prominent New York attorney and fund-raiser for a number of Jewish causes, Frieda Lorber accomplished much during her long and distinguished legal career.

Frieda Levin Lorber was born in New York City on May 7, 1899, to Sigmund Levin, a real estate developer, and Clara (Bergman) Levin. In her early years, Frieda was extremely interested in classical music. She studied voice at the Institute of Musical Art and sang with the chorus of the Metropolitan Opera. On December 7, 1924, she married Albert Lorber. The Lorbers, who divorced in the early 1940s, had one child, Mortimer, who became a doctor.

Frieda Lorber had always excelled academically. She was valedictorian of her high school class and graduated summa cum laude from New York University in 1936. Lorber's younger brother, Emil Levin, was a lawyer. Admiring him and observing that he enjoyed the legal profession, she decided to attend law school. She received her law degree from New York University Law School in 1938 and was admitted to the bar two years later. She and her brother, former commissioner of the State Human Rights Appeals Board, practiced commercial and real estate law together for many years. In 1959, she obtained a master's degree in law from Columbia University.

A few years after graduation, Lorber became the director of the division of coordination and research for the Department of Investigation of the City of New York. She held this position from 1944 to 1946. Other prominent positions followed in quick succession. From 1949 to 1951, she served as the president of the New York Women's Bar Association. In 1956, she became an arbitrator in the small claims section of the Brooklyn civil court. She was chair of the Women's Bar Association's judiciary committee from 1955 to 1958, and of its equal opportunity for women committee in 1960. In 1961, she was a delegate of the International Federation of Women Lawyers to the United Nations nongovernment organizations section and later was a representative to the United Nations Human Rights Commission. Additionally, she served as chair of the house committee of the New York County Lawyers Association and was a member of several other bar associations.

In addition to her legal career, Lorber devoted a substantial amount of time to fund-raising for Jewish causes. In 1949, she served as chair of the women lawyers' committee of the United Jewish Appeal–Federation of Jewish Philanthropies and was cochair of the State of Israel Bond Campaign. Reflecting her lifelong love for music, she sponsored an international music competition for the Federation of Jewish Philanthropies in 1961. She was also a member of HADASSAH.

Frieda Lorber died on September 28, 1976, at age seventy-seven. Her life reflected a blend of dedication to professional goals, concern about the welfare of others, and an abiding interest in Jewish causes.

BIBLIOGRAPHY

AJYB, 78:543; Lorber, Mortimer. Telephone interview by author, June 19, 1996; Obituary. *NYTimes*, September 30, 1976, 44:3; *Who's Who of American Women* (1964–1965, 1968–1969).

LAURA J. LEVINE

LOUIS, MINNIE DESSAU (1841–1922)

Minnie Dessau Louis was one of the most active and important Jewish communal workers on the American scene from the 1880s through the early 1900s.

Born in Philadelphia on June 21, 1841, the second daughter of Fannie (Zachariah) and Abraham Dessau, Minnie moved to Georgia with her family when she was four months old. She returned north to attend Brooklyn's Packer Collegiate Institute in 1857 and 1858, and in 1866 married businessman Adolph H. Louis.

Louis was an essayist, journalist, and poet (publishing her poems in private editions and newspapers such as the *American Hebrew* and *Jewish Messenger*), but she is best known for her philanthropic work in the Jewish community, largely focusing on women and children. She began her career as a volunteer, teaching at the Sunday school of Temple Emanu-El in New York City, and after teaching there for five years opened her own school in 1880. The school was incorporated as the Louis Downtown Sabbath School in 1884 and changed its name to the Hebrew Technical School for Girls in 1895. Even as she was acting as president of the school, Louis still found time for other Jewish communal activities. She was acting president of the Hebrew Free School kindergarten from 1882 to 1883, and a leader of the Mount Sinai Training School for Nurses, serving as the secretary for its executive committee from 1882 to 1886 and president of the school from 1886 to 1889.

Already a recognized leader among American Jewish women by the time of the World's Columbian Exposition in 1893, Louis spoke at the Jewish Women's Congress, and shortly thereafter was instrumental in founding the NATIONAL COUNCIL OF JEWISH WOMEN (NCJW), as well as its New York City section, in 1894. Also in the 1890s, Louis served as an NCJW national board member (1893–1895), as chair of its first national committee on religion (1894), and as a district inspector for New York's public schools (1894–1897).

Certainly her husband's death in 1897 did not slow down Louis's communal activities. In 1897 and 1898, she was director of the Clara de Hirsch Home for Girls, and from 1900 to 1901 was the field secretary for the Jewish Chautauqua Society. She also served as editor for the Personal Service Department of the *American Hebrew* (1901–1903). In 1900, Louis retired from her position at the Hebrew Technical School, though she returned to the school in 1906.

Minnie Dessau Louis began her communal career at the beginning of mass immigration from Eastern Europe and died on March 12, 1922, just before mass immigration came to an end. Louis herself perfectly embodied the contradictions of German Jewish philanthropy on behalf of Eastern European immigrants. Today, for instance, the Hebrew Technical School's instruction in morals, hygiene, and trades is likely to be seen as precisely the type of social control detested by the immigrants. Nevertheless, Louis was extremely committed to Judaism and the Jewish people, and devoted her adult life to improving their lot in America.

SELECTED WORKS BY MINNIE DESSAU LOUIS

Hannah and Her Seven Sons: An Incident of the Persecution of the Jews by the Syrian Monarch Antiochus Epiphanes, 167 B.C. (1902); "What It Is to Be a Jew." In Souvenir Book, Fair in Aid of the Educational Alliance and the Hebrew Technical Institute (1895).

BIBLIOGRAPHY

AJYB 7 (1905–1906): 83–84, 24:102; Kohns, Lee. "Minnie D. Louis." *PAJHS* 29 (1925): 178–179; *National Cyclopaedia of American Biography*, vol. 18; Obituary. *NYTimes*, March 13, 1922, 15:6; *Woman's Who's Who of America: A Biographical Dictionary of Contemporary Women in the United States and Canada, 1914–15* (1914).

SETH KORELITZ

LOVEMAN, AMY (1881–1955)

Amy Loveman, as described in the reminiscences of her friends, was optimistic without being foolish, incisive without being unkind, hardworking without being self-righteous, and the embodiment of unfailing integrity. As one of the founding editors of the *Saturday Review of Literature* and an important member of the Book-of-the-Month Club staff, Loveman applied those extraordinary personal qualities to her lifelong work of evaluating literature. Harry Scherman, the originator of Book-of-the-Month Club, once explained that she rarely read fewer than thirty books a month, and the books she read were placed in a context that was extraordinarily broad, balanced, realistic, and generous.

Loveman was born in New York City, on May 16, 1881, the daughter of Adolph P. and Adassa (Heilprin) Loveman. Amy Loveman's maternal grandfather, Michael Heilprin, himself the son of a rabbi, was a noted encyclopedist, linguist, regular contributor to *The Nation*, outspoken foe of slavery, and supporter of Jewish immigrants to the United States. Adassa Heilprin apparently shared in her family's tradition of learning and writing. Her brother-in-law Gustav Pollak notes in his biography *Michael Heilprin and His Sons*, "Girls and boys alike picked up languages very much as their father had done in his youth," and wrote of Adassa that "in former years she wrote casually for the press." Loveman's father, who came to the United States from Hungary around 1850, was a cotton broker. He was also a lover of books and spoke six languages.

The eldest child in the Loveman family was a daughter who died in infancy; Amy was second, followed by three brothers, Herbert, Ernest, and Michael. The family was a primary source of Loveman's education. She noted in *Current Biography* (1943) that "the family discussions of an intellectual nature" in which she had participated from childhood proved valuable later in life when she became a book reviewer.

She attended the Horace Mann School, graduating in 1897, and Barnard College, from which she graduated at age twenty, Phi Beta Kappa. (At Barnard, Loveman took no literature courses, convinced that her love of books would always inspire her to read and that her time in school should be devoted to other studies.)

Loveman's first literary work was as assistant to her uncle Louis Heilprin, who was revising *The New International Encyclopaedia* and *Lippincott's Pronouncing Gazetteer of the World*. Later, she worked at the *New York Evening Post* with another uncle, Gustav Pollak, helping prepare a special anniversary issue of *The Nation*. She was invited to remain at the *Post* as a book reviewer. In 1920, she helped to found the *Post's Literary Review*, with Henry Seidel Canby, Christopher Morley, and William Rose Benét. In 1924, with that same group of associates, she left to form an independent literary magazine, the *Saturday Review of Literature* (*SR*). Amy Loveman was named on the masthead as associate editor.

Close to eight hundred contributions by Amy Loveman are listed in the *Saturday Review of Literature Index 1924–1944*: editorials, reviews, and "The Clearing House," the column of answers to readers' queries on books she wrote for each issue from 1933 to 1937. Writing, however, was only a small part of what she did for the magazine. Norman Cousins described the breadth of Loveman's contribution to *SR* in the tribute he wrote after her death: "During the first fifteen years Amy Loveman assigned most of the books for review, wrote reviews of her own, handled a regular department in the magazine . . . , edited copy, pinned up the dummy, read page proofs, and put the magazine to bed at the printer's." She was the person who saw to it that the office ran smoothly, finding lost copy, staying late, doing whatever needed to be done: "the *sine qua non, ne plus ultra*, and power behind the throne," in the words of Bennett Cerf. In 1950, after Benét's death, she also took up the duties of poetry editor.

Loveman filled a similar role at Book-of-the-Month Club. She became a member of the preliminary reading committee soon after the club's founding in 1926; in 1938, she was named head of the editorial department. She retained that position (giving her what could have been regarded as another full-time job) until 1951, when she became a member of the Board of Judges. During World War II, Loveman also was a member of the Armed Services Editions Committee of the Council of Books in War Time.

The quality of her work and the nature of her dedication were recognized and valued by colleagues. In June 1942, a small group of friends planned a surprise party to present her with a gold medal for her contribution to literature and culture. That small party never took place; so many people asked to be invited that the gathering grew to fill a ballroom. The gold medallion she received carried on one side the *Saturday Review* symbol and on the other the inscription: "To Amy Loveman / A Courageous Champion of Literature / From Her Devoted Friends / June 15, 1942."

Loveman also received the Columbia University Medal for Excellence (1946), the Constance Lindsay Skinner Achievement Award of the Women's National Book Association (1946), and honorary Litt.D. degrees from Wheaton College and Wilson College (both 1950).

Amy Loveman remained close to her family. She cared for her father in his old age and traveled to England with her brother Michael the summer before her death. She was operated on for cancer in 1954 and continued working until days before her death, on December 11, 1955, in New York City.

SELECTED WORKS BY AMY LOVEMAN

Designed for Reading: An Anthology Drawn from "The Saturday Review of Literature," 1924–1934, with Henry Seidel Canby, William Rose Benét, Christopher Morley, and May Lamberton Becker (1934); *I'm Looking for a Book* (1936); *Saturday Papers: Essays on Literature from "The Literary Review,"* with Henry Seidel Canby and William Rose Benét (1921); *Varied Harvest: A Miscellany of Writing by Barnard College Women*, with Fredrica Barach and Marjorie M. Mayer (1953).

BIBLIOGRAPHY

AJYB 24:176; Cerf, Bennett. "Trade Winds." *Saturday Review* (June 27, 1942), and "Take a Bow." *Publishers Weekly* (April 6, 1946), and "You Meet Such Interesting People." *Publishers Weekly* (March 3, 1951); Cousins, Norman. "Amy Loveman." *Saturday Review* (December 24, 1955), and *The Saturday Review Gallery* (1959); *Current Biography Yearbook* (1943); *DAB* 5; Morais, Henry Samuel. *The Jews of Philadelphia* (1894); *National Cyclopaedia of American Biography*. Vol. 44 (1962); *NAW* modern; Obituary. *NYTimes*, December 12, 1955, 31:3; Pollak, Gustav. *Michael Heilprin and His Sons* (1912); Shuler, M., R.A. Knight, and M. Fuller. *Lady Editor: Careers for Women in Publishing* (1941); Smith, Harrison, Henry Seidel Canby, Harry Scherman, and George Stevens. "The World of Amy Loveman." *Saturday Review* (December 31, 1955); *WWWIA* 3.

PAMELA MATZ

LOVENSTEIN, REBECCA PEARL (1888–1971)

In few states did the struggle for women's right to practice law on original jurisdiction take longer than in Virginia. The effort lasted from 1890 until June 1920 and required a change in the state bar admission statutes. Rebecca Lovenstein, who had campaigned for the statutory change, was the first woman admitted to practice in the state. She took the oath in Richmond on June 28, 1920. Rebecca Pearl Greenberg Lovenstein was the third Jewish woman to open a state bar for women.

Born in Vilna, Russia, on May 25, 1888, she was the third child in a family of four daughters and two sons born to Moses S. and Deborah (Dora) Greenberg. The youngest son, Henry Clay Greenberg, became one of the most honored justices of the New York State Supreme Court. Moses Greenberg, a surveyor, settled in Durham, North Carolina, where he opened a wholesale grocery. In the 1890s, he brought his family to the United States.

After public schooling in Durham, Rebecca attended Duke University for two years. Her mother, in poor health, wanted her daughter near her. Moses Greenberg hired tutors so that she could continue her education while caring for her mother.

Benjamin Lovenstein, born in Philadelphia in 1883, was studying law in Charlottesville, Virginia, and selling typewriters to earn tuition. On a trip through Durham, he met Rebecca. They were married on July 25, 1907. Admitted to the North Carolina bar, Benjamin Lovenstein was a highly successful trial lawyer in Durham. The Lovensteins had two sons, Meno (b. 1910), and Irving (b. 1911). After Benjamin suffered an overwhelming financial loss in a real estate venture, his family in Virginia asked him to move to Richmond. There, Rebecca gave birth to another son, Harold, in 1915. They were members of Temple Beth-El.

Beginning in 1917, Rebecca Lovenstein tried, with little success, to obtain a legal education. Law schools were closed to women, and enabling legislation had not yet been passed. Interestingly, woman suffrage associations did not support her. The dislocations resulting from World War I made it possible for her to attend law school at night while taking care of her children during the day. In 1920, the Nineteenth Amendment was passed, paving the way for legislation allowing women to become lawyers.

After being admitted to the bar, Lovenstein opened an office in her basement. In 1923, when her husband developed a kidney condition, she took over his office and cared for him until his death in 1956. Benjamin still maintained contact with clients, but trial practice was impossible for him. The Lovensteins practiced together for some years.

In 1934, they endured tragedy when their second son, Irving, committed suicide after losing a young woman he loved to another man. Meno became a professor of economics at Ohio State University and later at the University of Miami. Harold moved to New York City to work in publishing, and was for a time assistant editor of *American Weekly*.

Lovenstein's strong personality, gregarious nature, and love of her profession sustained her through good and bad years. In the late 1960s, she slipped into the lost world of Alzheimer's disease. She died on February 10, 1971, in a New York nursing home, watched over by her son Harold. Funeral services were held in Richmond, Virginia, and she is buried in Beth-El Cemetery.

BIBLIOGRAPHY

Green, Jean. Interview by author, NYC, September 11, 1996; Lovenstein, Rebecca. Interview by author, Richmond, Virginia, December 1959; *Richmond Times-Dispatch*, January 8, 1925, and February 12, 1971; Thomas, Dorothy. *Women, the Bench and the Bar* (forthcoming).

DOROTHY THOMAS

LOW, MINNIE (1867–1922)

Known as the "Jane Addams of the Jews," Minnie Low was a leader in the Jewish social service community. Born in New York City, on November 9, 1867, Low was the second of six children. When she was ten, Low's family moved to Chicago, where she completed grammar school. Unfortunately, she was forced to leave South Division High School during her first year due to poor health.

Low's first foray into the field of social work occurred during the 1893 economic depression when she cofounded the Maxwell Street Settlement House, an agency that served the needs of Eastern European Jewish immigrants in Chicago. Her lifelong friendship with social worker and Hull House Settlement director Jane Addams began during this period; the initial planning meetings for the Maxwell Street Settlement House were held at Hull House.

While organizing the Maxwell Street Settlement House, Low was employed as secretary to HANNAH GREENEBAUM SOLOMON, the philanthropist and social reformer who founded the NATIONAL COUNCIL OF JEWISH WOMEN (NCJW) in 1893. When Solomon and other members of Chicago's NCJW founded the Seventh Ward Bureau in 1897, later known as the Bureau of Personal Service, they appointed Low as executive director, a position she held until her death twenty-five years later. Under Low's direction, the organization helped immigrants to secure housing, medical care, legal aid, and loans. Although Low described the bureau as nonsectarian, the vast majority of the agency's clients were Russian Jews.

The bureau's goals and activities reflected Low's philanthropic philosophy. An adherent of scientific philanthropy, a popular late nineteenth-century philanthropic approach that emphasized the importance of helping the poor to become self-sufficient, Low discouraged bureau workers from dispensing monetary relief to their poor clients. Low viewed alms as psychologically degrading as well as dangerous to the poor because they encouraged dependency.

In addition to its goal of encouraging initiative and responsibility among the poor, the bureau was committed to maximizing efficiency among Chicago's social service agencies. The bureau conducted investigations of people who applied to other agencies such as the Woman's Loan Association, the School Children's Aid Society, Hull House, and Henry Booth House. The purpose of these investigations was to make sure that applicants were seeking aid for "worthy" purposes and that they were being truthful about their dire financial situations.

All of Low's philanthropic endeavors were shaped by her belief in scientific philanthropy. She was an advocate of friendly visitor programs whereby indigent people were provided with the counsel and friendship of middle-class women rather than with monetary doles. Under the auspices of the bureau, Low created a workroom for women where workers were paid for their labor with coal and secondhand shoes and clothes. Similarly, Low was committed to providing the poor with loans rather than with conventional alms. For Low, loans preserved recipients' dignity, while monetary gifts were humiliating. In a 1905 essay on philanthropy, Low wrote:

> Loan a small amount to a man struggling for existence . . . let him at the same time repay the loan in small installments, without flinching, and without shirking his responsibility, and what greater proof do we require that undaunted courage, ambition, honor, and manliness are virtues of the poor? (Bernheimer: 97).

Low transformed her beliefs about the merit of loans into practice when she helped found the Woman's Loan Association in 1897. Beginning with eighty-seven dollars in its treasury, by 1918 the loan society was disbursing as much as thirty-three thousand dollars per year in interest-free loans, primarily to Jewish immigrants who needed funds to create and maintain businesses.

An ardent supporter of women's rights, Low was proud that women administered this Chicago loan facility. At a 1914 national meeting on Jewish philanthropy, not long after the state of Illinois voted in favor of woman suffrage, Low boldly asserted that "no man has ever had an active voice in the affairs of this [Woman's Loan] Association. As contributing members, men have been granted the courtesy of affixing their names to the subscription list, otherwise all privileges have been denied them."

Along with a group of prominent Chicago social reformers and philanthropists including Sara Hart, Louise de Koven Bowen, Judge Julian Mack, Julia Lathrop, Lucy Flower, Solomon, and Addams, Low organized the Juvenile Court of Chicago (1899), the first separate juvenile court in the nation, where she served as a probation officer. To further aid the goal of juvenile justice, Low helped establish the Juvenile Protective Association, an organization devoted to delinquency prevention.

Low's sphere of social work activities also encompassed the Central Bureau of Jewish Charities, Desertion Bureau, Helen Day Nursery, Home for Jewish Friendless, and Jewish Home Finding Society. The latter agency helped widows with dependent children and served as an adoption agency. In addition, Low was involved in securing legislation aimed at eliminating white slave traffic. Her commitment to social reform caught the attention of wealthy Chicago philanthropists such as Julius Rosenwald, owner of the mail-order firm Sears, Roebuck and Company, who gave her money every month to help with individual cases that she brought to his attention.

Low achieved national recognition for her abilities when her colleagues elected her president of the National Conference of Jewish Charities in 1914, a position she held for two years. Within her leadership capacity, Low actively fought for women's equality within the field of Jewish social work. For example, when she found out that all thirty-one presenters scheduled to speak at a Conference of Jewish Social Workers were male, Low protested. David Bressler, the president of the National Association of Jewish Social Workers, defended the speaker selection process by saying that the executive committee used merit, not gender, as the basis of invitation. Low responded with the following letter:

> Women not only like to vote, but they like to talk once in a while, and particularly in the presence of a crowd of brilliant co-workers of the other sex. In fact, if you want to retain the interest of the rank and file, you must give women a chance to be heard. It is not a question of favoring my sex, but it is merely a question of justice, because surely you could have found one fair dame in the width and breadth of this land, who could bring something valuable to the Conference (Low to Bressler, February 16, 1915, NAJSW Papers).

In contrast to many of her female colleagues who were married, wealthy, and worked as unpaid volunteers, Low was single, self-supporting, and employed as a paid professional. Her relatively low social status may help to explain why, despite an impressive career, Low is virtually unknown. After a seven-month illness, Minnie Low died in Chicago's Michael Reese Hospital on May 28, 1922. She was buried at Oakwoods Cemetery.

SELECTED WORKS BY MINNIE LOW

"Chicago." In *The Russian Jew in the United States*, edited by Charles Bernheimer (1905); "Woman's Loan Association." *Proceedings of the Eighth Biennial Session*. National Conference of Jewish Charities, Memphis, 1914.

BIBLIOGRAPHY

AJYB 7 (1905–1906): 84, 24:102; Bogen, Boris. *Extent of Jewish Philanthropy in the United States* (1908); Hart, Sara. *The Pleasure Is Mine: An Autobiography* (1947); Low, Minnie. Archives. Julius Rosenwald Papers. Department of Special Collections, Regenstein Library, University of Chicago, and National Association of Jewish Social Workers Papers. American Jewish Historical Society, Waltham, Mass.; Meites, Hyman. *History of the Jews of Chicago* (1924); Obituaries. *Chicago Tribune*, May 29, 1922, 15, and *NYTimes*, May, 29, 1922, 11:4; Solomon, Hannah. *Fabric of My Life* (1946);

Tenenbaum, Shelly. *A Credit to their Community: Jewish Loan Societies, 1880–1945* (1993); Werner, M.R. *Julius Rosenwald: The Life of a Practical Humanitarian* (1939).

SHELLY TENENBAUM

LOWENSTEIN, ELIZABETH GELEERD *see* GELEERD, ELIZABETH ROZETTA

LOWENTHAL, ESTHER (1883–1980)

In 1960, Bryn Mawr College celebrated its seventy-fifth anniversary by honoring seventy-five of its most distinguished alumnae. Esther Lowenthal was lauded as "a lucid and lively teacher, an efficient, clear-headed dean, and a witty, warm-hearted, and invaluable member of the . . . community."

Lowenthal was born on September 15, 1883, in Rochester, New York, to Louise and Max Lowenthal. Her father was one of the founders of the Mechanics Institute, now the Rochester Institute of Technology.

Lowenthal graduated from Bryn Mawr College in 1905. After completing economic studies at Oxford University, she enrolled at Columbia University and, under the direction of Edwin R.A. Seligman, received her Ph.D. in 1911. The university published her dissertation *The Ricardian Socialists*, which examined the work of socialist economists, including William Thompson, John Grey, Thomas Hodgskin, and John Francis Bray, between 1820 and 1840, and the significant place they occupy in the history of socialist theory. Lowenthal's work attempted "to estimate the relative importance of the Utopian and the scientific elements in the reasoning of these socialists and to examine . . . their political and economic theories."

Lowenthal became a member of the economics faculty of Smith College in 1911, was made a full professor in 1921, and became the Robert A. Woods Professor of Economics in 1925. She served the college in a variety of other roles until her retirement in 1952. She stepped in to fill the newly defined position of dean of the faculty from 1946 to 1948, with a mission to revitalize educational policy and the curriculum after the war. Lowenthal also served as chair of the department of economics, the chair of the Council on Industrial Studies, and president of the Smith chapter of the American Association of University Professors.

A distinguished economist, Lowenthal was respected by her colleagues and students for the enthusiasm and imagination she brought to her discipline. She specialized in public finance, particularly government revenues and expenditures, and modern forms of taxation.

Lowenthal lived her philosophy as well as teaching it. She was an active speaker in the community on subjects such as taxes, New Deal programs, and the relation of government to industry. She adopted a Spanish girl through the Foster Parents' Plan for War Children, and her will included an endowment to the local United Way. Lowenthal followed her own advice to students: "Remember that your mind is your closest companion. Keep it interesting." In 1950, friends and former students established the Esther Lowenthal Scholarship, honoring a career that "steadily exemplified the virtues of clarity, reason, and liberality."

She died on May 18, 1980, in Rochester, New York.

SELECTED WORKS BY ESTHER LOWENTHAL

Foreword to "Shutdown in the Connecticut Valley: A Study of Worker Displacement in the Small Industrial Community," by Katharine D. Lumpkin. *Smith College Studies in History* 19 (1935): 141–144; "Labor Policy of Oneida Community, Ltd." *Journal of Political Economy* 35 (February 1927); "The Ricardian Socialists." *Columbia University Studies in History, Economics, and Public Law* 46 (1911).

BIBLIOGRAPHY
AJYB 24:177; Lowenthal, Esther. Papers. Smith College Archives, Northampton, Mass.; Obituary. *Smith Alumnae Quarterly* 71 (1980): 68; Records of the Office of the President. Smith College Archives; Retirement notice. *Smith Alumnae Quarterly* 43 (1952): 212; *WWWIA* 7.

MARGERY N. SLY

LOWEY, NITA M. (b. 1937)

As cochair of the Bipartisan Congressional Caucus for Women's Issues, Congresswoman Nita M. Lowey has made women's health issues a priority. In the fiscal year of 1995, when the National Institutes of Health received only a 3 percent increase in funding, Lowey secured a 17 percent increase in funding for breast cancer research. Also serving on the House Appropriations Subcommittee on Foreign Operations, Lowey is a staunch supporter of the State of Israel.

She was born Nita Melnikoff in the Bronx on July 5, 1937, to Beatrice and Jack Melnikoff, both natives of New York. She has one younger brother, Richard. She attended the Bronx High School of Science and received her bachelor's degree from Mount Holyoke College in 1959.

The Democratic congresswoman represents New York's Eighteenth District, which includes Westchester, Queens, and the Bronx. She was first elected to the House of Representatives in 1988. Prior to that, she served in the New York Department of State and was assistant secretary of state from 1985 to 1987. She also was one of the founders of the New York State Association of Women Office Holders.

During her tenure in Congress, Lowey has proved herself a strong advocate for women's issues. In 1993, she was appointed to the Appropriations Committee, and she is one of two women on the subcommittee that determines health, education, and labor spending. She is also cochair of the Bipartisan Congressional Caucus for Women's Issues. In this capacity, she has helped protect funding for breast and cervical cancer research, domestic violence awareness programs, and child support programs. Lowey also chairs the House Pro-Choice Task Force. Together with Representative Patricia Schroeder of Colorado, Lowey introduced the Women's Choice and Reproductive Health Protection Act in 1996. Lowey is a former member of the Education and Labor Committee and has fought for equity in education for girls and young women, as well as for economic security for older women. She is also a member of the Glass Ceiling Commission, working to promote women's advancement in the workplace, and cochair of the Congressional Advisory Panel to the Campaign to Prevent Teen Pregnancy.

In addition, Lowey's record shows a strong commitment to the State of Israel. As a member of the House Appropriations Subcommittee on Foreign Operations, she helped push through the $3 million aid package to Israel in 1995 and 1996. In 1995, the Lowey Amendment stated that United States officials could not meet with Palestinian officials in Jerusalem, demonstrating her belief in Israel's sovereignty over Jerusalem. In 1994, the Lowey-Specter Amendment, which she coauthored with Senator Arlen Specter of Pennsylvania, was to ensure that the Palestine Liberation Organization was complying with its end of the Oslo Agreements signed with Israel.

Lowey is active in the United Jewish Appeal and wears the "Lion of Judah" pin symbolizing her support for its work. She and her husband, attorney Stephen Lowey, live in Harrison, in Westchester County, and belong to the Jewish Community Center of Harrison, a Conservative synagogue. They have three grown children, Dana, Jacqueline, and Doug.

BIBLIOGRAPHY

Lowey, Nita M. Biography. Congressional office of Nita M. Lowey, Washington, D.C.; Solomon, Adam. Telephone interview with author. Office of Nita M. Lowey, Washington, D.C., September 1996.

ALEXANDRA J. WALL

LUST, ADELINE COHNFELDT (1860–?)

Adeline Cohnfeldt Lust wrote popular short stories, editorials, and articles for many newspapers, as well as a novel. She was born in Crefeld, Germany, on April 12, 1860, to Albert and Henrietta (Davis) Cohnfeldt, but left her birthplace at an early age and immigrated to England. There she attended boarding school and studied with private tutors. At age fifteen she was already a published journalist. In 1876, she came to America and settled in New York.

She was a talented musician with a beautiful singing voice and could have become a concert performer, but chose to focus on her writing instead. On September 17, 1884, Adeline Cohnfeldt married Philip G. Lust. She wrote "Features of New York Life" and short stories for the *New York Graphic* (*New York Illustrated Weekly Graphic*) in 1882. Her stories were so well received that leading newspapers throughout the United States reprinted them. Both the *Cincinnati Graphic* and the *New York Graphic* published *Harum Scarum* as a serial novel in 1885. She became a regular contributor to the American Press Association. *A Tent of Grace*, her only novel, was published in 1899. It recounts the life of Jette, a Jewish orphan, who grows up in a Christian village in Germany. The heroine struggles with assimilation and anti-Semitism.

The date of Adeline Lust's death is unknown.

BIBLIOGRAPHY

AJYB 6 (1904–1905): 146–147, 24:177; Lust, Adeline C. *A Tent of Grace* (1899); *WWWIA* 4.

ELANA SHEVER RIPPS